Lecture Notes in Computer Science

Commenced Publication in 1973
Founding and Former Series Editors:
Gerhard Goos, Juris Hartmanis, and Jan van Leeuwen

Martín Abadi   Luca de Alfaro (Eds.)

CONCUR 2005 – Concurrency Theory

16th International Conference, CONCUR 2005
San Francisco, CA, USA, August 23-26, 2005
Proceedings

Springer

Volume Editors

Martín Abadi
Luca de Alfaro
University of California at Santa Cruz
School of Engineering
Santa Cruz, CA 95064, USA
E-mail: {abadi, luca}@soe.ucsc.edu

Library of Congress Control Number: 2005930640

CR Subject Classification (1998): F.3, F.1, D.3, D.1, C.2

ISSN 0302-9743
ISBN-10 3-540-28309-9 Springer Berlin Heidelberg New York
ISBN-13 978-3-540-28309-6 Springer Berlin Heidelberg New York

Springer is a part of Springer Science+Business Media

springeronline.com

Printed in Germany

Typesetting: Camera-ready by author, data conversion by Scientific Publishing Services, Chennai, India
Printed on acid-free paper SPIN: 11539452 06/3142 5 4 3 2 1 0

Preface

This volume contains the papers presented at CONCUR 2005, the 16th International Conference on Concurrency Theory. The purpose of the CONCUR series of conferences is to bring together researchers, developers, and students in order to advance the theory of concurrency and to promote its applications. This year's conference was in San Francisco, California, from August 23 to August 26.

We received 100 submissions in response to a call for papers. Each submission was assigned to at least three members of the Program Committee; in many cases, reviews were solicited from outside experts. The Program Committee discussed the submissions electronically, judging them on their perceived importance, originality, clarity, and appropriateness to the expected audience. The Program Committee selected 38 papers for presentation. Because of the format of the conference and the high number of submissions, many good papers could not be included. Although submissions were read and evaluated, the papers that appear in this volume may differ in form and contents from the corresponding submissions. It is expected that many of the papers will be further revised and submitted to refereed archival journals for publication.

Complementing the contributed papers, the program of CONCUR 2005 included invited lectures by Rajeev Alur, Luca Cardelli, Dawson Engler, and Christos Papadimitriou. Rajeev Alur's and Dawson Engler's lectures were jointly for CONCUR 2005 and SPIN 2005, one of 11 affiliated workshops that enhanced the program:

- BioCONCUR: Concurrent Models in Molecular Biology
- DisCoVeri: Distributed Algorithms Meet Concurrency Theory
- EXPRESS: Expressivity in Concurrency
- FIT: Foundations of Interface Technology
- FOCLASA: Coordination Languages and Software Architectures
- GETCO: Geometric and Topological Methods in Concurrency
- GT-VC: Graph Transformation for Verification and Concurrency
- INFINITY: Verification of Infinite-State Systems
- MoChArt: Model Checking and Artificial Intelligence
- SecCo: Security Issues in Concurrency
- SPIN: Model Checking of Software

We would like to thank the members of the Program Committee for their hard and expert work. We would also like to thank the CONCUR Steering Committee, the workshop organizers, the external reviewers, the authors, and the local organizers for their contributions to the success of the conference. Finally, we gratefully acknowledge the generous support received from Cisco Systems and from Microsoft Research.

Martín Abadi and Luca de Alfaro

CONCUR Steering Committee

Roberto Amadio (Université de Provence)
Jos Baeten (Eindhoven University of Technology)
Eike Best (Oldenburg University)
Kim Larsen (Aalborg University)
Ugo Montanari (Università di Pisa)
Scott Smolka (SUNY Stony Brook)

CONCUR 2005 Organization

General Chair

Luca de Alfaro (University of California, Santa Cruz)

Program Committee Chairs

Martín Abadi (University of California, Santa Cruz)
Luca de Alfaro (University of California, Santa Cruz)

Program Committee

Christel Baier (Universität Bonn)
Jos Baeten (Eindhoven University of Technology)
Albert Benveniste (IRISA/INRIA)
Luis Caires (Universidade Nova de Lisboa)
Giuseppe Castagna (CNRS/École Normale Supérieure)
Marsha Chechik (University of Toronto)
Vincent Danos (CNRS/Université Paris VII)
Javier Esparza (University of Stuttgart)
Cédric Fournet (Microsoft Research, Cambridge)
Dimitra Giannakopoulou (NASA Ames Research Center)
Anna Ingólfsdóttir (Aalborg University)
Radha Jagadeesan (DePaul University)
Bengt Jonsson (Uppsala University)
Antonin Kucera (Masaryk University)
Orna Kupferman (Hebrew University)
Cosimo Laneve (Università di Bologna)
Kim Larsen (Aalborg University)
John Mitchell (Stanford University)
Ugo Montanari (Università di Pisa)
Catuscia Palamidessi (INRIA Futurs and LIX)
Prakash Panangaden (McGill University)
Shaz Qadeer (Microsoft Research, Redmond)
Vijay Saraswat (IBM T.J. Watson Research Center)
Vladimiro Sassone (University of Sussex)
Philippe Schnoebelen (CNRS/École Normale Supérieure de Cachan)
Frits Vaandrager (Radboud University Nijmegen)
Mahesh Viswanathan (University of Illinois at Urbana-Champaign)
Igor Walukiewicz (Université Bordeaux)
Glynn Winskel (University of Cambridge)

External Reviewers

Samy Abbes, Parosh Abdulla, Luca Aceto, Karine Altisen, Rajeev Alur, Paul Camille Attie, Eric Badouel, Michael Baldamus, Paolo Baldan, Emmanuel Beffara, Nick Benton, Bernard Berthomieu, Karthik Bhargavan, Stefano Bistarelli, Bruno Blanchet, Bernard Boigelot, Mikolaj Bojanczyk, Marcello Bonsangue, Michele Boreale, Ahmed Bouajjani, Gérard Boudol, Patricia Bouyer, Claus Brabrand, Tomáš Brázdil, Roberto Bruni, Peter Buchholz, Nadia Busi, Thierry Cachat, Marco Carbone, Rohit Chadha, Thomas Colcombet, Giovanni Conforti, Ricardo Corin, Flavio Corradini, Scott Cotton, Jean-Michel Couvreur, Silvia Crafa, Cas Cremers, Philippe Darondeau, Johan de Kleer, Yannick Delbecque, Yuxin Deng, Rocco De Nicola, Ewen Denney, Josée Desharnais, Erik de Vink, Ellie D'Hondt, Maria Rita di Berardini, Eric Fabre, Ulrich Fahrenberg, Alessandro Fantechi, Harald Fecher, Jérôme Feret, Marcelo Fiore, Emmanuel Fleury, Riccardo Focardi, Wan Fokkink, Pierre Ganty, Simon Gay, Blaise Genest, Mihaela Gheorghiu, Hugo Gimbert, Patrice Godefroid, Jens Chr. Godskesen, Georges Gonthier, Valentin Goranko, Andy Gordon, Daniele Gorla, Roberto Gorrieri, Vineet Gupta, Arie Gurfinkel, Stefan Haar, Frédéric Herbreteau, Thomas Hildebrandt, Dan Hirsch, Loïc Hélouët, Hans Hüttel, Bertrand Jeannet, Ole Jensen, Ken Kahn, Apu Kapadia, Christos Karamanolis, Yannis Kassios, Joost-Pieter Katoen, Lionel Khalil, Josva Kleist, Bartek Klin, Pavel Krčál, Steve Kremer, Jean Krivine, Karl Krukow, Viraj Kumar, Celine Kuttler, Barbara König, Anna Labella, Albert Lai, Yassine Lakhnech, Leslie Lamport, Ivan Lanese, François Laroussinie, Sławomir Lasota, Olivier Laurent, François Laviolette, Jamey Leifer, Didier Lime, Markus Lohrey, Etienne Lozes, Michael Luttenberger, Bas Luttik, Parthasarathy Madhusudan, Matteo Maffei, Andrea Maggiolo Schettini, Pritha Mahata, Ka Lok Man, Richard Mayr, Hernan Melgratti, Paul-André Melliès, José Meseguer, Marius Mikucionis, Michael Mislove, MohammadReza Mousavi, Venkatesh Mysore, Shiva Nejati, Uwe Nestmann, Mogens Nielsen, Marcus Nilsson, Dirk Nowotka, Luke Ong, Simona Orzan, Joel Ouaknine, Joachim Parrow, Corina Pasareanu, Dusko Pavlovic, Radek Pelánek, Paul Pettersson, Henrik Pilegaard, Michele Pinna, Damien Pous, Vinayak Prabhu, Rosario Pugliese, Sriram Rajamani, Julian Rathke, Martin Raussen, Antonio Ravara, Laurent Regnier, Michel Reniers, Arend Rensink, Shamim Ripon, Bill Rounds, Vojtěch Řehák, Mayank Saksena, Simonas Saltenis, Davide Sangiorgi, Zdeněk Sawa, Alan Schmitt, Johann Schumann, Stefan Schwoon, Koushik Sen, Pawel Sobocinski, Ana Sokolova, Jiří Srba, Sam Staton, Alin Stefanescu, Marielle Stoelinga, Oldřich Stražovský, Jan Strejček, Grégoire Sutre, Dejvuth Suwimonteerabuth, David Teller, P.S. Thiagarajan, Simone Tini, Tayssir Touili, Nikola Trčka, Stavros Tripakis, Bruno Tuffin, Emilio Tuosto, Franck van Breugel, Rob van Glabbeek, Michiel van Osch, Daniele Varacca, Abhay Vardhan, Moshe Y. Vardi, Björn Victor, Aymeric Vincent, Ramesh Viswanathan, Hagen Völzer, Tomáš Vojnar, Marc Voorhoeve, Sergei Vorobyov, Ou Wei, Lucian Wischik, Kidane Yemane, Wang Yi, Mingsheng Ying, Francesco Zappa Nardelli, Gianluigi Zavattaro, Axelle Ziegler, W.M. Zuberek

Local Organizers

Bo Adler, Leandro Dias Da Silva, Marco Faella, Jessica Gronski, Teresa La Femina, Axel Legay

Table of Contents

Invited Lectures

Contributed Papers

Static Analysis Versus Model Checking for Bug Finding

Dawson Engler

Computer Systems Laboratory,
Stanford University,
Stanford, CA 94305, U.S.A

Abstract. This talk tries to distill several years of experience using both model checking and static analysis to find errors in large software systems. We initially thought that the tradeoffs between the two was clear: static analysis was easy but would mainly find shallow bugs, while model checking would require more work but would be strictly better — it would find more errors, the errors would be deeper and the approach would be more powerful. These expectations were often wrong. This talk will describe some of the sharper tradeoffs between the two, as well as a detailed discussion of one domain — finding errors in file systems code — where model checking seems to work very well.

M. Abadi and L. de Alfaro (Eds.): CONCUR 2005, LNCS 3653, p. 1, 2005.

The Benefits of Exposing Calls and Returns

Rajeev Alur

University of Pennsylvania

Regular languages have robust theoretical foundations leading to numerous applications including model checking. Context-free languages and pushdown automata have been indispensable in program analysis due to their ability to model control flow in procedural languages, but the corresponding theory is fragile. In particular, non-closure under intersection and undecidability of the language inclusion problem disallows context-free specifications in model checking applications.

In the recently proposed definition of *visibly pushdown languages*, the set of input symbols is partitioned into *calls*, *returns*, and *local* symbols, and the type of the input symbol determines when the pushdown automaton can push or pop or swap. Exposing the matching structure of calls and returns is natural in associating a language with a sequential block-structured program or a document format with nested tags. When calls and returns are exposed in this manner, the language can be defined by a (stackless) finite-state *alternating* automaton that can jump from a call to the matching return. The resulting class of VPLs has many appealing theoretical properties:

Closure Properties: it is closed under a variety of operations such as union, intersection, complementation, renaming, concatenation, and Kleene-$*$;

Robustness: it has multiple equivalent characterizations using context-free grammars, using the monadic second order (MSO) theory over words augmented with a binary matching predicate, and using Myhill-Nerode-like characterization by syntactic congruences;

Decidability: problems such as language inclusion and equivalence are decidable for visibly pushdown automata (VPA);

Determinization: nondeterministic VPAs can be determinized;

Minimization: under some restrictions, deterministic VPAs can be minimized yielding a canonical VPA; and

ω-VPLs: most of the results generalize to the class of languages over infinite words defined by visibly pushdown automata with Büchi acceptance condition.

After reviewing the theory of VPLs, we show how it allows enhancing the expressiveness of specification languages used in software model checking. The *temporal logic of calls and returns* (CaRet) integrates Pnueli-style temporal modalities with Hoare-style reasoning by pre/post conditions, in a single algorithmic framework. Besides the standard global temporal modalities, CaRet admits the *local-next operator* that allows a path to jump from a call to the *matching* return. This operator can be used to specify a variety of non-regular properties such as

M. Abadi and L. de Alfaro (Eds.): CONCUR 2005, LNCS 3653, pp. 2–3, 2005.

partial and total correctness of program blocks with respect to pre and post conditions. The abstract versions of the other temporal modalities can be used to specify regular properties of *local* paths within a procedure that skip over calls to other procedures. CaRet also admits the *last-caller* modality that jumps to the most recent pending call, and such caller modalities allow specification of a variety of security properties that involve inspection of the call-stack. The set of models of a CaRet formula can be interpreted as a visibly pushdown ω-language, and generalization of the classical tableau construction allows model checking CaRet formulas against a pushdown model. The complexity of model checking CaRet formulas is the same as checking LTL formulas, namely, polynomial in the model and singly exponential in the size of the specification.

We conclude by discussing ongoing research on a fixpoint calculus that can specify local and global properties of program flows, and some open problems.

Acknowledgements

This talk is based on joint work with S. Chaudhuri, K. Etessami, V. Kumar, P. Madhusudan, and M. Viswanathan reported in the publications [AM04], [AEM04], [AKMV05], and [ACM05], and on research supported by NSF award CCR-0306382 and ARO URI award DAAD19-01-1-0473.

References

[ACM05] R. Alur, S. Chaudhuri, and P. Madhusudan. A fixpoint calculus for local and global program flows. Under submission, 2005.

[AEM04] R. Alur, K. Etessami, and P. Madhusudan. A temporal logic of nested calls and returns. In *TACAS'04: Tenth International Conference on Tools and Algorithms for the Construction and Analysis of Software*, LNCS 2988, pages 467–481. Springer, 2004.

[AKMV05] R. Alur, V. Kumar, P. Madhusudan, and M. Viswanathan. Congruences for visibly pushdown languages. In *Automata, Languages and Programming: Proceedings of the 32nd ICALP*, 2005.

[AM04] R. Alur and P. Madhusudan. Visibly pushdown languages. In *Proceedings of the 36th ACM Symposium on Theory of Computing*, pages 202–211, 2004.

A Compositional Approach to the Stochastic Dynamics of Gene Networks

Luca Cardelli

Microsoft Research, CB3 0FB Cambridge, United Kingdom

We propose a compositional approach to the dynamics of gene regulatory networks based on the stochastic π-calculus, and develop a representation of gene network elements which can be used to build complex circuits in a transparent and efficient way. To demonstrate the power of the approach we apply it to several artificial networks, such as the repressilator and combinatorial gene circuits first studied in Combinatorial Synthesis of Genetic Networks [GEHL2002]. For two examples of the latter systems, we point out how the topology of the circuits and the interplay of the stochastic gate interactions influence the circuit behavior. Our approach may be useful for the testing of biological mechanisms proposed to explain the experimentally observed circuit dynamics.

Joint work with Ralf Blossey and Andrew Phillips.

References

[GEHL2002] Călin C. Guet, Michael B. Elowitz, Weihong Hsing, Stanislas Leibler. Combinatorial Synthesis of Genetic Networks. Science, Vol 296, Issue 5572, 1466-1470 , 24 May 2002

M. Abadi and L. de Alfaro (Eds.): CONCUR 2005, LNCS 3653, p. 4, 2005.

Games Other People Play*

Christos H. Papadimitriou

University of California, Berkeley

Games were used by Wittgenstein as an example in the philosophy of language of a concept that can have many and dramatically divergent meanings in different contexts.

Case in point: Games are familiar in the Concurrency community as models of dynamic, multi-staged threats to correctness. In Economics, on the other hand, games refer to a family of mathematical models (including, strictly speaking, the games alluded to above) whose intention is to model the behavior of rational, selfish agents in the face of situations that are to varying degrees competitive and cooperative. In recent years there has been an increasingly active interface, motivated by the advent of the Internet, between the theory of games on the one hand, and the theory of algorithms and complexity on the other, and both with networking. This corpus of research problems and reults is already quite extensive, rich, and diverse; however, one can identify in it at least three salient themes: First, there is the endeavor of developing efficient algorithms for the fundamental computational problems associated with games, such as finding Nash and other equilibria; this quest is more than the predictable reflex of our research community, but it is arguably of fundamental value to Game Theory at large. There is also the field of algorithmic mechanism design, striving to devise computationally efficient methods for designing games whose equilibria are precisely the socially desirable outcomes (for example, that the person who has the highest personal appreciation for the item being auctioned actually wins the auction). And finally we have an ever-expanding family of problems collectively given the playful name "the price of anarchy," studying how much worse a system emerging from the spontaneous interaction of a group of selfish agents can be when compared with the ideal optimum design.

This talk will review recent results and open problems in these areas.

* Research supported by NSF ITR grant CCR-0121555 and a grant from Microsoft Research.

M. Abadi and L. de Alfaro (Eds.): CONCUR 2005, LNCS 3653, p. 5, 2005.

Type-Directed Concurrency

Deepak Garg and Frank Pfenning*

Carnegie Mellon University
{dg, fp}@cs.cmu.edu

Abstract. We introduce a novel way to integrate functional and concurrent programming based on intuitionistic linear logic. The functional core arises from interpreting proof reduction as computation. The concurrent core arises from interpreting proof search as computation. The two are tightly integrated via a monad that permits both sides to share the same logical meaning for the linear connectives while preserving their different computational paradigms. For example, concurrent computation synthesizes proofs which can be evaluated as functional programs. We illustrate our design with some small examples, including an encoding of the pi-calculus.

1 Introduction

At the core of functional programming lies the beautiful Curry-Howard isomorphism which identifies intuitionistic proofs with functional programs and propositions with types. In this paradigm, computation arises from proof reduction. One of the most striking consequences is that we can write functions and reason logically about their behavior in an integrated manner.

Concurrent computation has resisted a similarly deep, elegant, and practical analysis with logical tools, despite several explorations in this direction (see, for example, [4,15]). We believe the lack of a satisfactory Curry-Howard isomorphism is due to the limits inherent in complete proofs: they provide an analysis of constructive truth but not of the dynamics of interaction.

An alternative logical foundation for concurrency is to view computation as proof search [6]. In this paper we show that the two views of computation, via proof reduction and via proof search, are not inherently incompatible, but can coexist harmoniously in a language that combines functional and concurrent computation. We retain the strong guarantees for functional computation without unduly restricting the dynamism of concurrent computation.

In order to achieve this synthesis, we employ several advanced building blocks. The first is linearity: as has been observed [12], the evolution and communication of processes maps naturally to the single-use semantics of assumptions in linear logic. The second is dependency: we use dependent types to model communication channels and also to retain the precision of functional specifications for transmitted values. The third is monads: we use monadic types to encapsulate concurrent computation, so that the linear connectives can retain the same

* This work has been partially supported by NSF Grant CCR-0306313 Efficient Logical Frameworks.

M. Abadi and L. de Alfaro (Eds.): CONCUR 2005, LNCS 3653, pp. 6–20, 2005.

logical meaning on the functional and concurrent side without interference. The fourth is focusing [5]: we use it to enforce the atomicity of concurrent interactions during proof search.

The result is a tightly integrated language in which functional computation proceeds by reduction and concurrent computation proceeds by proof search. Concurrent computation thereby synthesizes proofs which can be evaluated as functional programs. We illustrate the design with some small examples, including an encoding of the π-calculus to help gauge its expressive power.

There has been significant prior work in combining functional and concurrent programming. One class of languages, including Facile [11], Concurrent ML [18,19], JOCaml [9], and Concurrent Haskell [13], adds concurrency primitives to a language with functional abstractions. While we share some ideas (such as the use of monadic encapsulation in Concurrent Haskell), the concurrent features in these languages are motivated operationally rather than logically and are only faintly reflected in the type system. Another class of languages start from a rich concurrent formalism such as the π-calculus and either add or encode some features of functional languages [17]. While operationally adequate, these encodings generally do not have a strong logical component. An interesting intermediate point is the applied π-calculus [2] where algebraic equations are added to the π-calculus. However, it is intended for reasoning about specifications rather than as a programming language.

Perhaps most closely related to our work is CLF [21] and the logic programming language LolliMon [14] based on its first-order fragment. Our type system is based on the common logic underlying both these systems. However, these systems are intended as a logical framework and concurrent logic programming language respectively and differ significantly from our language in the operational semantics. Another closely related line of work is Abramsky's computational interpretations of linear logic [3], but the discussion of concurrency there is based on classical rather than intuitionistic linear logic and lacks functional features.

The principal contributions of this paper are conceptual and foundational, although a simple prototype [1] indicates that there is at least some practical merit to the work. Owing to space constraints we omit the linear type constructors & and $\oplus$, recursive types and all proofs from this paper. These details can be found in the companion technical report [10].

In the remainder of the paper we present our language (called CLL) in three steps. First, we present the functional core (fCLL) which integrates linearity and a monad. Second, we present the concurrent core (lCLL), which is based on proof search, and which can call upon functional computation. Third, we complete the integration with one additional construct to allow functional computation to call upon concurrent computation. We call the complete language full-CLL. We conclude with some remarks about the limitations of our work.

Our main technical results are as follows. For the functional core fCLL, we prove type soundness by proving preservation and progress. For the concurrent core lCLL, we only formulate and prove a suitable notion of preservation. For full-CLL, we prove both preservation and progress, but the progress theorem is

Sorts	$\gamma ::= \mathtt{chan} \mid \ldots$
Index terms	$s, t ::= i \mid f(t_1, \ldots, t_n)$
Index variable contexts	$\Sigma ::= \cdot \mid \Sigma, i : \gamma$
Sorting judgment	$\Sigma \vdash t \in \gamma$
Kinds	$K ::= \mathtt{Type} \mid \gamma \rightarrow K$
Types	$T ::= A \mid S$
Asynchronous types	$A, B ::= C\ t_1 \ldots t_n \mid A \rightarrow B \mid A \multimap B \mid \forall i : \gamma.A(i) \mid \{S\}$
Synchronous types	$S ::= A \mid S_1 \otimes S_2 \mid \mathbf{1} \mid !A \mid \exists i : \gamma.S(i)$
Programs	$P ::= N \mid M \mid E$
Terms	$N ::= x \mid \lambda x : A.N \mid N_1\ N_2 \mid \hat{\lambda} x : A.N \mid N_1 \,\hat{}\, N_2$ $\mid \Lambda i : \gamma.N \mid N\ [t] \mid \{E\}$
Monadic-terms	$M ::= N \mid M_1 \otimes M_2 \mid \star \mid !N \mid [t, M]$
Patterns	$p ::= x \mid \star \mid p_1 \otimes p_2 \mid !x \mid [i, p]$
Expressions	$E ::= M \mid \underline{\mathtt{let}}\ \{p : S\} = N\ \underline{\mathtt{in}}\ E$

Fig. 1. fCLL syntax

weaker than that of fCLL. This is because in full-CLL concurrent computations started during functional computation can deadlock.

2 fCLL: Functional Core of CLL

Syntax. The functional core of CLL is a first-order dependently typed linear functional language called fCLL. It is an extension of a linear lambda calculus with first-order dependent types from DML [22] and a monad. Its type and term syntax is based largely on that of CLF [21]. The syntax of fCLL is summarized in figure 1. Types in fCLL can depend on index terms (denoted by s, t) that are divided into a number of disjoint sorts (γ). Index terms contain index variables ($i, j, k, \ldots$) and uninterpreted function symbols ($f, g, h, \ldots$). We assume the existence of a *sorting* judgment $\Sigma \vdash t \in \gamma$, where Σ is a context that mentions the sorts of all free index variables in t.

Type constructors (denoted by C) are classified into kinds. For every fCLL program we assume the existence of an implicit signature that mentions the kinds of all type constructors used in the program. An atomic type is formed by applying a type constructor C to index terms $t_1, \ldots, t_n$. If C has kind $\gamma_1 \rightarrow \ldots \rightarrow \gamma_n \rightarrow \mathtt{Type}$, we say that the atomic type $C\ t_1 \ldots\ t_n$ is well-formed in the index variable context Σ iff for $1 \leq i \leq n$, $\Sigma \vdash t_i \in \gamma_i$. In the following we assume that all atomic types in fCLL programs are well-formed.

Following CLF, types in fCLL are divided into two classes - asynchronous (A, B) and synchronous (S). Asynchronous types can be freely used as synchronous types. However, synchronous types must be coerced explicitly into asynchronous types using a monad $\{\ldots\}$, which is presented in a judgmental style [16].

Programs (P) are divided into three syntactic classes – terms (N), monadic-terms (M) and expressions (E). This classification is reminiscent of a similar

$$\Sigma ::= \cdot \mid \Sigma, i : \gamma \qquad \Delta ::= \cdot \mid \Delta, x : A$$
$$\Gamma ::= \cdot \mid \Gamma, x : A \qquad \Psi ::= \cdot \mid \Psi, p : S$$

$\boxed{\mathbf{\Sigma; \Gamma; \Delta \vdash N : A}}$

$$\frac{}{\Sigma; \Gamma; x : A \vdash x : A}\text{Hyp1} \qquad \frac{}{\Sigma; \Gamma, x : A; \cdot \vdash x : A}\text{Hyp2}$$

$$\frac{\Sigma; \Gamma, x : A; \Delta \vdash N : B}{\Sigma; \Gamma; \Delta \vdash \lambda x : A.N : A \to B}\to\text{I} \qquad \frac{\Sigma; \Gamma; \Delta, x : A \vdash N : B}{\Sigma; \Gamma; \Delta \vdash \hat{\lambda} x : A.N : A \multimap B}\multimap\text{I}$$

$$\frac{\Sigma, i : \gamma; \Gamma; \Delta \vdash N : A}{\Sigma; \Gamma; \Delta \vdash \Lambda i : \gamma.N : \forall i : \gamma.A}\forall\text{I} \qquad \frac{\Sigma; \Gamma; \Delta \vdash E \div S}{\Sigma; \Gamma; \Delta \vdash \{E\} : \{S\}}\{\}\text{I}$$

$\boxed{\mathbf{\Sigma; \Gamma; \Delta \vdash M \div S}}$

$$\frac{\Sigma; \Gamma; \cdot \vdash N : A}{\Sigma; \Gamma; \cdot \vdash !N \div !A}!\text{R} \qquad \frac{\Sigma; \Gamma; \Delta \vdash M \div S(t) \qquad \Sigma \vdash t \in \gamma}{\Sigma; \Gamma; \Delta \vdash [t, M] \div \exists i : \gamma.S(i)}\exists\text{R}$$

$$\frac{\Sigma; \Gamma; \Delta_1 \vdash M_1 \div S_1 \qquad \Sigma; \Gamma; \Delta_2 \vdash M_2 \div S_2}{\Sigma; \Gamma; \Delta_1, \Delta_2 \vdash M_1 \otimes M_2 \div S_1 \otimes S_2}\otimes\text{R}$$

$\boxed{\mathbf{\Sigma; \Gamma; \Delta \vdash E \div S}}$

$$\frac{\Sigma; \Gamma; \Delta_1 \vdash N : \{S\} \qquad \Sigma; \Gamma; \Delta_2; p : S \vdash E \div S'}{\Sigma; \Gamma; \Delta_1, \Delta_2 \vdash \underline{\texttt{let}}\ \{p : S\} = N\ \underline{\texttt{in}}\ E \div S'}\{\}\text{E}$$

$\boxed{\mathbf{\Sigma; \Gamma; \Delta; \Psi \vdash E \div S}}$

$$\frac{\Sigma; \Gamma; \Delta \vdash E \div S}{\Sigma; \Gamma; \Delta; \cdot \vdash E \div S}\div\div \qquad \frac{\Sigma; \Gamma, x : A; \Delta; \Psi \vdash E \div S}{\Sigma; \Gamma; \Delta; !x : !A, \Psi \vdash E \div S}!\text{L} \qquad \frac{\Sigma; \Gamma; \Delta; \Psi \vdash E \div S}{\Sigma; \Gamma; \Delta; \star : \mathbf{1}, \Psi \vdash E \div S}\mathbf{1}\text{L}$$

$$\frac{\Sigma; \Gamma; \Delta; p_1 : S_1, p_2 : S_2, \Psi \vdash E \div S}{\Sigma; \Gamma; \Delta; p_1 \otimes p_2 : S_1 \otimes S_2, \Psi \vdash E \div S}\otimes\text{L} \qquad \frac{\Sigma, i : \gamma; \Gamma; \Delta; p : S', \Psi \vdash E \div S}{\Sigma; \Gamma; \Delta; [i, p] : \exists i : \gamma.S', \Psi \vdash E \div S}\exists\text{L}\ (i\ \text{fresh})$$

Fig. 2. *f*CLL type system (selected rules)

classification in CLF's objects. Under the Curry-Howard isomorphism, terms are proofs of asynchronous types whereas monadic-terms and expressions are proofs of synchronous types that end with *introduction* rules and *elimination* rules respectively. A *f*CLL program is called closed if it does not contain any free term variables. Closed programs may contain free index variables.

Typing. Programs in *f*CLL are type-checked using four contexts – a context of index variables Σ, a context of linear variables Δ, a context of unrestricted variables Γ and a context of patterns Ψ. Only the last of these contexts is ordered. There are four typing judgments in the type system. We use the notation $N : A$, $M \div S$ and $E \div S$ for typing relations. Some interesting rules from these judgments are shown in figure 2. Type-checking for *f*CLL is decidable.

Operational Semantics. We use a call-by-value reduction semantics for *f*CLL. Figure 3 shows the definition of values in *f*CLL and some interesting reduction rules. The substitution relation $P[M_V/p]$ substitutes the monadic-value M_V for a pattern p in the program P. It is defined by induction on the pattern p. $P[V/x]$ and $P[t/i]$ are the usual capture avoiding substitutions for term and index variables respectively. In *f*CLL, the monad $\{E\}$ is a value because after we extend the language in section 4, expressions have effects. Reduction of the

Term values $V ::= \lambda x : A.N \mid \hat{\lambda} x : A.N \mid \{E\} \mid \Lambda i : \gamma.N$
Monadic values $M_V ::= V \mid M_{V_1} \otimes M_{V_2} \mid \star \mid !V \mid [t, M_V]$
Expression values $E_V ::= M_V$

$\boxed{\mathbf{P[M_V/p]}}$

$$P[\star/\star] = P \qquad P[[t, M_V]/[i, p]] = (P[t/i])[M_V/p]$$
$$P[!V/!x] = P[V/x] \qquad P[M_{V_1} \otimes M_{V_2}/p_1 \otimes p_2] = (P[M_{V_1}/p_1])[M_{V_2}/p_2]$$

$\boxed{\mathbf{N \rightsquigarrow N'}}$

$$\frac{}{(\Lambda i : \gamma.N)\ [t] \rightsquigarrow N[t/i]} \rightsquigarrow \Lambda \qquad \frac{}{(\lambda x : A.N)\ V \rightsquigarrow N[V/x]} \rightsquigarrow \lambda$$
$$\frac{}{(\hat{\lambda} x : A.N)\ \hat{}\ V \rightsquigarrow N[V/x]} \rightsquigarrow \hat{\lambda}$$

$\boxed{\mathbf{M \mapsto M'}}$

$$\frac{N \rightsquigarrow N'}{N \mapsto N'} \rightsquigarrow\mapsto \qquad \frac{N \rightsquigarrow N'}{!N \mapsto !N'} \mapsto ! \qquad \frac{M \mapsto M'}{[t, M] \mapsto [t, M']} \mapsto \exists$$
$$\frac{M_1 \mapsto M_1'}{M_1 \otimes M_2 \mapsto M_1' \otimes M_2} \mapsto \otimes_1 \qquad \frac{M_2 \mapsto M_2'}{M_1 \otimes M_2 \mapsto M_1 \otimes M_2'} \mapsto \otimes_2$$

$\boxed{\mathbf{\Sigma; E \hookrightarrow \Sigma; E'}}$

$$\frac{M \mapsto M'}{\Sigma; M \hookrightarrow \Sigma; M'} \mapsto\hookrightarrow \qquad \frac{}{\Sigma; \underline{\mathtt{let}}\ \{p : S\} = \{M_V\}\ \underline{\mathtt{in}}\ E \hookrightarrow \Sigma; E[M_V/p]} \hookrightarrow \mathit{LETRED}$$
$$\frac{N \rightsquigarrow N'}{\Sigma; \underline{\mathtt{let}}\ \{p : S\} = N\ \underline{\mathtt{in}}\ E \hookrightarrow \Sigma; \underline{\mathtt{let}}\ \{p : S\} = N'\ \underline{\mathtt{in}}\ E} \hookrightarrow \mathit{LET}_1$$
$$\frac{\Sigma; E \hookrightarrow \Sigma; E'}{\Sigma; \underline{\mathtt{let}}\ \{p : S\} = \{E\}\ \underline{\mathtt{in}}\ E_1 \hookrightarrow \underline{\mathtt{let}}\ \Sigma; \{p : S\} = \{E'\}\ \underline{\mathtt{in}}\ E_1} \hookrightarrow \mathit{LET}_2$$

Fig. 3. fCLL operational semantics (selected rules)

two components of a $\otimes$ can be interleaved arbitrarily, or it may performed in parallel.

Expressions are reduced in a context of index variables Σ. This context plays no role in fCLL, but when we extend fCLL to full-CLL in section 4, the context Σ becomes computationally significant. We state preservation and progress theorems for fCLL below.

Theorem 1 (Preservation for *f*CLL).
1. If $\Sigma; \Gamma; \Delta \vdash N : A$ and $N \rightsquigarrow N'$, then $\Sigma; \Gamma; \Delta \vdash N' : A$.
2. If $\Sigma; \Gamma; \Delta \vdash M \div S$ and $M \rightsquigarrow M'$, then $\Sigma; \Gamma; \Delta \vdash M' : S$.
3. If $\Sigma; \Gamma; \Delta \vdash E \div S$ and $\Sigma; E \hookrightarrow \Sigma; E'$, then $\Sigma; \Gamma; \Delta \vdash E' \div S$.

Theorem 2 (Progress for *f*CLL).
1. If $\Sigma; \cdot; \cdot \vdash N : A$ then either $N = V$ or $N \rightsquigarrow N'$ for some N'.
2. If $\Sigma; \cdot; \cdot \vdash M \div S$ then either $M = M_V$ or $M \mapsto M'$ for some M'.
3. If $\Sigma; \cdot; \cdot \vdash E \div S$ then either $E = E_V$ or $\Sigma; E \hookrightarrow \Sigma; E'$ for some E'.

Example 1 (Fibonacci numbers). As a simple example of programming in fCLL, we describe a function for computing Fibonacci numbers. These numbers are defined inductively as follows.

```
fib: int → {!int} = λn : int.
        if (n = 0 or n = 1) then {!1}
        else
        {
            let {!n₁} = fib (n − 1) in
            let {!n₂} = fib (n − 2) in
                !(n₁ + n₂)
        }
```

Fig. 4. The function `fib` in *f*CLL

$$fib(0) = fib(1) = 1 \qquad fib(n) = fib(n-1) + fib(n-2)$$

For implementing this definition as a function in *f*CLL, we assume that *f*CLL terms have been extended with integers having type `int`, named recursive functions and a conditional if-then-else construct. These can be added to *f*CLL in a straightforward manner. Figure 4 shows the *f*CLL function `fib` that computes the nth Fibonacci number. It has the type $\texttt{int} \to \{!\texttt{int}\}$. It is possible to write this function in a manner simpler than the one presented here, but we write it this way to highlight specific features of *f*CLL.

The most interesting computation in `fib`, including recursive calls, occurs inside the monad. Since the monad is evaluated lazily in *f*CLL, computation in `fib` will actually occur only when the caller of `fib` eliminates the monad from the returned value of type $\{!\texttt{int}\}$. Syntactically, elimination of the monadic constructor can occur only in expressions at the let construct. Hence the program that calls `fib` must be an expression. Here is an example of such a top level program that prints the 5th Fibonacci number: $\underline{\texttt{let}}\ \{!x\} = \texttt{fib}\ 5\ \underline{\texttt{in}}\ \texttt{print}(x)$.

3 *l*CLL: Concurrent Core of CLL

The concurrent core of CLL is called *l*CLL. It embeds the functional language *f*CLL directly. In the structure of concurrent computations *l*CLL is similar to the π-calculus. However it is different in other respects. First, it allows a direct representation of functional computation inside concurrent ones, as opposed to the use of complex encodings for doing the same in the π-calculus [20]. Second, the semantics of *l*CLL are directed by types, not terms. This, we believe, is a new idea that has not been explored before.

Syntax. We present *l*CLL as a chemical abstract machine (CHAM) [7]. *l*CLL programs are called configurations, denoted by $\mathcal{C}$. Figure 5 shows the syntax of *l*CLL configurations. Each configuration is made of four components, written $\Sigma; \hat{\sigma} \rhd \hat{\Gamma} \,\|\, \hat{\Delta}$. Σ is a context of index variables, as defined in section 2. $\hat{\sigma}$ is a sorted substitution mapping index variables to index terms. $\hat{\Gamma}$ is a set of closed *f*CLL term values along with their types. $\hat{\Delta}$ is a multiset of closed *f*CLL programs together with their types. We require that whenever $N : A \in \hat{\Delta}$, N have the type $A[\hat{\sigma}]$, where $A[\hat{\sigma}]$ is the result of applying the substitution $\hat{\sigma}$ to the type A. Similar conditions hold for monadic-terms and expressions in $\hat{\Delta}$ and term values in $\hat{\Gamma}$. Formally, a configuration $\Sigma; \hat{\sigma} \rhd \hat{\Gamma} \,\|\, \hat{\Delta}$ is said to be well-formed if it satisfies the following conditions.

Configurations	$\mathcal{C}$	$::= \Sigma; \hat{\sigma} \triangleright \hat{\Gamma} \parallel \hat{\Delta}$
Global index names	Σ	$::= \cdot \mid \Sigma, i : \gamma$
Local name substitutions	$\hat{\sigma}$	$::= \cdot \mid \hat{\sigma}, t/i : \gamma$
Unrestricted solutions	$\hat{\Gamma}$	$::= \cdot \mid \hat{\Gamma}, V : A$
Linear solutions	$\hat{\Delta}$	$::= \cdot \mid \hat{\Delta}, N : A \mid \hat{\Delta}, M \div S \mid \hat{\Delta}, E \div S$

Fig. 5. lCLL syntax

1. If $(t/i : \gamma) \in \hat{\sigma}$, then $i \notin \mathtt{dom}(\Sigma)$ and $\Sigma \vdash t \in \gamma$.
2. If P is a program in $\hat{\Gamma}$ or $\hat{\Delta}$, then $\mathtt{fv}(P) \cap \mathtt{dom}(\hat{\sigma}) = \phi$.
3. If $V : A \in \hat{\Gamma}$, then $\Sigma; \cdot; \cdot \vdash V : A[\hat{\sigma}]$.
4. If $N : A \in \hat{\Delta}$, then $\Sigma; \cdot; \cdot \vdash N : A[\hat{\sigma}]$.
5. If $M \div S \in \hat{\Delta}$, then $\Sigma; \cdot; \cdot \vdash M \div S[\hat{\sigma}]$.
6. If $E \div S \in \hat{\Delta}$, then $\Sigma; \cdot; \cdot \vdash E \div S[\hat{\sigma}]$.

We assume that all our configurations are well-formed. Programs in $\hat{\Delta}$ and values in $\hat{\Gamma}$ are collectively called processes. Intuitively, we view programs in $\hat{\Delta}$ as concurrent processes that are executing simultaneously. $\hat{\Delta}$ is called a linear solution because these processes are single-use in the sense that they can neither be replicated, nor destroyed. Term values in $\hat{\Gamma}$ are viewed as irreducible processes (like functional abstractions) that are replicable. For this reason $\hat{\Gamma}$ is also called an unrestricted solution. The context Σ can be viewed as a set of global index names, that are known to have specific sorts. The domain of the substitution $\hat{\sigma}$ can be viewed as a set of local (private) index names that are created during the evaluation of the configuration. The substitution $\hat{\sigma}$ maps these local index names to index terms that depend only on the global names (see condition (1) for well-formedness above).

3.1 Semantics of lCLL

The semantics of lCLL are rewrite rules that allow a configuration to step to other configuration(s). The specific rules that apply to a particular configuration are determined by the *types* of processes in that configuration. In this sense, these rules are type-directed. We classify rewrite rules into three classes – functional, structural and synchronization.

Functional rules. Functional rules allow reduction of programs in the linear solution $\hat{\Delta}$. We denote them using the arrow $\twoheadrightarrow$. Figure 6 shows the functional rewrite rules for lCLL configurations. There are three rules, one for reducing programs in each of the three syntactic classes of fCLL. Reductions of different programs in $\hat{\Delta}$ can be performed in parallel. This supports the idea that programs in $\hat{\Delta}$ can be viewed as processes executing simultaneously.

Structural rules. Structural rules apply to those irreducible programs in $\hat{\Delta}$ that have synchronous types. These are exactly the monadic values M_V. A structural rule decomposes a monadic value into smaller monadic values. We denote structural rules with the arrow $\rightharpoonup$. All structural rules for rewriting lCLL configurations are shown in figure 7. Unlike most CHAMs, our structural rules are not reversible.

$$\frac{N \rightsquigarrow N'}{\Sigma; \hat{\sigma} \triangleright \hat{\Gamma} \parallel \hat{\Delta}, N : A \twoheadrightarrow \Sigma; \hat{\sigma} \triangleright \hat{\Gamma} \parallel \hat{\Delta}, N' : A} \twoheadrightarrow\rightsquigarrow$$

$$\frac{M \mapsto M'}{\Sigma; \hat{\sigma} \triangleright \hat{\Gamma} \parallel \hat{\Delta}, M \div S \twoheadrightarrow \Sigma; \hat{\sigma} \triangleright \hat{\Gamma} \parallel \hat{\Delta}, M' \div S} \twoheadrightarrow\mapsto$$

$$\frac{\Sigma; E \hookrightarrow \Sigma; E'}{\Sigma; \hat{\sigma} \triangleright \hat{\Gamma} \parallel \hat{\Delta}, E \div S \twoheadrightarrow \Sigma; \hat{\sigma} \triangleright \hat{\Gamma} \parallel \hat{\Delta}, E' \div S} \twoheadrightarrow\hookrightarrow$$

Fig. 6. Functional rewrite rules for *l*CLL configurations

$$\begin{array}{rcll}
\Sigma; \hat{\sigma} \triangleright \hat{\Gamma} \parallel \hat{\Delta}, (M_{V_1} \otimes M_{V_2}) \div (S_1 \otimes S_2) & \rightharpoonup & \Sigma; \hat{\sigma} \triangleright \hat{\Gamma} \parallel \hat{\Delta}, M_{V_1} \div S_1, M_{V_2} \div S_2 & (\rightharpoonup \otimes) \\
\Sigma; \hat{\sigma} \triangleright \hat{\Gamma} \parallel \hat{\Delta}, \star \div \mathbf{1} & \rightharpoonup & \Sigma; \hat{\sigma} \triangleright \hat{\Gamma} \parallel \hat{\Delta} & (\rightharpoonup \mathbf{1}) \\
\Sigma; \hat{\sigma} \triangleright \hat{\Gamma} \parallel \hat{\Delta}, [t, M_V] \div \exists i : \gamma.S(i) & \rightharpoonup & \Sigma; \hat{\sigma}, t/i : \gamma \triangleright \hat{\Gamma} \parallel \hat{\Delta}, M_V \div S(i) & (\rightharpoonup \exists) \\
& & (i \text{ fresh}) & \\
\Sigma; \hat{\sigma} \triangleright \hat{\Gamma} \parallel \hat{\Delta}, !V \div !A & \rightharpoonup & \Sigma; \hat{\sigma} \triangleright \hat{\Gamma}, V : A \parallel \hat{\Delta} & (\rightharpoonup !) \\
\Sigma; \hat{\sigma} \triangleright \hat{\Gamma} \parallel \hat{\Delta}, V \div A & \rightharpoonup & \Sigma; \hat{\sigma} \triangleright \hat{\Gamma} \parallel \hat{\Delta}, V : A & (\rightharpoonup \div) \\
\Sigma; \hat{\sigma} \triangleright \hat{\Gamma} \parallel \hat{\Delta}, M_V \div S & \rightharpoonup & \Sigma; \hat{\sigma} \triangleright \hat{\Gamma} \parallel \hat{\Delta}, M_V \div S & (\rightharpoonup \div)
\end{array}$$

Fig. 7. Structural rewrite rules for *l*CLL configurations

The rule $\rightharpoonup \otimes$ splits the monadic value $M_{V_1} \otimes M_{V_2}$ of type $S_1 \otimes S_2$ into two monadic values M_{V_1} and M_{V_2} of types S_1 and S_2 respectively. Intuitively, we can view $M_{V_1} \otimes M_{V_2}$ as a parallel composition of the processes M_{V_1} and M_{V_2}. The rule $\rightharpoonup \otimes$ splits this parallel composition into its components, allowing each component to rewrite separately.

In the rule $\rightharpoonup \exists$, there is a side condition that i must be fresh i.e. it must not occur anywhere except in $S(i)$. Some α-renaming may have to be performed to enforce this. In *l*CLL, the $\exists$ type acts as a local index name creator. The rule $\rightharpoonup \exists$ creates the new index name i and records the fact that i is actually bound to the index term t in the substitution $\hat{\sigma}$.

The rule $\rightharpoonup !$ moves a program of type $!A$ to the unrestricted solution, thus allowing multiple uses of this program. For this reason, the type $!A$ serves as a replication construct in *l*CLL. The rules $\rightharpoonup \div$ and $\rightharpoonup \div$ change the type ascription for programs that have been coerced from one syntactic class to another.

Synchronization Rules. Synchronization rules act on values in $\hat{\Gamma}$ and $\hat{\Delta}$ having asynchronous types. These are exactly the term values V. Synchronization rules are denoted by the arrow $\longrightarrow$. Figure 8 shows the two synchronization rules. The rule $\longrightarrow \{\}$ eliminates the monadic constructor $\{\}$ from values $\{E\}$ of asynchronous type $\{S\}$.

The second rule $\longrightarrow\Longrightarrow$ performs synchronization of several term values at the same time. It uses an auxiliary judgment $\Sigma; \hat{\sigma} \triangleright \hat{\Gamma} \parallel \hat{\Delta} \Longrightarrow N : A$, which we call the sync judgment. The rules of this judgment are also shown in figure 8. The sync judgment links values in $\hat{\Gamma}$ and $\hat{\Delta}$ to form a more complex program N.

Synchronization rules, $\Sigma; \hat{\sigma} \triangleright \hat{\Gamma} \mid \hat{\Delta} \longrightarrow \Sigma; \hat{\sigma} \triangleright \hat{\Gamma} \mid \hat{\Delta}'$

$$\frac{}{\Sigma; \hat{\sigma} \triangleright \hat{\Gamma} \mid \hat{\Delta}, \{E\} : \{S\} \longrightarrow \Sigma; \hat{\sigma} \triangleright \hat{\Gamma} \mid \hat{\Delta}, E \div S} \longrightarrow \{\}$$

$$\frac{\Sigma; \hat{\sigma} \triangleright \hat{\Gamma} \mid \hat{\Delta} \Longrightarrow N : \{S\}}{\Sigma; \hat{\sigma} \triangleright \hat{\Gamma} \mid \hat{\Delta}, \hat{\Delta}' \longrightarrow \Sigma; \hat{\sigma} \triangleright \hat{\Gamma} \mid N : \{S\}, \hat{\Delta}'} \longrightarrow\Longrightarrow$$

Sync judgment, $\Sigma; \hat{\sigma} \triangleright \hat{\Gamma} \mid \hat{\Delta} \Longrightarrow N : A$

$$\frac{}{\Sigma; \hat{\sigma} \triangleright \hat{\Gamma} \mid V : A \Longrightarrow V : A} \Longrightarrow HYP1 \qquad \frac{}{\Sigma; \hat{\sigma} \triangleright \hat{\Gamma}, V : A \mid \cdot \Longrightarrow V : A} \Longrightarrow HYP2$$

$$\frac{\Sigma \cup \mathtt{dom}(\hat{\sigma}) \vdash t \in \gamma \qquad \Sigma; \hat{\sigma} \triangleright \hat{\Gamma} \mid \hat{\Delta} \Longrightarrow N : \forall i : \gamma. A(i)}{\Sigma; \hat{\sigma} \triangleright \hat{\Gamma} \mid \hat{\Delta} \Longrightarrow N\ [t[\hat{\sigma}]] : A(t)} \Longrightarrow \forall$$

$$\frac{\Sigma; \hat{\sigma} \triangleright \hat{\Gamma} \mid \hat{\Delta}_1 \Longrightarrow N_1 : A \qquad \Sigma; \hat{\sigma} \triangleright \hat{\Gamma} \mid \hat{\Delta}_2 \Longrightarrow N_2 : A \multimap B}{\Sigma; \hat{\sigma} \triangleright \hat{\Gamma} \mid \hat{\Delta}_1, \hat{\Delta}_2 \Longrightarrow N_2 \ \hat{}\ N_1 : B} \Longrightarrow\multimap$$

$$\frac{\Sigma; \hat{\sigma} \triangleright \hat{\Gamma} \mid \cdot \Longrightarrow N_1 : A \qquad \Sigma; \hat{\sigma} \triangleright \hat{\Gamma} \mid \hat{\Delta} \Longrightarrow N_2 : A \rightarrow B}{\Sigma; \hat{\sigma} \triangleright \hat{\Gamma} \mid \hat{\Delta} \Longrightarrow N_2\ N_1 : B} \Longrightarrow\rightarrow$$

Fig. 8. Synchronization rewrite rules for lCLL configurations

We call this process synchronization. Synchronization uses values in $\hat{\Delta}$ exactly once, while those in $\hat{\Gamma}$ may be used zero or more times.

In the rule $\longrightarrow\Longrightarrow$ shown in figure 8, $\hat{\Delta}$ denotes a subset of the linear solution that participates in the synchronization. The remaining solution $\hat{\Delta}'$ is kept as is. Some backward reasoning is performed in the judgment $\Longrightarrow$ to produce the linked program N of type $\{S\}$. This is the essential point here – the result of a synchronization must be of type $\{S\}$.

The semantic rewriting relation for lCLL is defined as $\rightrightarrows = \twoheadrightarrow \cup \rightharpoonup \cup \longrightarrow$. It satisfies the following type preservation theorem.

Theorem 3 (Preservation for lCLL). If $\mathcal{C}$ is a well-formed configuration and $\mathcal{C} \rightrightarrows \mathcal{C}'$, then $\mathcal{C}'$ is also well-formed.

Concurrent computation as proof search. Given a lCLL configuration $\mathcal{C} = \Sigma; \hat{\sigma} \triangleright \hat{\Gamma} \mid \hat{\Delta}$, types in $\hat{\Delta}[\hat{\sigma}]$ and $\hat{\Gamma}[\hat{\sigma}]$ can be viewed as propositions that are *simultaneously true*, in a linear and unrestricted sense respectively. Using the Curry-Howard isomorphism, the corresponding programs in $\hat{\Delta}[\hat{\sigma}]$ and $\hat{\Gamma}[\hat{\sigma}]$ can be seen as specific proofs of these propositions. The sync judgment (figure 8) is actually a linear entailment judgment – if $\Sigma; \hat{\sigma} \triangleright \hat{\Gamma} \mid \hat{\Delta} \Longrightarrow N : A$, then from the unrestricted assumptions in $\hat{\Gamma}[\hat{\sigma}]$ and linear assumptions in $\hat{\Delta}[\hat{\sigma}]$, $A[\hat{\sigma}]$ can be proved in linear logic. The term N synthesized by this judgment is a proof of the proposition $A[\hat{\sigma}]$. As a result, each use of the synchronization rule $\longrightarrow\Longrightarrow$ can be viewed as a step of proof search in linear logic that uses several known facts to conclude a new fact, together with its proof term. By the Curry-Howard isomorphism, the proof term is a well-typed program that can be functionally reduced again.

More specifically, each use of $\longrightarrow\!\!\!\Longrightarrow$ corresponds to a single focusing step for eliminating asynchronous constructors from a proposition that has $\{S\}$ in the head position. For a detailed description of this see [10].

Example 2 (Client-Server Communication). We illustrate concurrent programming in *l*CLL with an example of a client-server interaction. The server described here listens to client requests to compute Fibonacci numbers. Each request contains an integer n. Given a request, the server computes the nth Fibonacci number and returns this value to the client.

We model communication through asynchronous message passing. Assume that all clients and the server have unique identities, which are index names from a special sort called `procid`. The identity of the server is *serv*. A message from one process to another contains three parts – the identity of the sender, the identity of the recipient and an integer, which is the content of the message. Messages are modeled using a type constructor `mess` and a term constructor `message` having the kind and type shown in figure 9. For every pair of index terms i and j of sort `procid` and every integer n, we view the value (`message` $[i]$ $[j]$ n) of type (`mess` i j) as a message having content n from the process with identity i to the process with identity j. In order to extract the integer content of a message, we use the destructor `fetchmessage` that has the reduction rule `fetchmessage` $[i]$ $[j]$ ^ (`message` $[i]$ $[j]$ n) $\rightsquigarrow$ $\{!n\}$.

The server program called `fibserver` is shown in figure 9. It waits for a message m from any client i. Then it extracts the content n from the message, computes the nth Fibonacci number using the function `fib` defined in example 1 and returns this computed value to the client i as a message. `fibserver` has the type `fibservtype` $= \forall i:$ `procid`. `mess` i $serv \multimap \{$`mess` $serv$ $i\}$.

A sequence of rewrite steps in *l*CLL using `fibserver` is shown in figure 9. The initial configuration contains `fibserver` and a message to `fibserver` containing the integer 6 from a client having identity k. For brevity, we omit the client process. The crucial rewrite in this sequence is the first one, where the synchronization rule $\longrightarrow\!\!\!\Longrightarrow$ is used to link the `fibserver` program with the message for it. Rewriting ends with a message containing the value of the 6th Fibonacci number (namely 13) from `fibserver` to the requesting client k.

3.2 An Encoding of the π-Calculus in *l*CLL

We describe a translation of a variant of the asynchronous π-calculus [8] to *l*CLL. The syntax and semantics of this variant are shown in figure 10. It extends the asynchronous π-calculus with a nil process 0. The replication operator ! is restricted to actions only.

Two translations $\ulcorner \cdot \urcorner$ and $\ulcorner\!\ulcorner \cdot \urcorner\!\urcorner$ are shown in figure 11. They map π-calculus entities to programs and types of *fCLL* respectively. We model channels as index terms of a specific sort `chan`. In order to translate $\bar{x}y$, which is an output message, we introduce a type constructor `out` and a related term constructor `output`, whose kind and type are shown in figure 11. The translations of $\bar{x}y$ to terms and types are `output` $[x]$ $[y]$ and `out` x y respectively.

Additional Signature

$$\begin{array}{l} \texttt{procid: sort} \\ serv : \texttt{procid} \\ \texttt{mess: procid} \to \texttt{procid} \to \texttt{Type} \\ \texttt{message: } \forall i : \texttt{procid}.\ \forall j : \texttt{procid}.\ \texttt{int} \to \texttt{mess}\ i\ j \\ \texttt{fetchmessage: } \forall i : \texttt{procid}.\ \forall j : \texttt{procid}.\ \texttt{mess}\ i\ j \multimap \{!\texttt{int}\} \\ \texttt{fetchmessage}\ [i]\ [j]\ \hat{}\ (\texttt{message}\ [i]\ [j]\ n) \ \leadsto\ \{!n\} \end{array}$$

Fibonacci Server

$$\begin{array}{l} \texttt{fibservtype} = \forall i : \texttt{procid}.\ \texttt{mess}\ i\ serv \multimap \{\texttt{mess}\ serv\ i\} \\ \texttt{fibserver: fibservtype} = \Lambda i : \texttt{procid}.\ \hat{\lambda} m : \texttt{mess}\ i\ serv. \\ \quad \{ \\ \qquad \underline{\texttt{let}}\ \{!n\} = \texttt{fetchmessage}\ [i]\ [serv]\ \hat{}\ m\ \underline{\texttt{in}} \\ \qquad \underline{\texttt{let}}\ \{!v\} = \texttt{fib}\ (n)\ \underline{\texttt{in}} \\ \qquad\quad (\texttt{message}\ [serv]\ [i]\ v) \\ \quad \} \end{array}$$

Sample Execution ($\Sigma = serv : \texttt{procid},\ k : \texttt{procid}$)

$$\begin{array}{ll} & \Sigma; \cdot \rhd \cdot \,\|\, \texttt{fibserver} : \texttt{fibservtype},\ (\texttt{message}\ [k]\ [serv]\ 6) : \texttt{mess}\ k\ serv \\ \longrightarrow & \Sigma; \cdot \rhd \cdot \,\|\, \texttt{fibserver}\ [k]\ \hat{}\ (\texttt{message}\ [k]\ [serv]\ 6) : \{\texttt{mess}\ serv\ k\} \\ \twoheadrightarrow^* & \Sigma; \cdot \rhd \cdot \,\|\, \left(\begin{array}{l} \{\ \underline{\texttt{let}}\ \{!n\} = \texttt{fetchmessage}\ [k]\ [serv]\ \hat{}\ (\texttt{message}\ [k]\ [serv]\ 6)\ \underline{\texttt{in}} \\ \quad \underline{\texttt{let}}\ \{!v\} = \texttt{fib}\ (n)\ \underline{\texttt{in}}\ (\texttt{message}\ [serv]\ [k]\ v) \\ \}\ :\ \{\texttt{mess}\ serv\ k\} \end{array} \right) \\ \longrightarrow & \Sigma; \cdot \rhd \cdot \,\|\, \left(\begin{array}{l} (\ \underline{\texttt{let}}\ \{!n\} = \texttt{fetchmessage}\ [k]\ [serv]\ \hat{}\ (\texttt{message}\ [k]\ [serv]\ 6)\ \underline{\texttt{in}} \\ \quad \underline{\texttt{let}}\ \{!v\} = \texttt{fib}\ (n)\ \underline{\texttt{in}}\ (\texttt{message}\ [serv]\ [k]\ v) \\ )\ \div\ \texttt{mess}\ serv\ k \end{array} \right) \\ \twoheadrightarrow^* & \Sigma; \cdot \rhd \cdot \,\|\, (\underline{\texttt{let}}\ \{!v\} = \texttt{fib}\ (6)\ \underline{\texttt{in}}\ (\texttt{message}\ [serv]\ [k]\ v)) \div \texttt{mess}\ serv\ k \\ \twoheadrightarrow^* & \Sigma; \cdot \rhd \cdot \,\|\, (\texttt{message}\ [serv]\ [k]\ 13) \div \texttt{mess}\ serv\ k \\ \rightharpoonup^2 & \Sigma; \cdot \rhd \cdot \,\|\, (\texttt{message}\ [serv]\ [k]\ 13) : \texttt{mess}\ serv\ k \end{array}$$

Fig. 9. Server for computing Fibonacci numbers in lCLL

Syntax

$$\begin{array}{lrl} \text{Actions} & A & ::= \bar{x}y \mid x(y).P \\ \text{Processes} & P, Q & ::= A \mid !A \mid P|P \mid \nu x.P \mid 0 \\ \text{Molecules} & m & ::= P \mid \nu x.S \\ \text{Solutions} & S & ::= \phi \mid S \uplus \{m\} \end{array}$$

Equations on terms and solutions

$$\nu x.P = \nu y.P[y/x] \quad (y \notin P) \qquad\qquad \nu x.S = \nu y.S[y/x] \quad (y \notin S)$$

CHAM semantics

$$\begin{array}{lll} P_1|P_2 \rightleftharpoons P_1, P_2 & x(y).P\ ,\ \bar{x}z \to & P[z/y] \\ 0 \rightleftharpoons & \nu x.P & \rightleftharpoons \nu x.\{P\} \\ !A \rightleftharpoons !A, A & (\nu x.P)|Q & \rightleftharpoons \nu x.(P|Q) \qquad (x \notin Q) \end{array}$$

Reduction semantics

$$P \equiv P' \ \Leftrightarrow\ P \rightleftharpoons^* P' \qquad\qquad P \to P' \ \Leftrightarrow\ P \rightleftharpoons^* \to \rightleftharpoons^* P'$$

Fig. 10. A variant of the asynchronous π-calculus

To translate $x(y).P$, we introduce a term destructor `destroyout` corresponding to the constructor `output`. Its type and reduction rule are shown in figure 11. The translation $\ulcorner x(y).P \urcorner$ waits for two inputs – the channel name y and a mes-

Additional Signature

$\texttt{chan}$: sort
$\texttt{out}$: $\texttt{chan} \rightarrow \texttt{chan} \rightarrow \texttt{Type}$
$\texttt{output}$: $\forall x : \texttt{chan}.\ \forall y : \texttt{chan}.\ \texttt{out}\ x\ y$
$\texttt{destroyout}$: $\forall x : \texttt{chan}.\ \forall y : \texttt{chan}.\ \texttt{out}\ x\ y \multimap \{\mathbf{1}\}$
$\texttt{destroyout}\ [x]\ [y]\ \hat{}\ (\texttt{output}\ [x]\ [y]) \rightsquigarrow \{\star\}$
$c_{\texttt{chan}} : \texttt{chan}$

A/P	fCLL Type, $\ulcorner\ulcorner A/P \urcorner\urcorner$	fCLL Program, $\ulcorner A/P \urcorner$
$\bar{x}y$	$\texttt{out}\ x\ y$	$\texttt{output}\ [x]\ [y]$
$x(y).P$	$\forall y : \texttt{chan}.\ \texttt{out}\ x\ y \multimap \{\ulcorner\ulcorner P \urcorner\urcorner\}$	$\Lambda y : \texttt{chan}.\ \hat{\lambda} m : \texttt{out}\ x\ y.$ $\{$ $\underline{\texttt{let}}\ \{\star\} = \texttt{destroyout}\ [x]\ [y]\ \hat{}\ m$ $\underline{\texttt{in}}\ \ulcorner P \urcorner$ $\}$
0	$\mathbf{1}$	$\star$
$!A$	$!\ \ulcorner\ulcorner A \urcorner\urcorner$	$!\ \ulcorner A \urcorner$
$P_1 \mid P_2$	$\ulcorner\ulcorner P_1 \urcorner\urcorner \otimes \ulcorner\ulcorner P_2 \urcorner\urcorner$	$\ulcorner P_1 \urcorner \otimes \ulcorner P_2 \urcorner$
$\nu x.P$	$\exists x : \texttt{chan}.\ulcorner\ulcorner P \urcorner\urcorner$	$[c_{\texttt{chan}},\ (\ulcorner P \urcorner [c_{\texttt{chan}}/x])]$

Fig. 11. Translation of the π-calculus

sage m that corresponds to the translation of $\bar{x}y$. It then discards the message m and starts the process P.

Translations of $!A$, $P_1|P_2$ and 0 are straightforward. We translate $\nu x.P$ to the type $\exists x : \texttt{chan}.\ulcorner\ulcorner P \urcorner\urcorner$. To translate $\nu x.P$ to a program, we assume that there is an index constant $c_{\texttt{chan}}$ of sort $\texttt{chan}$. Then we translate $\nu x.P$ to $[c_{\texttt{chan}},\ (\ulcorner P \urcorner [c_{\texttt{chan}}/x])]$, which has the type $\exists x : \texttt{chan}.\ulcorner\ulcorner P \urcorner\urcorner$.

For any π-calculus process P, $\texttt{fn}(P) : \texttt{chan}; \cdot; \cdot \vdash \ulcorner P \urcorner \div \ulcorner\ulcorner P \urcorner\urcorner$. The translation of a π-calculus process P to lCLL is defined as the configuration $\langle P \rangle = \texttt{fn}(P) : \texttt{chan}; \cdot \rhd \cdot \parallel \ulcorner P \urcorner \div \ulcorner\ulcorner P \urcorner\urcorner$. Although we have not formally proved it, we believe that the following correctness result holds for this translation: $P \rightarrow^* P'$ iff there is a lCLL configuration $\mathcal{C}$ such that $\langle P \rangle \rightrightarrows^* \mathcal{C}$ and $\langle P' \rangle \rightharpoonup^* \mathcal{C}$.

4 Full-CLL: The Complete Language

Full-CLL is an extension of fCLL that allows lCLL's concurrent computations inside functional ones. This is done by extending fCLL expressions by a single construct – $\underline{\texttt{link}}\ E \div S\ \underline{\texttt{to}}\ G$. $G \in \{A, !A, \mathbf{1}\}$ is called a goal type. Additional syntax and semantics for this construct are shown in figure 12. Other than the $\underline{\texttt{link}}$ construct, full-CLL inherits all of fCLL's syntax, typing rules and semantics.

$\underline{\texttt{link}}\ E \div S\ \underline{\texttt{to}}\ G$ is evaluated in a context of index variables Σ as follows. First, the lCLL configuration $\mathcal{C} = \Sigma; \cdot \rhd \cdot \parallel E \div S$ is created and allowed to rewrite according to the relation $\rightrightarrows$ till it reaches a *quiescent* configuration $\mathcal{C}'$. By quiescent we mean that no rewrite rule applies to $\mathcal{C}'$ i.e. $\mathcal{C}'$ is in $\rightrightarrows$-normal form. After $\mathcal{C}'$ is obtained, the result of evaluating $\underline{\texttt{link}}\ E \div S\ \underline{\texttt{to}}\ G$ depends on the goal type G.

Syntax

$$\text{Expressions } E ::= \ldots \mid \underline{\texttt{link}}\ E \div S\ \underline{\texttt{to}}\ G$$
$$\text{Goal Types } G ::= A \mid !A \mid \mathbf{1}$$

Typing rules

$$\frac{\Sigma; \Gamma; \Delta \vdash E \div S}{\Sigma; \Gamma; \Delta \vdash (\underline{\texttt{link}}\ E \div S\ \underline{\texttt{to}}\ G) \div G}\ \textit{LINK}$$

Operational Semantics

$$\frac{\Sigma; \cdot \rhd \cdot \mid E \div S \rightrightarrows^* \Sigma; \hat{\sigma} \rhd \hat{\Gamma} \mid V : A}{\Sigma; \underline{\texttt{link}}\ E \div S\ \underline{\texttt{to}}\ A \hookrightarrow \Sigma; V} \hookrightarrow_1 \qquad \frac{\Sigma; \cdot \rhd \cdot \mid E \div S \rightrightarrows^* \Sigma; \hat{\sigma} \rhd \hat{\Gamma}, V : A \mid \cdot}{\Sigma; \underline{\texttt{link}}\ E \div S\ \underline{\texttt{to}}\ A \hookrightarrow \Sigma; V} \hookrightarrow_2$$

$$\frac{\Sigma; \cdot \rhd \cdot \mid E \div S \rightrightarrows^* \Sigma; \hat{\sigma} \rhd \hat{\Gamma}, V : A \mid \cdot}{\Sigma; \underline{\texttt{link}}\ E \div S\ \underline{\texttt{to}}\ !A \hookrightarrow \Sigma; !V} \hookrightarrow_3 \qquad \frac{\Sigma; \cdot \rhd \cdot \mid E \div S \rightrightarrows^* \Sigma; \hat{\sigma} \rhd \hat{\Gamma} \mid \cdot}{\Sigma; \underline{\texttt{link}}\ E \div S\ \underline{\texttt{to}}\ \mathbf{1} \hookrightarrow \Sigma; \star} \hookrightarrow_4$$

Fig. 12. Full-CLL syntax and semantics

1. If $G = A$ and $\mathcal{C}' = \Sigma; \hat{\sigma} \rhd \hat{\Gamma} \mid V : A$ or $\mathcal{C}' = \Sigma; \hat{\sigma} \rhd \hat{\Gamma}, V : A \mid \cdot$, then $\underline{\texttt{link}}\ E \div S\ \underline{\texttt{to}}\ G$ evaluates to V.
2. If $G = !A$ and $\mathcal{C}' = \Sigma; \hat{\sigma} \rhd \hat{\Gamma}, V : A \mid \cdot$, then $\underline{\texttt{link}}\ E \div S\ \underline{\texttt{to}}\ G$ evaluates to $!V$.
3. If $G = \mathbf{1}$ and $\mathcal{C}' = \Sigma; \hat{\sigma} \rhd \hat{\Gamma} \mid \cdot$, then $\underline{\texttt{link}}\ E \div S\ \underline{\texttt{to}}\ G$ evaluates to $\star$.

All these conditions are summarized in figure 12. If none of these conditions hold, evaluation of the $\underline{\texttt{link}}$ construct fails and computation deadlocks. We call this condition *link failure.* Since expressions are coerced into terms through a monad, link failure never occurs during evaluation of terms and monadic-terms. As a result, full-CLL has the following progress theorem.

Theorem 4 (Progress for full-CLL).
1. If $\Sigma; \cdot; \cdot \vdash N : A$ then either $N = V$ or $N \rightsquigarrow N'$ for some N'.
2. If $\Sigma; \cdot; \cdot \vdash M \div S$ then either $M = M_V$ or $M \mapsto M'$ for some M'.
3. If $\Sigma; \cdot; \cdot \vdash E \div S$ then either $E = E_V$ or $\Sigma; E \hookrightarrow \Sigma; E'$ for some E' or reduction of $\Sigma; E$ deadlocks due to link failure.

Link failure is easy to detect at runtime and can be handled, for example, by throwing an exception. For all practical problems that we encountered, we found it possible to write programs in which link failure never occurs. fCLL's preservation theorem (theorem 1) holds for full-CLL also.

Example 3 (Fibonacci numbers in full-CLL). Figure 13 shows a concurrent implementation of Fibonacci numbers in full-CLL. The function `fibc` uses the additional signature from example 2 and assumes that the sort `procid` contains at least three constants k_1, k_2 and k. `fibc` has the type `int` $\rightarrow$ {`!int`}. Given an input integer $n \geq 2$, `fibc` computes the nth Fibonacci number using a $\underline{\texttt{link}}$ construct that starts concurrent computation with a tensor of three processes having identities k_1, k_2 and k respectively. The first two processes recursively compute $fib(n-1)$ and $fib(n-2)$ and send these values as messages to the third process. The third process waits for these messages (m_1 and m_2), extracts their integer contents and adds them together to obtain $fib(n)$. This becomes the result of evaluation of the $\underline{\texttt{link}}$ construct.

During the evaluation of `fibc`, each of the two recursive calls can encounter a $\underline{\texttt{link}}$ construct and create a nested lCLL concurrent computation. Since the two

```
fibc = λn : int.
  if (n = 0 or n = 1) then {!1}
  else
  { link
     (
          {let {!n1} = fibc (n − 1) in (message [k1] [k] n1)}
        ⊗ {let {!n2} = fibc (n − 2) in (message [k2] [k] n2)}
        ⊗ λ̂m1 : mess k1 k. λ̂m2 : mess k2 k.
          {
             let {!x} = fetchmessage [k1] [k] ^ m1 in
             let {!y} = fetchmessage [k2] [k] ^ m2 in
               !(x + y)
          }
     ) ÷ {mess k1 k} ⊗ {mess k2 k} ⊗ (mess k1 k ⊸ mess k2 k ⊸ {!int})
     to !int
  }
```

Fig. 13. The function `fibc` in full-CLL

recursive calls can be executed simultaneously, there may actually be more than one nested *l*CLL configuration at the same time. However, these configurations are distinct – processes in one configuration cannot synchronize with those in another. In general, full-CLL programs can spawn several nested concurrent computations that are completely disjoint from each other.

5 Conclusion

We have presented a language that combines functional and concurrent computation in a logically motivated manner. It requires linearity, a restricted form of dependent types, a monad, and focusing, in order to retain the desirable properties of each paradigm in their combination.

Perhaps the biggest limitation of our work is that the logic underlying the type system is not strong enough to express many useful properties of concurrent programs like deadlock freedom. This is clearly visible in the fact that full-CLL does not have a progress theorem as strong as that of its functional core *f*CLL. Our types represent only basic structural properties of concurrent processes. At the same time, due to the presence of dependent and linear types, the type system can be used to express very strong functional guarantees about various components of a concurrent program. Finding a logic that can express useful properties of both functional and concurrent computation and converting it to a programming language using the Curry-Howard isomorphism is a challenge at present. Another challenge is to build a realistic implementation of CLL, including a more complete functional language and type reconstruction to see if our ideas scale in practice. Since concurrency in CLL is somewhat low-level, it will be important to build up libraries of common idioms in order to write large programs conveniently.

References

1. CLL implementation. Available electronically from http://www.cs.cmu.edu/~dg.
2. M. Abadi and C. Fournet. Mobile values, new names, and secure communication. In *Proc. of POPL'01*, pages 104–115, 2001.
3. S. Abramsky. Computational interpretations of linear logic. *Theoretical Computer Science*, 111(1–2):3–57, 1993.
4. S. Abramsky, S. Gay, and R. Nagarajan. Specification structures and propositions-as-types for concurrency. In *Logics for Concurrency: Structure vs. Automata—Proc. of the VIIIth Banff Higher Order Workshop*, volume 1043 of *Lecture Notes in Computer Science*. Springer-Verlag, 1996.
5. J.-M. Andreoli. Logic programming with focusing proofs in linear logic. *Journal of Logic and Computation*, 2(3):297–347, 1992.
6. J.-M. Andreoli and R. Pareschi. Communication as fair distribution of knowledge. Technical Report ECRC-91-12, European Computer-Industry Research Centre, 1991.
7. G. Berry and G. Boudol. The chemical abstract machine. *Theoretical Computer Science*, 96:217–248, 1992.
8. G. Boudol. Asynchrony and the pi-calculus. Technical Report RR-1702, INRIA SofiaAntipolis, 1992.
9. S. Conchon and F. L. Fessant. Jocaml: Mobile agents for objective-caml. In *Proc. of ASAMA'99*. IEEE Computer Society, 1999.
10. D. Garg. CLL: A concurrent language built from logical principles. Technical Report CMU-CS-05-104, Computer Science Department, Carnegie Mellon University, January 2005.
11. A. Giacalone, P. Mishra, and S. Prasad. Facile: A symmetric integration of concurrent and functional programming. *International Journal of Parallel Programming*, 18(2):121–160, 1989.
12. J.-Y. Girard. Linear logic. In *Theoretical Computer Science*, volume 5, 1987.
13. S. P. Jones, A. Gordon, and S. Finne. Concurrent Haskell. In *Proc. of POPL'96*, 1996.
14. P. López, F. Pfenning, J. Polakow, and K. Watkins. Monadic concurrent linear logic programming. In *Proc. of PPDP'05*, 2005. To appear.
15. M. Nygaard and G. Winskel. Domain theory for concurrency. *Theor. Comput. Sc.*, 316(1-3), 2004.
16. F. Pfenning and R. Davies. A judgmental reconstruction of modal logic. *Math. Struc. in Comp. Sci.*, 11(4):511–540, 2001.
17. B. C. Pierce and D. N. Turner. Pict: a programming language based on the pi-calculus. In *Proof, language, and interaction: essays in honour of Robin Milner*, pages 455–494. MIT Press, 2000.
18. J. H. Reppy. CML: A higher-order concurrent language. In *Proc. of PLDI'91*, 1991.
19. J. H. Reppy. *Concurrent programming in ML*. Cambridge University Press, 1999.
20. D. Sangiorgi and D. Walker. *The π-calculus: A Theory of Mobile Processes*. Cambridge University Press, 2001. Chapters 15–17.
21. K. Watkins, I. Cervesato, F. Pfenning, and D. Walker. A concurrent logical framework I: Judgements and properties. Technical Report CMU-CS-02-101, Computer Science Department, Carnegie Mellon University, May 2003.
22. H. Xi and F. Pfenning. Dependent types in practical programming. In *Proc. of POPL'99*, 1999.

Multiport Interaction Nets and Concurrency
(Extended Abstract)

Damiano Mazza

Institut de Mathématiques de Luminy
mazza@iml.univ-mrs.fr
http://iml.univ-mrs.fr/~mazza

Abstract. We consider an extension of Lafont's Interaction Nets, called Multiport Interaction Nets, and show that they are a model of concurrent computation by encoding the full π-calculus in them. We thus obtain a faithful graphical representation of the π-calculus in which every reduction step is decomposed in fully local graph-rewriting rules.

1 Introduction

Lafont's Interaction Nets [1] are a model of sequential computation inspired by proof-nets for Multiplicative Linear Logic that can be seen as distributed Turing machines: as in these latter, transitions are local, but may be performed in parallel. They have been explicitly designed to be strongly deterministic, so no truly concurrent behavior can be expressed within them.

In this paper, we consider a non-deterministic extension[1] of Interaction Nets, called *Multiport Interaction Nets*, and show that they are an expressive model of concurrent computation by encoding the full π-calculus in them.

A considerable number of graphical representations of the π-calculus (or other process calculi) can be found in the existing literature. Let us mention for example Milner's π-nets [2], Parrow's Interaction Diagrams [3], and Fu's Reaction Graphs [4]. All these approaches succeed in describing concurrent dynamics as graph rewriting, but the treatment of prefixing is not very natural (in π-nets and Reaction Graphs, some form of "guarded box" is used, while Interaction Diagrams use polyadicity to encode causal dependency), and they all need boxes to represent replication, so that duplication is seen as a synchronous, global operation. It must also be observed that none of the existing graphical representations is ever shown to cover the π-calculus in all of its features, including sums and match prefix.

More recently, Laneve et al. proposed Solo Diagrams [5] as a graphical presentation of the *solos calculus* [6]. They too use replication boxes, but show that these can be limited to certain configurations which ensure constant-time reductions, and thus locality.

[1] It would actually be fairer to put it the other way around: Lafont intentionally restricted to one principal port because this yields systems with very nice properties.

M. Abadi and L. de Alfaro (Eds.): CONCUR 2005, LNCS 3653, pp. 21–35, 2005.

Much closer to the spirit of Interaction Nets, a nice graphical representation of (an extension of) the *fusion calculus* has been given by Beffara and Maurel [7], in which nevertheless replication must be accommodated using boxes. In view of our results, it does not seem unlikely that Multiport Interaction Nets can provide both an alternative, "box-less" graphical encoding for the solos calculus and a purely local version of Beffara and Maurel's Concurrent Nets.

It is worth mentioning the comparison between Interaction Nets and concurrent systems done by Yoshida [8], who found that, when seen from the point of view of Interaction Nets, the graphical representation for her concurrent combinators amounts more or less to allow *hyperwires* connecting cells, i.e., wires that link together more than two ports. This is also explicitly seen in Beffara and Maurel's Concurrent Nets. As a matter of fact, our approach "internalizes" these hyperconnections, extending Lafont's systems not with respect to the topology of the connections between cells but to the nature of the cells themselves.

Multiport Interaction Nets have already been considered by Vladimir Alexiev in his Ph.D. thesis [9] as one of several possible non-deterministic extensions of Interaction Nets; they are obtained from these latter by allowing cells to have more than one principal port.[2] Alexiev proved that this extension is as expressive as the "hyperwire" extension mentioned above, and defined in it a graphical encoding of the finite π-calculus, leaving open the problem of extending it to replication. These systems have also been the object of Lionel Khalil's Ph.D. thesis [10], in which he proved that it is actually sufficient to add to Lafont's Interaction Nets a single cell with two principal ports and two auxiliary ports, called amb, to obtain the full power of Multiport Interaction Nets. In spite of Khalil's result, it is still useful from the point of view of conciseness to consider cells with an arbitrary number of principal ports, as we shall do in this paper.

Our encoding (quite different from Alexiev's one, even in the finite case) covers every single feature of the π-calculus, in particular replication, which is crucial in terms of expressiveness. Compared to the aforementioned graphical formalisms, ours has an exceptional advantage: no "box" or other global notion is needed, i.e., the dynamics is fully local. In other words, our encoding may be seen as the equivalent of *sharing graphs* for the λ-calculus. In perspective, this opens the possibility for a new semantical study of concurrency, as the algebraic semantics enjoyed by Lafont's original systems (the Geometry of Interaction [11]) might be extended to Multiport Interaction Nets (this is not developed in the paper though).

We also stress the fact that, unlike virtually any other graphical system proposed for concurrency, Multiport Interaction Nets *are not* built around the π-calculus, or any other process calculus. On the contrary, they must be seen as an independent, alternative model of concurrency, which is shown here to be equivalent to the π-calculus; our result ought to be read more in this sense than as "yet-another-graphical-representation-of-π".

[2] Alexiev calls them **INMPP**, *Interaction Nets with Multiple Principal Ports.*

Another advantage of Multiport Interaction Nets lies in their logical roots: as extensions of multiplicative proof-nets, they can be endowed with a very natural type discipline, which makes programming much easier and more robust.

2 Multiport Interaction Net Systems

Cells. The basic elements of (multiport) interaction nets are *cells*. A cell has a distinct symbol identifying it (usually ranged over by $\alpha, \beta, \ldots$), and a finite number of *ports*, partitioned into *auxiliary ports*, the number of which is called the *arity* of the cell, and *principal ports*, the number of which is called the *co-arity* of the cell. Cells whose co-arity is 1 will be called *monocells*; cells with greater co-arities will instead be called *multicells*. Here is how we usually represent cells:

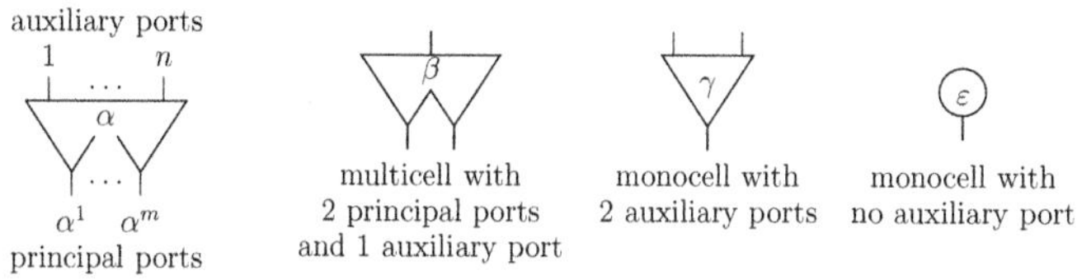

Nets. Given several occurrences[3] of cells, we use *wires* to connect their ports, and build a *net*. For example, here is a net that uses the three cells drawn above:

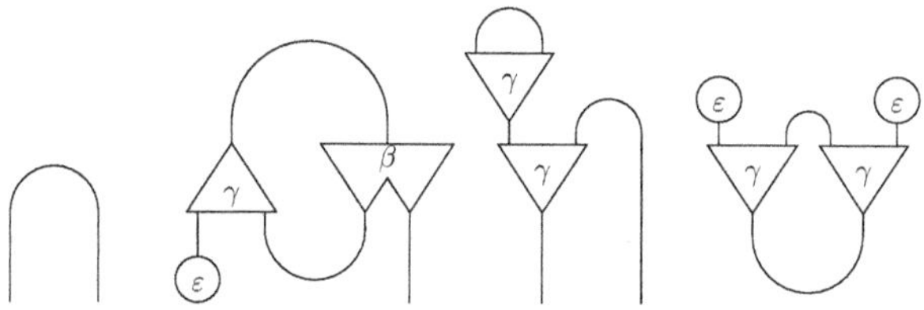

Nets are usually ranged over by $\mu, \nu, \ldots$ Notice that wires may be left "dangling", with one or both of their extremities not connected to any cell. In particular, a single wire is itself a net. These dangling wires are called *free ports* of the net. A free port can be principal or auxiliary, or neither, as in the case of an isolated wire. For example, the net above has 5 free ports, 2 of which are principal and 1 auxiliary. The free ports of a net form what is said to be its *interface*, since each of them is a "branching point" that can be used to connect the net to other nets, in a compositional/modular way.

Interaction. Nets become computational objects through *graph rewriting*. The fundamental *interaction principle* is that rewriting can occur only when two principal ports of two *distinct* occurrences of cells are connected; such a connection is called a *cut*. As a consequence, all rewriting rules will be of the form

[3] This is one of the very few times we will be pedantic about the distinction between cells and their occurrences; unless when strictly needed, we will usually make systematic confusion between the two concepts.

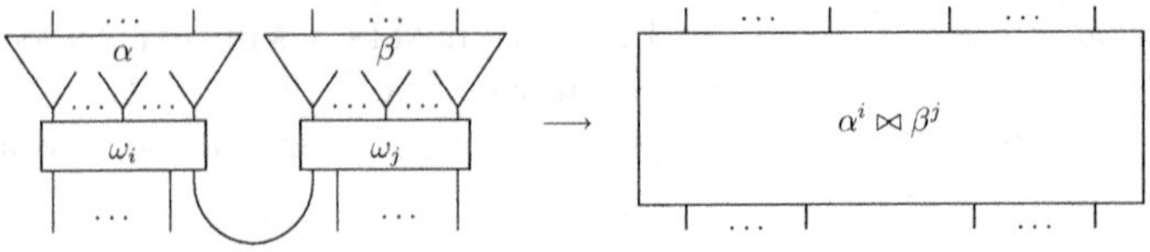

where, for graphical convenience, we have used two permutations ω_i and ω_j that "isolate" resp. the i-th principal port of α and the j-th principal port of β, i.e.

The left member is an *active pair*, and the right member its reduct. The reduct must be a net respecting the interface of the active pair, i.e., there must be a bijection between the free ports of the right and left members of each rule; this bijection will always be clear from the graphical representation.

The interface being respected, the active pair can be "disconnected" from the net and be replaced by its reduct. This is the basic rewriting step, and it is written $\mu \to \mu'$ (net μ *reduces* to μ'). We denote by $\to^*$ the reflexive and transitive closure of $\to$, and if $\mu \to^* \mu'$, we say that μ' is a *reduct* of μ. Notice that a multicell can in general be involved in several active pairs; the choice of which one is reduced is non-deterministic.

There are some additional constraints on interaction rules: first of all, there may be *at most* one rule for each pair of principal ports; allowing non-deterministic rules only complicates the definition without adding expressive power. We also observe that active pairs intrinsically lack an orientation, so the reduct $\beta^j \bowtie \alpha^i$ must be essentially the same as $\alpha^i \bowtie \beta^j$, just "flipped over"; we write this as $\beta^j \bowtie \alpha^i = \overline{\alpha^i \bowtie \beta^j}$. Moreover, reducts cannot contain active pairs (this does not prevent the possibility of infinite reductions).[4]

The Formal Definition. We are now ready to introduce the formal definition of a multiport Interaction Net System (mINS):

Definition 1 (Multiport Interaction Net System (mINS)). *A* multiport Interaction Net System *$\mathcal{S}$ is a couple $(\Sigma, \bowtie)$, where:*

- *Σ is a (possibly denumerably infinite) set of cells, called the* alphabet *of $\mathcal{S}$;*
- *$\bowtie$ is a (partial) function taking an active pair and yielding a cut-free net with the same interface, such that, if $\alpha^i \bowtie \beta^j$ is defined, then $\beta^j \bowtie \alpha^i = \overline{\alpha^i \bowtie \beta^j}$;*

A mINS is said to be finite *or* infinite *according to the cardinality of its alphabet.*

Since interaction is local, any rule of a finite mINS can be performed in constant time. However, in the rest of the paper we shall use only infinite systems, which make the presentation more readable. Nevertheless, everything we do can be done in finite mINS's; this will be detailed in the full version of the paper.

[4] Actually, reducts should be *reduced nets*, i.e., cut-free and *vicious-circle-free*. The definition of vicious circle is irrelevant for our present purposes, so we shall content ourselves with cut-free reducts.

Types. mINS's can be provided with a *type discipline*: given a system $\mathcal{S}$, we consider a set of *constant types*, ranged over by T, and to each port of the cells of $\mathcal{S}$ we assign an *input type* (T^-) or an *output type* (T^+). We say that a net is *well typed* if inputs are connected to outputs of the same type; a rule is well typed if both its left and right members are well typed, and the typing of the interface is preserved. If all rules of $\mathcal{S}$ are well typed, and if every well typed cut has a corresponding rule, we say that $\mathcal{S}$ is a *typed* mINS.

In a typed mINS, it is sometimes useful to have *overloaded* cells, i.e., cells which admit more than one typing for their ports; the typical example is a *duplicator cell*, which can duplicate no matter what and must therefore be capable of interacting with any cell of any type (see Fig. 3 and 4 below).

The type discipline can be useful to guarantee certain correctness properties of the system, mainly that "unreasonable" cuts never arise through reduction, like, say, that a cell representing integer addition never interacts with a string constructor.

3 mINS's and the π-Calculus

3.1 The Finite π-Calculus

Our first step will be to find a mINS which implements the *finite π-calculus*, or Fπ. By finite π-calculus we mean the simplest subcalculus of π, modeling only name-passing and name-restriction, without any other construct (in particular without either replication or recursion). The prefixes and processes of Fπ are resp. generated by the following grammars:

$$\pi ::= \overline{x}y \mid x(z)$$

$$P, Q ::= \mathbf{0} \mid \pi.P \mid P \mid Q \mid \boldsymbol{\nu}(z)P \ .$$

The basic Fπ reduction rule is

$$\overline{x}y.P \mid x(z).Q \longrightarrow P \mid Q\{y/z\} \ .$$

The set of free names of a process P is denoted $\mathsf{fn}(P)$. Structural congruence is defined, as usual, by the axioms making the set of processes a commutative monoid with respect to parallel composition (the neutral element being $\mathbf{0}$), plus the three standard axioms concerning name restriction: $\boldsymbol{\nu}(z)\boldsymbol{\nu}(w)P \equiv \boldsymbol{\nu}(w)\boldsymbol{\nu}(z)P$, $\boldsymbol{\nu}(z)\mathbf{0} \equiv \mathbf{0}$, and, if $z \notin \mathsf{fn}(P_1)$, $z(P_1 \mid P_2) \equiv P_1 \mid \boldsymbol{\nu}(z)P_2$. The observability predicate is written $\downarrow_\mu$, where μ is either a name x (input action), or a co-name $\overline{x}$ (output action); the invisible transition relation is written $\xrightarrow{\tau}$, and its reflexive and transitive closure $\Rightarrow$.

Now consider the infinite typed mINS $\mathcal{F}_\infty$ whose alphabet and rules are given resp. in Fig. 1 and Fig. 2. Types have been omitted in the rules, but the reader can check that they are all well typed. The first rule of Fig. 2 is an example of "template rule": for a fixed $m \geq 0$, it actually condenses $2(m+1)$ rules. Template rules, the fact that ϵ ranges over $\{+, -\}$, and the permutations σ^ϵ will be notational conventions constantly adopted throughout the rest of the paper.

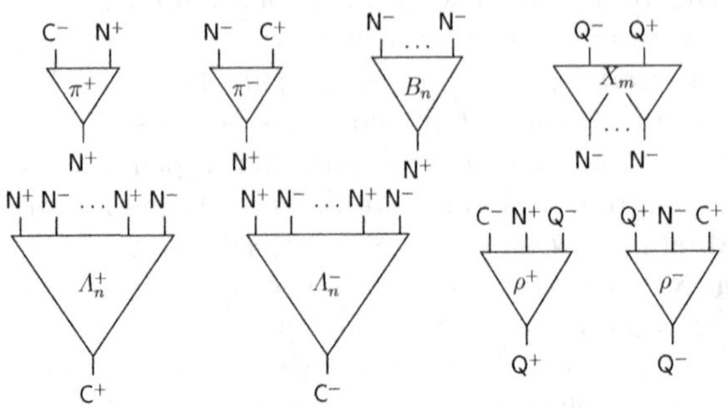

Fig. 1. The alphabet of $\mathcal{F}_\infty$

- Types N, C, and Q represent resp. *names*, *continuations*, and *queues*.
- π^+ and π^- cells will implement resp. output and input prefixes; each of them is ready to make a request on a name, and bears a continuation and another name (either the name being sent or the place-holder for substitution).
- B_n is a monocell with n auxiliary ports, with $n \geq 0$; this family of cells will be needed to bind the occurrences of the name used by an input prefix.
- X_m is a cell with m principal ports ($m \geq 1$) and 2 auxiliary ports. We stipulate that X_0 is just a wire of type Q. The cells belonging to this family will implement names: they are capable of concurrently handling several requests coming from π^+ and π^- cells, and they have two FIFO queues (one for inputs, the other for outputs) that will be used to store prefixes waiting for interaction. They also handle requests from B_n cells; the interaction with these cells models name-passing and the associated substitution.
- Λ_n^+ and Λ_n^- are monocells of arity $2n$, $n \geq 0$. These two families will implement the blocking function of prefixes: they "suspend" a connection until they interact.
- ρ^+ and ρ^- cells will be needed to represent resp. output and input queues on channels; they bear the same information as π^ϵ cells, plus a pointer to the rest of the queue. Their interaction synchronizes two prefixes: the name being sent is connected to the place-holder for substitution, and their two continuations are connected, so that they can be unblocked.

We shall now define a translation $\langle\cdot\rangle$ of Fπ processes into $\mathcal{F}_\infty$ nets. This encoding enjoys a clear correspondence with the interactive structure of processes, but accounts only for certain kinds of transitions. The free ports of $\langle P\rangle$ will be labelled with names: there will be one free port labelled x for each free occurrence of x in P. In particular, the presence of a free principal port labelled by x will mean that x is the subject of a prefix, i.e., $P \downarrow_{\overline{x}}$ or $P \downarrow_x$. In our graphical representations, we will always collect principal and auxiliary free ports resp. to the bottom and to the top of the net, so if P is a process with k observables, $\langle P\rangle$ will be pictured as a net with k free ports on the bottom.

$\langle P\rangle$ might as well contain cuts; if we need to translate $\pi.P$, we must "inhibit" such cuts to correctly represent prefixing. So we introduce the nets $.P^\epsilon$ as follows:

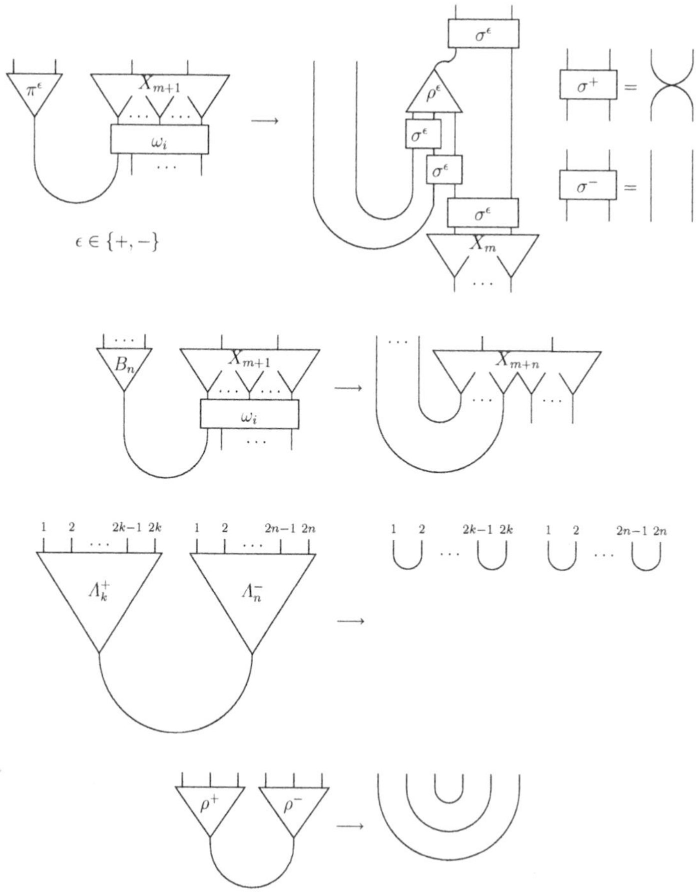

Fig. 2. The rules of $\mathcal{F}_\infty$

An important case is $\mathbf{.0}^\epsilon$, which is just a single 0-ary Λ_0^ϵ cell.

Definition 2 (Translation $\langle\cdot\rangle$ for Fπ). *We define $\langle P\rangle$ by induction on P:*

- $\langle \mathbf{0}\rangle$ *is the empty net.*
- $\langle \pi.P\rangle$ *is the following net, depending on the nature of π:*

$\langle \overline{x}y.P \rangle =$ 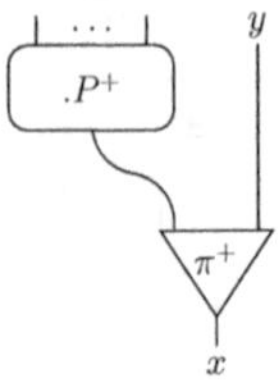

$\langle x(z).P \rangle =$ 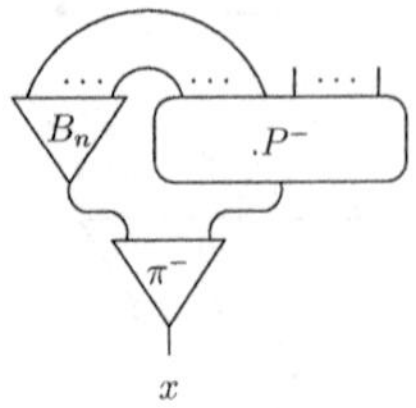

In the encoding of the input prefix, the n *free ports of* $.P^-$ *labelled by* z *are connected to the* B_n *cell.*

- $\langle P \mid Q \rangle$ *is the net obtained by juxtaposing* $\langle P \rangle$ *and* $\langle Q \rangle$*.*
- *If* $\langle P \rangle$ *has* m *free ports labelled by* z*, then* $\langle \boldsymbol{\nu}(z)P \rangle$ *is the net obtained from* $\langle P \rangle$ *by connecting all such free ports to the free ports of the following net:*

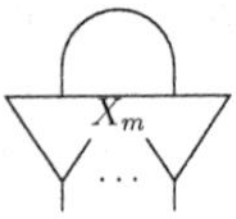

Notice that this is the only case in which cuts may be introduced.

If $\langle P \rangle$ *has a free port labelled by* x *which is the principal port of a* π^+ *(resp.* π^-*) cell, we write* $\langle P \rangle \downarrow_{\overline{x}}$ *(resp.* $\langle P \rangle \downarrow_x$*).*

We have not mentioned types, but the reader can check that all the nets of Definition 2 are well typed. Also, the encoding is defined modulo the ordering of the connections to the ports of B_n, Λ_n^ϵ, and X_m cells, which is irrelevant.

The translation $\langle \cdot \rangle$ has already some interesting properties:

Proposition 1. *If* $P \equiv Q$*, then* $\langle P \rangle = \langle Q \rangle$*.*

Definition 3 (Fully invisible actions). *We say that a process* P *is capable of evolving to* Q *through a* fully invisible action, $P \xrightarrow{\bar{\tau}} Q$*, if* $P \xrightarrow{\tau} Q$ *and the subject name used in the transition is under the scope of a restriction.*

Theorem 1 (Weak completeness of the encoding). *Let* P *be a process.*

1. *If* $P \downarrow_\mu$*, then* $\langle P \rangle \downarrow_\mu$*.*
2. *If* $P \xrightarrow{\bar{\tau}} Q$*, then* $\langle P \rangle \to^* \langle Q \rangle$*.*

Notice that the converse of Proposition 1 is false; in fact, whenever z does not appear in the prefix π, $\langle \boldsymbol{\nu}(z)\pi.P \rangle = \langle \pi.\boldsymbol{\nu}(z)P \rangle$, but the two processes are not structurally congruent (they are strong full bisimilar though).

To prove part 2 of Theorem 1 (part 1 is trivial), one just observes that $P \xrightarrow{\bar{\tau}} Q$ means that $P \equiv \boldsymbol{\nu}(z, \widetilde{w})(\overline{z}x.R_1 \mid z(y).R_2 \mid S)$ and $Q \equiv \boldsymbol{\nu}(z, \widetilde{w})(R_1 \mid R_2\{x/y\} \mid S)$ (this is the Harmony Lemma [12]), so, using Proposition 1, $\langle P \rangle$ contains a π^+ and a π^- cell cut to the same X_m cell; knowing this, one easily finds a chain of 5 reductions leading to $\langle Q \rangle$.

Another translation, noted $[\cdot]$, is needed if we want to account for τ transitions which are not fully invisible, i.e., which are due to synchronization on free channels. Basically, $[P]$ is a sort of "closure" of $\langle P \rangle$, i.e., $[P]$ is practically identical to $\langle \boldsymbol{\nu}(\widetilde{x})P \rangle$, where $\widetilde{x}$ are the free names of P, the only difference being that we want to remember the names we artificially bound:

Definition 4 (Translation $[\cdot]$ for Fπ). *Let x range over $\mathsf{fn}(P)$; if in $\langle P \rangle$ there are m free ports labelled by x, we define $[P]$ as the net obtained from $\langle P \rangle$ by connecting all such ports to a X_{m+1} cell, which will be left with one free port labelled by x:*

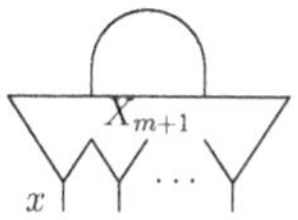

Hence, in general, $[P]$ has as many free ports as the number of free names in P. Notice that Proposition 1 transfers to $[\cdot]$ without any problem.

Now, free ports are stable under reduction, while free names are not (some might disappear); therefore, a statement like

$$\text{if } P \xrightarrow{\tau} Q, \text{ then } [P] \to^{*} [Q]$$

might fail for trivial reasons. In order to cope with this, and because it will be useful in other circumstances, we introduce the notion of *readback*.

Definition 5 (Bureaucratic cuts). *Cuts between B_n and X_m cells and between Λ_n^{ϵ} cells are called* bureaucratic, *and so are their respective reductions (which are resp. the second and third from the top in Fig. 2). We call* bureau-free *a net which contains no bureaucratic cut.*

The following is immediate:

Lemma 1. *Bureaucratic reduction is (strongly) confluent; hence, any net μ has a unique associated* bureau-free *form μ^{b}.*

Definition 6 (Readback). *Let μ be any reduct of a net of the form $[P]$ for some process P. The* readback *of μ, noted $\widehat{\mu}$, is the net obtained by taking μ^{b} and applying, until no longer possible, the following replacements:*

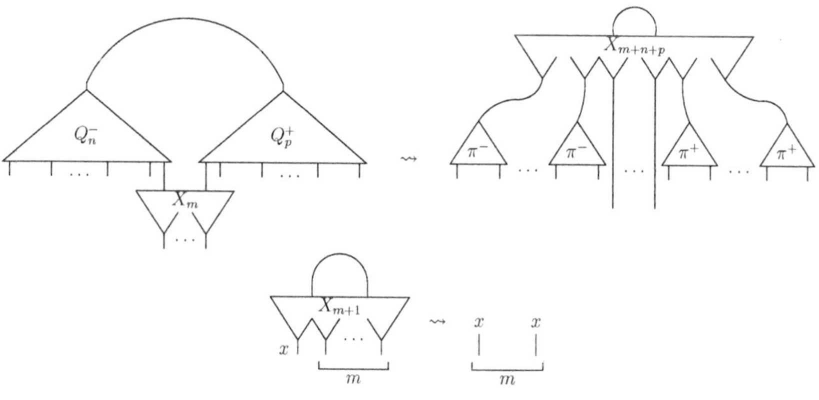

where Q_k^ϵ, for $k \geq 1$, is a tree of k ρ^ϵ cells (built in the only possible way induced by the typing). Notice that, in the second substitution, we start with 1 free port labelled by x and we end up with m free ports all labelled by x as well; as in Definition 4, x ranges over $\mathsf{fn}(P)$.

Basically, the readback procedure "undoes" the choices made in queuing up prefixes and removes the artificial closure of free names. It is evident from Definition 6 that $\widehat{[P]} = \langle P \rangle$. Now we can state the following, which follows immediately from Theorem 1 and the definition of readback:

Theorem 2 (Completeness of the encoding). *If $P \xrightarrow{\tau} Q$, then $[P] \to^* \nu$ such that $\widehat{\nu} = \langle Q \rangle$.*

The converse also holds:

Theorem 3 (Soundness of the encoding). *Let P be a process.*

1. *If $\langle P \rangle \downarrow_\mu$, then $P \downarrow_\mu$.*
2. *If $[P] \to^* \nu$, then $P \Rightarrow Q$ such that $\langle Q \rangle = \widehat{\nu}$.*

While part 1 is trivial, part 2 requires some work. We can reason by induction on the number s of reduction steps applied to get from $[P]$ to ν. If $s = 0$, then the statement follows from the above remark that $\widehat{[P]} = \langle P \rangle$. If $s > 0$, we call μ the reduct of $[P]$ after $s - 1$ steps, and we analyze the reduction $\mu \to \nu$. If this last transition results from applying a bureaucratic rule, then μ is not bureau-free, and (by Lemma 1) $\nu^{\mathsf{b}} = \mu^{\mathsf{b}}$, hence $\widehat{\nu} = \widehat{\mu}$ and we conclude using the induction hypothesis. If the last step is a π^ϵ/X_m rule (top of Fig. 2), the readback "undoes" the reduction and we have again $\widehat{\nu} = \widehat{\mu}$. The only case where something really happens, i.e., $\widehat{\nu} \neq \widehat{\mu}$, is when the last step is a ρ^ϵ rule (bottom of Fig. 2). We need here the following lemmas, the (not difficult) proofs of which are omitted:

Lemma 2. *Let P be a process, and μ a reduct of $[P]$. If μ contains a cut between a ρ^+ and a ρ^- cell, then the corresponding π^+ and π^- cells in $\widehat{\mu}$ are either cut to the same X_m multicell, or have their principal ports free and labelled with the same name.*

Lemma 3. *The reduction relation consisting of bureaucratic reductions and the ρ^ϵ reduction is (strongly) confluent.*

By the induction hypothesis, we know that $\widehat{\mu} = \langle Q \rangle$ for some Q such that $P \Rightarrow Q$; by Lemma 2, we also know that this Q contains an output and an input prefix acting on the same channel, i.e., $Q \equiv \boldsymbol{\nu}(\widetilde{w})(\overline{x}y.R_1 \mid x(z).R_2 \mid S)$. The ρ^ϵ reduction leading to ν introduces (at most) two bureaucratic cuts; by Lemma 3, we can assume these to be the only bureaucratic cuts in ν, for if μ was not bureau-free, reducing its cuts before or after the application of the ρ^ϵ rule has no effect on ν^{b} (and thus on $\widehat{\nu}$). It is then just a matter of applying a few rewriting rules to check that $\widehat{\nu} = \langle \boldsymbol{\nu}(\widetilde{w})(R_1 \mid R_2\{y/z\} \mid S) \rangle$, as needed to prove our statement. The typing discipline followed by $\mathcal{F}_\infty$ assures us that no cut other than those considered can arise through reduction, so we are done.

Of course the Soundness Theorem has a weaker version, stating that if $\langle P \rangle \to^* \nu$, then there are a process Q such that $\langle Q \rangle = \widehat{\nu}$ and a number of fully invisible transitions (including zero) leading from P to Q.

3.2 Adding Replication

The fact that mINS's are able to faithfully encode Fπ is already meaningful from the point of view of concurrent computation, but is extremely poor in terms of expressive power. In this section we shall give a stronger result by showing that the mINS $\mathcal{F}_\infty$ can be extended into a mINS $\mathcal{C}_\infty$ that encodes a fragment of the π-calculus, called here the "core" π-calculus, or Cπ, which adds the replication operator to Fπ. One could see Cπ basically as a synchronous and extended version of the Pict language [13].

A well known fact is that the replication operator is not needed everywhere in the definition of processes: *replicated prefixes* suffice to give universal computational power to the π-calculus. This is why we introduce *extended prefixes*

$$\kappa ::= \overline{x}(z) \;\big|\; \pi \qquad \text{(where } \pi \text{ is a prefix of F}\pi) ,$$

which add the bound-output prefix to the "standard" prefixes of Fπ, and we define the processes of Cπ to be those generated by the following grammar:

$$P, Q ::= \mathbf{0} \;\big|\; \pi.P \;\big|\; P \mid Q \;\big|\; \boldsymbol{\nu}(z)P \;\big|\; \kappa \triangleright P .$$

In the traditional syntax, if π is an Fπ prefix, we would write $\pi \triangleright P$ as $!\pi.P$, while $\overline{x}(z) \triangleright P$ would be written as $!\boldsymbol{\nu}(z)\overline{x}z.P$. Here, we choose this alternative syntax since we *do not* consider the standard axiom for structural congruence $!P \equiv P \mid !P$; structural congruence on Cπ processes is thus the same relation we defined on Fπ (see page 25). To recover the adequate notion of transition relation, we add the following rules:

$$\frac{}{\overline{x}y \triangleright P \xrightarrow{\overline{x}y} \overline{x}y \triangleright P \mid P} \qquad \frac{}{x(z) \triangleright P \xrightarrow{xy} x(z) \triangleright P \mid P\{y/z\}} \qquad \frac{}{\overline{x}(z) \triangleright P \xrightarrow{\overline{x}(z)} \overline{x}(z) \triangleright P \mid P}$$

The reduction relation is defined in the same way; so, for example, we have

$$\overline{x}y.P \mid x(z) \triangleright Q \longrightarrow P \mid Q\{y/z\} \mid x(z) \triangleright Q .$$

The alphabet of the (infinite) typed mINS $\mathcal{C}_\infty$ is defined by adding to the alphabet of $\mathcal{F}_\infty$ the cells of Fig. 3, whose interactions are given by the rules of Fig. 4:

- There is an additional type, R, which represents *name restrictions.*
- $!\pi^\epsilon$ and $!\rho^\epsilon$ cells play the same role resp. as π^ϵ and ρ^ϵ cells: the first represent replicated prefixes, the second *enqueued* replicated prefixes. They carry two additional pieces of information: another name, and a restriction. The first is a *potential occurrence* of the subject of the prefix, which is needed since a replicated prefix whose subject is x potentially generates a new occurrence of x after replication. The second is a sort of pointer to the restricted names which are under the scope of the replication; these names are not usable until replication takes place.

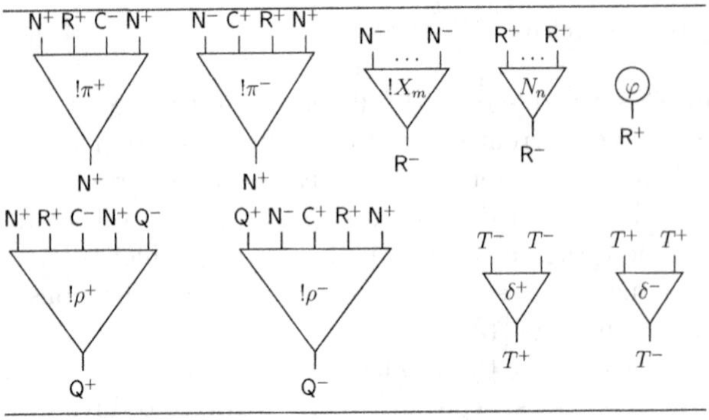

Fig. 3. Additional cells for $\mathcal{C}_\infty$

- A cell belonging to the $!X_m$ family (m auxiliary ports, $m \geq 1$) represents a restricted name with m occurrences blocked under a replicated prefix.
- Cells belonging to the N_n family (n auxiliary ports, $n \geq 0$) "collect" $!X_m$ cells and pass them to $!\pi^\epsilon$ cells.
- The φ cell "unblocks" restricted names whenever a copy of a replicated process is activated.
- δ^ϵ cells are *duplicators*: they implement (local) replication of processes. They are *overloaded* cells, i.e., their ports can be typed with any type T, provided the typing respects the input/output specifications of Fig. 3.

Definition 7 (Translations $\langle\cdot\rangle$ and $[\cdot]$ for Cπ). *We extend the translation $\langle\cdot\rangle$ of Definition 2 to Cπ processes in the following way. Suppose that $.P^\epsilon$ (as always, $\epsilon \in \{+,-\}$) is a net containing n X-cells and (among others) k free ports labelled with the name z:*

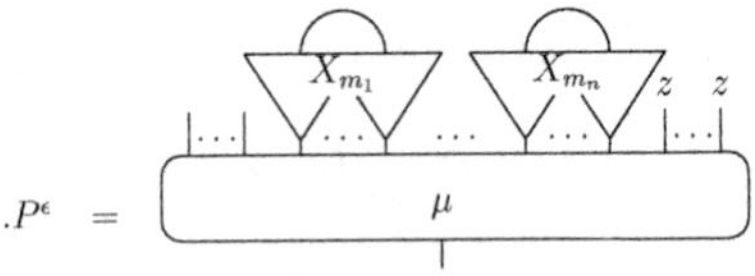

Then, we define $\rhd P^\epsilon$ and $\rhd P^z$ as follows:

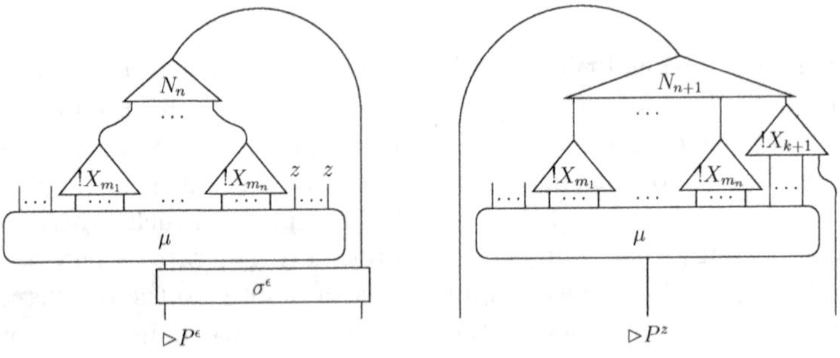

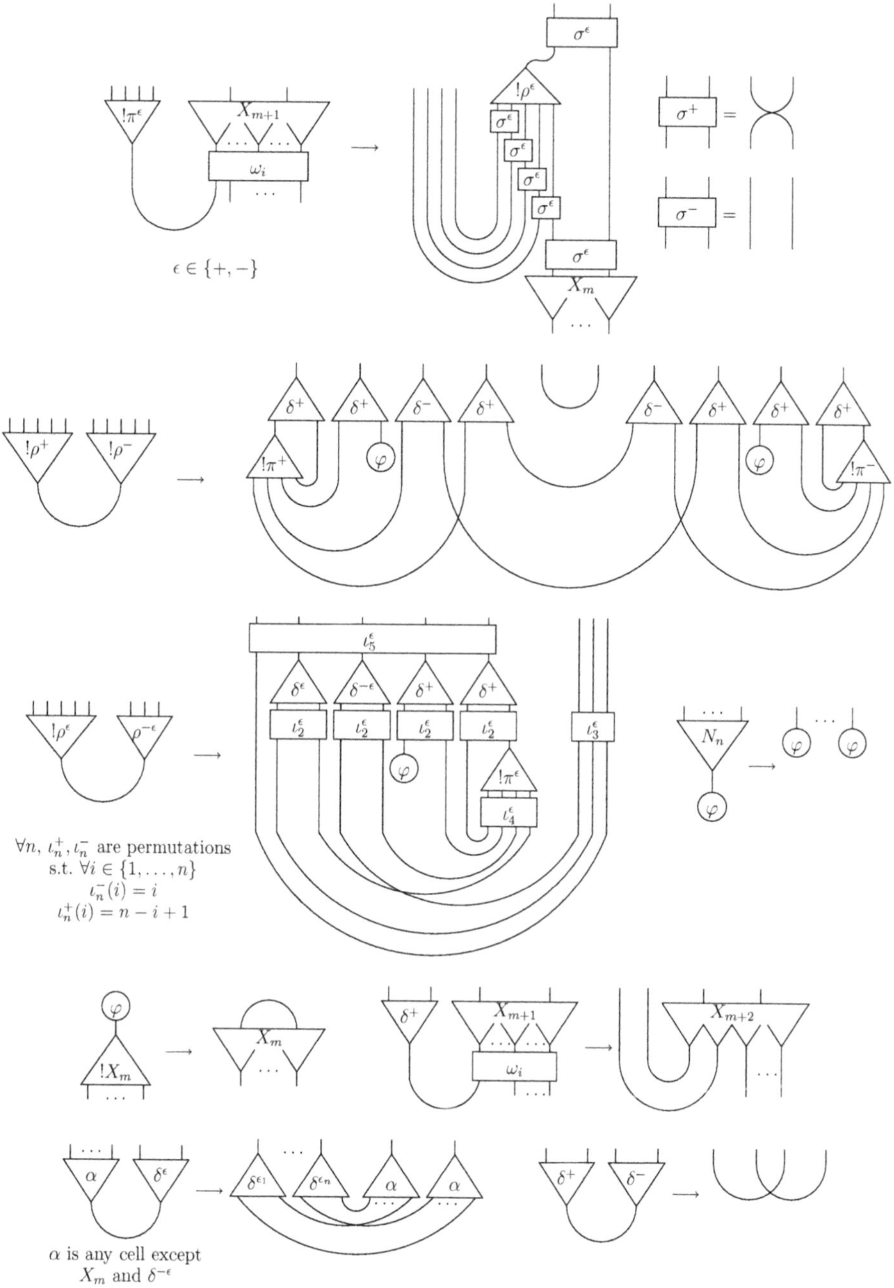

Fig. 4. Rules for the additional cells of $\mathcal{C}_\infty$

where, as usual, σ^- *is the identity permutation and* σ^+ *is the "twist" permutation. We can now define* $\langle \kappa \rhd P \rangle$*:*

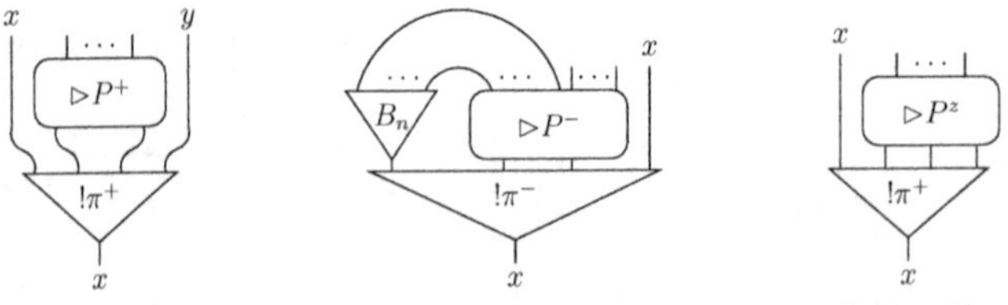

$\langle \overline{x}y \triangleright P \rangle$ $\langle x(z) \triangleright P \rangle$ $\langle \overline{x}(z) \triangleright P \rangle$

If $\langle P \rangle$ has a free port labelled by x which is the principal port of a π^+ or $!\pi^+$ (resp. π^- or $!\pi^-$) cell, we write $\langle P \rangle \downarrow_{\overline{x}}$ (resp. $\langle P \rangle \downarrow_x$).

The translation $[P]$ is obtained from $\langle P \rangle$ exactly as in Definition 4.

Notice that it is no longer the case that each free occurrence of x in P corresponds to a free port labelled by x in $\langle P \rangle$; here, a free occurrence of x as subject of a replicated prefix generates *two* free ports. It is still the case though that the free *principal* ports of $\langle P \rangle$ are in bijection with the observables of P. We also remark that Proposition 1 holds trivially for both of the extended translations; this would of course be impossible if we admitted that $!P \equiv P \mid !P$.

Definition 5 can be extended to $\mathcal{C}_\infty$ by considering as bureaucratic the last 5 cuts of Fig. 4, i.e., all cuts involving φ and δ^ϵ cells; it is immediate to verify that Lemma 1 still holds. We can then define the readback $\widehat{\mu}$ of a $\mathcal{C}_\infty$ net μ which is the reduct of a net $[P]$: simply take its bureau-free form μ^{b}, and apply the substitutions of Definition 6, where this time the queues might contain $!\rho^\epsilon$ cells, which need to be replaced by the corresponding $!\pi^\epsilon$ cells.

With all the definitions extended to $\mathcal{C}_\infty$, it is not hard to prove the following:

Theorem 4 (Faithfullness of the encoding of Cπ). *Let P be a Cπ process.*

1. *$P \downarrow_\mu$ iff $\langle P \rangle \downarrow_\mu$.*
2. *If $P \xrightarrow{\tau} Q$, then $[P] \to^* \nu$ and $\widehat{\nu} = \langle Q \rangle$.*
3. *If $[P] \to^* \nu$, then $P \Rightarrow Q$ and $\langle Q \rangle = \widehat{\nu}$.*

The proof follows a similar argument to that given for Theorem 2 and Theorem 3. The fundamental issue concerning replication is that neither cuts, nor X_m or δ^ϵ cells can be duplicated by δ^ϵ cells. This is why $\triangleright P^\epsilon$ and $\triangleright P^z$ are introduced: such nets are cut-free, and do not contain either X_m or δ^ϵ cells, so they can be safely duplicated. Then, φ cells extract P from $\triangleright P^\epsilon$ or $\triangleright P^z$. We also observe that, thanks to the encoding, nested replication poses no problem. The other two important points are that duplication is completely bureaucratic (therefore strongly confluent), and that it stops on free channels; this assures us that the replication process does not interfere with prefix synchronization.

4 Conclusions

We have seen how one can find an infinite typed mINS $\mathcal{C}_\infty$ which is able to faithfully encode a quite expressive fragment of the π-calculus, equivalent to a synchronous and extended version of the Pict language. As a matter of fact, much more can be done: one can enrich $\mathcal{C}_\infty$ in order to represent any other feature of the π-calculus, in particular guarded choice and match prefix. This will be shown in the full version of the paper.

We also remark that the systems introduced in Sect. 3 can easily be adapted to encode any kind of *typed* π-calculus. To see this, just notice, for example, that X_m cells can be overloaded by uniformly instantiating the type N into any type V belonging to the grammar $V ::= B \mid \sharp V$, where B ranges over some set of basic types. We can then proceed to overload π^ϵ cells so that if their two auxiliary ports have types V^ϵ and $\mathsf{C}^{-\epsilon}$, then the principal port has type $\sharp V^+$. If we apply similar changes to $!\pi^\epsilon$, ρ^ϵ and $!\rho^\epsilon$ cells, we obtain a mINS for the simply typed π-calculus [12]. Of course, the original system $\mathcal{C}_\infty$ is retrievable by typing everything with a fixpoint type N such that $\mathsf{N} = \sharp\mathsf{N}$.

Acknowledgments. We would like to thank Laurent Regnier and the anonymous referees for their useful comments and suggestions.

References

1. Lafont, Y.: Interaction Nets. In: Conference Record of POPL'90, ACM Press (1990) 95–108
2. Milner, R.: Pi-nets: A graphical form of π-calculus. In: Proceedings of ESOP'94. Volume 788 of Lecture Notes in Computer Science., Springer (1994) 26–42
3. Parrow, J.: Interaction diagrams. Nordic Journal of Computing **2** (1995) 407–443 A previous version appeared in *Proceedings of A Decade in Concurrency*, LNCS 803: 477–508, 1993.
4. Fu, Y.: Reaction Graph. Journal of Computer Science and Technology **13** (1998) 510–530
5. Laneve, C., Parrow, J., Victor, B.: Solo Diagrams. In: Proceedings of TACS'01. Volume 2215 of Lecture Notes in Computer Science., Springer-Verlag (2001) 127–144
6. Laneve, C., Victor, B.: Solos in Concert. In: Proceedings of ICALP'99. Volume 1644 of LNCS., Springer-Verlag (1999) 513–523
7. Beffara, E., Maurel, F.: Concurrent nets: a study of prefixing in process calculi. In: Proceedings of EXPRESS 2004. Volume 128 of ENTCS., Elsevier (2005) 67–86
8. Yoshida, N.: Graph Notation for Concurrent Combinators. In: Proceedings of TPPP'99. Volume 907 of LNCS., Springer (1995) 393–412
9. Alexiev, V.: Non-deterministic Interaction Nets. Ph.D. Thesis, University of Alberta (1999)
10. Khalil, L.: Généralisation des Réseaux d'Interaction avec amb, l'agent de McCarthy: propriétés et applications. Ph.D. Thesis, École Normale Supérieure de Paris (2003)
11. Lafont, Y.: Interaction combinators. Information and Computation **137** (1997) 69–101
12. Sangiorgi, D., Walker, D.: The π-calculus — A Theory of Mobile Processes. Cambridge University Press (2001)
13. Pierce, B., Turner, D.: Pict: A Programming Language Based on the Pi-Calculus. CSCI Technical Report 476, Indiana University (1997)

Model Checking for π-Calculus Using Proof Search

Alwen Tiu

INRIA Lorraine, 615 rue du Jardin Botanique,
54602 Villers-lès-Nancy, France
Alwen.Tiu@loria.fr

Abstract. Model checking for transition systems specified in π-calculus has been a difficult problem due to the infinite-branching nature of input prefix, name-restriction and scope extrusion. We propose here an approach to model checking for π-calculus by encoding it into a logic which supports reasoning about bindings and fixed points. This logic, called $FO\lambda^{\Delta\nabla}$, is a conservative extension of Church's Simple Theory of Types with a "generic" quantifier. By encoding judgments about transitions in pi-calculus into this logic, various conditions on the scoping of names and restrictions on name instantiations are captured naturally by the quantification theory of the logic. Moreover, standard implementation techniques for (higher-order) logic programming are applicable for implementing proof search for this logic, as illustrated in a prototype implementation discussed in this paper. The use of logic variables and eigenvariables in the implementation allows for exploring the state space of processes in a symbolic way. Compositionality of properties of the transitions is a simple consequence of the meta theory of the logic (i.e., cut elimination). We illustrate the benefits of specifying systems in this logic by studying several specifications of modal logics for pi-calculus. These specifications are also executable directly in the prototype implementation of $FO\lambda^{\Delta\nabla}$.

1 Introduction

The π-calculus [16] provides a simple yet powerful framework for specifying communication systems with evolving communication structures. Its expressiveness derives mainly from the possibility of passing communication channels (names), restricting the scope of channels and scope extrusion. These are precisely the features that make model checking for π-calculus difficult. Model checking has traditionally been done with transitions which have finite state models. The name passing feature alone (input prefix) in π-calculus would yield infinite-branching transition systems, if implemented naively. Scope and scope extrusion add another significant layer of complexity, since in model checking the transition systems one has to take into account the exact scope and identity of various channel names. This is a problem which has been studied extensively, of course, due to the importance of π-calculus. A non-exhaustive list of existing

M. Abadi and L. de Alfaro (Eds.): CONCUR 2005, LNCS 3653, pp. 36–50, 2005.

works includes the work on *history dependent automata* [6] model of mobile processes, specific programming logics and decision procedures for model checking mobile processes [3,4], the spatial logic model checker [2] using Gabbay-Pitts permutation techniques [7], and implementation using logic programming [27].

The approach to model checking π-caculus (or mobile processes in general) taken in this paper is based on the proof theory of sequent calculus, by casting the problem of reasoning about scoping and name-instantiation into the more general setting of proof theory for quantifiers in formal logic. More specifically, we encode judgments about transitions in π-calculus and several modal logics for π-calculus [17] into a meta logic, and proof search is used to model the operational semantics of these judgments. This meta logic, called $FO\lambda^{\Delta\nabla}$ [15], is an extension of Church's Simple Theory of Types (but without quantification over propositions, so the logic is essentially first-order) with a proof theoretical notion of *definitions* [22] and a new "generic" quantifier, ∇. The quantifier ∇, roughly summarized, facilitates reasoning about binders (more details will be given later). We summarize our approach as follows.

λ-tree syntax. We use the λ-tree syntax [14] to encode syntax with bindings. It is a variant of higher-order abstract syntax, where syntax of arbitrary system is encoded as λ-terms and the λ-abstraction is used to encode bindings within expressions. One of the advantages of adopting λ-tree syntax, or higher-order abstract syntax in general, is that all the side conditions involving bindings such as scoping of variables, α-conversion, etc., are handled uniformly at the level of the abstract syntax, using the known notions in λ-calculus. Another one is that efficient implementation techniques for manipulating this abstract syntax are well-understood, e.g., algorithms for doing pattern-matching and unification of simply typed λ-terms.

Definitional reflection. Proof search in traditional logics, e.g., variants of Gentzen's LJ or LK, is limited to model the *may-behaviour* of computation system. *Must-behaviour*, eg., notions like bisimulations, or in the interest of this paper, satisfiability of modal formulae, cannot be expressed directly in these logics. To encode such notions, it is necessary to move to a richer logic. Recent developments in the proof theory of *definitions* [10,11] have shown that must-behaviour can indeed be captured in logics extended with this proof-theoretical notion of definitions. In a logic with definitions, an atomic proposition may be "defined" by another formula (which may contain the atomic proposition itself). Thus, a definition can be seen as expressing a fixed point equation. Proof search for a defined atomic formula is done by unfolding the definition of the formula. In the logic with definitions used in this paper, a provable formula like $\forall x.px \supset qx$, where p and q are some defined predicates, expresses the fact that for every term t and for every proof (computation) of pt, there is a proof (computation) of qt. If p and q are predicates encoding one-step transitions, then this formula expresses one-step simulation. If q is an encoding of some assertion in modal logics, then the formula expresses the fact that the modal assertion is true for all reachable "next states" associated with the transition relation encoded by p.

Eigenvariables and ∇. In proof search for a universal quantified formula, e.g., $\forall x.Bx$, the quantified variable x is replaced by a new constant c, and proof search is continued on Bc. Such constants are called *eigenvariables*, and in traditional intuitionistic or classical logic, they play the role of scoped constants as they are created dynamically as proof search progresses and are not instantiated during the proof search. In the meta theory of the logic, eigenvariables play the role of place holder for values, since from a proof for Bc where c is an eigenvariable, one can obtain a proof of Bt for any term t by substituting t into c. In the proof theory of definitions, these dual roles of eigenvariables are internalized in the proof rules of the logic. In particular, in unfolding a definition in a negative context (left-hand side of a sequent), eigenvariables are treated as variables, and in the positive context they are treated as scoped constants. Computation (or transition) states can be encoded using eigenvariables. This in conjunction with definitions allows for exploring the state space of a transition system symbolically.

Since eigenvariables are not used here entirely as scoped constants, to account for scoped names we make use of the ∇-quantifier, first introduced in the logic $FO\lambda^{\Delta\nabla}$ [15], to help encode the notion of "generic judgment" that occurs commonly when reasoning with λ-tree syntax. The ∇ quantifier is used to introduce new elements into a type within a given scope. In particular, a reading of the truth condition for $\nabla x_\gamma.Bx$ is something like: if given a new element, say c, of type γ, then check the truth of Bc. The difference between ∇ and $\forall$ appears in their interaction with definition rules: the constants introduced by ∇ are not subject to instantiation. Note that intended meaning of the ∇-quantifier is rather different from the "new" quantifier of Gabbay and Pitts [7], although they both address the same issue from a pragmatic point of view. In particular, in Gabbay-Pitts setting, an infinite number of names is assumed to be given, and equality between two names are decidable. In our approach here, no such assumptions are made concerning the type of names, not even the assumption that it is non-empty. Instead, new names are generated dynamically when needed, such as when inferring a transition involving extrusion of scopes.

An implementation of proof search. Proof search for $FO\lambda^{\Delta\nabla}$ can be implemented quite straightforwardly, using only the standard tools and techniques used in higher-order logic programming and theorem provers. An automated proof search engine for a fragment of $FO\lambda^{\Delta\nabla}$ has been implemented [24]. It was essentially done by plugging together different existing implementation: higher-order pattern unification [12,18], stream-based approach to back-tracking, and parser for λ-terms. On top of this prototype implementation several specifications of process calculi and bisimulation have been implemented.[1] In most cases, the specifications are implemented almost without any modifications (except for the type-setting of course). A specification of modal logics has also been implemented in this prototype.

---

[1] The prototype implementation along with the example specifications can be downloaded from the author's website: `http://www.loria.fr/~tiu`.

Outline of the papers. The rest of the paper is organized as follows. In Section 2, an overview of the meta logic $FO\lambda^{\Delta\nabla}$ is given. This is followed by the specification of the operational semantics of the late π-calculus in Section 3. The materials in these two sections have appeared in [15,26]; they are included here since the main results of this paper are built on them. Section 4 presents the specification of modal logics introduced in [17] along with the adequacy results. Section 5 gives an overview of a prototype implementation of $FO\lambda^{\Delta\nabla}$ in which the specification of modal logics is implemented. These two sections constitute the main contribution of this paper. Section 6 discusses related and future work. An extended version of this paper containing detailed proofs is available on the web.

2 Overview of the Meta Logic

The logic $FO\lambda^{\Delta\nabla}$ (pronounced"fold-nabla") is presented using a sequent calculus that is an extension of Gentzen's system LJ for first-order intuitionistic logic. A *sequent* is an expression of the form $B_1, \ldots, B_n \vdash B_0$ where $B_0, \ldots, B_n$ are formulas and the elongated turnstile $\vdash$ is the sequent arrow. To the left of the turnstile is a multiset: thus repeated occurrences of a formula are allowed. If the formulas $B_0, \ldots, B_n$ contain free variables, they are considered universally quantified outside the sequent, in the sense that if the above sequent is provable than every instance of it is also provable. In proof theoretical terms, such free variables are called *eigenvariables.*

A first attempt at using sequent calculus to capture judgments about the π-calculus could be to use eigenvariables to encode names in π-calculus, but this is certainly problematic. For example, if we have a proof for the sequent $\vdash Pxy$, where x and y are different eigenvariables, then logic dictates that the sequent $\vdash Pzz$ is also provable (given that the reading of eigenvariables is universal). If the judgment P is about, say, bisimulation, then it is not likely that a statement about bisimulation involving two different names x and y remains true if they are identified to the same name z. To address this problem, the logic $FO\lambda^{\Delta\nabla}$ extends sequents with a new notion of "local scope" for proof-level bound variables (originally motivated in [15] to encode "generic judgments"). In particular, sequents in $FO\lambda^{\Delta\nabla}$ are of the form

$$\Sigma\,;\,\sigma_1 \triangleright B_1, \ldots, \sigma_n \triangleright B_n \vdash \sigma_0 \triangleright B_0$$

where Σ is a *global signature*, i.e., the set of eigenvariables whose scope is over the whole sequent, and σ_i is a *local signature*, i.e., a list of variables scoped over B_i. We shall consider sequents to be binding structures in the sense that the signatures, both the global and local ones, are abstractions over their respective scopes. The variables in Σ and σ_i will admit α-conversion by systematically changing the names of variables in signatures as well as those in their scope, following the usual convention of the λ-calculus. The meaning of eigenvariables is as before, only that now instantiation of eigenvariables has to be capture-avoiding, with respect to the local signatures. The variables in local signatures act as locally scoped *generic constants*, that is, they do not vary in proofs since they will not be instantiated. The expression $\sigma \triangleright B$ is called a *generic judgment* or simply a *judgment*. We use script letters $\mathcal{A}$, $\mathcal{B}$, etc. to denote judgments. We write simply B instead of $\sigma \triangleright B$ if the signature σ is empty. We shall often write the list σ as a string of variables, e.g., a judgment $(x_1, x_2, x_3) \triangleright B$ will be written as $x_1 x_2 x_3 \triangleright B$. If the list x_1, x_2, x_3 is known from context we shall also abbreviate the judgment as $\bar{x} \triangleright B$.

The logical constants of $FO\lambda^{\Delta\nabla}$ are $\forall$ (universal quantifier), $\exists$ (existential quantifier), ∇, $\wedge$ (conjunction), $\vee$ (disjunction), $\supset$ (implication), $\top$ (true) and $\bot$ (false). The inference rules for the quantifiers are given in Figure 1. The complete set of inference rules can be found in [15]. Since we do not allow quantification over predicates, this logic is proof-theoretically similar to first-order logic (hence, the letters FO in $FO\lambda^{\Delta\nabla}$).

$$\frac{\Sigma, \sigma \vdash t : \gamma \qquad \Sigma ; \sigma \triangleright B[t/x], \Gamma \longrightarrow \mathcal{C}}{\Sigma ; \sigma \triangleright \forall_\gamma x.B, \Gamma \longrightarrow \mathcal{C}} \; \forall\mathcal{L} \qquad \frac{\Sigma, h ; \Gamma \longrightarrow \sigma \triangleright B[(h\ \sigma)/x]}{\Sigma ; \Gamma \longrightarrow \sigma \triangleright \forall x.B} \; \forall\mathcal{R}$$

$$\frac{\Sigma, h ; \sigma \triangleright B[(h\ \sigma)/x], \Gamma \longrightarrow \mathcal{C}}{\Sigma ; \sigma \triangleright \exists x.B, \Gamma \longrightarrow \mathcal{C}} \; \exists\mathcal{L} \qquad \frac{\Sigma, \sigma \vdash t : \gamma \qquad \Sigma ; \Gamma \longrightarrow \sigma \triangleright B[t/x]}{\Sigma ; \Gamma \longrightarrow \sigma \triangleright \exists_\gamma x.B} \; \exists\mathcal{R}$$

$$\frac{\Sigma ; (\sigma, y) \triangleright B[y/x], \Gamma \longrightarrow \mathcal{C}}{\Sigma ; \sigma \triangleright \nabla x\ B, \Gamma \longrightarrow \mathcal{C}} \; \nabla\mathcal{L} \qquad \frac{\Sigma ; \Gamma \longrightarrow (\sigma, y) \triangleright B[y/x]}{\Sigma ; \Gamma \longrightarrow \sigma \triangleright \nabla x\ B} \; \nabla\mathcal{R}$$

Fig. 1. The quantifier rules of $FO\lambda^{\Delta\nabla}$.

During the search for proofs (reading rules bottom up), inference rules for $\forall$ and $\exists$ quantifier place new eigenvariables into the global signature while the inference rules for ∇ place them into the local signature. In the $\forall\mathcal{R}$ and $\exists\mathcal{L}$ rules, raising [13] is used when moving the bound variable x, which can range over the variables in both the global signature and the local signature σ, with the variable h that can only range over variables in the global signature: so as not to miss substitution terms, the variable x is replaced by the term $(h\, x_1 \ldots x_n)$, which we shall write simply as $(h\, \sigma)$, where σ is the list $x_1, \ldots, x_n$ (h must not be free in the lower sequent of these rules). In $\forall\mathcal{L}$ and $\exists\mathcal{R}$, the term t can have free variables from both Σ and σ. This is presented in the rule by the typing judgment $\Sigma, \sigma \vdash t : \tau$. The $\nabla\mathcal{L}$ and $\nabla\mathcal{R}$ rules have the proviso that y is not free in $\nabla x\ B$.

The standard inference rules of logic express introduction rules for logical constants. The full logic $FO\lambda^{\Delta\nabla}$ additionally allows introduction of atomic judgments, that is, judgments which do not contain any occurrences of logical constants. To each atomic judgment, $\mathcal{A}$, we associate a defining judgment, $\mathcal{B}$, the *definition* of $\mathcal{A}$. The introduction rule for the judgment $\mathcal{A}$ is in effect done by replacing $\mathcal{A}$ with $\mathcal{B}$ during proof search. This notion of definitions is an extension of work by Schroeder-Heister [22], Eriksson [5], Girard [8], Stärk [23] and McDowell and Miller [10]. These inference rules for definitions allow for modest reasoning about the fixed points of definitions.

Definition 1. *A* definition clause *is written* $\forall \bar{x}[p\,\bar{t} \triangleq B]$*, where* p *is a predicate constant, every free variable of the formula* B *is also free in at least one term in the list* $\bar{t}$ *of terms, and all variables free in* $p\,\bar{t}$ *are contained in the list* $\bar{x}$ *of variables. The atomic formula* $p\,\bar{t}$ *is called the* head *of the clause, and the formula* B *is called the* body*. The symbol* $\triangleq$ *is used simply to indicate a definitional clause: it is not a logical connective. The predicate* p *occurs strictly positively in* B*, that is, it does not occur to the left of any* $\supset$ *(implication).*

Let $\forall_{\tau_1} x_1 \ldots \forall_{\tau_n} x_n.H \triangleq B$ *be a definition clause. Let* $y_1, \ldots, y_m$ *be a list of variables of types* $\alpha_1, \ldots, \alpha_m$*, respectively. The* raised definition clause *of* H *with respect to the signature* $\{y_1 : \alpha_1, \ldots, y_m : \alpha_m\}$ *is defined as*

$$\forall h_1 \ldots \forall h_n.\bar{y} \triangleright H\theta \triangleq \bar{y} \triangleright B\theta$$

where θ *is the substitution* $[(h_1\,\bar{y})/x_1, \ldots, (h_n\,\bar{y})/x_n]$ *and* h_i*, for every* $i \in \{1, \ldots, n\}$*, is of type* $\alpha_1 \rightarrow \ldots \rightarrow \alpha_m \rightarrow \tau_i$*. A* definition *is a set of definition clauses together with their raised clauses.*

The introduction rules for a defined judgment are as follow. When applying the introduction rules, we shall omit the outer quantifiers in a definition clause and assume implicitly that the free variables in the definition clause are distinct from other variables in the sequent.

$$\frac{\{\Sigma\theta\,;\,\mathcal{B}\theta, \Gamma\theta \longrightarrow \mathcal{C}\theta \mid \theta \in CSU(\mathcal{A}, \mathcal{H}) \text{ for some clause } \mathcal{H} \triangleq \mathcal{B}\}}{\Sigma\,;\,\mathcal{A}, \Gamma \longrightarrow \mathcal{C}}\; def\mathcal{L}$$

$$\frac{\Sigma\,;\,\Gamma \longrightarrow \mathcal{B}\theta}{\Sigma\,;\,\Gamma \longrightarrow \mathcal{A}}\; def\mathcal{R}, \quad \text{where } \mathcal{H} \triangleq \mathcal{B} \text{ is a definition clause and } \mathcal{H}\theta = \mathcal{A}$$

In the above rules, we apply substitution to judgments. The result of applying a substitution θ to a generic judgment $x_1, \ldots, x_n \triangleright B$, written as $(x_1, \ldots, x_n \triangleright B)\theta$, is $y_1, \ldots, y_n \triangleright B'$, if $(\lambda x_1 \ldots \lambda x_n.B)\theta$ is equal (modulo λ-conversion) to $\lambda y_1 \ldots \lambda y_n.B'$. If Γ is a multiset of generic judgments, then $\Gamma\theta$ is the multiset $\{J\theta \mid J \in \Gamma\}$. In the $def\mathcal{L}$ rule, we use the notion of *complete set of unifiers* (CSU) [9]. We denote by $CSU(\mathcal{A}, \mathcal{H})$ the complete set of unifiers for the pair $(\mathcal{A}, \mathcal{H})$, that is, for any substitution θ such that $\mathcal{A}\theta = \mathcal{H}\theta$, there is a substitution $\rho \in CSU(\mathcal{A}, \mathcal{H})$ such that $\theta = \rho \circ \theta'$ for some substitution θ'. In all the applications of $def\mathcal{L}$ in this paper, the set $CSU(\mathcal{A}, \mathcal{H})$ is either empty (the two judgments are not unifiable) or contains a single substitution denoting the most general unifier. The signature $\Sigma\theta$ in $def\mathcal{L}$ denotes a signature obtained from Σ by removing the variables in the domain of θ and adding the variables in the range of θ. In the $def\mathcal{L}$ rule, reading the rule bottom-up, eigenvariables can be instantiated in the premise, while in the $def\mathcal{R}$ rule, eigenvariables are not instantiated. The set that is the premise of the $def\mathcal{L}$ rule means that that rule instance has a premise for every member of that set: if that set is empty, then the premise is proved.

3 Logical Specification of One-Step Transition

We consider the late transition system for the π-calculus in [16], but we shall follow the operational semantics of π-calculus presented in [21]. The syntax of processes is defined as follows

$$\mathtt{P} ::= 0 \mid \bar{x}y.\mathtt{P} \mid x(y).\mathtt{P} \mid \tau.\mathtt{P} \mid (x)\mathtt{P} \mid [x=y]\mathtt{P} \mid \mathtt{P}|\mathtt{P} \mid \mathtt{P}+\mathtt{P} \mid !P.$$

We use the notation $\mathtt{P}$, $\mathtt{Q}$, $\mathtt{R}$, $\mathtt{S}$ and $\mathtt{T}$ to denote processes. Names are denoted by lower case letters, e.g., a, b, c, d, x, y, z. The occurrence of y in the process $x(y).\mathtt{P}$ and $(y)\mathtt{P}$ is a binding occurrence, with $\mathtt{P}$ as its scope. The set of free names in $\mathtt{P}$ is denoted by $\mathrm{fn}(\mathtt{P})$, the set of bound names is denoted by $\mathrm{bn}(\mathtt{P})$. We write $\mathrm{n}(\mathtt{P})$ for the set $\mathrm{fn}(\mathtt{P}) \cup \mathrm{bn}(\mathtt{P})$. We consider processes to be syntactically equivalent up to renaming of bound names.

One-step transition in the π-calculus is denoted by $\mathtt{P} \xrightarrow{\alpha} \mathtt{Q}$, where $\mathtt{P}$ and $\mathtt{Q}$ are processes and α is an action. The kinds of actions are *the silent action* τ, *the free input action* xy, *the free output action* $\bar{x}y$, *the bound input action* $x(y)$ and *the bound output action* $\bar{x}(y)$. The name y in $x(y)$ and $\bar{x}(y)$ is a binding occurrence. Just like we did with processes, we use $\mathrm{fn}(\alpha)$, $\mathrm{bn}(\alpha)$ and $\mathrm{n}(\alpha)$ to denote free names, bound names, and names in α. An action without binding occurrences of names is a *free action*, otherwise it is a *bound action.*

We encode the syntax of process expressions using higher-order syntax as follows. We shall require three primitive syntactic categories: n for names, p for processes, and a for actions, and the constructors corresponding to the operators in π-calculus. We do not assume any inhabitants of type n, therefore in our encoding a free name is translated to a variable of type n, which can later be either universally quantified or ∇-quantified, depending on whether we want to treat a certain name as instantiable or not. In this paper, however, we consider only ∇-quantified names. Universally quantified names are used in the encoding of open bisimulation in [26]. Since the rest of this paper is about the π-calculus, the ∇ quantifier will from now on only be used at type n. To encode actions, we use $\tau : a$ (for the silent action), and the two constants $\downarrow$ and $\uparrow$, both of type $n \to n \to a$ for building input and output actions. The free output action $\bar{x}y$, is encoded as $\uparrow xy$ while the bound output action $\bar{x}(y)$ is encoded as $\lambda y\, (\uparrow xy)$ (or the η-equivalent term $\uparrow x$). The free input action xy, is encoded as $\downarrow xy$ while the bound input action $x(y)$ is encoded as $\lambda y\, (\downarrow xy)$ (or simply $\downarrow x$). The process constructors are encoded using the following constants:

$$0 : p \qquad \tau : p \to p \qquad \mathit{out} : n \to n \to p \to p \qquad \mathit{in} : n \to (n \to p) \to p$$
$$+ : p \to p \to p \qquad | : p \to p \to p \qquad ! : p \to p$$
$$\mathit{match} : n \to n \to p \to p \qquad \nu : (n \to p) \to p$$

We use two predicates to encode the one-step transition semantics for the π-calculus. The predicate $\cdot \xrightarrow{\cdot} \cdot$ of type $p \to a \to p \to o$ encodes transitions involving free values and the predicate $\cdot \stackrel{\cdot}{\rightharpoonup} \cdot$ of type $p \to (n \to a) \to (n \to p) \to o$ encodes transitions involving bound values. The precise translation of π-calculus syntax into simply typed λ-terms is given in the following definition.

Definition 2. *The following function* $[\![.]\!]$ *translates from process expressions to* $\beta\eta$*-long normal terms of type* p.

$$\begin{array}{lll} [\![0]\!] = 0 & [\![\mathtt{P}+\mathtt{Q}]\!] = [\![\mathtt{P}]\!] + [\![\mathtt{Q}]\!] & [\![\mathtt{P}|\mathtt{Q}]\!] = [\![\mathtt{P}]\!] \mid [\![\mathtt{Q}]\!] \\ [\![\tau.\mathtt{P}]\!] = \tau\,[\![\mathtt{P}]\!] & [\![[x=y]\mathtt{P}]\!] = match\ x\ y\ [\![\mathtt{P}]\!] & [\![\bar{x}y.\mathtt{P}]\!] = out\ x\ y\ [\![\mathtt{P}]\!] \\ [\![x(y).\mathtt{P}]\!] = in\ x\ \lambda y.[\![\mathtt{P}]\!] & [\![(x)\mathtt{P}]\!] = \nu\lambda x.[\![\mathtt{P}]\!] & [\![!\mathtt{P}]\!] = ![\![\mathtt{P}]\!] \end{array}$$

The one-step transition judgments are translated to atomic formulas as follows (we overload the symbol $[\![.]\!]$*).*

$$\begin{array}{ll} [\![\mathtt{P} \xrightarrow{\bar{x}y} \mathtt{Q}]\!] = [\![\mathtt{P}]\!] \xrightarrow{\uparrow xy} [\![\mathtt{Q}]\!] & [\![\mathtt{P} \xrightarrow{x(y)} \mathtt{Q}]\!] = [\![\mathtt{P}]\!] \xrightharpoonup{\downarrow x} \lambda y.[\![\mathtt{Q}]\!] \\ [\![\mathtt{P} \xrightarrow{\tau} \mathtt{Q}]\!] = [\![\mathtt{P}]\!] \xrightarrow{\tau} [\![\mathtt{Q}]\!] & [\![\mathtt{P} \xrightarrow{\bar{x}(y)} \mathtt{Q}]\!] = [\![\mathtt{P}]\!] \xrightharpoonup{\uparrow x} \lambda y.[\![\mathtt{Q}]\!] \\ [\![\mathtt{P} \xrightarrow{xy} \mathtt{Q}]\!] = [\![\mathtt{P}]\!] \xrightarrow{\downarrow xy} [\![\mathtt{Q}]\!] & \end{array}$$

We abbreviate $\nu\lambda x.P$ as simply $\nu x.P$. Notice that when τ is written as a prefix, it has type $p \to p$, and when it is written as an action, it has type a.

The operational semantics of the late transition system for π-calculus is given as a definition, called $\mathbf{D}_\pi$, in Figure 2. In the figure, we omit the symmetric cases for par, sum, close and com. In this specification, free variables are schema variables that are assumed to be universally scoped over the definition clause in which they appear. These schema variables have primitive types such as a, n, and p as well as functional types such as $n \to a$ and $n \to p$.

Notice that as a consequence of the use of HOAS in the encoding, the complicated side conditions in the original specifications of π-calculus [16] are no longer present. For example, the side condition that $X \neq y$ in the open rule is implicit, since X is outside the scope of y and therefore cannot be instantiated with y. The adequacy of our encoding is stated in the following lemma and proposition (their proofs can be found in [25]).

Lemma 3. *The function* $[\![.]\!]$ *is a bijection between* α*-equivalence classes of expressions.*

Proposition 4. *Let* P *and* Q *be processes and* α *an action. Let* $\bar{n}$ *be a list of free names containing the free names in* P, Q, *and* α. *The transition* $\mathtt{P} \xrightarrow{\alpha} \mathtt{Q}$ *is derivable in* π*-calculus if and only if* $.\,;\,.\ \vdash \nabla\bar{n}.[\![\mathtt{P} \xrightarrow{\alpha} \mathtt{Q}]\!]$ *in* $FO\lambda^{\Delta\nabla}$ *with the definition* $\mathbf{D}_\pi$.

Note that since in the translation from π-calculus to $FO\lambda^{\Delta\nabla}$ free names are translated to ∇-quantified variables, to get the completeness of the encoding, it is necessary to show that the transition in π-calculus is invariant under free-name renaming. This has been shown in [16]. In fact, most of the properties of interest in π-calculus, such as bisimulation and satisfiability of modal formulae, are closed under free-name renaming [17].

4 Specification of Modal Logics

We now consider the modal logics for π-calculus introduced in [17]. In order not to confuse meta-level ($FO\lambda^{\Delta\nabla}$) formulas (or connectives) with the formulas

$$
\begin{array}{rl}
\text{TAU:} & \tau\, P \xrightarrow{\tau} P \triangleq \top \\
\text{IN:} & in\ X\ M \stackrel{\downarrow X}{\rightharpoonup} M \triangleq \top \\
\text{OUT:} & out\ x\ y\ P \xrightarrow{\uparrow xy} P \triangleq \top \\
\text{MATCH:} & match\ x\ x\ P \xrightarrow{A} Q \triangleq P \xrightarrow{A} Q \\
 & match\ x\ x\ P \stackrel{A}{\rightharpoonup} Q \triangleq P \stackrel{A}{\rightharpoonup} Q \\
\text{SUM:} & P + Q \xrightarrow{A} R \triangleq P \xrightarrow{A} R \\
 & P + Q \stackrel{A}{\rightharpoonup} R \triangleq P \stackrel{A}{\rightharpoonup} R \\
\text{PAR:} & P \mid Q \xrightarrow{A} P' \mid Q \triangleq P \xrightarrow{A} P' \\
 & P \mid Q \stackrel{A}{\rightharpoonup} \lambda n(M\,n \mid Q) \triangleq P \stackrel{A}{\rightharpoonup} M \\
\text{RES:} & \nu n.Pn \xrightarrow{A} \nu n.Qn \triangleq \nabla n(Pn \xrightarrow{A} Qn) \\
 & \nu n.Pn \stackrel{A}{\rightharpoonup} \lambda m\ \nu n.P'nm \triangleq \nabla n(Pn \stackrel{A}{\rightharpoonup} P'n) \\
\text{OPEN:} & \nu y.My \stackrel{\uparrow X}{\rightharpoonup} M' \triangleq \nabla y(My \xrightarrow{\uparrow Xy} M'y) \\
\text{CLOSE:} & P \mid Q \xrightarrow{\tau} \nu y.My \mid Ny \triangleq \exists X.P \stackrel{\downarrow X}{\rightharpoonup} M \wedge Q \stackrel{\uparrow X}{\rightharpoonup} N \\
\text{COM:} & P \mid Q \xrightarrow{\tau} MY \mid Q' \triangleq \exists X.P \stackrel{\downarrow X}{\rightharpoonup} M \wedge Q \xrightarrow{\uparrow XY} Q' \\
\text{REP-ACT:} & !P \xrightarrow{A} P' |!P \triangleq P \xrightarrow{A} P' \\
 & !P \stackrel{X}{\rightharpoonup} \lambda y(My|!P) \triangleq P \stackrel{X}{\rightharpoonup} M \\
\text{REP-COM:} & !P \xrightarrow{\tau} (P' \mid M\ Y)|!P \triangleq \exists X.P \xrightarrow{\uparrow XY} P' \wedge P \stackrel{\downarrow X}{\rightharpoonup} M \\
\text{REP-CLOSE:} & !P \xrightarrow{\tau} \nu z.(Mz \mid Nz)|!P \triangleq \exists X.P \stackrel{\uparrow X}{\rightharpoonup} M \wedge P \stackrel{\downarrow X}{\rightharpoonup} N
\end{array}
$$

Fig. 2. Definition clauses for the late transition system.

(connectives) of modal logics under consideration, we shall refer to the latter as object formulas (respectively, object connectives). We shall work only with object formulas which are in negation normal form, i.e., negation appears only at the level of atomic object formulas. As a consequence, we introduce explicitly each dual pair of the object connectives. Note that since the only atomic object formulas are either true or false, by de Morgan duality $\neg$true $\equiv$ false and $\neg$false $\equiv$ true. Therefore we are in effect working with positive formulas only. The syntax of the object formulas is given by

$$
\begin{array}{rl}
\mathtt{A} ::= & \text{true} \mid \text{false} \mid \mathtt{A} \wedge \mathtt{A} \mid \mathtt{A} \vee \mathtt{A} \mid [x = z]\mathtt{A} \mid \langle x = z \rangle \mathtt{A} \\
 & \mid \langle \alpha \rangle \mathtt{A} \mid [\alpha]\mathtt{A} \mid \langle \bar{x}(y) \rangle \mathtt{A} \mid [\bar{x}(y)]\mathtt{A} \mid \langle x(y) \rangle \mathtt{A} \mid [x(y)]\mathtt{A} \\
 & \mid \langle x(y) \rangle^L \mathtt{A} \mid [x(y)]^L \mathtt{A} \mid \langle x(y) \rangle^E \mathtt{A} \mid [x(y)]^E \mathtt{A}
\end{array}
$$

In each of the formulas (and their dual 'boxed'-formulas) $\langle \bar{x}(y) \rangle \mathtt{A}$, $\langle x(y) \rangle \mathtt{A}$, $\langle x(y) \rangle^L \mathtt{A}$ and $\langle x(y) \rangle^E \mathtt{A}$, the occurrence of y in parentheses is a binding occurrence whose scope is $\mathtt{A}$. We use $\mathtt{A}, \mathtt{B}, \mathtt{C}, \mathtt{D}$, possibly with subscripts or primes, to range over object formulas. Note that we consider only finite conjunction since the transition system we are considering is finitely branching, and therefore (as noted in [17]) infinite conjunction is not needed. Note also that we do not

(a) Propositional connectives and *basic* modality:

$$
\begin{array}{lll}
(\text{true}:) & P \models \text{true} & \triangleq \top. \\
(\text{and}:) & P \models A\&B & \triangleq P \models A \wedge P \models B. \\
(\text{or}:) & P \models A\hat{\vee}B & \triangleq P \models A \vee P \models B. \\
(\text{match}:) & P \models \langle X \dot{=} X\rangle A & \triangleq P \models A. \\
(\text{match}:) & P \models [X \dot{=} Y]A & \triangleq (X = Y) \supset P \models A. \\
(\text{free}:) & P \models \langle X\rangle A & \triangleq \exists P'(P \xrightarrow{X} P' \wedge P' \models A). \\
(\text{free}:) & P \models [X]A & \triangleq \forall P'(P \xrightarrow{X} P' \supset P' \models A). \\
(\text{out}:) & P \models \langle \uparrow X\rangle A & \triangleq \exists P'(P \xrightarrow{\uparrow X} P' \wedge \nabla y.P'y \models Ay). \\
(\text{out}:) & P \models [\uparrow X]A & \triangleq \forall P'(P \xrightarrow{\uparrow X} P' \supset \nabla y.P'y \models Ay). \\
(\text{in}:) & P \models \langle \downarrow X\rangle A & \triangleq \exists P'(P \xrightarrow{\downarrow X} P' \wedge \exists y.P'y \models Ay). \\
(\text{in}:) & P \models [\downarrow X]A & \triangleq \forall P'(P \xrightarrow{\downarrow X} P' \supset \forall y.P'y \models Ay).
\end{array}
$$

(b) *Late* modality:

$$
\begin{array}{l}
P \models \langle \downarrow X\rangle^l A \triangleq \exists P'(P \xrightarrow{\downarrow X} P' \wedge \forall y.P'y \models Ay). \\
P \models [\downarrow X]^l A \triangleq \forall P'(P \xrightarrow{\downarrow X} P' \supset \exists y.P'y \models Ay).
\end{array}
$$

(c) *Early* modality:

$$
\begin{array}{l}
P \models \langle \downarrow X\rangle^e A \triangleq \forall y \exists P'(P \xrightarrow{\downarrow X} P' \wedge P'y \models Ay). \\
P \models [\downarrow X]^e A \triangleq \exists y \forall P'(P \xrightarrow{\downarrow X} P' \supset P'y \models Ay).
\end{array}
$$

Fig. 3. Modal logics for π-calculus in λ-tree syntax

consider free input modality $\langle xy\rangle$ since we restrict ourselves to late transition system (but adding early transition rules and free input modality does not pose any difficulty). We consider object formulas equivalent up to renaming of bound variables.

We introduce the types o' to denote object-level propositions, and the following constants for encoding the object connectives.

$$
\begin{array}{llll}
\text{true} : o', & \text{false} : o', & \& : o' \to o' \to o', & \hat{\vee} : o' \to o' \to o' \\
\multicolumn{2}{r}{\langle \cdot \dot{=} \cdot \rangle \cdot : n \to n \to o' \to o',} & \multicolumn{2}{l}{[\cdot \dot{=} \cdot] \cdot : n \to n \to o' \to o',} \\
\multicolumn{2}{r}{\langle \cdot \rangle \cdot : a \to o' \to o',} & \multicolumn{2}{l}{[\cdot] \cdot : a \to o' \to o',} \\
\multicolumn{2}{r}{\langle \downarrow \cdot \rangle \cdot : n \to (n \to o') \to o',} & \multicolumn{2}{l}{[\downarrow \cdot] \cdot : n \to \to (n \to o') \to o'} \\
\multicolumn{2}{r}{\langle \downarrow \cdot \rangle^l \cdot : n \to (n \to o') \to o',} & \multicolumn{2}{l}{[\downarrow \cdot]^l \cdot : n \to (n \to o') \to o'} \\
\multicolumn{2}{r}{\langle \downarrow \cdot \rangle^e \cdot : n \to (n \to o') \to o',} & \multicolumn{2}{l}{[\downarrow \cdot]^e \cdot : n \to (n \to o') \to o'}
\end{array}
$$

The precise translation from object-level modal formulas to λ-tree syntax is given in the following.

Definition 5. *The following function* $[\![.]\!]$ *translates from object formulas to* $\beta\eta$*-long normal terms of type* o'*.*

$$
\begin{array}{ll}
[\![true]\!] = true & [\![false]\!] = false \\
[\![\mathtt{A} \wedge \mathtt{B}]\!] = [\![\mathtt{A}]\!] \& [\![\mathtt{B}]\!] & [\![\mathtt{A} \vee \mathtt{B}]\!] = [\![\mathtt{A}]\!] \hat{\vee} [\![\mathtt{B}]\!] \\
[\![[x = y]\mathtt{A}]\!] = [x \dot{=} y][\![\mathtt{A}]\!] & [\![\langle x = y \rangle \mathtt{A}]\!] = \langle x \dot{=} y \rangle [\![\mathtt{A}]\!] \\
[\![\langle \alpha \rangle \mathtt{A}]\!] = \langle \alpha \rangle [\![\mathtt{A}]\!] & [\![[\alpha]\mathtt{A}]\!] = [\alpha][\![\mathtt{A}]\!] \\
[\![\langle x(y) \rangle \mathtt{A}]\!] = \langle \downarrow x \rangle (\lambda y [\![\mathtt{A}]\!]) & [\![[x(y)]\mathtt{A}]\!] = [\downarrow x](\lambda y [\![\mathtt{A}]\!]) \\
[\![\langle x(y) \rangle^L \mathtt{A}]\!] = \langle \downarrow x \rangle^l (\lambda y [\![\mathtt{A}]\!]) & [\![[x(y)]^L \mathtt{A}]\!] = [\downarrow x]^l (\lambda y [\![\mathtt{A}]\!]) \\
[\![\langle x(y) \rangle^E \mathtt{A}]\!] = \langle \downarrow x \rangle^e (\lambda y [\![\mathtt{A}]\!]) & [\![[x(y)]^E \mathtt{A}]\!] = [\downarrow x]^e (\lambda y [\![\mathtt{A}]\!])
\end{array}
$$

The satisfaction relation $\models$ between processes and formulas are encoded using the same symbol, which is given the type $p \to o' \to o$. The inference rules for this satisfaction relation are given as definition clauses in Figure 3. Some of the definition clauses make use of the syntactic equality predicate, which is defined as the definition: $X = X \stackrel{\triangle}{=} \top$. Note that the symbol $=$ here is a predicate symbol written in infix notation. The inequality $x \neq y$ is an abbreviation for $x = y \supset \bot$.

We refer to the definition shown in Figure 3 as $\mathcal{DA}$. This definition corresponds to the modal logic $\mathcal{A}$ defined in [17]. However, this definition is not complete, in the sense that there are true assertion of modal logics which are not provable using this definition alone. For instance, the modal judgment

$$x(y).x(z).0 \models \langle x(y) \rangle \langle x(z) \rangle (\langle x = z \rangle \text{true} \ \hat{\vee} \ [x = z]\text{false})$$

is valid, but its encoding in $FO\lambda^{\Delta\nabla}$ is not provable without additional assumptions. It turns out that the only assumption we need to get completeness is the axiom of excluded middle on names:

$$\forall x \forall y. x = y \vee x \neq y.$$

Note that since we allow dynamic creation of scoped names (via ∇), we must also state this axiom for arbitrary extension of local signatures. We therefore define the following set of excluded middles on arbitrary finite extension of local signatures

$$\mathcal{E} = \{\nabla n_1 \cdots \nabla n_k \forall x \forall y (x = y \vee x \neq y) \mid k \geq 0\}$$

We shall write $\mathcal{X} \subseteq_f \mathcal{E}$ to indicate that $\mathcal{X}$ is a finite subset of $\mathcal{E}$.

We shall now state the adequacy of the encoding of modal logics. The proof of the adequacy result can be found in the extended version of this paper.

Proposition 6. *Let* $\mathtt{P}$ *be a process, let* $\mathtt{A}$ *be an object formula. Then* $\mathtt{P} \models \mathtt{A}$ *if and only if for some list* $\bar{n}$ *containing the free names of* $(\mathtt{P}, \mathtt{A})$ *and some* $\mathcal{X} \subseteq_f \mathcal{E}$*, the sequent* $\mathcal{X} \longrightarrow \nabla \bar{n}.([\![\mathtt{P}]\!] \models [\![\mathtt{A}]\!])$ *is provable in* $FO\lambda^{\Delta\nabla}$ *with definition* $\mathcal{DA}$.

Note that we quantify free names in the process-formula pair in the above proposition since, as we have mentioned previously, we do not assume any constants of type n. Of course, such constants can be introduced without affecting the provability of the satisfaction judgments, but for simplicity in the meta-theory we consider the more uniform approach using ∇-quantified variables to encode names in process and object formulas. Note that adequacy result stated in Proposition 6 subsumes the adequacy for the specifications of the sublogics of $\mathcal{A}$.

$$
\begin{array}{lcl}
P \models_L \langle\uparrow X\rangle A & \triangleq & \exists P'(P \xrightarrow{\uparrow X} P' \wedge \nabla y.P'y \models_{y::L} Ay).\\
P \models_L [\uparrow X]A & \triangleq & \forall P'(P \xrightarrow{\uparrow X} P' \supset \nabla y.P'y \models_{y::L} Ay).\\
P \models_L \langle\downarrow X\rangle A & \triangleq & \exists P'(P \xrightarrow{\downarrow X} P' \wedge \nabla z \exists y.y \in (z :: L) \wedge P'y \models_{z::L} Ay).\\
P \models_L [\downarrow X]A & \triangleq & \forall P'(P \xrightarrow{\downarrow X} P' \supset \nabla z \forall y.y \in (z :: L) \supset P'y \models_{z::L} Ay).\\
P \models_L \langle\downarrow X\rangle^l A & \triangleq & \exists P'(P \xrightarrow{\downarrow X} P' \wedge \nabla z \forall y.y \in (z :: L) \supset P'y \models_{z::L} Ay).\\
P \models_L [\downarrow X]^l A & \triangleq & \forall P'(P \xrightarrow{\downarrow X} P' \supset \nabla z \exists y.y \in (z :: L) \wedge P'y \models_{z::L} Ay).
\end{array}
$$

Fig. 4. A more concrete specification with explicit names representation.

5 Implementation of Proof Search

We now give an overview of a prototype implementation of a fragment of $FO\lambda^{\Delta\nabla}$, in which the specification of modal logics given in the previous section is implemented. This implementation, called *Level 0/1 prover* [24], is based on the duality of finite success and *finite failure* in proof search, or equally, the duality of proof and refutation. In particular, the finite failure in proving a goal $\exists x.G$ should give us a proof of $\neg(\exists x.G)$ and vice versa. We experiment with a simple class of formulae which exhibits this duality. This class of formulae is given by the following grammar:

$$
\begin{array}{ll}
\text{Level 0:} & G := \top \mid \bot \mid A \mid G \wedge G \mid G \vee G \mid \exists x.G \mid \nabla x.G\\
\text{Level 1:} & D := \top \mid \bot \mid A \mid D \wedge D \mid D \vee D \mid G \supset D \mid \exists x.D \mid \nabla x.D \mid \forall x.D\\
\text{atomic:} & A := p\, t_1 \ldots t_n
\end{array}
$$

Notice that the level-0 formula is basically Horn-goal extended with ∇ to allow dynamic creation of names. Level-0 formula is used to encode transition systems (via definitions). Level-1 formula allows for reflecting on the provability of level-0 formulae, and hence exploring all the paths of the transition systems encoded at level-0.

The proof search implementation for level-0 formula is the standard logic-programming implementation. It is actually a subset of λProlog (with $\forall$ replacing ∇). That is, existentially quantified variables are replaced by logic variables, ∇-quantified variables are replaced with (scoped) constants. The non-standard part in Level 0/1 prover is the proof search for level-1 goals. Proof search for a level-1 goal $G_1 \supset G_2$ proceeds as follows:

1. Run the prover with the goal G_1, treating eigenvariables as logic variables.
2. If Step 1 fails, then proof search for $G_1 \supset G_2$ succeeds. Otherwise, collect all answer substitutions produced in Step 1, and for each answer susbtitution θ, proceed with proving $G_2\theta$

There is some restriction on the occurrence of logic variables in Step 2, which however does not affect the encoding of modal logics considered in this paper. We refer the interested readers to [24] for more details.

We now consider the problem of automating model-checking for a given process P against a given assertion A of sublogics of $\mathcal{A}$. There are two main difficulties in automating the model checking: when to use the excluded middle on names, and guessing how many names to be provided in advance. There seems to be two extremes in dealing with these problems: one in which excluded middles are omitted and the set of names are fixed to the free names of the processes and assertions involved, the other is to keep track of the set of free names explicitly and to instantiate any universally quantified name with all the names in this set. For the former, the implementation is straightforward: we simply use the specification given in Figure 3. The problem is of course that it is incomplete, although it may cover quite a number of interesting cases. We experiment here on the second approach using explicit handling of names which is complete but less efficient. The essential modifications to the specification in Figure 3 are those concerning input modalities. We list some modified clauses in Figure 4, the complete "implementation" can be found in an extended version of this paper. We shall refer to this definition as $\mathcal{DA}'$ The satisfiability relation $\models$ now takes an extra argument which is a list of names. The empty list is denoted with nil and the list constructor with ::. Here we use an additional defined predicate for list membership. It is defined in the standard way (writing the membership predicate in infix notation): $X \in (X :: L) \stackrel{\triangle}{=} \top$ and $X \in (Y :: L) \stackrel{\triangle}{=} X \in L$.

Proposition 7. *Let* P *be a process, let* A *be an object formula and let* $\bar{n}$ *be a list containing the free names of* (P, A). *Then* $\mathtt{P} \models \mathtt{A}$ *if and only the formula* $\nabla\bar{n}.[\![\mathtt{P}]\!] \models_{\bar{n}} [\![\mathtt{A}]\!]$ *is provable in* $FO\lambda^{\Delta\nabla}$ *with definition* $\mathcal{DA}'$. *Moreover, proof search in the Level 0/1 prover for the formula terminates.*

6 Related and Future Work

Perhaps the closest to our approach is Mads Dam's work on model checking mobile processes [3,4]. However, our approach differs from his work in that the proof system we introduce is modular; different transition systems can be incorporated via definitions, while in his system, specifications of transition systems (π-calculus) are tightly integrated into the proof rules of the logic. Another difference is that we use the labelled transitions to encode the operational semantics which yields a simpler formalization (not having to deal with structural congruence) while Dam uses commitment relation with structural congruence. Another notable difference is that the use of relativised correctness assertions in his work which make explicit various conditions on names. In our approach, the conditions on names are partly taken care of implicitly by the meta logic (e.g., scoping, α-conversion, "newness"). However, Dam's logic is certainly more expressive in the sense that it can handle modal μ-calculus as well, via some global discharge conditions in proofs. We plan to investigate how to extend $FO\lambda^{\Delta\nabla}$ with such global discharge conditions.

History dependent automata (see, e.g., [6]) is a rather general model theoretic approach to model checking mobile processes. Its basis in automata models makes it closer to existing efficient implementation of model checkers. Our approach is certainly different from a conceptual view, so the sensible comparison would be in terms of performance comparison. However, at the current stage of our implementation, meaningful comparison cannot yet be made. A point to note, however, is that in the approach using history dependent automata, the whole state space of a process is constructed before checking the satisfiability of an assertion. In our approach, states of processes are constructed only when needed, that is, it is guided by the syntax of the process and the assertion it is being checked against.

Model checkers for π-calculus have also been implemented in XSB tabled logic programming [27]. The logic programming language used is a first-order one, and consequently, they have to encode bindings, α-conversion, etc. using first-order syntax. Such encodings make it hard to reason about the correctness of their specification. Compared to this work, our approach here is more declarative and meta theoretic analysis on the specification of the model checkers is available. Model checking for a richer logic than the modal logics we consider has been done in [2]. In this work, the issue concerning fresh names generation is dealt with using the permutation techniques of Gabbay-Pitts [7]. As in Dam's work, names here are dealt with explicitly via some algorithms for computing fresh names, while in our approach, the notion of freshness of names is captured implicitly by their scoping. More in-depth comparison is left for future work.

We plan to improve our current implementation to use the tabling methods in logic programming. Its use in implementing model checkers has been demonstrated in XSB [27] and also in [20]. Implementation of tabled deduction for higher-order logic programming has also been studied in [19], which can potentially be used in the implementation of $FO\lambda^{\Delta\nabla}$. We also plan to study other process calculi and their related notions of equivalences and modal logics, in particular the spi-calculus [1] and its related notions of bisimulation.

Acknowledgment. The author would like to thank the anonymous referees for useful comments and suggestions. This work is based partly on a joint work with Dale Miller (INRIA Futurs/École polytechnique).

References

1. M. Abadi and A. D. Gordon. A calculus for cryptographic protocols: The spi calculus. *Information and Computation*, 148(1):1–70, 99.
2. L. Caries. Behavioral and spatial observations in a logic for the pi-calculus. In I. Walukiewicz, editor, *Proc. of FoSSaCs 2004*, 2004.
3. M. Dam. Model checking mobile processes. *Inf. Comput.*, 129(1):35–51, 1996.
4. M. Dam. Proof systems for pi-calculus logics. *Logic for concurrency and synchronisation*, pages 145–212, 2003.
5. L.-H. Eriksson. A finitary version of the calculus of partial inductive definitions. Vol. 596 of *LNAI*, pages 89–134. Springer-Verlag, 1991.
6. G.-L. Ferrari, S. Gnesi, U. Montanari, and M. Pistore. A model-checking verification environment for mobile processes. *ACM Trans. Softw. Eng. Methodol.*, 12(4):440–473, 2003.

7. M. J. Gabbay and A. M. Pitts. A new approach to abstract syntax with variable binding. *Formal Aspects of Computing*, 13:341–363, 2001.
8. J.-Y. Girard. A fixpoint theorem in linear logic. Email to the linear@cs.stanford.edu mailing list, February 1992.
9. G. Huet. A unification algorithm for typed λ-calculus. *Theoretical Computer Science*, 1:27–57, 1975.
10. R. McDowell and D. Miller. Cut-elimination for a logic with definitions and induction. *Theoretical Computer Science*, 232:91–119, 2000.
11. R. McDowell, D. Miller, and C. Palamidessi. Encoding transition systems in sequent calculus. *Theoretical Computer Science*, 294(3):411–437, 2003.
12. D. Miller. A logic programming language with lambda-abstraction, function variables, and simple unification. Vol. 475 of *LNAI*, pp. 253–281. Springer, 1991.
13. D. Miller. Unification under a mixed prefix. *J. of Symboluc Computation*, 14(4):321–358, 1992.
14. D. Miller and C. Palamidessi. Foundational aspects of syntax. *ACM Comp. Surveys Symp. on Theoretical Computer Science: A Perspective*, vol. 31. ACM, 1999.
15. D. Miller and A. Tiu. A proof theory for generic judgments: An extended abstract. In *Proc. of LICS 2003*, pages 118–127. IEEE, June 2003.
16. R. Milner, J. Parrow, and D. Walker. A calculus of mobile processes, Part II. *Information and Computation*, pages 41–77, 1992.
17. R. Milner, J. Parrow, and D. Walker. Modal logics for mobile processes. *Theoretical Computer Science*, 114(1):149–171, 1993.
18. T. Nipkow. Functional unification of higher-order patterns. In M. Vardi, editor, *Proc. of LICS'93*, pages 64–74. IEEE, June 1993.
19. B. Pientka. *Tabled Higher-Order Logic Programming*. PhD thesis, Carnegie Mellon University, December 2003.
20. Y. S. Ramakrishna, C. R. Ramakrishnan, I. V. Ramakrishnan, S. A. Smolka, T. Swift, and D. S. Warren. Efficient model checking using tabled resolution. In *Proc. of CAV97*, vol. 1254 of LNCS, pages 143–154, 1997.
21. D. Sangiorgi and D. Walker. *π-Calculus: A Theory of Mobile Processes*. Cambridge University Press, 2001.
22. P. Schroeder-Heister. Rules of definitional reflection. In M. Vardi, editor, *Proc. of LICS'93*, pages 222–232. IEEE, June 1993.
23. R. F. Stärk. Cut-property and negation as failure. *International Journal of Foundations of Computer Science*, 5(2):129–164, 1994.
24. A. Tiu. *Level 0/1 Prover: A tutorial*, September 2004. Available online.
25. A. Tiu. *A Logical Framework for Reasoning about Logical Specifications*. PhD thesis, Pennsylvania State University, May 2004.
26. A. Tiu and D. Miller. A proof search specification of the π-calculus. In *3rd Workshop on the Foundations of Global Ubiquitous Computing*, Sept. 2004.
27. P. Yang, C. Ramakrishnan, and S. Smolka. A logical encoding of the π-calculus: model checking mobile processes using tabled resolution. *International Journal on Software Tools for Technology Transfer (STTT)*, 6(1):38–66, July 2004.

A Game Semantics of the Asynchronous π-Calculus

Jim Laird*

Dept. of Informatics, University of Sussex, UK
jiml@sussex.ac.uk

Abstract. This paper studies the denotational semantics of the typed asynchronous π-calculus. We describe a simple game semantics of this language, placing it within a rich hierarchy of games models for programming languages,

A key element of our account is the identification of suitable categorical structures for describing the interpretation of types and terms at an abstract level. It is based on the notion of *closed Freyd category*, establishing a connection between our semantics, and that of the λ-calculus. This structure is also used to define a *trace operator*, with which name binding is interpreted. We then show that our categorical characterization is sufficient to prove a weak soundness result.

Another theme of the paper is the correspondence between justified sequences, on which our model is based, and traces in a labelled transition system in which only bound names are passed. We show that the denotations of processes are equivalent, via this correspondence, to their sets of traces. These results are used to show that the games model is fully abstract with respect to may-equivalence.

1 Introduction

The π-calculus [23] is an elegant and powerful formalism offering a flexible description of name mobility; it can be used to give detailed descriptions of concurrent systems, whilst its conceptual and formal simplicity suggest a route to capturing an underlying "logical structure" of information flow. By investigating the semantics of π-calculus at both abstract and more concrete levels, we aim to develop a model of concurrent, mobile behaviour with both of these features.

In this paper, we describe approaches via category theory and denotational (games) semantics. These complement each other well; the former yields an abstract account of the structure of the π-calculus, whilst the latter gives more concrete representations of processes, closely linked to games models of higher-order programmming and logical systems, and also to other process models such as labelled transition systems. Moreover, their rôles in this paper are interlinked — we define the games model in terms of its categorical structure, whilst the

* Supported by EU FET-GC 'MyThS: Models and Types for Security in Mobile Distributed Systems' IST-2001-32617.

M. Abadi and L. de Alfaro (Eds.): CONCUR 2005, LNCS 3653, pp. 51–65, 2005.

existence of a concrete instance demonstrates the consistency and relevance of the notion of categorical model.

Game semantics already contains a strong element of concurrency: programs (or proofs) are interpreted as strategies, which are basically processes of a particular form, described via their traces. Moreover, π-calculus terms have already been proposed as an elegant formalism for describing strategies in games models of functional languages such as PCF [11,3]. One of the objectives of this paper is to clarify and generalize this relationship between games and the π-calculus (by showing that justified sequences of moves in the former correspond to traces in a labelled transition system for the latter). This should enable the use of the π-calculus to describe and reason about games models to be extended in a methodical way — to imperative features such as state, for example.

On the other hand, given the connections between justifed sequences and traces, what is the advantage of the former to model the π-calculus itself? If we simply regard games as an abstract and mathematically precise representation of trace semantics, this is already a useful development; for example, abstract interpretation [21] and model-checking techniques [6,7] based on HO game semantics are available. Moreover, since our games model is constructed in a purely compositional way, it can be generalized to more "truly concurrent" representations of interaction — we sketch such a pomset model in Section 3.1.

A further important characteristic of game semantics is that it imposes a higher-order, typed structure on the more chaotic world of processes, allowing us to identify a deeper "logical structure" within it. It is this structure which we aim to describe using categorical notions. In particular, our account is based on *closed Freyd categories* [24] which are categorical models of the computational λ-calculus, making a semantic connection between the π-calculus and higher-order functional computation (which is implicit in existing translations of the latter into the former). We also show that adding a simple distributivity condition yields a natural definition of a *trace operator*, which we use to interpret new-name binding, conforming to the intuition that this corresponds to a "plugging in" of input and output. More generally, our account is part of an investigation of the logical structure of higher-order imperative/concurrent computation [17].

1.1 Related Work

Hennessey [9], Stark [26] and Fiore, Moggi and Sangiorgi [20] have described domain-theoretic models of the π-calculus, which are fully abstract with respect to various notions of process equivalence. These works differ from the semantics described here in aspects of the language and equivalence studied (synchronous versus asynchronous, untyped versus typed, bisimulation versus may-testing). One may also contrast the nature of the description of processes obtained: the domain theoretic models represent name-passing quite directly, whereas the games model breaks it down into a smaller atoms. (Giving an equally natural characterization of agent mobility.)

A closer parallel is with the data-flow semantics of the π-calculus given by Jagadeesan and Jagadeesan [12], in which dynamic binding is described using notions from the Geometry of Interaction, analogous to our use of the trace operator. Viewed in the light of the correspondence between game semantics and the labelled transition system described in Section 4, our work is also related to Jeffrey and Rathke's may-testing semantics of concurrent objects [14]. The characterization of may-testing equivalence for the asynchronous π-calculus obtained via interpretatation in the fully abstract model is essentially as described (for a somewhat different LTS) by Boreale, de Nicola and Pugliese in [19].

Connections between Hyland-Ong games and the π-calculus were initially investigated by Hyland and Ong themselves, who described a translation of PCF into the π-calculus derived from the representation of innocent strategies as π-calculus terms. This work was developed by Honda, Berger and Yoshida [3,4], who developed a typing system for the π-calculus identifying sequential processes, and showed that the translation of PCF into this fragment is fully abstract. This research has many parallels with the work described here.

2 A Simply-Typed Asynchronous π-Calculus

We recall the polyadic asynchronous π-calculus [10,5], of which the key operations are the asynchronous output $\overline{x}\langle \boldsymbol{y} \rangle$ of the tuple of names $\boldsymbol{y}$ on channel x, and bound input $x(\boldsymbol{y}).P$ — reception of a tuple of names on channel x which are then substituted for $\boldsymbol{y}$ in P. Our denotational semantics will be made clearer and simpler by a small departure from the original syntax: instead of a single name having distinct input and output capabilities, names will come in complementary pairs $(x, \overline{x})$ of an input name and the corresponding output name $\overline{x}$. New name binding $\nu x.P$ binds both x and $\overline{x}$, but abstraction binds input and output names separately.[1] By convention, we write tuples of names as pairs $(\boldsymbol{y}, \overline{\boldsymbol{z}})$ of tuples of input names $\boldsymbol{x}$ and output names $\overline{\boldsymbol{y}}$. Clearly, we can represent a tuple of names with both input and output capabilities as the pair $(\boldsymbol{x}, \overline{\boldsymbol{x}})$. However, there is no way to guarantee to the receiver of such a tuple that input and output capabilities refer to the same channels. (The difficulties inherent in doing so, in the denotational semantics, are similar to the "bad variable" problem for imperative functional languages.) For related reasons we have neither matching nor mismatching constructs (another point of difference with previous denotational models). We adopt the convention of restricting replication to input-processes, from which we may derive replication of general processes. So the terms of our calculus are given by the grammar:

$$P, Q ::= \mathbf{0} \mid \overline{x}\langle \boldsymbol{y}, \overline{\boldsymbol{z}} \rangle \mid x(\boldsymbol{y}, \overline{\boldsymbol{z}}).P \mid !x(\boldsymbol{y}, \overline{\boldsymbol{z}}).P \mid \nu x.P \mid P|Q$$

Our semantics will be given for a simply-typed version of the π-calculus. Channel types take the form $(\boldsymbol{S}, \boldsymbol{T})$, being a pair of sequences of types (possibly empty) representing the input and output capabilities of the channel (we write

[1] So, in particular, any α-conversion which replaces an input name x with y must replace $\overline{x}$ with $\overline{y}$ (and vice-versa) if x is bound by ν but need not if x is free or bound in an abstraction.

Table 1. Typing Judgements for processes

$$\frac{\Gamma,x{:}T,y{:}T \vdash P;\Sigma}{\Gamma,z{:}T \vdash P\{z/x,z/y\};\Sigma} \qquad \frac{\Gamma \vdash P;\Sigma,\overline{x}{:}T,\overline{y}{:}T}{\Gamma \vdash P\{\overline{z}/\overline{x},\overline{z}/\overline{y}\};\Sigma,\overline{z}{:}T}$$

$$\frac{\Gamma,x{:}S,y{:}T,\Gamma' \vdash P;\Sigma}{\Gamma,y{:}T,x{:}s,\Gamma' \vdash P;\Sigma} \qquad \frac{\Gamma \vdash P;\Sigma,\overline{x}{:}S,\overline{y}{:}T,\Sigma'}{\Gamma \vdash P;\Sigma,\overline{y}{:}T,\overline{x}{:}S,\Sigma'}$$

$$\frac{}{\Gamma \vdash \mathbf{0};\Sigma} \qquad \frac{\Gamma \vdash P;\Sigma \quad \Gamma' \vdash Q;\Sigma'}{\Gamma,\Gamma' \vdash P|Q;\Sigma,\Sigma'}$$

$$\frac{}{\Gamma,\boldsymbol{y}{:}\boldsymbol{S} \vdash \overline{x}\langle \boldsymbol{y},\overline{\boldsymbol{z}}\rangle;\Sigma,\overline{x}{:}(\boldsymbol{S},\boldsymbol{T}),\overline{\boldsymbol{z}}{:}\boldsymbol{T}} \qquad \frac{\Gamma,\boldsymbol{y}{:}\boldsymbol{S} \vdash P;\Sigma,\overline{\boldsymbol{z}}{:}\boldsymbol{T}}{\Gamma,x{:}(\boldsymbol{S},\boldsymbol{T}) \vdash x(\boldsymbol{y},\overline{\boldsymbol{z}}).P;\Sigma}$$

$$\frac{\Gamma,\boldsymbol{y}{:}\boldsymbol{S} \vdash P;\Sigma,\overline{\boldsymbol{z}}{:}\boldsymbol{T}}{\Gamma,x{:}(\boldsymbol{S},\boldsymbol{T}) \vdash !x(\boldsymbol{y},\overline{\boldsymbol{z}}).P;\Sigma} \qquad \frac{\Gamma,x{:}T \vdash P;\Sigma,\overline{x}{:}T}{\Gamma \vdash \nu x.P;\Sigma}$$

() for the empty type $(\_,\_)$). Typing judgements take the form $\Gamma \vdash P;\Sigma$, where Γ is a sequence of typed input names, and Σ is a sequence of typed output names. Derivation rules are given in Table 1; we include explicit structural rules as this simplifies the description of the categorical semantics.

We adopt a reduction semantics based on the standard rules for the π-calculus, except that we require that communication only takes place over *bound* channels. (Note that this is implied by the fact that α-equivalence allows us to replace free input and output names separately: it is at the binding stage that output is "plugged in" to input.) Thus the reduction rule for communication is as follows:

$$\nu \boldsymbol{a}.\nu x.(x(\boldsymbol{y},\overline{\boldsymbol{z}}).P)|\overline{x}\langle \boldsymbol{b},\overline{\boldsymbol{c}}\rangle|Q) \longrightarrow \nu \boldsymbol{a}.\nu x.(P\{\boldsymbol{b}/\boldsymbol{y},\overline{\boldsymbol{c}}/\overline{\boldsymbol{z}}\}|Q)$$

We define the reduction relation $\twoheadrightarrow$ to be the reflexive, transitive closure of (the union of) one-step reduction and structural equivalence, where the latter is defined (standardly) as the smallest congruence containing α-equivalence together with the following rules:

$$\begin{array}{ccc} P|Q \equiv Q|P & \mathbf{0}|P \equiv P & (P|Q)|R \equiv P|(Q|R) \\ \nu x.\nu y.P \equiv \nu y.\nu x.P & (\nu x.P)|Q \equiv \nu x.(P|Q)\ (x \notin FN(Q)) & P \equiv P|!P \end{array}$$

We will show that our semantics is fully abstract with respect to *may-testing equivalence*. Although it is rather coarse, may-equivalence is useful in describing safety properties, and in the study of *deterministic* programming languages via translation.

We test processes in the π-calculus by observing whether they may produce output on a distinguished channel. For a specified (output) name $\overline{x} : ()$, we write $P \downarrow$ if P is structurally equivalent to a process of the form $\overline{x}\langle\rangle|Q$, and $P \Downarrow$ if $P \twoheadrightarrow P'$ such that $P' \downarrow$.

Definition 1. *Assuming that our testing channel x does not occur in P or Q, we define $P \lesssim Q$ if for all contexts $C[\cdot]$, $C[P] \Downarrow$ implies $C[Q] \Downarrow$, and $P \simeq Q$ if $P \lesssim Q$ and $Q \lesssim P$.*

3 Game Semantics

An *arena* [11] is a forest in which the nodes or *moves* are labelled as belonging to either Player or Opponent. Thus an arena A is specified as a triple $(M_A, \lambda_A, \vdash_A)$ consisting of a set of moves, a labelling function $\lambda_A : M_A \to \{P, O\}$ and a set of directed edges $\vdash_A \subseteq M_A \times M_A$ or *enabling relation*[2]. The root nodes of A are called *initial* moves: an arena in which all initial moves are O-moves is said to be *negative*. The *dual* $A^\perp$ of the arena A is obtained by swapping Player and Opponent moves: $A^\perp = (M_A, \lambda_A^\perp, \vdash_A)$, where $\lambda_A^\perp(m) = P$ if $\lambda_A(m) = O$ and vice-versa.

A *justified sequence* s over an arena A is a sequence of moves of A, together with a pointer from each non-initial move in s to some preceding move which enables it. A justified sequence s may be represented as a sequence of moves s together with a (partial) justification function $j_s : \mathbb{N} \to \mathbb{N}$ such that $j_s(k) = i$ if the kth move in s is justified by the ith move. We represent processes as sets of justified sequences or *strategies*. We stipulate that strategies are closed under a preorder $\preceq$, which allows us to give a sequential representation of parallel processes by accounting for the fact that moves of the same polarity (input or output actions) are independent events; their ordering is not (directly) observable, whilst if a process responds to a sequence of actions by the environment (O-moves), then it must make at least the same response to any sequence with more or earlier O-moves. The preorder is based on that introduced in [16], but similar relations are well-established in concurrency theory, in particular we note their use in a LTS characterisation of may-equivalence for the π-calculus [19].

Definition 2. *Let $\preceq$ be the least preorder on justified sequences such that:*

- *If $\lambda(a) = O$ then $sabt \preceq sbat$ and if $\lambda^{OP}(a) = P$ then $sbat \preceq sabt$.*
- *If $\lambda(a) = O$ then $sat \preceq st$, and if $\lambda(a) = P$, then $t \preceq sat$.*

In other words, $s \preceq t$ if s can be obtained from t by removing P-moves or migrating them forwards, and adding O-moves or migrating them backwards. The label-inversion operation $(\_)^\perp$ extends pointwise to justified sequences and is antitone with respect to $\preceq$ — $s \preceq t$ if and only $t^\perp \preceq s^\perp$.

Definition 3. *A strategy $\sigma : A$ is a non-empty subset of J_A which is prefix-closed — i.e. $s \sqsubseteq t \in \sigma$ implies $s \in \sigma$ — and $\preceq$-closed — i.e. $s \preceq t$ and $t \in \sigma$ implies $s \in \sigma$.*

Given any set $S \subseteq J_A$, we may form a strategy $\widehat{S}$ by taking the $\preceq$-closure of the prefix-closure of S: $\widehat{S} = \{t \in J_A \mid \exists s \in S, r \in J_A . t \in S . t \preceq r \sqsubseteq s\}$.

We now define a category of processes $\mathcal{P}$ in which the objects are negative arenas, and morphisms from A to B are strategies on the "function-space" $A^\perp \odot B$, where $\odot$ is the disjoint union of forests:

$$A \odot B = \langle M_A + M_B, [\lambda_A, \lambda_B], [\vdash_A, \vdash_B] \rangle$$

[2] Unlike games models of functional languages, we do not require that non-initial O moves are enabled by P-moves and vice-versa.

Composition of $\sigma : A \to B$ and $\tau : B \to C$ is by "parallel composition plus hiding" [1]:

$$\sigma;\tau = \{s \in J_{A^\perp \odot C} \mid \exists t \in J_{A \odot B \odot C}.t{\restriction}A^\perp, B \in \sigma \wedge t{\restriction}B^\perp, C \in \tau \wedge t{\restriction}A^\perp, C = s\}$$

(where $t \restriction A^\perp, B$ means t restricted to moves from A and B, with the former relabelled by swapping Player and Opponent labels). The identity strategy on A is determined by its set of $\preceq$-maximal sequences, which are the sequences which "copycat" between the two components:

$$\mathtt{id}_A = \{s \in J_{A^\perp \odot A} \mid \forall t \widehat{\sqsubseteq^{even}} .t{\restriction}A^\perp = (t{\restriction}A)^\perp\}$$

We show that $\mathcal{P}$ is a well-defined category following proofs for similar categories of games [2,11,16].

We observe that $\odot$ acts as a symmetric monoidal product[3] on $\mathcal{P}$ with the empty arena I as its identity element, and an action on functions taking $\sigma : A \to C$ and $\tau : B \to D$ to:

$$\sigma \odot \tau = \{s \in A^\perp \odot B^\perp \odot C \odot D \mid s{\restriction}A^\perp \odot C \in \sigma \wedge s{\restriction}B^\perp \odot D \in \tau\}$$

We also note that $\mathcal{P}$ is (pointed) cpo-enriched with the inclusion order on strategies, the least element of each hom-set being the $\preceq$-closure of the set containing only the empty sequence.

We will interpret each process $x_1 : S_1, \ldots, x_m : S_m \vdash P; \overline{y_1} : T_1, \ldots, \overline{y_n} : T_n$ as a morphism from $[\![T_1]\!] \odot \ldots \odot [\![T_n]\!]$ to $[\![S_1]\!] \odot \ldots \odot [\![S_m]\!]$ in $\mathcal{P}$. This may seem counterintuitive: why not interpret P as a morphism from inputs to outputs in the *dual* of $\mathcal{P}$? The reason is that we will interpret the type-structure of the π-calculus using structure defined on $\mathcal{P}$, rather than on its dual. We will show that we can define a *closed Freyd Category* [24] based on $(\mathcal{P}, I, \odot)$. Closed Freyd categories are models of Moggi's computational λ-calculus (in a canonical sense); thus we have the basis for a categorical analysis of the relationship between higher-order functional behaviour and name mobility. A Freyd category is determined by a symmetric premonoidal category of "computations" (in this case the SMC of processes $\mathcal{P}$), a Cartesian category of "values", and an identity-on-objects, symmetric (pre)monoidal functor from the latter to the former. The closure property operates via this functor.

We define a category of values or *abstractions* using the notion of *well-opened* strategy, adapted from [22].

Definition 4. *A legal sequence on a justified arena A is* well-opened *if it is empty, or contains precisely one initial O-move, which is the first move.*

In other words, the set W_A of well-opened sequences of A consists of sequences of the form as, where a is an O-move and s contains no initial O-moves. A well-opened strategy σ is a non-empty and $\sqsubseteq$ and $\preceq$-closed subset of W_A.

[3] For the sake of simplicity, we shall not henceforth mention associativity and unit isomorphisms, as if in a strict monoidal category.

We may think of a well-opened strategy $\sigma : A \to B$ as a process which receives a single input at B, and then produces multiple outputs at A. Thus to define composition of σ with $\tau : B \to C$, we form the "parallel composition plus hiding" of τ with the replication ad libitum of σ.

Definition 5. *Let $s|t$ denote the set of interleavings of the justified sequences s and t. Given a set X of (justified) sequences, we may define the set $!X$ consisting of interleavings of elements of X — i.e. $s \in !X$ if there exists $t_1, \ldots, t_n \in \sigma$ such that $s \in t_1|\ldots|t_n$. Note that if σ is a strategy, then $!\sigma$ is a strategy, and that $!$ is idempotent.*

Composition of σ and τ is now defined:

$$\sigma;\tau = \{s \in W_{A^\perp \odot C} \mid \exists t \in W_{A \odot B \odot C}.t\lceil A^\perp, B \in !\sigma \wedge t\lceil B^\perp, C \in \tau \wedge t\lceil A^\perp, C = s\}$$

Thus we may form a category of abstractions, $\mathcal{A}$ in which the objects are negative arenas, and the morphisms from A to B are well-opened strategies on $A^\perp \odot B$. The well-opened identity on A is the well-opened subset of $\mathtt{id}^{\mathcal{P}}_A$ — i.e. $\mathtt{id}^{\mathcal{A}}_A : A \to A = \mathtt{id}^{\mathcal{P}}_A \cap W_{A^\perp \odot A}$.

Lemma 1. *$\mathcal{A}$ is a well-defined category, with finite products given by $\odot$.*

Proof. We prove that $!$, $\mathtt{id}^{\mathcal{A}}$ have the following properties:

- If $\sigma : A \to B$ is well-opened, then $!\sigma; \mathtt{id}^{\mathcal{A}}_B = \sigma$,
- $!\mathtt{id}^{\mathcal{A}}_A = \mathtt{id}^{\mathcal{P}}_A$,
- If σ, τ are well-opened, then $!\sigma; \tau$ is well-opened, and $!(!\sigma; \tau) = !\sigma; !\tau$.

We also note that every well-opened strategy $\sigma : A \to B$ determines a unique morphism from A to B in $\mathcal{P}$ as its $\preceq$-closure. In particular, we shall write the $\preceq$-closure of the well-opened identity as $\mathsf{der}_A : A \to A$ and use the fact that $\mathsf{der}_A \subseteq \mathtt{id}_A$.

The proof of Lemma 1 also establishes that $!$ acts as a (identity-on-objects) functor from $\mathcal{A}$ to $\mathcal{P}$ such that $!(\sigma \odot \tau) = !\sigma \odot !\tau$ (and $!I = I$) and so $!$. The Cartesian structure of $\mathcal{A}$ gives projection maps $\pi_l : A_1 \odot A_2 \to A_1$ and $\pi_r : A_1 \odot A_2 \to A_2$, and a diagonal map $\Delta_A : A \to A \odot A$. We use the fact that each hom-set of $\mathcal{A}$ is a join semilattice with respect to the inclusion order to define $\nabla_A : A \odot A \to A = \pi_l \cup \pi_r$. This has the defining properties $!\Delta_A; !\nabla_A = !((\Delta; \pi_l) \cup (\Delta; \pi_r)) = !\mathtt{id}^{\mathcal{A}}_A = \mathtt{id}^{\mathcal{P}}_A$ and $\mathtt{id}^{\mathcal{P}}_{A \odot A} \subseteq !\nabla_A; !\Delta_A$.

We have established that the SMC $(\mathcal{P}, I, \odot)$, the Cartesian category $\mathcal{A}$, and the functor $!$ form a Freyd Category in which the product is monoidal rather than premonoidal. Moreoever, it is a *closed* Freyd Category — i.e. the functor $A \odot !\_ : \mathcal{A} \to \mathcal{P}$ has a right-adjoint $A \rightharpoonup \_$. We define $A \rightharpoonup B$ to be $\uparrow (A^\perp \odot B)$, where $\uparrow \_$ is the *lifting* operation which converts a forest to a tree by adding an edge into each of its roots from a single, new (O-labelled) root.

$$\uparrow A = (M_A + \{*\}, [\lambda_A, \{\langle *, O \rangle\}], [\vdash_A, \varnothing] \cup \{\langle *, m \rangle \mid \vdash_A m\})$$

Proposition 1. *For any arena B, $B \multimap \_$ is right-adjoint to $!\_ \odot B : \mathcal{A} \to \mathcal{P}$.*

Proof. There is a simple bijection taking justified sequences in $(A \odot B)^{\perp} \odot C$ to well-opened sequences in $A^{\perp} \odot \uparrow (B^{\perp} \odot C)$: prefix a single initial move in $\uparrow (B^{\perp}, C)$, with justification pointers from the initial moves in $(B^{\perp}, C)$. This acts on strategies to yield a natural isomorphism $\Lambda : \mathcal{P}(!A \odot B, C) \to \mathcal{A}(!A, B \multimap C)$

We use the following additional property of the adjunction: for any A, B, $(\mathsf{der}_{A \multimap B} \odot \mathtt{id}_A); \mathsf{app}_{A,B} = \mathsf{app}_{A,B}$, where $\mathsf{app}_{A,B} : (A \multimap B) \odot A \to B$ is the co-unit. (Since $\mathsf{app}_{A,B}$ only makes the initial move in $A \multimap B$ once.)

We will interpret output as app, and input as the operation Λ, composed with a natural transformation expressing a distributivity property for the exponential over the tensor.

Definition 6. *A Freyd category may be said to be* distributive-closed *if it is closed, and there is a natural transformation: $\varrho_{A,B,C} : !(A \multimap (B \odot C)) \to B \odot !(A \multimap C)$ satisfying the following properties:*

- $(\varrho_{A,B,C} \otimes \mathtt{id}_A); (\mathtt{id}_B \odot \mathsf{app}_{A,C}) = \mathsf{app}_{A,B\odot C}$,
- $\varrho_{A,B,C\otimes D}; (\mathtt{id}_B \otimes \varrho_{A,C,D}) = \varrho_{A,B\otimes C,D}$

In $\mathcal{P}$, ϱ is induced by the map from justified sequences on $A \multimap (B \odot C)$ to justified sequences on $(A \multimap B) \odot C$ which relabels initial moves and removes the justification pointers from the initial moves in C.

In any distributive-closed Freyd category, including $\mathcal{P}$, we may define a *trace operator* $\mathsf{Tr}^{B}_{A,C} : \mathcal{P}(A \odot B, C \odot B) \to \mathcal{P}(B, C)$ making $\mathcal{P}$ a traced monoidal category [15]. This provides a natural notion of "feedback" connecting input to output, with which we interpret new-name binding. We define the trace of $f : A \odot B \to C \odot B$:

$$\mathsf{Tr}^{B}_{A,C}(f) = !\Lambda(f; \theta_{B,C}); \varrho_{B,B,C}; \theta_{B,B \multimap C}; \mathsf{app}_{B,C}$$

Using naturality of the constituent operations, together with the axioms for ϱ, we prove the following lemma.

Lemma 2. Tr *is a trace operator for $\mathcal{P}$ in the sense of [15].*

We may now give the interpretation of the π-calculus in $\mathcal{P}$. The type $(\boldsymbol{S}, \boldsymbol{T})$ is interpreted as the negative arena $[\![\boldsymbol{T}]\!] \multimap [\![\boldsymbol{S}]\!]$ — i.e. $\uparrow ([\![T_1]\!]^{\perp} \odot \ldots [\![T_n]\!]^{\perp} \odot [\![S_1]\!] \odot \ldots \odot [\![S_m]\!])$. Terms-in-context $\Gamma \vdash P; \Sigma$ are interpreted as morphisms $[\![\Gamma \vdash P; \Sigma]\!] : [\![\Sigma]\!] \to [\![\Gamma]\!]$ using the structure of a symmetric monoidal, distributive-closed Freyd category, according to the rules in Table 2. (More precisely, Table 2 gives rules for interpreting each typing-judgement *derivation* as a morphism; we show that every derivation of the same term receives the same denotation.)

We will now use the categorical structure of our model to establish a weak soundness result with respect to the reduction semantics: if M may reduce to N, then $[\![N]\!]$ is included in $[\![M]\!]$. We first show soundness with respect to structural equivalence.

Table 2. Interpretation of processes

$$
\begin{array}{c}
[\![\Gamma, y : T, x : S, \Gamma' \vdash P; \Sigma]\!] = [\![\Gamma, x : S, y : T, \Gamma' \vdash P; \Sigma]\!]; (\mathtt{id}_{[\![\Gamma]\!]} \odot \theta_{[\![T]\!],[\![S]\!]} \odot \mathtt{id}_{[\![\Gamma']\!]}) \\
[\![\Gamma \vdash P; \Sigma, \overline{y} : T, \overline{x} : S, \Sigma']\!] = (\mathtt{id}_{[\![\Sigma]\!]} \odot \theta_{[\![S]\!],[\![T]\!]} \odot \mathtt{id}_{[\![\Sigma']\!]}); [\![\Gamma \vdash P; \Sigma, \overline{x} : S, \overline{y} : T, \Sigma']\!] \\
[\![\Gamma, z : T \vdash P\{z/x, z/y\}; \Sigma]\!] = [\![\Gamma, x : T, y : T \vdash P; \Sigma]\!]; (\mathtt{id}_{[\![\Gamma]\!]} \odot !\Delta_{[\![T]\!]}) \\
[\![\Gamma \vdash P\{\overline{z}/\overline{x}, \overline{z}/\overline{y}\}; \Sigma, \overline{z} : T]\!] = (\mathtt{id}_{[\![\Sigma]\!]} \odot !\nabla_{[\![T]\!]}); [\![\Gamma \vdash P; \Sigma, \overline{x} : S, \overline{y} : T]\!] \\
\Gamma \vdash \mathbf{0}; \Sigma = \bot_{\Sigma,\Gamma} \\
[\![\Gamma, \Gamma' \vdash P|Q; \Sigma, \Sigma']\!] = [\![\Gamma \vdash P, \Sigma]\!] \odot [\![\Gamma' \vdash Q; \Sigma']\!] \\
[\![\Gamma, x : (\boldsymbol{S}, \boldsymbol{T}) \vdash x(\boldsymbol{y}, \overline{\boldsymbol{z}}).P; \Sigma]\!] = !\Lambda([\![\Gamma, \boldsymbol{y} : \boldsymbol{S} \vdash P; \Sigma, \overline{\boldsymbol{z}} : \boldsymbol{T}]\!]); \varrho_{[\![\boldsymbol{S}]\!],[\![\Gamma]\!],[\![\boldsymbol{T}]\!]}; (\mathsf{der}_{[\![(\boldsymbol{S},\boldsymbol{T})]\!]} \odot \mathtt{id}_{[\![\Gamma]\!]}) \\
[\![\Gamma, x : (\boldsymbol{S}, \boldsymbol{T}) \vdash !x(\boldsymbol{y}, \overline{\boldsymbol{z}}).P; \Sigma]\!] = !\Lambda([\![\Gamma, \boldsymbol{y} : \boldsymbol{S} \vdash P; \Sigma, \overline{\boldsymbol{z}} : \boldsymbol{T}]\!]); \varrho_{[\![\boldsymbol{S}]\!],[\![\Gamma]\!],[\![\boldsymbol{T}]\!]} \\
[\![\Gamma, \boldsymbol{y} : \boldsymbol{S} \vdash \overline{x}\langle \boldsymbol{y}, \overline{\boldsymbol{z}}\rangle; \Sigma, \overline{x} : (\boldsymbol{S}, \boldsymbol{T}), \overline{\boldsymbol{z}} : \boldsymbol{T}]\!] = \bot_{\Sigma,\Gamma} \odot \mathsf{app}_{[\![\boldsymbol{S}]\!],[\![\boldsymbol{T}]\!]} \\
[\![\Gamma \vdash \nu x.P; \Sigma]\!] = \mathsf{Tr}^{[\![T]\!]}_{[\![\Sigma]\!],[\![\Gamma]\!]}([\![\Gamma, x : T \vdash P; \Sigma, \overline{x} : T]\!])
\end{array}
$$

Lemma 3. *If $M \equiv N$, then $[\![M]\!] = [\![N]\!]$.*

Proof. The equivalences for parallel composition follow directly from the analogous properties of $\odot$. Those for new-name binding follow from its interpretation as a trace operator — e.g. scope extrusion follows from "tightening"; naturality of $tr^X_{A,B}$ with respect to A, B. For replication, we use the fact that $!f = !\Delta; ((!f; \mathsf{der}) \odot !f); \pi_r \subseteq !\Delta; ((!f; \mathsf{der}) \odot !f); !\nabla \subseteq !\Delta; (!f \odot !f); !\nabla$.

Proposition 2. *If $M \longrightarrow N$, then $[\![N]\!] \subseteq [\![M]\!]$.*

Proof. To show soundness of the reduction rule, we first observe that for any process $\Gamma, x : B, y : B \vdash P; \Sigma, \overline{x} : B, \overline{y} : B$, $[\![\nu x.\nu y.P]\!] \subseteq [\![\nu x.P\{x/y, \overline{x}/\overline{y}\}]\!]$:

By sliding (naturality of the trace operator in B) we have $[\![\nu x.P\{x/y, \overline{x}/\overline{y}\}]\!] = \mathsf{Tr}^B_{[\![\Sigma,\Gamma]\!]}((\mathtt{id}_{[\![\Sigma]\!]} \odot !\Delta_B); [\![P]\!]; (\mathtt{id}_{[\![\Gamma]\!]} \odot !\nabla_B)) = \mathsf{Tr}^{B\odot B}_{[\Sigma]\!],[\![\Gamma]\!]}((\mathtt{id}_{[\![\Sigma]\!]} \odot (!\nabla; !\Delta)); [\![P]\!])$. Since $\mathtt{id}_B \subseteq !\nabla_B; !\Delta_B$, we have $[\![\nu x.\nu y.P]\!] = \mathsf{Tr}^B_{[\![\Sigma]\!],[\![\Gamma]\!]}(\mathsf{Tr}^B_{[\![\Sigma]\!]\odot B,[\![\Gamma]\!]\odot B}([\![P]\!])) = \mathsf{Tr}^{B\odot B}_{[\![\Sigma]\!],[\![\Gamma]\!]}([\![P]\!]) \subseteq [\![\nu x.P\{x/y, \overline{x}/\overline{y}\}]\!]$ as required.

We then show that if c is not free in P, Q, then $[\![\nu c.(\overline{c}\langle \boldsymbol{a}, \overline{\boldsymbol{b}}\rangle | c(\boldsymbol{y}, \overline{\boldsymbol{z}}).P]\!] = [\![P\{\boldsymbol{a}/\boldsymbol{y}, \overline{\boldsymbol{b}}/\overline{\boldsymbol{z}}\}]\!]$, since $[\![\nu c.(\overline{c}\langle \boldsymbol{a}, \overline{\boldsymbol{b}}\rangle | c(\boldsymbol{y}, \overline{\boldsymbol{z}}).P]\!] = \mathsf{Tr}^B_{[\![\Sigma]\!],[\![\Gamma]\!]}(\mathsf{app} \odot (!\Lambda([\![P]\!]); \mathrm{dist}; (\mathsf{der} \odot \mathtt{id}))); \theta) = (!\Lambda([\![P]\!]) \odot \mathtt{id}); \mathrm{dist}; (\mathtt{id} \odot \mathtt{id})(\mathtt{id}_\Gamma \odot \mathsf{app}) = (!\Lambda([\![\mathrm{P}]\!]) \odot \mathtt{id}); \mathsf{app}) = [\![\mathrm{P}\{\boldsymbol{a}/\boldsymbol{y}, \overline{\boldsymbol{b}}/\overline{\boldsymbol{z}}\}]\!]$ (by the "generalized yanking" property for trace operators).

So $[\![\nu x.P\{\boldsymbol{a}/\boldsymbol{y}, \overline{\boldsymbol{b}}/\overline{\boldsymbol{z}}\} | Q]\!] = [\![\nu x.(\nu c.\overline{c}\langle \boldsymbol{a}, \overline{\boldsymbol{b}}\rangle | c(\boldsymbol{y}, \overline{\boldsymbol{z}}).P) | Q]\!] \subseteq [\![\nu x.\overline{x}\langle \boldsymbol{a}, \overline{\boldsymbol{b}}\rangle | x(\boldsymbol{y}, \overline{\boldsymbol{z}}).P | Q]\!]$ as required.

3.1 More Categorical Models

Any semantics based on a distributive-closed Freyd category satisfying the properties used in the proof will also satisfy weak soundness: we have instances reflecting both finer and weaker notions of process equivalence.

Justified Pomsets. By moving to a representation of interaction in terms of pomsets rather than sequences, we may define a finer "true-concurrency-style" version of our games model. Its relationship to the pomset semantics of the synchronous π-calculus in [12] is still under investigation.

A *justified* pomset over an arena A is a finite pomset p for which the labels are elements of M_A, and for each event $e \in p$ with a non-initial label, a pointer to an event e' such that $e' < e$ and $\mathsf{label}(e') \vdash \mathsf{label}(e)$. A pomset over A is alternating, if whenever e' is a maximal element of the set $\{d \in p \mid d <_p e\}$ then $\lambda_A(\mathsf{label}(e)) = \lambda_A^\perp(\mathsf{label}(e'))$.

Note that each justified sequence $s \in J_A$ may be viewed as a (non-alternating), justified *total* pomset: we may say that the justified sequence s is a *sequentialization* of the justified pomset p if there is a order, pointer and label-preserving bijection from p to s. The sequentialization of a set X of pomsets is the set of justified sequences which are the sequentialization of some $p \in \sigma$.

Let O_p and P_p be the restrictions of P to Opponent and player moves, respectively. We define the saturation order on justified, alternatin pomsets thus: $p \preceq q$ if there exist injective functions $f : O_q \to O_p$ and $g : P_p \to P_q$ whicch preserve and reflect order and labelling, and such that if $f(a)$ justifies b, then a justifies $g(b)$, if a justifies $f(b)$ then $g(a)$ justifies b, and if $f(a) < b$ then $a < g(b)$.

Using the constructions $(\_)^\perp$, $\odot$ and $\uparrow(\_)$, we may construct a distributive-closed Freyd category of arenas and pomset-strategies (sets of justified, alternating pomsets, closed under $\preceq$), and thus a semantics of the π-calculus. Denotational equivalence in this model is strictly finer than the interleaving semantics: the justified sequence denotation of any term is the sequentialization of its denotation in the justified pomset model.

Unjustified Sequences. On the other hand, we may construct models which are coarser (not being *adequate* with respect to may-testing) but do have somewhat simpler structure and might therefore be used as *abstract interpretations.* One example is obtained by simply forgetting the justification-pointers in the games model. Given an arena A, an "unjustified sequence" over A is simply a sequence in M_A^* such that every non-initial move is preceded by at least one move which enables it.We may define strategies and their composition exactly as for the justified model, yielding a symmetric monoidal distributive-closed Freyd category. With limited forms of recursion (iteration rather than general replication) we may describe unjustified strategies as regular grammars [6].

We have further instances of "event-structure" like models in which morphisms represent reachable positions, and compositional is wholly relational. In this case we also lose some information about the sequential ordering of events.

4 Full Abstraction

We will now show that our game semantics is fully abstract with respect to may-equivalence. The difficult part of the proof is to show that it is *adequate*: any process $\_ \vdash P; \overline{x} : ()$ which has a non-empty denotation will produce a corresponding output on x. To show this we will relate our game semantics to a *labelled transition system* for the asynchonous π-calculus. We show that traces in our LTS are in bijective correspondence with justified sequences over the associated arenas, and that this extends to relate traces of terms to their denotations as strategies. Rather than the standard LTS for the π-calculus, we use one in which only bound names may be passed. This corresponds to labelled transition systems for HOπ [25,13], in which messages are fresh names used as "triggers".

Actions α are either silent (τ) or take the form $x\langle \boldsymbol{k}, \overline{\boldsymbol{l}}\rangle$ (input) or $\overline{x}\langle \overline{\boldsymbol{k}}, \boldsymbol{l}\rangle$ (the complementary output) where $\boldsymbol{k}, \boldsymbol{l}$ are distinct names such that if $x : (\boldsymbol{S}, \boldsymbol{T})$, then $\boldsymbol{k} : \boldsymbol{T}$ and $\boldsymbol{l} : \boldsymbol{S}$. We refer to x (resp. $\overline{x}$) as the *channel* of α, or $\kappa(\alpha)$, and to $\boldsymbol{k}, \overline{\boldsymbol{l}}$ (resp. $\overline{\boldsymbol{k}}, \boldsymbol{l}$) as the *contents* of α or $\epsilon(\alpha)$. We require that the channel of any action performed by P *must* occur free in P, and that its contents, and their complements, *must not* occur free in P — i.e. the rules of Table 3 all have as an implicit side condition that $P \xrightarrow{\alpha} Q$ only if $\kappa(\alpha) \in FN(P)$ and $(\epsilon(\alpha) \cup \epsilon(\overline{\alpha})) \cap FN(P) = \varnothing$. We write $[x \mapsto \overline{y}]$ for the "persistent forwarder" $!x(\boldsymbol{a}, \overline{\boldsymbol{b}}).\overline{y}\langle \boldsymbol{a}, \overline{\boldsymbol{b}}\rangle$.

Table 3. LTS for bound name passing

$$x(\boldsymbol{y}, \overline{\boldsymbol{z}}).P \xrightarrow{x\langle \boldsymbol{k}, \overline{\boldsymbol{l}}\rangle} P\{\boldsymbol{k}/\boldsymbol{y}, \overline{\boldsymbol{l}}/\overline{\boldsymbol{z}}\} \qquad \overline{x}\langle \boldsymbol{y}, \overline{\boldsymbol{z}}\rangle \xrightarrow{\overline{x}\langle \overline{\boldsymbol{k}}, \boldsymbol{l}\rangle} [\boldsymbol{y} \mapsto \overline{\boldsymbol{k}}] | [\boldsymbol{l} \mapsto \overline{\boldsymbol{z}}]$$

$$\frac{P \xrightarrow{\alpha} P'}{P|Q \xrightarrow{\alpha} P'|Q} \qquad \frac{P \xrightarrow{\alpha} P'}{\nu x.P \xrightarrow{\alpha} \nu x.P'}$$

$$\frac{P \xrightarrow{\alpha} Q \qquad P \equiv P'}{P' \xrightarrow{\alpha} Q} \qquad \frac{P \xrightarrow{x\langle \boldsymbol{k}, \overline{\boldsymbol{l}}\rangle} P' \qquad Q \xrightarrow{\overline{x}\langle \overline{\boldsymbol{k}}, \boldsymbol{l}\rangle} Q'}{\nu x.(P|Q) \xrightarrow{\tau} \nu x.\nu \boldsymbol{k}.\nu \boldsymbol{l}.(P'|Q')}$$

We write $\mathtt{trace}(P)$ for the set of traces of the process P, with the τ-actions erased. If P is typable as $\Gamma \vdash P; \Sigma$, then every member of $\mathtt{trace}(P)$ is a (τ-free) *well-formed trace* over (Γ, Σ) — a sequence of actions α such that:

- The channel of α either occurs as a free name in P — in which case we shall say that α is *initial* — or in the contents of some unique previous action in the trace, which we may call the *justifier* of α.
- The contents of α and their complements do not appear in Γ, Σ, or previously in the trace.

We note also that the set of well-formed traces is closed under α-equivalence, and that if $M \equiv_\alpha N$, then $\forall t \in \mathtt{trace}(M).\exists t' \in N$ such that $t \equiv_\alpha t'$, and vice-versa.

We may now observe that there is a simple correspondence between the traces over (Γ, Σ) and the justified sequences on $[\![\Sigma]\!]^\perp \odot [\![\Gamma]\!]$: we replace each output action with a Player move and each input action with an Opponent move, and retain the justification structure. To determine which move replaces a given action, we note that the justification history of each action determines a unique path through the syntax forest of (Γ, Σ) (which is isomorphic to the forest of moves $[\![\Sigma]\!]^\perp \odot [\![\Gamma]\!]$), and this path determines a unique move in the arena. More precisely, for each action α (with $\kappa(\alpha) : T$) in a trace s over (Γ, Σ) we define a map $\psi_{s,\alpha}$ from $M_{[\![T]\!]}$ to $M_{[\![\Sigma]\!]^\perp \odot [\![\Gamma]\!]}$:

If α is initial then if $\kappa(\alpha) = \overline{x_i} : S_i$, then $\psi_{s,\alpha}(m) = (\mathrm{in_l}(\mathrm{in_i}(\mathrm{m}))$, and if $\kappa(\alpha) = y_i : T_i$, then $\psi_{s,\alpha}(m) = \mathrm{in_r}(\mathrm{in_i}(\mathrm{m}))$.

If α is justified by β, then if $\kappa(\alpha) = \overline{x_i} : S_i$, then $\psi_{s\alpha}(m) = \psi_{s,\beta}(\mathrm{in_l}(\mathrm{in_i}(\mathrm{m}))$, and if $\kappa(\alpha) = y_i : T_i$, then $\psi_{s,\alpha}(m) = \psi_{s,\beta}(\mathrm{in_r}(\mathrm{in_i}(\mathrm{m})))$.

Thus we may define a map ϕ from traces over (Γ, Σ) to justified sequences over $(\llbracket \Sigma \rrbracket^{\perp} \odot \llbracket \Gamma \rrbracket)$ by replacing each action α in s with $\psi_{s,\alpha}(*)$, and defining a justification function so that $j_{\phi(s)}(k) = i$ if the kth action in s is the justifier of the ith action.

It is easy to see that ϕ sends α-equivalent traces to the same justified sequence: the following lemma is then straightforward to prove.

Lemma 4. *For any context (Γ, Σ), (α-equivalence classes of) traces over (Γ, Σ), and justified sequences over the arena $\llbracket \Gamma \rrbracket^{\perp} \odot \llbracket \Sigma \rrbracket$ are in bijective correspondence.*

What is the relationship between $\phi(\mathtt{trace}(P))$ and the denotation of P in the games model? They are not equal in general; for example, the nil process has no non-empty traces, but is not represented by the empty strategy. However, by inductive characterization of $\mathtt{trace}(P)$ we may prove the following.

Proposition 3. *For any process P, $\llbracket P \rrbracket = \phi(\widehat{\mathtt{trace}(P)})$.*

We now use our weak soundness result, and the correspondence between traces and justified sequences to prove that the denotational semantics is sound and adequate with respect to may-testing in the the reduction semantics. To complete the proof, we need to show that if a process may perform an input action in the LTS, then it may perform the same action in the reduction semantics. First, we prove the following equivalences by showing that the smallest precongruence containing them is preserved by reduction.

Lemma 5. *For any process $\Gamma \vdash P; \Sigma$, if $k \notin \Gamma$ then $P\{k/x\} \lesssim \nu x.(P|[k \mapsto \overline{x}])$, and if $\overline{k} \notin \Sigma$, then $P\{\overline{k}/\overline{x}\} \lesssim \nu x.(P|[x \mapsto \overline{k}])$.*

Lemma 6. *For any process $\_ \vdash P; \overline{x} : ()$, if $P \xrightarrow{\tau^*} P' \xrightarrow{\overline{x}\langle\rangle} Q$ then $P \Downarrow$.*

Proof. By induction on the number of silent actions in $P \xrightarrow{\tau^*} P'$. If $P = P'$, then we show by induction on the derivation of $P \xrightarrow{x\langle\rangle} Q$ that $P \downarrow$.

Otherwise, $P \xrightarrow{\tau} P'' \xrightarrow{\tau^*} P' \xrightarrow{x\langle\rangle} Q$. We prove by induction on the derivation of $P \xrightarrow{\tau} P''$ that there are terms R_1, R_2 such that $P \equiv \nu \boldsymbol{y}.(\overline{y_i}\langle \boldsymbol{c}, \overline{\boldsymbol{d}}\rangle | y_i(\boldsymbol{a}, \overline{\boldsymbol{b}}).R_1 | R_2)$, and $P'' \equiv \nu \boldsymbol{y}.\nu \boldsymbol{k}.\nu \boldsymbol{l}.([\boldsymbol{c} \mapsto \overline{\boldsymbol{k}}] | [\boldsymbol{l} \mapsto \overline{\boldsymbol{d}}] | R_1\{\boldsymbol{k}/\boldsymbol{a}, \overline{\boldsymbol{l}}/\overline{\boldsymbol{b}}\} | R_2)$. Hence P reduces to $\nu \boldsymbol{y}.(R_1\{\boldsymbol{c}/\boldsymbol{a}, \overline{\boldsymbol{d}}/\overline{\boldsymbol{b}}\} | R_2)$, and by Lemma 5, $P'' \lesssim \nu \boldsymbol{y}.(R_1\{\boldsymbol{c}/\boldsymbol{a}, \overline{\boldsymbol{d}}/\overline{\boldsymbol{b}}\} | R_2)$. By induction hypothesis, $P'' \Downarrow$, and hence $P \Downarrow$ as required.

Proposition 4. *For any process $\_ \vdash P; \overline{x} : ()$, $P \Downarrow$ if and only if $\llbracket P \rrbracket \neq \perp$.*

Proof. From left-to-right, this follows from weak soundness by induction on derivation length. From right-to left, this follows from Proposition 3 and Lemma 6: if $\llbracket P \rrbracket \neq \perp$, then $\mathtt{trace}(P) \neq \varnothing$, and hence $P \Downarrow$ as required.

To prove full abstraction, we now show that for any terms with distinct denotations, we may define a distinguishing context. It is sufficient to show that strategies which test for the existence of a given trace are definable, for which we need to prove that for any sequence $s \in [\![\Sigma]\!]^\perp \odot [\![\Gamma]\!]$, the strategy $\widehat{\{s\}}$ is the denotation of a term $\Gamma \vdash P; \Sigma$. In contrast to previous such "definability results" for games models, this is straightforward to prove, since from any trace we may extract a ("minimal") term which generates it (following proofs of similar results for the higher-order π-calculus [25]).

Proposition 5. *For every justified sequence $s \in [\![\Sigma]\!]^\perp \odot [\![\Gamma]\!]$, there exists a process $\Gamma \vdash P; \Sigma$ such that $[\![P]\!] = \widehat{\{s\}}$.*

Proof. By induction on the length of s. Suppose the first move in s is an Opponent move. We suppose without loss of generality that this move is the initial move in the final conjunct of $\Gamma = \Gamma', x : (\boldsymbol{S}, \boldsymbol{T})$. By removing it, and relabelling moves hereditarily justified by it as moves in $[\![\boldsymbol{S}]\!]$ and $[\![\boldsymbol{T}]\!]^\perp$, we may define a justified sequence t on the arena $[\![\Sigma, \boldsymbol{S}]\!] \odot [\![\Gamma, \boldsymbol{T}]\!]^\perp$. By induction hypothesis, the strategy $\widehat{\{t\}}$ is definable as a term $\Gamma, \boldsymbol{y} : \boldsymbol{S} \vdash P; \Sigma, \overline{\boldsymbol{z}} : \boldsymbol{T}$ and hence $\widehat{\{s\}}$ is definable as $x(\boldsymbol{y}, \overline{\boldsymbol{z}}).P$.

If the first move is a Player move (initial in the final component of $\Sigma = \Sigma', \overline{x} : (\boldsymbol{S}, \boldsymbol{T})$), then by removing it and relabelling as above, we obtain a sequence t such that $\widehat{\{t\}}$ is definable as a process $\Gamma, \boldsymbol{y} : \boldsymbol{T} \vdash P; \Sigma, \overline{\boldsymbol{z}} : \boldsymbol{T}$. Then $\widehat{\{s\}} = [\![\nu \boldsymbol{y}.\nu \boldsymbol{z}.(P|\overline{x}\langle \boldsymbol{z}, \overline{\boldsymbol{y}}\rangle)]\!]$.

Theorem 1. *For any processes $\Gamma \vdash P, Q; \Sigma$, $P \lesssim Q$ if and only if $[\![P]\!] \subseteq [\![Q]\!]$.*

Proof. From right-to left (inequational soundness) this follows from soundness and adequacy (Proposition 4). We prove the converse for processes P, Q with a single (input) name y, which implies the general case as $P(\boldsymbol{a}, \overline{\boldsymbol{b}})$ may be recovered from $y(\boldsymbol{a}, \overline{\boldsymbol{b}}).P$. So suppose $[\![y : T \vdash P]\!] \not\subseteq [\![y : T \vdash Q]\!]$. Then there exists $s \in [\![T]\!]$ such that $s \in [\![P]\!]$ and $s \notin [\![Q]\!]$. By Proposition 5, the strategy $\widehat{\{s^\perp *\}}$ on $[\![T]\!]^\perp \odot (\uparrow I)^\perp$ (where $*$ is the unique move in $\uparrow I$) is definable as a process $\vdash R; \overline{y} : T, \overline{x} : ()$. Then $[\![\nu y.(P|R)]\!] = \{*\}$ and hence by adequacy, $\nu y.(P|R) \Downarrow$. But $[\![\nu y.(Q|R)]\!] = \perp$, since for all $t* \in \lceil s^\perp * \rceil$ we have $t \preceq s^\perp$ and hence $s \preceq t^\perp$ and so by assumption $t^\perp \notin [\![Q]\!]$. Hence $\nu y.(Q|R) \not\Downarrow$, and $P \not\lesssim Q$ as required.

5 Conclusions and Further Directions

For the sake of simplicity, we have restricted our semantics to simple types, but it is possible to extend it with recursive types, using the methodology developed by McCusker for solving recursive domain equations in a functional setting [22]. In particular, we may construct a model of the standard, untyped π-calculus, based on the type $\mu X.(X, X)$.

Our semantics represents names implicitly, via information flow. So, for instance, it does not provide a natural way to interpret matching and mismatching constructs, or the association of input and output capabilities to a single name. We could, however introduce the capacity to represent names explicitly into our model using the techniques described in [18] based on a category of games acted on by the group of natural number permutations.

The representation of processes via their traces, is probably suitable only for characterizing testing equivalences. A natural extension of the current research would be to construct a model of must-testing, by recording traces resulting in divergence, as in [8,16] and deadlock. However, there are many technical complications. We have also sketched "true concurrency" and "abstract interpretation" examples of our categorical semantics which require further investigation. Alternatively, we may use π-calculus terms themselves to represent strategies, in which case we may ask which notions of equivalence yield a distributive-closed Freyd category. We may also attempt to develop domain-theoretic instances of our categorical constructions and relate them to other such models of the π-calculus.

References

1. S. Abramsky, R. Jagadeesan. Games and full completeness for multiplicative linear logic. *Journal of Symbolic Logic*, 59:543–574, 1994.
2. S. Abramsky, R. Jagadeesan and P. Malacaria. Full abstraction for PCF. *Information and Computation*, 163:409–470, 2000.
3. M. Berger, K. Honda, and N. Yoshida. Sequentiality and the π-calculus. In *Proceedings of TLCA 2001*, volume 2044 of *Lecture Notes in Computer Science*. Springer-Verlag, 2001.
4. M. Berger, K. Honda, and N. Yoshida. Strong normalization in the π-calculus. In *Proceedings of LICS 2001*. IEEE Press, 2001.
5. G. Boudol. Asynchrony in the pi-calculus. Technical Report 1702, INRIA, 1992.
6. D. Ghica and G. McCusker. The regular language semantics of second-order Idealised Algol. *Theoretical Computer Science (To appear)*, 2003.
7. D. Ghica and A. Murawski. Angelic semantics of fine-grained concurrency. In *Proceedings of FOSSACS '04*, number 2987 in LNCS, pages 211–225. Springer, 2004.
8. R. Harmer and G. McCusker. A fully abstract games semantics for finite nondeterminism. In *Proceedings of the Fourteenth Annual Symposium on Logic in Computer Science, LICS '99*. IEEE Computer Society Press, 1998.
9. M. Hennessy. A fully abstract denotational semantics for the π-calculus. Technical Report 041996, University of Sussex (COGS), 2996.
10. K. Honda and M. Tokoro. An object calculus for asynchronous communication. In *Proceedings of ECOOP '91*, number 512 in LNCS, pages 133–147, 1991.
11. J. M. E. Hyland and C.-H. L. Ong. On full abstraction for PCF: I, II and III. *Information and Computation*, 163:285–408, 2000.
12. L. J. Jagadeesan and R. Jagadeesan. Causality and true concurrency: A data-flow analysis of the pi-calculus. In *Proceedings of AMAST '95*, 1995.
13. A. S. A. Jeffrey and J. Rathke. Contextual equivalence for higher-order pi-calculus revisited. Technical Report 0402, University of Sussex (COGS), 2002.
14. A. S. A. Jeffrey and J. Rathke. A fully abstract may-testing semantics for concurrent objects. In *Proceedings of LICS '02*, pages 101–112, 2002.
15. A. Joyal, R. Street, and D. Verity. Traced monoidal categories. *Math. Proc. Camb. Phil. Soc.*, 119:447 – 468, 1996.

16. J. Laird. A game semantics of ICSP. In *Proceedings of MFPS XVII*, number 45 in Electronic notes in Theoretical Computer Science. Elsevier, 2001.
17. J. Laird. A categorical semantics of higher-order store. In *Proceedings of CTCS '02*, number 69 in ENTCS. Elsevier, 2002.
18. J. Laird. A game semantics of local names and good variables. In *Proceedings of FOSSACS '04*, number 2987 in LNCS, pages 289–303. Springer, 2004.
19. R. de Nicola M. Boreale and R. Pugliese. Trace and testing equivalence on asynchronous processes. *Information and Computation*, 172(2):139–164, 2002.
20. E. Moggi M. Fiore and D. Sangiorgi. A fully abstract model for the π-calculus. In *Proceedings of LICS '96*, 2996.
21. P. Malacaria and C. Hankin. Generalised flowcharts and games. In *Proceedings of the 25th International Colloquium on Automata, Langugages and Programming*, 1998.
22. G. McCusker. *Games and full abstraction for a functional metalanguage with recursive types.* PhD thesis, Imperial College London, 1996. Published by Cambridge University Press.
23. R. Milner. Polyadic π-calculus: a tutorial. In *Proceedings of the Marktoberdorf Summer School on Logic and Algebra of Specification*, 1992.
24. J. Power and H. Thielecke. Environments in Freyd categories and κ-categories. In *Proceedings of ICALP '99*, number 1644 in LNCS. Springer, 1999.
25. D. Sangiorgi. *Expressing Mobility in Process Algebras: First-Order and Higher-Order Paradigms.* PhD thesis, University of Edinburgh, 1993.
26. I. Stark. A fully abstract domain model for the π-calculus. In *Proceedings of LICS '96*, 1996.

Efficient On-the-Fly Algorithms for the Analysis of Timed Games

Franck Cassez[1,*], Alexandre David[2], Emmanuel Fleury[2], Kim G. Larsen[2], and Didier Lime[2]

[1] IRCCyN, UMR 6597, CNRS, France
Franck.Cassez@irccyn.ec-nantes.fr
[2] Computer Science Department,
CISS (Center for Embedded Software Systems), Aalborg University, Denmark
{adavid, fleury, kgl, didier}@cs.aau.dk

Abstract. In this paper, we propose the first efficient on-the-fly algorithm for solving games based on timed game automata with respect to reachability and safety properties

The algorithm we propose is a symbolic extension of the on-the-fly algorithm suggested by Liu & Smolka [15] for linear-time model-checking of finite-state systems. Being on-the-fly, the symbolic algorithm may terminate long before having explored the entire state-space. Also the individual steps of the algorithm are carried out efficiently by the use of so-called zones as the underlying data structure.

Various optimizations of the basic symbolic algorithm are proposed as well as methods for obtaining time-optimal winning strategies (for reachability games). Extensive evaluation of an experimental implementation of the algorithm yields very encouraging performance results.

1 Introduction

On-the-fly algorithms offer the benefit of settling properties of individual system states (*e.g.* an initial state) in a local fashion and without necessarily having to generate or examine the entire state-space of the given model. For finite-state (untimed) systems the search for optimal (linear) on-the-fly or local algorithms has been a very active research topic since the end of the 80's [12,4,15] and is one of the most important techniques applied in finite-state model-checkers using enumerative or explicit state-space representation, as is the case with SPIN [10], which performs on-the-fly model-checking of LTL properties.

Also for timed systems, on-the-fly algorithms have been absolutely crucial to the success of model-checking tools such as KRONOS [8] and UPPAAL [13] in their analysis of timed automata based models [2]. Both reachability, safety as well as general liveness properties of such timed models may be decided using on-the-fly algorithms exploring the reachable state-space in a (symbolic) forward manner with the possibility of early termination. More recently, timed automata technology has been successfully applied to optimal scheduling problems with

* Work supported by ACI Cortos, a program of the French government. Visits to Aalborg supported by CISS, Aalborg University, Denmark.

M. Abadi and L. de Alfaro (Eds.): CONCUR 2005, LNCS 3653, pp. 66–80, 2005.

guiding and pruning heuristics being added to yield on-the-fly algorithms which quickly lead to near-optimal (time- or cost-wise) schedules [5,3,11,18].

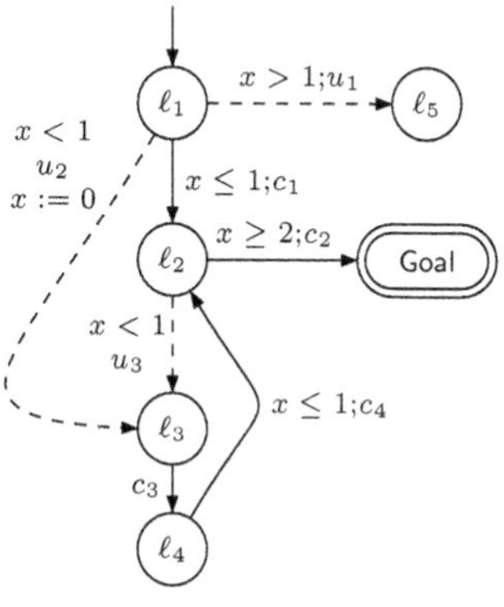

Fig. 1. A Timed Game Automaton

We consider timed game automata and how to decide the existence of a winning strategy *w.r.t.* reachability or safety. As an example, consider the timed game automaton A of Fig. 1 consisting of a timed automaton with one clock x and two types of edges: controllable (c_i) and uncontrollable (u_i). The reachability game consists in finding a strategy for a controller, *i.e.* when to take the controllable transitions that will guarantee that the system, regardless of when and if the opponent chooses to take uncontrollable transitions, will eventually end up in the location Goal. Obviously, for all initial states of the form (ℓ_1, x) with $x \le 1$ there is such a winning strategy[3].

Though such timed game automata for long have been known to be decidable [16,6,9] there is still a lack of efficient and truly on-the-fly algorithms for their analysis. Most of the suggested algorithms are based on backwards fix-point computations of the set of winning states [16,6,9]. In contrast, the on-the-fly algorithms used for model-checking timed automata models (*w.r.t.* reachability) make a forward symbolic state-space exploration resulting in the so-called *simulation graph*. However, the simulation graph is by itself too abstract to be used as the basis for an on-the-fly algorithm for computing winning strategies. Fig. 2 (a) gives the simulation graph of the timed game automata of Fig. 1, which incorrectly classifies the initial state as being uncontrollable when viewed as a finite-state game.

As a remedy to this problem, the authors of [20,1] propose a partially on-the-fly method for solving reachability games for a timed game automaton A. However, this method involves an extremely expensive preprocessing step in which the quotient graph of the dense time transition system S_A *w.r.t.* time-abstracted bisimulation[4] needs to be built. Once obtained this quotient graph may be used with any on-the-fly game-solving algorithm for untimed (finite-state) systems. As an illustration, Fig. 2 (b) gives the time abstracted quotient graph for the timed game automaton of Fig. 1. It should be easy for the reader to see that the initial state will now (correctly) be classified as controllable.

In this paper, we propose an efficient, truly on-the-fly algorithm for the computation of winning states for timed game automata. Our algorithm is a symbolic extension of the on-the-fly algorithm suggested by Liu & Smolka [15] for

---

[3] A winning strategy would consist in taking c_1 immediately in all states (ℓ_1, x) with $x \le 1$; taking c_2 immediately in all states (ℓ_2, x) with $x \ge 2$; taking c_3 immediately in all state (ℓ_3, x) and delaying in all states (ℓ_4, x) with $x < 1$ until the value of x is 1 at which point the edge c_4 is taken.

[4] A time-abstracted bisimulation is a binary relation on states preserving discrete states and abstracted delay-transitions.

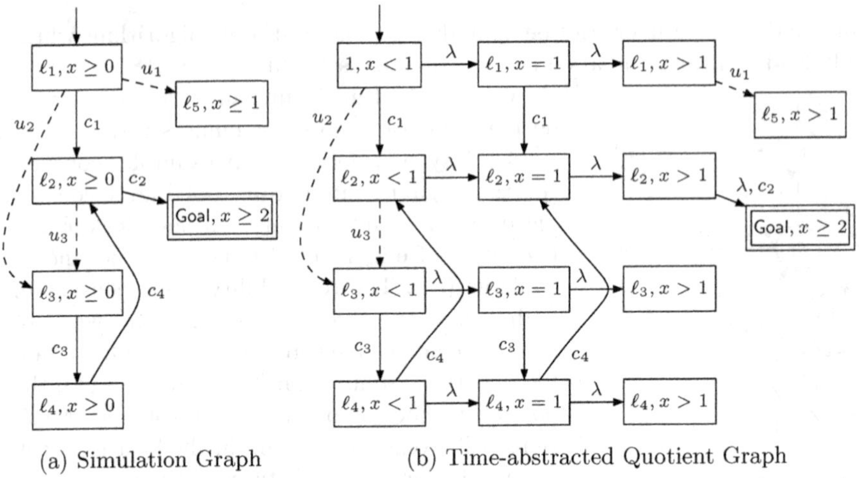
$\ell_1, x \geq 0$
u_1
$\ell_5, x \geq 1$
u_2
c_1
$\ell_2, x \geq 0$
c_2
Goal, $x \geq 2$
u_3
$\ell_3, x \geq 0$
c_4
c_3
$\ell_4, x \geq 0$
(a) Simulation Graph
$1, x < 1$
λ
$\ell_1, x = 1$
$\ell_1, x > 1$
$\ell_5, x > 1$
$\ell_2, x < 1$
$\ell_2, x = 1$
$\ell_2, x > 1$
λ, c_2
$\ell_3, x < 1$
$\ell_3, x = 1$
$\ell_3, x > 1$
$\ell_4, x < 1$
$\ell_4, x = 1$
$\ell_4, x > 1$
(b) Time-abstracted Quotient Graph

Fig. 2. Simulation and time-abstracted quotient graph of Fig. 1 (λ is for time elapsing)

linear-time model-checking of finite-state systems. Being on-the-fly, the symbolic algorithm may terminate before having explored the entire state-space, *i.e.* as soon as a winning strategy has been identified. Also the individual steps of the algorithm are carried out efficiently by the use of so-called zones as the underlying data structure.

The rest of the paper is organized as follows. Section 2 provides definitions and preliminaries about timed game automata and the classic backwards algorithm for solving them. Section 3 presents our instantiation of the general on-the-fly algorithm of Liu & Smolka [15] to untimed reachability games. Then, in Section 4, we present our symbolic extension of this algorithm, providing a first forward, zone-based and fully on-the-fly algorithm for solving timed reachability games. Section 5 discusses few optimizations of the basic algorithm and how to apply the algorithm to determine time-optimal winning strategies. Section 6 presents experimental evaluation of an efficient implementation of the algorithm to determine (time-optimal) winning strategies. The performance results obtained are very encouraging. Finally, Section 7 presents conclusion and future work.

2 Backward Algorithms for Solving Timed Games

Timed Game Automata [16] (TGA) were introduced for control problems on timed systems. This section recalls basic results of controller synthesis for TGA.

Let X be a finite set of real-valued variables called clocks. We note $\mathcal{C}(X)$ the set of constraints φ generated by the grammar: $\varphi ::= x \sim k \mid x - y \sim k \mid \varphi \wedge \varphi$ where $k \in \mathbb{Z}$, $x, y \in X$ and $\sim \in \{<, \leq, =, >, \geq\}$. $\mathcal{B}(X)$ is the subset of $\mathcal{C}(X)$ that uses only rectangular constraints of the form $x \sim k$. A *valuation* of the variables in X is a mapping $X \mapsto \mathbb{R}_{\geq 0}$ (thus $\mathbb{R}_{\geq 0}^X$). We write $\mathbf{0}$ for the valuation that assigns 0 to each clock. For $Y \subseteq X$, we denote by $v[Y]$ the valuation assigning 0 (*resp.* $v(x)$) for any $x \in Y$ (*resp.* $x \in X \setminus Y$). We denote $v + \delta$ for $\delta \in \mathbb{R}_{\geq 0}$

the valuation *s.t.* for all $x \in X$, $(v+\delta)(x) = v(x)+\delta$. For $g \in \mathcal{C}(X)$ and $v \in \mathbb{R}_{\geq 0}^X$, we write $v \models g$ if v satisfies g and $[\![g]\!]$ denotes the set of valuations $\{v \in \mathbb{R}_{\geq 0}^X \mid v \models g\}$. A *zone* Z is a subset of $\mathbb{R}_{\geq 0}^X$ *s.t.* $[\![g]\!] = Z$ for some $g \in \mathcal{C}(X)$.

2.1 Timed Game Automata and Simulation Graph

Definition 1 (Timed Automaton [2]). *A* Timed Automaton *(TA) is a tuple* $A = (L, \ell_0, \mathsf{Act}, X, E, \mathsf{Inv})$ *where* L *is a finite set of* locations, $\ell_0 \in L$ *is the* initial *location,* Act *is the set of* actions, X *is a finite set of* real-valued clocks, $E \subseteq L \times \mathcal{B}(X) \times \mathsf{Act} \times 2^X \times L$ *is a finite set of* transitions, $\mathsf{Inv} : L \to \mathcal{B}(X)$ *associates to each location its* invariant.

A *state* of a TA is a pair $(\ell, v) \in L \times \mathbb{R}_{\geq 0}^X$ that consists of a discrete part and a valuation of the clocks. From a state $(\ell, v) \in L \times \mathbb{R}_{\geq 0}^X$ *s.t.* $v \models \mathsf{Inv}(\ell)$, a TA can either let time progress or do a discrete transition and reach a new state. This is defined by the transition relation $\longrightarrow$ built as follows: for $a \in \mathsf{Act}$, $(\ell, v) \xrightarrow{a} (\ell', v')$ if there exists a transition $\ell \xrightarrow{g,a,Y} \ell'$ in E *s.t.* $v \models g$, $v' = v[Y]$ and $v' \models \mathsf{Inv}(\ell')$; for $\delta \geq 0$, $(\ell, v) \xrightarrow{\delta} (\ell, v')$ if $v' = v + \delta$ and $v, v' \in [\![\mathsf{Inv}(\ell)]\!]$. Thus the semantics of a TA is the labeled transition system $S_A = (Q, q_0, \longrightarrow)$ where $Q = L \times \mathbb{R}_{\geq 0}^X$, $q_0 = (\ell_0, \mathbf{0})$ and the set of labels is $\mathsf{Act} \cup \mathbb{R}_{\geq 0}$. A *run* of a timed automaton A is a sequence of alternating time and discrete transitions in S_A. We use $\mathsf{Runs}((\ell, v), A)$ for the set of runs that start in (ℓ, v). We write $\mathsf{Runs}(A)$ for $\mathsf{Runs}((\ell_0, \mathbf{0}), A)$. If ρ is a finite run we denote $last(\rho)$ the last state of the run and $\mathsf{Duration}(\rho)$ the total elapsed time all along the run.

The analysis of TA is based on the exploration of a finite graph, the *simulation graph*, where the nodes are *symbolic states*; a symbolic state is a pair (ℓ, Z) where $\ell \in L$ and Z is a zone of $\mathbb{R}_{\geq 0}^X$. Let $X \subseteq Q$ and $a \in \mathsf{Act}$ we define the a-successor of X by $\mathsf{Post}_a(X) = \{(\ell', v') \mid \exists (\ell, v) \in X, (\ell, v) \xrightarrow{a} (\ell', v')\}$ and the a-predecessor $\mathsf{Pred}_a(X) = \{(\ell, v) \mid \exists (\ell', v') \in X, (\ell, v) \xrightarrow{a} (\ell', v')\}$. The timed successors and predecessors of X are respectively defined by $X^{\nearrow} = \{(\ell, v+d) \mid (\ell, v) \in X \cap [\![\mathsf{Inv}(\ell)]\!], (\ell, v+d) \in [\![\mathsf{Inv}(\ell)]\!], d \in \mathbb{R}_{\geq 0}\}$ and $X^{\swarrow} = \{(\ell, v-d) \mid (\ell, v) \in X, d \in \mathbb{R}_{\geq 0}\}$. Let $\rightarrow$ be the relation defined on symbolic states by: $(\ell, Z) \xrightarrow{a} (\ell', Z')$ if $(\ell, g, a, Y, \ell') \in E$ and $Z' = ((Z \cap [\![g]\!])[Y])^{\nearrow}$. The simulation graph $SG(A)$ of A is defined as the transition system $(Z(Q), S_0, \rightarrow)$, where $Z(Q)$ is the set of zones of Q, $S_0 = ((\{\ell_0, \mathbf{0}\}^{\nearrow}) \cap [\![\mathsf{Inv}(\ell_0)]\!]$ and $\rightarrow$ defined as above.

Definition 2 (Timed Game Automaton [16]). *A* Timed Game Automaton (TGA) G *is a timed automaton with its set of actions* Act *partitioned into* controllable *(*Act_c*) and* uncontrollable *(*Act_u*) actions.*

2.2 Safety and Reachability Games

Given a TGA G and a set of states $K \subseteq L \times \mathbb{R}_{\geq 0}^X$ the *reachability control problem* consists in finding a *strategy* f s.t. G supervised by f enforces K. The *safety control problem* is the dual asking for the strategy to constantly avoid K. By "a reachability game (G, K)" (*resp.* safety) we refer to the reachability (*resp.* safety) control problem for G and K.

Let (G, K) be a reachability (resp. safety) game. A finite or infinite (ruling out runs with an infinite number of consecutive time transitions of duration 0) run $\rho = (\ell_0, v_0) \xrightarrow{e_0} (\ell_1, v_1) \xrightarrow{e_1} \cdots \xrightarrow{e_n} (\ell_{n+1}, v_{n+1}) \cdots$ in $\mathsf{Runs}(G)$ is *winning* if there is some $k \geq 0$ *s.t.* $(\ell_k, v_k) \in K$ (resp. for all $k \geq 0$ *s.t.* $(\ell_k, v_k) \in K$). The set of winning runs in G from (ℓ, v) is denoted $\mathsf{WinRuns}((\ell, v), G)$.

For reachability games we assume w.l.o.g. that the goal is a particular location Goal. For safety games the goal is a set a locations to avoid.

The formal definition of the control problems is based on the definitions of *strategies* and *outcomes*. A strategy [16] is a function that during the course of the game constantly gives information as to what the controller should do in order to win the game. In a given situation, the strategy could suggest the controller to either i) "do a particular controllable action" or ii) "do nothing at this point in time, just wait" which will be denoted by the special symbol λ.

Definition 3 (Strategy). *Let* $G = (L, \ell_0, \mathsf{Act}, X, E, \mathsf{Inv})$ *be a TGA. A* strategy f *over* G *is a partial function from* $\mathsf{Runs}(G)$ *to* $\mathsf{Act}_c \cup \{\lambda\}$ s.t. *for every finite run* ρ, *if* $f(\rho) \in \mathsf{Act}_c$ *then* $last(\rho) \xrightarrow{f(\rho)}_{S_G} (\ell', v')$ *for some* (ℓ', v').

We denote $\mathsf{Strat}(G)$ the set of strategies over G. A strategy f is *state-based* whenever $\forall \rho, \rho' \in \mathsf{Runs}(G)$, $last(\rho) = last(\rho')$ implies that $f(\rho) = f(\rho')$. State-based strategies are also called *memoryless* strategies in game theory [9,19].

The restricted behavior of a TGA G controlled with some strategy f is defined by the notion of *outcome* [9].

Definition 4 (Outcome). *Let* $G = (L, \ell_0, \mathsf{Act}, X, E, \mathsf{Inv})$ *be a TGA and* f *a strategy over* G. *The* outcome $\mathsf{Outcome}(q, f)$ *of* f *from* q *in* S_G *is the subset of* $\mathsf{Runs}(q, G)$ *defined inductively by:*

- $q \in \mathsf{Outcome}(q, f)$,
- *if* $\rho \in \mathsf{Outcome}(q, f)$ *then* $\rho' = \rho \xrightarrow{e} q' \in \mathsf{Outcome}(q, f)$ *if* $\rho' \in \mathsf{Runs}(q, G)$ *and one of the following three conditions hold:*
  1. $e \in \mathsf{Act}_u$,
  2. $e \in \mathsf{Act}_c$ *and* $e = f(\rho)$,
  3. $e \in \mathbb{R}_{\geq 0}$ *and* $\forall 0 \leq e' < e, \exists q'' \in Q$ s.t. $last(\rho) \xrightarrow{e'} q'' \wedge f(\rho \xrightarrow{e'} q'') = \lambda$.
- *for an infinite run* ρ, $\rho \in \mathsf{Outcome}(q, f)$ *if all the finite prefixes of* ρ *are in* $\mathsf{Outcome}(q, f)$.

We assume that uncontrollable actions can only spoil the game and the controller has to do some controllable action to win [6,16,11]. In other words, an uncontrollable action cannot be forced to happen in G. Thus, a run may end in a state where only uncontrollable actions can be taken. Moreover we focus on reachability games and assume $K = \{\mathsf{Goal}\} \times \mathbb{R}^X_{\geq 0}$. A *maximal run* ρ is either an infinite run (supposing no infinite sequence of delay transitions of duration 0) or a finite run ρ that satisfies either i) $last(\rho) \in K$ or ii) if $\rho \xrightarrow{a}$ then $a \in \mathsf{Act}_u$ (*i.e.* the only possible next discrete actions from $last(\rho)$, if any, are uncontrollable actions).

A strategy f is *winning* from q if all maximal runs in $\mathsf{Outcome}(q, f)$ are in $\mathsf{WinRuns}(q, G)$. A state q in a TGA G is *winning* if there exists a winning strategy f from q in G. We denote by $\mathcal{W}(G)$ the set of winning states in G and $\mathsf{WinStrat}(q, G)$ the set of winning strategies from q over G.

2.3 Backwards Algorithms for Solving Timed Games

Let $G = (L, \ell_0, \mathsf{Act}, X, E, \mathsf{Inv})$ be a TGA. For reachability games, the computation of the winning states is based on the definition of a *controllable predecessor* operator [9,16]. The controllable and uncontrollable discrete predecessors of X are defined by $\mathsf{cPred}(X) = \bigcup_{c \in \mathsf{Act}_c} \mathsf{Pred}_c(X)$ and $\mathsf{uPred}(X) = \bigcup_{u \in \mathsf{Act}_u} \mathsf{Pred}_u(X)$. A notion of *safe* timed predecessors of a set X *w.r.t.* a set Y is also needed. Intuitively a state q is in $\mathsf{Pred}_t(X, Y)$ if from q we can reach $q' \in X$ by time elapsing and along the path from q to q' we avoid Y. Formally this is defined by:

$$\mathsf{Pred}_t(X,Y) = \{q \in Q \mid \exists \delta \in \mathbb{R}_{\geq 0} \ s.t.\ q \xrightarrow{\delta} q', q' \in X \text{ and } \mathsf{Post}_{[0,\delta]}(q) \subseteq \overline{Y}\} \quad (1)$$

where $\mathsf{Post}_{[0,\delta]}(q) = \{q' \in Q \mid \exists t \in [0, \delta] \ s.t.\ q \xrightarrow{t} q'\}$ and $\overline{Y} = Q \setminus Y$. The *controllable predecessors* operator π is defined as follows[5]:

$$\pi(X) = \mathsf{Pred}_t\left(X \cup \mathsf{cPred}(X), \mathsf{uPred}(\overline{X})\right) \quad (2)$$

Let (G, K) be a reachability game, if S is a finite union of symbolic states, then $\pi(S)$ is again a finite union of symbolic states. Moreover the iterative process given by $W^0 = K$ and $W^{n+1} = \pi(W^n)$ will converge after finitely many steps for TGA [16] and the least fixed point obtained is W^*. It is also proved in [16] that $W^* = \mathcal{W}(G)$. Note also that W^* is the maximal set of winning states of G *i.e.* a state is winning iff it is in W^*. Thus there is a winning strategy in G iff $(\ell_0, \mathbf{0}) \in W^*$. Altogether this gives a symbolic algorithm for solving reachability games. Extracting strategies can be done using the winning set of states W^*. For safety games (G, K), it suffices to swap the roles of the players leading to a game $\overline{G}$ and solve a reachability game $(\overline{G}, \overline{K})$. If the winning set of states for $(\overline{G}, \overline{K})$ is W then the winning set of states of (G, K) is $\overline{W}$.

3 On-the-Fly Algorithm for Untimed Games

For finite-state systems, on-the-fly model-checking algorithms has been an active and successful research area since the end of the 80's, with the algorithm proposed by Liu & Smolka [15] being particularly elegant (and optimal). We present here our instantiation of this algorithm to untimed reachability games.

We consider untimed games as a restricted class of timed games with only finitely many states Q and with only discrete actions, *i.e.* the set of labels is Act. Hence (memoryless) strategies simplifies to a choice of controllable action given the current state, *i.e.* $f : Q \to \mathsf{Act}_c$. For (untimed) *reachability games* we assume a designated set Goal of goal-states and the purpose of the analysis is to decide the existence of a strategy f where all runs contains at least one state from Goal

[5] Note that π is defined here such that uncontrollable actions cannot be used to win.

Initialization:
$Passed \leftarrow \{q_0\};$
$Waiting \leftarrow \{(q_0, \alpha, q') \mid \alpha \in Act\ q \xrightarrow{\alpha} q'\};$
$Win[q_0] \leftarrow (q_0 \in \mathsf{Goal}\ ?\ 1 : 0);$
$Depend[q_0] \leftarrow \emptyset;$

Main:
while $((Waiting \neq \emptyset) \wedge Win[q_0] \neq 1))$ **do**
$e = (q, \alpha, q') \leftarrow pop(Waiting);$
if $q' \notin Passed$ **then**
$Passed \leftarrow Passed \cup \{q'\};$
$Depend[q'] \leftarrow \{(q, \alpha, q')\};$
$Win[q'] \leftarrow (q' \in \mathsf{Goal}\ ?\ 1 : 0);$
$Waiting \leftarrow Waiting \cup \{(q', \alpha, q'') \mid q' \xrightarrow{\alpha} q''\};$
if $Win[q']$ **then** $Waiting \leftarrow Waiting \cup \{e\};$
else (* reevaluate *)
$Win^* \leftarrow \bigwedge_{q \xrightarrow{u} u} Win[u] \wedge \bigvee_{q \xrightarrow{c} w} Win[w];$
if Win^* **then**
$Waiting \leftarrow Waiting \cup Depend[q];\ Win[q] \leftarrow 1;$
if $Win[q'] = 0$ **then** $Depend[q'] \leftarrow Depend[q'] \cup \{e\};$
endif
endwhile

Fig. 3. OTFUR: **O**n-**T**he-**F**ly Algorithm for **U**ntimed **R**eachability Games

(once again, safety games are solved by swapping the roles of the controller and the environment).

Now, our instantiation OTFUR of the local algorithm by Liu & Smolka to untimed reachability games is given in Fig. 3. This algorithm is based on a waiting-list, $Waiting \subseteq E$ of *edges* waiting to be explored together with a passed-list $Passed \subseteq Q$ containing the states that have been encountered so far. Information about the current winning status of a state is given by a function $Win : Passed \rightarrow \{0,1\}$, where $Win[q]$ is initialized to 0 and later potentially upgraded to 1 when the winning status of successors to q change from 0 to 1. To activate the reevaluation of the winning status of states, each state q has an associated set of edges $Depend[q]$ *depending* on it: at any stage $Depend[q]$ contains all edges (q', α, q) that were encountered at a moment when $Win[q] = 0$ and where the winning status of the source state q' must be scheduled for reevaluation when $Win[q] = 1$ becomes true. We refer to [15] for the formal proof of correctness of this algorithm summarized by the following theorem:

Theorem 1 ([15]). *Upon termination of running the algorithm* OTFUR *on a given untimed game G the following holds:*

1. *If $q \in Passed$ and $Win[q] = 1$ then $q \in \mathcal{W}(G)$;*
2. *If $Waiting = \emptyset$ and $Win[q] = 0$ then $q \notin \mathcal{W}(G)$.*

In fact, the first property is an invariant of the **while**-statement holding after each iteration. Also, the algorithm is optimal in that it has linear time complexity in the size of the underlying untimed game: it is easy to see that each edge $e = (q, \alpha, q')$ will be added to $Waiting$ at most twice, the first time q is encountered (and added to *Passed*) and the second time when $Win[q']$ changes winning status from 0 to 1[6].

4 On-the-Fly Algorithm for Timed Games

Now let us turn our attention to the timed case and present our symbolic extension of the algorithm of Liu & Smolka providing a zone-based forward and on-the-fly algorithm for solving timed reachability games. The algorithm, SOTFTR, is given in Fig. 4 and may be viewed as an interleaved combination of *forward computation* of the *simulation graph* of the timed game automaton together with *back-propagation* of information *of winning states.* As in the untimed case the algorithm is based on a waiting-list, $Waiting$, of edges in the simulation-graph to be explored, and a passed-list, *Passed*, containing all the symbolic states of the simulation-graph encountered so far by the algorithm.

The crucial point of our symbolic extension is that the winning status $Win[q]$ of an individual state q is replaced by a set $Win[S] \subseteq S$ identifying the *subset* of the symbolic state S which is currently known to be winning. The set *Depend*$[S]$ indicates the set of edges (or predecessors of S) which must be reevaluated (*i.e.* added to $Waiting$) when new information about $Win[S]$ is obtained (*i.e.* when $Win[S] \subsetneq Win^*$). Whenever an edge $e = (S, \alpha, S')$ is considered with $S' \in$ *Passed*, the edge e is added to the dependency set of S' in order that possible future information about additional winning states within S' may also be back-propagated to S. In Table 1, we illustrate the forward exploration and backwards propagation steps of the algorithm.

The correctness of the symbolic on-the-fly algorithm SOTFTR is given by the following lemma and theorem, the rigorous proofs of which can be found in the appendix.

Lemma 1. *The* **while**-*loop of algorithm* SOTFTR *has the following invariance properties when running on a timed game automaton G:*

1. *For any $S \in Passed$ if $S \xrightarrow{\alpha} S'$ then either $(S, \alpha, S') \in Waiting$ or $S' \in Passed$ and $(S, \alpha, S') \in Depend[S']$*
2. *If $q \in Win[S]$ for some $S \in Passed$ then $q \in \mathcal{W}(G)$*
3. *If $q \in S \setminus Win[S]$ for some $S \in Passed$ then either*
   - *$e \in Waiting$ for some $e = (S, \alpha, S')$ with $S' \in Passed$,*

     or
   - *$q \notin \mathsf{Pred}_t\big[Win[S] \cup \bigcup_{S \xrightarrow{c} T} \mathsf{Pred}_c(Win[T]), \bigcup_{S \xrightarrow{u} T} \mathsf{Pred}_u(T \setminus Win[T])\big]$.*

[6] To obtain an algorithm running in linear time in the size of G (*i.e.* $|Q| + |E|$) it is important that the reevaluation of the winning status of a state q does not directly involve (repeated and expensive) evaluation of the large boolean expression for Win^*. In a practice, this may be avoided by adding a boolean b_q and a counter c_q recording the existence of a winning, controllable successor of q, and the number of winning, uncontrollable successor of q.

Initialization:

$Passed \leftarrow \{S_0\}$ **where** $S_0 = \{(\ell_0, \mathbf{0})\}^{\nearrow}$;
$Waiting \leftarrow \{(S_0, \alpha, S') \mid S' = \mathsf{Post}_\alpha(S_0)^{\nearrow}\}$;
$Win[S_0] \leftarrow S_0 \cap (\{\mathsf{Goal}\} \times \mathbb{R}^X_{\geq 0})$;
$Depend[S_0] \leftarrow \emptyset$;

Main:

```
while ((Waiting ≠ ∅) ∧ (s₀ ∉ Win[S₀])) do
    e = (S, α, S') ← pop(Waiting);
    if S' ∉ Passed then
      Passed ← Passed ∪ {S'};
      Depend[S'] ← {(S, α, S')};
      Win[S'] ← S' ∩ ({Goal} × R^X_{≥0});
      Waiting ← Waiting ∪ {(S', α, S'') | S'' = Post_α(S')^↗};
      if Win[S'] ≠ ∅ then Waiting ← Waiting ∪ {e};
    else (* reevaluate *)^a
      Win* ← Pred_t(Win[S] ∪ ⋃_{S -c-> T} Pred_c(Win[T]),
                          ⋃_{S -u-> T} Pred_u(T \ Win[T])) ∩ S;
      if (Win[S] ⊊ Win*) then
        Waiting ← Waiting ∪ Depend[S]; Win[S] ← Win*;
      Depend[S'] ← Depend[S'] ∪ {e};
    endif
endwhile
```

[a] When $T \notin Passed, Win[T] = \emptyset$

Fig. 4. SOTFTR: **S**ymbolic **O**n-**T**he-**F**ly Algorithm for **T**imed **R**eachability Games

Theorem 2. *Upon termination of running the algorithm* SOTFTR *on a given timed game automaton* G *the following holds:*

1. *If* $q \in Win[S]$ *for some* $S \in Passed$ *then* $q \in \mathcal{W}(G)$*;*
2. *If* $Waiting = \emptyset$*,* $q \in S \setminus Win[S]$ *for some* $S \in Passed$ *then* $q \notin \mathcal{W}(G)$*.*

Termination of the algorithm SOTFTR is guaranteed by the finiteness of symbolic states[7] and the fact that each edge (S, α, T) will be present in the *Waiting*-list at most $1 + |T|$ times, where $|T|$ is the number of regions of T: (S, α, T) will be in *Waiting* the first time that S is encountered and subsequently each time the value of $Win[T]$ increases. Now, any given region may be contained in several symbolic states of the simulation graph (due to overlap). Thus the SOTFTR algorithm is *not* linear in the region-graph and hence not theoretically optimal, as an algorithm with linear worst-case time-complexity could be obtained by applying the untimed algorithm directly to the region-graph. However, this is only a theoretical result and, as we shall see, the use of

[7] Strictly speaking, this requires that we either transforms the given TGA into an equivalent one in which all location-invariants insist on an upper bound on all clocks or, alternatively, that we apply standard extrapolation *w.r.t.* maximal constant occurring in the TGA (which is correct up to time-abstracted bisimulation).

Table 1. Running SOTFTG

Steps #	S	S'	Waiting	Passed	*Depend*	*Win*
0	-	-	$(S_0,u_1,S_1),(S_0,u_2,S_2),(\mathbf{S_0},\mathbf{c_1},\mathbf{S_3})$	S_0	-	$(S_0,\emptyset)$
1	S_0	S_3	$(S_0,u_1,S_1),(S_0,u_2,S_2)$ $+(\mathbf{S_3},\mathbf{c_2},\mathbf{S_4}),(S_3,u_3,S_2)$	S_3	$S_3 \mapsto (S_0,c_1,S_3)$	$(S_3,\emptyset)$
2	S_3	S_4	$(S_0,u_1,S_1),(S_0,u_2,S_2),(S_3,u_3,S_2)$ $+(\mathbf{S_3},\mathbf{c_2},\mathbf{S_4})$	S_4	$S_4 \mapsto (S_3,c_2,S_4)$	(S_4,S_4)
3	S_3	S_4	$(S_0,u_1,S_1),(S_0,u_2,S_2),(S_3,u_3,S_2)$ $+(\mathbf{S_0},\mathbf{c_1},\mathbf{S_3})$	-	-	$(S_3,x\geq 1)$
4	S_0	S_3	$(S_0,u_1,S_1),(S_0,u_2,S_2),(\mathbf{S_3},\mathbf{u_3},\mathbf{S_2})$	S_4	$S_3 \mapsto (S_0,c_1,S_3)$	$(S_0,x=1)$
5	S_3	S_2	$(S_0,u_1,S_1),(S_0,u_2,S_2)$ $+(\mathbf{S_2},\mathbf{c_3},\mathbf{S_5})$	S_2	$S_2 \mapsto (S_3,u_3,S_2)$	$(S_2,\emptyset)$
6	S_2	S_5	$(S_0,u_1,S_1),(S_0,u_2,S_2)$ $+(\mathbf{S_5},\mathbf{c_4},\mathbf{S_3})$	S_5	$S_5 \mapsto (S_2,c_3,S_2)$	$(S_5,\emptyset)$
7	S_5	S_3	$(S_0,u_1,S_1),(S_0,u_2,S_2)$ $+(\mathbf{S_2},\mathbf{c_3},\mathbf{S_5})$	-	$S_3 \mapsto$ (S_2,c_3,S_2) (S_5,c_4,S_3)	$(S_5,x\leq 1)$
8	S_2	S_5	$(S_0,u_1,S_1),(S_0,u_2,S_2)$ $+(\mathbf{S_3},\mathbf{u_3},\mathbf{S_2})$	-	$S_5 \mapsto (S_2,c_3,S_2)$	$(S_2,x\leq 1)$
9	S_3	S_2	$(S_0,u_1,S_1),(\mathbf{S_0},\mathbf{u_2},\mathbf{S_2})$ $+(S_0,c_1,S_3),(S_5,c_4,S_3)$	-	-	(S_3,S_3)
10	S_0	S_2	$(S_0,u_1,S_1),(S_0,c_1,S_3),(\mathbf{S_5},\mathbf{c_4},\mathbf{S_3})$	-	$S_2 \mapsto$ (S_3,u_3,S_2) (S_0,u_2,S_2)	$(S_0,x\leq 1)$
11	S_5	S_3	$(S_0,u_1,S_1),(\mathbf{S_0},\mathbf{c_1},\mathbf{S_3})$	-	-	-
12	S_0	S_3	$(\mathbf{S_0},\mathbf{u_1},\mathbf{S_1})$	-	-	-
13	S_0	S_1	$\emptyset$	S_1	$S_1 \mapsto (S_0,u_1,S_1)$	$(S_1,\emptyset)$

At step n, $(\mathbf{S},\alpha,\mathbf{S'})$ is the transition popped at step $n+1$;
At step n, $+(S,\alpha,S')$ the transition added to *Waiting* at step n;
Symbolic States: $S_0=(\ell_1,x\geq 0)$, $S_1=(\ell_5,x>1)$, $S_2=(\ell_3,x\geq 0)$, $S_3=(\ell_2,x\geq 0)$, $S_4=(\mathsf{Goal},x\geq 2)$, $S_5=(\ell_4,x\geq 0)$

zones yields very encouraging performance results in practice, as is the case for reachability analysis of timed automata.

5 Implementation, Optimizations and Extensions

5.1 Implementation of the Pred_t Operator with Zones

In order to be efficient, the algorithm SOTFTR manipulates zones. However, while a forward step always gives a single zone as a result, the Pred_t operator does not. So, given a symbolic state S, $Win[S]$ is, in general, an union of zones (and so is $S \setminus Win[S]$). As a consequence, we now give two results, which allow us to handle unions of zones (Theorem 3) and to define the computation of Pred_t in terms of basic operations on zones (Theorem 4).

Theorem 3. *The following distribution law holds:*

$$\mathsf{Pred}_t(\bigcup_i G_i, \bigcup_j B_j) = \bigcup_i \bigcap_j \mathsf{Pred}_t(G_i, B_j) \tag{3}$$

Theorem 4. *If B is a convex set, then the Pred_t operator defined in equation (1) can be expressed as:*

$$\mathsf{Pred}_t(G,B) = (G^{\swarrow} \setminus B^{\swarrow}) \cup ((G \cap B^{\swarrow}) \setminus B)^{\swarrow} \tag{4}$$

5.2 Optimizations

Zone Inclusion. When we explore forward the automaton, we check if any newly generated symbolic state S' belongs to the passed list: $S' \in Passed$. As an optimization we may instead use the classical inclusion check: $\exists S'' \in Passed$ s.t. $S' \subseteq S''$, in which case, S' is discarded and we update the dependency graph as well. Indeed, new information learned from the successors of S'' can be new information on S' but not necessarily. This introduces an overhead in the sense that we may back-propagate information for nothing.

On the other hand, back-propagating only the relevant information would be unnecessarily complex and would void most of the memory gain introduced by the use of inclusion. In practice, the reduction of the number of forward steps obtained by the inclusion check pays off for large systems and is a little overhead otherwise, as shown in our experiments.

Losing States. In the case of *reachability*, our games being determined, we can sometimes decide at an early stage that a state q is losing (*i.e.* $q \notin \mathcal{W}(S_G)$), either because it is given as a part of the model in the same way as goal states, or because it is deadlock state, which is not in the set of goal states.

The detection of such losing states has a two-fold benefit. First, we can stop the forward exploration on these states, since we know that we have lost (in the case of a user-defined non-deadlock losing state). Second, we can back-propagate these losing states in the same way as we do for winning states and stop the algorithm if we have the initial state $s_0 \in Lose[S_0]$, where $Lose[S]$ is the subset of the symbolic state S currently known to be losing. In some cases, this can bring a big benefit, illustrated by Fig. 1, if the guard $x < 1$ is changed to true in the edge from ℓ_1 to ℓ_5.

Pruning. In the basic algorithm early termination takes place when the initial state is known to be winning (*i.e.* $s_0 \in Win[S_0]$). However, we may extend this principle to other parts of the algorithm. In particular, we can add the condition that whenever an edge $e = (S, \alpha, S')$ is selected and it turns out that $Win[S] = S$ then we may safely skip the rest of the **while** loop as we know that no further knowledge on the winning states of S can be gained. In doing so, we prune unnecessary continued forward exploration and/or expensive reevaluation. When we back-propagate losing states as described previously, the condition naturally extends to $Win[S] \cup Lose[S] = S$.

5.3 Time Optimal Strategy Synthesis

Time-optimality for reachability games consists in computing the best (optimal) time the controller can guarantee to reach the Goal location: if t^* is the optimal-time, the controller has a strategy that guarantees to reach location Goal within t^* time units whatever the opponent is doing, and moreover, the controller has no strategy to guarantee this for any $t < t^*$.

First consider the following problem: decide whether the controller has a strategy to reach location Goal within B time units. To solve this problem, we

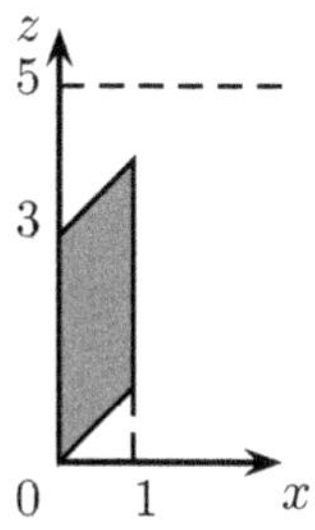

Fig. 5. Winning subset of the initial zone of the TGA of Fig. 1 with clock z added

just add a fresh clock z to the TGA G and the invariant $\mathsf{Inv}(\ell) \equiv z \leq B$ for all locations ℓ with z being unconstrained in the initial state. Then we compute the set of winning states of this game and check that $(\ell_0, \mathbf{0}, z = 0)$ is actually a winning state. If not, try with some $B' > B$. Otherwise we know that the controller can guarantee to reach Goal within B time units ... but in addition we have the optimal-time to reach Goal[8]. Indeed, when computing the winning set of states W^* on the TGA G augmented with the z clock (being initially unconstrained), we have the maximal set of winning states. This means that we obtain some $(\ell_0, Z_0) \in W^*$ and $(\ell_0, \mathbf{0}, z = 0) \in (\ell_0, Z_0)$. But $Z_0 \cap \{(\ell_0, \mathbf{0})\}$ gives us for free the optimal-time to reach Goal. Assume $I = Z_0 \cap \{(\ell_0, \mathbf{0})\}$, then $0 \in I$ and the upper bound of I is less than B. This means that starting in $(\ell_0, \mathbf{0})$ with $z \in I$ the controller can guarantee to reach Goal within B time units. And as W^* is the maximal set of winning states, starting with $z \notin I$ cannot guarantee this any more. Assume $I = [0, b]$. The optimal-time is then $t^* = B - b$. If it turns out that I is right open $[0, b[$, we even know more: that this optimal time t^* cannot be achieved by any strategy, but we can reach Goal in a time arbitrarily close to t^*. On the example of Fig. 1, if we choose $B = 5$ we obtain a closed interval $I = [0, 3]$ giving the optimal time $t^* = 2$ to reach Goal (Fig. 5). Moreover we know that there is a strategy that guarantees this optimal.

6 Experiments

Several versions of the described timed game reachability algorithm have been implemented: with or without inclusion checking between zones, with or without back-propagation of the losing states, and with or without pruning. To benchmark the implementations we used the Production Cell [14,17] case study (Fig. 6). Unprocessed plates arrive on a feeding belt, are taken by a robot to a press, are processed, and are taken away to a departure belt. The robot has two arms (A and B) to take and release the plates and its actions are controllable, except for the time needed to rotate. The arrival of the plates and the press are uncontrollable.

We run experiments on a dual-Xeon 2.8GHz equipped with 3GB of RAM running Linux 2.4.21. Table 2 shows the obtained results. The tests are done with varying number of plates from 2 to 7, and with controllable (win) and uncontrollable (lose) configurations. The models contain one clock for the controller and one clock for each plate. An extra clock is added in the case of timed optimal strategy.

[8] To get an optimum, the condition of the **while**-loop must be $Waiting \neq \emptyset$ alone in the algorithm, disabling early termination.

The inclusion checking of zones is shown to be an important optimization. Furthermore, activating pruning, which really exploits that the algorithm is *on-the-fly*, is useful in practice: the algorithm really terminates earlier. The results for time optimal reachability confirm that the algorithm is exploring the whole state-space and is comparable to exploring without pruning. We stress in the tables the best result obtained for every configuration: it turns out that propagating back the losing states has a significant overhead that pays off for large systems, *i.e.* it is clearly better from 6 plates.

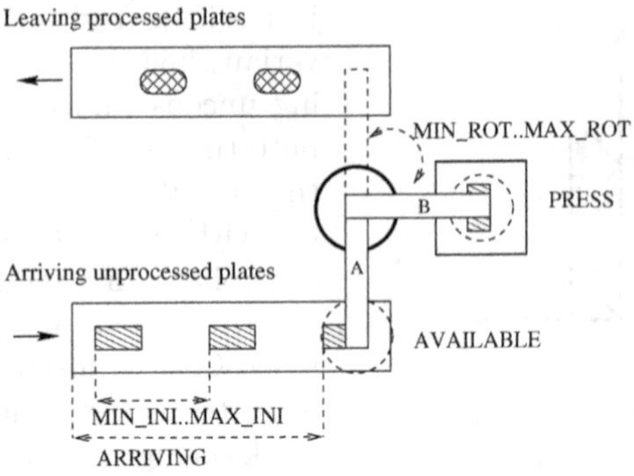

Fig. 6. The production cell

The state-space grows exponentially with respect to the number of plates but the algorithm keeps up linearly with it, which is shown on Fig. 7 that depicts $pre + post$[9]. These results show that the algorithm based on zones behaves well despite the fact that zones are (in theory) worse than Alur & Dill's regions.

Table 2. Results for the different implementations: basic algorithm, then with inclusion checking (inc), pruning (pruning), back propagation of losing states (backlose) and time optimal strategy generation (topt, only for "win", and pruning has little effect). For each number of plates, the tests are done with a controllable (win) and an uncontrollable (lose) configuration. Time (user process) is given in seconds (s) rounded to 0.1s and memory in megabytes (M). '-' denotes a failed run (not enough memory). Results in bold font are the best ones.

Plates		Basic		Basic +inc		Basic +inc +pruning		Basic +backlose +inc +pruning		Basic+backlose +inc +topt	
		time	mem	time	mem	time	mem	time	mem	time	mem
2	win	0.0s	1M	0.0s	1M	**0.0s**	**1M**	0.0s	1M	0.04s	1M
	lose	0.0s	1M	0.0s	1M	**0.0s**	**1M**	0.0s	1M	n/a	n/a
3	win	0.5s	19M	0.0s	1M	**0.0s**	**1M**	0.1s	1M	0.27s	4M
	lose	1.1s	45M	0.1s	1M	**0.0s**	**1M**	0.2s	3M	n/a	n/a
4	win	33.9s	1395M	0.2s	8M	**0.1s**	6M	0.4s	**5M**	1.88s	13M
	lose	-	-	0.5s	11M	**0.4s**	10M	0.9s	**9M**	n/a	n/a
5	win	-	-	3.0s	31M	**1.5s**	22M	2.0s	**16M**	13.35s	59M
	lose	-	-	11.1s	61M	**5.9s**	46M	7.0s	**41M**	n/a	n/a
6	win	-	-	89.1s	179M	38.9s	121M	**12.0s**	**63M**	220.3s	369M
	lose	-	-	699s	480M	317s	346M	**135.1s**	**273M**	n/a	n/a
7	win	-	-	3256s	1183M	1181s	786M	**124s**	**319M**	6188s	2457M
	lose	-	-	-	-	16791s	2981M	**4075s**	**2090M**	n/a	n/a

7 Conclusion and Future Work

In this paper we have introduced what we believe is the first completely on-the-fly algorithm for solving timed games. For its efficient implementation we have

[9] $pre + post$ represents the number of iterations of the algorithm and is therefore an abstraction in both time and space of the implementation.

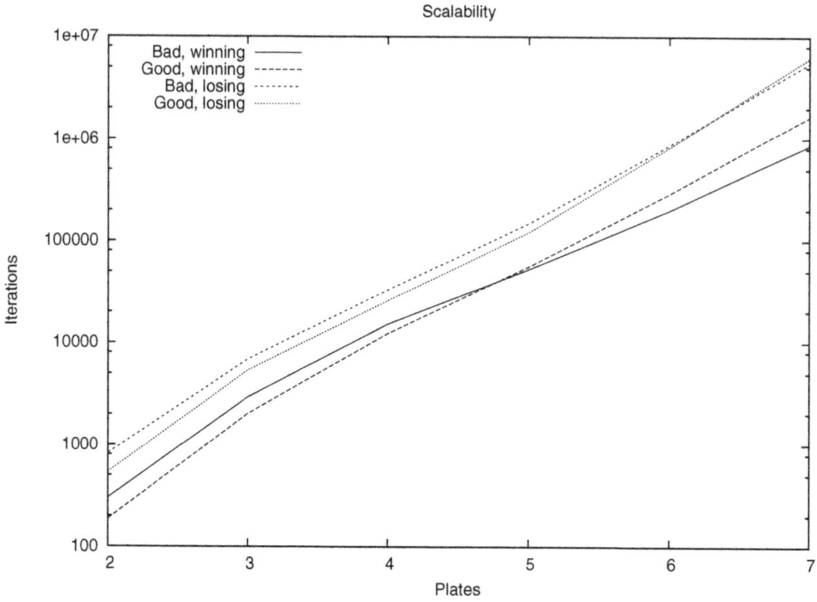

Fig. 7. Scalability of the algorithm. The scale is logarithmic.

used zones as the main datastructure, and we have applied decisive optimizations to take full advantage of the on-the-fly nature of our algorithm and its zone representation. Experiments have shown that an implementation based on zones is feasible and with encouraging performances *w.r.t.* the complexity of the problem. Finally, we have exhibited how to obtain the time optimal strategies with minor additions to our algorithm (essentially book-keeping).

We are working on an improved version of the implementation to distribute it and use the UPPAAL GUI augmented with (un)controllable transitions. We are investigating more aggressive abstractions for the underlying simulation graph computed by our algorithm and efficient guiding of the search, in particular for optimal strategies. Our algorithm is well suited for distributed implementation by its use of unordered waiting-list and there are plans to pursue this directions as has been done for UPPAAL [7]. We are also investigating how to extract strategies and represent them compactly with CDDs (Clock Decision Diagrams).

Acknowledgments. The authors want to thank Patricia Bouyer and Gerd Behrmann for inspiring discussions on the topic of timed games.

References

1. K. Altisen and S. Tripakis. Tools for controller synthesis of timed systems. In *Proc. 2nd Work. on Real-Time Tools (RT-TOOLS'02)*, 2002. Proc. published as Technical Report 2002-025, Uppsala University, Sweden.
2. R. Alur and D. Dill. A theory of timed automata. *Theoretical Computer Science*, 126(2):183–235, 1994.

3. R. Alur, S. La Torre, and G. J. Pappas. Optimal Paths in Weighted Timed Automata. In *Proc. of 4th Work. Hybrid Systems: Computation and Control (HSCC'01)*, volume 2034 of *LNCS*, pages 49–62. Springer, 2001.
4. Henrik R. Andersen. Model Checking and Boolean Graphs. *Theoretical Computer Science*, 126(1):3–30, 1994.
5. E. Asarin and O. Maler. As Soon as Possible: Time Optimal Control for Timed Automata. In *Proc. 2nd Work. Hybrid Systems: Computation & Control (HSCC'99)*, volume 1569 of *LNCS*, pages 19–30. Springer, 1999.
6. E. Asarin, O. Maler, A. Pnueli, and J. Sifakis. Controller Synthesis for Timed Automata. In *Proc. IFAC Symp. on System Structure & Control*, pages 469–474. Elsevier Science, 1998.
7. Gerd Behrmann. Distributed reachability analysis in timed automata. *Journal of Software Tools for Technology Transfer (STTT)*, 7(1):19–30, 2005.
8. M. Bozga, C. Daws, O. Maler, A. Olivero, S. Tripakis, and S. Yovine. KRONOS: a Model-Checking Tool for Real-Time Systems. In *Proc. 10th Conf. on Computer Aided Verification (CAV'98)*, volume 1427 of *LNCS*, pages 546–550. Springer, 1998.
9. L. De Alfaro, T. A. Henzinger, and R. Majumdar. Symbolic Algorithms for Infinite-State Games. In *Proc. 12th Conf. on Concurrency Theory (CONCUR'01)*, volume 2154 of *LNCS*, pages 536–550. Springer, 2001.
10. Gerard J. Holzmann. *The SPIN Model Checker.* Addison-Wesley, 2003.
11. S. La Torre, S. Mukhopadhyay, and A. Murano. Optimal-Reachability and Control for Acyclic Weighted Timed Automata. In *Proc. 2nd IFIP Conf. on Theoretical Computer Science (TCS 2002)*, volume 223, pages 485–497. Kluwer, 2002.
12. K. G. Larsen. Efficient Local Correctness Checking. In *Proc. of Conf. of Computer Assisted Verification (CAV'92)*, volume 663 of *LNCS*, pages 30–43. Springer, 1992.
13. K. G. Larsen, P. Pettersson, and W. Yi. UPPAAL in a Nutshell. *Journal of Software Tools for Technology Transfer (STTT)*, 1(1-2):134–152, 1997.
14. C. Lewerentz and T. Lindner. Production Cell: A Comparative Study in Formal Specification and Verification. In *Methods, Languages & Tools for Construction of Correct Software*, volume 1009 of *LNCS*, pages 388–416. Springer, 1995.
15. X. Liu and S. Smolka. Simple Linear-Time Algorithm for Minimal Fixed Points. In *Proc. 26th Conf. on Automata, Languages and Programming (ICALP'98)*, volume 1443 of *LNCS*, pages 53–66. Springer, 1998.
16. O. Maler, A. Pnueli, and J. Sifakis. On the synthesis of discrete controllers for timed systems. In *Proc. 12th Symp. on Theoretical Aspects of Computer Science (STACS'95)*, volume 900, pages 229–242. Springer, 1995.
17. H. Melcher and K. Winkelmann. Controller Synthesis for the "Production Cell" Case Study. In *Proc. of 2nd Work. on Formal Methods in Software Practice*, pages 24–36. ACM Press, 1998.
18. J. Rasmussen, K. G. Larsen, and K. Subramani. Resource-optimal scheduling using priced timed automata. In *Proc. 10th Conf. on Tools and Algorithms for the Construction and Analysis of Systems (TACAS'04)*, volume 2988 of *LNCS*, pages 220–235. Springer, 2004.
19. W. Thomas. On the Synthesis of Strategies in Infinite Games. In *Proc. 12th Symp. on Theoretical Aspects of Computer Science (STACS'95)*, volume 900, pages 1–13. Springer, 1995. Invited talk.
20. S. Tripakis and K. Altisen. On-the-Fly Controller Synthesis for Discrete and Timed Systems. In *Proc. of World Congress on Formal Methods (FM'99)*, volume 1708 of *LNCS*, pages 233–252. Springer, 1999.

Modal Logics for Timed Control*

Patricia Bouyer[1], Franck Cassez[2], and François Laroussinie[1]

[1] LSV, UMR 8643, CNRS & ENS de Cachan, France
{bouyer, fl}@lsv.ens-cachan.fr
[2] IRCCyN, UMR 6597, CNRS, France
cassez@irccyn.ec-nantes.fr

Abstract. In this paper we use the timed modal logic L_ν to specify control objectives for timed plants. We show that the control problem for a large class of objectives can be reduced to a model-checking problem for an extension (L_ν^{cont}) of the logic L_ν with a new modality.

More precisely we define a fragment of L_ν, namely L_ν^{det}, such that any control objective of L_ν^{det} can be translated into a L_ν^{cont} formula that holds for the plant if and only if there is a controller that can enforce the control objective.

We also show that the new modality of L_ν^{cont} strictly increases the expressive power of L_ν while model-checking of L_ν^{cont} remains EXPTIME-complete.

1 Introduction

Control Problem. The *control problem* (CP) for discrete event systems was first studied by Ramadge & Wonham in [RW89]. The CP is the following: "Given a finite-state model of a *plant P* (*open system)* with controllable and uncontrollable discrete actions, a *control objective* Φ, does there exist a *controller* f such that the plant supervised by f (*closed system*) satisfies Φ?" The *dense-time* version of the CP with an *untimed* control objective has been investigated and solved in [MPS95]. In this seminal paper, Maler *et al.* consider a plant P given by a *timed game automaton* which is a standard timed automaton [AD94] with its set of discrete actions partitioned into controllable and uncontrollable actions. They give an algorithm to decide whether a controller exists or not, and show that if one such controller exists a witness can be effectively computed. In [WT97] a semi-algorithm has been proposed to solve the CP when the plant is defined by a hybrid (game) automaton.

Specification of Control Properties. In the aforementioned papers the control objective is either a *safety* or *reachability* property (or some simple Büchi conditions). In [dAHM01] the authors give an algorithm to deal with general ω-regular control objectives. It is to be noticed that those control objectives are often called *internal* in the sense that they refer to the state properties (and clocks) of the system to be controlled. In the case of timed systems they only

* Work supported by ACI Cortos, a program of the French government.

M. Abadi and L. de Alfaro (Eds.): CONCUR 2005, LNCS 3653, pp. 81–94, 2005.

refer to the untimed sequences of states of the system and thus have a restrictive expressiveness: it is possible to specify a property like "after p has been reached q will be reached" but nothing like "after p has been reached, q will be reached within less than d time units" (*bounded liveness*). Moreover, in the verification methodology for closed systems, one usually models (and thinks of) the plant P and the controller f as a closed system $f(P)$, and specifies a property φ with a suitable timed temporal logic and check whether the closed system $f(P)$ satisfies φ. It is then very natural to have similar logics in the game framework to specify timed control objectives for *open* systems.

Our Contribution. The logic L_ν [LL95] is a subset of the timed μ-calculus that can be used for specifying timed safety properties of closed timed systems. Modalities of L_ν seem to be appropriate to specify timed control objectives as well because we can use existential and universal quantifications over *discrete* actions (as it is used in the untimed framework of [AVW03, RP03]), and also over time *delays*. The control problem CP for a plant (specified as a timed automaton) and a control objective in L_ν expresses as folloes:

> *Given a timed automaton P, the* plant, *and a L_ν formula φ, the* safety control objective, *is there a* controller *f s.t. $f(P) \models \varphi$?* (CP)

So far there is no constraint neither on the structure nor on the power of the controller f we are looking for: it may even require unbounded memory or arbitrary small delays between two consecutive controllable actions. In this paper we focus on controllability (CP) and not on the controller synthesis problem (*i.e.* exhibit a witness controller).

The main result of the paper is that we can reduce CP for a plant P and an L_ν control objective φ, to a standard *model-checking* problem on the plant P and a formula φ_c of a more expressive logic L_ν^{cont}, that extends L_ν with a new modality. More precisely we exhibit a *deterministic* fragment of L_ν, namely L_ν^{det}, s.t. for all $\varphi \in L_\nu^{\text{det}}$, the following reduction (RED) holds:

$$\left(\textit{There exists a controller } f \textit{ s.t. } f(P) \models \varphi \right) \iff P \models \varphi_c \qquad \text{(RED)}$$

where φ_c is a formula of L_ν^{cont}. We also give an effective procedure to obtain φ_c from φ.

Further on we study the logic L_ν^{cont} and prove that it is strictly more expressive than L_ν, which is a technically involved result on its own. We also show that the new modality of L_ν^{cont} is not necessary when we restrict our attention to *sampling* control (the controller can do an action every Δ time units) or to *Known Switch Conditions Dense-Time* control (where time elapsing is uncontrollable [CHR02]). A natural question following equation (RED) above is to study the model-checking problem for timed automata against L_ν^{cont} specifications. In the paper we prove that *i)* the model-checking of L_ν^{cont} over timed automata is EXPTIME-complete; *ii)* L_ν^{cont} inherits the *compositionality* property of L_ν.

Related Work. In the discrete (untimed) case many logics used to specify *correctness* properties of closed systems have been extended to specify *control objectives* of open systems. ATL [AHK02] (resp. ATL*) is the *control* version of CTL (resp. CTL*). More recently [AVW03, RP03] have considered a more general framework in which properties of the controlled system are specified in various extensions of the μ-calculus: *loop* μ-calculus for [AVW03] and *quantified* μ-calculus for [RP03]. In both cases the control problem is reduced to a model-checking (or satisfiability) problem as in equation (RED). In the timed framework, external specifications have been studied in [DM02]: properties of the controlled system are specified with timed automata, and in [FLTM02], the control objective is given as a formula of the logic TCTL.

Outline of the Paper. In section 2 we define basic notions used in the paper: timed systems, logic L_ν and variants and the control problem. In section 3 we prove that (RED) holds and also that φ_c is in L_ν for two simpler control problems. Section 4 is devoted to the study of the logic L_ν^{cont} (expressiveness, decidability, and compositionality).

The proofs are omitted and can be found in [BCL05].

2 Timed Automata and the Timed Modal Logic L_ν

We consider as time domain the set $\mathbb{R}_{\geq 0}$ of non-negative reals. Act is a finite set of *actions*.[1] We consider a finite set X of variables, called *clocks*. A *clock valuation* over X is a mapping $v : X \to \mathbb{R}_{\geq 0}$ that assigns to each clock a time value. The set of all clock valuations over X is denoted $\mathbb{R}_{\geq 0}^X$. Let $t \in \mathbb{R}_{\geq 0}$, the valuation $v + t$ is defined by $(v+t)(x) = v(x) + t$ for all $x \in X$. For $Y \subseteq X$, we denote by $v[Y \leftarrow 0]$ the valuation assigning 0 (resp. $v(x)$) for any $x \in Y$ (resp. $x \in X \setminus Y$).

We denote $\mathcal{C}(X)$ the set of *clock constraints* defined as the conjunctions of atomic constraints of the form $x \bowtie c$ with $x \in X$, $c \in \mathbb{Q}_{\geq 0}$ and $\bowtie \in \{<, \leq, =, \geq, >\}$. For $g \in \mathcal{C}(X)$ and $v \in \mathbb{R}_{\geq 0}^X$, we write $v \models g$ if v satisfies g and $[\![g]\!]$ denotes the set $\{v \in \mathbb{R}_{\geq 0}^X \mid v \models g\}$.

2.1 Timed Transition Systems and Timed Automata

Timed Transition Systems. A *timed transition system* (TTS) is a tuple $S = (Q, q_0, \mathsf{Act}, \longrightarrow_S)$ where Q is a set of states, $q_0 \in Q$ is the initial state, and $\longrightarrow_S \subseteq Q \times (\mathsf{Act} \cup \mathbb{R}_{\geq 0}) \times Q$ is a set of transitions. If $(q, e, q') \in \longrightarrow_S$, we also write $q \xrightarrow{e}_S q'$. The transitions labeled by $a \in \mathsf{Act}$ (resp. $t \in \mathbb{R}_{\geq 0}$) are called *action* (resp. *delay*) transitions. We make the following common assumptions about TTSs [Yi90]:

- 0-delay: $q \xrightarrow{0}_S q'$ if and only if $q = q'$,
- Additivity: if $q \xrightarrow{d}_S q'$ and $q' \xrightarrow{d'}_S q''$ with $d, d' \in \mathbb{R}_{\geq 0}$, then $q \xrightarrow{d+d'}_S q''$,

[1] We assume that Act and $\mathbb{R}_{\geq 0}$ are disjoint.

– Continuity: if $q \xrightarrow{d}_S q'$, then for every d' and d'' in $\mathbb{R}_{\geq 0}$ such that $d = d' + d''$, there exists q'' such that $q \xrightarrow{d'}_S q'' \xrightarrow{d''}_S q'$,
– Time-determinism: if $q \xrightarrow{e}_S q'$ and $q \xrightarrow{e}_S q''$ with $e \in \mathbb{R}_{\geq 0}$, then $q' = q''$.

A *run* is a finite or infinite sequence $\rho = s_0 \xrightarrow{e_1}_S s_1 \xrightarrow{e_2}_S \cdots \xrightarrow{e_n} s_n \cdots$ We denote by $\mathit{first}(\rho) = s_0$. If ρ is finite, $\mathit{last}(\rho)$ denotes the last state of ρ. $\mathsf{Runs}(q, S)$ is the set of runs in S starting from q and $\mathsf{Runs}(S) = \mathsf{Runs}(q_0, S)$. We use $q \xrightarrow{e}_S$ as a shorthand for "$\exists q'$ s.t. $q \xrightarrow{e}_S q'$" and extend this notation to finite runs $\rho \xrightarrow{e}_S$ whenever $\mathit{last}(\rho) \xrightarrow{e}_S$.

Timed Automata. A *timed automaton (TA)* [AD94] is a tuple $\mathcal{A} = (L, \ell_0, \mathsf{Act}, X, \mathsf{inv}, T)$ where L is a finite set of locations, $\ell_0 \in L$ is the initial location, X is a finite set of clocks, $\mathsf{inv} : L \to \mathcal{C}(X)$ is a mapping that assigns an invariant to each location, and $T \subseteq L \times [\mathcal{C}(X) \times \mathsf{Act} \times 2^X] \times L$ is a finite set of transitions[2]. The semantics of a TA $\mathcal{A} = (L, \ell_0, \mathsf{Act}, X, \mathsf{inv}, T)$ is a TTS $S_\mathcal{A} = (L \times \mathbb{R}^X_{\geq 0}, (\ell_0, v_0), \mathsf{Act}, \longrightarrow_{S_\mathcal{A}})$ where $v_0(x) = 0$ for all $x \in X$ and $\longrightarrow_{S_\mathcal{A}}$ consists of: *i)* action transition: $(\ell, v) \xrightarrow{a}_{S_\mathcal{A}} (\ell', v')$ if there exists a transition $\ell \xrightarrow{g,a,Y} \ell'$ in T s.t. $v \models g$, $v' = v[Y \leftarrow 0]$ and $v' \models \mathsf{inv}(\ell')$; *ii)* delay transitions: $(\ell, v) \xrightarrow{t}_{S_\mathcal{A}} (\ell, v')$ if $t \in \mathbb{R}_{\geq 0}$, $v' = v + t$ and $v, v' \in \mathsf{inv}(\ell)$.

A TA is *deterministic* w.r.t. $\Sigma \subseteq \mathsf{Act}$ if for all $a \in \Sigma$, if $(\ell, g_1, a, Y_1, \ell_1) \in T$ and $(\ell, g_2, a, Y_2, \ell_2) \in T$ then $[\![g_1]\!] \cap [\![g_2]\!] = \emptyset$.

2.2 The Modal Logics L_ν, L_ν^{det} and L_ν^{cont}

The Modal Logic L_ν [LL95, LL98]. The logic L_ν over the finite set of clocks K, the set of identifiers Id, and the set of actions Act is defined as the set of formulae generated by the following grammar:

$$\begin{aligned}\varphi ::= \mathtt{tt} \mid \mathtt{ff} \mid \varphi \wedge \varphi \mid \varphi \vee \varphi \mid x \ \underline{\mathsf{in}} \ \varphi \mid x \bowtie c \mid [a]\, \varphi \mid \langle a \rangle\, \varphi \mid \\ [\delta]\ \varphi \mid \langle \delta \rangle\, \varphi \mid Z\end{aligned}$$

where $a \in \mathsf{Act}$, $x \in K$, $\bowtie \in \{<, \leq, =, \geq, >\}$, $c \in \mathbb{Q}_{\geq 0}$, $Z \in \mathsf{Id}$.

The meaning of the identifiers is specified by a declaration $\mathcal{D}$ assigning a L_ν formula to each identifier. When $\mathcal{D}$ is understood we write $Z =_\nu \Psi_Z$ if $\mathcal{D}(Z) = \Psi_Z$. We define the following shorthands in L_ν: $r \ \underline{\mathsf{in}}\ \varphi \overset{def}{=} x_1 \ \underline{\mathsf{in}}\ x_2 \ \underline{\mathsf{in}} \cdots \underline{\mathsf{in}}\ x_n \ \underline{\mathsf{in}}\ \varphi$ if $r = \{x_1, \cdots, x_n\} \subseteq K$.

Let $S = (Q, q_0, \mathsf{Act}, \longrightarrow_S)$ be a TTS. L_ν formulae are interpreted over extended states (q, v) where for $q \in Q$ and $v \in \mathbb{R}^K_{\geq 0}$. We write "$S, (q, v) \models \varphi$" when an extended state (q, v) satisfies φ in the TTS S. This satisfaction relation is defined as the largest relation satisfying the implications in Table 1. The modalities $\langle e \rangle$ with $e \in \mathsf{Act} \cup \{\delta\}$ correspond to existential quantification over action or delay transitions, and $[e]$ is the counterpart for universal quantification. An extended state satisfies an identifier Z (denoted $S, (q, v) \models Z$) if it belongs to the

[2] We often write $\ell \xrightarrow{g,a,Y} \ell'$ instead of simply the tuple (ℓ, g, a, Y, ℓ').

maximal fixedpoint of the equation $Z =_\nu \Psi_Z$. Finally the formula clocks are used to measure time elapsing in properties. We define $[\![\varphi]\!]_S = \{(q,v) \mid S,(q,v) \models \varphi\}$. We write $S \models \varphi$ for $S,(q_0,v_0) \models \varphi$ where $v_0(x) = 0$ for all $x \in K$. The logic L_ν allows us to express many behavioural properties of timed systems [LL98]. For example the formula Z defined by $\Psi_Z = (\bigwedge_{a\in\mathsf{Act}}[a]\, Z \wedge [\delta]\, Z \wedge \varphi)$ holds when all reachable states satisfy φ. Other examples of formulae will be given later on in the paper.

Table 1. Satisfaction implications for L_ν

$$
\begin{array}{l}
S,(q,v) \models \alpha \implies \alpha \text{ with } \alpha \in \{\mathtt{tt},\mathtt{ff}\}\\
S,(q,v) \models x \bowtie c \implies v(x) \bowtie c\\
S,(q,v) \models Z \implies S,(q,v) \models \Psi_Z\\
S,(q,v) \models \varphi_1\ op\ \varphi_2, \implies S,(q,v) \models \varphi_1 \quad op \quad S,(q,v) \models \varphi_2 \text{ with } \ op \in \{\wedge,\vee\}\\
S,(q,v) \models x\ \underline{\mathsf{in}}\ \varphi \implies S,(q,v[x \leftarrow 0]) \models \varphi\\
S,(q,v) \models [a]\,\varphi \implies \text{for all } q \xrightarrow{a}_S q',\ S,(q',v) \models \varphi\\
S,(q,v) \models \langle a\rangle\,\varphi \implies \text{there is some } q \xrightarrow{a}_S q',\ S,(q',v) \models \varphi\\
S,(q,v) \models [\delta]\,\varphi \implies \text{for all } t \in \mathbb{R}_{\geq 0} \text{ s.t. } q \xrightarrow{t}_S q',\ S,(q',v+t) \models \varphi\\
S,(q,v) \models \langle\delta\rangle\,\varphi \implies \text{there is some } t \in \mathbb{R}_{\geq 0} \text{ s.t. } q \xrightarrow{t}_S q',\ S,(q',v+t) \models \varphi
\end{array}
$$

The Modal Logic L_ν^{cont}**.** As we will see later in the paper, the modal operators of L_ν are not sufficient to express dense-time control. Indeed we need to express the persistence (w.r.t. time elapsing) of a property **until** a controllable action is performed: we thus need to express that some property is true only for a subset of the states of the plant which are reachable by time elapsing **before** a controllable action leading to good states is possible. This kind of property cannot be expressed using the $[\delta]$ and $\langle\delta\rangle$ operators. This is why we define the new modality $[\delta\rangle$, the semantics of which is defined over an extended configuration (q,v) of a TTS S as follows:

$$
\begin{aligned}
S,(q,v) \models \varphi\,[\delta\rangle\,\psi \Leftrightarrow\ & \text{either } \forall t \in \mathbb{R}_{\geq 0},\ q \xrightarrow{t}_S q' \Rightarrow S,(q',v+t) \models \varphi\\
& \text{or } \exists t \in \mathbb{R}_{\geq 0} \text{ s.t. } q \xrightarrow{t}_S q' \text{ and } S,(q',v+t) \models \psi \text{ and} \qquad (1)\\
& \forall 0 \leq t' < t,\ q \xrightarrow{t'}_S q'' \text{ we have } S,(q'',v+t') \models \varphi
\end{aligned}
$$

Let L_ν^{cont} be the timed modal logic which extends L_ν by adding the modality $[\delta\rangle$. This operator is some kind of "Until" modality over delays. In [HNSY94] the timed μ-calculus which is studied contains a modality $\rhd$ the semantics of which is close to the semantics of $[\delta\rangle$ (the main difference between $\rhd$ and $[\delta\rangle$ is that $\rhd$ may include an action transition after the delay).

A Deterministic Fragment of L_ν**,** L_ν^{det}**.** In the following we will restrict the possible control objectives to properties expressed in a subset L_ν^{det} of L_ν. Indeed, we want to define a transformation such that equation (RED) given in the introduction holds, the restriction is then motivated by the following remark:

Remark 1. A control objective of L_ν like $\varphi_1 \wedge \varphi_2$ intuitively requires to find a controller that both ensures φ_1 and φ_2. In an inductive construction, this amounts to build a controller that ensures $\varphi_1 \wedge \varphi_2$ from two controllers: one that ensures φ_1 and an other that ensures φ_2. This means that we must be able to merge controllers in a suitable manner. The definition of L_ν^{det} will syntactically ensure that the conjunctions of L_ν^{det} formulae can be merged safely, *i.e.* that they are in some sense *deterministic.*

Indeed, any (first-level) subformula of a conjunction in L_ν^{det} will be prefixed by a modal operator with a particular action, and then the existence of a controller for φ_1 and another one for φ_2 entails the existence of a controller for $\varphi_1 \wedge \varphi_2$.

In the untimed case, some kind of "deterministic" form is also used (the so-called *disjunctive normal form*), but this is not a restriction as all formulae of the μ-calculus can be rewritten in a disjunctive normal form [JW95]. One hope could be to be able to transform any formula of L_ν into an equivalent formula of L_ν^{det}, but we do not know yet if this is possible. Note that in the untimed framework, transforming formulae of the μ-calculus into formulae in disjunctive normal form is strongly related to the satisfiability problem, and in the timed case, the satisfiability problem for L_ν is still an open problem [LLW95].

We first define *basic* terms B_ν by the following grammar:

$$\alpha ::= \mathtt{tt} \mid \mathtt{ff} \mid x \bowtie c \mid r \ \underline{\mathsf{in}} \ \langle a \rangle \varphi \mid r \ \underline{\mathsf{in}} \ [a] \varphi$$

with $x \in K$, $r \subseteq K$, $c \in \mathbb{Q}$ and $a \in \mathsf{Act} \cup \{\delta\}$ and $\varphi \in L_\nu^{\mathrm{det}}$ (L_ν^{det} is defined hereafter). A set of basic terms $A = \{\alpha_1, \alpha_2, \cdots, \alpha_n\}$ is *deterministic* if for all $\sigma \in \mathsf{Act} \cup \{\delta\}$ there is at most one i s.t. $\alpha_i = r \ \underline{\mathsf{in}} \ \langle \sigma \rangle \varphi$ or $\alpha_i = r \ \underline{\mathsf{in}} \ [\sigma] \varphi$. We then define L_ν^{det} as the deterministic fragment of L_ν inductively defined as follows:

$$L_\nu^{\mathrm{det}} \ni \varphi, \psi ::= X \mid \varphi \vee \psi \mid \bigwedge_{\alpha \in A} \alpha$$

with $X \in \mathsf{Id}$ and A a (finite) deterministic set of basic terms. With this restriction on the conjunctions, if there are controllers f_α for all $\alpha \in A$, we can merge them to obtain a controller for $\bigwedge_{\alpha \in A} \alpha$ (see remark 1 above).

Note that already many properties can be expressed in the fragment L_ν^{det}, for example safety and bounded liveness properties:

$$X_1 = [\mathsf{Bad}]\, \mathtt{ff} \wedge \bigwedge_{\mathsf{a} \neq \mathsf{Problem}, \mathsf{Bad}} [\mathsf{a}]\, \mathsf{X}_1 \wedge [\mathsf{Problem}]\, (\mathsf{z}\ \underline{\mathsf{in}}\ \mathsf{X}_2) \wedge [\delta]\, \mathsf{X}_1$$

$$X_2 = z < d_{\max} \wedge [\mathsf{Bad}]\, \mathtt{ff} \wedge [\mathsf{Alarm}]\, \mathsf{X}_1 \wedge \bigwedge_{\mathsf{a} \neq \mathsf{Alarm}, \mathsf{Bad}} [\mathsf{a}]\, \mathsf{X}_2 \wedge [\delta]\, \mathsf{X}_2$$

The above formula expresses that the system is always safe (represented by property $[\mathsf{Bad}]\, \mathtt{ff}$), and that every $\mathsf{Problem}$ is followed in less than $d_{\max}$ time units by the Alarm. The previous formula can also be specified using simpler formalism (*e.g. test automaton* [ABBL03]) but this is not the case for every L_ν^{det} formula. The formula $X = [\delta]\, X \wedge \bigwedge_{a \in \mathsf{Act}} [a]\, X \wedge \langle \delta \rangle \langle b \rangle \mathtt{tt}$ for some $b \in \mathsf{Act}$, which means that there is always some delay s.t. b is enabled cannot be expressed with test automata.

2.3 The Control Problem

Definition 1 (Live Plant). *A* live plant *(plant in the sequel) P is a TA where* Act *is partitionned into* Act_u *and* Act_c *and s.t. 1) it is deterministic w.r.t. every* $a \in \mathsf{Act}_c$*; 2) in every state* (ℓ, v) *the TA P can let time elapse or do an uncontrollable action.*

A *controller* [MPS95] for a plant, is a function that during the evolution of the system constantly gives information as to what should be done in order to ensure a control objective Φ. In a given state the controller can either *i)* "enable some particular *controllable* action" or *ii)* "do nothing at this point in time, just wait" which will be denoted by the special symbol λ. Of course a controller cannot prevent uncontrollable actions from occurring. Nevertheless, we assume that the controller can **disable** a controllable action at any time, and this will not block the plant because the plant is *live*.

Definition 2 (Controller). *Let* $P = (L, \ell_0, \mathsf{Act}, X, \mathsf{inv}, T)$ *be a plant. A* controller[3] *f over P is a partial function from* $\mathsf{Runs}(S_P)$ *to* $\mathsf{Act}_c \cup \{\lambda\}$ *s.t. for any finite run* $\rho \in \mathsf{Runs}(S_P)$*, if $f(\rho)$ is defined* [4] *then* $f(\rho) \in \{e \mid \rho \xrightarrow{e}_{S_P}\}$.

The purpose of a controller f for a plant P is to restrict the set of behaviours in S_P in order to ensure that some property holds. Closing the plant P with f produces a TTS (set of runs) corresponding to the controlled plant:

Definition 3 (Controlled plant). *Let* $P = (L, \ell_0, \mathsf{Act}, X, \mathsf{inv}, T)$ *be a plant,* $q \in S_P$ *and f a controller over P. The* controlled plant $f(S_P, q)$ *is the TTS* $(Q, q, \mathsf{Act}, \longrightarrow_f)$ *defined inductively by:*

- $q \in Q$,
- *if* $\rho \in \mathsf{Runs}(f(S_P, q))$*, then* $last(\rho) \xrightarrow{e}_f q'$ *and* $q' \in Q$*, if* $last(\rho) \xrightarrow{e}_{S_P} q'$ *and one of the following three conditions hold:*
  1. $e \in \mathsf{Act}_u$,
  2. $e \in \mathsf{Act}_c$ *and* $e = f(\rho)$,
  3. $e \in \mathbb{R}_{\geq 0}$ *and* $\forall 0 \leq e' < e, \exists last(\rho) \xrightarrow{e'}_{S_P} q''$ *s.t.* $\lambda = f(\rho \xrightarrow{e'}_{S_P} q'')$.

We note $f(P)$ the controlled plant P by controller f from initial state of P.

The Δ-dense-time control problem amounts to finding a controller for a system s.t. at least $\Delta \geq 0$ time units elapse between two consecutive control actions. Such a controller is called a Δ-*controller* and can prevent time elapsing and force a controllable action to happen at any point in time if the time elapsed since the last controllable move is more than Δ. If $\Delta = 0$ we admit controllers that can do two consecutive actions separated by arbitrary small delays (even 0-delay), *i.e.* controllers that have infinite speed. If $\Delta > 0$, the Δ-controllers are forced to be *strongly non-zeno*. We note $\mathsf{Contr}_\Delta(P)$ the set of Δ-controllers for plant P.

---

[3] The notation f comes from the fact that a controller is specified as a function, as strategies in game theory.

[4] $\rho \xrightarrow{\lambda}_{S_P}$ stands here for $\exists t > 0$ s.t. $last(\rho) \xrightarrow{t}_{S_P} s'$.

Definition 4 (Δ-Dense-Time Control Problem). *Let* $P = (L, \ell_0, \mathsf{Act}, X, \mathsf{inv}, T)$ *be a plant,* $\varphi \in L_\nu^{\mathrm{det}}$, *a (deterministic)* safety control objective, *and* $\Delta \in \mathbb{Q}_{\geq 0}$. *The* Δ-Dense-Time Control Problem *(Δ-CP for short) asks the following:*

$$\textit{Is there a } \text{controller } f \in \mathsf{Contr}_\Delta(P) \textit{ such that } f(P) \models \varphi? \qquad (\Delta\text{-CP})$$

Remark 2. In the above Δ-CP, we look for controllers which can do a controllable action only if the time elapsed since the last controllable action is at least Δ. We could specify many other classes of controllers: for example we could impose the controller doing controllable actions exactly every Δ units of time (this is called *sampling control* — see later), or to alternate controllable actions. Notice that this fits very well in our framework as we will see in section 4 that L_ν^{det} is *compositional*: any reasonable constraint on the controller can be given as an extra (timed) automaton and taken into account simply by synchronizing it with the plant P. For example the Δ-controllers can be specified by an extra self-loop automaton where the loop is constrained by a guard $x \geq \Delta$, any controllable action can be done, and clock x is reset.

In the following we note P_Δ the synchronized product of P with this self-loop automaton (see [AD94] for the definition of the classical synchronisation product).

3 From Control to Model Checking

In this section, we prove that for any control objective defined as a L_ν^{det} formula φ, we can build an L_ν^{cont} formula $\overline{\varphi}$ that holds for P_Δ iff there exists a Δ-controller which supervises plant P in order to satisfy φ. This corresponds to equation (RED) we have settled in the introduction.

3.1 Dense-Time Control Problem

Let φ be a L_ν^{det} formula and $\sigma \in \mathsf{Act}_c \cup \{\lambda\}$, we define the formula $\overline{\varphi}^{\,\sigma}$ by the inductive translation of Fig. 1. Intuitively, formula $\overline{\varphi}^{\,a_c}$ will hold when there is a controller which ensures φ and which starts by enforcing controllable action a_c whereas formula $\overline{\varphi}^{\,\lambda}$ will hold when there is a controller which ensures φ and which starts by delaying. We use the shortcut $\overline{\varphi}$ to express that nothing is required for the strategy, which will correspond to $\bigvee_{\sigma \in \mathsf{Act}_c \cup \{\lambda\}} \overline{\varphi}^{\,\sigma}$.We also use $\langle\lambda\rangle\, \mathtt{tt}$ as a shortcut for $\bigwedge_{a_c \in \mathsf{Act}_c} [a_c]\, \mathtt{ff}$. Note that the new operator $[\delta\rangle$ is used in the formula $\overline{[\delta]\,\varphi}^{\,\sigma}$. This translation rule introduces the superscript a_c in the disjunctive right argument of $[\delta\rangle$. This just means that we can actually prevent time from elapsing at some point, if we perform a controllable action.

We can now state our main theorem about controllability:

Theorem 1. *Given P a plant, $\varphi \in L_\nu^{\mathrm{det}}$ a control objective, $\Delta \in \mathbb{Q}_{\geq 0}$, we then have:*

$$\Big(\exists f \in \mathsf{Contr}_\Delta(P) \text{ s.t. } f(P) \models \varphi\Big) \iff P_\Delta \models \overline{\varphi} \qquad (2)$$

$\overline{\bigwedge_{\alpha\in A}\alpha}^{\sigma} \stackrel{def}{=} \bigwedge_{\alpha\in A}\overline{\alpha}^{\sigma}$	$\overline{\bigvee_{\alpha\in A}\alpha}^{\sigma} \stackrel{def}{=} \bigvee_{\alpha\in A}\overline{\alpha}^{\sigma}$
$\overline{\langle a\rangle\,\varphi}^{\sigma} \stackrel{def}{=} \begin{cases}\mathtt{ff} & \text{if } \sigma, a\in \mathsf{Act}_c \wedge \sigma\neq a\\ \langle a\rangle\,\overline{\varphi}\wedge\langle\sigma\rangle\,\mathtt{tt} & \text{if } a\in\mathsf{Act}_u\\ \langle a\rangle\,\overline{\varphi} & \text{otherwise}\end{cases}$	$\overline{x\sim c}^{\sigma} \stackrel{def}{=} x\sim c\wedge\langle\sigma\rangle\,\mathtt{tt}$
$\overline{\langle\delta\rangle\,\varphi}^{\sigma} \stackrel{def}{=} \begin{cases}\langle\delta\rangle\,\overline{\varphi} & \text{if } \sigma=\lambda\\ \overline{\varphi}^{\sigma} & \text{if } \sigma\in\mathsf{Act}_c\end{cases}$	$\overline{r\ \underline{\mathsf{in}}\ \varphi}^{\sigma} \stackrel{def}{=} r\ \underline{\mathsf{in}}\ \overline{\varphi}^{\sigma}$
$\overline{[a_c]\,\varphi}^{\sigma} \stackrel{def}{=} \begin{cases}\langle\sigma\rangle\,\mathtt{tt} & \text{if } a_c\neq\sigma\\ \langle a_c\rangle\,\overline{\varphi} & \text{if } a_c=\sigma\end{cases}$	$\overline{[a_u]\,\varphi}^{\sigma} \stackrel{def}{=} [a_u]\,\overline{\varphi}\wedge\langle\sigma\rangle\,\mathtt{tt}$
$\overline{[\delta]\,\varphi}^{\sigma} \stackrel{def}{=} \begin{cases}\overline{\varphi}^{\sigma} & \text{if } \sigma\in\mathsf{Act}_c\\ \overline{\varphi}^{\lambda}\,[\delta\rangle\left(\bigvee_{a_c\in\mathsf{Act}_c}\overline{\varphi}^{a_c}\right) & \text{otherwise}\end{cases}$	$\overline{X}^{\sigma} \stackrel{def}{=} X_{\sigma}\wedge\langle\sigma\rangle\,\mathtt{tt}$

Fig. 1. Definition of $\overline{\varphi}^{\sigma}$, $\varphi\in L_{\nu}^{\mathrm{det}}$ and $\sigma\in\mathsf{Act}_c\cup\{\lambda\}$

The proof of Theorem 1 can be done by induction on the structure of the formula and is given in [BCL05].

This theorem reduces the *controllability* problem for properties expressed in L_{ν}^{det} to some *model-checking* problem for properties expressed in L_{ν}^{cont}. Note however that this theorem does not provide a method to synthesize controllers: indeed L_{ν} and L_{ν}^{cont} are compositional logics (see in the next section), controller synthesis is thus equivalent to model synthesis. But, as already said, the satisfiability problem (or model synthesis) for L_{ν}^{det} or L_{ν} is still open (see [LLW95] for partial results about this problem). Note also that as L_{ν}^{cont} is compositional (see next section), verifying $P_{\Delta}\models\overline{\varphi}$ reduces to checking $P\models\overline{\varphi}\,/S_{\Delta}$ where S_{Δ} is the self-loop automaton mentioned before.

3.2 Known-Switch Condition Dense-Time Control

Known-switch condition (KSC) dense-time control [CHR02] corresponds to the control of the time-abstract model of a game: intuitively this assumes that time elapsing is not controllable. A controller can thus choose to do a controllable action $a\in\mathsf{Act}_c$ or to do nothing (λ), but in the latter case the controller does not control the duration of the next continuous move.

To see that L_{ν} is sufficient to express KSC dense-time control, we just need to focus on formula of the type $[\delta]\,\varphi$ as this is the only formula that may need the use of the $[\delta\rangle$ operator when translated into a model-checking formula. More precisely we only need to focus on the translation of $\overline{[\delta]\,\varphi}^{\lambda}$ as this is the only case that can generate a $[\delta\rangle$ formula. It is then clear that if the controller chooses λ, and as it has no way of controlling time-elapsing in the time-abstract system, it must ensure φ in all possible future positions in S. Thus $\overline{[\delta]\,\varphi}^{\lambda}$ simply reduces to $[\delta]\,\overline{\varphi}^{\lambda}$. Thus L_{ν} is sufficient to express KSC dense-time control.

3.3 Sampling Control

The *sampling* control problem is a version of the control problem where the controller can perform a controllable action only at dates $k.\Delta$ for $k \in \mathbb{N}$ and $\Delta \in \mathbb{Q}$. Δ is the sampling *rate* of the controller. Let P be a plant. As emphasized earlier in this section for the Δ-dense-time control, we can build a plant P_Δ where all the controllable actions are required to happen at multiple values of the sampling rate Δ. This can be done by defining a timed automaton $\mathcal{B}_\Delta$ with one location ℓ_0, a fresh clock y, the invariant $\mathsf{inv}(\ell_0) \equiv y \leq \Delta$ and a number of loops on ℓ_0: for each $a_c \in \mathsf{Act}_c$ there is a loop $(\ell_0, y = \Delta, a_c, \{y\}, \ell_0)$. Moreover we want to leave the controller free to do nothing. To this end we add a new controllable action *reset* and a loop $(\ell_0, y = \Delta, \mathit{reset}, \{y\}, \ell_0)$. As this action is not in P, it is harmless to do it and when the controller does not want to do an action, it can always choose to do *reset*.
Thus we can design an equivalent version of the sampling control where the controller is bound to do a controllable action at each date $k.\Delta$ with $k \in \mathbb{N}$. As in the previous case of KSC dense-time control problem, we just modify the definition of $\overline{[\delta]\,\varphi}^{\lambda}$ with:

$$\overline{[\delta]\,\varphi}^{\lambda} \stackrel{def}{=} [\delta]\left(([\mathit{reset}]\,\mathtt{ff} \wedge \overline{\varphi}^{\lambda}) \vee \bigvee_{a_c \in \mathsf{Act}_c} \overline{\varphi}^{a_c}\right)$$

which is equivalent to $[\delta]\overline{\varphi}$. Indeed the formula $[\mathit{reset}]\,\mathtt{ff}$ holds precisely when no controllable action can be perfomed by the controller; and when $\langle \mathit{reset}\rangle\,\mathtt{tt}$ holds, a controllable move has to be performed.

4 The Timed Modal Logic L_ν^{cont}

In this section we focus on the logic L_ν^{cont} and prove several properties of this logic, namely its expressive power, its decidability and compositionality.

L_ν^{cont} is More Expressive Than L_ν. The modality "$[\delta\rangle$" has been introduced for expressing control properties of open systems. We now prove that this operator adds expressive power to L_ν, *i.e.* it can not be expressed with L_ν. As usual we say that two formulae φ and ψ are equivalent for a class of systems $\mathcal{S}$ (we then write $\varphi \equiv_{\mathcal{S}} \psi$) if for all $s \in \mathcal{S}$, $s \models \varphi$ iff $s \models \psi$. A logic L is said to be as expressive as L' over $\mathcal{S}$ (denoted $L \succeq_{\mathcal{S}} L'$) if for every $\varphi \in L'$, there exists $\psi \in L$ s.t. $\varphi \equiv_{\mathcal{S}} \psi$. And L is said to be strictly more expressive than L' if $L \succeq_{\mathcal{S}} L'$ and $L' \not\succeq_{\mathcal{S}} L$. We have the following result:

Theorem 2. *The logic L_ν^{cont} is strictly more expressive than L_ν over timed automata.*

The full proof is long and technical, we give it in [BCL05]. Here we just give the techniques which we have used. Let φ be the L_ν^{cont} formula $([a]\,\mathtt{ff})\ [\delta\rangle\ (\langle b\rangle\,\mathtt{tt})$ stating that no a-transition can be performed as long as (*via* delay transitions) no b has been enabled. The core of the proof is based on the fact that there is no L_ν formula equivalent to φ.

The difficult point is that it is not possible to find two TAs A and A' such that $A \models \varphi$, $A' \not\models \varphi$ and $A \models \psi \Leftrightarrow A' \models \psi$ for any $\psi \in L_\nu$. Indeed L_ν allows us to build a characteristic formula for a TA [LLW95] (*i.e.* a formula which describes the behaviour of A w.r.t. strong timed bisimulation) and clearly the two TAs A and A' wouldn't be bisimilar. This is a classical problem in temporal logic [Eme91] where one shows that two temporal logics may have different expressive power even if they have the same *distinguishing power*. This makes the proof more difficult. Such expressiveness problems are not much considered in the timed framework. Up to our knowledge this is one of the first proofs of that type for timed logics.

To prove the result, we build two families of TAs $(A_i)_{i\geq 1}$ and $(A'_i)_{i\geq 1}$ such that for every integer i, $A_i \models \varphi$ whereas $A'_i \not\models \varphi$. We then prove that if φ can be expressed equivalently as formula $\Phi \in L_\nu$ (over timed automata), then there must exist some integer $i \geq 1$ such that $A'_i \models \Phi$, which will be a contradiction. The behaviours of automata A_i and A'_i can be represented by (and infered from) the following picture.

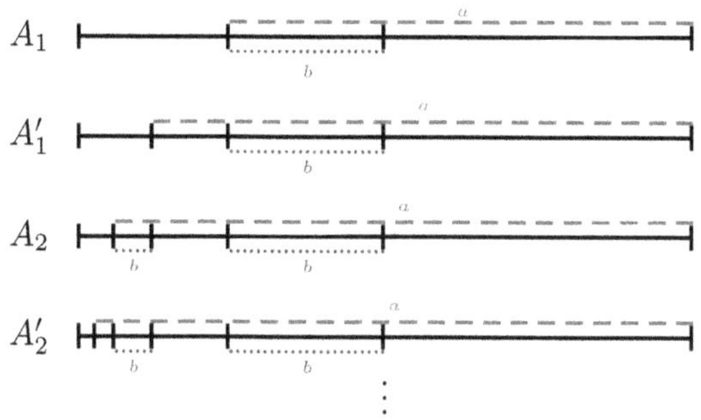

Model-Checking L_ν^{cont}**.** Model-checking of L_ν over TAs is an EXPTIME-complete problem [AL02]. Adding the modality $[\delta\rangle$ does not change this result, we have:

Theorem 3. *The model-checking of* L_ν^{cont} *over timed automata is EXPTIME-complete.*

Proof (Sketch). The EXPTIME-hardness comes from the EXPTIME-hardness of the model-checking of L_ν. For the EXPTIME-easyness, we just have to explain how to handle the $[\delta\rangle$ modality. Let A be a TA and $\Phi \in L_\nu^{\text{cont}}$. We consider the region graph [AD94] R_A associated with A and the set of formula clocks K. Clearly the classical notion of region can be used for $[\delta\rangle$: two states in a region r satisfy the same L_ν^{cont} formulae (the semantics of $[\delta\rangle$ can be defined in term of regions as well). Then we can define procedures to label R_A states with the Φ subformulae they satisfy. We can use the same algorithms as for L_ν to label $[\delta]\,\varphi$, $\langle\delta\rangle\,\varphi$, $\langle a\rangle\,\varphi, \ldots$ and define a new procedure for the $\varphi\,[\delta\rangle\,\psi$ subformulae. This can be done easily (as soon as φ and ψ have already been labeled) and it consists in a classical "Until" over the delay transitions (see below a way of computing

$\varphi\,[\delta\rangle\,\psi$ with DBMs). The complexity of the algorithm will remain linear in the size of R_A and Φ, and finally exponential in the size of A and Φ [AL02]. □

Instead of considering region techniques, classical algorithms for timed model-checking use *zones* (*i.e.* convex sets of valuations, defined as conjunctions of $x - y \bowtie c$ constraints and implemented with DBMs [Dil90, Bou04]). This makes verification more efficient in practice. In this approach $[\![\varphi]\!]$ is defined as sets of pairs (q, z) where z is a zone and q is a control state of the TA. This approach is also possible for L_ν^{cont}. Indeed we can define $[\![\varphi[\delta\rangle\psi]\!]$ when $[\![\varphi]\!]$ and $[\![\psi]\!]$ are already defined as sets of symbolic configurations (q, z). We use standard operations on zones: $\overleftarrow{z}$ (resp. $\overrightarrow{z}$, z^c) denotes the past (resp. future, complement) of z, and z^+ represents the set $z \cup \{v \mid \exists t > 0 \text{ s.t. } v - t \in z \text{ and } \forall 0 \leq t' < t,\ v - t' \in z\}$ (if z is represented by a DBM in normal form, z^+ is computed by relaxing constraints $x < c$ to $x \leq c$). It is then easy to prove that:

$$[\![\varphi\,[\delta\rangle\,\psi]\!] = \left(\overleftarrow{[\![\varphi]\!]^c}\right)^c \cup \left[\left(\overleftarrow{\left(\overrightarrow{[\![\psi]\!]} \cup [\![\varphi]\!]\right)^c}\right)^c \cap \left([\![\psi]\!] \cup \left([\![\varphi]\!] \cap \left(\overleftarrow{[\![\varphi]\!]^+ \cap [\![\psi]\!]}\right)\right)\right)\right]$$

L_ν^{cont} is Compositional. An important property of L_ν is that it is *compositional* [LL95, LL98] for timed automata. This is also the case for L_ν^{cont}.

A logic L is said to be *compositional* for a class $\mathcal{S}$ of models if, given an instance $(s_1|\cdots|s_n) \models \varphi$ with $s_i \in \mathcal{S}$ and $\varphi \in L$, it is possible to build a formula φ/s_1 (called a *quotient* formula) s.t. $(s_1|\cdots|s_n) \models \varphi \Leftrightarrow (s_2|\cdots|s_n) \models \varphi/s_1$. This can be viewed as an encoding of the behaviour of s_1 into the formula. Of course this also depends on the synchronization function, but we will not enter into the details here.

For $\varphi \in L_\nu$, A a TA, it is possible to define inductively a *quotient formula* φ/A (we refer to [LL98] for a complete description of this technique). In order to prove that L_ν^{cont} is compositional it is sufficient to define the quotient formula for the new modality $\varphi\,[\delta\rangle\,\psi$. We define the quotient of $\varphi_1\,[\delta\rangle\,\varphi_2$ for a location ℓ of a TA A in the following way:

$$\Big(\varphi_1\,[\delta\rangle\,\varphi_2\Big)/\ell \overset{def}{=} \Big(\mathsf{inv}(\ell) \Rightarrow (\varphi_1/\ell)\Big)\,[\delta\rangle\,\Big(\mathsf{inv}(\ell) \wedge (\varphi_2/\ell)\Big)$$

With such a quotient construction we get the following proposition:

Proposition 1. *The logic L_ν^{cont} is compositional for the class of timed automata.*

We have discussed a little bit in previous sections why the property is very useful and important. In particular, the new modality of L_ν^{cont} has been added to the model-checker CMC [LL98] which implements a compositional model-checking algorithm: it first computes a quotient formula of the system and the property and then check for the satisfiability of the formula. We have added to CMC the quotient rule for the operator $[\delta\rangle$ and thus we can use CMC for checking controllability properties. We do not provide here our experimental results but better refer to the web page of the tool: `http://www.lsv.ens-cachan.fr/ fl/cmcweb.html`.

5 Conclusion

In this paper we have used the logic L_ν to specify control objectives on timed plants. We have proved that a deterministic fragment of L_ν allows us to reduce control problems to a model-checking problem for an extension of L_ν (denoted L_ν^{cont}) with a new modality. We have also studied the properties of the extended logic L_ν^{cont} and proved that *i)* L_ν^{cont} is strictly more expressive than L_ν; *ii)* the model-checking of L_ν^{cont} over timed automata is EXPTIME-complete; *iii)* L_ν^{cont} inherits the *compositionality* property of L_ν.

Our current and future work is many-fold:

- extend our work to the synthesis of controllers. Note that this problem is strongly related to the satisfiability problem for L_ν^{det} and L_ν which is still open [LLW95].
- use the features of the logic L_ν to express more general types of control objectives *e.g.* to take into account dynamic changes of the set of controllable events as in [AVW03].

References

[ABBL03] Luca Aceto, Patricia Bouyer, Augusto Burgueño, and Kim G. Larsen. The power of reachability testing for timed automata. *Theoretical Computer Science*, 300(1–3):411–475, 2003.

[AD94] Rajeev Alur and David Dill. A theory of timed automata. *Theoretical Computer Science*, 126(2):183–235, 1994.

[AHK02] Rajeev Alur, Thomas A. Henzinger, and Orna Kupferman. Alternating-time temporal logic. *Journal of the ACM*, 49:672–713, 2002.

[AL02] Luca Aceto and François Laroussinie. Is your model-checker on time ? on the complexity of model-checking for timed modal logics. *Journal of Logic and Algebraic Programming (JLAP)*, 52–53:7–51, 2002.

[AVW03] André Arnold, Aymeric Vincent, and Igor Walukiewicz. Games for synthesis of controllers with partial observation. *Theoretical Computer Science*, 1(303):7–34, 2003.

[BCL05] Patricia Bouyer, Franck Cassez, and François Laroussinie. Modal logics for timed control. Research Report LSV-05-04, Laboratoire Spécification & Vérification, ENS de Cachan, France, 2005.

[Bou04] Patricia Bouyer. Forward analysis of updatable timed automata. *Formal Methods in System Design*, 24(3):281–320, 2004.

[CHR02] Franck Cassez, Thomas A. Henzinger, and Jean-François Raskin. A comparison of control problems for timed and hybrid systems. In *Proc. 5th International Workshop on Hybrid Systems: Computation and Control (HSCC'02)*, volume 2289 of *LNCS*, pages 134–148. Springer, 2002.

[dAHM01] Luca de Alfaro, Thomas A. Henzinger, and Rupak Majumdar. Symbolic algorithms for infinite-state games. In *Proc. 12th International Conference on Concurrency Theory (CONCUR'01)*, volume 2154 of *Lecture Notes in Computer Science*, pages 536–550. Springer, 2001.

[Dil90] David Dill. Timing assumptions and verification of finite-state concurrent systems. In *Proc. of the Workshop on Automatic Verification Methods for Finite State Systems (1989)*, volume 407 of *Lecture Notes in Computer Science*, pages 197–212. Springer, 1990.

[DM02] Deepak D'Souza and P. Madhusudan. Timed control synthesis for external specifications. In *Proc. 19th International Symposium on Theoretical Aspects of Computer Science (STACS'02)*, volume 2285 of *Lecture Notes in Computer Science*, pages 571–582. Springer, 2002.

[Eme91] E. Allen Emerson. *Temporal and Modal Logic*, volume B (Formal Models and Semantics) of *Handbook of Theoretical Computer Science*, pages 995–1072. MIT Press Cambridge, 1991.

[FLTM02] Marco Faella, Salvatore La Torre, and Aniello Murano. Dense real-time games. In *Proc. 17th Annual Symposium on Logic in Computer Science (LICS'02)*, pages 167–176. IEEE Computer Society Press, 2002.

[HNSY94] Thomas A. Henzinger, Xavier Nicollin, Joseph Sifakis, and Sergio Yovine. Symbolic model-checking for real-time systems. *Information and Computation*, 111(2):193–244, 1994.

[JW95] David Janin and Igor Walukiewicz. Automata for the modal mu-calculus and related results. In *Proc. 20th International Symposium on Mathematical Foundations of Computer Science (MFCS'95)*, volume 969 of *Lecture Notes in Computer Science*, pages 552–562. Springer, 1995.

[LL95] François Laroussinie and Kim G. Larsen. Compositional model-checking of real-time systems. In *Proc. 6th International Conference on Concurrency Theory (CONCUR'95)*, volume 962 of *Lecture Notes in Computer Science*, pages 27–41. Springer, 1995.

[LL98] François Laroussinie and Kim G. Larsen. CMC: A tool for compositional model-checking of real-time systems. In *Proc. IFIP Joint International Conference on Formal Description Techniques & Protocol Specification, Testing, and Verification (FORTE-PSTV'98)*, pages 439–456. Kluwer Academic, 1998.

[LLW95] François Laroussinie, Kim G. Larsen, and Carsten Weise. From timed automata to logic – and back. In *Proc. 20th International Symposium on Mathematical Foundations of Computer Science (MFCS'95)*, volume 969 of *Lecture Notes in Computer Science*, pages 529–539. Springer, 1995.

[MPS95] Oded Maler, Amir Pnueli, and Joseph Sifakis. On the synthesis of discrete controllers for timed systems. In *Proc. 12th Annual Symposium on Theoretical Aspects of Computer Science (STACS'95)*, volume 900 of *Lecture Notes in Computer Science*, pages 229–242. Springer, 1995.

[RP03] Stéphane Riedweg and Sophie Pinchinat. Quantified mu-calculus for control synthesis. In *Proc. 28th International Symposium on Mathematical Foundations of Computer Science (MFCS'03)*, volume 2747 of *Lecture Notes in Computer Science*, pages 642–651. Springer, 2003.

[RW89] P.J.G. Ramadge and W.M. Wonham. The control of discrete event systems. *Proc. of the IEEE*, 77(1):81–98, 1989.

[WT97] Howard Wong-Toi. The synthesis of controllers for linear hybrid automata. In *Proc. 36th IEEE Conference on Decision and Control*, pages 4607–4612. IEEE Computer Society Press, 1997.

[Yi90] Wang Yi. Real-time behaviour of asynchronous agents. In *Proc. 1st International Conference on Theory of Concurrency (CONCUR'90)*, volume 458 of *Lecture Notes in Computer Science*, pages 502–520. Springer, 1990.

Timed Shuffle Expressions[⊛]

Cătălin Dima

Laboratoire d'Algorithmique, Complexité et Logique,
Université Paris XII – Val de Marne, 61 av. du Général de Gaulle, 94010 Créteil Cedex, France

Abstract. We show that stopwatch automata are equivalent to timed shuffle expressions, an extension of timed regular expressions with the shuffle operation. This implies that the emptiness problem for timed shuffle expressions is undecidable. The result holds for both timed state sequence semantics and timed event sequence semantics of automata and expressions.

Similarly to timed regular expressions, our timed shuffle expressions employ renaming. But we show that even when renaming is not used, shuffle regular expressions still have an undecidable emptiness problem. This solves in the negative a conjecture of Asarin on the possibility to use shuffle to define timed regular languages.

We also define a subclass of timed shuffle expressions which can be used to model preemptive scheduling problems. Expressions in this class are in the form $(E_1 \sqcup\!\sqcup \ldots \sqcup\!\sqcup E_n) \wedge E$, where E_i and E do not use shuffle. We show that emptiness checking within this class is undecidable too.

1 Introduction

Regular expressions are an important and convenient formalism for the specification of sets of discrete behaviors. Their connection to automata is one of the cornerstones of theoretical computer science, relating the class of behaviors recognizable by a finite-memory device to those that can be characterized as regular.

In the past decade several results have been lifted to the theory of timed systems over a continuous time domains. Several classes of regular expressions have been devised [4,5,6,7], but the connection between automata and regular expressions is less elegant than in classical automata theory. For example, the timed regular expressions of [4] need intersection and renaming in order to be equivalent to the timed automata of [1].

Eugene Asarin has recently asked [2] a series of questions whose answers would hopefully "substantially improve our understanding of the area" of timed systems. One of these questions is whether the shuffle of two timed regular languages is always regular. It was observed that, e.g. $5 \sqcup\!\sqcup 3 = 8$ and that $5a \sqcup\!\sqcup 3b$ is a timed regular language. A positive answer to this question might have helped the development of an alternative set of regular expressions for timed automata, with the hope that shuffle would eventually replace intersection and/or renaming.

In this paper we show that timed regular expressions (in the sense of [4] or [3]) extended with shuffle are equivalent to stopwatch automata [9], when they employ renaming. This result implies that they are strictly more powerful than timed regular

[⊛] Partially supported by the PAI "Brancusi" no. 08797XL.

M. Abadi and L. de Alfaro (Eds.): CONCUR 2005, LNCS 3653, pp. 95–109, 2005.

expressions, at least because the emptiness problem for stopwatch automata is undecidable. We then show that even without renaming, timed regular expressions extended with shuffle have an undecidable emptiness problem. These results rely on the possiblity to encode non-difference constraints with a combination of shuffle and intersection. An example of such a combination gives a negative answer to the question of Asarin.

We also define a subclass of timed shuffle expressions which could be regarded as a "specification language" for preemptive scheduling problems. Our expressions, called *preemptive scheduling expressions*, are in the form $(E_1 \sqcup\!\sqcup \ldots \sqcup\!\sqcup E_n) \wedge E$, where E_i and E do not use shuffle. We show that emptiness checking within this class is undecidable too. This result complements results of [12] on the undecidability of emptiness checking for some class of timed automata augmented with preemptive jobs and different types of scheduling strategies. We note here that the expressive power of our preemptive scheduling expressions is not an issue in this paper, though it is an interesting question in itself.

Our proofs work for both state-based (i.e. signals or timed state sequences) and action-based (i.e. timed words) semantics. When presenting our undecidability result, we concentrate on state-based semantics, since preempting a job is somewhat equivalent to a "state change" in the system. But we also give an encoding of state-based expressions into action-based expressions, since the original conjecture of Asarin was stated on action-based semantics. However our undecidability results for action-based semantics rely on a "weakly monotonic semantics", that is, we allow two actions to occur at the same instant, but in a certain order. The restriction to strongly monotonic time is an open question.

The paper is divided as follows: in the second section we recall the timed event sequence (or *timed words*) framework and the timed state sequence (or *signals*) framework for the semantics of timed systems. Then, in the third section we recall the notion of stopwatch automata and the undecidability of their emptiness problem. The fourth section serves for the introduction of the timed shuffle expressions and for the proof of the Kleene theorem relating them to stopwatch automata. The fifth section presents the new undecidability results and the preemptive scheduling expressions, while the sixth section gives the translation of our results to action-based semantics. We end with a short section containing conclusions and further directions of study.

2 Timed Languages

Timed event sequences and timed state sequences are the two alternative models for the behavior of timed systems. While timed event sequences put the accent on actions that a system is executing and on moments at which actions take place, timed state sequences put the accent on states in which the system is and on state durations.

A **signal** (or **timed state sequence**) is a finite sequence of pairs of symbols from Σ and nonnegative numbers. For example, the signal $(s, 1.2)\,(t, 1.3)\,(s, 0.1)$ denotes a behavior in which the *state* s holds for 1.2 time units, then is followed by the state t for another 1.3 time units, and ends with the state s again, which holds for 0.1 time units. For easier readability, we denote this signal as follows: $s^{1.3}t^{1.2}s^{0.1}$. The set of timed state sequences over Σ can be organized as a monoid, denoted $\mathsf{Sig}(\Sigma)$. Note that in this monoid, concatenation of identical signals amounts to the addition of their exponents, hence $s^{1.3}t^{0.3} \cdot t^{0.9}s^{0.1} = s^{1.3}t^{1.2}s^{0.1}$. And also $s^0 = \varepsilon$, the empty signal. The length $\ell(\omega)$ of a signal ω is the sum of all the numbers occurring in it, e.g. $\ell(s^{1.3}t^{1.2}s^{0.1}) = 1.2+1.3+0.1=2.6$. **Timed (signal) languages** are then sets of signals.

We will also work with **timed event sequences** (or **timed words**) which are finite sequences of nonnegative numbers and symbols from Σ. For example, the sequence $1.2\,a\,1.3\,b$ denotes a behavior in which an *action* a occurs 1.2 time units after the beginning of the observation, and after another 1.3 time units action b occurs. The set of timed words over Σ can be organized as a monoid w.r.t. concatenation; we denote this monoid as $\mathsf{TW}(\Sigma)$. Note that in this monoid, concatenation of two reals amounts to summation of the reals, hence, $a\,1.3 \cdot 1.7\,b = a(1.3+1.7)b = a\,3\,b$. The length $\ell(w)$ of a timed word w is the sum of all the reals in it, e.g. $\ell(1.2\,a\,1.3\,b) = 1.2+1.3 = 2.5$. **Timed event languages** are then sets of timed words.

Besides concatenation, we will be interested in the *shuffle* operation, which is the generalization of shuffle on Σ^*. Formally, given $w_1, w_2 \in \mathsf{Sig}(\Sigma)$

$$w_1 \sqcup\!\sqcup w_2 = \{u_1v_1 \ldots u_nv_n \mid w_1 = u_1 \ldots u_n, w_2 = v_1 \ldots v_n\} \qquad (1)$$

A shuffle operation with the same definition as above can be defined on timed words.

Shuffle can be extended as a set operation to languages: given $L_1, L_2 \subseteq \mathsf{Sig}(\Sigma)$ (or $L_1, L_2 \subseteq \mathsf{TW}(\Sigma)$) $L_1 \sqcup\!\sqcup L_2 = \bigcup\{w_1 \sqcup\!\sqcup w_2 \mid \sigma_1 \in L_1, \sigma_2 \in L_2\}$.

Another useful operation on timed languages is *renaming*: it simply replaces some symbols with some others, while keeping durations the same. The renaming of $a \in \Sigma$ with $b \in \Sigma$ is denoted $[a/b]$, For signals, renaming cannot delete symbols. An example of renaming on signals is $t^{2.5}u^{0.1} = [s/t](s^{1.3}t^{1.2}u^{0.1})$.

For timed words, we may also employ symbol deletion. The deletion of a symbol $a \in \Sigma$ is denoted $[a/\varepsilon]$. By abuse of notation (and of naming), we will call *renaming* also an operation in which some of the *action* symbols are deleted (but not time passage!). For example, $[a/c][b/\varepsilon](1.3\,a\,1.2\,b\,0.1\,a) = 1.3\,c\,1.3\,c$.

3 Stopwatch Automata

We recall here the definition of stopwatch automata [9], adapted such that they accept signals in our setting.

A **stopwatch automaton** [9] is a tuple $\mathcal{A} = (Q, \mathcal{X}, \Sigma, \eta, \lambda, \delta, Q_0, Q_f)$ where Q is a finite set of *states*, $\mathcal{X}$ is a finite set of *stopwatches*, Σ is a finite set of *state symbols*, $Q_0, Q_f \subseteq Q$ are sets of *initial*, resp. *final* states, $\lambda : Q \to \Sigma$ is the location labeling mapping, $\eta : Q \to \mathcal{P}(\mathcal{X})$ is a mapping assigning to each state the set of stopwatches that are active in that state. Finally, δ is a finite set of tuples (i.e. *transitions*), of the form (q, C, X, q'), where $q, q' \in Q$, $X \subseteq \mathcal{X}$, and C is a finite conjunction of *stopwatch constraints*. Stopwatch constraints that can be used in transitions are of the form $x \in I$, where $x \in \mathcal{X}$ and $I \subseteq [0, \infty[$ is an interval with integer (or infinite) bounds.

For each transition $(q, C, X, r) \in \delta$, the component C is called the *guard* of the transition, and X is called the *reset component* of the transition.

The semantics of the automaton $\mathcal{A}$ is given in terms of a *timed transition system* $\mathcal{T}(\mathcal{A}) = (\mathcal{Q}, \theta, \mathcal{Q}_0, \mathcal{Q}_f)$ where $\mathcal{Q} = Q \times \mathbb{R}^n_{\geq 0}$, $\mathcal{Q}_0 = Q_0 \times \{\mathbf{0}_n\}$, $\mathcal{Q}_f = Q_f \times \mathbb{R}^n_{\geq 0}$ and

$$\theta = \big\{(q,v) \xrightarrow{\tau} (q,v') \mid v'_i = v_i + \tau,\ \forall i \in [n] \text{ with } x_i \in \eta(q), v'_i = v_i \text{ otherwise.}\big\}$$
$$\cup \big\{(q,v) \to (q',v') \mid \exists (q,C,X,q') \in \delta \text{ such that } v \models C \text{ and } \forall 1 \le i \le n, \quad (2)$$
$$\text{if } i \in X \text{ then } v'_i = 0 \text{ and if } i \notin X \text{ then } v'_i = v_i\big\}$$

In the line (2) of the definition of θ we say that the transition $q \xrightarrow{C,X} q' \in \delta$ *generates* the transition $(q,v) \to (q',v') \in \theta$.

Informally, the automaton can make time passage transitions (without changing location), in which all stopwatches *that are active in that location* advance by τ, and discrete transitions, in which location changes. The discrete transitions are enabled when the "current stopwatch valuation" v satisfies the guard C of a certain tuple $(q,C,X,q')\in \delta$, and when they are executed, the stopwatches in the reset component X are set to zero.

The **label** of a discrete transition $(q,v) \to (q',v')$ is ε, the empty sequence. The **label** of a time passage transition $(q,v) \xrightarrow{\tau} (q,v')$ is $\lambda(q)^\tau$.

A *run* in $\mathcal{T}(\mathcal{A})$ is a chain $\rho = \Big((q_{i-1},v_{i-1}) \xrightarrow{\xi_i} (q_i,v_i)\Big)_{1\le i\le k}$ of transitions from θ, while a *run* in $\mathcal{A}$ is a chain of transitions $\rho' = \Big(q_{i-1} \xrightarrow{C_i,X-i} q_i\Big)_{1\le i\le k'}$ in δ. The two runs ρ, ρ' are **associated** iff the i-th discrete transition in ρ is generated by the i-th transition of ρ'. An **accepting run** in $\mathcal{T}(\mathcal{A})$ is a run which starts in $\mathcal{Q}_0$, ends in $\mathcal{Q}_f$ and *does not end with a time passage transition.* An accepting run **accepts** a signal w iff w represents the formal concatenation of the labels of the transitions in the run.

The **language accepted by** $\mathcal{A}$ is then the set of signals which are accepted by some accepting run of $\mathcal{T}(\mathcal{A})$. The language accepted by $\mathcal{A}$ is denoted $L(\mathcal{A})$. Two timed automata are called **equivalent** iff they have the same language.

The Figure 1 gives an example of a stopwatch automaton. The active stopwatches in each location are identified as having derivative one; hence in location q_1 only stopwatch x is active. The language of this automaton is

$$\big\{s^{t_1}u^{t_2}\dots s^{t_{2k-1}}u^{t_{2k}}s^t \mid \sum t_{2i-1} \in [2,3], \sum t_{2i} \in [3,4[\,,\ t + \sum t_{2i-1} = 3\big\}$$

(recall that accepting runs cannot end with time passage transitions, hence the label ν of the final state may never occur in any accepted signal!)

A stopwatch automaton in which all stopwatches are active in each location is a *timed automaton*. In this case we will speak of *clocks* instead of stopwatches.

The *underlying untimed automaton* for a stopwatch automaton $\mathcal{A}$ is the automaton that keeps only the information regarding the transitions between states, and "forgets" all about stopwatch values and constraints. Hence, if $\mathcal{A} = (Q,\mathcal{X},\Sigma,\eta,\lambda,\delta,Q_0,Q_f)$ then the underlying untimed automaton for $\mathcal{A}$ is $\hat{\mathcal{A}} = (Q,\emptyset,\Sigma,\eta,\lambda,\delta',Q_0,Q_f)$ where

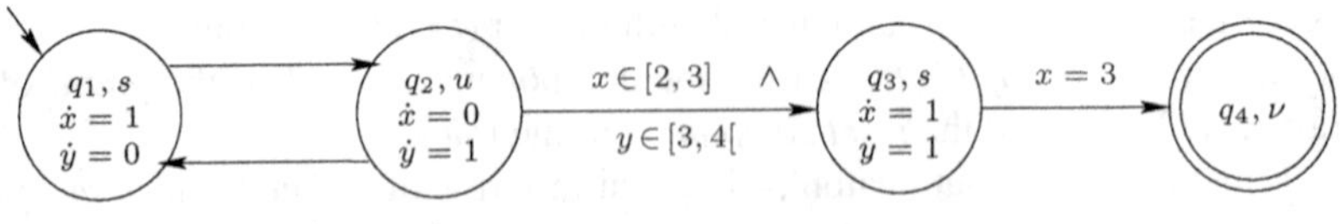

Fig. 1. A stopwatch automaton on signals

$(q, \mathsf{true}, \emptyset, r) \in \delta'$ if and only if $(q, C, X, r) \in \delta$ for some constraint C and subset of stopwatches $X \subseteq \mathcal{X}$.

Theorem 1 ([9]). *The emptiness problem for stopwatch automata is undecidable.*

The essential property that induces this undecidability is the fact that division by two, resp. doubling the value of a stopwatch can be simulated in stopwatch automata.

4 Timed Shuffle Expressions

In this section we introduce the class of timed shuffle expressions and prove their equivalence with stopwatch automata.

The syntax of **timed shuffle expressions** is the following:

$$E ::= s \mid E + E \mid E \cdot E \mid E \wedge E \mid E^* \mid \langle E \rangle_I \mid E \sqcup\!\sqcup E \mid [s/s']E$$

Here I is an interval and $s,s' \in \Sigma$. An expression not using shuffle is a **timed regular expression**.

The *semantics* of a timed shuffle expression (with renaming) is given by the following rules:

$$\begin{aligned} \|s\| &= \{s^l \mid l \in \mathbb{R}_{\geq 0}\} & \|[s/u]E\| &= \{[s/u](w) \mid w \in \|E\|\} \\ \|E_1 + E_2\| &= \|E_1\| \cup \|E_2\| & \|E^*\| &= \|E\|^* \\ \|E_1 \wedge E_2\| &= \|E_1\| \cap \|E_2\| & \|\langle E \rangle_I\| &= \{w \in \|E\| \mid \ell(w) \in I\} \\ \|E_1 \cdot E_2\| &= \|E_1\| \cdot \|E_2\| & \|E_1 \sqcup\!\sqcup E_2\| &= \|E_1\| \sqcup\!\sqcup \|E_2\| \end{aligned}$$

For example, the following expression is equivalent to the automaton in Figure 1:

$$[s_1/s]\Big(\Big(\big\langle \langle s_1 \rangle_{[2,3]} s \big\rangle_3 \sqcup\!\sqcup u\Big) \wedge \Big(\langle u \rangle_{[3,4[} s \sqcup\!\sqcup s_1\Big) \wedge (s_1 u)^* s\Big) \tag{3}$$

Theorem 2. *Timed shuffle expressions with renaming have the same expressive power as stopwatch automata.*

Proof. For the direct inclusion, the union, intersection, concatenation, star, time binding and renaming constructions from [4] can be easily extended to stopwatch automata. We will only give here the construction for the shuffle of two automata. The basic idea is to put together the two automata, making the control pass nondeterministically from one automaton to the other; moreover, to accept a timed word, the run must pass through an initial location and a final location in both automata.

So take two automata $\mathcal{A}_i = (Q_i, \mathcal{X}_i, \Sigma, \eta_i, \lambda_i, \delta_i, Q_0^i, Q_f^i)$ $(i = 1, 2)$. The automaton accepting $L(\mathcal{A}_1) \sqcup\!\sqcup L(\mathcal{A}_2)$ is then $\mathcal{A} = (Q, \mathcal{X}, \Sigma, \eta, \lambda, \delta, Q_0, Q_f)$ where

- $Q = Q_1 \times Q_2 \times \{1, 2\}$ and $\mathcal{X} = \mathcal{X}_1 \cup \mathcal{X}_2$.
- $Q_0 = Q_0^1 \times Q_0^2 \times \{1, 2\}$ and $Q_f = Q_f^1 \times Q_f^2 \times \{1, 2\}$.
- $\lambda : Q \to \Sigma$ is defined by $\lambda(q_1, q_2, i) = \lambda_i(q_i)$, while $\eta : Q \to \mathcal{P}(\mathcal{X}_1 \cup \mathcal{X}_2)$ is defined by $\eta(q_1, q_2, i) = \eta_i(q_i)$.

- the transition relation is defined as follows:

$$\begin{aligned}\delta = & \{(q_1, q, 1) \xrightarrow{C,X} (q_2, q, 1) \mid q_1 \xrightarrow{C,X} q_2 \in \delta_1\} \\ & \cup \{(q, q_1, 2) \xrightarrow{C,X} (q, q_2, 2) \mid q_1 \xrightarrow{C,X} q_2 \in \delta_2\} \\ & \cup \{(q_1, q_2, 1) \xrightarrow{\mathsf{true},\emptyset} (q_1, q_2, 2), (q_1, q_2, 2) \xrightarrow{\mathsf{true},\emptyset} (q_1, q_2, 1) \mid q_1 \in Q_1, q_2 \in Q_2\}\end{aligned}$$

The proof of the reverse inclusion is a two-step proof: the first step involves the decomposition of each stopwatch automaton with n stopwatches into the intersection of n one-stopwatch automata – similarly to the proof of the Kleene theorem for timed automata [4]. The second step shows how to associate a timed shuffle expression to an automaton with one stopwatch, by generalizing the construction of the expression (3) associated to the automaton in Figure 1.

The decomposition step requires a relabeling of the states of $\mathcal{A}$ such that two different states bear different labels. To do this, we simply replace Σ with Q as state labels, and put the identity function $id : Q \to Q$ as the state labeling function. Hence, if $\tilde{\mathcal{A}} = (Q, \mathcal{X}, Q, \eta, id, \delta, Q_0, Q_f)$ is the result of the above transformation, then $L(\mathcal{A}) = \lambda^{\#}(L(\tilde{\mathcal{A}})$ where $\lambda^{\#}$ is the renaming defined by $\lambda : Q \to \Sigma$.

Then we decompose $\tilde{\mathcal{A}}$ into n automata $\mathcal{A}_i = (Q, \{x_i\}, Q, \eta_i, id, \delta_i, Q_0, Q_f)$ having a single stopwatch; here $\eta_i(q) = \eta(q) \cap \{x_i\}$ and δ_i is a copy of δ in which the guard and the reset component of each tuple is a projection on $\{x_i\}$. Then

$$L(\mathcal{A}) = \lambda^{\#}\big(L(\mathcal{A}_1) \cap \ldots \cap L(\mathcal{A}_n)\big)$$

For the second step, suppose that $\mathcal{B}$ is an automaton with a single stopwatch in which all states have distinct state labels, $\mathcal{B} = (Q, \{x\}, Q, \eta, id, \delta, Q_0, Q_f)$. The following terminology will be used throughout the rest of this proof: we will speak of a state q as being *x-active* if $\eta(q) = x$; otherwise, we will say q is *x-inactive*. A run that passes through x-inactive states – excepting perhaps the starting and the ending state – is called a *x-inactive run*.

We will decompose $\mathcal{B}$ into three automata such that:

$$L(\mathcal{B}) = \big(L(\mathcal{B}_1) \sqcup\!\sqcup L(\mathcal{B}_2)\big) \cap L(\hat{\mathcal{B}})$$

In this decomposition, $\mathcal{B}_1$ is a one-clock timed automaton, while $\mathcal{B}_2$ is an untimed automaton and $\hat{\mathcal{B}}$ is the underlying untimed automaton for $\mathcal{B}$. $\mathcal{B}_1$ will carry the duration constraints of x, the stopwatch of $\mathcal{B}$, while $\mathcal{B}_2$ will carry the sequential properties within the states in which x is inactive. The task of $\hat{\mathcal{B}}$ is to correctly connect the sequences of states in which x is active with those in which x is inactive. The ideas of this decomposition can be traced to the expression (3) associated to the automaton in Figure 1.

Consider then an x-inactive run $\rho = \big(q_{i-1} \xrightarrow{C_i,\emptyset} q_i\big)_{1 \leq i \leq k}$, in which x is never reset. Note that $C_i = (x \in I_i)$ for some nonnegative interval I_i. Throughout this run, the value of the stopwatch x remains unchanged, hence all the guards could be replaced with a single guard $x \in I_\rho := \bigcap_{1 \leq i \leq k} I_i$, which can be placed on any of the transitions. This implies that, in order to construct $\mathcal{B}_1$, we need to consider all sub-runs that contain only states inactive for x; then, for each such run, construct the intersection of the intervals on their guards.

Note further that we do not need to take into consideration runs with circuits: if ρ is a run from q to q' and $\overline{\rho}$ is another run that was constructed from ρ by adding a circuit in a state of ρ, then $I_\rho \supseteq I_{\overline{\rho}}$, hence a transition from q to q' labeled with $I_{\overline{\rho}}$ is superfluous. The consequence of this observation is that, given any two transitions $\tau, \tau' \in \delta$, the set of all non-superfluous intervals I_ρ associated to runs that start with τ and end in τ' can be computed by a Dijkstra-like algorithm. Let us denote then

$$\mathcal{I}_{\tau\tau'} = \big\{ I_\rho \mid \rho \text{ is an } x\text{-inactive run without circuits that starts with transition } \tau, \\ \text{ends with } \tau' \text{ and contains no transition resetting } x \big\}.$$

When $\tau = \tau' = q \xrightarrow{x \in I, \emptyset} q'$ we put $\mathcal{I}_{\tau\tau'} = \{I\}$.

The above remarks deal with x-inactive runs that do not pass through a transition resetting x. Taking into consideration resetting transitions can be done as follows: consider $\rho = \big(q_{i-1} \xrightarrow{C_i, X_i} q_i\big)_{1 \leq i \leq k}$ an x-inactive run in which the first transition which resets x is $q_{j-1} \xrightarrow{C_j, \{x\}} q_j$. This run is unfeasible if there exists a guard $C_i : (x \in I_i)$ with $i > j$ for which $0 \notin I_i$. Hence, for all feasible runs ρ we can replace all C_i with $i > j$ with $x = 0$ while all the guards C_i with $i \leq j$ could be replaced with $x \in \bigcap_{1 \leq i \leq j} I_i$. Thence, given $q' \in Q$ and a transition $\tau \in \delta$, we do the following constructions:

1. Build $(q') = \big\{ \tau' \in \delta \mid \tau' = r \xrightarrow{x \in J, \{x\}} r' \text{ and } q' \text{ is reachable from } r'$ through an x-inactive run whose clock constraints all contain $0. \big\}$

   This set is computable by backward reachability analysis on $\mathcal{B}$.
2. For each $\tau' = r \xrightarrow{x \in J, \{x\}} r' \in (q')$ and $\tau'' = r'' \xrightarrow{C, X} r \in \delta$, compute $\mathcal{I}_{\tau\tau''}$ as above.
3. Then compute $\mathcal{J}_{\tau\tau'} := \big\{ I \cap J \mid I \in \mathcal{I}_{\tau\tau''} \big\}$. where J is the interval labeling $\tau' = r \xrightarrow{x \in J, \{x\}} r'$.
4. If $\tau = \tau'$ then we put $\mathcal{J}_{\tau\tau'} = \big\{J\big\}$ (similarly to the fact that circuits can be ignored when computing $\mathcal{I}$).

The timed automaton $\mathcal{B}_1$ is then $\mathcal{B}_1 = \big(Q_1 \cup Q_f, \{x\}, Q, \eta_1, id, \delta_1, Q_0^1, Q_f\big)$ where

$$Q_1 = \big\{ q \in Q \mid q \text{ is } x\text{-active} \big\} \text{ and } \eta_1(q) = \{x\} \text{ for all } q \in Q_1 \cup Q_f$$

$$Q_0^1 = \big\{ q \in Q_1 \mid \exists \rho \ x\text{-inactive run starting in } q_0 \in Q_0 \text{ and ending in } q \text{ and} \\ \text{whose clock constraints all contain } 0 \big\}$$

$$\delta_1 = \big\{ q \xrightarrow{C, X} q' \in \delta \mid q, q' \in Q_1 \big\}$$

$$\cup \big\{ q \xrightarrow{x \in I, X} q' \mid q, q' \in Q_1, \exists \tau_1 = q \xrightarrow{x \in I_1, \emptyset} r_1 \in \delta, \tau_2 = r_2 \xrightarrow{x \in I_2, X} q' \in \delta \text{ s.t.} \\ \eta(r_1) = \eta(r_2) = \emptyset \text{ and } I \in \mathcal{I}_{\tau_1\tau_2} \big\} \tag{4}$$

$$\cup \big\{ q \xrightarrow{x \in I, \{x\}} q' \mid q, q' \in Q_1, \exists \tau_1 = q \xrightarrow{x \in I_1, X_1} r_1 \in \delta, \tau_2 = r_2 \xrightarrow{C, z, \{x\}} r_3, \\ \tau_2 \in (q') \text{ s.t. } \eta(r_1) = \eta(r_2) = \emptyset, \tau_2 \in (q') \text{ and } I \in \mathcal{J}_{\tau_1\tau_2} \big\} \tag{5}$$

$$\cup \big\{ q \xrightarrow{x \in I, \emptyset} q_f \mid q_f \in Q_f, \exists \tau_1 = q \xrightarrow{x \in I, X_1} q_1, \tau_2 = q_2 \xrightarrow{x \in J, X_2} q_3 \in \delta \text{ and} \\ \text{either } I \in \mathcal{I}_{\tau_1\tau_2} \text{ and } q_3 = q_f \text{ or } I \in \mathcal{J}_{\tau_1\tau_2} \text{ and } \tau_2 \in (q_f) \big\} \tag{6}$$

Note that the components 4 and 5, are used for assembling pieces of x-active parts in an accepting run in $\mathcal{B}$.

The timed automaton $\mathcal{B}_2$ is then $\mathcal{B}_2 = \big(Q_2, \emptyset, Q_2, \eta_2, id, \delta_2, Q_0^2, Q_f^2\big)$ where

$$\begin{aligned}
Q_2 =& \{q \in Q \mid \eta(q) = \emptyset\} \text{ and } \eta_2(q) = \emptyset \text{ for all } q \in Q_2 \\
Q_0^2 =& \{q \in Q_2 \mid q \in Q_0 \text{ or there exists an } x\text{-active run } \rho \text{ starting in } Q_0 \text{ and ending in } q\} \\
Q_f^2 =& \{q \in Q_2 \mid q \in Q_f \text{ or there exists an } x\text{-active run } \rho \text{ starting in } q \text{ and ending in } Q_f\} \\
\delta_2 =& \{q \xrightarrow{\mathsf{true},\emptyset} q' \in \delta \mid q, q' \in Q_2\} \cup \\
& \{q \xrightarrow{\mathsf{true},\emptyset} q' \mid \text{there exists an } x\text{-active run } \rho \text{ starting in } q \text{ and ending in } q' \}
\end{aligned}$$

Hence, $\mathcal{B}_2$ keeps track of the x-inactive parts of each accepting run of $\mathcal{B}$. To correctly combine runs in $\mathcal{B}_1$ with runs in $\mathcal{B}_2$ we further intersect their shuffle with $L(\hat{\mathcal{B}})$, the language of the underlying untimed automaton for $\hat{\mathcal{B}}$. This final intersection forbids incorrect "plugging" of parts of x-active runs, as provided by $\mathcal{B}_1$, with parts of x-inactive runs, as found in $\mathcal{B}_2$.

The Kleene theorem for timed automata [3] assures then the existence of timed regular expressions equivalent to each of the three automata ($\mathcal{B}_1$. $\mathcal{B}_2$ and $\hat{\mathcal{B}}$), fact which ends our proof. □

Note that the equivalence in Theorem 2 is effective, i.e. all the constructions in the proof are algorithmic. This ensures then the following

Corollary 1. *The emptiness problem for timed shuffle expressions with renaming is undecidable.*

5 Timed Shuffle Expressions Without Renaming Are Undecidable

The technique used in the papers [3,10] can be adapted to show that intersection and renaming are necessary for the Theorem 2 to hold. However we will be interested here in a different problem: can we diminish the expressive power of the timed shuffle expressions (without giving up the shuffle!) such that they be comparable to timed automata? And the first natural question is to compare timed shuffle expressions without renaming and timed regular expressions.

In this section we will show that the emptiness problem remains undecidable even for s timed shuffle expressions without renaming. Recall that the essential property that gives the undecidability is the fact that we may "double" the value of a stopwatch. We will adapt this property to timed shuffle expressions without renaming.

Remark 1. We start with an example showing that timed shuffle expressions may induce more general linear constraints than those induced by timed regular expressions. Namely, for any timed word in the semantics of the following expression:

$$E_{1/2} = \langle \mathbf{ps} \rangle_1 \mathbf{uvz} \wedge \big(\mathbf{p}\langle \mathbf{suz} \rangle_1 \sqcup\!\sqcup \mathbf{v}\big) \wedge \mathbf{ps}\langle \mathbf{uv} \rangle_1 \mathbf{z} \wedge \mathbf{psu}\langle \mathbf{vz} \rangle_1$$

the duration of the state symbol $\mathbf{p}$ represents twice the duration of the state symbol $\mathbf{u}$:

$$\|E_{1/2}\| = \{\mathbf{p}^{t_1}\mathbf{s}^{t_2}\mathbf{u}^{t_3}\mathbf{v}^{t_4}\mathbf{z}^{t_5} \mid t_1 = 2t_3, t_1 + t_2 = 1 = t_3 + t_4, t_3 = t_5\} \quad (7)$$

Note that t_2 is used as a reference for asserting that t_1 and $t_3 + t_5$ must be equal, and similarly for t_4, which asserts that t_3 and t_5 are equal. On the other hand, t_5 is used as a "divisor".

The main result of this section is the following:

Theorem 3. *The emptiness problem for timed shuffle expressions without renaming is undecidable.*

Proof. The proof goes by reduction of the problem of the existence of a terminating computation of a Minsky machine [11]. We will show that, for each 2-counter (Minsky) machine M, the computation of M can be encoded into a timed shuffle expression E. To this end, we encode the value of each counter of the machine M in some configuration as the duration of a certain state symbol. The value of the counter x, denoted x too, will be encoded by the signal $\mathbf{s}^{2^{-x}} = \mathbf{s}^{\frac{1}{2^x}}$ and similarly, y is encoded by $\mathbf{u}^{2^{-y}}$. Then, decrementing the counter x amounts to "doubling the length" of the state symbol $\mathbf{s}$ whereas incrementing x amounts to "dividing the length" of $\mathbf{s}$ by two, along the idea presented in the remark 1.

The encoding of a configuration (q, x, y) will consist of the set of timed state sequences of the type $q^{l_0} s_1^{l_1} \mathbf{s}^{2^{-x}} u_1^{l_2} \mathbf{u}^{2^{-y}}$ where $s_1, u_1, \mathbf{s}, \mathbf{u}$ are distinct symbols ($i \in [1 \ldots 3]$) and l_0, l_1, l_2 are some nonnegative numbers.

So suppose the 2-counter machine is $M = (Q, \theta, q_0, Q_f)$ where

$$\theta \subseteq Q \times \left\{x^{++}, y^{++}, x^{--}, y^{--}, x = 0?, y = 0?\right\} \times Q$$

Remind that we may consider M being *deterministic*, in a sense that implies that between two states q, r, at most one transition could occur in δ.

We will first associate to each transition $\tau = (q, op, r) \in \delta$ four timed regular expressions, $E^x_{(q,op,r)}$, $E^y_{(q,op,r)}$, $E^0_{(q,op,r)}$ and $E^\wedge_{(q,op,r)}$, with the aim to encode in the following expression:

$E_{(q,op,r)} := \left(E^x_{(q,op,r)} \sqcup\!\sqcup E^y_{(q,op,r)} \sqcup\!\sqcup E^0_{(q,op,r)}\right) \wedge E^\wedge_{(q,op,r)}$ the sequentialization of an encoding of a configuration (q, x, y) before taking τ with an encoding of the resulting configuration (q, x', y'), the result of τ. The desired expressions, for $op = x^{++}$, are:

$$E^x_{(q,x^{++},r)} = \langle q\rangle_1 s_1 \big\langle \mathbf{s}\langle r\rangle_1 s_1\big\rangle_3 \mathbf{s} s_3 \Big(\big\langle \mathbf{s} s_3\big\rangle_2 \langle r\rangle_1 \mathbf{s} \wedge \mathbf{s}\big\langle s_3 r \mathbf{s}\big\rangle_3\Big)$$

$$E^y_{(q,x^{++},r)} = \langle q\rangle_1 u_1 \big\langle \mathbf{u}\langle r\rangle_1 u_1\big\rangle_3 \big\langle \mathbf{u}\langle r\rangle_1 u_1\big\rangle_3 \mathbf{u} \wedge q u_1 \mathbf{u} r \big\langle u_1 \mathbf{u}\big\rangle_2 r \big\langle u_1 \mathbf{u}\big\rangle_2$$

$$E^0_{(q,x^{++},r)} = \langle q\rangle_1 s_2 s_3 u_2 u_3 \langle r\rangle_1 s_2 u_2 u_3 \langle r\rangle_1 s_1$$

$$E^\wedge_{(q,x^{++},r)} = \langle q\rangle_3 s_1 \mathbf{s} s_2 s_3 u_1 \mathbf{u} u_2 u_3 \langle r\rangle_3 \Big(\big\langle s_1 \mathbf{s} s_2\big\rangle_2 s_3 \wedge s_1 \mathbf{s}\big\langle s_2 s_3\big\rangle_2\Big) u_1 \mathbf{u} u_2 u_3 \langle r\rangle_3 s_1 \mathbf{s} u_1 \mathbf{u}$$

Note that if $q^3 s_1^{l_1} \mathbf{s}^l s_2^{l_2} s_3^{l_3} u_1^{m_1} \mathbf{u}^m u_2^{m_2} u_3^{m_3} r^3 s_1^{l_4} \mathbf{s}^{l'} s_2^{l_5} s_3^{l_6} u_1^{m_4} \mathbf{u}^{m'} u_2^{m_5} u_3^{m_6} r^3 s_1^{l_7} \mathbf{s}^{l''} u_1^{m_7}$ $\mathbf{u}^{m''}$ belongs to $\|E_{(q,x^{++},r)}\|$, then

- $l + l_4 = l_4 + l' + l_5 = 2$ (by $E^x_{(q,x^{++},r)}$ and $E^\wedge_{(q,x^{++},r)}$).
- $l' + l_6 = l_5 + l_6 = l_6 + l'' = 2$ (again by $E^x_{(q,x^{++},r)}$ and $E^\wedge_{(q,x^{++},r)}$), hence $l = 2l' = 2l''$.
- $m + m_4 = m_4 + m' = m' + m_7 = m_7 + m'' = 2$ (by $E^y_{(q,x^{++},r)}$), hence $m = m' = m''$.

Hence if $q^3 s_1^{l_1}\mathbf{s}^l u_1^{m_1}\mathbf{u}^m$ encodes some configuration (q,x,y) then $q^3 s_1^{l_7}\mathbf{s}^{l''} u_1^{m_7}\mathbf{u}^{m''}$ encodes $(r, x+1, y)$, which is the result of the transition (q, op, r).

The subexpressions for $E_{(q,x--,r)}$ are:

$$
\begin{aligned}
E^x_{(q,x--,r)} &= \langle q\rangle_1 \big\langle s_1 s_2\big\rangle_2 \langle r\rangle_1 \Big(s_1 \big\langle \mathbf{s} r s_1\big\rangle_3 \mathbf{s}\Big)\\
E^y_{(q,x--,r)} &= \langle q\rangle_1 u_1 \big\langle \mathbf{u}\langle r\rangle_1 u_1\big\rangle_3 \big\langle \mathbf{u}\langle r\rangle_1 u_1\big\rangle_3 \mathbf{u} \wedge q u_1 \mathbf{u} r \big\langle u_1 \mathbf{u}\big\rangle_2 \langle r\rangle_1 \big\langle u_1\mathbf{u}\big\rangle_2 r \big\langle u_1\mathbf{u}\big\rangle_2\\
E^0_{(q,x--,r)} &= \langle q\rangle_1 s_2 s_3 \mathbf{u} u_3 \langle r\rangle_1 s_2 s_3 u_2 u_3 \langle r\rangle_1\\
E^\wedge_{(q,x--,r)} &= \langle q\rangle_3 \Big(\big\langle s_1\mathbf{s}\big\rangle_2 s_2 \big\langle s_3 u_1 \mathbf{u} u_2 u_3\big\rangle_4 \langle r\rangle_3 \big\langle s_1 \mathbf{s}\big\rangle_2 \wedge s_1 \big\langle \mathbf{s} s_2 s_3\big\rangle_2 \big\langle u_1 \mathbf{u} u_2 u_3 r s_1\big\rangle_7 \mathbf{s}\Big)\\
&\qquad \cdot s_2 s_3 u_1 \mathbf{u} u_2 u_3 \langle r\rangle_3 s_1 \mathbf{s} u_1 \mathbf{u}
\end{aligned}
$$

Note that if $q^3 s_1^{l_1}\mathbf{s}^l s_2^{l_2} s_3^{l_3} u_1^{m_1}\mathbf{u}^m u_2^{m_2} u_3^{m_3} r^3 s_1^{l_4}\mathbf{s}^{l'} s_2^{l_5} s_3^{l_6} u_1^{m_4}\mathbf{u}^{m'} u_2^{m_5} u_3^{m_6} r^3 s_1^{l_7}\mathbf{s}^{l''} u_1^{m_7}$ $\mathbf{u}^{m''}$ belongs to $\|E_{(q,x++,r)}\|$ then

- $l_1 + l = l_1 + l_2 = 2$ (by $E^x_{(q,x--,r)}$ and $E^\wedge_{(q,x--,r)}$), hence $l = l_2$.
- $m + m_4 = m_4 + m' = m' + m_7 = m_7 + m'' = 2$ (as implied by $E^y_{(q,x--,r)}$), hence $m = m' = m''$.
- $l + l_2 + l_3 = l_4 + l' = l' + l_7 = l_7 + l'' = 2$ and $l_3 + m_1 + m + m_2 + m_3 = m_1 + m + m_2 + m_3 + l_4 = 4$ (as implied by $E^x_{(q,x--,r)}$ and $E^\wedge_{(q,x--,r)}$), hence $l + l_2 = 2l = l' = l''$.

Finally, the subexpressions for $E_{(q,x=0?,r)}$ are the following:

$$
\begin{aligned}
E^x_{(q,x=0?,r)} &= \langle q\rangle_1 s_1 \langle \mathbf{s}\rangle_1 \langle r\rangle_1 s_1 \langle \mathbf{s}\rangle_1 \langle r\rangle_1 s_1 \langle \mathbf{s}\rangle_1\\
E^y_{(q,x=0?,r)} &= \langle q\rangle_1 u_1 \big\langle \mathbf{u}\langle r\rangle_1 u_1\big\rangle_3 \big\langle \mathbf{u}\langle r\rangle_1 u_1\big\rangle_3 \mathbf{u} \wedge q u_1 \mathbf{u} r \big\langle u_1\mathbf{u}\big\rangle_2 \langle r\rangle_1 \big\langle u_1 \mathbf{u}\big\rangle_2\\
E^0_{(q,x=0?,r)} &= \langle q\rangle_1 s_2 s_3 u_2 u_3 \langle r\rangle_1 s_2 s_3 u_2 u_3 \langle r\rangle_1\\
E^\wedge_{(q,x=0?,r)} &= \langle q\rangle_3 s_1 \mathbf{s} s_2 s_3 u_1 \mathbf{u} u_2 u_3 \langle r\rangle_3 \Big(\big\langle s_1 \mathbf{s} s_2\big\rangle_2 s_3 \wedge s_1 \mathbf{s} \big\langle s_2 s_3\big\rangle_2\Big) u_1 \mathbf{u} u_2 u_3 \langle r\rangle_3 s_1 \mathbf{s} u_1 \mathbf{u}
\end{aligned}
$$

Along the same lines, we want to construct an expression $E = \big(E_x \sqcup\!\sqcup E_y \sqcup\!\sqcup E_0\big) \wedge E_\wedge$, such that E_x gives the (encoding of the) projection of the run of M onto the counter x, E_y does the same for y, E_0 inserts some "locally unused" symbols, while $E_\wedge$ ensures that E_x and E_y apply synchronously the same transition of M.

Let us denote

$$
E^x_\delta = \sum\nolimits_{(q,op,r)\in\delta} E^x_{(q,op,r)}, \qquad E^y_\delta = \sum\nolimits_{(q,op,r)\in\delta} E^y_{(q,op,r)},
$$
$$
E^0_\delta = \sum\nolimits_{(q,op,r)\in\delta} E^0_{(q,op,r)}, \qquad E^\wedge_\delta = \sum\nolimits_{(q,op,r)\in\delta} E^\wedge_{(q,op,r)}
$$

An important remark to make here is that for all $\sigma \in \Big\|\big(E^x_\delta \sqcup\!\sqcup E^y_\delta \sqcup\!\sqcup E^0_\delta\big) \wedge E^\wedge_\delta\Big\|$ we have in fact that $\sigma \in \Big\|\big(E^x_{(q,op,r)} \sqcup\!\sqcup E^x_{(q,op,r)} \sqcup\!\sqcup E^x_{(q,op,r)}\big) \wedge E^x_{(q,op,r)}\Big\|$ for *the same* $(q, op, r) \in \delta$. (Remind that the Minsky machine was deterministic.)

To see this, note that $E^\wedge_\delta$ requires that σ contain only two state symbols $q, r \in Q$, both of which last for 3 time units. But then, if E^x_δ, E^y_δ and E^0_δ choose different transitions, i.e., if we pick $\sigma_1 \in E^x_{(q_1,op_1,r_1)}$, $\sigma_2 \in E^y_{(q_2,op_2,r_2)}$, $\sigma_3 \in E^0_{(q_3,op_3,r_3)}$, where at least two of the three transitions are distinct, then $\sigma_1 \sqcup\!\sqcup \sigma_2 \sqcup\!\sqcup \sigma_3$ contains three distinct state symbols of non-zero length from the set $\{(q_1)^1, (q_2)^1, (q_3)^1, (r_1)^1, (r_2)^1, (r_3)^1\}$. Hence, $\sigma_1 \sqcup\!\sqcup \sigma_2 \sqcup\!\sqcup \sigma_3 \notin \| E_\delta^\wedge \|$.

Thence, the expression $\Big((E_\delta^x)^* \sqcup\!\sqcup (E_\delta^y)^* \sqcup\!\sqcup (E_\delta^0)^* \Big) \wedge (E_\delta^\wedge)^*$ encodes sequences of arbitrary transitions in M, but imposes no connection between two consecutive transitions either by state symbols or by counter values. We will then have to add more constraints to the subexpressions E_δ^x and E_δ^y, in order to ensure proper "propagation" of states and counter values.

For each $q \in Q$, consider the following expressions:

$$E_q^x = \langle q \rangle_1 (\varepsilon + s_1) \Big(\big\langle \mathbf{s} \langle q \rangle_1 s_1 \big\rangle_3 (\mathbf{s} + s_2) \wedge \mathbf{s} q \big\langle s_1 (\mathbf{s} + s_2) \big\rangle_2 \Big)$$
$$E_q^x = \langle q \rangle_1 (\varepsilon + u_1) \Big(\big\langle \mathbf{u} \langle q \rangle_1 u_1 \big\rangle_3 (\mathbf{u} + u_2) \wedge \mathbf{u} q \big\langle u_1 (\mathbf{u} + u_2) \big\rangle_2 \Big)$$

These expressions will be essential in asserting correct connection of intermediary states and counter values. Note that, for example, in each $\sigma = q^1 \mathbf{s}^m q^1 s_1^{l_2} \mathbf{s}^{m'} \in \| E_q^x \|$, we have that $m = m'$, and similarly with $\sigma' = q^1 s_1^{l_1} \mathbf{s}^m q^1 s_1^{l_2} s_2^{m'} \in \| E_q^x \|$, and all the other types of signals in $\| E_q^x \|$.

Let us denote further

$$E_x = (E_\delta^x)^* \wedge q_0 s_1 \mathbf{s} \Big(\sum\nolimits_{q \in Q} q s_1 \mathbf{s} (s_3 + \varepsilon) E_q^x \Big)^* \cdot \sum\nolimits_{q \in Q_f} q s_1 \mathbf{s} (\varepsilon + s_3) q (\varepsilon + s_1) \mathbf{s}$$
$$E_y = (E_\delta^y)^* \wedge q_0 u_1 \mathbf{u} \Big(\sum\nolimits_{q \in Q} q u_1 \mathbf{u} (s_3 + \varepsilon) E_q^y \Big)^* \cdot \sum\nolimits_{q \in Q_f} q u_1 \mathbf{u} (\varepsilon + u_3) q (\varepsilon + u_1) \mathbf{u}$$
$$E_0 = (E_\delta^0)^*, \qquad E_\wedge = (E_\delta^\wedge)^*$$

Observe now that, in the expression E_x, we ensure correct connection of the intermediary states of M and of the counter values for x. This remark follows by a case study for each of the possibilities of having two successive transitions. For example, if $\sigma_1 \sigma_2, \ldots, \sigma_k \in E_x$ with $\sigma_i = q_i^{l_1^i} s_1^{l_2^i} \mathbf{s}^{m_i} r_i^{l_3^i} s_1^{l_4^i} \mathbf{s}^{m_i'} s_3^{l_5^i} r_i^{l_6^i} s_1^{l_7^i} \mathbf{s}^{m_i''} \in \| E_\delta^x \|$ for $1 \leq i \leq k$, then we must have that $r_{i-1} = q_i$ and $m_{i-1}' = m_{i-1}'' = m_i$, that is, two consecutve signals represent part of the encoding of two consecutive transitions that share the intermediary state and the counter value for x.

Another example is when some σ_i is of the form $q_i^{l_1^i} s_1^{l_2^i} s_2^{m_i} r_i^{l_3^i} s_1^{l_4^i} \mathbf{s}^{m_i'} r_i^{l_6^i} s_1^{l_7^i} \mathbf{s}^{m_i''} \in \| E_\delta^x \|$. This situation occurs when $\sigma_i \in \Big\| E^x_{(q_{i-1}, x^{--}, q_i)} \Big\|$. We have again $r_{i-1} = q_i$ and $m_{i-1}' = m_i$, but this time it is the length of s_2 in σ_i that copies the duration of the last $\mathbf{s}$ in σ_{i-1}. But this is ok, if we recall from the definition of $E_{(q, x^{--}, r)}$ that the length of the first s_2 and the length of the first $\mathbf{s}$ in σ_i are equal. Hence, again two consecutive signals represent part of the encoding of two consecutive transitions that share the intermediary state and the counter value for x. All the other cases lead to similar conclusions about the correct connection of intermediary states and counter values.

The expression that encodes the (unique!) run of M is the following:

$$E_\rho = \Big(E_x \sqcup\!\sqcup E_y \sqcup\!\sqcup E_0 \Big) \wedge E_\wedge \tag{8}$$

Then $\| E_\rho \| = \emptyset$ iff M does not have a finite run. □

The particularity of the proof of Theorem 3 suggests us that shuffle expressions without renaming are not the only interesting strict subclass of expressions that have an undecidable emptiness problem.

Preemptive scheduling expressions are timed shuffle expressions of the form

$$E \wedge (E_1 \sqcup\!\sqcup \ldots \sqcup\!\sqcup E_k)$$

where $E, E_1, \ldots, E_k$ are *timed regular expressions* – i.e. do not contain shuffle (but may contain renaming). Their name comes from the fact that $E_1, \ldots, E_k$ may be considered as expressions defining the behavior of some (preemptive) jobs, encapsulating duration constraints within each job, whereas E can be regarded as an expression embodying overall timing constraints for each job and the scheduling policy.

As an example, consider the following expressions:

$$E_1 = \big(s_1 \langle s_2 s_3 \rangle_2\big)^*, \quad E_2 = \big(u_1 \langle u_2 u_3 \rangle_2\big)^*$$
$$E = \big(\langle s_1 s_2 \rangle_2 (s_3 + u_1 + u_2 + u_3)^*\big)^* \wedge \big(\langle u_1 (s_1 + s_2 + s_3)^* u_2 \rangle_2 (s_1 + s_2 + s_3 + u_3)^*\big)^*$$

The expression $E \wedge (E_1 \sqcup\!\sqcup E_2)$ can be regarded as a specification of (the solution of) a two-job scheduling problem, in which

1. In the job E_1, the duration of s_2 plus s_3 equals 2 time units;
2. In the job E_2, the duration of u_2 plus u_3 equals 2 time units;
3. The part $s_1 s_2$ of E_1 cannot be preempted, hence has higher priority over E_2 and must be executed within 2 time units of the starting of signal state s_1.
4. The part $u_1 u_2$ of E_2 must be executed within 2 time units of the starting of signal state u_1, regardless of the interruptions.

The proof of Theorem 3 implies also the following:

Theorem 4. *Preemptive shuffle expressions have an undecidable emptiness problem.*

As we may see from the proof of Theorem 3, expressions with three "components" – that is, expressions of the form $E \wedge (E_1 \sqcup\!\sqcup E_2 \sqcup\!\sqcup E_3)$ – already have an undecidable emptiness problem. It is an open question whether two components would suffice.

6 Action-Based Semantics for Automata and Expressions

Throughout this section we show that all the results in this paper also apply to automata and expressions with timed word semantics.

Let us review in more detail the definition of stopwatch automata with action semantics: a **stopwatch automaton** is a tuple $\mathcal{A} = (Q, \mathcal{X}, \Sigma, \eta, \delta, Q_0, Q_f)$ where Q, Σ, $\mathcal{X}$, η, Q_0 and Q_f have the same meaning as in Section 3, while δ is a finite set of tuples (i.e. *transitions*), of the form (q, C, a, X, q'), where $q, q' \in Q$, $X \subseteq \mathcal{X}$, $a \in \Sigma$ and C is a finite conjunction of stopwatch constraints.

Similarly to automata with signal semantics, the timed word semantics of a stopwatch automaton is given in terms of a *timed transition system* $\mathcal{T}(\mathcal{A}) = (\mathcal{Q}, \theta, \mathcal{Q}_0, \mathcal{Q}_f)$ where $\mathcal{Q} = Q \times \mathbb{R}^n_{\geq 0}$, $\mathcal{Q}_0 = Q_0 \times \{\mathbf{0}_n\}$, $\mathcal{Q}_f = Q_f \times \mathbb{R}^n_{\geq 0}$ and

$$\begin{aligned}
\theta = \big\{(q, v) \xrightarrow{\tau} (q, v') \mid v'_i = v_i + \tau,\ \forall i \in [n] \text{ with } x_i \in \eta(q), v'_i = v_i \text{ otherwise.}\big\} \\
\cup \big\{(q, v) \xrightarrow{a} (q', v') \mid \exists (q, C, a, X, q') \in \delta \text{ such that } v \models C \text{ and for all } i \in [n], \\
\text{if } i \in X \text{ then } v'_i = 0 \text{ and if } i \notin X \text{ then } v'_i = v_i\big\}
\end{aligned}$$

The **label** of a discrete transition $(q, v) \xrightarrow{a} (q', v')$ is the symbol a that lies on the arrow. The **label** of a time passage transition $(q, v) \xrightarrow{\tau} (q, v')$ is τ.

A *run* in $\mathcal{T}(\mathcal{A})$ is a chain $\rho = \Big((q_{i-1}, v_{i-1}) \xrightarrow{\xi_i} (q_i, v_i) \Big)_{1 \leq i \leq k}$ of transitions from θ, while a *run* in $\mathcal{A}$ is a chain of transitions $\rho' = \Big(q_{i-1} \xrightarrow{C_i, a_i, X_i} q_i \Big)_{1 \leq i \leq k'}$. The two runs ρ, ρ' are **associated** iff the i-th discrete transition in ρ is generated by the i-th transition of ρ'. An **accepting run** in $\mathcal{T}(\mathcal{A})$ is a run which starts in $\mathcal{Q}_0$, ends in $\mathcal{Q}_f$ and *does not end with a time passage transition*. An accepting run **accepts** a timed word w iff w represents the formal concatenation of the labels of the transitions in the run.

The Figure 2 gives an example of a stopwatch automaton whose language is

$$L(\mathcal{A}) = \big\{ t_1 a t_2 b t_3 c \mid t_1 + t_3 = 1 \big\}.$$

Recall that the last transition in an accepting run cannot be a time passage transition and hence the automaton cannot spend any time in the last state q_4 when accepting a timed word.

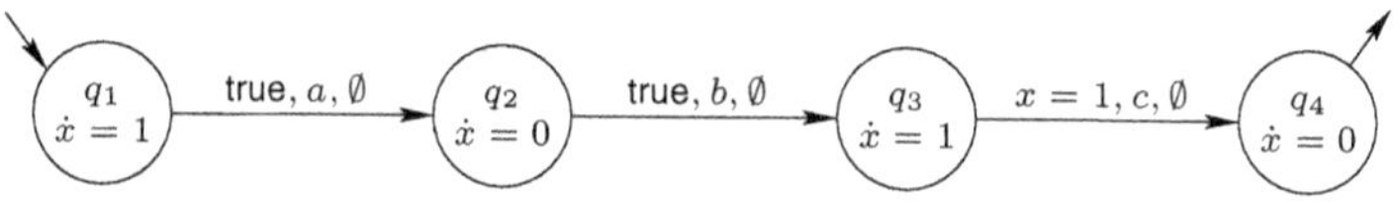

Fig. 2. A stopwatch automaton with action semantics.

The syntax of **timed action shuffle expressions** is the following:

$$E ::= a \mid \underline{t} \mid E + E \mid E \cdot E \mid E \wedge E \mid E^* \mid \langle E \rangle_I \mid E \sqcup\!\sqcup E \mid [a/b]E$$

where I is an interval, $a \in \Sigma$ and $b \in \Sigma \cup \{\varepsilon\}$.

Their semantics follows the same compositional rules as the semantics of timed shuffle expressions over signals, with the only difference on the rules on atoms, which, for timed action shuffle expressions are the following:

$$\|a\| = \{a\}, \quad \|\underline{t}\| = \{t \mid t \in \mathbb{R}_{\geq 0}\}$$

For example, the expression $E_1 = [z_1/\varepsilon][z_2/\varepsilon]\big((\langle z_1 \underline{t} a z_1 \underline{t} c \rangle_1 \sqcup\!\sqcup z_2 \underline{t} b) \wedge z_1 \underline{t} a z_2 \underline{t} b z_1 \underline{t} c\big)$ represents the language of the automaton $\mathcal{A}$ from Figure 2. Note the need to "duplicate" each transition label: if we do not make use of the additional symbols z_1 and z_2, we would not be able to correctly "insert" the first subexpression of the shuffle "within" the second. That is, the following shuffle expression is not equivalent to the automaton in Figure 2:

$$E_2 = \big(\langle \underline{t} a \underline{t} c \rangle_1 \sqcup\!\sqcup \underline{t} b\big) \wedge \underline{t} a \underline{t} b \underline{t} c$$

(E_2 was obtained from E_1 by removing all occurrences of z_1 and z_2.) This expression is equivalent to the timed expression $E_3 = \langle \underline{t} a \underline{t} b \underline{t} c \rangle_{]1,\infty[}$, which is obviously not what is needed. The problem lies in the fact that the duration before b in the subexpression $\underline{t} b$ must not "mix" with the other durations. The use of the additional symbols z_1 and z_2 is essential in forbidding this mixing.

In order to compare the expressive power of state based and action based semantics, note that the "division" expression from Identity 7 can be converted to action-based semantics:

$$E^a_{1/2} = \langle a\underline{t}\hat{a}\, b\underline{t}\hat{b}\rangle_1 c\underline{t}\hat{c}\, d\underline{t}\hat{d}\, e\underline{t}\hat{e} \wedge \big(a\underline{t}\hat{a}\langle b\underline{t}\hat{b}\, c\underline{t}\hat{c}\, e\underline{t}\hat{e}\rangle_1 \sqcup\!\sqcup d\underline{t}\hat{d}\big) \wedge$$
$$a\underline{t}\hat{a}\, b\underline{t}\hat{b}\langle c\underline{t}\hat{c}\, d\underline{t}\hat{d}\rangle_1 e\underline{t}\hat{e} \wedge a\underline{t}\hat{a}\, b\underline{t}\hat{b}\, c\underline{t}\hat{c}\langle d\underline{t}\hat{d}\, e\underline{t}\hat{e}\rangle_1 \quad (9)$$

Here, the duration of the time interval between a and $\hat{a}$ represents twice the duration of the interval between c and $\hat{c}$:

$$\|E^a_{1/2}\| = \{at_1\hat{a}\, bt_2\hat{b}\, ct_3\hat{c}\, dt_4\hat{d}\, et_5\hat{e} \mid t_1 = 2t_3, t_1 + t_2 = 1 = t_3 + t_4, t_3 = t_5\}$$

Given a set of symbols Σ, consider a copy $\hat{\Sigma}$ of it, and denote $\hat{s}$ the copy of the symbol $s \in \Sigma$. Consider then the following morphism $\varphi : \mathsf{Sig}(\Sigma) \to \mathsf{TW}(\Sigma)$, defined by

$$\varphi(s^\alpha) = st^\alpha\hat{s}, \quad \varphi(w_1w_2) = \varphi(w_1)\varphi(w_2) \text{ for all } w_1, w_2 \in \mathsf{Sig}(\Sigma)$$

Then, given any stopwatch automaton $\mathcal{A}$ with signal semantics, we may associate to it a stopwatch automaton $\mathcal{B}$ with action semantics such that $L(\mathcal{B}) = \varphi(L(\mathcal{A}))$. A similar result can be provided for expressions E with signals semantics, by constructing an expression with action semantics E' such that $\|E'\| = \varphi(\|E\|)$.

We give here the construction for shuffle expressions, since the respective construction for automata can be derived by the Kleene theorem. This construction is straightforward: given a timed shuffle expression over signals E, we replace each atom $a \in \Sigma$ with $a\underline{t}\hat{a}$. We denote the resulting expression $\varphi(E)$.

Remark 2. Note that $\|\varphi(E)\| \neq \emptyset$ iff $\|E\| \neq \emptyset$ and that, if we apply this construction to an expression without renaming or to a preemptive scheduling expression, the resulting expression remains in the same class.

Also note that $\varphi\Big([\mathbf{p}/a][\mathbf{s}/b][\mathbf{u}/c][\mathbf{v}/d][\mathbf{z}/e](E_{1/2})\Big) = E^a_{1/2}$

Theorem 5. *Emptiness checking for timed action shuffle expressions without renaming or for preemptive shuffle expressions with action semantics is undecidable.*

We end with the sketch of the proof that timed action shuffle expressions without intersection are more expressive than timed regular expressions. Our example is:

$$E_0 = \langle a\underline{t}\hat{a}b\underline{t}\hat{b}\rangle_1 c\underline{t}\hat{c} \wedge \big(\langle a\underline{t}\hat{a}c\underline{t}\hat{c}\rangle_1 \sqcup\!\sqcup b\underline{t}\hat{b}\big)$$

We also rely on the following observation (that is proved e.g. in [13,8]) saying roughly that timed words having $n+1$ action symbols and whose time intervals belong to the same $(n+1)$-dimensional region cannot be distinguished by timed automata:

Remark 3. For any timed regular expression E and $w = a_0t_1a_1 \ldots a_{n-1}t_na_n \in \|E\|$ if we have $w' = a_0t'_1a_1 \ldots a_{n-1}t'_na_n$ $(a_i \in \Sigma, t_i, t'_i \in \mathbb{R}_{\geq 0})$ such that for all $1 \leq i \leq j \leq n$,

$$\Big[\sum_{i\leq k\leq j} t_k\Big] = \Big[\sum_{i\leq k\leq j} t'_k\Big] \text{ and } \mathsf{frac}\Big(\sum_{i\leq k\leq j} x_k\Big) = \mathsf{frac}\Big(\sum_{i\leq k\leq j} x'_k\Big) \quad (10)$$

then $w' \in \|E\|$. Here $[\alpha]$ is the integral part and $\mathsf{frac}(\alpha)$ is the fractional part of $\alpha \in \mathbb{R}$.

Hence, we may see that $w_1 = a\,0.5\,\hat{a}\,b\,0.5\,\hat{b}\,c\,0.5\,\hat{c} \in \|E_0\|$, $w_2 = a\,0.3\,\hat{a}\,b\,0.7\,\hat{b}\,c\,0.3\,\hat{c} \notin \|E_0\|$, and w_1 and w_2 meet the condition (10). Therefore no timed regular expression can be equivalent to E_0.

7 Conclusions and Comments

We have seen that shuffle regular expressions with renaming are equivalent to stopwatch automata, and that, even without renaming, they still have an undecidable emptiness problem. The use of weakly monotonic time was essential in the proof of the last result. We do not know whether, in a strongly monotonic time setting, this theorem still holds.

Note that the automata encodings of [9] for the undecidability for stopwatch automata cannot be directly transformed into expressions without renamings or into preemptive scheduling expressions: the paper [9] utilizes a technique called "wrapping of clock values" which, when translated to shuffle expressions, require renamings.

An interesting direction of study concerns the expressive power of shuffle expressions w.r.t. preemptive scheduling problems, especially on defining of a class of expressions embodying *scheduling strategies*.

Finally, it is not very hard to figure out that shuffle regular expressions without intersection have a decidable emptiness problem. The the proof idea would proceed in a "compositional" manner along the following three observations:

- $\|E_1E_2\| \neq \emptyset$ iff $\|E_1\| \neq \emptyset$ and $\|E_1\| \neq \emptyset$, and similarly for $E_1 \sqcup\!\sqcup E_2$.
- $\|E_1 + E_2\| \neq \emptyset$ iff $\|E_1\| \neq \emptyset$ or $\|E_1\| \neq \emptyset$.
- $\|E\| \neq \emptyset$ iff $\|E^*\| \neq \emptyset$.

References

1. R. Alur and D. Dill. A theory of timed automata. *Theoretical Computer Science*, 126:183–235, 1994.
2. E. Asarin. Challenges in timed languages. *Bulletin of EATCS*, 83, 2004.
3. E. Asarin, P. Caspi, and O. Maler. A Kleene theorem for timed automata. In *Proceedings of LICS'97*, pages 160–171, 1997.
4. E. Asarin, P. Caspi, and O. Maler. Timed regular expressions. *Journal of ACM*, 49:172–206, 2002.
5. P. Bouyer and A. Petit. Decomposition and composition of timed automata. In *Proceedings of ICALP'99*, volume 1644 of *LNCS*, pages 210–219, 1999.
6. C. Dima. Kleene theorems for event-clock automata. In *Proceedings of FCT'99*, volume 1684 of *LNCS*, pages 215–225, 1999.
7. C. Dima. Real-time automata. *Journal of Automata, Languages and Combinatorics*, 6:3–23, 2001.
8. C. Dima. A nonarchimedian discretization for timed languages. In *Proceedings of FORMATS'03*, volume 2791 of *LNCS*, pages 161–181, 2003.
9. T.A. Henzinger, P.W. Kopke, A. Puri, and P. Varaiya. What's decidable about hybrid automata. *J. Comput. Syst. Sci*, 57:94–124, 1998.
10. P. Herrmann. Renaming is necessary in timed regular expressions. In *Proceedings of FST&TCS'99*, volume 1738 of *LNCS*, pages 47–59, 1999.
11. J.E. Hopcroft and J.D. Ullman. *Introduction to Automata Theory, Languages and Computation*. Addison-Wesley/Narosa Publishing House, 1992.
12. P. Krcál and Wang Yi. Decidable and undecidable problems in schedulability analysis using timed automata. In *Proceedings of TACAS'04*, volume 2988 of *LNCS*, pages 236–250, 2004.
13. J. Ouaknine and James Worrell. Revisiting digitization, robustness, and decidability for timed automata. In IEEE Computer Society Press, editor, *Proceedings of LICS'03*, pages 198–207, 2003.

A New Modality for Almost Everywhere Properties in Timed Automata*

Houda Bel Mokadem[1], Béatrice Bérard[2], Patricia Bouyer[1], and François Laroussinie[1]

[1] LSV, CNRS & ENS de Cachan,
61 av. du Président Wilson, 94235 Cachan Cedex, France
{mokadem, bouyer, fl}@lsv.ens-cachan.fr
[2] LAMSADE, CNRS & Université Paris-Dauphine,
Place du Maréchal de Lattre de Tassigny, 75775 Paris Cedex 16, France
berard@lamsade.dauphine.fr

Abstract. The context of this study is timed temporal logics for timed automata. In this paper, we propose an extension of the classical logic TCTL with a new Until modality, called "Until almost everywhere". In the extended logic, it is possible, for instance, to express that a property is true at all positions of all runs, except on a negligible set of positions. Such properties are very convenient, for example in the framework of boolean program verification, where transitions result from changing variable values. We investigate the expressive power of this modality and in particular, we prove that it cannot be expressed with classical TCTL modalities. However, we show that model-checking the extended logic remains PSPACE-complete as for TCTL.

1 Introduction

Verification of Timed Temporal Logic Properties. Temporal logic provides a fundamental framework for formally specifying systems and reasoning about them. Furthermore, model-checking techniques lead to the automatic verification that a finite-state model of a system satisfies some temporal logic specification. Since the introduction of timed automata [AD90,AD94] and timed logics like MITL, L_ν or TCTL [AH92,LLW95,AFH96], model-checking has been extended to real-time models [HNSY94] and analysis tools have been developed [DOTY96,HHWT95,LPY97] and successfully applied to numerous case studies.

Among these case studies, some examples concern the verification of programs which handle boolean or integer variables. The usual way to build a (possibly timed) model of the program consists in defining the discrete control states as tuples of variable values. The transitions are thus equipped with updates for the variables (and possibly time constraints). In such a model, a variable may change its value exactly upon leaving a control state and reaching another one,

* Work partially supported by the project VSMT of ENS de Cachan.

M. Abadi and L. de Alfaro (Eds.): CONCUR 2005, LNCS 3653, pp. 110–124, 2005.

which gives an ambiguous semantics: a variable can have several different values at a given time. This may lead to detect errors in the system, which are only due to the modeling phase. Such problems occur in the area of industrial automation, for the verification of Programmable Logic Controllers. In this case, programs are written from a set of languages described by the IEC-61131-3 specification [IEC93].

Example. Consider the SFC (Sequential Function Chart, one of the languages of the IEC standard) in Figure 1 below. It describes the control program of a device, designed to start some machine when two buttons (`L` and `R` for left and right button respectively) are pushed within 0.5 seconds. If only one button is pushed (then `L`+`R` is true) and the 0.5 seconds delay is reached (time-out `Et` has occurred), then the whole process must be started again. After the machine has started, it stops as soon as one button is released, and it can start again only after both buttons have been released ($\overline{\texttt{L}}.\overline{\texttt{R}}$ is true).

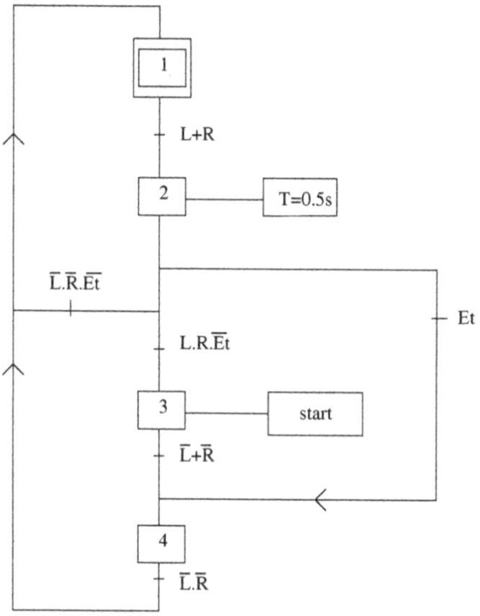

Fig. 1. SFC program for the two button machine

This device can be modeled with three timed automata (Figure 2), which communicate through the boolean variables `L` and `R`. The two automata for the buttons simply give arbitrary values in $\{0, 1\}$ to `L` and `R`, while the automaton for the control program is a straightforward translation of the SFC, with the only addition of an initialization step. The latter automaton handles a clock to measure the time interval of length 0.5. Note that some transitions must be urgent: for instance, the transition into state `running`, which sets the output variable `s` to 1, must be taken as soon as both buttons are pushed (if $t < 0.5$).

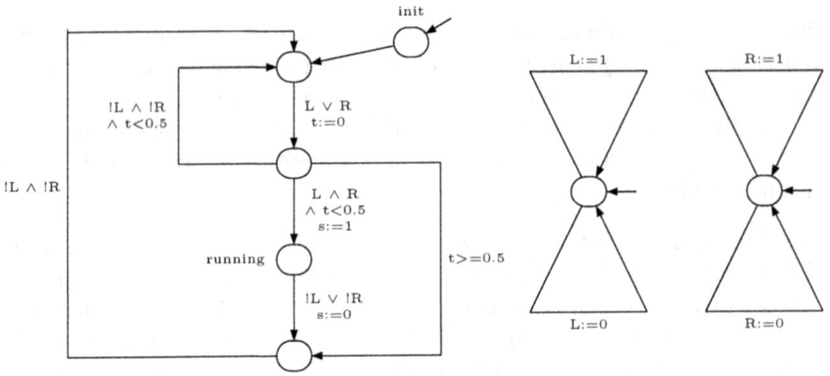

Fig. 2. Timed automata for the control program and the buttons

Consider now the following property: *it is always true that the machine has started only if both buttons have been pushed*, *i.e.* if `s=1` then `L=1` and `R=1`. This property does not hold because the automaton is still in state `running` when one of the buttons has been released, even if the transition into the next state will occur instantaneously afterward. What we should require instead is that this property be true *almost everywhere*, meaning that it could be false only on intervals with null duration.

A similar problem can occur when a sequence of transitions must be executed in an atomic way. To this purpose, a convenient feature was introduced in UPPAAL: when a location of a timed automaton is labeled as *committed*, no time delay is permitted in this location and a new action transition has to be performed to leave this location. This mechanism is used in particular to obtain n-ary synchronization when only binary synchronization is possible. For example, the sequence $s_1 \xrightarrow{a_1} s_2 \xrightarrow{a_2} s_3$ executes atomically if location s_2 is committed. Like above, a given property may be true before s_1 and after s_3 but false in the intermediate location s_2 where the control stays for a null duration. Again in this case, a property true "almost everywhere" would be sufficient.

Some Solutions. A basic method to solve the particular example of the "two buttons machine" described above would be to synchronize the update transitions of the L and R variables with the control transitions. This would amount to remove the variables in the model, introducing synchronizing channels instead. However, the resulting models do not faithfully represent the control program of the device, which receives the values of L and R by intermediate variables updated through sensors. Since the control program may later be translated into some other language of the standard (like Ladder Diagram), the model should remain as close as possible to the original specification.

A simple way of dealing with the general case consists in defining restricted semantics for timed automata, requiring that at most one configuration be associated with a given time. This holds for instance when only strictly increasing time sequences are permitted. However, when practical issues are considered, it is often useful to assume that several actions are executed in an atomic way (as described above for synchronization), which leads to simpler models. Restricting the expressive power of a model is generally not a good idea. When such atomicity hypotheses are made, it is then possible to modify the property to be checked, requiring it to be true only in specified states where no ambiguity can occur. Such methods were used for instance in the verification with HyTech of the ABR protocol [BFKM03]. But this is an *ad-hoc* construction, where all the details of the system must be carefully investigated.

Finally, one could think of introducing an observer automaton. For example, to test if some atomic proposition a is true almost everywhere, such an automaton would move to an error state if it has stayed in $\neg a$ for a non null duration. However, it is well known that this method does not apply to full TCTL, but is restricted to a fragment expressing safety properties [ABBL03].

Contribution. In this paper, we propose a solution that does not depend on the model, which can thus remain as it was originally designed (often in a long and difficult process) for a given system. This solution consists in extending the syntax of the TCTL logic with an *almost everywhere* until modality U^{a}. We obtain for instance formulae like $\mathsf{AG}^{\mathsf{a}}\varphi$, meaning that property φ is true almost everywhere.

Section 2 recalls the main features of the timed automata model and gives definitions for the syntax and semantics of our extended logic. In Section 3, we investigate the expressive power of this extension, comparing it with TCTL. In particular, we prove that the modality U^{a} cannot be expressed with TCTL operators and conversely that U^{a} cannot express TCTL modalities. Finally, in the last section, we show that model-checking the extended logic $\mathsf{TCTL}^{\mathsf{ext}}$ is decidable by some labeling procedure, with the same complexity as TCTL.

Some proofs are omitted and can be found in the research report [BMBBL05].

2 Timed Automata and $\mathsf{TCTL}^{\mathsf{ext}}$

Let $\mathbb{N}$ and $\mathbb{R}_{\geq 0}$ denote respectively the sets of natural and non-negative real numbers. Let X be a set of real valued clocks. The set of *valuations* is the set $\mathbb{R}_{\geq 0}^X$ of mappings from X to $\mathbb{R}_{\geq 0}$. We write $\mathcal{C}(X)$ for the set of boolean expressions over atomic formulae of the form $x \sim k$ with $x \in X$, $k \in \mathbb{N}$, and $\sim \in \{<, \leq, =, \geq, >\}$. Constraints of $\mathcal{C}(X)$ are interpreted over clock valuations. For every $v \in \mathbb{R}_{\geq 0}^X$ and $d \in \mathbb{R}_{\geq 0}$, we use $v + d$ to denote the time assignment which maps each clock $x \in X$ to the value $v(x) + d$. For a subset r of X, we write $v[r \leftarrow 0]$ for the valuation which maps each clock in r to the value 0 and agrees with v over $X \setminus r$. Let AP be a set of atomic propositions.

2.1 Timed Automata

Definition 1. *A* timed automaton *(TA) is a tuple* $A = \langle X, Q_A, q_{init}, \rightarrow_A, \mathsf{Inv}_A, l_A\rangle$ *where* X *is a finite set of clocks,* Q_A *is a finite set of* locations or control states *and* $q_{init} \in Q_A$ *is the* initial location. *The set* $\rightarrow_A \subseteq Q_A \times \mathcal{C}(X) \times 2^X \times Q_A$ *is a finite set of* action transitions: *for* $(q, g, r, q') \in \rightarrow_A$, g *is the enabling condition* *and r is a set of clocks to be reset with the transition (we write $q \xrightarrow{g,r}_A q'$).* $\mathsf{Inv}_A : Q_A \to \mathcal{C}(X)$ *assigns an* invariant *to each control state. Finally $l_A : Q_A \to 2^{\mathsf{AP}}$ labels every location with a subset of* AP.

A *configuration* of a TA A is a pair (q, v), where $q \in Q_A$ is the current location and $v \in \mathbb{R}^X_{\geq 0}$ is the current clock valuation. The initial state of A is (q_{init}, v_0) with $v_0(x) = 0$ for any x in X. There are two kinds of transition. From (q, v), it is possible to perform the *action transition* $q \xrightarrow{g,r}_A q'$ if $v \models g$ and $v[r \leftarrow 0] \models \mathsf{Inv}_A(q')$ and then the new configuration is $(q', v[r \leftarrow 0])$. It is also possible to let time elapse, and reach $(q, v + t)$ for some $t \in \mathbb{R}$ whenever the invariant is satisfied along the delay. Formally the semantics of a TA A is given by a Timed Transition System (TTS) $\mathcal{T}_A = (S, s_{\text{init}}, \to_{\mathcal{T}_A}, l)$ where:

- $S = \{(q, v) \mid q \in Q_A \text{ and } v \in \mathbb{R}^X_{\geq 0} \text{ s.t. } v \models \mathsf{Inv}_A(q)\}$ and $s_{\text{init}} = (q_{\text{init}}, v_0)$.
- $\to_{\mathcal{T}_A} \subseteq S \times S$ and we have $(q, v) \to_{\mathcal{T}_A} (q', v')$ iff
  - either $q' = q$, $v' = v + t$ and $v + t' \models \mathsf{Inv}_A(q)$ for any $t' \leq t$. This is a delay transition, written $(q, v) \xrightarrow{t} (q, v + t)$,
  - or $\exists q \xrightarrow{g,r}_A q'$ and $v \models g$, $v' = v[r \leftarrow 0]$ and $v' \models \mathsf{Inv}_A(q')$. This is an action transition, written $(q, v) \to_a (q', v')$.
- $l : S \to 2^{\mathsf{AP}}$ labels every state (q, v) with the subset $l_A(q)$ of AP .

A run of A is an infinite path $s_0 \to_{\mathcal{T}_A} s_1 \to_{\mathcal{T}_A} s_2 \ldots$ in $\mathcal{T}_A$ such that (1) time diverges and (2) there are infinitely many action transitions. Note that a run can always be described as an alternating infinite sequence $s_0 \xrightarrow{t_0}\to_a s_1 \xrightarrow{t_1}\to_a \cdots$ for some $t_i \in \mathbb{R}$. Such a run ρ goes through any configuration s' reachable from some s_i by a delay transition of duration $t \in [0, t_i]$. We write Exec(s) for the set of all runs starting from s. A configuration can occur several times along some run ρ. A particular occurrence p of a configuration is called a *position*, we write $p \in \rho$. For such a p, the corresponding configuration is denoted by s_p.

The standard notions of prefix, suffix and subrun apply for paths in TTS: given a position $p \in \rho$, $\rho^{\leq p}$ is the prefix leading to p, $\rho^{\geq p}$ is the suffix issued from p. Finally a subrun σ from p to p' is denoted by $p \overset{\sigma}{\mapsto} p'$.

Given two positions p and p', we say that p *precedes strictly* p' along ρ (written $p <_\rho p'$) iff there exists a finite subrun σ of ρ s.t. $p \overset{\sigma}{\mapsto} p'$ and σ contains at least one non null delay transition **or** one action transition (*i.e.* σ is not reduced to $\xrightarrow{0}$). Note that the set of positions along ρ is totally ordered by $<_\rho$, independently of the representation of the run.

Given a position $p \in \rho$, the prefix $\rho^{\leq p}$ has a *duration*, $\mathsf{Time}(\rho^{\leq p})$, defined as the sum of all delays along $\rho^{\leq p}$. Since time diverges along an execution, we have: for any $t \in \mathbb{R}$, there exists $p \in \rho$ such that $\mathsf{Time}(\rho^{\leq p}) > t$. For a subset $P \subseteq \rho$ of positions in ρ, we define a natural measure $\hat{\mu}(P) = \mu\{\mathsf{Time}(\rho^{\leq p}) \mid p \in P\}$, where μ is Lebesgue measure on the set of real numbers.

2.2 Definition of $\mathsf{TCTL}^{\mathsf{ext}}$.

We extend the syntax of TCTL to express that a formula holds almost everywhere: $\mathsf{TCTL}^{\mathsf{ext}}$ is obtained by adding the two modalities $\mathsf{E\_U}^{\mathsf{a}}_{\sim c}\_$ and $\mathsf{A\_U}^{\mathsf{a}}_{\sim c}\_$ to TCTL.

Definition 2 (Syntax of $\mathsf{TCTL}^{\mathsf{ext}}$). *$\mathsf{TCTL}^{\mathsf{ext}}$ formulae are given by the following grammar:*

$$\varphi, \psi ::= P_1 \mid P_2 \mid \ldots \mid \neg\varphi \mid \varphi \wedge \psi \mid \mathsf{E}\varphi\mathsf{U}_{\sim c}\psi \mid \mathsf{A}\varphi\mathsf{U}_{\sim c}\psi \mid \mathsf{E}\varphi\mathsf{U}^{\mathsf{a}}_{\sim c}\psi \mid \mathsf{A}\varphi\mathsf{U}^{\mathsf{a}}_{\sim c}\psi$$

where $P_i \in \mathsf{AP}$, $\sim$ belongs to the set $\{<, >, \leq, \geq, =\}$ and $c \in \mathbb{N}$.

Standard abbreviations include $\top, \bot, \varphi \vee \psi, \varphi \Rightarrow \psi, \ldots$ as well as :

$$\mathsf{EF}^{a}_{\sim c}\,\varphi \stackrel{def}{=} \mathsf{E}(\top\,\mathsf{U}^{\mathsf{a}}_{\sim c}\,\varphi) \qquad \mathsf{AF}^{\mathsf{a}}_{\sim c}\,\varphi \stackrel{def}{=} \mathsf{A}(\top\,\mathsf{U}^{\mathsf{a}}_{\sim c}\,\varphi)$$
$$\mathsf{EG}^{\mathsf{a}}_{\sim c}\,\varphi \stackrel{def}{=} \neg\mathsf{AF}^{\mathsf{a}}_{\sim c}\neg\varphi \qquad \mathsf{AG}^{\mathsf{a}}_{\sim c}\,\varphi \stackrel{def}{=} \neg\mathsf{EF}^{\mathsf{a}}_{\sim c}\neg\varphi$$

Definition 3 (Semantics of $\mathsf{TCTL}^{\mathsf{ext}}$). *The following clauses define when a state s of some TTS $\mathcal{T} = \langle S, s_{init}, \rightarrow, l\rangle$ satisfies a $\mathsf{TCTL}^{\mathsf{ext}}$ formula φ, written $s \models \varphi$, by induction over the structure of φ (the semantics of boolean operators is omitted).*

$s \models \mathsf{E}\varphi\mathsf{U}_{\sim c}\psi$ *iff* $\exists\,\rho \in Exec(s)$ *s.t.* $\rho \models \varphi\mathsf{U}_{\sim c}\psi$
$s \models \mathsf{A}\varphi\mathsf{U}_{\sim c}\psi$ *iff* $\forall\,\rho \in Exec(s)$ *we have* $\rho \models \varphi\mathsf{U}_{\sim c}\psi$
$s \models \mathsf{E}\varphi\mathsf{U}^{\mathsf{a}}_{\sim c}\psi$ *iff* $\exists\,\rho \in Exec(s)$ *s.t.* $\rho \models \varphi\mathsf{U}^{\mathsf{a}}_{\sim c}\psi$
$s \models \mathsf{A}\varphi\mathsf{U}^{\mathsf{a}}_{\sim c}\psi$ *iff* $\forall\,\rho \in Exec(s)$ *we have* $\rho \models \varphi\mathsf{U}^{\mathsf{a}}_{\sim c}\psi$

$\rho \models \varphi\mathsf{U}_{\sim c}\psi$ *iff* $\exists p \in \rho$ *s.t.* $\mathsf{Time}(\rho^{\leq p}) \sim c \wedge s_p \models \psi \wedge \forall p' <_\rho p,\ s_{p'} \models \varphi$
$\rho \models \varphi\mathsf{U}^{\mathsf{a}}_{\sim c}\psi$ *iff there exists a subrun* σ *s.t.* $\hat{\mu}(\sigma) > 0, \exists p \in \sigma,\ \mathsf{Time}(\rho^{\leq p}) \sim c,$ $\forall p' \in \sigma, s_{p'} \models \psi,\ \hat{\mu}(\{p' \mid p' <_\rho p \wedge s_{p'} \not\models \varphi\}) = 0$

Note that in the case of the *almost* modality U^{a}, we ask that φ holds almost everywhere before ψ occurs. Moreover, we require that ψ holds not only at a single position (which has a measure equal to 0), like in the usual framework, but on a whole interval around the position satisfying the time constraint.

For example, $\mathsf{AG}^{a}_{\geq 0}\varphi$ specifies that along every run, the set of positions at which φ does not hold has a measure equal to 0, *i.e.* φ holds *almost everywhere* along all paths. It was precisely this kind of property we wanted to be able to express. Note that the positions where some formula φ does not hold are not restricted to discrete transitions, contrary to some intuition. Indeed, consider the automaton below, with two atomic propositions a and b, and the formula $\varphi = \mathsf{E}a\mathsf{U}_{=1}b$. Let ρ be a run starting in $(q_0, 0)$. Clearly, the only position where φ is satisfied is $(q_0, 1)$, which does not correspond to a discrete transition. In this case, we have $(q_0, 0) \models \mathsf{AG}^{a}(\neg\varphi)$ (but $(q_0, 0) \not\models \mathsf{AG}(\neg\varphi)$).

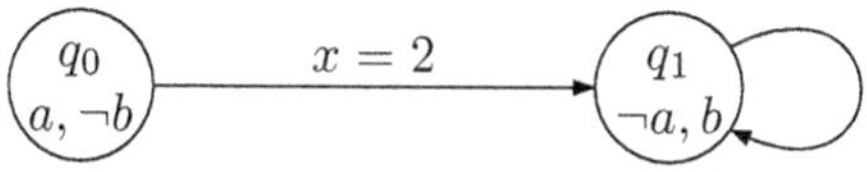

The standard TCTL logic is the fragment of $\mathsf{TCTL}^{\mathsf{ext}}$ without $\mathsf{E\_U}^{\mathsf{a}}_{\sim c}\_$ and $\mathsf{A\_U}^{\mathsf{a}}_{\sim c}\_$, while the logic $\mathsf{TCTL}^{\mathsf{a}}$ is the restriction of $\mathsf{TCTL}^{\mathsf{ext}}$ where classical $\mathsf{E\_U}_{\sim c}\_$ and $\mathsf{A\_U}_{\sim c}\_$ are forbidden.

The size $|\varphi|$ of a formula φ is defined in the standard way, with constants written in binary notation.

3 Expressiveness of $\mathsf{U^a}$ Modality

In this section we show that the modality $\mathsf{U^a}$ cannot be expressed with TCTL operators and conversely that $\mathsf{U^a}$ cannot express TCTL modalities.

Formally we say that two formulae φ and ψ are *equivalent* for a class of models C whenever their truth value is the same for any element of C, this is denoted $\varphi \overset{C}{\equiv} \psi$ or just $\varphi \equiv \psi$ when C is clear from the context. Let $\mathcal{L}$ and $\mathcal{L}'$ be two logical languages interpreted over the same models. $\mathcal{L}'$ is said to be *as expressive as* $\mathcal{L}$ (denoted $\mathcal{L} \preceq \mathcal{L}'$) iff for any formula $\varphi \in \mathcal{L}$ there exist $\varphi' \in \mathcal{L}'$ s.t. $\varphi \equiv \varphi'$. Moreover $\mathcal{L}'$ is *strictly more expressive* than $\mathcal{L}$ (written $\mathcal{L} \prec \mathcal{L}'$) iff $\mathcal{L} \preceq \mathcal{L}'$ and $\mathcal{L}' \not\preceq \mathcal{L}$.

3.1 TCTL $\prec$ TCTL^{ext}

First we show that $\mathsf{U^a}$ cannot be expressed with standard U modality. The proof is based on classical techniques used in untimed temporal logics (see for ex. [Eme91,EH86]). However, adapting them to the timed framework results in more involved constructions.

Let Ψ be the TCTL^{a} formula $\mathsf{E}(a\mathsf{U}^{\mathsf{a}}_{>0}\mathsf{b})$. We will prove that there is no TCTL formula equivalent to Ψ. Consider the timed automata M_i and N_i with $i \geq 1$ in Figure 3. Clearly we have $M_i,(q_i,0) \models \Psi$ while $N_i,(q'_i,0) \not\models \Psi$. The next lemma states that M_i and N_i satisfy the same TCTL formula whose size is less than i.

We first introduce some notations. Given two configurations s and s', we write $s \equiv^k_{\mathsf{TCTL}} s'$ iff for any $\varphi \in \mathsf{TCTL}$ with $|\varphi| \leq k$, we have $s \models \varphi \Leftrightarrow s' \models \varphi$. We write $s \equiv_{\mathsf{TCTL}} s'$ iff $s \equiv^k_{\mathsf{TCTL}} s'$ for any $k \geq 1$.

Automata M_i and N_i contain only one clock, any configuration is then defined as a pair (ℓ, t) where ℓ is a location and $t \in \mathbb{R}_{\geq 0}$ is a value for x. Moreover the automata have only one cycle on r_0: for any configuration of the form (q_j,t), (q'_j,t), (r_j,t), or (r'_j,t) with $j \geq 1$, there is at most one such position along ρ.

Proof of expressiveness will be a consequence of the following Lemma:

Lemma 4. *Given the automata described in Figure 3, $\forall k \geq 1$, $\forall i \geq k$ and $\forall t \in \mathbb{R}$, we have:*

$$(q_i,t) \equiv^k_{\mathsf{TCTL}} (q'_i,t) \qquad\qquad (r_i,t) \equiv^k_{\mathsf{TCTL}} (r'_i,t)$$

Let ρ be a run starting in (q'_i,t) in N_i with $i > 0$. The run ρ is characterized by the time elapsed δ_0 in q'_i, the time elapsed δ_1 in r'_i and a suffix ρ_1 in N_{i-1} or M_{i-1}. Then ρ has the following structure:

$$(q'_i,t) \xrightarrow{\delta_0} (q'_i,\delta_0+t) \rightarrow_a (r'_i,0) \xrightarrow{\delta_1} (r'_i,\delta_1) \rightarrow_a \overset{\rho_1}{\mapsto}$$

Note that the suffix ρ_1 is in M_{i-1} only if $\delta_1 > 0$. Let $f_{M_i}(\rho)$ be the run of M_i defined by: $(q_i,t) \xrightarrow{\delta_0} (q_i,\delta_0+t) \rightarrow_a (r_i,0) \xrightarrow{\delta_1} (r_i,\delta_1) \rightarrow_a \overset{\rho_1}{\mapsto}$. The same can be done for a run issued from (r'_i,t), but in this case there is only the delay transition labeled by δ_1. Note that ρ and $f_{M_i}(\rho)$ share the same suffix ρ_1.

Given a run ρ in M_i from (q_i,t) or (r_i,t), one can also define a corresponding run $f_{N_i}(\rho)$ in N_i whenever the delay δ_1 spent in r_i is strictly positive.

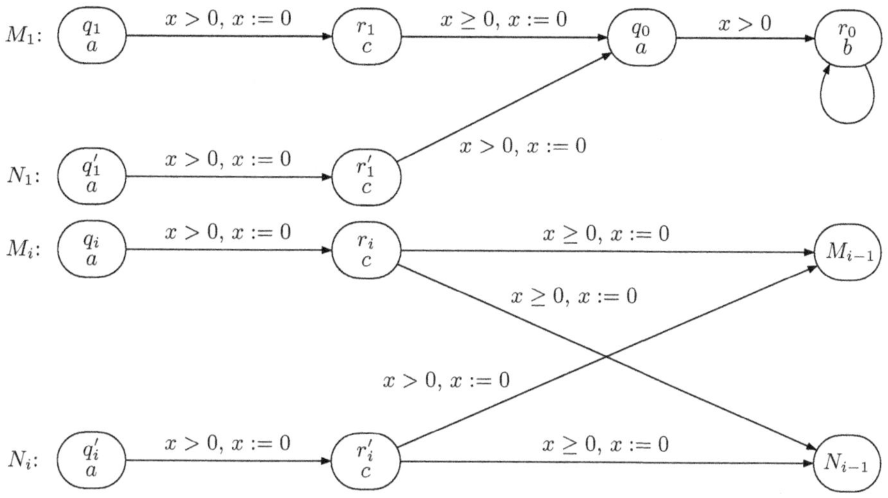

Fig. 3. Automata M_i and N_i, $i = 1, 2, \dots$

Proof (of Lemma 4). The proof is done by induction over k, the size of formulae.

First note that, given the guards and the resets on transitions of M_i and N_i, we clearly have for every $j \geq 0$ and locations $\ell \in \{q_j, r_j, q'_j, r'_j\}$

$$(r_j, 0) \equiv_{\mathsf{TCTL}} (r_j, t) \qquad \forall t > 0 \tag{1}$$

$$(\ell, t) \equiv_{\mathsf{TCTL}} (\ell, t') \qquad \forall t, t' > 0 \tag{2}$$

For formulae of size $k = 1$, the equivalences of the lemma hold because q_i and q'_i (resp. r_i and r'_i) are labeled by the same atomic propositions.

We assume now that $k > 1$ and that equivalences of the lemma hold for formulae with size $< k$. The case of boolean combinations is obvious, so we now concentrate on formulae $\mathsf{A}(\varphi_1 \mathsf{U}_{\sim c} \varphi_2)$ and $\mathsf{E}(\varphi_1 \mathsf{U}_{\sim c} \varphi_2)$.

From equivalences (1) and (2) and from induction hypothesis, if ρ is a run in N_i, then $f_{M_i}(\rho)$ exists and $\rho \models (\varphi_1 \mathsf{U}_{\sim c} \varphi_2) \iff f_{M_i}(\rho) \models (\varphi_1 \mathsf{U}_{\sim c} \varphi_2)$. Similarly, if ρ is a run in M_i and if $f_{N_i}(\rho)$ exists, then $\rho \models (\varphi_1 \mathsf{U}_{\sim c} \varphi_2) \iff f_{N_i}(\rho) \models (\varphi_1 \mathsf{U}_{\sim c} \varphi_2)$. Note that there exist some runs ρ in M_i for which there is no corresponding $f_{N_i}(\rho)$ (when there is no delay in location r_i).

We thus deduce immediately that

$$\begin{cases} (q_i, t) \models \mathsf{A}(\varphi_1 \mathsf{U}_{\sim c} \varphi_2) \implies (q'_i, t) \models \mathsf{A}(\varphi_1 \mathsf{U}_{\sim c} \varphi_2) \\ (r_i, t) \models \mathsf{A}(\varphi_1 \mathsf{U}_{\sim c} \varphi_2) \implies (r'_i, t) \models \mathsf{A}(\varphi_1 \mathsf{U}_{\sim c} \varphi_2) \\ \\ (q'_i, t) \models \mathsf{E}(\varphi_1 \mathsf{U}_{\sim c} \varphi_2) \implies (q_i, t) \models \mathsf{E}(\varphi_1 \mathsf{U}_{\sim c} \varphi_2) \\ (r'_i, t) \models \mathsf{E}(\varphi_1 \mathsf{U}_{\sim c} \varphi_2) \implies (r_i, t) \models \mathsf{E}(\varphi_1 \mathsf{U}_{\sim c} \varphi_2) \end{cases}$$

To get all equivalences of Lemma 4, we need some extra work for several implications.

– Assume that $(q_i, t) \models \mathsf{E}(\varphi_1 \mathsf{U}_{\sim c} \varphi_2)$ and take a run ρ from state (q_i, t) satisfying $\varphi_1 \mathsf{U}_{\sim c} \varphi_2$ with no corresponding run $f_{N_i}(\rho)$ (the delay in location r_i is thus 0). We note (ℓ, v) the position along ρ which satisfies φ_2 while all previous positions satisfy φ_1. If that position is before $(q_{i-1}, 0)$, then taking a run which starts with the prime version of the prefix of ρ ending in (ℓ, v), by induction hypothesis, we get a run which satisfies $\varphi_1 \mathsf{U}_{\sim c} \varphi_2$. Otherwise we need to change delays in ρ (to get a run ρ') as follows: on ρ, there is no delay in location r_i, we add one small delay in this state, small enough such that the run is unchanged after state r_{i-1} (the accumulated delays in states r_i and q_{i-1} in ρ' corresponds to the delay in q_{i-1} on run ρ, see the figure below) and such that if $\ell = q_{i-1}$ (in which case $v > 0$ by assumption), then the corresponding position on ρ' is some (q_{i-1}, v') with $v' > 0$.

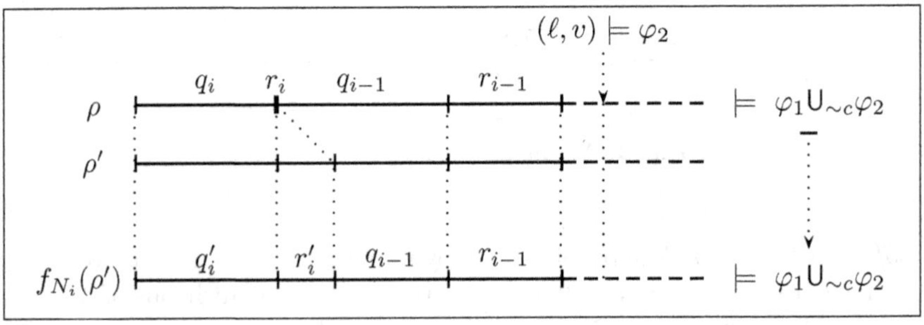

The run ρ' then satisfies $\varphi_1 \mathsf{U}_{\sim c} \varphi_2$: the position which corresponds to (ℓ, v) on ρ' also satisfies φ_2, and all previous positions satisfy φ_1 (using equivalences (1) and (2)). We thus get that $f_{N_i}(\rho')$ also satisfies $\varphi_1 \mathsf{U}_{\sim c} \varphi_2$. Thus, $(q'_i, t) \models \mathsf{E}(\varphi_1 \mathsf{U}_{\sim c} \varphi_2)$.

A similar construction can be done to prove that $(r_i, 0) \models \mathsf{E}(\varphi_1 \mathsf{U}_{\sim c} \varphi_2)$ implies $(r'_i, 0) \models \mathsf{E}(\varphi_1 \mathsf{U}_{\sim c} \varphi_2)$.

– For the formula $\mathsf{A}(\varphi_1 \mathsf{U}_{\prec c} \varphi_2)$ where $\prec$ is either $<$ or $\leq$ and $c > 0$, we consider a location $\ell \in \{q_i, r_i, q'_i, r'_i\}$. The following then holds:
  - if $t > 0$, $(\ell, t) \models \mathsf{A}(\varphi_1 \mathsf{U}_{\prec c} \varphi_2)$ iff $(\ell, t) \models \varphi_2$ as we can take a run waiting at least c time units in location ℓ, and for some delay $d \prec c$, $(\ell, t + d)$ will have to satisfy φ_2 (which entails by (2) that (ℓ, t) must satisfy φ_2)
  - similarly $(\ell, 0) \models \mathsf{A}(\varphi_1 \mathsf{U}_{\prec c} \varphi_2)$ iff $(\ell, 0) \models \varphi_2$ or $((\ell, 0) \models \varphi_1$ and $(\ell, t) \models \varphi_2$ for every $t > 0)$

  Using induction hypothesis (on formulae φ_1 and φ_2), we get that $(\ell', t) \models \mathsf{A}(\varphi_1 \mathsf{U}_{\prec c} \varphi_2)$ implies $(\ell, t) \models \mathsf{A}(\varphi_1 \mathsf{U}_{\prec c} \varphi_2)$ if $\ell \in \{q_i, r_i\}$.

– We consider formula $\mathsf{A}(\varphi_1 \mathsf{U}_{=c} \varphi_2)$ with $c > 0$. Any reachable state from some (ℓ, t) can be reached in exactly c units of time and in strictly less than c units of time (because there is no real constraints on delays in states). This formula is then equivalent to $\varphi_1 \wedge \varphi_2$ over states (ℓ, t) with $\ell \in \{q_i, r_i, q'_i, r'_i\}$ and $t > 0$, and $(\ell, 0) \models \mathsf{A}(\varphi_1 \mathsf{U}_{=c} \varphi_2)$ iff $(\ell, 0) \models \varphi_1$ and all reachable states from $(\ell, 0)$ satisfy $\varphi_1 \wedge \varphi_2$ (ℓ is in $\{q_i, r_i, q'_i, r'_i\}$). Using induction hypothesis, we get that $(\ell', t) \models \mathsf{A}(\varphi_1 \mathsf{U}_{=c} \varphi_2)$ implies $(\ell, t) \models \mathsf{A}(\varphi_1 \mathsf{U}_{=c} \varphi_2)$ for $\ell \in \{q_i, r_i\}$.

– We assume that $(q'_i, t) \models \mathsf{A}(\varphi_1 \mathsf{U}_{\geq c} \varphi_2)$ and we want to prove that $(q_i, t) \models \mathsf{A}(\varphi_1 \mathsf{U}_{\geq c} \varphi_2)$. We consider a run ρ in M_i starting in (q_i, t) such that $f_{N_i}(\rho)$ is not defined (the delay in state r_i is 0). We will construct a run in N_i from state (q'_i, t) "equivalent" to ρ, and distinguish two cases, depending on the delay δ in location q_i. We first consider the case where $\delta < c$.

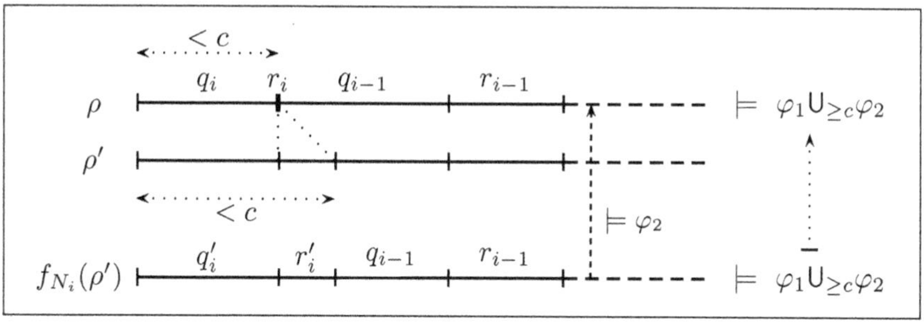

In ρ, the delay in q_i is $< c$ whereas the delay in r_i is null. We first construct a run ρ' with a positive delay in r_i (however smaller than the initial delay of ρ in state q_{i-1}) such that the accumulated delay in q_i and r_i is still $< c$ (see the figure above). From ρ' we construct run $f_{N_i}(\rho')$ in N_i. Using induction hypothesis, at all positions, the two runs ρ' and $f_{N_i}(\rho')$ agree on properties φ_1 and φ_2. As $(q'_i, t) \models \mathsf{A}(\varphi_1 \mathsf{U}_{\geq c} \varphi_2)$, this implies that $f_{N_i}(\rho') \models \varphi_1 \mathsf{U}_{\geq c} \varphi_2$, and thus that $\rho' \models \varphi_1 \mathsf{U}_{\geq c} \varphi_2$. In particular, φ_1 has to hold in states (r_i, t) for every $t \geq 0$. Moreover, property φ_2 holds at some position along ρ', and φ_2 will also hold at the same position on ρ. We thus get that ρ also satisfies property $\varphi_1 \mathsf{U}_{\geq c} \varphi_2$.

We now assume that $\delta \geq c$. From ρ which does not delay in state r_i, we construct a run ρ' which waits a small amount of time (as in the previous case), and then consider the corresponding run $f_{N_i}(\rho')$ in N_i. By assumption, this runs satisfies $\varphi_1 \mathsf{U}_{\geq c} \varphi_2$. Then several cases can happen: (i) the property φ_2 holds in some $(q'_i, t+d)$ with $d \geq c$, in which case φ_2 also holds in $(q_i, t+d)$ by induction hypothesis, and φ_1 holds in all $(q_i, t+d')$ for $d' < d$ (also by induction hypothesis) which implies that $\rho \models \varphi_1 \mathsf{U}_{\geq c} \varphi_2$; (ii) the property holds in some (r'_i, d) for some $d \geq 0$, which implies that φ_2 also holds in (r_i, d) by i.h. and thus that $(r_i, 0) \models \varphi_2$ using (1), thus $\rho \models \varphi_1 \mathsf{U}_{\geq c} \varphi_2$; (iii) the property φ_2 holds for some other state (ℓ, d), which will be also true on run ρ, thus in that case also $\rho \models \varphi_1 \mathsf{U}_{\geq c} \varphi_2$.

In both cases we can conclude that $(q_i, t) \models \mathsf{A}(\varphi_1 \mathsf{U}_{\geq c} \varphi_2)$.

Similar constructions can be done to prove that $(r'_i, t) \models \mathsf{A}(\varphi_1 \mathsf{U}_{\geq c} \varphi_2)$ implies $(r_i, t) \models \mathsf{A}(\varphi_1 \mathsf{U}_{\geq c} \varphi_2)$.

– Formula $\mathsf{A}(\varphi_1 \mathsf{U}_{>c} \varphi_2)$ is almost handled in a similar way as $\mathsf{A}(\varphi \mathsf{U}_{\geq c} \varphi_2)$. Like before, we consider a run ρ in M_i which has no corresponding run $f_{N_i}(\rho)$. If δ is the delay in location q_i, we have also to distinguish three cases (instead of two): cases where $\delta < c$ or $\delta > c$ can be done exactly as previously. The only different case is when $\delta = c$. As previously we first construct a run ρ' which waits some positive delay in location r_i, and then consider run $f_{N_i}(\rho')$ which has to satisfy $\varphi_1 \mathsf{U}_{>c}\varphi_2$, and then using induction hypothesis we get that $\rho' \models \varphi_1 \mathsf{U}_{>c}\varphi_2$, from which we get that $\rho \models \varphi_1 \mathsf{U}_{>c}\varphi_2$ (using equivalences (1) and (2)). In that case, the delay in location q_i is shortened, and the accumulated delay in q_i and r_i (in run ρ') is precisely c, as seen in the figure below.

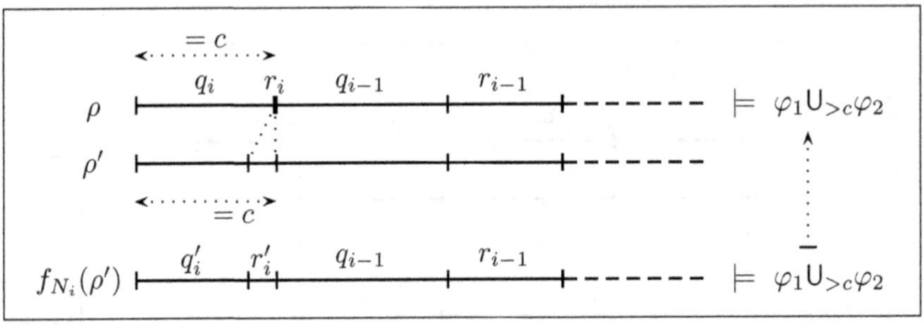

– It is easy to see that formula $\mathsf{A}(\varphi_1 \mathsf{U}_{=0}\varphi_2)$ is equivalent to φ_2 over states of M_i and N_i. □

Now we have the following result:

Theorem 5. $\mathsf{TCTL}^{\mathsf{ext}}$ *is strictly more expressive than* TCTL.

Proof. This is a consequence of Lemma 4: assume that there exists a TCTL formula Φ equivalent to formula $\mathsf{E}(a\mathsf{U}^{\mathsf{a}}_{>0}\mathsf{b})$. Then $(q_i, 0) \models \Phi$ and $(q'_i, 0) \not\models \Phi$ for any $i \geq 0$, but this contradicts $(q_i, 0) \equiv^{|\Phi|}_{\mathsf{TCTL}} (q'_i, 0)$ for any $i \geq |\Phi|$ provided by Lemma 4. □

3.2 $\mathsf{TCTL}^{\mathsf{a}} \prec \mathsf{TCTL}^{\mathsf{ext}}$

However, modality U^{a} is no help to express the classical U modality:

Theorem 6. $\mathsf{TCTL}^{\mathsf{ext}}$ *is strictly more expressive than* $\mathsf{TCTL}^{\mathsf{a}}$.

Proof. Let A be the automaton described in Figure 4. It can be easily proven that (q_0, t) and (q'_0, t) agree on the same $\mathsf{TCTL}^{\mathsf{a}}$ formulae. Indeed the only difference is that the state $(r'_0, 0)$ belongs to any run from q'_0. But this state has to be left immediately and then this position has a measure null along any run and cannot have an effect on the truth value of $\mathsf{TCTL}^{\mathsf{a}}$ formulae. □

4 Model-Checking $\mathsf{TCTL}^{\mathsf{ext}}$

We now address the model-checking problem for $\mathsf{TCTL}^{\mathsf{ext}}$: given a TA A and a formula $\Phi \in \mathsf{TCTL}^{\mathsf{ext}}$, we want to decide whether Φ holds for A or not. The number of states of the TTS $\mathcal{T}_A$ is infinite, we then use the standard *region graph* technique introduced by Alur, Courcoubetis and Dill [ACD93] for TCTL model-checking. This method consists in defining an equivalence $\cong$ over clocks valuations such that (1) (q, v) and (q, v') satisfy the same formulae when $v \cong v'$,

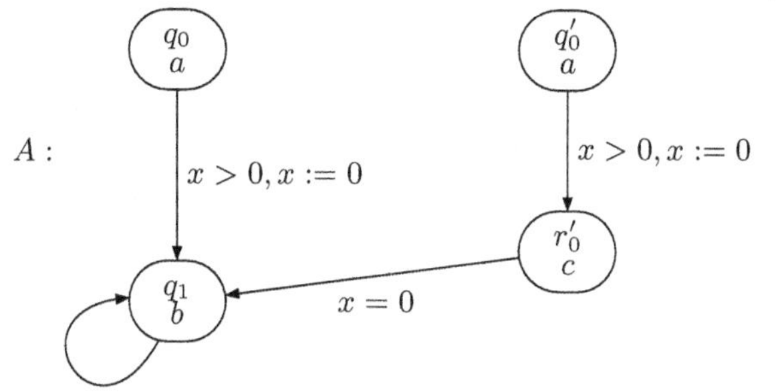

Fig. 4. $(q_0, 0) \models \mathsf{E}(a\mathsf{U}b)$, $(q'_0, 0) \not\models \mathsf{E}(a\mathsf{U}b)$, but $(q_0, 0) \equiv_{\mathsf{TCTL^a}} (q'_0, 0)$

and (2) the quotient $\mathbb{R}^X_{\geq 0}/\cong$ is finite. Then model-checking TCTL reduces to model-checking a CTL-like logic over a (finite) abstracted graph. This technique can be extended to $\mathsf{TCTL^{ext}}$ by using the same equivalence over valuations as the one used for TCTL.

Given A and some clock $x \in X$, we use $c_x \in \mathbb{N}$ to denote the maximal constant that x is compared with in the guards and invariants of A. Let $\cong$ be the following equivalence [AD90] over clocks valuations of $v, v' \in \mathbb{R}^X_{\geq 0}$: $v \cong v'$ iff (1) $\lfloor v(x) \rfloor = \lfloor v'(x) \rfloor \vee (v(x) > c_x \wedge v'(x) > c_x)$ for any $x \in X$, and (2) for any $x, y \in X$ s.t. $v(x) \leq c_x$ and $v(y) \leq c_y$, we have: $\mathsf{frac}(v(x)) \leq \mathsf{frac}(v(y)) \Leftrightarrow \mathsf{frac}(v'(x)) \leq \mathsf{frac}(v'(y))$ and $\mathsf{frac}(v(x)) = 0 \Leftrightarrow \mathsf{frac}(v'(x)) = 0$. This equivalence is of finite index. An equivalence class of $\cong$ is called a *region* and $[v]$ denotes the class of v. Now we can show that this equivalence is consistent with the truth values of $\mathsf{TCTL^{ext}}$ formulae:

Lemma 7. *Given a TA* $A = \langle X, Q_A, q_{init}, \rightarrow_A, \mathsf{Inv}_A, l_A \rangle$, $q \in Q_A$, *a formula* $\Phi \in \mathsf{TCTL^{ext}}$ *and* $v, v' \in \mathbb{R}^X_{\geq 0}$ *s.t.* $v \cong v'$, *we have:* $(q, v) \models \Phi \;\Leftrightarrow\; (q, v') \models \Phi$.

Proof (sketch). The proof follows the same steps as the corresponding one for TCTL. First, given a run $\rho \in \text{Exec}(q, v)$, we can build a run $\rho' \in \text{Exec}(q, v')$ where the same action transitions are taken at "almost" the same times and where the regions visited for a duration strictly positive are the same. Let $\rho \in \text{Exec}(q, v)$ be the run $(q_0, v_0) \xrightarrow{t_0}\rightarrow_a (q_1, v_1) \xrightarrow{t_1}\rightarrow_a \ldots$ with $q_0 = q$ and $v_0 = v$. Let $\delta_i = \sum_{j<i} t_j$ be the time at which the i-th action transition takes place, and $\delta_0 = 0$. Let v^*_i be the extended valuation over $X \cup \{\delta\}$ – where δ is a new symbol – defined by $v^*_i(x) = v_i(x)$ and $v^*_i(\delta) = \delta_i$. Now we consider the equivalence $\cong$ extended to valuations over $X \cup \{\delta\}$ by assuming $c_\delta = \infty$. Like in [ACD93], we can build a run $\rho' \in \text{Exec}(q, v')$ of the form $(q_0, v'_0) \xrightarrow{t'_0}\rightarrow_a (q_1, v'_1) \xrightarrow{t'_1}\rightarrow_a \ldots$ with $v'_0 = v'$ such that for any i we have: $v^*_i \cong v'^*_i$. This clearly entails that there is no strictly positive delay between the i-th and $(i+1)$-th action transitions in ρ iff there is no strictly positive delay between the i-th and $(i+1)$-th action transitions in ρ'.

We now prove the lemma by structural induction over the $\mathsf{TCTL^{ext}}$ formulae. Since the property holds for TCTL formulae, we only have to consider the $\mathsf{U^a}$ modalities.

Assume $(q,v) \models \mathsf{E}\varphi\mathsf{U}^{\mathsf{a}}_{\sim\mathsf{c}}\psi$ and assume that the truth value of φ and ψ are homogeneous over regions $(q,[u])$ (*i.e.* for any region γ, they hold for any valuation of γ, or for no valuation of γ). There exists some run $\rho \in \mathrm{Exec}(q,v)$ with a subrun σ s.t. : $\hat{\mu}(\sigma) > 0$, $\exists p \in \sigma$ s.t. $\mathsf{Time}(\rho^{\leq p}) \sim c$, $\forall p' \in \sigma$ we have $s_{p'} \models \psi$ and $\hat{\mu}(\{p' \mid p' <_\rho p \wedge s_{p'} \not\models \varphi\}) = 0$. Now consider a run ρ' corresponding to ρ as described above. Clearly there exists a subrun σ' in ρ' corresponding to the same regions as σ, and then these regions also satisfy ψ. Moreover, like for the TCTL case, there exists some position p' in ρ' s.t. $\mathsf{Time}(\rho'^{\leq p'}) \sim c \Leftrightarrow \mathsf{Time}(\rho^{\leq p}) \sim c$. The set of positions $\{p' \mid p' <_\rho p \wedge s_{p'} \not\models \varphi\}$ corresponds to a set of regions along ρ where no time elapses. In ρ' the same regions are visited and no delay transition occur. Then this set will also have a null measure. Thus $(q,v') \models \mathsf{E}\varphi\mathsf{U}^{\mathsf{a}}_{\sim\mathsf{c}}\psi$.
The same argument can be used for $\mathsf{A}\varphi\mathsf{U}^{\mathsf{a}}_{\sim\mathsf{c}}\psi$ because any run from (q,v) has a corresponding run from (q,v') and vice versa. □

Given some region $\gamma \in \mathbb{R}^X_{\geq 0}/\cong$, the *successor* region of γ, when it exists, is the region distinct from γ s.t. for any $v \in \gamma$, there exists some $t \in \mathbb{R}_{\geq 0}$ s.t. $v+t \in \mathsf{Succ}(\gamma)$ and $v+t' \in \gamma \cup \mathsf{Succ}(\gamma)$ for any $0 \leq t' < t$. We will write $\gamma(x) \sim c$ when any valuation v in γ satisfies $v(x) \sim c$. Finally the region $\gamma[r \leftarrow 0]$ denotes the region $[v[r \leftarrow 0]]$ for any $v \in \gamma$.

Model-checking $\mathsf{TCTL}^{\mathsf{ext}}$ reduces to a model-checking problem for a CTL-like logic over a finite graph, called the *region graph*. Let X^* be the set of clocks $X \cup \{x_\Phi\}$. The new clock x_Φ is used to handle subscripts $\sim c$ in U modalities, the value c_{x_Φ} is the maximal constant occurring in a subscript. For any subscript $\sim c$ in Φ we add new atomic propositions $p_{<c}$, $p_{>c}$ and $p_{=c}$, that hold for regions γ s.t. $\gamma(x_\Phi) \sim c$. Let p_b be another proposition that holds for *boundary regions*: $\gamma \models p_b$ iff there is some clock $x \in X^*$ with $\mathsf{frac}(x) = 0$ in γ. Let $\mathsf{AP}^+ = \mathsf{AP} \cup \{p_b, p_{<c}, \ldots\}$ be the extended set of atomic propositions.

We can now recall the region graph of [ACD93]: For a TA $A = \langle X, Q_A, q_{\mathrm{init}}, \rightarrow_A, \mathsf{Inv}_A, l_A \rangle$ and a $\mathsf{TCTL}^{\mathsf{ext}}$ formula Φ, the region graph $\mathcal{R}_{A,\Phi}$ is the finite fair graph $(V, \rightarrow, l, F)$ with:

- $V = \{(q,\gamma) \mid q \in Q_A \text{ and } \gamma \in \mathbb{R}^{X^*}_{\geq 0}/\cong\}$
- The set of transitions $\rightarrow = \rightarrow_t \cup \rightarrow_a$ contains two kinds of transitions:
  - $(q,\gamma) \rightarrow_t (q, \mathsf{Succ}(\gamma))$ if $\mathsf{Succ}(\gamma) \models \mathsf{Inv}_A(q)$.
  - $(q,\gamma) \rightarrow_a (q,\gamma')$ s.t. there exists $q \xrightarrow{g,r}_A q'$ with $\gamma \models g$, $\gamma' = \gamma[r \leftarrow 0]$ and $\gamma' \models \mathsf{Inv}_A(q')$.
- $l : V \rightarrow 2^{\mathsf{AP}^+}$ labels the vertices with the atomic propositions it satisfies: $l(q,\gamma)$ contains $l_A(q)$ and the propositions for γ.
- F is a set of fairness constraints: $F = \{F_x \mid x \in X^*\}$ with $F_x = \{(q,\gamma) \mid \gamma(x) = 0 \vee \gamma(x) > c_x\}$. A fair path in $\mathcal{R}_{A,\Phi}$ has to visit infinitely often a configuration in F_x for any $x \in X^*$.

We now define $\mathcal{R}^+_{A,\Phi}$ an extension of $\mathcal{R}_{A,\Phi}$ where we consider the transitive closure of $\rightarrow_a$: $\mathcal{R}^+_{A,\Phi} = (V, \rightarrow, l, F)$ where V, l and F are defined as for $\mathcal{R}_{A,\Phi}$, and $\rightarrow = \rightarrow_t \cup \rightarrow^+_a$. Then an action transition in $\mathcal{R}^+_{A,\Phi}$ $(q,\gamma) \rightarrow^+_a (q',\gamma')$ corresponds to a sequence of action transitions in A which can be performed with no delay in between. Note that all the intermediate configurations along such a sequence are visited but the set of their positions is of measure 0 w.r.t. $\hat{\mu}$. We call these configurations *transient* configurations, and more formally, a configuration along a run ρ is non-transient iff its region is non-boundary and the previous or the next transition on ρ is a delay transition (a strictly positive delay has to elapse in the state along ρ). We will use this extended region graph when looking for the existence of a run satisfying $\varphi \mathsf{U}^{\mathsf{a}}_{\sim c} \psi$ because we do not need to consider such intermediate transient configuration.

We reduce model-checking $\mathsf{TCTL}^{\mathsf{ext}}$ to model-checking CTL over $\mathcal{R}^+_{A,\Phi}$. We will use the classical $\mathsf{E}\_\mathsf{U}\_$ and $\mathsf{A}\_\mathsf{U}\_$ operators where E and A deal with paths in $\mathcal{R}_{A,\Phi}$, whereas E^+ and A^+ deal with paths in $\mathcal{R}^+_{A,\Phi}$, that is when transitions corresponding to transitive closure of action transitions in $\mathcal{R}_{A,\Phi}$ are allowed. Finally we also assume that for any state (q,γ) of $\mathcal{R}_{A,\Phi}$, there is a fair path rooted at (q,γ).

It remains to describe a labeling procedure to label every state of $\mathcal{R}_{A,\Phi}$ with the Φ-subformulae it satisfies. This is done by adapting the procedure for the TCTL case [ACD93], using the graphs $\mathcal{R}_{A,\Phi}$ and $\mathcal{R}^+_{A,\Phi}$. For example, in the case of formula $\mathsf{EG}^{\mathsf{a}}_{\leq c}\varphi$, a state (q,γ) is labeled by $\mathsf{EG}^{\mathsf{a}}_{\leq c}\varphi$ iff $(q,\gamma[x_\Phi \leftarrow 0])$ satisfies the CTL formula:

$$\mathsf{E}^+(p_b \vee \varphi)\mathsf{U}\Big(p_{=c} \wedge \big((\varphi \wedge \mathsf{EX}p_{>c}) \vee \mathsf{EX}(p_{>c} \wedge \varphi)\big)\Big)$$

where the next operator (EX) ensures that the position for which the right-hand side of the Until has to hold, is the last position at duration $= c$ along a run.

This leads to the following result:

Theorem 8. *Given a TA A and a* $\mathsf{TCTL}^{\mathsf{ext}}$ *formula* Φ*, deciding whether* Φ *holds for A is a PSPACE-complete problem.*

5 Conclusion

In this work, we studied the extension $\mathsf{TCTL}^{\mathsf{ext}}$ of the classical logic TCTL, obtained by introducing a new modality $\mathsf{U}^{\mathsf{a}}_{\sim c}$. The superscript a means "almost everywhere" and expresses the fact that a property must be true except on a negligible set of positions. We proved that this modality cannot be expressed by the classical ones, and conversely. We also proposed a model-checking procedure for $\mathsf{TCTL}^{\mathsf{ext}}$, with the same complexity result than TCTL, where the classical constructions must be adapted to take into account the set of negligible positions on a run. Further work could consist in extending this new modality for the verification of "permanent" properties, *i.e.* properties that hold on an sufficiently large interval, the length of which could be a parameter.

References

[ABBL03] L. Aceto, P. Bouyer, A. Burgueño, and K.G. Larsen. The power of reachability testing for timed automata. *Theoretical Computer Science*, 300(1–3):411–475, 2003.

[ACD93] R. Alur, C. Courcoubetis, and D. Dill. Model-checking in dense real-time. *Information and Computation*, 104(1):2–34, 1993.

[AD90] R. Alur and D. Dill. Automata for modeling real-time systems. In *Proc. 17th International Colloquium on Automata, Languages and Programming (ICALP'90)*, vol. 443 of *LNCS*, pp. 322–335. Springer, 1990.

[AD94] R. Alur and D. Dill. A theory of timed automata. *Theoretical Computer Science*, 126(2):183–235, 1994.

[AFH96] R. Alur, T. Feder, and T.A. Henzinger. The benefits of relaxing punctuality. *Journal of the ACM*, 43(1):116–146, 1996.

[AH92] R. Alur and T.A. Henzinger. Logics and models of real-time: a survey. In *Real-Time: Theory in Practice, Proc. REX Workshop 1991*, vol. 600 of *LNCS*, pp. 74–106. Springer, 1992.

[BMBBL05] H. Bel Mokadem, B. Bérard, P. Bouyer, and F. Laroussinie. A new modality for almost everywhere properties in timed automata. Research Report LSV-05-06, LSV, ENS de Cachan, France, 2005.

[BFKM03] B. Bérard, L. Fribourg, F. Klay, and J.-F. Monin. A compared study of two correctness proofs for the standardized algorithm of abr conformance. *Formal Methods in System Design*, 22(1):59–86, 2003.

[DOTY96] C. Daws, A. Olivero, S. Tripakis, and S. Yovine. The tool KRONOS. In *Proc. Hybrid Systems III: Verification and Control (1995)*, vol. 1066 of *LNCS*, pp. 208–219. Springer, 1996.

[EH86] E.A. Emerson and J.Y. Halpern. "Sometimes" and "not never" revisited: On branching versus linear time temporal logic. *Journal of the ACM*, 33(1):151–178, 1986.

[Eme91] E.A. Emerson. *Temporal and Modal Logic*, vol. B (Formal Models and Semantics) of *Handbook of Theoretical Computer Science*, pp. 995–1072. MIT Press Cambridge, 1991.

[HHWT95] T.A. Henzinger, P.-H. Ho, and H. Wong-Toi. HyTech: the next generation. In *Proc. 16th IEEE Real-Time Systems Symposium (RTSS'95)*, pp. 56–65. IEEE Computer Society Press, 1995.

[HNSY94] T.A. Henzinger, X. Nicollin, J. Sifakis, and Sergio Yovine. Symbolic model-checking for real-time systems. *Information and Computation*, 111(2):193–244, 1994.

[IEC93] IEC (International Electrotechnical Commission). *IEC Standard 61131-3: Programmable controllers - Part 3*, 1993.

[LLW95] F. Laroussinie, K.G. Larsen, and C. Weise. From timed automata to logic – and back. In *Proc. 20th International Symposium on Mathematical Foundations of Computer Science (MFCS'95)*, vol. 969 of *LNCS*, pp. 529–539. Springer, 1995.

[LPY97] K.G. Larsen, P. Pettersson, and W. Yi. UPPAAL in a nutshell. *Journal of Software Tools for Technology Transfer*, 1(1–2):134–152, 1997.

The Coarsest Congruence for Timed Automata with Deadlines Contained in Bisimulation*

Pedro R. D'Argenio[1,**] and Biniam Gebremichael[2]

[1] CONICET – FaMAF, Universidad Nacional de Córdoba, Ciudad Universitaria, 5000 Córdoba, Argentina
[2] Institute for Computing and Information Sciences. Radboud University Nijmegen, P.O. Box 9010, 6500 GL Nijmegen, The Netherlands
dargenio@famaf.unc.edu.ar
B.Gebremichael@cs.ru.nl

Abstract. Delaying the synchronization of actions may reveal some hidden behavior that would not happen if the synchronization met the specified deadlines. This precise phenomenon makes bisimulation fail to be a congruence for the parallel composition of timed automata with deadlines, a variant of timed automata where time progress is controlled by deadlines imposed on each transition. This problem has been known and unsolved for several years. In this paper we give a characterization of the coarsest congruence that is included in the bisimulation relation. In addition, a symbolic characterization of such relation is provided and shown to be decidable. We also discuss the pitfalls of existing parallel compositions in this setting and argue that our definition is both reasonable and sufficiently expressive as to consider the modeling of both soft and hard real-time constraints.

1 Introduction

Design and specification languages allow to model systems in a modular manner by linking small modules or components using the language operations —such as the sequential composition or the parallel composition— in order to build larger modules. Hence a desirable requirement is that the language is *compositional* with respect to its semantics. By compositional we mean that components can be replaced by behaviorally equivalent components without changing the properties of the larger model in which they are embedded. The preservation of such properties can be guaranteed by means of semantic equivalences or preorders. For example branching bisimulation preserves CTL* [11], language inclusion preserves LTL [22] and, in particular, timed bisimulation preserves (timed) properties expressed in logics such as TCTL [27]. Hence, compositionality amounts to requiring that relations like these are *congruences* (or precongruences) for the different operations of the language.

Timed automata [1,18] are used to model real-time systems and have become popular as modeling language for several model checkers because of its simplicity and tractability [2,9,10]. Timed automata are automata with the additional ingredients of

* Supported by the EC project IST-2001-35304 AMETIST, URL: ametist.cs.utwente.nl.
** Also at Formal Methods and Tools, Dep. of Comp. Sci. University of Twente. Supported by the NWO Vernieuwingsimpuls and the ANPCyT project PICT 11-11738.

M. Abadi and L. de Alfaro (Eds.): CONCUR 2005, LNCS 3653, pp. 125–140, 2005.

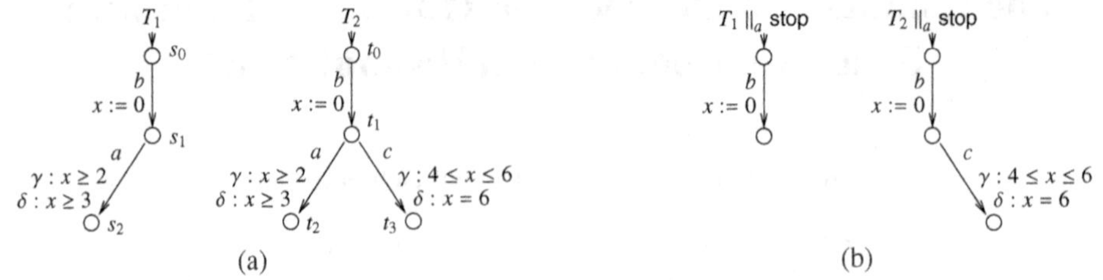

Fig. 1. TAD and compositionality

clocks. Clocks are variables that increase at the same rate in order to register time progress. Transitions are labeled with constraints on clocks, called *guards*, that indicate when such transition *may* take place. Usually timed automata are used to model real-time systems with *hard* constraints. In this cases, timed automata are equipped with an *invariant*, which is a constraint on clocks that limits time progress in each control state [18]: the system is obliged to leave such state before invalidating the invariant.

Because of the nature of invariants, time is allowed to progress in the composed timed automaton only if time is allowed to progress in all component automata. Therefore, if one of the automaton fails to meet the deadline imposed by a partner in a synchronisation, then the entire system crashes (which is represented by the so called *time deadlock*: the composed system has reached a state where time is blocked forever). This is the nature of hard deadlines. But it is debatable whether hard deadlines are always appropriate to model synchronisation in real-time systems. An alternative composition is, a composition with *soft* deadlines that allows the fast partner to wait the slow partner if nothing else is possible. In this case the deadlines can be violated, but the synchronisation is performed urgently whenever possible.

Timed automata with deadlines (TAD for short) [26,7,5,6] were introduced for these reasons. Parallel compositions with hard and soft deadlines as well as urgency can be naturally defined in TAD. At the same time, the TAD model ensures, under reasonable assumption, what is called time reactivity in [6] and time lock freedom in [8], that is, whenever time progress stops there exists at least one transition enabled. (Note that time reactivity and hard constraints are not fully compatible.) This model is nowadays embedded in modeling languages such as IF [10] and MoDeST [16,4], and urgent transitions in UPPAAL [3] can be seen as a particular instance of TAD transitions.

TADs do not have invariants. Instead, a TAD transition has associated a second clock constraint, called *deadline*, that indicates in which moment such transition *must* be taken. As a consequence, a deadline is required to hold *only if* the corresponding guard holds ensuring the transition can be taken after the deadline is reached. In this sense, the deadline impose an *urgency constraint*.

Contrary to the traditional timed automata setting, bisimulation in the TAD model *is not* preserved by parallel composition [6]. This is illustrated in the following example. T_1 in Fig. 1.(a) depicts a TAD in which circles represent control state and arrows are control transitions. In particular the small incoming arrow identifies the initial state. T_1 performs first an action b at any moment and sets clock x to 0. As time progresses, the value of x increases and when it takes value 2 action a becomes enabled. This is controlled by guard $\gamma : x \geq 2$. At any point after x takes value 2, this transition may take place, but as time continues to progress and x takes value 3, the deadline $\delta : x \geq 3$ obliges the execution of the transition. Notice that T_2 shows a similar behavior since action c cannot be executed: the deadline of a obliges its execution before the guard of c becomes enabled. In fact, T_1 and T_2 are timed bisimilar in the sense of [6].

Suppose now that T_1 is composed in parallel with the automaton stop requiring synchronization on action a. (stop is the automaton with a single location and no transition; hence, it does not do anything but idling.) This blocks the execution of action a in T_1. The resulting automaton $T_1 \parallel_a \mathsf{stop}$ is depicted in Fig. 1.(b). Similarly, the composition of T_2 with stop in $T_2 \parallel_a \mathsf{stop}$ also blocks the execution of a, but in this case time progresses beyond 3 time units allowing the execution of c after 4 time units (see Fig. 1.(b)). As a consequence $T_1 \parallel_a \mathsf{stop}$ and $T_2 \parallel_a \mathsf{stop}$ are not bisimilar.

To the best of our knowledge there is no characterization of a congruence for parallel composition on TADs. The only exception is what is called strong congruence in [6], which is the usual bisimulation applied directly on TADs. This relation is, however, far too strong as it requires the syntactic equality of guards, deadlines, and clock resets.

In this paper we present a congruence relation for parallel composition and prove that it is the coarsest congruence included in the bisimulation relation. This new relation, which we call ∇-bisimulation (read "drop-bisimulation"), is in fact the usual bisimulation on an extended semantics of TAD. Such semantics allows for time progressing beyond deadlines but carefully accounting the actions whose deadline have been overruled. We also give a symbolic characterization of ∇-bisimulation, that is, a relation defined directly on TADs. As a corollary of this characterization we obtain that ∇-bisimulation is decidable. Another particular contribution of this paper is that the proof of congruence is entirely carried out at symbolic level (i.e., without resorting to the underlying transition system in which ∇-bisimulation is defined). We finally discuss different kind of parallel compositions on TADs (mostly defined already in the literature) reporting which of them preserves ∇-bisimulation and which do not and why.

Related Work. The failure of bisimulation to be a congruence becomes apparent when soft deadlines are considered, that is actions that may be urgent in isolation are required to wait if they are intended for synchronization i.e. synchronizing actions need to be *patient*. This problem has appeared in the context of stochastic process algebra where synchronization is required to be patient (e.g. [20,19,14]). It becomes evident (in a similar manner as above) if bisimulation is considered for the underlying probabilistic transition system rather than for the finer symbolic model [14]. The problem of compositionality also showed up in other process algebras for performance behavior [13].

In [21], compositionality is studied on timed automata with urgent actions w.r.t. simulation. (An urgent action corresponds to an action in TADs for which guard and deadline are the same.) In this case, it suffices to add a condition of readiness on the urgent actions to achieve precongruence. Recently, [17] defined a variant of TADs where actions are distinguished between input and output following the model of [25] and for which bisimulation *is* a congruence for the parallel composition. This is possible due to input enabling and to the fact that only output actions are allowed to be urgent (i.e. to have deadline.) Therefore there is no need to wait for synchronization as it is always possible. Though the restrictions imposed by [17] makes the new model much simpler and tractable, using it to describe soft real-time systems may result in complex models.

In addition to the solution for the compositionality problem, we also give a symbolic characterization of the congruence. Our work is based on the result of Lin & Yi [23] who gave a symbolic characterization of the bisimulation for timed automata. In turn, their result is based on Čerāns' who determined that bisimulation for timed automata is decidable [12]. We use also this result to show the decidability of the ∇-bisimulation.

Paper Outline. The paper is organized as follows. Section 2 gives the preliminaries recalling timed automata with deadlines, its semantics in terms of transition systems, the definition of bisimulation, and particularly, the definition of parallel composition. In Section 3 we discuss the pitfalls of the composition and progressively construct the semantics that leads to the definition of ∇-bisimulation. The symbolic characterization is provided in Section 4 and shown to be the coarsest congruence in Section 5. We conclude in Section 6 discussing decidability of ∇-bisimulation and the different kind of synchronization in parallel composition. A full version of this paper appeared as [15].

2 Preliminaries

Timed Automata with Deadlines. A *clock* is a non-negative real-valued variable, which can be reset to zero at the occurrence of an event, and between two resets, its derivative with respect to time is equal to 1. We denote $C = \{x_1, \ldots, x_N\}$ to be a finite set of clocks. A *clock constraint* $\mathcal{F}(C)$ is a conjunction of formula(s) of atomic constraints in the form of $x_i \bowtie n$ or $x_i - x_j \bowtie m$, where x_i and x_j are clocks in C, $\bowtie \in \{<, >, \leq, \geq, =\}$ and n, m are natural numbers. The constraints **tt** and **ff** are used to denote, respectively, the atomic constraints which are constantly true and false. We will assume that there is a global finite set of actions $\mathcal{A}$ for all timed automata with deadlines.

Definition 1. *A* timed automaton with deadlines *[6] (TAD for short) is a structure $T = (\mathcal{L}, \mathsf{l}^0, C, \twoheadrightarrow)$ where (i) $\mathcal{L}$ is a finite set of locations, (ii) $\mathsf{l}^0 \subseteq \mathcal{L}$ is the set of initial locations, (iii) C is a finite set of clocks, (iv) $\twoheadrightarrow \subseteq \mathcal{L} \times (\mathcal{A} \times \mathcal{F}(C) \times \mathcal{F}(C) \times 2^C) \times \mathcal{L}$, is a finite set of edges. If $(s, a, \gamma, \delta, \mathbf{x}, s') \in \twoheadrightarrow$ we write $s \xrightarrow{a,\gamma,\delta,\mathbf{x}} s'$ and require that $\delta \Rightarrow \gamma$ holds, moreover we assume δ is left-closed (left-closure is formally defined in Def. 2).*

The notion $s \xrightarrow{a,\gamma,\delta,\mathbf{x}} s'$ represents an edge from location s to s' that executes action a whenever *guard* γ becomes true. In addition, *deadline* predicate δ impose an urgency condition: the transition cannot be delayed whenever δ is satisfied. When executing the transition, clocks in $\mathbf{x}$ are set to 0.

Parallel Composition of TADs. Parallel composition allows the independent execution of the activity of the component automata except if they are intended to synchronize. We assume CSP synchronization in which actions with equal name synchronize if and only if they belong to a set of *synchronizing actions* $B \subseteq \mathcal{A}$. Since enabling of actions is determined by guards, we define the guard on the synchronized transition to be the conjunction of the guards on the synchronizing transitions. Therefore synchronization takes place only if both partners are able to execute the same synchronizing action. (Other compositions of guards are discussed in Sec. 6). Similarly, the deadlines of the synchronizing transitions should affect the deadline of the synchronization. In this case, we do not fix any particular operation. Instead, we assume a given operator $\otimes$ that, when applied to guards and deadlines of the synchronizing transitions, returns the deadline of the synchronization. We require that $\otimes$ satisfies the following:

1. $(\delta_1, \gamma_1) \otimes (\delta_2, \gamma_2) \Rightarrow (\gamma_1 \wedge \gamma_2)$ whenever $\delta_1 \Rightarrow \gamma_1$ and $\delta_2 \Rightarrow \gamma_2$
2. $\otimes$ preserves *left-closure*, that is, if δ_1 and δ_2 are left closed, so is $(\delta_1, \gamma_1) \otimes (\delta_2, \gamma_2)$
3. $\otimes$ distributes with respect to $\vee$ in all its arguments, that is $\left(\bigvee_i \left(\delta_1^i, \gamma_1^i\right) \otimes \left(\delta_2^i, \gamma_2^i\right)\right) \Leftrightarrow \left(\bigvee_i \delta_1^i, \bigvee_i \gamma_1^i\right) \otimes \left(\bigvee_i \delta_2^i, \bigvee_i \gamma_2^i\right)$
4. There exists a constraint $\mathbf{0}_\delta$ such that $(\mathbf{0}_\delta, \mathbf{tt})$ acts as a neutral element for $\otimes$ in the following sense: $((\delta_1, \gamma_1) \otimes (\mathbf{0}_\delta, \mathbf{tt})) \Leftrightarrow \delta_1$

$(\delta_1, \gamma_1) \otimes (\delta_2, \gamma_2)$ has to imply the guard $\gamma_1 \wedge \gamma_2$ of the resulting transition in order to preserve this property on the composed TAD. This is required in 1. Similarly, condition 2 ensures that deadlines of the composed TAD are left-closed. The distributivity of 3 is needed to prove congruence (see proof of Theorem 2). As we will see in the next section, time passage in a location is limited by the complement of the disjunction of the outgoing deadlines. Therefore condition 3 states compositionality for $\otimes$, allowing to represent the deadline of a synchronized action in terms of the deadlines and guards of the component automata. Constraint 4 is only necessary to show that our definition is the coarsest congruence included in the bisimulation (see Lemma 6). For operators not meeting this condition there may exist coarser congruences than ours that are also bisimulation. Constraint 4 guarantees a way to test the validity of the original deadline in a component's transition by means of a synchronization. In Sec. 6 we discuss different implementations of $\otimes$.

Let $T_i = (\mathcal{L}_i, \mathsf{l}^0{}_i, C_i, \twoheadrightarrow_i)$, such that $C_1 \cap C_2 = \emptyset$ for $i \in \{1,2\}$, and let $B \subseteq \mathcal{A}$ be a set of *synchronizing actions*, and $\otimes$ be an operation for synchronizing deadlines. The *parallel composition* $T_1 \parallel_B^\otimes T_2$ is defined by the TAD $(\mathcal{L}_1 \times \mathcal{L}_2, \mathsf{l}^0{}_1 \times \mathsf{l}^0{}_2, C_1 \cup C_2, \twoheadrightarrow)$ where $\twoheadrightarrow$ is defined as the smallest relation satisfying:

$$\frac{s_i \xrightarrow{a,\gamma,\delta,\mathbf{x}}_i s_i' \quad s_j = s_j' \quad \{i,j\}=\{1,2\} \quad a \notin B}{(s_1, s_2) \xrightarrow{a,\gamma,\delta,\mathbf{x}} (s_1', s_2')} \qquad \frac{s_1 \xrightarrow{a,\gamma_1,\delta_2,\mathbf{x}_1}_1 s_1' \quad s_2 \xrightarrow{a,\gamma_2,\delta_2,\mathbf{x}_2}_2 s_2' \quad a \in B}{(s_1, s_2) \xrightarrow{a,\gamma_1 \wedge \gamma_2,(\delta_1,\gamma_1)\otimes(\delta_2,\gamma_2),\mathbf{x}_1 \cup \mathbf{x}_2} (s_1', s_2')}$$

The rules are fairly standard. Notice, in particular, that the last rule only allows to synchronize guards when both of them are valid. This is a significant restriction w.r.t. [6]. We later argue that this is nevertheless reasonable and discuss the feasibility of compositions not consider here. From now on, subscripts on edges will be omited.

Transition Systems and Bisimulation. A *transition system (TS for short)* is a structure $TS = (\mathcal{S}, \mathsf{s}^0, \Sigma, \longrightarrow)$ where $\mathcal{S}$ is an infinite set of states, s^0 is the set of initial states, Σ is a set of labels, and $\longrightarrow \subseteq (\mathcal{S} \times \Sigma \times \mathcal{S})$ is a set of transitions. Since we use TSs to model timed systems, we consider two kind of labels: those representing the execution of discrete actions and those representing the passage of time. Then $\Sigma = \mathcal{A} \cup \mathbb{R}_{\geq 0}$.

A *bisimulation* [24] is a symmetric relation $R \in \mathcal{S} \times \mathcal{S}$ such that for all $a \in \Sigma$, whenever $(p,q) \in R$ and $p \xrightarrow{a} p'$ then $q \xrightarrow{a} q'$ and $(p', q') \in R$ for some q'. We write $p \sim q$ if $(p,q) \in R$ for some bisimulation relation R on TS. Given two TSs TS_1 and TS_2 with set of initial states $\mathsf{s}^0{}_1$ and $\mathsf{s}^0{}_2$, respectively, we say that they are bisimilar (notation $TS_1 \sim TS_2$) if there is a bisimulation R in the disjoint union of $TS_1 \uplus TS_2$ such that $s^0{}_j \subseteq R(s^0{}_i)$ for $\{i, j\} = \{1, 2\}$, i.e. every initial state of TS_1 is related to some initial state of TS_2 and vice-versa.

Semantics of TADs. In the following we recall the semantics of TADs in terms of TSs. A state of the timed system is divided in two parts, one indicating the current control location in the TAD, and the other the current time values. This last part is represented by means of a *clock valuation* which is a function $\rho : C \to \mathbb{R}_{\geq 0}$ mapping to each clock the time elapsed since the last time it was reset to 0. Given a clock valuation ρ and $d \in \mathbb{R}_{\geq 0}$ the function $\rho + d$ denotes the valuation such that for each clock $x \in C$, $(\rho + d)(x) = \rho(x) + d$. The function $\rho\{\mathbf{x}{:=}0\}$ denotes the valuation such that for each clock $x \in \mathbf{x} \cap C$, $\rho\{\mathbf{x}{:=}0\}(x) = 0$, otherwise $\rho\{\mathbf{x}{:=}0\}(x) = \rho(x)$. We first define what it means for a constraint to be left-closed, followed by the semantics of TADs.

Definition 2. *A constraint ϕ is called* left closed *if and only if for all valuations ρ, $\rho \models \neg\phi \;\Rightarrow\; \exists\varepsilon > 0 : \forall\varepsilon' \leq \varepsilon : \rho + \varepsilon' \models \neg\phi$.*

Definition 3. *Let $T = (\mathcal{L}, \mathsf{l}^0, C, \dashrightarrow)$ be a TAD. Its semantics is given by $TS(T) = (\mathcal{L} \times (C \mapsto \mathbb{R}_{\geq 0}), \mathsf{l}^0 \times (C \mapsto 0), \mathcal{A} \cup \mathbb{R}_{\geq 0}, \longrightarrow)$, where $\longrightarrow$ is the smallest relation satisfying:*

A1: discrete transition $s \xrightarrow{a,\gamma,\delta,\mathbf{x}} s'$ *and* $\rho \models \gamma$ *implies* $s\rho \xrightarrow{a} s'\rho\{\mathbf{x}{:=}0\}$; *and*

A2: delay transition $\forall d' < d : \rho + d' \models tpc(s)$ *implies* $s\rho \xrightarrow{d} s(\rho + d)$

where $tpc(s) = \neg \bigvee\{\delta \mid \exists a, \gamma, \mathbf{x}, s' : s \xrightarrow{a,\gamma,\delta,\mathbf{x}} s'\}$ *is the* time progress condition *in* s.

Rule **A1** states that an edge $s \xrightarrow{a,\gamma,\delta,\mathbf{x}} s'$ defines a discrete transition in current location s whenever the guard holds in current valuation ρ. After the transition is taken clocks in $\mathbf{x}$ are set to 0 in the new valuation. According to **A2**, time can progress in s only when $tpc(s)$ is true, that is as long as no deadline of an edge leaving s becomes true. Notice that $tpc(s)$ is required to hold for all $d' < d$ but not for d itself. Therefore it is indistinguishable whether $tpc(s)$ holds in the limit or not. For instance, if $\rho(x) = 0$ both $x < 3$ and $x \leq 3$ hold in all $\rho + d'$ with $d' < 3$. Thus our assumption that deadline has to be specified as left-closed predicate is not a limitation but a preference to avoid technical complications which do not contribute to the work.

As a consequence of Def. 3 the notion of bisimulation extends to TADs straightforwardly: two TADs T_1 and T_2 are bisimilar (notation $T_1 \sim T_2$) if $TS(T_1) \sim TS(T_2)$.

Example. Consider automata T_1 and T_2 of Fig. 1. Using Def. 3 it is routine to check that relation $\{(s_0\{x{:=}d\}, t_0\{x{:=}d\}) \mid 0 \leq d\} \cup \{(s_1\{x{:=}d\}, t_1\{x{:=}d\}) \mid 0 \leq d \leq 3\} \cup \{(s_2\{x{:=}d\}, t_2\{x{:=}d\}) \mid 2 \leq d\}$ is a bisimulation witnessing $T_1 \sim T_2$. Besides, if $\mathsf{stop} = (\{r\}, \{r\}, \varnothing, \varnothing)$, then $T_2 \mathbin{\|_a^{\circledast}} \mathsf{stop}$ can execute the trace $b\,5\,c$, which is not possible in $(s_0, r)\{x{:=}0\}$. Consequently, $T_1 \mathbin{\|_a^{\circledast}} \mathsf{stop} \not\sim T_2 \mathbin{\|_a^{\circledast}} \mathsf{stop}$.

3 Towards a Congruence Relation

In the following we discuss different proposals for congruence until finding a satisfactory definition. All proposals are bisimulation relations on different modifications of the transition system underlying the TAD.

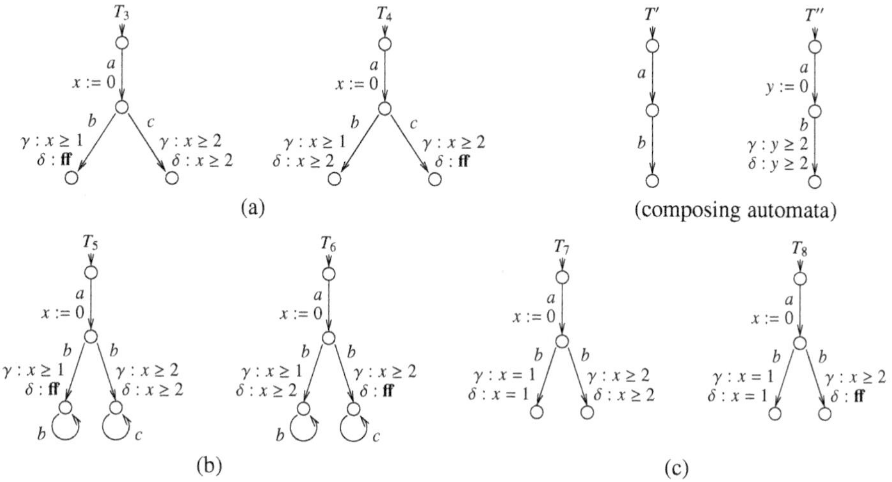

Fig. 2. (Counter)examples for congruence

The example in Fig. 1 suggests that action c could be distinguished if time would be allowed to elapse beyond the deadline. Therefore, a first naive proposal would be to let time progress beyond the time progress condition but this would not be compatible with the bisimulation since TADs with different deadlines but equal guards may become equated. So, a modification of this semantics could consider separately a potential time progress by adding a new kind of transition: $s\rho \xrightarrow{[d]} s(\rho + d)$ for all $d \geq 0$. Though clearly stronger than bisimulation —notice that it would distinguish T_1 and T_2 in Fig. 1— it fails to be a congruence. This is shown in Fig. 2(a). The relation would equate T_3 and T_4, but not their compositions $T_3 \mathbin{\|^{\circledast}_{B}} T'$ and $T_4 \mathbin{\|^{\circledast}_{B}} T'$ with $B = \{a, b, c\}$. Notice that after realization of action a, $T_3 \mathbin{\|^{\circledast}_{B}} T'$ lets (non-potential) time progress beyond 2 time units while this is not possible in $T_4 \mathbin{\|^{\circledast}_{B}} T'$ due to the deadline in b.

As a consequence, we may think to consider different potential time progress transition for each edge in the TAD, but this turns to be too strong (apart from cumbersome). See automata T_5 and T_6 in Fig. 2(b) which share some similitude with the previous example, only that c has been renamed to b. They are expected to be congruent.

The new example suggests that time can potentially progress differently for every action name since they can be delayed or preempted independently. A possible solution seems to consider a different kind of potential time progress for each action. Since time progress is associated to deadlines, we follow a different approach: instead of considering potential time progress, we consider a new type of discrete action ∇_D, $D \subseteq \mathcal{A}$, that indicates that from the moment action ∇_D is issued, deadlines of actions in D would be disregarded. We call this type of action "drop" (since it drops the deadline). Notice that a drop action can be performed at any moment.

Let $\mathcal{A}_\nabla = \{\nabla_D \mid D \subseteq \mathcal{A}\}$. To keep track of which deadlines have to be disregarded, states also need to book keep the current set of actions whose deadlines were dropped. The extended semantics of $T = (\mathcal{L}, l^0, C, \twoheadrightarrow)$ is then given by the TS $(\mathcal{L} \times 2^{\mathcal{A}} \times (C \mapsto \mathbb{R}_{\geq 0}), l^0 \times \{\varnothing\} \times (C \mapsto 0), \mathcal{A} \cup \mathcal{A}_\nabla \cup \mathbb{R}_{\geq 0}, \longrightarrow)$, where $\longrightarrow$ is the smallest relation satisfying:

A1$_\nabla$: discrete transition $s \xrightarrow{a,\gamma,\delta,\mathbf{x}} s'$ and $\rho \models \gamma$ implies $(s, D)\rho \xrightarrow{a} (s', \emptyset)\rho\{\mathbf{x}{:=}0\}$
A2$_\nabla$: delay transition $\forall d'{<}d : \rho{+}d' \models \neg dl(s, \mathcal{A} - D)$ implies $(s, D)\rho \xrightarrow{d} (s, D)(\rho{+}d)$
A3: drop transition $(s, D)\rho \xrightarrow{\nabla_E} (s, D \cup E)\rho$

where $dl(s, A)$ is the deadline collected by actions in $A \subseteq \mathcal{A}$ in location s and is defined by $dl(s, A) = \bigvee\{\delta \mid s \xrightarrow{a,\gamma,\delta,\mathbf{x}} s'$ and $a \in A$ for some $a, \gamma, \mathbf{x}, s'\}$. Bisimulation in this new semantics distinguishes automata in Figs. 1(a) and 2(a), and equates those in Fig. 2(b). Regarding to the new predicate $dl(s, A)$ notice that for any location s, $tpc(s) = \neg dl(s, \mathcal{A})$.

Notice that once a deadline is dropped, it cannot be observed anymore. Example in Fig. 2(c) shows that this semantics does not yet yields a congruence. According to this semantics T_7 and T_8 are equated. However, under the assumption that deadlines of synchronizing transitions are arranged in a conjunction (i.e. $\otimes$ is $\wedge$), the compositions $T_7 \parallel_B^\otimes T''$ and $T_8 \parallel_B^\otimes T''$, with $B = \{a, b\}$, are distinguished by the usual bisimulation: after executing action a, $T_8 \parallel_B^\otimes T''$ let time progress beyond 2 time units while this is not the case in $T_7 \parallel_B^\otimes T''$ due to the composed deadline $(x \geq 2) \wedge (y \geq 2)$ in b.

This phenomenon is due to the fact that after action a is performed, automaton T'' *temporarily* disregard the deadline of b during the first 2 units of time, but later it allows to observe it again. As a consequence, we introduce a new action Δ (read "undrop") which indicates that in the future all deadlines will be consider again.

Definition 4. *The extended semantics of* $T = (\mathcal{L}, l^0, C, \twoheadrightarrow)$ *is given by* $TS_\nabla(T) = (\mathcal{L} \times 2^{\mathcal{A}} \times (C \mapsto \mathbb{R}_{\geq 0}), l^0 \times \{\emptyset\} \times (C \mapsto 0), \mathcal{A} \cup \mathcal{A}_\nabla \cup \{\Delta\} \cup \mathbb{R}_{\geq 0}, \longrightarrow)$*, where* $\longrightarrow$ *is the smallest relation satisfying* **A1$_\nabla$**, **A2$_\nabla$**, *and* **A3** *above plus*

A4: undrop transition $(s, D)\rho \xrightarrow{\Delta} (s', \emptyset)\rho$

Notice that the undrop action can be performed at any moment. Notice also that the execution sequence $a\, \nabla_{\{b\}}\, 2\, \Delta\, 1$ is possible in T_8 but not in T_7. Hence, a bisimulation in this setting distinguishes T_7 from T_8. We define such a relation as follows.

Definition 5 (∇-bisimulation). *We say that automata* T_1 *and* T_2 *are* ∇-bisimilar, *notation* $T_1 \sim^\nabla T_2$, *if* $TS_\nabla(T_1) \sim TS_\nabla(T_2)$. *We also say that locations* s *and* t *are* ∇-bisimilar *in some valuation* ρ, *notation* $s\rho \sim^\nabla t\rho$, *if* $(s, \emptyset)\rho \sim (t, \emptyset)\rho$.

Notice that two ∇-bisimilar automata are also bisimilar. We conclude this section by stating two basic properties (lemmas) of ∇-bisimulation. They are needed to prove Theorem 1 which relates $\sim^\nabla$ to a symbolic bisimulation.

Notice that the ability of dropping all the deadlines, letting time pass, and then undropping the deadlines, ensures that if two locations are ∇-bisimilar at a certain moment, no matter how long the activity is blocked, this two locations will still be ∇-bisimilar. This is stated in Lemma 1. Moreover, if two locations are ∇-bisimilar at some given valuation ρ then both satisfy the deadline associated to some action in valuation ρ, or none of them does. This is easy to check by dropping all the deadlines except those associated to the action of interest. This is formally stated in Lemma 2.

Lemma 1. *If* $t\rho \sim^\nabla u\rho$ *then* $t(\rho + d) \sim^\nabla u(\rho + d)$*, for all* $d \geq 0$.

Lemma 2. *If* $t\rho \sim^\nabla u\rho$ *then* $\rho \models dl(t, D) \Leftrightarrow dl(u, D)$*, for any* $D \subseteq \mathcal{A}$.

4 Symbolic Characterization of ∇-Bisimulation

We postpone the proof that ∇-bisimulation is a congruence until Sec. 5 and give first a symbolic characterization of $\sim^{\nabla}$. That is, we give a relation directly in TADs which does not resort to the underlying transition system and equates exactly the same automata as $\sim^{\nabla}$ does. The symbolic bisimulation we propose works in a similar fashion to that of [23]. The construction of such relation is based on zone and region manipulation. A clock region or *region* for short, is a consistent conjunction of atomic constraints of the form, $\psi \equiv \bigwedge_{x\in C} \psi_x \wedge \bigwedge_{\{x,y\}\subseteq C, x\neq y} \psi_{\{x,y\}}$ where

- each ψ_x is either $x = n$, $m < x < m + 1$ or $x > N$, and
- each $\psi_{\{x,y\}}$ is either $x-y = n$, $m < x-y < m + 1$ or $x-y > N$.

with n, m, N non-negative integers such that $0 \leq n \leq N$, and $0 \leq m < N$. Regions can be expressed by constraints as we defined above, and any constraint can be expressed as a disjunction of regions. Similar to the clock resetting ($\rho\{\mathbf{x} := 0\}$) and time successor ($\rho{+}d$) of the clock valuation defined earlier, we define below their symbolic counterpart.

Reset: For a constraint ϕ and a set of clocks $\mathbf{x}$, the reset $\phi{\downarrow_{\mathbf{x}}}$ is a predicate such that for all ρ, $\rho \models \phi{\downarrow_{\mathbf{x}}}$ iff $\rho = \rho'\{\mathbf{x} := 0\}$ and $\rho' \models \phi$ for some ρ'

Time successor: For a constraint ϕ, the time successor $\phi{\Uparrow}$ is a predicate such that for all ρ, $\rho \models \phi{\Uparrow}$ iff $\rho = \rho' + d$ and $\rho' \models \phi$ for some ρ' and $d \geq 0$

A constraint ϕ *is* $\Uparrow$*-closed* if and only if $\phi{\Uparrow} \Leftrightarrow \phi$ is valid (i.e. a tautology). The operations above distribute on disjunction and are expressible in terms of constraints (see e.g. [28,23].) The following facts can be derived from the definitions or have already appear elsewhere [28,23].

Fact 1. *(1)* Let ψ and ϕ be regions. Let ρ and ρ' be valuations s.t. $\rho \models \psi$ and $\rho' \models \psi$. If $\rho{+}d \models \phi$ for some $d \geq 0$, there exists $d' \geq 0$ s.t. $\rho'{+}d' \models \phi$. *(2)* If ϕ is a region then, for any constraint ψ, either $\phi \Rightarrow \psi$ is valid or $\phi \wedge \psi$ is a contradiction. *(3)* If ϕ is a region, so does $\phi{\downarrow_{\mathbf{x}}}$. *(4)* $\rho \models \phi$ implies $\rho \models \phi{\Uparrow}$. *(5)* $\phi{\Uparrow}$ is $\Uparrow$-closed. *(6)* If ϕ is $\Uparrow$-closed then $\rho \models \phi$ implies $\rho + d \models \phi$ for all $d \in \mathbb{R}_{\geq 0}$. *(7)* If ϕ_1 and ϕ_2 are $\Uparrow$-closed (resp. left-closed), so are $\phi_1 \wedge \phi_2$ and $\phi_1 \vee \phi_2$.

Given a constraint ϕ, a ϕ-partition [23] is a finite set of constraints Φ if $\bigvee \Phi \Leftrightarrow \phi$ and for any two distinct $\psi, \psi' \in \Phi$, ψ and ψ' are disjoint (i.e. $\psi \wedge \psi'$ is a contradiction). A ϕ-partition Φ is called *finer* than another ϕ-partition Ψ if Φ can be obtained from Ψ by decomposing some of its elements. $\mathcal{RC}(\phi)$ denotes the set of all regions that constitute ϕ. Notice that $\phi \Leftrightarrow \bigvee \mathcal{RC}(\phi)$ and that $\mathcal{RC}(\phi)$ is the finest of all ϕ-partitions.

Lemma 3. *Let ψ be a region and ρ be such that $\rho \models \psi$. For all $\phi \in \mathcal{RC}(\psi{\Uparrow})$ exists $d \geq 0$ such that $\rho + d \models \phi$.*

The definition of symbolic bisimulation we propose is based on Lin & Yi's definition [23], which in turns is based on Čerāns' result [12]. A symbolic bisimulation is a relation containing tuples (s, t, ϕ) meaning that locations s and t are related in any valuation that satisfies constraint ϕ. Here ϕ is a constraint over the disjoint union of the set of clocks of the two automata. In this way, the relation ensures that clocks in both automata progress at the same rate. In turn, this guarantees that the related locations can idle the same time until some given deadline becomes true.

Definition 6 (Symbolic Bisimulation). *Let T_1 and T_2 be two TADs with disjoint set of clocks C_1 and C_2 and disjoint set of locations $\mathcal{L}_1$ and $\mathcal{L}_2$ respectively. A relation $S \subseteq (\mathcal{L}_1 \times \mathcal{L}_2 \cup \mathcal{L}_2 \times \mathcal{L}_1) \times \mathcal{F}(C_1 \cup C_2)$ (where $\mathcal{F}(C)$ denotes the set of all constraints with clocks in C) is a* symbolic bisimulation *if for all $(t, u, \phi) \in S$,*

(1) $(u, t, \phi) \in S$, (2) ϕ is $\Uparrow$-closed,
(3) whenever $t \xrightarrow{a,\gamma,\delta,\mathbf{x}} t'$, there is a $(\phi \wedge \gamma)$-partition Φ such that for each $\phi' \in \Phi$, $u \xrightarrow{a,\gamma',\delta',\mathbf{y}} u'$, $\phi' \Rightarrow \gamma'$ and $(t', u', \phi'{\downarrow_{\mathbf{xy}}}\Uparrow) \in S$, for some γ', δ', $\mathbf{y}$ and u'; and
(4) $\phi \Rightarrow (dl(t, A) \Leftrightarrow dl(u, A))$ is valid for all $A \subseteq \mathcal{A}$.

We write $t \sim^{\phi} u$ if $(t, u, \phi) \in S$ for some symbolic bisimulation S. We also write $T_1 \sim^{\phi} T_2$ if for every initial location t of T_1 there is an initial location u in T_2 such that $t \sim^{\phi} u$, and the same with the roles of T_1 and T_2 exchanged.

Property 1 states the symmetric characteristics of a bisimulation. The requirement that ϕ is $\Uparrow$-closed (property 2) ensures that location t and u show an equivalent behavior any time in the future which is necessary if deadlines are dropped. Property 3 ensures the transfer properties of discrete transitions. This is similar to [23] except that there is no invariant to consider. Finally, property 4 states that any possible combination of deadlines should match under the assumption that ϕ holds. This ensures that the time elapsed until a deadline associated to a given action is the same in both locations. Notice that property 4 is equivalent to requiring that $\phi \Rightarrow (dl(t, \{a\}) \Leftrightarrow dl(u, \{a\}))$ for all $a \in \mathcal{A}$. This makes evident that deadlines may be "changed" from one edge to another as long as both edges are labeled with the same action (see Fig. 2(b)). Moreover property 4 is comparable to the property of invariants in [23]. Like in [23], the use of partitioning allows that one edge is matched by several edges as is the case in Fig. 3 where both $T_9 \sim^{\nabla} T_{10}$ and $T_9 \sim^{x=y} T_{10}$.

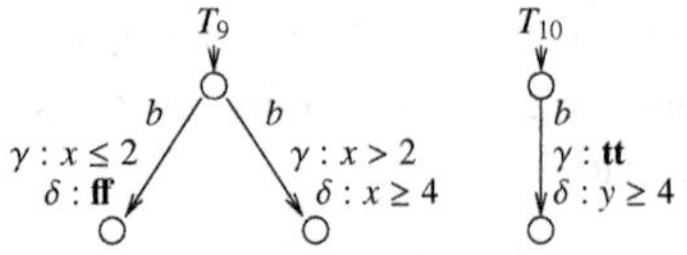

Fig. 3. $T_9 \sim^{x=y} T_{10}$

The following theorem states that symbolic bisimulation completely captures the notion of ∇-bisimulation.

Theorem 1. *For $\Uparrow$-closed ϕ, $t \sim^{\phi} u$ iff $t\rho \sim^{\nabla} u\rho$ for any $\rho \models \phi$*

Proof (Sketch). From the results exposed above, it follows that if S be a symbolic bisimulation, then $\{((t, D)\rho, (u, D)\rho) \mid \exists\phi : \rho \models \phi : (t, u, \phi) \in S \text{ and } D \subseteq \mathcal{A}\}$ is a bisimulation up to $\sim$ [24], which proves the "only if". Moreover, it also follows that $\{(t, u, \phi) | \phi \text{ is } \Uparrow\text{-closed and } \forall\psi \in \mathcal{RC}(\phi) : \exists\rho : \rho \models \psi : t\rho \sim^{\nabla} u\rho\}$ is a symbolic bisimulation, which proves the other implication. □

Corollary 1. *Let $\phi_0 \equiv \bigwedge_{x,y \in C_1 \cup C_2}(0 \leq x = y)$. $T_1 \sim^{\phi_0} T_2$ iff $T_1 \sim^{\nabla} T_2$.*

5 The Coarsest Congruence Included in ~

In this section, we show that $\sim^{\phi_0}$ (and hence $\sim^{\nabla}$, too) is the coarsest congruence for the parallel composition included in bisimulation. The first part of the section is devoted to prove that $\sim^{\phi_0}$ is a congruence. It is interesting to notice that the proof of congruence is carried out fully at symbolic level (in contrast to the usual proof using the underlying transition system). To the best of our knowledge, this is a novel approach. In the second part we show that $\sim^{\nabla}$ is the coarsest congruence included in $\sim$.

The next two lemmas are required for the proof of congruence. Lemma 4 implies that a deadline of a set of actions can be decomposed as a disjunction of the deadlines of each of the actions. Lemma 5 states that if two locations t and u are symbolically bisimilar under a constraint ϕ, then a given action a is enabled in t if and only if it is enabled in u for all valuations that satisfy constraint ϕ.

Lemma 4. $dl(s, D \cup E) \Leftrightarrow (dl(s, D) \vee dl(s, E))$

Lemma 5. *Define* $gd(s, a) = \bigvee\{\gamma \mid s \xrightarrow{a,\gamma,\delta,\mathbf{x}} s'$ *for some* $\delta, \mathbf{x}, s'\}$. *If* S *is a symbolic bisimulation s.t.* $(t, u, \phi) \in S$, *then* $\phi \Rightarrow (gd(t, a) \Leftrightarrow gd(u, a))$ *is valid for all* $a \in \mathcal{A}$.

In particular, these lemmas are needed to check that property 4 of the symbolic bisimulation is preserved in the congruence.

Now, we are in conditions to prove that $\sim^{\phi}$ is a congruence for any parallel composition defined as in Sec. 2. In particular, we notice that the proof does not use constraints 1 and 4 imposed on $\otimes$.

Theorem 2. *Let* $T_i^j = (\mathcal{L}_i^j, \mathsf{l}_i^{0j}, C_i^j, \longrightarrow)$, *for* $i, j \in \{1, 2\}$ *such that* $C_i^j \cap C_k^l = \varnothing$ *if* $i \neq k$ *or* $j \neq l$. *Then* $T_1^1 \sim^{\phi} T_2^1$ *and* $T_1^2 \sim^{\phi} T_2^2$ *imply* $T_1^1 \|_B^{\otimes} T_1^2 \sim^{\phi} T_2^1 \|_B^{\otimes} T_2^2$ *for all* $B \in \mathcal{A}$, *operation* $\otimes$ *and constraint* ϕ.

Proof (Sketch). Let S_1 and S_2 be symbolic bisimulations witnessing $T_1^1 \sim^{\phi_1} T_2^1$ and $T_1^2 \sim^{\phi_2} T_2^2$, resp. The proof checks that $S = \{((t_1, t_2), (u_1, u_2), \phi_1 \wedge \phi_2) \mid (t_1, u_1, \phi_1) \in S_1$ and $(t_2, u_2, \phi_2) \in S_2\}$ is also a symbolic bisimulation. Properties 1 and 2 in Def. 6 follow easily since S_1 and S_2 also satisfy them. Property 3 follows from the definitions of parallel composition and symbolic bisimulation making careful manipulations of constraints, regions, and partitions using Fact 1. Because of Lemma 4, property 4 is a consequence of implication $(\phi_1 \wedge \phi_2) \Rightarrow (dl((t_1, t_2), \{a\}) \Leftrightarrow dl((u_1, u_2), \{a\}))$, which, for $a \notin B$, follows from the definitions. For $a \in B$, conditions 2 and 3 on $\otimes$ allow to show that $dl((t_1, t_2), \{a\})$ is equivalent to $(dl(t_1, \{a\}), gd(t_1, a)) \otimes (dl(t_2, \{a\}), gd(t_2, a))$, and similarly for (u_1, u_2). Then, by Lemma 5, and since S_1 and S_2 are symbolic bisimulations, $dl((t_1, t_2), \{a\})$ and $dl((u_1, u_2), \{a\})$ can be proved equivalent. □

Because of Corollary 1 and Theorem 2, $\sim^{\nabla}$ is also a congruence.

The next lemma is core for the proof that $\sim^{\nabla}$ is the coarsest congruence included in $\sim$. We notice that it does not use constraints 1, 2, and 3 imposed on $\otimes$. The lemma exhibits a test automata T_t that distinguish, modulo bisimulation, two automata that are not ∇-bisimilar. Automata T_t is built by adding extra actions in such a way that, when composed with an automata T, the composition can mimic in the original semantics the behavior of T in the extended semantics. In fact, the extra actions are the same drop (∇_D) and undrop (Δ) actions of the extended semantics.

Lemma 6. *Define the test automata* T_t *with set of locations* $\mathcal{L}_t = \{s_D \mid D \subseteq \mathcal{A}\}$, $\mathsf{l}^0{}_t = \{s_\varnothing\}$, *set of clocks* $C_t = \varnothing$, *set of actions* $\mathcal{A} \cup \mathcal{A}_\nabla \cup \{\Delta\}$ *and, for all* $D, D' \subseteq \mathcal{A}$, $a \notin D$, *define* $s_D \xrightarrow{a,\mathit{tt},\mathbf{0}_\delta,\varnothing} s_\varnothing$, $s_D \xrightarrow{\nabla_{D'},\mathit{tt},\mathit{ff},\varnothing} s_{D\cup D'}$, *and* $s_D \xrightarrow{\Delta,\mathit{tt},\mathit{ff},\varnothing} s_\varnothing$. *Let* T_1 *and* T_2 *be TADs with set of locations* $\mathcal{L}_1$ *and* $\mathcal{L}_2$ *respectively. Suppose that* $T_1 \|^{\otimes}_{\mathcal{A}} T_t \sim T_2 \|^{\otimes}_{\mathcal{A}} T_t$. *Then,* $R = \{((t_1, D)\rho_1, (t_2, D)\rho_2) \mid t_1 \in \mathcal{L}_1,\ t_2 \in \mathcal{L}_2,\ s_D \in \mathcal{L}_t, \text{ and } (t_1, s_D)\rho_1 \sim (t_2, s_D)\rho_2\}$ *is a bisimulation relation that witnesses* $T_1 \sim^\nabla T_2$.

The proof of the lemma is fairly straightforward except in the case of the delay transition. Notice that a delay transition from (t, D) is governed by satisfaction of $\neg dl(t, \mathcal{A}{-}D)$ (by $\mathsf{A2}_\nabla$) while in (t, s_D), it is governed by $tpc(t, s_D)$. To show that both predicates are equivalent it is necessary that $(\mathbf{0}_\delta, \mathbf{tt})$ is neutral for $\otimes$.

From Lemma 6, it follows that $\sim^\nabla$ and $\sim^{\phi_0}$ are the coarsest congruence in $\sim$:

Theorem 3. *Fix* $\otimes$ *satisfying conditions 1 and 2 in Sec. 2. Then* $\sim^\nabla$ *(and hence* $\sim^{\phi_0}$*) is the coarsest congruence included in* $\sim$ *for the family of operators* $\|^{\otimes}_{B}$, *with* $B \subseteq \mathcal{A}$.

6 Concluding Remarks

On Deciding ∇-Bisimulation. Our symbolic characterisation is based on [23] and [12]. In particular, [12] states that bisimulation is decidable for timed automata. The same applies to our relation. Since the number of regions is finite so is the number of (relevant) constraints (modulo logic equivalence) and as a consequence also the number of relevant $\Uparrow$-closed constraints. Therefore, any possible symbolic bisimulation relating two TADs will also be finite. Besides, operations $\downarrow_{\mathbf{x}}$ and $\Uparrow$ are expressible in terms of constraints, and it is possible to decide validity of the constraints on clocks. Following [12], checking that two TADs T_1 and T_2 are ∇-bisimilarity is then possible by taking relation $S = \{(t, u, \phi\Uparrow) \mid \phi \in \mathcal{RC}(\mathbf{tt})\}$ (which is the finest partition possible since $\mathcal{RC}(\mathbf{tt})$ is the set of all regions) and checking that the transfer rules in Def. 6 hold for all tuples reachable from some set $I \subseteq (S \cap (\mathsf{ini}_1 \times \mathsf{ini}_2 \times \mathcal{RC}(\phi_0)))$ such that it relates all initial states of T_1 (resp. T_2) with some initial state of T_2, (resp. T_1).

A Remark on Symbolic Bisimulation. The third constraint in the definition of symbolic bisimulation (Def. 6) can be relaxed as follows:

whenever $t \xrightarrow{a,\gamma,\delta,\mathbf{x}} t'$, there is a $(\phi\wedge\gamma)$-partition Φ s.t. for each $\phi' \in \Phi$, $u \xrightarrow{a,\gamma',\delta',\mathbf{y}} u'$, $\phi' \Rightarrow \gamma'$, $\phi'\downarrow_{\mathbf{xy}}\Uparrow \Rightarrow \psi$, and $(t', u', \psi) \in S$, for some ψ, γ', δ', $\mathbf{y}$ and u'.

the difference being on the existence of ψ such that $\phi'\downarrow_{\mathbf{xy}}\Uparrow \Rightarrow \psi$. It is not difficult to check that the new characterisation is equivalent to the original definition. This modification is important since it allows to obtain smaller relations due to the fact that a tuple $(t, u, \phi) \in S$ is redundant if there is a different tuple $(t, u, \phi') \in S$ such that $\phi \Rightarrow \phi'$.

On Synchronising Constraints in Parallel Compositions. In [6] the synchronisation of guards and deadlines of synchronising actions are defined by two operations which we call here $\oplus$ and $\otimes$ respectively. Some conditions are imposed in $\oplus$ and the only condition imposed in $\otimes$ is that $(\delta_1, \gamma_1) \otimes (\delta_2, \gamma_2) \Rightarrow (\gamma_1 \oplus \gamma_2)$ whenever $\delta_1 \Rightarrow \gamma_1$ and $\delta_2 \Rightarrow \gamma_2$ ([6] also suggest that $(\delta_1, \gamma_1) \otimes (\delta_2, \gamma_2) \Rightarrow (\delta_1 \vee \delta_2)$ should hold). We will only discuss here some particular examples that have recurred on the works of Sifakis et al. (see, e.g. [7,5,6]). We first focus on the guard:

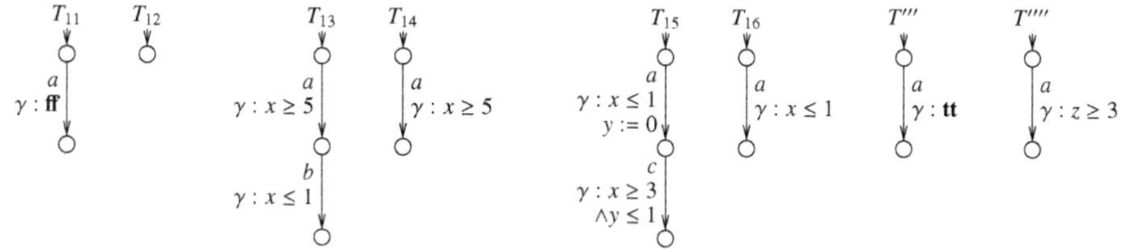

Fig. 4. $T_{11} \sim^{\nabla} T_{12}$, $T_{13} \sim^{\nabla} T_{14}$, and $T_{15} \sim^{\nabla} T_{16}$

$\oplus = \wedge$. This is the one we use and amounts to check that both guards are enables in order to enable the synchronised transition.

$\oplus = \vee$. The synchronised transition can execute if any of the partners can do so.

$\oplus = \mathsf{max}$, where $\gamma_1 \mathsf{max} \gamma_2 = (\gamma_1 \wedge \gamma_2 \Uparrow) \vee (\gamma_2 \wedge \gamma_1 \Uparrow)$. In this case, a component is willing to synchronise if the synchronising transition was enabled in the past and the other component is ready to synchronise now.

$\oplus = \mathsf{min}$, where $\gamma_1 \mathsf{min} \gamma_2 = (\gamma_1 \wedge \gamma_2 \Downarrow) \vee (\gamma_2 \wedge \gamma_1 \Downarrow)$ with $\Downarrow$ being the *time predecessor* operator (the dual of $\Uparrow$). In this case, the synchronised guard anticipates the execution of the synchronising transitions.

Our congruence relation only works for $\wedge$. It is debatable how reasonable are the other operations. Synchronisation through $\vee$ is highly questionable. It is expected that automata T_{11} and T_{12} in Fig. 4 are equivalent under any reasonable criterion. Nevertheless, the composition $T_{11} \parallel_a^{\otimes} T'''$ can perform action a at any moment while $T_{12} \parallel_a^{\otimes} T'''$ cannot.

Under min, a component may anticipate the future behaviour of the synchronising partner. [7] and [6] suggest that the intention of this synchronisation is that the earliest synchronising transition makes irrelevant the second one (e.g. a tramway leaves a crossing and after a while it signals to allow the change of the traffic light though it may be ignored if the light has already changed [6]). This intuition does not completely match the behaviour of min which will speed up the slower component allowing it to do activity otherwise impossible. This is observed when automata T''' is composed with T_{13} and with T_{14} synchronising on a (see Fig. 4). Notice that T_{13} and T_{14} exhibit an apparent equal behaviour since action a in T_{13} is always too late to execute b. However, the composition $T_{13} \parallel_a^{\otimes} T'''$ may hasten the synchronisation on a making b apparent.

Dually, under max, an automata may allow the execution of the synchronising action if it was enabled in the past. Notice that T_{15} and T_{16} in Fig. 4 exhibit equivalent behaviour: c cannot be executed in T_{15} since clock y is always set too early. Instead, the composition with T'''' synchronising on a will delay the execution long enough as to set y sufficiently late to enable the c transition. The intention behind this form of synchronisation is that the fastest component can always wait for the slowest. This design choice seems an adequate choice to use with soft deadlines. Notice also that the appearance of new activity is reasonable since it may be important to cope with the occasional delay. What is debatable is the need of max since this type of synchronisation can easily be represented using $\wedge$: Notice that the max synchronisation does not allow any test automata to distinguish between γ and $\gamma \Uparrow$. Hence, it is more reasonable to model this kind of synchronisation using $\wedge$ instead of max and let all guards be $\Uparrow$-closed.

With respect to deadlines, [6] is more liberal. The two type of synchronising deadlines that stand out are:

Patient synchronisation: $(\delta_1, \gamma_1) \otimes (\delta_2, \gamma_2) = \delta_1 \wedge \delta_2$ with $\mathbf{0}_\delta = \mathbf{tt}$, and
Impatient synchronisation: $(\delta_1, \gamma_1) \otimes (\delta_2, \gamma_2) = (\delta_1 \vee \delta_2) \wedge (\gamma_1 \wedge \gamma_2)$ with $\mathbf{0}_\delta = \mathbf{ff}$.

The nomenclature corresponds to [16] but these definitions are already introduced in [26] with the names of *flexible* and *stiff* respectively. Patient synchronisation allows to model soft deadlines, in the sense that one of the components is always willing to wait for the other (as long as its guards remain valid). On the other hand, impatient synchronisation impose urgency and obliges the execution as soon as both partners are ready to execute the synchronising transition. Both [26] and [16,4] give a weaker definition of impatient synchronisation: $(\delta_1, \gamma_1) \otimes (\delta_2, \gamma_2) = \delta_1 \vee \delta_2$. Taking $\mathbf{0}_\delta = \mathbf{ff}$, our result is also valid for this definition. The only problem with it is that it does not preserve time reactivity, i.e. condition 1 on $\otimes$ (see Sec. 2) does not hold[1].

We finally mention that ∇-bisimulation is still a congruence for $||_B^\otimes$ if condition 4 on $\otimes$ is dropped. However, it is *not* the coarsest congruence in $\sim$ any longer. (This can easily be seen by taking $(\delta_1, \gamma_1) \otimes (\delta_2, \gamma_2) = \mathbf{ff}$).

Conclusions. We have characterised the coarsest congruence for parallel compositions of TADs with soft and hard deadline synchronisation that is included in bisimulation. We also gave a symbolic characterisation of it and show that it is decidable. An aside novelty in our result is that the proof of congruence was entirely carried out in the symbolic semantics rather than resorting to the underlying transition system. The choice on this strategy is not fortuitous. It is mainly due to the complexity on defining an equivalent parallel composition on transition systems. To begin with, any possible definition needs to be tailored for a particular choice of deadline. Besides, it would need complex bookkeeping to know which possible deadline is blocking the passage of time. Many other different complications appear depending on the choice of $\otimes$.

We finally discussed different types of synchronisation in parallel composition and conclude that our choice is both reasonable and sufficiently expressive as to consider the modelling of both soft and hard real-time constraints.

Acknowledgments. We thank Frits Vaandrager for his remarks on early drafts that helped to improve the quality of the paper. Referees are also acknowledged for their useful remarks.

References

1. R. Alur and D. Dill. A theory of timed automata. *TCS*, 126:183–235, 1994.
2. G. Behrmann, A. David, K.G. Larsen, O. Möller, P. Pettersson, and Wang Yi. UPPAAL – present and future. In *Proc. of 40th IEEE Conf. on Decision and Control*. IEEE Press, 2001.
3. J. Bengtsson, K.G. Larsen, F. Larsson, P. Pettersson, and Wang Yi. UPPAAL - A tool suite for automatic verification of real-time systems. In R. Alur, T.A. Henzinger, and E.D. Sontag, eds., *Hybrid Systems III: Verification and Control*, *LNCS* 1066, pp. 232–243. Springer, 1996.

[1] To strictly model hard deadlines, this composition requires some modification on the rules in order to ensure the time-blockage produced when a component is ready to synchronise but the other cannot do it at all. A possible solution appears in [4].

4. H. Bohnenkamp, P.R. D'Argenio, H. Hermanns, and J.-P. Katoen. MoDeST: A compositional modeling formalism for real-time and stochastic systems. CTIT Tech. Rep. 04-46, University of Twente, 2004. Submitted for publication.
5. S. Bornot and J. Sifakis. On the composition of hybrid systems. In Thomas A. Henzinger and Shankar Sastry, eds., *Hybrid Systems: Computation and Control, First International Workshop, HSCC'98, LNCS* 1386, pp. 49–63. Springer, 1998.
6. S. Bornot and J. Sifakis. An algebraic framework for urgency. *Inf. & Comp.*, 163:172–202, 2000.
7. S. Bornot, J. Sifakis, and S. Tripakis. Modeling urgency in timed systems. In Roever W.-P. de, H. Langmaack, and A. Pnueli, eds., *Compositionality: The Significant Difference, LNCS* 1536, pp. 103–129. Springer, 1998.
8. H. Bowman. Modelling timeouts without timelocks. In J.-P. Katoen, ed., *Formal Methods for Real-Time and Probabilistic Systems, 5th International AMAST Workshop, ARTS'99, LNCS* 1601, pp. 334–353. Springer, 1999.
9. M. Bozga, C. Daws, O. Maler, A. Olivero, S. Tripakis, and S. Yovine. Kronos: A model-checking tool for real-time systems. In A.J. Hu and M. Vardi, eds., *Procs. of 10th CAV, LNCS* 1427, pp. 546–550. Springer, 1998.
10. M. Bozga and L. Mounier S. Graf. IF-2.0: A validation environment for component-based real-time systems. In E. Brinksma and K.G. Larsen, eds., *Procs. of 14th CAV, LNCS* 2404, pp. 343–348. Springer, 2002.
11. M.C. Browne, E.M. Clarke, and O. Grumberg. Characterizing finite Kripke structures in propositional temporal logic. *TCS*, 59(1,2):115–131, 1988.
12. K. Čerāns. Decidability of bisimulation equivalences for parallel timer processes. In G. von Bochmann and D.K. Probst, eds., *Procs. of 4th CAV, LNCS* 663, pp. 302–315. Springer, 1992.
13. F. Corradini. On performance congruences for process algebras. *Inf. & Comp.*, 145(2):191–230, 1998.
14. P.R. D'Argenio. *Algebras and Automata for Timed and Stochastic Systems*. PhD thesis, Department of Computer Science, University of Twente, 1999.
15. P.R. D'Argenio and B. Gebremichael. The coarsest congruence for timed automata with deadlines contained in bisimulation. Tech. Rep. ICIS-R05015. Radboud University Nijmegen, 2005.
16. P.R. D'Argenio, H. Hermanns, J.-P. Katoen, and R. Klaren. MoDeST - a modelling and description language for stochastic timed systems. In L. de Alfaro and S. Gilmore, eds., *Procs. of PAPM-PROBMIV 2001, LNCS* 2165, pp. 87–104. Springer, 2001.
17. B. Gebremichael and F.W. Vaandrager. Specifying urgency in timed I/O automata. To appear *In Procs. of* 3rd *IEEE Conference on Software Engineering and Formal Methods*, 2005.
18. T.A. Henzinger, X. Nicollin, J. Sifakis, and S. Yovine. Symbolic model checking for real-time systems. *Inf. & Comp.*, 111:193–244, 1994.
19. H. Hermanns. *Interactive Markov Chains : The Quest for Quantified Quality, LNCS* 2428. Springer, 2002.
20. J. Hillston. *A Compositional Approach to Performance Modelling*. Distinguished Dissertation in Computer Science. Cambridge University Press, 1996.
21. H.E. Jensen, K.G. Larsen, and A. Skou. Scaling up Uppaal automatic verification of real-time systems using compositionality and abstraction. In M. Joseph, ed., *Procs. of FTRTFT 2000, LNCS* 1926, pp. 19–30. Springer, 2000.
22. L. Lamport. What good is temporal logic? In R.E. Mason, ed., *Information Processing 83*, pp. 657–668. North-Holland, 1983.
23. H. Lin and W. Yi. Axiomatizing timed automata. *Acta Informatica*, 38(4):277–305, 2002.
24. R. Milner. *Communication and Concurrency*. Prentice Hall, 1989.
25. R. Segala, R. Gawlick, J.F. Søgaard-Andersen, and N.A. Lynch. Liveness in timed and untimed systems. *Inf. & Comp.*, 141(2):119–171, 1998.

26. J. Sifakis and S. Yovine. Compositional specification of timed systems. In *Procs. of the STACS'96, LNCS* 1046, pp. 347–359, Grenoble, France, 1996. Springer.
27. S. Tripakis and S. Yovine. Analysis of timed systems using time-abstracting bisimulations. *Formal Methods in System Design*, 18(1):25–68, 2001.
28. S. Yovine. Model checking timed automata. In G. Rozenberg and F.W. Vaandrager, eds., *Lectures on Embedded Systems, LNCS* 1494, pp. 114–152. Springer, 1998.

A Behavioural Pseudometric for Metric Labelled Transition Systems

Franck van Breugel*

Department of Computer Science, York University,
4700 Keele Street, Toronto, Ontario M3J 1P3, Canada
franck@cs.yorku.ca

Abstract. Metric labelled transition systems are labelled transition systems whose states and actions form (pseudo)metric spaces. These systems can capture a large class of timed transition systems, including systems with uncountably many states and uncountable nondeterminism. In this paper a behavioural pseudometric is introduced for metric labelled transition systems. The behavioural distance between states, a nonnegative real number, captures the similarity of the behaviour of those states. The smaller the distance, the more alike the states are. In particular, the distance between states is 0 iff they are bisimilar. Three different characterisations of this pseudometric are given: a fixed point, a logical and a coinductive characterisation. These generalise the fixed point, logical and coinductive characterisations of bisimilarity.

1 Introduction

Concurrent systems are often modelled by *labelled transition systems* in which bisimilar states are considered behaviourally indistinguishable. *Bisimilarity* can be characterised in different ways. Park [24] showed that bisimilarity can be captured as the greatest *fixed point* of a monotone selfmap on a complete lattice of relations. Hennessy and Milner [19] introduced a modal *logic* and showed that states are bisimilar iff they satisfy the same formulae. A *coalgebraic* characterisation of bisimilarity was given by Aczel and Mendler in [1]. For more about bisimilarity, we refer the reader to, for example, [23,25].

In this paper, we study labelled transition systems whose states and actions contain quantitative data, like, for example, time. Notions of bisimilarity have been adapted for these systems. However, such a discrete notion (states are either bisimilar or they are not) sits uneasily with models featuring quantitative data. If some of the quantities change a little bit—these quantities are often obtained experimentally and, hence, are usually approximations—states that used to be bisimilar may not be anymore or vice versa. In summary, bisimilarity is not *robust* for these types of systems.

To address this problem, Giacalone, Jou and Smolka [16] suggested to exploit *pseudometrics* that assign a distance, a nonnegative real number, to each pair

* Supported by the Natural Sciences and Engineering Research Council of Canada.

M. Abadi and L. de Alfaro (Eds.): CONCUR 2005, LNCS 3653, pp. 141–155, 2005.

of states of a system. Such a pseudometric yields a quantitative analogue of bisimilarity in that the distances between states express the similarity of the behaviour of those states. The smaller the distance, the more the states behave alike. In particular, the distance between states is 0 if they are bisimilar.

Recently, there has been a renewed interest in such *behavioural pseudometrics*. Most work has focused on different types of probabilistic systems (see, for example, the work of Desharnais, Gupta, Jagadeesan and Panangaden [13,14,15], de Alfaro, Henzinger and Majumdar [9,11] and Van Breugel and Worrell [6,7,8]). Behavioural pseudometrics for so-called action-labelled quantitative transition systems have been proposed by Deng, Chothia, Palamidessi and Pang in [12]. Time has been considered by Ying and Wirsing [29,30] and Gupta, Jagadeesan and Panangaden have studied a combination of time and probability in [18]. Behavioural pseudometrics for so-called quantitative transition systems have been put forward by de Alfaro, Faella and Stoelinga [10]. Related systems have been considered by Girard and Pappas [17]. We will discuss some related work in more detail in the concluding section.

Here, we consider *metric labelled transition systems.* These are labelled transition systems the states of which are endowed with a pseudometric and the actions of which are endowed with a metric. Each labelled transition system can be turned into a metric labelled transition system by endowing both the states and the actions with the discrete metric. Metric labelled transition systems can capture a large class of *timed transition systems*, including systems with uncountably many states and uncountable nondeterminism.

Three different approaches have been put forward to define behavioural pseudometrics. Desharnais, Gupta, Jagadeesan and Panangaden [14] defined a behavioural pseudometric for probabilistic transition systems as the greatest fixed point of a monotone selfmap on a complete lattice of pseudometrics. Desharnais et al. [13,15] also defined a behavioural pseudometric for probabilistic transition systems in terms of a real-valued interpretation of a modal logic. Van Breugel and Worrell [7,8] gave a coalgebraic definition of a behavioural pseudometric for probabilistic transition systems and showed that it coincides with the logical definition of Desharnais et al.

In this paper, we apply these three approaches to metric labelled transition systems. The three approaches are shown to give rise to the same behavioural pseudometric. This behavioural pseudometric captures bisimilarity since states have distance 0 iff they are bisimilar. Therefore, the fixed point, logical and coalgebraic definition of the behavioural pseudometric can be viewed as a quantitative generalisation of the characterisations of bisimilarity mentioned in the first paragraph of this introduction. Because of lack of space, no proofs are given. These can be found in [4].

2 Metric Labelled Transition Systems

Labelled transition systems are generalised to *metric labelled transition systems* by augmenting them with some additional structure. The states are endowed with a pseudometric and the actions are endowed with a metric. Before formally defining metric labelled transition systems, let us first introduce the notions of a pseudometric space and a metric space.

Definition 1. *A pseudometric space is a pair (X, d_X) consisting of a set X and a distance function $d_X : X \times X \to [0, \infty]$ satisfying*

1. *for all $x \in X$, $d_X(x, x) = 0$,*
2. *for all x, $y \in X$, $d_X(x, y) = d_X(y, x)$,*
3. *for all x, y, $z \in X$, $d_X(x, z) \leq d_X(x, y) + d_X(y, z)$.*

If the distance function d_X also satisfies

4. *for all x, $y \in X$, if $d_X(x, y) = 0$ then $x = y$,*

then (X, d_X) is a metric space.

Instead of (X, d_X) we often write X and we denote the distance function of a space X by d_X. Note that we allow infinite distances[1]. Also observe that in pseudometric spaces different elements may have distance zero.

In the examples below, we will use the following two distance functions.

Example 1. Let X be a set. The *discrete* metric $d_X : X \times X \to [0, \infty]$ is defined by

$$d_X(x, y) = \begin{cases} 0 & \text{if } x = y \\ \infty & \text{otherwise.} \end{cases}$$

The *Euclidean* metric $d_{[0,\infty]} : [0, \infty] \times [0, \infty] \to [0, \infty]$ is defined by

$$d_{[0,\infty]}(r, s) = |r - s|.$$

Definition 2. *A metric labelled transition system is a triple $\langle S, A, \to \rangle$ consisting of*

- *a pseudometric space S of states,*
- *a metric space A of actions, and*
- *a labelled transition relation $\to \subseteq S \times A \times S$.*

Instead of $\langle s, a, s' \rangle \in \to$ we often write $s \xrightarrow{a} s'$. We will restrict our attention to a particular class of metric labelled transition systems. To capture this class, we introduce two constructions on pseudometric spaces.

Given pseudometric spaces X and Y, the pseudometric space $X \otimes Y$ consists of the Cartesian product[2] of the sets underlying the pseudometric spaces X and Y endowed with the following distance function.

---

[1] $\infty + \infty = \infty$ and $\infty - \infty = 0$.

[2] The Cartesian product can be endowed with many different distance functions. The distance function introduced in Definition 3 corresponds to the tensor product (see Section 6). The distance function corresponding to the product is considered in the concluding section of this paper.

Definition 3. *The distance function* $d_{X \otimes Y} : (X \times Y) \times (X \times Y) \to [0, \infty]$ *is defined by*

$$d_{X \otimes Y}(\langle u, v \rangle, \langle x, y \rangle) = d_X(u, x) + d_Y(v, y).$$

We write $\mathcal{P}(X)$ for the set of subsets of a pseudometric space X. This set is endowed with the following distance function.

Definition 4. *The distance function* $d_{\mathcal{P}(X)} : \mathcal{P}(X) \times \mathcal{P}(X) \to [0, \infty]$ *is defined by*

$$d_{\mathcal{P}(X)}(A, B) = \max \left\{ \sup_{a \in A} \inf_{b \in B} d_X(a, b), \sup_{b \in B} \inf_{a \in A} d_X(a, b) \right\}.$$

Note that $\inf \emptyset = \infty$ and $\sup \emptyset = 0$. The distance function $d_{\mathcal{P}(X)}$ is known as the *Hausdorff* metric.[3]

Next, we generalise the condition of finitely branching from labelled transition systems to metric labelled transition systems. Recall that a subset A of a pseudometric space X is compact if each sequence in A has a subsequence that is convergent in A. Also recall that a function $f : X \to Y$ is nonexpansive if it does not increase any distances, that is, $d_Y(f(x), f(y)) \leq d_X(x, y)$ for all x, $y \in X$.

Definition 5. *A metric labelled transition system* $\langle S, A, \rightarrow \rangle$ *is compactly branching if for each* $s \in S$*, the set*

$$\{ \langle a, s' \rangle \in A \otimes S \mid s \xrightarrow{a} s' \}$$

is compact. A metric labelled transition system $\langle S, A, \rightarrow \rangle$ *is nonexpansive if the function* $t : S \to \mathcal{P}(A \otimes S)$ *defined by*

$$t(s) = \{ \langle a, s' \rangle \in A \otimes S \mid s \xrightarrow{a} s' \}$$

is nonexpansive.

Example 2. Let $\langle S, A, \rightarrow \rangle$ be a finitely branching labelled transition system. If we endow both the states and the actions with the discrete metric, then we obtain a compactly branching and nonexpansive metric labelled transition system.

3 A Fixed Point Characterisation

Bisimilarity can be characterised as the greatest fixed point of a monotone selfmap on a complete lattice of relations. Here we generalise that characterisation by capturing the behavioural pseudometric as the greatest fixed point of a monotone selfmap on a complete lattice of pseudometrics. For the rest of this section, we fix a metric labelled transition system $\langle S, A, \rightarrow \rangle$.

---

[3] One could also consider an assymmetric version of the Hausdorff metric, by dropping the second half of the maximum. This gives rise to a quantitative analogue of similarity (see, for example, [10]).

Pseudometrics on the set (underlying the pseudometric space) S can be viewed as a quantitative generalisation of equivalence relations on S.[4] The smaller the distance between states, the more they are related. In the characterisation of bisimilarity as a greatest fixed point, the relations are ordered by inclusion. This order can be generalised[5] as follows.

Definition 6. *The relation $\sqsubseteq$ on pseudometrics on S is defined by*

$$d_1 \sqsubseteq d_2 \text{ if } d_1(s_1, s_2) \geq d_2(s_1, s_2) \text{ for all } s_1, s_2 \in S.$$

Note the reverse direction of $\sqsubseteq$ and $\geq$ in the above definition (so that $\sqsubseteq$ generalises $\subseteq$). The set of pseudometrics on S endowed with the order $\sqsubseteq$ forms a complete lattice.

Definition 7. *Let d be a pseudometric on the set (underlying the pseudometric space) S of states of the metric labelled transition system and let d_A be the metric on the set A of actions of the system. The distance function $\Delta(d) : S \times S \to [0, \infty]$ is defined by*

$$\Delta(d)(s_1, s_2) = \max \left\{ \begin{array}{l} \sup\limits_{s_1 \xrightarrow{a_1} s_1'} \inf\limits_{s_2 \xrightarrow{a_2} s_2'} d_A(a_1, a_2) + d(s_1', s_2'), \\[2ex] \sup\limits_{s_2 \xrightarrow{a_2} s_2'} \inf\limits_{s_1 \xrightarrow{a_1} s_1'} d_A(a_1, a_2) + d(s_1', s_2') \end{array} \right\}.$$

The suprema and infima in the above definition are the quantitative analogues of universal and existential quantifiers, respectively. $\Delta(d)$ is a pseudometric on S and Δ is monotone. According to Tarski's fixed point theorem, a monotone selfmap on a complete lattice has a greatest fixed point. We denote the greatest fixed point of Δ by $gfp(\Delta)$.

Definition 8. *The distance function $d_f : S \times S \to [0, \infty]$ is defined by*

$$d_f = gfp(\Delta).$$

Definition 7 and 8 are quantitative analogues of the characterisation of bisimilarity as the greatest fixed of a monotone selfmap on a complete lattice of relations (see, for example, [22, Section 4.6]).

The behavioural pseudometric d_f is a quantitative analogue of bisimilarity. In particular, states are bisimilar iff they have distance 0, provided that the metric labelled transition system is compactly branching.

---

[4] An equivalence relation R on S can be viewed as the pseudometric d_R defined by

$$d_R(s_1, s_2) = \begin{cases} 0 & \text{if } s_1 \, R \, s_2 \\ \infty & \text{otherwise.} \end{cases}$$

[5] Let R_1 and R_2 be equivalence relations on S with $R_1 \subseteq R_2$. Then $d_{R_1} \sqsubseteq d_{R_2}$.

Theorem 1. *1. If s_1 and s_2 are bisimilar then $d_f(s_1, s_2) = 0$.*
2. If $\langle S, A, \rightarrow \rangle$ is compactly branching and $d_f(s_1, s_2) = 0$ then s_1 and s_2 are bisimilar.

The next examples show that the second part of the above theorem does not hold for arbitrary metric labelled transition systems, not even for those satisfying obvious weakenings of the compactly branching condition. Recall that a subset of a complete pseudometric space is compact iff it is closed and totally bounded (see, for example, [26]).

Example 3. Consider the metric labelled transition system $\langle \{s_1, s_2, s_3\}, [0,1], \rightarrow \rangle$. The set $\{s_1, s_2, s_3\}$ of states is endowed with the discrete metric and the set $[0,1]$ of labels is endowed with the Euclidean metric. The system has the following transitions.

$$\begin{aligned} s_1 &\xrightarrow{r} s_3 \text{ for all } r \in [0,1] \\ s_2 &\xrightarrow{r} s_3 \text{ for all } r \in (0,1) \end{aligned}$$

Since the states are endowed with the discrete metric, the metric labelled transition system is obviously nonexpansive. However, the metric labelled transition system is not compactly branching, since the set $t(s_2)$ is not closed. Note that the sets $t(s_1)$, $t(s_2)$ and $t(s_3)$ are totally bounded. Obviously, s_1 and s_2 are not bisimilar, but one can easily verify that $d_f(s_1, s_2) = 0$.

Example 4. Consider the metric labelled transition system $\langle \omega + 1 \cup \{s_0, s_1, s_2\}, [0,1], \rightarrow \rangle$. The states are endowed with the discrete metric and the labels are endowed with the Euclidean metric. The system has the following transitions (where we assume $2^{-\omega} = 0$)

$$\begin{aligned} s_1 &\xrightarrow{0} n && \text{for all } n \in \omega \\ s_2 &\xrightarrow{0} n && \text{for all } n \in \omega + 1 \\ n &\xrightarrow{2^{-n}} s_0 && \text{for all } n \in \omega + 1 \end{aligned}$$

Trivially, the metric labelled transition system is nonexpansive. However it is not compactly branching, since the sets $t(s_1)$ and $t(s_2)$ are closed but not totally bounded. Let d be a pseudometric on $\omega + 1 \cup \{s_0, s_1, s_2\}$ such that

$$\begin{aligned} d(m,n) &= |2^{-m} - 2^{-n}| \text{ for all } m, n \in \omega + 1 \\ d(s_1, s_2) &= 0 \end{aligned}$$

and all other distances are ∞. One can easily verify that $\Delta(d) = d$. Since d_f is the greatest fixed point, $d \sqsubseteq d_f$ and, hence, $d_f(s_1, s_2) \leq d(s_1, s_2) = 0$, but s_1 and s_2 are clearly not bisimilar.

According to Tarski's fixed point theorem, the greatest fixed point of a monotone selfmap from on complete lattice can be obtained by iteration of the function starting from the greatest element. In our setting, this iteration boils down to the following.

Definition 9. *The distance function* $d_f^0 : S \times S \to [0, \infty]$ *is defined by*

$$d_f^0(s_1, s_2) = 0.$$

For each ordinal α*, the distance function* $d_f^{\alpha+1} : S \times S \to [0, \infty]$ *is defined by*

$$d_f^{\alpha+1} = \Delta(d_f^\alpha).$$

For each limit ordinal α*, the distance function* $d_f^\alpha : S \times S \to [0, \infty]$ *is defined by*

$$d_f^\alpha = \prod_{\beta \in \alpha} d_f^\alpha.$$

If the metric labelled transition system is not only compactly branching but also nonexpansive, then the greatest fixed point is reached in at most ω iterations. This can be viewed as a quantitative analogue of, for example, [22, Section 10.4].

Theorem 2. *If* $\langle S, A, \to \rangle$ *is compactly branching and nonexpansive then* $\Delta\left(d_f^\omega\right) = d_f^\omega$.

Without restricting to nonexpansiveness the above result does not hold in general as is demonstrated by the following example.

Example 5. Consider the metric labelled transition system $\langle \{ 2^{-n} \mid n \in \omega + 1 \} \cup \{s_0, s_1, s_2\}, \{a\}, \to \rangle$. The states $\{ 2^{-n} \mid n \in \omega + 1 \}$ are endowed with the Euclidean metric and the states s_0, s_1 and s_2 have distance ∞ to all other states. The system contains the following transitions.

$$\begin{aligned} 2^{-(n+1)} &\xrightarrow{a} 2^{-n} \text{ for all } n \in \omega \\ s_1 &\xrightarrow{a} 2^{-n} \text{ for all } n \in \omega + 1 \\ s_2 &\xrightarrow{a} 2^{-n} \text{ for all } n \in \omega + 1 \\ s_2 &\xrightarrow{a} s_0 \\ s_0 &\xrightarrow{a} s_0 \end{aligned}$$

One can verify that the metric labelled transition system is compactly branching. However the system is not nonexpansive, since states $\frac{1}{2}$ and $\frac{1}{4}$ are $\frac{1}{4}$ apart but $t(\frac{1}{2})$ and $t(\frac{1}{4})$ are $\frac{1}{2}$ apart. One can prove that for all $m \in \omega + 1$ and $n \in \omega$,

$$d_f^n(2^{-m}, s_0) = \begin{cases} 0 & \text{if } m < n \\ \infty & \text{otherwise} \end{cases}$$

by induction on n. Hence, for all $n \in \omega$, $d_f^{n+1}(s_1, s_2) = \inf_{m \in \omega+1} d_f^n(2^{-m}, s_0) = 0$. Obviously, s_1 and s_2 are not bisimilar. Hence, from Theorem 1 we can conclude that $d_f(s_1, s_2) \neq 0$. Therefore, $d_f \neq d_f^\omega$.

4 A Logical Characterisation

In this section we show that our behavioural pseudometric admits a logical characterisation. This is motivated by the well-known characterisation of bisimilarity in terms of Hennessy-Milner logic. The logic we consider is syntactically almost identical to Hennessy-Milner logic. However, we change its semantics by interpreting the logic in the interval $[0, \infty]$.

For the rest of this section, we fix a metric labelled transition system $\langle S, A, \rightarrow \rangle$.

Definition 10. *The logic $\mathcal{L}$ is defined by*

$$\varphi ::= \text{true} \mid \langle a \rangle \varphi \mid [a]\varphi \mid \varphi + r \mid \bigwedge_{i \in I} \varphi \mid \bigvee_{i \in I} \varphi$$

where $a \in A$, $r \in [0, \infty]$ and I is an index set.

Next, we provide a real-valued interpretation of the logic. For each formula φ and state s, the real number $\varphi(s)$ provides a quantitative measure of the validity of φ in s. The smaller $\varphi(s)$, the more φ is valid in s.[6]

Definition 11. *For each $\varphi \in \mathcal{L}$, the function $\varphi : S \rightarrow [0, \infty]$ is defined by*

$$\begin{aligned}
\text{true}(s) &= 0 \\
(\langle a \rangle \varphi)(s) &= \inf\{\, \varphi(s') + d_A(a, b) \mid s \xrightarrow{b} s' \,\} \\
([a]\varphi)(s) &= \sup\{\, \varphi(s') \ominus d_A(a, b) \mid s \xrightarrow{b} s' \,\} \\
(\varphi + r)(s) &= \varphi(s) + r \\
(\textstyle\bigwedge_{i \in I} \varphi_i)(s) &= \sup_{i \in I} \varphi_i(s) \\
(\textstyle\bigvee_{i \in I} \varphi_i)(s) &= \inf_{i \in I} \varphi_i(s)
\end{aligned}$$

where

$$r \ominus s = \begin{cases} r - s & \textit{if } r \geq s \\ 0 & \textit{otherwise.} \end{cases}$$

Notice how the interpretation of the possibility modality $\langle a \rangle$ and the necessity modality $[a]$ reflect the pseudometric on actions. In the clause for $([a]\varphi)(s)$, in any transition $s \xrightarrow{b} s'$, the further b is from a the lesser the requirement on $\varphi(s')$. Dually[7], in the clause for $(\langle a \rangle \varphi)(s)$, in any transition $s \xrightarrow{b} s'$, the further b is from a the greater the requirement on $\varphi(s')$.

Given the logic and its real-valued interpretation, we can define a behavioural pseudometric as follows.

---

[6] In contrast with the real-valued interpretations of probabilistic modal logics in, for example, [15], we use 0 to represent true and ∞ to represent false. Consequently, existential and universal quantification are interpreted as infimum and supremum, respectively.

[7] For each $r \in [0, \infty]$, $\cdot \ominus r$ and $\cdot + r$ form an adjunction: for all r_1, $r_2 \in [0, \infty]$, $r_1 \geq r_2 \ominus r$ iff $r_1 + r \geq r_2$.

Definition 12. *The distance function* $d_\ell : S \times S \to [0, \infty]$ *is defined by*

$$d_\ell(s_1, s_2) = \sup_{\varphi \in \mathcal{L}} |\varphi(s_1) - \varphi(s_2)|.$$

To show that the behavioural pseudometrics d_f and d_ℓ coincide, for each state s and ordinal α we introduce a characteristic formula φ_s^α.

Definition 13. *For each* $s \in S$, *the formula* φ_s^0 *is defined by*

$$\varphi_s^0 = \text{true}.$$

For each $s \in S$ *and ordinal* α, *the formula* $\varphi_s^{\alpha+1}$ *is defined by*

$$\varphi_s^{\alpha+1} = \left(\bigwedge_{s \xrightarrow{a} s'} \langle a \rangle \varphi_{s'}^\alpha \right) \wedge \left(\bigwedge_{b \in A} [b] \bigvee_{s \xrightarrow{a} s'} \varphi_{s'}^\alpha + d_A(a, b) \right).$$

For each $s \in S$ *and limit ordinal* α, *the formula* φ_s^α *is defined by*

$$\varphi_s^\alpha = \bigwedge_{\beta \in \alpha} \varphi_s^\beta.$$

The formula φ_s^α shows similarities to the characteristic formula in Hennessy-Milner logic that captures bisimilarity (see, for example, [27, Definition 4.1]). Note that $\varphi_s^{\alpha+1}$ contains a subformula of the form $\varphi + r$. The formula φ_s^α provides an upper bound for the d_f^α-distances from state s to any other state.

Proposition 1. *For each* s_1, $s_2 \in S$ *and ordinal* α,

$$\varphi_{s_1}^\alpha(s_1) = 0$$
$$\varphi_{s_1}^\alpha(s_2) \geq d_f^\alpha(s_1, s_2)$$

The above proposition is one of the key ingredients of the proof of

Theorem 3. $d_f = d_\ell$.

Next, we restrict our attention to the sublogic with finite conjunctions and disjunctions.

Definition 14. *The logic* $\mathcal{L}_\omega$ *is defined by*

$$\varphi ::= \text{true} \mid \langle a \rangle \varphi \mid [a]\varphi \mid \varphi + r \mid \varphi \wedge \varphi \mid \varphi \vee \varphi.$$

This sublogic gives rise to the same behavioural pseudometric if the metric labelled transition system is compactly branching and nonexpansive.

Theorem 4. *If* $\langle S, A, \rightarrow \rangle$ *is compactly branching and nonexpansive, then for all* s_1, $s_2 \in S$,

$$d_\ell(s_1, s_2) = \sup_{\varphi \in \mathcal{L}_\omega} |\varphi(s_1) - \varphi(s_2)|.$$

The above result can be seen as a generalisation of the result of Hennessy and Milner [19, Theorem 2.2] in the discrete setting. Without nonexpansiveness the result does not hold in general (an example very similar to Example 5 can be constructed that shows this).

5 A Coalgebraic Characterisation

Below, we present yet another characterisation of the behavioural pseudometric. This characterisation is based on the theory of coalgebra. In this section, however, we do not refer to that theory. The details will be provided in the next section.

Definition 15. *Let $\langle S_1, A, \rightarrow_1 \rangle$ and $\langle S_2, A, \rightarrow_2 \rangle$ be compactly branching and nonexpansive metric labelled transition systems. A* zigzag map *from $\langle S_1, A, \rightarrow_1 \rangle$ to $\langle S_2, A, \rightarrow_2 \rangle$ is a nonexpansive function $h : S_1 \rightarrow S_2$ satisfying*

- *if $s_1 \xrightarrow{a}_1 s_1'$ then $h(s_1) \xrightarrow{a}_2 h(s_1')$ and*
- *if $h(s_1) \xrightarrow{a}_2 s_2'$ then $s_1 \xrightarrow{a}_1 s_1'$ for some s_1' such that $h(s_1') = s_2'$.*

A zigzag map preserves and reflects transitions (see, for example, [28]) and it does not increase any distances.

Theorem 5. *Given a metric space A, there exists a compactly branching and nonexpansive metric labelled transition system $\langle S_A, A, \rightarrow_A \rangle$ such that*

(1) for every compactly branching and nonexpansive metric labelled transition system $\langle S, A, \rightarrow \rangle$ there exists a unique zigzag map from $\langle S, A, \rightarrow \rangle$ to $\langle S_A, A, \rightarrow_A \rangle$.

For the rest of this section, we fix a compactly branching and nonexpansive metric labelled transition system $\langle S, A, \rightarrow \rangle$. Given a compactly branching and nonexpansive metric labelled transition system $\langle S_A, A, \rightarrow_A \rangle$ satisfying (1) of Theorem 5, we can define a behavioural pseudometric on S as follows.

Definition 16. *The distance function $d_c : S \times S \rightarrow [0, \infty]$ is defined by*

$$d_c(s_1, s_2) = d_{S_A}(h(s_1), h(s_2)),$$

where h is the unique zigzag map from $\langle S, A, \rightarrow \rangle$ to $\langle S_A, A, \rightarrow_A \rangle$.

There is more than one compactly branching and nonexpansive metric labelled transition system satisfying (1) of Theorem 5. However, the definition of the behavioural pseudometric d_c does not depend on the choice of $\langle S_A, A, \rightarrow_A \rangle$. Assume that the compactly branching and nonexpansive metric labelled transition systems $\langle S_A^1, A, \rightarrow_A^1 \rangle$ and $\langle S_A^2, A, \rightarrow_A^2 \rangle$ both satisfy (1) of Theorem 5. Consider the following unique zigzag maps.

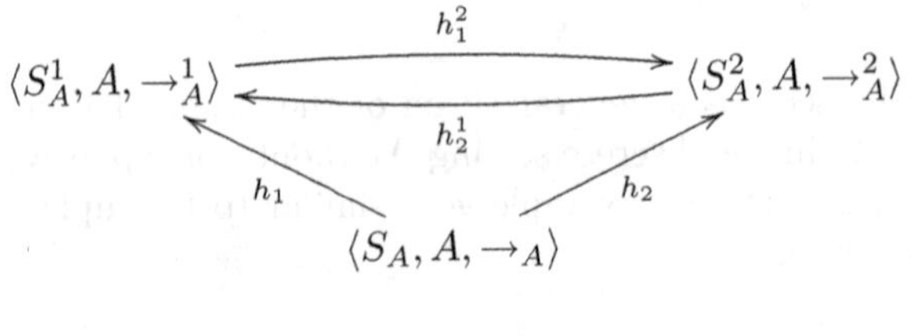

By uniqueness, we can conclude that $h_1 = h_2^1 \circ h_2$ and $h_2 = h_1^2 \circ h_1$. Hence, for all s_1, $s_2 \in S$,

$$\begin{aligned} d_c^1(s_1, s_2) &= d_{S_A^1}(h_1(s_1), h_1(s_2)) \\ &= d_{S_A^1}(h_2^1(h_2(s_1)), h_2^1(h_2(s_2))) \\ &\leq d_{S_A^1}(h_2(s_1), h_2(s_2)) \quad [h_2^1 \text{ is nonexpansive}] \\ &= d_c^2(s_1, s_2). \end{aligned}$$

Therefore, $d_c^1 \sqsupseteq d_c^2$. Similarly, we can show that $d_c^1 \sqsubseteq d_c^2$.

Note that the definition of the behavioural pseudometric d_c is restricted to compactly branching and nonexpansive metric labelled transition systems. For these systems, the behavioural pseudometrics d_c, d_f and d_ℓ coincide.

Theorem 6. $d_c = d_f$.

6 Terminal Coalgebras and Accessible Categories

In this section, we capture some of the results presented in the previous section in categorical terms. In particular, we exploit the theory of coalgebra to prove Theorem 5.

Definition 17. *Let $\mathbb{C}$ be a category. Let $\mathcal{F} : \mathbb{C} \to \mathbb{C}$ be a functor. An $\mathcal{F}$-coalgebra consists of an object C in $\mathbb{C}$ together with a morphism $f : C \to \mathcal{F}(C)$ in $\mathbb{C}$. An $\mathcal{F}$-homomorphism from $\mathcal{F}$-coalgebra $\langle C, f \rangle$ to $\mathcal{F}$-coalgebra $\langle D, g \rangle$ is a morphism $h : C \to D$ in $\mathbb{C}$ such that $\mathcal{F}(h) \circ f = g \circ h$.*

$$\begin{array}{ccc} C & \xrightarrow{\ h\ } & D \\ {\scriptstyle f}\downarrow & & \downarrow{\scriptstyle g} \\ \mathcal{F}(C) & \xrightarrow[\mathcal{F}(h)]{} & \mathcal{F}(D) \end{array}$$

The $\mathcal{F}$-coalgebras and $\mathcal{F}$-homomorphisms form a category. If this category has a terminal object, then this object is called a terminal $\mathcal{F}$-coalgebra.

For more details about the theory of coalgebra, we refer the reader to, for example, [20].

As we will see, compactly branching and nonexpansive metric labelled transition systems can be viewed as coalgebras. Next, we introduce the ingredients of the functor that induces those coalgebras.

The category $\mathbb{PM}et$ has pseudometric spaces as objects and nonexpansive functions as morphisms. We denote the identity functor on $\mathbb{PM}et$ by $\mathrm{Id}_{\mathbb{PM}et}$. Let A be a metric space. The constant functor $A : \mathbb{PM}et \to \mathbb{PM}et$ maps each pseudometric space to the space A and each nonexpansive function to the identity function on A. The operation $\otimes$ introduced in Definition 3 can be extended to a bifunctor as follows.

Definition 18. *Let $f : U \to X$ and $g : V \to Y$ be nonexpansive functions. The function $f \otimes g : (U \times V) \to (X \times Y)$ is defined by*

$$(f \otimes g)\langle u, v\rangle = \langle f(u), g(v)\rangle.$$

For a pseudometric space X, the subspace of $\mathcal{P}(X)$ consisting of the compact subsets of X endowed the Hausdorff metric introduced in Definition 4 is denoted by $\mathcal{H}(X)$. This operation can also be extended to a functor.

Definition 19. *Let $f : X \to Y$ be a nonexpansive function. The function $\mathcal{H}(f) : \mathcal{H}(X) \to \mathcal{H}(Y)$ is defined by*

$$\mathcal{H}(f)(A) = \{\, f(a) \mid a \in A \,\}.$$

Combining the above ingredients, we obtain the following functor.

Definition 20. *Given a metric space A, the functor $\mathcal{T}_A : \mathbb{PM}et \to \mathbb{PM}et$ is defined by*

$$\mathcal{T}_A = \mathcal{H}(A \otimes Id_{\mathbb{PM}et}).$$

One can easily verify that the $\mathcal{T}_A$-coalgebras exactly capture the compactly branching and nonexpansive metric labelled transition systems whose action space is A, and that the $\mathcal{T}_A$-homomorphisms are the zigzag maps of Definition 15. Hence, to prove Theorem 5, it suffices to prove

Theorem 7. *For each metric space A, a terminal $\mathcal{T}_A$-coalgebra exists.*

To prove the above theorem, we exploit the theory of accessible categories (see, for example, [21]). In particular, we apply the following terminal coalgebra theorem: If the category $\mathbb{C}$ is accessible and complete and the functor $\mathcal{F} : \mathbb{C} \to \mathbb{C}$ is accessible, then a terminal $\mathcal{F}$-coalgebra exists. This theorem is implicit in [21] (see also [5, Theorem 1]). The category $\mathbb{PM}et$ is complete (see, for example, [2, Chapter 4]) and the functor $\mathcal{T}_A$ is accessible (see [5, Section 4 and 5]). Hence, Theorem 7 follows from the above terminal coalgebra theorem.

Theorem 7 can be viewed as a generalisation of [3, Example 4.6]. There, a functor on the category of sets and functions is introduced whose coalgebras can be viewed as finitely branching labelled transition systems. This functor has a terminal coalgebra as well. Given any finitely branching labelled transition system, there exists a unique zigzag map from the system to the terminal one. The kernel of this zigzap map is bisimilarity.

7 Conclusion

Before discussing related and future work, we first briefly review our main contributions. We have presented a behavioural pseudometric for compactly branching and nonexpansive metric labelled transition systems. These systems capture a large class of timed transition systems. In particular, systems with uncountably many states and uncountable nondeterminism can be captured. Both are essential features of many timed transition systems. As we will see below, most related work restricts to finite nondeterminism or even to finite state spaces. Furthermore, we have painted a fairly complete picture by showing that the fixed point, logical, and coalgebraic characterisation of the behavioural pseudometric coincide. As a consequence, we can exploit the advantages of all three approaches. Most related work only provides one or two characterisations. Our three characterisations generalise the corresponding characterisations of bisimilarity. In particular, we have shown that states have distance 0 iff they are bisimilar.

7.1 Related Work

In the introductory section we have already mentioned some related work. Here, we discuss that work which is most relevant to ours.

Our work is most closely related to that of Ying and Wirsing [29,30]. Given a labelled transition system $\langle S, A, \rightarrow \rangle$ and a binary relation R on S, they introduce a bisimulation index i_R which is a nonnegative real number. Its definition shows similarities with the Hausdorff metric. The smaller i_R, the more R resembles a bisimulation. They also define an approximate notion of bisimilarity. For each $\lambda \in [0, \infty]$, the binary relation $\sim_\lambda$ on S is defined by $s_1 \sim_\lambda s_2$ if $s_1 \; R \; s_2$ for some R such that $i_R \leq \lambda$. Ordinary bisimilarity corresponds to $\sim_0$. Ying and Wirsing provide a fixed point characterisation of $\sim_\lambda$. They introduce a logic similar to Hennessy-Milner logic with the modality $\langle \boldsymbol{a} \rangle_r \varphi$, where $\boldsymbol{a}$ is a sequence of actions and r is a nonnegative real number. A logical characterisation is only given when either $\lambda = 0$ or the set of actions is endowed with an ultrametric (the Euclidean metric is not an ultrametric). Hence, this logic may not be very suitable for approximate reasoning (corresponding to the case $\lambda \neq 0$) of timed transition systems (where the actions usually carry the Euclidean metric). We conjecture that our behavioural pseudometric and their approximate notion of bisimilarity are related as follows: $d(s_1, s_2) = \inf\{ \lambda \mid s_1 \sim_\lambda s_2 \}$.

Also the work of Deng, Chothia, Palamidessi and Pang [12] is closely related to ours. They consider a more general type of system (they not only consider nondeterminism but also probabilistic nondeterminism), but they restrict themselves to finite state spaces and finite action spaces (and, hence, to finite nondeterminism). Deng et al. only provide a fixed point definition of their behavioural pseudometric. We conjecture that their behavioural pseudometric can be characterised coalgebraically by means of the functor $\mathcal{H}(\mathcal{K}(A \times \mathrm{Id}_{\mathbb{PM}et}))$, where $\mathcal{K}$ denotes the Kantorovich functor studied in [5].

De Alfaro, Faella and Stoelinga [10] consider a different type of system: finitely branching transition systems (and, hence, finite nondeterminism), the states of which are labelled (rather than the transitions). For these systems they define behavioural pseudometrics as fixed points and they also characterise them logically. We conjecture that their behavioural pseudometrics can be characterised coalgebraically by the functor $A \times \mathcal{H}(\mathrm{Id}_{\mathbb{PM}et})$ and variations thereof.

Very recently, Girard and Pappas [17] introduced behavioural pseudometrics for systems with continuous state spaces. Their distance functions are similar to the ones of de Alfaro, Faella and Stoelinga.

7.2 Future Work

If we replace the tensor product $\otimes$ with the product $\times$ in the functor $\mathcal{H}(A \otimes \mathrm{Id}_{\mathbb{PM}et})$, we obtain the functor $\mathcal{H}(A \times \mathrm{Id}_{\mathbb{PM}et})$. The corresponding coalgebras represent a class of metric labelled transition systems. For this functor, also a terminal coalgebra exists and, hence, it induces a behavioural pseudometric as well. Whereas the behavioural pseudometric studied in this paper accumulates differences, the proposed modification does not. This behavioural pseudometric can also be characterised as a fixed point. Modifying the logic and its interpretation so that we obtain a logical characterisation of the behavioural pseudometric is left as future work.

Logical formulae of the form $\varphi + r$ play a key role in the characteristic formula $\varphi_s^{\alpha+1}$ introduced in Definition 13. It is, however, not clear to us yet whether the logic $\mathcal{L}$ of Definition 10 and the logic $\mathcal{L}$ without formulae of the form $\varphi + r$ give rise to different behavioural pseudometrics.

Developing an algorithm to approximate our behavioural pseudometric is another topic for further research. The algorithms of [6,10] cannot be adapted in a straightforward way to our setting.

Acknowledgements

The author thanks Marcelo Fiore, Claudio Hermida, Robin Milner, Glynn Winskel and James Worrell for discussion and the referees for their constructive feedback.

References

1. P. Aczel and N. Mendler. A final coalgebra theorem. In *Proceedings of CTCS*, volume 389 of *LNCS*, pages 357–365, 1989. Springer-Verlag.
2. M.A. Arbib and E.G. Manes. *Arrows, Structures, and Functors: the categorical imperative*, Academic Press, 1975.
3. M. Barr. Terminal coalgebras in well-founded set theory. *Theoretical Computer Science*, 114(2):299–315, 1993.
4. F. van Breugel. A behavioural pseudometric for metric labelled transition systems. Technical Report CS-2005-11, York University, 2005.
5. F. van Breugel, C. Hermida, M. Makkai, and J. Worrell. An accessible approach to behavioural pseudometrics. In *Proceedings of ICALP*, volume 3580 of *LNCS*, pages 1018–1030, 2005. Springer-Verlag.
6. F. van Breugel and J. Worrell. An algorithm for quantitative verification of probabilistic transition systems. In *Proceedings of CONCUR*, volume 2154 of *LNCS*, pages 336–350, 2001. Springer-Verlag.
7. F. van Breugel and J. Worrell. Towards quantitative verification of probabilistic transition systems. In *Proceedings of ICALP*, volume 2076 of *LNCS*, pages 421–432, 2001. Springer-Verlag.

8. F. van Breugel and J. Worrell. A behavioural pseudometric for probabilistic transition systems. *Theoretical Computer Science*, 331(1):115–142, 2005.
9. L. de Alfaro. Quantitative verification and control via the mu-calculus. In *Proceedings of CONCUR*, volume 2761 of *LNCS*, pages 102–126, 2003. Springer-Verlag.
10. L. de Alfaro, M. Faella, and M. Stoelinga. Linear and branching metrics for quantitative transition systems. In *Proceedings of ICALP*, volume 3142 of *LNCS*, pages 97–109, 2004. Springer-Verlag.
11. L. de Alfaro, T.A. Henzinger, and R. Majumdar. Discounting the future in systems theory. In *Proceedings of ICALP*, volume 2719 of *LNCS*, pages 1022–1037, 2003. Springer-Verlag.
12. Y. Deng, T. Chothia, C. Palamidessi, and J. Pang. Metrics for action-labelled quantitative transition systems. In *Proceedings of QAPL*, ENTCS, 2005. Elsevier.
13. J. Desharnais, V. Gupta, R. Jagadeesan, and P. Panangaden. Metrics for labeled Markov systems. In *Proceedings of CONCUR*, volume 1664 of *LNCS*, pages 258–273, 1999. Springer-Verlag.
14. J. Desharnais, V. Gupta, R. Jagadeesan, and P. Panangaden. The metric analogue of weak bisimulation for probabilistic processes. In *Proceedings of LICS*, pages 413–422, 2002. IEEE.
15. J. Desharnais, V. Gupta, R. Jagadeesan, and P. Panangaden. Metrics for labelled Markov processes. *Theoretical Computer Science*, 318(3):323–354, 2004.
16. A. Giacalone, C.-C. Jou, and S.A. Smolka. Algebraic reasoning for probabilistic concurrent systems. In *Proceedings of PROCOMET*, pages 443–458, 1990. North-Holland.
17. A. Girard and G.J. Pappas. Approximation metrics for discrete and continuous systems. Technical Report MS-CIS-05-10, University of Pennsylvania, 2005.
18. V. Gupta, R. Jagadeesan, and P. Panangaden. Approximate reasoning for real-time probabilistic processes. In *Proceedings of QEST*, pages 304–313, 2004. IEEE.
19. M. Hennessy and R. Milner. Algebraic laws for nondeterminism and concurrency. *Journal of the ACM*, 32(1):137–161, 1985.
20. B. Jacobs and J.J.M.M. Rutten. A tutorial on (co)algebras and (co)induction. *Bulletin of the EATCS*, 62:222–259, 1997.
21. M. Makkai and R. Paré. *Accessible Categories: The Foundation of Categorical Model Theory*, American Mathematical Society, 1989.
22. R. Milner. *Communication and Concurrency*, Prentice Hall International, 1989.
23. R. Milner. David Michael Ritchie Park (1935–1990) in memoriam. *Theoretical Computer Science*, 133(2):187–200, 1994.
24. D. Park. Concurrency and automata on infinite sequences. In *Proceedings of 5th GI-Conference on Theoretical Computer Science*, volume 104 of *LNCS*, pages 167–183, 1981. Springer-Verlag.
25. D. Sangiorgi. Bisimulation: from the origins to today. In *Proceedings of LICS*, pages 298–302. IEEE, 2004.
26. M.B. Smyth. Topology. In *Handbook of Logic in Computer Science*, volume 1, pages 641–761. Oxford University Press, 1992.
27. B. Steffen and A. Ingólfsdóttir. Characteristic formulae for processes with divergence. *Information and Computation*, 110(1):149–163, 1994.
28. G. Winskel and M. Nielsen. Models for concurrency. In *Handbook of Logic in Computer Science*, volume 4, pages 1–148. Oxford University Press, 1995.
29. M. Ying. Bisimulation indexes and their applications. *Theoretical Computer Science*, 275(1/2):1–68, 2002.
30. M. Ying and M. Wirsing. Approximate bisimilarity. In *Proceedings of AMAST*, volume 1816 of *LNCS*, pages 309–322, 2000. Springer-Verlag.

On Probabilistic Program Equivalence and Refinement*

Andrzej S. Murawski and Joël Ouaknine

Oxford University Computing Laboratory,
Wolfson Building, Parks Road, Oxford OX1 3QD, UK

Abstract. We study notions of *equivalence* and *refinement* for probabilistic programs formalized in the second-order fragment of Probabilistic Idealized Algol. Probabilistic programs implement randomized algorithms: a given input yields a probability distribution on the set of possible outputs. Intuitively, two programs are equivalent if they give rise to identical distributions for all inputs. We show that equivalence is decidable by studying the fully abstract game semantics of probabilistic programs and relating it to probabilistic finite automata. For terms in β-normal form our decision procedure runs in time exponential in the syntactic size of programs; it is moreover fully compositional in that it can handle *open* programs (probabilistic modules with unspecified components).

In contrast, we show that the natural notion of program refinement, in which the input-output distributions of one program uniformly dominate those of the other program, is undecidable.

1 Introduction

Ever since Michael Rabin's seminal paper on probabilistic algorithms [1], it has been widely recognized that introducing randomization in the design of algorithms can yield substantial improvements in time and space complexity. There are by now dozens of randomized algorithms solving a wide range of problems much more efficiently than their 'deterministic' counterparts—see [2] for a good textbook survey of the field.

Unfortunately, these advantages are not without a price. Randomized algorithms can be rather subtle and tricky to understand, let alone prove correct. Moreover, the very notion of 'correctness' slips from the Boolean to the probabilistic. Indeed, whereas traditional deterministic algorithms associate to each input a given output, randomized algorithms yield for each input a *probabilistic distribution* on the set of possible outputs.

The main focus of this paper is the study of *probabilistic equivalence*. Intuitively, two algorithms are equivalent if they give rise to identical distributions for all inputs. To this end, we introduce (second-order) Probabilistic Idealized

* Work supported by the UK EPSRC (GR/R88861/01) and St John's College, Oxford.

M. Abadi and L. de Alfaro (Eds.): CONCUR 2005, LNCS 3653, pp. 156–170, 2005.

Algol, a programming language which extends Idealized Algol[1] by allowing *(fair) coin-tossing* as a valid expression. It can be shown that, in the presence of loop constructs, this notion of randomization is as powerful as any other 'reasonable' one. Any randomized algorithm can therefore be coded in Probabilistic Idealized Algol. An important consequence of our work is to enable the automated comparison of different randomized algorithms against each other.

We study program equivalence through fully abstract game models, and obtain EXPTIME decidability by recasting the problem in terms of probabilistic automata. We also investigate *program refinement*, a notion intended to capture the relationship that an implementation should enjoy with respect to its specification, and prove undecidability. Our paper continues the algorithmic line of research in game semantics initiated in [4,5], which aims to exploit the fully abstract character of the game models. These provide exact accounts of extensional behaviour and lead to models of programs that are much different from the traditional approaches to program verification. Their distinctive feature is the absence of explicit reference to state (state manipulations are hidden) which leads to precise and compact summaries of observable program behaviour.

Related Work. Much previous work in probabilistic program verification has focussed on *probabilistic model checking*, whereby a probabilistic program is checked against a probabilistic temporal logic specification—see, e.g., [6,7] and references within. Probabilistic behavioural equivalences have also been studied in the context of process algebra, both from an operational (e.g., [8]) and a denotational (e.g., [9]) perspective.

2 Probabilistic Idealized Algol

The subject of this paper is the finitary version $\mathsf{PA_f}$ of Probabilistic Idealized Algol. Its types θ are generated by the grammar

$$\beta ::= com \,|\, exp \,|\, var \qquad \theta ::= \beta \,|\, \theta \to \theta$$

where β stands for base types: *com* is the command type, *exp* is the *finite* type of expressions ($exp = \{\,0, \cdots, max\,\}$ for $max > 0$), *var* is the type of assignable variables in which one can store values of type *exp*. The order of a type, written $\mathsf{ord}(\theta)$ is defined by: $\mathsf{ord}(\beta) = 0$, $\mathsf{ord}(\theta \to \theta') = \max(\mathsf{ord}(\theta) + 1, \mathsf{ord}(\theta'))$. $\mathsf{PA_f}$ enables probabilistic functional and imperative programming. Recursion is allowed only in the strictly restricted form of **while**-loops. The complete syntax is shown in Figure 1. We will say that a term-in-context $\Gamma \vdash M : \theta$ is of order i provided $\mathsf{ord}(\theta) \leq i$ and identifiers from Γ have types of order strictly less than i. The big-step operational semantics is defined for terms $\Gamma \vdash M : \theta$, where $\Gamma =$

[1] Devised by Reynolds [3], Idealized Algol augments a Pascal-like procedural language with functional programming constructs. We consider a finitary version in which variables range over a bounded set of integers, terms are parameterized by the allowable higher-order types of their free identifiers, and neither recursion nor pointers are allowed.

$$\frac{}{\Gamma \vdash \mathit{skip} : \mathit{com}} \qquad \frac{i \in \{0, \cdots, \mathit{max}\}}{\Gamma \vdash i : \mathit{exp}} \qquad \frac{}{\Gamma \vdash \mathit{coin} : \mathit{exp}}$$

$$\frac{}{\Gamma, x : \theta \vdash x : \theta} \qquad \frac{\Gamma \vdash M : \mathit{exp}}{\Gamma \vdash \mathbf{succ}(M) : \mathit{exp}} \qquad \frac{\Gamma \vdash M : \mathit{exp}}{\Gamma \vdash \mathbf{pred}(M) : \mathit{exp}}$$

$$\frac{\Gamma \vdash M : \mathit{exp} \quad \Gamma \vdash N_0 : \beta \quad \Gamma \vdash N_1 : \beta}{\Gamma \vdash \mathbf{ifzero}\, M\, N_0\, N_1 : \beta}$$

$$\frac{\Gamma \vdash M : \mathit{com} \quad \Gamma \vdash N : \beta}{\Gamma \vdash M; N : \beta} \qquad \frac{\Gamma \vdash M : \mathit{exp} \quad \Gamma \vdash N : \mathit{com}}{\Gamma \vdash \mathbf{while}\ M\ \mathbf{do}\ N : \mathit{com}}$$

$$\frac{\Gamma \vdash M : \mathit{var}}{\Gamma \vdash !M : \mathit{exp}} \qquad \frac{\Gamma \vdash M : \mathit{var} \quad \Gamma \vdash N : \mathit{exp}}{\Gamma \vdash M := N : \mathit{com}}$$

$$\frac{\Gamma, X : \mathit{var} \vdash M : \mathit{com}, \mathit{exp}}{\Gamma \vdash \mathbf{new}\ X\ \mathbf{in}\ M : \mathit{com}, \mathit{exp}}$$

$$\frac{\Gamma, x : \theta \vdash M : \theta'}{\Gamma \vdash \lambda x^{\theta}.M : \theta \to \theta'} \qquad \frac{\Gamma \vdash M : \theta \to \theta' \quad \Gamma \vdash N : \theta}{\Gamma \vdash MN : \theta'}$$

Fig. 1. Syntax of $\mathsf{PA_f}$

$x_1 : \mathit{var}, \cdots, x_n : \mathit{var}$, through judgments of the shape $(s, M) \Downarrow^p (s', V)$, where s, s' are functions from $\{x_1, \cdots, x_n\}$ to $\{0, \cdots, \mathit{max}\}$. Whenever an evaluation tree ends in $(s, M) \Downarrow^p (s', V)$ we can interpret that as "the associated evaluation of M from state s has probability p". Because of *coin*, M may have countably many evaluations from a given s. We shall write $(s, M) \downarrow^p V$ iff $p = \sum p_i$ and the sum ranges over all evaluations of the form $(s, M) \Downarrow^{p_i} (s', V)$ (for some s'). If there are no such reductions, we simply have $(s, M) \downarrow^0 V$. The judgment $(s, M) \downarrow^p V$ thus denotes the fact that the probability of evaluating M in state s to V is p. When M is closed we write $M \downarrow^p V$, because s is then trivial. For instance, we have $\mathit{coin} \downarrow^{0.5} 0$ and $\mathit{coin} \downarrow^{0.5} 1$.

We can now define the induced notion of contextual equivalence: the terms-in-context $\Gamma \vdash M_1 : \theta$ and $\Gamma \vdash M_2 : \theta$ are *equivalent* (written $\Gamma \vdash M_1 \cong M_2$) if for all contexts $\mathcal{C}[-]$ such that $\vdash \mathcal{C}[M_1], \mathcal{C}[M_2] : \mathit{com}$ we have $\mathcal{C}[M_1] \downarrow^p \mathit{skip}$ if and only if $\mathcal{C}[M_2] \downarrow^p \mathit{skip}$. Danos and Harmer gave a fully abstract game model for $\cong$ in [10], which we review in the following section.

As stated in the Introduction, randomized algorithms can readily be coded in Probabilistic Idealized Algol. Under mild conditions[2], contextual equivalence then precisely corresponds to the natural notion of equivalence for randomized algorithms: identical input/output distributions.

3 Probabilistic Game Semantics

The games needed to interpret probabilistic programs are played in arenas as in the sequential case. An arena A is a triple $\langle M_A, \lambda_A, \vdash_A \rangle$, where M_A is the set of

[2] Essentially syntactic restrictions aimed at preventing undesirable side-effects.

moves, $\lambda_A : M_A \to \{\,O, P\,\} \times \{\,Q, A\,\}$ indicates to which of the two players (O or P) each move belongs and whether it is a question- or an answer-move, and $\vdash_A$ is the so-called *enabling* relation between $\{\,\star\,\} + M_A$ and M_A. $\vdash_A$ is required to satisfy a number of technical conditions: for instance, moves enabled by $\star$, called *initial* and collected in the set called I_A, must be O-questions and whenever one move enables another they have to belong to different players. Here are the arenas used to interpret base types:

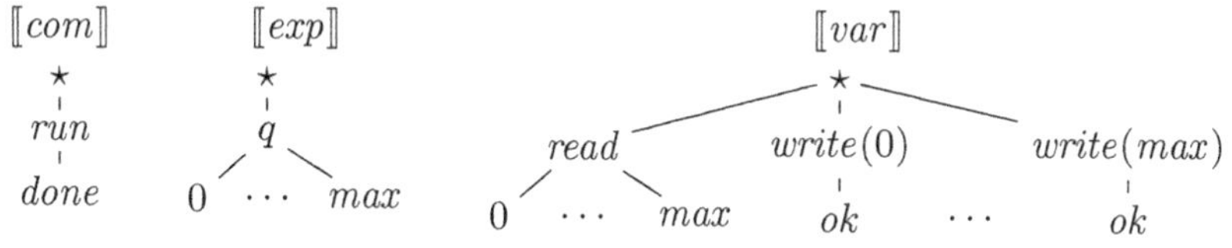

The moves $run, q, read$ and $write(i)$ $(0 \le i \le max)$ are initial O-questions, the rest are P-answers enabled by the respective O-questions.

Arenas can be combined to form *product* and *arrow* arenas as follows[3].

$$\begin{aligned} M_{A\times B} &= M_A + M_B \\ \lambda_{A\times B} &= [\lambda_A, \lambda_B] \\ \vdash_{A\times B} &= \vdash_A + \vdash_B \end{aligned}$$

$$\begin{aligned} M_{A\Rightarrow B} &= M_A + M_B \\ \lambda_{A\Rightarrow B} &= [\overline{\lambda}_A, \lambda_B] \\ \vdash_{A\Rightarrow B} &= (\vdash_A \cap (M_A \times M_A)) \ + \ (I_B \times I_A) + \ \vdash_B \end{aligned}$$

The allowable exchanges of moves in an arena A are *justified sequences*, which are sequences of moves of A such that each occurrence of a non-initial move n is equipped with a pointer to an earlier move m such that $m \vdash_A n$. In order for a justified sequence to become a *play*, the moves must alternate between the two players (O necessarily begins then) and the standard conditions of visibility and bracketing must be satisfied [11,12]. The set of plays over A will be denoted by $\mathcal{L}_A$, that of odd- and even-length ones by $\mathcal{L}_A^{\mathsf{odd}}$ and $\mathcal{L}_A^{\mathsf{even}}$ respectively.

The notion of a probabilistic strategy makes a departure from sequential game semantics. A strategy σ is a function $\sigma : \mathcal{L}_A^{\mathsf{even}} \to [0,1]$ such that $\sigma(\varepsilon) = 1$ and for any $s \in \mathcal{L}_A^{\mathsf{even}}, sa \in \mathcal{L}_A^{\mathsf{odd}}$ we have $\sigma(s) \ge \sum_{\{\, sab \in \mathcal{L}_A^{\mathsf{even}} \,\}} \sigma(sab)$. Let $\mathcal{T}_\sigma$ be the set of all even-length plays s such that $\sigma(s) > 0$. In the following they will be called the *traces* of σ. To interpret *coin* one takes the strategy $\sigma : [\![exp]\!]$ such that $\sigma(qi_1 \cdots qi_n) = (1/2)^n$ where $i_1, \cdots, i_n \in \{\,0, 1\,\}$ and $\sigma(s) = 0$ otherwise.

The above definition of a strategy describes the global probabilistic behaviour. Providing $s \in \mathcal{T}_\sigma$ and $sa \in \mathcal{L}_A^{\mathsf{odd}}$ the conditional (local) probability of sab given sa can be calculated by taking $\sigma(sab)/\sigma(s)$.

Probabilistic strategies are composed by considering interaction sequences between them. Suppose u is a sequence of moves from arenas A, B, C together with unique pointers from all moves except those initial in C. We define $u \upharpoonright B, C$

[3] $\overline{\lambda}_A$ works like λ_A except that it reverses the ownership of moves.

by deleting from u all moves from A together with associated pointers. $u \upharpoonright A, B$ is defined in a similar way. $u \upharpoonright A, C$ works analogously except that whenever there was a pointer from an A-move m_A to a B-move m_B and a pointer from m_B to a C-move m_C, we introduce a pointer from m_A to m_C. u is called an *interaction sequence* of A, B, C provided $u \upharpoonright A, B \in \mathcal{L}_{A \Rightarrow B}$ and $u \upharpoonright B, C \in \mathcal{L}_{B \Rightarrow C}$. The set of interaction sequences is then denoted by $\mathcal{I}(A, B, C)$. If $s \in \mathcal{L}^{\mathsf{even}}_{A \Rightarrow C}$, the set of B-witnesses of s, written $\mathsf{wit}_B(s)$, is defined to be $\{ u \in \mathcal{I}(A, B, C) \mid u \upharpoonright A, C = s \}$. Finally, given $\sigma : A \Rightarrow B$ and $\tau : B \Rightarrow C$, one defines $\sigma; \tau : A \Rightarrow C$ by

$$(\sigma; \tau)(s) = \sum_{u \in \mathsf{wit}_B(s)} \sigma(u \upharpoonright A, B) \cdot \tau(u \upharpoonright B, C).$$

4 Inside the Game Model

In general, plays may contain several occurrences of initial moves. Such occurrences define *threads* within the play in the following way: two moves are in the same thread if they are connected via chains of pointers to the same occurrence of an initial move. Plays that contain just one occurrence of an initial move (and consequently consist of one thread only) are called *well-opened* (we write $\mathcal{L}^{\mathsf{wo}}_A$ for the set containing them)[4].

Because plays satisfy the visibility condition, responses by P are always in the same thread as the preceding O-move, a condition known as *well-threadedness*. A stricter class of *single-threaded* strategies arises when one requires that P-responses depend on the thread of play of the preceding O-move. This behaviour is formally captured by the notion of a comonoid homomorphism in [10] and can be summed up in two points. Firstly, the threads occurring in a trace are also traces, so we can regard traces as interleavings of well-opened ones (such that only O can switch between threads). Secondly, whenever a trace s is an interleaving of well-opened $s_1, \cdots, s_n$, we have $\sigma(s) = \sigma(s_1) \cdot \ldots \cdot \sigma(s_n)$. As shown in [10], arenas and single-threaded strategies, quotiented by the *intrinsic preorder*, constitute a fully abstract model for $\cong$. Next we give a more direct full abstraction result based on comparing probabilities in special kinds of plays rather than quotienting them.

Our analysis will also capture a notion of probabilistic refinement defined as follows: $\Gamma \vdash M_1 : \theta$ *refines* $\Gamma \vdash M_2 : \theta$, written $\Gamma \vdash M_1 \precsim M_2$, iff for all contexts $\mathcal{C}[-]$ such that $\vdash \mathcal{C}[M_1], \mathcal{C}[M_2] : com$ if $\mathcal{C}[M_1] \Downarrow^{p_1} skip$ then $\mathcal{C}[M_2] \Downarrow^{p_2} skip$ and $p_1 \leq p_2$. Note that $M_1 \cong M_2$ iff $M_1 \precsim M_2$ and $M_2 \precsim M_1$. We are going to show that, like in the sequential second-order case [4], $\cong$ is decidable. However, in contrast, $\precsim$ will turn out undecidable.

[4] Equivalently, one can present the model in the style of [12], where terms induce well-opened sequences only and the interpretation of function spaces adheres to the decomposition $A \Rightarrow B = !A \multimap B$. In this paper we stick to the presentation of [10], where the induced plays do not have to be well-opened, but the strategies are restricted to be single-threaded.

Definition 1. *A play* $s \in \mathcal{L}_A^{\mathsf{even}}$ *is* **complete** *iff all questions in* s *are answered. The set of complete plays of* A *is denoted by* $\mathcal{L}_A^{\mathsf{comp}}$. *Suppose* $\sigma_1, \sigma_2 : A$ *are single-threaded strategies. We then define:*

$$\sigma_1 \leq_\pi \sigma_2 \stackrel{\text{def}}{\Longleftrightarrow} \sigma_1(s) \leq \sigma_2(s) \text{ for all } s \in \mathcal{L}_A^{\mathsf{wo}} \cap \mathcal{L}_A^{\mathsf{comp}}.$$

Lemma 1. *Let* $\vdash M_1, M_2 : \theta$ *and* $\sigma_i = [\![\vdash M_i]\!]$ $(i = 1, 2)$. *Then* $\vdash M_1 \sqsubsetapprox M_2$ *if and only if* $\sigma_1 \leq_\pi \sigma_2$.

Proof. Suppose $\vdash M_1 \sqsubsetapprox M_2$. Let $s \in \mathcal{L}_{[\![\theta]\!]}^{\mathsf{wo}} \cap \mathcal{L}_{[\![\theta]\!]}^{\mathsf{comp}}$ and $\sigma_1(s) = p_1$. By the definability result for (sequential) Idealized Algol in [12] there exists a *deterministic* context $x : \theta \vdash \mathcal{C}[x] : com$ such that the only well-opened complete play in $[\![x : \theta \vdash \mathcal{C}[x] : com]\!]_{\mathsf{IA}}$ is *run s done*. Then in the probabilistic game model we have $[\![x : \theta \vdash \mathcal{C}[x] : com]\!](run\ s\ done) = 1$ and $[\![x : \theta \vdash \mathcal{C}[x] : com]\!](run\ s'\ done) = 0$ whenever $s \neq s'$. So:

$$[\![\vdash \mathcal{C}[M_1] : com]\!](run\ done) = (\sigma_1; [\![x : \theta \vdash \mathcal{C}[x] : com]\!])(run\ done) = p_1.$$

By adequacy (Theorem 3.2 in [10]) $\mathcal{C}[M_1] \Downarrow^{p_1} skip$. Because $\vdash M_1 \sqsubsetapprox M_2$ we have $\mathcal{C}[M_2] \Downarrow^{p_2} skip$ and $p_1 \leq p_2$. By soundness for evaluation (Theorem 3.2 in [10]) $\sigma_2(run\ done) = p_2$. Because $[\![\vdash \mathcal{C}[M_2]]\!] = \sigma_2; [\![x : \theta \vdash \mathcal{C}[x] : com]\!]$ and $\mathcal{C}$ is deterministic, we have $\sigma_2(s) = p_2$. Hence, $\sigma_1 \leq_\pi \sigma_2$.

Now we prove the contrapositive of the converse. Suppose we do not have $\vdash M_1 \sqsubsetapprox M_2$, i.e. there exists a context $\mathcal{C}[-]$ such that $\vdash \mathcal{C}[M_i] : com$, $\mathcal{C}[M_i] \Downarrow^{p_i} skip$ for $i = 1, 2$ and $p_1 > p_2$. By soundness, compositionality and the composition formula we have

$$p_i = [\![\vdash \mathcal{C}[M_i]]\!](run\ done) = (\sigma_i; [\![x : \theta \vdash \mathcal{C}[x] : com]\!])(run\ done) =$$
$$= \sum_{u \in \mathsf{wit}_{[\![\theta]\!]}(run\ done)} \sigma_i(u \upharpoonright 1, [\![\theta]\!]) \cdot [\![x : \theta \vdash \mathcal{C}[x] : com]\!](u \upharpoonright [\![\theta]\!], [\![com]\!]).$$

Since $p_1 > p_2$, there must exist $u \in \mathsf{wit}_{[\![\theta]\!]}(run\ done)$ such that $\sigma_1(u \upharpoonright 1, [\![\theta]\!]) > \sigma_2(u \upharpoonright 1, [\![\theta]\!])$. Let $s = u \upharpoonright 1, [\![\theta]\!]$. Because *run done* is complete, so is s. In general s might be an interleaving of several well-opened complete plays, let us call them $s_1, \cdots, s_k$. Because σ_i is single-threaded, we then have $\sigma_i(s) = \prod_{j=1}^k \sigma_i(s_j)$ and, further, because $\sigma_1(s) > \sigma_2(s)$, we must have $\sigma_1(s_j) > \sigma_2(s_j)$ for some j. Consequently, $\sigma_1 \not\leq_\pi \sigma_2$. □

The Lemma generalizes to open terms (by observing that $\Gamma \vdash M_1 \sqsubsetapprox M_2$ is equivalent to $\vdash \lambda\Gamma.M_1 \sqsubsetapprox \lambda\Gamma.M_2$) and implies the following result for program equivalence. Given single-threaded strategies $\sigma_1, \sigma_2 : A$ we write $\sigma_1 =_\pi \sigma_2$ iff $\sigma_1(s) = \sigma_2(s)$ for all $s \in \mathcal{L}_A^{\mathsf{wo}} \cap \mathcal{L}_A^{\mathsf{comp}}$.

Lemma 2. *Let* $\vdash M_1, M_2 : \theta$ *and* $\sigma_i = [\![\vdash M_i]\!]$ $(i = 1, 2)$. *Then* $\vdash M_1 \cong M_2$ *if and only if* $\sigma_1 =_\pi \sigma_2$.

5 Probabilistic Automata

Probabilistic automata (PA) generalize finite automata in that probability distributions are imposed on transitions. Their first definition goes back to Rabin's work in the 1960s [13] (see Paz [14] for a textbook treatment). Various modifications of the automata have recently reappeared in research on probabilistic systems (see e.g. [15,16]).

Let X be a finite set. A *subprobability* over X is a function $\omega : X \to [0,1]$ such that $\sum_{x\in X}\omega(x) \leq 1$. A *probabilistic distribution* over X is a subprobability such that $\sum_{x\in X}\omega(x) = 1$. We write $\mathcal{S}(X), \mathcal{P}(X)$ respectively for the sets of all subprobabilities and probabilistic distributions over X.

Definition 2. *A* **probabilistic automaton** *is a tuple* $\mathcal{A} = \langle Q, \Sigma, i, F, \delta \rangle$, *where* Q *is a finite set of states,* Σ *is the alphabet,* $i \in Q$ *is the initial state,* $F \subseteq Q$ *is the set of final states and* δ *is the transition function, which can take one of the following two shapes: either* $\delta : Q \times \Sigma \to \mathcal{P}(Q)$ *or* $\delta : Q \to \mathcal{P}(\Sigma \times Q)$. *In the former case* $\mathcal{A}$ *is called* **reactive**, *in the latter* **generative**.

The different shapes of the transition function reflect the typical scenarios which the two kinds of automata are used to model. Reactive automata describe probabilistic reactions to given symbols, while for generative ones the symbol is viewed as part of the probabilistic response. The automata we are going to use to model probabilistic programs will turn out to combine the features of the two. O-moves will adhere to a restricted form of the reactive framework, whereas P-moves will be generative.

We refer to transitions by writing $q \xrightarrow{x,p} q'$ whenever $\delta(q,x)(q') = p$ (the reactive case) or $\delta(q)(x,q') = p$ (the generative case). A run r of a probabilistic automaton is a sequence of transitions

$$i \xrightarrow{x_1,p_1} q_1 \xrightarrow{x_2,p_2} \cdots \xrightarrow{x_k,p_k} q_k.$$

Let us write $P_{\mathcal{A}}(r)$ for the probability of the run r, i.e. $P_{\mathcal{A}}(r) = \prod_{i=1}^{k} p_i$. The word associated with the run r will be denoted by $W_{\mathcal{A}}(r)$, i.e. $W_{\mathcal{A}}(r) = x_1 \cdots x_k$. A run is accepting if $q_k \in F$. Let $Acc_{\mathcal{A}}(w)$ be the set of accepting runs r such that $W_{\mathcal{A}}(r) = w$. For a given automaton $\mathcal{A}$ we define a function $\mathcal{A} : \Sigma^\star \to [0,1]$ as follows

$$\mathcal{A}(w) = \sum_{r \in Acc_{\mathcal{A}}(w)} P_{\mathcal{A}}(r).$$

$\mathcal{A}(w)$ denotes the probability that the automaton reaches a final state and reads the string w.

From now on we restrict our attention to automata in which the probabilities associated with transitions are rational numbers. We shall also often consider automata where the requisite distributions are in fact only subprobabilities on the understanding that they can be extended to probability distributions by adding a dummy "sink" state and dummy transitions. In this sense generative automata can be considered special cases of reactive ones. Note also that a reactive automaton $\mathcal{A}$ can be converted to a generative one, which we denote $\mathcal{A}/|\Sigma|$, by dividing all probabilities occurring in transitions by the size of the alphabet. We introduce the following two decision problems.

Definition 3. *Suppose $\mathcal{A}_1, \mathcal{A}_2$ are probabilistic automata of the same kind.*

- EQUIVALENCE*: $\mathcal{A}_1(w) = \mathcal{A}_2(w)$ for all $w \in \Sigma^*$.*
- REFINEMENT*: $\mathcal{A}_1(w) \leq \mathcal{A}_2(w)$ for all $w \in \Sigma^*$.*

EQUIVALENCE for reactive automata was already considered by Paz in [14] (in a slightly different setting) and shown decidable. His proof relies on the observation that in order to prove two automata equivalent it suffices to verify equivalence for strings of length $n_1 + n_2 - 1$, where n_1, n_2 are the respective numbers of states. This leads to an NP algorithm. Paz's result was subsequently refined by Tzeng [17], who presented a PTIME algorithm based on a search for a basis in a vector space. Note that the decidability of EQUIVALENCE for reactive automata implies decidability for generative automata as well.

In contrast, we next show that REFINEMENT is undecidable by reducing the following problem to it:

> NONEMPTINESS WITH THRESHOLD: Given a reactive automaton $\mathcal{A}$ and a rational $0 \leq \lambda \leq 1$, there exists $w \in \Sigma^*$ such that $\mathcal{A}(w) > \lambda$.

NONEMPTINESS WITH THRESHOLD was introduced by Rabin [13] and proved undecidable by Paz [14]. More recently, Blondel and Canterini [18] gave a more elementary proof based on Post's Correspondence Problem. Observe that the complement of NONEMPTINESS WITH THRESHOLD reduces to REFINEMENT (for reactive automata) by considering the automaton $\mathcal{A} = \langle \{ i, f \}, \Sigma, i, \{ f \}, \delta \rangle$ below which accepts every non-empty word with probability λ.

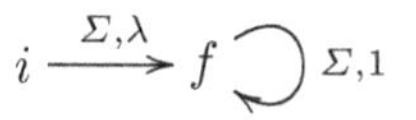

Then we have $\mathcal{A}(w) = \lambda$ for any $w \in \Sigma^+$, which implies undecidability of REFINEMENT in the reactive case.

The undecidability carries over to the generative case, because the refinement of $\mathcal{A}_1$ by $\mathcal{A}_2$, where both are reactive, is equivalent to the refinement of $\mathcal{A}_1/|\Sigma|$ by $\mathcal{A}_2/|\Sigma|$ (both generative). Furthermore, refinement remains undecidable for pairs of generative automata in which all probabilities in $\mathcal{A}_1$ and $\mathcal{A}_2$ are of the form $m/2^n$. To see this, observe that refinement of $\mathcal{A}_1$ by $\mathcal{A}_2$ is equivalent to that of $v\mathcal{A}_1$ by $v\mathcal{A}_2$, where $v \in (0, 1]$ and $v\mathcal{A}$ is obtained from $\mathcal{A}$ by multiplying all probabilities on transitions by v. Now given $\mathcal{A}_1$ and $\mathcal{A}_2$, choose $v = d/2^n$, where d is the least common denominator of all the probabilities appearing in both $\mathcal{A}_1$ and $\mathcal{A}_2$, and 2^n is the smallest power of two that exceeds d. Every weight in $v\mathcal{A}_1$ and $v\mathcal{A}_2$ is now of the form $m/2^n$ for some integer m. We are interested in restricting the probabilities to this form, because later on we are going to simulate generative automata in $\mathsf{PA_f}$. Although it was shown in [10] that the strategy representing *coin* is universal, the proof relied on infinitary features such as infinite datatypes and recursion. By contrast, distributions based on probabilities of the shape $m/2^n$ can be simulated in a small fragment of $\mathsf{PA_f}$ that does not even require **while**.

Another problem from the theory of probabilistic automata that will be useful in our work concerns ε-transitions. Note that the definitions of probabilistic automata (as well as those of $P_{\mathcal{A}}(r), W_{\mathcal{A}}(r)$ and $\mathcal{A}(w)$) can easily be extended to encompass ε-transitions. Then it is natural to ask whether and how ε-transitions can be removed in such a way as to yield an equivalent automaton. This problem was investigated by Mohri in the general setting of weighted automata, where the weights come from a variety of semirings [19,20]. The probabilistic case then falls into the case of *closed* semirings, which require a special approach based on a decomposition into strongly-connected components and a generalization of the Floyd-Warshall all-pairs shortest-path algorithm. This decomposition is designed to handle the problematic ε-cycles, as it is easier to deal with them in a strongly-connected component. A consequence of the algorithm is the fact that rationality of weights is preserved after ε-removal, which should be contrasted with the general failure of compositionality for rational strategies pointed out in [10].

6 Second-order Program Equivalence is Decidable

Recall that a $\mathsf{PA_f}$ term $\Gamma \vdash M : \theta$ is a second-order term if $\mathsf{ord}(\theta) \leq 2$ and the type of each identifier from Γ is either a base type or a first-order type. We show that program equivalence for second-order $\mathsf{PA_f}$ terms is decidable. The argument will be based on a reduction to EQUIVALENCE for reactive automata via Lemma 2. More precisely, we show that for any second-order $\mathsf{PA_f}$ term there exists a reactive automaton which accepts (the sequences of moves that occur in) well-opened complete plays with the same probabilities as those assigned to them by the corresponding probabilistic strategy. As we are interested in the second-order terms only, it is not necessary to represent pointers, because they can be uniquely reconstructed [4]. Consequently, we ignore them completely in what follows.

The automata corresponding to programs will be special instances of reactive automata. Their sets of states will be partitioned into O-states and P-states: only transitions on O-moves (respectively P-moves) will be available from O-states (respectively P-states). Moreover, at O-states, there can only be at most one transition for a given input letter (its probability is then 1). For P-states, however, the probabilities of all outgoing transitions will have to add up to at most 1, which is consistent with the generative framework. This pattern of behaviour is captured by the definition below (M_A^O and M_A^P stand for the sets of O-moves and P-moves respectively).

Definition 4. *An A-automaton is a tuple* $\mathcal{A} = \langle\, Q, M_A, i, f, \delta\,\rangle$, *where:*

1. $Q = Q^O + Q^P$ *is the set of states (elements of* Q^O, Q^P *are called O-states and P-states respectively);*
2. i *has no incoming transitions,* f *has no outgoing transitions;*

3. $\{i, f\} \subseteq Q^O$;
4. $\delta = \delta^O + \delta^P$, where $\delta^O : Q^O \times M_A^O \rightharpoonup Q^P$ ($\delta(q,m) = q'$ is taken to mean $\delta(q,m)(q') = 1$) and $\delta^P : Q^P \rightharpoonup \mathcal{S}(M_A^P \times Q^O)$;
5. sequences of moves determined by runs of $\mathcal{A}$ are plays of A, accepting runs are complete positions.

Example 1. *coin* : *exp* will be interpreted by the automaton $i \xrightarrow{q,1} \circ \overset{0,\frac{1}{2}}{\underset{1,\frac{1}{2}}{\rightrightarrows}} f$.

Definition 5. *A* $[\![\Gamma \vdash \theta]\!]$*-automaton* $\mathcal{A}$ *represents* $\Gamma \vdash M : \theta$ *iff*

$$\mathcal{A}(w) = \begin{cases} [\![\Gamma \vdash M : \theta]\!](w) & w \in \mathcal{L}^{\mathsf{wo}}_{[\![\Gamma\vdash\theta]\!]} \cap \mathcal{L}^{\mathsf{comp}}_{[\![\Gamma\vdash\theta]\!]} \\ 0 & \text{otherwise} \end{cases}$$

In the rest of this section we set out to prove that any second-order $\mathsf{PA_f}$ term is represented by an automaton as specified in the definition above. It suffices to prove that this is the case for terms in β-normal form, since β-equivalent terms are also $\cong$-equivalent (the fully abstract model [10] is a cartesian-closed category). The most difficult stage in the construction is the interpretation of the application rule

$$\frac{\Gamma \vdash M : \theta \to \theta' \quad \Gamma \vdash N : \theta}{\Gamma \vdash MN : \theta'}$$

which will be split into two simpler rules, multiplicative application and contraction respectively:

$$\frac{\Gamma \vdash M : \theta \to \theta' \quad \Delta \vdash N : \theta}{\Gamma, \Delta \vdash MN : \theta'} \qquad \frac{\Gamma, x : \theta, y : \theta \vdash M : \theta'}{\Gamma, x : \theta \vdash M[x/y] : \theta'}.$$

The former is simply interpreted by composition, because (up to currying) $[\![\Gamma, \Delta \vdash MN : \theta']\!]$ is equal to $[\![\Delta \vdash N : \theta]\!]\,;[\![\, \vdash \lambda x^\theta.\lambda\Gamma.Mx : \theta \to (\Gamma \to \theta')]\!]$. Hence, in order to interpret application we need to be able to handle composition and contraction. Other term constructs (except λ-abstraction) can also be interpreted through application by introducing special constants for each of them [12]. For instance, assignment then corresponds to the constant $(:=)$: *var* $\to$ *exp* $\to$ *com* so that $((:=)M)N$ corresponds to $M := N$. For local variables one uses $\mathsf{new}_\beta : (\mathit{var} \to \beta) \to \beta$ so that **new** X **in** M is equivalent to $\mathsf{new}_\beta(\lambda X.M)$.

Theorem 1. *For any second-order term* $\Gamma \vdash M : \theta$ *there exists a* $[\![\Gamma \vdash \theta]\!]$*-automaton representing* $\Gamma \vdash M : \theta$.

Proof. We construct the automata by induction on the structure of β-normal terms. The base cases are ground-type constants (*coin*, *skip*, i : *exp*), free identifiers (of base type or first-order type) and the constants corresponding to **succ**, **pred**, **ifzero**, ;, **while**, !, :=, **new**. The automaton for *coin* was given in Example 1. The shape of the strategies corresponding to other constants and free identifiers is already known from work on sequential Algol (see e.g. [21]). Because the strategies are all deterministic, the probabilistic automata representing them can be obtained by assigning probability 1 to all transitions of the finite automata associated with them. Thus it remains to interpret λ-abstraction and application. The former is trivial in game semantics, because currying amounts to the identity operation (up to associativity of the disjoint sum), so we only need to concentrate on application, i.e. composition and contraction.

Let $\sigma = [\![\Delta \vdash N : \theta]\!]$ and $\tau = [\![x : \theta \vdash \lambda\Gamma.Mx : \Gamma \to \theta']\!]$. Suppose $\mathcal{A}_1 = \langle Q_1, M_{[\![\Delta]\!]} + M_{[\![\theta]\!]}, i_1, f_1, \delta_1 \rangle$ and $\mathcal{A}_2 = \langle Q_2, M_{[\![\theta]\!]} + M_{[\![\Gamma]\!]} + M_{[\![\theta']\!]}, i_2, f_2, \delta_2 \rangle$ represent $\Delta \vdash N$ and $x \vdash \lambda\Gamma.Mx$ respectively. Because we consider β-normal terms of second order only, well-opened complete traces of $\sigma;\tau$ can arise only from interaction sequences which involve well-opened complete traces from τ and iterated well-opened complete traces from σ. Thus, as a first step, we have to construct a probabilistic automaton that accepts iterated well-complete traces from σ with the same probabilities as those assigned to them by σ. Since σ is well-threaded, we would like the probability of accepting a complete trace which is not well-opened to be equal to the product of probabilities with which the automaton accepts the constituent well-opened traces. This is achieved simply by identifying f_1 with i_1, because i_1 does not have any incoming transitions and f_1 has no outgoing ones. We write $\mathcal{A}_1^*$ for the automaton obtained from $\mathcal{A}_1$ in this way. Let $A = [\![\Delta]\!]$, $B = [\![\theta]\!]$ and $C = [\![\Gamma \to \theta']\!]$. We define another automaton

$$\mathcal{A}_{||} = \langle Q_{||}, M_A + M_B + M_C, (i_1, i_2), (f_1, f_2), \delta \rangle,$$

where $Q_{||} = (Q_1^O \times Q_2^O) + (Q_1^O \times Q_2^P + Q_1^P \times Q_2^O)$, which will model all the interactions that may result in well-opened complete plays of $\sigma;\tau$. This is done by parallel composition of $\mathcal{A}_1^*$ with $\mathcal{A}_2$ synchronized on moves from B. The function δ is defined by the transitions given below (q_1^O, q_1^P below range over O-states and P-states of $\mathcal{A}_1^*$ respectively; q_2^O, q_2^P are used analogously for $\mathcal{A}_2$):

- for any $q_1^O \in Q_1^O$ and $x \in M_C$

$$\begin{array}{ll} (q_1^O, q_2^O) \xrightarrow{x,1} (q_1^O, q_2^P) & \text{if } q_2^O \xrightarrow{x,1} q_2^P \\ (q_1^O, q_2^P) \xrightarrow{x,p} (q_1^O, q_2^O) & \text{if } q_2^P \xrightarrow{x,p} q_2^O \end{array}$$

- for any $q_2^O \in Q_2^O$ and $x \in M_A$

$$\begin{array}{ll} (q_1^O, q_2^O) \xrightarrow{x,1} (q_1^P, q_2^O) & \text{if } q_1^O \xrightarrow{x,1} q_1^P \\ (q_1^P, q_2^O) \xrightarrow{x,p} (q_1^O, q_2^O) & \text{if } q_1^P \xrightarrow{x,p} q_1^O \end{array}$$

- for any $x \in M_B$

$$\begin{array}{ll} (q_1^O, q_2^P) \xrightarrow{x,p} (q_1^P, q_2^O) & \text{if } q_1^O \xrightarrow{x,1} q_1^P \text{ and } q_2^P \xrightarrow{x,p} q_2^O \\ (q_1^P, q_2^O) \xrightarrow{x,p} (q_1^O, q_2^P) & \text{if } q_1^P \xrightarrow{x,p} q_1^O \text{ and } q_2^O \xrightarrow{x,1} q_2^P. \end{array}$$

By the structure of interaction sequences (as described, for instance, by the state diagram in Figure 2 of [10]) each run of $\mathcal{A}_{||}$ determines an interaction sequence of σ and τ. Moreover, because accepting runs of $\mathcal{A}_1^*$ and $\mathcal{A}_2$ determine complete plays in the respective games (well-opened for $\mathcal{A}_2$), the accepting runs of $\mathcal{A}_{||}$ determine interactions that, when projected onto $M_A + M_C$ yield well-opened complete plays in $A \Rightarrow C$. Note that the probability of an accepting run of $\mathcal{A}_{||}$ is the product of probabilities associated with the corresponding runs of $\mathcal{A}_1^*$ and $\mathcal{A}_2$. Because interaction sequences are uniquely determined by the constituent plays, for any $w \in \mathcal{L}^{\mathsf{wo}}_{[\![\Delta\to(\Gamma\to\theta')]\!]} \cap \mathcal{L}^{\mathsf{comp}}_{[\![\Delta\to(\Gamma\to\theta')]\!]}$ we get

$$\begin{aligned}\mathcal{A}_{||}(w) &= \sum_{r\in Acc_{\mathcal{A}_{||}}(w)} P_{\mathcal{A}_{||}}(r)\\ &= \sum_{r_1\in Acc_{\mathcal{A}_1^*}(w\restriction A,B)}\ \sum_{r_2\in Acc_{\mathcal{A}_2^*}(w\restriction B,C)} P_{\mathcal{A}_1^*}(w\restriction A,B)\cdot P_{\mathcal{A}_2}(w\restriction B,C)\\ &= \mathcal{A}_1^*(w\restriction A,B)\cdot\mathcal{A}_2(w\restriction B,C) = \sigma(w\restriction A,B)\cdot\tau(w\restriction B,C).\end{aligned}$$

By the composition formula for $\sigma;\tau$, in order to construct an $A \Rightarrow C$-automaton for $\Delta \vdash \lambda\Gamma.MN$, it now suffices to relabel all transitions on B-moves as ε-transitions and subsequently replace them using Mohri's algorithm [19] (in fact, the full power of the algorithm is needed to handle composition with **while** and **new**, other cases can be easily solved "by hand"). Because B-moves are only available from states in $(Q_1^O \times Q_2^P + Q_1^P \times Q_2^O)$, the automaton after the ε-removal will be an $A \Rightarrow C$-automaton with the partition of states given before.

Finally, we discuss contraction. It is interpreted simply by identifying moves originating from the two contracted copies of θ, i.e. by relabelling. To complete the argument, we only need to show that the transition function retains the shape required in A-automata. This is obvious for P-states but (at least in principle) the relabelling might produce an O-state with two outgoing transitions on the same O-move. Then we claim that the O-state is unreachable and, consequently, can be deleted. Indeed, if it were reachable, there would exist a position s such that the automaton representing the term before contraction would read both $s\,o_1$ and $s\,o_2$, where o_1 and o_2 are O-moves from the two different copies of θ. By 5. both so_1 and so_2 would be plays then, but this is impossible because only one of them can satisfy visibility (since the questions justifying o_1 and o_2 cannot appear in the O-view at the same time). Consequently, contraction can be interpreted in such a way that we get an automaton of the required shape.

By Lemma 2, the Lemma above and the decidability of EQUIVALENCE we have:

Theorem 2. $\cong$ *is decidable for second-order* $\mathsf{PA_f}$ *terms.*

Note that the size of the automaton produced in the above proof will be exponential in the size of the β-normal term. Because ε-removal and equivalence testing work in polynomial time, equivalence of β-normal second-order $\mathsf{PA_f}$ terms can be decided in EXPTIME.

7 Probabilistic Program Refinement Is Undecidable

Probabilistic program refinement at second order will be shown undecidable by reducing REFINEMENT for generative probabilistic automata to probabilistic program refinement. To this end, for each generative automaton where the probabilities are of the form $m/2^n$, we construct a $\mathsf{PA_f}$ term representing it in a way to be described later.

First we discuss how to model the special distributions in $\mathsf{PA_f}$. Let us define a family of terms $\mathsf{choice}_n(M_0, \cdots, M_{2^n-1})$ which evaluate to each of the terms M_i with the same probability $\frac{1}{2^n}$:

$$\mathsf{choice}_0(M_0) = M_0$$
$$\mathsf{choice}_{n+1}(M_0, \cdots, M_{2^{n+1}-1}) = \\ \quad \mathbf{ifzero}\ coin\ (\mathsf{choice}_n(M_0, \cdots, M_{2^n-1}))\ (\mathsf{choice}_n(M_{2^n}, \cdots, M_{2^{n+1}-1})).$$

Observe that by using the same term M as M_i for several i's we can vary (increase) the probability of $\mathsf{choice}_n(M_0, \cdots, M_{2^n-1})$ being equivalent to M_i. Suppose that, given terms $N_1, \cdots, N_k$, we are to construct another term $\widehat{N}$ which evaluates to N_i ($1 \le i \le k$) with probability $p_i = \frac{m_i}{2^n}$, where $m_i \in \mathbb{N}$ and $\sum_{i=1}^{k} p_i = 1$. This can be done by taking $\widehat{N}$ to be $\mathsf{choice}_n(M_0, \cdots, M_{2^n-1})$ where for $M_0, \cdots, M_{2^n-1}$ we take m_i copies of N_i for each $i = 1, \cdots, k$ (the order is irrelevant). Then the probability of N_i being selected is $\frac{m_i}{2^n}$.

In order to complete the encoding of the special generative automata we have to define how strings are interpreted. Suppose $\Sigma = \{x_1, \cdots, x_m\}$. A string $w = x_{j_1} \cdots x_{j_l}$ is then interpreted by the position $\widehat{w}$:

$$run\,run_f(run_{f,1}run_{x_{j_1}}\,done_{x_{j_1}}\,done_{f,1}) \cdots (run_{f,1}run_{x_{j_l}}\,done_{x_{j_l}}\,done_{f,1})done_f\,done$$

in the game $[\![com_{x_1}, \cdots, com_{x_m}, com_{f,1} \to com_f \vdash com]\!]$, where we have used subscripts to indicate the origin of moves from the various occurrences of com.

Lemma 3. *Suppose $\mathcal{A} = \langle Q, \Sigma, i, F, \delta \rangle$ is a generative automaton and $\Sigma = \{x_1, \cdots, x_m\}$. There exists a term-in-context $\Gamma \vdash M_{\mathcal{A}} : com$, where*

$$\Gamma = x_1 : com, \cdots, x_m : com, f : com \to com,$$

such that for all $s \in \mathcal{L}^{\mathsf{wo}}_{[\![\Gamma \vdash com]\!]} \cap \mathcal{L}^{\mathsf{comp}}_{[\![\Gamma \vdash com]\!]}$:

$$[\![\Gamma \vdash M_{\mathcal{A}}]\!](s) = \begin{cases} \mathcal{A}(w) & \exists_{w \in \Sigma^*}\ s = \widehat{w} \\ 0 & \text{otherwise.} \end{cases}$$

Proof. We will construct $M_{\mathcal{A}}$ in such a way that its induced plays will emulate runs of $\mathcal{A}$. The state of $\mathcal{A}$ will be kept in a variable ST. If $|Q| > max$ we will use sufficiently large tuples of variables, which we also denote by ST. Using branching we can easily define a case distinction construct $\mathsf{case}[!ST](\cdots, H_q, \cdots)$ which for each $q \in Q$ selects H_q if $!ST$ represents q. We will use the first-order identifier $f : com \to com$ for iterating the transitions. $M_{\mathcal{A}}$ has the shape

$$\mathbf{new}\ ST\ \mathbf{in}\ ST := i; f(\mathsf{case}[!ST](\cdots, H_q, \cdots)); [!ST \in F]$$

where $[condition] \equiv$ **if** *condition* **then** *skip* **else** *div* and $div \equiv$ **while** 1 **do** *skip*. The condition $!ST \in F$ can also be implemented via branching. Finally, the terms H_q will have the shape $\widehat{N}$ and will be constructed for the distribution $\delta(q) \in \mathcal{P}(\Sigma \times Q)$. Recall that in order to complete the definition of $\widehat{N}$ we need to specify the terms $N_1, \cdots, N_k$. They are defined as follows: if $\delta(q)(x_j, q') = p_i$ then $N_i \equiv (x_j; ST := q')$. □

Theorem 3. $\precsim$ *is undecidable.*

Proof. Let $\mathcal{A}_1, \mathcal{A}_2$ be generative automata. By the above Lemma and Lemma 1 the refinement of $\mathcal{A}_1$ by $\mathcal{A}_2$ is equivalent to $\Gamma \vdash M_{\mathcal{A}_1} \precsim M_{\mathcal{A}_2}$. Because REFINEMENT is undecidable, so is $\precsim$.

Note that the terms used for simulating generative automata are of second order (the types of free identifiers have order 0 or 1) and that the encoding does not rely on **while**. Accordingly, the undecidability result applies not only to $\mathsf{PA_f}$ but also to its **while**-free fragment. Note however that the above argument did depend on free first-order identifiers. If we leave them as well as **while** out, the problem becomes decidable as the length of the induced well-opened traces is then bounded (the corresponding automata have no cycles).

8 Conclusion and Future Work

The main result of this paper is an EXPTIME algorithm for deciding probabilistic contextual equivalence of β-normal second-order Probabilistic Idealized Algol terms. Subject to mild conditions, this corresponds to the natural notion of equivalence for randomized algorithms, namely identical input/output distributions, and therefore enables the comparison of different randomized algorithms against each other.

It can be shown that probabilistic equivalence is PSPACE-hard, since it subsumes the deterministic case, which itself is PSPACE-complete [22]. We conjecture that probabilistic equivalence is in fact also PSPACE-complete. In any case, even the EXPTIME bound is quite encouraging within the realm of verification, and we therefore intend to implement our algorithm to conduct a number of experimental case studies.

An interesting alternative to (exact) probabilistic equivalence is that of *approximate* probabilistic equivalence, parameterized by some small 'tolerance margin' ε. Such a notion would allow us to quantitatively compare two randomized algorithms, or a randomized and a deterministic algorithm, by checking whether their input/output distributions remain within a predetermined small bound of each other. Unfortunately, the most natural interpretation of approximate equivalence is already undecidable for reactive probabilistic automata, by a simple reduction from NONEMPTINESS WITH THRESHOLD. Moreover, *contextual* approximate equivalence for programs seems difficult to define sensibly: if two non-divergent programs fail to be *exactly* equivalent, then a context can always be manufactured that, through some kind of 'statistical testing', can magnify the differences between the two programs to arbitrarily large values. We would like to investigate this question in greater detail, perhaps by restricting contexts to using their arguments only a bounded number of times. We would also like to discover conditions under which such problems become decidable (cf. [17]), or alternatively develop efficient semi-algorithms for them.

References

1. Rabin, M.O.: Algorithms and Complexity. Academic Press, 1976.
2. Motwani, R., Raghavan, P.: Randomized Algorithms. CUP, 1995.
3. Reynolds, J.: The essence of Algol. In Jaco W. de Bakker and J. C. van Vliet, eds.: Algorithmic Languages. North-Holland, 1981.
4. Ghica, D.R., McCusker, G.: Reasoning about Idealized Algol using regular expressions. In ICALP 2000, LNCS 1853.
5. Abramsky, S., Ghica, D.R., Murawski, A.S., Ong, C.H.L.: Applying game semantics to compositional software modelling and verification. In TACAS 2004, LNCS 2988.
6. Kwiatkowska, M., Norman, G., Parker, D.: Probabilistic symbolic model checking with PRISM: a hybrid approach. In TACAS 2002, LNCS 2280.
7. Bustan, D., Rubin, S., Vardi, M.: Verifying ω-regular properties of Markov chains. In CAV 2004, LNCS 3114.
8. Giacalone, A., Jou, C., Smolka, S.A.: Algebraic reasoning for probabilistic concurrent systems. In IFIP WG 2.2/2.3 Conference on Programming Concepts and Methods, 1990.
9. Lowe, G.: Probabilistic and prioritized models of Timed CSP. Theoretical Computer Science **138(2)**, 1995.
10. Danos, V., Harmer, R.: Probabilistic game semantics. ACM Trans. on Comp. Logic **3(3)**, 2002.
11. Hyland, J.M.E., Ong, C.H.L.: On Full Abstraction for PCF. Information and Computation **163(2)**, 2000.
12. Abramsky, S., McCusker, G.: Linearity, sharing and state: a fully abstract game semantics for Idealized Algol with active expressions. In O'Hearn, P.W., Tennent, R.D., eds.: Algol-like languages, Birkhaüser, 1997.
13. Rabin, M.O.: Probabilistic automata. Information and Control **6(3)**, 1963.
14. Paz, A.: Introduction to Probabilistic Automata. Academic Press, 1971.
15. Segala, R.: Modeling and Verification of Randomized Distributed Real-Time Systems. PhD thesis, MIT. Available as Technical Report MIT/LCS/TR-676, 1995.
16. Stoelinga, M.I.A.: An introduction to probabilistic automata. In Rozenberg, G., ed.: EATCS bulletin. Volume 78, 2002.
17. Tzeng, W.G.: A polynomial-time algorithm for the equivalence of probabilistic automata. SIAM Journal on Computing **21**, 1992.
18. Blondel, V.D., Canterini, V.: Undecidable problems for probabilistic automata of fixed dimension. Theoretical Computer Science **36(3)**, 2003.
19. Mohri, M.: Generic e-removal and input e-normalization algorithms for weighted transducers. International Journal of Foundations of Computer Science **13**, 2002.
20. Mohri, M.: Semiring frameworks and algorithms for shortest-distance problems. Journal of Automata, Languages and Combinatorics **7**, 2002.
21. Abramsky, S.: Algorithmic games semantics: a tutorial introduction. In Schwichtenberg, H., Steinbruggen, R., eds.: Proof and System Reliability. Kluwer, 2002.
22. Murawski, A.: Games for complexity of second-order call-by-name programs. Theoretical Computer Science, to appear.

Probabilistic Anonymity*

Mohit Bhargava[1,**] and Catuscia Palamidessi[2]

[1] Indian Institute of Technology Delhi
[2] INRIA Futurs and LIX, École Polytechnique

Abstract. The concept of anonymity comes into play in a wide range of situations, varying from voting and anonymous donations to postings on bulletin boards and sending mails. The systems for ensuring anonymity often use random mechanisms which can be described probabilistically, while the agents' interest in performing the anonymous action may be totally unpredictable, irregular, and hence expressable only nondeterministically.

Formal definitions of the concept of anonymity have been investigated in the past either in a totally nondeterministic framework, or in a purely probabilistic one. In this paper, we investigate a notion of anonymity which combines both probability and nondeterminism, and which is suitable for describing the most general situation in which both the systems and the user can have both probabilistic and nondeterministic behavior. We also investigate the properties of the definition for the particular cases of purely nondeterministic users and purely probabilistic users.

We formulate our notions of anonymity in terms of observables for processes in the probabilistic π-calculus, whose semantics is based on Probabilistic Automata.

We illustrate our ideas by using the example of the dining cryptographers.

1 Introduction

The concept of *anonymity* comes into play in those cases in which we want to keep secret the identity of the agent participating to a certain event. There is a wide range of situations in which this property may be needed or desirable; for instance: delation, voting, anonymous donations, and posting on bulletin boards.

An important characteristic of anonymity is that it is usually relative to a particular point of view. In general an event can be observed from various viewpoints - differing in the information they give access to, and therefore, the anonymity property depends on the view from which the event is being looked at (that is the exact information available to the observer). For example, in the situation of electronic bulletin boards, a posting by one member of the group is kept anonymous to the other members; however, it may be possible that the administrator of the board has access to some privileged information and can determine the member who posted the message(s), either directly or indirectly.

* This work has been partially supported by the Project Rossignol of the ACI Sécurité Informatique (Ministère de la recherche et nouvelles technologies).

** This work has been carried out during the visit of Mohit Bhargava at INRIA, which has been supported by the INRIA/DREI programme for International Internship.

M. Abadi and L. de Alfaro (Eds.): CONCUR 2005, LNCS 3653, pp. 171–185, 2005.

In general anonymity may be required for a subset of the agents only. In order to completely define anonymity for a system it is therefore necessary to specify which set(s) of members has to be kept anonymous. A further generalization is the concept of *group anonymity*: the members are divided into a number of sets, and it is revealed which of the groups is responsible for an event, but the information as to which particular member has performed the event must be hidden. In this paper, however, we do not consider the notion of group anonymity, we leave it for further work.

Various formal definitions and frameworks for analyzing anonymity have been developed in literature. They can be classified into approaches based on process-calculi ([24,22]), epistemic logic ([26,11]), and "function views" ([13]). In this paper, we focus on the approach based on process-calculi.

The framework and techniques of process calculi have been used extensively in the area of security, to formally define security properties, and to verify cryptographic protocols. See, for instance, [2,15,21,23,3]. The common denominator is that the various entities involved in the system to verify are specified as concurrent processes and present typically a nondeterministic behavior. In [24,22], the nondeterminism plays a crucial role to define the concept of anonymity. More precisely, this approach to anonymity is based on the so-called "principle of confusion": a system is anonymous if the set of the possible outcomes is saturated with respect to the intended anonymous users, i.e. if one such user can cause a certain observable trace in one possible computation, then there must be alternative computations in which each other anonymous user can give rise to the same observable trace (modulo the identity of the anonymous users).

The principle of anonymity described above is very elegant and general, however it has a limitation: Many systems for anonymity use random mechanisms. See, for example, Crowds ([20]) and Onion Routing ([27]). If the observer has the means to repeat the experiment and perform statistical analysis, he may be able to deduce certain quantitative information on the system. In particular, he may be able to compute the probability of certain observables and from that infer the probability of the relation between users and observables. Now, the situation of perfect anonymity can be only achieved when one cannot differenciate the agents by the observable. However this condition cannot be expressed in the nondeterministic approach, since the latter is based on set-theoretic notions, and it is therefore only able to detect the difference between possible and impossible (which in the finite case correspond to positive and zero probability respectively). Even the case in which one user has probability close to 1 will be considered acceptable by the definition of anonymity based on nondeterminism, provided that all the other users have positive probability.

Probabilistic information also allows to classify various notions of anonymity according to their strength. See for instance the hierarchy proposed by Reiter and Robin ([20]). In this paper we explore a notion of anonymity which corresponds to the strongest one (perfect anonymity: from the observables we deduce no information about the possible user).

A probabilistic notion of anonymity was developed (as a part of a general epistemological approach) in [11]. The approach there is purely probabilistic, in the sense that both the system and the users are assumed to act probabilistically. In particular the emphasis is on the probabilistic behavior of the users.

In this work, we take the opposite point of view, namely we assume that nothing may be known about the relative frequency by which the users perform the anonymous action. More precisely, the users can in principle be totally unpredictable and change intention every day, so that their behavior cannot be described probabilistically, not even by repeating statistical observations. The mechanisms of the systems, on the contrary, are like coin tossing, or random selection of a nearby node, are supposed to exhibit a certain regularity and obey a probabilistic distribution. Hence, we investigate a notion of anonymity which combines both probability and nondeterminism, and which is suitable for describing the most general situation in which both the systems and the user can have both probabilistic and nondeterministic behavior. We also investigate the properties of the definition for the particular cases of purely nondeterministic users and purely probabilistic users.

In order to define the notion of probability we need, of course, a model of computation able to express both probabilistic and nondeterministic choices. This kind of systems is by now well established in literature, see for instance the probabilistic automata of [25], and have been provided with solid mathematical foundations and sophisticated tools for verification. These models have practically replaced nowadays the purely probabilistic models since it was recognized that nondeterministic behavior is not "probabilistic behavior with unknown probabilities", but rather a phenomenon on its own, which is needed to describe situations in which an entity has a completely unpredictable and irregular behavior.

For reasons of space we omit the proofs and we only sketch the preliminary notions. The full details can be found on the report version of this paper, available on line ([4]).

2 The Nondeterministic Approach to Anonymity

In this section we briefly recall the approach in [24,22]. In these works, the actions of a system S are classified into three sets which determine the "point of view":

- A: the actions that are intended to be known anonymously by the observer,
- B: the actions that are intended to be known completely by the observer,
- C: the actions that are intended to be abstracted (hidden) to the observer.

Typically the set A consists of actions of the form $a.i$, where a is a fixed "abstract" action (the same for all the elements of A), and i represents the identity of an anonymous user. Hence $A = \{a.i \mid i \in I\}$., where I is the set of all the identities of the anonymous users.

Consider a dummy action d (different from all actions in S) and let f be the function on the actions of $A \bigcup B$ defined by $f(\alpha) = d$ if $\alpha \in A$, and $f(\alpha) = \alpha$ otherwise. Then S is said to be (strongly) anonymous on the actions in A if $f^{-1}(f(S\backslash C)) \sim_T S\backslash C$, where, following the CSP notation ([5]), $S\backslash C$ is the system resulting from hiding C in S, $f(S')$ is the system obtained from S' by applying the relabeling f to each (visible) action, f^{-1} is the relation inverse of f, and $\sim_T$ represents trace equivalence.

Intuitively, the above definition means that for any action sequence $\vec{\alpha} \in A^*$, if an observable trace t containing $\vec{\alpha}$ (not necessarily as a consecutive sequence) is a possible

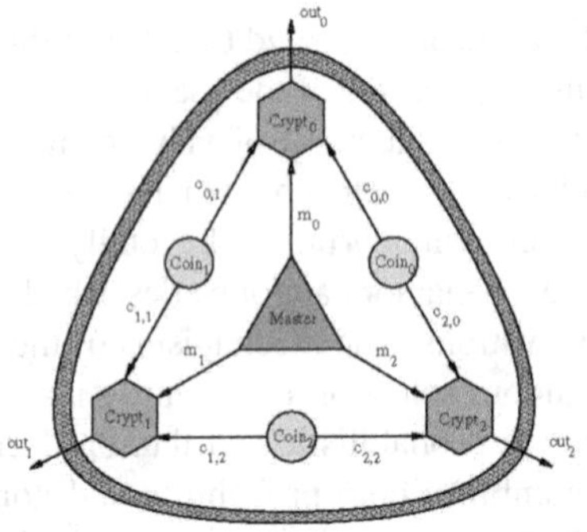

Fig. 1. Chaum's system for the Dining Cryptographers ([7,22])

outcome of $S \backslash C$, then, any trace t' obtained from t by replacing $\vec{\alpha}$ with an arbitrary $\vec{\alpha}' \in A^*$ must also be a possible outcome of $S \backslash C$.

We now illustrate the above definition on the example of the Dining Cryptographers.

3 The Dining Cryptographers' Problem

This problem, described by Chaum in [7], involves a situation in which three cryptographers are dining together. At the end of the dinner, each of them is secretly informed by a central agency (master) whether she should pay the bill, or not. So, either the master will pay, or one of the cryptographers will be asked to pay. The cryptographers (or some external observer) would like to find out whether the payer is one of them or the master. However, if the payer is one of them, they also wish to maintain anonymity over the identity of the payer.

A possible solution to this problem, described in [7], is that each cryptographer tosses a coin, which is visible to herself and her neighbor to the right. Each cryptographer observes the two coins that she can see and announces *agree* or *disagree*. If a cryptographer is not paying, she will announce *agree* if the two sides are the same and *disagree* if they are not. However, the paying cryptographer will say the opposite. It can be proved that if the number of *disagrees* is even, then the master is paying; otherwise, one of the cryptographers is paying. Furthermore, if one of the cryptographers is paying, then neither an external observer nor the other two cryptographers can identify, from their individual information, who exactly his paying.

The Dining Cryptographers (DC) will be a running example through the paper.

3.1 Nondeterministic Dining Cryptographers

In this approach the outcome of the coin tossing and the decision of the master regarding the payment of bill are considered to be nondeterministic ([24,22]).

The specification of the solution can be given in a process calculus style as illustrated below. In the original works ([24,22]) the authors used CSP. For the sake of uniformity we use here the π-calculus ([18]). We recall that $+$ ($\sum$) is the nondeterministic sum and $|$ (Π) is the parallel composition. 0 is the empty process. τ is the silent

Table 1. The dining cryptographer protocol specified in π-calculus

$$
\begin{aligned}
Master &= \textstyle\sum_{i=0}^{2} \tau \,.\, \overline{m}_i \mathsf{p} \,.\, \overline{m}_{i\oplus 1} \mathsf{n} \,.\, \overline{m}_{i\oplus 2} \mathsf{n} \,.\, 0 \\
&\quad + \ \tau . \overline{m}_0 \mathsf{n} \,.\, \overline{m}_1 \mathsf{n} \,.\, \overline{m}_2 \mathsf{n} \,.\, 0 \\
Crypt_i &= m_i(x) \,.\, c_{i,i}(y) \,.\, c_{i,i\oplus 1}(z) \,. \\
&\qquad \text{if } x = \mathsf{p} \\
&\qquad\quad \text{then } \overline{pay}_i \ .\text{if } y = z \\
&\qquad\qquad \text{then } \overline{out_i} disagree \\
&\qquad\qquad \text{else } \overline{out_i} agree \\
&\qquad\quad \text{else if } y = z \\
&\qquad\qquad \text{then } \overline{out_i} agree \\
&\qquad\qquad \text{else } \overline{out_i} disagree \\
Coin_i &= \tau \,.\, Head_i + \tau \,.\, Tail_i \\
Head_i &= \overline{c}_{i,i} head \,.\, \overline{c}_{i\ominus 1,i} head \,.\, 0 \\
Tail_i &= \overline{c}_{i,i} tail \,.\, \overline{c}_{i\ominus 1,i} tail \,.\, 0 \\
DCP &= (\nu \vec{m})(Master \\
&\qquad \mid \ (\nu \vec{c})(\Pi_{i=0}^{2} Crypt_i \ \mid \ \Pi_{i=0}^{2} Coin_i)\ )
\end{aligned}
$$

(or internal) action. $\bar{c}m$ and $c(x)$ are, respectively, send and receive actions on channel c, where m is the message being transmitted and x is the formal parameter. ν is an operator that, in the π-calculus, has multiple purposes: it provides abstraction (hiding), enforces synchronization, and generates new names. For more details on the π-calculus and its semantics, we refer to [18,17].

In the code, given in Table 1, $\oplus$ and $\ominus$ represent the sum and the subtraction modulo 3. Messages p and n sent by the master are the requests to pay or to not pay, respectively. $\overline{pay}_i$ is the action of paying for cryptographer i.

We remark that we do not need all the expressive power of the π-calculus for this program. More precisely, we do not need guarded choice (all the choices are internal because they start with τ), and we do not need neither name-passing nor scope extrusion, thus ν is used just like the restriction operator of CCS ([16]).

Let us consider the point of view of an external observer. The actions that are to be hidden (set C) are the communications of the decision of the master and the results of the coins ($\vec{m}$, $\vec{c}$). These are already hidden in the definition of the system DCP. The anonymous users are of course the cryptographers, and the anonymous actions (set A) is constituted by the $\overline{pay}_i$ actions, for $i = 0, 1, 2$. The set B is constituted by the actions of the form $\overline{out_i} agree$ and $\overline{out_i} disagree$, for $i = 0, 1, 2$.

Let f be the function $f(\overline{pay}_i) = \overline{pay}$ and $f(\alpha) = \alpha$ for all the other actions. It is possible to check that $f^{-1}(f(DCP))) \sim_T DCP$, where we recall that $\sim_T$ stands for trace equivalence. Hence the nondeterministic notion of anonymity, as defined in Section 2, is verified.

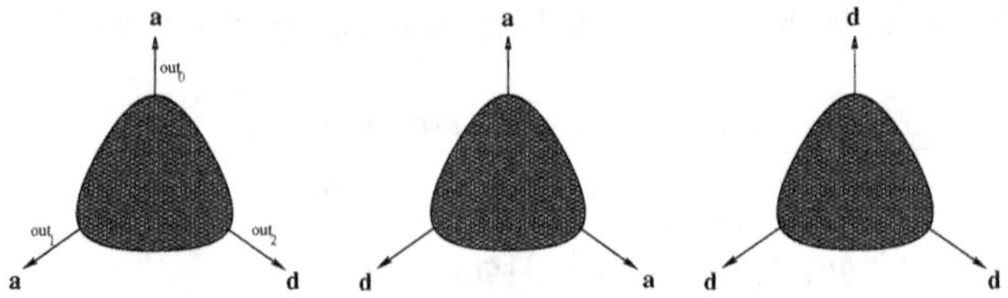

Fig. 2. Illustration of Example 1: the results that are observed with high frequency

3.2 Limitations of the Nondeterministic Approach

As a result of the nondeterminism, we cannot differentiate between a fair coin and an unfair one. However, it is evident that the fairness of the coins is essential to ensure the anonymity property in the system, as illustrated by the following example.

Example 1. Assume that, whenever a cryptographer pays, an external observer obtains *almost always* (i.e. with high frequency, say 99% of the times) one of the three outcomes represented in Figure 2, where a stands for *agree* and d for *disagree*. What can the observer deduce? By examining all possible cases, it is easy to see that the coins must be biased, and more precisely, $Coin_0$ and $Coin_1$ must produce almost always *head*, and $Coin_2$ must produce almost always *tail* (or vice-versa). From this estimation, it is immediate to conclude that, in the first case, the payer is *almost for sure* $Crypt_1$, in the second case $Crypt_2$, and in the third case $Crypt_0$.

In the situation illustrated in the above example, clearly, the system does not provide anonymity. However the nondeterministic definition of anonymity is still satisfied (as long as "almost always" is not "always", which in terms of observations means that the fourth configuration d, a, a must also appear, from time to time). The problem is that that definition can only express whether or not it is possible to have a particular trace, but cannot express whether one trace is more likely than the other.

3.3 Probabilistic Dining Cryptographers

The probabilistic version of the system can be obtained from the nondeterministic one by attaching probabilities to the the outcome of the coin tossing. We wish to remark that this is the essential change in perspective: the *random mechanisms internal to the system* which is designed to ensure anonymity are assumed to have a probabilistic behavior. As for the choices of the master, those are in a sense external to the system, and it is secondary whether they are nondeterministic or probabilistic.

We start by considering a nondeterministic master, which is in a sense the basic case: the fact that the master is nondeterministic means that we cannot assume any regularity in its behavior, nobody has any information about it, not even a probabilistic one. The anonymity system must then assure that this complete lack of knowledge be preserved through the observations of the possible outcomes (except, of course, for gaining the information on whether the payer is one of the cryptographers or not).

We use the probabilistic π-calculus (π_p) introduced in [12,19] to represent the probabilistic system. The essential difference with respect to the π-calculus is the presence of a *probabilistic choice operator* of the form $\sum_i p_i \alpha_i . P_i$, where the p_i's represents probabilities, i.e. they satisfy $p_i \in [0,1]$ and $\sum_i p_i = 1$, and the α_i's are non-output prefixes, i.e. either input or silent prefixes. (Actually, for the purpose of this paper, only silent prefixes are used.) For the detailed presentation of this calculus we refer to [12,19,4].

The only difference with respect to the program presented in Section 1 is the definition of the $Coin_i$'s, which is as follows (p_h and p_t represent the probabilities of the outcome of the coin tossing):

$$Coin_i = p_h \tau \,.\, Head_i + p_t \tau \,.\, Tail_i$$

It is clear that the system obtained in this way combines probabilistic and nondeterministic behavior, not only because the master is nondeterministic, but also because the various components of the system and their internal interactions can follow different scheduling policies, selected nondeterministically (although it can be proved that this latter form of nondeterminism is not relevant for this particular problem).

This kind of systems (combining probabilistic and nondeterministic choices) is by now well established in literature, see for instance the probabilistic automata of [25], and have been provided with solid mathematical foundations and sophisticated tools for verification. In particular, we are interested here in the definition of the probability associated to a certain observable. The canonical way of defining such a probability is the following: First we *solve* the nondeterminism, i.e. we determine a function (*scheduler*) which, for each nondeterministic choice in the the computation tree, selects one alternative. After pruning the tree from all the non-selected alternatives, we obtain a *fully probabilistic automaton*, and we can define the probabilities of (measurable) sets of runs (and therefore of the intended observables) in the standard way. See [4] for the details.

One thing that should be clear, from the description above, is that in general the probability of an observable *depends on the given scheduler*.

4 Probabilistic Anonymity for Nondeterministic Users

In this section we propose our notion of probabilistic anonymity for the case in which the anonymous user is selected nondeterministically.

The system in which the anonymous users live and operate is modeled as a probabilistic automaton M ([25], see [4]. Following [24,22] we classify the actions of M into the three sets A, B and C (cfr. Section 2). As before, these three sets are determined by the set of the anonymous users, the specific type of action on which we want anonymity, and the observer. We only change notation slightly:

- The set of the anonymous actions: $A = \{a(i) \mid i \in I\}$, where I is the set of the identities of the anonymous users and a is an injective functions from I to the set of actions which we call *abstract action*. We also call the pair (I, a) *anonymous action generator*.
- The set of the actions that we observe entirely, B. We will use b, b', ... to denote the elements of this set.
- The set of the hidden actions C.

It should be remarked the the term "observable" here is relative: we assume that the observer can observe only B and a, but, to the purpose of defining anonymity and checking whether a system is anonymous, we need the elements of A to be visible outcomes of the system.

Definition 1. *An anonymity system is a tuple* (M, I, a, B, Z, p), *where* M *is a probabilistic automaton which we assume already restricted (abstracted) on* C, (I, a) *is an anonymous action generator,* B *is a set of observable actions,* Z *is the set of all possible schedulers for* M, *and for every* $\varsigma \in Z$, p_ς *is a probability measure on the event space generated by the execution tree of* M *under* ς *(denoted by* $etree(M, \varsigma)$*), i.e. the* σ*–field generated by the cones in* $etree(M, \varsigma)$ *(cfr. [4]).*

Note that, as expressed by the above definition, given a scheduler ς, an *event* is a set of executions in $etree(M, \varsigma)$. We introduce the following notation to represent the events of interest:

- $a(i)$: all the executions in $etree(M, \varsigma)$ containing the action $a(i)$
- a : all the executions in $etree(M, \varsigma)$ containing an action $a(i)$ for an arbitrary i
- o : all the executions in $etree(M, \varsigma)$ containing as their maximal sequence of observable actions the sequence o (where o is of the form $\langle b_1, b_2, \ldots, b_n \rangle$ for some $b_1, b_2, \ldots, b_n \in B$). We denote by O the set of all such o's (*observables*).

We use the symbols $\cup$, $\cap$ and $\neg$ to represent the union, the intersection, and the complement of events, respectively.

We wish to keep the notion of observables as general as possible, but we still need to make some assumptions on them. First, we want the observables to be disjoint events. Second, they must cover all possible outcomes. Third, an observable o must indicate unambiguously whether a has taken place or not, i.e. it either implies a, or it implies $\neg a$. In set-theoretic terms it means that either o is contained in a or in the complement of a. Formally:

Assumption 1 (Assumptions on the observables) *1.* $\forall \varsigma \in Z.\, \forall o_1, o_2 \in O.\ o_1 \neq o_2 \Rightarrow p_\varsigma(o_1 \cup o_2) = p_\varsigma(o_1) + p_\varsigma(o_2)$
2. $\forall \varsigma \in Z.\ p_\varsigma(O) = 1$
3. $\forall \varsigma \in Z.\, \forall o \in O.\ p_\varsigma(o \cap a) = p_\varsigma(o) \vee p_\varsigma(o \cap \neg a) = p_\varsigma(o)$

Analogously, we need to make some assumption on the anonymous actions. We consider here conditions tailored for the nondeterministic users: Each scheduler determines completely whether an action of the form $a(i)$ takes place or not, and in the positive case, there is only one such i. Formally:

Assumption 2 (Assumption on the anonymous actions for nondeterministic users)

$$\forall \varsigma \in Z.\ p_\varsigma(a) = 0 \vee (\exists i \in I.\ (p_\varsigma(a(i)) = 1 \ \wedge\ \forall j \in I.\ j \neq i \Rightarrow p_\varsigma(a(j)) = 0))$$

We are now ready to give the definition of anonymity for the case in which the anonymous user is selected nondeterministically:

Definition 2 (Probabilistic anonymity for nondeterministic users).
A system (M, I, a, B, Z, p) *is anonymous if*

$$\forall \varsigma, \vartheta \in Z.\, \forall o \in O.\ p_\varsigma(a) = p_\vartheta(a) = 1 \Rightarrow p_\varsigma(o) = p_\vartheta(o)$$

Intuitively, the above definition expresses the fact that, for every two possible nondeterministic choices ς and ϑ which both select a, (say $a(i)$ and $a(j)$, with i and j possibly different) it should not be possible to detect from the probabilistic measure of the observables whether the choice was ς or ϑ (i.e. whether the user was i or j).

Example 2. Consider the DC with probabilistic coins and nondeterministic master. If the coins can give both *head* and *tail*, then, for each scheduler which chooses a (i.e. $\overline{m}_i\mathsf{p}$ for some i), the possible observable events are $\langle a, a, d\rangle$, $\langle a, d, a\rangle$, $\langle d, a, a\rangle$, and $\langle d, d, d\rangle$ ($\langle r_0, r_1, r_2\rangle$ here represents the collective result $\overline{out_0}r_0$, $\overline{out_1}r_1$, and $\overline{out_2}r_2$). In principle different schedulers would affect also the order in which the outputs are emitted, but it is easy to see that the order, in this system, does not matter.

Consider the case in which the coins are totally fair, i.e. each of them gives *head* and *tail* with $1/2$ probability each. By considering all the 8 possible configurations of the coins, $\langle h, h, h\rangle$, $\langle h, h, t\rangle$, $\ldots \langle t, t, t\rangle$, it is easy to see that, for each possible payer i, each of the above observables is produced by exactly two configurations and hence has probability $1/4$. Hence Definition 2 is verified.

Consider now the case in which the coins are biased. Say, $Coin_0$ and $Coin_1$ give *head* with probability $9/10$ and *tail* with probability $1/10$, and vice-versa $Coin_2$ gives *head* with probability $1/10$ and *tail* with probability $9/10$. (This case is analogous to that illustrated in Example 1). Let us consider the observable $\langle a, a, d\rangle$. In case $Crypt_1$ is the payer, then the probability to get $\langle a, a, d\rangle$ is equal to the probability that the result of the coins is $\langle h, h, t\rangle$, plus the the probability that the result of the coins is $\langle t, t, h\rangle$, which is $9/10 * 9/10 * 9/10 + 1/10 * 1/10 * 1/10 = 730/1000$. In case $Crypt_2$ is the payer, then the probability to get $\langle a, a, d\rangle$ is equal to the probability that the result of the coins is $\langle h, h, h\rangle$, plus the the probability that the result of the coins is $\langle t, t, t\rangle$, which is $9/10 * 9/10 * 1/10 + 1/10 * 1/10 * 9/10 = 90/1000$.

Hence, in the biased case, Definition 2 is not verified. And this is what we expect, because the system, intuitively, is not anonymous: when we observe $\langle a, a, d\rangle$, $Crypt_1$ is much more likely to be the payer than $Crypt_2$.

As proved in the example above, the DC with fair coins are anonymous.

Proposition 1. *The DC with probabilistic fair coins and nondeterministic master are probabilistically anonymous.*

5 Probabilistic Anonymity for Users with Combined Probabilistic and Nondeterministic Behavior

In this section we develop a notion of anonymity for the more general case in which also the users may be selected according to some probabilistic distribution, possibly combined with a nondeterministic selection.

An example of such kind of behavior in the DC can be obtained by specifying the master as making first a nondeterministic choice on which probabilistic distribution to apply for selecting the payer, and then a probabilistic choice.

An example of such a master in π_p would be the following ($p_0, \ldots, p_3, q_0, \ldots, q_3$ represent the probabilities of the various decisions of the master)

$$\begin{aligned} Master &= \tau.Master_1 + \tau.Master_2 \\ Master_1 &= \textstyle\sum_{i=0}^{2} p_i\ \tau\,.\,\overline{m}_i\mathsf{p}\,.\,\overline{m}_{i\oplus 1}\mathsf{n}\,.\,\overline{m}_{i\oplus 2}\mathsf{n}\,.\,0 \\ &\quad +\ p_3\tau.\overline{m}_0\mathsf{n}\,.\,\overline{m}_1\mathsf{n}\,.\,\overline{m}_2\mathsf{n}\,.\,0 \\ Master_2 &= \textstyle\sum_{i=0}^{2} q_i\ \tau\,.\,\overline{m}_i\mathsf{p}\,.\,\overline{m}_{i\oplus 1}\mathsf{n}\,.\,\overline{m}_{i\oplus 2}\mathsf{n}\,.\,0 \\ &\quad +\ q_3\tau.\overline{m}_0\mathsf{n}\,.\,\overline{m}_1\mathsf{n}\,.\,\overline{m}_2\mathsf{n}\,.\,0 \end{aligned}$$

Note that the choice in *Master* is nondeterministic while the choices in $Master_1$ and $Master_2$ are probabilistic.

While the assumptions on the observables remain the same, the assumption on the anonymous actions in this case is much weaker: the scheduler does not determine completely, in general, whether a is executed or not, and who is the user. However, we still require that there be at most an user which performs a for each computation, i.e. $a(i)$ and $a(j)$ must be disjoint for $i \neq j$. Formally:

Assumption 3 (Assumption on the anonymous actions for users with combined probabilistic and nondeterministic behavior)

$$\forall \varsigma \in Z.\, \forall i, j \in I.\ i \neq j \Rightarrow p_\varsigma(a(i) \cup a(j)) = p_\varsigma(a(i)) + p_\varsigma(a(j))$$

The notion of anonymity, in this case, must take into account the probabilities of the $a(i)$'s. When we observe a certain event o, the probability of o having been induced by $a(i)$ must be the same as the probability of o having been induced by $a(j)$ for any other $j \in I$. To formalize this notion, we need the concept of *conditional probability*. Given two events x and y with $p(y) > 0$, the conditional probability of x given y is defined as $p(x \,|\, y) = \frac{p(x \cap y)}{p(y)}$.

Definition 3 (Probabilistic anonymity for users with combined probabilistic and nondeterministic behavior). *A system* (M, I, a, B, Z, p) *is anonymous if*

$$\forall \varsigma, \vartheta \in Z.\, \forall i, j \in I.\, \forall o \in O.$$
$$(p_\varsigma(a(i)) > 0 \wedge p_\vartheta(a(j)) > 0) \Rightarrow p_\varsigma(o \,|\, a(i)) = p_\vartheta(o \,|\, a(j))$$

Example 3. Consider the DC with probabilistic coins and the nondeterministic and probabilistic master illustrated above. Assume that the coins are totally fair. Consider a scheduler ς which selects $Master_1$ and assume that $Master_1$ selects $i \in I$ as the payer, with probability p_i. Consider now a scheduler ϑ which selects $Master_2$, and assume that $Master_2$ selects $j \in I$ as the payer, with probability q_j. Again, the possible observable events are $\langle a, a, d\rangle$, $\langle a, d, a\rangle$, $\langle d, a, a\rangle$, and $\langle d, d, d\rangle$. By considering all the 8 possible configurations of the coins, it is easy to see that if the scheduler is ς and the payer is i, each of the above observables is produced by exactly two configurations and hence the conditional probability of that observable, given that i is the payer, is $1/4$. The same holds for ϑ and j, hence Definition 3 is verified.

The behavior of a master which combines nondeterministic and probabilistic behavior can be much more complicated than the one illustrated above. However it is easy to see that as long as the master does not influence the behavior of the coins, and these are fair, the conditional probability of each observable for a given payer is $1/4$.

Proposition 2. *The DC with probabilistic fair coins and nondeterministic and probabilistic master are probabilistically anonymous.*

We terminate this section by giving an alternative characterization of anonymity.

Theorem 1. *A system (M, I, a, B, Z, p) is anonymous iff*

$$\forall \varsigma, \vartheta \in Z.\, \forall i \in I.\, \forall o \in O.\ \ (p_\varsigma(a(i)) > 0 \wedge p_\vartheta(a) > 0) \Rightarrow p_\varsigma(o \,|\, a(i)) = p_\vartheta(o \,|\, a)$$

6 Probabilistic Anonymity for Fully Probabilistic Users

In this section we consider the case of a totally probabilistic system. For instance, in the case of the dining philosophers, the master would be of the form

$$\begin{aligned} Master = & \textstyle\sum_{i=0}^{2} p_i\ \tau\,.\,\overline{m}_i\mathsf{p}\,.\,\overline{m}_{i\oplus 1}\mathsf{n}\,.\,\overline{m}_{i\oplus 2}\mathsf{n}\,.\,0 \\ & +\ \ p_3\tau.\overline{m}_0\mathsf{n}\,.\,\overline{m}_1\mathsf{n}\,.\,\overline{m}_2\mathsf{n}\,.\,0 \end{aligned}$$

Furthermore, we would fix the scheduling of the parallel activities, so that each step in the computation would be either deterministic or probabilistic.

Since there is no nondeterminism, there is no choice of scheduler either, so we can eliminate Z from the tuple and we can write $p(x)$ instead of $p_\varsigma(x)$. The definition of probabilistic anonymity given in previous section simplifies into the following:

Definition 4 (Probabilistic anonymity for probabilistic users).
A system (M, I, a, B, p) is anonymous if

$$\forall i, j \in I.\, \forall o \in O.\ \ (p(a(i)) > 0 \wedge p(a(j)) > 0) \Rightarrow p(o \,|\, a(i)) = p(o \,|\, a(j))$$

Furthermore, the alternative characterization in Theorem 1 reduces to the following:

Corollary 1. *A system (M, I, a, B, p) is anonymous iff*

$$\forall i \in I.\, \forall o \in O.\ \ (p(a(i)) > 0 \wedge p(a) > 0) \Rightarrow p(o \,|\, a(i)) = p(o \,|\, a)$$

In the fully probabilistic case there are two other interesting characterizations: The first is based on the intuition that a system is anonymous if the observations do not change the probability of $a(i)$: we may know the probability of $a(i)$ by some means external to the system, but the system should not increase our knowledge about it (cfr. [11]). The second is based on the (similar) idea that observing o rather than o' should not change our knowledge of the probability of $a(i)$. Formally:

Proposition 3. *The following conditions are equivalent, and are equivalent to the condition of anonymity.*

1. $\forall i \in I.\, \forall o \in O.\;\; p(o \cap a) > 0 \;\Rightarrow\; p(a(i) \,|\, o) = p(a(i))/p(a)$
2. $\forall i \in I.\, \forall o, o' \in O.\;\; (p(o \cap a) > 0 \wedge p(o' \cap a) > 0) \;\Rightarrow\; p(a(i) \,|\, o) = p(a(i) \,|\, o')$.

Proposition 3 can be reformulated as a general property of probablistic spaces, independent from anonymity. Similar results have been presented in [10] and in [9].

6.1 Characterizations Given by Proposition 3 and Nondeterminism

It is not clear whether the characterizations expressed in Proposition 3 can be generalized to the case of the users with combined nondeterministic and probabilistic behavior. The "naive" extensions obtained by introducing the scheduler in the formulae would not work. Let us consider the first characterization in Proposition 3 (the other would be analogous). One possible way of reintroducing the notion of scheduler is

$$\forall \varsigma, \vartheta \in Z.\, \forall i \in I.\, \forall o \in O.$$
$$(p_\varsigma(o \cap a) > 0 \wedge p_\vartheta(a) > 0) \Rightarrow p_\varsigma(a(i) \,|\, o) = p_\vartheta(a(i))/p_\vartheta(a)$$

However this condition is too strong because it implies that $p_\vartheta(a(i))/p_\vartheta(a)$ is the same for every ϑ, and this is clearly not the case for instance for the nondeterministic and probabilistic master specified in Section 5.

On the other hand, if we weaken the condition by identifying ς and ϑ:

$$\forall \varsigma \in Z.\, \forall i \in I.\, \forall o \in O.\;\; p_\varsigma(o \cap a) > 0 \Rightarrow p_\varsigma(a(i) \,|\, o) = p_\varsigma(a(i))/p_\varsigma(a)$$

then the condition would be too weak to ensure anonymity, as shown by next example:

Example 4. Consider a system in which the master influences the behavior of the coins somehow, in such a way that when $Crypt_i$ is chosen as the payer (say, purely nondeterministically, by ς_i) the result is always $o_0 = \langle d, a, a \rangle$ for $i = 0$, $o_1 = \langle a, d, a \rangle$ for $i = 1$, and $o_2 = \langle a, a, d \rangle$ for $i = 2$. Then we would have $p_{\varsigma_i}(o_j \cap a) > 0$ only if $j = i$, and $p_{\varsigma_i}(a(i) \,|\, o_i) = 1 = p_{\varsigma_i}(a(i))/p_{\varsigma_i}(a)$. Hence the above condition would be verified, but the system is not be anonymous at all: whenever we observe $\langle d, a, a \rangle$, for instance, we are sure that $Crypt_0$ is the payer.

6.2 Independence from the Probability Distribution of the Users

One important property of Definition 4 is that it is independent from the probability distribution of the users. Intuitively, this is due to the fact that the condition of anonymity implies that $p(o \,|\, a(i)) = p(o)/p(a)$, hence it is independent from $p(a(i))$.

Theorem 2. *If (M, I, a, B, p) is anonymous (according to Definition 4) then for any p' which differs from p only on the $a(i)$'s, (M, I, a, B, p') is anonymous.*

Also the characterizations of anonymity given in Proposition 3 are (obviously) independent from the probability distribution of the users. It should be remarked, however, that their correspondence with Definition 4, and the property of independence from the probability of the users, only holds under the hypothesis that there is at most one agent performing a. (Assumption 3.)

7 Related work

The work [13] presents a modular framework to formalize a range of properties (including numerous flavors anonymity and privacy) of computer systems in which an observer has only partial information about system behavior, thereby combining the benefits of the knowledge-based approach (natural specification of information-hiding) and the algebra-based approach (natural specification of system behavior). It proposes the notion of *function view* to represent a mathematical abstraction of partial knowledge of a function. The logical formulas describing a property are characterized as *opaqueness* of certain function views, converted into predicates over observational equivalence classes, and verified, when possible, using the proof techniques of the chosen process formalism.

In [11,26] epistemic logic is used to characterize a number of information-hiding requirements (including anonymity). In particular, [26] introduces the notion of a *group principal* and an associated model, language and logic to axiomatize anonymity. The main advantage of modal logic is that even fairly complex properties can be stated directly as formulas in the logic. On the other hand, [11] uses a completely semantic approach and provides an appropriate semantic framework in which to consider anonymity. It also propose notions of probabilistic anonymity in a purely probabilistic framework. In particular, it propose a notion of conditional probability (cfr. Definition 4.4 in [11]) which is similar to the first characterization in Proposition 3, if we interpret the formula φ in [11] as the occurrence of the event a.

The first characterization in Proposition 3 was also implicitly used by Chaum in [7] (in which he considered a purely probabilistic system) as definition of anonymity. The factor $p(a)$ is not present in the formula of Chaum, but that's probably a typo, because in the informal explanation he gives, that factor is taken into account.

In literature there have been other works involving the use of variants of the π-calculus for formalizing protocols providing anonymity or similar properties. See for example [1,14].

8 Conclusion and Future Work

We have proposed a new notion of anonymity based on a model which combines probability and nondeterminism, and we have shown that it can be regarded as a generalization of the probabilistic one given in [11].

We have formulated the notion of anonymity in terms of observables for processes in the probabilistic π-calculus, whose semantics is based on the probabilistic automata of [25]. This opens the way to the automatic verification of the property. We are currently developing a model checker for the probabilistic π-calculus.

We are currently investigating weaker versions of our notion of anonymity, and studying their application to protocols like Crowds [8,6].

References

1. Martín Abadi and Cédric Fournet. Private authentication. *Theoretical Computer Science*, 322(3):427–476, 2004.
2. Martín Abadi and Andrew D. Gordon. A calculus for cryptographic protocols: The spi calculus. *Information and Computation*, 148(1):1–70, 10 January 1999

3. Roberto M. Amadio and Denis Lugiez. On the reachability problem in cryptographic protocols. In *Proceedings of CONCUR 00*, volume 1877 of *Lecture Notes in Computer Science*. Springer, 2000. INRIA Research Report 3915, march 2000.
4. Mohit Bhargava and Catuscia Palamidessi. Probabilistic anonymity. Technical report, INRIA Futurs and LIX, 2005. To appear in the proceedings of CONCUR 2005. Report version available at `www.lix.polytechnique.fr/~catuscia/papers/Anonymity/report.ps`.
5. S.D. Brookes, C.A.R. Hoare, and A.W. Roscoe. A theory of communicating sequential processes. *Journal of the ACM*, 31(3):560–599, 1984.
6. Kostantinos Chatzikokolakis and Catuscia Palamidessi. Probable innocence revisited. Technical report, INRIA Futurs and LIX, 2005. `www.lix.polytechnique.fr/~catuscia/papers/Anonymity/reportPI.pdf`.
7. David Chaum. The dining cryptographers problem: Unconditional sender and recipient untraceability. *Journal of Cryptology*, 1:65–75, 1988.
8. Yuxin Deng, Catuscia Palamidessi, and Jun Pang. Weak probabilistic anonymity. Technical report, INRIA Futurs and LIX, 2005. Submitted for publication. `www.lix.polytechnique.fr/~catuscia/papers/Anonymity/reportWA.pdf`.
9. R.D. Gill, M. van der Laan, and J. Robins. Coarsening at random: Characterizations, conjectures and counterexamples. In D.Y. Lin and T.R. Fleming, editors, *Proceedings of the First Seattle Symposium in Biostatistics*, Lecture Notes in Statistics, pages 255–294. Springer-Verlag, 1997.
10. P. D. Grunwald and J. Y. Halpern. Updating probabilities. *Journal of Artificial Intelligence Research*, 19:243–278, 2003.
11. Joseph Y. Halpern and Kevin R. O'Neill. Anonymity and information hiding in multiagent systems. In *Proc. of the 16th IEEE Computer Security Foundations Workshop*, pages 75–88, 2003.
12. Oltea Mihaela Herescu and Catuscia Palamidessi. Probabilistic asynchronous π-calculus. In Jerzy Tiuryn, editor, *Proceedings of FOSSACS 2000 (Part of ETAPS 2000)*, volume 1784 of *Lecture Notes in Computer Science*, pages 146–160. Springer-Verlag, 2000.
13. Dominic Hughes and Vitaly Shmatikov. Information hiding, anonymity and privacy: a modular approach. *Journal of Computer Security*, 12(1):3–36, 2004.
14. Steve Kremer and Mark D. Ryan. Analysis of an electronic voting protocol in the applied pi-calculus. In Mooly Sagiv, editor, *Programming Languages and Systems – Proceedings of the 14th European Symposium on Programming (ESOP'05)*, volume 3444 of *Lecture Notes in Computer Science*, pages 186–200, Edinburgh, U.K., April 2005. Springer.
15. Gavin Lowe. Casper: A compiler for the analysis of security protocols. In *Proceedings of 10th IEEE Computer Security Foundations Workshop*, 1997. Also in Journal of Computer Security, Volume 6, pages 53-84, 1998.
16. R. Milner. *Communication and Concurrency*. International Series in Computer Science. Prentice Hall, 1989.
17. Robin Milner. *Communicating and mobile systems: the π-calculus*. Cambridge University Press, 1999.
18. Robin Milner, Joachim Parrow, and David Walker. A calculus of mobile processes, I and II. *Information and Computation*, 100(1):1–40 & 41–77, 1992. A preliminary version appeared as Technical Reports ECF-LFCS-89-85 and -86, University of Edinburgh, 1989.
19. Catuscia Palamidessi and Oltea M. Herescu. A randomized encoding of the π-calculus with mixed choice. *Theoretical Computer Science*, 335(2-3):73–404, 2005. To appear.
20. Michael K. Reiter and Aviel D. Rubin. Crowds: anonymity for Web transactions. *ACM Transactions on Information and System Security*, 1(1):66–92, 1998.

21. A. W. Roscoe. Modelling and verifying key-exchange protocols using CSP and FDR. In *Proceedings of the 8th IEEE Computer Security Foundations Workshop*, pages 98–107. IEEE Computer Soc Press, 1995.
22. Peter Y. Ryan and Steve Schneider. *Modelling and Analysis of Security Protocols*. Addison-Wesley, 2001.
23. S. Schneider. Security properties and csp. In *Proceedings of the IEEE Symposium Security and Privacy*, 1996.
24. Steve Schneider and Abraham Sidiropoulos. CSP and anonymity. In *Proc. of the European Symposium on Research in Computer Security (ESORICS)*, volume 1146 of *Lecture Notes in Computer Science*, pages 198–218. Springer-Verlag, 1996.
25. Roberto Segala and Nancy Lynch. Probabilistic simulations for probabilistic processes. *Nordic Journal of Computing*, 2(2):250–273, 1995. An extended abstract appeared in *Proceedings of CONCUR '94*, LNCS 836: 481-496.
26. Paul F. Syverson and Stuart G. Stubblebine. Group principals and the formalization of anonymity. In *World Congress on Formal Methods (1)*, pages 814–833, 1999.
27. P.F. Syverson, D.M. Goldschlag, and M.G. Reed. Anonymous connections and onion routing. In *IEEE Symposium on Security and Privacy*, pages 44–54, Oakland, California, 1997.

Secrecy Despite Compromise: Types, Cryptography, and the Pi-Calculus

Andrew D. Gordon[1] and Alan Jeffrey[2,*]

[1] Microsoft Research
[2] DePaul University and Bell Labs, Lucent Technologies

Abstract. A realistic threat model for cryptographic protocols or for language-based security should include a dynamically growing population of principals (or security levels), some of which may be compromised, that is, come under the control of the adversary. We explore such a threat model within a pi-calculus. A new process construct records the ordering between security levels, including the possibility of compromise. Another expresses the expectation of conditional secrecy of a message—that a particular message is unknown to the adversary unless particular levels are compromised. Our main technical contribution is the first system of secrecy types for a process calculus to support multiple, dynamically-generated security levels, together with the controlled compromise or downgrading of security levels. A series of examples illustrates the effectiveness of the type system in proving secrecy of messages, including dynamically-generated messages. It also demonstrates the improvement over prior work obtained by including a security ordering in the type system. Perhaps surprisingly, the soundness proof for our type system for symbolic cryptography is via a simple translation into a core typed pi-calculus, with no need to take symbolic cryptography as primitive.

1 Introduction

Ever since the Internet entered popular culture it has had associations of insecurity. The Morris worm of 1989 broke the news by attacking vulnerable computers on the network and exploiting them to attack others. At least since then, compromised hosts and untrustworthy users have been a perpetual presence on the Internet, and, perhaps worse, inside many institutional intranets. Hence, like all effective risk management, good computer security does not focus simply on prevention, but also on management and containment.

There is by now a substantial literature on language-based techniques to prevent disclosure of secrets [21]. This paper contributes new language constructs to help manage and contain the impact of partial compromise on a system: we generalize the attacker model from a completely untrusted outsider to include attacks mounted by compromised insiders. We use the pi-calculus [17], a theory of concurrency that already supports reasoning about multiple, dynamically generated identities, and security based on

* This material is based upon work supported by the National Science Foundation under Grant No. 0208549.

M. Abadi and L. de Alfaro (Eds.): CONCUR 2005, LNCS 3653, pp. 186–201, 2005.

abstract channels or symbolic cryptography [1,4]. We formalize the new idea of *conditional secrecy*, that a message is secret unless particular principals are compromised. We describe a type system that checks conditional secrecy, and hence may help assess the containment of compromise within a system.

Specifying Compromise and Conditional Secrecy. We model systems as collections of processes, that interact by exchanging messages on named channels. Most of the examples in the paper rely on channel abstractions for security, but our methods also handle protocols that rely on cryptography. The opponent is an implicit process that runs alongside the processes making up the system under attack, and may interact with it using channels (or keys) in its possession. We say a message is *public* if it may come into the possession of the opponent (possibly after a series of interactions).

We base our model of partially compromised systems on a *security ordering* between abstract *security levels*. Secrecy levels model individual (or groups of) principals, hosts, sessions, and other identifiers. For instance, the level of the opponent is the distinguished lowest security level $\perp$.

The process construct $L_1 \leq L_2$, called a *statement*, declares that level L_1 is less than level L_2. Hence, any process defines a security ordering between levels; it is given by the set of active statements occurring in the process, closed under a set of inference rules including reflexivity and transitivity. (Statements are akin to the use of process constructs to describe the occurrence of events [6,14] or to populate a database of facts [10].) We say a level L is *compromised* when $L \leq \perp$. Compromise may arise indirectly: if $L_1 \leq L_2$ and subsequently L_2 is compromised, then so too is L_1, by transitivity. So $L_1 \leq L_2$ can be read "L_1 is at risk from L_2" as well as "L_1 is less secure than L_2."

Compromise may be contained or non-catastrophic in the sense that despite the compromise of one part of a system, another part may reliably keep messages secret. For example, key establishment protocols often have the property that A and B can keep their session key secret even though a session key established between B and a compromised party C has become public. However, as soon as either A or B is compromised, their session key may become public.

The process construct **secret** M **amongst** L, called an *expectation of conditional secrecy*, declares the invariant "M is secret unless L is compromised". For example, the process **secret** S **amongst** (A, B) asserts that S is secret unless the composite security level (A,B) has been compromised, which occurs if either A or B has been compromised. This definition of conditional secrecy via a syntactic process construct is new and may be of interest independently of our type system. By embedding falsifiable expectations within processes, we can express the conditional secrecy of freshly generated messages, unlike previous definitions [2]. Our trace-based notion of secrecy concerns direct flows to an active attacker; we do not address indirect flows or noninterference.

Checking Conditional Secrecy by Typing. Our main technical contribution is the first system of secrecy types for a process calculus that supports multiple, dynamically-generated security levels, together with compromise or downgrading of security levels. Abadi's original system [1] of secrecy types for cryptographic protocols, and its descendants, are limited to two security levels, and therefore cannot conveniently model the dynamic creation and compromise of security levels, or the possibility of attack from compromised insiders. Our treatment of asymmetric communication channels builds on our recent work on types for authentication properties [13].

Our main technical result, Theorem 2, is that no expectation of conditional secrecy is ever falsified when a well-typed process interacts with any opponent process.

We anticipate applications of this work both in the design of security-typed languages and in the verification of cryptographic protocols. Security types with multiple security levels are common in the literature on information flow in programming languages, but ours is apparently the first use in the analysis of cryptographic protocols.

Section 2 describes our core pi-calculus. Section 3 exhibits a series of example protocols that make use of secure channels. Theorem 2 can be applied to show these protocols preserve the secrecy of dynamically generated data. Previous type systems yield unconditional secrecy guarantees, and therefore cannot handle the dynamic declassification of data in these protocols. Section 4 presents our type system formally. Section 5 outlines the extension of our results to a pi-calculus with symbolic cryptography. Section 6 discusses related work, and Section 7 concludes.

A companion technical report [15] includes further explanations and examples, an extension of the core calculus and type system to cover symbolic cryptography, and proofs. Notably, the soundness of the extended type system follows via a straightforward translation into our core pi-calculus. We represent ciphertexts as processes, much like the encoding [17] of other data structures in the pi-calculus. Although such a representation of ciphertexts is well known to admit false attacks in general, it is adequate in our typed setting.

2 A Pi Calculus with Expectations of Conditional Secrecy

Our core calculus is an asynchronous form of Odersky's polarized pi-calculus [19] extended with secrecy expectations and security levels.

Computation is based on communication of messages between processes on named channels. The calculus is polarized in the sense that there are separate capabilities to send and receive on each channel. The send capability $k!$ confers the right to send (but not receive) on a channel k. Conversely, the receive capability $k?$ confers the right to receive (but not send) on k. The asymmetry of these capabilities is analogous to the asymmetry between public encryption and private decryption keys, and allows us to write programs with the flavour of cryptographic protocols in a small calculus.

Messages are values communicated over channels between processes. As well as send and receive capabilities, messages include names, pairs, tagged messages, and the distinguished security levels $\top$ and $\bot$.

Processes include the standard pi-calculus constructs plus operations to access pairs and tagged unions. To track direct flows of messages, each output is tagged with its security level; for instance, an output by the opponent may be tagged $\bot$. The only new process constructs are statements $M \leq N$ and expectations **secret** M **amongst** L.

Names, Messages, Processes:

$a,\ldots,n,v,\ldots,z$	names and variables
$L,M,N ::=$	message, security level
x	name, variable
$M?$	capability to input on M
$M!$	capability to output on M
(M,N)	message pair
inl M	left injection
inr M	right injection
$\top$	highest security
$\bot$	lowest security
$C ::= M \leq N$	clause: level M less secure than level N
$\vec{M},\vec{N} ::= M_1,\ldots,M_m$	sequence of messages ($m \geq 0$)
T,U	type: defined in Section 4
$P,Q,R ::=$	process
out $M\ N :: L$	asynchronous output at level L
inp $M(x{:}T);P$	input (scope of x is P)
new $x{:}T;P$	name generation (scope of x is P)
repeat P	replication
$P \mid Q$	parallel composition
stop	inactivity
split M **is** $(x \leq y{:}T, z{:}U);P$	pair splitting (scope of x,y is U, P, of z just P)
match M **is** $(x \leq N{:}T, z{:}U);P$	pair matching (scope of x is U, P, of z just P)
case M **is inl** $(x{:}T)$ P **is inr** $(y{:}U)$ Q	union case (scope of x is P, of y is Q)
C	statement of clause C
secret M **amongst** L	expectation of conditional secrecy

We write $P \rightarrow Q$ to mean P may reduce to Q, and $P \equiv Q$ to mean P and Q are structurally equivalent. The mostly standard definitions of these relations are in [15]. The only nonstandard reductions are for **split** and the first-component-matching operation **match**, which bind an extra variable. (We motivate the use of this variable in Section 3).

$$\textbf{split } (M,N) \textbf{ is } (x \leq y{:}T, z{:}U);P \rightarrow P\{x\leftarrow M\}\{y\leftarrow M\}\{z\leftarrow N\}$$
$$\textbf{match } (M,N) \textbf{ is } (x \leq M, z{:}U);P \rightarrow P\{x\leftarrow M\}\{z\leftarrow N\}$$

Any message M can be seen as a *security level*. Levels are ordered, with bottom element $\bot$, top element $\top$, and meet given by (M,N). We write S for a set of clauses of the form $M \leq N$, and write $S \vdash M \leq N$ when $M \leq N$ is derivable from hypotheses S.

Set of Clauses:

$S ::= \{C_1,\ldots,C_n\}$	set of clauses
$\{C_1,\ldots,C_n\} \triangleq C_1 \mid \cdots \mid C_n \mid$ **stop**	when considered as a process

Preorder on Security Levels: $S \vdash M \leq N$

$C \in S \Rightarrow S \vdash C$	(Order Id)
$S \vdash M \leq M$	(Order Refl)
$S \vdash L \leq M \wedge S \vdash M \leq N \Rightarrow S \vdash L \leq N$	(Order Trans)
$S \vdash \bot \leq M$	(Order Bot-L)
$S \vdash M \leq \top$	(Order Top-R)
$S \vdash (M,N) \leq M$	(Order Meet-L-1)
$S \vdash (M,N) \leq N$	(Order Meet-L-2)
$S \vdash L \leq M \wedge S \vdash L \leq N \Rightarrow S \vdash L \leq (M,N)$	(Order Meet-R)

Since processes contain ordering statements, we can derive $P \vdash M \leq N$ whenever P contains statements S, and $S \vdash M \leq N$.

Security Order Induced by a Process: $P \vdash M \leq N$

Let $P \vdash M \leq N$ if and only if $P \equiv \mathbf{new}\ \vec{x}{:}\vec{T}; (S \mid Q)$ and $S \vdash M \leq N$ and $\mathsf{fn}(M,N) \cap \{\vec{x}\} = \varnothing$.

An expectation **secret** M **amongst** N in a process is justified if every output of M is at a level L such that $N \leq L$. That is, the secret M may flow up, not down. We say P is *safe for conditional secrecy* to mean no unjustified expectation exists in any process reachable from P. The "robust" extension of this definition means the process is safe when composed with any opponent process, much as in earlier work [12].

Safety:

A process P is *safe for conditional secrecy* if and only if
whenever $P \rightarrow^* \mathbf{new}\ \vec{x}{:}\vec{T}; (\mathbf{secret}\ M\ \mathbf{amongst}\ N \mid \mathbf{out}\ !x\ M :: L \mid Q)$, we have $Q \vdash N \leq L$.

Opponent Processes and Robust Safety:

A process O is **Un**-*typed* if and only if every type occurring in O is **Un**.
Write $\mathsf{erase}(P)$ for the **Un**-typed process given by replacing all types in P by **Un**.
A process O is **secret**-*free* if any only if there are no **secret** expectations in O.
A process $O\{\vec{x}\}$ with $\mathsf{fn}(O\{\vec{x}\}) = \{\vec{x}\}$ is an *opponent* if and only if it is **Un**-typed and **secret**-free.
A process P is *robustly safe for conditional secrecy despite* $\vec{L}$ if and only if
$P \mid O\{\vec{L}\}$ is safe for secrecy for all opponents $O\{\vec{x}\}$.

3 Examples of Secrecy Despite Compromise

The examples in this section illustrate some protocols and their secrecy properties, and also informally introduce some aspects of our type system. We use mostly standard abbreviations for common message and process idioms, such as arbitrary-length tuples. These are much the same as in previous work [13], and are given in [15].

A Basic Example. Consider a world with just the two security levels $\top$ and $\bot$. The following processes, at level $\top$, communicate along a shared channel k. (We use the keyword **process** to declare non-recursive process abbreviations.)

process Sender(k:**Ch**(**Secret**{ $\top$ })) =
  new s:**Secret**{ $\top$ }; **out** k!(s) :: $\top$ | **secret** s **amongst** $\top$.
process Receiver(k:**Ch**(**Secret**{ $\top$ })) =
  inp k?(s:**Secret**{ $\top$ }); **secret** s **amongst** $\top$.

The parallel composition Sender(k) | Receiver(k) is robustly safe despite $\varnothing$ but not, for example, despite either {k!} (because the attacker can send public data to falsify the receiver's expectation) or {k?} (because the attacker can obtain the secret s to falsify the sender's expectation).

Our type system can verify the robust safety property of this system based on its type annotations. Messages of type **Secret**$\{L\}$ are secrets at level L. Messages of type **Ch** T are channels for exchanging messages of type T. Later on, we use types ?**Ch** T and !**Ch** T for the input and output capabilities on channels of T messages.

An Example of Secrecy Despite Host Compromise. To establish secrecy properties (for example, that A and B share a secret) in the presence of a compromised insider (for example C, who also shares a secret with B) requires more security levels than just $\top$ and $\bot$. For example, consider the following variant on an example of Abadi and Blanchet [3] (rewritten to include the identities of the principals).

process Sender(a:**Un**, b:**Un**, cA:Type2(a,b), cB:Type1(b)) =
  new k:**Secret**{a,b}; **secret** k **amongst** (a,b);
  new s:**Secret**{a,b}; **secret** s **amongst** (a,b);
  out cB (a, k, cA!) :: a |
  inp cA? (**match** k, cAB:!Type3(a,b)); // pattern-matching syntax
  out cAB (s) :: a.

process Receiver(b:**Un**, cB:Type1(b)) =
  inp cB? (a$\leq$a$'$:**Un**, k:**Secret**{a,b}, cA:!Type2(a,b)); // pattern-matching syntax
  new cAB:Type3(a,b);
  out cA (k, cAB!) :: b |
  inp cAB? (z:**Secret**{a,b}); **stop**.

Here, sender A sends to receiver B a tuple (A,k,cA!), along a trusted output channel cB, whose matching input channel is known only to B. She then waits to receive a message of the form (k,cAB), whose first component matches the freshly generated name k, along the channel cA?, which must have come from B, as only A and B know k. Hence, A knows that cAB is a trusted channel to B, and so it is safe to send s along cAB.

Receiver B runs the matching half of the protocol, but gets much weaker guarantees, as the output channel cB is public, and so anyone (including an attacker) can send messages along it. When B receives (A,k,cA?), he knows that it claims to be from A, and binds a$'$ to A's security level. However, he does not know who the message really came from: it could be A, or it could be an attacker masquerading as A. All B knows is that there is some security level a$\leq$a$'$ indicating who really sent the message.

When a process such as Receiver receives an input such as (A,k,cA!), it binds two variables a$\leq$a$'$ reflecting the actual and claimed security level of the message. This is reflected in the dependent type $(\pi x \leq y : T, U)$, which binds two variables in U. The variable x is bound to the actual security level, and the variable y is bound to the claimed security level. At run-time, the binding for x is unknown, so it is restricted to only being used in types, not in messages. In examples, we often elide x when it is unused.

Processes have two ways of accessing a pair: they may use the **split** construct to extract the components of the pair, or they may use the **match** construct to match the first element of the pair against a constant. For example, the Sender process above contains the input **inp** ca?(**match** k, cAB:!Type3(a,b)), which requires the first component to match the known name k, or else fails, and (implicitly) uses **split** to bind the second component to cAB. (We are using pattern-matching abbreviations to avoid introducing large numbers of temporary variables, as discussed in [15].) These two forms of access to tuples are not new, and have formed the basis of our previous work on typechecking cryptographic protocols [12,13]. What is new is that these forms of access are reflected in the types. We tag fields with a marker π, which is either **split** or **match**, to indicate how they are used.

The types for this example are:

type Type3(a,b) = **Ch** (**Secret**{a,b})
type Type2(a,b) = **Ch** (**match** k:**Secret**{a,b}, **split** cAB:!Type3(a,b))
type Type1(b) = **Ch** (**split** a$\leq$a′:**Un**, **split** k:**Secret**{a,b}, **split** cA:!Type2(a,b))

Given the environment:

A:**Un**, CA:Type2(A,B), B:**Un**, CB:Type1(B), C:**Un**, CC:Type2(C,B)

we can typecheck:

repeat Sender(A,B,CA,CB!) | **repeat** Receiver(B,CB) |
repeat Sender(C,B,CC,CB!) | C$\leq\bot$

Hence, soundness of the type system (Theorem 2) implies the system is robustly safe for secrecy despite {A,B,C,CA!,CB!,CC}. The statement C$\leq\bot$ represents the compromise of C. Thus, A and B are guaranteed to preserve their secrecy, even though compromised C shares a secret CC with B.

An Example of Secrecy Despite Session Compromise. Finally, we consider an adaption of the previous protocol to allow for declassification of secrets. Declassification may be deliberate, or it may model the consequences of an exploitable software defect. We regard the session identifier k as a new security level, that may be compromised independently of A and B. We modify the example by allowing the sender to declassify the secret after receiving a message on channel d.

process Sender(a:**Un**, b:**Un**, cA:Type2(a,b), cB:Type1(b), d:**Un**) =
  new k:**Secret**{a,b}; **secret** k **amongst** (a,b);
  new s:**Secret**{a,b,k}; **secret** s **amongst** (a,b,k);
  out cB (a, k, cA!) :: a |
  inp cA? (**match** k, cAB:!Type3(a,b));
  out cAB (s) :: a |
  inp d?(); k$\leq\bot$; **out** d!(s) :: a

Here, the sender declassifies s by the statement k $\leq \bot$. Since k is mentioned in the security level of s, this statement allows s to be published on public channel d. The rest of the system remains unchanged and the types are now:

type Type3(a,b,k) = **Ch** (**Secret**{a,b,k})
type Type2(a,b) = **Ch** (**match** k:**Secret**{a,b}, **split** cAB:!Type3(a,b,k))
type Type1(b) = **Ch** (**split** a $\leq$ a′:**Un**, **split** k:**Secret**{a,b}, **split** cA:!Type2(a,b))

Theorem 2 now gives us not only that A and B can maintain secrecy despite compromise of C, but also that it is possible to compromise one session k, and hence declassify the matching secret s, without violating secrecy of the other sessions.

4 A Type System for Checking Conditional Secrecy

A basic idea in our type system is to identify classes of public and tainted types [13]. Intuitively, messages of public type can flow to the opponent, while messages of tainted type may flow from the opponent. More formally, if **Un** is the type of all messages known to the opponent and <: is the subtype relation, a type T is *public* just when T <: **Un**, and a type T is *tainted* just when **Un** <: T.

Both classes depend on the security ordering. Just as the attacker encroaches on the compromised parts of a system over time, types may become public or tainted over time. We reflect this dependency syntactically by decorating types with symbolic kinds. A *kind* K is a pair $\{?M, !N\}$ of security levels. A message of a type decorated $\{?M, !N\}$ can be assumed to flow from a source at level M (or higher), and is allowed to flow to a target at level N (or higher). If $M \leq \bot$ the type is tainted; if $N \leq \bot$ the type is public. We often write shorthand such as {A, ?B, !C} for the kind {?(A,B), !(A,C)}.

Kinds:

$K ::= \{?M, !N\}$	tainted if $M \leq \bot$, public if $N \leq \bot$

Write $\{L_1, \ldots, L_l, ?M_1, \ldots, ?M_m, !N_1, \ldots, !N_n\}$
for $\{?(L_1, \ldots, L_l, M_1, \ldots, M_m), !(L_1, \ldots, L_l, N_1, \ldots, N_n)\}$.

Our language of types consists of standard constructs for channels with optional read-only and write-only attributes, sum types, and **Ok** types [11]. The only non-standard types are the dependent pairs $(\pi x \leq y : T, U)$, discussed previously in Section 3.

Types:

$\nu ::= ? \mid !$	input-only (?) or output-only (!) attribute
$\pi ::=$ **split** | **match**	split-only or match-only attribute
$T, U ::=$	type
Ch $K\ T$	channel for T messages
ν**Ch** $K\ T$	input or output capability on channel for T messages
$(\pi x \leq y{:}T, U)$	split-only or match-only dependent pair (scope of x, y is U)
$T + U$	tagged sum type
Ok S	proof of security ordering

Our judgments are defined with respect to an *environment*, a list of all names in scope, paired with their types. A generative type is one that can be freshly generated.

Environments:

$E ::= \varnothing \mid E, x{:}T$	environment: list of name typings

$\mathsf{dom}(\varnothing) = \varnothing \quad \mathsf{dom}(E, x{:}T) = \mathsf{dom}(E) \cup \{x\}$

$\mathsf{clauses}(\varnothing) = \varnothing \quad \mathsf{clauses}(E, x{:}T) = \mathsf{clauses}(E) \cup \{C_1, \ldots, C_n \mid T \text{ is } \mathbf{Ok}\{C_1, \ldots, C_n\}\}$

Generative Types and Environments:

Let a type be *generative* if and only if it is a channel type $\mathbf{Ch}\ K\ T$.
Let an environment E be *generative* if and only if $E(x)$ is generative for each $x \in \mathsf{dom}(E)$.

Judgments of the Type System:

$E \vdash \diamond$	good environment
$E \vdash \mathit{Public}(T)$	public type: T data may flow to the opponent
$E \vdash \mathit{Tainted}(T)$	tainted type: T data may flow from the opponent
$E \vdash T <: T'$	subtype
$E \vdash M : T$	good message of type T
$E \vdash P$	good process

Next, we present the rules defining these judgments. We rely on several abbreviations.

Abbreviations:

Write E, S for the environment $E, x : \mathbf{Ok}\ S$ where x is fresh.
Write $E \vdash M$ for $E \vdash \diamond$ and $\mathsf{fn}(M) \subseteq \mathsf{dom}(E)$.
Write $E \vdash M \leq N$ for $E \vdash (M, N)$ and $\mathsf{clauses}(E) \vdash M \leq N$.
Write $E \vdash S$ for $E \vdash M \leq N$ for every $(M \leq N) \in S$.
Write $E \vdash M \leftrightarrow N$ for $E \vdash M \leq N$ and $E \vdash N \leq M$.
Write $E \vdash T <:> U$ for $E \vdash T <: U$ and $E \vdash U <: T$.

The following standard rules state that in a good environment, each declared name must be fresh, and each name occurring in a type must be declared previously.

Good Environment:

(Env $\varnothing$)
$$\frac{}{\varnothing \vdash \diamond}$$

(Env x)
$$\frac{E \vdash \diamond \quad x \notin \mathsf{dom}(E) \quad \mathsf{fn}(T) \subseteq \mathsf{dom}(E)}{E, x{:}T \vdash \diamond}$$

The judgments $E \vdash \mathit{Public}(T)$ and $E \vdash \mathit{Tainted}(T)$ formalize the classes of public and tainted types. The rules follow the pattern of previous work [13]. The most interesting rules are those for determining when a dependent pair $(\pi x \leq y{:}T, U)$ is tainted. If data of this type has been received from the opponent, then we know that the real security level of the term is $\bot$, and so when we check U for taintedness, we first replace x by $\bot$. In the case when π is **match**, we can be even more liberal, and add into the environment extra clauses generated by tainting the type T: for example ($\mathbf{match}\ x \leq y{:}\mathbf{Secret}\{a\}, \mathbf{Secret}\{a\}$) is tainted, because we add the clause $a \leq \bot$ to the environment before checking taintedness of the type $\mathbf{Secret}\{a\}$.

Extracting a Set of Clauses from a Tainted Type:

$\mathsf{taint}(\mathbf{Ch}\{?M, !N\}\ T) \triangleq \{M \leq \bot, N \leq \bot\}$
$\mathsf{taint}(\nu\mathbf{Ch}\ \{?M, !N\}\ T) \triangleq \{M \leq \bot\}$
$\mathsf{taint}(\pi x \leq y{:}T, U) \triangleq \mathsf{taint}(T + U) \triangleq \mathsf{taint}(\mathbf{Ok}\ S) \triangleq \varnothing$

Public and Tainted Types:

(Public I/O)
$$\frac{E \vdash M \leftrightarrow \bot \quad E \vdash N \leftrightarrow \bot \quad E \vdash \mathit{Public}(T) \quad E \vdash \mathit{Tainted}(T)}{E \vdash \mathit{Public}(\mathbf{Ch}\ \{?M, !N\}\ T)}$$

(Tainted I/O)
$$\frac{E \vdash M \leftrightarrow \bot \quad E \vdash N \leftrightarrow \bot \quad E \vdash \mathit{Public}(T) \quad E \vdash \mathit{Tainted}(T)}{E \vdash \mathit{Tainted}(\mathbf{Ch}\ \{?M, !N\}\ T)}$$

(Public I)
$$\frac{E \vdash M \quad E \vdash N \leftrightarrow \bot \quad E \vdash \mathit{Public}(T)}{E \vdash \mathit{Public}(?\mathbf{Ch}\ \{?M, !N\}\ T)}$$

(Tainted I)
$$\frac{E \vdash M \leftrightarrow \bot \quad E \vdash N \quad E \vdash \mathit{Tainted}(T)}{E \vdash \mathit{Tainted}(?\mathbf{Ch}\ \{?M, !N\}\ T)}$$

(Public O)
$$\frac{E \vdash M \quad E \vdash N \leftrightarrow \bot \quad E \vdash \mathit{Tainted}(T)}{E \vdash \mathit{Public}(!\mathbf{Ch}\ \{?M, !N\}\ T)}$$

(Tainted O)
$$\frac{E \vdash M \leftrightarrow \bot \quad E \vdash N \quad E \vdash \mathit{Public}(T)}{E \vdash \mathit{Tainted}(!\mathbf{Ch}\ \{?M, !N\}\ T)}$$

(Public Split)
$$\frac{E \vdash \mathit{Public}(T) \quad E, x{:}T, y{:}T, x \leq y \vdash \mathit{Public}(U)}{E \vdash \mathit{Public}((\mathbf{split}\ x \leq y{:}T, U))}$$

(Tainted Split)
$$\frac{E \vdash \mathit{Tainted}(T) \quad E, y{:}T \vdash \mathit{Tainted}(U\{x \leftarrow \bot\})}{E \vdash \mathit{Tainted}((\mathbf{split}\ x \leq y{:}T, U))}$$

(Public Match)
$$\frac{E \vdash \mathit{Public}(T) \quad E, x{:}T, y{:}T, x \leq y \vdash \mathit{Public}(U)}{E \vdash \mathit{Public}((\mathbf{match}\ x \leq y{:}T, U))}$$

(Tainted Match)
$$\frac{E, \mathsf{taint}(T) \vdash \mathit{Tainted}(T) \quad E, y{:}T, \mathsf{taint}(T) \vdash \mathit{Tainted}(U\{x \leftarrow \bot\})}{E \vdash \mathit{Tainted}((\mathbf{match}\ x \leq y{:}T, U))}$$

(Tainted Sum)
$$\frac{E \vdash \mathit{Tainted}(T) \quad E \vdash \mathit{Tainted}(U)}{E \vdash \mathit{Tainted}(T + U)}$$

(Public Sum)
$$\frac{E \vdash \mathit{Public}(T) \quad E \vdash \mathit{Public}(U)}{E \vdash \mathit{Public}(T + U)}$$

(Public Order)
$$\frac{E \vdash \diamond \quad \mathsf{fn}(S) \subseteq \mathsf{dom}(E)}{E \vdash \mathit{Public}(\mathbf{Ok}\ S)}$$

(Tainted Order)
$$\frac{E \vdash \diamond \quad E \vdash M_i \leftrightarrow \bot \quad E \vdash N_i \quad \forall i \in 1..n}{E \vdash \mathit{Tainted}(\mathbf{Ok}\ \{M_1 \leq N_1, \ldots, M_n \leq N_n\})}$$

The rules for subtyping are mostly taken from [13]. The main exception is the rule for ($\mathbf{match} x \leq y{:}T, U$), which requires an extra condition to ensure that subtyping preserves the taint function used in the definition of $E \vdash \mathit{Tainted}(T)$.

Subtyping:

(Sub Public/Tainted)
$$\frac{E \vdash \mathit{Public}(T) \quad E \vdash \mathit{Tainted}(U)}{E \vdash T <: U}$$

(Sub I/O)
$$\frac{E \vdash M \leftrightarrow M' \quad E \vdash N \leftrightarrow N' \quad E \vdash T <:> T'}{E \vdash \mathbf{Ch}\ \{?M, !N\}\ T <: \mathbf{Ch}\ \{?M', !N'\}\ T'}$$

(Sub I)
$$\frac{E \vdash M' \leq M \quad E \vdash N \leq N' \quad E \vdash T <: T'}{E \vdash ?\mathbf{Ch}\ \{?M, !N\}\ T <: ?\mathbf{Ch}\ \{?M', !N'\}\ T'}$$

(Sub O)
$$\frac{E \vdash M' \leq M \quad E \vdash N \leq N' \quad E \vdash T' <: T}{E \vdash !\mathbf{Ch}\ \{?M, !N\}\ T <: !\mathbf{Ch}\ \{?M', !N'\}\ T'}$$

(Sub Split)
$$\frac{\begin{array}{c} E \vdash T <: T' \\ E, x{:}T, y{:}T, x \leq y \vdash U <: U' \end{array}}{E \vdash (\mathbf{split}\ x \leq y{:}T, U) <: (\mathbf{split}\ x \leq y{:}T', U')}$$

(Sub Match)
$$\frac{\begin{array}{c} E \vdash T <: T' \quad E, \mathsf{taint}(T') \vdash \mathsf{taint}(T) \\ E, x{:}T, y{:}T, x \leq y \vdash U <: U' \end{array}}{E \vdash (\mathbf{match}\ x \leq y{:}T, U) <: (\mathbf{match}\ x \leq y{:}T', U')}$$

(Sub Sum)
$$\frac{E \vdash T <: T' \quad E \vdash U <: U'}{E \vdash T + U <: T' + U'}$$

(Sub Hierarchy)
$$\frac{E \vdash \diamond \quad E, S \vdash S'}{E \vdash \mathbf{Ok}\ S <: \mathbf{Ok}\ S'}$$

To illustrate the judgments defined so far, we derive the types **Un** and **Secret**K, used already in examples. (Our examples rely also on standard abbreviations, such as tuple types encoded using pair types. Full details are in [15].)

Abbreviations for Un and Secret$K$:

$\mathbf{Un} \triangleq \mathbf{Ch}\ \{\bot\}\ (\mathbf{Ok}\ \{\})$	generative type of messages known to opponent
$\mathbf{Secret}\,K \triangleq ?\mathbf{Ch}\ K\ \mathbf{Un}$	type of secrets at kind K

Given these derived types, the four types $\mathbf{Secret}\{?M, !N\}$ where $M, N \in \{\top, \bot\}$ have the following properties, assuming that $\bot < \top$. Moreover, the subtype ordering induces a diamond lattice, with Any at the top, and Empty at the bottom. The Empty type is uninhabited, and the remaining inhabited types are exactly those of Abadi [1].

The Four Types Secret$\{?M, !N\}$ with $M, N \in \{\top, \bot\}$:

$\mathrm{Any} \triangleq \mathbf{Secret}\{?\bot, !\top\}$	tainted, not public
$\mathrm{Pub} \triangleq \mathbf{Secret}\{?\bot, !\bot\}$	tainted, public
$\mathrm{Sec} \triangleq \mathbf{Secret}\{?\top, !\top\}$	not tainted, not public
$\mathrm{Empty} \triangleq \mathbf{Secret}\{?\top, !\bot\}$	not tainted, public

Next, here are the type assignment rules for messages.

Good Message:

(Msg Subsum)
$$\frac{E \vdash M : T \quad E \vdash T <: T'}{E \vdash M : T'}$$

(Msg x)
$$\frac{E \vdash \diamond \quad (x{:}T) \in E}{E \vdash x : T}$$

(Msg I)
$$\frac{E \vdash L : \mathbf{Ch}\ \{?M, !N\}\ T}{E \vdash L? : ?\mathbf{Ch}\ \{M\}\ T}$$

(Msg O)
$$\frac{E \vdash L : \mathbf{Ch}\ \{?M, !N\}\ T}{E \vdash L! : !\mathbf{Ch}\ \{N\}\ T}$$

(Msg Pair)
$$\frac{E \vdash M : T \quad E \vdash N : U\{x \leftarrow M\}\{y \leftarrow M\}}{E \vdash (M, N) : (\pi x \leq y{:}T, U)}$$

(Msg $\bot$)
$$\frac{E \vdash \diamond}{E \vdash \bot : \mathbf{Un}}$$

(Msg Inl)
$$\frac{E \vdash M : T \quad \mathsf{fn}(U) \subseteq \mathsf{dom}(E)}{E \vdash \mathbf{inl}\, M : T + U}$$

(Msg Inr)
$$\frac{E \vdash N : U \quad \mathsf{fn}(T) \subseteq \mathsf{dom}(E)}{E \vdash \mathbf{inr}\, N : T + U}$$

(Msg Ok)
$$\frac{E \vdash \diamond \quad E \vdash S}{E \vdash \top : \mathbf{Ok}\ S}$$

The type rules for processes are standard, with two exceptions. The rule for output performs an extra check on the security level of the output, to ensure that the data can be published at that level: the assumption $E, L \leq \bot \vdash \mathit{Public}(T)$ can be read "if the level L were compromised, the type T would be public". The rule for composition typechecks each component in an environment extended with any top-level statement $M \leq N$ occurring in the other component.

Extracting Environments from Processes:

$\mathsf{env}(P \mid Q) = \mathsf{env}(P), \mathsf{env}(Q)$
$\mathsf{env}(\mathbf{repeat}\ P) = \mathsf{env}(P)$
$\mathsf{env}(M \leq N) = x{:}\mathbf{Ok}\ \{M \leq N\}$ for fresh x
$\mathsf{env}(\mathbf{new}\ x{:}T; P) = y{:}T, \mathsf{env}(P\{x \leftarrow y\})$ for fresh y
$\mathsf{env}(P) = \varnothing$ otherwise

Good Process:

(Proc Output)
$$\frac{E, L \leq \bot \vdash \mathit{Public}(T) \qquad E \vdash M : !\mathbf{Ch}\ K\ T \quad E \vdash N : T}{E \vdash \mathbf{out}\ M\ N :: L}$$

(Proc Input)
$$\frac{E \vdash M : ?\mathbf{Ch}\ K\ T \qquad E, x{:}T \vdash P}{E \vdash \mathbf{inp}\ M(x{:}T); P}$$

(Proc Res)
$$\frac{E, x{:}T \vdash P \quad T \text{ generative}}{E \vdash \mathbf{new}\ x{:}T; P}$$

(Proc Repl)
$$\frac{E \vdash P}{E \vdash \mathbf{repeat}\ P}$$

(Proc Par Mutual)
$$\frac{E, \mathsf{env}(Q) \vdash P \quad E, \mathsf{env}(P) \vdash Q}{E \vdash P \mid Q}$$

(Proc Stop)
$$\frac{E \vdash \diamond}{E \vdash \mathbf{stop}}$$

(Proc Split)
$$\frac{x \notin \mathsf{fn}(\mathsf{erase}(P)) \qquad E \vdash M : (\mathbf{split}\ x \leq y{:}T, U) \qquad E, x{:}T, y{:}T, x \leq y, z{:}U \vdash P}{E \vdash \mathbf{split}\ M\ \mathbf{is}\ (x \leq y{:}T, z{:}U); P}$$

(Proc Match)
$$\frac{x \notin \mathsf{fn}(\mathsf{erase}(P)) \qquad E \vdash M : (\mathbf{match}\ x \leq y{:}T, U) \quad E \vdash N : T \qquad E, x{:}T, x \leq N, z{:}U\{x \leftarrow N\} \vdash P}{E \vdash \mathbf{match}\ M\ \mathbf{is}\ (x \leq N, z{:}U\{y \leftarrow N\}); P}$$

(Proc Case)
$$\frac{E \vdash M : T + U \quad E, x{:}T \vdash P \quad E, y{:}U \vdash Q}{E \vdash \mathbf{case}\ M\ \mathbf{is\ inl}\ (x{:}T)\ P\ \mathbf{is\ inr}\ (y{:}U)\ Q}$$

(Proc Clause)
$$\frac{E \vdash M \quad E \vdash N}{E \vdash M \leq N}$$

(Proc Secret Cap)
$$\frac{E \vdash M : \nu\mathbf{Ch}\ \{?L\}\ T}{E \vdash \mathbf{secret}\ M\ \mathbf{amongst}\ L}$$

We can now state the main result of the paper, that the type system is sound with respect to robust safety. (Proofs are in [15].)

Theorem 1 (Safety). *If $E \vdash P$ and E is generative then P is safe for conditional secrecy.*

Theorem 2 (Robust Safety). *If $E \vdash P$, E is generative, and $E \vdash \vec{M}$:* **Un** *then P is robustly safe for conditional secrecy despite $\vec{M}$.*

5 An Extended Calculus with Symbolic Cryptography (Outline)

To express cryptographic protocols, we can add symbolic encryption and decryption operations to our core calculus to obtain a form of the spi-calculus [5]. We can easily extend our type system to accommodate these operations, much as in previous work [13]; for example, encryption and decryption keys are treated analogously to the output and input capabilities in our core calculus. Somewhat surprisingly, we can prove soundness of the extended type system by a straightforward translation into the core calculus. Keys are translated to channels, encryption keys to output channels, decryption keys to input channels, and ciphertexts to the constant $\perp$. The translation is not fully abstract, but preserves typings and reflects safety, which suffices to establish that well-typed spi-calculus processes are robustly safe. (The companion report [15] has full details of the extended calculus, type system, and the translation.) As an example of using the extended calculus, consider Lowe's variant of the Needham–Schroeder public key protocol:

Message 1. A $\rightarrow$ B: $\{\!|$msg1(A,sA)$|\!\}$kB
Message 2. B $\rightarrow$ A: $\{\!|$msg2(B,sA,sB)$|\!\}$kA
Message 3. A $\rightarrow$ B: $\{\!|$msg3(sB)$|\!\}$kB

In [15] we show that this protocol robustly preserves conditional secrecy of sA and sB amongst $\{A, B\}$, in the presence of compromised insiders. The proof is based on the type for a key for use by principal p:

type NS(p) = **Key**(msg1(**split** a $\leq$ a$'$:**Un**, **split** sa:**Secret**$\{$a,p$\}$)
| msg2(**match** b:**Un**, **match** sa:**Secret**$\{$p,b$\}$, **split** sb:**Secret**$\{$p,b$\}$)
| msg3(**match** sb:**Secret**$\{?\perp$,!p$\}$)).

Abadi and Blanchet [3] consider the same protocol, under similar assumptions of compromise, but rely on two separate typing derivations to prove the secrecy of sA and sB.

6 Related Work

Abadi [1] proposes the use of security types for establishing secrecy properties in cryptographic protocols expressed in the spi-calculus [5]. Abadi takes a fixed, binary view of security, where the world is divided into system and attacker, and a secret is something the attacker does not have. We are the first to generalize his work to multiple security levels and to allow the boundary between system and attacker to shift as levels are created and compromised. Another generalization of Abadi's work is the type system of Bugliesi, Focardi, and Maffei [8], which checks security properties in the presence of a fixed set of compromised hosts, but assumes this set is known during typechecking.

Abadi's type system establishes an equationally-defined secrecy property of Abadi and Gordon [5], that prevents some indirect flows as well as direct flows. Our expectations of conditional secrecy generalize the notion of explicit flow introduced by Abadi [2], and since used in several papers on process calculi [6,9].

The decentralized label model (DLM) of Myers and Liskov [18] is the basis of the Jif language in which security types track ownership and possible compromise of data.

DLM policies govern which principals can downgrade data—the system of the present paper does not address this question. A "declassify" expression converts the level of a whole expression, but it does not alter the security ordering. Since they convert high data into low data, programs using declassification typically falsify noninterference properties; there have been several proposals of modified noninterference properties to handle declassification [22].

Pottier and Simonet's Flow Caml [23], has global, static declarations of flows, but no local or dynamic declarations.

Two recent papers consider dynamic additions to the security ordering. Boudol and Matos [7] introduce block-structured declarations of orderings, in which edges may temporarily be added to the security ordering. They present a type and effect system that establishes a form of noninterference. They do not consider dynamic creation of security levels and they do not associate levels with code. Tse and Zdancewic [24] consider dynamic creation and communication of principal identities, and propose a delegation operation that allows temporary modification of the lattice of security levels.

We mention a couple of the many studies of security orderings within process calculi. Hennessy and Riely [20] study mobile agents migrating between locations, that may or may not be compromised. By a combination of static and dynamic checks they prevent type violations at uncompromised sites. Hoshina, Sumii, and Yonezawa [16] introduce a security order between protection domains in a process calculus. They use a type system with dependent types to prevent access violations. To the best of our knowledge, the present paper is the first to consider runtime compromise of security levels in the setting of a process calculus.

Finally, many of the techniques for the Dolev-Yao model other than type systems deal with host compromise and insider attacks; type systems such as ours do require some human effort to construct type annotations, but given these annotations admit automatic, efficient protocol checking.

7 Conclusion

This paper introduces a mutable security ordering into a process calculus, in order to model a dynamically growing population of principals, some of which may become compromised. We advocate the placement of conditional secrecy annotations in processes to express containment of compromise; that particular messages are kept secret, unless particular principals are compromised. We describe a type system for checking that no opponent can interact with the system to falsify these annotations. As well as proving a soundness theorem for the type system, we assess our proposal by exhibiting a series of typed examples, showing an improvement over prior work. Our system verifies versions of all the examples considered by Abadi and Blanchet [3] (modified to include multiple principals, and multiple simultaneous runs of the protocols).

We end by discussing three criticisms. First, our present system tracks only secrecy properties. We expect it is possible to combine our system with prior constructs expressing authentication and authorization properties [10,14]. Second, our type system allows any process to augment any part of the security ordering. This is acceptable in short programs modelling cryptographic protocols, but for larger programs there should be an enforceable policy governing additions to the security ordering. Prior work on policies for declassification may be applicable. Third, our type-based verification method requires the programmer to supply type annotations. A type inference algorithm would lessen this burden, although the lack of principal types would make such an algorithm non-trivial. A complementary approach may be to adapt logic programming interpretations of the pi-calculus [4] to obtain a logic-based method for checking conditional secrecy. We leave these directions for future work.

Acknowledgements. We thank Gérard Boudol, Ana Matos, Andrei Sabelfeld, and Dave Sands for sending us previews of their CSFW'05 papers [7,22]. Thanks also to Tony Hoare and the anonymous reviewers for useful comments.

References

1. M. Abadi. Secrecy by typing in security protocols. *J. ACM*, 46(5):749–786, Sept. 1999.
2. M. Abadi. Security protocols and their properties. In *Foundations of Secure Computation*, pages 39–60. IOS Press, Amsterdam, 2000.
3. M. Abadi and B. Blanchet. Secrecy types for asymmetric communication. *Theoretical Comput. Sci.*, 298(3):387–415, 2003.
4. M. Abadi and B. Blanchet. Analyzing Security Protocols with Secrecy Types and Logic Programs. *Journal of the ACM*, 52(1):102–146, 2005.
5. M. Abadi and A. D. Gordon. A calculus for cryptographic protocols: The spi calculus. *Information and Computation*, 148:1–70, 1999.
6. B. Blanchet. From secrecy to authenticity in security protocols. In *9th International Static Analysis Symposium (SAS'02)*, volume 2477 of *LNCS*, pages 242–259. Springer, 2002.
7. G. Boudol and A. Matos. On declassification and the non-disclosure policy. In *18th IEEE Computer Security Foundations Workshop*. IEEE Computer Society Press, 2005. To appear.
8. M. Bugliesi, R. Focardi, and M. Maffei. Authenticity by tagging and typing. In *Formal Methods in Security Engineering (FMSE'04)*, pages 1–12, 2004.
9. L. Cardelli, G. Ghelli, and A. D. Gordon. Secrecy and group creation. *Information and Computation*, 196(2):127–155, 2005.
10. C. Fournet, A. D. Gordon, and S. Maffeis. A type discipline for authorization policies. In *European Symposium on Programming (ESOP'05)*, LNCS, pages 141–156. Springer, 2005.
11. A. D. Gordon and A. Jeffrey. Typing one-to-one and one-to-many correspondences in security protocols. In *Software Security—Theories and Systems*, volume 2609 of *LNCS*, pages 270–282. Springer, 2002.
12. A. D. Gordon and A. Jeffrey. Authenticity by typing for security protocols. *Journal of Computer Security*, 11(4):451–521, 2003.
13. A. D. Gordon and A. Jeffrey. Types and effects for asymmetric cryptographic protocols. *Journal of Computer Security*, 12(3/4):435–484, 2003.
14. A. D. Gordon and A. Jeffrey. Typing correspondence assertions for communication protocols. *Theoretical Computer Science*, 300:379–409, 2003.
15. A. D. Gordon and A. Jeffrey. Secrecy despite compromise: Types, cryptography, and the pi-calculus. Technical Report MSR–TR–2005–76, Microsoft Research, 2005.
16. D. Hoshina, E. Sumii, and A. Yonezawa. A typed process calculus for fine-grained resource access control in distributed computation. In *4th International Symposium on Theoretical Aspects of Computer Software (TACS 2001)*, volume 2215 of *LNCS*, pages 64–81. Springer, 2001.

17. R. Milner. *Communicating and Mobile Systems: the π-Calculus*. CUP, 1999.
18. A. C. Myers and B. Liskov. Protecting privacy using the decentralized label model. *ACM Transactions on Software Engineering and Methodology*, 9(4):410–442, 2000.
19. M. Odersky. Polarized name passing. In *Foundations of Software Technology and Theoretical Computer Science*, volume 1026 of *LNCS*, pages 324–335. Springer, 1995.
20. J. Riely and M. Hennessy. Trust and partial typing in open systems of mobile agents. In *26th ACM Symposium on Principles of Programming Languages*, pages 93–104, 1999.
21. A. Sabelfeld and A. C. Myers. Language-based information-flow security. *IEEE Journal on Selected Areas in Communications*, 21(1):5–19, 2003.
22. A. Sabelfeld and D. Sands. Dimensions and principles of declassification. In *18th IEEE Computer Security Foundations Workshop*. IEEE Computer Society Press, 2005. To appear.
23. V. Simonet. The Flow Caml system: documentation and user's manual. Technical Report 0282, INRIA, 2003.
24. S. Tse and S. Zdancewic. Run-time principals in information-flow type systems. In *IEEE Computer Society Symposium on Research in Security and Privacy*, 2004.

Timed Spi-Calculus with Types for Secrecy and Authenticity*

Christian Haack[1] and Alan Jeffrey[1,2]

[1] CTI, DePaul University,
[2] Bell Labs, Lucent Technologies

Abstract. We present a discretely timed spi-calculus. A primitive for key compromise allows us to model key compromise attacks, thus going beyond the standard Dolev–Yao attacker model. A primitive for reading a global clock allows us to express protocols based on timestamps, which are common in practice. We accompany the timed spi-calculus with a type system, prove that well-typed protocols are robustly safe for secrecy and authenticity and present examples of well-typed protocols as well as an example where failure to typecheck reveals a (well-known) flaw.

1 Introduction

Models for cryptographic protocols often assume perfect cryptography— an example is the spi-calculus [3]— and ignore the fact that session keys can be compromised given a sufficient amount of time. Yet typical protocols for the distribution of session keys are careful to prevent attacks that fool honest agents into accepting compromised session keys. A security goal of such protocols is that after the end of a protocol run each principal possesses a session key that is currently secret (and will remain secret until its expiration time). This goal could not be expressed, for instance, in [11], which instead uses injective agreement as a security goal for key distribution protocols. In this paper, we extend the spi-calculus with a simple notion of time so that we can express such security goals. We also add a primitive for key compromise, which allows us to express key compromise attacks, thus going beyond the Dolev–Yao attacker model. A primitive for reading a global clock allows us to express protocols based on timestamps, which are common in practice.

Our model of time is very coarse and simple. A clock-tick represents the end of an epoch. Protocol designers may specify that a key is a short-term secret and a key compromise primitive cracks keys that are short-terms secrets. Cracking uses up all time of the current epoch (and not more than that) moving on to the next epoch. So after a clock-tick short-term secrets cannot be considered secret anymore and expire. Cracking a key is the only interesting action that uses up time. The usual spi-calculus actions are instantaneous. The safety of cryptographic protocols often depends on the fact that sessions expire when waiting for input for too long. We model this by letting input and most other statements expire with a clock-tick.

* This material is based upon work supported by the National Science Foundation under Grant No. 0208459.

M. Abadi and L. de Alfaro (Eds.): CONCUR 2005, LNCS 3653, pp. 202–216, 2005.

We think that our simple model of time is enough to capture important aspects of security protocols in the presence of key compromise. On the other hand, because of its simplicity reasoning in this model remains tractable. In order to make this point, we have accompanied our timed spi-calculus with a type system for secrecy and authenticity and prove its robust safety. We show how an attempt to typecheck the Needham–Schroeder Symmetric Key Protocol [20] reveals its flaw and typecheck Denning–Sacco's fix [8] of this protocol. It turns out that proving our type system safe for short-term assertions is considerably simpler than the proofs for injective agreement in [11], which may suggest that short-term assertions are easier to reason about than injective agreement.

2 Syntax

Our protocol description language is an extension of the spi-calculus. In this section, we define its syntax: Messages are built from variables, time constants and the empty message by concatenation, symmetric encryption and message tagging. Unlike some other versions of the spi-calculus, we do not distinguish between variables and names. The ciphertext $\{M\}_K$ represents M encrypted with symmetric key K. Key K may be an arbitrary message, but the typing rules for honest agents require K to be a variable. The term $L(M)$ represents M tagged by label L. Label L may be an arbitrary message, but the typing rules for honest agents require L to be a variable. Message tagging is a common technique for avoiding type confusion attacks [17,4] and is often treated explicitly in typed spi-calculi. A ciphertext that is formed by honest principals is typically of the form $\{l(M)\}_k$, where k is a secret key and l is a public message tag, whose purpose it is to distinguish the plaintext $l(M)$ from other plaintexts that are encrypted by the same key k.

Messages:

x,y,z,k,l,m,n	variables and names
$s,t \in \mathbb{N}$	discrete time
$K,L,M,N ::=$	message
x	variable or name
t	time
$()$	empty message
(M,N)	M concatenated with N
$\{M\}_K$	M encrypted with symmetric key K
$L(M)$	M tagged by L

As usual for spi-calculi, the process language includes a π-calculus extended with primitives for encryption. The importance of this paper is the inclusion of the operation crack M is $\{x{:}T\}_{y:U}$. This operation gives attackers the capability of cracking short-term keys given a sufficient amount of time. Thus, the attacker capabilities that we model go beyond the standard Dolev–Yao model. We also include an operation clock$(x{:}T)$ for reading a global clock. This clock-operation permits to express protocols with timestamps, which are quite common in practice.

For specification purposes, secrecy and correspondence assertions may be inserted into programs. The meaning of secrecy assertions is the intuitive one. Correspondence assertions are a standard method for specifying authenticity. They specify that in every protocol run every $\mathsf{end}(M)$-assertion must have been *recently* preceded by a corresponding $\mathsf{begin!}(M)$-assertion. In this paper, we restrict our attention to short-term, many-to-one correspondences for short-term, non-injective agreement.

Processes with Assertions:

$\vec{x}{:}\vec{T}$	type-annotated variables, $\lvert\vec{x}\rvert = \lvert\vec{T}\rvert$
$\tau \in \{\mathsf{lt}, \mathsf{st}\}$	long/short qualifier (long-term or short-term)
$O, P, Q, R ::=$	process
$P \mid Q$	parallel composition
$!P$	replication
$\mathbf{0}$	inactivity
$\mathsf{out}\ N\ M$	asynchronous output of message M on channel N
$\pi; P$	prefix π followed by P
A	assertion
$\pi ::=$	prefix
$\mathsf{inp}\ N\ (x{:}T)$	input x from channel N (binding x in P)
$\mathsf{new}(n{:}T)$	generating name n (binding n in P)
$\mathsf{decrypt}\ M\ \mathsf{is}\ \{x{:}T\}_K$	decrypting M (binding x in P)
$\mathsf{untag}\ M\ \mathsf{is}\ L(x{:}T)$	untagging M (binding x in P)
$\mathsf{split}\ M\ \mathsf{is}\ (x{:}T, y{:}U)$	splitting M (binding x in U and x, y in P)
$\mathsf{match}\ M\ \mathsf{is}\ (N, x{:}T)$	matching M against (N, x) (binding x in P)
$\mathsf{crack}\ M\ \mathsf{is}\ \{x{:}T\}_{y:U}$	cracking key y of ciphertext M (binding x, y in P)
$\mathsf{clock}(x{:}T)$	reading current time into x (binding x in P)
$\mathsf{begin!}(M)$	short-term begin-assertion: begin session M
$A, B, C ::=$	assertions
$\mathsf{end}(M)$	short-term end-assertion: session M has recently begun
$\theta(M)$	secrecy assertion
$\theta ::=$	secrecy predicates
$\tau\text{-}\mathsf{secret}$	$\tau = \mathsf{st}$: secret for the current epoch; $\tau = \mathsf{lt}$: secret forever
public	public

Prefixing and replication bind more tightly than parallel composition. We often elide $\mathbf{0}$ from the end of processes, write $(\mathsf{out}\ N\ M; P)$ for $(\mathsf{out}\ N\ M \mid P)$, write $(A; P)$ for $(A \mid P)$, and write $(\mathsf{new}\ \theta\ (n{:}T); P)$ for $(\mathsf{new}(n{:}T); \theta(n); P)$. We write $\mathit{fv}(P)$ for the set of free variables of P; similarly for messages and other objects that may contain variables.

3 Semantics

The architecture of our operational semantics is inspired by [18]. It is defined as a reduction relation on states of the form $(t; \vec{n}; \bar{A} \parallel P)$, where t is a natural number representing the global time, $\vec{n}$ is a binder for $(\bar{A}, P)$'s free names, $\bar{A}$ is the set of correspondences that can be ended in the particular run, and P is the process that remains to be executed. The reduction rules are divided into a set of *instantaneous reductions*, which are assumed to take no time, and a set of *tick-reductions*, which use up all time in the current epoch moving on to the next epoch. The instantaneous reductions are pretty standard:

Structural Process Equivalence, $P \equiv Q$:

$P \equiv P$	(Struct Refl)
$P \equiv Q \Rightarrow Q \equiv P$	(Struct Symm)
$P \equiv Q, Q \equiv R \Rightarrow P \equiv R$	(Struct Trans)
$Q \equiv R \Rightarrow P \mid Q \equiv P \mid R$	(Struct Par)
$P \mid \mathbf{0} \equiv P$	(Struct Par Zero)
$P \mid Q \equiv Q \mid P$	(Struct Par Comm)
$(P \mid Q) \mid R \equiv P \mid (Q \mid R)$	(Struct Par Assoc)
$!P \equiv P \mid !P$	(Struct Repl Par)

Instantaneous Reductions, $(t;\vec{n};\bar{A} \parallel P) \to (t;\vec{m};\bar{B} \parallel Q)$:

$P \equiv P', (t;\vec{n};\bar{A} \parallel P') \to (t;\vec{m};\bar{B} \parallel Q'), Q' \equiv Q \;\Rightarrow\; (t;\vec{n};\bar{A} \parallel P) \to (t;\vec{m};\bar{B} \parallel Q)$	(Redn Equiv)
$m \notin fv(\vec{n}, Q) \;\Rightarrow\; (t;\vec{n};\bar{A} \parallel \mathsf{new}(m{:}T);P \mid Q) \to (t;\vec{n},m;\bar{A} \parallel P \mid Q)$	(Redn New)
$(t;\vec{n};\bar{A} \parallel \mathsf{out}\, N\, M \mid \mathsf{inp}\, N\, (x{:}T);P \mid Q) \to (t;\vec{n};\bar{A} \parallel P\{x \leftarrow M\} \mid Q)$	(Redn IO)
$(t;\vec{n};\bar{A} \parallel \mathsf{decrypt}\ \{M\}_K \text{ is } \{x{:}T\}_K;P \mid Q) \to (t;\vec{n};\bar{A} \parallel P\{x \leftarrow M\} \mid Q)$	(Redn Decrypt)
$(t;\vec{n};\bar{A} \parallel \mathsf{untag}\ L(M) \text{ is } L(x{:}T);P \mid Q) \to (t;\vec{n};\bar{A} \parallel P\{x \leftarrow M\} \mid Q)$	(Redn Untag)
$(t;\vec{n};\bar{A} \parallel \mathsf{split}\ (M,N) \text{ is } (x{:}T,y{:}U);P \mid Q) \to (t;\vec{n};\bar{A} \parallel P\{x,y \leftarrow M,N\} \mid Q)$	(Redn Split)
$(t;\vec{n};\bar{A} \parallel \mathsf{match}\ (M,N) \text{ is } (M,x{:}T);P \mid Q) \to (t;\vec{n};\bar{A} \parallel P\{x \leftarrow N\} \mid Q)$	(Redn Match)
$(t;\vec{n};\bar{A} \parallel \mathsf{clock}(x{:}T);P \mid Q) \to (t;\vec{n};\bar{A} \parallel P\{x \leftarrow t\} \mid Q)$	(Redn Clock)
$(t;\vec{n};\bar{A} \parallel \mathsf{begin!}(M);P \mid Q) \to (t;\vec{n};\bar{A},\mathsf{end}(M) \parallel P \mid Q)$	(Redn Begin)

Tick-Reductions, $(t;\vec{n};\bar{A} \parallel P) \xrightarrow{\sigma} (t+1;\vec{n};\emptyset \parallel Q)$:

(Tick Par)

$$\frac{(t;\vec{n};\bar{A} \parallel P) \xrightarrow{\sigma} (t+1;\vec{n};\emptyset \parallel P') \quad (t;\vec{n};\bar{A} \parallel Q) \xrightarrow{\sigma} (t+1;\vec{n};\emptyset \parallel Q')}{(t;\vec{n};\bar{A} \parallel P \mid Q) \xrightarrow{\sigma} (t+1;\vec{n};\emptyset \parallel P' \mid Q')}$$

(Tick Crack)

$$\frac{P = (\mathsf{st\text{-}secret}(K) \mid \mathsf{crack}\ \{M\}_K \text{ is } \{x{:}T\}_{y:U};Q)}{(t;\vec{n};\bar{A} \parallel P) \xrightarrow{\sigma} (t+1;\vec{n};\emptyset \parallel Q\{x,y \leftarrow M,K\})}$$

(Tick Remain)

$$\frac{P \text{ is } !Q,\ (\mathsf{out}\ N\ M),\ \mathsf{public}(M) \text{ or } \mathsf{lt\text{-}secret}(M)}{(t;\vec{n};\bar{A} \parallel P) \xrightarrow{\sigma} (t+1;\vec{n};\emptyset \parallel P)}$$

(Tick Expire)

$$\frac{}{(t;\vec{n};\bar{A} \parallel P) \xrightarrow{\sigma} (t+1;\vec{n};\emptyset \parallel \mathbf{0})}$$

We write $\Rightarrow$ for the reflexive and transitive closure of $(\to \cup \xrightarrow{\sigma})$.

The tick-reduction rule (Tick Par) ensures that a clock-tick happens simultaneously in every branch of a parallel composition. crack operates as expected and uses up time. Process replication and output remain alive in the next epoch. Importantly, every other syntactic form expires with a clock-tick, degenerating to the null-process. In particular, if a process waits for input for more than one epoch it aborts and declines to accept later incoming messages. Many security protocols depend on this kind of behavior, and we have decided to make *expiring input* the default in our process calculus. Because process replication survives clock-ticks, we can express the capability to start a session at any time in the future. Our choice to let asynchronous output survive clock-ticks is a bit arbitrary. A language where output expires would probably have been equally suitable for modeling security protocols.

Definition 1 (Safety). P is *safe for secrecy* iff $(s;fv(P);\emptyset \mid\mid P) \not\Rightarrow (t;\vec{n};\bar{A} \mid\mid \mathsf{public}(N) \mid \tau\text{-}\mathsf{secret}(M) \mid \mathsf{out}\ N\ M \mid Q)$. P is *safe for authenticity* iff $(s;fv(P);\emptyset \mid\mid P) \Rightarrow (t;\vec{n};\bar{A} \mid\mid \mathsf{end}(M) \mid Q)$ implies $\mathsf{end}(M) \in \bar{A}$. P is *safe* iff it is both safe for secrecy and authenticity.

Definition 2 (Opponent Processes). A process is an *opponent process* iff its only assertions are of the form $\mathsf{public}(M)$ and all its type annotations are the special type Un.

Definition 3 (Robust Safety). A process P is *robustly safe* iff $(P \mid O)$ is safe for all opponent processes O.

Our type system is designed so that well-typed processes with public free names are robustly safe:

Theorem (Robust Safety) *If* $(\vec{n}{:}\vec{T} \vdash \mathsf{public}(\vec{n}))$ *and* $(\vec{n}{:}\vec{T} \vdash P)$, *then P is robustly safe.*

4 Examples

We will use derived forms for lists and matching against tagged lists. Their definition uses derived forms for list types as type annotations. Type annotations have no impact operationally and the definition of list types is postponed to the type system.

Derived Forms for Lists and Matching Against Lists:

$$\langle\rangle \triangleq () \qquad \langle M\rangle \triangleq (M,()) \qquad \langle M,\vec{N}\rangle \triangleq (M,\langle\vec{N}\rangle)$$
$$\mathsf{match}\ M\ \mathsf{is}\ \langle N\rangle[\bar{A}] \triangleq \mathsf{match}\ M\ \mathsf{is}\ (N,x{:}\langle\rangle[\bar{A}])$$
$$\mathsf{match}\ M\ \mathsf{is}\ \langle x{:}T\rangle[\bar{A}] \triangleq \mathsf{split}\ M\ \mathsf{is}\ (x{:}T,y{:}\langle\rangle[\bar{A}])$$
$$\mathsf{match}\ M\ \mathsf{is}\ \langle x{:}T,nxts\rangle[\bar{A}] \triangleq \mathsf{split}\ M\ \mathsf{is}\ (x{:}T,y{:}\langle nxts\rangle[\bar{A}]);\ \mathsf{match}\ y\ \mathsf{is}\ \langle nxts\rangle[\bar{A}]$$
$$\mathsf{match}\ M\ \mathsf{is}\ \langle N,nxts\rangle[\bar{A}] \triangleq \mathsf{match}\ M\ \mathsf{is}\ (N,y{:}\langle nxts\rangle[\bar{A}]);\ \mathsf{match}\ y\ \mathsf{is}\ \langle nxts\rangle[\bar{A}]$$
$$\mathsf{match}\ M\ \mathsf{is}\ L\langle nxts\rangle[\bar{A}] \triangleq \mathsf{untag}\ M\ \mathsf{is}\ L(x{:}\langle nxts\rangle[\bar{A}]);\ \mathsf{match}\ x\ \mathsf{is}\ \langle nxts\rangle[\bar{A}]$$

Example 1: Establishing a session key using a nonce.

B generates nonce *n*
$B \to A \quad n$
A generates short-term secrets *kab* and *m*
A begins! "*A* sending session key *kab* to *B*" and "*A* sending secret message *m* to *B*"
$A \to B \quad \{msg_1\langle n,kab\rangle\}_{lab},\ \{msg_2\langle m\rangle\}_{kab}$
B asserts $\mathsf{st\text{-}secret}(kab)$ and ends "*A* sending session key *kab* to *B*"
B asserts $\mathsf{st\text{-}secret}(m)$ and ends "*A* sending secret message *m* to *B*"

Bob wants to receive a secret message from Alice. To this end, he sends Alice a freshly generated nonce *n*. In reply, Alice generates a short-term session key *kab* and sends it to Bob together with *n* and encrypted by their shared long-term key *lab*. Alice also sends the secret message *m* encrypted by *kab*. The names msg_1 and msg_2 are used as tags.

To express this protocol in spi, we assume that X is some finite set of principal names and abbreviate $\mathsf{new}_{a,b\in X}$ $\mathsf{lt\text{-}secret}$ $(lab{:}?)$ for the generation of their long-term keys and $\prod_{x,y\in X} P(x,y)$ for the parallel composition of all processes $P(x,y)$. We use the additional tags *key* and *sec* in our correspondence assertions.

$$P \triangleq \mathsf{public}(net) \mid \mathsf{new}_{a,b\in X}\ \mathsf{lt\text{-}secret}\ (lab{:}?);\ \textstyle\prod_{a,b\in X}(!P_A(a,b,lab) \mid !P_B(a,b,lab))$$

$$P_A(a:?,b:?,lab:?) \triangleq$$
$$\mathsf{inp}\ net\ (n{:}?);\ \mathsf{new}\ \mathsf{st\text{-}secret}\ (kab{:}?);\ \mathsf{begin!}(key(a,kab,b));\ \mathsf{new}\ \mathsf{st\text{-}secret}\ (m{:}?);$$
$$\mathsf{begin!}(sec(a,m,b));\mathsf{out}\ net\ (\{msg_1\langle n,kab\rangle\}_{lab}, \{msg_2\langle m\rangle\}_{kab})$$

$$P_B(a:?,b:?,lab:?) \triangleq$$
$$\mathsf{new}\ \mathsf{public}\ (n{:}?);\ \mathsf{out}\ net\ n;\ \mathsf{inp}\ net\ (x{:}?,u{:}?);\ \mathsf{decrypt}\ x\ \mathsf{is}\ \{y{:}?\}_{lab};$$
$$\mathsf{match}\ y\ \mathsf{is}\ msg_1\langle n,kab{:}?\rangle[?];\ \mathsf{st\text{-}secret}(kab);\ \mathsf{end}(key(a,kab,b));$$
$$\mathsf{decrypt}\ u\ \mathsf{is}\ \{v{:}?\}_{kab};\ \mathsf{match}\ v\ \mathsf{is}\ msg_2\langle m{:}?\rangle[?];\ \mathsf{st\text{-}secret}(m);\ \mathsf{end}(sec(a,m,b))$$

This protocol is robustly safe: Bob only accepts the session key *kab* if received shortly after he generated nonce n. Because the ciphertext contains the fresh nonce, Bob knows that it must have been formed recently and that it is not a replay of an old message. Consequently, the session key that is contained in the ciphertext is still a secret and A has recently begun the $key(A,kab,B)$-session. Bob's second secrecy and end-assertions are safe, because Bob's session expires before opponents can possibly have cracked the session key. With appropriate type annotations this protocol typechecks.

Example 2: Needham–Schroeder Symmetric Key Protocol (NSSK). In this protocol, Alice and Bob want to establish a short-term session key *kab* via key server S using long-term keys *las* and *lbs*. NSSK is not robustly safe and, by the robust safety theorem, does not typecheck.

A generates nonce *na*
$A \rightarrow S$ $\quad A,B,na$
S generates short-term secret *kab*
S begins! $init(kab,A,B)$ and $resp(kab,B,A)$
$S \rightarrow A$ $\quad \{msg_2\langle na,B,kab,\{msg_3\langle A,kab\rangle\}_{lbs}\rangle\}_{las}$
A asserts $\mathsf{st\text{-}secret}(kab)$ and ends $init(kab,A,B)$
$A \rightarrow B$ $\quad \{msg_3\langle A,kab\rangle\}_{lbs}$
B generates nonce *nb*
$B \rightarrow A$ $\quad \{msg_4\langle nb\rangle\}_{kab}$
$A \rightarrow B$ $\quad \{msg_5\langle nb\rangle\}_{kab}$
B asserts $\mathsf{st\text{-}secret}(kab)$ and ends $resp(kab,B,A)$

Alice's secrecy- and end-assertions are safe. Bob's secrecy and end-assertions, however, are unsafe. The problem is that msg_3 may be a replay from an old protocol run. Here is an opponent process O that compromises this protocol; $(NSSK \mid O)$ is unsafe for both secrecy and authenticity:

$O \triangleq$ $\mathsf{inp}\ net\ (m_3{:}\mathsf{Un});\ \mathsf{out}\ net\ m_3;$ // monitoring msg_3
$\mathsf{inp}\ net\ (m_4{:}\mathsf{Un});\ \mathsf{out}\ net\ m_4;$ // monitoring msg_4
$\mathsf{crack}\ m_4\ \mathsf{is}\ \{x{:}\mathsf{Un}\}_{kab:\mathsf{Un}};$ // cracking short-term key *kab*
$\mathsf{inp}\ net\ (m_3'{:}\mathsf{Un});$ // intercepting msg_3 from a later protocol run
$\mathsf{out}\ net\ m_3;$ // sending m_3 instead of m_3' to Bob
$\mathsf{out}\ net\ kab$ // publishing old key *kab*

The output statement (out *net* m_3) results in a violation of Bob's end-assertion, because Bob wants to end an old $resp(kab,B,A)$-session, but is only entitled to end a $resp(kab',B,A)$-session, where kab' is the new session key that is contained in message m_3'. The output statement (out *net kab*) obviously violates Bob's secrecy assertion st-secret(kab).

5 Type System

For the type system we extend the set of assertions from Section 2:

Type-Level Assertions:

$A,B,C ::=$	assertions	
...		as defined in Section 2
$M : T$		M has type T
$\mathsf{fresh}(N)$		N is a fresh nonce
$\mathsf{now}(N)$		N is the current time
$N\text{-}\mathsf{stamped}_\mathsf{t}(A)$		A is stamped by time N
$N\text{-}\mathsf{stamped}_\mathsf{n}(A)$		A is stamped by nonce N

Type-level assertions are needed to define type environments: An *environment* is simply an assertion set. Let $E,F,G,\bar{A},\bar{B},\bar{C}$ range over *environments*. An important judgment of our system is *assertion entailment*, $E \vdash \bar{A}$. We usually use meta-variables E,F,G left of $\vdash$ and $\bar{A},\bar{B},\bar{C}$ right of $\vdash$. We define the *subjects* of environments: $subj(\emptyset) \triangleq \emptyset$; $subj(E,M{:}T) \triangleq subj(E) \cup \{M\}$; $subj(E,A) \triangleq subj(E)$ otherwise. Let $(E \vdash \diamond)$ iff $fv(E) \subseteq fv(subj(E))$. We often write $(M_1,\ldots,M_n){:}(T_1,\ldots,T_n)$ for $\{M_1{:}T_1,\ldots,M_n{:}T_n\}$, write $\vec{M}{:}T$ for $\{M{:}T \mid M \in \vec{M}\}$, write $\theta\{\vec{M}\}$ for $\{\theta(M) \mid M \in \vec{M}\}$, write $\mathsf{end}\{\vec{M}\}$ for $\{\mathsf{end}(M) \mid M \in \vec{M}\}$, write $\mathsf{fresh}\{\vec{N}\}$ for $\{\mathsf{fresh}(N) \mid N \in \vec{N}\}$, and write $N\text{-}\mathsf{stamped}_i(\bar{A})$ for $\{N\text{-}\mathsf{stamped}_i(A) \mid A \in \bar{A}\}$ if $i \in \{\mathsf{t},\mathsf{n}\}$.

Types:

$T,U,V,W ::=$	types	
Top		well-typed text
Un		public text
τ-Secret		τ-secret
$\tau\text{-}\mathsf{Key}(\vec{M})$		principals $\vec{M}$'s shared τ-key
$\mathsf{Tag}(X)$		tag of type-scheme X
$\tau\text{-}\mathsf{Auth}(K,\vec{M})$		plaintext to be authenticated by principals $\vec{M}$'s shared τ-key K
$(x{:}T,U)$		T-text paired with U-text (binding x in U)
$\mathsf{Ok}(\bar{A})$		empty text with precondition $\bar{A}$
$X,Y,Z ::=$	type-schemes for tags	
$T \to \tau\text{-}\mathsf{Auth}(k{:}U,\vec{x}{:}\vec{V})$		text T to tagged text $\tau\text{-}\mathsf{Auth}(k,\vec{x})$ (binding $k,\vec{x}$ in $T,U,\vec{V}$)

A type T is called *generative* iff $T \neq \mathsf{Ok}(\bar{A})$ for all $\bar{A}$. Names generated by new are required to have generative types.

Types include a top type, dependent pair types, a type Un for public messages and types τ-Secret (where $\tau \in \{\mathsf{lt},\mathsf{st}\}$) for long- or short-term secrets. In addition, there are the following types:

- The *key type* $\tau\text{-Key}(\vec{M})$ is the type of secret keys shared by principals $\vec{M}$.
- The *ok-type* $\mathsf{Ok}(\bar{A})$ is a type for the empty message. In order to assign this type to the empty message in environment E, it is required that $(E \vdash \bar{A})$.
- The *authentication type* $\tau\text{-Auth}(K,\vec{M})$ is a type of tagged messages that require authentication by principals $\vec{M}$'s shared τ-key K.
- The *tag type* $\mathsf{Tag}(T \to \tau\text{-Auth}(k{:}U,\vec{x}{:}\vec{V}))$ is a type of tags l that may tag messages M of type $T\{k,\vec{x}\leftarrow K,\vec{N}\}$. The type of the resulting tagged message $l(M)$ is $\tau\text{-Auth}(K,\vec{N})$.

For instance, consider the following tag:

$$l : \mathsf{Tag}(\ (x{:}\text{st-Secret}, \mathsf{Ok}(\mathsf{end}(sec(p,x,q)))) \to \text{st-Auth}(k{:}\text{st-Key}(p,q), p{:}\mathsf{Un}, q{:}\mathsf{Un})\ )$$

In environment $E = (A{:}\mathsf{Un}, B{:}\mathsf{Un}, kab{:}\text{st-Key}(A,B), m{:}\text{st-Secret}, \mathsf{end}(sec(A,m,B)))$, this tag can be used to tag message $\langle m\rangle$ $(= (m,()))$ forming $l\langle m\rangle$ of type $\text{st-Auth}(kab,A,B)$, which can then be authenticated by encryption with kab resulting in $\{l\langle m\rangle\}_{kab}$. Type-schemes for tags are a form of dependent types. Technically, they resemble type-schemes for polymorphic data constructors in languages like Haskell or ML (with the difference that binders range over messages instead of types).

Ok-types are important as a tool to "statically communicate" assertions between parallel processes for the purpose of typechecking. Typically, the set $\bar{A}$ in $\mathsf{Ok}(\bar{A})$ contains assertions of the form $\mathsf{end}(M)$ indicating that it is safe to end M-sessions. When typechecking a *sender* of the empty message at type $\mathsf{Ok}(\mathsf{end}(M))$, the typechecker is *required to prove* that it is safe to end M-sessions. On the other hand, when typechecking a *receiver* of a message of type $\mathsf{Ok}(\mathsf{end}(M))$, the typechecker *may use* that it is safe to end M-sessions.

Subtyping, $T \leq U$:

(Sub Refl) $\dfrac{}{T \leq T}$ (Sub Top) $\dfrac{}{T \leq \mathsf{Top}}$ (Sub Key) $\dfrac{}{\tau\text{-Key}(\vec{M}) \leq \tau\text{-Secret}}$ (Sub Tag) $\dfrac{}{\mathsf{Tag}(X) \leq \mathsf{Un}}$ (Sub Pair) $\dfrac{T \leq T' \quad U \leq U'}{(x{:}T,U) \leq (x{:}T',U')}$

(Sub Pair Un) $\dfrac{T \leq \mathsf{Un} \quad U \leq \mathsf{Un}}{(x{:}T,U) \leq \mathsf{Un}}$ (Sub Ok Un) $\dfrac{}{\mathsf{Ok}() \leq \mathsf{Un}}$ (Sub Env) $\dfrac{E \vdash \diamond \quad fv(T,U) \subseteq fv(E) \quad T \leq U}{E \vdash T \leq U}$

The rule (Sub Key) expresses that long- or short-term keys are long- or short-term secrets, and (Sub Tag) expresses that tags are public. Pair types are covariant, by (Sub Pair). The rules (Sub Ok Un) and (Sub Pair Un) express that the empty message and pairs of public messages may be published.

Step-Function, $step(\bar{A})$:

$step(T) \triangleq \mathsf{Un}$, if $T \leq \text{st-Secret}$ or $T = \text{st-Auth}(K,\vec{M})$; $step(\mathsf{Ok}(\bar{A})) \triangleq \mathsf{Ok}(step(\bar{A}))$;
$step(x{:}T,U) \triangleq (x{:}step(T), step(U))$; $step(T) \triangleq T$, otherwise; $step(\mathsf{end}(M)) \triangleq \emptyset$;
$step(\text{st-secret}(M)) \triangleq \{\mathsf{public}(M)\}$; $step(\mathsf{fresh}(N)) \triangleq step(\mathsf{now}(N)) \triangleq \emptyset$;
$step(M{:}T) \triangleq \{M{:}step(T)\}$; $step(A) \triangleq \{A\}$, otherwise; $step(\bar{A}) \triangleq \cup\{step(A) \mid A \in \bar{A}\}$

The *step*-function maps an assertion set to the assertion set that it evolves into with a clock-tick: assertions $\mathsf{fresh}(N)$ or $\mathsf{now}(N)$ are dropped, $\mathsf{st\text{-}secret}(M)$ is mapped to $\mathsf{public}(M)$, short-term types are mapped to Un, and all other clauses are the identity or defined by structural induction. We call an assertion set $\bar{A}$ *long-term* if $step(\bar{A}) = \bar{A}$, and *short-term* otherwise.

Assertion Entailment, $E \vdash \bar{A}$:

(Id)
$$\frac{E, A \vdash \diamond}{E, A \vdash A}$$

(And)
$$\frac{E \vdash \diamond \quad E \vdash A_1 \cdots E \vdash A_n}{E \vdash A_1, \ldots, A_n}$$

(Public)
$$\frac{E \vdash M : \mathsf{Un}}{E \vdash \mathsf{public}(M)}$$

(Secret)
$$\frac{E \vdash M : \tau\text{-}\mathsf{Secret}}{E \vdash \tau\text{-}\mathsf{secret}(M)}$$

(Time)
$$\frac{E \vdash \diamond}{E \vdash t : \mathsf{Un}}$$

(Nonce Stamp)
$$\frac{E \vdash N : \mathsf{Top}, A}{E \vdash N\text{-}\mathsf{stamped_n}(A)}$$

(Time Stamp)
$$\frac{E \vdash N : \mathsf{Top}, \mathsf{now}(N), A}{E \vdash N\text{-}\mathsf{stamped_t}(A)}$$

(Sub)
$$\frac{E \vdash M : T \quad E \vdash T \leq U}{E \vdash M : U}$$

(Encrypt)
$$\frac{E \vdash K : \tau\text{-}\mathsf{Key}(\vec{N}), M : \tau\text{-}\mathsf{Auth}(K, \vec{N})}{E \vdash \{M\}_K : \mathsf{Un}}$$

(Encrypt Un)
$$\frac{E \vdash K : \mathsf{Un}, M : \mathsf{Un}}{E \vdash \{M\}_K : \mathsf{Un}}$$

(Tag Un)
$$\frac{E \vdash L : \mathsf{Un}, M : \mathsf{Un}}{E \vdash L(M) : \mathsf{Un}}$$

(Tag) $\rho = (k, \vec{x} \leftarrow K, \vec{N})$
$$\frac{\tau = \mathsf{st} \Rightarrow step(T) \leq \mathsf{Un} \quad \tau = \mathsf{lt} \Rightarrow step(T, U, \vec{V}) = (T, U, \vec{V}) \quad E \vdash L : \mathsf{Tag}(T \rightarrow \tau\text{-}\mathsf{Auth}(k{:}U, \vec{x}{:}\vec{V})), M{:}T\{\rho\}, K{:}U\{\rho\}, \vec{N}{:}\vec{V}\{\rho\}}{E \vdash L(M) : \tau\text{-}\mathsf{Auth}(K, \vec{N})}$$

(Pair)
$$\frac{E \vdash M : T, N : U\{x \leftarrow M\}}{E \vdash (M, N) : (x{:}T, U)}$$

(Empty)
$$\frac{E \vdash \bar{A}}{E \vdash () : \mathsf{Ok}(\bar{A})}$$

The rule (Time) expresses that time values are public. (Nonce Stamp) is typically used to stamp short-term assertions. Importantly, stamped assertions are long-term. Thus, the rule (Nonce Stamp) turns short-term assertions into long-term assertions by associating them with a nonce N. The rule (Time Stamp) is similar. The process-level typing rules (Nonce Unstamp) and (Time Unstamp) presented below, then permit a "receiver" of an assertion $N\text{-}\mathsf{stamped}_i(A)$ to use A, if he can validate that N is a fresh nonce or the current time. Note that the rule (Time Stamp) requires that the "creator" of a timestamped assertion knows that the stamp is current: it would be dangerous if he used a future timestamp. The rule (Encrypt) is consistent with our informal interpretation of authentication types; ciphertexts are public. (Encrypt Un) and (Tag Un) allow us to typecheck Dolev–Yao attackers; typically, these rules are not used for type-checking honest agents. Perhaps the most interesting typing rule is (Tag) for formation of trusted tagged messages. The premise for $\tau = \mathsf{st}$ enforces that short-term keys may not encrypt long-term secrets; a requirement that is obviously needed for long-term secrecy. The premise for $\tau = \mathsf{lt}$ enforces that long-term keys may not encrypt messages of short-term types. Without this premise the system would be unsafe because a receiver of a short-term assertion under a long-term key has no guarantee that the short-term assertion is still valid at the time of reception. It is still possible to communicate short-term assertions under long-term keys, provided the short-term assertions are associated with nonces or timestamps using (Nonce Stamp) and (Time Stamp). The rule (Pair) is the standard rule for dependent pair types.

Well-Typed Processes, $E \vdash P$**:**

(Par)
$$\frac{E \vdash P \quad E \vdash Q}{E \vdash P \mid Q}$$

(Repl)
$$\frac{E \vdash P \quad step(E) \vdash P}{E \vdash !P}$$

(Zero)
$$\frac{E \vdash \diamond}{E \vdash \mathbf{0}}$$

(Begin)
$$\frac{E, \mathsf{end}(M) \vdash P}{E \vdash \mathsf{begin!}(M); P}$$

(Out)
$$\frac{E \vdash N : \mathsf{Un}, M : \mathsf{Un}}{E \vdash \mathsf{out}\, N\, M}$$

(In) $x \notin fv(E)$
$$\frac{E \vdash N : \mathsf{Un} \quad E, x : \mathsf{Un} \vdash P}{E \vdash \mathsf{inp}\, N\, (x{:}\mathsf{Un}); P}$$

(New) $n \notin fv(E)$, T generative
$$\frac{E, n : T, \mathsf{fresh}(n) \vdash P}{E \vdash \mathsf{new}(n{:}T); P}$$

(Clock) $x \notin fv(E)$
$$\frac{E, x : \mathsf{Un}, \mathsf{now}(x) \vdash P}{E \vdash \mathsf{clock}(x{:}\mathsf{Un}); P}$$

(Crack) $x, y \notin fv(E)$
$$\frac{E \vdash M : \mathsf{Un} \quad step(E), x : \mathsf{Un}, y : \mathsf{Un} \vdash P}{E \vdash \mathsf{crack}\, M\, \mathsf{is}\, \{x{:}\mathsf{Un}\}_{y:\mathsf{Un}}; P}$$

(Decrypt) $x \notin fv(E)$
$$\frac{E \vdash M : \mathsf{Un}, K : \tau\text{-}\mathsf{Key}(\vec{N}) \quad E, x : \tau\text{-}\mathsf{Auth}(K, \vec{N}) \vdash P}{E \vdash \mathsf{decrypt}\, M\, \mathsf{is}\, \{x : \tau\text{-}\mathsf{Auth}(K, \vec{N})\}_K; P}$$

(Decrypt Un) $x \notin fv(E)$
$$\frac{E \vdash M : \mathsf{Un}, K : \mathsf{Un} \quad E, x : \mathsf{Un} \vdash P}{E \vdash \mathsf{decrypt}\, M\, \mathsf{is}\, \{x{:}\mathsf{Un}\}_K; P}$$

(Untag Un) $x \notin fv(E)$
$$\frac{E \vdash M : \mathsf{Un}, L : \mathsf{Un} \quad E, x : \mathsf{Un} \vdash P}{E \vdash \mathsf{untag}\, M\, \mathsf{is}\, L(x{:}\mathsf{Un}); P}$$

(Untag) $x \notin fv(E) \quad \rho = (k, \vec{y} \leftarrow K, \vec{N}) \quad E \vdash T\{\rho\} \leq U$
$$\frac{E \vdash M : \tau\text{-}\mathsf{Auth}(K, \vec{N}), L : \mathsf{Tag}(T \to \tau\text{-}\mathsf{Auth}(k{:}U, \vec{y}{:}\vec{V})) \quad E, x : U \vdash P}{E \vdash \mathsf{untag}\, M\, \mathsf{is}\, L(x{:}U); P}$$

(Split) $x, y \notin fv(E)$
$$\frac{E \vdash M : (x{:}T, U) \quad E, x : T, y : U \vdash P}{E \vdash \mathsf{split}\, M\, \mathsf{is}\, (x{:}T, y{:}U); P}$$

(Split Un) $x, y \notin fv(E)$
$$\frac{E \vdash M : \mathsf{Un} \quad E, x : \mathsf{Un}, y : \mathsf{Un} \vdash P}{E \vdash \mathsf{split}\, M\, \mathsf{is}\, (x{:}\mathsf{Un}, y{:}\mathsf{Un}); P}$$

(Match) $y \notin fv(E) \quad \rho = (x \leftarrow N)$
$$\frac{E \vdash M : (x{:}\mathsf{Top}, T), N : \mathsf{Top} \quad E, y : T\{\rho\} \vdash P}{E \vdash \mathsf{match}\, M\, \mathsf{is}\, (N, y{:}T\{\rho\}); P}$$

(Match Un) $x \notin fv(E)$
$$\frac{E \vdash M : \mathsf{Un}, N : \mathsf{Un} \quad E, x : \mathsf{Un} \vdash P}{E \vdash \mathsf{match}\, M\, \mathsf{is}\, (N, x{:}\mathsf{Un}); P}$$

(Nonce Unstamp) $E, A \vdash P$
$$\frac{E \vdash \mathsf{fresh}(N), N\text{-}\mathsf{stamped}_{\mathsf{n}}(A)}{E \vdash P}$$

(Time Unstamp) $E, A \vdash P$
$$\frac{E \vdash \mathsf{now}(N), N\text{-}\mathsf{stamped}_{\mathsf{t}}(A)}{E \vdash P}$$

(Ok) $E, \bar{A} \vdash P$
$$\frac{E \vdash M : \mathsf{Ok}(\bar{A})}{E \vdash P}$$

Among the process rules, (Repl) for process replication is noteworthy, because it requires to typecheck the body P of a replicated process $!P$ both in the current environment E and the future environment $step(E)$. Checking P in E is needed because replicated processes unfold instantaneously (by (Redn Equiv)); checking P in $step(E)$ is needed because replicated processes survive clock-ticks (by (Tick Remain)); because the $step$-function is idempotent, it suffices to check P in environment $step(E)$ instead of $step^n(E)$ for all $n \geq 1$. For typechecking the process continuation P in $(\mathsf{new}(x{:}T);P)$ or $(\mathsf{clock}(x{:}\mathsf{Un});P)$, we may assume that x is fresh or current. Remember that specification processes $\mathsf{end}(M)$ and $\theta(M)$ are both processes and assertions, so their typing rules are given with the rules for assertion entailment.

6 Typed Examples

We will annotate the earlier example with types using these derived forms:

Derived Forms for List Types:

$$\langle\rangle[\bar{A}] \triangleq \mathsf{Ok}(\bar{A}); \quad \langle x{:}T\rangle[\bar{A}] \triangleq (x{:}T, \mathsf{Ok}(\bar{A})); \quad \langle N\rangle[\bar{A}] \triangleq (x{:}\mathsf{Top}, \mathsf{Ok}(\bar{A}));$$
$$\langle x{:}T, nxts\rangle[\bar{A}] \triangleq (x{:}T, \langle nxts\rangle[\bar{A}]); \quad \langle N, nxts\rangle[\bar{A}] \triangleq (x{:}\mathsf{Top}, \langle nxts\rangle[\bar{A}])$$

Example 1: Establishing a session key using a nonce. Recall Example 1 from Section 4. Here are the types for the global names:

$$net : \mathsf{Un} \qquad \bar{A}(n,k,p,q) \triangleq n\text{-}\mathsf{stamped}_{\mathsf{n}}(k{:}\mathsf{st\text{-}Key}(p,q), \mathsf{end}(key(p,k,q)))$$
$$msg_1 : \mathsf{Tag}(\langle n{:}\mathsf{Un}, k{:}\mathsf{Top}\rangle[\bar{A}(n,k,p,q)] \to \mathsf{lt\text{-}Auth}(l{:}\mathsf{lt\text{-}Key}(p,q), p{:}\mathsf{Un}, q{:}\mathsf{Un}))$$
$$msg_2 : \mathsf{Tag}(\langle m{:}\mathsf{st\text{-}Secret}\rangle[\mathsf{end}(sec(p,m,q))] \to \mathsf{st\text{-}Auth}(k{:}\mathsf{st\text{-}Key}(p,q), p{:}\mathsf{Un}, q{:}\mathsf{Un}))$$

In the type of msg_1, note that the typing rules force us to stamp the type assertion $k{:}\mathsf{st\text{-}Key}(p,q)$. If we directly annotated the binder k by short-term type $\mathsf{st\text{-}Key}(p,q)$, then the protocol would not typecheck: Alice would not be permitted to form the message $msg_1\langle t, kab\rangle$ because $step(\mathsf{st\text{-}Key}(p,q)) \neq \mathsf{st\text{-}Key}(p,q)$ in violation to the premise for $\tau = \mathsf{lt}$ in the (Tag)-rule. Here is the type-annotated spi-calculus specification:

$$
\begin{array}{l}
P_A(a{:}\mathsf{Un}, b{:}\mathsf{Un}, lab{:}\mathsf{lt\text{-}Key}(a,b)) \triangleq \\
\quad \mathsf{inp}\ net\ (n{:}\mathsf{Un});\ \mathsf{new\ st\text{-}secret}\ (kab{:}\mathsf{st\text{-}Key}(a,b));\ \mathsf{begin!}(key(a,kab,b)); \\
\quad \mathsf{new\ st\text{-}secret}\ (m{:}\mathsf{st\text{-}Secret});\ \mathsf{begin!}(sec(a,m,b)); \\
\quad \mathsf{out}\ net\ (\{msg_1\langle n,kab\rangle\}_{lab}, \{msg_2\langle m\rangle\}_{kab}) \\
P_B(a{:}\mathsf{Un}, b{:}\mathsf{Un}, lab{:}\mathsf{lt\text{-}Key}(a,b)) \triangleq \\
\quad \mathsf{new\ public}\ (n{:}\mathsf{Un});\ \mathsf{out}\ net\ n;\ \mathsf{inp}\ net\ (x{:}\mathsf{Un}, u{:}\mathsf{Un}); \\
\quad \mathsf{decrypt}\ x\ \mathsf{is}\ \{y{:}\mathsf{lt\text{-}Auth}(lab,a,b)\}_{lab}; \\
\quad \mathsf{match}\ z\ \mathsf{is}\ msg_1\langle n, kab{:}\mathsf{Top}\rangle[\bar{A}(n,kab,a,b)];\ \mathsf{st\text{-}secret}(kab);\ \mathsf{end}(key(a,kab,b)); \\
\quad \mathsf{decrypt}\ u\ \mathsf{is}\ \{v{:}\mathsf{st\text{-}Auth}(kab,a,b)\}_{kab}; \\
\quad \mathsf{match}\ v\ \mathsf{is}\ msg_2\langle m{:}\mathsf{st\text{-}Secret}\rangle[\mathsf{end}(sec(a,m,b))]; \\
\quad \mathsf{st\text{-}secret}(m);\ \mathsf{end}(sec(a,m,b))
\end{array}
$$

Example 2: Needham–Schroeder Symmetric Key Protocol (NSSK). This protocol is unsafe and, hence, does not typecheck. The problem is msg_3:

$$
\begin{array}{ll}
\ldots & \\
A \to B & \{msg_3\langle A, kab\rangle\}_{lbs} \\
\ldots &
\end{array}
$$

Here is the type that we want to give to the message tag:

$$msg_3 : \mathsf{Tag}(\langle p{:}\mathsf{Un}, k{:}\mathsf{st\text{-}Key}(p,q)\rangle[] \to \mathsf{lt\text{-}Auth}(l{:}\mathsf{lt\text{-}Key}(p,q), p{:}\mathsf{Un}, q{:}\mathsf{Un}))$$

However, this type does not permit Alice to form the tagged message $msg_3\langle A, kab\rangle$ because $step(\text{st-Key}(p,q)) \neq \text{st-Key}(p,q)$ in violation to the premises of (Tag).

Example 3: Denning–Sacco Protocol with acknowledgment. The Denning–Sacco protocol for establishing a short-term session key avoids the key compromise attack on NSSK by including a timestamp. We have added to the Denning–Sacco protocol Bob's acknowledgment for receipt of session key *kab*, which is achieved by Bob using *kab* to encrypt a tagged null-message.

$A \to S \quad A, B$
S generates short-term secret *kab* and timestamp t
S begins! $init(S, kab, A, B)$ and $resp(S, kab, B, A)$
$S \to A \quad \{msg_2\langle t, B, kab, \{msg_3\langle t, A, kab\rangle\}_{lbs}\rangle\}_{las}$
A asserts $\text{st-secret}(kab)$ and ends $init(S, kab, A, B)$
$A \to B \quad \{msg_3\langle t, A, kab\rangle\}_{lbs}$
B asserts $\text{st-secret}(kab)$ and ends $resp(S, kab, B, A)$
B begins! $ack(B, kab, A)$
$B \to A \quad \{msg_4\langle\rangle\}_{kab}$
A ends $ack(B, kab, A)$

The types for the long-term keys are $las{:}\text{lt-Key}(A,S)$ and $lbs{:}\text{lt-Key}(B,S)$. Here are the tag types:

$$\begin{aligned}
msg_2 &: \text{Tag}(\,\langle t{:}\text{Un}, q{:}\text{Un}, k{:}\text{Top}, x{:}\text{Un}\rangle[t\text{-stamped}_{\text{t}}(k{:}\text{st-Key}(p,q), \text{end}(init(s,k,p,q)))] \\
&\qquad \to \text{lt-Auth}(l{:}\text{lt-Key}(p,s), p{:}\text{Un}, s{:}\text{Un})\,) \\
msg_3 &: \text{Tag}(\,\langle t{:}\text{Un}, p{:}\text{Un}, k{:}\text{Top}\rangle[t\text{-stamped}_{\text{t}}(k{:}\text{st-Key}(p,q), \text{end}(resp(s,k,q,p)))] \\
&\qquad \to \text{lt-Auth}(l{:}\text{lt-Key}(q,s), q{:}\text{Un}, s{:}\text{Un})\,) \\
msg_4 &: \text{Tag}(\,\langle\rangle[\text{end}(ack(q,k,p))] \to \text{st-Auth}(k{:}\text{st-Key}(p,q), p{:}\text{Un}, q{:}\text{Un})\,)
\end{aligned}$$

7 Type Preservation

Like in other type systems for spi-calculi, robust safety is a consequence of a type preservation theorem. In this section, we present this theorem and a few selected lemmas that are needed to prove it. Proofs and additional lemmas are omitted and given in an extended version of this paper. In order to define well-typed computation states, we extend the judgment for assertion entailment: Let $(E \vdash^+ \bar{A})$ iff it is derivable by the $\vdash$-rules plus the rules (Useless Nonce) and (Useless Time) below. The relation $\leq$ in (Useless Time) is defined by: $M \leq N$ iff either $M = N$ or $M = s \leq t = N$ for times $s, t \in \mathbb{N}$.

Well-typed Computation States, $(t; \vec{n}; \text{end}\{\vec{M}\} \parallel P) : \diamond$**:**

(Good State) $E = (\vec{n}{:}\vec{T}, \text{end}\{\vec{M}\}, \text{fresh}\{\vec{N}\}, \text{now}(t))$

$$\frac{E \vdash^+ \bar{A} \quad \bar{A} \vdash P \quad \vec{n} \text{ distinct} \quad \vec{T} \text{ generative}}{(t; \vec{n}; \text{end}\{\vec{M}\} \parallel P) : \diamond}$$

(Useless Nonce) $fv(A) \subseteq fv(E)$

$$\frac{\text{fresh}(N) \notin E \quad E \vdash^+ N : \text{Top}}{E \vdash^+ N\text{-stamped}_{\text{n}}(A)}$$

(Useless Time) $fv(A) \subseteq fv(E)$

$$\frac{(\forall M)(\text{now}(M) \in E \Rightarrow M \not\leq N) \quad E \vdash^+ N : \text{Top}}{E \vdash^+ N\text{-stamped}_{\text{t}}(A)}$$

The additional rules (Useless Nonce) and (Useless Time) allow to stamp assertions with messages that are neither fresh nonces nor current or future times. This is safe because the typing rules for unstamping are not applicable in such cases. Technically, these rules are needed to prove the following lemma.

Lemma (Step Invariance). If E is basic and $(E \vdash^{+} \bar{A})$, then $(\mathit{step}^{+}(E) \vdash^{+} \mathit{step}(\bar{A}))$.

Proof $\mathit{step}^{+}/\mathit{step}$ maps (Nonce Stamp) to (Useless Nonce), and (Time Stamp) to (Useless Time). (Encrypt) is mapped to itself if $\tau = \mathsf{lt}$ and to (Encrypt Un) if $\tau = \mathsf{st}$. (Tag) is mapped to itself if $\tau = \mathsf{lt}$ and to (Tag Un) if $\tau = \mathsf{st}$. □

Here are the definitions that are needed to fully understand the step invariance lemma: We call environment E *basic* iff it is of the form $E = (\vec{n}{:}\vec{T}, \mathsf{end}\{\vec{M}\}, \mathsf{fresh}\{\vec{N}\}, \mathsf{now}(t))$ for distinct $\vec{n}$ and generative $\vec{T}$. Let $\mathit{step}^{+}(E, \mathsf{now}(t)) \triangleq (\mathit{step}(E), \mathsf{now}(t+1))$.

Lemma (Cut). *If E is basic, $(E \vdash^{+} \bar{A})$ and $(\bar{A} \vdash \bar{B})$, then $(E \vdash^{+} \bar{B})$.*

This cut lemma is not hard to prove. Step invariance and cut are used to prove that tick-reductions preserve well-typedness. More generally, we obtain the following theorem.

Theorem (Type Preservation). *If $((t;\vec{n};\bar{A} \mid\mid P) : \diamond)$ and $(t;\vec{n};\bar{A} \mid\mid P) \Rightarrow (s;\vec{m};\bar{B} \mid\mid Q)$, then $((s;\vec{m};\bar{B} \mid\mid Q) : \diamond)$.*

8 Conclusion

Related Work. Compared to other work on the spi-calculus [3,1,11,12,10,2,16], the novelty of this paper is the addition of time, key-compromising attackers and short-term assertions for secrecy and authenticity. To the best of our knowledge, this is the first spi-calculus type system for reasoning about short-term assertions.

There are some formal models for cryptographic protocols that deal with recency or key compromise implicitly (without explicitly modeling time): BAN logic [5] has a primitive formula for freshness, which allows reasoning about recency. Guttman shows how to reason about recency for nonce-based protocols within the strand space model [15]. Both these works are based on the assumption that protocol sessions time out before short-term keys can possibly get compromised. Paulson's inductive method [21] models key compromise by a rule called "Oops" for leaking short-term keys, and his safety theorems typically require premises that certain data has not been leaked to dishonest principals. Recently, Gordon and Jeffrey [13] have presented a type system for proving conditional secrecy that models key compromise in a similar way.

There are also some models that deal with time more explicitly: Evans and Schneider [9] analyze time dependent security properties in tock-CSP using theorem proving with the rank function method. Rank functions have similarities with type systems: on the one hand, both rank functions and type systems are designed to prove safety properties without assuming a bounded number of sessions and, on the other hand, both require less help from protocol specifiers than general theorem proving—the supply of a rank-function or type-annotations is enough. Gorrieri, Locatelli and Martinelli [14] present the process algebra tCryptoSPA with event-based time for expressing cryptographic protocols. Both tock-CSP and tCryptoSPA seem a bit more expressive than our timed spi-calculus. For instance, these languages can express processes that patiently wait for input arbitrarily long, whereas it is not obvious how to express this in our language. On the other hand, both tock-CSP and tCryptoSPA allow some anomalies, like timestops, that our language omits. Bozga, Ene and Lakhnech [19] and Delzanno and Ganty [7] model real time and present symbolic procedures for checking time sensitive safety properties. These procedures are more automatic than typechecking; they do not require help in the form of type annotations. On the other hand, they assume a bounded number of sessions [19] or do not guarantee termination [7]. The Casper model checker is based on discretely timed CSP and can analyze protocols for timed agreement and timed secrecy [22]. It requires bounds on the size of protocols. Most of the languages discussed in this paragraph, with the exception of [19], do not explicitly model key compromising attackers. [19] models key compromising attackers by creating for each short-term key a key-cracking process that accepts messages encrypted under this key, then waits for a while and then publishes the key. In this model, attackers can crack keys by directing ciphertexts to key-cracking processes. Key compromising attackers could probably be modeled similarly in the other languages above, but we expect that key-cracking processes create additional problems for some of the verification methods.

Limitations of our Model of Time. A limitation is that we cannot distinguish between the amounts of time that it takes to timeout and the time needed for cracking short-term keys. In reality, the former is usually much shorter than the latter. While it is often safe to assume that timeout happens later than it really does, it sometimes prevents us from expressing attacks. Consider, for instance, the Wide Mouthed Frog protocol (WMF):

$$\begin{array}{ll} \multicolumn{2}{l}{A \text{ generates short-term key } kab} \\ A \to S & A, \{t_i, B, kab\}_{kas} \\ S \to B & \{t_s, A, kab\}_{kbs} \\ \multicolumn{2}{l}{B \text{ asserts } \mathsf{st\text{-}secret}(kab)} \end{array}$$

There is a type confusion attack on WMF, where the attacker repeatedly intercepts the second message and plays it back to the server as the first message of another run. The attacker, thus, always has a message of the correct format that contains a current timestamp and after cracking *kab* he can fool either principal to accept the compromised *kab* as recent. In our model, the server's timestamp t_s will always be equal to the initiator's timestamp t_i. Therefore, the attack is not possible in the model. (Fortunately, WMF still does not typecheck, though.) While it would not be hard to refine our model of time, it is less clear how to refine the type system.

Future Work. Although this article deals with symmetric cryptography only, we expect no problems to integrate this work into a more general system with public cryptography and other cryptographic operators [12,16]. Our type system is simple and can typecheck many key distribution protocols from the literature [6]. While we plan to investigate how it can be extended to verify protocols with additional intricacies, like Yahalom [5], we do not think that such extensions are of utmost importance, because often similar, sometimes simpler, protocols exist that achieve the same security goals and obey our type discipline, for instance BAN's Yahalom simplification [5]. More interestingly, we plan to investigate if we can find similar type systems for refined models of time.

References

1. M. Abadi. Secrecy by typing in security protocols. *Journal of the ACM*, 46(5):749–786, September 1999.
2. M. Abadi and B. Blanchet. Secrecy types for asymmetric communication. In *Foundations of Software Science and Computation Structures*, volume 2030 of *LNCS*. Springer, 2001.
3. M. Abadi and A.D. Gordon. A calculus for cryptographic protocols: The spi calculus. *Information and Computation*, 148:1–70, 1999.
4. M. Abadi and R. Needham. Prudent engineering practice for cryptographic protocols. *IEEE Transactions on Software Engineering*, 22(1):6–15, 1996.
5. M. Burrows, M. Abadi, and R.M. Needham. A logic of authentication. *Proceedings of the Royal Society of London A*, 426:233–271, 1989.
6. J. Clark and J. Jacob. A survey of authentication protocol literature. Unpublished report. University of York, 1997.
7. G. Delzanno and P. Ganty. Automatic verification of time sensitive cryptographic protocols. In K. Jensen and A. Podelski, editors, *Tools and Algorithms for the Construction and Analysis of Systems*, volume 2988 of *LNCS*, pages 342–356. Springer, 2004.
8. D.E. Denning and G.M. Sacco. Timestamps in key distribution protocols. *Communications of the ACM*, 24(8):533–536, 1981.
9. N. Evans and S. Schneider. Analysing time dependent security properties in CSP using PVS. In F. Cuppens, Y. Deswarte, D. Gollmann, and M. Waidner, editors, *ESORICS*, volume 1895 of *LNCS*, pages 222–237. Springer, 2000.
10. A. D. Gordon and A.S.A. Jeffrey. Typing one-to-one and one-to-many correspondences in security protocols. In *Proc. Int. Software Security Symp.*, volume 2609 of *Lecture Notes in Computer Science*, pages 263–282. Springer-Verlag, 2002.
11. A.D. Gordon and A.S.A. Jeffrey. Authenticity by typing for security protocols. *J. Computer Security*, 11(4):451–521, 2003.
12. A.D. Gordon and A.S.A. Jeffrey. Types and effects for asymmetric cryptographic protocols. *J. Computer Security*, 12(3/4):435–484, 2003.
13. A.D. Gordon and A.S.A. Jeffrey. Secrecy despite compromise: Types, cryptography and the pi-calculus. In *CONCUR 2005: Concurrency Theory*, LNCS. Springer, 2005.
14. R. Gorrieri, E. Locatelli, and F. Martinelli. A simple language for realtime cryptographic protocol analysis. In P. Degano, editor, *12th European Symposium on Programming*, volume 2618 of *LNCS*, pages 114–128. Springer, 2003.
15. Joshua D. Guttman. Key compromise, strand spaces, and the authentication tests. *Electr. Notes Theor. Comput. Sci.*, 45, 2001.
16. C. Haack and A.S.A. Jeffrey. Pattern-matching spi-calculus. In *2nd IFIP Workshop on Formal Aspects in Security and Trust*, volume 173 of *IFIP*. Kluwer Academic Press, 2004.
17. J. Heather, G. Lowe, and S. Schneider. How to prevent type flaw attacks on security protocols. In *13th IEEE Computer Security Foundations Workshop*, pages 255–268. IEEE Computer Society Press, 2000.
18. M. Hennessy and T. Regan. A process algebra for timed systems. *Information and Computation*, 117(2):221–239, 1995.
19. Y. Lakhnech L. Bozga, C. Ene. A symbolic decision procedure for cryptographic protocols with time stamps. In *CONCUR 2004: Concurrency Theory*, volume 3170 of *LNCS*, pages 177–192. Springer, 2004.
20. R.M. Needham and M.D. Schroeder. Using encryption for authentication in large networks of computers. *Communications of the ACM*, 21(12):993–999, 1978.
21. L.C. Paulson. The inductive approach to verifying cryptographic protocols. *Journal of Computer Security*, 6:85–128, 1998.
22. P. Ryan and S. Schneider. *Modelling and Analysis of Security Protocols*. Addison-Wesley, 2001.

Selecting Theories and Recursive Protocols*

Tomasz Truderung

LORIA-INRIA-Lorraine, France
Institute of Computer Science, Wrocław University, Poland

Abstract. Many decidability results are known for non-recursive cryptographic protocols, where the protocol steps can be expressed by simple rewriting rules. Recently, a tree transducer-based model was proposed for *recursive* protocols, where the protocol steps involve some kind of recursive computations. This model has, however, some limitations: (1) rules are assumed to have linear left-hand sides (so no equality tests can be performed), (2) only finite amount of information can be conveyed from one receive-send action to the next ones. It has been proven that, in this model, relaxing these assumptions leads to undecidability.

In this paper, we propose a formalism, called *selecting theories*, which extends the standard non-recursive term rewriting model and allows participants to compare and store arbitrary messages. This formalism can model recursive protocols, where participants, in each protocol step, are able to send a number of messages unbounded w.r.t. the size of the protocol. We prove that insecurity of protocols with selecting theories is decidable in NEXPTIME.

1 Introduction

Formal verification of cryptographic protocols has been very successful in finding flaws in published cryptographic protocols (see [14,7] for an overview). Although the general verification problem is undecidable [10,1,11], there are important decidable variants [9,10,16]. One of them is the insecurity problem of protocols analyzed w.r.t. a bounded number of sessions, in presence of the so-called Dolev-Yao intruder [16,6,5,8]. In this case, one assumes that actions performed by participants during the course of the protocol execution are simple and can be described by single rewrite rules of the form $t \to s$. Such a rule is intended to specify receive-send action of a principal who after receiving a message $t\theta$, for some ground substitution θ, replies $s\theta$. However, in many protocols, participants perform more complicated, recursive computations which cannot be expressed by simple rewrite rules. Examples of protocols of this kind are Internet Key Exchange Protocol (IKE), the Recursive Authentication (RA) protocol [4], and the A-GDH.2 protocol [2]. We will call protocols that involve some kind of iterative or recursive computations *recursive protocols*.

Recently, a tree transducer-based model was proposed for recursive protocols [13,12]. Tree transducers seem to be a natural choice in the context of recursive cryptographic protocols. The proposed model has, however, the following limitations: (1) rules are assumed to have linear left-hand sides, so no equality tests can be performed,

* Partially supported by the RNTL project PROUVE-03V360 and by SATIN Project of ACI Sécurité Informatique.

M. Abadi and L. de Alfaro (Eds.): CONCUR 2005, LNCS 3653, pp. 217–232, 2005.

(2) only finite amount of information can be conveyed from one receive-send action to the next ones. Moreover, these assumptions cannot be relaxed without losing decidability. In some cases, these limitations can make modeling of protocols inconvenient or even impossible. For example, the RA protocol, which was chosen in [13] and [12] to illustrate the tree transducer-based protocol model, has rules with non-linear left-hand sides and had to be slightly modified. It should be mentioned that both equality tests for messages of arbitrary size and the possibility of storing arbitrary messages can be easily expressed in the standard term rewriting-based model.

The goal of this paper is to provide a model which can express some recursive computations, without limiting the possibility of compare and store messages. In fact, in many cases the expression power of tree transducers is more than sufficient, so one could ask, whether there is some restricted class of tree transducers which can be used to model protocols, preserving the ability of parties to compare and store messages. One can, however, prove that these assumption cannot be relaxed even, if we consider very weak forms of tree transducers (or any similar formalism) which allow us to model the following basic kinds of computations:

(a) *list mapping* — for an input which is an encoded list $\{[t_1, \ldots t_n]\}_k$, produce an encoded list $\{[t'_1, \ldots, t'_n]\}_{k'}$, where, for each $i = 1, \ldots, n$, the term t'_i is the result of applying some simple rewrite rule to t_i,

(b) *mapping functional symbols* — replace functional symbols of a given term with functional symbols of the same arity, preserving the exact structure of the term (distinct occurrences of a symbol need not be replaced with the same symbol).

The model presented in this paper can express recursive protocols, where participants, in each protocol step, can send a number of messages unbounded w.r.t. the size of the protocol. Each of these messages is the result of applying some simple rewriting rule to some subterm of the messages received so far. So called *selecting theories* are used to determine which rewriting rule should be applied to which terms. Participants are able to store and compare arbitrary messages, like in the case of standard term rewriting-based approach. We assume that keys used in symmetric and public key encryption are constants. Clearly, in our model, one cannot model computations described in the items (a) and (b) above. One can, however, model actions like for instance: for a list $[t_1, \ldots, t_n]$ produce and send the list $[t'_1, \ldots, t'_n]$, where, for each $i = 1, \ldots, n$, the term t'_i is the result of applying some simple rewrite rule to t_i. It is possible, because from the point of view of the Dolev-Yao intruder, the effect of sending $[t'_1, \ldots, t'_n]$ is the same as the effect of sending terms $t'_1, \ldots, t'_n$ separately. The key fact here is that the result list is not encrypted, which is the case, when protocols like IKE or RA are considered. In the paper, we show how to model the RA protocol in our framework. Because the formalism can express protocols with non-linear left-hand sides of rules, we model this protocol without changes.

We prove that insecurity of protocols with selecting theories with respect to bounded number of sessions decidable in NEXPTIME.

Structure of the Paper. Section 2 contains some basic definitions. In Section 3, the model is introduced. It is also showed how to model the RA protocol in the proposed framework. Section 4 contains the proof of the main result of the paper, decidability of protocols with selecting theories.

2 Preliminaries

Let $T(\Sigma, V)$ denote the set of terms over the signature Σ and the set of variables V. A term is *ground*, if it does not contain variables. A (ground) *substitution* is a mapping from variables to (ground) terms, which, in a natural way, is extended to a mapping from term to terms. We denote the set of subterms of t by $sub(t)$.

For a given signature Σ, a *term*-DAG D is a labelled directed acyclic ordered graph such that, if a node v is labelled with a function symbol f of arity n, then it has n ordered immediate successors $v_1, \ldots, v_n$. In such a case we write $v =_D f(v_1, \ldots, v_n)$, and we say that v is a *parent* of v_i (for each $i = 1, \ldots, n$), and v_i is a *child* of v. We define also the notion of *descendant* in the usual way. For a term-DAG D, and a vertex $v =_D f(v_1, \ldots, v_n)$, we recursively define the *term* $t(v, D)$ *represented by* v *in* D by the equation $t(v, D) = f(t(v_1, D), \ldots, t(v_n, D))$. For $s = t(v, D)$, we will write $v \rightrightarrows_D s$, or $v \rightrightarrows s$, if D is known from the context.

Let Σ be a signature, V be a set of variables, and P be a set of unary predicate symbols. If $p \in P$, and $t \in T(\Sigma, V)$, then $p(t)$ is an *atomic formula*. An atomic formula $p(t)$ is *ground*, if t is ground. A *unary Horn theory* is a finite set of *clauses* of the form $a_0 \leftarrow a_1, \ldots, a_n$, where $a_0, \ldots, a_n$ are atomic formulas.

We will use the following notation. Let T be a unary Horn theory, let A, B be sets of ground atomic formulas. We write $A \vdash_T B$, if there exists *a proof of* B *with respect to* T *assuming* A, i.e. a sequence $a_1, \ldots, a_n$ of atomic formulas such that each element of B occurs in $a_1, \ldots, a_n$, and, for each $i = 1, \ldots, n$, we have either (i) $a_i \in A$, or (ii) there exists a clause $b_0 \leftarrow b_1, \ldots, b_m$ in T and a substitution θ such that $a_i = b_0\theta$, and each of $b_1\theta, \ldots, b_m\theta$ occurs in $a_1, \ldots, a_{i-1}$. For a set of atomic formulas A, and an atomic formula a, we write $A \vdash_T a$ for $A \vdash_T \{a\}$.

3 The Formal Model

Protocols with Selecting Theories. *Messages* are ground terms over the signature Σ consisting of constants (*atomic messages* such as principal names, nonces, keys), the unary function symbol $\mathsf{hash}(\cdot)$ (*hashing*), and the following binary function symbols: $\langle \cdot, \cdot \rangle$ (*pairing*), $\{\cdot\}.$ (*symmetric encryption*), and $\{\!|\cdot|\!\}.$ (*public key encryption*). We assume that keys used to encrypt messages are constants[1]. We assume that there is a bijection $\cdot^{-1}$ on atomic messages which maps every public (private) key k to its corresponding private (public) key k^{-1}. We assume that Σ contains the constant c_0 known to the intruder and the constant *Sec* (a secret). We will sometimes omit $\langle \cdot, \cdot \rangle$ and write, for instance, $\{t, s\}_k$ instead of $\{\langle t, s\rangle\}_k$.

Let Q and R be disjoint sets of *pop predicate symbols* and *push predicate symbols*, respectively. A *selecting theory* Φ over (Q, R) is a set of clauses of the forms

$$q_1(x_1), \ldots, q_n(x_n) \Rightarrow q(f(x_1, \ldots, x_n)), \quad (1)$$

$$q_1(t), \ldots, q_l(t), r(t) \Rightarrow r'(x) \quad \text{where } x \in \mathit{Var}(t) \quad (2)$$

$$q_1(t), \ldots, q_l(t), r(t) \Rightarrow I(s) \quad \text{where } \mathit{Var}(s) \subseteq \mathit{Var}(t), \quad (3)$$

[1] In the case of the NP-completeness result for non-recursive protocols [16], only keys used in public-key cryptography are assumed to be constants.

where $I \notin Q \cup R$ is a predicate symbol, $q, q_1, \ldots, q_n \in Q$, $r, r' \in R$, $f \in \Sigma$ is a function symbol of arity n, and $x, x_1, \ldots, x_n$ are variables. Clauses of the form (1), called *pop clauses*, have an auxiliary role: they can simulate runs of any finite tree automaton. The information about which states (predicate symbols) can be assigned to a term can be used in (2) and (3), which provides a regular look-ahead. Clauses of the form (2), called *push clauses*, transfer some information (predicate symbols) from a term to its subterms. Clauses of the form (3), called *send clauses*, select terms to be sent (the predicate symbol I means that the term is sent and thus it is known to the intruder).

Let Φ be a selecting theory over (Q, R). For a term t and $r \in R \cup \{I\}$, we define the set of *terms selected by* Φ, $[\![r(t)]\!]_\Phi = \{s \mid r(t) \vdash_\Phi I(s)\}$. A *rule over* (Q, R) has the form $t \to r(s)$, where t, s are terms and $r \in R \cup \{I\}$. The intended meaning of such a rule is that a principal, after receiving a term $t\theta$, for some ground substitution θ, sends all the terms from the set $[\![r(s\theta)]\!]_\Phi$. Note that the number of terms which are sent in one step of a protocol is not bounded by the size of the protocol, it is only bounded by the size of the message $s\theta$. Because (for any Φ) we have $[\![I(s)]\!]_\Phi = \{s\}$, each simple non-recursive rewrite rule $t \to s$ can be easily expressed in our formalism by $t \to I(s)$.

A *principal* Π *over* (Q, R) is a sequence $(t_i \to r_i(s_i))_{i=1}^n$ of rules over (Q, R) such that, for each $i = 1, \ldots, n$, we have $t_i, s_i \in T(\Sigma, V)$, for a set of variables V, and every variable in s_i occurs in $t_1, \ldots, t_i$. A *protocol over* (Q, R) is a pair (P, Φ), where P is a finite set of principals over (Q, R) and Φ is a selecting theory over (Q, R).

Example. Now, we show how to model the *Recursive Authentication* (RA) protocol [4] in our formalism. This protocol has been analyzed using theorem provers [15,3]. In [13] and [12] a version of this protocol has been expressed in the tree transducer-based model (the original version has rules with non-linear left hand sides which cannot be expressed in this model). In the presentation of the protocol we follow [13] and [12]. Because, as it was mentioned above, non-recursive receive-send actions can be modeled in our formalism in a straightforward way, we will only describe the only recursive action of the protocol. In this action, the server S receives a sequence of requests of pairs of principals who want to obtain session keys. In response, S generates certificates containing the sessions keys. For instance, suppose that S receives

$$m = h_{K_c}(C, S, N_c, h_{K_b}(B, C, N_b, h_{K_a}(A, B, N_a, -))),$$

where N_a, N_b, N_c are nonces generated by A, B, C, respectively, K_a, K_b, K_c are long-term keys shared between S and A, B, C, and $h_k(m)$ stands for the term $\langle \mathsf{hash}(k, m), m\rangle$. The constant '$-$' marks the end of the sequence of requests. In general, messages sent to S may contain an arbitrary number of requests. In response to m, the server generates two certificates for C: $\{K_{cs}, S, N_c\}_{K_c}$ and $\{K_{bc}, B, N_c\}_{K_c}$, two certificates for B: $\{K_{bc}, C, N_b\}_{K_b}$ and $\{K_{ab}, A, N_b\}_{K_b}$, and one certificate for A: $\{K_{ab}, B, N_a\}_{K_a}$.

So, suppose that $P_0, \ldots, P_n$ are principals, $S = P_n$, and K_i is the long-term key shared by P_i and S. The recursive action of S can be described by the rule $x \to r(x)$ with the selecting theory over $(\emptyset, \{r\})$ given by the following set of clauses.

$$I(x), I(y) \Rightarrow I(\langle x, y\rangle), \qquad I(x), I(k) \Rightarrow I(\{x\}_k), \tag{4}$$
$$I(x) \Rightarrow I(\mathsf{hash}(x)) \qquad I(x), I(k) \Rightarrow I(\{\!|x|\!\}_k), \tag{5}$$
$$I(\langle x, y\rangle) \Rightarrow I(x), \qquad I(\{x\}_k), I(k) \Rightarrow I(x), \tag{6}$$
$$I(\langle x, y\rangle) \Rightarrow I(y), \qquad I(\{\!|x|\!\}_k), I(k^{-1}) \Rightarrow I(x) \qquad \text{(for each key } k\text{)} \tag{7}$$

Fig. 1. T_I — The Intruder Theory

$$r\big(h_{K_i}(P_i, P_j, x, y)\big) \Rightarrow r(y)$$
$$r\big(h_{K_i}(P_i, P_j, x,\ h_{K_l}(P_l, P_i, x', y))\big) \Rightarrow I\big(\{K_{ij}, P_j, x\}_{K_i}\big), I\big(\{K_{il}, P_l, x\}_{K_i}\big)$$
$$r\big(h_{K_i}(P_i, P_j, x,\ -)\big) \Rightarrow I\big(\{K_{ij}, P_j, x\}_{K_i}\big),$$

where the constant K_{ij} is the key for secure communication of P_i and P_j. Note that this theory does not use a regular look-ahead, and uses only one push symbol r.

Attacks. In the Dolev-Yao model [9], the intruder have the entire control over the network. He can intercept and memorize messages, generate new messages and send them to participants with a false identity. We express the ability of the intruder to generate (derive) new messages from a given set of messages by the theory T_I in Figure 1, where the predicate symbol I is intended to describe the intruder knowledge. For a set A of messages, let $I(A) = \{I(t) \mid t \in A\}$. We will say that the intruder can *derive a message t from messages A*, if $I(A) \vdash_{T_I} I(t)$.

Now, we give a definition of an *attack for a bounded number of sessions*. In an attack, the intruder nondeterministically chooses an execution order for the protocol steps and then produces input messages for the protocol rules. These input messages have to be derived from the intruder's initial knowledge and the output messages obtained so far. The aim of the intruder is to derive the secret message *Sec*. If some number of interleaving sessions of a protocol is to be analyzed, then these sessions have to be encoded into the protocol, which is the standard approach when protocols are analyzed w.r.t. a bounded number of sessions (see, for instance [16,6]).

Formally, given a protocol $(\{\Pi_1, \ldots, \Pi_l\}, \Phi)$, a *protocol execution scheme* is a sequence of rules $\pi = \pi_1, \ldots, \pi_n$ such that each element of π can be assigned to one of the participants $\Pi_1, \ldots, \Pi_l$, and, for each participant Π_k $(k = 1, \ldots, l)$, the subsequence of the elements of π assigned to Π_k is $\Pi_k^1, \ldots, \Pi_k^m$, for some $m \leq |\Pi_k|$, where Π_k^i is the i-th rule of Π_k.[2] An *attack* is a pair (π, σ), where $\pi = (t_i \rightarrow r_i(s_i))_{i=1}^n$ is a protocol execution scheme, and σ is a ground substitution such that

$$I(c_0), I([\![r_1(s_1\sigma)]\!]_\Phi), \ldots, I([\![r_{i-1}(s_{i-1}\sigma)]\!]_\Phi) \vdash_{T_I} I(t_i\sigma), \quad \text{for all } i = 1, \ldots, n \tag{8}$$
$$I(c_0), I([\![r_1(s_1\sigma)]\!]_\Phi), \ldots, I([\![r_n(s_n\sigma)]\!]_\Phi) \vdash_{T_I} I(\mathit{Sec}). \tag{9}$$

[2] More formally, a sequence $\pi_1, \ldots, \pi_n$ of rules is a protocol execution scheme, if there is a function $f : \{1, \ldots, n\} \rightarrow \{1, \ldots, l\}$ such that, for each $k = 1, \ldots, l$, assuming that integers $i_1 < \cdots < i_m$ are all the elements of $f^{-1}(k)$, we have $\pi_{i_j} = \Pi_k^j$, for each $j = 1, \ldots, m$.

Recall that c_0 is the only constant initially known to the intruder[3]. A protocol is *insecure*, if there exists an attack on it.

We end this section with the following, easy to prove lemma.

Lemma 1. *$A \vdash_{T_I} B$ iff there exists a proof of B with respect to T_I assuming A such that all the facts obtained by rules* (6), (7) *are before the facts obtained by rules* (4), (5).

4 Main Result

Theorem 1. *Insecurity of protocols with selecting theories w.r.t. a bounded number of sessions is decidable in nondeterministic exponential time.*

The remainder of this section is devoted to prove Theorem 1. In Subsections 4.1 and 4.2, the existence of an attack is expressed in a way which is more appropriate for the rest of the proof. In Subsection 4.3 we introduce the key notion of ADAG. ADAGs are labelled term-DAGs which can represent attacks. We show how to minimize ADAG, so that, if an ADAG exists, then there exists an ADAG of an exponential size, which gives rise to the nondeterministic exponential time algorithm for the insecurity problem.

4.1 The Theory of a Protocol

In this section we express the existence of an attack in a more uniform way, without using expressions of the form $[\![r(s)]\!]_\Phi$. We use here the fact that both selecting theories and the intruder theory are unary horn theories. Moreover, Lemma 1 allows us to extend selecting theories in such a way that the clauses (6) and (7) of T_I are not necessary.

In the following, $Acc(t)$ denotes the set of elements of the form $s/_K$, where s is a subterm of t and K is a minimal set of keys sufficient to access s providing t is known. For example, if $t = \{c, \{d\}_b\}_a$, then $Acc(t) = \{t/_\emptyset, c/_{\{a\}}, \{d\}_b/_{\{a\}}, d/_{\{a,b\}}\}$. Formally, we define Acc by the equations $Acc(\langle t_1, t_2\rangle) = \{\langle t_1, t_2\rangle/_\emptyset\} \cup Acc(t_1) \cup Acc(t_2)$, $Acc(\{t\}_k) = \{\{t\}_k/_\emptyset\} \cup \{s/_{\{k\}\cup K} \mid s/_K \in Acc(t))\}$, and $Acc(\{\!|t|\!\}_k) = \{\{\!|t|\!\}_k/_\emptyset\} \cup \{s/_{\{k^{-1}\}\cup K} \mid s/_K \in Acc(t))\}$. Note that $t/_\emptyset \in Acc(t)$, for each term t.

Definition 1. Let (P, Φ) be a protocol over (Q, R). Let r_I be a fresh predicate symbol. *The theory Φ_I of the protocol P* consists of the rules given in Fig. 2.

Note that the theory Φ_I consists of rules of three types: (a) rules (10) and (11), called the *intruder pop rules*, (b) pop rules, (c) rules of the form $I(k_1), \ldots, I(k_n), q_1(t), \ldots, q_l(t), r(t) \Rightarrow r'(x)$, called *generalized push rules*, and (d) rules of the form $I(k_1), \ldots, I(k_n), q_1(t), \ldots, q_l(t), r(t) \Rightarrow I(s)$, called *generalized send rules*. Note also that Φ_I contains all the rules of Φ. By Lemma 1, rules (12)–(14) and (16) can simulate the intruder rules (6) and (7). Thus, one can prove the following characterization of the existence of an attack.

[3] If we want to consider an initial knowledge of the intruder given by a finite set $\{t_1, \ldots, t_m\}$, we can add a principal with the rule $c_0 \rightarrow I(\langle t_1, \ldots, t_m\rangle)$.

$$I(x), I(y) \Rightarrow I(\langle x, y \rangle), \qquad I(x), I(k) \Rightarrow I(\{x\}_k), \tag{10}$$
$$I(x) \Rightarrow I(\mathsf{hash}(x)) \qquad I(x), I(k) \Rightarrow I(\{\!|x|\!\}_k), \tag{11}$$
$$r_I(x) \Rightarrow I(x), \tag{12}$$
$$r_I(\langle x, y \rangle) \Rightarrow r_I(x), \qquad r_I(\{x\}_k), I(k) \Rightarrow r_I(x), \tag{13}$$
$$r_I(\langle x, y \rangle) \Rightarrow r_I(y), \qquad r_I(\{\!|x|\!\}_k), I(k^{-1}) \Rightarrow r_I(x) \quad \text{(for each key } k) \tag{14}$$
$$\varphi, \qquad \text{for each pop or push rule } \varphi \text{ of } \Phi \tag{15}$$
$$I(k_1), \ldots, I(k_n), q_1(t), \ldots, q_l(t), r(t) \Rightarrow p(s'), \tag{16}$$

for each send rule $q_1(t), \ldots, q_l(t), r(t) \Rightarrow I(s)$ of Φ, for each $s'/_K \in Acc(s)$ with $K = \{k_1, \ldots, k_n\}$, where $p = I$, if s' is not a variable, and $p = r_I$, otherwise.

Fig. 2. Φ_I — the theory of the protocol (P, Φ)

Lemma 2. *Let (P, Φ) be a protocol over (Q, R), let $\pi = (t_i \to r_i(s_i))_{i=1}^n$ be a protocol execution scheme for P and σ be a substitution. The pair (π, σ) is an attack iff we have*

$$I(c_0), \hat{r}_1(s_1\sigma), \ldots, \hat{r}_{i-1}(s_{i-1}\sigma) \vdash_{\Phi_I} I(t_i\sigma), \quad \textit{for all } i = 1, \ldots, n \tag{17}$$
$$I(c_0), \hat{r}_1(s_1\sigma), \ldots, \hat{r}_n(s_n) \vdash_{\Phi_I} I(Sec), \tag{18}$$

where, for each $i = 1, \ldots, n$, we put $\hat{r}_i = r_I$, if $r_i = I$, and $\hat{r}_i = r_i$, otherwise.

4.2 Stage Theories

In this subsection, we express the existence of an attack using *a stage theory of a protocol.* In this theory, instead of representing the knowledge of the intruder by the predicate symbol I, the family of predicate symbols $I^{(0)}, \ldots, I^{(m)}$ is used to represent his knowledge at different stages of an attack.

Let (P, Φ) be a protocol over (Q, R) and $\pi = (t_i \to r_i(s_i))_{i=1}^n$ be a protocol execution scheme. Let $\mathcal{K}$ be the set containing the constant *Sec* and all the keys of P. A sequence $\boldsymbol{e} = e_1, \ldots, e_m$ of elements of $\mathcal{K} \cup \{1, \ldots, n\}$ is called a *stage sequence for* π, if $\boldsymbol{e}$ contains all the elements *Sec*, $1, \ldots, n$, and whenever $e_i = k$ and $e_j = l$, for $i < j$, then $k < l$. A stage sequence represents key elements of the intruder knowledge at consecutive stages of an attack. An element e_i of such a sequence either represents a new key that can be used by the intruder at the i-th stage (if e_i is a key), or, if $e_i = j$, it express progress in the protocol execution, and it means that at the i-th stage the j-th step of the protocol has been executed, so the intruder can use terms from $[\![r_j(s_j\sigma)]\!]_\Phi$.

Let $\mathcal{K}_i = \{a \in \mathcal{K} \mid a = e_j \text{ for some } j \leq i\}$. The *stage theory for Φ and* $\boldsymbol{e}$, denoted by $\Phi_{\boldsymbol{e}}$, is given in Figure 3, where $p^{(i)}$, for $i = 0, \ldots, m$, and $p \in R \cup \{r_I, I\}$, are fresh predicate symbols. The predicate symbol $I^{(k)}$ is intended to describe the intruder knowledge at the k-th stage of an attack. The intended meaning of $r^{(k)}(t)$ is that the intruder is able to prove $r(t)$ at the k-th stage.

$$q_1(x_1), \ldots, q_n(x_n) \Rightarrow q(f(x_1, \ldots, x_n)), \tag{19}$$

for each pop rule $q_1(x_1), \ldots, q_n(x_n) \Rightarrow q(f(x_1, \ldots, x_n))$ of Φ_I,

$$q_1(t), \ldots, q_l(t), r^{(j)}(t) \Rightarrow p^{(i)}(s), \tag{20}$$

for each (generalized) push or send rule $I(k_1), \ldots, I(k_m), q_1(t), \ldots, q_l(t), r(t) \Rightarrow p(s)$ of Φ_I, for $i \geq j$, and $k_1, \ldots, k_m \in \mathcal{K}_i$,

$$I^{(j)}(x), I^{(k)}(y) \Rightarrow I^{(i)}(\langle x, y\rangle) \quad I^{(j)}(x) \Rightarrow I^{(i)}(\mathsf{hash}(x)) \quad \text{if } i \geq j, k \tag{21}$$

$$I^{(j)}(x) \Rightarrow I^{(i)}(\{x\}_a), \quad I^{(j)}(x) \Rightarrow I^{(i)}(\{\!|x|\!\}_a) \quad \text{if } i \geq j, \text{ and } a \in \mathcal{K}_i. \tag{22}$$

Fig. 3. Φ_e — The Stage Theory for Φ and $\boldsymbol{e}$

Lemma 3. *Let* $\pi = (t_i \to r_i(s_i))_{i=1}^n$ *be a protocol execution scheme and* σ *be a ground substitution. The pair* (π, σ) *is an attack iff there is a stage sequence* $\boldsymbol{e} = e_1, \ldots, e_m$ *for* π *such that*

$$I^{(0)}(c_0), \psi_1, \ldots, \psi_m \vdash_{\Phi_e} \varphi_1, \ldots, \varphi_m, \tag{23}$$

where $\varphi_1, \ldots, \varphi_m$ *and* $\psi_1, \ldots, \psi_m$ *are defined as follows. If* $e_i = j \in \{1, \ldots, n\}$, *then* $\varphi_i = I^{(i-1)}(t_j\sigma)$, *and* $\psi_i = \hat{r}_j^{(i)}(s_j\sigma)$, *where* $\hat{r}$ *is defined like in Lemma 2. If* $e_i = a \in \mathcal{K}$, *then* $\varphi_i = I^{(i-1)}(a)$ *and* $\psi_i = I^{(0)}(c_0)$.

Proof. First, suppose that (23) holds, for some π, $\boldsymbol{e}$, and σ, and that Γ is a proof of it. Let Γ_0 denotes the subsequence of Γ containing only facts of the form $q(t)$, for $q \in Q$. Let Γ_i denotes the subsequence of Γ containing only facts of the form $p^{(i)}(t)$, and let $\Gamma_{\leq i}$ be the concatenation of $\Gamma_0, \ldots, \Gamma_i$. Let $\Gamma^*_{\leq i}$ be the sequence obtained from $\Gamma_{\leq i}$ by substituting each $p^{(k)}$ by p. One can show that $\Gamma^*_{\leq i-1}$ is a proof of (17), and $\Gamma^*_{\leq m}$ is a proof of (18). Hence, (π, σ) is an attack.

Now, suppose that we have an attack (π, σ). By Lemma 2, (17) and (18) hold. So, let Π_i be a proof of (17), for $i = 1, \ldots, n$, and let Π_{n+1} be a proof of (18). We split each Π_k (for $k = 1, \ldots, (n+1)$) into the maximal (w.r.t. its length) sequence $\Pi_k^1, \ldots, \Pi_k^{m_k}$ such that the last element of Π_k^i, for $1 \leq i < m_k$, is of the form $I(a)$, for $a \in \mathcal{K}$, and this occurrence of $I(a)$ is the only one in $\Pi_1, \ldots, \Pi_{k-1}, \Pi_k^1, \ldots, \Pi_k^i$. We want to re-index the obtained sequence of Π_k^i, so let $\hat{\Pi}_1, \ldots, \hat{\Pi}_N = \Pi_1^1, \ldots, \Pi_1^{m_1}, \ldots, \Pi_{n+1}^1, \ldots, \Pi_{n+1}^{m_{n+1}}$.

For $i = 1, \ldots, N$, let Γ_i be the sequence of facts obtained from $\hat{\Pi}_i$ by substituting each $p(t)$, for $p \in R \cup \{r_I, I\}$, by $p^{(i-1)}(t)$, and let e_i be equal to k, if $\hat{\Pi}_i = \Pi_k^{m_k}$, for some k, and, otherwise, let e_i be a, where $I(a)$ is the last element of $\hat{\Pi}_i$. One can prove that the concatenation of $\Gamma_1, \ldots, \Gamma_n$ is a proof of (23). □

We say that a fact $I^{(i)}(t)$ is *stronger than* $I^{(j)}(t)$, if $i \leq j$. A proof is *normal*, if for each term t, it contains at most one fact of the form $I^{(i)}$. The following lemma is easy to prove.

Lemma 4. *It holds* (23) *iff there is a normal proof of*

$$I^{(0)}(c), \psi_1, \ldots, \psi_m \vdash_{\Phi_e} \varphi'_1, \ldots, \varphi'_m, \tag{24}$$

where, for each $k = 1, \ldots, m$, *the fact* φ'_k *is stronger than* φ_k.

4.3 ADAGs

This section is the central part of the proof of Theorem 1. We give here the definition of an ADAG and link the existence of ADAGs with the existence of attacks (Lemma 5). Next, we show that if there exists an ADAG which represents an attack on a protocols, then there exists an ADAG of exponential size. Finally, as a consequence of the above, we obtain an NEXPTIME algorithm for deciding insecurity of protocols.

We will assume that selecting theories have the following property: the push rules are *flat*, i.e. are of the form (2) with $t = f(x_1, \ldots, x_n)$, where $x_1, \ldots, x_n$ are variables. We can do it without loss of generality, because, for any selecting theory, one can easily obtain an equivalent selecting theory with this property.

Definition 2. Let D be a term-DAG over Σ with the set V of vertices, and let T be a set of terms over Σ and $\mathbb{V}$. A function $\theta : sub(T) \to V$ is a *D-embedding for* T, if $\theta(f(t_1, \ldots, t_n)) = v$ implies that $v =_D f(v_1, \ldots, v_n)$ and $\theta(t_i) = v_i$, for $i = 1, \ldots, n$. Embeddings θ_1 and θ_2 are *compatible*, if for each variable x which is in the domain of both θ_1 and θ_2, we have $\theta_1(x) = \theta_2(x)$.

Let $v \in V$, and $t \in T(\Sigma, \mathbb{V})$. By $\text{emb}(t \mapsto v)$ we denote the unique embedding θ for $\{t\}$ such that $\theta(t) = v$ (if it exists). Let $v_1, v_2 \in V$, and $t_1, t_2 \in T(\Sigma, \mathbb{V})$. The terms (t_1, t_2) *embeds to* (v_1, v_2), if the embeddings $\text{emb}(t_1 \mapsto v_1)$ and $\text{emb}(t_2 \mapsto v_2)$ exist and are compatible.

Definition 3. Let Φ and Ψ be stage theories over (Q, R). The theory Ψ is an *instance of* Φ, if each clause in Ψ is an instance of a clause in Φ.

Definition 4. Let (P, Φ) be a protocol over (Q, R), let $\pi = (t_i \to r_i(s_i))_{i=1}^n$ be a protocol execution scheme, and $\boldsymbol{e} = e_1, \ldots, e_m$ be a stage sequence for π. Let $\mathcal{T}_P$ denote the set $\{t_i, s_i\}_{i=1}^n \cup \{c_0\} \cup \mathcal{K}$, and $Q_{\boldsymbol{e}}$ denote the set of predicate symbols of $\Phi_{\boldsymbol{e}}$.

A DAG *of the attack* (an ADAG for short) for $(\Phi, \pi, \boldsymbol{e})$ is a tuple $\mathcal{D} = \langle D, \alpha, \beta, \Psi, \delta \rangle$ where D is a term-DAG over Σ with the set of vertices V, $\delta : V \to 2^{Q_{\boldsymbol{e}}}$, α is a D-embedding for $\mathcal{T}_P$, a stage theory Ψ is an instance of Φ, and β is a partial function from $V \times Q_{\boldsymbol{e}}$ to $V \times \Psi_{\boldsymbol{e}}$, called a *witness function*, such that

(i) if $v = \alpha(t_j)$, then $I^{(i')} \in \delta(v)$, for some $i' < i$, where i is the integer such that $e_i = j$,

(ii) for each vertex v, the set $\delta(v)$ contains at most one element of the form $I^{(i)}$,

(iii) if $p \in \delta(v)$ then one of the following conditions holds:

   (a) $v = \alpha(c_0)$ and $p = I^{(l)}$ (for some l), or $v = \alpha(s_j)$ and $p = \hat{r}_j^{(i)}$, for some i, j such that $e_i = j$,

   (b) $v =_D f(v_1, \ldots, v_n)$, and $\Psi_{\boldsymbol{e}}$ contains the clause $p_1(x_1), \ldots, p_n(x_n) \Rightarrow p(f(x_1, \ldots, x_n))$, for some $p_1 \in \delta(v_1), \ldots, p_n \in \delta(v_n)$,

   (c) $\beta(v, p) = (v', \varphi)$, where $\varphi = (p_1(t), \ldots, p_l(t) \Rightarrow p(x_i))$, for $t = f(x_1, \ldots, x_j)$, is a push clause of $\Psi_{\boldsymbol{e}}$, $\{p_1, \ldots, p_l\} \subseteq \delta(v')$, and $v' =_D f(v_1, \ldots, v_n)$ with $v_i = v$, or

   (d) $\beta(v, p) = (v', \varphi)$, where $\varphi = \big(p_1(t'), \ldots, p_l(t') \Rightarrow p(t)\big)$ is a send clause of $\Psi_{\boldsymbol{e}}$ (so $p = I^{(j)}$), $\{p_1, \ldots, p_l\} \subseteq \delta(v')$, and (t, t') embeds to (v, v').

Lemma 5. *If there is an attack (π, σ) on a protocol (P, Φ) then there is an* ADAG $\langle D, \alpha, \beta, \Psi, \delta \rangle$ *for $(\Phi, \pi, \boldsymbol{e})$, for some stage sequence $\boldsymbol{e}$ for π, such that $\Psi = \Phi$. If there exists an* ADAG *for $(\Phi, \pi, \boldsymbol{e})$ then there exists an attack (π, σ), for some substitution σ.*

Proof. Suppose that there is an attack (π, σ). By Lemma 3 and Lemma 4, there is a sequence $\boldsymbol{e}$ and a normal proof Γ of (24). Let D be the DAG representing all the terms of the form $t\sigma$, where $t \in \mathcal{T}_P$. For $t \in \mathcal{T}_P$, let $\alpha(t)$ be the vertex v such that $v \rightrightarrows t\sigma$. For a vertex v of D, let $\delta(v)$ be the set of the predicate symbols $p \in Q_{\boldsymbol{e}}$ such that $p(t_v)$ occurs in Γ, for $v \rightrightarrows t_v$. Further, if we have $p(t_v)$ in Γ, because $\varphi = \big(q_1(s'), \ldots, q_l(s'), p'(s') \Rightarrow p(s)\big)$ is a push or send clause of $\Phi_{\boldsymbol{e}}$, $t_v = s\sigma$, for some substitution σ, and $q_1(s'\sigma), \ldots, q_l(s'\sigma), p'(s'\sigma)$ occur in Γ before $p(t_v)$, then let $\beta(v, p) = (v', \varphi)$, where v' is the vertex of D such that $v' \rightrightarrows s'\sigma$ (such a vertex exists, because $s'\sigma$ has to be a subterm of some $s_i\sigma$). One can show that $\langle D, \alpha, \beta, \Phi, \delta \rangle$ is an ADAG.

Now, suppose that $\langle D, \alpha, \beta, \Psi, \delta \rangle$ is an ADAG for $(\Phi, \pi, \boldsymbol{e})$. Let $\sigma(x) = t$, where t is the term such that $\alpha(x) \rightrightarrows t$. We produce the following sequence of facts: First, we put all the facts of the form $q(t)$, where $v \rightrightarrows t$ and $q \in \delta(v)$, for $q \in Q$, in such a way that $q(t)$ is before $q'(t')$, if $t < t'$. Second, we put all the fact of the form $r^{(i)}(t)$, where $v \rightrightarrows t$ and $r^{(i)} \in \delta(v)$, for $r \in R \cup \{r_I\}$, in such a way that $p(t)$ is before $p'(t')$, if $t > t'$. Finally, we put all the fact of the form $I^{(i)}(t)$, where $v \rightrightarrows t$ and $I^{(i)} \in \delta(v)$, in such a way that $p(t)$ is before $p'(t')$, if $t < t'$. One can prove that this sequence is a normal proof of (24) (note that Ψ is an instance of Φ, so each clause of $\Psi_{\boldsymbol{e}}$ is an instance of a clause of $\Phi_{\boldsymbol{e}}$), which by Lemma 3 and Lemma 4, implies that there exists an attack. □

Lemma 5 is a crucial step of our construction, because it characterizes the existence of an attack by a structure which is defined by some local properties. Now, we will describe how to minimize ADAGs, roughly speaking, by merging vertices which are indistinguishable from the point of view of this local properties. We proceed in three steps given by Lemmas 6, 7, and 8 below (proofs of these lemmas are given in the separate sections). To formulate these lemmas we need the following definitions.

Let (P, Φ) be a protocol, and let $\mathcal{D} = \langle D, \alpha, \beta, \Psi, \delta \rangle$ be an ADAG for $(\Phi, \pi, \boldsymbol{e})$. A vertex v of $\mathcal{D}$ is *bounded*, if $v = \alpha(t)$, for some $t \in \mathit{sub}(\mathcal{T}_P)$. Otherwise, v is *free*. Let $\mathcal{B}(\mathcal{D})$ be the set of vertices which can be reached from bounded vertices, moving from a vertex to its child, in less than $|P| \cdot |\Phi|$ steps. Note that $\mathcal{B}(\mathcal{D})$ is exponentially bounded with respect to the size of the protocol.

A *goal* is a vertex v with $I^{(i)} \in \delta(v)$, for some i, such that the item (iii,d) of Definition 4 holds for v and $p = I^{(i)}$. Let $G(\mathcal{D})$ be the set of goals of $\mathcal{D}$. For a stage sequence $\boldsymbol{e}$, let $G_k(\mathcal{D}) = \{v \mid v \in G(\mathcal{D})$, and $I^{(i)} \in \delta(v)$ for $\boldsymbol{e}^{-1}(k) \le i < \boldsymbol{e}^{-1}(k+1)\}$, where $\boldsymbol{e}^{-1}(0) = 0$, $\boldsymbol{e}^{-1}(n+1) = \infty$, and, for $k = 1, \ldots, n$, let $\boldsymbol{e}^{-1}(k)$ be the integer i such that $e_i = k$. Let $G_{>k}(\mathcal{D}) = \bigcup_{i>k} G_i(\mathcal{D})$.

An ADAG $\mathcal{D}$ is *simple*, if, whenever $u \notin \mathcal{B}(\mathcal{D})$ is a descendant of $v \in G_i(\mathcal{D})$, then $u \notin G_{>i}(\mathcal{D})$. Let $\hat{\Phi} = \Phi \cup \{C' \mid C'$ is an instance of a send clause $C \in \Phi$ of the form $(\ldots \Rightarrow I^{(i)}(s))$, and the depth of C' is not greater than $|P| \cdot i\}$.

Lemma 6. *Let (P, Φ) be a protocol. If $\mathcal{D} = \langle D, \alpha, \beta, \Phi, \delta \rangle$ is an* ADAG *for $(\Phi, \pi, \boldsymbol{e})$, then there exists a simple* ADAG $\mathcal{D}' = \langle D', \alpha', \beta', \hat{\Phi}, \delta' \rangle$ *for $(\Phi, \pi, \boldsymbol{e})$.*

Lemma 6 states that each ADAG can be transformed to a simple ADAG. Having a simple ADAG, we can minimize the number of its goals, which is expressed by the following lemma. It allows us to minimize the size of the whole ADAG, as is stated in Lemma 8.

Lemma 7. *Let* (P, Φ) *be a protocol. If* $\mathcal{D} = \langle D, \alpha, \beta, \hat{\Phi}, \delta \rangle$ *is a simple* ADAG *for* $(\Phi, \pi, \boldsymbol{e})$*, then there exists an* ADAG $\mathcal{D}' = \langle D', \alpha', \beta', \hat{\Phi}, \delta' \rangle$ *such that the set of goals of* $\mathcal{D}'$ *is exponentially bounded w.r.t. the size of* (P, Φ)*.*

Lemma 8. *Let* (P, Φ) *be a protocol over* (Q, R)*. If* $\mathcal{D}_0 = \langle D, \alpha, \beta, \hat{\Phi}, \delta \rangle$ *(for some* D, α, β, δ*) is an* ADAG *for* $(\Phi, \pi, \boldsymbol{e})$ *with an exponentially bounded set of goals (w.r.t. the size of* (P, Φ)*), then there is an* ADAG *for* $(\Phi, \pi, \boldsymbol{e})$ *of an exponentially bounded size.*

Lemmas 5, 6, 7, and 8 have the following consequence.

Corollary 1. *Let* (P, Φ) *be a protocol, and let* π *be a protocol execution scheme. There is an attack* (π, σ)*, for some* σ*, iff there exists an* ADAG *for* $(\Phi, \pi, \boldsymbol{e})$*, for some* $\boldsymbol{e}$*, of an exponential size w.r.t. the size of the protocol.*

The Algorithm. To decide insecurity of a given protocol (P, Φ), we guess an attack skeleton π, a stage sequence $\boldsymbol{e}$, and an ADAG for $(\Phi, \pi, \boldsymbol{e})$ of exponential size w.r.t. the size of the protocol. Correctness of this algorithm is given by the Corollary 1. The algorithm works in NEXPTIME, which concludes the proof of Theorem 1. □

An easy to obtain lower bound is DEXPTIME, because the problem of the emptiness of the intersection of regular tree languages, which is DEXPTIME-hard, can be easily reduced to the problem of deciding protocols with selecting theories (in the reduction, pop-clauses of selecting theories are used).

4.4 Proof of Lemma 6

We start this section with technical definitions used in this section and in the following ones. For an ADAG $\mathcal{D}$, let $S^i_{\mathcal{D}}$ denote the set of descendants of $\alpha(c_0), \alpha(t_j), \alpha(s_j)$, for $j \leq i$. For a goal u, we define sets of vertices $B^u_{\mathcal{D}}$ and $F^u_{\mathcal{D}}$ in the following way. Let $\beta(u, I^{(i)}) = (u', \varphi)$, with $\varphi = \big(q_1(t'), \ldots, q_l(t'), r(t') \Rightarrow I^{(i)}(t)\big)$, $\theta = \mathrm{emb}(t \mapsto u)$, and $\theta' = \mathrm{emb}(t' \mapsto u')$. $B^u_{\mathcal{D}} = \{\theta(s) \mid s \text{ is a subterm of } t \text{ or } t'\}$. $F^u_{\mathcal{D}} = \{\theta(x) \mid x \in \mathrm{dom}(\theta) \cap \mathrm{dom}(\theta')\}$ (note that θ and θ' are compatible, so $\theta(x) = \theta'(x)$).

We write $(v', p') \overset{\mathcal{D}}{\leadsto} (v, p)$, if $\beta(v, p) = (v', \varphi)$, for $\varphi = \big(q_1(t'), \ldots, q_l(t'), p'(t') \Rightarrow p(t)\big)$. Let $\overset{\mathcal{D}}{\leadsto}{}^*$ denotes the transitive closure of $\overset{\mathcal{D}}{\leadsto}$. If u is a goal and $I^{(i)} \in \delta(u)$, then we can write $(v, p) \overset{\mathcal{D}}{\leadsto}{}^* u$ instead of $(v, p) \overset{\mathcal{D}}{\leadsto}{}^* (u, I^{(i)})$, and $v \overset{\mathcal{D}}{\leadsto}{}^* u$, if, for some p', we have $(v, p') \overset{\mathcal{D}}{\leadsto}{}^* (u, I^{(i)})$.

In order to prove Lemma 6, we construct a sequence $\mathcal{D}_0, \ldots, \mathcal{D}_n = D'$ of ADAGs such that $\mathcal{D}_0 = \langle D, \alpha, \beta, \hat{\Psi}, \delta \rangle$ and, for each $\mathcal{D}_i$ $(i = 0, \ldots, n)$, we have

- $(*)$ if $u \notin \mathcal{B}(\mathcal{D}_i)$ is a descendant of $v \in G_j(\mathcal{D}_i)$, for $j = 1, \ldots, i$, then $u \notin G_{>j}(\mathcal{D}_i)$, and
- $(**)$ if $u \in G_{>i}(\mathcal{D}_i)$ and $\beta(u) = (u', \varphi)$, then either $\varphi \in \Phi$, or $F^u_{\mathcal{D}_i} \subseteq S^i_{\mathcal{D}_i}$.

It is easy to show that $\mathcal{D}_0$ is an ADAG for $(\Phi, \pi, \boldsymbol{e})$ and $(*)$, $(**)$ hold for $\mathcal{D}_0$. Now, assume that $(*)$ and $(**)$ hold for $\mathcal{D}_{i-1} = \langle D_{i-1}, \alpha, \beta_{i-1}, \hat{\Phi}, \delta_{i-1}\rangle$. We will construct $\mathcal{D}_i = \langle D_i, \alpha, \beta_i, \hat{\hat{\Phi}}, \delta_i\rangle$. Let V_{i-1} and V_i denote the sets of vertices of D_{i-1} and D_i, respectively. Let $A = \{u \mid u$ is a descendant of some $u' \in G_i(\mathcal{D}_{i-1})$, $u \notin G_i(\mathcal{D}_{i-1})$, $u \notin S^i_{\mathcal{D}_{i-1}}\}$. Let X be the least set of vertices of $\mathcal{D}_{i-1}$ such that (i) if $u \in A$ and u is bounded, then $u \in X$, (ii) if $u \in X$ and $u' \in A$ is a child of u, then $u' \in X$.

The construction of D_i. Let $V_i = V_{i-1} \cup W_i$, where W_i is the set of fresh vertices of the form $\hat{v}$, for $v \in A$. Now, suppose that $v =_{D_{i-1}} f(v_1, \ldots, v_n)$. For each $i = 1, \ldots, n$, we define $h(v, i)$ as follows. If $v \notin A$, $v_i \in A$, $v \notin G_{\leq i}(\mathcal{D}_{i-1})$, and v or v_i is free, then $h(v, i) = \hat{v}_i$. Otherwise, $h(v, i) = v_i$. We put $v =_{D_i} f(h(v, 1), \ldots, h(v, n))$. For $v \in A$ with $v =_{D_{i-1}} f(v_1, \ldots, v_n)$ we put $\hat{v} =_{D_i} f(v'_1, \ldots, v'_n)$, where, for each $i = 1, \ldots, n$, $v'_i = \hat{v}_i$, if $v_i \in A$, and $v'_i = v_i$, otherwise. Note that $S^i_{\mathcal{D}_{i-1}} = S^i_{\mathcal{D}_i}$.

The construction of δ_i. For $v \in A$ we define the set $R(u) \subseteq R \cup \{r_I\}$ by the following equivalence: $r \in R(u)$ iff there exist vertices $w \notin A$ and $v \in A$ such that $h(w, k) = \hat{v}$, for some k, and $(w, r'') \overset{\mathcal{D}_{i-1}}{\rightsquigarrow} (v, r') \overset{\mathcal{D}_{i-1}}{\rightsquigarrow}{}^{*} (u, r)$, for some r', r''. For $v \notin A$, let $\delta_i(v) = \delta_{i-1}(v)$. For $v \in A$, we define $\delta_i(v)$ and $\delta_i(\hat{v})$ as follows: $\delta_Q = \{q \in Q \mid q \in \delta_{i-1}(v)\}$, $\delta_i(v) = \delta_Q \cup \{r \in R \mid r \in \delta_{i-1}(v), r \notin R(v)\} \cup \{I^{(j)} \mid I^{(j)} \in \delta_{i-1}(v)$, and either $j \leq i$, or $v \in X\}$, and $\delta_i(\hat{v}) = \delta_Q \cup \{r \in R \mid r \in \delta_{i-1}(v), r \in R(v)\} \cup \{I^{(j)} \mid I^{(j)} \in \delta_{i-1}(v)\}$. It is easy to check that $\delta_{i-1}(v) = \delta_i(v) \cup \delta_i(\hat{v})$.

The construction of β_i. If v is a vertex of $\mathcal{D}_{i-1}$ and $r \in R \cup \{r_I\}$, $r \in \delta_i(v)$, then let $\beta_i(v, r) = \beta_{i-1}(v, r)$. If $v \in A$ and $r \in R \cup \{r_I\}$, $r \in \delta_i(\hat{v})$, then let $\beta_i(\hat{v}, r) = (w, r')$, where $\beta_{i-1}(v, r) = (u, r')$, and $w = u$, if $u \notin A$, and $w = \hat{u}$, otherwise.

For $v \in V_i$, let us define $\check{v} \in V_{i-1}$ as follows: $\check{v} = v$, if $v \in V_{i-1}$, and $\check{v} = u$, if $v = \hat{u}$. For $v \in V_{i-1}$, and $r \in \delta_{i-1}(v)$, we define $g(v, r) \in V_i$ as follows: $g(v, r) = v$, if $r \in \delta_i(v)$, and $g(v, r) = \hat{v}$, otherwise.

Let $v \in V_i$ with $I^{(j)} \in \delta_i(v)$. We will define $\beta_i(v, I^{(j)})$. Let $(v', \varphi) = \beta_{i-1}(\check{v}, I^{(j)})$, with $\varphi = \big(q_1(t'), \ldots, q_l(t'), r(t') \Rightarrow I^{(j)}(t)\big)$. Let $w = g(v', r)$. Note that, because $r \in \delta_i(u)$, we have $r \in \delta_{i+1}(w)$. Since, by the inductive hypothesis, $(**)$ holds for $\mathcal{D}_{i-1}$, it is enough to consider two cases:

1. $B^{\check{v}}_{\mathcal{D}_{i-1}} \cap A = \emptyset$, or $F^{\check{v}}_{\mathcal{D}_{i-1}} \subseteq S^i_{\mathcal{D}_i}$. In this case, let $\beta_i(v, I^{(j)}) = (w, \varphi)$.
2. $B^{\check{v}}_{\mathcal{D}_{i-1}} \cap A \neq \emptyset$, and $\varphi \in \Phi$. In this case we proceed as follows. Let $\theta_{\check{v}} = \mathrm{emb}(t \mapsto \check{v})$. We define a substitution σ with the domain $\mathrm{dom}(\sigma) = \{x \mid x \in \mathit{Var}(t),\ \theta_{\check{v}}(x) \in A\}$ as follows. Let $x \in \mathrm{dom}(\sigma)$. Let u be an (arbitrarily chosen) vertex in $G_i(\mathcal{D}_{i-1})$ such that $\theta_{\check{v}}(x)$ is a descendant of u (such a vertex exists, because $\theta_{\check{v}}(x) \in A$). Let $\beta_i(u, I^{(i)}) = (u', \psi)$, with ψ of the form $(\ldots \Rightarrow I^{(i)}(s))$, $\theta_u = \mathrm{emb}(s \mapsto u)$. One can show that there exists a subterm s'' of s such that $\theta_{\check{v}}(x) = \theta_u(s'')$. We define $\sigma(x) = s''$. Let $\varphi' = \varphi\sigma$. One can show that $\varphi' \in \hat{\Phi}$. Finally, let $\beta_i(v, I^{(j)}) = (w, \varphi')$.

One can prove that $\mathcal{D}_i$ is an ADAG and $(**)$ holds. Now we will show that $(*)$ holds. Let $u \notin \mathcal{B}(\mathcal{D}_i)$ be a descendant of some $v \in G_j(\mathcal{D}_i)$, for some $j = 1, \ldots, i$. Note that $u \notin \mathcal{B}(\mathcal{D}_i)$ implies $u \notin X$. For $j < i$, if we suppose that $u \in G_{>j}(\mathcal{D}_i)$, then we have $\check{v} \in G_j(\mathcal{D}_{i-1})$ and $\check{u} \in G_{>j}(\mathcal{D}_{i-1})$. We also have that $\check{u}$ is a descendant of $\check{v}$, which contradicts the inductive hypothesis.

Now, assume that $j = i$. Note that, for any $v \in A$, the vertex $\hat{v}$ is not a descendant of any $v' \in G_i(\mathcal{D}_i)$. So, suppose that $u \in A$. In this case the definition of δ_i guarantees that $u \notin G_{>j}(\mathcal{D}_i)$. Second, suppose that $u \notin A$. In this case $u \in S^i_{\mathcal{D}_i}$, and because $u \notin \mathcal{B}(\mathcal{D}_i)$, u is free and u is reachable from $\alpha(t_i)$. It means that there is a path $v_1, \ldots, v_M$ in $\mathcal{D}_i$, such that $v_1 = \alpha(t_i)$, v_M is a leaf, and $u = v_k$, for some k. Because $I^{(i-1)} \in \delta_i(v_1)$, then there exists an index l such that $v_l \in G_{i-1}(\mathcal{D}_i)$ and, for each $l' = 1, \ldots, l$, $I^{(i-1)} \in \delta_i(v_{l'})$. So, if $k \leq l$, then $u \notin G_{>j}(D_i)$ ($\delta_i(v)$ contains $I^{(i-1)}$, so it cannot contain $I^{(j)}$ for any $j \neq i-1$), and if $k > l$, then by inductive hypothesis, we also have $u \notin G_{>j}(D_i)$. It concludes the proof of Lemma 6. □

One can also prove, using very similar argumentation to the one in the last paragraph of the proof above, the following fact.

Lemma 9. *If $\mathcal{D}$ is a simple* ADAG, *$u \in S^i_{\mathcal{D}}$ and $u \notin \mathcal{B}(\mathcal{D})$, then $u \notin G_{\geq i}(\mathcal{D})$.*

4.5 Proof of Lemma 7

We will construct a sequence $\mathcal{D}_n, \ldots, \mathcal{D}_0$ of ADAGs, starting with $\mathcal{D}_n = \mathcal{D}$. We will show that $G_{\geq i}(\mathcal{D}_i)$ is exponentially bounded, which, for $i = 0$, means that the set of goals of $\mathcal{D}_0$ is exponentially bounded. All the ADAGs of this family share the same α, $\hat{\Phi}$, and the same set of vertices. So, let $\mathcal{D}_{i+1} = \langle \mathcal{D}_{i+1}, \alpha, \beta, \delta_{i+1} \rangle$. We will construct $\mathcal{D}_i = \langle \mathcal{D}_i, \alpha, \beta, \delta_i \rangle$. By induction, we assume that $G_{>i}(\mathcal{D}_{i+1})$ is exponentially bounded.

For $v_1, v_2 \in G_i(\mathcal{D}_{i+1})$, let $v_1 \sim v_2$ iff $\delta_{i+1}(v_1) = \delta_{i+1}(v_2)$. Let h be a function which for the equivalence class $[v]_\sim$ of v, gives some vertex $h([v]_\sim) \in [v]_\sim$ such that no vertex $v' \in [v]_\sim$ is a descendant of $h([v]_\sim)$. Let $H = \{v \in G_i(\mathcal{D}_{i+1}) \mid h([v]_\sim) = v\}$. Let $\mathcal{G}$ be the least subset of $G_i(\mathcal{D}_{i+1})$ such that:

(a) if $u \in G_i(\mathcal{D}_{i+1})$ is an element of $\mathcal{B}(\mathcal{D}_{i+1}) \cup H$, then $u \in \mathcal{G}$,
(b) if $u \in B^v_{\mathcal{D}_{i+1}}$, for some $v \in G_{>i}(\mathcal{D}_{i+1})$, then $u \in \mathcal{G}$,
(c) if $u \overset{\mathcal{D}_{i+1}}{\rightsquigarrow}{}^* u'$, for some $u' \in G_{>i}(\mathcal{D}_{i+1})$, then $u \in \mathcal{G}$,
(d) if $u \in G_i(\mathcal{D}_{i+1})$ is a descendant of some $u' \in \mathcal{G}$, then $u \in \mathcal{G}$.

Using Lemma 9 and the fact that, for $u \in G_i(\mathcal{D}_{i+1})$, we have $F^u_{\mathcal{D}_{i+1}} \subseteq S^i_{\mathcal{D}_{i+1}}$, one can show that each $u \in G_i(\mathcal{D}_{i+1})$ can have at most exponentially many descendants in $\mathcal{G}$, and hence, the size of $\mathcal{G}$ is exponentially bounded as well. Let $\bar{\mathcal{G}} = G_i(\mathcal{D}_{i+1}) \setminus \mathcal{G}$.

The construction of $\mathcal{D}_i$. We define $\delta_i(v)$ as follows. Let $\delta_Q(v) = \delta_{i+1}(v) \cap Q$, let $\delta_R(v) = \{r^{(j)} \mid r^{(j)} \in \delta_{i+1}(v),$ and $(v, r^{(j)}) \overset{\mathcal{D}_{i+1}}{\rightsquigarrow} u,$ for some $u \notin \bar{\mathcal{G}}\}$, and let $\delta_I(v) = \{I^{(j)} \mid I^{(j)} \in \delta_{i+1}(v)\}$. If $v \in \bar{\mathcal{G}}$, then let $\delta_i(v) = \delta_Q(v) \cup \delta_R(v)$. Otherwise, let $\delta_i(v) = \delta_Q(v) \cup \delta_R(v) \cup \delta_I(v)$. To define the term-DAG D_i, let $v =_{\mathcal{D}_{i+1}} f(v_1, \ldots, v_k)$. For each $i = 1, \ldots, k$, we define v'_i: If $I^{(j)} \in \delta(v)$, $v \notin G_j(\mathcal{D}_{i+1})$, and $v_i \in \bar{\mathcal{G}}$, then $v'_i = h([v_i]_\sim)$. Otherwise, $v'_i = v_i$. Note that because $G_i(\mathcal{D}_i) = \mathcal{G}$, the size of $G_i(\mathcal{D}_i)$ is exponentially bounded. Note also that the number of goals from $G_{>i}(\mathcal{D}_i) \cup G_{<i}(\mathcal{D}_i)$ has not been changed.

One can show that $\mathcal{D}_i$ it is an ADAG. The most difficult thing to prove is that the item (iii,d) of Definition 4 holds for each vertex $v \in G_j(\mathcal{D}_i)$ (for some j). So suppose that $v \in G_j(\mathcal{D}_i)$. Clearly, $v \in G_j(\mathcal{D}_{i+1})$. Let $(v', \varphi) = \beta(v, I^{(j)})$ with $\varphi = (q_1(t'), \ldots, q_l(t'), r(t') \Rightarrow I^{(j)}(t))$. We have (t, t') embeds to (v, v') in $\mathcal{D}_{i+1}$.

If $B^v_{\mathcal{D}_{i+1}}$ does not contain any $u \in \bar{\mathcal{G}}$, then $B^v_{\mathcal{D}_{i+1}}$ and $B^v_{\mathcal{D}_i}$ have exactly the same structure and clearly (t, t') embeds to (v, v') in $\mathcal{D}_i$. So suppose that there exists $u \in B^v_{\mathcal{D}_{i+1}}$ such that $u \in \bar{\mathcal{G}}$. Because $u \notin \mathcal{G}$, we have $v \notin G_{>i}(\mathcal{D}_{i+1})$ (see (b) above). We consider two cases. In the both we get a contradiction.

1. *u is a descendant of v.* Then $v \notin G_{<i}(\mathcal{D}_{i+1})$, because $\mathcal{D}_{i+1}$ is simple and, by (a), $u \notin \mathcal{B}(\mathcal{D}_{i+1})$. So, $v \in G_i$. But in this case we cannot have $v \in \mathcal{G}$ (because u would be in $\mathcal{G}$ too; see (d)), and v cannot be in $G_i(\mathcal{D}_i)$.
2. *u is not a descendant of v.* By Lemma 9, either $u \in \mathcal{B}(\mathcal{D}_{i+1})$ and $u \in \mathcal{G}$ (see (a)), or $u \notin S^i_{\mathcal{D}_{i+1}}$ which implies $v' \notin S^i_{\mathcal{D}_{i+1}}$ and $v \notin G_{\leq i}(\mathcal{D}_{i+1})$. □

4.6 Proof of Lemma 8

For an ADAG $\mathcal{D}$ let $U(\mathcal{D})$ be the set of free vertices which are not in $B^v_{\mathcal{D}}$, for any goal v of $\mathcal{D}$, and let $\overline{U}(\mathcal{D})$ denote the set of vertices of $\mathcal{D}$ which are not in $U(\mathcal{D})$. One can check that the size of $\overline{U}(\mathcal{D}_0)$ is exponentially bounded.

Now, consider the following procedure. For an input ADAG $\mathcal{D} = \langle D, \alpha, \beta, \Psi, \delta \rangle$ such that some vertex $u \in U(\mathcal{D})$ has more than one parent, we construct an ADAG $\mathcal{D}' = \langle D', \alpha, \beta', \Psi, \delta' \rangle$ in the following way. Let $v_1, \ldots, v_k$ be the parents of u ($k > 1$). We construct the term-DAG D' from D by splitting u into $u_1, \ldots, u_k$ and making v_i the only parent of u_i. If $u' \neq u$, then we put $\delta'(u') = \delta(u)$ and $\beta'(u') = \beta(u')$. We put $\delta'(u_i) = \{p \in \delta(u) \mid \text{either } p \in Q,\ p \text{ is of the form } I^{(j)}, \text{ or } (p', v_i) \overset{\mathcal{D}}{\rightsquigarrow} (p, u), \text{ for some } p'\}$. For $r \in R \cup \{r_I\}, r \in \delta'(u_i)$, we put also $\beta'(u_i, r) = \beta(u, r)$. One can verify, that $\mathcal{D}'$ is in fact an ADAG. Note also that $\overline{U}(\mathcal{D}') = \overline{U}(\mathcal{D})$.

Starting with $\mathcal{D}_0$, we can repeat this procedure until we obtain an ADAG $\mathcal{D}_1 = \langle D_1, \alpha, \beta_1, \hat{\Phi}, \delta_1 \rangle$ for $(\Phi, \pi, \boldsymbol{e})$ such that each $v \in U(\mathcal{D}_1)$ has at most one parent and, because $\overline{U}(\mathcal{D}_0) = \overline{U}(\mathcal{D}_1)$, the number of goals is exponentially bounded. Now, we will minimize the number of vertices in $U(\mathcal{D}_1)$. Let V denotes the set of vertices of $\mathcal{D}_1$, let $U = U(\mathcal{D}_1)$, and $\overline{U} = \overline{U}(\mathcal{D}_1)$. Let $\prec$ be a linear ordering on V compatible with the DAG ordering (i.e. if v is a descendant of v' then $v \prec v'$). Let $v_1 \prec \cdots \prec v_{N-1}$ be all the vertices of $\overline{U}$. For $k = 0, \ldots, N$, we define the k-th segment U_k of $\mathcal{D}$ by the following equations: $U_0 = \{u \in U \mid u \prec v_1\}$, $U_N = \{u \in U \mid v_{N-1} \prec u\}$, and for $k = 1, \ldots, (N-1)$, $U_k = \{u \in U \mid v_{k-1} \prec u \prec v_k\}$. Note that $\bigcup_{k=1}^{N} U_k = U$.

For a vertex v, let $\rho(v) = \{u \mid u \text{ is a goal and } v \overset{\mathcal{D}_1}{\rightsquigarrow} {*} u\}$. Let $v, v' \in U_k$ (for $k = 0, \ldots, N$). Suppose that $\rho(v) = \rho(v')$ and $\delta(v) = \delta(v')$. Then we have either $v < v'$ or $v' < v$. Let us assume that $v < v'$ holds. Let us remove v and replace it by v' (i.e. whenever v was a child of u, we make v' a child of u instead). For each $r \in \delta(v')$, let $\beta(v', r) = \beta(v, r)$. One can prove that what we have obtained is an ADAG. We repeat this procedure until the ADAG has no two distinct vertices $v, v' \in U_k$, for some k, with $\rho(v) = \rho(v')$ and $\delta(v) = \delta(v')$.

Because $|\overline{U}| = |\overline{U}(\mathcal{D}_0)|$ is exponentially bounded and $N = |\overline{U}|$, to complete the proof it is enough to show that each U_k is exponentially bounded. Let M denote the number of goals of the resulting ADAG (which is equal to the number of goals of $\mathcal{D}_0$) and K denote the number of distinct possible values of δ. One can show that each path in U_k is not longer than $M \cdot K$ (since vertices from U_k can have at most one parent, the values of $\rho(u)$ can only decrease along a path). One can also show that, if $v, v' \in U_k$ are not on the same path, then $\rho(v) \cap \rho(v') = \emptyset$, and thus, the number of distinct (maximal) paths in U_k is bounded by M. Hence, the size of U_k is bounded by $M^2 \cdot K$ which is exponential w.r.t. the size of (P, Φ). □

5 Conclusions

We have introduced a new formalism to model recursive cryptographic protocols. In this formalism, one can express protocols such that participants are able to send many messages in one step, to compare, and to store messages. Usefulness of the proposed model is illustrated by an example. We have proven that the insecurity problem of protocols with selecting theories w.r.t. a bounded number of sessions is decidable in NEXPTIME.

The proof technique used in this paper (stage theories, representing attacks by ADAGs) is, in its outline, an adaptation of the method used in [17] to prove NP-completeness of insecurity of (non-recursive) protocols, where the initial knowledge of the intruder is a regular language of terms. In [17], however, the minimization of an ADAG is relatively simple and straightforward, whereas in this paper, it is the main technical difficulty.

Future work. The exact complexity of the problem of deciding protocols with selecting theories is not known. Another open problem is decidability of security of protocols with selecting theories and *with complex keys*.

References

1. Roberto M. Amadio and Witold Charatonik, *On name generation and set-based analysis in the Dolev-Yao model*, CONCUR, Lecture Notes in Computer Science, vol. 2421, Springer, 2002, pp. 499–514.
2. G. Ateniese, M. Steiner, and G. Tsudik, *Authenticated group key agreement and friends*, Proceedings of the 5th ACM Conference on Computer and Communication Serucity (CCS'98), ACM Press, 1998.
3. J. Bryans and S.A. Schneider, *CSP, PVS, and a recursive authentication protocol*, DIMACS Workshop on Formal Verification of Security Protocols, 1997.
4. J.A. Bull and D.J. Otway, *The authentication protocol*, Technical Report DRA/CIS3/PROJ/CORBA/SC/1/CSM/436-04/-03, Defence Research Agency, Malvern, UK, 1997.
5. Y. Chevalier, R. Küsters, M. Rusinowitch, and M. Turuani, *Deciding the security of protocols with Diffie-Hellman exponentiation and products in exponents*, FSTTCS, 2003.
6. ———, *An NP decision procedure for protocol insecurity with XOR*, LICS, 2003.
7. H. Comon and V. Shmatikov, *Is it possible to decide whether a cryptographic protocol is secure or not?*, Journal of Telecommunications and Information Technology, special issue on cryptographic protocol verification **4** (2002), 5–15.
8. H. Comon-Lundh and V. Shmatikov, *Intruder deductions, constraint solving and indecurity decision in presence of exclusive or*, LICS, 2003.
9. D. Dolev and A.C. Yao, *On the security of public-key protocols*, IEEE Transactions on Information Theory **29** (1983), 198–208.
10. N.A. Durgin, P.D. Lincoln, J.C. Mitchell, and A. Scedrov, *Undecidability of bounded security protocols*, Workshop on Formal Methods and Security Protocols (FMSP'99), 1999.

11. S. Even and O. Goldreich, *On the security of multi-party ping-pong protocols*, Technical Report 285, Israel Institute of Technology, 1983.
12. Ralf Küsters and Thomas Wilke, *Automata-based analysis of recursive cryptographic protocols*, Technical Report IFI 0311, CAU Kiel, 2003.
13. ______, *Automata-based analysis of recursive cryptographic protocols*, STACS, Lecture Notes in Computer Science, vol. 2996, Springer, 2004, pp. 382–393.
14. Catherine Meadows, *Formal methods for cryptographic protocol analysis: Emerging issues and trends*, IEEE Journal on Selected Areas in Communication **21** (2003), no. 1, 44–54.
15. L.C. Paulson, *Mechanized proofs for a recursive authentication protocol*, 10th IEE Computer Security Foundations Workshop (CSFW-10), IEEE Press, 1997.
16. Michaël Rusinowitch and Mathieu Turuani, *Protocol insecurity with a finite number of sessions, composed keys is NP-complete*, Theor. Comput. Sci. **1-3** (2003), no. 299, 451–475.
17. Tomasz Truderung, *Regular protocols and attacks with regular knowledge*, Proceedings of CADE 2005, LNCS, Springer, 2005, to appear.

Constraint Solving for Contract-Signing Protocols

Detlef Kähler and Ralf Küsters

Institut für Informatik und Praktische Mathematik,
Christian-Albrechts-Universität zu Kiel, 24098 Kiel, Germany
{kaehler, kuesters}@ti.informatik.uni-kiel.de

Abstract. Research on the automatic analysis of cryptographic protocols has so far mainly concentrated on reachability properties, such as secrecy and authentication. Only recently it was shown that certain game-theoretic security properties, such as balance for contract-signing protocols, are decidable in a Dolev-Yao style model with a bounded number of sessions but unbounded message size. However, this result does not provide a practical algorithm as it merely bounds the size of attacks. In this paper, we prove that game-theoretic security properties can be decided based on standard constraint solving procedures. In the past, these procedures have successfully been employed in implementations and tools for reachability properties. Our results thus pave the way for extending these tools and implementations to deal with game-theoretic security properties.

1 Introduction

One of the central results in the area of automatic analysis of cryptographic protocols is that the security of cryptographic protocols is decidable when analyzed w.r.t. a finite number of sessions, without a bound on the message size, and in presence of the so-called Dolev-Yao intruder (see, e.g., [14,1]). Based on this result, many fully automatic tools (see, e.g., [2,7,13]) have been developed and successfully been applied to find flaws in published protocols, where many of these tools employ so-called *constraint solving procedures* (see, e.g., [13,7,4]). However, the mentioned decidability result and tools are restricted to security properties such as authentication and secrecy which are reachability properties of the transition system associated with a given protocol. In contrast, crucial properties required of contract-signing and related protocols (see, e.g., [9,3]), for instance abuse-freeness [9] and balance [5], are game-theoretic properties of the structure of the transition system associated with a protocol. Balance, for instance, requires that in no stage of a protocol run, the intruder or a dishonest party has both a strategy to abort the run and a strategy to successfully complete the run and thus obtain a valid contract.

Only recently [11], the central decidability result mentioned above was extended to such game-theoretic security properties, including, for instance, balance. However, similar to the result by Rusinowitch and Turuani [14] for reachability properties, the decision algorithm presented in [11] is merely based on the fact that the size of attacks can be bounded, and hence, all potential attacks up to a certain size have to be enumerated and checked. Clearly, just as in the case of reachability properties, this is completely impractical. For reachability properties, one has therefore developed the mentioned constraint solving procedures to obtain practical decision algorithms.

M. Abadi and L. de Alfaro (Eds.): CONCUR 2005, LNCS 3653, pp. 233–247, 2005.

The main contribution of the present work is a *constraint-based* decision algorithm for the game-theoretic security properties of the kind considered in [11]. The main feature of our algorithm is that it can be built on top of *standard constraint solving procedures* (see, e.g., [13,7,4] and references therein). As mentioned, such procedures have successfully been employed for reachability properties in the past and proved to be a good basis for practical implementations. Hence, our algorithm paves the way for extending existing implementations and tools for reachability properties to deal with game-theoretic security properties.

In a nutshell, our constraint-based algorithm works as follows: Given a protocol along with the considered game-theoretic security property, first the algorithm guesses what we call a symbolic branching structure. This structure represents a potential attack on the protocol and corresponds to the interleavings, which are, however, linear structures, guessed for reachability properties. In the second step of the algorithm, the symbolic branching structure is turned into a constraint system. This step requires some care due to the branching issue and write-protected channels considered in our model (also called secure channels here), i.e., channels that are not under the control of the intruder. Then, a standard constraint solving procedure is used to compute a finite sound and complete set of so-called simple constraint systems. A simple constraint system in such a set represents a (possibly infinite) set of solutions of the original constraint system and the sound and complete set of these simple constraint systems represents the set of *all* solutions of the original constraint system. Finally, it is checked whether (at least) one of the computed simple constraint systems in the sound and complete set passes certain additional tests.

There are some crucial differences of our constraint-based algorithm to algorithms for reachability properties: First, as mentioned, instead of symbolic branching structures, for reachability properties only interleavings, i.e., linear structures, need to be guessed. Turning these interleavings into constraint systems is immediate due to the absence of the branching issue and the absence of secure channels. Second, and more importantly, for reachability properties it suffices if the constraint solving procedure only returns one simple constraint system, rather than a sound and complete set. Third, the final step of our constraint-based algorithm—performing additional tests on the simple constraint system—is not required for reachability properties.

We emphasize that even though for reachability properties it suffices if the constraint solving procedure returns only one simple constraint system, standard constraint solving procedures are typically capable of computing sound and complete sets of simple constraint systems. Any such procedure can be used by our constraint-based algorithm as a black-box for solving constraint systems. This makes it possible to extend existing implementations and tools for reachability properties to deal with game-theoretic properties since the core of the algorithms—solving constraint systems—remains the same, provided that the considered cryptographic primitives can be dealt with by the constraint solving procedure (see Section 4).

The protocol and intruder model that we use is basically the one proposed in [11], which in turn is the "bounded session" version of a model proposed in [5]. We slightly modify the model of [11]—without changing its expressivity and accuracy—in order to simplify our constraint-based algorithm (see Section 2 and 3).

Further Related Work. Contract-signing and related protocols have been analyzed both manually [5], based on a relatively detailed model (as mentioned before, our model is a "bounded session" version of this model), and using finite-state model checking (see, e.g., [15,12]), based on a coarser finite-state model. Drielsma and Mödersheim [8] were the first to apply an automatic tool based on constraint solving to the contract-signing protocol by Asokan, Shoup, and Waidner [3]. Their analysis is, however, restricted to reachability properties since game-theoretic properties cannot be handled by their tool. The results shown in the present work pave the way for extending such tools in order to be able to analyze game-theoretic properties.

Structure of This Paper. We first introduce our protocol and intruder model (Section 2) as well as intruder strategies and game-theoretic properties (Section 3). Section 4 provides the necessary background on constraint solving. In Section 5, we present our constraint-based decision algorithm along with an example and state our main result—soundness, completeness, and termination of the algorithm. We conclude in Section 6. Full definitions and proofs can be found in our technical report [10].

2 The Protocol and Intruder Model

The protocol and intruder model that we use basically coincides with the model first introduced in [11], which in turn is the "bounded session" version of the model proposed in [5]. We only slightly modify the model in [11] in that we impose a restriction on principals which is necessary for principals to perform feasible computations.

In our model, a protocol is a finite set of principals and every principal is a finite tree, which represents all possible behaviors of the principal, including all subprotocols a principal can carry out. Each edge of such a tree is labeled by a rewrite rule, which describes the receive-send action that is performed when the principal takes this edge in a run of the protocol.

When a principal carries out a protocol, it traverses its tree, starting at the root. In every node, the principal takes its current input, chooses one of the edges leaving the node, matches the current input with the left-hand side of the rule the edge is labeled with, sends out the message which is determined by the right-hand side of the rule, and moves to the node the chosen edge leads to. While in the standard Dolev-Yao model (see, e.g., [14]) inputs to principals are always provided by the intruder, in our model inputs can also come from the secure channel. Secure channels are typically used by principals in contract-signing protocols to communicate with a trusted third party. The important point is that these channels are not controlled by the intruder, i.e., the intruder cannot delay, duplicate, remove messages, or write messages onto this channel under a fake identity (unless he has corrupted a party). However, just as in [5], the intruder can read the messages written onto the secure channel. We note that our results also hold in case of read-protected secure channels. Another difference to standard Dolev-Yao models is that, in order to be able to formulate game-theoretic properties, we explicitly describe the behavior of a protocol as an infinite-state transition graph which comprises all runs of a protocol.

We now describe the model in more detail by defining terms and messages, the intruder, principals and protocols, and the transition graph.

Terms and Messages. As usual, we have a finite set $\mathcal{V}$ of variables, a finite set $\mathcal{A}$ of atoms, a finite set $\mathcal{K}$ of public and private keys equipped with a bijection $\cdot^{-1}$ assigning public to private keys and vice versa. In addition, we have a finite set $\mathcal{N}$ of *principal addresses* for the secure channels and an *infinite* set $\mathcal{A}_I$ of *intruder atoms*, containing nonces and symmetric keys the intruder can generate. All of the mentioned sets are assumed to be disjoint.

We define two kinds of terms by the following grammar, namely *plain terms* and *secure channel terms*:

$$\begin{aligned} \textit{plain-terms} &::= \mathcal{V} \mid \mathcal{A} \mid \mathcal{A}_I \mid \langle \textit{plain-terms}, \textit{plain-terms} \rangle \mid \{\textit{plain-terms}\}^s_{\textit{plain-terms}} \mid \\ &\qquad \{\textit{plain-terms}\}^a_{\mathcal{K}} \mid \mathsf{hash}(\textit{plain-terms}) \mid \mathsf{sig}_{\mathcal{K}}(\textit{plain-terms}) \\ \textit{sec-terms} &::= \mathsf{sc}(\mathcal{N}, \mathcal{N}, \textit{plain-terms}) \\ \textit{terms} &::= \textit{plain-terms} \mid \textit{sec-terms} \mid \mathcal{N} \end{aligned}$$

While the plain terms are standard in Dolev-Yao models, a secure channel term of the form $\mathsf{sc}(n, n', t)$ stands for feeding the secure channel from n to n' with t. Knowing n grants access to secure channels with sender address n. A *(plain/secure channel) message* is a (plain/secure channel) ground term, i.e., a term without variables.

Intruder. Given a set $\mathcal{I}$ of messages, the (infinite) set $d(\mathcal{I})$ of messages the intruder can derive from $\mathcal{I}$ is the smallest set satisfying the following conditions: $\mathcal{I} \subseteq d(\mathcal{I})$; if $m, m' \in d(\mathcal{I})$, then $\langle m, m' \rangle \in d(\mathcal{I})$; if $\langle m, m' \rangle \in d(\mathcal{I})$, then $m \in d(\mathcal{I})$ and $m' \in d(\mathcal{I})$; if $m, m' \in d(\mathcal{I})$, then $\{m\}^s_{m'} \in d(\mathcal{I})$; if $\{m\}^s_{m'} \in d(\mathcal{I})$ and $m' \in d(\mathcal{I})$, then $m \in d(\mathcal{I})$; if $m \in d(\mathcal{I})$ and $k \in d(\mathcal{I}) \cap \mathcal{K}$, then $\{m\}^a_k \in d(\mathcal{I})$; if $\{m\}^a_k \in d(\mathcal{I})$ and $k^{-1} \in d(\mathcal{I})$, then $m \in d(\mathcal{I})$; if $m \in d(\mathcal{I})$, then $\mathsf{hash}(m) \in d(\mathcal{I})$; if $m \in d(\mathcal{I})$ and $k^{-1} \in d(\mathcal{I}) \cap \mathcal{K}$, then $\mathsf{sig}_k(m) \in d(\mathcal{I})$ (the signature contains the public key but can only be generated if the corresponding private key is known); if $m \in d(\mathcal{I})$, $n \in d(\mathcal{I}) \cap \mathcal{N}$, and $n' \in \mathcal{N}$, then $\mathsf{sc}(n, n', m) \in d(\mathcal{I})$ (*writing onto the secure channel*); $\mathcal{A}_I \subseteq d(\mathcal{I})$ (*generating fresh constants*).

Intuitively, $n \in d(\mathcal{I}) \cap \mathcal{N}$ means that the intruder has corrupted the principal with address n and therefore can impersonate this principal when writing onto the secure channel.

In our model, all (strongly) dishonest parties are subsumed in the intruder. Weakly dishonest parties can be modeled as principals whose specification deviates from the specification of the protocol.

Principals and Protocols. Principal rules are of the form $L \Rightarrow R$ where L is a term or ε and R is a term.

A *rule tree* $\Pi = (V, E, r, \ell)$ is a finite tree rooted at $r \in V$ where ℓ maps every edge $(v, v') \in E$ of Π to a principal rule $\ell(v, v')$.

A *principal* is a tuple consisting of a rule tree $\Pi = (V, E, r, \ell)$ and a finite set of plain messages, the *initial knowledge of the principal*. Similar to models for reachability properties, we require that every variable occurring on the right-hand side of a principal rule $\ell(v, v')$ in Π also occurs on the left-hand side of $\ell(v, v')$ or on the left-hand side of a principal rule on the path from r to v. In addition, and unlike [11], we require a condition necessary for the principal to perform a feasible computation: The decryption and signature verification operations performed when receiving a message can actually be carried out, i.e., terms in key positions (t' in $\{t\}^s_{t'}$, k^{-1} in $\{t\}^a_k$, and k in $\mathsf{sig}_k(t)$) on the left-hand side of principal rules can be derived from the set consisting of the left-hand side of the current principal rule, the left-hand sides of preceeding rules, and the initial knowledge of the principal. Obviously, the above condition is satisfied for all realistic principals. Moreover, it allows to simplify the constraint-based algorithm (Section 5).

For $v \in V$, we write $\Pi{\downarrow}v$ to denote the subtree of Π rooted at v. For a substitution σ, we write $\Pi\sigma$ for the principal obtained from Π by substituting all variables x occurring in the principal rules of Π by $\sigma(x)$.

A *protocol* $P = ((\Pi_1, \ldots, \Pi_n), \mathcal{I})$ consists of a finite sequence of principals Π_i and a finite set $\mathcal{I}$ of messages, the *initial intruder knowledge*. We require that each variable occurs in the rules of only one principal, i.e., different principals must have disjoint sets of variables. We assume that intruder atoms, i.e., elements of $\mathcal{A}_I$, do not occur in P.

As an example protocol, let us consider P_{ex} as depicted in Figure 1. This protocol consists of two principals Π_1 and Π_2 and the initial knowledge $\mathcal{I}_0 = \{\{a\}^s_k, \{b\}^s_k\}$ of the intruder. Informally speaking, Π_2 can, without waiting for input from the secure channel or the intruder, decide whether to write $\langle a, b\rangle$ or $\langle b, b\rangle$ into the secure channel from Π_2 to Π_1. While the intruder can read the message written into this channel, he cannot modify or delay this message. Also, he cannot insert his own message into this channel as he does not have the principal address 2 in his intruder knowledge, and hence, cannot generate messages of the form $\mathsf{sc}(2, \cdot, t)$. Consequently, such messages must come from Π_2. Principal Π_1 first waits for a message of the form $\langle x, b\rangle$ in the secure channel from Π_2 to Π_1. In case Π_2 wrote, say, $\langle a, b\rangle$ into this channel, x is substituted by a, and this message is written into the network, and hence, given to the intruder. Next, Π_1 waits for input of the form $\{y\}^s_k$. This is not a secure channel term, and thus, comes from the intruder. In case the intruder sends $\{b\}^s_k$, say, then y is substituted by b. Finally, Π_1 waits for input of the form a (in the edges from f_3 to f_4 and f_3 to f_5) or b (in the edge from f_3 to f_6). Recall that x was substituted by a and y by b. If the intruder sends b, say, then Π_2 takes the edge from f_3 to f_6 and outputs c_2 into the network. If the intruder had sent a, Π_1 could have chosen between the first two edges. We note that this protocol is not meant to perform a useful task. It is rather used to illustrate different aspects of our constraint-based algorithm ([11] contains a formal specification of the contract-signing protocol by Asokan, Shoup, and Waidner [3] in our model).

2.1 Transition Graph Induced by a Protocol

A transition graph $\mathcal{G}_P$ induced by a protocol P comprises all runs of a protocol. To define this graph, we first introduce states and transitions between these states.

A *state* is of the form $((\Pi_1, \ldots, \Pi_n), \sigma, \mathcal{I}, \mathcal{S})$ where σ is a ground substitution, for each i, Π_i is a rule tree such that $\Pi_i\sigma$ is a principal, $\mathcal{I}$ is a finite set of messages, the *intruder knowledge*, and $\mathcal{S}$ is a finite multi-set of secure channel messages, the *secure channel*. The idea is that when the transition system gets to such a state, then the substitution σ has been performed, the accumulated intruder knowledge is what can

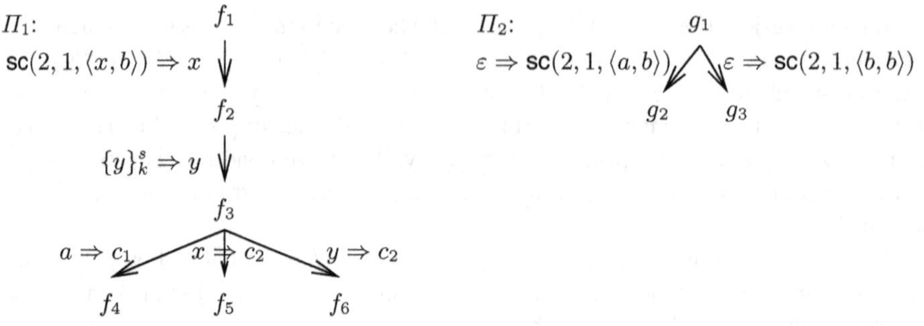

Fig. 1. Protocol $P_{ex} = (\{\Pi_1, \Pi_2\}, \mathcal{I}_0)$ with $\mathcal{I}_0 = \{\{a\}^s_k, \{b\}^s_k\}$, initial knowledge $\{1, a, b, k, c_1, c_2\}$ of Π_1 and initial knowledge $\{2, a, b\}$ of Π_2.

be derived from $\mathcal{I}$, the secure channels hold the messages in $\mathcal{S}$, and for each i, Π_i is the "remaining protocol" to be carried out by principal i. This also explains why $\mathcal{S}$ is a multi-set: messages sent several times should be delivered several times. Given a protocol $P = ((\Pi_1, \ldots, \Pi_n), \mathcal{I})$ the *initial state of* P is $((\Pi_1, \ldots, \Pi_n), \sigma, \mathcal{I}, \emptyset)$ where σ is the substitution with empty domain.

We have three kinds of transitions: intruder, secure channel, and ε-transitions. In what follows, let $\Pi_i = (V_i, E_i, r_i, \ell_i)$ and $\Pi'_i = (V'_i, E'_i, r'_i, \ell'_i)$ denote rule trees. We define under which circumstances there is a transition

$$((\Pi_1, \ldots, \Pi_n), \sigma, \mathcal{I}, \mathcal{S}) \xrightarrow{\tau} ((\Pi'_1, \ldots, \Pi'_n), \sigma', \mathcal{I}', \mathcal{S}') \qquad (1)$$

with τ an appropriate label.

1. *Intruder transitions:* The transition (1) with label i, m, I exists if there exists $v \in V_i$ with $(r_i, v) \in E_i$ and $\ell_i(r_i, v) = L \Rightarrow R$, and a substitution σ'' of the variables in $L\sigma$ such that (a) $m \in d(\mathcal{I})$, (b) $\sigma' = \sigma \cup \sigma''$, (c) $L\sigma' = m$, (d) $\Pi'_j = \Pi_j$ for every $j \neq i$, $\Pi'_i = \Pi_i{\downarrow}v$, (e) $\mathcal{I}' = \mathcal{I} \cup \{R\sigma'\}$ if $R \neq \mathsf{sc}(\cdot,\cdot,\cdot)$, and $\mathcal{I}' = \mathcal{I} \cup \{t\sigma'\}$ if $R = \mathsf{sc}(\cdot,\cdot,t)$ for some t, (f) $\mathcal{S}' = \mathcal{S}$ if $R \neq \mathsf{sc}(\cdot,\cdot,\cdot)$, and $\mathcal{S}' = \mathcal{S} \cup \{R\sigma'\}$ otherwise. This transition models that principal i reads the message m from the intruder (i.e., the public network).
2. *Secure channel transitions:* The transition (1) with label i, m, sc exists if there exists $v \in V_i$ with $(r_i, v) \in E_i$ and $\ell_i(r_i, v) = L \Rightarrow R$, and a substitution σ'' of the variables in $L\sigma$ such that $m \in \mathcal{S}$, (b)–(e) from 1., and $\mathcal{S}' = \mathcal{S} \setminus \{m\}$ if $R \neq \mathsf{sc}(\cdot,\cdot,\cdot)$, and $\mathcal{S}' = (\mathcal{S} \setminus \{m\}) \cup \{R\sigma'\}$ otherwise. This transition models that principal i reads message m from the secure channel.
3. *ε-transitions:* The transition (1) with label i exists if there exists $v \in V_i$ with $(r_i, v) \in E_i$ and $\ell_i(r_i, v) = \varepsilon \Rightarrow R$ such that $\sigma' = \sigma$ and (d), (e), (f) from above. This transition models that i performs a step where neither a message is read from the intruder nor from the secure channel.

Given a protocol P, the *transition graph* $\mathcal{G}_P$ *induced by* P is the tuple (S_P, E_P, q_P) where q_P is the initial state of P, S_P is the set of states reachable from q_P by a sequence of transitions, and E_P is the set of all transitions among states in S_P. We write $q \in \mathcal{G}_P$ if q is a state in $\mathcal{G}_P$ and $q \xrightarrow{\tau} q' \in \mathcal{G}_P$ if $q \xrightarrow{\tau} q'$ is a transition in $\mathcal{G}_P$.

We note that $\mathcal{G}_P$ is a DAG since by performing a transition, the size of the first component of a state decreases. While the graph may be infinite branching, the maximal length of a path in this graph is bounded by the total number of edges in the principals Π_i of P.

3 Intruder Strategies and Strategy Properties

We now define intruder strategies on transition graphs and the goal the intruder tries to achieve following his strategy. To define intruder strategies, we introduce the notion of a strategy tree, which captures that the intruder has a way of acting such that regardless of how the other principals act he achieves a certain goal, where goal in our context means that a state will be reached where the intruder can derive certain constants and cannot derive others (e.g., for balance, the intruder tries to obtain IntruderHasContract but tries to prevent HonestPartyHasContract from occurring).

More concretely, let us consider the protocol P_{ex} depicted in Figure 1. We want to know if the intruder has a strategy to get to a state where he can derive atom c_2 but not atom c_1 (no matter what the principals Π_1 and Π_2 do). Such a strategy of the intruder has to deal with both decisions principal Π_2 may make in the first step because the intruder cannot control which edge is taken by Π_2. It turns out that regardless of which message is sent by principal Π_2 in its first step, the following simple strategy allows the intruder to achieve his goal: The intruder can send $\{b\}_k^s$ to principal Π_1 in the second step of Π_1 and in the last step of Π_1, the intruder sends b to principal Π_1. This guarantees that in the last step of Π_1, the left-most edge is never taken, and thus, c_1 is not returned, but at least one of the other two edges can be taken, which in any case yields c_2. Formally, such strategies are defined as trees. In our example, the strategy tree corresponding to the strategy informally explained above is depicted in Figure 2.

Definition 1. *For $q \in \mathcal{G}_P$ a q-*strategy tree *$\mathcal{T}_q = (V, E, r, \ell_V, \ell_E)$ is an unordered tree where every vertex $v \in V$ is mapped to a state $\ell_V(v) \in \mathcal{G}_P$ and every edge $(v, v') \in E$ is mapped to a label of a transition such that the following conditions are satisfied for all $v, v' \in V$, principals j, messages m, and states q', q'':*

1. *$\ell_V(r) = q$.*
2. *$\ell_V(v) \xrightarrow{\ell_E(v,v')} \ell_V(v') \in \mathcal{G}_P$ for all $(v, v') \in E$. (Edges correspond to transitions.)*
3. *If $\ell_V(v) = q'$ and $q' \xrightarrow{j} q'' \in \mathcal{G}_P$, then there exists $v'' \in V$ such that $(v, v'') \in E$, $\ell_V(v'') = q''$, and $\ell_E(v, v'') = j$. (All ε-transitions originating in q' must be present in $\mathcal{T}_q$.)*
4. *If $\ell_V(v) = q'$ and $q' \xrightarrow{j,m,\mathsf{sc}} q'' \in \mathcal{G}_P$, then there exists $v'' \in V$ such that $(v, v'') \in E$, $\ell_V(v'') = q''$, and $\ell_E(v, v'') = j, m,$ sc. (The same as 3. for secure channel transitions.)*
5. *If $(v, v') \in E$, $\ell_E(v, v') = j, m, I$, and there exists $q'' \neq \ell_V(v')$ with $\ell_V(v) \xrightarrow{j,m,I} q'' \in \mathcal{G}_P$, then there exists v'' with $(v, v'') \in E$, $\ell_E(v, v'') = j, m, I$ and $\ell_V(v'') = q''$. (The intruder cannot choose which principal rule is taken by j if several are possible given the input provided by the intruder.)*

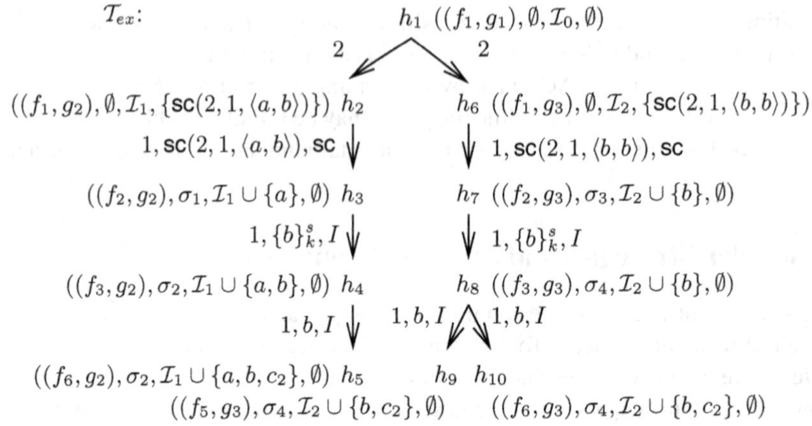

Fig. 2. Strategy tree $\mathcal{T}_{ex}$ for P_{ex} with $\mathcal{I}_1 = \mathcal{I}_0 \cup \{\langle a, b\rangle\}$, $\mathcal{I}_2 = \mathcal{I}_0 \cup \{\langle b, b\rangle\}$, $\sigma_1 = \{x \mapsto a\}$, $\sigma_2 = \sigma_1 \cup \{y \mapsto b\}$, $\sigma_3 = \{x \mapsto b\}$, and $\sigma_4 = \sigma_3 \cup \{y \mapsto b\}$. Also, for brevity of notation, in the first component of the states we write, for instance, f_1 instead of $\Pi_1{\downarrow}f_1$. The strategy property we consider is $((C_{ex}, C'_{ex})) = ((\{c_2\}, \{c_1\}))$.

A *strategy property*, i.e., the goal the intruder tries to achieve, is a tuple $((C_1, C'_1), \ldots, (C_l, C'_l))$ where $C_i, C'_i \subseteq \mathcal{A} \cup \mathcal{K} \cup \mathcal{N}$. A state $q \in \mathcal{G}_P$ satisfies $((C_1, C'_1), \ldots, (C_l, C'_l))$ if there exist q-strategy trees $\mathcal{T}_1, \ldots, \mathcal{T}_l$ such that every $\mathcal{T}_i$ satisfies (C_i, C'_i) where $\mathcal{T}_i$ satisfies (C_i, C'_i) if for all leaves v of $\mathcal{T}_i$ all elements from C_i can be derived by the intruder and all elements from C'_i cannot, i.e., $C_i \subseteq d(\mathcal{I})$ and $C'_i \cap d(\mathcal{I}) = \emptyset$ where $\mathcal{I}$ denotes the intruder knowledge in state $\ell_V(v)$.

The decision problem STRATEGY asks, given a protocol P and a strategy property $((C_1, C'_1), \ldots, (C_l, C'_l))$, whether there exists a state $q \in \mathcal{G}_P$ that satisfies the property. In this case we write $(P, (C_1, C'_1), \ldots, (C_l, C'_l)) \in$ STRATEGY.

Note that in a q-strategy tree $\mathcal{T}_q$ there may exist vertices $v' \neq v$ with $\ell_V(v') = \ell_V(v)$ such that the subtrees $\mathcal{T}_q{\downarrow}v$ and $\mathcal{T}_q{\downarrow}v'$ of $\mathcal{T}_q$ rooted at v and v', respectively, are not isomorphic. In other words, the intruder's strategy may depend on the path that leads to a state (i.e., the history) rather than on the state alone, as is the case for positional strategies. We note that the strategies defined in [11] are positional. However, it is easy to see that in our setting both notions of strategies are equivalent. The motivation for using history dependent strategies is that the constraint-based algorithm (Section 5) becomes considerably simpler.

4 Constraint Solving

In this section, we introduce constraint systems and state the well-known fact that procedures for solving these systems exist (see, e.g., [13,10] for more details). In Section 5, we will then use such a procedure as a black-box for our constraint-based algorithm.

A *constraint* is of the form $t : T$ where t is a plain term and T is a finite non-empty set of plain terms. Since we will take care of secure channel terms when turning the symbolic branching structure into a constraint system, we can disallow secure channel terms in constraints.

A *constraint system* **C** is a tuple consisting of a sequence $s = t_1 : T_1, \ldots, t_n : T_n$ of constraints and a substitution τ such that i) the domain of τ is disjoint from the set of variables occurring in s and, ii) for all x in the domain of τ, $\tau(x)$ only contains variables also occurring in s. We call **C** *simple* if t_i is a variable for all i. We call **C** *valid* if it satisfies the origination and monotonicity property as defined in [13]. The precise definition of valid constraint systems is not needed for the rest of the paper. Let us only note that origination and monotonicity are standard restrictions on constraint systems imposed by constraint solving procedures. Valid constraint systems are all that is needed in our setting.

A ground substitution σ where the domain of σ is the set of variables in $t_1 : T_1, \ldots, t_n : T_n$ is a *solution* of **C** ($\sigma \vdash \mathbf{C}$) if $t_i\sigma \in d(T_i\sigma)$ for every i. We call $\sigma \circ \tau$ (the composition of σ and τ read from right to left) a *complete* solution of **C** ($\sigma \circ \tau \vdash_c \mathbf{C}$) with τ as above.

A simple constraint system **C** obviously has a solution. One such solution, which we denote by σ_C, replaces all variables in **C** by new intruder atoms $a \in \mathcal{A}_I$ where different variables are replaced by different atoms. We call σ_C the *solution associated with* **C** and $\sigma_C \circ \tau$ the *complete solution associated with* **C**.

Given a constraint system **C**, a finite set $\{\mathbf{C}_1, \ldots, \mathbf{C}_n\}$ of simple constraint systems is called a *sound and complete solution set for* **C** if $\{\nu \mid \nu \vdash_c \mathbf{C}\} = \{\nu \mid \exists i \text{ s.t. } \nu \vdash_c \mathbf{C}_i\}$. Note that **C** does not have a solution iff $n = 0$.

From results shown, for example, in [7,13,4] it follows:

Fact 1. *There exists a procedure which given a valid constraint system* **C** *outputs a sound and complete solution set for* **C**.

While different constraint solving procedures (and implementations thereof) may compute different sound and complete solution sets, our constraint-based algorithm introduced in Section 5 works with any of these procedures. It is only important that the set computed is sound and complete. As already mentioned in the introduction, to decide reachability properties it suffices if the procedure only returns one simple constraint system in the sound and complete set. However, the constraint solving procedures proposed in the literature are typically capable of returning a sound and complete solution set.

In what follows, we fix one such procedure and call it the *constraint solver*. More precisely, w.l.o.g., we consider the constraint solver to be a non-deterministic algorithm which non-deterministically chooses a simple constraint system from the sound and complete solution set and returns this system as output. We require that for every simple constraint system in the sound and complete solution set, there is a run of the constraint solver that returns this system. If the sound and complete set is empty, the constraint solver always returns no.

We note that while standard constraint solving procedures can deal with the cryptographic primitives considered here, these procedures might need to be extended when adding further cryptographic primitives. For example, this is the case for private contract signatures, which are used in some contract signing protocols [9] and were taken into account in [11]. However, constraint solving procedures can easily be extended to deal with these signatures. We have not considered them here for brevity of presentation and since the main focus of the present work is not to extend constraint solving procedures but to show how these procedures can be employed to deal with game-theoretic security properties.

5 The Constraint-Based Algorithm

We now present our constraint-based algorithm, called SolveStrategy, for deciding STRATEGY. As mentioned, it uses a standard constraint solver (Fact 1) as a subprocedure.

In what follows, we present the main steps performed by SolveStrategy, with more details given in subsequent sections. The input to SolveStrategy is a protocol P and a strategy property $((C_1, C_1'), \ldots, (C_l, C_l'))$.

1. Guess a symbolic branching structure $\mathbf{B}$, i.e., guess a symbolic path π^s from the initial state of P to a symbolic state q^s and a symbolic q^s-strategy tree $\mathcal{T}^s_{i,q^s}$ for every (C_i, C_i') starting from this state (see Section 5.1 for more details).
2. Derive from $\mathbf{B} = \pi^s, \mathcal{T}^s_{1,q^s}, \ldots, \mathcal{T}^s_{l,q^s}$ and the strategy property $((C_1, C_1'), \ldots, (C_l, C_l'))$ the induced and valid constraint system $\mathbf{C} = \mathbf{C_B}$ (see Section 5.2 for the definition). Then, run the constraint solver on $\mathbf{C}$. If it returns no, then halt. Otherwise, let $\mathbf{C}'$ be the simple constraint system returned by the solver. (Recall that $\mathbf{C}'$ belongs to the sound and complete solution set and is chosen non-deterministically by the solver.)
3. Let ν be the complete solution associated with $\mathbf{C}'$. Check whether ν when applied to $\mathbf{B}$ yields a valid path in $\mathcal{G}_P$ from the initial state of P to a state q and q-strategy trees $\mathcal{T}_{i,q}$ satisfying (C_i, C_i') for every i. If so, output yes and $\mathbf{B}$ with ν applied, and otherwise return no (see Section 5.3 for more details). In case yes is returned, $\mathbf{B}$ with ν applied yields a concrete solution of the problem instance $(P, (C_1, C_1'), \ldots, (C_l, C_l'))$.

We emphasize that, for simplicity of presentation, SolveStrategy is formulated as a non-deterministic algorithm. Hence, the overall decision of SolveStrategy is yes if there exists at least one computation path where yes is returned. Otherwise, the overall decision is no (i.e., $(P, (C_1, C_1'), \ldots, (C_l, C_l')) \notin$ STRATEGY).

In the following three sections, the three steps of SolveStrategy are further explained. Our main result is the following theorem:

Theorem 1. *SolveStrategy is a decision procedure for* STRATEGY.

Recall that decidability of STRATEGY was already shown in [11]. The main point of Theorem 1 is that SolveStrategy uses standard constraint solving procedures as a black-box, and as such, is a good basis for extending existing practical constraint-based algorithms for reachability properties to deal with game-theoretic security properties.

The proof of Theorem 1 is quite different from the cut-and-paste argument in [11] where, similar to [14], it was shown that an attack can be turned into a "small" attack. Here we rather make use of the fact that procedures for computing sound and complete

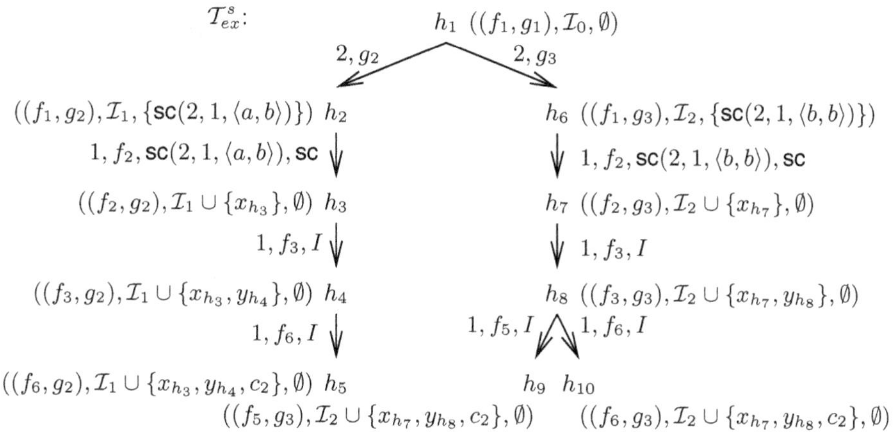

Fig. 3. Symbolic strategy tree $\mathcal{T}^s_{ex}$ for the protocol P_{ex} where $\mathcal{I}_1 = \mathcal{I}_0 \cup \{\langle a, b\rangle\}$ and $\mathcal{I}_2 = \mathcal{I}_0 \cup \{\langle b, b\rangle\}$. For brevity of notation, in the first component of the symbolic states we write, for instance, f_1 instead of $\Pi_1 \downarrow f_1$.

solution sets exist, which makes our proof (and also our algorithm) more modular and easier to extend.

We note that if we used positional strategies as in [11], SolveStrategy would have to be extended to guess the symbolic states of symbolic branching structures that coincide after the substitution ν is applied. To avoid this, we employ the strategies with history as explained above.

5.1 Guess the Symbolic Branching Structure

To describe the first step of SolveStrategy in more detail, we first define symbolic branching structures, which consist of symbolic paths and symbolic strategy trees. To define symbolic paths and strategy trees, we need to introduce symbolic states, transitions, and trees (see [10] for full details). These notions will be illustrated by the example in Figure 1.

A *symbolic state* $q^s = ((\Pi_1, \ldots, \Pi_n), \mathcal{I}, \mathcal{S})$ is defined just as a concrete state (see Section 2.1) except that the substitution is omitted and the intruder knowledge $\mathcal{I}$ and the secure channel $\mathcal{S}$ may contain terms (with variables) instead of only messages. The *symbolic initial state* of a protocol $P = ((\Pi_1, \ldots, \Pi_n), \mathcal{I}_0)$ is $((\Pi_1, \ldots, \Pi_n), \mathcal{I}_0, \emptyset)$.

A *symbolic transition*, analogously to concrete transitions, is a transition between symbolic states and is of the form

$$((\Pi_1, \ldots, \Pi_n), \mathcal{I}, \mathcal{S}) \xrightarrow{\ell} ((\Pi'_1, \ldots, \Pi'_n), \mathcal{I}', \mathcal{S}') \qquad (2)$$

with ℓ an appropriate label where again we distinguish between symbolic intruder, secure channel, and ε-transitions. Informally speaking, these transitions are of the following form (see [10] for details and the example below): For *symbolic intruder transitions* the label ℓ is of the form i, f, I where now f is not the message delivered by the intruder, as was the case for concrete intruder transitions, but a direct successor of the root r_i of Π_i. The intuition is that the principal rule $L \Rightarrow R$ the edge (r_i, f) is labeled with in Π_i is applied. The symbolic state $((\Pi_1, \ldots, \Pi_n), \mathcal{I}, \mathcal{S})$ is updated accordingly to $((\Pi'_1, \ldots, \Pi'_n), \mathcal{I}', \mathcal{S}')$ (see the example below). We call $L \Rightarrow R$ the *principal rule associated with the symbolic transition*. Similarly, the label of a *symbolic secure channel transition* is of the form i, f, L', sc where f is interpreted as before and L' is the term read from the secure channel. If $L \Rightarrow R$ is the principal rule associated with the transition, then $\mathcal{S}'$ is obtained by removing L' from $\mathcal{S}$ and adding R if R is a secure channel term. When constructing the constraint system, we will guarantee that L' unifies with L. Finally, the label of *symbolic ε-transitions* is of the form i, f with the obvious meaning.

A *symbolic q^s-tree* $\mathcal{T}^s_{q^s} = (V, E, r, \ell_V, \ell_E)$ is an unordered finite tree where the vertices are labeled with symbolic states, the root is labeled with q^s, and the edges are labeled with labels of symbolic transitions such that an edge (v, v') of the tree, more precisely, the labels of v and v' and the label of (v, v') correspond to symbolic transitions. We call the principal rule associated with such a symbolic transition *the principal rule associated with* (v, v'). Note that the symbolic transitions of different edges may be associated with the same principal rule. Now, since the same rule may occur at different positions in the tree, its variables may later be substituted differently. We therefore need a mechanism to consistently rename variables.

Figure 3 depicts a symbolic q^s_0-tree $\mathcal{T}^s_{ex}$ for protocol P_{ex} (Figure 1) where $q^s_0 = (\{\Pi_1, \Pi_2\}, \mathcal{I}_0, \emptyset)$ is the symbolic initial state of P_{ex}. For brevity of notation, just as in the case of the strategy tree in Figure 1, the first component of the symbolic states in this tree does not contain the principals but only their corresponding roots. Note that the principal rules of Π_1 are applied at different places in this tree. Therefore, different copies of the variables x and y need to be introduced, which we do by indexing the variables by the name of the vertex where the rule is applied. This yields the variables $x_{h_3}, x_{h_7}, y_{h_4}, y_{h_8}$ in $\mathcal{T}^s_{ex}$.

A *symbolic path* π^s of a protocol P is a symbolic q^s_0-tree where every vertex has at most one successor and q^s_0 is the symbolic initial state of P.

A *symbolic q^s-strategy tree* $\mathcal{T}^s_{q^s} = (V, E, r, \ell_V, \ell_E)$ is a symbolic q^s-tree which satisfies additional conditions. Among others, we require that in one node of this tree the intruder may only send a message to one principal Π_i; we show that this is w.l.o.g. Also, all ε-transitions applicable in one node are present. Symbolic strategy trees are defined in such a way that for every symbolic state q^s the number of symbolic q^s-strategy trees is finite and all such trees can effectively be generated. The tree depicted in Figure 3 is a symbolic q^s_0-strategy tree.

For a protocol P and strategy property $((C_1, C'_1), \ldots, (C_l, C'_l))$, a *symbolic branching structure* is of the form $\mathbf{B}^s = \pi^s, \mathcal{T}^s_1, \ldots, \mathcal{T}^s_l$ where π^s is a symbolic path of P and the $\mathcal{T}^s_i$ are symbolic q^s-strategy trees where q^s is the symbolic state the leaf of π^s is labeled with. Given a protocol and a strategy property, there are only a finite number of symbolic branching structures and these structures can be generated by an algorithm. In particular, there is a non-deterministic algorithm which can guess one symbolic branching structure $\mathbf{B}^s$ among all possible such structures.

For the strategy property $((C_{ex}, C'_{ex})) = ((\{c_2\}, \{c_1\}))$, we can consider $\mathcal{T}^s_{ex}$ in Figure 3 also as a symbolic branching structure $\mathbf{B}^s_{ex}$ of P_{ex} where the path π^s is empty and the number of symbolic strategy trees in $\mathbf{B}^s_{ex}$ is $l = 1$.

5.2 Construct and Solve the Induced Constraint System

We now show how the constraint system $\mathbf{C} = \mathbf{C_B}$ is derived from the symbolic branching structure $\mathbf{B} = \pi^s, \mathcal{T}_1^s, \ldots, \mathcal{T}_l^s$ (guessed in the first step of SolveStrategy) and the given strategy property $((C_1, C'_1), \ldots, (C_l, C'_l))$. This constraint system can be shown to be valid, and hence, by Fact 1, a constraint solver can be used to solve it. In this extended abstract, we only illustrate how $\mathbf{C}$ is derived from $\mathbf{B}$ and the strategy property by the example in Figure 1 (see [10] for full definitions).

Before turning to the example, we informally explain how to encode in a constraint system communication involving the secure channel. (Another, somewhat less interesting issue is how to deal with secure channel terms generated by the intruder. This is explained in our technical report [10].) The basic idea is that we write messages intended for the secure channel into the intruder's knowledge and let the intruder deliver these messages. The problem is that while every message in the secure channel can only be read once, the intruder could try to deliver the same message several times. To prevent this, every such message when written into the intruder's knowledge is encrypted with a *new* key not known to the intruder and this key is also (and only) used in the principal rule which according to the symbolic branching structure is supposed to read the message. This guarantees that the intruder cannot abusively deliver the same message several times to unintended recipients or make use of these encrypted messages in other contexts. Here we use the restriction on principals introduced in Section 2, namely that decryption keys can be derived by a principal. Without this condition, a principal rule of the form $\{y\}^s_x \Rightarrow x$ would be allowed even if the principal does not know (i.e., cannot derive) x. Such a rule would equip a principal with the unrealistic ability to derive any secret key from a ciphertext. Hence, the intruder, using this principal as an oracle, could achieve this as well and could potentially obtain the new keys used to encrypt messages intended for the secure channel.

We now turn to our example and explain how the (valid) constraint system, called $\mathbf{C}_{ex}$, derived from $\mathbf{B}^s_{ex}$ and $((C_{ex}, C'_{ex}))$ looks like and how it is derived from $\mathbf{B}^s_{ex}$, where $\mathbf{B}^s_{ex}$, as explained above, is simply the symbolic strategy tree $\mathcal{T}^s_{ex}$ (Figure 3): $\mathbf{C}_{ex}$ is the following sequence of constraints with an empty substitution where $k_1, k_2, k_3 \in \mathcal{A}$ are new atoms and we write $t_1, \ldots, t_n$ instead of $\{t_1, \ldots, t_n\}$.

1. $\{\langle x_{h_3}, b\rangle\}^s_{k_1} : \mathcal{I}_1, \{\langle a, b\rangle\}^s_{k_1}$	6. $x_{h_7} : \mathcal{I}_2, \{\langle b, b\rangle\}^s_{k_2}, x_{h_7}, y_{h_8}$
2. $\{\langle x_{h_7}, b\rangle\}^s_{k_2} : \mathcal{I}_2, \{\langle b, b\rangle\}^s_{k_2}$	7. $y_{h_8} : \mathcal{I}_2, \{\langle b, b\rangle\}^s_{k_2}, x_{h_7}, y_{h_8}$
3. $\{y_{h_4}\}^s_k : \mathcal{I}_1, \{\langle a, b\rangle\}^s_{k_1}, x_{h_3}$	8. $c_2 : \mathcal{I}_1, \{\langle a, b\rangle\}^s_{k_1}, x_{h_3}, y_{h_4}, c_2$
4. $\{y_{h_8}\}^s_k : \mathcal{I}_2, \{\langle b, b\rangle\}^s_{k_2}, x_{h_7}$	9. $c_2 : \mathcal{I}_2, \{\langle b, b\rangle\}^s_{k_2}, x_{h_7}, y_{h_8}, c_2$
5. $y_{h_4} : \mathcal{I}_1, \{\langle a, b\rangle\}^s_{k_1}, x_{h_3}, y_{h_4}$	10. $c_2 : \mathcal{I}_2, \{\langle b, b\rangle\}^s_{k_2}, x_{h_7}, y_{h_8}, c_2$

This constraint system is obtained from $\mathbf{B}^s_{ex}$ as follows: We traverse the vertices of $\mathbf{B}^s_{ex}$ in a top-down breadth first manner. Every edge induces a constraint except those edges which correspond to symbolic ε-transitions. This is how the constraints 1.–7. come about where 1., 3., and 5. are derived from the left branch of $\mathbf{B}^s_{ex}$ and 2., 4., 6., and 7. from the right branch. Note that in 1. and 2. we encode the communication with the secure channel by encrypting the terms with new keys k_1 and k_2. The terms $\{\langle a,b\rangle\}^s_{k_1}$ and $\{\langle b,b\rangle\}^s_{k_2}$ are not removed anymore from the right-hand side of the constraints, i.e., from the intruder knowledge, in order for $\mathbf{C}_{ex}$ to satisfy the monotonicity property of constraint systems (recall that monotonicity is necessary for the validity of constraint systems). As explained above, since we use *new* keys and due to the restriction on principals, this does not cause problems. The constraints 8.–10. are used to ensure that c_2 can be derived at every leaf of $\mathcal{T}^s_{ex}$, a requirement that comes from our example security property $((C_{ex}, C'_{ex}))$ where $C_{ex} = \{c_2\}$. In vertex h_8 of $\mathcal{T}^s_{ex}$, two symbolic intruder transitions leave the vertex, which, as explained above, means that the associated principal rules should both be able to read the message delivered by the intruder.

Let $\mathbf{C}_1$ and $\mathbf{C}_2$ be constraint systems with empty sequences of constraints and the substitution $\nu_1 = \{x_{h_3} \mapsto a, x_{h_7} \mapsto b, y_{h_4} \mapsto a, y_{h_8} \mapsto b\}$ and $\nu_2 = \{x_{h_3} \mapsto a, x_{h_7} \mapsto b, y_{h_4} \mapsto b, y_{h_8} \mapsto b\}$, respectively. It is easy to see that $\{\mathbf{C}_1, \mathbf{C}_2\}$ is a sound and complete solution set for $\mathbf{C}_{ex}$. Since $\mathbf{C}_{ex}$ is valid, such a set can be computed by the constraint solver (Fact 1).

5.3 Check the Induced Substitutions

Let $\mathbf{B}^s = \pi^s, \mathcal{T}^s_1, \ldots, \mathcal{T}^s_l$ be the symbolic branching structure obtained in the first step of SolveStrategy and let $\mathbf{C}'$ be the simple constraint system returned by the constraint solver when applied to $\mathbf{C} = \mathbf{C}_{\mathbf{B}^s}$ in the second step of SolveStrategy. Let ν be the complete solution associated with $\mathbf{C}'$ (see Section 5.2). We emphasize that for our algorithm to work, it is important that ν replaces the variables in $\mathbf{C}'$ by *new* intruder atoms from $\mathcal{A}_I$ not occurring in $\mathbf{B}^s$.

Basically, we want to check that when applying ν to $\mathbf{B}^s$, which yields $\mathbf{B}^s\nu = \pi^s\nu, \mathcal{T}^s_1\nu, \ldots, \mathcal{T}^s_l\nu$, we obtain a solution of the problem instance $(P, (C_1, C'_1), \ldots, (C_l, C'_l))$. Hence, we need to check whether i) $\pi^s\nu$ corresponds to a path in $\mathcal{G}_P$ from the initial state of $\mathcal{G}_P$ to a state $q \in \mathcal{G}_P$ and ii) $\mathcal{T}^s_i\nu$ corresponds to a q-strategy tree for (C_i, C'_i) for every i. However, since ν is a complete solution of $\mathbf{C}$, some of these conditions are satisfied by construction. In particular, $\pi^s\nu$ is guaranteed to be a path in $\mathcal{G}_P$ starting from the initial state. Also, the conditions 1.–3. of strategy trees (Definition 1) do not need to be checked and we know that $\mathcal{T}^s_i\nu$ satisfies $(C_i, \emptyset)$. Hence, SolveStrategy only needs to make sure that 4. and 5. of Definition 1 are satisfied for every $\mathcal{T}^s_i\nu$ and that $\mathcal{T}^s_i\nu$ fulfills $(\emptyset, C'_i)$. Using that the derivation problem is decidable in polynomial time [6] (given a message m and a finite set of messages $\mathcal{I}$, decide whether $m \in d(\mathcal{I})$), all of these remaining conditions can easily be checked (see [10] for details).

In our example, the induced substitution for $\mathbf{C}_i$ is ν_i as $\mathbf{C}_i$ does not contain any variables. It can easily be verified that with $\mathbf{C}' = \mathbf{C}_2$ and the induced substitution ν_2, the above checks are all successful. However, they fail for $\mathbf{C}' = \mathbf{C}_1$ and ν_1 because in h_4 the rule $a \Rightarrow c_1$ could also be applied but it is not present in $\mathbf{B}^s_{ex}$. This violates Definition 1, 5. In fact, $\mathbf{B}^s_{ex}\nu_1$ would not yield a solution of the instance $(P_{ex}, ((C_{ex}, C'_{ex})))$. This example illustrates that in SolveStrategy one cannot dispense with the last step, namely checking the substitutions, and that one has to try the different constraint systems in the sound and complete solution set for $\mathbf{C}$.

6 Conclusion

We have shown that certain game-theoretic security properties, such as balance, of contract-signing and related protocols can be decided using standard constraint solving procedures as a black-box. This opens the way for extending existing constraint-based implementations and tools, which have successfully been employed for reachability properties, to deal with game-theoretic security properties. As future work, we plan to implement our algorithm, which will probably require some optimizations, and evaluate the algorithm on existing contract-signing and related protocols.

References

1. R.M. Amadio, D. Lugiez, and V. Vanackere. On the symbolic reduction of processes with cryptographic functions. *Theoretical Computer Science*, 290(1):695–740, 2002.
2. A. Armando, D. Basin, M. Bouallagui, Y. Chevalier, L. Compagna, S. Mödersheim, M. Rusinowitch, M. Turuani, L. Viganò, and L. Vigneron. The AVISS Security Protocol Analysis Tool. In *CAV 2002*, LNCS 2404, pages 349–353. Springer, 2002.
3. N. Asokan, V. Shoup, and M. Waidner. Asynchronous protocols for optimistic fair exchange. In *Security&Privacy 2002*, pages 86–99, 1998.
4. D. Basin, S. Mödersheim, and L. Viganò. An On-The-Fly Model-Checker for Security Protocol Analysis. In *ESORICS 2003*, LNCS 2808, pages 253–270. Springer, 2003.
5. R. Chadha, M.I. Kanovich, and A.Scedrov. Inductive methods and contract-signing protocols. In *CCS 2001*, pages 176–185. ACM Press, 2001.
6. Y. Chevalier, R. Küsters, M. Rusinowitch, and M. Turuani. An NP Decision Procedure for Protocol Insecurity with XOR. In *LICS 2003*, pages 261–270. IEEE, Computer Society Press, 2003.
7. Y. Chevalier and L. Vigneron. A Tool for Lazy Verification of Security Protocols. In *ASE 2001*, pages 373–376. IEEE CS Press, 2001.
8. P. H. Drielsma and S. Mödersheim. The ASW Protocol Revisited: A Unified View. In *ARSPA*, 2004.
9. J.A. Garay, M. Jakobsson, and P. MacKenzie. Abuse-free optimistic contract signing. In *CRYPTO'99*, LNCS 1666, pages 449–466. Springer-Verlag, 1999.
10. D. Kähler and R. Küsters. A Constraint-Based Algorithm for Contract-Signing Protocols. Technical report, IFI 0503, CAU Kiel, Germany, 2005. Available from http://www.informatik.uni-kiel.de/reports/2005/0503.html
11. D. Kähler, R. Küsters, and Th. Wilke. Deciding Properties of Contract-Signing Protocols. In *STACS 2005*, LNCS 3404, pages 158–169. Springer, 2005.
12. S. Kremer and J.-F. Raskin. Game analysis of abuse-free contract signing. In *CSFW 2002*, pages 206–220. IEEE Computer Society, 2002.
13. J. K. Millen and V. Shmatikov. Constraint solving for bounded-process cryptographic protocol analysis. In *CCS 2001*, pages 166–175. ACM Press, 2001.
14. M. Rusinowitch and M. Turuani. Protocol insecurity with a finite number of sessions, composed keys is NP-complete. *Theoretical Computer Science*, 299(1–3):451–475, 2003.
15. V. Shmatikov and J.C. Mitchell. Finite-state analysis of two contract signing protocols. *Theoretical Computer Science*, 283(2):419–450, 2002.

A Ground-Complete Axiomatization of Finite State Processes in Process Algebra

Jos C.M. Baeten[1] and Mario Bravetti[2]

[1] Division of Computer Science,Technische Universiteit Eindhoven
josb@win.tue.nl
[2] Department of Computer Science,Università di Bologna
bravetti@cs.unibo.it

Abstract. We consider a generic process algebra of which the standard process algebras ACP, CCS and CSP are subalgebras of reduced expressions. In particular such an algebra is endowed with a recursion operator which computes minimal fixpoint solutions of systems of equations over processes. As model for processes we consider finite-state transition systems modulo Milner's observational congruence and we define an operational semantics for the process algebra. Over such a generic algebra we show the following. We provide a syntactical characterization (allowing as many terms as possible) for the equations involved in recursion operators, which guarantees that transition systems generated by the operational semantics are indeed finite-state. Vice-versa we show that every process admits a specification in terms of such a restricted form of recursion. We then present an axiomatization which is ground-complete over such a restricted signature: an equation can be derived from the axioms between closed terms exactly when the corresponding finite-state transition systems are observationally congruent. Notably, in presenting such an axiomatization, we also show that the two standard axioms of Milner for weakly unguarded recursion can be expressed by using just a single axiom.

1 Introduction

The problem of developing a sound and complete axiomatization for a weak form of bisimulation (abstracting from internal τ activities) over a process algebra expressing finite-state processes with both guarded and (weakly and fully) unguarded recursion has been solved by Robin Milner [16]. His solution has been developed in the context of a basic process algebra (basic CCS) made up of visible prefix $a.t$, silent prefix $\tau.t$, summation $t' + t''$ and recursion $recX.t$ (based on least transition system solution), whose model is assumed to be finite-state transition systems modulo observational congruence (rooted weak bisimulation). Such a solution is crucially based on three axioms: one for fully unguarded recursion

$$(FUng)\ recX.(X + t) = recX.t$$

and two for weakly unguarded recursion

M. Abadi and L. de Alfaro (Eds.): CONCUR 2005, LNCS 3653, pp. 248–262, 2005.

$$(WUng1)\ recX.(\tau.X + t) = recX.\tau.t$$
$$(WUng2)\ recX.(\tau.(X + t) + s) = recX.(\tau.X + t + s).$$

The idea is that by means of the three axioms above we are able to turn each (weakly or fully) unguarded process algebraic term into an equivalent guarded one. Then the proof of completeness just works on normal forms where recursion is assumed to be guarded, i.e. it is shown that if two guarded terms are equivalent then they can be equated by the axiomatization. This is done by exploiting the two crucial axioms

$$(Unfold)\ recX.t = t\{recX.t/X\}$$
$$(Fold)\ t' = t\{t'/X\} \ \Rightarrow\ t' = recX.t \quad \text{if } X \text{ is guarded in } t$$

However Milner's result is crucially based on the fact that the signature of the process algebra under consideration is very simple. For example if we extend the signature to full CCS (by e.g. considering parallel composition and restriction), we have that the axioms above are no longer sufficient to get rid of unguarded recursion. In other words, even if two CCS terms are both finite-state it may be that they are not equated by an axiomatization including the standard CCS axioms (the axioms for CCS without the $recX.t$ recursion operator) plus the axioms for unguarded and guarded recursion above. An example is the following:

$$(\,(recX.a.X) \mid (recX.a.X)\,)\setminus a$$

where "$|$" and "$\setminus$" denote CCS parallel composition and restriction, respectively. The model of such a term has just one state with a τ self-loop, but cannot be equated by the axiomatization to the equivalent term $recX.\tau.X$ or to $\tau.\underline{0}$. The problem is that, since the process above produces unguarded recursion (a loop with only τ transitions in the transition system), we cannot apply the folding axiom $(Fold)$. We should first remove unguarded recursion, but the three axioms $(FUng)$, $(WUng1)$, $(WUng2)$ only work with the restricted signature (which does not include the parallel and restriction operators).

In this paper we consider a generic process algebra of which the standard process algebras ACP, CCS and CSP are subalgebras of reduced expressions. More precisely such an algebra is an extension of the algebra TCP [1,2] (which extends ACP by including successful termination ϵ and prefixing à la CCS) with a recursion operator $\langle X|E\rangle$ which computes minimal fixpoint solutions of systems of equations (denoted by $E = \{X = t_X, Y = t_Y, \dots\}$) over processes and consider an initial variable X among variables V defined by the system of equations E. Such an operator (which extends the similar operator introduced in [8] with the possibility of nesting recursion operators inside recursion operators) encompasses both the CCS $recX.t$ operator (which is obtained by taking $E = \{X = t\}$) and the standard way to express recursion in ACP (where usually only guarded recursion is considered via systems of equations E). As we will see, such an algebra, called TCP+REC, is endowed with sequencing "$t' \cdot t''$", hiding "$\tau_I(t)$", restriction "$\partial_H(t)$", relabeling "$\rho_f(t)$", and parallel composition "$t' \parallel t''$" à la ACP (where a communication function γ is assumed to compute the type of communicating actions).

As model for processes we consider finite-state transition systems modulo Milner's observational congruence and we define an operational semantics for such a process algebra.

In order to guarantee that transition systems generated by the operational semantics are indeed finite-state, we provide a syntactical constraint for the systems of equations $E = E(V)$ involved in recursion operators $\langle X|E\rangle$. Such a constraint is similar to that considered in [9]: in essence we disallow variables in V occurring in the right-hand side of equations in E (that are bound by the $\langle X|E\rangle$ operator) to be in the scope of static operators like hiding, restriction, relabeling and parallel composition or in the left-hand side of a sequencing operator. For example $\langle X|\{X = \tau_I(a.X)\}\rangle$ for any hiding set I, which produces an infinite-state transition system, is a term rejected by the constraint that we consider. Note however that recursion can be included in the scope of static operators (or in the left-hand side of sequencing) as in the case of the CCS term $((recX.a.X)|(recX.a.X))\backslash a$ shown before (it is simple to express such a term in terms of our generic process algebra by using ACP parallel, hiding and restriction). We also show that the syntactical constraint that we propose is somehow the weakest: if a (reachable) variable which is bound by an outer recursion operator occurs in the scope of a static operator or in the lefthand-side of sequencing then it produces an infinite-state transition system. We call TCP+REC$_f$ the process algebra which extends TCP with the recursion operator $\langle X|E\rangle$, where E satisfies the constraint above.

Vice-versa we show that in the considered context of finite-state models every process admits a specification in terms of TCP+REC$_f$.

The main result of the paper is the introduction of an axiomatization that is ground-complete over the signature of TCP+REC$_f$: an equation can be derived from the axioms between closed terms exactly when the corresponding finite-state transition systems are observationally congruent.

This axiomatization is based on the introduction of the new axiom

$$\tau_I(\langle X|X = t\rangle) = \langle X|X = \tau_I(t)\rangle$$

which allows the hiding operator (the only static operator which may generate unguarded recursion) to be exchanged with the recursion operator. We will show that by using such a crucial axiom, that was previously considered also in [14] (where the author just showed it to be sound), it is possible to achieve completeness in the finite-state case when static operators are considered, thus extending Milner's result. The main idea is that, by means of this axiom, we can first move the hiding operator inside recursion and more generally outside-in traversing the whole syntactic structure of the term considered (so to get the effect of hiding on the actions syntactically occurring in the term), and then (by applying it in the reversed way) inside-out again. Supposing that we are turning the term into normal form (essentially basic CCS where recursion is guarded) by means of syntactical induction, once we have done the procedure above we can apply Milner's rule for unguarded recursion in the term inside the hiding operator, thus getting a term in normal form on which the hiding operator has no longer any effect. As a consequence we can get rid of it like we do with any other static operator by using the Fold axiom.

Notably, in the axiomatization that we present we also make use of the following result that we introduce here. The two axioms of Milner for getting rid of weakly unguarded recursion presented above (WUng1 and WUng2) can be equivalently expressed by means of the following single axiom:

$$\langle X|X = \tau.(X + t) + s\rangle = \langle X|X = \tau.(t + s)\rangle$$

The paper is structured as follows. In Sect. 2 we present the model of processes that we consider (finite state transition systems) and the notion of observational congruence. In Sect. 3 we present the process algebra TCP and its operational semantics. In Sect. 4 we introduce the recursion operator, its operational semantics, the considered syntactical constraint over sets of equations and the full syntax of TCP+REC$_f$. Moreover we prove that: (i) TCP+REC$_f$ terms produce finite-state transitions systems only, (ii) the constraint that we consider is the weakest and (iii) every finite-state transition system can be expressed in terms of a TCP+REC$_f$ term. In Sect. 5 we present the axiomatization and we show that it is sound and ground-complete for observational congruence over the TCP+REC$_f$ signature. Sect. 6 concludes the paper.

2 Finite Behaviours

In this paper, we consider finite behaviours: the model of finite state transition systems modulo Milner's observational congruence.

Definition 1 (Transition-system space). A *transition-system space* over a set of labels L is a set S of *states*, equipped with one ternary relation $\rightarrow$ and one subset $\downarrow$:

1. $\rightarrow \subseteq S \times L \times S$ is the set of *transitions*;
2. $\downarrow \subseteq S$ is the set of *terminating* or *final* states.

The notation $s \xrightarrow{\alpha} t$ is used for $(s, \alpha, t) \in \rightarrow$ and $s \downarrow$ for $s \in \downarrow$.

Here, we will always assume the sets S and L are finite, and the set of labels will consist of a set of actions A and a special label $\tau \notin A$.

In the remainder, assume that $(S, L, \rightarrow, \downarrow)$ is a transition-system space. Each state $s \in S$ can be identified with a transition system that consists of all states and transitions reachable from s. The notion of reachability is defined as usual.

Definition 2 (Weak Bisimilarity). Define $s \Rightarrow t$ if there is a sequence of 0 or more τ-steps from s to t. A symmetric binary relation R on the set of states S of a transition-system space is a *weak bisimulation* relation if and only if the following so-called *transfer conditions* hold:

1. for all states $s, t, s' \in S$, whenever $(s,t) \in R$ and $s \xrightarrow{\alpha} s'$ for some $\alpha \in L$, then either $\alpha = \tau$ and $(s',t) \in R$ or there are states t^*, t'', t' such that $t \Rightarrow t^* \xrightarrow{a} t'' \Rightarrow t'$ and $(s',t') \in R$;

2. whenever $(s,t) \in R$ and $s \downarrow$ then there is a state t^* such that $t \Rightarrow t^* \downarrow$;

Two transition systems $s,t \in S$ are *weak bisimulation equivalent* or *weakly bisimilar*, notation $s \leftrightarrows_w t$, if and only if there is a weak bisimulation relation R on S with $(s,t) \in R$.

The pair (s,t) in a weak bisimulation R *satisfies the root condition* if whenever $s \xrightarrow{\tau} s'$ there are states t'', t' such that $t \xrightarrow{\tau} t'' \Rightarrow t'$ and $(s',t') \in R$. Two transition systems $s,t \in S$ are *rooted weak bisimulation equivalent, observationally congruent* or *rooted weakly bisimilar*, notation $s \leftrightarrows_{rw} t$, if and only there is a weak bisimulation relation in which the pair (s,t) satisfies the root condition.

3 Process Algebra

We consider the process algebra TCP (Theory of Communicating Processes), introduced in [1] and completely worked out in [2], of which the standard process algebras ACP, CCS and CSP are subalgebras of reduced expressions.

Our theory has two parameters: the set of actions A, and a *communication function* $\gamma : A \times A \to A$. The function γ is partial, commutative and associative. The signature elements are the following. Constant δ denotes *inaction* (or deadlock), and is the neutral element of alternative composition: process δ cannot execute any action, and cannot terminate. Constant ϵ denotes the *empty process* or *skip* and is the neutral element of sequential composition: process ϵ cannot execute any action, but terminates successfully. For each $a \in A$, there is the unary *prefix operator* $a.\_$: process $a.x$ executes action a and then proceeds as x. There is the additional prefix operator $\tau.\_$. Here, $\tau \notin A$ is the *silent step*, that cannot be observed directly. Binary operator $+$ denotes *alternative composition* or choice: process $x + y$ executes either x or y, but not both (the choice is resolved upon execution of the first action). Binary operator $\cdot$ denotes *sequential composition*: having sequential composition as a basic operator, makes it necessary to have a difference between successful termination (ϵ) and unsuccessful termination (δ). Sequential composition is more general than action prefixing. Binary operator $\|$ denotes *parallel composition*. In order to give a finite axiomatization of parallel composition, there are two variations on this operator, the auxiliary operators $\lfloor\!\lfloor$ (left-merge) and $|$ (synchronization merge). In the parallel composition $x \parallel y$, the separate components may execute a step independently (denoted by $x \lfloor\!\lfloor y$ resp. $y \lfloor\!\lfloor x$), or they may synchronize in executing a communication action (when they can execute actions for which γ is defined), or they may terminate together (the last two possibilities given by $x \mid y$). Unary operator ∂_H denotes *encapsulation* or *restriction*, for each $H \subseteq A$: actions from H are blocked, cannot be executed. Unary operator τ_I denotes *abstraction* or *hiding*, for each $I \subseteq A$: actions from I are turned into τ, and are thus made unobservable. Unary operator ρ_f denotes *renaming* or *relabeling*, for each $f : A \to A$.

In the following we will use meta-variables x, y to range over processes of our process algebra, i.e. finite-state transition-systems possibly denoted via a term over the signature of the algebra, a, b, c to range over A and α to range over $A \cup \{\tau\}$.

We turn the set of closed terms (i.e. terms containing no variables) over the signature of the algebra into a transition-system space by providing so-called operational rules. See Table 1. States in the transition-system space are denoted by closed terms over the signature. These rules give rise to a finite transition system, without cycles, for each closed term.

Table 1. Deduction rules for TCP

$$
\begin{array}{cccc}
\epsilon\downarrow & \alpha.x \xrightarrow{\alpha} x & & \\[2ex]
\dfrac{x \xrightarrow{\alpha} x'}{x+y \xrightarrow{\alpha} x'} & \dfrac{y \xrightarrow{\alpha} y'}{x+y \xrightarrow{\alpha} y'} & \dfrac{x\downarrow}{x+y\downarrow} & \dfrac{y\downarrow}{x+y\downarrow} \\[2ex]
\dfrac{x \xrightarrow{\alpha} x'}{x\cdot y \xrightarrow{\alpha} x'\cdot y} & \dfrac{x\downarrow, y \xrightarrow{\alpha} y'}{x\cdot y \xrightarrow{\alpha} y'} & \dfrac{x\downarrow, y\downarrow}{x\cdot y\downarrow} & \\[2ex]
\dfrac{x \xrightarrow{a} x', y \xrightarrow{b} y', \gamma(a,b)=c}{x \parallel y \xrightarrow{c} x' \parallel y'} & \dfrac{x\downarrow, y\downarrow}{x \parallel y\downarrow} & \dfrac{x \xrightarrow{\alpha} x'}{x \parallel y \xrightarrow{\alpha} x' \parallel y} & \dfrac{y \xrightarrow{\alpha} y'}{x \parallel y \xrightarrow{\alpha} x \parallel y'} \\[2ex]
\dfrac{x \xrightarrow{a} x', y \xrightarrow{b} y', \gamma(a,b)=c}{x \mid y \xrightarrow{c} x' \parallel y'} & \dfrac{x\downarrow, y\downarrow}{x \mid y\downarrow} & \dfrac{x \xrightarrow{\alpha} x'}{x \mathbin{\|\!\lfloor} y \xrightarrow{\alpha} x' \parallel y} & \\[2ex]
\dfrac{x \xrightarrow{\tau} x', x' \mid y \xrightarrow{\alpha} z}{x \mid y \xrightarrow{\alpha} z} & \dfrac{y \xrightarrow{\tau} y', x \mid y' \xrightarrow{\alpha} z}{x \mid y \xrightarrow{\alpha} z} & \dfrac{x \xrightarrow{\tau} x', x' \mid y\downarrow}{x \mid y\downarrow} & \dfrac{y \xrightarrow{\tau} y', x \mid y'\downarrow}{x \mid y\downarrow} \\[2ex]
\dfrac{x \xrightarrow{\alpha} x', \alpha \notin H}{\partial_H(x) \xrightarrow{\alpha} \partial_H(x')} & \dfrac{x\downarrow}{\partial_H(x)\downarrow} & \dfrac{x \xrightarrow{\alpha} x', \alpha \notin I}{\tau_I(x) \xrightarrow{\alpha} \tau_I(x')} & \dfrac{x \xrightarrow{a} x', a \in I}{\tau_I(x) \xrightarrow{\tau} \tau_I(x')} \\[2ex]
\dfrac{x\downarrow}{\tau_I(x)\downarrow} & \dfrac{x \xrightarrow{a} x'}{\rho_f(x) \xrightarrow{f(a)} \rho_f(x')} & \dfrac{x \xrightarrow{\tau} x'}{\rho_f(x) \xrightarrow{\tau} \rho_f(x')} & \dfrac{x\downarrow}{\rho_f(x)\downarrow}
\end{array}
$$

We can provide an axiomatization that is *ground-complete*, i.e. an equation can be derived from the axioms between two closed terms exactly when the corresponding transition systems are observationally congruent. The basic set of axioms is presented in Table 2.

This process algebra is *generic*, in the sense that most features of commonly used process algebras can be embedded in it. In the following, we made use of [13,14] and [4].

We consider a subtheory corresponding to CCS, see [17]. This is done by omitting the signature elements $\epsilon, \cdot, \mathbin{\|\!\lfloor}, \mid$. Next, we specialize the parameter set A by separating it into three parts: a set of names $\mathcal{A}$, a set of co-names $\bar{\mathcal{A}}$ and a set of communications $\mathcal{A}^*$ such that for each $a \in \mathcal{A}$ there is exactly one $\bar{a} \in \bar{\mathcal{A}}$ and exactly one $a^* \in \mathcal{A}^*$. The communication function γ is specialized to having as the only defined communications $\gamma(a, \bar{a}) = \gamma(\bar{a}, a) = a^*$, and then the CCS parallel composition operator $\mid_{CCS}$ can be defined by the formula

$$x \mid_{CCS} y = \tau_{\mathcal{A}^*}(x \parallel y).$$

We consider a subtheory corresponding to ACP$_\tau$, see [7]. This is done by defining, for each $a \in A$, a new constant a by $a = a.\epsilon$, and then omitting the signature elements $\epsilon, ., \rho_f$.

Table 2. Axioms of TCP

$x + y = y + x$	A1	$x \parallel y = x \llcorner\!\llcorner y + y \llcorner\!\llcorner x + x \mid y$	M
$(x + y) + z = x + (y + z)$	A2		
$x + x = x$	A3	$\delta \llcorner\!\llcorner x = \delta$	LM1
$(x + y) \cdot z = x \cdot z + y \cdot z$	A4	$\epsilon \llcorner\!\llcorner x = \delta$	LM2
$(x \cdot y) \cdot z = x \cdot (y \cdot z)$	A5	$\alpha.x \llcorner\!\llcorner y = \alpha.(x \parallel y)$	LM3
$x + \delta = x$	A6	$(x + y) \llcorner\!\llcorner z = x \llcorner\!\llcorner z + y \llcorner\!\llcorner z$	LM4
$\delta \cdot x = \delta$	A7		
$\epsilon \cdot x = x$	A8	$x \mid y = y \mid x$	SM1
$x \cdot \epsilon = x$	A9	$\delta \mid x = \delta$	SM2
$(\alpha.x) \cdot y = \alpha.(x \cdot y)$	A10	$\epsilon \mid \epsilon = \epsilon$	SM3
		$a.x \mid b.y = c.(x \parallel y)$ if $\gamma(a, b) = c$	SM4
$\partial_H(\delta) = \delta$	D1	$a.x \mid b.y = \delta$ otherwise	SM5
$\partial_H(\epsilon) = \epsilon$	D2	$a.x \mid \epsilon = \delta$	SM6
$\partial_H(a.x) = \delta$ if $a \in H$	D3	$(x + y) \mid z = x \mid z + y \mid z$	SM7
$\partial_H(\alpha.x) = \alpha.\partial_H(x)$ otherwise	D4		
$\partial_H(x + y) = \partial_H(x) + \partial_H(y)$	D5	$\rho_f(\delta) = \delta$	RN1
		$\rho_f(\epsilon) = \epsilon$	RN2
$\tau_I(\delta) = \delta$	TI1	$\rho_f(a.x) = f(a).\rho_f(x)$	RN3
$\tau_I(\epsilon) = \epsilon$	TI2	$\rho_f(\tau.x) = \tau.\rho_f(x)$	RN4
$\tau_I(a.x) = \tau.\tau_I(x)$ if $a \in I$	TI3	$\rho_f(x + y) = \rho_f(x) + \rho_f(y)$	RN5
$\tau_I(\alpha.x) = \alpha.\tau_I(x)$ otherwise	TI4		
$\tau_I(x + y) = \tau_I(x) + \tau_I(y)$	TI5		
$\alpha.\tau.x = \alpha.x$	T1	$\tau.x + x = \tau.x$	T2
$\alpha.(\tau.x + y) = \alpha.(\tau.x + y) + \alpha.x$	T3	$\tau.x \mid y = x \mid y$	T4

We consider a subtheory corresponding to CSP, see [15]. The *non-deterministic choice* operator $\sqcap$ can be defined by

$$x \sqcap y = \tau.x + \tau.y,$$

but the *external choice* operator $\Box$ cannot be defined directly, as possible non-determinism is removed at the start of the process. It can be axiomatized as shown by Brookes in [10]. The parameter set A is specialized into two parts: a set of names $\mathcal{A}$ and a set of communications $\mathcal{A}^*$ such that for each $a \in \mathcal{A}$ there is exactly one $a^* \in \mathcal{A}^*$. The communication function γ is specialized to having as the only defined communications $\gamma(a, a) = a^*$, and further, we use the renaming function f that has $f(a^*) = a$. Then, the CSP parallel composition operator $\|_S$, parametrized by a set of names $S \subseteq \mathcal{A}$, can be defined by the formula

$$x \parallel_S y = \rho_f(\partial_S(x \parallel y)).$$

4 Recursion

We proceed to define recursion in our setting, in order to obtain also finite-state transition systems with cycles.

Let V be a set of variables ranging over processes, ranged over by X, Y. According to a terminology which is usual in the ACP setting, a *recursive specification* $E = E(V)$ is a set of equations $E = \{X = t_X \mid X \in V\}$ where each t_X is a term over the signature in question and variables from V. A *solution* of a recursive specification $E(V)$ is a set of transition systems $\{y_X \mid X \in V\}$ such that the equations of $E(V)$ correspond to equivalent transition systems, if for all $X \in V$, y_X is substituted for X. Mostly, we are interested in one particular variable $X \in V$, called the *initial* variable.

Let t be a term containing a variable X. We call an occurrence of X in t *guarded* if this occurrence of X is in the scope of an action prefix operator (not τ prefix) and *not* in the scope of an abstraction operator.

We call a recursive specification *guarded* if all occurrences of all its variables in the right-hand sides of all its equations are guarded or it can be rewritten to such a recursive specification using the axioms of the theory and the equations of the specification.

Now, in the models obtained by adding rules for recursion to the operational semantics given above, and dividing out one of the congruence relations strong bisimulation, or observational congruence, guarded recursive specifications have unique solutions, so we can talk about *the* process given by a guarded recursive specification. On the other hand, unguarded recursive specifications usually have several solutions. Thus, the specification $\{X = X\}$ will have every transition system as a solution, and the specification $\{X = \tau.X\}$ will have multiple solutions under observational congruence, as any transition system with a τ-step as only initial step will satisfy this equation.

The process algebras ACP, CCS and CSP handle this situation in different ways. In ACP, variables occurring in unguarded recursive specifications are treated as (constrained) variables, and not as processes. In CCS, where recursive specifications are made via so-called "*constants*", ranged over by $A, B, ..$, or equivalently by the $recX.t$ operator, where t is a term containing variable X, from the set of solutions the solution will be chosen that has the least transitions in the generated transition system. Thus, the solution chosen for the equation $\{X = X\}$ has no transitions, is the process δ, and the solution chosen for $\{X = \tau.X\}$ has only a τ-transition to itself, a process that is bisimilar to $\tau.\delta$ in observational congruence. Finally, also in CSP a solution will be chosen, but a different one, the least deterministic one. Thus, both CCS and CSP use a least fixed point construction, but with respect to a different ordering relation. In CSP, the solution chosen for the equation $\{X = X\}$ is the *chaos* process $\perp$, a process that satisfies $x + \perp = \perp$ for all processes x (for an extension of TCP with such a process, see [2], based on [3]).

Here we will introduce in TCP the possibility of performing (not guarded) recursive specifications by means of an operator $\langle X|E\rangle$ (where $E = E(V)$ is a recursive specification and X a variable in V which acts as the initial variable) which, similarly as in CCS, yields the least transitions in the generated transition system. Note that our approach also encompasses recursive specifications in ACP which are usually assumed to be guarded. The extended signature gives rise to a process algebra that we call TCP+REC.

More precisely, the set of terms of TCP+REC is generated by the following syntax:

$$t ::= \delta \mid \epsilon \mid a.t \mid \tau.t \mid t + t \mid t \cdot t \mid t \parallel t \mid t \llcorner\!\llcorner t \mid t \,|\, t \mid \partial_H(t) \mid \tau_I(t) \mid \rho_f(t) \mid X \mid \langle X | E \rangle$$

where $E = E(V)$ is a set of equations $E = \{X = t \mid X \in V\}$.

Note that terms t included in recursive specifications are again part of the same syntax, i.e. they may include again recursive specifications. In the following we will use t_X to denote the term defining variable X (i.e. $X = t_X$) in a given recursive specification.

As usual, in the following, we will use, as terms representing processes, closed terms over the syntax above. In the setting above a closed term is a term in which every variable X occurs in the scope of a binding recursive specification $E(V)$ such that $X \in V$. Note that the binding recursive specification may not be the one that directly includes the equation which contains the occurrence of X in the right-hand term, but X may be bound by an outer recursive specification, as e.g. in:

$$\langle\, X \mid \{\, X = a.\langle Y | \{Y = X + Y\}\rangle \,\}\, \rangle$$

Table 3 provides deduction rules for recursive specifications. Such rules are similar to those in [11], but we have the additional possibility of nesting recursion operators inside recursion operators. They come down to looking upon $\langle X|E\rangle$ as the process $\langle t_X|E\rangle$, which is defined as follows.

Definition 3. Given a recursive specification $\langle X|E\rangle$ with the syntax above, where $E = E(V)$, we define $\langle t_X|E\rangle$ to be t_X where, for all $Y \in V$, all free occurrences of Y in t_X are replaced by $\langle Y|E\rangle$.

Note that in $\langle t_X|E\rangle$ we replace not only variables $Y \in V$ occurring directly in t_X, but even Y occurring freely inside inner recursive specifications, e.g. in

$$\langle\ a.\langle Y | \{Y = X + Y\}\rangle \mid \{\, X = a.\langle Y | \{Y = X + Y\}\rangle \,\}\ \rangle$$

variable X of $a.\langle Y|\{Y = X+Y\}\rangle$ is replaced by $\langle X|\{\, X = a.\langle Y|\{Y = X+Y\}\rangle \,\}\rangle$ yielding:

$$a.\langle\ Y \mid \{Y = \langle X|\{\, X = a.\langle Y|\{Y = X + Y\}\rangle \,\}\rangle + Y\}\ \rangle$$

Table 3. Deduction rules for recursion

$$\frac{\langle t_X|E\rangle \xrightarrow{\alpha} y}{\langle X|E\rangle \xrightarrow{\alpha} y} \quad \frac{\langle t_X|E\rangle \downarrow}{\langle X|E\rangle \downarrow}$$

In order to remain in the setting of processes with a finite-state model we now consider a restricted syntax for constants $\langle X|E\rangle$ which guarantees that transition systems generated by the operational rules are indeed finite-state.

Definition 4. Let E be a recursive specification over a set of variables V. We call E *essentially finite state* if E has only finitely many equations and all variables in all right-hand sides of all equations of E do not occur in the scope of one of the operators $\|, \lfloor\!\lfloor, \mid, \partial_H, \tau_I, \rho_f$ or on the left-hand side of the operator $\cdot$. We call E *regular* if E has only finitely many equations and each equation is of the form

$$X = \sum_{1 \leq i \leq n} \alpha_i.X_i + \{\epsilon\},$$

where an empty sum stands for δ and the ϵ summand is optional, for certain $n \in \mathbb{N}, \alpha_i \in A \cup \{\tau\}, X_i \in V$. It is immediate that every regular recursive specification is essentially finite-state.

Now it is a well-known fact that each finite state process allows a regular recursive specification. But also in the other direction, every process specified by a term including essentially finite state recursive specifications only has finitely many states in the transition system generated by the operational rules.

Proposition 5. Given a term t such that every recursive specification E included in t is essentially finite state. Then the transition system generated by the operational rules has only finitely many states.

Proof. See [5] for a complete proof. □

The following proposition shows that the definition of essentially finite state does not disregard unnecessarily terms which generate finite-state transition systems. In the proposition we assume that an occurrence of a variable X is reachable, if, once such an occurrence of X is replaced by $a_X.\delta$, there is a path that leads to the execution of the action a_X.

Proposition 6. Let t be a term that includes a recursion $\langle X|E\rangle$ such that the recursive specification E has finitely many equations but is not essentially finite state. If one of the occurrences of variables in V which violate the condition, i.e. which are in the scope of one of the operators $\|, \lfloor\!\lfloor, \mid, \partial_H, \tau_I, \rho_f$ or on the left-hand side of the operator $\cdot$, is reachable from $\langle X|E\rangle$, then t has infinitely many states.

Proof. It is just a matter of showing that, since there is a variable which violates the condition and is reachable, then there is a loop where every time a new copy of the static operator is produced (or of the righthand-side of the sequencing), hence the transition system produced is infinite. □

In the rest of this paper, we will consider the process algebra TCP+REC$_f$ obtained by extending the signature of TCP with essentially finite state recursive specifications, i.e. we consider closed terms in the syntax above, where we additionally require that every recursive specification included is essentially finite-state. Together Table 1 and Table 3 provide a transition system space over the signature of TCP+REC$_f$.

Table 4. Axioms for recursion

$\langle X \mid E \,\tilde{\cup}\, \{Y = t\}\rangle = \langle X \mid E\{\langle Y \mid Y = t\rangle / Y\}\rangle$ if $X \neq Y$	Dec
$\langle X \mid X = t\rangle = t\{\langle X \mid X = t\rangle / X\}$	Unf
$y = t\{y/X\} \quad \Rightarrow \quad y = \langle X \mid X = t\rangle$ if $X = t$ guarded	Fold
$\langle X \mid X = X + t\rangle = \langle X \mid X = t\rangle$	Ung
$\langle X \mid X = \tau.(X + t) + s\rangle = \langle X \mid X = \tau.(t + s)\rangle$	WUng
$\tau_I(\langle X \mid X = t\rangle) = \langle X \mid X = \tau_I(t)\rangle$	Hid

5 Axiomatization

Now we will present a sound axiomatization which is ground-complete for the process algebra TCP+REC$_f$. The axioms in Table 2 together with the axioms in Table 4 form such an axiomatization. In the axioms of Table 4 we use the usual operation $\{t/X\}$ for expressing syntactical replacement of a closed term t for every free occurrence of variable X. Such an operation can be applied to a term t' or to the righthand-side of all equations in a recursive specification $E = E(V)$ such that $X \notin V$ by writing $t'\{t/X\}$ and $E\{t/X\}$, respectively. Moreover the symbol $\tilde{\cup}$ stands for disjoint union. Note that the axioms in Table 4 are *axiom schemes*: we have these axioms for each possible term t.

The axiom Dec is used to decompose recursive specifications E made up of multiple (finitely-many) equations into several recursive specifications made up of single equations. For example the process

$$\langle\ X \mid \{X = a.X + b.Y, Y = c.X + d.Y\}\ \rangle$$

is turned into

$$\langle\ X \mid \{X = a.X + b.\langle Y \mid \{Y = c.X + d.Y\}\rangle\}\ \rangle$$

The unfolding axiom (Unf) is Milner's standard one. In ACP, where usually there is no explicit recursion operator, it corresponds to the *Recursive Definition Principle*: it states that the constant $\langle X \mid E\rangle$ is a solution of the recursive specification E. Thus, each recursive specification has a solution. The folding axiom (Fold) is Milner's standard one: it states that if y is a solution for X in E, and E is guarded, then $y = \langle X \mid E\rangle$. In ACP, where usually there is no explicit recursion operator, it corresponds to the *Recursive Specification Principle*: it says that each guarded recursive specification has at most one solution.

Axioms Ung, WUng, Hid are used to deal with unguarded specifications. Ung, which is the same as in Milner's axiomatization, is the axiom that deals with variables not in the scope of any prefix operator (fully unguarded recursion). WUng and Hid are instead needed to get rid of weakly unguarded recursion. As far as WUng is concerned, it gets rid of weakly unguarded recursion arising from just prefixing and summation. It is easy to see that it replaces the two axioms of Milner:

$$\langle X|X = \tau.X + t\rangle = \langle X|X = \tau.t\rangle$$
$$\langle X|X = \tau.(X + t) + s\rangle = \langle X|X = \tau.X + t + s\rangle$$

The first one is obtained from (WUng) by just taking $t = \delta$. The second one is obtained from (WUng) as follows:

$$\langle X|X = \tau.(X + t) + s\rangle = \langle X|X = \tau.(t + s)\rangle$$

by directly applying (WUng) and then

$$\langle X|X = \tau.(t + s)\rangle = \langle X|X = \tau.X + t + s\rangle$$

by applying (WUng) where we take $s = t + s$ and $t = \delta$.

As explained in the introduction, the axiom (Hid) is used to get rid of weak unguardedness generated by the hiding operator. It allows to turn a term into such a form that the standard axioms for weak unguardedness can be used (see the proof of the following Proposition 8).

Note that if we want to derive a ground-complete axiomatization in a setting where no construct is added for recursion, as usually done in the context of the ACP process algebra (so we just have closed terms over the syntax of TCP and we just consider sets of recursion equations over this syntax), then in order to achieve the effect of our axiom Hid we have to add a much more complex set of conditional equations called CFAR (Cluster Fair Abstraction Rule) introduced in [18]. CFAR is a generalisation of the KFAR (Koomen's Fair Abstraction Rule) introduced in [6].

Proposition 7. The axiomatization formed by the axioms in Table 2 and by the axioms in Table 4 is sound for the model of transition systems modulo observational congruence generated by the rules in Tables 1 and 3.

Proof. Most of the axioms are standard. See [14] for the axiom (Hid). □

Proposition 8. The axiomatization formed by the axioms in Table 2 and by the axioms in Table 4 is ground-complete for the model of transition systems modulo observational congruence generated by the rules in Tables 1 and 3.

Proof. We show, by structural induction over the syntax of (possibly open) terms t of TCP+REC$_f$ such that free variables do not occur in the scope of one of the operators $\|$, $\lfloor\!\lfloor$, $|$, $\partial_H, \tau_I, \rho_f$ or on the left-hand side of the operator $\cdot$, that t can be turned into normal form, where normal forms are defined as follows. A term is normal form if it is made up of only δ,ϵ,X,$a.t'$,$\tau.t'$,$t' + t''$ and $\langle X|E\rangle$, where E is guarded and contains one equation only. Proving this yields ground-completeness; this because normal forms are like terms of basic CCS (with the only difference that we have two non equivalent kinds of terminating processes δ and ϵ, instead of just one) and completeness over such terms has been proved by Milner (since we do not have $\cdot$ or $\|$ operators in normal forms the presence of the two ways of termination does not change the proof).

The base cases of the induction ($t \equiv \delta$ or $t \equiv \epsilon$ or $t \equiv X$) are trivial because they are in normal form already.

The inductive cases of the induction are the following ones:

- if $t \equiv a.t'$ or $t \equiv \tau.t'$ or $t \equiv t' + t''$ then t can be turned into normal form by directly exploiting the inductive argument over t' and t''.

- if $t \equiv t' \parallel t''$ or $t \equiv t' \lfloor\!\lfloor t''$ or $t \equiv t' \,|\, t''$ or $t \equiv \partial_H(t')$ or $t \equiv \rho_f(t')$, then we can turn t into normal form as follows. By exploiting the inductive argument over t' and t'', and by observing that t cannot include free variables, we know that t has a finite transition system. Let $t_1 \dots t_n$ be the states of the transition system of t, $t_n \equiv t$. It can be easily seen that, for each $i \in \{1 \dots n\}$, there exist m_i, $\{\alpha^i_j\}_{j \leq m_i}$ (denoting actions), $\{k^i_j\}_{j \leq m_i}$ (denoting natural numbers) s.t. we can derive $t_i = \sum_{j \leq m_i} \alpha^i_j.t_{k^i_j} + \{\epsilon\}$. Hence we can characterize the behavior of t by means of a set of equations similarly as in [16]. Moreover, similarly as for the unique solution of equations theorem of [16], we have that there is a term t''' in normal form such that we can derive $t''' = t_n \equiv t$. This can be shown as follows. For each i, from 1 to n, we do the following. If i is such that $\exists j \leq m_i : k^i_j = i$ we have, by applying $Fold$, that $t_i = \langle X | X = \sum_{j \leq m_i : k^i_j \neq i} \alpha^i_j.t_{k^i_j} + \sum_{j \leq m_i : k^i_j = i} \alpha^i_j.X + \{\epsilon\} \rangle$. Note that axiom $Fold$ is applicable because, by exploiting the inductive argument, t' and t'' are in normal form and contain guarded recursion only, hence (since the operators considered cannot turn visible actions into τ ones) every cycle in the derived transition system contains at least a visible action. Then we replace each subterm t_i occurring in the equations for $t_{i+1} \dots t_n$ with its equivalent term. When, in the equation for $t_n \equiv t$, we have replaced t_{n-1}, we are done.
- if $t \equiv t' \cdot t''$ then t is turned into normal form similarly as in the previous item. The only difference is that t'' may include free variables. Supposing that $c(t'')$ denotes the closed term obtained from t'' by replacing each free occurrence of a variable X by $a_X.\delta$, the procedure for obtaining the normal form from $t \equiv t' \cdot t''$ is the same followed for $t' \cdot c(t'')$ with the procedure of the previous item (note that when a state is reached such that any actions a_X corresponding to free variables X in t'' are immediately executable, the $\cdot$ operator has disappeared already).
- if $t \equiv \langle X | E \rangle$ then t is turned into normal form by first exploiting the inductive argument over terms t_Y where $Y \in V$, assuming $E = E(V)$, and then by applying axioms Ung and $WUng$ to get rid of generated unguarded recursion as in the standard approach of Milner (after decomposing multi-variable recursion with axiom Dec).
- if $t \equiv \tau_I(t')$ then t is turned into normal form as follows. By exploiting the inductive argument over t', we consider term t'' which is obtained by turning t' into normal form. Observe that t' (hence t'') cannot include free variables and that it has a finite transition system.
  We first show, by structural induction on term t'', that $\tau_I(t'')$ can be turned into $\tau_I(t''')$, where t''' is obtained from t'' by syntactically replacing each occurrence of an action in I with τ.
  The base cases of the induction ($t'' \equiv \delta$ or $t'' \equiv \epsilon$ or $t'' \equiv X$) are trivial because no action in I is included.
  The inductive cases of the induction are the following ones:
  - if $t'' \equiv a.t''_1$ then we have the following two cases:
    * if $a \in I$ then, since $\tau_I(a.t''_1)$ can be turned into $\tau.\tau_I(t''_1)$, which by induction hypothesis can be turned into $\tau.\tau_I(t'''_1)$, with t'''_1 such that

each occurrence of an action in I is replaced with τ, we obtain term t''' by the final transformation into $\tau_I(\tau.t_1''')$.
  * if $a \notin I$ then it is a repetition of the previous case where a is not turned into τ.
- if $t'' \equiv \tau.t_1''$ it is a repetition of the previous item where τ is not affected by the transformation.
- if $t'' \equiv t_1'' + t_2''$ then, since $\tau_I(t_1'' + t_2'')$ can be turned into $\tau_I(t_1'') + \tau_I(t_2'')$, which by induction hypothesis can be turned into $\tau_I(t_1''') + \tau_I(t_2''')$, with t_1''' and t_2''' such that each occurrence of an action in I is replaced with τ, we obtain term t''' by the final transformation into $\tau_I(t_1''' + t_2''')$.
- if $t'' \equiv \langle X|\{X = t_1''\}\rangle$ then, since $\tau_I(\langle X|\{X = t_1''\}\rangle)$ can be turned into $\langle X|\{X = \tau_I(t_1'')\}\rangle$ by means of axiom Hid, which by induction hypothesis can be turned into $\langle X|\{X = \tau_I(t_1''')\}\rangle$, with t_1''' such that each occurrence of an action in I is replaced with τ, we obtain term t''' by the final transformation into $\tau_I(\langle X|\{X = t_1'''\}\rangle)$ by means again of axiom Hid.

Then we use Ung and $WUng$ to get rid of generated unguarded recursion into t''' as in Milner's standard approach, thus getting a guarded t''''. Finally we consider $\tau_I(t'''')$ and we apply the same technique as for, e.g., the $||$ operator to turn it into normal form (exploiting the fact that t'''' is guarded, finite state and does not include free variables). In particular now we can do that because the application of the hiding operator has no effect on labels of transitions, hence it cannot generate cycles made up of only τ actions when the semantics is considered. □

6 Conclusion

We just make some commentary about future work. First of all, we claim that the axiomatization that we presented is complete over all terms in the signature of TCP plus the recursion operator $\langle X|E\rangle$ (without syntactical restriction) which are finite state, i.e. we can include also terms with variables bound by an outer recursion operator that are in the scope of static operators (or in the lefthand-side of a sequence) provided that they are not reachable. Moreover, we plan to rebuild the whole machinery we showed here in the case of branching bisimulation instead of considering observational congruence. In particular we claim that we can find a ground-complete axiomatization for essentially finite state behaviours modulo branching bisimulation by taking the axiomatization of [12], extending the syntax as we have done, and adding as only extra axiom our axiom (Hid).

Acknowledgements

We thank Rob van Glabbeek (NICTAustralia) and the anonymous reviewers for their useful remarks and suggestions. The replacement of the two axioms of Milner for weakly guarded recursion by just one axiom was also found independently by Rob van Glabbeek, but never published.

References

1. J.C.M. Baeten. Embedding untimed into timed process algebra: The case for explicit termination. *Mathematical Structures in Computer Science*, 13(4):589–618, 2003.
2. J.C.M. Baeten, T. Basten, and M.A. Reniers. *Algebra of Communicating Processes.* Cambridge Tracts in Theoretical Computer Science. Cambridge University Press, 2005.
3. J.C.M. Baeten and J.A. Bergstra. Process algebra with propositional signals. *Theoretical Computer Science*, 177(2):381–406, 1997.
4. J.C.M. Baeten, J.A. Bergstra, C.A.R. Hoare, R. Milner, J. Parrow, and R. de Simone. The variety of process algebra. Deliverable ESPRIT Basic Research Action 3006, CONCUR, 1991.
5. J.C.M. Baeten and M. Bravetti. A ground-complete axiomatization of finite state processes in process algebra. Technical Report CS Report 05-18, Technische Universiteit Eindhoven, Department of Mathematics and Computer Science, 2005.
6. J. A. Bergstra and J. W. Klop. Verification of an alternating bit protocol by means of process algebra. In Wolfgang Bibel and Klaus P. Jantke, editors, *Proc. Mathematical Methods of Specification and Synthesis of Software Systems*, volume 215 of *LNCS*, pages 9–23. Springer, 1986.
7. J.A. Bergstra and J.W. Klop. Algebra of communicating processes with abstraction. *Theoretical Computer Science*, 37(1):77–121, 1985.
8. J.A. Bergstra and J.W. Klop. A complete inference system for regular processes with silent moves. In F.R. Drake and J.K. Truss, editors, *Proc. Logic Colloquium'86*, pages 21–81. North-Holland, 1988.
9. M. Bravetti and R. Gorrieri. Deciding and axiomatizing weak st bisimulation for a process algebra with recursion and action refinement. *ACM Transactions on Computational Logic*, 3(4):465–520, 2002.
10. S.D. Brookes. On the relationship of CCS and CSP. In J. Diaz, editor, *Proceedings ICALP'83*, number 154 in LNCS, pages 83–96. Springer Verlag, 1983.
11. R.J. van Glabbeek. Bounded nondeterminism and the approximation induction principle in process algebra. In F.J. Brandenburg, G. Vidal-Naquet, and M. Wirsing, editors, *Proceedings STACS'87*, number 247 in Lecture Notes in Computer Science, pages 336–347. Springer Verlag, 1987.
12. R.J. van Glabbeek. A complete axiomatization for branching bisimulation congruence of finite-state behaviours. In A.M. Borzyszkowski and S. Sokolowski, editors, *Proc. MFCS'93*, volume 711 of *LNCS*, pages 473–484. Springer, 1993.
13. R.J. van Glabbeek. On the expressiveness of ACP (extended abstract). In A. Ponse, C. Verhoef, and S.F.M. van Vlijmen, editors, Proceedings First Workshop on the *Algebra of Communicating Processes,* ACP94, Utrecht, The Netherlands, May 1994, Workshops in Computing, pages 188–217, 1994. Available at `http://boole.stanford.edu/pub/acp.ps.gz`.
14. R.J. van Glabbeek. Notes on the methodology of CCS and CSP. *Theoretical Computer Science*, 177(6):329–349, 1997.
15. C.A.R. Hoare. *Communicating Sequential Processes.* Prentice Hall, 1985.
16. R. Milner. A complete inference system for a class of regular behaviours. *Journal of Comput. System Sci.*, 28(3):439–466, 1984.
17. R. Milner. *Communication and Concurrency.* Prentice Hall, 1989.
18. F.W. Vaandrager. Verification of two communication protocols by means of process algebra. Technical Report report CS-R8608, CWI Amsterdam, 1986.

Decomposition and Complexity of Hereditary History Preserving Bisimulation on BPP*

Sibylle Fröschle and Sławomir Lasota**

Institute of Informatics, Warsaw University,
02–097 Warszawa, Banacha 2, Poland
{sib, sl}@mimuw.edu.pl

Abstract. We propose a polynomial-time decision procedure for hereditary history preserving bisimilarity (hhp-b) on Basic Parallel Processes (BPP). Furthermore, we give a sound and complete equational axiomatization for the equivalence. Both results are derived from a decomposition property of hhp-b, which is the main technical contribution of the paper. Altogether, our results complement previous work on complexity and decomposition of classical and history-preserving bisimilarity on BPP.

1 Introduction

The success of automatic verification in the finite-state world is contrasted by the reality that in practice most processes have either an infinite or an extremely large state space. Thus, it is important to clarify: how far can the automatic methods of the finite-state world be extended to infinite-state processes? It is folklore that full process calculi such as CCS are too expressive to allow for a decidable theory. However, there is now a standard hierarchy of restricted processes, the *Process Rewrite Systems* (*PRS*) hierarchy, along which the borderlines of decidability and complexity with respect to the major verification problems are well-investigated [19]. One central category of the PRS-hierarchy is *Basic Parallel Processes* (*BPP*): it can be seen as an extension of finite automata by a parallel composition operator. One of the major verification problems is to check whether two processes are equivalent under a given bisimulation equivalence.

With the recent addition of two more results our understanding of the computational power of bisimulation equivalences on BPP is now almost complete. On the one hand, the complexity of classical bisimilarity on BPP has finally been settled to be PSPACE-complete [18,11]. On the other hand, [16] has established that truly-concurrent bisimulation equivalences, such as *history preserving bisimilarity* (*hp-b*), are P-complete for this class; in [12] the upper bound has been improved to $O(n^3)$, building on the technique of [11]. Together, these results indicate the following trend: while in the finite-state world truly-concurrent verification problems are at least as hard as their interleaving counterparts (e.g. [13,15]), in the infinite-state world this effect seems reversed. The same trend has also been revealed in model-checking [4], and linear-time equivalence checking [20].

* This work is supported by the European Community Research Training Network GAMES.
** Partially supported by Polish KBN grant No. 4 T11C 042 25.

M. Abadi and L. de Alfaro (Eds.): CONCUR 2005, LNCS 3653, pp. 263–277, 2005.

One gap remains in our understanding of bisimilarities on BPP: the complexity of *hereditary history preserving bisimilarity* (*hhp-b*) [2,14]. Hhp-b is known to coincide with hp-b for *simple BPP* (*SBPP*) [6], and is thus polynomial-time decidable here. For full BPP it was shown to be decidable [5], but the proof left the complexity open. This paper fills this gap: we establish that hhp-b is polynomial-time decidable on BPP. Thereby we settle that hhp-b conforms to the positive trend for true-concurrency in the infinite-state world. This is particularly interesting since hhp-b takes a special position among bisimilarities: it is often considered to be *the* bisimulation equivalence for true-concurrency [14,8]. Unlike all the other equivalences it is undecidable for finite-state systems [15]; only a few positive results could be achieved for restricted classes [7].

The reason behind the positive trend for true-concurrency in the infinite-state world seems to be the following: BPP processes have natural decomposition characteristics; these may translate into decomposition results for truly-concurrent equivalences, and allow us to decide the respective concept by a 'divide and conquer' approach. There are two kinds of decomposition results that one can consider. The classical question is [17]: given a process class and an equivalence, is each process term uniquely, up to the equivalence, represented as a parallel composition of prime processes? A process is prime if it cannot be expressed, up to the equivalence, as a non-trivial parallel composition. This type of decomposition stands behind the polynomial-time algorithm for bisimilarity on normed BPP by Hirshfeld et. al. [10]. Unique decomposition has also been shown for BPP with respect to distributed bisimilarity [3] (which coincides with hp-b for BPP).

As recently advocated in [6], in a truly-concurrent framework one can also consider whether a given equivalence is decomposable with respect to the independent components of the processes to be compared. If two processes P and Q are equivalent then we ask whether there is a one-to-one correspondence between the components of P and those of Q such that related components are equivalent. This kind of decomposition stands behind the coincidence of hhp-b with hp-b on SBPP: decomposition was proved for hp-b and hhp-b for a class that subsumes SBPP (and incomparable to BPP) [6]. Hp-b is not decomposable in general, and, as we will see later, neither is it for BPP.

As our core result, we will resolve that, modulo hhp-bisimilar choices (a concept to be explained later), hhp-b on BPP is indeed decomposable in the second sense. We will also show that an analogue for the choice operator holds. Building on our decomposition theory we will design a decision procedure for hhp-b on BPP, running in $O(n^2 \log n)$ time. Further, we will give a complete equational theory for hhp-b. The latter connects to work of Christensen, who presented equational theories for classical and distributed bisimilarity for BPP [3]. We proceed as follows. Section 2 contains the necessary definitions. In particular, we define hhp-b in terms of a *step game*. In Section 3 we prove our decomposition results. In Section 4 we present the algorithm and in Section 5 the equational theory. In Section 6 we discuss the consequences of our results, and highlight some further directions. Some proofs, missing here, can be found in [9].

2 Preliminaries

BPP. In the following assume a countably infinite set of actions $Act = \{a, b, \ldots\}$ and a countably infinite set of process variables $Vars = \{X, X_1, \ldots\}$. *BPP expressions* are given by the following grammar:

$$E ::= \mathbf{0} \mid X \mid a.E \mid E{+}E \mid E||E,$$

where $\mathbf{0}$ is the empty process, X is a process variable, $a.X$ is action prefix, $E{+}E$ denotes nondeterministic choice, and $E||E$ parallel composition. We usually consider BPP expressions modulo associativity and commutativity of choice and parallel composition, and $\mathbf{0}$ as unit for these operators. A *BPP definition* Δ is a finite family of recursive equations $X \stackrel{\text{def}}{=} E_X$, where the X are distinct variables, and each E_X is a BPP expression that only contains variables defined by Δ and where each variable occurrence is guarded, i.e., within the scope of action prefix. (This ensures that recursive definitions yield unique solutions.) The set of variables occurring in Δ is denoted by $Vars_\Delta$. A *BPP process* is a pair (Δ, E), where Δ is a BPP definition, and E is an expression that only contains variables of $Vars_\Delta$. If Δ is clear from the context, we denote (Δ, E) simply by E.

Execution Normal Form. We will mainly work with BPP in *Execution Normal Form (ENF)*. *BPP expressions in ENF (ENF expressions)* are defined by:

$$E ::= \mathbf{0} \mid a.X \mid E{+}E \mid E||E.$$

Each BPP process (E, Δ) can easily be transformed into a process in ENF, $\texttt{enf}(E)$. During the transformation, always work modulo $\mathbf{0}$ as unit for '+' and '||': remove all superfluous occurrences of $\mathbf{0}$ in the expressions. Translate E and all defining expressions of Δ into ENF expressions by replacing each subexpression $a.E'$ by $a.X_{E'}$. Add new equations $X_{E'} \stackrel{\text{def}}{=} E'$ to Δ. E' is possibly unguarded. Therefore, replace each unguarded occurrence of a variable Y by E_Y. Treat such newly created defining expressions as the original ones, until finally all defining expressions will be in ENF. Note that this transformation only makes use of operations such as unfolding of variables and introduction of new variables for subexpressions, which will be respected by any behavioural equivalence.

Transition-Based ENF. For our definition of hhp-b, given a BPP E, we need to be able to uniquely identify each occurrence of an action prefix within E. A convenient way to do so is to work with labelled transitions rather than actions. In the following, for each $a \in Act$, assume a countably infinite set of transitions labelled by a, $T_a = \{t^a, t^a_1, \ldots\}$. Let $T = T_a \cup T_b \cup \ldots$ be the set of all transitions. Let $t, t_1, \ldots$ range over T, and set $l(t) = a$ if $t \in T_a$. *Transition-based ENF (T-ENF) expressions* are defined as follows:

$$E ::= \mathbf{0} \mid t.X \mid E{+}E \mid E||E,$$

where $t.X$ is transition prefix. We denote the set of transitions occurring in E by T_E. We only consider T-ENF expressions E that are *transition-genuine* in that every $t \in T_E$ appears syntactically only once in E. Given $t \in T_E$, there will be exactly one X such that '$t.X$' is a subexpression of E; denote X by X_t. Given a definition Δ, by $T\text{-}ENF_\Delta$ we denote all T-ENF expressions E such that E only contains variables of $Vars_\Delta$.

Proviso. In the following, we mainly work with T-ENF processes. We allow us to assume that all defining expressions in a definition Δ are in T-ENF, and that $\texttt{enf}(E)$ is in

T-ENF as well. Clearly, whatever we state for T-ENF processes can be carried over to ENF processes obtained by replacing all transitions with their labels.

Steps of T-ENF Processes. Rather than providing an operational semantics for T-ENF processes we prefer to capture the *concurrent steps* of a T-ENF expression E, i.e., the sequences of pairwise concurrent transitions initially enabled at E. This will be sufficient for our definition of hhp-b.

We say a transition t is enabled at E, written $E \xrightarrow{t}$, iff $t \in T_E$. If $E \xrightarrow{t}$ then the *parallel remainder* of E wrt. t, written $pR(E,t)$, is inductively defined as follows, where we work modulo $\mathbf{0}$ as unit for '$+$' and '$||$':

$$\begin{aligned} pR(t.X,t) &= \mathbf{0}, \\ pR(E+F,t) &= \texttt{if } t \in T_E \texttt{ then } pR(E,t) \texttt{ else } pR(F,t), \\ pR(E||F,t) &= \texttt{if } t \in T_E \texttt{ then } pR(E,t)||F \texttt{ else } E||pR(F,t). \end{aligned}$$

We say $r = t_1 \dots t_n \in T_E^*$ is a *concurrent step* of E, denoted by $r \in \mathit{steps}(E)$, iff there is a sequence $E_1, \dots, E_n$ such that $E = E_1$, and $\forall i \in [1,n]$, $E_i \xrightarrow{t_i}$ and $E_{i+1} = pR(E_i, t_i)$. We generalize $pR(E,t)$ to steps in the obvious way. Given $r \in \mathit{steps}(E)$ and $t \in T_E$, we say t is enabled at r, written $r \xrightarrow{t}$, iff $E' \xrightarrow{t}$, where $E' = pR(E,r)$. E' is a parallel remainder of E, written $E' \in pR(E)$, iff $E' = pR(E,r)$ for some $r \in \mathit{steps}(E)$.

Step Game and Hhp-b. The usual way to define hhp-b for BPP would be to proceed as follows: first, give the standard definition of hhp-b for, say, 1-safe Petri nets; second, define true-concurrency semantics for BPP so that each BPP is interpreted as a (typically infinite) 1-safe Petri net; and third, define two BPP to be hhp-bisimilar iff their interpretations as 1-safe Petri nets are hhp-bisimilar ([5]). To avoid the bulk of definitions this would require, we define hhp-b in a non-standard way, making use of a characterization of [5]: two T-ENF processes E and F are hhp-bisimilar iff: (1) Duplicator has a winning strategy $\mathcal{H}$ in a bisimulation game with backtracking, which is *only* played in the scope of the concurrent steps of E and F; and (2) whenever two transitions t_E and t_F are related by $\mathcal{H}$ then X_{t_E} and X_{t_F} are hhp-bisimilar.

Let E be a T-ENF expression, and $r = t_1 t_2 \dots t_n \in \mathit{steps}(E)$. Write $|r|$ for the length of r, that is $|r| = n$. Given $k \in [1,|r|]$, we define $\delta(r,k)$ to be the result of backtracking the kth transition in r, that is $\delta(r,k) = t_1 \dots t_{k-1} t_{k+1} \dots t_n$. Observe that we have $\delta(r,k) \in \mathit{steps}(E)$. Given $\mathcal{H} \subseteq \mathit{steps}(E) \times \mathit{steps}(F)$, we define $\mathit{Matches}(\mathcal{H})$ to be the set $\{(t_E, t_F) \mid (r_E t_E r'_E, r_F t_F r'_F) \in \mathcal{H},\ \text{where } |r_E| = |r_F|\}$.

Let E and F be T-ENF expressions. The $(E,F)_{\mathit{step}}$*-game* between Spoiler and Duplicator is played as follows. Configurations are pairs $(r_E, r_F) \in \mathit{steps}(E) \times \mathit{steps}(F)$ with $|r_E| = |r_F|$. The initial configuration is $(\varepsilon, \varepsilon)$. A play proceeds from (r_E, r_F) by the following rules:

1. Spoiler chooses one of E or F, say E, and picks a transition $t_E \in T_E$ that is enabled at r_E. Duplicator has to respond by executing a transition t_F in F that is enabled at r_F and satisfies $l(t_E) = l(t_F)$. Play continues at $(r_E t_E, r_F t_F)$.

2. Alternatively, Spoiler chooses one of E or F, say E; he picks $k \in [1, |r_E|]$, and backtracks the kth transition in r_E. Duplicator has to backtrack the corresponding transition in r_F. Play resumes at $(\delta(r_E, k), \delta(r_F, k))$.
3. The play continues like this forever, in which case Duplicator wins, or until either Spoiler or Duplicator is unable to move, in which case the other participant wins.

Note that a play can continue indefinitely only because of repeated backward and forward steps which may undo each other.

A winning strategy for Duplicator in the $(E, F)_{step}$-game is a set of configurations $\mathcal{H}$ such that $(\varepsilon, \varepsilon) \in \mathcal{H}$ and whenever Spoiler has a move at some $(r_E, r_F) \in \mathcal{H}$ then Duplicator has a response and the accordingly updated configuration is in $\mathcal{H}$.

Let Δ be a BPP definition in T-ENF. We map a relation $\sim \subseteq \textit{T-ENF}_\Delta \times \textit{T-ENF}_\Delta$ to a relation $\dot{\sim} \subseteq \textit{T-ENF}_\Delta \times \textit{T-ENF}_\Delta$ as follows: $E \dot{\sim} F$ iff Duplicator has a winning strategy $\mathcal{H}$ in the $(E, F)_{step}$-game such that for all $(t_E, t_F) \in \textit{Matches}(\mathcal{H})$, $X_{t_E} \sim X_{t_F}$ (by convention, for variables X and Y we write $X \sim Y$ if $E_X \sim E_Y$). In [9] it is proved that the standard definition of hhp-b on BPP (e.g. [5]) is equivalent to:

Definition 1. *Hhp-b, denoted by $\sim_{hhp}$, is the greatest relation $\sim$ such that $\sim = \dot{\sim}$. We carry over $\sim_{hhp}$ to all BPP processes: $E \sim_{hhp} F$ iff* $\texttt{enf}(E) \sim_{hhp} \texttt{enf}(F)$.

3 Decomposition

Let Δ be a BPP definition in T-ENF. All processes that appear in this section are assumed to be in $\textit{T-ENF}_\Delta$. We define the *summands* and *factors* of a process inductively as follows:

$$\texttt{summands}(E_1+E_2) = \texttt{summands}(E_1) \cup \texttt{summands}(E_2) \quad \texttt{summands}(t.X) = \{t.X\}$$
$$\texttt{summands}(E_1||E_2) = \{E_1||E_2\} \quad \texttt{summands}(\mathbf{0}) = \emptyset$$
$$\texttt{factors}(E_1+E_2) = \{E_1+E_2\} \quad \texttt{factors}(t.X) = \{t.X\}$$
$$\texttt{factors}(E_1||E_2) = \texttt{factors}(E_1) \cup \texttt{factors}(E_2) \quad \texttt{factors}(\mathbf{0}) = \emptyset.$$

We investigate whether hhp-b is decomposable wrt. parallel composition in the following sense: whenever E and F are hhp-bisimilar is there a bijection between the factors of E and those of F such that related factors are hhp-bisimilar? We also ask whether hhp-b is decomposable wrt. choice in the analogous sense. In view of Section 4 we prove our decomposition results in a more general formulation: we work with $\dot{\sim}$ rather than $\sim_{hhp}$, where we assume $\sim \subseteq \textit{T-ENF}_\Delta \times \textit{T-ENF}_\Delta$ to be an arbitrary equivalence.

A first observation is that we will have to work modulo choices that are trivial wrt. $\dot{\sim}$: let $P = E||F$ and $Q = P'+P''$ such that $P \dot{\sim} P' \dot{\sim} P''$; clearly P is equivalent to Q under any reasonable behavioural equivalence, but there is no bijection between the factors of P and those of Q. Formally, we capture trivial choices as follows.

Definition 2. *We say that E* contains a trivial choice wrt. $\dot{\sim}$ *if it contains, up to associativity and commutativity of $+$, a subexpression E_1+E_2 with $E_1 \dot{\sim} E_2$. When $\dot{\sim} = \sim_{hhp}$, we say that E* contains a hhp-bisimilar choice.

We will prove that, modulo trivial choices, $\dot{\sim}$ is indeed decomposable wrt. both operators. The proof of decomposition wrt. parallel composition relies on three lemmas. The first is a cancellation lemma, which holds in general.

Lemma 1. $F||E \dot{\sim} G||E \Longrightarrow F \dot{\sim} G$.

Proof. For shorter notation we set $L = F||E$ and $R = G||E$. Assume a winning strategy $\mathcal{H}$ for Duplicator in the $(L, R)_{step}$-game such that for all $(t_L, t_R) \in \mathit{Matches}(\mathcal{H})$, $X_{t_L} \sim X_{t_R}$.

Based on $\mathcal{H}$ we exhibit a winning strategy $\mathcal{H}'$ for Duplicator in the $(F, G)_{step}$-game. The idea behind the construction of $\mathcal{H}'$ is as follows. Assume, in the $(F, G)_{step}$-game, Spoiler picks a transition in F, say t_F, as his first move. This move can be copied to the $(L, R)_{step}$-game. According to $\mathcal{H}$, Duplicator has a reply, say t_m, either in E or in G. If the latter holds then Duplicator can copy t_m straight to the (F, G)-game. But what to do if t_m is in E? Then Duplicator can obtain her answer to t_F by the following 'zig-zag'-strategy. Spoiler can choose t_m in L as his next move in the $(L, R)_{step}$-game. If, according to $\mathcal{H}$, Duplicator's answer, say t'_m, is in G, take t'_m to be her reply to t_F in the $(F, G)_{step}$-game. Otherwise, let Spoiler perform t'_m in L as his next move in the $(L, R)_{step}$-game, and check whether this time Duplicator's answer is in G. We repeat this procedure, until, finally, we hit a match in G. In this manner, we will exhibit answers for Duplicator not only to Spoiler's first moves but to all of his moves.

We will make use of the following two observations, where $r_L \in \mathit{steps}(L)$, $r_R \in \mathit{steps}(R)$, $r_F \in \mathit{steps}(F)$, and $r_G \in \mathit{steps}(G)$. We use a notation $r \restriction T$ for projection of a concurrent step r on a set of transitions T, i.e., $r \restriction T$ is a concurrent step obtained by dropping all transitions of r that are not in T.

1. If $r_L \restriction T_E = r_R \restriction T_E$ then $\forall t_E \in T_E, r_L \stackrel{t_E}{\rightarrow} \iff r_R \stackrel{t_E}{\rightarrow}$.
2. If $r_L \restriction T_F = r_F$ then $\forall t_F \in T_F, r_L \stackrel{t_F}{\rightarrow} \iff r_F \stackrel{t_F}{\rightarrow}$. And, in analogy:
   If $r_R \restriction T_G = r_G$ then $\forall t_G \in T_G, r_R \stackrel{t_G}{\rightarrow} \iff r_G \stackrel{t_G}{\rightarrow}$.

Formally, we construct $\mathcal{H}'$ inductively from the initial configuration while preserving the following property:

Property P. Let $(r_F, r_G) \in \mathcal{H}'$; (r_F, r_G) is of the form $(t_F^1 \dots t_F^m, t_G^1 \dots t_G^m)$, where $m \geq 0$ and $\forall i \in [1, m]$, $t_F^i \in T_F$, $t_G^i \in T_G$. Then there is $(r_L, r_R) \in \mathcal{H}$ such that $r_L = w_L^1 \dots w_L^m$, $r_R = w_R^1 \dots w_R^m$, and $\forall i \in [1, m]$, w_L^i and w_R^i are of the form

$$\begin{aligned} w_L^i &= t_F^i t_E^1 \dots t_E^n, \\ w_R^i &= t_E^1 \dots t_E^n t_G^i, \end{aligned} \qquad \text{or} \qquad \begin{aligned} w_L^i &= t_E^1 \dots t_E^n t_F^i, \\ w_R^i &= t_G^i t_E^1 \dots t_E^n, \end{aligned}$$

where $n \geq 0$ and $\forall j \in [1, n]$, $t_E^j \in T_E$.

Base case. We start with $(\varepsilon, \varepsilon) \in \mathcal{H}'$. Property (P) trivially holds since $(\varepsilon, \varepsilon) \in \mathcal{H}$.

Inductive case. Let $(r_F, r_G) \in \mathcal{H}'$. Spoiler chooses his next move according to rule (1) or (2) of the game. Assume $(r_L, r_R) \in \mathcal{H}$ as given by (P). In either case, we construct a response for Duplicator such that (P) is preserved.

(1) Spoiler chooses one of F or G, say F, and performs a transition t_F of F that is enabled at r_F. Consider the $(L, R)_{step}$-game. Let Spoiler perform t_F at (r_L, r_R); this is possible by Observation (2). Say Duplicator's response according to $\mathcal{H}$ is t_m. We obtain a match for t_F in the $(F, G)_{step}$-game by the following 'zig-zag' algorithm:

> $r_L := r_L t_F; r_R := r_R t_m;$ -- update the configuration
> `while` $t_m \notin T_G$ `do`
> let Spoiler perform t_m in L;
> set t'_m to be Duplicator's response according to $\mathcal{H}$;
> $r_L := r_L t_m; r_R := r_R t'_m;$ -- update the configuration
> $t_m := t'_m;$ -- update the match
> `return` t_m;

The following is an invariant of the while-loop: let r'_R be given by r_R minus Duplicator's last match; (a) $r_L \upharpoonright T_E = r'_R \upharpoonright T_E$, and (b) $r'_R \upharpoonright T_G = r_G$. By (a) and Observation (1), the first instruction of the while-loop is indeed a valid move in the $(L, R)_{step}$-game. The algorithm clearly terminates: there is only a finite number of transitions in T_E. We take t_m to be Duplicator's response to t_F in the $(F, G)_{step}$-game; by (b) and Observation (2) this is a legal move. Thus, we extend $\mathcal{H}'$ by $(r_F t_F, r_G t_m)$. Property (P) will be preserved: at the last stage of the algorithm (r_L, r_R) is a configuration as required.

(2) Spoiler chooses one of F or G, say F; he picks $k \in [1, |r_F|]$, and backtracks the kth transition in r_F. Duplicator must backtrack the kth transition in r_G. We add $(\delta(r_F, k), \delta(r_G, k))$ to $\mathcal{H}'$. Property (P) will be preserved by this addition. In the $(L, R)_{step}$-game, at (r_L, r_R), let Spoiler backtrack all the w_L^k-transitions. Then $(w_L^1 \ldots w_L^{k-1} w_L^{k+1} \ldots w_L^m, w_R^1 \ldots w_R^{k-1} w_R^{k+1} \ldots w_R^m) \in \mathcal{H}$; but this is exactly a configuration as required.

It remains to check whether for all $(t_F, t_G) \in \mathit{Matches}(\mathcal{H}')$, $X_{t_F} \sim X_{t_G}$. Let $(t_F, t_G) \in \mathit{Matches}(\mathcal{H}')$. If $(t_F, t_G) \in \mathit{Matches}(\mathcal{H})$ then $X_{t_F} \sim X_{t_G}$ is immediate. Otherwise, wlog. assume (P) gives us $(t_F, t_E^1), (t_E^1, t_E^2), \ldots, (t_E^n, t_G) \in \mathit{Matches}(\mathcal{H})$, where $n > 0$, and $\forall i \in [1, n]$, $t_E^i \in T_E$. We know that $X_{t_F} \sim X_{t_E^1}$, $\forall i \in [1, n-1]$, $X_{t_E^i} \sim X_{t_E^{i+1}}$, and $X_{t_E^n} \sim X_{t_G}$. But then $X_{t_F} \sim X_{t_G}$ follows by transitivity of $\sim$. □

Relation $\dot{\sim}$ is a congruence with respect to parallel composition; hence we also obtain:

Corollary 1. *$(E \dot{\sim} E')$ & $(F||E \dot{\sim} F'||E') \Longrightarrow F \dot{\sim} F'$.*

The second lemma implies: if a choice and a parallel composition are related by $\dot{\sim}$ then the choice must be trivial wrt. $\dot{\sim}$.

Lemma 2. *If $E \dot{\sim} F$ and $|\mathtt{factors}(F)| \geq 2$ then for each $G \in \mathtt{summands}(E)$, $G \dot{\sim} F$.*

Proof. Let E and F be given as above. If $|\mathtt{summands}(E)| < 2$ then the lemma is immediate. Otherwise, let $\mathcal{H}$ be a winning strategy for Duplicator in the $(E, F)_{step}$-game such that for all $(t_E, t_F) \in \mathit{Matches}(\mathcal{H})$, $X_{t_E} \sim X_{t_F}$. Choose any $G \in \mathtt{summands}(E)$. We will exhibit a winning strategy $\mathcal{H}'$ for Duplicator in the $(G, F)_{step}$-game such that

$(t_G, t_F) \in \mathit{Matches}(\mathcal{H}')$ only if $(t_G, t_F) \in \mathit{Matches}(\mathcal{H})$. This will clearly yield $G \dot{\sim} F$.

If Spoiler picks a transition in G as his first move then Duplicator can copy her response and all subsequent moves straight from $\mathcal{H}$. This is so because: once we have decided for G, the other E-summands become disabled, and, from this point onwards, the $(E, F)_{step}$-game corresponds exactly to the $(G, F)_{step}$-game. Similarly, if Spoiler picks a transition in F as his first move, and, according to $\mathcal{H}$, Duplicator responds with a G-transition then she can copy this response and all subsequent moves from $\mathcal{H}$. The difficult case is when Spoiler performs his first move in F, say he executes t_F, and $\mathcal{H}$ prescribes a match in a E-summand other than G. We show that, in this case, Duplicator has an alternative match in G: we exhibit $t_E \in G$ such that $(t_E, t_F) \in \mathcal{H}$.

Consider the $(E, F)_{step}$-game. At $(\varepsilon, \varepsilon)$, let Spoiler perform a transition in G, say t_G; this is clearly possible. Assume, according to $\mathcal{H}$, Duplicator answers this move by t'_F. There are three cases:

(a) $t'_F = t_F$, (b) t'_F and t_F are concurrent in F, (c) t'_F and t_F are in conflict in F.

(Given an expression E, two distinct transitions $t, t' \in T_E$ are in conflict in E if there is a subexpression $E_1 + E_2$ of E with $t \in T_{E_1}$ and $t' \in T_{E_2}$; otherwise t, t' are concurrent in E.)

If (a) holds then t_G is a match as required. In case (b) Spoiler can perform t_F as his next move. Duplicator must match t_F by a transition in G, say t'_G. Let Spoiler backtrack t'_F. Duplicator must backtrack t_G. We arrive at $(t'_G, t_F) \in \mathcal{H}$, and thus t'_G is a match as required. Finally, assume (c) holds. t_F and t'_F must belong to the same factor of F, say H. There must be a further factor of F, say H'. Spoiler can perform a transition in H', say t''_F, as his next move. Duplicator must match t''_F by a G-transition, say t'_G. Let Spoiler backtrack t'_F. Duplicator must backtrack t_G. We arrive at $(t'_G, t''_F) \in \mathcal{H}$; but from here we can proceed exactly as in (b). □

With the help of the previous lemma we will show: given $E \dot{\sim} F$, where E and F are non-zero and contain no trivial choice, we can always find a factor G of E and a factor H of F such that $G \dot{\sim} H$. This will ensure that we can apply Corollary 1 consecutively to obtain our decomposition result.

Lemma 3. *Assume that E and F contain no trivial choice wrt. $\dot{\sim}$, and $E \neq \mathbf{0}$ or $F \neq \mathbf{0}$. If $E \dot{\sim} F$ then there exist $G \in \texttt{factors}(E)$ and $H \in \texttt{factors}(F)$ such that $G \dot{\sim} H$.*

Proof. Wlog. assume $E \neq \mathbf{0}$. Let $\mathcal{H}$ be a winning strategy for Duplicator in the $(E, F)_{step}$-game such that for all $(t_E, t_F) \in \mathit{Matches}(\mathcal{H})$, $X_{t_E} \sim X_{t_F}$. Choose any $G \in \texttt{factors}(E)$, and consider $r_E \in \mathit{steps}(E)$ such that $pR(E, r_E) = G$; this is clearly possible. There must be $r_F \in \mathit{steps}(F)$ such that $(r_E, r_F) \in \mathcal{H}$. Set $F' = pR(F, r_F)$. It is straightforward to derive $G \dot{\sim} F'$. One of the following three cases will hold:

1. $F' \in \texttt{factors}(F)$.
2. $F' \in pR(H)$ and $F' \neq H$ for some $H \in \texttt{factors}(F)$.

3. $F' = H'_1 || \dots || H'_n$, where $n \geq 2$ and $\forall i \in [1, n]$, $H'_i \neq \mathbf{0}$ and $H'_i \in pR(H)$ for some $H \in \texttt{factors}(F)$.

If (1) holds then G and F' are factors as required. If (2) applies, at (r_E, r_F), let Spoiler backtrack all the H-transitions in r_F. Duplicator must backtrack the corresponding transitions. The new configuration, say (r'_E, r'_F), satisfies: $pR(F, r'_F) = H$ and $pR(E, r'_E) = G||G'_1|| \dots ||G'_n$, where $n \geq 1$ and $\forall i \in [1, n]$, $G'_i \neq \mathbf{0}$ and $G'_i \in pR(G')$ for some $G' \in \texttt{factors}(E)$. But this means (2) reduces to (3): wlog. we can exchange G by H. Finally, assume (3) holds. G cannot be of the form $t.X$: we have $G \dot{\sim} F'$ but there are at least two concurrent transitions in F' for Duplicator to match. Since G cannot be a parallel composition either, we conclude $|\texttt{summands}(G)| \geq 2$. But then we can apply Lemma 2 to obtain a contradiction with our assumption that E does not contain any trivial choice wrt. $\dot{\sim}$. □

Now, we are ready to prove decomposition wrt. parallel composition.

Theorem 1. *Assume E and F contain no trivial choice wrt. $\dot{\sim}$. If $E \dot{\sim} F$ then there exists a bijection $\beta : \texttt{factors}(E) \rightarrow \texttt{factors}(F)$ such that $G \dot{\sim} \beta(G)$ for each $G \in \texttt{factors}(E)$.*

Proof. Set $m = |\texttt{factors}(E)|$. The proof is by induction on m. If $m = 0$ then we must also have $|\texttt{factors}(F)| = 0$, and a bijection as required is trivially given. If $m > 0$, we can apply Lemma 3 to obtain $G \in \texttt{factors}(E)$ and $H \in \texttt{factors}(F)$ such that $G \dot{\sim} H$. Let E' be given by $E = E'||G$, and F' by $F = F'||H$. Corollary 1 gives us $E' \dot{\sim} F'$, and, applying the induction hypothesis, we easily obtain a bijection as required. □

Decomposition wrt. choice is not as involved to prove. It is a consequence of the following theorem.

Theorem 2. *If $E \dot{\sim} F$ then*

- *for each $G \in \texttt{summands}(E)$ there is $H \in \texttt{summands}(F)$ such that $G \dot{\sim} H$,*
- *for each $H \in \texttt{summands}(F)$ there is $G \in \texttt{summands}(E)$ such that $G \dot{\sim} H$.*

Corollary 2. *Assume E and F contain no trivial choice wrt. $\dot{\sim}$. If $E \dot{\sim} F$ then there exists a bijection $\beta : \texttt{summands}(E) \rightarrow \texttt{summands}(F)$ such that $G \dot{\sim} \beta(G)$ for each $G \in \texttt{summands}(E)$.*

Although we will build on Theorem 1 and Corollary 2 it is worth spelling them out for the special case $\sim = \sim_{hhp}$. By definition of hhp-b all the previous results carry over, and we obtain decomposition of hhp-b wrt. all BPP operators.

Corollary 3. *Assume E and F contain no hhp-bisimilar choice. If $E \sim_{hhp} F$ then*

- *there exists a bijection $\beta : \texttt{factors}(E) \rightarrow \texttt{factors}(F)$ such that $G \sim_{hhp} \beta(G)$ for each $G \in \texttt{factors}(E)$;*
- *there exists a bijection $\beta : \texttt{summands}(E) \rightarrow \texttt{summands}(F)$ such that $G \sim_{hhp} \beta(G)$ for each $G \in \texttt{summands}(E)$.*

Note that $\dot{\sim}$, including $\sim_{hhp}$, is clearly compositional, i.e., preserved by '$+$' and '$||$'; hence the opposite directions of Theorems 1, 2 and Corollaries 2, 3 hold as well.

4 Algorithm

Let Δ be a BPP definition in T-ENF. By convention, let E_X denote the defining expression of a variable X. Let n be the size of Δ, i.e., the sum of lengths of all E_X. We will concentrate on relations $\sim \subseteq Vars_\Delta \times Vars_\Delta$ between variables in this section. Hence, in the following, symbol $\sim_{hhp}$ is used to denote hhp-b restricted to variables. We will show that $\sim_{hhp}$ can be computed in time polynomial wrt. n.

Define an operator $\mathcal{F}$ that given $\sim \subseteq Vars_\Delta \times Vars_\Delta$ yields a relation $\mathcal{F}(\sim) \subseteq Vars_\Delta \times Vars_\Delta$, defined by: $\langle X, Y \rangle \in \mathcal{F}(\sim)$ iff $E_X \mathrel{\dot{\sim}} E_Y$. $\mathcal{F}$ can be seen as the restriction of the mapping $\sim \mapsto \dot{\sim}$ to variables. In particular, $\mathcal{F}$ is monotonic: if $\sim_1 \subseteq \sim_2$ then $\mathcal{F}(\sim_1) \subseteq \mathcal{F}(\sim_2)$. By Definition 1 we get:

Proposition 1. *$\sim_{hhp}$ is the greatest fixed point of $\mathcal{F}$.*

Hence, $\sim_{hhp}$ is the limit of the following sequence of approximants, where $\sim_0 = Vars_\Delta \times Vars_\Delta$:

$$\sim_0 \supseteq \mathcal{F}(\sim_0) \supseteq \mathcal{F}^2(\sim_0) \supseteq \ldots .$$

In other words, $\sim_{hhp}$ equals the first $\mathcal{F}^i(\sim_0)$ with $\mathcal{F}^i(\sim_0) = \mathcal{F}^{i+1}(\sim_0)$. It can easily be shown, by induction on i, that all the approximants are equivalence relations; hence the number of iterations is not greater than the number of variables. We only need to show that computing $\mathcal{F}^{i+1}(\sim_0)$ from $\mathcal{F}^i(\sim_0)$ can be done in polynomial time. We will prove:

Lemma 4. *Given an equivalence $\sim \subseteq Vars_\Delta \times Vars_\Delta$, relation $\mathcal{F}(\sim)$ can be computed in time $\mathcal{O}(n \log n)$.*

We will also show that checking whether the limit has been reached can be done without any extra cost. Thus, altogether we obtain:

Theorem 3. *Relation $\sim_{hhp}$ can be computed in time $\mathcal{O}(n^2 \log n)$.*

In the rest of this section we describe the algorithm announced in Lemma 4. It is inspired by the standard algorithm solving tree isomorphism (e.g. [1]). Our algorithm assigns an integer $i(v)$ to each node v of the syntactic trees corresponding to the defining expressions of Δ such that for any two nodes v_1, v_2 we have: $i(v_1) = i(v_2)$ iff the expressions represented by v_1 and v_2 are related by $\dot{\sim}$.

The nodes of the syntactic trees are of three types: prefix, '+' and '||'; the leaves are precisely the nodes of type prefix. We assume that the trees are constructed up to associativity and commutativity of '+' and '||'. In particular, if a node has type '+', its parent has type '||', and vice versa. The trees can be constructed in time $\mathcal{O}(n)$.

The algorithm works in bottom-up manner, visiting each of the nodes once. It starts in the leaves and each non-leaf is processed after all its children have been visited. In each node v, a sorted list l_v is computed. To start off with, l_v exactly contains the child nodes of v. To notionally remove trivial choices from the trees, l_v is processed such that: (1) if v is of type '+' then, for any integer j, l_v will contain at most one node v' with $i(v') = j$; (2) if v is of type '||' and some child v' of v has been identified as a trivial choice, i.e., v' is of type '+' and $l_{v'}$ contains only one node, say v'', then the nodes of

$l_{v''}$ will be inserted into l_v in place of v'. For convenience, we assume $l_v = \{v\}$ at each leaf v. A table T is used to store triples (j, x, t), where j is an integer assigned to some non-leaf node v, x is the type of v, and $t = i(l_v)$ is the sorted tuple of integers assigned to the nodes of l_v. The table T is initially empty.

Assign integers to all leaves such that two leaves $t.X$ and $t'.X'$ have the same integer iff $l(t) = l(t')$ and $X \sim X'$. This can clearly be done in time $\mathcal{O}(n)$. The processing of a non-leaf v depends on its type. First, we do the following:

```
let l_v be a tuple containing all child nodes of v
if v is of type '+'
    sort l_v wrt. the integers assigned to the nodes
    remove duplicates from l_v:                                        (*)
        as long as v_1, v_2 ∈ l_v, v_1 ≠ v_2 and i(v_1) = i(v_2), remove one of v_1, v_2
    if l_v contains only one node, mark node v 'trivial choice'
else                            -- i.e., v is of type '||'
    for each node v' ∈ l_v marked 'trivial choice'
        replace v' by the elements of l_v'', where {v''} = l_v'         (**)
    sort l_v wrt. the integers assigned to the nodes.
```

If v is marked 'trivial choice' then we assign to v the integer that has been given to the unique element of l_v. Otherwise, we perform a look-up in T. If a triple (j, x, t) is found with $t = i(l_v)$ and x the type of v, assign j to v. Otherwise, assign to v a fresh number j' and update T by inserting $(j', x', i(l_v))$ into T, where x' is the type of v.

After all nodes have been processed we assign to each variable X of Δ the integer assigned to the root of the tree that represents E_X. This yields a representation of $\mathcal{F}(\sim)$.

The correctness of the algorithm follows from Lemma 5 below. For its formulation and proof we adopt some conventions. Given an expression E, define the *children* of E, denoted by $\texttt{children}(E)$, as follows: if E is a choice then set $\texttt{children}(E) = \texttt{summands}(E)$, otherwise define $\texttt{children}(E) = \texttt{factors}(E)$. (If E is a prefix this implies $\texttt{children}(E) = \{E\}$.) Given a processed node v, let l_v^r be the 'real' tuple of v: if v is marked 'trivial choice' set l_v^r to be $l_{v'}$ where $\{v'\} = l_v$, otherwise set l_v^r to be l_v. We carry over $\dot{\sim}$ to nodes in the obvious way: e.g., given a node v, we write $E \dot{\sim} v$ iff E and the expression represented by v are related by $\dot{\sim}$.

Lemma 5. *Let v, v_1, v_2 be nodes of the trees after termination of the algorithm.*

1. *$v \dot{\sim} E$ for some process E such that*
   (a) *E does not contain any trivial choice;*
   (b) *there exists a bijection $\beta : l_v^r \to \texttt{children}(E)$ such that $v' \dot{\sim} \beta(v')$ for each $v' \in l_v^r$;*
   (c) *if there is no entry for $i(v)$ in T then E is a prefix, otherwise E is of type x, where x is given by $(i(v), x, i(l_v^r)) \in T$.*
2. *$v_1 \dot{\sim} v_2$ iff $i(v_1) = i(v_2)$.*

Proof (Sketch). The lemma follows by induction on the number of nodes that have already been processed. (1) If v is a prefix then take E to be v. Otherwise, for each $v_i \in l_v^r$ assume E_i such that $E_i \dot{\sim} v_i$ as given by the induction hypothesis. Let x be defined by $(i(v), x, i(l^r_v)) \in T$. If $x =$ '$||$' then take E to be the parallel composition of the E_i, otherwise take E to be the choice of the E_i. Using the induction hypothesis of (2) it is routine to check that $E \dot{\sim} v$ and that conditions (a)–(c) are satisfied.

(2)($\Rightarrow$) Assume E_1 and E_2 such that $E_1 \dot{\sim} v_1$ and $E_2 \dot{\sim} v_2$ as given by (1). Since E_1 and E_2 do not contain any trivial choice we can apply Theorem 1 and Corollary 2 to obtain: E_1 and E_2 must be of the same type, and there is a bijection between the children of E_1 and those of E_2 such that related children are in $\dot{\sim}$. If E_1 and E_2 are of type prefix then $i(v_1) = i(v_2)$ can be derived immediately. Otherwise, using the induction hypothesis, we first obtain $i(l^r_{v_1}) = i(l^r_{v_2})$, and then conclude $i(v_1) = i(v_2)$. ($\Leftarrow$) By a converse argument using congruence rather than decomposition. □

Finally, we provide a cost estimation of the algorithm.

Claim. The algorithm runs in time $\mathcal{O}(L \cdot \log n)$, where $L = \sum_v |l_v|$ is the sum of lengths of all tuples l_v. (When v is a '+' node, we consider the length of l_v *before* removing duplicates in $(*)$.)

Indeed: sorting l_v requires $\mathcal{O}(|l_v| \cdot \log |l_v|)$ time; each look-up and update can be done in time $\mathcal{O}(|l_v| \cdot \log n)$ by bisection: T never contains more than n entries, and equality test for l_v requires at most time $|l_v|$ since all tuples are sorted. The crucial observation for the total cost estimation is the following:

Claim. L is $\mathcal{O}(n)$.

Each node w belongs to a tuple l_v of its parent v (before w may be removed from l_v during $(*)$). Moreover, a node can belong to several other tuples $l_{v'}$, due to the replacement $(**)$ in the algorithm. Obviously, L is equal to the total number of pairs $(w, v) : w \in l_v$. There are at most n such pairs with v being the parent of w. We will show that there are also at most n pairs with v *not* the parent of w. Concretely, we will injectively assign to each such pair a node in the tree.

Consider stage $(**)$ of the algorithm: assume a '$||$' node v with one of its children v' marked 'trivial choice'; let $l_{v'} = \{v''\}$, and assume $w \in l_{v''}$. Node v' has type '+' and v'' can either be of type prefix or of type '$||$'. We will assign to the pair (w, v) a node as follows. There must be a second child $\bar{v}''$ of v' which satisfies $i(\bar{v}'') = i(v'')$; $\bar{v}''$ must have been removed from $l_{v'}$ at an earlier stage of the algorithm. We have $i(l_{v''}) = i(l_{\bar{v}''})$. Assign to (w, v) a corresponding node $\bar{w}$ in $l_{\bar{v}''}$. (Note that $\bar{w}$ is not necessarily a child of $\bar{v}''$.) In total, all pairs (w, v) with $w \in l_{v''}$ can be assigned injectively to the nodes of $l_{\bar{v}''}$. The crucial observation is that a node from $l_{\bar{v}''}$ will not be assigned to any other pair again later, since $\bar{v}''$ has been removed from $l_{v'}$. This implies that the mapping is injective.

To complete the cost estimation, we note that checking whether $\sim = \mathcal{F}(\sim)$ can be done without any extra cost. It can be shown that, as long as the limit has not been reached, in each iteration of the algorithm the set of nodes marked 'trivial choice' is a strict subset of the nodes thus marked in the previous iteration. Hence, let the overall algorithm terminate when no node is 'unmarked' during the current iteration.

5 Equational Theory

In this section we work with general BPP expressions. We give a complete equational theory for hhp-b. That is to say, $E \sim_{hhp} F$ if and only if $\vdash E = F$ can be derived within the theory. Our approach is sequent-based (similarly to [3]), i.e., we provide a set of axioms of the form $\Gamma \vdash E = F$, to be read as "$E = F$ is provable under assumption Γ", where Γ is a finite set of equations. We write $\vdash E = F$ when Γ is empty. Interestingly, our axiomatization is essentially the same as that given by [3] for hp-b on SBPP, a subclass for which hhp-b and hp-b coincide [6]. We work relative to a BPP definition Δ.

Summation

(S1) $\Gamma \vdash E{+}F = F{+}E$

(S2) $\Gamma \vdash E{+}(F{+}G) = (E{+}F){+}G$

(S3) $\Gamma \vdash E{+}\mathbf{0} = E$

(S4) $\Gamma \vdash E{+}E = E$

Composition

(P1) $\Gamma \vdash E \| F = F \| E$

(P2) $\Gamma \vdash E \| (F \| G) = (E \| F) \| G$

(P3) $\Gamma \vdash E \| \mathbf{0} = E$

Recursion

(R1) $\Gamma, E = F \vdash E = F$

(R2) $$\frac{\Gamma, X = F \vdash E_X = F}{\Gamma \vdash X = F} \quad (X \stackrel{\text{def}}{=} E_X) \in \Delta$$

Axioms (S1)-(S3) and (P1)-(P3) are the commutative monoid laws for summation and parallel composition. Axiom (S4) is idempotency for summation. Rules (R1)-(R2) are laws for recursion and can be seen as an instance of fixed-point induction. In particular, Rule (R2) says that in order to prove a goal $X = F$ under assumption Γ, one is allowed to replace X by its defining expression. Moreover, the additional assumption $X = F$ is added to Γ, which guarantees immediate termination of the proof, by (R1), whenever a subgoal $X = F$ is to be proved again.

In addition, we need standard equivalence rules (E1)-(E3) and substitutivity rules (C1)-(C3):

Equivalence

(E1) $\Gamma \vdash E = E$ (E2) $$\frac{\Gamma \vdash E = F}{\Gamma \vdash F = E}$$ (E3) $$\frac{\Gamma \vdash E = F \quad \Gamma \vdash F = G}{\Gamma \vdash E = G}$$

Congruence

(C1) $$\frac{\Gamma \vdash E = F}{\Gamma \vdash a.E = a.F}$$ (C2) $$\frac{\Gamma \vdash E = F}{\Gamma \vdash E \| G = F \| G}$$ (C3) $$\frac{\Gamma \vdash E = F}{\Gamma \vdash E{+}G = F{+}G}$$

A proof of $\Gamma \vdash E = F$ is in the form of a finite tree, whose root is labelled by $\Gamma \vdash E = F$, leaves are instances of axioms and the children of each non-leaf are determined by an instance of some rule (in fact, only (E3) admits more than one child). We write $\Gamma \vdash E = F$ when such a proof exists. (It would be more precise to write $\Gamma \vdash_\Delta E = F$; however, we assume that Δ is clear from the context.)

Soundness of the theory for hhp-b is intuitively clear: one would expect each rule to be respected by any behavioural equivalence. Completeness follows from the strong decomposition characteristics of hhp-b on BPP. A formal proof of soundness and completeness is provided in [9].

Theorem 4 (soundness, completeness). $\vdash E = F$ *if and only if* $E \sim_{hhp} F$.

6 Conclusions

We have provided a polynomial-time procedure (working in time $\mathcal{O}(n^2 \log n)$) to compute hhp-b on BPP. Our algorithm takes a BPP definition in T-ENF as input. Transformation to T-ENF can easily be done in time quadratic wrt. the size of the input; the size of the definition may also grow by that factor during the transformation. Furthermore, we have proposed a sound and complete equational axiomatization of the equivalence. The crucial insight behind both of these results is that, modulo hhp-bisimilar choices, hhp-b is decomposable wrt. parallel composition and choice. Our results highlight that, modulo trivial choices, hhp-b fully reflects the structure of BPP expressions. One could argue that this is what one would intuitively expect of a truly-concurrent bisimulation equivalence. In particular, it does not imply that hhp-b is trivial on BPP: hhp-bisimilar choices may be hidden deeply within the process definition.

One could ask whether hhp-b also satisfies the unique decomposition property usually investigated in the interleaving setting: is each BPP process uniquely, up to hhp-b, represented as a parallel composition of primes? A process is prime if it cannot be expressed, up to hhp-b, as a non-trivial parallel composition. Indeed, from our results it is straightforward to derive that hhp-b does satisfy unique decomposition in this sense: Lemma 2 ensures that there is a one-to-one correspondence between prime factors wrt. hhp-b and factors that do not contain any hhp-bisimilar choices.

As mentioned in the introduction, unique decomposition with respect to distributed bisimilarity, and hence with respect to hp-b, has been established for BPP [3]. It has also been proved that cancellation (c.f. Lemma 1) does hold for distributed bisimilarity [3]. However, the following example of [3] shows that hp-b is *not* decomposable wrt. $||$ or $+$, in the sense of Section 3.

$$E = (a.\mathbf{0} + b.\mathbf{0})||a.\mathbf{0} + a.\mathbf{0}||a.\mathbf{0} \qquad\qquad F = (a.\mathbf{0} + b.\mathbf{0})||a.\mathbf{0}.$$

Both E and F have no hp-bisimilar choices, and $E \sim_{hp} F$. But $\mathtt{summands}(E)$ and $\mathtt{factors}(F)$ have two elements while $\mathtt{summands}(F)$ and $\mathtt{factors}(E)$ are singletons. In particular, the example illustrates that Lemma 2 fails for hp-b. An interesting question that remains open is whether, modulo hhp-bisimilar choices, hhp-b is decomposable with respect to prime decompositions of labelled asynchronous transition systems (c.f. [6]).

Our algorithm is a natural complement of the polynomial-time procedures for hp-b on BPP [16,12]. However, in the case of hhp-b the good complexity is due to its very strong decomposition properties; the technique of [11] seems not to be applicable here. Both algorithms can be carried over to CPP, an extension of BPP that allows for synchronization between processes in CCS style but disallows a silent action τ to appear explicitly inside expressions. It is not clear whether a polynomial-time procedure exists for hhp-b or hp-b on BPP_τ, which extends CPP by allowing explicit τ-actions. Preliminary investigations give hope that polynomial-time complexity of hhp-b on BPP_τ can indeed be achieved;—this issue will be treated in detail in a full version of this paper.

References

1. A.V. Aho, J.E. Hopcroft, and J.D. Ullman. *The Design and Analysis of Computer Algorithms*. Addison-Wesley Publishing Co., 1974.
2. M. Bednarczyk. Hereditary history preserving bisimulation or what is the power of the future perfect in program logics. Technical report, Polish Academy of Sciences, Gdansk, 1991.
3. S. Christensen. *Decidability and Decomposition in process algebras*. PhD thesis, Dept. of Computer Science, University of Edinburgh, UK, 1993.
4. J. Esparza and A. Kiehn. On the model checking problem for branching time logics and basic parallel processes. In *CAV'95*, volume 939 of *LNCS*, pages 353–366. Springer-Verlag, 1995.
5. S. Fröschle. Decidability of plain and hereditary history-preserving bisimulation for BPP. In *Proc. EXPRESS'99, volume 27 of ENTCS*, 1999.
6. S. Fröschle. Composition and decomposition in true-concurrency. In *Proc. FOSSACS'05*, LNSC. Springer-Verlag, to appear, 2005.
7. S. Fröschle. The decidability border of hereditary history preserving bisimilarity. *Information Processing Letters*, to appear, 2005.
8. S. Fröschle and T. Hildebrandt. On plain and hereditary history-preserving bisimulation. In *MFCS'99*, volume 1672 of *LNCS*, pages 354–365. Springer-Verlag, 1999.
9. S. Fröschle and S. Lasota. Decomposition and complexity of hereditary history preserving bisimulation on BPP. Technical Report 280, Institute of Informatics, Warsaw University, Poland, 2005.
10. Y. Hirshfeld, M. Jerrum, and F. Moller. A polynomial time algorithm for deciding bisimulation equivalence of normed basic parallel processes. *Mathematical Structures in Computer Science*, 6:251–259, 1996.
11. P. Jančar. Bisimilarity of basic parallel processes is PSPACE-complete. In *Proc. LICS'03*, pages 218–227, 2003.
12. P. Jančar and Z. Sawa. On distributed bisimilarity over Basic Parallel Processes. In *Proc. AVIS2'05*, 2005.
13. L Jategaonkar and A. R. Meyer. Deciding true concurrency equivalences on safe, finite nets. *Theoretical Computer Science*, 154:107–143, 1996.
14. A. Joyal, M. Nielsen, and G. Winskel. Bisimulation from open maps. *Information and Computation*, 127:164–185, 1996.
15. Marcin Jurdziński, Mogens Nielsen, and J. Srba. Undecidability of domino games and hhp-bisimilarity. *Inform. and Comput.*, 184:343–368, 2003.
16. S. Lasota. A polynomial-time algorithm for deciding true concurrency equivalences of Basic Parallel Processes. In *Proc. MFCS'03*, LNCS 2747, pages 521–530. Springer-Verlag, 2003.
17. R. Milner and F. Moller. Unique decomposition of processes. *TCS*, 107(2):357–363, 1993.
18. J. Srba. Strong bisimilarity and regularity of Basic Parallel Processes is PSPACE-hard. In *Proc. STACS'02, LNCS 2285*, 2002.
19. J. Srba. *Roadmap of Infinite Results*, volume 2: Formal Models and Semantics. World Scientific Publishing Co., 2004.
20. K. Sunesen and M. Nielsen. Behavioural equivalence for infinite systems—partially decidable! In *ICATPN'96*, volume 1091 of *LNCS*, pages 460–479. Springer-Verlag, 1996.

Bisimulations Up-to for the Linear Time Branching Time Spectrum*

David de Frutos Escrig and Carlos Gregorio Rodríguez

Department of Sistemas Informáticos y Programación,
Universidad Complutense de Madrid
{defrutos, cgr}@sip.ucm.es

Abstract. Coinductive definitions of semantics based on bisimulations have rather pleasant properties and are simple to use. In order to get coinductive characterisations of those semantic equivalences that are weaker than strong bisimulation we use a variant of the bisimulation up-to technique in which we allow the use of a given preorder relation. We prove that under some technical conditions our bisimulations up-to characterise the kernel of the given preorder. It is remarkable that the adequate orientation of the ordering relation is crucial to get this result. As a corollary, we get nice coinductive characterisations of all the axiomatic semantic equivalences in Van Glabbeek's spectrum. Although we first prove our results for finite processes, reasoning by induction, then we see, by using continuity arguments, that they are also valid for infinite (finitary) processes.

1 Introduction

Along the years a great variety of concurrent process semantics have been proposed under different settings and from quite dissimilar points of view. The comparative study of concurrency semantics tries to shed light on this heterogeneous field to bring up differences and similarities that will allow to order and classify the variety of semantics, in spite of the different ways they are defined.

Clearly, the thorough work of Van Glabbeek is a cornerstone in the field of comparative concurrency semantics. In [Gla01] he presents the well known linear time-branching time spectrum for processes without internal transitions. There, fifteen different semantics are defined and ordered by their inclusion relations. Besides, for each equivalence a motivating testing scenario is provided, and for most of them, a complete axiomatisation for basic processes is given. Figure 1 shows these axiomatised semantics (but tree semantics) ordered by inclusion.

Not just because it is the strongest one of them, bisimulation [Par81, Mil89] merits a special attention. Bisimulation is a mathematically elegant concept that is recursively defined over the intensional description of processes. Its stability and elegance have been shown by several characterisations, for instance in terms

* Partially supported by the projects TERMAS TIC2003-07848-C02-01, MIDAS TIC2003-01000, PAC-03-001 and MRTN-CT-2003-505121/TAROT.

M. Abadi and L. de Alfaro (Eds.): CONCUR 2005, LNCS 3653, pp. 278–292, 2005.

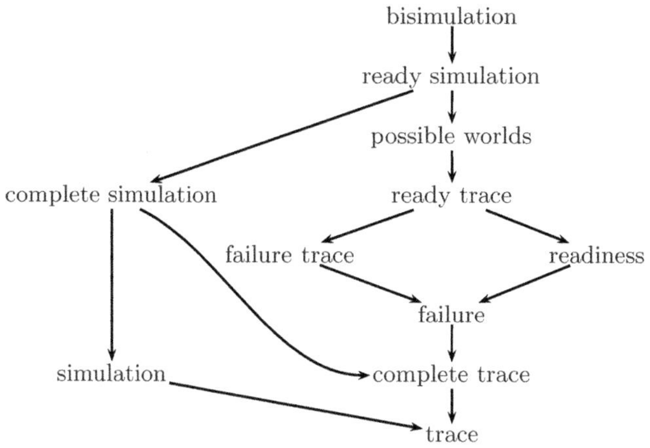

Fig. 1. Axiomatic Semantics in the Linear Time-Branching Time Spectrum I

of modal logic, final coalgebras, testing, etc. There also exist efficient algorithms to decide bisimulation equivalence and several tools that can effectively check process bisimilarity.

However, bisimulation is also too strong, and in many cases it is enough to take into account some weaker semantics. But, most of the semantics in Fig. 1 are extensional ([CS96]) and none of them has a symmetric, coinductive definition as bisimulation does. It is true that all the simulation semantics (simulation, ready simulation and so on) are intensional and quite close to bisimulation, but the induced equivalences are just the kernel of the corresponding preorder and do not admit a direct single symmetric definition. Could these semantics be somehow characterised by a symmetric definition? And for the other extensional semantics? Could they be expressed in a coinductive way?

In this paper we propose a way to weaken the definition of bisimulation by using a preorder relation, what we call *bisimulation up-to* the preorder. In this way we obtain a conductively and symmetrically defined equivalence, parameterised by preorders. As main results we prove that, under quite sensible assumptions on the considered preorder, bisimulation up-to such a preorder defines exactly the same equivalence that the kernel of the preorder does. These results are quite general and can be applied to all the semantics in Fig. 1 (and beyond), so that we get symmetric, coinductive, bisimulation-like definitions for nearly any reasonable semantics.

With these results we have answered the questions we left open in [dFG04], where we studied ready simulation as a representative example. There, we defined our *global bisimulations* that are indeed closely related to bisimulations up-to. They were previously introduced in a different context in [dFLN99].

There have been indeed some other previous approaches to the problem of getting coinductive characterisations of extensional semantics. Most of them study the question in a rather coalgebraic framework [JH03, KS03, Kli04, Jac04] and, in many cases, are based on relatively complex categorical concepts. These works aim generality and their results are rather general, but just because of that the machinery to apply them in particular cases can be rather complex. Instead, our results, at least as presented here, can only be applied to transition systems but they are quite simple to state and to apply.

Rutten [Rut03] has also made a coalgebraic approach to the subject but based on the novel concept of *behavioural differential equations*. Boreale and Gadducci in [BG03] have applied this technique to define a fully abstract model for the failures semantics. However the extension to other semantics seems not easy.

A different approach is presented in [Gar03] where the author uses predicate transformers to get a variant of the bisimulation equivalence that gives rise to both trace and failure preorders. However, for each of these preorders an ad-hoc construction is needed and it is not clear how to extend it to cover other semantics.

The rest of the paper is structured as follows. In Sec. 2 definitions and notations on processes and preorders are presented. In Sec. 3 we define bisimulations up-to a preorder and present the main results of the paper, namely Theorems 1 and 2. As a corollary of Theorem 1 all the semantics in Fig. 1 can be expressed by a bisimulation-like definition. Some examples help to clarify the role of the conditions in the theorems. In Sec. 4 the results of the previous section are extended to infinite finitary tree-like processes. In Sec. 5 we discuss a simple application example. Finally, in Sec. 6 we present some conclusions and lines for future work.

Along this paper we make use of the semantics in Fig. 1. Most of them can be considered *classical* and are well known, anyway we refer to [Gla01] for formal definition of each semantics and to Tables 2 and 3 in that paper for the complete axiomatisation for the equivalences and preorders, respectively, that we use in some of our examples and proofs.

2 Processes and Preorders

The behaviour of processes is usually described using the well-established formalism of *labelled transition systems* [Plo81] or lts for short.

Definition 1. *A labelled transition system is a structure* $\mathcal{T} = (\mathcal{P}, Act, \rightarrow)$ *where*

- $\mathcal{P}$ *is a set of processes, agents or states,*
- Act *is a set of actions and*
- $\rightarrow \subseteq \mathcal{P} \times Act \times \mathcal{P}$ *is a transition relation.*

A rooted lts is a pair $(\mathcal{T}, p_0)$ *with* $p_0 \in \mathcal{P}$.

Act is the set of actions that processes can perform and the relation $\rightarrow$ describes the process transitions after the execution of actions. The triple $\langle p, a, q\rangle$ is represented by $p \xrightarrow{a} q$, indicating that process p performs action a evolving to process q. A rooted lts describe the semantics of a process: that corresponding to its initial state p_0.

Some usual notations on lts are used. We write $p \xrightarrow{a}$ if there exists a process q such that $p \xrightarrow{a} q$ and, on the contrary, we write $p \not\xrightarrow{a}$ if there exists no process q such that $p \xrightarrow{a} q$. For a string of actions $\sigma = a_1 a_2 \cdots a_n$, $a_i \in Act$, $p \xrightarrow{\sigma} q$ means that there exist processes $q_1 \ldots q_{n-1}$, such that $p \xrightarrow{a_1} q_1 \xrightarrow{a_2} q_2 \xrightarrow{a_3} \cdots q_{n-1} \xrightarrow{a_n} q$. The function I calculates the set of initial actions of a process, $I(p) = \{a \mid a \in Act \text{ and } p \xrightarrow{a}\}$.

Lts's for finite processes are just finite trees, which can be syntactically described by a basic process algebra BCCSP, which was also used in [Gla01].

Definition 2. *Given a set of actions Act, the set of BCCSP processes is defined by the following BNF-expression:*

$$p ::= \mathbf{0} \mid ap \mid p + q$$

where $a \in Act$. $\mathbf{0}$ represents the process that performs no action; for every action in Act, there is a prefix operator; and + is a choice operator.

Therefore, BCCSP is just the term algebra for the signature $(\mathbf{0}, a \in Act, +)$. The set of rooted lts's is also the support of such an algebra, by defining prefix and choice operators in the natural way. All the definitions in the paper are valid for arbitrary processes, that is, for arbitrary rooted lts's. However we are going to prove the main results in the paper in two steps. First, we reason by induction on the depth of processes, and therefore the results would only be valid, at the moment, for BCCSP processes. Second, we use continuity arguments to extend these results to a general class of infinite tree-like processes.

The operational semantics for the BCCSP terms is defined in Fig. 2. The depth of a BCCSP process is the depth of the tree it denotes.

$$ap \xrightarrow{a} p \qquad \frac{p \xrightarrow{a} p'}{p + q \xrightarrow{a} p'} \qquad \frac{q \xrightarrow{a} q'}{p + q \xrightarrow{a} q'}$$

Fig. 2. Operational Semantics for BCCSP Terms

As usual, trailing occurrences of the constant **0** are omitted. By using $\sum$ as a shorthand for multiple choice (which is commutative and associative) we can write any process as $\sum_i \sum_j a_i p_{ij}$. A process aq' is a summand of the process q if and only if $q \xrightarrow{a} q'$. Given $a \in Act$ we define $p|_a$ as the (sub)process we get by adding all the a-summands of p. That is, if $p = \sum_i \sum_j a_i p_{ij}$, then $p|_{a_i} = \sum_j a_i p_{ij}$.

Preorders, that we represent by $\sqsubseteq$, are reflexive and transitive relations. We use the symbol $\sqsupseteq$ to represent the preorder relation $\sqsubseteq^{-1}$. Every preorder induces an equivalence relation that we denote by $\equiv$; that is, $p \equiv q$ if and only if $p \sqsubseteq q$ and $q \sqsubseteq p$. We will denote by $=_B$ the bisimulation equivalence. We are interested on preorders that are weaker than it.

Definition 3. *A preorder relation* $\sqsubseteq$ *over processes is a* behaviour preorder *when it is weaker than the bisimulation equivalence, i.e.* $p =_B q \Rightarrow p \sqsubseteq q$, *and it is a precongruence with respect to the prefix and choice operators, i.e. if* $p \sqsubseteq q$ *then* $ap \sqsubseteq aq$; *and if* $p \sqsubseteq q$ *then* $p + r \sqsubseteq q + r$.

Definition 4. *A behaviour preorder* $\sqsubseteq$ *is* initials preserving *when* $p \sqsubseteq q$ *implies* $I(p) \subseteq I(q)$. *It is* action factorised *(or just* factorised*) when* $p \sqsubseteq q$ *implies* $p|_a \sqsubseteq q|_a$, *for all* $a \in I(p)$.

Initials preservation and factorisation are natural properties that are satisfied by any of the behaviour preorders corresponding to the semantics in Fig. 1, from trace preorder to ready simulation preorder (Table 3 in [Gla01] shows the axiomatisation of these preorders).

There are other properties that a behaviour preorder can satisfy and that are going to play an important role in the rest of the paper. We say that a behaviour preorder $\sqsubseteq$ satisfies the property

(S)	if for all p and q, $p \sqsubseteq p + q$
(CS)	if for all a, p and q, $ap \sqsubseteq ap + q$
(RS)	if for all a, p and q, $ap \sqsubseteq ap + aq$

These axioms characterise the simulation preorder, the complete simulation preorder and the ready simulation preorder, respectively.

We finish this section by introducing another interesting property.

Definition 5. *Let* $\sqsubseteq$ *be a behaviour preorder and* $\equiv$ *the induced equivalence. Then* $\sqsubseteq$ *has the* Hoare equivalence property[1] *(HE for short) whenever*

$$\left.\begin{array}{r} \text{for all } p \xrightarrow{a} p' \text{ there exists } q', q \xrightarrow{a} q' \text{ and } p' \sqsubseteq q' \\ \text{and for all } q \xrightarrow{a} q' \text{ there exists } p', p \xrightarrow{a} p' \text{ and } q' \sqsubseteq p' \end{array}\right\} \text{ then } p \equiv q$$

3 Bisimulation Up-to a Preorder

In Sec. 2 the behaviour of processes is described in terms of the actions they can perform, so it is natural to define the process equivalence in terms of these action transitions. That is precisely what bisimulations do: they inductively explore the intensional behaviour of processes. Bisimulation was introduced in [Par81] and it has became one of the fundamental notions in the theory of concurrent processes. It is defined as follows.

Definition 6 ([Mil89]). *A binary relation* $\mathcal{R}$ *is called a (strong)* bisimulation *if for all* p, q *processes such as* $p \,\mathcal{R}\, q$, *and for all* $a \in Act$, *the following properties are satisfied:*

- *Whenever* $p \xrightarrow{a} p'$ *there exists some* q' *such that* $q \xrightarrow{a} q'$ *and* $p' \,\mathcal{R}\, q'$.
- *Whenever* $q \xrightarrow{a} q'$ *there exists some* p' *such that* $p \xrightarrow{a} p'$ *and* $p' \,\mathcal{R}\, q'$.

[1] The name comes from Hoare's powerdomain construction.

Two processes p and q are bisimilar, *notation* $p =_B q$, *if there exists a bisimulation containing the pair* $\langle p, q \rangle$.

Let us recall that the definition imposes *simultaneous simulations* by means of a single symmetrical definition of bisimulations. If instead, *separated simulations* are considered, the induced equivalence relation, that we call mutual simulation, is weaker than bisimulation equivalence (see [Gla01] for details).

In [Mil89], in order to make bisimilarity easier to decide, Milner introduced the notion of *bisimulation up-to* (strong) bisimilarity. This is a useful technique, but care must be taken when generalising it. It is well known that the original (simple and natural!) definition of weak bisimulation up-to weak bisimulation, that appeared in [Mil89], was wrong. Later, in [SM92] two new up-to (now correct, but more involved!) techniques were proposed. Sangiorgi continued with the study of up-to techniques in [San98], but focusing on reducing the size of the bisimulation relations to prove that two given processes are bisimilar.

In this paper we retake the concept of bisimulation up-to but we use it with a different goal. We are looking for the adequate way to weaken the definition of bisimulation in such a manner that weaker equivalences can be captured by a coinductive definition.

Definition 7. *Let* $\sqsubseteq$ *be a behaviour preorder. Then a binary relation S over processes is a* bisimulation up-to $\sqsubseteq$, *if pSq implies that:*

- *For every a, if* $p \xrightarrow{a} p'_a$, *then there exist* q' *and* q'_a, $q \sqsupseteq q' \xrightarrow{a} q'_a$ *and* $p'_a S q'_a$;
- *For every a, if* $q \xrightarrow{a} q'_a$, *then there exist* p' *and* p'_a, $p \sqsupseteq p' \xrightarrow{a} p'_a$ *and* $p'_a S q'_a$.

Two processes are bisimilar up-to $\sqsubseteq$, *written* $p \approx_{\sqsubseteq} q$, *if there exists a bisimulation up-to* $\sqsubseteq$, *S, such that pSq.*

The key point in the previous definition is that the process that has to mimic the movement of the other is allowed to: first, to transform itself according to the inverse of the considered preorder relation; second, to execute the corresponding action. The added capability generalises the original definition of bisimulation, so that we have now more chances to prove the equivalence between processes. When the behaviour preorder is just the identity relation we get the bisimulation equivalence, but, as we are going to prove below, considering other behaviour preorders we will be able to get other interesting semantics (traces, failures, ready simulation and so on).

For the sake of simplicity, we often drop the subscript, and use $\approx$ instead of $\approx_{\sqsubseteq}$, when the behaviour preorder is clear from the context.

Proposition 1. *For every behaviour preorder* $\sqsubseteq$, *if* $p \equiv q$ *then* $p \approx q$.

Proof. If $p \equiv q$ *then* $p \sqsubseteq q$ *and* $q \sqsubseteq p$. *For every transition* $p \xrightarrow{a} p'_a$, *then* $q \sqsupseteq p \xrightarrow{a} p'_a$ *and, symmetrically, for every transition* $q \xrightarrow{a} q'_a$, *then* $p \sqsupseteq q \xrightarrow{a} q'_a$.

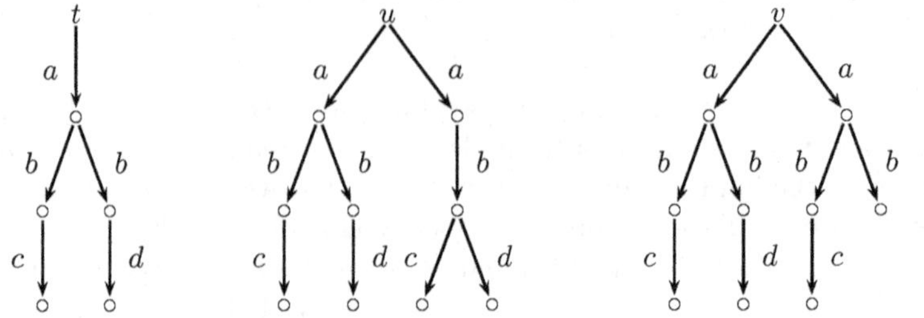

$a(bc+bd)$ $a(bc+bd)+ab(c+d)$ $a(bc+bd)+a(bc+b)$

Fig. 3. Examples of Processes

Example 1. Let us consider processes t and v in Fig. 3. Let $\sqsubseteq_S$ be the simulation preorder, $=_S$ the induced equivalence, and $=_B$ the (strong) bisimulation equivalence. Processes t and v are not (strongly) bisimilar, $t \neq_B v$, but they are bisimilar up-to the simulation preorder, $t \precsim_{\sqsubseteq_S} v$. The only difficult point to find a bisimulation up-to between t and v corresponds to the case when v starts executing a and evolves into $v' = bc + b$. Then t can be reduced to abc, since $abc \sqsubseteq_S t$, and then performing the action a the process evolves into $t' = bc$. Now, by using the fact that $b \sqsubseteq_S bc$ one can check in a similar way that v' and t' are bisimilar up-to the simulation preorder, and conclude the proof.

Lemma 1. *For every initials preserving behaviour preorder* $\sqsubseteq$, *if* $p \precsim q$ *then* $I(p) = I(q)$.

Proof. It is enough to show that $I(p) \subseteq I(q)$. *For any* $a \in I(p)$, *since* $q \sqsupseteq q' \xrightarrow{a} q'_a$, $a \in I(q')$, *and therefore* $a \in I(q)$, *due to the initials preservation property of* $\sqsubseteq$.

Theorem 1. *For every behaviour preorder* $\sqsubseteq$, *that is initials preserving, action factorised and satisfying the axiom (RS), we have that* $p \precsim q$ *if and only if* $p \equiv q$.

Proof. If $p \equiv q$ *then* $p \precsim q$ *is proved in Proposition 1. We prove the reverse implication, if* $p \precsim q$ *then* $p \equiv q$. *We proceed by induction on the depth of process* p *and prove that if* $p \precsim q$ *then* $p \sqsubseteq q$.

By definition of $p \precsim q$, *if* $p \xrightarrow{a} p'_a$ *then* $q \sqsupseteq q' \xrightarrow{a} q'_a$ *and* $p'_a \precsim q'_a$. *By induction hypothesis* $p'_a \equiv q'_a$, *in particular it is also true that* $p'_a \sqsubseteq q'_a$, *and, since* $\sqsubseteq$ *is a precongruence,* $ap'_a \sqsubseteq aq'_a$. *On the other hand,* $q \sqsupseteq q'$ *and, due to the factorised property,* $q|_a \sqsupseteq q'|_a$.

We would like to establish the order relation between $q'|_a$ *and* aq'_a. *In fact,* $q'|_a = aq'_a + r$, *and given that* $I(q'|_a) = \{a\}$ *we have also* $I(r) = \{a\}$. *Then we can use the axiom (RS)* $ax + ay \sqsupseteq ax$, *to conclude that* $q'|_a \sqsupseteq aq'_a$. *All together:*

$$ap'_a \sqsubseteq aq'_a \sqsubseteq q'|_a \sqsubseteq q|_a$$

Considering now the general definition of $p = \sum_i \sum_j a_i p_{ij}$, *we can write for every* i *and* j *the following sequence of relations*

$$a_i p_{ij} \sqsubseteq a_i q^{ij}_{a_i} \sqsubseteq q^{ij}|_{a_i} \sqsubseteq q|_{a_i}$$

and therefore

$$p = \sum_i \sum_j a_i p_{ij} \sqsubseteq \sum_i q|_{a_i}$$

Finally, by Lemma 1, $I(p) = I(q)$ *and we conclude that* $\sum_i q|_{a_i} = q$ *and therefore* $p \sqsubseteq q$.

This result even if simple is rather general, all the preorders for the semantics in Fig. 1 below the ready simulation satisfy the axiom (RS) and therefore the corresponding bisimulations up-to characterise each equivalence. That is, this theorem provides a symmetric, bisimulation-like characterisation for any equivalence in the linear time-branching time spectrum from trace equivalence to ready simulation equivalence. Besides, as a corollary, we get that for any of the equivalence relations, defined by the semantics in Fig. 1, it is true also that $\approx_{\equiv}$ is equal to $\equiv$.

Example 2. Let us retake again our Example 1. As the simulation preorder is one of those in the conditions of Theorem 1, the fact that $t \approx v$ is enough to conclude that t and v are simulation equivalent, that is, we have proved it by constructing a single bisimulation instead of two simulations $t \sqsubseteq_S v$ and $v \sqsubseteq_S t$.

The conditions imposed to the behaviour preorders in Theorem 1 suggest that not every preorder is adequate to get the induced equivalence by means of a bisimulation up-to. Next we comment some examples.

Example 3. Let us consider the behaviour preorder defined by the following axiom: $p + q \sqsubseteq p$. This preorder relation is the inverse of the simulation preorder ($\sqsubseteq_S$) and therefore its kernel is also the simulation equivalence. However, bisimulation up-to $\sqsubseteq$ is far from being equal to the simulation equivalence. In fact it relates any two processes: for every p and q whenever $p \xrightarrow{a} p'$, $q \sqsupseteq q + p \xrightarrow{a} p'$ and conversely, whenever $q \xrightarrow{a} q'$, $p \sqsupseteq p + q \xrightarrow{a} q'$. Note that we have not contradicted Theorem 1 because the preorder $\sqsubseteq$ is not initials preserving.

There exist also other preorders which do not allow bisimulation up-to characterization via Theorem 1 because they do not fulfil the axiom (RS) as shown by the next example.

Example 4. Let us consider the behaviour preorder relation that is induced by the axiom $a(p + q) \sqsubseteq ap + aq$. Obviously, by definition, this relation is action factorised and initials preserving, but does not satisfy the axiom (RS). Let us consider the processes t and u in Fig. 3. Let us take $t' = bc{+}bd$ and $u' = b(c{+}d)$. It is true that $u \sqsubseteq t$ ($t = a(bc{+}bd) \sqsubseteq a(bc{+}bd){+}a(bc{+}bd) \sqsubseteq a(bc{+}bd){+}ab(c{+}d) = u$), but $t \not\sqsubseteq u$, (because the application of the axiom only allows to take choices earlier, but never to delay them as in the right subprocess of u). However, t and u are bisimilar up-to $\sqsubseteq$:

- Any action transition of t can be trivially simulated by u because t is a subprocess of u;
- If u performs action a and evolves into t', then t can trivially simulate that movement;
- If u performs action a and evolves into u', then t can delay its choice and reduces to $ab(c+d)$, then performing action a, evolves also into u'.

Although the range from trace equivalence to ready simulation equivalence is quite wide and most of the classic semantics fall into it, we have studied whether the use of the bisimulations up-to is also possible outside these margins. We have found that there is a family of semantic preorders for which the bisimulations up-to work properly. Any preorder in this family is a simulation (see, for instance, [Gla01]).

Lemma 2. *For every behaviour preorder* $\sqsubseteq$ *being a simulation, whenever* $p \sqsupseteq p' \xrightarrow{a} p'_a$*, there exists* p_a *such that* $p \xrightarrow{a} p_a \sqsupseteq p'_a$.

Proof. By definition of simulation.

For behaviour preorders that are simulations and satisfy the Hoare Equivalence property, we have the following result:

Theorem 2. *For every behaviour preorder* $\sqsubseteq$*, being a simulation and satisfying the Hoare equivalence property,* $p \precapprox q$ *if and only if* $p \equiv q$.

Proof. If $p \equiv q$ *then* $p \precapprox q$ *is proved by Proposition 1. The reverse implication, if* $p \precapprox q$ *then* $p \equiv q$*, is proved by induction on the depth of the first process.*

Let us consider $p \precapprox q$*. Then whenever* $p \xrightarrow{a} p'_a$ *there exist* q' *and* q'_a *such that* $q \sqsupseteq q' \xrightarrow{a} q'_a$ *and* $p'_a \precapprox q'_a$ *and, by induction hypothesis,* $p'_a \equiv q'_a$*. As the behaviour preorder is a simulation, by Lemma 2, there exists* q_a *such that* $q \xrightarrow{a} q_a \sqsupseteq q'_a$*. Therefore, for some process* r*, it is true that* $q = aq_a + r \sqsupseteq aq'_a + r \equiv ap'_a + r$*. That is, for every* $p \xrightarrow{a} p'_a$ *there exists* q_a *such that* $q_a \sqsupseteq p'_a$*.*

Symmetrically, we can prove that for every $q \xrightarrow{a} q'_a$ *there exists* p_a *such that* $p_a \sqsupseteq q'_a$*. These are the premises for the HE property that our behaviour preorder satisfies, and so we conclude that* $p \equiv q$*.*

Both the simulation preorder and the ready simulation preorder are simulations and satisfy the HE property, so for these preorders Theorem 2 provides an alternative proof to that of Theorem 1. But there are other interesting preorders that induce equivalences between strong bisimulation and ready simulation equivalence for which Theorem 2 provide a characterisation in terms of bisimulation up-to.

Example 5. Let us consider the preorder $\sqsubseteq_{FS}$ defined as $p \sqsubseteq_{FS} q$ if there exist a binary relation S over processes such that pSq implies

- For every a, $p \xrightarrow{a} p'$, there exists q', $q \xrightarrow{a} q'$ and $p'Sq'$;
- $F(p) = F(q)$.

where $F(p) = \{(a, X) \mid a \in I(p), X \subset Act\, p \xrightarrow{a} p' \text{ and } X \cap I(p') = \emptyset\}$

That is, $\sqsubseteq_{FS}$ is much alike the ready simulation preorder but instead of checking the equality of initial actions, we check the equality of the *failures* immediately below the root of the processes.

The preorder $\sqsubseteq_{FS}$ satisfies the conditions to apply Theorem 2: obviously it is a simulation and it can be easily checked that satisfies the HE property. Therefore, bisimulation up-to $\sqsubseteq_{FS}$ defines the same equivalence relation as $\sqsubseteq_{FS} \cap \sqsubseteq_{FS}^{-1}$. To check that the induced equivalence is finer than the ready simulation equivalence let us consider, for instance, the processes $p = a(bc + bd)$ and $q = abc + a(bc + bd)$, that are ready simulation equivalent but $q \not\sqsubseteq_{FS} p$.

Following the ideas in the previous example it is quite easy to find other *constrained* simulations in the conditions of Theorem 2 that define equivalences between the ready simulation and strong bisimilarity. Some of them can be defined axiomatically in an easy way, as that in the following example.

Example 6. Let us consider the axiom $a(p+q) \sqsubseteq a(p+q) + ap$ and the induced behaviour preorder. This preorder refines the axiom of the simulation preorder, and satisfies the HE property.

Next example points out the necessity of the HE property in the conditions of Theorem 2.

Example 7. Let us consider the axiom $ap \sqsubseteq ap + a(p + q)$ and the induced behaviour preorder. This preorder refines the axiom of the simulation preorder but it does not satisfies the HE property. We will see that there exist some pairs of processes which are not related by the induced equivalence relation but however are bisimilar up-to that preorder. For instance, let us consider $m = a(bc + b(c + d)) + abc$ and $n = a(bc + b(c + d))$, we have that $n \sqsubseteq m$ and $m \not\sqsubseteq n$ but m and n are bisimilar up-to $\sqsubseteq$:

- m can trivially simulate n;
- If m performs action a and evolves into $bc + b(c + d)$ then n can trivially simulate that movement;
- If m performs action a and evolves into bc then n can be reduced by the preorder to $a(bc + b(c + d)) \sqsubseteq abc$, and then, performing a, it evolves into bc.

4 Bisimulations Up-to for Infinite Processes

The results in the previous sections were proved for BCCSP processes. In this section we extend these results, considering processes to be (possibly) infinite finitary trees. We will use the same notation as for finite trees (prefix, choice, multiple choice...) extended in the natural way.

To reduce infinite trees to (collections of) finite trees, we define an adequate notion of approximation, that we call *level continuity*, and prove how level continuous behaviour preorders give way to level continuous bisimulations up-to. Once this result is stated, Theorems 1 and 2 can also be proved for level continuous behaviour preorders, using simple continuity reasonings. The definition of level continuity is rather natural, so that every behaviour preorder for the semantics in Fig. 1 is indeed level continuous.

Definition 8. *A behaviour preorder is level continuous if* $p \sqsubseteq q$ *if and only if for all* n $p\downarrow_n \sqsubseteq q\downarrow_n$ *where* $p\downarrow_n$ *is the result of pruning process* p *below level* n*, that is:*

- $p\downarrow_0 = \mathbf{0}$
- $(\sum ap_a)\downarrow_{n+1} = \sum a(p_a)\downarrow_n$

Note that $p\downarrow_n$ is always a finite process having depth at most n. Next we prove a technical lemma stating that the number of equivalence classes, with respect to the bisimulation equivalence, of processes having bounded depth is finite. We use $|A|$ to denote the cardinal of a set A and $[p]_{=_B}$ to denote the equivalence class of p with respect to bisimulation equivalence, $=_B$.

Lemma 3. *If the alphabet of actions Act is finite, for any natural number* n *we have*

$$|\{[p]_{=_B} \mid depth(p) \leq n\}| < \infty$$

Proof. *By induction on* n*. For* $n = 0$, $p = \mathbf{0}$*. For* $n > 0$*, if* $p = \sum_i ap^i_a$ *and* $q = \sum_j aq^j_a$*, then* $p =_B q$ *iff*

- *for all* a *and* i *there exists* j *such that* $p^i_a =_B q^j_a$,
- *for all* a *and* j *there exists* i *such that* $p^i_a =_B q^j_a$.

Thus, $p =_B q$ *iff for any* a *action,* $\{[p^i_a]_{=_B}\} = \{[q^j_a]_{=_B}\}$*, therefore, the elements of* $\{[p]_{=_B} \mid depth(p) \leq n+1\}$ *are in one to one correspondence with functions in* $Act \longrightarrow \mathcal{P}(\{[p]_{=_B} \mid depth(p) \leq n\})$*. And thus we conclude the proof by applying the induction hypothesis.*

Then, for every behaviour preorder stronger than the trace preorder we have the following finiteness result:

Lemma 4. *If a behaviour preorder* $\sqsubseteq$ *is stronger than the trace preorder* ($\sqsubseteq \Rightarrow \sqsubseteq_T$)*, for any finite process* q*, then the set of bisimilarity classes* $\{[p]_{=_B} \mid p \sqsubseteq q\}$ *is finite.*

Proof. *Since* $\sqsubseteq \Rightarrow \sqsubseteq_T$ *we have that* $p \sqsubseteq q \Rightarrow depth(p) \leq depth(q)$ *and that any action in the alphabet of process* p *is also in that of process* q*. We are then in the hypothesis of Lemma 3.*

Proposition 2. *For every behaviour preorder* $\sqsubseteq$*, and the corresponding bisimulation up-to* $\sqsubseteq$, $\eqsim$*, if* $\sqsubseteq$ *is level continuous then* $\eqsim$ *is level continuous too.*

Proof. *According to the definition, we have to prove that* $p \eqsim q$ *iff for all* n, $p\downarrow_n \eqsim q\downarrow_n$*. First we prove the left to right implication.*

Let S *be a bisimulation up-to* $\sqsubseteq$*, then* $S_f = \{(p\downarrow_n, q\downarrow_n) \mid pSq\}$ *is also a bisimulation up-to* $\sqsubseteq$*. Whenever* $p\downarrow_n \xrightarrow{a} p'_a\downarrow_{n-1}$*, because of the level continuity of* $\sqsubseteq$, $q\downarrow_n \sqsupseteq q'\downarrow_n \xrightarrow{a} q'_a\downarrow_{n-1}$*, and since* $p'_a S q'_a$ *then* $p'_a\downarrow_{n-1} S_f\, q'_a\downarrow_{n-1}$.

Now we prove the right to left implication. Let us define the relation $R = \{(p, q) \mid$ *for all* n $p\downarrow_n \eqsim q\downarrow_n\}$*. We will see that it is a bisimulation up-to* $\sqsubseteq$*. We* *have that* $p \xrightarrow{a} p'_a$ *iff* $p\downarrow_n \xrightarrow{a} p'_a\downarrow_{n-1}$, *and then there exists* $q\downarrow_n \sqsubseteq q'_n \xrightarrow{a} q'_{n,a}$ *with* $p'_a\downarrow_{n-1} \precsim q'_{n,a}$.

It is easy to check that for all $m > n$, $p'_a\downarrow_{n-1} \precsim q'_{m,a}\downarrow_{n-1}$. *Then, we define* $Q_n^m = \{q'_m\downarrow_n \mid q\downarrow_m \sqsupseteq q'_m \xrightarrow{a} q'_{m,a}$ *and* $p'_a\downarrow_{n-1} \precsim q'_{m,a}\}$ *and because* $\sqsubseteq$ *is weaker than bisimulation equivalence, we have that* Q_n^m *is closed under* $=_B$. *We can now check that for all* $m' > m, Q_n^{m'} \subseteq Q_n^m$ *since if* $q'_{m'}\downarrow_n \in Q_n^{m'}$ *then* $(q'_{m'}\downarrow_m)\downarrow_n = q'_{m'}\downarrow_n$ *and* $(q'_{m'}\downarrow_m)\downarrow_n \in Q_n^m$. *Now, applying Lemma 4,* $Q_n^{m'}/_{=_B} \subseteq Q_n^m/_{=_B}$ *and therefore* $0 < |Q_n^m/_{=_B}| < \infty$

We conclude that there exists a natural number m *such that for any other natural number* m', $Q_n^{m'} = Q_n^m$. *Defining* $Q_n = Q_n^m$ *for such an* m, *we also have* $Q_n = Q_{n'}\downarrow_n$ *for all* $n' \geq n$. *Then it is clear that there exists some process* q' *such that for all* n $q'\downarrow_n \in Q_n$ *and therefore for all* n $q\downarrow_n \sqsubseteq q'\downarrow_n$ *and* $q'\downarrow_n \xrightarrow{a} q'_{n,a}$ *with* $p'_a\downarrow_{n-1} \precsim q'_{n,a}$, *so that we have both* $q \sqsupseteq q'$ *and* $q' \xrightarrow{a} q'_a$ *with* $p'_a\downarrow_{n-1} \precsim q'_a\downarrow_{n-1}$, *thus proving that the pair* $(p'_a, q'_a) \in R$, *so that* R *is indeed a bisimulation up-to* $\sqsubseteq$.

All the preorders for the semantics in Fig. 1 are level continuous. We give the proof for two representative examples.

Proposition 3. *The trace preorder* $\sqsubseteq_T$ *is level continuous.*

Proof. $p \sqsubseteq_T q$ *iff whenever* $p \xrightarrow{\sigma}$ *then* $q \xrightarrow{\sigma}$ *iff for all* n, $p\downarrow_n \xrightarrow{\sigma}$ *then* $q\downarrow_n \xrightarrow{\sigma}$, *iff for all* n, $p\downarrow_n \sqsubseteq_T q\downarrow_n$.

Proposition 4. *The ready simulation preorder* $\sqsubseteq_R$ *is level continuous.*

Proof. $p \sqsubseteq_R q$ *iff for all* n, $p\downarrow_n \sqsubseteq_R q\downarrow_n$. *For the left to right implication we define the relation* $R = \{(p\downarrow_n, q\downarrow_n) \mid p \sqsubseteq_R q\}$ *that is a ready simulation since* $I(p) = I(q)$ *implies that* $I(p\downarrow_n) = I(q\downarrow_n)$ *and if* $p \xrightarrow{a} p'$ *then* $p\downarrow_n \xrightarrow{a} p'\downarrow_{n-1}$.

For the other implication we define $R = \{(p,q) \mid$ *for all* $n, p\downarrow_n \sqsubseteq_R q\downarrow_n\}$, *and show that it is a ready simulation. Firstly,* $I(p) = I(p\downarrow_1)$, *so that, whenever* pRq *we have* $I(p) = I(q)$. *Then, whenever* $p \xrightarrow{a} p'$, *we know* $p\downarrow_n \xrightarrow{a} p'\downarrow_{n-1}$ *for all* $n \geq 1$ *and therefore there exists* q''_n *such that* $q\downarrow_n \xrightarrow{a} q''_n$ *with* $p'\downarrow_{n-1} \sqsubseteq_R q''_n$. *Obviously, there exists some descendent of* q *that extends* q''_n, *that is there exists* $q'_{i(n)}$ *such that* $q \xrightarrow{a} q'_{i(n)}$ *and* $q'_{i(n)}\downarrow_{n-1} = q''_n$.

Since q *is finitely branching there exists some* q', *such that* $q' = q'_{i(n)}$ *for infinitely many* n, *and therefore, we can take as* $q'_{i(n)}$ *this* q' *for any* n. *Then,* $p'\downarrow_n \sqsubseteq_R q'\downarrow_n$ *for all* n *and then* $p'Rq'$, *proving that* R *is a ready simulation containing the pair* (p,q).

Thus for any level continuous preorder verifying the hypothesis of any of the theorems in Sec. 3 the results of these theorems are also valid for infinite processes.

5 A Simple Application Example

As a simple application we present the same example used by Klin in [Kli04]. We prove that any process has the same traces as its deterministic form. This result can be easily proved, by induction, for finite processes. But we need care when coping with infinite processes. As Klin, we use here a coalgebraic reasoning to do it, but our proof is simpler than that in [Kli04], although it is true that Klin develops his approach in a broader framework than ours.

Definition 9. *For any process* $p = \sum_a \sum_i ap_{a,i}$ *the* deterministic form *of* p *is defined as* $Det(p) = \sum_a aDet(\sum_i p_{a,i})$.

We wish to prove that p and $\mathrm{Det}(p)$ are trace equivalent. We will do it by using our bisimulation up-to technique. First we prove the following lemma.

Lemma 5. *For any processes* p *and* q *we have that* $Det(p) \sqsubseteq_T Det(p+q)$.

Proof. *We prove something stronger, in fact* $Det(p)$ *is simulated by* $Det(p+q)$. *As* $Det(p) = \sum_a aDet(\sum_i p_{a,i})$ *whenever* $Det(p) \xrightarrow{a} Det(\sum_i p_{a,i})$ *we have also* $Det(p+q) \xrightarrow{a} Det(\sum_i p_{a,i} + \sum_j q_{a,j})$.

Proposition 5. *For any process* p, $p \approx_{\sqsubseteq_T} Det(p)$.

Proof. *We will prove that the relation* $R = \{(p, Det(p)) \mid p \text{ is a process }\}$ *is a bisimulation up-to* $\sqsubseteq_T$. *Whenever* $p \xrightarrow{a} p_{a,i}$, *then, by using Lemma 5,* $Det(p) = \sum_a aDet(\sum_i p_{a,i}) \sqsupseteq_T aDet(p_{a,i}) \xrightarrow{a} Det(p_{a,i})$. *Besides, if* $Det(p) \xrightarrow{a} Det(\sum p_{a,i})$, *applying the axioms that characterise the trace preorder* ($x \sqsubseteq_T x + y$, $a(x+y) =_T ax + ay$) *we have that* $p \sqsupseteq_T \sum_i ap_{a,i} \sqsupseteq_T a\sum_i p_i$ *and therefore* $p \sqsupseteq_T a\sum p_{a,i} \xrightarrow{a} \sum p_{a,i}$.

It is important to note that even if in the definition of bisimulation up-to we have the full power of the trace preorder, we just use a simple part of it, namely that corresponding to the result of Lemma 5. As a matter of fact, we are just transferring the way *bisimulation up-to bisimulation* is used to prove bisimilarity between processes. Therefore, we are just proving the initial part of the property in which we are interested and coinduction makes the rest, by means of bisimulation up-to.

6 Conclusions and Future Work

We have defined the notion of bisimulation up-to a preorder. This settles a framework in which to define, in a coalgebraic flavour, many of the classical equivalences of process semantics, and therefore, the possibility of reasoning about them by using coinduction.

We have also transferred the up-to preorder technique to the simulation framework. Using simulations up-to preorders we have obtained coinductive characterisations of the considered preorders. Besides, simulations up-to and bisimulations up-to can be related concluding that, under similar conditions than those in the results in the paper, two processes are bisimilar up-to a preorder if and only if they are mutually similar up-to it. Due to lack of space it has not been possible to reproduce here these results.

Although, obviously, it is not possible to avoid the high complexity of the equivalence problem with respect to most of the classical semantics, our results open the door for using the tools to check bisimilarity to decide other equivalences. In fact, some results already exist in that direction. A seminal paper relating testing semantics and bisimulation is [CH92]. There the authors change the transition system defining the operational semantics of processes, to get a more complex and (bigger) transition system where bisimulation corresponds to the original testing semantics. More recently, Kucera and Mayr have related simulation and bisimulation. First, in [KM02a] they prove that bisimulation can be easily translated into simulation, so proving that to decide the latter is at least as expensive as the former. In [KM02b] the opposite reduction is studied, and the results are similar to those in [CH92], but for the simulation semantics. They use an ad-hoc technique to transform the original transition system into a suitable transition system that, in this case, is smaller than the original one, but much more difficult to obtain, although they also prove that for a class of Petri Nets with at most one unbounded place the transformation can be effectively done.

As work in progress, we are studying the other semantics in the linear time-branching time not discussed in this paper, namely, the nested simulation semantics. They are the only ones for which Van Glabbeek provides no axiomatisation.

Moreover, the study of bisimulations up-to has showed us that all the semantics in Van Glabbeek's spectrum have always a simulation part, corresponding to axioms such as $p \sqsubseteq p + q$, that characterises the intensional behaviour and, possibly, another component that characterises the extensional behaviour, for instance, $a(p + q) = ap + aq$ for the trace semantics. In particular, we are interested in the axiomatisations and we are looking for a systematic way to relate the axioms of the preorders with those of the corresponding equivalences.

References

[BG03] Michele Boreale and Fabio Gadducci. Denotational testing semantics in coinductive form. In Branislav Rovan and Peter Vojtás, editors, *28th International Symposium, MFCS 2003*, volume 2747 of *Lecture Notes in Computer Science*, pages 279–289. Springer, 2003.

[CH92] Rance Cleaveland and Matthew Hennessy. Testing equivalence as a bisimulation equivalence. *Formal Aspects of Computing*, 3:1–21, 1992.

[CS96] Rance Cleaveland and Scott A. Smolka. Strategic directions in concurrency research. *ACM Computing Surveys.*, 28(4):607–625, 1996.

[dFG04] David de Frutos-Escrig and Carlos Gregorio-Rodríguez. Semantics equivalences defined with global bisimulations. Annual meeting of the IFIP Working Group 2.2, Bertinoro, Italy, September 2004.

[dFLN99] David de Frutos-Escrig, Natalia López, and Manuel Núñez. Global timed bisimulation: An introduction. In *Formal Methods for Protocol Engineering and Distributed Systems, FORTE XII / PSTV XIX*, pages 401–416. Kluwer Academic Publishers, 1999.

[Gar03] Paul Gardiner. Power simulation and its relation to traces and failures refinement. *Theoretical Computer Science*, 309:157–176, 2003.

[Gla01] Rob J. van Glabbeek. *Handbook of Process Algebra*, chapter The Linear Time – Branching Time Spectrum I: The Semantics of Concrete, Sequential Processes, pages 3–99. Elsevier, 2001.

[Jac04] Bart Jacobs. Trace semantics for coalgebras. In *CMCS'04: 7th International Workshop on Coalgebraic Methods in Computer Science*, volume 106 of *Electronic Notes in Theoretical Computer Science*. Elsevier, 2004.

[JH03] Bart Jacobs and Jesse Hughes. Simulations in coalgebra. In *CMCS'03: 6th International Workshop on Coalgebraic Methods in Computer Science*, volume 82 of *Electronic Notes in Theoretical Computer Science*. Elsevier, 2003.

[Kli04] Bartek Klin. A coalgebraic approach to process equivalence and a coinductive principle for traces. In *CMCS'04: 7th International Workshop on Coalgebraic Methods in Computer Science*, volume 106 of *Electronic Notes in Theoretial Computer Science*. Elsevier, 2004.

[KM02a] Antonín Kucera and Richard Mayr. Why is simulation harder than bisimulation? In *CONCUR 2002 - Concurrency Theory, 13th International Conference, Proceedings*, volume 2421 of *Lecture Notes in Computer Science*, pages 594–610. Springer, 2002.

[KM02b] Antonín Kucera and Richard Mayr. Simulation preorder over simple process algebra. *Information and Computation*, 173(2):184–198, 2002.

[KS03] Bartek Klin and Pawel Sobocinski. Syntactic formats for free. In *14th International Conference, CONCUR 2003 - Concurrency Theory, Proceedings*, volume 2761 of *Lecture Notes in Computer Science*, pages 72–86. Springer, 2003.

[Mil89] Robin Milner. *Communication and Concurrency*. Prentice Hall, 1989.

[Par81] David M.R. Park. Concurrency and automata on infinite sequences. In *Theoretical Computer Science, 5th GI-Conference*, volume 104 of *Lecture Notes in Computer Science*, pages 167–183. Springer, 1981.

[Plo81] Gordon D. Plotkin. A structural approach to operational semantics. Technical Report DAIMI FN-19, Computer Science Department, Aarhus University, 1981.

[Rut03] Jan J. M. M. Rutten. Behavioural differential equations: a coinductive calculus of streams, automata, and power series. *Theoretical Computer Science*, 308(1-3):1–53, 2003.

[San98] Davide Sangiorgi. On the bisimulation proof method. *Journal of Mathematical Structures in Computer Science*, 8(5):447–479, 1998.

[SM92] D. Sangiorgi and R. Milner. The problem of "Weak Bisimulation up to". In W.R. Cleveland, editor, *Proc. CONCUR '92*, volume 630 of *Lecture Notes in Computer Science*, pages 32–46. Springer, 1992.

Deriving Weak Bisimulation Congruences from Reduction Systems*

Roberto Bruni, Fabio Gadducci, Ugo Montanari, and Paweł Sobociński

Dipartimento di Informatica, Università di Pisa, Italia

Abstract. The focus of process calculi is *interaction* rather than *computation*, and for this very reason: (i) their operational semantics is conveniently expressed by labelled transition systems (LTSs) whose labels model the possible interactions with the environment; (ii) their abstract semantics is conveniently expressed by observational congruences. However, many current-day process calculi are more easily equipped with reduction semantics, where the notion of *observable action* is missing. Recent techniques attempted to bridge this gap by synthesising LTSs whose labels are process contexts that enable reactions and for which bisimulation is a congruence. Starting from Sewell's set-theoretic construction, category-theoretic techniques were defined and based on Leifer and Milner's *relative pushouts*, later refined by Sassone and the fourth author to deal with structural congruences given as *groupoidal 2-categories*.

Building on recent works concerning observational equivalences for *tile logic*, the paper demonstrates that *double categories* provide an elegant setting in which the aforementioned contributions can be studied. Moreover, the formalism allows for a straightforward and natural definition of weak observational congruence.

1 Introduction

Since Milner's proposal of an alternative semantics for the π-calculus [14] based on reactive rules modulo a suitable structural congruence, ongoing research focused on the investigation of the relationship between the *labelled transition system* (LTS) based semantics for process calculi and the more abstract *reduction semantics*.

Early attempts by Sewell [19] devised a strategy for obtaining an LTS from a *reduction relation* by adding suitable contexts as labels on transitions. The technique was further refined by Leifer and Milner [11] who introduced the notion of *relative pushout* (RPO) in order to capture the notion of *minimal contexts*. Such attempts share the basic property of a congruent bisimulation equivalence.

In this paper we pursue the comparison between these two different semantic styles, using categorical tools to model and to relate the possible approaches. The result is a schema for the translation of reductions semantics into LTS semantics such that their natural bisimulation equivalences are indeed congruences with respect to the state structure. In particular, we show that double categories provide a uniform framework for experimenting with different constructions of observational models out of reactive systems, accounting for both weak and strong bisimulation congruences.

* This work has been partly supported by the EU within the project HPRN-CT-2002-00275 SEGRAVIS (*Syntactic and Semantic Integration of Visual Modelling Techniques*).

M. Abadi and L. de Alfaro (Eds.): CONCUR 2005, LNCS 3653, pp. 293–307, 2005.

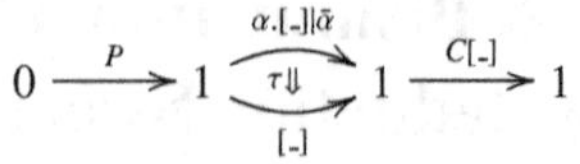

Fig. 1. The reduction $C[\alpha.P|\bar{\alpha}] \Rightarrow C[P]$.

Reduction semantics. The dynamics of many calculi is often defined in terms of reduction relations. For example, the λ-calculus has the β-reduction $(\lambda x.M)N \Rightarrow M[N/x]$ that models the application of a functional process $\lambda x.M$ to the actual argument N. Usually, this kind of rules can be freely instantiated and contextualised because they represent *internal reductions* of a system component. For example the reduction rule $\alpha.P|\bar{\alpha} \Rightarrow P$ for asynchronous CCS-like communication can be instantiated to $P = \bar{\beta}$ and contextualised in the unary context $C[\_] = \beta.nil|[\_]$ yielding the rewrite sequent

$$\beta.nil|\alpha.\bar{\beta}|\bar{\alpha} \Rightarrow \beta.nil|\bar{\beta}$$

illustrated in Fig. 1 with a standard notation: natural numbers represents the number of context-holes, hence an arrow from 0 to 1 is a ground process, while an arrow from 1 to 1 is a context with a unique hole. Processes and contexts compose horizontally, while reductions proceed vertically.

Observational semantics. Reduction semantics have the advantage of conveying the semantics of calculi with relatively few compact rules. The main drawback of reduction semantics is poor compositionality, in the sense that the dynamic behaviour of arbitrary stand alone terms (like $\alpha.P$ in the example above) can be interpreted only by inserting them in the appropriate context (i.e., $[\_]|\bar{\alpha}$), where a reduction may take place. Instead, in LTS semantics, transitions are labelled over suitable *observable actions*; these are intended to capture the potential interactions of each process with any environment. Because interaction is explicit, this approach has proven to be flexible in defining various notions of process equivalence.

Reductions vs. Labelled Transitions, or Cells vs. Double Cells. Both reductions and labeled transitions have a strong set-theoretic flavour. Nevertheless, both logical and categorical presentations for these paradigms have been proposed in the literature. Concerning reduction semantics, it is agreed that *enriched categories* (more specifically, *2-categories*) are a suitable model [16, 17], and *rewriting logic* [13] a successful logical framework for interpreting many computational formalisms. Concerning LTSs, *tile logic* [8] offers a uniform approach to system specifications, admitting both a sequent calculus presentation (with rules accounting for side-effects and synchronisations) and a categorical semantics in terms of *double categories*. Moreover, tile logic yields a natural notion of observational equivalence, *tile bisimulation*, for which congruence proofs can be carried out in a purely diagrammatic way. Our belief is that the comparison between reduction semantics and LTS semantics can be conveniently pursued at the level of their categorical representatives.

Indeed, Leifer and Milner's notion of reactive system can be seen as a 2-category in which the 2-cells are freely generated from a set of basic ground *reaction rules*. This treatment generalises to Sassone and the fourth author's work, where the starting point is a special kind of 2-category that accounts for structural congruences, called a G-category, and adds such reductions freely to obtain a 2-category.

In order to study the derivations on a LTS, we construct the *observational double category* out of a reduction system, which expresses the orthogonality of reactions (the vertical dimension of the double category) and contexts (the horizontal dimension). This double category unites all of the structure (terms, contexts, structural congruence and reductions) in the same categorical universe, and it allows us to recover Leifer and Milner's notion of strong bisimilarity. More interestingly, the ordinary notion of tile bisimilarity turns out to define a congruent *weak* bisimilarity which promises to be an operationally more natural equivalence.

Structure of the Paper. In Section 2 we recall the definitions of double categories, 2-categories and tile bisimulation. In Section 3 we recall the definition of reactive system and show how the theory can be reconciled with traditional 2-categorical approaches to rewriting. Section 4 is devoted to the main contribution of the paper, showing that: (1) depth preserving tile bisimulation over observational double categories is a congruence which corresponds to Leifer and Milner's strong bisimilarity, and (2) ordinary tile bisimilarity results in a notion of weak bisimulation congruence. In the Conclusion we summarise the results and point out further extensions and other possible applications of our framework. In the Appendix we give some technical background on previous work relating to the notions of reactive systems and relative pushouts.

2 Background

Double Categories. This section presents a minimal introduction to double categories; we refer the reader to [2, 8] for further details. Throughout the paper we shall follow the convention of denoting composition in the diagrammatic order.

Concisely, a *double category* is simply an internal category in **Cat** (the category of small categories and functors). This means that a double category contains two categorical structures, called *horizontal* and *vertical* respectively, defined over the same set of cells. More explicitly, double categories admit the following, naïve definition.

Definition 1 (Double category). *A* double category $\mathcal{D}$ *consists of a collection of* cells $\alpha, \beta, \gamma, ...$ *such that*

1. *cells form the* horizontal category $\mathcal{D}^*$, *where* $*$ *denotes horizontal cell composition;*
2. *cells form the* vertical category $\mathcal{D}^\bullet$, *where* $\bullet$ *denotes vertical cell composition;*
3. *the objects of* $\mathcal{D}^*$, *ranged by* $v, u, w, ...$, *are called* observations *and form the* vertical 1-category $\mathcal{V}$ *over the objects in* O, *ranged by* $a, b, c, ...$;
4. *the objects of* $\mathcal{D}^\bullet$, *ranged by* $h, g, f, ...$, *are called* configurations *and form the* horizontal 1-category $\mathcal{H}$ *over the same objects* O *of* $\mathcal{V}$;
5. *both the vertical and horizontal composition of cells are* functorial *with each other and w.r.t. the corresponding compositions in the underlying 1-categories.*

We shall often use ';' to denote composition in both the horizontal and vertical 1-categories. A cell α with horizontal source v, horizontal target u, vertical source h

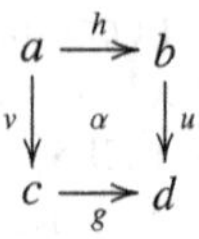

Fig. 2. Graphical representation of a cell

and vertical target g is written $\alpha : h \xrightarrow[u]{v} g$ and depicted as in Fig. 2—its sources and targets must be *compatible*, in the sense that h and v must have the same domain a, the codomain of v must coincide with the domain of g and so on, as illustrated in Fig. 2.

The functoriality requirement amounts to impose the convenient *exchange law*

$$(\alpha \bullet \gamma) * (\beta \bullet \delta) = (\alpha * \beta) \bullet (\gamma * \delta)$$

for any composable cells $\alpha : h \xrightarrow[u]{v} g, \beta : f \xrightarrow[w]{u} l, \gamma : g \xrightarrow[x]{z} h'$, and $\delta : l \xrightarrow[y]{x} f'$.

To substantiate the definition of a double category, we give some basic examples.

Example 1 (Square category). Given a category C, the corresponding *double category of squares* is defined by taking the objects of C as objects, C as both the horizontal 1-category and vertical 1-category, and the set of *square diagrams* formed by compatible arrows (in the sense explained above) as cells.

Example 2 (Quartet category). Cells of a square category are compatible, but not necessarily commuting. Given a category C, we denote by $\Box\, C$ the *double category of quartets* of C: its objects are the objects of C, its horizontal and vertical arrows are the arrows of C, and its cells are the *commuting* square diagrams of arrows in C (i.e., such that $h; u = v; g$ with reference to Fig. 2). The quartet category is therefore a sub-double category of the square category.

Since any square in the square category over C is uniquely characterised by its "border" (i.e., any two squares with the same border are equal), it is immediate that in all the examples above the exchange law is trivially satisfied. Note that in general a double category can have many different cells with the same border. Indeed, when considering double categories which arise from 2-categories using a generalisation of the quartet construction, we shall consider two cells to be equal if they have equal border *and* equal internal 2-cells (Definition 10).

2-Categories. A *2-category* is described concisely as a double category whose underlying vertical 1-category is discrete (i.e., it only contains identity arrows). In other terms a *2-category* C is a category where every homset (the collections of arrows between any pair of objects a and b) is the class of objects of some category $C(a, b)$ and, correspondingly, whose composition "functions" $C(a, b) \times C(b, c) \to C(a, c)$ are functors.

Definition 2 (2-category). *A 2-category C consists of*

1. *a class of* objects $a, b, c, \ldots$;
2. *for each $a, b \in C$ a category $C(a, b)$. The objects of $C(a, b)$ are called* 1-cells, *or simply arrows, and denoted by $f : a \to b$. Its morphisms are called* 2-cells, *and are written $\alpha : f \Rightarrow g : a \to b$. Composition in $C(a, b)$ is denoted by $\bullet$ and referred to as* vertical *composition. Identity 2-cells are denoted by $1_f : f \Rightarrow f$;*

3. *for each* $a, b, c \in C$ *a functor* $*\colon C(a,b) \times C(b,c) \to C(a,c)$, *called* horizontal *composition. Horizontal composition is associative and admits* 1_{id_a} *as identities.*

Definition 3 (G-category). *A* groupoidal category *(or G-category) is a 2-category where all 2-cells are invertible.*

Starting from [16, 17, 13], 2-categories have been the chosen formalism for the algebraic presentation of the reduction semantics for many term-like structures [5, 7]–the 2-cells of such 2-categories model reduction. The idea is to start from an abstract presentation of the basic reduction steps of a system: the closure with respect to contexts is then precisely obtained by the 2-categorical operation of whiskering [20]. Here, the relevant notion is that of *(G-)computad*: a (G-)category enriched with a relation on homsets, each pair representing a basic reduction step of the system. Via a well-known construction, a 2-category can be freely generated from any (G-)computad.

Definition 4 (G-computad). *A* G-computad *is a pair* $\langle \mathcal{H}, T\rangle$, *where* $\mathcal{H}$ *is a G-category and* $T = \bigcup_{a,b\in\mathcal{H}} T_{a,b}$ *is a family of relations on arrows* $T_{a,b} \subseteq \mathcal{H}(a,b) \times \mathcal{H}(a,b)$.

When writing $f\ T\ g$ we assume that f, g belong to the same homset. G-computads are slightly more general than computads, in that $\mathcal{H}$ is a G-category instead of an ordinary category (which itself can be seen as a G-category whose 2-cells are all identities).

Ground Tile Bisimilarity. When used as a semantic foundation for computational models as tile logic, double categories allow for a suitable notion of behavioural equivalence which is reminiscent of the well-known technique of *bisimulation*. This notion can be lifted to a more abstract level of generic double categories without much effort.

The general definition of tile bisimulation establishes a family of equivalences for each homset in the horizontal category $\mathcal{D}^*$. A restricted variant, called *ground tile bisimulation* in [4], focuses just on the suitable homset of *closed* processes; it is relevant for us because reactive systems (in the sense of Leifer and Milner, see Definition 7) are designed for closed systems. In our framework, closed systems correspond to horizontal arrows which cannot be left-instantiated, except in trivial ways.

In the following we shall assume that our horizontal 1-category has a distinguished *ground object* ι: we require that for all objects a, if there exists $f : a \to \iota$ then $f = id_\iota$. The closed systems we shall consider are then characterised by having a ground object in their left interface and we simply write $t \xrightarrow[v]{} t'$ for a cell with horizontal source id_ι.

Definition 5 (Ground Tile Bisimulation). *Let* $\mathcal{D}$ *be a double category with a ground object* ι. *A symmetric relation* B *on closed configurations (arrows in the homsets* $\mathcal{H}[\iota, a]$ *for any object* a*) is called a* ground tile bisimulation *if whenever* $s\ B\ t$ *and* $s \xrightarrow[v]{} s' \in \mathcal{D}$, *then* t' *exists such that* $t \xrightarrow[v]{} t' \in \mathcal{D}$ *and* $s'\ B\ t'$.

The maximal ground tile bisimulation is denoted by $\approx$, and two closed configurations s and t are *ground tile bisimilar* if $s \approx t$. Note that $\approx$ only relates arrows within the same homset. Bisimilarity is said to be *congruent* when $s \approx t$ implies $s; c \approx t; c$ for any arrow c in $\mathcal{D}^*$. The following property on $\mathcal{D}$ is known to be sufficient for congruence.

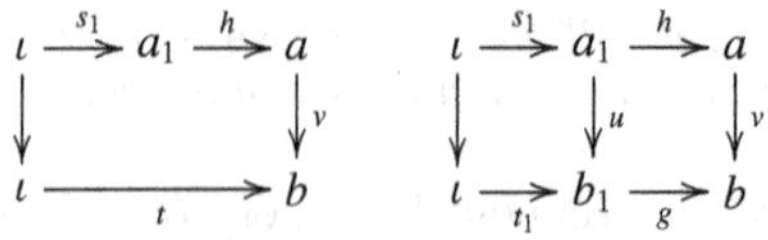

Fig. 3. Ground decomposition

Definition 6 (Ground decomposition). *A double category $\mathcal{D}$ enjoys the* ground decomposition property *if for any ground configuration $s : \iota \to a$ and any cell $s_1; h \xrightarrow[v]{} t \in \mathcal{D}$ such that $s = s_1; h$, there exists an observation u, a ground configuration t_1 and a configuration g such that $s_1 \xrightarrow[u]{} t_1 \in \mathcal{D}$ and $h \xrightarrow[v]{u} g$, with $t = t_1; g$.*

The situation is depicted in Fig. 3. The observation u defines the amount of interaction between s_1 and the environment h that is needed to perform the effect v. In general u is not uniquely determined, as s_1 and h can interact in many ways. For example, it can be that $u = id$ if h can perform v without interacting with s_1. The key point about the (ground) decomposition property is that a transition of the whole can always be expressed as a suitable combination of the transitions of its parts.

Theorem 1 (Cfr. [4]). *The ground decomposition property implies that ground tile bisimilarity is a congruence.*

3 From Reactive Systems to 2-Categories

Reactive systems were proposed by Leifer and Milner as a general framework for the study of simple formalisms equipped with a reduction semantics [11]. The setting was extended by Sassone and the fourth author [18] in order to treat the situation where the contexts of a formalism are equipped with a structural congruence relation. For instance, in examples which contain a parallel composition operator, it is usually not satisfactory to simply quotient out terms with respect to its commutativity—intuitively, it is important to know the precise location within the term where the reaction occurs. This information is expressed in a natural way as a 2-dimensional structure, where the 2-cells are isomorphisms which "permute" the structure of the term.

Definition 7 (Reactive system). *A* reactive system $\mathbb{C}$ *consists of*

1. *a G-category C of* context;
2. *a distinguished object $\iota \in C$;*
3. *a composition-reflecting, 2-full 2-subcategory $\mathcal{E}$ of* evaluation contexts[1]*;*
4. *a set of pairs $R \subseteq \bigcup_{a \in \mathcal{E}} C(\iota, a) \times C(\iota, a)$ called the* reaction rules.

Reaction rules are closed with respect to evaluation contexts in order to obtain the reaction relation on the closed terms (arrows with domain ι) of C.

[1] That is, $\mathcal{E}$ is full on the two-dimensional structure and $e_1; e_2 \in \mathcal{E} \Rightarrow e_1 \in \mathcal{E}$ and $e_2 \in \mathcal{E}$.

A Calculus with Restriction. As a running example, we shall first define a G-category C, the arrows of which shall represent the terms of a simple process calculus with a restriction operator. Adding the expected reaction rules, we shall obtain a reactive system.

Objects. Two objects: 0, 1.

Arrows. The homset $C(0, 0)$ is the singleton containing only the identity arrow. There are no arrows from 1 to 0. Fixing a set A of channel names, we construct the terms of our simple calculus as specified by the grammar below

$$P \quad ::= \quad \epsilon \ \mid \ a \ \mid \ \overline{a} \ \mid \ - \ \mid \ P \mid P \ \mid \ \nu a.P \qquad (a \in A)$$

Although the parallel composition '|' is a binary operator, we shall consider terms to be quotiented with respect to its associativity. The set of closed terms (those terms containing no occurrences of the hole '–') is the homset $C(0, 1)$. The set of terms which contain precisely one hole forms the homset $C(1, 1)$.

Composition of C arrows (either an arrow $t : 0 \to 1$ with an arrow $c : 1 \to 1$, or two arrows $c : 1 \to 1$ and $d : 1 \to 1$) is substitution of the first term for the unique hole within the second term. Note that the hole in an open term is allowed to be within the scope of a restriction, and thus substitution can involve capturing.

2-Cells. Roughly, the structural isomorphisms between terms of our G-category C correspond to the usual axioms describing the commutativity of '|', while at the same time respecting the scopes of any present restriction.

More concretely, 2-cells between terms without restriction are permutations which swap parallel components (where by 'component' we mean an occurrence of an input/output on a channel or a hole). Thus, for instance, there are two automorphisms on $a \mid a : 0 \to 1$, the identity, and the automorphism which swaps the two copies of a.[2]

The restriction $\nu a.P$ reduces the allowed permutations in any context: an input or output on a within the scope of the restriction νa is not allowed to be taken outside the scope, and dually, an input or an output on a not within the scope of a restriction νa is not allowed to be taken into its scope. In open terms (members of the homset $C(1, 1)$), holes are not allowed to cross any scoping boundaries.

In order to check whether there exists a structural isomorphism between two arrows s and t it is enough to erase all occurrences of ν, check for the existence of a permutation, reintroduce the instances of ν and check whether the permutation respects their scope. Two 2-cells are equal if and only if their domains and codomains coincide, and their underlying permutations are equal. Moreover, we postulate that an automorphism is the identity 2-cell if and only if its underlying permutation is the identity permutation.

Thus, there are six automorphisms on $a \mid a \mid a$ but only two on $a \mid \nu a.(a \mid a)$. However, there is an invertible 2-cell $\nu a.(b \mid a) \to b \mid \nu a.a$, induced by the identity permutation, capturing the usual structural congruence rule. Similarly, there are invertible 2-cells $\nu a.b \to b$ and $\nu a.a \mid b \to b \mid \nu a.a$, but no 2-cell $\nu a.a \mid \nu a.a \to \nu a.(a \mid a)$.

[2] We do not quotient the terms with respect to the commutativity of '|' because it is important not to lose the concrete position of a redex within a term when considering interaction with arbitrary contexts – in contrast, the associativity of '|' plays no role and can be quotiented out.

Vertical composition of 2-cells in the 2-category is the obvious composition of permutations and horizontal composition of 2-cells is defined as expected.

Reactive System. It is a simple exercise to show that all of the data defines a G-category C. We construct a reactive system $\mathbb{C}_{cal}$ by adding rules $\{ \langle a \mid \overline{a}, \epsilon \rangle \mid a \in A \}$ and taking all contexts to be the set of evaluation contexts. The reader will notice that the resulting reduction relation (obtained by instantiating the rules with all contexts) is as expected.

In order to keep the example as simple as possible, we add neither extra axioms or structural rules which guarantee that the null process ϵ is the identity for parallel composition nor do we require any notions of α-equivalence; we note, however, that any derived operational equivalence we shall consider relates terms which would be equated via such axioms. For instance, any arrow P is related with $\epsilon \mid P$ and any two α-equivalent (closed) terms are related.

The 2-Category of Computations. We shall now show that a reactive system can be used to generate 2-categories in two relevant ways. The first of the two constructions is the classic one, but it does not have an immediate computational intuition associated with the 2-dimensional structure. In the following, all definitions are parametric w.r.t. a reactive systems $\mathbb{C}$, with components $\langle C, \iota, \mathcal{E}, R \rangle$.

Definition 8 (2-category of interactions). *Let C_i denote the 2-category freely generated from the G-computad $\langle C, R \rangle$.*

Indeed, the 2-cells in C_i are generated freely from the original G-category C and the reaction rules R. Thus, in general, a 2-cell of C_i does not denote a meaningful computation in $\mathbb{C}$ as it allows reduction even in non-evaluation contexts.

Definition 9 (2-category of computations). *Let C_c denote the smallest sub-2-category of C_i which includes the reaction rules R and the cells of the G-category $\mathcal{E}$.*

The 2-cells in C_c are generated by extending the original structural isomorphisms in C with the 2-cells corresponding to computations. It is easy to show that there is a close relationship with Leifer and Milner's reaction relation because we use the 2-category $\mathcal{E}$ of *evaluation* contexts in the construction of C_c.

4 From 2-Categories to Double Categories

In Definition 8 we defined the 2-category of interactions. In this section we shall associate to such a 2-category C a double category $\widehat{C}$ that simulates also the potential reductions of partial redexes in C. We start by recalling a construction which lifts the quartet category approach in order to obtain a double category from a 2-category.

Definition 10 (Quartet double category). *Let C be a 2-category. The quartet double category $\square C$ is obtained decomposing each cell as in Fig. 4, and defining horizontal and vertical composition as sketched in Fig. 5.*

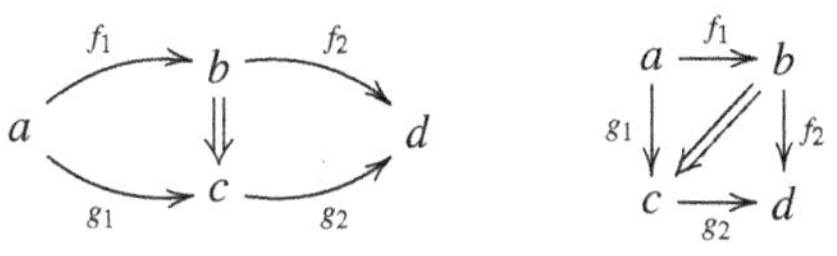

Fig. 4. A 2-cell and a tile associated to it

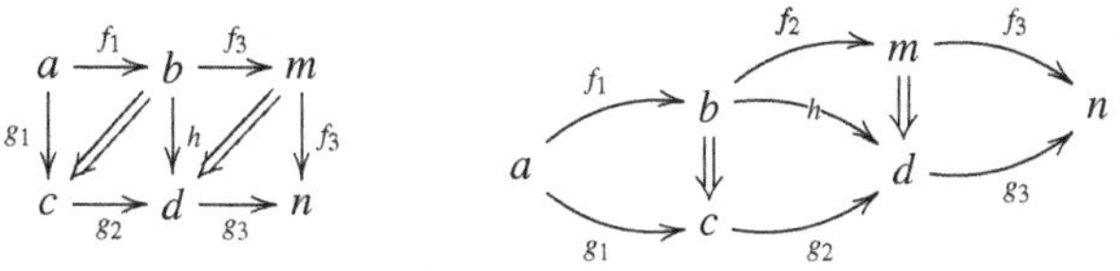

Fig. 5. Horizontal composition, and the corresponding 2-cell

A check is enough to guarantee that the resulting structure is indeed a double category, and both vertical and horizontal 1-categories coincide with the category underlying C (even if the exchange law becomes more difficult to prove).

As for Example 2, also the previous construction is folklore, the standard reference being probably [15]. It appears implicitly in recent works on tile bisimilarity [4]. From our perspective, it suggests an automatic generation of a labeled relation (abstracting a double category), starting from an unlabelled one (abstracting a 2-category).

From Computads to Double Categories. The mechanism we propose for synthesising labeled transition systems is an instantiation of the general construction of the quartet category: It takes into account the cells of the original G-computad, closing them with just enough information for obtaining the right closure of the resulting double category.

We shall use the notion of *groupoidal idempushouts* [18] (GIPOs), an extension to G-categories of Leifer and Milner's [11] notion of *idempushout* (IPO), in the central construction of Definition 11. Here we shall briefly recall a definition of (G)IPOs, directing to the appendix for further results and their use in the theory of reactive systems.

Intuitively, a (G)IPO refers to a commutative (up to an isomorphic 2-cell α) square as illustrated in Fig. 6, in which the arrows $g_1 : b \to d$ and $g_2 : c \to d$ are minimal, in the sense that there is no non-trivial arrow $h : e \to d$ and arrows $h_1 : b \to e$, $h_2 : c \to e$ such that $f_1; h_1$ is (up to an isomorphic 2-cell) $f_2; h_2$, $h_1; h$ is (up to an isomorphic 2-cell) g_1 and $h_2; h$ is (up to an isomorphic 2-cell) g_2. When working with G-categories, these isomorphisms are required to paste together to obtain the original isomorphism α.

Given arbitrary f_1 and f_2, it is usual for categories of contexts to have more than one such closure—i.e., there is more than one (G)IPO that has f_1 and f_2 as its lower compo-

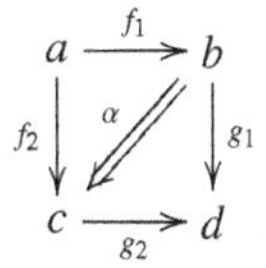

Fig. 6. A GIPO

nents. It turns out that to obtain a (G)IPO one constructs a (bi)pushout in a (pseudo) slice category. Such pushouts have been dubbed (groupoidal) relative pushouts, or (G)RPOs.

Example 3. Consider the reactive system $\mathbb{C}_{cal}$ previously defined. The underlying category of terms has GRPOs. Diagram (*i*), below, is a simple example of a GIPO, while diagram (*ii*), with $\sigma : \nu a.(a \mid \overline{a}) \mid b \to b \mid \nu a.(a \mid \overline{a})$ the unique 2-cell between these two terms is not, since $- \mid b$ is unnecessary and may be factored out. Diagrams (*iii*) (where $\tau : a \mid \overline{a} \mid b \mid \overline{a} \to a \mid \overline{a} \mid b \mid \overline{a}$ is the permutation which swaps the two copies of $\overline{a}$) and (*iv*) are both GIPOs, which illustrates our previous remark that two arrows may have several different minimal closures. Diagram (*v*) is also an example of a GIPO, which is less interesting since the terms $a \mid \overline{a}$ and b are disjoint.

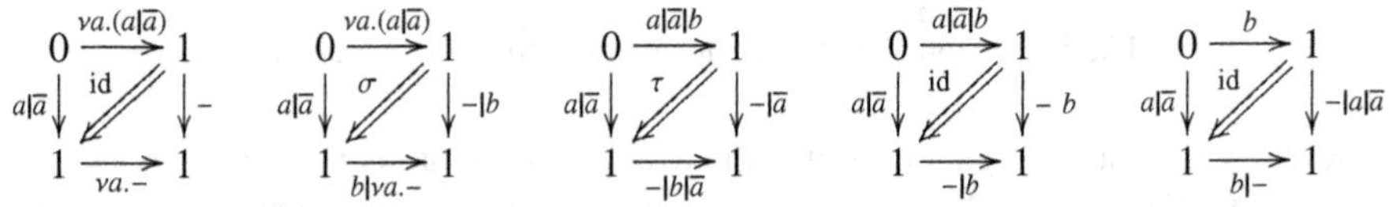

(*i*) (*ii*) (*iii*) (*iv*) (*v*)

Definition 11 (Observational double category). *Let* $\mathbb{C} = \langle C, \iota, \mathcal{E}, R\rangle$ *be a reactive system. The* observational double category *of* $\mathbb{C}$*, denoted* $O(\mathbb{C})$*, is the smallest sub-double category of the quartet double category* $\Box\, C_\iota$ *which includes the double cells*

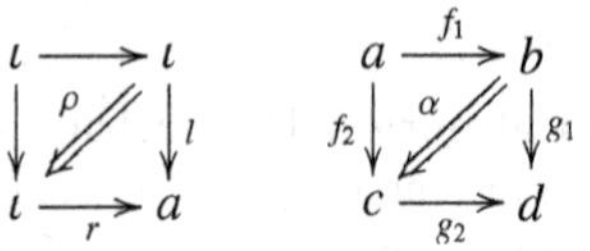

(*i*) (*ii*)

where the tiles of type (i) correspond to the rules of R, and the tiles of type (ii) correspond to GIPOs in C, with $g_2 \in \mathcal{E}$*.*

Remark 1. Notice that while the observational double category is a sub-double category of the quartet double category $\Box\, C_\iota$, the resulting cells are filled in with 2-cells of C_c, as a consequence of requiring g_2 to be an evaluation context. The advantage of working within $\Box C_\iota$ is that our congruence results (Corollaries 1 and 2) hold w.r.t. all contexts, not just the evaluation contexts.

Thanks to the properties of GIPOs, it is easy to check that the resulting 1-categories coincide with the category underlying C. Later we will show that the proof of decomposition property can be carried out rather easily for the observational double category because of the above facts. Before proving that the decomposition property holds, though, we introduce the notion of depth of a double-cell.

Definition 12 (Depth of a cell). *A cell in* $O(\mathbb{C})$ has depth *n if it contains n occurrences of* ρ *tiles, defined according to Definition 11 (i.e., the cells* ρ *modelling the rules).*

The definition is meaningful, since the closure of the quartet construction allows for no equivalence between cells containing a different number of such basic cells (while this is not the case for those associated with GIPOs).

Example 4. As an example of a cell of depth 2 in the observational double category which results from the reactive system $\mathbb{C}_{cal}$ previously defined, consider the cell illustrated in the diagram below left, which factorises into the rules ρ, ρ' and GIPOs obtained by taking the unique choices for α and α'.

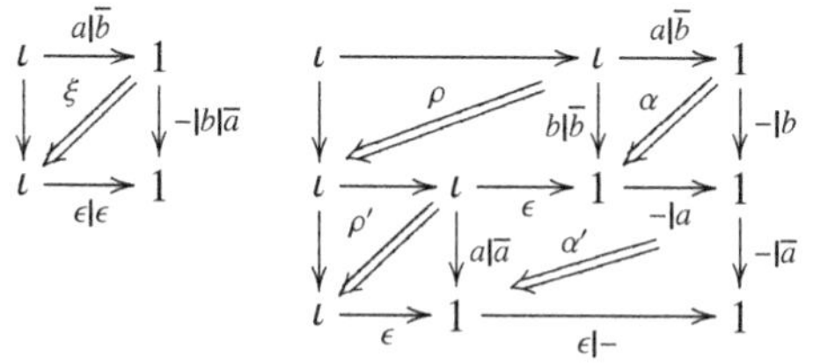

First, we offer an analysis of the labels of the observational double category. The following lemma is similar in nature to Melliès' Verticalization Theorem [12–Theorem 2] and states that any cell can be decomposed into 'elementary' cells – that is, cells which result from the composition of a single reduction (diagram (*i*) of Definition 11) with a minimal context (diagram (*ii*) of Definition 11).

Lemma 1 (Characterisation). *Let* $f \underset{u}{\longrightarrow} g$ *be a cell of depth n in* $O(\mathbb{C})$*. Then*

- *either* $n \geq 1$ *and there exists cells* $f_{i-1} \underset{u_i}{\longrightarrow} f_i$ *of depth 1 for* $i = 1 \ldots n$ *with* $f_0 = f$ *and* $f_n = g$*, such that* $u = u_1; \ldots; u_n$*;*
- *or* $n = 0$ *and u is an equivalence and* $f, g : \iota \to a$ *are related by an invertible cell in* C_c*.*

The special case for $n = 0$ is a basic consequence of the fact that the square below is always a GIPO, for any invertible cell α relating f and g in C_c.

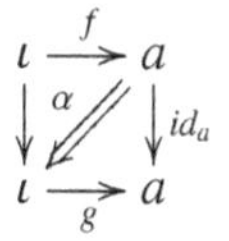

Next we can prove the key result.

Lemma 2 (Ground decomposition). $O(\mathbb{C})$ *satisfies ground decomposition.*

Proof. By induction on the depth of a cell $\tau : s \underset{h}{\longrightarrow} t$. If τ has depth 0 then decomposition holds by the decomposition properties of GIPOs (see Lemma 5 in Appendix). Suppose τ has depth $n > 0$, then by Lemma 1 τ decomposes as shown in Fig. 7(i), where (*a*) α and β are GIPOs; (*b*) ρ models a rewrite rule; and (*c*) τ' has depth $n - 1$.

Using the fact that GIPOs decompose (see Lemma 5 in the Appendix), we obtain α_1, α_2 such that $\alpha_1 * \alpha_2 = \alpha$ and β_1, β_2 such that $\beta_1 * \beta_2 = \beta$ (see Fig. 7(ii)). The remainder of the decomposition follows via the inductive hypothesis on τ' (along the decomposition of its vertical source $r; g$ in $r; g_1$ and g_2). □

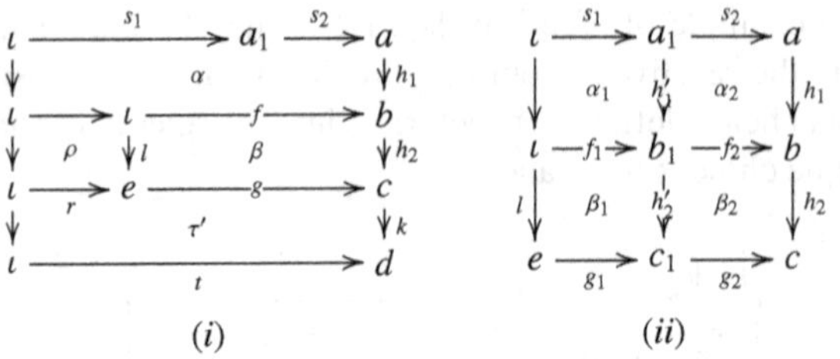

Fig. 7. Ground decomposition, diagrammatically

Depth-Preserving Bisimulation. We exploit the definition of depth in order to offer a refined notion of tile bisimulation.

Definition 13 (Depth-preserving tile bisimulation). *A (ground) tile bisimulation B on* $O(\mathbb{C})$ is depth-preserving *if whenever s B t for* $s, t \in C$, *then for any cell* $s \xrightarrow[v]{} s'$ of depth *n there exists* $t' \in C$ *and a cell* $t \xrightarrow[v]{} t'$ of the same depth *such that* $s'\ B\ t'$.

We shall denote the largest depth-preserving tile bisimulation by $\sim$ and refer to it as *depth-preserving bisimilarity*. It yields Leifer and Milner's semantics for a given reactive system; we include a definition of the latter in the Appendix (Definition 14).

Lemma 3. *Depth preserving tile bisimilarity on* $O(\mathbb{C})$ *defines the same relation as strong bisimilarity on* LTS($\mathbb{C}$) *(as defined in Definition 14).*

Indeed, as a direct consequence of Lemma 2 we have the following corollary.

Corollary 1. *Depth preserving tile bisimilarity on* $O(\mathbb{C})$ *is a congruence.*

Tile Bisimilarity as a Weak Bisimulation. We shall now look at the results of considering ordinary tile bisimilarity and, in particular, we shall argue that it amounts to a notion of weak bisimulation. This follows straightforwardly from Lemma 1.

Thus, in the bisimulation game, a minimal context which sets off a chain of reactions on f may be matched by the minimal context for another chain of reactions as long as the results are a bisimilar pair of terms. The fact that internal reaction (i.e. only the identity context is provided) can be matched either by internal reaction or no reaction is reminiscent of Milner's original formulation of weak bisimilarity for CCS in which a τ action can be matched by *zero or more* τ's.

Jensen has carried out a preliminary study [9] of defining the notion of weak bisimilarity for reactive systems, and specifically, for bigraphs [10]. We plan to study the relationship between the two bisimilarities as future work.

By definition of depth preserving tile bisimilarity we have the result below.

Lemma 4. *Depth preserving tile bisimilarity* $\sim$ *on an observational double category implies tile bisimilarity* $\approx$ *over that double category.*

The case study which follows shows that, in general, $\sim$ is strictly finer than $\approx$ (see hence Example 5). As a direct consequence of Lemma 2 we have the corollary below.

Corollary 2. *Tile bisimilarity $\approx$ on an observational double category is a congruence.*

We conclude by illustrating how the constructions we have seen so far can be applied to the simple process algebra previously introduced.

Example 5. Let $\mathbb{C}_{cal}$ be the reactive system defined in our running example, and let $a \in A$ be a name. Then $\nu a.(a \mid \overline{a}) \not\sim 0$ while $\nu a.(a \mid \overline{a}) \approx 0$. For the first part, note that $\nu a.(a \mid \overline{a}) \overrightarrow{_{\text{id}}} \nu a.0$ via a cell of depth 1, which cannot be matched by 0. For the second part, observe instead that $\nu a.(a \mid \overline{a}) \overrightarrow{_{\text{id}}} \nu a.0$ can be matched by the depth 0 cell $0 \overrightarrow{_{\text{id}}} 0$.

5 Conclusions

In this paper we presented a novel approach to the synthesis of a labelled transition system out of reactive system. Our proposal builds on the results by Leifer and Milner, later refined by Sassone and the fourth author, since in order to obtain the contexts necessary for the observation we rely on (groupoidal) relative pushouts. However, we dispense with any set-theoretical presentation. We show instead how the mechanism of synthesising can be obtained as an instance of the classical construction of the quartet category, relating 2-categories and double categories, considered as abstract presentations for reactive and labelled transition systems, respectively.

Our work was also inspired by a series of papers on tile logic, the proof-theoretic counterpart of double categories. The associated tile bisimulation often fails to be a congruence, and the research focused on the characterisation of syntactical constraints for proving when the property holds. One approach has been the saturation of the category with additional cells, thus recovering e.g. (ground) dynamic congruence [4]. The methodology has been applied for recovering s-semantics for logic programming of [3].

We feel confident that our contribution streamlines former results on tile logic and synthesised labelled transition systems, and highlights what we consider the basic ingredient on both approaches, namely, the *decomposition property*. In fact, relative pushouts decompose, and this is the reason why the bisimulation on the observational double category is a congruence. Note also that both [3, 4] can be considered as instances of the general approach proposed in the paper since all pushouts are also IPOs.

Future Directions. We envision two clear roads for further development. First of all, we would like to tackle open tile bisimulation, in order to lift the restriction to ground reactive systems since, after all, usually a presentation is given in terms of under-specified components, which should be also instantiated, besides being contextualised. Groundness is clearly effective for proving that a bisimulation is a congruence, but of course double categories, with their obvious notion of triggering for a cell, seem to offer a mathematically sound environment where to consider the most general case of open systems. After all, the quartet construction has no restriction whatsoever, and in fact it has a much more general, and stimulating, theory underlying it [15].

The second path to follow concerns the chance of synthesising adequate *concurrent semantics*. Usually, the concurrent semantics for a reactive system is obtained by considering some notion of *permutation equivalence* on reductions; while on labelled transition systems it is usually recovered by capturing some notion of independence on the labels. Thus, the quartet construction appears to be a general mechanism that is well-suited, especially if categories with structure (i.e. either monoidal or cartesian categories) are considered, and the structure on the arrows is lifted to the observations). After all, tile logic has been successfully applied to term and graph rewriting, and the decomposition property has been established in many different settings [1, 6, 12].

References

1. R. Bruni, D. de Frutos-Escrig, N. Martí-Oliet, and U. Montanari. Bisimilarity congruences for open terms and term graphs via tile logic. In *Proc. of CONCUR 2000*, vol. 1877 of *Lect. Notes in Comp. Sci.*, pp. 259–274. Springer, 2000.
2. R. Bruni, J. Meseguer, and U. Montanari. Symmetric and cartesian double categories as a semantic framework for tile logic. *Mathematical Structures in Computer Science*, 12:53–90, 2002.
3. R Bruni, U. Montanari, and F. Rossi. An interactive semantics of logic programming. *Theory and Practice of Logic Programming*, 1:647–690, 2001.
4. R. Bruni, U. Montanari, and V. Sassone. Observational congruences for dynamically reconfigurable tile systems *Theor. Comp. Sci.*, 335(2-3):331-372, 2005.
5. A. Corradini and F. Gadducci. Rewriting on cyclic structures: Equivalence between the operational and the categorical description. *Informatique Théorique et Applications/Theoretical Informatics and Applications*, 33:467–493, 1999.
6. G. Ferrari and U. Montanari. Tile formats for located and mobile systems. *Inform. and Comput.*, 156:173–235, 2000.
7. F. Gadducci, R. Heckel, and M. Llabrés. A bi-categorical axiomatisation of concurrent graph rewriting. In *Proc. of CTCS'99*, vol. 29 of *Electr. Notes in Theor. Comp. Sci.*, Elsevier, 1999.
8. F. Gadducci and U. Montanari. The tile model. In *Proof, Language and Interaction: Essays in Honour of Robin Milner*, pp. 133–166. MIT Press, 2000.
9. O. H. Jensen. Bigraphs and weak bisimilarity. Talk at Dagstuhl Seminar 04241, June 2004.
10. O. H. Jensen and R. Milner. Bigraphs and mobile processes. Technical Report 570, Computer Laboratory, University of Cambridge, 2003.
11. J. Leifer and R. Milner. Deriving bisimulation congruences for reactive systems. In *Proc. of CONCUR 2000*, vol. 1877 of *Lect. Notes in Comp. Sci.*, pp. 243–258. Springer, 2000.
12. P. A. Melliès. Double categories: A modular model of multiplicative linear logic. *Mathematical Structures in Computer Science*, 12:449–479, 2002.
13. J. Meseguer. Conditional rewriting logic as a unified model of concurrency. *Theor. Comp. Sci.*, 96:73–155, 1992.
14. R. Milner. The polyadic π-calculus: A tutorial. In *Logic and Algebra of Specification*, vol. 94 of *Nato ASI Series F*, pp. 203–246. Springer, 1993.
15. P.H. Palmquist. The double category of adjoint squares. In *Midwest Category Seminar*, vol. 195 of *Lectures Notes in Mathematics*, pp. 123–153. Springer, 1971.
16. A.J. Power. An abstract formulation for rewrite systems. In *Category Theory and Computer Science*, vol. 389 of *Lect. Notes in Comp. Sci.*, pp. 300–312. Springer, 1989.
17. D.E. Rydehard and E.G. Stell. Foundations of equational deductions: A categorical treatment of equational proofs and unification algorithms. In *Category Theory and Computer Science*, vol. 283 of *Lect. Notes in Comp. Sci.*, pp. 114–139. Springer, 1987.
18. V. Sassone and P. Sobociński. Deriving bisimulation congruences using 2-categories. *Nordic Journal of Computing*, 10:163–183, 2003.
19. P. Sewell. From rewrite rules to bisimulation congruences. *Theor. Comp. Sci.*, 274:183–230, 2004.
20. R.H. Street. Categorical structures. *Handbook of Algebra*, vol. 1, pp. 529–577. North-Holland, 1996.

Appendix: (G)IPOs

Using the universal properties of (bi)colimits, one can prove that (G)IPOs satisfy several basic properties reminiscent of ordinary pushouts.

Lemma 5 (Composition and decomposition of (G)IPOs). *Let C be a (G-)category which has (G)RPOs. Then*

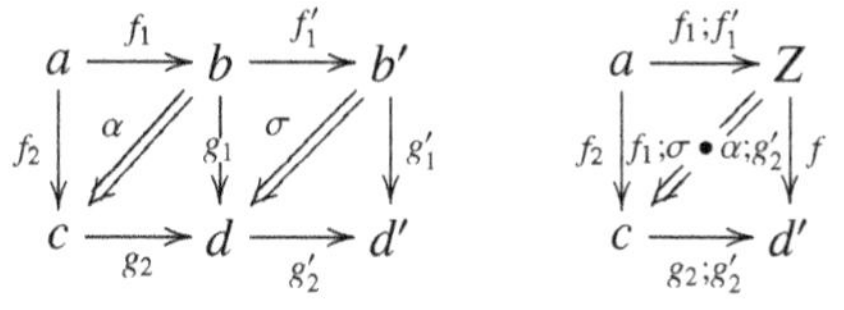

(*i*) (*ii*)

1. *if both squares α and β in diagram (i) are (G)IPOs then the exterior (see diagram (ii)) is also a (G)IPO;*
2. *if the left square α and the exterior (see diagram (ii)) of diagram (i) are (G)IPOs then so is the right square.*

The basic idea, originally due to Sewell [19], is that the labels are the smallest contexts which allow a reaction to occur.

Definition 14 (LTS). *Let $\mathbb{C}$ be a reactive system. The associated labelled transition systems* LTS($\mathbb{C}$) *is given by*

1. *the states of* LTS($\mathbb{C}$) *are arrows $s\colon \iota \to a$ in C*
2. *there is a transition $s \xrightarrow{f} t'$ iff there exists $\langle l, r\rangle \in R$, $t \in \mathcal{E}$ and a 2-cell $\alpha : s; f \Rightarrow l; t$ such that the square below is a GIPO and $t' = r; t$.*

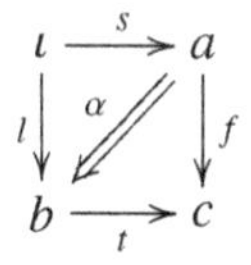

In the case of G-categories, one normally quotients the states and the transitions of the LTS with respect to isomorphism—in other words, the 2-dimensional structure is no longer necessary and may be discarded.

One of the main results that holds for such an LTS is that when the underlying (G-)category has enough (G)RPOs (one only has to require so-called *redex*-GRPOs to exist), then bisimilarity is a congruence. This was originally shown by Leifer and Milner [11] and extended to the more general setting by Sassone and the fourth author [18].

SOS for Higher Order Processes (Extended Abstract)

MohammadReza Mousavi[1], Murdoch J. Gabbay[2], and Michel A. Reniers[1]

[1]Department of Computer Science, Eindhoven University of Technology, Eindhoven, The Netherlands
[2]Department of Computer Science, King's College London, London, UK

Abstract. We lay the foundations for a Structural Operational Semantics (SOS) framework for higher order processes. Then, we propose a number of extensions to Bernstein's *promoted tyft/tyxt* format which aims at proving congruence of strong bisimilarity for higher order processes. The extended format is called *promoted PANTH*. This format is easier to apply and strictly more expressive than the *promoted tyft/tyxt* format. Furthermore, we propose and prove a congruence format for a notion of *higher order bisimilarity* arising naturally from our SOS framework. To illustrate our formats, we apply them to Thomsen's Calculus of Higher Order Communicating Systems (CHOCS).

Keywords: Formal Semantics, Structural Operational Semantics, Bisimulation, Congruence, Congruence Rule Formats.

1 Introduction

Bisimilarity, in its different flavors, is a central notion to concurrency theory. Congruence is a very much desired property for bisimilarity which does not generally hold. Congruence is essential for algebraic treatment of bisimilarity as well as for using it in a compositional manner. Thus, it is an interesting question whether a notion of bisimilarity is a congruence for a particular language or not.

This question has been addressed in a great depth and breadth for languages endowed with a Structural Operational Semantics (SOS) [17] (see [1] for an overview). These studies are usually formulated in terms of syntactic formats that induce congruence for a notion of bisimilarity once the SOS rules conform to the formats.

For languages with a higher order notion of behavior (which may emit and receive their own terms as labels), a few proposals exist in the literature [3,14,19]. This work's most direct inspiration is from Bernstein's *promoted tyft/tyxt* format [3] which aims at proving congruence of strong bisimilarity for higher order processes. We lay the foundations for an SOS framework for higher order processes and extend Bernstein's *promoted tyft/tyxt*, making it both easier to use and strictly more expressive.

M. Abadi and L. de Alfaro (Eds.): CONCUR 2005, LNCS 3653, pp. 308–322, 2005.

For processes with a higher order behavior, strong bisimilarity might be too restrictive since it requires the emitted or received processes (shown as labels) to be syntactically the same. In practice, however, processes are considered important up to their behavior and hence they should be related using a behavioral (and not syntactic) notion of equality. This leads to a *higher order notion of bisimilarity* [2,6,22]. In this paper, we also present and prove a novel format that induces congruence for higher order bisimilarity.

This paper is organized as follows: In the next section, we give more details of our contribution in the context of the literature. Section 3 formally defines our SOS framework and defines the intended notions of bisimilarity and congruence. Based on these concepts, our *promoted PANTH* format is presented in Section 4. Section 5 studies higher order bisimilarity and proposes the *higher order PANTH* format which induces congruence for this notion. We conclude the paper and comment on future work in Section 6.

2 Related Work

From Tyft/tyxt to PANTH. The *tyft/tyxt* format [13] is aimed at proving congruence of strong bisimilarity and it allows for SOS rules of the following forms:

$$\frac{\{t_i \xrightarrow{l_i} y_i \mid i \in I\}}{f(\overrightarrow{x_j}) \xrightarrow{l} t}, \qquad \frac{\{t_i \xrightarrow{l_i} y_i \mid i \in I\}}{x \xrightarrow{l} t},$$

where x_j and y_i are distinct variables ranging over process terms, f is a function symbol or operator (e.g., sequential composition, parallel composition, etc.), I is a (possibly infinite) set of indices and t and t_i's are process terms.

In [12], negative premises of the form $t_i \stackrel{l_i}{\nrightarrow}$ were added to the *tyft/tyxt* format, resulting in the *ntyft/ntyxt* format. The format guarantees the congruence property in this extended setting provided that the transition system specification is *stratified.* Stratification is concerned with defining a measure that decreases from the conclusion to negative premises and does not increase from the conclusion to positive premises. Note that the addition of negative premises to the *tyft/tyxt* format is a non-trivial extension in that it increases expressiveness and introduces technical complications with respect to existence and uniqueness of an intended model for the semantics.

Finally, the *PANTH* format [23] (for Predicates And Negative Tyft/tyxt Hybrid format) extends the *ntyft/ntyxt* format. A deduction rule in the *PANTH* format may have predicates, negative predicates, transitions and negative transitions in its premises and a predicate or a transition in its conclusion.

Promoted Tyft/tyxt. Bernstein in [3] proposes the *promoted tyft/tyxt* format which extends the *tyft/tyxt* format by allowing for the use of terms as labels. Rules in this format have the following form:

$$\frac{\{t_i \xrightarrow{t'_i} y_i \mid i \in I\}}{f(\overrightarrow{x_j}) \xrightarrow{g(\overrightarrow{z_k})} t}, \quad \frac{\{t_i \xrightarrow{t'_i} y_i \mid i \in I\}}{f(\overrightarrow{x_j}) \xrightarrow{z} t}, \quad \frac{\{t_i \xrightarrow{t'_i} y_i \mid i \in I\}}{x \xrightarrow{g(\overrightarrow{z_k})} t}, \quad \frac{\{t_i \xrightarrow{t'_i} y_i \mid i \in I\}}{x \xrightarrow{z} t}.$$

The intuition behind the symbols in common with the *tyft/tyxt* format remains unchanged. For the rest, g is a function symbol, z_k's and z are variables, variables in the source and label of the conclusion and targets of the premises are all distinct and furthermore, all t_i''s (labels of premises) are assumed to contain at least one function symbol, i.e., they are not variables. Bernstein proves congruence of strong bisimilarity for SOS specifications conforming to the *promoted tyft/tyxt* format.

Promoted PANTH. In this paper, we show that most of the restrictions on labels imposed above are not necessary in general and propose a more general and relaxed format based on the *promoted tyft/tyxt* format of [3]. We call our new format for strong bisimilarity *promoted PANTH*. Furthermore, the *promoted PANTH* format extends syntactic capabilities of the *promoted tyft/tyxt* format by allowing for predicates, negative premises and lists of terms as labels. We show that the *promoted PANTH* format is strictly more expressive than the *promoted tyft/tyxt* format and point out some usual patterns of SOS rules that the *promoted tyft/tyxt* format cannot deal with and the *promoted PANTH* format can.

Proof Methods for Evaluation Systems. The proof method of Howe [14] and related methods such as those proposed in [18] have been used for proving congruence of applicative bisimulation for functional languages. Sangiorgi also proposes a similar framework in [19] for concurrent extensions of lambda-calculi. Although some of the standard concepts of Howe's method, such as abstraction and evaluation structures, are not explicitly present in our framework, as shown by [3], we can still model the systems studied by [14,18,19] and obtain similar results using our formats.

Higher Order Bisimulation and Higher Order PANTH. It was first noted in [2,6] that there is a need for a notion of behavioral equivalence that relates the behavior of labels instead of their syntax. This notion was also used in [21,22] for the Calculus of Higher Order Communicating Systems (CHOCS).

In this paper, we give a general framework for defining the semantics of such systems and proving congruence for the higher order notion of bisimilarity. We also specify CHOCS [22] in our framework, show that the higher order bisimilarity of [22] trivially coincides with ours and conclude that bisimilarity in this framework is indeed a congruence. This way, one can save pages of proof (such as those given explicitly in [22]) for proving congruence.

In [20], it is argued that the higher order notion of bisimilarity may be still too strong for systems with static restriction while it works fine with dynamic restriction of names. It goes beyond the scope of this paper to discuss this issue but the techniques developed here can be useful in formulating congruence meta-theorems for other notions of bisimilarity for higher order processes (e.g., normal and context bisimilatities of [20]).

It is worth mentioning that in [3], the *promoted tyft/tyxt* format is used to prove that higher order bisimilarity is a congruence for CHOCS. But to do so, the semantics of CHOCS is translated into a new semantics and it is shown that higher order bisimilarity in CHOCS coincides with strong bisimilarity in the new semantics. Using our approach, one can save these intermediate steps and arrive at the desired result directly.

Other SOS Frameworks. Our SOS framework is closest to that of [8] (simplified by omitting the binding signatures) for which no known congruence format exists. The *generalized PANTH* format [15] includes variable binding operators (which are not addressed in this paper), but does not allow for terms as labels and hence cannot deal with higher order process algebras such as CHOCS directly. Galpin in [10] defines a multi-sorted SOS framework with terms as labels. However there, the sort of labels is necessarily different from the sort of processes. Thus higher order processes and higher order bisimilarity do not have a natural presentation in the *extended TSS* framework of [10].

3 Preliminaries

3.1 SOS with First Order Labels

Fix an infinite set of **variables** $x, y, \ldots \in V$. A **signature** is a collection of **function symbols** f, g, each with an associated **arity** $ar(f)$ which is the number of arguments of f. We call f a **constant** when $ar(f) = 0$.

(Process) terms $t, t', t_0 \ldots \in \mathcal{T}(\Sigma)$ are inductively defined in the standard way given variables and a signature. Terms $p, q, \ldots \in \mathcal{C}(\Sigma)$ are **closed** when they mention no variables. We tend to write $p, q, p_0, \ldots$ for closed terms. We shall keep Σ fixed but arbitrary henceforth, so we may drop it. Write $\mathcal{L}$ for the set of **finite lists of terms** (of possibly zero length). We write L, L', or (if we want to refer to elements) $\overrightarrow{t_i}$ for lists. Finally, we write $f(\overrightarrow{t_i})$ and by that we mean $f(t_0, \ldots, t_{ar(f)-1})$ by an implicit assumption that the list $\overrightarrow{t_i}$ is of the right length, i.e., $ar(f)$.

A substitution σ replaces variables in a term with other terms. The set of variables appearing in term t is denoted by $vars(t)$. Two substitutions σ and σ' **respect** relation R when for all $x \in V$, $(\sigma(x), \sigma'(x)) \in R$.

A transition system specification, defined below, is a logical way of defining transition relations and predicates on (closed) terms. We need some important basic definitions first:

For a (transition) relation $r \in Rel$ of arity n, $t, t' \in \mathcal{T}$, and $\overrightarrow{t_i} \in \mathcal{L}$ of length n, call $t \xrightarrow{\overrightarrow{t_i}}_r t'$ a **positive** and $t \overset{\overrightarrow{t_i}}{\nrightarrow}_r$ a **negative transition formula**. We call t the **source** of both transitions and t' the **target** of the positive one.

For a predicate $P \in Pred$ of arity n, $t \in \mathcal{T}$, and $\overrightarrow{t_i} \in \mathcal{L}$ of length n, we call $P(\overrightarrow{t_i})\ t$ a **positive predicate formula** and $\neg P(\overrightarrow{t_i})\ t$ a **negative predicate formula**. A (positive or negative) **formula** is a (positive or negative) transition or predicate formula.

We say formulae are **closed** when all the terms they mention are.

A **deduction rule** $dr \in D$ is a tuple (H, c) where H is a set of formulae and c is a positive formula. We call c the **conclusion** and formulae in H **premises**. We write (H, c) as $\frac{H}{c}$.

Definition 1 (Transition System Specification (TSS)). A **transition system specification** is a tuple $(\Sigma, Rel, Pred, D)$ consisting of a signature Σ, disjoint sets of relations Rel and predicates $Pred$ on terms with fixed arities, and a set of deduction rules D.

Note that a transition relation of arity n can be viewed as a predicate of arity $n+1$. [23] also shows how to code predicate formulae as transition formulae with dummy right-hand sides.

In the following example, we give the TSS of a higher order process algebra called CHOCS [22] which serves as a running example throughout the rest of the paper.

Example 1 (Calculus of Higher Order Communicating Systems (CHOCS)) The signature of CHOCS consists of the following operators: 0, a, $\tau.\_$, $c!\_.\_$, $c?a.\_$, $\_ + \_$, $\_ \mid \_$, $\_ \setminus c$ and $\_[S]$ where c is taken from the set C of *channel names*, a from the set A of *atoms* and $S : C \to C$ is a function on channel names. (In [22], atoms are called process variables. To avoid confusion with variables in our SOS setting, we use the term *atom* instead.)

Process 0 is a deadlocking process. An atom a is supposed to represent a "hole" in the process description which can be substituted by another process term. Other than being substituted by a term, an atom does not have any other observable behavior. Internal action prefixing $\tau.p$ first performs a τ-step and then behaves as p. A send prefixed process $c!p.p'$ sends process p along the channel c and becomes p' afterwards. A receive prefixed process $c?a.p$, receives a process along c and substitutes it for atom a in p. Choice is denoted by $+$ and parallel composition by $\mid$. To make a channel name c internal to process p the restriction expression $p \setminus c$ is used. Finally, renaming expression $p[S]$ renames all channel names of p as specified by the the renaming function S.

The transition relations for this formalism are classes of unary substitution $\xrightarrow{t}_{/a}$, send $\xrightarrow{t}_{c!}$ and receive $\xrightarrow{t}_{c?}$ transitions and a nullary internal action $\rightarrow_\tau$ transition. Substitution transition $p \xrightarrow{p'}_{/a} p''$ stands for "substituting a with p' in p results in p''". Send transition $p \xrightarrow{p'}_{c!} p''$ means that process p emits process p' along channel c and arrives in p'', similarly $p \xrightarrow{p'}_{c?} p''$ means that p receives p' along channel c and becomes p''. No predicates are used in the TSS of CHOCS.

The deduction rules of the CHOCS semantics are given in Figure 1. For brevity, we have omitted the rules dedicated to commutativity of choice and parallel composition. Also, we assume that processes are written in such a way that the substitution happening in the receive rule avoids capture of bound atoms. This can be dealt with explicitly in our SOS framework (cf. [3]) but it will only clutter our presentation and hence we dispense with it.

$$
\frac{}{a \stackrel{z}{\rightarrow}_{/a} z} \qquad
\frac{}{b \stackrel{z}{\rightarrow}_{/a} b}\, a \neq b \qquad
\frac{x_0 \stackrel{z}{\rightarrow}_{/a} y_0 \quad x_1 \stackrel{z}{\rightarrow}_{/a} y_1}{c!x_0.x_1 \stackrel{z}{\rightarrow}_{/a} c!y_0.y_1} \qquad
\frac{x \stackrel{z}{\rightarrow}_{/b} y}{c?a.x \stackrel{z}{\rightarrow}_{/b} c?a.y}\, a \neq b
$$

$$
\frac{x_0 \stackrel{z}{\rightarrow}_{/a} y_0 \quad x_1 \stackrel{z}{\rightarrow}_{/a} y_1}{x_0 + x_1 \stackrel{z}{\rightarrow}_{/a} y_0 + y_1} \quad
\frac{x_0 \stackrel{z}{\rightarrow}_{/a} y_0 \quad x_1 \stackrel{z}{\rightarrow}_{/a} y_1}{x_0 \mid x_1 \stackrel{z}{\rightarrow}_{/a} y_0 \mid y_1} \quad
\frac{x_0 \stackrel{z}{\rightarrow}_{/a} y_0}{x_0 \setminus c \stackrel{z}{\rightarrow}_{/a} y_0 \setminus c} \quad
\frac{x_0 \stackrel{z}{\rightarrow}_{/a} y_0}{x_0[S] \stackrel{z}{\rightarrow}_{/a} y_0[S]}
$$

$$
\frac{}{\tau.x \rightarrow_{\tau} x} \qquad
\frac{}{c!x_0.x_1 \stackrel{x_0}{\rightarrow}_{c!} x_1} \qquad
\frac{x_1 \stackrel{z}{\rightarrow}_{/a} y_1}{c?a.x_1 \stackrel{z}{\rightarrow}_{c?} y_1}
$$

$$
\frac{x_0 \rightarrow_{\tau} y_0}{x_0 + x_1 \rightarrow_{\tau} y_0} \qquad
\frac{x_0 \stackrel{z}{\rightarrow}_{c!} y_0}{x_0 + x_1 \stackrel{z}{\rightarrow}_{c!} y_0} \qquad
\frac{x_0 \stackrel{z}{\rightarrow}_{c?} y_0}{x_0 + x_1 \stackrel{z}{\rightarrow}_{c?} y_0}
$$

$$
\frac{x_0 \rightarrow_{\tau} y_0}{x_0 \mid x_1 \rightarrow_{\tau} y_0 \mid x_1} \quad
\frac{x_0 \stackrel{z}{\rightarrow}_{c?} y_0 \quad x_1 \stackrel{z}{\rightarrow}_{c!} y_1}{x_0 \mid x_1 \rightarrow_{\tau} y_0 \mid y_1} \quad
\frac{x_0 \stackrel{z}{\rightarrow}_{c!} y_0}{x_0 \mid x_1 \stackrel{z}{\rightarrow}_{c!} y_0 \mid x_1} \quad
\frac{x_0 \stackrel{z}{\rightarrow}_{c?} y_0}{x_0 \mid x_1 \stackrel{z}{\rightarrow}_{c?} y_0 \mid x_1}
$$

$$
\frac{x_0 \rightarrow_{\tau} y_0}{x_0 \setminus c \rightarrow_{\tau} y_0 \setminus c} \qquad
\frac{x_0 \stackrel{z}{\rightarrow}_{c'!} y_0}{x_0 \setminus c \stackrel{z}{\rightarrow}_{c'!} y_0 \setminus c}\, c \neq c' \qquad
\frac{x_0 \stackrel{z}{\rightarrow}_{c'?} y_0}{x_0 \setminus c \stackrel{z}{\rightarrow}_{c'?} y_0 \setminus c}\, c \neq c'
$$

$$
\frac{x_0 \rightarrow_{\tau} y_0}{x_0[S] \rightarrow_{\tau} y_0[S]} \qquad
\frac{x_0 \stackrel{z}{\rightarrow}_{c!} y_0}{x_0[S] \stackrel{z}{\rightarrow}_{S(c)!} y_0[S]} \qquad
\frac{x_0 \stackrel{z}{\rightarrow}_{c?} y_0}{x_0[S] \stackrel{z}{\rightarrow}_{S(c)?} y_0[S]}
$$

Fig. 1. Deduction Rules for CHOCS

Not all TSS's induce a unique set of transition relations and predicates. However, in this paper and in all practical cases, it is essential to make sure that a TSS uniquely defines the intended semantics. A criterion that helps in this respect is *stratification* [12] which guarantees that a TSS uniquely defines an intuitive model, called its *stable model*. Since it plays no role in the technical development of this paper, we do not give the details about stratification and only use it in our proofs. Henceforth and without comment, we assume all TSS's under study are stratified and consequently, induce a unique stable model.

Definition 2 (Proof). We say a positive closed formula ϕ is **provable** from a set of positive formulae T and a TSS tss, denoted by $(T, tss) \vdash \phi$ when there is a well-founded upwardly branching tree with nodes labelled by closed formulae such that:

- the root node is labelled by ϕ, and
- if the label of a node q, denoted by ψ, is a positive formula and $\{\psi_i \mid i \in I\}$ is the set of labels of the nodes directly above q, then there is a deduction rule $\dfrac{\{\chi_i \mid i \in I\}}{\chi}$ in tss (N.B. χ_i can be a positive or a negative formula) and a substitution σ such that $\sigma(\chi) = \psi$ and for all $i \in I$, $\sigma(\chi_i) = \psi_i$;
- if the label of a node q, denoted by $p \stackrel{L}{\nrightarrow}$, is a negative formula then there exists no p' such that $p \stackrel{L}{\rightarrow} p' \in T$ (or similarly, if it is of the form $\neg P(L)p$ then $P(L)p \notin T$).

Definition 3 (Stable Model). A **stable model** defined by tss is a set of positive formulae T such that $\phi \in T$ if and only if $(T, tss) \vdash \phi$, for all closed positive formulae ϕ.

3.2 Bisimilarity

Strong bisimilarity is a natural behavioral equivalence. It is generally too fine-grained (it does not equate enough terms) but it can serve as a basis for other weaker equivalences (e.g., those ignoring internal actions [11]). Congruence formats for weak equivalences (e.g. [4]) are often based on those for strong bisimilarity. Hence, we start with studying strong bisimilarity as an important notion of behavioral equivalence.

We may write pRq for $(p,q) \in R$, or even $\overrightarrow{p_i} R \overrightarrow{q_i}$ to say $\overrightarrow{p_i}$ and $\overrightarrow{q_i}$ have the same length and $p_i R q_i$, for each i.

Definition 4 (Strong Bisimulation and Bisimilarity). Given a TSS $(\Sigma, \mathit{Rel}, \mathit{Pred}, D)$ which induces a unique set of transition relations and predicates, a relation $R \subseteq \mathcal{C} \times \mathcal{C}$ is a **strong simulation** relation if and only if $\forall_{p,q \in \mathcal{C}}\ pRq \Rightarrow$

1. $\forall_{r \in \mathit{Rel}, L \in \mathcal{L}, p' \in \mathcal{C}}\ p \xrightarrow{L}_r p' \Rightarrow \exists_{q' \in \mathcal{C}}\ q \xrightarrow{L}_r q' \wedge p'Rq'$;
2. $\forall_{P \in \mathit{Pred}, L \in \mathcal{L}}\ P(L)p \Rightarrow P(L)q$.

A *strong bisimulation* relation is a symmetric strong simulation relation. Closed terms p and q are strongly bisimilar, denoted by $p \leftrightarroweq_s q$, if and only if there exists a strong bisimulation relation R such that pRq.

We treat this notion in Section 4 and there, we formulate a congruence meta-theorem for it in Theorem 1.

On one hand, our SOS framework allows for processes as labels. On the other hand processes are usually considered important up to their behavior (and not up to their syntax). Hence, it seems more natural to use a different notion of bisimilarity, rather than the strong one, which not only relates the behavior of source and target processes but also the behavior of label processes. This way, we come to the notion of higher order bisimilarity defined below.

Definition 5 (Higher Order Bisimulation and Bisimilarity [2]). Given a TSS $(\Sigma, \mathit{Rel}, \mathit{Pred}, D)$ which induces a unique set of transition relations and predicates, a relation $R \subseteq \mathcal{C} \times \mathcal{C}$ is a **higher order simulation** relation if and only if $\forall_{p,q \in \mathcal{C}}\ pRq \Rightarrow$

1. $\forall_{r \in \mathit{Rel}, L \in \mathcal{L}, p' \in \mathcal{C}}\ p \xrightarrow{L}_r p' \Rightarrow \exists_{L' \in \mathcal{L}, q' \in \mathcal{C}}\ q \xrightarrow{L'}_r q' \wedge LRL' \wedge p'Rq'$;
2. $\forall_{P \in \mathit{Pred}, L \in \mathcal{L}}\ P(L)p \Rightarrow \exists_{L' \in \mathcal{L}}\ P(L')q \wedge LRL'$.

A *higher order bisimulation* relation is a symmetric higher order simulation relation. Closed terms p and q are higher order bisimilar, denoted by $p \leftrightarroweq_h q$, if and only if there exists a higher order bisimulation relation R such that pRq.

We treat this notion in Section 5 and the corresponding congruence results are given in Theorem 3.

Note that higher order bisimilarity is sometimes required to be closed under substitution of atoms [6,22]. Here, we do not add this requirement for the sake of generality but in the coming examples, we show that this additional constraint can easily be coded in the semantic model.

It is also worth noting that higher order bisimilarity, though more natural in our setting, does not make strong bisimilarity obsolete. In some cases, the labels have a syntactic structure and use terms from the language but do not show any behavior, or alternatively, scrutinizing their behavior is a very complex task. In other words, not always terms on the labels are processes or treated as such. In cases, where labels are indeed terms but do not show any observable behavior, all labels are considered equal from a bisimilarity viewpoint and hence higher order bisimilarity renders very weak and impractical. Thus, presenting a meta-theorem for congruence of bisimilarity is interesting even in the presence of terms as labels.

As one might expect, higher order bisimilarity is strictly coarser than strong bisimilarity, i.e., it identifies more processes. Examples of this are shown in the remainder. In Section 5, we also give some sufficient criteria for the two notions to coincide.

3.3 Congruence for Bisimilarity

Next, we define the concept of congruence which is of central importance to our topic.

Definition 6 (Congruence). For a TSS with signature Σ, an equivalence relation $R \subseteq T(\Sigma) \times T(\Sigma)$ is a **congruence** when for all function symbols $f \in \Sigma$ and for all terms $p_i, q_i \in T(\Sigma)$ $(0 \leq i < ar(f))$, if $\overrightarrow{p_i} R \overrightarrow{q_i}$ then $f(\overrightarrow{p_i}) R f(\overrightarrow{q_i})$.

None of the notions of bisimilarity are necessarily a congruence. In the rest of this paper, we endeavor to find sufficient conditions that guarantee them to be a congruence. After all, it turns out that the sufficient conditions for the two notions are somewhat different. A natural question is whether this difference is genuine or not. In the following two examples we show that the notions of congruence for these two equivalences are indeed unrelated, i.e., for neither of the two equivalences, congruence of one implies congruence for the other.

Example 2 . $\dfrac{}{f(a) \xrightarrow{a}_r a} \quad \dfrac{}{a \xrightarrow{a}_r a} \quad \dfrac{}{b \xrightarrow{b}_r b}$

Consider the above set of deduction rules defined on the signature a, b and $f(\_)$. In the above TSS, it holds that $a \leftrightarrow_h b$ but not $f(a) \leftrightarrow_h f(b)$ since $f(a)$ can make an r-transition with label a but $f(b)$ cannot make any transition. Higher order bisimilarity is not a congruence for the above TSS. As for strong bisimilarity, it does not hold that $a \leftrightarrow_s b$ in the first place and hence, strong bisimilarity is trivially a congruence.

Example 3 . $\dfrac{}{f(a) \xrightarrow{a}_r a} \quad \dfrac{}{f(b) \xrightarrow{b}_r a} \quad \dfrac{}{a \xrightarrow{a}_r a} \quad \dfrac{}{b \xrightarrow{a}_r b}$

Consider the above set of deduction rules defined on the same signature as of Example 2. This time, higher order bisimilarity is a congruence since $a \underline{\leftrightarrow}_h b$ and $f(a) \underline{\leftrightarrow}_h f(b)$. However, strong bisimilarity is not a congruence since $a \underline{\leftrightarrow}_s b$ but not $f(a) \underline{\leftrightarrow}_s f(b)$.

4 Congruence for Strong Bisimilarity

In this section, we propose a syntactic restriction on TSSs, in the form of a format, that guarantees strong bisimilarity is a congruence. To begin with, we define the auxiliary notion of volatile operators.

4.1 Volatile Operators

Due to the possible interaction between terms and labels, for some operators, it is essential to make sure that transitions with these operators (as labels) are always possible under the change of their arguments by bisimilar ones. First, we give a simple example motivating this concept and then we present the formal definition.

Example 4 . $\dfrac{a \xrightarrow{g(x)}_r y}{f(x) \xrightarrow{a}_{r'} y} \quad \dfrac{}{a \xrightarrow{g(a)}_r a} \quad \dfrac{}{b \xrightarrow{g(a)}_r a}$

Consider the above TSS with a and b as constants and f and g as unary function symbols. It holds that $a \underline{\leftrightarrow}_s b$ but it does not hold that $f(a) \underline{\leftrightarrow}_s f(b)$ and hence strong bisimilarity is not a congruence.

In this case, we call g *volatile* for r transitions because in the premise of the left-most rule, g appears as a label with an argument that comes from the source of the conclusion of this rule and as such can be replaced by different terms. In order for strong bisimilarity to be a congruence, we require that r-transitions with g in the label should be indifferent to replacing arguments of g by bisimilar ones. However, this is clearly not the case for the middle and rightmost rules since for both an r transition with $g(a)$ is allowed while the same transitions with $g(b)$ are prohibited, thus causing the anomaly.

Definition 7 (Volatile Operators)**.** Given a TSS $(\Sigma, Rel, Pred, D)$ an operator $f \in \Sigma$ is called **volatile** for $r \in Rel$ (similarly for $P \in Pred$) when there exists a rule $d \in D$ of the following form:

$$\frac{\{P_i(L_i)t_i \text{ or } t_i \xrightarrow{L_i}_{r_i} t'_i \mid i \in I\} \quad \{\neg P_j(L_j)t_j \text{ or } t_j \stackrel{L_j}{\nrightarrow}_{r_j} \mid j \in J\}}{P'(L)t \text{ or } t \xrightarrow{L}_{r'} t'}$$

and $f(\overrightarrow{t_k})$ is a subterm of a component of L_m for some $m \in I \cup J$ such that $r = r_m$ $(P = P_m)$ and $vars(\overrightarrow{t_k}) \cap vars(t) \neq \emptyset$ or $\exists_{i \in I} vars(\overrightarrow{t_k}) \cap vars(t'_i) \neq \emptyset$.

It trivially follows from the above definition that no constant can be volatile.

4.2 Promoted PANTH Format

Next, we formulate our congruence format for strong bisimilarity.

Definition 8 (Promoted PANTH Format). A deduction rule is in the **promoted PANTH** format when it is of the following form

$$\frac{\{P_i(L_i)t_i \text{ or } t_i \xrightarrow{L_i}_{r_i} y_i \mid i \in I\} \quad \{\neg P_j(L_j)t_j \text{ or } t_j \stackrel{L_j}{\nrightarrow}_{r_j} \mid j \in J\}}{P(L)f(\overrightarrow{x_i}) \text{ or } f(\overrightarrow{x_i}) \xrightarrow{L}_r t'}$$

and first, all the variables x_i and y_j ($0 \leq i < ar(f)$ and $j \in I$) and the variables in L are pairwise distinct, second, if a component of L_k ($k \in I \cup J$) is a variable (i.e., does not have any function symbol) then it is not among x_i's and y_j's and third, for all components t of L:

1. if t contains a volatile $g \in \Sigma$ for r (for P) then t is of the form $g(\overrightarrow{z_l})$ where all z_l's are distinct variables and for all $k \in I \cup J$, all components of L_k containing a variable among $\overrightarrow{z_l}$ are of the form $g'(\overrightarrow{t_m})$ where g' is volatile for r_k (for P_k),
2. if there is a volatile operator for r (for P) in the signature and if t is a variable z then for all $k \in I \cup J$, all components of L_k containing z are either z itself or are of the form $g'(\overrightarrow{t_n})$ where g' is volatile for r_k (for P_k).

A TSS is in the *promoted PANTH* format when all its deduction rules are.

Observe that if there is no volatile operator in the signature then none of the two checks on the labels are needed. Volatile operators are very rare in process-algebraic formalisms as it can be observed in the coming examples. Hence, most of the times, the above format can be simplified and checks on the labels can be saved. Surprisingly, the *promoted tyft/tyxt* format is formulated in such a way that all operators can be considered volatile and thus, it turns out to be more restrictive and less expressive than ours. Examples of these phenomena are pointed out next.

Example 5 (Congruence of Strong Bisimilarity for CHOCS). Consider the TSS of CHOCS given in Example 1. No operator in this language is not volatile. All the deduction rules of this TSS are in the *promoted PANTH* format but the one concerning the send operator $c!\_.\_$. This rule violates the format by exploiting variable x_0 in both the source and the label of the conclusion. All the other rules, having a premise are *not* in the *promoted tyft/tyxt* format since they have variables as labels of premises. Note that this restriction of the *promoted tyft/tyxt* format can be seen as a disadvantage since using this format, one cannot deal with ordinary process algebraic operators (e.g., choice and parallel composition) by replacing variables for constant labels. This restriction is not present in the *promoted PANTH* format.

Hitherto, one can imagine two scenarios. Either our format is too weak to capture the congruence of strong bisimilarity for CHOCS (since syntactic formats only give sufficient and not necessary conditions) or strong bisimilarity for

CHOCS is not a congruence in the first place. Fortunately, the latter is the case and this can be shown by a very simple example.

Consider two processes 0 and 0+0. It clearly holds that $0 \leftrightarrow_s 0{+}0$ and $0 \leftrightarrow_s 0$ but it does not hold that $c!0.0$ is bisimilar to $c!(0+0).0$ as the former can only perform a $\stackrel{0}{\rightarrow}_{c!}$ transition but the latter can only make a $\stackrel{0+0}{\rightarrow}_{c!}$ a transition and 0 and $0+0$ are not (syntactically) the same terms.

However, one can change the language a bit so that strong bisimilarity becomes a congruence. One such approach is presented in [3] and with a proof of more than a page, it is shown that strong bisimilarity in the new language coincides with a notion of higher order bisimilarity [22] in the original semantics and hence, it is concluded that this notion of higher order bisimilarity for the original language is a congruence. In Section 5, we propose a congruence format for higher order bisimilarity and using that we give a direct proof for congruence of higher order bisimilarity. So, we do not take the approach of [3] in this section.

Alternatively, in order to make the strong bisimilarity a congruence, we propose to change the send operator as follows. First, we change the syntax of a send operator to be a class of unary send operators $c!p.\_$ for given closed terms $p \in P$. Then, we change the semantics of the send operator and replace it with this rule: $\dfrac{}{c!p.x_0 \stackrel{p}{\rightarrow}_{c!} x_0}$.

Note that in the above rule the p in the source of the conclusion is part of the function symbol while the p in the label is a term. To check that this rule fits in the *promoted PANTH* format one has to check the following two conditions: first, the set of variables appearing in p and $c!p.x_0$ should be disjoint which holds trivially since the former p is a closed term and second, either p contains no volatile operator or it is of the form $g(\overrightarrow{x})$ for a volatile g. Since the language contains no volatile operator the second obligation is also discharged and hence, we can conclude that strong bisimilarity is a congruence for this slightly modified language. Note that one cannot get a similar result by using the *promoted tyft/tyxt* format for it only allows for labels of the form x or $g(\overrightarrow{x})$ in the conclusion.

Next, by a simple and abstract example, we show that our format is strictly more expressive than the *promoted tyft/tyxt* format of [3].

Example 6 . $\dfrac{x \stackrel{z}{\rightarrow}_r y}{f(x) \stackrel{z}{\rightarrow}_r y} \quad \dfrac{}{a \stackrel{f(a)}{\rightarrow}_r b} \quad \dfrac{}{b \stackrel{f(a)}{\rightarrow}_r b}$

Consider a TSS defined by signature $\{a, b, f(\_)\}$, a unary transition relation $\rightarrow_r$, no predicate and the deduction rules given above. None of the three deduction rules are in the *promoted tyft/tyxt* format while they are all in the *promoted PANTH* format and one can check that strong bisimilarity is indeed a congruence. Our claim is that there exists no TSS in the *promoted tyft/tyxt* format that induces the same transition relation as the one induced by the above TSS.

The proof of our claim is quite simple and follows from the proof of Theorem 2.1 in [3]. There, it is shown that, for a TSS in the *promoted tyft/tyxt* format, for all terms $f(\overrightarrow{p_i})$ and $g(\overrightarrow{q_j})$ if there exists $p' \in \mathcal{C}$ and $\overrightarrow{p_i'}, \overrightarrow{q_j'} \in \mathcal{L}$ such that $f(\overrightarrow{p_i}) \xrightarrow{g(\overrightarrow{q_j})}_r p'$, $\overrightarrow{p_i} \leftrightarrow_s \overrightarrow{p_i'}$ and $\overrightarrow{q_j} \leftrightarrow_s \overrightarrow{q_j'}$ then there exists a $p'' \in \mathcal{C}$ such that $f(\overrightarrow{p_i'}) \xrightarrow{g(\overrightarrow{q_j'})}_r p''$. Getting back to our example, suppose that there exists a TSS in the *promoted tyft/tyxt* format that induces the same transition relation as the one induced by the above TSS. Then, since $a \leftrightarrow_s b$ and $f(a) \xrightarrow{f(a)}_r b$, it should hold that $f(b) \xrightarrow{f(b)}_r p''$ for some $p'' \in \mathcal{C}$ such that $b \leftrightarrow_s p''$. But note that in the transition relation induced by the above TSS, no transition with label $f(b)$ is provable. Q.E.D.

4.3 Characteristic Theorem

Common to [3], we impose an extra constraint on the *promoted PANTH* format to prove congruence, namely the well-foundedness of the TSS under consideration.

Definition 9 (P-Well-Foundedness)**.** For a deduction rule, the **p-variable ordering** $\leq_p$ is an ordering among variables. We wrie $x \leq_p y$, for two variables x and y, when x appears in the source or the label of a premise of the deduction rule and y in the target of the same premise. A TSS is called **p-well-founded** when for all deduction rules in TSS, there is no infinite backward chain of variables with respect to $\leq_p$.

Note that in [7] it has been shown that the well-foundedness assumption, although being very convenient for proofs, is not essential for the *PANTH* format. Indeed, for each non-well-founded TSS in the *PANTH* format, one can construct a well-founded one in a subset of this format (called NTree rules format) that induces the same transition relations and predicates. We leave it open whether the results of [7] carries over to our settings or not.

Theorem 1 (Congruence for Promoted PANTH)**.** For a p-well-founded TSS in the *promoted PANTH* format, strong bisimilarity is a congruence.

5 Congruence for Higher Order Bisimilarity

5.1 Persistency

In this section, we seek sufficient syntactic criteria for the higher order bisimilarity induced by a TSS to be a congruence.

We begin with an auxiliary definition that has the same spirit as that for volatile operators. It is supposed to capture that the labels of a transition can be replaced by bisimilar ones.

Definition 10. Consider a TSS $(\Sigma, \mathit{Rel}, \mathit{Pred}, D)$ and a set Ps of tuples (U, L) where $U \in \mathit{Rel} \cup \mathit{Pred}$ and $L \in \mathcal{L}$. We call Ps a **persistent set** when for all

$(U, L) \in Ps$ and all deduction rules $d \in D$ if d has U in its conclusion then it is of the following form:

$$\frac{\{P(L_i)t_i \text{ or } t_i \xrightarrow{L_i}_{r_i} y_i \mid i \in I\} \quad \{\neg P(L_j)t_j \text{ or } t_j \stackrel{L_j}{\nrightarrow}_{r_j} \mid j \in J\}}{U(L')f(\overrightarrow{x}) \text{ or } f(\overrightarrow{x}) \xrightarrow{L'}_U t'}$$

where $L = \sigma(L')$ for some substitution σ and

1. all x_i's, y_j's ($0 \leq i < ar(f)$ and $j \in I$) and variables appearing in L' are pairwise distinct;
2. for all $k \in I \cup J$, $(r_k, \sigma(L_k)) \in Ps$ (or $(P_k, \sigma(L_k)) \in Ps$).

If a set Ps is persistent and $(U, L) \in Ps$ then we say that **U-transitions (predicates) are persistent for L labels**. A transition relation (predicate) is **persistent** if it is persistent for a label of the form $\overrightarrow{z_i}$ where z_i are distinct variables.

The following theorem gives an idea about the intuition behind persistency.

Theorem 2. If for a TSS all its transition relations and predicates are persistent then:

1. higher order bisimilarity is a congruence;
2. higher order and strong bisimilarity coincide.

Example 7 (Persistency for CHOCS)**.** Substitution, receive and τ-transitions are all persistent in CHOCS, i.e., substitution and receive are persistent for a variable.

5.2 Higher Order PANTH Format

Our criteria are formulated as a syntactic format which we call *higher order PANTH*.

Definition 11 (Higher Order PANTH Format)**.** A deduction rule is in the **higher order PANTH** format when it is of the following form

$$\frac{\{P(L_i)t_i \text{ or } t_i \xrightarrow{L_i}_{r_i} y_i \mid i \in I\} \quad \{\neg P(L_j)t_j \text{ or } t_j \stackrel{L_j}{\nrightarrow}_{r_j} \mid j \in J\}}{P(L)f(\overrightarrow{x_i}) \text{ or } f(\overrightarrow{x_i}) \xrightarrow{L}_r t'}$$

where variables x_i's and y_j's ($0 \leq i < ar(f)$ and $j \in I$) are all pairwise distinct and for all $k \in I \cup J$

1. r_k-transitions (predicates) are persistent for L_k labels (Definition 10);
2. or alternatively, $k \in I$, L_k is a list of distinct variables $\overrightarrow{z_{km}}$ that are distinct from labels of other non-persistent transitions and predicates and are different from x_i's and y_j's.

A TSS is in the *higher order PANTH* format when all its rules are.

Next, we define the notion of well-foundedness for TSS's in the *higher order PANTH* format.

Definition 12 (H-Well-Foundedness). An **h-variable ordering** $\leq_h$ with respect to a deduction rule is an ordering on variables. For two variables x and y, $x \leq_h y$ if x appears in the source of a premise of the rule and y appears in its label or target. A TSS is **h-well-founded** when for all deduction rules in TSS, there is no infinite backward chain of variables with respect to $\leq_h$.

We believe that well-foundedness for this format is a convenience for our proofs and is not a necessary ingredient for congruence but this remains to be formally checked.

Theorem 3 (Congruence for Higher Order PANTH). For an h-well-founded TSS in the *higher order PANTH* format, higher order bisimilarity is a congruence.

Example 8 (Congruence of Higher Order Bisimilarity for CHOCS). The semantics of CHOCS as given in Example 1 conforms to our format. To verify this claim we have to check that in the conclusion of each deduction rule mentions only one function symbol, the targets of premises mention distinct variables and the label of premises either mention distinct variables or are persistent. The first two checks are straightforward. For the third, the only problem arises from the rules having two premises mentioning the same label z. Two of such rules appear in the definition of substitution transitions which is shown to be persistent, so they conform to our format. The only other rule having the same condition is the one defining communication for parallel composition. But in that rule, the receive transition is persistent and hence, the only non-persistent premise (the send transition) trivially satisfies the second criterion of Definition 11. Note that the notion of higher order bisimilarity in [22] also requires that bisimilarity should be closed under substitution of atoms. Our notion does not require this in general, but in the case of CHOCS semantics, the addition of substitution, makes sure that bisimilar terms always have the same "substitution behavior". Hence, the two notions trivially coincide.

6 Conclusion

In this paper, we presented two syntactic formats that guarantee congruence for two notions of strong and higher order bisimilarity. We applied these formats to the CHOCS process algebra [22].

Due to the abundant presence of notions of names and binders in the formalisms with higher order behavior, the addition of these notions to our formats is a very natural and useful extension. We are currently considering this extension and we try to exploit the Gabbay-Pitts Nominal Techniques [9,16] for this purpose.

References

1. L. Aceto, W. J. Fokkink, and C. Verhoef. Structural operational semantics. In *Handbook of Process Algebra, Chapter 3*, pages 197–292. Elsevier Science, 2001.
2. E. Astesiano, A. Giovini, and G. Reggio, Generalized bisimulation in relational specifications. In *Proc. of STACS'88*, volume 294 of *LNCS*, pages 207–226, Springer, 1988.
3. K. L. Bernstein. A congruence theorem for structured operational semantics of higher-order languages. In *Proc. of LICS'98*, pages 153–164. IEEE CS, 1998.
4. B. Bloom. Structural operational semantics for weak bisimulations. *TCS*, 146:25–68, 1995.
5. R. Bol and J. F. Groote. The meaning of negative premises in transition system specifications. *JACM*, 43(5):863–914, 1996.
6. G. Boudol. Towards a lambda-calculus for concurrent and communicating systems. In *Proc. of TAPSOFT'89*, volume 351 of *LNCS*, pages 149–161, Springer, 1989.
7. W. J. Fokkink and R. J. van Glabbeek. Ntyft/ntyxt rules reduce to ntree rules. *I&C*, 126(1):1–10, 1996.
8. W. J. Fokkink and C. Verhoef. A conservative look at operational semantics with variable binding. *I&C*, 146(1):24–54, 1998.
9. M. J. Gabbay and J. Cheney. A Sequent Calculus for Nominal Logic, In *Proc. of LICS'04*, pages 139–148, IEEE CS, 2004.
10. V. Galpin. A format for semantic equivalence comparison, *TCS*, 309(1-3):65–109, 2003.
11. R. J. van Glabbeek and W. P. Weijland. Branching Time and Abstraction in Bisimulation Semantics. *JACM*, 43(3):555–600, 1996.
12. J. F. Groote. Transition system specifications with negative premises. *TCS*, 118(2):263–299, 1993.
13. J. F. Groote and F. W. Vaandrager. Structured operational semantics and bisimulation as a congruence. *I&C*, 100(2):202–260, 1992.
14. D. J. Howe. Proving congruence of bisimulation in functional programming languages. I&C, 124:103–112, 1996.
15. C. A. Middelburg. Variable binding operators in transition system specifications. *JLAP*, 47(1):15–45, 2001.
16. A. M. Pitts. Nominal logic, a first order theory of names and binding. *I&C*, 186(2):165–193, 2003.
17. G. D. Plotkin. A structural approach to operational semantics. *JLAP*, 60:17–139, 2004.
18. D. Sands. From SOS rules to proof principles: An operational metatheory for functional languages. *Proc. of POPL'97*, pages 428-441, ACM Press, 1997.
19. D. Sangiorgi. The Lazy lambda calculus in a concurrency scenario. *I&C*, 111(1):120–153, 1994.
20. D. Sangiorgi. Bisimulation for Higher-Order Process Calculi. *I&C*, 131(2):141–178, 1996.
21. B. Thomsen. Plain CHOCS a second generation calculus for higher order processes. *Acta Informatica*, 30(1):1–59, 1993.
22. B. Thomsen. A theory of higher order communicating systems. *I&C*, 116:38–57, 1995.
23. C. Verhoef. A congruence theorem for structured operational semantics with predicates and negative premises. *Nordic Journal of Computing*, 2(2):274–302, 1995.

The Individual and Collective Token Interpretations of Petri Nets

Robert Jan van Glabbeek

National ICT Australia
and School of Computer Science and Engineering,
The University of New South Wales
rvg@cs.stanford.edu

Abstract. Starting from the opinion that the standard firing rule of Petri nets embodies the collective token interpretation of nets rather than their individual token interpretation, I propose a new firing rule that embodies the latter. Also variants of both firing rules for the self-sequential interpretation of nets are studied. Using these rules, I express the four computational interpretations of Petri nets by semantic mappings from nets to labelled step transition systems, the latter being event-oriented representations of higher dimensional automata. This paper totally orders the expressive power of the four interpretations, measured in terms of the classes of labelled step transition systems up to isomorphism of reachable parts that can be denoted by nets under each of the interpretations. Furthermore, I extend the unfolding construction of place/transition nets into occurrence net to nets that may have transitions without incoming arcs.

1 Introduction

In the literature on Petri nets $2 \times 2 = 4$ computational interpretations of nets can be distinguished, that in VAN GLABBEEK & PLOTKIN [6] were called the *individual token* and the *collective token* interpretation, and, orthogonally, the *self-sequential* and the *self-concurrent* interpretation. The differences show up only when dealing with non-safe place/transition nets and, as far as the individual/collective token dichotomy concerns, only when precisely keeping track of causal dependencies between action occurrences.

The individual token interpretation has been formalised by the notion of a *process*, described in GOLTZ & REISIG [7]. A causality respecting bisimulation relation based on this approach was proposed by BEST, DEVILLERS, KIEHN & POMELLO [3] under the name fully concurrent bisimulation. ENGELFRIET [4] and MESEGUER *et al.* [8] define an unfolding of Petri nets into occurrence nets that preserves this interpretation. BEST & DEVILLERS [2] adapted the process concept of [7] to fit the collective token philosophy. Equivalence relations on Petri nets based on the collective token interpretation were proposed in [6].

In older papers on Petri nets a multiset of transitions was allowed to fire only if it was a set, i.e., no transition could fire multiple times concurrent with

M. Abadi and L. de Alfaro (Eds.): CONCUR 2005, LNCS 3653, pp. 323–337, 2005.

itself. The argument for this restriction was that a transition can be thought of as a subsystem like a printer, that can only print one file at a time. When there are enough tokens in its preplaces (representing print-requests and other preconditions for printing) to handle two files, these have to be printed one by one. GOLTZ & REISIG [7] exemplified that not all subsystems suffer from such limitations; when one does, this is a matter of scarcity of recourses that can be modelled by an extra place. Since [7] multisets are generally allowed to fire. Nevertheless, for the sake of completeness, I take both interpretations into account.

The present work can be understood as a way of formally pinpointing the differences between these computational interpretations. This is done by formulating four different firing rules, and by giving four translations from Petri nets into labelled step transition systems, one for each interpretation. *Labelled step transition systems* arose from discussions with Vaughan Pratt in 1991 as an event-oriented representation of *higher dimensional automata* [10], an angle that will not be pursued here. Step transition systems were used to describe the operational behaviour of Petri nets in MUKUND [9]. In the form proposed here, but without the labelling, they appear in BADOUEL [1].

I compare the expressive power of classes of Petri nets under each of the four interpretations in terms of the labelled step transition systems they can denote up to isomorphism of reachable parts, and find that the class of all Petri nets under either one of the individual token interpretations is equally expressive as a subclass of nets on which all four interpretations coincide. Likewise, the class of all Petri nets under the self-concurrent collective token interpretation is equally expressive as a subclass of nets on which both collective token interpretations coincide. This gives rise to the following hierarchy:

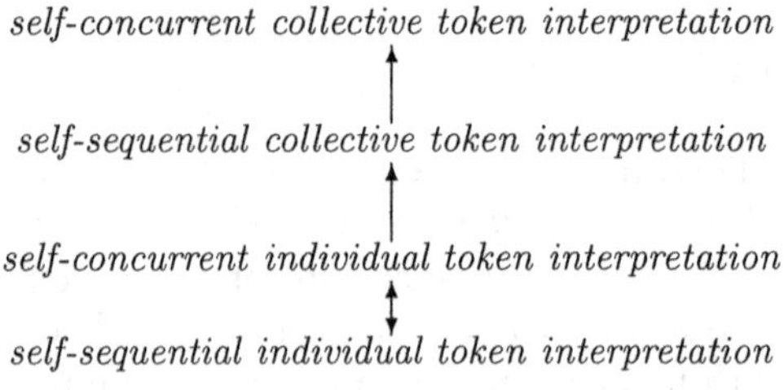

Fig. 1. Relative expressiveness of four computational interpretations of Petri nets

The expressiveness results above were first claimed by me in [5], using a different model of higher dimensional automata for interpreting the dynamic behaviour of Petri nets, namely *cubical sets* instead of labelled step transition systems. However, the individual token interpretations of [5] apply to *standard nets* only, nets in which each transition has at least one incoming arc, and a proof is given for the expressiveness result relating the two self-concurrent interpretations only.

As a spin-off, this study provides a particularly simple definition of the unfolding of an arbitrary place/transition net into an occurrence net. My construction extends the constructions of [11], [4] and [8] by including non-standard nets.

2 Petri Nets and the Firing Rule

Definition 1. A (labelled, marked) *Petri net* is a tuple (S, T, F, I, l) with

- S and T two disjoint sets of *places* (*Stellen* in German) and *transitions*,
- $F : (S \times T \cup T \times S) \to \mathbb{N}$, the *flow relation*,
- $I : S \to \mathbb{N}$, the *initial marking*,
- and $l : T \to A$, for A a set of *actions*, the *labelling function*.

Petri nets are pictured by drawing the places as circles and the transitions as boxes, containing their label. For $x, y \in S \cup T$ there are $F(s,t)$ *arcs* from x to y. When a Petri net represents a concurrent system, a global state of this system is given as a *marking*, a function $M : S \to \mathbb{N}$. Such a state is depicted by placing $M(s)$ dots (*tokens*) in each place s. The initial state is given by the marking I. In order to describe the behaviour of a net, one defines the *step transition relation* between markings.

Definition 2. A *multiset* over a set S is a function $M : S \to \mathbb{N}$, i.e. $M \in \mathbb{N}^S$. For multisets M and N over S write $M \leq N$ if $M(s) \leq N(s)$ for all $s \in S$. $M + N \in \mathbb{N}^S$ is the multiset with $(M + N)(s) = M(s) + N(s)$, and $M - N$ is the function given by $(M - N)(s) = M(s) - N(s)$—it is not always a multiset. The function $0 : S \to \mathbb{N}$ given by $0(s) = 0$ for all $s \in S$ is the *empty* multiset. A multiset $M \in \mathbb{N}^S$ with $M(s) \leq 1$ for all $s \in S$ is identified with the set $\{s \in S \mid M(s) = 1\}$. A multiset M over S is *finite* if $\{s \in S \mid M(s) > 0\}$ is finite. Let $\mathcal{M}(S)$ denote the collection of finite multisets over S.

Definition 3. For a finite multiset $U : T \to \mathbb{N}$ of transitions in a Petri net, let ${}^\bullet U,\ U^\bullet : S \to \mathbb{N}$ be the multisets of *input* and *output places* of U, given by

$${}^\bullet U(s) = \sum_{t \in T} F(s,t) \cdot U(t) \quad \text{and} \quad U^\bullet(s) = \sum_{t \in T} U(t) \cdot F(t,s) \quad \text{for all } s \in S.$$

U is *enabled* under a marking M if ${}^\bullet U \leq M$. In that case U can *fire* under M, yielding the marking $M' = M - {}^\bullet U + U^\bullet$, written $M \xrightarrow{U} M'$.

If a multiset U of transitions fires, for every transition t in U and every arc from a place s to t, a token moves along that arc from s to t. These tokens are consumed by the firing, but also new tokens are created, namely one for every outgoing arc of t. These end up in the places at the end of those arcs. If t occurs several times in U, all this happens several times (in parallel) as well. The firing of U is only possible if there are sufficiently many tokens in the preplaces of U (the places where the incoming arcs come from).

The components of a net N are called S^{N}, T^{N}, F^{N}, I^{N} and l^{N}, a convention that also applies to other structures given as tuples. When clear from context, the index N is omitted.

Two nets P and Q are *isomorphic*, written $P \cong Q$, if they differ only in the names of their places and transitions, i.e. if there are bijections $\beta : S^{\mathrm{P}} \to S^{\mathrm{Q}}$ and $\eta : T^{\mathrm{P}} \to T^{\mathrm{Q}}$ such that, for $s \in S^{\mathrm{P}}$ and $t \in T^{\mathrm{P}}$: $I^{\mathrm{Q}}(\beta(s)) = I^{\mathrm{P}}(s)$, $F^{\mathrm{Q}}(\beta(s), \eta(t)) = F^{\mathrm{P}}(s,t)$, $F^{\mathrm{Q}}(\eta(t), \beta(s)) = F^{\mathrm{P}}(t,s)$ and $l^{\mathrm{Q}}(\eta(t)) = l^{\mathrm{P}}(t)$.

3 The Individual and Collective Token Interpretations

In the *individual token interpretation* of Petri nets one distinguishes different tokens residing in the same place, keeping track of where they come from. If a transition fires by using a token that has been produced by another transition, there is a causal link between the two. Consequently, the causal relations between the transitions in a run of a net can always be described by means of a partial order. In the *collective token interpretation*, on the other hand, tokens cannot be distinguished: if there are two tokens in a place, all that is present there is the number 2. This gives rise to more subtle causal relationships between transitions in a run of a net, which cannot be expressed by partial orders.

The following example illustrates the difference between the two interpretations.

A: 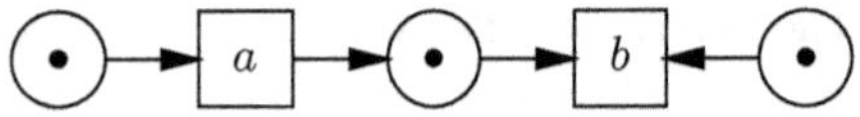

In this net, the transitions labelled a and b can fire once each. After a has fired, there are two tokens in the middle place. According to the individual token philosophy, it makes a difference which of these tokens is used in firing b. If the token that was there already is used (which must certainly be the case if b happens before the token from a arrives), the transitions a and b are causally independent. If the token that was produced by a is used, b is causally dependent on a. Thus, the net A above has two maximal executions, that can be characterised by the partial orders $\begin{smallmatrix} a \\ b \end{smallmatrix}$ and $a \rightarrow b$ According to the collective token philosophy on the other hand, all that is present in the middle place after the occurrence of a is the number 2. The preconditions for b to fire do not change, and consequently b is always causally independent of a.

The following illustrates that both philosophies yield incomparable notions of equivalence.

B: 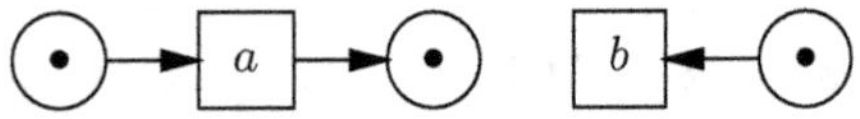

In the collective token philosophy the precondition of b expressed by the place in the middle is redundant, and hence A must be equivalent to B. However, A and B are not *fully concurrent bisimulation equivalent* (a causality respecting equivalence based on the individual token approach [3]), as B lacks the execution $a \rightarrow b$ On the other hand, A is fully concurrent bisimulation equivalent with C below.

C: 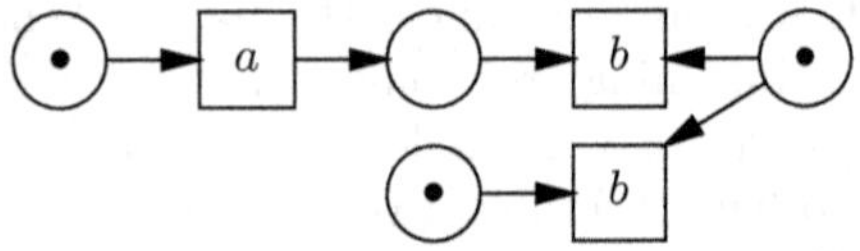

In fact, C is the occurrence net obtained from A by the unfolding of [4,8]. In the individual token philosophy, both A and C have the executions $a \rightarrow b$ and $\begin{smallmatrix} a \\ b \end{smallmatrix}$. However, in the collective token philosophy A does not have a run $a \rightarrow b$ and can therefore not be equivalent to C in any causality preserving way.

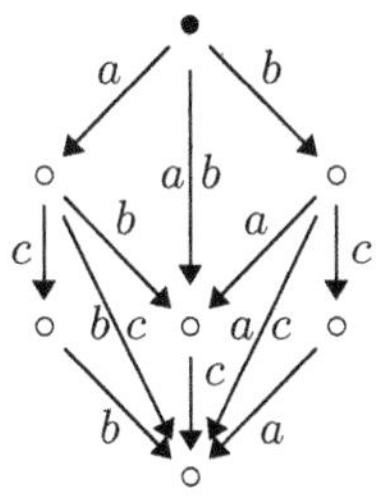

$\mathcal{H}_{\text{CT}}(\text{D})$

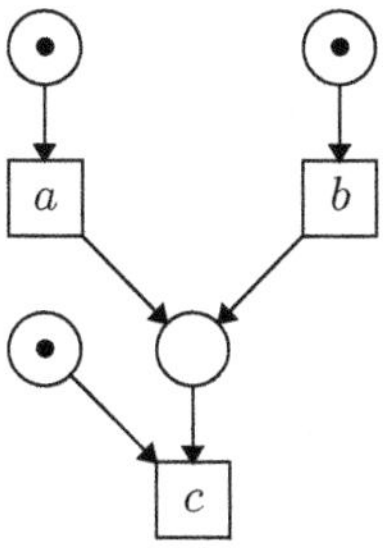

D

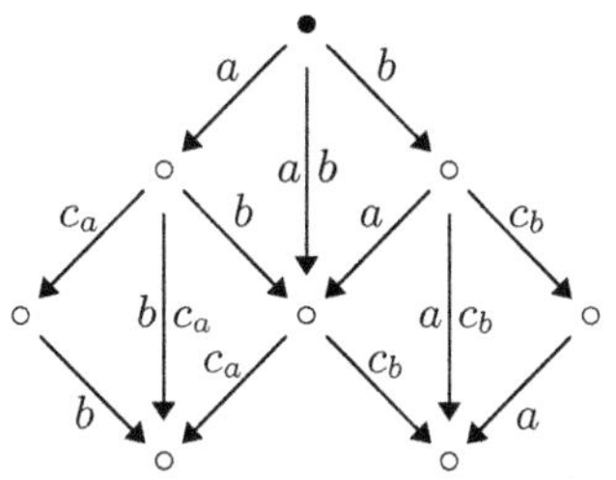

$\mathcal{H}_{\text{IT}}(\text{D})$

The Petri net D above (ignore $\mathcal{H}_{\text{CT}}(\text{D})$ and $\mathcal{H}_{\text{IT}}(\text{D})$ for now) illustrates how the collective token interpretation gives rise to causal relationships that cannot be expressed by partial orders. Under the collective token interpretation this net features *disjunctive causality*: c is causally dependent on $a \vee b$. In contrast, under the individual token interpretation D admits two executions, one in which c depends only on a, and one in which c depends only on b.

Antoni Mazurkiewicz once argued for the collective reading of this net by letting a and b be £1 contributions of two school children to buy a present for their teacher. The act of buying the present, which only costs £1, is represented by c. Now the individual token interpretation suggests that the present is bought from the contribution from either one child or the other, whereas the collective token interpretation admits only one complete execution, in which the buying of the present is caused by the disjunction of the two contributions. The latter would be a fairer description of the intended state of affairs.

4 A Firing Rule for the Individual Token Interpretation

In my opinion, the standard definition of a marking and the corresponding firing rule (Def. 3) embody the collective token interpretation rather than the individual one. Here I will redefine these concepts in a way that embodies the individual token interpretation. To this end I define the notion of a token as it could occur in a Petri net, in such a way that all possible token occurrences have a different name. A token will be a triple (t', k, s), with s the place where the token occurs, and t' the transition firing that brought it there. For tokens that are in s initially, I take $t' = *$. When the number of tokens that t' deposits in s in n, I distinguish these tokens by giving them ordinal numbers $k = 0, 1, 2, \ldots, n-1$. In order to define tokens as announced above I need to define transition firings simultaneously. These will be pairs (X, t) with t the transition that fires, and X the set of tokens that is consumed in the firing. Transitions t that can fire without consuming tokens can fire multiple times on the same (empty) input; these firings will be called (k, t) with $k \in \mathbb{N}$ instead of $(\emptyset, t)$. I define the functions β from tokens to the places where they occur by $\beta(x, k, s) = s$, and η from transition firings to the transition that fires by $\eta(x, t) = t$. The function β extends to a function from sets of tokens X to multisets of places $\beta(X) : S \to \mathbb{N}$, by $\beta(X)(s) = |\{s' \in X \mid \beta(s') = s\}|$.

Definition 4. Given a Petri net $\mathrm{N} = (S, T, F, I, l)$, the sets of *tokens* $S_\bullet$ and *transition firings* $T_\bullet$ of N are recursively defined by

- $(*, k, s) \in S_\bullet$ for $s \in S$ and $k < I(s)$;
- $(t', k, s) \in S_\bullet$ for $s \in S$, $t' \in T_\bullet$ and $k < F(\eta(t'), s)$;
- $(X, t) \in T_\bullet$ for $t \in T$ and $X \subseteq S_\bullet$ such that $\beta(X) = {}^\bullet t \neq 0$;
- $(k, t) \in T_\bullet$ for $k \in \mathbb{N}$ and $t \in T$ such that ${}^\bullet t = 0$.

The labelling function $l_\bullet : T_\bullet \rightarrow A$ on transition firings is given by $l_\bullet(t) = l(\eta(t))$. An *individual marking* of N is a multiset $M : S_\bullet \rightarrow \mathbb{N}$ of tokens. The *initial* individual marking $I_\bullet : S_\bullet \rightarrow \mathbb{N}$ is given by $I_\bullet(*, k, s) = 1$ and $I_\bullet(t', k, s) = 0$.

Standard Nets. A *standard net* is a net N in which each transition has at least one incoming arc: $\forall t \in T.\ {}^\bullet t > 0$. A net is standard iff its set of *spontaneous transition firings* $T_\circ = \{(k, t) \in T_\bullet \mid k \in \mathbb{N}\}$ is empty. I define the firing rule embodying the individual token interpretation for standard nets first.

Definition 5. For a finite set $U \subseteq T_\bullet$ of transition firings in a standard net, let

$$ {}^\bullet U = \sum_{(X,t) \in U} X \quad \text{and} \quad U^\bullet = \{(t', k, s) \mid t' \in U \wedge k < F(\eta(t'), s)\} $$

be the multiset of *input tokens* and the set of *output tokens* of U. The set U is *enabled* under an individual marking $M \in \mathbb{N}^{S_\bullet}$ if ${}^\bullet U \leq M$. In that case U can *fire* under M, yielding $M' = M - {}^\bullet U + U^\bullet \in \mathbb{N}^{S_\bullet}$, written $M \xrightarrow{U}_\bullet M'$.
A chain $I_\bullet \xrightarrow{U_1}_\bullet M_1 \xrightarrow{U_2}_\bullet \cdots \xrightarrow{U_n}_\bullet M_n$ is called a *firing sequence.* An individual marking $M \in \mathbb{N}^{S_\bullet}$ is *reachable* if there is such a sequence ending in $M = M_n$.

The following proposition says that I succeeded in giving all possible token occurrences a different name.

Proposition 1. *In a standard net, any reachable multiset of tokens is a set.*

Proof. I show that in a firing sequence $I_\bullet \xrightarrow{U_1}_\bullet M_1 \xrightarrow{U_2}_\bullet \cdots \xrightarrow{U_n}_\bullet M_n$ the multiset $I_\bullet + \sum_{i=1}^n U_i^\bullet$, which includes M_n, is a set. Applying induction on n, the base case holds by the definition of $I_\bullet$. For the induction step, if a token occurs twice in $I_\bullet + \sum_{i=1}^n U_i^\bullet$, the definitions of $I_\bullet$ and $U^\bullet$ imply that it has the form (t', k, s), hence the transition firing t' occurs twice in $\sum_{i=1}^n U_i$. As t' is not spontaneous, it has the form (X, t) with X a nonempty set of tokens. By the definition of ${}^\bullet U$, a token in X occurs twice in $I_\bullet + \sum_{i=1}^{n-1} U_i^\bullet$. □

Prop. 1 also shows that there is no point in upgrading Def. 5 to *multi*sets U.

Non-Standard Nets. For arbitrary nets, the definition of $U^\bullet$, for U a finite set of transitions, remains the same, but in the definition of ${}^\bullet U$ one needs to decide on the input conditions of spontaneous transition firings. The simplest solution would be to treat k as $\emptyset$ in the definition of ${}^\bullet U$ or, equivalently, to let the sum range over the non-spontaneous transition firings in U only. However, this would lead to a failure of Prop. 1 for non-standard nets, as a spontaneous transition firing (k,t) could occur multiple times in a firing sequence, leaving multiple copies of its output tokens in the resulting reachable marking. A solution for this problem would be to upgrade the definition of a firing sequence with the requirement that each spontaneous transition firing may only occur once in it. This condition would be motivated by the idea that every time a transition t with ${}^\bullet t = 0$ fires, its firing gets a different identifier.

Here I aim at the same result by using a notion of state that consists of an individual marking, together with the set names of spontaneous transition firings that may still fire. I could just as well have taken the set of spontaneous transition firings that have already occurred, this set being equally rich in information content, but the choice above allows me to combine both components of a state into one set of resources that need to be available for transition firings to occur.

Definition 6. Let N be a Petri net. Let $S_\bullet^+ = S_\bullet \cup \{t_k \mid (k,t) \in T_\circ\}$ be the set of *resources* of N. An *individual state* $M \in \mathbb{N}^{S_\bullet^+}$ of N is the union of an individual marking and a multiset of names t_k of spontaneous transition firings (k,t). The *initial state* $I_\bullet^+ = \{(*,k,s) \mid k < I(s)\} \cup \{t_k \mid (k,t) \in T_\circ\}$ is the union of $I_\bullet$ and the set of names of all spontaneous transition firings. The multiset of *input resources* of a finite set of transition firings $U \subseteq T_\bullet$ is given by

$$^\bullet U = \sum_{(X,t)\in U - T_\circ} X + \{t_k \mid (k,t) \in U \cap T_\circ\}.$$

All other elements of Def. 5 apply unchanged, but using individual states instead of individual markings, and $I_\bullet^+$ instead of $I_\bullet$.

Corollary 1. *In any Petri net, all reachable individual states are sets.*

5 The Individual and Collective Firing Rules Agree

Having defined a new firing rule that caters to the individual token interpretation, I now show how it is consistent with the standard firing rule of Definition 3. I use variables $M_\bullet$ to range over individual states, and $U_\bullet$ to range over sets of transition firings. The function η from transition firings to the transition that fires extends to a function from sets of transition firings $U_\bullet$ to multisets of transitions $\eta(U_\bullet) : T \to \mathbb{N}$, by $\eta(U_\bullet)(t) = |\{t' \in U_\bullet \mid \eta(t') = t\}|$. Moreover, the function β from tokens to the places where they occur extends to a function from individual states (multisets of resources) to markings (multisets of places) by $\beta(M_\bullet)(s) = \sum_{s' \in \beta^{-1}(s)} M_\bullet(s')$ (where non-token resources are ignored).

Now the following theorem, whose proof is trivial, says that the functions β and η constitute a *bisimulation* between the step transition relations of a given net under the individual and collective token interpretations.

Theorem 1. $\beta(I_\bullet^+) = I$ *and for any individual states* $M_\bullet$ *and markings* M'*:*

$$\beta(M_\bullet) \xrightarrow{U} M' \Leftrightarrow \exists U_\bullet, M'_\bullet : M_\bullet \xrightarrow{U_\bullet}_\bullet M'_\bullet \wedge \eta(U_\bullet) = U \wedge \beta(M'_\bullet) = M'.$$

6 Firing Rules for the Self-sequential Interpretations

The firing rules of Sections 2 and 4 embody the *self-concurrent* interpretations of Petri nets, allowing a transition to fire concurrently with itself. Here I investigate how they need to be adapted to obtain firing rules for the *self-sequential* interpretations, excluding transitions from firing concurrently with themselves.

The firing rule for the self-sequential collective token interpretation is evident: a multiset U of transitions is *enabled* under the self-sequential interpretation of nets if it is enabled in the sense of Def. 3 and U is a set. The *self-sequential step transition relation* $\rightarrow^{ss}$ between markings is given by $M \xrightarrow{U}{}^{ss} M'$ iff $M \xrightarrow{U} M'$ and U is a set.

On standard nets, a firing rule for the self-sequential individual token interpretation can be obtained in the same way: a multiset U of transition firings is *enabled* under the self-sequential interpretation of nets if it is enabled in the sense of Def. 5 and U is a set with the property that if $(X,t),(Y,t) \in U$ for $t \in T$ then $X = Y$. Thus, all transition firings in U should be firings of different transitions. One defines $\rightarrow_\bullet^{ss}$ by imposing the same requirement.

On non-standard nets, before employing the same definitions, I take the opportunity to rectify an unfortunate design decision that was unavoidable under the self-concurrent interpretation. Namely, if a net contains a transition t without input places, Def. 6 yields an infinitely branching transition relation: there is a transition $I_\bullet \xrightarrow{\{(k,t)\}}_\bullet M_{(k,t)}$ for any $k \in \mathbb{N}$. The reason this was unavoidable under the self-concurrent interpretation is that any number of transition firings (k,t) can happen simultaneously, and I want to preserve the fundamental property of Petri nets that whenever a number of transition firings can happen in one step, they can happen in any order; so any of the firings (k,t) can happen first. Under the self-sequential interpretation, on the other hand, it is much more natural so take the point of view that although the transition t allows arbitrary many firings to occur sequentially, there is no point in distinguishing different kinds of first firings. Thus, I will use k not merely as a label taken from an arbitrary countable set, but as an actual number, (k,t) denoting the $k{+}1^{th}$ firing of transition t. The set $S_\bullet^+$ of resources of a net and the individual states $M \in \mathbb{N}^{S_\bullet^+}$ are as in Def. 6, but this time the presence of t_k in a state signifies that the $k{+}1^{th}$ firing of t is enabled. The multiset of input resources remains the same as in Def. 6, but the notions of initial state and output resources need to be adapted.

Definition 7. Let N be a Petri net. The *initial state* of N under the self-sequential interpretation is $I_\bullet^{ss} = \{(*,k,s) \mid k < I(s)\} \cup \{t_0 \mid t{\in}T \wedge {}^\bullet t = 0\}$, and the set of *output resources* of a finite set of transition firings $U \subseteq T_\bullet$ is

$$U_{ss}^\bullet = \{(t',k,s) \mid t' \in U \wedge k < F(\eta(t'),s)\} \cup \{t_{k+1} \mid (k,t) \in U \cap T_\circ\}.$$

The set U is *enabled* in an individual state $M : S_\bullet^+ \rightarrow \mathbb{N}$ under the self-sequential interpretation if ${}^\bullet U \leq M$ and $\forall t((x,t),(y,t) {\in} U \Rightarrow x = y)$. In that case U can *fire* under M, yielding the state $M' = M - {}^\bullet U + U_{ss}^\bullet$, written $M \xrightarrow{U}{}_\bullet^{ss} M'$.

Again, it is trivial to check that all $\rightarrow_{\bullet}^{ss}$-reachable individual states are sets, and β and η constitute a bisimulation between the step transition relations of a net under the self-sequential individual and collective token interpretations.

Theorem 2. *$\beta(I_{\bullet}^{ss}) = I$ and for any individual states $M_{\bullet}$ and markings M':*

$$\beta(M_{\bullet}) \xrightarrow{U}{}^{ss} M' \Leftrightarrow \exists U_{\bullet}, M'_{\bullet} : M_{\bullet} \xrightarrow{U_{\bullet}}{}_{\bullet}^{ss} M'_{\bullet} \wedge \eta(U_{\bullet}) = U \wedge \beta(M'_{\bullet}) = M'.$$

7 Labelled Step Transition Systems

Definition 8. A *labelled step transition system* is a tuple $(Q, E, \rightarrow, I, l)$ with

- Q and E are two disjoint sets of *states* and *events*,
- $\rightarrow \subseteq Q \times \mathcal{M}(E) \times Q$, the *step transition relation*, satisfying

(1)	if $(p, u, q), (p, u, q') \in \rightarrow$ then $q = q'$	(determinism)
(2)	$(p, 0, p) \in \rightarrow$	(trivial step)
(3)	if $(p, u + v, r) \in \rightarrow$ then $\exists q : (p, u, q), (q, v, r) \in \rightarrow$	(asynchronousness)

- $I \in Q$, the *initial state*,
- and $l : E \rightarrow A$, for A a set of *actions*, the *labelling function*.

Henceforth, write $p \xrightarrow{u} q$ for $(p, u, q) \in \rightarrow$.

Notes. A *labelled transition system* (LTS) is a quadruple $(Q, \Sigma, \rightarrow, I)$ with Q a set of states, Σ a set of *labels*, $\rightarrow \subseteq Q \times \Sigma \times Q$, and $I \in Q$. An LTS is *deterministic*, if it satisfies (1) above; in that case the *transition relation* $\rightarrow$ is really a *partial function* from $Q \times \Sigma$ to Q. A *step transition system* is an LTS whose labels are *sets* or *multisets* of actions, rather than single actions. Here $p \xrightarrow{u} q$ means that the represented system can transition from state p to state q by performing the actions in u in *one step*, meaning simultaneously or concurrently. Property (2) says that in any state p it is possible to do nothing and stay in p. Together with (1), property (2) implies that $p \xrightarrow{0} q$ iff $q = p$, so without performing actions it is not possible to move to another state. The information content would be the same if in Def. 8 instead of (2) it would be required that transitions are labelled by *nonempty* multisets.

A step transition system is *asynchronous* if it satisfies (3). This requirement represents the postulate that different action occurrences do not synchronise in any way; they can happen simultaneously *only* if they are causality independent, and in that case they can also happen in any order.

Now a *labelled step transition system* (LSTS) is a *doubly* labelled transition system. First of all the arrows are labelled by sets of *events*, and secondly the events are labelled by actions. This double layer of labelling is reflected in the name, as the word "step" already implies "labelled". The creation of events as an intermediate concept between transitions and actions is a trick that allows me to control the non-determinism of concurrent systems on the level of actions. I want to be able to model that a system in state p has a choice between two a-actions, leading to different successor states, and at the level of abstraction at which the system is represented there is no way to tell the two as apart (or influence the choice). However, optionally based on the belief that the world is not truly nondeterministic, the nondeterminism can be attributed to a difference between the two a actions that, although not observable, does account for the fact that they lead to different successor states. An *event* is now an action together with all its subtle qualities that influence which state it leads to when executed in a given state. Thus, an action is an equivalence class of events that are indistinguishable at the chosen level of abstraction.

When used for representing concurrent systems, LSTSs need to be considered modulo a suitable semantic equivalence. One the finest possible candidates is the following notion of *isomorphism of reachable parts*, $\cong_{\mathcal{R}}$:

Definition 9. Two LSTSs A and B are *isomorphic*, written A $\cong$ B, if they differ only in the names of their states and events, i.e. if there are bijections $\beta : Q^{\mathrm{A}} \to Q^{\mathrm{B}}$ and $\eta : E^{\mathrm{A}} \to E^{\mathrm{B}}$ such that $\beta(I^{\mathrm{A}}) = I^{\mathrm{B}}$, and, for $p, q \in Q^{\mathrm{A}}$, $u : E^{\mathrm{A}} \to \mathbb{N}$ and $e \in E^{\mathrm{A}}$: $\beta(p) \stackrel{\eta(u)}{\longrightarrow} \beta(q)$ iff $p \stackrel{u}{\longrightarrow} q$ and $l^{\mathrm{B}}(\eta(e)) = l^{\mathrm{A}}(e)$.

The set $R(Q)$ of *reachable states* in $\mathrm{A} = (Q, E, \to, I, l)$ is the smallest set such that I is reachable and whenever p is reachable and $p \stackrel{u}{\longrightarrow} q$ then q is reachable. The *reachable part* of A is the LSTS $\mathcal{R}(\mathrm{A}) = (R(Q), E, \to\restriction R(Q), I, l)$.

Write A $\cong_{\mathcal{R}}$ B if $\mathcal{R}(\mathrm{A})$ and $\mathcal{R}(\mathrm{B})$ are isomorphic.

To check A $\cong_{\mathcal{R}}$ B it suffices to restrict to subsets of Q^{A} and Q^{B} that contain all reachable states, and construct an isomorphism between the resulting LSTSs.

8 Interpreting Petri Nets in LSTSs

I now give four translations from Petri nets into labelled step transition systems, one for each of the computational interpretations of this paper. This is a way of formally pinpointing the differences between these interpretations; it amounts to giving four different semantics of Petri nets.

Definition 10. Let $\mathrm{N} = (S, T, F, I, l)$ be a net. Then $\mathcal{H}_{\mathrm{CT}}(\mathrm{N}) = (\mathbb{N}^S, T, \to, I, l)$ is the LSTS associated to N under the self-concurrent collective token interpretation, and $\mathcal{H}_{\mathrm{IT}}(\mathrm{N}) = (\mathbb{N}^{S^+_\bullet}, T_\bullet, \to_\bullet, I^+_\bullet, l_\bullet)$ is the LSTS associated to N under the self-concurrent collective token interpretation. $\mathcal{H}^{ss}_{\mathrm{CT}}(\mathrm{N}) = (\mathbb{N}^S, T, \to^{ss}, I, l)$ and $\mathcal{H}^{ss}_{\mathrm{IT}}(\mathrm{N}) = (\mathbb{N}^{S^+_\bullet}, T_\bullet, \to^{ss}_\bullet, I^{ss}_\bullet, l_\bullet)$ are the LSTSs associated to N under the self-sequential interpretations.

Example 1. The LSTSs below express the collective and individual token interpretation of the net A from Sect. 3, respectively. The equivalence of A and B

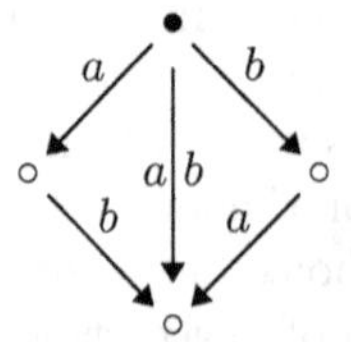

$\mathcal{H}_{\mathrm{CT}}(\mathrm{A}) \cong_{\mathcal{R}} \mathcal{H}_{\mathrm{CT}}(\mathrm{B}) \cong_{\mathcal{R}} \mathcal{H}_{\mathrm{IT}}(\mathrm{B})$

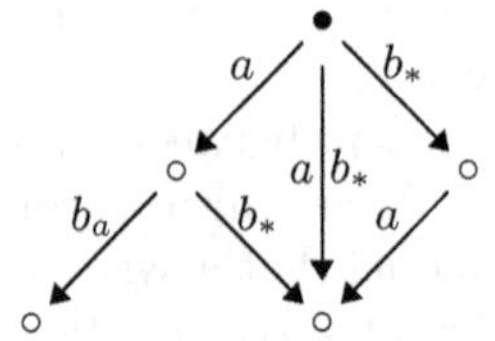

$\mathcal{H}_{\mathrm{IT}}(\mathrm{A}) \cong_{\mathcal{R}} \mathcal{H}_{\mathrm{IT}}(\mathrm{C}) \cong_{\mathcal{R}} \mathcal{H}_{\mathrm{CT}}(\mathrm{C})$

under the collective token interpretation, and of A and C under the individual token interpretation, manifests itself as isomorphism of reachable parts of the associated LSTSs.

The pictures above display LSTSs up to isomorphism of reachable parts. Letters like b_a and b_* stand for "different events labelled b". In fact, if the places of A are called s_1, s_2 and s_3, respectively, and its transitions a and b, then the event b_* is $(\{(*,0,s_2),(*,0,s_3)\},b)$, whereas $b_a = (\{((\{(*,0,s_1)\},a),0,s_2),(*,0,s_3)\},b)$.

Example 2. The LSTSs associated to the net D of Sect. 3 under the the collective and individual token interpretations can be found right next to it.

Example 3. In the previous examples there was no difference between the self-sequential and the self-concurrent interpretations. The following shows, however, that in general all four interpretations yield a different result.

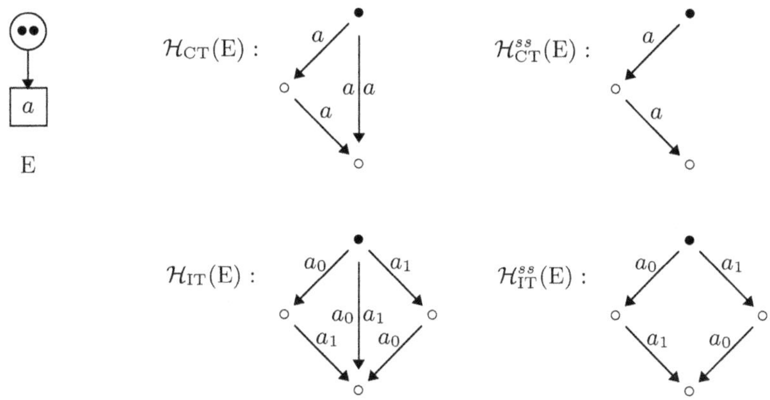

9 The Relative Expressiveness of the Four Interpretations

Each of the four computational interpretations above makes a different model of concurrency out of Petri nets. These models can now be compared with respect to their expressive power in denoting labelled step transition systems.

9.1 The Individual Versus Collective Token Interpretations

The following theorem says that Petri nets under the self-concurrent collective token interpretation are at least as expressive as Petri nets under the self-concurrent individual token interpretation, in the sense that any LSTS that can be denoted by a net under the latter interpretation can also be a denoted by a net under the former interpretation. On the other hand, the LSTS $\mathcal{H}_{\mathrm{CT}}(\mathrm{D})$ in Sect. 3 cannot be denoted by a Petri net under the individual token interpretation.

Theorem 3. *For every net* N *there is a net* $\mathrm{N}_\bullet$ *such that* $\mathcal{H}_{\mathrm{CT}}(\mathrm{N}_\bullet) = \mathcal{H}_{\mathrm{IT}}(\mathrm{N})$.

Proof. $\mathrm{N}_\bullet = (S^+_\bullet, T_\bullet, F_\bullet, I^+_\bullet, l_\bullet)$ with $S^+_\bullet$, $T_\bullet$, $I^+_\bullet$ and $l_\bullet$ as in Def. 4 and 6, and

- $F_\bullet(s',t') = 1$ if $t' = (X,t)$ with $s' \in X$, or $t' = (k,t) \in T_\circ$ and $s' = t_k$; $F_\bullet(s',t') = 0$ otherwise;
- $F_\bullet(t',s') = 1$ if s' has the form (t',k,s); $F_\bullet(t',s') = 0$ otherwise.

That $\mathcal{H}_{\mathrm{CT}}(\mathrm{N}_\bullet) = \mathcal{H}_{\mathrm{IT}}(\mathrm{N})$ is straightforward. □

The net $\mathrm{N}_\bullet$ constructed above is a close relative of the *unfolding* of a Petri net into an *occurrence net*, as defined in [11,4,8] (see Sect. 10). The difference is that I have not bothered to eliminate unreachable places and transitions.

9.2 The Self-sequential Versus Self-concurrent Interpretations

In general, results as strong as the one above can not be obtained: in order to compare expressiveness in a meaningful way, processes represented by LSTSs, Petri nets, or other models of concurrency should be regarded modulo some semantic equivalence relation. A particularly fine equivalence relation that allows me to totally order the computational interpretations of Petri nets is isomorphism of reachable parts of LSTSs (see Def. 9 in Sect. 7).

The following theorem shows that the behaviour of nets under the self-sequential interpretations can easily be encoded into the behaviour of nets under the corresponding self-concurrent interpretation.

Theorem 4. *For every net* N *there is a net* N^{ss} *such that* $\mathcal{H}_{\mathrm{CT}}(\mathrm{N}^{ss}) \cong_{\mathcal{R}} \mathcal{H}^{ss}_{\mathrm{CT}}(\mathrm{N})$ *and* $\mathcal{H}_{\mathrm{IT}}(\mathrm{N}^{ss}) \cong_{\mathcal{R}} \mathcal{H}^{ss}_{\mathrm{IT}}(\mathrm{N})$.

Proof. Following [7], N^{ss} is obtained from N by adding for every transition t a *self-loop*, consisting of a place s_t with $I(s_t) = F(s_t,t) = F(t,s_t) = 1$ and $F(s_t,u) = F(u,s_t) = 0$ for all $u \neq t$. Write S_{new} for the set of new places s_t.

To check that $\mathcal{H}_{\mathrm{CT}}(\mathrm{N}^{ss}) \cong_{\mathcal{R}} \mathcal{H}^{ss}_{\mathrm{CT}}(\mathrm{N})$, restrict the states of $\mathcal{H}_{\mathrm{CT}}(\mathrm{N}^{ss})$, i.e. the markings M of N^{ss}, to the ones with $M(s_t) = 1$ for all $s_t \in S_{new}$; this set of states surely contains all reachable ones. Let $\overline{\beta}(M) \in \mathbb{N}^S$ be obtained by restricting the domain of $M \in \mathbb{N}^{S \cup S_{new}}$ to S, and $\overline{\eta}$ be the identity. Now the bijections $\overline{\beta}$ and $\overline{\eta}$ constitute an isomorphism of reachable parts between $\mathcal{H}_{\mathrm{CT}}(\mathrm{N}^{ss})$ and $\mathcal{H}^{ss}_{\mathrm{CT}}(\mathrm{N})$.

To check that $\mathcal{H}_{\mathrm{IT}}(\mathrm{N}^{ss}) \cong_{\mathcal{R}} \mathcal{H}^{ss}_{\mathrm{IT}}(\mathrm{N})$, restrict the states of $\mathcal{H}_{\mathrm{IT}}(\mathrm{N}^{ss})$ to the individual states $M_\bullet$ of N^{ss} that contain exactly one token of the form $(x,0,s_t)$ for each $s_t \in S_{new}$; this set of states surely contains all reachable ones. Also, in view of Cor. 1, the states of $\mathcal{H}_{\mathrm{IT}}(\mathrm{N}^{ss})$ and $\mathcal{H}^{ss}_{\mathrm{IT}}(\mathrm{N})$ may be restricted to *sets* of resources rather than multisets. Let $S_\circ = \{s_t \in S_{new} \mid {}^\bullet t = 0 \text{ (in N)}\}$. For $s_t \in S_\circ$, let $s_t^0 = (*,0,s_t)$ and $s_t^{k+1} = ((\{s_t^k\},t),0,s_t)$. Then all tokens (x,k,s_t) of N^{ss} are of the form s_t^k for $k \in \mathbb{N}$. Now the mappings $\overline{\eta}$ from the transition firings in N^{ss} to the transition firings in N, for convenience extended with $\overline{\eta}(*) = *$, and $\overline{\beta}$ from sets of individual tokens in N^{ss} to sets of individual resources in N, are defined with recursion on the structure of transition firings and sets of tokens by $\overline{\eta}(X,t) = \begin{cases} (\overline{\beta}(X),t) & \text{if } {}^\bullet t \neq 0 \\ (k,t) & \text{if } {}^\bullet t = 0 \wedge X = \{s_t^k\} \end{cases}$
and $\overline{\beta}(X) = \{(\overline{\eta}(x),k,s) \mid (x,k,s) \in X \wedge s \notin S_{new}\} \cup \{t_k \mid s_t^k \in X \wedge s_t \in S_\circ\}$.
Again, the bijections $\overline{\beta}$ and $\overline{\eta}$ constitute an isomorphism between the reachable parts of $\mathcal{H}_{\mathrm{IT}}(\mathrm{N}^{ss})$ and $\mathcal{H}^{ss}_{\mathrm{IT}}(\mathrm{N})$. □

The construction of N^{ss} above, reducing the self-sequential to the self-concurrent interpretation of nets is well known [7]. The point of the proof above is to some extent just a sanity check on the definitions of $\mathcal{H}_{CT}$, $\mathcal{H}_{CT}^{ss}$, $\mathcal{H}_{IT}$ and $\mathcal{H}_{IT}^{ss}$.

By Theorem 4, any LSTS that can be denoted by a Petri nets under the self-sequential collective token interpretation, can also be denoted by a net under the self-concurrent collective token interpretation, and likewise for nets under the individual token interpretations. On the other hand, the LSTS $\mathcal{H}_{CT}(E)$ of Example 3 cannot be denoted by a Petri net under the self-sequential collective token interpretation.

9.3 Subsumption

So far, I proved the expressiveness results $\mathcal{H}_{IT}^{ss} \preceq \mathcal{H}_{IT} \prec \mathcal{H}_{CT} \succ \mathcal{H}_{CT}^{ss}$, where $\mathcal{J} \prec \mathcal{K}$ means that up to $\cong_{\mathcal{R}}$ the class of LSTSs that can be denoted by Petri nets under the computational interpretation $\mathcal{J}$ is a proper subclass of the class that can be denoted by Petri nets under the computational interpretation $\mathcal{K}$. Here I will strengthen and augment these results by considering the following *subsumption* relation between computational interpretations and classes of nets.

Definition 11. Write $\mathcal{J} \preceq_{\mathbf{C}} \mathcal{K}$ if $\mathbf{C}$ is a class of Petri nets such that

- for any net $N \in \mathbf{C}$ one has $\mathcal{J}(N) \cong_{\mathcal{R}} \mathcal{K}(N)$ and
- for any net N there is a net $N' \in \mathbf{C}$ such that $\mathcal{J}(N') \cong_{\mathcal{R}} \mathcal{J}(N)$.

If $\mathcal{J} \preceq_{\mathbf{C}} \mathcal{K}$, then up to $\cong_{\mathcal{R}}$, the class of all Petri nets under interpretation $\mathcal{J}$ is equally expressive as the subclass $\mathbf{C}$ on which the two interpretations coincide.

Observation 1. If $\mathcal{J} \preceq_{\mathbf{C}} \mathcal{K} \preceq_{\mathbf{D}} \mathcal{L}$ and $\mathbf{C} \subseteq \mathbf{D}$ then $\mathcal{J} \preceq_{\mathbf{C}} \mathcal{L}$.

Observation 2. If $\mathcal{J} \preceq_{\mathbf{C}} \mathcal{K} \preceq_{\mathbf{C}} \mathcal{L}$ then $\mathcal{K} \preceq_{\mathbf{C}} \mathcal{J}$.

Moreover, $\mathcal{J} \preceq_{\mathbf{C}} \mathcal{K}$ implies $\mathcal{J} \preceq \mathcal{K}$. Also note that in the presence of the first clause, the second clause of Def. 11 is equivalent with

- for any net N there is a net $N' \in \mathbf{C}$ such that $\mathcal{K}(N') \cong_{\mathcal{R}} \mathcal{J}(N)$.

9.4 Self-sequential Petri Nets

Definition 12. A Petri net is *self-sequential* if, using the standard firing rule of Def. 3, under no reachable marking a proper multiset of transitions is enabled, i.e. a transition is doubly enabled. Let **SS** be the class of self-sequential nets.

Theorem 5. *$\mathcal{H}_{CT}^{ss} \preceq_{\mathbf{SS}} \mathcal{H}_{CT}$ and $\mathcal{H}_{IT}^{ss} \preceq_{\mathbf{SS}} \mathcal{H}_{IT}$.*

Proof. If N is self-sequential, trivially $\mathcal{R}(\mathcal{H}_{CT}^{ss}(N)) = \mathcal{R}(\mathcal{H}_{CT}(N))$, and therefore $\mathcal{H}_{CT}^{ss}(N) \cong_{\mathcal{R}} \mathcal{H}_{CT}(N)$. Likewise, $\mathcal{R}(\mathcal{H}_{IT}^{ss}(N)) = \mathcal{R}(\mathcal{H}_{IT}(N))$, considering that self-sequential nets can have no transitions t with ${}^\bullet t = 0$. The second clause of Def. 11 is satisfied because the net N^{ss} constructed in the proof of Theorem 4 is self-sequential.

9.5 Unique-Occurrence Nets

Definition 13. A Petri net is a *unique-occurrence net* if $\forall t \in T.\ {}^\bullet t > 0$ (i.e. it is a standard net), $\forall s \in S.\ I(s) + \Sigma_{t \in T} F(t,s) = 1$ and the flow relation F is well-founded, i.e. there is no infinite alternating sequence $x_0, x_1, \ldots$ of places and transitions such that $F(x_{i+1}, x_i) > 0$ for $i \in \mathbb{N}$. Let **UO** be the class of unique-occurrence nets.

This class of nets is a close relative of the class of *occurrence nets* of WINSKEL [11]; it just lacks the requirements that cause the elimination of unreachable places and transitions (see Sect. 10).

Proposition 2. *For every Petri net* N*, the net* $\mathrm{N}_\bullet$ *is an unique-occurrence net. Moreover, if* N *is an unique-occurrence net, then* $\mathrm{N}_\bullet \cong \mathrm{N}$.

Proof. The first statement follows immediately from the construction of $N_\bullet$, the well-foundedness of F being a consequence of the recursive nature of Def. 4.

The second statement follows with induction on the well-founded order F, using the mappings β and η of Sect. 4. □

Prop. 2 tells that in a unique-occurrence net there is a bijective correspondence between places and token occurrences, and between transitions and transition firings. In particular, in a run of a net each place will be visited at most once, and each transition will fire at most once. Hence the name "unique-occurrence nets". It follows that unique-occurrence nets are self-sequential.

Theorem 6. $\mathcal{H}_{\mathrm{IT}} \preceq_{\mathbf{UO}} \mathcal{H}_{\mathrm{CT}}$.

Proof. Let N be a unique-occurrence net. Then $\mathcal{H}_{\mathrm{IT}}(\mathrm{N}) = \mathcal{H}_{\mathrm{CT}}(\mathrm{N}_\bullet) \cong \mathcal{H}_{\mathrm{CT}}(\mathrm{N})$, using Theorem 3, Prop. 2 and the observation $\mathrm{N}_\bullet \cong \mathrm{N} \Rightarrow \mathcal{H}_{\mathrm{CT}}(\mathrm{N}_\bullet) \cong \mathcal{H}_{\mathrm{CT}}(\mathrm{N})$. Now let N be any Petri net. Then $\mathrm{N}_\bullet \in \mathbf{UO}$ by Prop. 2 and $\mathcal{H}_{\mathrm{CT}}(\mathrm{N}_\bullet) \cong \mathcal{H}_{\mathrm{IT}}(\mathrm{N})$ by Theorem 3.

Theorem 7. $\mathcal{H}^{ss}_{\mathrm{IT}} \preceq_{\mathbf{UO}} \mathcal{H}_{\mathrm{IT}} \preceq_{\mathbf{UO}} \mathcal{H}^{ss}_{\mathrm{CT}}$ *and* $\mathcal{H}_{\mathrm{IT}} \preceq_{\mathbf{UO}} \mathcal{H}^{ss}_{\mathrm{IT}} \preceq_{\mathbf{UO}} \mathcal{H}_{\mathrm{CT}}$.

Proof. Let N be a unique-occurrence net. As unique-occurrence nets are self-sequential, Theorems 5 and 6 yield $\mathcal{H}^{ss}_{\mathrm{IT}}(\mathrm{N}) \cong_{\mathcal{R}} \mathcal{H}_{\mathrm{IT}}(\mathrm{N}) \cong_{\mathcal{R}} \mathcal{H}_{\mathrm{CT}}(\mathrm{N}) \cong_{\mathcal{R}} \mathcal{H}^{ss}_{\mathrm{CT}}(\mathrm{N})$. Now let N be any Petri net. Then $(\mathrm{N}^{ss})_\bullet$ is a unique-occurrence net by Prop. 2 and $\mathcal{H}^{any}_{any}((\mathrm{N}^{ss})_\bullet) \cong_{\mathcal{R}} \mathcal{H}_{\mathrm{CT}}((\mathrm{N}^{ss})_\bullet) \cong_{\mathcal{R}} \mathcal{H}_{\mathrm{IT}}(\mathrm{N}^{ss}) \cong_{\mathcal{R}} \mathcal{H}^{ss}_{\mathrm{IT}}(\mathrm{N})$ by Theorems 3 and 4.

This yields the expressiveness hierarchy of Fig. 1.

10 Unfolding into Occurrence Nets

Definition 14 ([11]). An *occurrence net* is a unique-occurrence net such that
- the *conflict relation* $\# \subseteq T \times T$ is irreflexive, where

$$x \# y \Leftrightarrow \exists t, t' \in T.\ t \neq t',\ {}^\bullet t \cap {}^\bullet t' \neq \emptyset,\ tF^*x,\ tF^*y$$

- and $\forall t \in T.\ \{t' \mid t'F^*t\}$ is finite.

Here F^* denotes the reflexive and transitive closure of the *flow relation*, given by xFy iff $F(x,y) > 0$. It is easy to see that transitions in a unique-occurrence net that violate the conditions above can never fire, and in fact an occurrence net is a unique-occurrence net with the property that every place occurs in a reachable marking and every transition in a firing sequence. Therefore, any unique-occurrence net can be converted into an occurrence net by the operation $\mathcal{R}$ that omits all transitions t that violate the requirements above, together with all places and transitions x with tF^*x. The net $\mathcal{R}(\mathrm{N})$ consists of the *reachable* places and transitions in N, and $\mathcal{H}(\mathcal{R}(\mathrm{N})) \cong_{\mathcal{R}} \mathcal{H}(\mathrm{N})$ for $\mathcal{H} \in \{\mathcal{H}_{\mathrm{CT}}, \mathcal{H}_{\mathrm{IT}}, \mathcal{H}^{ss}_{\mathrm{CT}}, \mathcal{H}^{ss}_{\mathrm{IT}}\}$. This allows me to define an *unfolding operator* $\mathcal{U}$, turning any given Petri net N into an occurrence net $\mathcal{U}(\mathrm{N})$ with $\mathcal{H}_{\mathrm{IT}}(\mathcal{U}(\mathrm{N})) \cong_{\mathcal{R}} \mathcal{H}_{\mathrm{IT}}(\mathrm{N})$, as follows.

Definition 15. Let N be a Petri net. The unfolding $\mathcal{U}(\mathrm{N})$ of N is $\mathcal{R}(\mathrm{N}_\bullet)$.

This construction extends the prior unfolding constructions of WINSKEL [11], ENGELFRIET [4] and MESEGUER, MONTANARI & SASSONE [8]. The latter, and most general, was given for standard nets only. Instead of restricting to reachable transitions at the end, these approaches do so on the fly. The same could be done here, by applying the two requirements of Def. 14 in the third clause of Def. 4.

References

1. E. BADOUEL (1996): *Splitting of actions, higher-dimensional automata, and net synthesis.* Technical Report RR-3490, Inria, France.
2. E. BEST & R. DEVILLERS (1987): *Sequential and concurrent behavior in Petri net theory.* Theoretical Computer Science 55(1), pp. 87–136.
3. E. BEST, R. DEVILLERS, A. KIEHN & L. POMELLO (1991): *Concurrent bisimulations in Petri nets.* Acta Informatica 28, pp. 231–264.
4. J. ENGELFRIET (1991): *Branching processes of petri nets.* Acta Informatica 28(6), pp. 575–591.
5. R.J. VAN GLABBEEK (2005): *On the expressiveness of higher dimensional automata (extended abstract).* Available at `http://boole.stanford.edu/pub/hda-ea.pdf`. *Electronic Notes in Theoretical Computer Science* 128(2): Proc. 11th International Workshop on *Expressiveness in Concurrency*, EXPRESS 2004, pp. 5–34.
6. R.J. VAN GLABBEEK & G.D. PLOTKIN (1995): *Configuration structures (extended abstract).* In D. Kozen, editor: Proceedings 10th Annual IEEE Symposium on *Logic in Computer Science*, LICS'95, San Diego, USA, IEEE Computer Society Press, pp. 199–209. Available at `http://boole.stanford.edu/pub/conf.ps.gz`.
7. U. GOLTZ & W. REISIG (1983): *The non-sequential behaviour of Petri nets.* Information and Computation 57, pp. 125–147.
8. J. MESEGUER, U. MONTANARI & V. SASSONE (1997): *On the semantics of place/transition Petri nets.* Mathematical Structures in Computer Science 7, pp. 359–397.
9. M. MUKUND (1992): *Petri nets and step transition systems.* International Journal of Foundations of Computer Science 3(4), pp. 443–478.
10. V.R. PRATT (1991): *Modeling concurrency with geometry.* In *Proc. 18th Ann. ACM Symposium on Principles of Programming Languages*, pp. 311–322.
11. G. WINSKEL (1987): *Event structures.* In W. Brauer, W. Reisig & G. Rozenberg, editors: *Petri Nets: Applications and Relationships to Other Models of Concurrency, Advances in Petri Nets 1986, Part II,* Proceedings of an Advanced Course, Bad Honnef, September 1986, LNCS 255, Springer, pp. 325–392.

Merged Processes — A New Condensed Representation of Petri Net Behaviour

Victor Khomenko[1], Alex Kondratyev[2], Maciej Koutny[1], and Walter Vogler[3]

[1] School of Computing Science, University of Newcastle, NE1 7RU, U.K.
[2] Cadence Berkeley Labs, Berkeley, CA 94704, USA
[3] Institut für Informatik, Universität Augsburg, D-86135 Germany

Abstract. Model checking based on Petri net unfoldings is an approach widely applied to cope with the state space explosion problem.

In this paper we propose a new condensed representation of a Petri net's behaviour called *merged processes*, which copes well not only with concurrency, but also with other sources of state space explosion, viz. sequences of choices and non-safeness. Moreover, this representation is sufficiently similar to the traditional unfoldings, so that a large body of results developed for the latter can be re-used. Experimental results indicate that the proposed representation of a Petri net's behaviour alleviates the state space explosion problem to a significant degree and is suitable for model checking.

Keywords: Merged processes, Petri net unravelling, Petri net unfolding, state space explosion, model checking, formal verification.

1 Introduction

A reactive system is commonly described by a set of concurrent processes that interact with each other. Processes typically have descriptions which are short and manageable, and the complexity of the behaviour of the system as a whole comes from highly complicated interactions between them. One way of coping with this complexity problem is to use formal methods and, especially, computer aided verification tools implementing model checking (see, e.g., [1]) — a technique in which the verification of a system is carried out using a finite representation of its state space.

The main drawback of model checking is that it suffers from the *state space explosion* problem [16]. That is, even a relatively small system specification can (and often does) yield a very large state space. To cope with this, several techniques have been developed, which usually aim either at a compact representation of the full state space of the system, or at the generation of a reduced state space (that is still sufficient for a given verification task). Among them, a prominent technique is McMillan's (finite prefixes of) Petri net unfoldings (see, e.g., [5,7,11]). They rely on the partial order view of concurrent computation, and represent system states implicitly, using an acyclic *unfolding prefix*.

M. Abadi and L. de Alfaro (Eds.): CONCUR 2005, LNCS 3653, pp. 338–352, 2005.

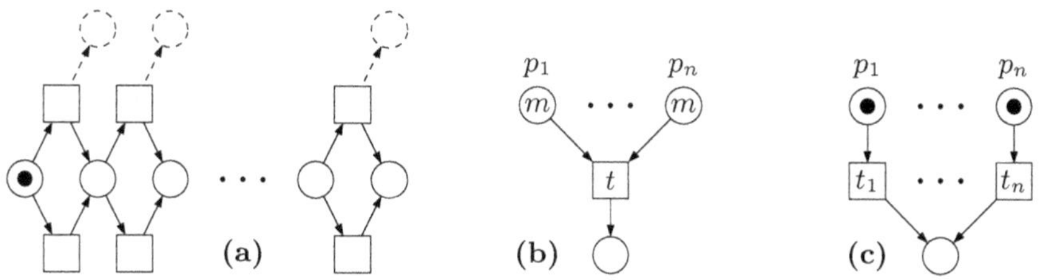

Fig. 1. Examples of Petri nets

There are several common sources of state space explosion. One of them is concurrency, and the unfolding techniques were primarily designed for efficient verification of highly concurrent systems. Indeed, complete prefixes are often exponentially smaller than the corresponding reachability graphs, because they represent concurrency directly rather than by multidimensional 'diamonds' as it is done in reachability graphs. For example, if the original Petri net consists of 100 transitions which can fire once in parallel, the reachability graph will be a 100-dimensional hypercube with 2^{100} vertices, whereas the complete prefix will be isomorphic to the net itself. However, unfoldings do not cope well with some other important sources of state space explosion, in particular with sequences of choices and non-safeness. Below we consider examples illustrating this problem.

First, consider Figure 1(a) with the dashed part not taken into account. The cut-off condition proposed in [5] copes well with this Petri net (since the marking reached after either choice on each stage is the same — in fact, the Petri net has very few reachable markings), and the resulting prefix is linear in the size of the original Petri net. However, if the dashed part of the figure is taken into account, the smallest complete prefix is exponential in the size of the Petri net, since no event can be declared a cut-off (intuitively, each reachable marking of the Petri net 'remembers' its past). Thus Petri nets performing a sequence of choices leading to different markings may yield exponential prefixes.

Another problem arises when one tries to unfold non-safe Petri nets. Consider the Petri net in Figure 1(b). Its smallest complete unfolding prefix contains m^n instances of t, since the unfolding *distinguishes between different tokens on the same place*. One way to cope with non-safe nets is to convert them into safe ones and unfold the latter, as was proposed in [5]. However, such an approach destroys the concurrency and can lead to very large prefixes; e.g., this approach applied to the Petri net in Figure 1(c) would yield a prefix exponential in the size of the original Petri net, while the traditional unfolding technique would yield a prefix which is linear in its size [5].

The described problems with Petri net unfoldings should be viewed in the light of the fact that all the above examples have a very simple structure — viz. they are all acyclic, and thus many model checking techniques, in particular those based on the *marking equation* [7,13,15], could be applied *directly to the original Petri nets*. And so it may happen that a prefix exponential in the size of the Petri net is built for a relatively simple problem!

In this paper we propose a new condensed representation of a Petri net's behaviour called *merged processes,* which remedies the problems described above. It copes well not only with concurrency, but also with other sources of state space explosion we mentioned, viz. sequence of choices and non-safeness. Moreover, this representation is sufficiently similar to the traditional unfoldings, so that a large body of results developed for unfoldings can be re-used.

The main idea behind this representation is to fuse some equally labelled nodes in the complete prefix of the Petri net being verified, and use the resulting net as the basis for verification. For example, the unfolding of the Petri shown in Figure 1(a) (even with the dashed part taken into account) will collapse back to the original net after the fusion. In fact, this will happen in all the examples considered above. Of course, such a fusion can result in various problems, in particular cycles can appear and the marking equation alone is not sufficient for verification of such nets. The rest of this paper is devoted to formally defining this transformation and solving some of the arising problems. The experimental results indicate that the proposed representation of a Petri net's behaviour alleviates the state space explosion problem to a significant degree and is suitable for model checking.

All the proofs and further examples can be found in the technical report [8] (available on-line).

2 Basic Notions

In this section we introduce the basic notions concerning Petri nets and their unfoldings (see also [5,7,9,11,13-15])

Petri Nets. A *net* is a triple $N \stackrel{\text{df}}{=} (P, T, F)$ such that P and T are disjoint sets of respectively *places* and *transitions*, and $F \subseteq (P \times T) \cup (T \times P)$ is a *flow relation.* A *marking* of N is a multiset M of places, i.e., $M : P \to \mathbb{N} \stackrel{\text{df}}{=} \{0, 1, 2, \ldots\}$. The standard rules about drawing nets are adopted in this paper, viz. places are represented as circles, transitions as boxes, the flow relation by arcs, and the marking is shown by placing tokens within circles. As usual, ${}^{\bullet}z \stackrel{\text{df}}{=} \{y \mid (y, z) \in F\}$ and $z^{\bullet} \stackrel{\text{df}}{=} \{y \mid (z, y) \in F\}$ denote the *pre-* and *postset* of $z \in P \cup T$. In this paper, the presets of transitions are restricted to be non-empty, i.e., ${}^{\bullet}t \neq \varnothing$ for every $t \in T$. A *net system* (or *Petri net*) is a pair $\Sigma \stackrel{\text{df}}{=} (N, M_0)$ comprising a finite net N and an *initial* marking M_0. It is assumed that the reader is familiar with the standard notions of Petri net theory, such as the *enabledness* and *firing* of a transition, *reachability* of a marking, the *marking equation*, *safe Petri net* and *deadlock* (see, e.g., [15] for a brief introduction).

Branching Processes. A *branching process* [5,7] β of a Petri net Σ is a finite or infinite acyclic net which can be obtained through unfolding Σ, by successive firings of transition, under the following assumptions: (i) for each new firing a fresh transition (called an *event*) is generated; and (ii) for each newly produced token a fresh place (called a *condition*) is generated. There exists a unique (up to isomorphism) maximal (w.r.t. the prefix relation) branching process of Σ called the *unfolding* of Σ. For example, the unfolding of the Petri net in Figure 2(a) is shown in part (b) of this figure (with the dashed lines ignored).

The unfolding is infinite whenever Σ has an infinite run; however, if Σ has finitely many reachable states then the unfolding eventually starts to repeat itself and can be truncated (by identifying a set of *cut-off* events) without loss of essential information. The sets of conditions, events, arcs and cut-off events of β will be denoted by B, E, G and E_{cut}, respectively, (note that $E_{cut} \subseteq E$), and the labelling function mapping the nodes of β to the corresponding nodes of Σ will be denoted by h.

Since β is acyclic, the transitive closure of its flow relation is a partial order $<$ on $B \cup E$, called the *causality relation*. (The reflexive order corresponding to $<$ will be denoted by $\leq$.) Intuitively, all the events which are smaller than an event $e \in E$ w.r.t. $<$ must precede e in any valid execution of β containing e. To make this precise, consider the implicit initial marking of β, obtained by putting a single token in each condition which does not have an incoming arc. Note that h is a *homomorphism*, i.e., it maps the conditions in the preset (postset resp.) of an event e bijectively to the preset (postset resp.) of $h(e)$ and, intuitively, it maps the (implicit) initial marking of β to the initial marking of Σ. Such as any homomorphism, h maps runs of β to runs of Σ. It is known that in acyclic nets like β, a marking is reachable if and only if the corresponding marking equation has a solution [15], and hence branching processes can be used for efficient model checking [6,7,10,11,12,13].

Two nodes $x, y \in B \cup E$ are in *conflict*, denoted $x\#y$, if there are distinct events $e, f \in E$ such that $^\bullet e \cap {}^\bullet f \neq \varnothing$ and $e \leq x$ and $f \leq y$. Intuitively, no valid execution of β can contain two events in conflict. Two nodes $x, y \in B \cup E$ are *concurrent*, denoted x *co* y, if neither $y\#y'$ nor $y \leq y'$ nor $y' \leq y$. Intuitively, two concurrent events can be enabled simultaneously, and executed in any order, or even concurrently. For example, in the branching process shown in Figure 2(b) the following relationships hold: $e_1 < e_5$, $e_3\#e_4$ and c_1 *co* c_4.

Due to structural properties of branching processes (such as acyclicity), the reachable markings of Σ can be represented using *configurations* of β. A *configuration* is a finite set of events $C \subseteq E$ such that for all $e, f \in C$, $\neg(e\#f)$ and, for every $e \in C$, $f < e$ implies $f \in C$. For example, in the branching process shown in Figure 2(b) $\{e_1, e_3, e_5\}$ is a configuration whereas $\{e_1, e_2, e_3\}$ and $\{e_1, e_5\}$ are not (the former includes events in conflict, $e_1\#e_2$, while the latter does not include e_3, a causal predecessor of e_5). Intuitively, a configuration is a partial-order execution, i.e., an execution where the order of firing of some of its events is not important.

After starting β from the implicit initial marking and executing all the events in C, one reaches the marking denoted by *Cut*(C). *Mark*(C) denotes the corresponding marking of Σ, reached by firing a transition sequence corresponding to the events in C. A branching process β is *marking-complete w.r.t. a set* $E_{cut} \subseteq E$ if for every reachable marking M of Σ there is a configuration C of β such that $C \cap E_{cut} = \varnothing$ and *Mark*$(C) = M$; moreover, β is *complete* if it is marking-complete and for each configuration C of β such that $C \cap E_{cut} = \varnothing$ and each event $e \notin C$ of the unfolding such that $C \cup \{e\}$ is a configuration of the unfolding, e is in β (e may be in E_{cut}); this additional *preservation of firings* is sometimes used for deadlock detection. Complete branching processes are often called complete (unfolding) *prefixes.* One can build such a complete prefix ensuring that the number of non-cut-off events $|E \setminus E_{cut}|$ in it does not exceed the number of reachable markings of Σ [5,7].

3 Merged Processes

In this section we introduce the notion of a *merged process,* which is the main construction investigated in this paper.

Definition 1 (occurrence-depth). *Let β be a branching process of a Petri net Σ, and x be one of its nodes (condition or event). The* occurrence-depth *of x is defined as the maximum number of $h(x)$-labelled nodes on any directed path starting at a minimal (w.r.t. $<$) condition and terminating at x in the directed graph representing β.*

The above notion is well-defined since there is always at least one directed path starting at a minimal (w.r.t. $<$) condition and terminating at x, and the number of all such paths is finite. In Figure 2(b) the occurrence-depths of conditions are shown in brackets.

Definition 2 (merged process). *Given a branching process β, the corresponding* merged process $\mu = \mathfrak{Merge}(\beta)$ *is a Petri net which is obtained in two steps, as follows:*

Step 1: *the places of μ, called* mp-conditions, *are obtained by fusing together all the conditions of β which have the same labels and occurrence-depths; each mp-condition inherits its label and arcs from the fused conditions, and its initial marking is the total number of minimal (w.r.t. $<$) conditions which were fused into it.*
Step 2: *the transitions of μ, called* mp-events, *are obtained by merging all the events which have the same labels, presets and postsets (after step 1 was performed); each mp-event inherits its label from the merged events (and has exactly the same connectivity as either of them), and it is declared cut-off iff all the events merged into it were cut-off events in β.*

Figure 2(b,c) illustrates this notion. In the sequel, $\hbar$ will denote the homomorphism mapping the nodes of β to the corresponding nodes of μ, and $\widehat{E}$, $\widehat{B}$, $\widehat{G}$, $\widehat{M_0}$, $\widehat{E_{cut}}$ and $\widehat{h}$ will denote the set of its mp-events, the set of its mp-conditions, its flow relation, its initial marking, the set of its cut-off events and the homomorphism mapping the nodes of μ to the corresponding nodes of Σ (note that $\widehat{h} \circ \hbar = h$). The merged process corresponding to the (full) unfolding of Σ will be called the *unravelling* of Σ. A few simple properties of merged processes are listed below:

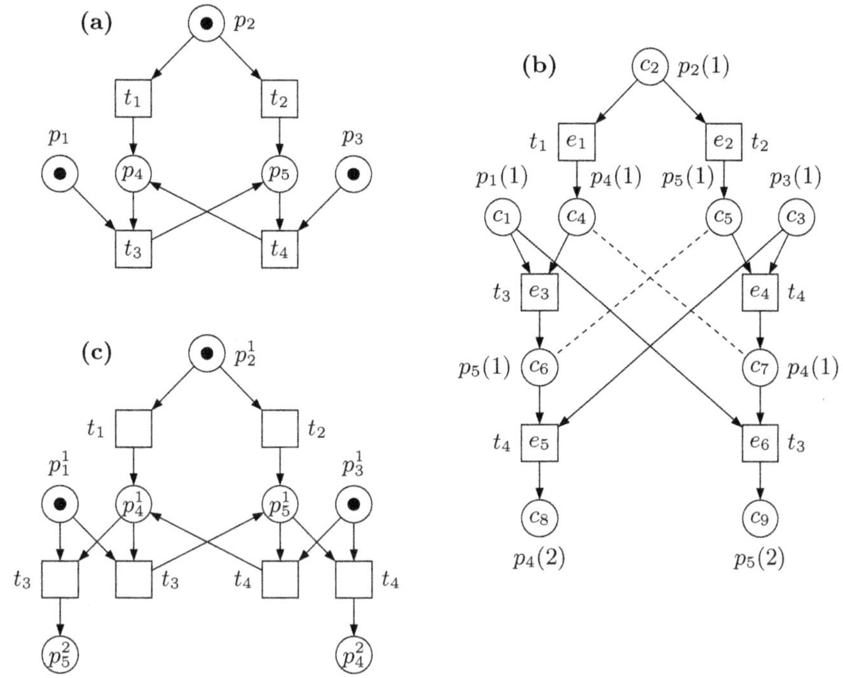

Fig. 2. A Petri net **(a)**, its unfolding with the occurrence-depths of conditions shown in brackets and the conditions to be fused connected by dashed lines **(b)**, and its unravelling **(c)**.

1. There is at most one mp-condition p^k resulting from the fusion of conditions labelled by place p of Σ occurring at depth $k \geq 1$.
2. Two distinct conditions in β having the same label and occurrence-depth are either concurrent or in conflict. Hence, if the original Petri net was safe then all the conditions in β which were fused into the same mp-condition p^k of μ were in conflict.
3. For two mp-conditions, p^k and p^{k+1}, there is a directed path from the former to latter. Moreover, if p^{k+1} is present and $k \geq 1$ then p^k is also present.
4. In general, μ is not acyclic (cycles can arise due to criss-cross fusions of conditions, as illustrated in Figure 2(b,c)). This, in turn, leads to complications for model checking, in particular the marking equation can have *spurious* solutions, i.e., solutions which do not correspond to any reachable marking. To simplify model checking, one could stop fusing conditions in Definition 2 when this leads to cycles, but this is not a satisfactory solution, since μ is not uniquely defined in such a case; moreover, this would lead to lower compression. So we chose to allow cycles, and strengthen the marking equation with additional constraints excluding spurious solutions (see Proposition 6).
5. There can be events consuming conditions in the postset of a cut-off mp-event.

6. There is a strong correspondence between the runs of Σ and those of its unravelling: σ is a run of Σ iff $\sigma = \widehat{h}(\widehat{\sigma})$ for some run $\widehat{\sigma}$ of the unravelling of Σ.

A multiset $\widehat{C}$ of mp-events is an *mp-configuration* of μ if $\widehat{C} = \hbar(C)$ for some configuration C of the unfolding of Σ (that we refer to the full unfolding rather than β here is a subtle point explained in [8]). If $\widehat{C}$ is an mp-configuration then the corresponding *mp-cut* $Cut(\widehat{C})$ is defined as the marking of μ reached by executing all the events of $\widehat{C}$ starting from the initial marking $\widehat{M_0}$. ($Cut(\widehat{C})$ can be efficiently computed using, e.g., the marking equation.) Moreover, $Mark(\widehat{C})$ is defined as $\widehat{h}(Cut(\widehat{C}))$. Note that if $\widehat{C} = \hbar(C)$ then $Mark(\widehat{C}) = Mark(C)$.

Canonical Merged Processes. Since $\mathfrak{Merge}$ is a deterministic transformation, one can easily define the *canonical* merged process as $\mathfrak{Merge}(\beta)$, where β is the canonical unfolding prefix [9]. This allows for an easy import of the results of [7,9] related to the canonicity.

The Size of a Merged Process. One can see that in Definition 2 the fusion of conditions can only decrease the number of conditions without affecting the number of events or arcs; moreover, merging events can only decrease the number of events and arcs, without affecting the number of conditions. Hence, the following result holds:

Proposition 1 (size). *If β is finite then μ is finite and $|\widehat{B}| \leq |B|$, $|\widehat{E}| \leq |E|$ and $|\widehat{G}| \leq |G|$.*

This result allows to import all the upper bounds proved for unfolding prefixes [5,7,9]; in particular, since for every safe Petri net Σ one can build a marking-complete branching process with the number of events not exceeding the number of reachable markings of Σ, the corresponding merged process μ has the same upper bound on the number of its events. However, the upper bound given by Proposition 1 is rather pessimistic; in practice, merged processes turn out to be much more compact than the unfolding prefixes.

Tables 1 and 2 show the results of our experiments. The popular set of benchmarks collected by J.C. Corbett [2] has been attempted. The meaning of the columns is as follows (from left to right): the name of the problem; the number of places and transitions in the original Petri net; the number of conditions, events and cut-off events in the unfolding prefix; the time taken by deadlock checking based on unfoldings (discussed in the next section); the number of mp-conditions and mp-events in the corresponding merged process; the time taken by deadlock checking based on merged processes (discussed in the next section); and the ratios $|\widehat{E}|/|T|$ and $|E|/|\widehat{E}|$ giving measures of compactness of the merged process relative to the original Petri net and its unfolding prefix, respectively. The unfolding prefixes in our experiments were built using the algorithm described in [5,7,9], and the corresponding merged processes were obtained by application of the algorithm given by Definition 2. (The time taken by this algorithm is

Table 1. Experimental results for benchmarks with deadlocks

Problem	Net		Unfolding				Unravelling				
	$\|P\|$	$\|T\|$	$\|B\|$	$\|E\|$	$\|E_{cut}\|$	MC [s]	$\|\widehat{B}\|$	$\|\widehat{E}\|$	MC [s]	$\|\widehat{E}\|/\|T\|$	$\|E\|/\|\widehat{E}\|$
Q	163	194	16123	8417	1188	<1	248	256	<1	1.32	32.88
SPEED	33	39	4929	2882	1219	<1	92	175	<1	4.49	16.47
DAC(6)	42	34	92	53	0	<1	42	35	<1	1.03	1.51
DAC(9)	63	52	167	95	0	<1	63	53	<1	1.02	1.79
DAC(12)	84	70	260	146	0	<1	84	71	<1	1.01	2.06
DAC(15)	105	88	371	206	0	<1	105	89	<1	1.01	2.31
DP(6)	36	24	204	96	30	<1	60	37	<1	1.54	2.59
DP(8)	48	32	368	176	56	<1	80	49	<1	1.53	3.59
DP(10)	60	40	580	280	90	<1	100	61	<1	1.53	4.59
DP(12)	72	48	840	408	132	<1	120	73	<1	1.52	5.59
ELEV(1)	63	99	296	157	59	<1	73	89	<1	0.90	1.76
ELEV(2)	146	299	1562	827	331	<1	150	241	<1	0.81	3.43
ELEV(3)	327	783	7398	3895	1629	<1	304	588	<1	0.75	6.62
ELEV(4)	736	1939	32354	16935	7337	<1	634	1387	<1	0.72	12.21
HART(25)	127	77	179	102	1	<1	153	102	<1	1.32	1.00
HART(50)	252	152	354	202	1	<1	303	202	<1	1.33	1.00
HART(75)	377	227	529	302	1	<1	453	302	<1	1.33	1.00
HART(100)	502	302	704	402	1	<1	603	402	<1	1.33	1.00
KEY(2)	94	92	1310	653	199	<1	147	402	<1	4.37	1.62
KEY(3)	129	133	13941	6968	2911	<1	201	1086	11	8.17	6.42
KEY(4)	164	174	135914	67954	32049	<1	255	2054	69	11.80	33.08
MMGT(1)	50	58	118	58	20	<1	61	58	<1	1.00	1.00
MMGT(2)	86	114	1280	645	260	<1	111	282	<1	2.47	2.29
MMGT(3)	122	172	11575	5841	2529	2	159	662	<1	3.85	8.82
MMGT(4)	158	232	92940	46902	20957	10	207	1206	<1	5.20	38.89
SENT(25)	104	55	383	216	40	<1	120	81	<1	1.47	2.67
SENT(50)	179	80	458	241	40	<1	195	106	<1	1.33	2.27
SENT(75)	254	105	533	266	40	<1	270	131	<1	1.25	2.03
SENT(100)	329	130	608	291	40	<1	345	156	<1	1.20	1.87

not included in the tables because it was negligible.) The algorithm for building merged processes directly from Petri nets is a matter of future research [8] (significant progress has already been made).

One can see that merged processes can be by orders of magnitude smaller than unfolding prefixes, and, in many cases, are just slightly greater than the original Petri nets. In fact, in some of the examples merged processes are *smaller than the original Petri nets* due to the elimination of dead transitions. However, merged processes are much more amenable to model checking than general safe Petri nets — e.g., most of 'interesting' behaviourial properties are known to be $\mathcal{PSPACE}$-complete for safe Petri nets [4], whereas in Section 4 we develop a non-deterministic polynomial-time algorithm for checking reachability-like properties of merged processes, i.e., many behaviourial properties of merged processes are in $\mathcal{NP}$. Since many such properties are known to be $\mathcal{NP}$-complete already for unfolding prefixes, the complexity class is not worsened if one uses merged processes rather than unfolding prefixes.

Since merged processes are inherently more compact than unfolding prefixes, it would be natural to seek sharper upper bounds than the trivial ones given by Proposition 1. In particular, it would be interesting to identify subclasses of Petri nets whose unfolding prefixes can be exponential in the size of the original Petri net, but whose merged prefixes are guaranteed to be only polynomial. Below, we present two such results.

Table 2. Experimental results for deadlock-free benchmarks

Problem	Net		Unfolding				Unravelling				
	$\|P\|$	$\|T\|$	$\|B\|$	$\|E\|$	$\|E_{cut}\|$	MC [s]	$\|\widehat{B}\|$	$\|\widehat{E}\|$	MC [s]	$\|\widehat{E}\|/\|T\|$	$\|E\|/\|\widehat{E}\|$
ABP	43	95	337	167	56	<1	75	83	<1	0.87	2.01
BDS	53	59	12310	6330	3701	<1	145	359	<1	6.08	17.63
FTP	176	529	178085	89046	35197	16	304	875	<1	1.65	101.77
CYCLIC(3)	23	17	52	23	4	<1	39	21	<1	1.24	1.10
CYCLIC(6)	47	35	112	50	7	<1	84	45	<1	1.29	1.11
CYCLIC(9)	71	53	172	77	10	<1	129	69	<1	1.30	1.12
CYCLIC(12)	95	71	232	104	13	<1	174	93	<1	1.31	1.12
DME(2)	135	98	487	122	4	<1	309	98	<1	1.00	1.24
DME(3)	202	147	1210	321	9	<1	463	148	<1	1.01	2.17
DME(4)	269	196	2381	652	16	<1	617	197	<1	1.01	3.31
DME(5)	336	245	4096	1145	25	<1	771	246	<1	1.00	4.65
DME(6)	403	294	6451	1830	36	<1	925	295	<1	1.00	6.20
DME(7)	470	343	9542	2737	49	<1	1079	344	<1	1.00	7.96
DME(8)	537	392	13465	3896	64	<1	1233	393	<1	1.00	9.91
DME(9)	604	441	18316	5337	81	<1	1387	442	<1	1.00	12.07
DME(10)	671	490	24191	7090	100	2	1541	491	<1	1.00	14.44
DME(11)	738	539	31186	9185	121	2	1695	540	<1	1.00	17.01
DPD(4)	36	36	594	296	81	<1	81	78	<1	2.17	3.79
DPD(5)	45	45	1582	790	211	<1	102	100	<1	2.22	7.90
DPD(6)	54	54	3786	1892	499	<1	123	122	<1	2.26	15.51
DPD(7)	63	63	8630	4314	1129	<1	144	144	<1	2.29	29.96
DPFM(2)	7	5	12	5	2	<1	10	5	<1	1.00	1.00
DPFM(5)	27	41	67	31	20	<1	31	31	<1	0.76	1.00
DPFM(8)	87	321	426	209	162	<1	89	209	<1	0.65	1.00
DPFM(11)	1047	5633	2433	1211	1012	<1	313	1211	<1	0.21	1.00
DPH(4)	39	46	680	336	117	<1	87	108	<1	2.35	3.11
DPH(5)	48	67	2712	1351	547	<1	129	293	<1	4.37	4.61
DPH(6)	57	92	14590	7289	3407	<1	198	904	2313	9.83	8.06
DPH(7)	66	121	74558	37272	19207	1	277	2773	>10 hrs	22.92	13.44
FURN(1)	27	37	535	326	189	<1	70	98	<1	2.65	3.33
FURN(2)	40	65	4573	2767	1750	<1	121	432	<1	6.65	6.41
FURN(3)	53	99	30820	18563	12207	<1	180	1224	<1	12.36	15.17
GASNQ(2)	71	85	338	169	46	<1	87	103	<1	1.21	1.64
GASNQ(3)	143	223	2409	1205	401	<1	173	325	<1	1.46	3.71
GASNQ(4)	258	465	15928	7965	2876	6	308	748	21	1.61	10.65
GASNQ(5)	428	841	100527	50265	18751	321	505	1449	4455	1.72	34.69
GASQ(1)	28	21	43	21	4	<1	35	21	<1	1.00	1.00
GASQ(2)	78	97	346	173	54	<1	96	111	<1	1.14	1.56
GASQ(3)	284	475	2593	1297	490	<1	316	509	<1	1.07	2.55
GASQ(4)	1428	2705	19864	9933	4060	9	1540	3004	34	1.11	3.31
OVER(2)	33	32	83	41	10	<1	51	39	<1	1.22	1.05
OVER(3)	52	53	369	187	53	<1	89	97	<1	1.83	1.93
OVER(4)	71	74	1536	783	237	<1	138	217	<1	2.93	3.61
OVER(5)	90	95	7266	3697	1232	<1	186	375	<1	3.95	9.86
RING(3)	39	33	97	47	11	<1	58	40	<1	1.21	1.18
RING(5)	65	55	339	167	37	<1	110	97	<1	1.76	1.72
RING(7)	91	77	813	403	79	<1	160	146	<1	1.90	2.76
RING(9)	117	99	1599	795	137	<1	210	194	<1	1.96	4.10
RW(6)	33	85	806	397	327	<1	51	85	<1	1.00	4.67
RW(9)	48	181	9272	4627	4106	<1	75	181	<1	1.00	25.56
RW(12)	63	313	98378	49177	45069	<1	99	313	<1	1.00	157.12

Proposition 2 (unravelling of an acyclic Petri net). *If Σ is an acyclic Petri net then its unravelling is isomorphic to the Petri net obtained from Σ by removing all its dead transitions and unreachable places.*

This result easily follows from the fact that no token in an acyclic Petri net can 'visit' a place more than once, and thus the occurrence-depth of every condition

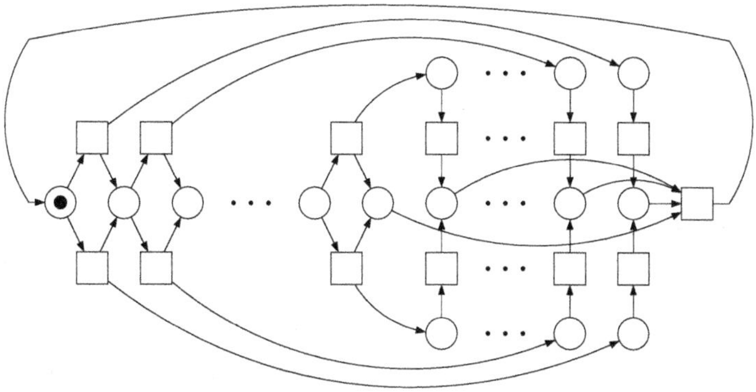

Fig. 3. An $LSFC^2$ Petri net whose unfolding prefix is exponential in its size

in the unfolding of Σ is 1. On the other hand, unfolding prefixes of even safe acyclic Petri nets can be exponential in the size of the original nets, e.g., this is the case for the acyclic Petri net in Figure 1(a) with the dashed part taken into account.

In the discussion below, $LSFC^k$ denotes the class of live and safe free-choice Petri nets [3] whose transitions' postsets have cardinality less than or equal to $k \in \mathbb{N} \cup \{\infty\}$; hence, $LSFC^\infty$ denotes the whole class of live and safe free-choice Petri nets. It turns out that if $k \neq \infty$ then the marking-complete merged processes for the nets in $LSFC^k$ are polynomial in the size of the original nets, even though their unfolding prefixes can be exponential; e.g., one can make the Petri net in Figure 1(a) (with the dashed part taken into account) live by adding a subnet 'gathering' tokens at the end of the execution and returning a token to the initial place, as shown in Figure 3. This net is in $LSFC^2$ and its complete prefix is exponential in its size.

Proposition 3 (merged processes of $LSFC^k$-nets [8]). *For any $k \in \mathbb{N}$, there exist marking-complete merged processes of $LSFC^k$-nets polynomial in the sizes of the original nets.*

This result is unlikely to be generalised to $LSFC^\infty$ [8]. However, one should note that the expressive power of $LSFC^k$ for $k \geq 2$ is comparable with that of $LSFC^\infty$, since every transition of an $LSFC^\infty$-net with postset of cardinality greater than k can be replaced by a tree of transitions with postsets of cardinality not exceeding k, and the resulting Petri net will be in $LSFC^k$.

Finiteness of a Merged Process. In view of Proposition 1, μ is finite if β is. However, it is not obvious that the reverse holds, since, in general, infinitely many nodes of β can correspond to a single node of μ [8]. However, by the analog of König's lemma for branching processes [7,9], if β is infinite then there exists an infinite path in β. Since the number of places in Σ is finite, some place $p \in P$ is repeated infinitely many times along this path, and so the occurrence-depth of its instances grows unboundedly in β. Thus there are infinitely many instances of p after fusion, and the following result holds:

Proposition 4. *μ is finite iff β is finite.*

Again, this result allows to import into the new framework all the finiteness results proved for unfolding prefixes [5,7,9].

Completeness of a Merged Process. The marking-completeness of a merged process is defined similarly to the marking-completeness of a branching process. A merged process μ is *marking-complete w.r.t. a set* $\widehat{E_{cut}} \subsetneq \widehat{E}$ if for every reachable marking M of Σ there exists an mp-configuration $\widehat{C}$ of μ such that $\widehat{C} \cap \widehat{E_{cut}} = \varnothing$ and $Mark(\widehat{C}) = M$.

Let C be a configuration of β and $\widehat{C} = \hbar(C)$ be the corresponding configuration in μ. One can easily show that if C contains no cut-off event then $\widehat{C}$ contains no cut-off mp-events, and that $Mark(C) = Mark(\widehat{C})$. Hence:

Proposition 5. *If β is marking-complete then μ is marking-complete.*

However, no such result holds for full completeness [8]; therefore, model checking algorithms developed for unfolding prefixes relying on the preservation of firings (e.g., some of the deadlock checking algorithms in [6,7,11-13]) cannot be easily transferred to merged processes. However, marking-completeness is sufficient for most purposes, as the transitions enabled by the final state of an mp-configuration can be easily found using the original Petri net. The model checking algorithm proposed in the next section does not make use of cut-off mp-events, and so they can be removed from the merged process before model checking.

4 Model Checking Based on Merged Processes

Model checking algorithms [6,7,10-13] working on complete prefixes of Petri net unfoldings are usually based on the following non-deterministic algorithm:

> **choose** a set of events $C \subseteq E \setminus E_{cut}$
> **if** C is a configuration violating the property (e.g., deadlock-freeness)
> **then accept** /* C is a certificate convertible to a witness trace */
> **else reject**

Various kinds of solvers have been employed to implement it, e.g., ones based on mixed-integer programming [13], stable models of logic programs [6], integer programming [7] and Boolean satisfiability (SAT) [10]. More precisely, a system of constraints having for each non-cut-off event e of the prefix a variable conf_e is built (it might also contain other variables), and for every satisfying assignment A, the set of events $C \stackrel{\text{df}}{=} \{e \mid A(\mathsf{conf}_e) = 1\}$ is a configuration such that $Mark(C)$ violates the property being checked. This system of constraints usually has the form $\mathcal{CONF}\&\mathcal{VIOL}$. The role of the *configuration constraint,* $\mathcal{CONF}$, is to ensure that C is a configuration of the prefix (not just an arbitrary set of events), and the role of the *violation constraint,* $\mathcal{VIOL}$, is to capture the property violation condition for a configuration C, so that if a configuration C satisfying this constraint is found then the property (e.g., deadlock-freeness) does not hold, and any ordering of events in C consistent with the causal order on the events of the prefix is a violation trace.

It is natural to follow a similar approach for verification based on merged processes. However, one should bear in mind the following complications:

- An mp-configuration is generally a multiset (rather than a set) of mp-events. Though this is not a major problem, it does hamper verification employing Boolean solvers, as associating a single Boolean variable with each mp-event is no longer sufficient for representing an mp-configuration. But if the original Petri net is safe, the mp-configurations of its merged processes are sets.
- An easily testable characterisation of an mp-configuration is necessary (our 'indirect' definition of an mp-configuration as an $\hbar$-image of some configuration of the unfolding is not of much use for model checking). In what follows we develop such a characterisation for mp-configurations of merged processes of safe Petri nets. Some issues make it non-trivial to develop such a characterisation:

  Spurious Solutions of the Marking Equation. Many model checking algorithms working on unfolding prefixes [6,7,10,13] are based on the marking equation (perhaps expressed not as integer linear constraints but in some other form, e.g., as a Boolean formula) and the fact that for acyclic Petri nets it cannot have spurious solutions [15]. Since merged processes are not generally acyclic, the marking equation *can* have spurious solutions. For example, the associated marking equations for the unravelling shown in Figure 2(c) has a spurious solution: if one 'borrows' a token in p_4^1 then the t_3- and t_4-labelled mp-events forming a cycle can be executed, returning the borrowed token to p_4^1 and leading to the spurious marking $\{p_2^1\}$.

  Spurious Runs. The correspondence between the runs and mp-configurations of μ is not very straightforward: some of its runs (e.g., the run comprised of the instance of t_1 followed by the left instance of t_3 in Figure 2(c)) do not form mp-configurations.

Below we solve these problems for merged processes of safe Petri nets.

The Case of Safe Petri Nets

To capture the notion of an mp-configuration in the case when the original Petri net Σ is safe, we proceed as follows. Let C be a configuration of β, and $\widehat{C}$ be a set of mp-events of μ. Below, $\mathcal{G}(C)$ and $\mathcal{G}(\widehat{C})$ will denote two graphs induced by the events of C together with their adjacent conditions and the minimal (w.r.t. $<$) conditions of β and by the mp-events of $\widehat{C}$ together with their adjacent mp-conditions and the initially marked mp-conditions of μ, respectively.

We say that $\widehat{C}$ satisfies: (a) $\mathcal{ME}$ if it is a solution of the marking equation for μ; (b) $\mathcal{ACYCLIC}$ if $\mathcal{G}(\widehat{C})$ is acyclic; and (c) $\mathcal{NG}$ (no-gap) if, for all $k > 1$

and all places p of Σ, the following holds: if p^k is a node in $\mathcal{G}(\widehat{C})$ then p^{k-1} is also a node in $\mathcal{G}(\widehat{C})$. Note that if $\widehat{C} = \hbar(C)$ then $\mathcal{G}(C)$ is isomorphic to $\mathcal{G}(\widehat{C})$ (including the labelling in terms of places and transitions). The next result gives a direct characterisation of mp-configurations and is crucial for model checking:

Proposition 6 (mp-configurations in the safe case [8]). *A set of mp-events $\widehat{C}$ is an mp-configuration iff $\mathcal{ME}\&\mathcal{ACYCLIC}\&\mathcal{NG}$ holds for $\widehat{C}$.*

Hence it is enough for model checking to take $\mathcal{CONF} \stackrel{\text{df}}{=} \mathcal{ME}\&\mathcal{ACYCLIC}\&\mathcal{NG}$ and apply an algorithm similar to that described in the beginning of this section for unfolding prefixes.

We implemented a deadlock checking algorithm based on merged processes using zCHAFF [14] as the underlying SAT solver. (Note that other reachability-like properties can also be implemented simply by adjusting the $\mathcal{VIOL}$ constraint.) All the experiments were conducted on a PC with a PENTIUM^{TM} IV/2.8GHz processor and 512M RAM.

The implementation of the $\mathcal{ME}$ and $\mathcal{VIOL}$ constraints as Boolean formulae is very similar to that for unfoldings and not discussed here. The $\mathcal{NG}$ constraint has been implemented as a conjunction of implications of the form $\mathsf{conf}_{p^k} \to \mathsf{conf}_{p^{k-1}}$, for all mp-conditions p^k such that $k > 1$. (Intuitively, $\mathsf{conf}_{p^k} = 1$ conveys that p^k is in $\mathcal{G}(\widehat{C})$; similarly, $\mathsf{conf}_{\widehat{e}} = 1$ conveys that $\widehat{e}$ is in $\mathcal{G}(\widehat{C})$, for each non-cut-off mp-event $\widehat{e}$ of μ.)

The implementation of $\mathcal{ACYCLIC}$ constraint is different from that in [8] (and so we report better results for deadlock checking). The problem can be re-formulated as follows: given a digraph $G = (V, E)$ (representing μ) with a boolean variable conf_v associated with each vertex $v \in V$, construct a boolean formula $\mathcal{ACYCLIC}$ (depending on the variables conf_* and, perhaps, other variables) such that, given an assignment to variables conf_*, the formula obtained from $\mathcal{ACYCLIC}$ by substituting the variables conf_* by their values is satisfiable iff the subgraph of G induced by the vertices whose corresponding variables were assigned to 1 is acyclic. (Note that $\mathcal{ME}$, $\mathcal{NG}$ and $\mathcal{VIOL}$ also contain the variables conf_*.)

Since each cycle is contained in some strongly connected component of G, one can partition G into its strongly connected components, generate such a constraint for each of them separately and form $\mathcal{ACYCLIC}$ as their conjunction. For each strongly connected component $G_k = (V_k, E_k)$ of $G = (V, E)$, the vertices are sorted to heuristically minimise the number of *feedback vertices*, i.e., vertices $v \in V_k$ for which there exists $w \in V_k$ such that $(w, v) \in E_k$ and $w > v$ (since the vertices of G_k are ordered, we identify each vertex $v \in V_k$ with its position in this order). Then for each such a feedback vertex $v \in V_k$ the following formula is generated (reach_* are auxiliary variables created separately for each such v):

$$(\mathsf{conf}_v \to \mathsf{reach}_v) \wedge \bigwedge_{\substack{(x,y)\in E_k \\ x \geq v \wedge y > v}} ((\mathsf{reach}_x \wedge \mathsf{conf}_y) \to \mathsf{reach}_y) \wedge \bigwedge_{\substack{(w,v)\in E_k \\ w > v}} \neg \mathsf{reach}_w \, .$$

The idea behind this formula is to perform a reachability analysis in G_k starting from v and ignoring all the vertices which precede v in the chosen order or are not selected. Note that if the values of the variables conf_* are fixed then this formula is unsatisfiable iff at least one of the sources of the feedback arcs ending at v is reachable from v (and hence there is a cycle); moreover, the unsatisfiability can be proven by unit resolution alone, i.e., one can setup the solver not to branch on the variables reach_*.

The experimental results in Tables 1 and 2 show that the developed model checking algorithm is quite practical and it even outperformed the one working on unfolding prefixes on some of the benchmarks. On the other hand, its performance deteriorated on the DPH and GASNQ series. We reckon that this is due to our still inefficient implementation of the $\mathcal{ACYCLIC}$ constraint, and that this can be significantly improved (major improvements over the results reported in [8] have already been achieved due to a different implementation of $\mathcal{ACYCLIC}$).

The point we are making with these results is: merged processes are a more compact behaviour representation than unfolding prefixes, but still allow model checking of reachability-like properties in at least comparable time. Since space considerations are of utmost importance in model checking, we regard this as very promising — although, to make merged processes practical, we still have to develop an *unravelling algorithm* that builds them directly from Petri nets instead of deriving them from unfolding prefixes (significant progress has already been made).

5 Conclusions and Future Work

We proposed the notion of a merged process — a new condensed representation of a Petri net's behaviour allowing one to contain state space explosion arising not only from concurrency, but also from a sequence of choices and from non-safeness of the Petri net. Experimental results show that merged processes can be smaller by orders of magnitude than the corresponding unfolding prefixes, and are in many cases not much bigger than the original Petri nets. Many results developed for Petri net unfoldings (related to canonicity, finiteness, completeness and size) have been transferred to the new framework. Moreover, we proved sharper upper bounds for some of the net subclasses and directly characterised the mp-configurations of merged processes of safe Petri nets, which allowed us to develop a model checking algorithm.

We now identify possible directions for future study (see also the discussion in [8]): (i) direct characterisation of merged processes (cf. the characterisation of branching processes by occurrence nets); (ii) direct characterisation of (general) mp-configurations (for non-safe Petri nets this is still an open problem); (iii) more efficient model checking; and (iv) direct unravelling algorithm.

Acknowledgements. The authors would like to thank Keijo Heljanko for a helpful discussion about expressing $\mathcal{ACYCLIC}$ and Javier Esparza for sharing his expertise on $LSFC$ nets. This research was supported by the EC IST grant 511599 (RODIN).

References

1. E. M. Clarke, O. Grumberg and D. Peled: *Model Checking.* MIT Press (1999).
2. J. C. Corbett: Evaluating Deadlock Detection Methods for Concurrent Software. *IEEE Transactions on Software Engineering* 22 (1996) 161–180.
3. J. Desel and J. Esparza: *Free Choice Petri Nets.* Cambridge Tracts in Theoretical Computer Science 40, Cambridge University Press (1995).
4. J. Esparza: Decidability and Complexity of Petri Net Problems — an Introduction. In: *Lectures on Petri Nets I: Basic Models*, LNCS 1491 (1998) 374–428.
5. J. Esparza, S. Römer and W. Vogler: An Improvement of McMillan's Unfolding Algorithm. *Formal Methods in System Design* 20 (2002) 285–310.
6. K. Heljanko: Using Logic Programs with Stable Model Semantics to Solve Deadlock and Reachability Problems for 1-Safe Petri Nets. *Fundamenta Informatica* 37 (1999) 247–268.
7. V. Khomenko: *Model Checking Based on Prefixes of Petri Net Unfoldings.* PhD Thesis, School of Computing Science, University of Newcastle upon Tyne (2003).
8. V. Khomenko, A. Kondratyev, M. Koutny and V. Vogler: Merged Processes — a New Condensed Representation of Petri Net Behaviour. Technical Report CS-TR-884, School of Computing Science, University of Newcastle (2005). URL: `http://homepages.cs.ncl.ac.uk/victor.khomenko/home.formal/papers/CS-TR-884.pdf`
9. V. Khomenko, M. Koutny and V. Vogler: Canonical Prefixes of Petri Net Unfoldings. *Acta Informatica* 40 (2003) 95–118.
10. V. Khomenko, M. Koutny and A. Yakovlev: Detecting State Coding Conflicts in STG Unfoldings Using SAT. *Fundamenta Informatica* 62 (2004) 221–241.
11. K. L. McMillan: Using Unfoldings to Avoid State Explosion Problem in the Verification of Asynchronous Circuits. Proc. of *CAV'1992*, LNCS 663 (1992) 164–174.
12. K. L. McMillan: *Symbolic Model Checking: an Approach to the State Explosion Problem.* PhD thesis, CMU-CS-92-131 (1992).
13. S. Melzer and S. Römer: Deadlock Checking Using Net Unfoldings. Proc. of *Computer Aided Verification (CAV'97)*, LNCS 1254 (1997) 352–363.
14. S. Moskewicz, C. Madigan, Y. Zhao, L. Zhang and S. Malik: CHAFF: Engineering an Efficient SAT Solver. Proc. of *DAC'2001*, ASME Tech. Publ. (2001) 530–535.
15. T. Murata: Petri Nets: Properties, Analysis and Applications. *Proceedings of the IEEE* 77 (1989) 541–580.
16. A. Valmari: The State Explosion Problem. In: *Lectures on Petri Nets I: Basic Models*, LNCS 1491 (1998) 429–528.

Concurrent Clustered Programming*
(Extended Abstract)

Vijay Saraswat[1,**] and Radha Jagadeesan[2,***]

[1] IBM T.J. Watson Research Lab
[2] School of CTI, DePaul University

Abstract. We present the concurrency and distribution primitives of X10, a modern, statically typed, class-based object-oriented (OO) programming language, designed for high productivity programming of scalable applications on high-end machines. The basic move in the X10 programming model is to reify locality through a notion of *place*, which hosts multiple data items and activities that operate on them. Aggregate objects (such as arrays) may be distributed across multiple places. Activities may dynamically spawn new activities in mulitple places and sequence them through a `finish` operation that detects termination of activities. Atomicity is obtained through the use of *atomic blocks*. Activities may repeatedly detect quiescence of a data-dependent collection of (distributed) activities through a notion of *clocks*, generalizing barriers. Thus X10 has a handful of orthogonal constructs for *space*, *time*, *sequencing* and *atomicity*. X10 smoothly combines and generalizes the current dominant paradigms for shared memory computing and message passing.

We present a bisimulation-based operational semantics for X10 building on the formal semantics for "Middleweight Java". We establish the central theorem of X10: programs without conditional atomic blocks do not deadlock.

1 Introduction

A holy grail of concurrency and theoretical programming languages is the development of clean but real concurrent languages. Real enough that they can be used for regular programming tasks by millions of programmers. Clean enough that they can be formalized, theorems proven, and correct compilers, transformation systems, program development methodologies and interactive refactoring tools developed.

There has always been considerable theoretical research in concurrency – CCS, CSP, process algebras, CCP, π-calculus etc. On the practical front, in imperative languages, CILK[1,2] has introduced some novel ideas such as work-stealing for symmetric multi-processors (SMPs). Titanium [3], Co-Array Fortran [4] and Unified Parallel C [5] (UPC) have introduced the *Partitioned Global Address Space* (PGAS) model [6] in JAVA, Fortran and C respectively, albeit in a Single Program Multiple Data (SPMD)

* We thank Bard Bloom, Philippe Charles, Christopher Donawa, Kemal Ebcioglu, Christian Grothoff, Allan Kielstra, Doug Lea, Maged Michael, Robert O'Callahan, Christoph von Praun, Vivek Sarkar, and Jan Vitek for many discussions on the topic of this paper.

** Research supported in part by DARPA No. NBCH30390004.

*** Research supported in part by NSF 0430175.

M. Abadi and L. de Alfaro (Eds.): CONCUR 2005, LNCS 3653, pp. 353–367, 2005.

framework. However, the state of the art in concurrent high performance computing continues to be library-based (e.g. OpenMP [7] for shared-memory concurrency and MPI [8] for message-passing) rather than language-based. Mainstream languages have been slow to adopt concurrency. JAVA^{TM} [9] has the best thought out model (some recent work has been proposed on a memory model for C++ [10]), but it suffers from several problems. A single global heap does not scale – complex memory models [11] are needed to enable efficient implementation on modern multi-processors. As is widely accepted, lock-based synchronization is very brittle – leading to underlocking/overlocking and bugs that are very hard to find. For high performance (HPCS) computation, JAVA does not support multidimensional arrays, user-definable value types, relaxed exception model, aggregate operations etc [12,13].

A number of ideas have come together now which promise a breakthrough. The exciting new idea of *atomic blocks* [14,15,16] has raised the possibility that the promise of robust, reliable parallel imperative programming may be at hand. A fundamental new opportunity presents itself with the development of the next generation of high performance computers (e.g. capable of $\approx 10^{15}$ operations per second). These will be based on scale-out techniques rather than clock rate increases (because of power and heat dissipation issues). This leads to a notion of *clustered computing*: a single computer may contain hundreds of thousands of tightly coupled (multi-threaded/SMP) nodes. Unlike a distributed model, failure of a single node is tantamount to failure of the entire machine (and all nodes may be assumed to lie in the same trust boundary). However because of latency and bandwidth, the notion of a single uniform shared memory is no longer appropriate for such machines.

Together with our colleagues, we have have designed an explicitly parallel programming language for clustered computing, X10 [17], under the aegis of the DARPA HPCS programme. The fundamental goal of X10 is to enable scalable, high-performance, high-productivity programming for high-end computers – for traditional numerical computation workloads (such as weather simulation, molecular dynamics, particle transport problems etc) as well as commercial server workloads. X10 is explicitly parallel because of our unwillingness to rely on heroic compilers to automatically extract enough parallelism to keep hundreds of thousands of nodes busy. For productivity, we have chosen to design X10 in the familiar statically typed, class-based, object-oriented programming mould; X10 is intended to be readily accessible to programmers in JAVA-like languages. Thus X10 is intended to support in an integrated fashion the set of problems that are today addressed by libraries such as OpenMP and MPI bolted onto base programming languages such as Fortran or C.

A reference manual for the language has been completed [17]. The language has been implemented via a translator to JAVA, developed using the Polyglot compiler framework. A number of programs have been written in X10 and preliminary productivity measures are reported in [18]. In this paper we lay out the basic semantic foundations of X10.

1.1 Basic Paradigm

Space. Local vs remote memory latency and bandwidth ratios for large scale-out machines are often higher than two, perhaps three orders of mangitude. Another problem is that current architecture research has not yet established the efficiency of sequentically consistent (SC) execution of threads. Attempts to provide a "weaker" semantics have proven very difficult to formalize and understand (cf the work on the Java memory model [9,11]).

Our approach to this dilemma is to introduce the notion of a *place*. A place consists of a collection of data and activities that operate on the data. (A computation may consist of millions of places.) A programmer may think of a place as an MPI task or a node in a distributed Java Virutal Machine (JVM) with its own heap and collection of threads.

An asynchronous activity is created by a statement `async (p) s` where `p` is a place expression and `s` is a statement. Such a statement is executed by spawning an activity at the place designated by `p` to execute statement `s`. An activity is created in a place and remains resident at that place for its lifetime. `s` (and `p`) may access lexically scoped `final` variables.

Each activity has a sequentially consistent view of the data at that place and may operate only on the data at the place. It may reference data at other places, but must operate on them only by launching asynchronous activities (at the place where the data lives). Thus X10 supports a *globally asynchronous, locally synchronous* (GALS) computation model, familiar from hardware design and embedded systems research. Unlike other PGAS languages, X10 is not SPMD – different (collections of) activities may run at each place.

Any activity may use the place expression `here` to reference the current place. Places are assumed to be totally ordered; if `p` is a place expression, then `p.next` is a place expression denoting the next place in the order. There are no expressions for creating a new place, rather each computation is initiated with a fixed number of places.[1] Each object carries its location through a final field `location`. Access to non-final fields is permitted only for objects at the same place. Any attempt to access remote mutable data results in a `BadPlaceException` (`BPE`).

EXAMPLE 1 (LATCH). A latch is an object which is initially *unlatched*, and may become latched. Once it is latched it stays latched. It may be implemented in X10 thus:[2]

```
class Latch {
 boolean forced = false;
 nullable Object result = null;
 atomic  boolean setValue(nullable Object val) {
   if (forced) return false;
   this.result = val; this.forced = true; return true;
 }
 Object force() {when (forced) {return result;}}
}
```

[1] This is consistent with most MPI programs that are started with a fixed number of processes.

[2] In X10, reference types do not contain `null` by default (unlike JAVA), instead the `nullable` type constructor must be used to construct a type with the value `null`. This is one of the sequential features of X10 we do not discuss in this paper for lack of space.

Sequencing. Since X10 supports fine-grained asynchronous, parallel activities – even a remote read is an activity – a reliable mechanism is needed to detect termination. X10 provides a `finish` construct (Section 2.4). Intuitively, `finish S` executes `S` and suspends until all activities created while doing so have terminated (normally or abruptly).

EXAMPLE 2 (FUTURES). Consider a new expression of the form `future (p){e}` where `e` is of type `T`. It is desired that this stand for a value of type `future<T>`. When this is `forced`, it will return a value of type `T` which is the result of evaluating the expression `e` in the place `p`. Such an expression may be implemented as a new latch `L`, with the following statement executed in parallel:

```
async(p){finish T X = e; async(L.location){L.setValue(X);}}
```

This example shows how distributed datastructures may be created in X10 (even without using distributed arrays); the field of an object may contain a reference to an object at a different place.

Atomicity. How can multiple activities running in the same place reliably access shared data? JAVA-like languages support a notion of monitors – the programmer must write code that explicitly obtains and releases *locks* [9]. Our experience is that locks are a very low-level and error-prone synchronization mechanism, making it very easy for programmers to write erroneous code that underlocks (causing race conditions) or overlocks (causing deadlock). Instead X10 supports *atomic blocks* (cf. [15,19,20]) (Section 2.2). The statement `when(c) s` where `s` is a statement blocks until (if ever) a state is reached in which `c` evaluates to `true`; in this state `s` is executed atomically – in a single step as if all other activities are frozen.

`when` is the only construct for atomicity and mutual exclusion in X10: constructs such as clocks (Section 2.5) can be expressed using `when`. This power comes at the cost of potential deadlock, a risk that can be avoided by using the more restrictive clocks.

We use the shorthand `atomic s` for `when(true) s`. We permit the modifier `atomic` on method definitions and take that to mean that the body of the method is enclosed in an `atomic`.

EXAMPLE 3 (CAS). The following class implements a *compare and swap* (CAS) operation, the basis for many highly concurrent, non-blocking (lock-free, wait-free) datastructures (e.g. [21,22]). In the code below `target` is defined in the lexically enclosing environment.

```
atomic boolean CAS(Object old, Object new){
 if (target.equals(old)){target = new;return true;}
 return false;
 }
```

Time. Thus an X10 computation consists of a large number of asynchronous activities scattered across space. We now introduce a notion of *time*. Many scientific computations need to progress in a sequence of *phases*. In each phase, activities (scattered across multiple places) read and write shared data (e.g. a distributed array). Once all activities have performed one phase of their calculations, each is informed of this global quiescence and computation moves to the next phase, and the process repeats. For instance, in a molecular dynamics application, it may be necessary for a controller activity to determine that (the activity associated with) each molecule has computed the force incident on it from all other molecules, and hence its instantaneous acceleration a. The controller may then advance simulation time, causing each molecule to determine its new position p and velocity v (as a function of its mass m, a and old p and v).

In SPMD languages this phasing is accomplished using the notion of a (split-phase) *barrier*. For instance, UPC provides a single barrier for all threads in a computation, accessed through `upc_notify` (signal that this thread has reached the barrier) and `upc_wait` (wait until all threads have reached this barrier).

X10 *clocks* (Section 2.5) can be thought of as obtained from split-phase barriers while (1) permitting dynamic creation, (2) permitting dynamic (de-) registration of activities, and (3) ensuring that operations are *race-free* (hence *determinate*). By race-free we mean that two operations on the same clock performed at the same time by two separate activities commute with each other (hence cannot conflict).

Concretely, a clock is a data-structure that may be dynamically created (`clock c is new`); an activity may create as many clocks as it wishes.[3] Conceptually each clock is associated with an integer that specifies the *current phase* of the clock; this integer is initially zero, and is incremented each time the clock *advances*. A clock is said to *advance* to the next phase when all activities *registered* with it have *quiesced* (see below).

The activity creating the clock is automatically registered with it. An activity A may at any time deregister itself from clock `c` by executing `c.drop();` any subsequent attempt by A to invoke an operation on `c` results in a `ClockUseException` (`CUE`) being thrown. A may indicate that it has *quiesced* on `c` (in its current phase) by executing `c.resume()`. It may suspend until *all* clocks it is registered with have moved to the next phase by executing the `next;` statement (this automatically resumes all clocks the activity is registered with). There is no statement allowing A to suspend until a *given* clock it is registered with has moved to the next phase; such a statement can easily cause deadlock.

An activity A may register a new activity it is spawning with clocks `c1, ..., cn` by executing `async(P) clocked (c1,...,cn) s`. We require the *Live Clock Condition* (LCC) to hold: A itself be *live* on `ci` (for `i` in `1,...,n`). That is, A should be registered with `ci` and not have quiesced on it. A `ClockUseException` is thrown if this condition is violated.

The LCC ensures that the only way an activity can be registered on a pre-existing clock `c` is if it is created by an activity that is live on `c`. While an activity is live on `c`, `c` cannot advance; hence X10 has no race conditions between registration and clock advance. (It is easy to see that permitting an activity to read a clock as the value of some field of some object and register itself on it could cause a race condition.) The execution of `c.resume()` (or `c.drop()`) operations by two activities commute, hence they do not constitute a race. Thus X10 clocks are race-free.

[3] In particular, we remark that clocks may be used to obtain oversampling through nesting.

A key semantic property of a clock is that clock quiescence is stable (Theorem 5): once every activity registered on the clock has quiesced, no further action by any activity can change this fact. Therefore when the *last* activity quiesces, it can trigger a clock advance.

`finish` interacts with clocks. `finish async clocked(c) next;` deadlocks when executed by an activity A registered on `c`. (A cannot advance till the `async` terminates; that cannot happen until A executes `c.resume()`.) To ensure deadlock freedom, X10 requires that the activity executing the body of a `finish` must not spawn a clocked async while doing so. This can be accomplished dynamically by throwing a `ClockUseException` in such a case (Section 2.5) or statically, with appropriate type rules.

The fundamental theorem of X10 is that these conditions are sufficient to ensure that programs without `when` are deadlock-free (Theorem 9).

EXAMPLE 4 (NOW). Imagine we wish to define a construct `now (c) s` intended to ensure that execution of statement `s` terminate completely in the current phase of the clock `c`. This may be accomplished by: `async clocked(c) finish async s;`

The outer activity is registered on `c`; hence `c` cannot advance until it performs a `next` or terminates. It cannot terminate until the `finish` is completed. An async is used to ensure that the execution of `s` is done in an activity which is not registered with any old clock. Thus any `next` performed by `s` will interact only with "new" clocks (produced during the execution of `s`).

1.2 Rest of This Paper

This completes a description of the basic concurrency and distribution primitives in X10. We briefly mention those aspects of X10 that are not covered in this abstract for reasons of space (details in [17]). X10 supports a *rooted, synchronous, non-resumptive* exception model, with a `try/catch/finally` construct. An exception thrown by an abruptly terminating activity A is caught by the enclosing activity suspended on a `finish` waiting for A to terminate. This paper, however, permits exceptions to be raised but not caught; thus any exception raised is fatal and terminates the entire computation. X10 supports a notion of immutable datastructures called *value types* and an explicit `nullable` type annotation (to specify that the type contains the value `null`). X10 supports multi-dimensional arrays that may be distributed across multiple places, using the concept of named *regions* (set of index points), and *distributions* (mapping of these points to places). X10 also has a static place-based type system (augmented with dynamic place-casts).

The rest of this paper presents a formal operational semantics for the concurrency and distribution features of X10. The semantics is intended to be used as a basis for informal reasoning with programs, program development methodologies, advanced compiler optimizations, and program refactoring.

The primary contributions of this paper are as follows. (1) We present a simple programming model for clustered computing. (2) We show that programs in a rich subset – including `finish` and nested clocks – cannot deadlock. (3) We formalize a compositional operational semantics based on bisimulation. (4) We establish other basic properties of the programming model: equational laws for various constructs; the correctness of programs is not affected by the number of places; clock quiescence is stable. We refer the reader to the sister paper [18] for a discussion of how lock-free computations, CILK programs, systolic arrays and MPI computations can be expressed in this subset.

The model is formalized in the style of previous JAVA-centric calculi focusing on types ([23]) and (sequential) imperative programming (MJ [24]).

1.3 Related Work

While there has been a lot of work on formal models for concurrency, there has been less work on formal models for real concurrent languages. We have chosen to design X10 on top of a modern OO language and present the semantics as such in this paper. However the core concurrency and distribution model can also be adapted for other imperative languages such as `C` or `Fortran`.

X10 is a member of the PGAS family of languages and is distinguished from them in not being based on an SPMD model, permitting multiple activities per locale or place, supporting very general notions of clocked computations, supporting sequencing of distributed computations (through `finish`), and using atomic blocks for mutual exclusion.

The X10 `async` and `finish` operations are related to CILK's `spawn` and `sync` constructs but are not arbitrarily scoped to methods. (CILK has no notion of places, distributed arrays, clocks or atomic blocks.)

While being similar to JAVA in its sequential aspects, X10 has a completely different concurrency and distribution model. All the Java Grande Forum benchmarks [25] that use threads (crypt, lufact, moldyn, montecarlo, raytracer, series, sor) have been ported to the deadlock-free fragment of X10.

An MPI program may be represented in X10 with a place per MPI process, running a single main activity. The MPI-2 communication primitives can be directly implemented with `asyncs`.

2 The X10 Programming Model

Our presentation is built on top of the MJ calculus [24]. It includes mutable state, block structured values and basic object-oriented features. Additional sequential constructs may be added in a routine fashion.

An MJ *configuration* consists of a quadruple (H, VS, s, FS) where:

- H represents the *heap* of objects. The heap is represented as a binding of object names to a pair of the class name and a finite function mapping field names to values (objects or basic values).
- VS, the *variable stack*, represents the block structure of the underlying programming language. The variable stack changes during reduction whenever a new scope is added or removed.
- s is the *statement* currently being executed.

- *FS* the *frame stack*, represents the continuation that follows the execution of s. In the case that s is an expression that evaluates to a value (say v), the head of the frame stack is an *open frame* with a hole to indicate the position at which v is to be substituted. Otherwise (s is a statement without a return value), the head of the frame stack is a closed frame without a hole.

This structure is changed for X10 by taking a configuration to be a triple (H,σ,Δ) where H is a heap (changed from MJ to include place information with each object), σ is a constraint store used to model clocks and Δ is a tree each of whose nodes is labeled with an *activity*. An activity is of the form $p:(s,(VS,FS,K))$ where p indicates the place of the activity, *VS* and *FS* are as above and K is a *clock-map* associating object id's representing clocks with their associated data structure (clock-counters, Section 2.5). These changes are summarized in Figure 1.

The Table is to be taken in conjunction with Figure 1 and the Table in Section 2.3 of [24]. The former defines the syntactic categories programs (p), class (cd), field (fd), constructor(cnd), method (md) definitions, expressions (*MJe* below), and statements (*MJs*). The latter defines MJ's Variable Stack (*MJVS*), Closed Frame (*MJCF*), and Open Frame (*MJOF*). We refer the reader to [24] for a detailed description of MJ.

Table 1. Syntax and Configurations for X10

`e` ::=pe $\mid$ MJe	(X10 Conf.)	Xc	::=	$(H,\sigma,\Delta) \mid E$
`s` ::=(Statement)	(Activity)	a	::=	$p:(s,(\mathrm{VS},\mathrm{FS},K)) \mid E$
`when(c) s`	(Term. Activity)	ta	::=	$p:(;,(\mathrm{VS},[],[])) \mid E$
`async(p)clocked(c̄)s`	(Frame Stack)	FS	::=	$F \circ \mathrm{FS} \mid []$
`finish` s	(Frame)	F	::=	CF $\mid$ OF
`next;`	(Variable Stack)	VS	::=	MJVS
`clock x is new`	(Places)	p,q	::=	*int*
`resume` c	(Closed Frame)	CF	::=	`waitn;`
`drop` c				`waitf;` $\mid$ MJCF
MJs	(Open Frame)	OF	::=	`async(•)` s
`pe`::=(Place Expression)				$\mid$ `when(•)` s $\mid$ MJOF
`here` $\mid$ `pe.next` $\mid$ `v.place`	(Values)	v	::=	`null` $\mid$ o $\mid$ p
	(Error)	E	::=	`BPE` $\mid$ `CUE` $\mid$ `FE` $\mid$ `NPE` $\mid$ `CCE`

The transition relation relates configurations. X10 specifies the top-level statement is executed implicitly in a `finish`.

Tree Transitions. The transition relation on composite configurations is described as a tree transformation. Let $\bar{\Delta}$ be the (possibly empty) sequence $\Delta_0,\ldots,\Delta_{k-1}$. We use the notation $n \rhd \bar{\Delta}$ to indicate a tree with root node n and subtrees $\Delta_0,\ldots,\Delta_{k-1}$.

A rule $\Delta[\Delta_1] \longrightarrow \Delta[\Delta_2]$ is understood as saying that a tree Δ containing a subtree Δ_1 can transition to a tree which is the same as Δ except that the subtree Δ_1 is replaced by Δ_2. Thus if Δ is the tree $A_1(A_2(A_3,A_4),A_5(A_6))$ then an application of the rule $\Delta[A_2] \longrightarrow \Delta[A_8(A_9)]$ gives the tree $A_1(A_8(A_9,A_3,A_4),A_5(A_6))$. An application of the rule $\Delta[A_2 \rhd \Delta'] \longrightarrow \Delta[A_8(A_9)]$ gives the tree $A_1(A_8(A_9),A_5(A_6))$ (the entire subtree at A_2 is replaced).

(COMPOSITE)

$$\frac{(H,\sigma,\Delta_1) \longrightarrow (H',\sigma',\Delta_2)}{(H,\sigma,\Delta[\Delta_1]) \longrightarrow (H',\sigma',\Delta[\Delta_2])}$$

MJ *Transitions.* The transition system incorporates *mutatis mutandis* all the MJ reduction and decomposition reduction rules ([24, Fig 2,3])) for the various MJ constructs, except for changes caused by the introduction of places. These changes are: the rule (E-New) is replaced by (New) below (to ensure the new object is created at the right place); the rules (E-Method), (E-MethodVoid), (E-FieldAccess) and (E-FieldWrite) are replaced by rules that check that the target object is local. We illustrate below with FieldAccess.

2.1 Places and Activities

The heap has place information for each object, recoverable using the final field `location`. Access to non-final fields is permitted only for objects at the same place. Access to objects located at a different place leads to a `BPE`.

(HERE)

$$\frac{}{(H,\sigma,p:(\texttt{here},S)) \longrightarrow (H,\sigma,p:(p,S))}$$

(NEW)

$$\frac{\begin{array}{l} cnBody(C) = (\bar{x},\bar{s}), \Delta_c(C) = \bar{C}, o \notin dom(H), \\ \mathcal{F} = [location \mapsto p, f \mapsto null, f \in fields(C)], BS = [this \mapsto (o,C), \bar{x} \mapsto (\bar{v},\bar{C})] \end{array}}{\begin{array}{l} (H,\sigma,p:(\texttt{new}\ C(\bar{v}),(VS,FS,K))) \\ \qquad \longrightarrow (H[o \mapsto p:(C,\mathcal{F})],\sigma,p:(\bar{s},((BS \circ []) \circ VS,(return\ o;) \circ FS),K)) \end{array}}$$

(FIELDACCESS)

$$\frac{H(o) = q:((C,\mathcal{F})), \mathcal{F}(f) = v, q = p \text{ or } f \text{ is final}}{(H,\sigma,p:(o.f,S)) \longrightarrow (H,\sigma,p:(v,S))}$$

(FIELDACCESSBPE)

$$\frac{H(o) = q:((C,\mathcal{F})), p \neq q \text{ and } f \text{ is not final}}{(H,\sigma,p:(o.f,S)) \longrightarrow \texttt{BPE}}$$

2.2 Atomic Blocks

`when`(e) s completes in one step if and when e evaluates to true in the current store and without interruption s completes execution. X10 syntax rules guarantee that an atomic block cannot execute an `async` or a clock operation; hence K remains unchanged in the antecedent of Rule Atomic1.

(ATOMIC1)

$$\frac{\begin{array}{l} (H,\sigma,p:(e,(VS,[],K))) \stackrel{\star}{\longrightarrow} (H_1,\sigma_1,p:(true,(VS_1,[],K)) \\ (H_1,\sigma_1,p:(s,(VS_1,[],K))) \stackrel{\star}{\longrightarrow} (H_2,\sigma_2,p:(;,(VS_2,[],K))) \mid E \end{array}}{(H,\sigma,p:(\texttt{when}(e)\ s,(VS,FS,K))) \longrightarrow (H_2,\sigma_2,p:(;,(VS_2,FS,K))) \mid E}$$

(ATOMIC2)

$$\frac{(H,\sigma,p:(e,(VS,[],K))) \stackrel{\star}{\longrightarrow} E}{(H,\sigma,p:(\texttt{when}(e)\ s,(VS,FS,K))) \longrightarrow E}$$

2.3 Asynchronous Activities

Async Without Clocks. In `async`(e) s, the expression e must be evaluated first. It is considered locally terminated after it has spawned the new activity. The spawned activity is started with an empty continuation, but is given the variable stack of the spawning environment (the static semantics ensures only `final` variables can be accessed in *VS*).

$$\frac{\text{(ASYNC1)}}{(H,\sigma,p:(\texttt{async}(e)\ s,(VS,FS,K))) \longrightarrow (H,\sigma,p:(e,(VS,\texttt{async}(\bullet)\ s\circ FS,K)))}$$

$$\frac{\text{(ASYNC2)}}{(H,\sigma,p:(\texttt{async}(q)\ s,(VS,FS,K)) \longrightarrow (H,\sigma,p:(;,(VS,FS,K))\rhd q:(s,(VS,[],[])))}$$

2.4 `finish`

The finish rule creates a nested activity, with the given variable stack and clocks but no continuation. [4] On termination of this activity and its subtree the parent activity may continue, with updated *VS* and *K*. The second and third rules replace an entire subtree of terminated activities with a single node. (For the purposes of the simpler exception semantics of this paper, the last rule could have been simplified to propagate exceptions more eagerly.)

$$\frac{\text{(FINISH1)}}{(H,\sigma,p:(\texttt{finish}(s),(VS,FS,K))) \longrightarrow (H,\sigma,p:(\texttt{waitf}\,;,([],FS,[]))\rhd p:(s,(VS,[],K)))}$$

$$\frac{\text{(FINISH2)}\quad \Delta \text{ is a tree of terminated activities w/ no exceptions}}{(H,\sigma,p:(\texttt{waitf}\,;,([],FS,[]))\rhd q:(;,(VS,[],K))\rhd\Delta) \longrightarrow (H,\sigma,p:(;,(VS,FS,K)))}$$

$$\frac{\text{(FINISH3)}\quad \Delta \text{ is a tree of terminated activities containing an exception}}{(H,\sigma,p:(\texttt{waitf}\,;,([],FS,[]))\rhd\Delta) \longrightarrow \texttt{FE}}$$

In the last rule the exception could have been propagated more eagerly; we choose the above formulation because it reflects the semantics of `finish` in the richer model in which exceptions are propagated and may be caught.

2.5 Clocks

To specify the semantics of clocks, we use the *streamed short circuit* technique for detecting stable properties of distributed systems from concurrent logic programming [26,27]. This technique makes the proof of the Clock Quiescence Stability theorem (Theorem 5) immediate. We note that this technique is used purely to specify the *semantics* of clocks.

In essence, the technique uses constraints to implement a *distributed stable counter* (henceforth: counter). A counter `X` is equipped with the following operations: (1) set

[4] This nesting is necessary: consider `finish {s1; finish {s2;} s3;}`. `s3` cannot be initiated until all the activities spawned by `s2` have terminated; but there is no requirement that activities spawned by `s1` have terminated.

Table 2. Clock Rules

(NEW CLOCK)

$$\frac{}{\begin{array}{l}(H,\sigma,p:(\texttt{clock x is new;},(VS,FS,K)))\\ \longrightarrow(H,\sigma+g,p:(;,(VS,FS,K[x\mapsto(g,g)])))\end{array}}$$

(CLOCK-ASYNC)

$$\frac{\begin{array}{l}\{c_0,\ldots,c_{n-1}\}\subseteq|K|,\texttt{waitf;}\text{ not in }FS,\\ K'=K[c_i\mapsto(K_g(c_i),X_i)\mid i<n],K''=[c_i\mapsto(K_g(c_i),Y_i)\mid i<n]\end{array}}{\begin{array}{l}(H,\sigma,p:(\texttt{async}(q)\texttt{clocked}(c_0,\ldots,c_{n-1})\ s,(VS,FS,K)))\\ \longrightarrow(H,\sigma\cup\{K_l(c_i)=X_i+Y_i\mid i<n\},p:(;,(VS,FS,K'))\rhd q:(s,(VS,[],K'')))\end{array}}$$

(CLOCK-ASYNC-EXCEPTION)

$$\frac{\{c_0,\ldots,c_{n-1}\}\not\subseteq|K|\ \textit{or}\ \texttt{waitf;}\text{ in }FS}{(H,\sigma,p:(\texttt{async}(q)\texttt{clocked}(c_0,\ldots,c_{n-1})\ s,(VS,FS,K)))\longrightarrow\text{CUE}}$$

(RESUME)

$$\frac{}{(H,\sigma,p:(\texttt{resume c},S))\longrightarrow(H,\sigma\cup\{K_l(c).\texttt{car}=0\},p:(;,S))}$$

(NEXT)

$$\frac{\sigma'=\sigma\cup\{K_l(c).\texttt{car}=0\mid c\in|K|\}}{(H,\sigma,p:(\texttt{next;},S))\longrightarrow(H,\sigma',p:(\texttt{waitn;},S))}$$

(WAITNEXT)

$$\frac{\begin{array}{l}\sigma\vdash K_g(c).\texttt{car}=0\quad(\forall c\in|K|)\\ K'=[c\mapsto(K_g(c).\texttt{cdr},K_l(c).\texttt{cdr})\mid c\in|K|]\end{array}}{(H,\sigma,p:(\texttt{waitn;},(VS,FS,K)))\longrightarrow(H,\sigma,p:(;,(VS,FS,K')))}$$

(DROP)

$$\frac{}{(H,\sigma,p:(\texttt{drop c},(VS,FS,K)))\longrightarrow(H,\sigma\cup\{0(K_l(c))\},p:(;,(VS,FS,K\setminus c)))}$$

(TERMINATE)

$$\frac{}{(H,\sigma,p:(;,(VS,[],K)))\longrightarrow(H,\sigma\cup\{0(K_l(c))\mid c\in|K|\},p:(;,(VS,[],[])))}$$

to zero, (2) split and (3) check if zero. A counter r can only be split if it is not zero; two new counters are created and when both reach zero, r is set to zero. Once zero, the counter stays at zero, hence the success of the check is stable. These operations may be implemented with constraints as follows: A counter is represented by a variable `X`, it is set to zero by asserting `X=0`, it is split by asserting `X=Y+Z`, where `Y` and `Z` are two new variables, and it is checked by asking if `X=0`.

Clocks require a check for quiescence in each phase, hence we need a *stream* of counters, a *counter-stream*.

Formally, a *constraint store* σ is a set of constraints, equipped with a function **var** which represents the set of variables over which the constraints are defined. If X does not occur in σ, then we write $\sigma+X$ to indicate a constraint store identical to σ except that $\mathbf{var}(\sigma+X)=\mathbf{var}(\sigma)\cup\{X\}$. The relevant constraints are:

$$\begin{array}{lrl}\textit{(Term)} & t & ::= \texttt{X}\mid\texttt{0}\mid\texttt{t}+\texttt{t}\mid\texttt{t.cdr}\mid\texttt{t.car}\\ \textit{(Constraint Store)} & \sigma & ::= \texttt{true}\mid\texttt{t}=\texttt{t}\mid\texttt{0(t)}\mid\sigma,\sigma\end{array}$$

with the obvious entailment relation, augmented with the axioms: `O(X), X.car = Z` $\vdash$ `Z=0` and `O(X), X.cdr = Z` $\vdash$ `O(Z)`.

A *clock-counter* is a pair of terms $\langle g,l \rangle$, where g is the *global* counter-stream and l the *local* counter-stream. We will arrange matters so that if the set of activities registered with a clock c is $A_1,\ldots,A_n$, then each A_i has a clock-counter (g,l_i), and the store has the constraint `g.car= l1.car+ ...+ ln.car`. When activity A_i performs a `resume` it asserts the constraint `li.car= 0`. A_i can determine when all activities have quiesced by checking `g=0`. It can move to the next phase by progressing with the clock-counter `(g.cdr, li.cdr)`. It can drop the counter by asserting `O(li)`. No separate active representation of a clock is needed.

In Table 2, we present the formal rules capturing these ideas. We augment the state of each activity with a *clock map* (henceforth: map) K (a finite partial function from oids to clock-counters). We use ε to indicate the unique map with empty domain. If $K(c) = (x,y)$, we use $K_g(c)$ for x and $K_l(c)$ for y. We use $|K|$ for the domain of K; $K[c \mapsto X_c \mid \phi]$ for K extended with the value X_c for each c satisfying ϕ (we drop K when it is ε, the empty map); and $K \setminus c$ for K with c removed from its domain.

In the rule for new clocks, we assume alpha renaming to ensure that x and g are new. Note that for a newly created clock the global counter-stream is the same as the local counter-stream, reflecting the fact that the clock has a single activity registered with it. Clocks may be transmitted to new activities when they are created.

THEOREM 5 (CLOCK QUIESCENCE IS STABLE). *Let configuration* (H,σ,Δ) *be such that* $\sigma \vdash \mathtt{X.car} = 0$ *where X is the global counter-stream of a clock in the clock set of some activity in* Δ. *Let* $(H,\sigma,\Delta) \longrightarrow (H',\sigma',\Delta')$. *Then* $\sigma' \vdash \mathtt{X.car} = 0$.

The only operations performed on the constraint store are Ask and Tell operations [27]. So, the theorem follows from the monotonicity of the constraint store.

3 Properties of X10 Programs

3.1 Bisimulation

We define a notion of bisimulation and show that it is a congruence. Our study of bisimulation focuses on issues relating to concurrency and shared memory. Thus, our treatment does not validate enough equations in the sequential subset, eg. those relating to garbage collection. However, even this weak notion of equality suffices to prove several basic laws relating the new control constructs that we have discussed in this paper.

The transition system defined so far is for closed programs. In order to get a notion of equality that is a congruence wrt shared memory concurrent programming, we need to model the transition relation for open programs. We use a notion of an *environment move* to model update of shared heap by a concurrent activity. For a heap H, an environment move $\lambda = (o,f,p,o')$ is the update of the field f in object o (if it exists) to o'. Formally, if $H(o) = (C,\mathcal{F}), f \in dom(\mathcal{F})$ then, the resulting heap is $\lambda H = H[o \mapsto p : (C,F[f \mapsto o'])]$. This notion of environment move is stronger than necessary, e.g. it does not respect the visibility constraints imposed by the underlying OO paradigm.

DEFINITION 6. A binary relation $\equiv$ on configurations is a bisimulation if the following holds. If $(H_1,\sigma_1,\Delta_1) \equiv (H_2,\sigma_2,\Delta_2)$, then:

- $H_1 = H_2$, $\sigma_1 = \sigma_2$.
- For all environment moves $\lambda = (o,f,p,o')$, if $(\lambda H_1,\sigma_1,\Delta_1) \longrightarrow (H_1',\sigma_1',\Delta_1')$, then there exists $(\lambda H_2,\sigma_2,\Delta_2) \stackrel{\star}{\longrightarrow} (H_2',\sigma_2',\Delta_2')$ such that $(H_1',\sigma_1',\Delta_1') \equiv (H_2',\sigma_2',\Delta_2')$.
- For all environment moves $\lambda = (o,f,p,o')$, if $(\lambda H_2,\sigma_2,\Delta_2) \longrightarrow (H_2',\sigma_2',\Delta_2')$, then there exists $(\lambda H_1,\sigma_1,\Delta_1) \stackrel{\star}{\longrightarrow} (H_1',\sigma_1',\Delta_1')$ such that $(H_2',\sigma_2',\Delta_2') \equiv (H_1',\sigma_1'\Delta_1')$.

Let $C[\cdot]$ be an activity context with a statement hole. Two statements s_1,s_2 are bisimilar, written $s_1 \equiv s_2$ if for all $C[\cdot]$ forall heaps H and forall σ , $(H,\sigma,C[s_1]) \equiv (H,\sigma,C[s_2])$. Similarly for two (promotable) expressions e_1,e_2, $e_1 \equiv e_2$ if for all $C[\cdot]$ with expression holes, forall heaps H and forall σ, $(H,\sigma,C[e_1]) \equiv (H,\sigma,C[e_2])$.

The definition of $\equiv$ quantifies over all sequential contexts. The use of environment moves in Definition 6 enables us to prove a congruence property for all contexts including tree contexts.

LEMMA 7. *Let $\Delta[\cdot]$ (resp. $\Delta'[\cdot]$) be a tree of open or closed activity contexts with a statement (resp. expression) hole. Then, for all heaps H and forall σ, if $s_1 \equiv s_2$, then: $(H,\sigma,\Delta[s_1]) \equiv (H,\sigma,\Delta[s_2])$ and $(H,\sigma,\Delta'[e_1]) \equiv (H,\sigma,\Delta'[e_2])$.*

The following equations hold upto bisimulation.

```
             when(c) when(d) s ≡ when(c&&d) s
       atomic { s1; atomic s2} ≡ atomic {s1; s2}
    async(P){s}; async(Q) {s1} ≡ async(Q){s1}; async(P){s}
     async(P){async(Q){s} s1} ≡ async(Q[here/P]){s}; async(P) {s1}
              finish{s; s1} ≡ finish{s}; finish{s1}
         finish{when(c){s}} ≡ when(c){finish{s}}
          finish async(p) {} ≡ {}
```

Additionally `finish s` is equal to `s` for `s` a `next`, `resume` or `drop` operation.

3.2 Monotonicity of Places

As an application of bisimulation, we show that FX10 programs are insensitive to the location of objects in the heap. For these programs, distribution may introduce efficiency but *does not affect correctness*. Let $S_{\texttt{Coord}} = \{\texttt{here}, \texttt{here.next}, \texttt{here.next.next}\ldots\}$. Let s be such that no transition sequence from $([],\sigma,p:([],s,[]))$ leads to an error.

LEMMA 8. *Let Θ be an operator on the set $S_{\texttt{Coord}}$. Let $\texttt{trans}(\Theta,s)$ be the result of replacing every subexpression* `async(p)` *in s by* `async(`$\Theta(e)$`)`. *Then: $([],\sigma,p:(s,([],[],[]))) \equiv ([],\sigma,p:(\texttt{trans}(\Theta,s),([],[],[])))$.*

When Θ is the constant function, we get a class of programs can be debugged and developed in a one-place execution environment before being deployed in a multi-place execution environment for efficiency.

3.3 Deadlock Freedom

For any configuration, define a *wait-for* graph as follows. There is a node for each clock and each activity that is suspended on a `next;` or a `finish`. There is an edge from each clock to an activity registered on that clock that is suspended on a `finish`. There is an edge from each activity suspended on a next to a clock the activity is registered on. There is an edge from each activity suspended on a `finishs` to each activity spawned by `s` that is suspended. A configuration is stuck iff it is terminal or there is a cycle in the wait-for graph.

Clocks (without finish) are deadlock free, since no activity has an incoming edge in this case. Deadlock-freedom holds for a larger language that encompasses lock-free computations, CILK programs, systolic arrays and MPI computations.

THEOREM 9. *There are no cycles in the wait-for graph for programs in the language with* `atomic`*, clocks, and* `finish`.

4 Conclusion and Future Research

We believe that X10 offers a simple, clean but real design for high-productivity, high-performance concurrent programming for high-end computers.

However, these are just the first stages of X10 development. Considerable additional work is needed to establish efficient compilers and multi-node virtual machines for X10.

References

1. CILK-5.3 reference manual. Technical report, Supercomputing Technologies Group (2000)
2. Blumofe, R., Leiserson, C.: Scheduling multithreaded computations by work stealing. In: Proceedings of the 35th Annual Symposium on the Foundations of Computer Science. (1994) 356–368
3. Yelick, K.A., Semenzato, L., Pike, G., Miyamoto, C., Liblit, B., Krishnamurthy, A., Hilfinger, P.N., Graham, S.L., Gay, D., Colella, P., Aiken, A.: Titanium: A high-performance java dialect. Concurrency - Practice and Experience **10** (1998) 825–836
4. Numrich, R., Reid, J.: Co-array Fortran for parallel programming. Fortran Forum **17** (1998)
5. El-Ghazawi, T., Carlson, W., Draper, J.: UPC Language Specification v1.1.1. Technical report, George Washington University (2003)
6. Carlson, W., El-Ghazawi, T., Numrich, B., Yelick, K.: Programming in the Partitioned Global Address Space Model (2003) Presentation at SC 2003, http://www.gwu.edu/ upc/ tutorials.html.
7. (Openmp specifications) www.openmp.org/specs.
8. Skjellum, A., Lusk, E., Gropp, W.: Using MPI: Portable Parallel Programming with the Message Passing Iinterface. MIT Press (1999)
9. Gosling, J., Joy, W., Steele, G., Bracha, G.: The Java Language Specification. Addison Wesley (2000)
10. Alexandrescu, A., Boehn, H., Henney, K., Lea, D., Pugh, B.: Memory model for multi-threaded c++. Technical report, metalanguage.com (2004) JTC1/SC22/WG21 – C++, Document Number: WG21/N1680=J16/04-0120.

11. Pugh, W.: Java Memory Model and Thread Specification Revision (2004) JSR 133, http://www.jcp.org/en/jsr/detail?id=133.
12. Moreira, J.E., Midkiff, S.P., Gupta, M., Artigas, P.V., Snir, M., Lawrence, R.D.: Java programming for high-performance numerical computing. IBM Systems Journal **39** (2000) 21–
13. Moreira, J., Midkiff, S., Gupta, M.: A comparison of three approaches to language, compiler, and library support for multidimensional arrays in java computing. In: Proceedings of the ACM Java Grande - ISCOPE 2001 Conference. (2001)
14. Flanagan, C., Freund, S.: Atomizer: A dynamically atomicity checker for multithreaded programs. In: Conference Record of POPL 04: The 31st ACM SIGPLAN-SIGACT Symposium on Principles of Programming Languages, Venice, Italy, New York, NY (2004)
15. Harris, T., Fraser, K.: Language support for lightweight transactions. In: OOPSLA. (2003) 388–403
16. Harris, T., Herlihy, M., Marlow, S., Jones, S.P.: Composable memory transaction. In: SIGPLAN Symposium on Principles and Practice of Parallel Programming. (2005)
17. Saraswat, V.: Report on the Experimental Language X10, v0.41. Technical report, IBM Research (2005)
18. Charles, P., Grothoff, C., Donawa, C., Ebcioglu, K., Kielstra, A., von Praun, C., Saraswat, V., Sarkar, V.: X10: An object-oriented approach to non-uniform cluster computing. Technical report, IBM Research (2005) To appear in OOPSLA 2005 Onwards! Track Proceedings.
19. Hansen, P.B.: Structured multiprogramming. CACM **15** (1972)
20. Hoare, C.: Monitors: An operating system structuring concept. CACM **17** (1974) 549–557
21. Herlihy, M.: Wait-free synchronization. ACM Transactions on Programming Languages and Systems **13** (1991) 124–149
22. Michael, M., Scott, M.: Simple, Fast and Practical Non-Blocking and Blocking Concurrent Queue Algorithms. In: Proceedings of the 15th ACM Annual Symposium on Principles of Distributed Computing. (1996) 267–275
23. Igarashi, A., Pierce, B.C., Wadler, P.: Featherweight java: a minimal core calculus for java and gj. ACM Trans. Program. Lang. Syst. **23** (2001) 396–450
24. G.M. Bierman, M.P., Pitts, A.: MJ: An imperative core calculus for Java and Java with effects. Technical Report 563, University of Cambridge Computer Laboratory (2003)
25. : (The java grande forum benchmark suite) www.epcc.ed.ac.uk/javagrande/javag.html.
26. Saraswat, V., Kahn, K., Shapiro, U., Weinbaum, D.: Detecting stable properties of networks in concurrent logic programming languages. In: Seventh Annual ACM Symposium on Principles of Distributed Computing. (1988) 210–222
27. Saraswat, V.: Concurrent Constraint Programming. Doctoral Dissertation Award and Logic Programming. MIT Press (1993)

A Theory of System Behaviour in the Presence of Node and Link Failures
(Extended Abstract)

Adrian Francalanza and Matthew Hennessy

University of Sussex, Falmer Brighton BN1 9RH, England
{adrianf, matthewh}@sussex.ac.uk

Abstract. We develop a behavioural theory of distributed programs in the presence of failures such as nodes crashing and links breaking. The framework we use is that of Dπ, a language in which located processes, or agents, may migrate between dynamically created locations. In our extended framework, these processes run on a distributed network, in which individual nodes may crash in fail-stop fashion or the links between these nodes may become permanently broken. The original language, Dπ, is also extended by a ping construct for detecting and reacting to these failures.

We define a bisimulation equivalence between these systems, based on labelled actions which record, in addition to the effect actions have on the processes, the effect on the actual state of the underlying network and the view of this state known to observers. We prove that the equivalence is *fully abstract*, in the sense that two systems will be differentiated if and only if, in some sense, there is a computational context, consisting of a surrounding network and an observer, which can see the difference.

1 Introduction

It is generally accepted that *partial failures* are one of the principal factors precluding location transparency in distributed settings such as *wide-area networks*, [4], large computational infrastructures which may even span the globe. Because of this, various *location-aware* calculi and programming languages have arisen in the literature to model the behaviour of distributed programs in the presence of failures, and to study the correctness of algorithms is such a setting. The purpose of this paper is to:

- invent a simple framework, a distributed process calculus, for describing computations over a distributed network in which individual *nodes* and *links* between the nodes are subject to failure
- use this framework to develop a behavioural theory of distributed systems in which these failures are taken into account.

Our point of departure is Dπ [12], a simple distributed version of the standard π-calculus [16], where the locations that host processes model closely physical network nodes. Ignoring the type system developed for Dπ, which is orthogonal to the issues addressed here, we consider the following three Dπ abstract server implementations as motivation:

M. Abadi and L. de Alfaro (Eds.): CONCUR 2005, LNCS 3653, pp. 368–382, 2005.

$$\mathsf{server} \Leftarrow (\nu\, data)\begin{pmatrix} l[\![req?(x,y).data!\langle x,y\rangle]\!] \\ \mid l[\![data?(x,y).y!\langle f(x)\rangle]\!] \end{pmatrix}$$

$$\mathsf{servD} \quad \Leftarrow \quad (\nu\, data)\begin{pmatrix} l[\![req?(x,y).\mathsf{go}\ k_1.data!\langle x,y\rangle]\!] \\ \mid k_1[\![data?(x,y).\mathsf{go}\ l.y!\langle f(x)\rangle]\!] \end{pmatrix}$$

$$\mathsf{servD2Rt} \Leftarrow (\nu\, data)\left(\begin{array}{l} l\left[\!\!\left[req?(x,y).(\nu sync)\begin{pmatrix} \mathsf{go}\ k_1.data!\langle x, sync\rangle \\ \mid \mathsf{go}\ k_2.\,\mathsf{go}\ k_1.\,data!\langle x, sync\rangle \\ \mid synch?(x).y!\langle x\rangle \end{pmatrix} \right]\!\!\right] \\ \mid k_1\left[\!\!\left[data?(x,y).\begin{pmatrix} \mathsf{go}\ l.\,y!\langle f(x)\rangle \\ \mathsf{go}\ k_2.\,\mathsf{go}\ l.\,y!\langle f(x)\rangle \end{pmatrix} \right]\!\!\right] \end{array}\right)$$

The three systems server, servD and servD2Rt implement a server that accepts a single request for processing on channel *req* at location l with two arguments, x being the value to be processed and y being the return channel on which to return the result of the processing. A typical client for these servers would have the form $l[\![req!\langle n, ret\rangle]\!]$, sending the name n as the value to be looked up and *ret* as the return channel.

Every server forwards the request to an internal database hidden from the client, denoted by the scoped channel *data*, which processes the value using an unspecified function $f(x)$. The three implementations differ by where the internal database is located and how it is handled. More specifically, server holds the database *locally* at l and carries out all the processing there; by contrast, servD and servD2Rt distribute the database *remotely* at location k_1. The latter two server implementations also differ by how the remote database is accessed: servD accesses the database using the direct route from l to k_1; servD2Rt forwards the service requests along two concurrent routes, that is the direct one from l to k_1 and an indirect route using an intermediary node k_2 and non-deterministically selects one of two results if both routes are active.Intuitively, these three server implementations are not equivalent because they exhibit distinct behaviour in a setting with node and link failure. For instance, if node k_1 fails, servD and servD2Rt may not be able to service a client request whereas server would continue to work seamlessly. Moreover, servD and servD2Rt are also distinct because if the link between l and k_1 breaks, servD may block and not serve a request while servD2Rt would still operate as intended. Despite the fact that these three implementations are qualitatively different, it is hard to distinguish between them in Dπ theories such as [10].

In this paper, we develop a behavioural theory that tells these three systems apart. We use extended Dπ configurations of the form $\Sigma \triangleright N$ where Σ is a representation of the current state of the network, and N consists of the systems such as those we have just seen, software executing in a distributed manner over Σ. Here Σ records the set of nodes in the network, their *status* (whether they are *alive* or *dead*), and their *connectivity* (the set of symmetric links between these nodes). This results in a succinct but expressive framework, in which many of the phenomena associated with practical distributed settings, such as routing algorithms and ad-hoc network discoveries, can be examined.

The corresponding behavioural theory takes the form of *(weak) bisimulation equivalence*, based on labelled actions

$$\Sigma \triangleright N \xrightarrow{\mu} \Sigma' \triangleright N' \tag{1}$$

where the label μ represents the manner in which an observer, also running on the network Σ, can interact with the system N. This interaction may not only change the state of the system, to N', in the usual manner, but also affect the nature of the underlying network. For instance, an observer may extend the network by creating new locations or otherwise induce faults in the network by killing sites or breaking links between sites, thereby capturing, at least, some of the reaction of N to dynamic failures.

It turns out that the definition of the actions in (1) needs to be relatively sophisticated: although the system and the observer may initially share the same view of the underlying network, Σ, interactions quickly give rise to situations in which these views *diverge*. More specifically, observers may learn of new nodes in the system as a result of interaction (scope extrusion), but at the same time, cannot determine the state of such nodes and the code executing at them either because the newly discovered nodes are *completely disconnected* or because the observer does not have enough information to *determine a route* which leads to these nodes. As a result, in (1) above, the network representation Σ needs to somehow record the actual full state of the underlying network, together with the *observer's partial view* of it.

We choose to develop the theory in terms of a representation with nodes and links, despite the widely held view that representation of nodes *only* is sufficient; this would typically entail encoding a link between location l and k as an intermediary node lk, encoding migration from l to k as a two step migration from l to lk and lk to k, and finally encoding link failure as the intermediary node lk failing. A network representation with partial connection between nodes is very natural in itself since WANs are often *not a clique*. The resulting calculus also gives rise to an interesting theory of partial views that deserves to be investigated in its own right. In addition, this setting allows us to study *directly* the interplay between node and link failure and their respective observation from the software's point of view. Finally, it is unlikely that a theory resulting from an encoding into a *nodes only* calculus would be fully abstract, due to the fact that any encoding would typically decomposes atomic reductions such as migration into sub-reductions, which in turn affects the resulting bisimulation equivalence; see [9].

The paper is organised as follows: Section 2 introduces DπF and the reduction semantics. In Section 3 we present an initial definition of actions for DπF, based on the general approach of [11]. The resulting bisimulation equivalence can be used to demonstrate equivalencies between systems, but we show, by a series of examples, that it is too discriminating. In Section 4, we revise the definition of these actions, by abstracting from internal information present in the action labels, and show that the resulting equivalence is *fully abstract* with respect to an intuitive form of *contextual equivalence*. This means that two systems will be differentiated by the bisimulation equivalence if and only if, in some sense, there is a computational context, consisting of a network and an observer, which can see the difference. The complete proofs, elaborate discussions and extensive examples may be found in the corresponding technical report [8].

2 The Language

We assume a set of *variables* VARS, ranged over by $x, y, z, \ldots$ and a separate set of *names*, NAMES, ranged over by $n, m, \ldots$, which is divided into locations, LOCS, ranged

Table 1. *Syntax of typed DπF*

Types

$\mathtt{T},\mathtt{U},\mathtt{W} ::= \mathtt{ch} \mid \mathtt{loc_S[C]} \qquad \mathtt{S} ::= \mathtt{a} \mid \mathtt{d} \qquad \mathtt{C},\mathtt{D} ::= \{u_1,\dots,u_n\}$

Processes

$P,Q ::= u!\langle V\rangle.P \mid u?(X).P \mid *\,u?(X).P \mid \mathsf{if}\ v{=}u\ \mathsf{then}\ P\ \mathsf{else}\ Q \mid \mathbf{0} \mid P|Q \mid (\nu n{:}\mathtt{T})P$
$\quad \mid \mathsf{go}\ u.P \mid \mathsf{kill} \mid \mathsf{break}\ u \mid \mathsf{ping}\ u.P\ \mathsf{else}\ Q$

Systems

$M,N,O ::= l[\![P]\!] \mid N|M \mid (\nu n{:}\mathtt{T})N$

over by $l, k, \dots$ and channels, Chans, ranged over by $a, b, c, \dots$. Finally we use $u, v, \dots$ to range over the set of *identifiers*, consisting of either variables and names.

The syntax of DπF is given in Figure 1, where the main syntactic category is that of *systems*, ranged over by M, N; these are essentially a collection of *located processes*, or *agents* $l[\![P]\!]$, but there may also be occurrences of typed *scoped names*, $(\nu n : \mathtt{T})N$. Although we could employ the full power of the type system for Dπ [10], for simplicity, we use a very simple notion of type and adapt it to the purpose at hand. Thus, if n is used as a channel in N, then T is simply ch; however if it is a location then $\mathtt{T} = \mathtt{loc_S[C]}$ records it's *status* S, whether it is alive a or dead d, and the set of locations C to which it is linked, $\{l_1, \dots, l_n\}$.

The syntax for agents, P, Q, is an extension of that in Dπ. There are input and output on channels; here V is a tuple of identifiers, and X a tuple of variables, to be interpreted as a pattern. We also have the standard forms of parallel, replicated input, local declarations, a test for equality between identifiers and an asynchronous migration construct. We also introduce a ping conditional construct, $l[\![\mathsf{ping}\ k.P\ \mathsf{else}\ Q]\!]$, in the style of [2,1,15], branching to $l[\![P]\!]$ or $l[\![Q]\!]$ depending on the *accessibility* of k from l. Finally we have two new constructs to simulate failures; $l[\![\mathsf{kill}]\!]$ kills the location l, while $k[\![\mathsf{break}\ l]\!]$ breaks the link between l and k, if it exists. We are not really interested in programming with these last two operators. Nevertheless, when we come to consider *contextual behaviour*, their presence will mean that the behaviour will take into account the effects of *dynamic* failures.

In this extended abstract, we will assume the standard notions of *free* and *bound* occurrences of both names and variables, together with the associated concepts of α-conversion and *substitution*. Furthermore, we will assume that all system terms are *closed*, that is they have no free occurrences of variables.

Reduction Semantics: This takes the form of a binary relation

$$\Delta \triangleright N \longrightarrow \Delta' \triangleright N' \qquad (2)$$

where Δ and Δ' are representations of the state of the network. Intuitively this must record the set of locations in existence, whether they are alive or dead, and any live links between them.

Definition 1 (Network Representation). *We first introduce some notation to represent the* links *in a network. A binary relation $\mathcal{L}$ over locations is called a* linkset *if it is:*

- *symmetric, that is,* $\langle l,k\rangle \in \mathcal{L}$ *implies* $\langle k,l\rangle$ *is also in* $\mathcal{L}$
- *reflexive, that is,* $\langle l,k\rangle \in \mathcal{L}$ *implies* $\langle l,l\rangle$ *and* $\langle k,k\rangle$ *are also in* $\mathcal{L}$.

A network representation, Δ, *is any triple* $\langle \mathcal{N}, \mathcal{D}, \mathcal{L}\rangle$ *where*

- $\mathcal{N}$ *is a set of names, divided into* $\mathbf{loc}(\mathcal{N})$ *(location names) and* $\mathbf{chan}(\mathcal{N})$ *(channel names)*
- $\mathcal{A} \subseteq \mathbf{loc}(\mathcal{N})$ *represents the set of live locations*
- $\mathcal{L} \subseteq \mathbf{loc}(\mathcal{N}) \times \mathbf{loc}(\mathcal{N})$ *is a linkset representing the set of live connections between locations*

In the sequel, we use the abbreviation $l \leftrightarrow k$ in linksets to denote the pairs $\langle l,l\rangle$, $\langle k,k\rangle$, $\langle l,k\rangle$, $\langle k,l\rangle$; we also denote the components of Δ as $\Delta_{\mathcal{N}}$, $\Delta_{\mathcal{A}}$ and $\Delta_{\mathcal{L}}$.

We may therefore take Δ and Δ' in (2) above to be network representations. Formally, we call pairs $\Delta \triangleright N$ *configurations*, whenever every free name in N occurs in the name component of Δ, and we define reductions to take place between such configurations. Since not all nodes are interconnected, the reduction semantics is based on the notions of *accessibility* and *reachability* between nodes: k is accessible from l in Δ, denoted as $\Delta \vdash k \leftarrow l$, if and only if k is alive ($k \in \Delta_{\mathcal{A}}$) and there is a (direct) live link between l and k ($\langle l,k\rangle \in \Delta_{\mathcal{L}}$); a node k is *reachable* from l in Δ, denotes as $\Delta \vdash k \leftsquigarrow l$, if there exists a *chain of live links* between the two nodes, where *every intermediate node is alive*.

The rules governing these reductions are given in Figures 2, 3 and 4. Figure 2 gives the standard rules for (local) communication, and the management of replication, matching and parallelism, derived from the corresponding rules for Dπ in [12]. Every rule depends on the requirement that l, the location of the activity, is currently alive; this is the intent of the predicate $\Delta \vdash l$: **alive**. The rules in Figure 3 are more interesting. Rules (r-go) and (r-ngo) state that a migration is successful depending on the accessibility of the destination. Similarly, (r-ping) and (r-nping) are subject to the same condition for the respective branchings. Note that $l[\![\mathsf{ping}\, k.P\ \mathsf{else}\ Q]\!]$ yields *partial information* about the state of the underlying network: it can only determine that k is inaccessible, but does not give information on whether this is caused by the failure of node k, the breaking of the link $l \leftrightarrow k$, or both. The rules (r-kill), (r-brk) make the obvious changes to the current network; $\Delta - l$ means changing l to be a dead site in Δ, while $\Delta - l \leftrightarrow k$ means breaking the link between l and k. Finally (r-newc) and (r-newl) regulates the generation of new names; for example, (r-newl) launches a new location with a declared type $\mathtt{loc_S[C]}$ using the function $\mathsf{inst}(\mathtt{loc_S[C]}, l, \Delta)$. Intuitively, this returns the location type $\mathtt{loc_S[D]}$, where the set of locations $\mathtt{D}$, is the subset of locations in $\mathsf{C}\cup\{l\}$ which are *reachable* from l. We refer the reader to the technical report, [8], for an example explaining how this function works.

Finally, in Figure 4 we have an adaptation of the standard *contextual* rules, which allow the basic reductions to occur in *evaluation contexts*. The rule (r-str) allows reductions up to a structural equivalence, in the standard manner, using the identities in Figure 5. The only non-trivial identities in Figure 5 are (s-flip-1) and (s-flip-2), where the types of the successively scoped locations need to be changed if they denote a link between them, thus avoiding unwanted name capture. The rules (r-ctxt-par) and (r-ctxt-rest) allow reductions to occur under contexts; note that the latter is somewhat non-standard,

Table 2. *Local Reduction Rules for DπF*

Assuming $\Delta \vdash l : \textbf{alive}$

(r-comm)
$$\overline{\Delta \triangleright l[\![a!\langle V\rangle.P]\!] \mid l[\![a?(X).Q]\!] \;\longrightarrow\; \Delta \triangleright l[\![P]\!] \mid l[\![Q\{^{V}\!/X\}]\!]}$$

(r-rep)
$$\overline{\Delta \triangleright l[\![*a?(X).P]\!] \;\longrightarrow\; \Delta \triangleright l[\![a?(X).(P \mid *a?(X).P)]\!]}$$

(r-fork)
$$\overline{\Delta \triangleright l[\![P|Q]\!] \;\longrightarrow\; \Delta \triangleright l[\![P]\!] \mid l[\![Q]\!]}$$

(r-eq)
$$\overline{\Delta \triangleright l[\![\mathsf{if}\ u = u\ \mathsf{then}\ P\ \mathsf{else}\ Q]\!] \longrightarrow \Delta \triangleright l[\![P]\!]}$$

(r-neq)
$$\overline{\Delta \triangleright l[\![\mathsf{if}\ u = v\ \mathsf{then}\ P\ \mathsf{else}\ Q]\!] \longrightarrow \Delta \triangleright l[\![Q]\!]}\ u \neq v$$

Table 3. *Network Reduction Rules for DπF*

Assuming $\Delta \vdash l : \textbf{alive}$

(r-go)
$$\overline{\Delta \triangleright l[\![\mathsf{go}\ k.P]\!] \longrightarrow \Delta \triangleright k[\![P]\!]}\ \Delta \vdash k \leftarrow l$$

(r-ngo)
$$\overline{\Delta \triangleright l[\![\mathsf{go}\ k.P]\!] \longrightarrow \Delta \triangleright k[\![\mathbf{0}]\!]}\ \Delta \nvdash k \leftarrow l$$

(r-ping)
$$\overline{\Delta \triangleright l[\![\mathsf{ping}\ k.P\ \mathsf{else}\ Q]\!] \longrightarrow \Delta \triangleright l[\![P]\!]}\ \Delta \vdash k \leftarrow l$$

(r-nping)
$$\overline{\Delta \triangleright l[\![\mathsf{ping}\ k.P\ \mathsf{else}\ Q]\!] \longrightarrow \Delta \triangleright l[\![Q]\!]}\ \Delta \nvdash k \leftarrow l$$

(r-kill)
$$\overline{\Delta \triangleright l[\![\mathsf{kill}]\!] \longrightarrow (\Delta - l) \triangleright l[\![\mathbf{0}]\!]}$$

(r-brk)
$$\overline{\Delta \triangleright l[\![\mathsf{break}\ k]\!] \longrightarrow (\Delta - l \leftrightarrow k) \triangleright l[\![\mathbf{0}]\!]}\ \Delta \vdash l \leftrightarrow k$$

(r-newc)
$$\overline{\Delta \triangleright l[\![(\nu c : \mathtt{ch})\, P]\!] \longrightarrow \Delta \triangleright (\nu c : \mathtt{ch})\, l[\![P]\!]}$$

(r-newl)
$$\overline{\Delta \triangleright l[\![(\nu k : \mathtt{loc_S[C]})\, P]\!] \longrightarrow \Delta \triangleright (\nu k : \mathtt{loc_S[D]})\, l[\![P]\!]}\ \mathtt{loc_S[D]} = \mathsf{inst}(\mathtt{loc_S[C]}, l, \Delta)$$

but as reductions may induce faults in the network, it may be that the status and connectivity of the scoped (location) name n is affected by the reduction, thereby changing T to U.

This completes our exposition of the reduction semantics. At this point, we should point out that in a configuration such as $\Delta \triangleright N$, contrary to what we have implied up to now, Δ does not give a completely true representation of the network on which the code in N is running; the type information associated with scoped locations encodes parts of the network Δ that is hidden from the observer.

Example 1 (Syntax). Let Δ represent the network $\langle\{l, a\}; \{l\}; \{l \leftrightarrow l\}\rangle$ consisting of a channel a and a live node l and M_1 the system

$$(\nu k_2 : \mathtt{loc_a}[\emptyset])\,(\nu k_1 : \mathtt{loc_d}[\{l, k_2\}])\,(l[\![a!\langle k_2\rangle.P]\!] \mid k_2[\![Q]\!])$$

Table 4. *Contextual Reduction Rules for DπF*

(r-str)
$$\frac{\Delta \triangleright N' \equiv \Delta \triangleright N \quad \Delta \triangleright N \longrightarrow \Delta' \triangleright M \quad \Delta' \triangleright M \equiv \Delta' \triangleright M'}{\Delta \triangleright N' \longrightarrow \Delta' \triangleright M'}$$

(r-ctxt-rest)
$$\frac{\Delta + n : \mathrm{T} \triangleright N \longrightarrow \Delta' + n : \mathrm{U} \triangleright M}{\Delta \triangleright (\nu n : \mathrm{T})N \longrightarrow \Delta' \triangleright (\nu n : \mathrm{U})M}$$

(r-ctxt-par)
$$\frac{\Delta \triangleright N \longrightarrow \Delta' \triangleright N'}{\Delta \triangleright N|M \longrightarrow \Delta' \triangleright N'|M} \; \Delta \vdash M$$

Table 5. *Structural Rules for DπF*

(s-comm)	$N\|M \equiv M\|N$	
(s-assoc)	$(N\|M)\|M' \equiv N\|(M\|M')$	
(s-unit)	$N\|l[\![\mathbf{0}]\!] \equiv N$	
(s-extr)	$(\nu n{:}\mathrm{T})(N\|M) \equiv N\|(\nu n{:}\mathrm{T})M$	$n \notin \mathbf{fn}(N)$
(s-flip-1)	$(\nu n{:}\mathrm{T})(\nu m{:}\mathrm{U})N \equiv (\nu m{:}\mathrm{U})(\nu n{:}\mathrm{T})N$	$n \notin \mathbf{fn}(\mathrm{U})$
(s-flip-2)	$(\nu n{:}\mathrm{T})(\nu m{:}\mathrm{U})N \equiv (\nu m : \mathrm{U}{-}n)(\nu n : \mathrm{T}{+}m)N$	$n \in \mathbf{fn}(\mathrm{U})$
(s-inact)	$(\nu n{:}\mathrm{T})N \equiv N$	$n \notin \mathbf{fn}(N)$

Here M_1 generates two new locations $k_1,\ k_2$, where k_1 is dead and linked to the existing node l and k_2 is alive linked to k_1. Although Δ only contains one node l, the located process $l[\![a!\langle k_2\rangle.P]\!]$ (as well as $k_2[\![Q]\!]$) is running on a network of *three nodes*, two of which, $k_1,\ k_2$ are scoped, that is not available to other systems. We can informally represent this network by

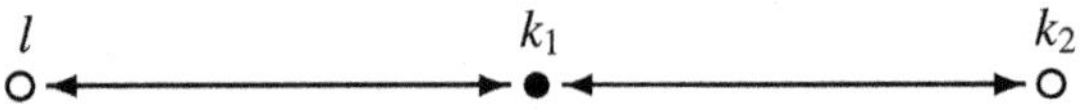

where the nodes ∘ and • denote live and dead nodes respectively. Note that the same network could be denoted by the system N_1

$$(\nu k_1 : \mathtt{loc_d}[\{l\}])\,(\nu k_2 : \mathtt{loc_a}[\{k_1\}])\;(l[\![a!\langle k_2\rangle.P]\!] \,|\, k_2[\![Q]\!])$$

Note also that the two systems are structurally equivalent, $M_1 \equiv N_1$, through (s-flip-2). As a notational abbreviation, in all future example we will omit the status annotation a in live location declarations; so for example system N_1 would be given as

$$(\nu k_1 : \mathtt{loc_d}[\{l\}])\,(\nu k_2 : \{k_1\})\;(l[\![a!\langle k_2\rangle.P]\!] \,|\, k_2[\![Q]\!])$$

3 A Labelled Transition System

In this section we give a labelled transition system for the language, in which the labelled actions are intended to mimic the possible interactions between a system and an observer; it is natural to assume that both share the same underlying network. However Example 2 below demonstrates that our representation of this joint network is no longer sufficient if we want to faithfully record the effect interactions have on systems, because they may lead to a discrepancy between the *system network view* and the *observer network view*.

Example 2 (Observer's Network view). Let Δ and M_1 be defined as in Example 1. An observer O at site l, such as $l[\![a?(x).P(x)]\!]$, can gain knowledge of the new location k_2, thereby evolving to $l[\![P(k_2)]\!]$. But even though it is in possession of the name k_2, it's knowledge of the state of the underlying network is no longer represented by Δ, and there is now a mismatch between the observer view of the network, and the system view. The system view is now $\Delta' = \langle\{a, l, k_2\}; \{l, k_2\}; \{l \leftrightarrow l,\ k_2 \leftrightarrow k_2\}\rangle$, that is Δ augmented by the scope extrusion of the *live* node k_2 linked to a private (dead) node k_1, which is, in turn, linked to l. But the observer's view is quite different: the node l is accessible to the observer, since it has code running there; nevertheless, even though the observer knows about k_2 at l in $P(k_2)$, it does not have enough information to *reach* k_2 from l. As a result, it has no means how to determine k_2's state (its status and connections) nor interact with any code at k_2. This means that the representation of the observers view, requires a new kind of annotation, for nodes such as k_2, whose name is known but cannot be *reached*.

Stated otherwise, in order to give an lts semantics, we need to refine our representations of networks.

Definition 2 (Effective Network Representations). *An* effective network representation *Σ is a triple $\langle \mathcal{N}, \mathcal{O}, \mathcal{H}\rangle$, where:*

- *$\mathcal{N}$ is a set of names, as before, divided into* $\mathbf{loc}(\mathcal{N})$ *and* $\mathbf{chan}(\mathcal{N})$
- *$\mathcal{O}$ is a* linkset, *denoting the live locations and links that are* observable *by the context*
- *$\mathcal{H}$ is another* linkset, *denoting the live locations and links that are* hidden *(or unreachable) to the context.*

We also assume three consistency requirements: (i) $\mathbf{dom}(\mathcal{O}) \subseteq \mathbf{loc}(\mathcal{N})$, *(ii)* $\mathbf{dom}(\mathcal{H}) \subseteq \mathbf{loc}(\mathcal{N})$ *and (iii)* $\mathbf{dom}(\mathcal{O}) \cap \mathbf{dom}(\mathcal{H}) = \emptyset$.

The intuition is that an observer running on a network representation Σ, knows about all the names in Σ, denoted as $\Sigma_{\mathcal{N}}$, and has access to all the locations in $\mathbf{dom}(\mathcal{O})$. As a result, it knows the state of every location in $\mathbf{dom}(\mathcal{O})$ and the live links between these locations. The observer, however, does not have access to the live locations in $\mathbf{dom}(\mathcal{H})$; as a result, it cannot determine the live links between them nor can it distinguish them from dead nodes. Σ, optimises on the previous (intuitive) network representation Δ in two ways: (1) It encodes the node and liveness using a single linkset, instead of two distinct sets, $\Delta_{\mathcal{A}}$ and $\Delta_{\mathcal{L}}$ (2) it does not represent unusable live links, that is links where either end point is a dead node. Summarising, Σ hold all the necessary information from the observer's point of view, that is, the known names, $\mathcal{N}$, the known state, $\mathcal{O}$, and the state that can potentially become known in future, as a result of scope extrusion, $\mathcal{H}$. For brevity, we omit channel names from any $\Sigma_{\mathcal{N}}$ in the remainder of the paper.

With this refined notion, we can now represent the observers view of Example 2 as $\mathcal{N} = \{l, k_2\}$, $\mathcal{O} = \{l \leftrightarrow l\}$ and $\mathcal{H} = \{k_2 \leftrightarrow k_2\}$. In the sequel, we use *configurations* of the form $\Sigma \triangleright N$, where Σ is a network representation, and N satisfies the previous consistency constraint, $\mathbf{fn}(N) \subseteq \Sigma_{\mathcal{N}}$.

We now define a labelled transition system for DπF, which consists of a collection of actions over configurations, $\Sigma \triangleright N \xrightarrow{\mu} \Sigma' \triangleright N'$, where μ can be an internal action, τ, a bound input, $(\tilde{n} : \tilde{\mathsf{T}})l : a?(V)$ or bound output, $(\tilde{n} : \tilde{\mathsf{T}})l : a!\langle V\rangle$, adopted from [11,10], or the new labels, $\mathsf{kill} : l$ and $l \not\leftrightarrow k$, denoting external location killing and link breaking respectively. These actions are defined by transition rules given in the full paper, [8]. In Figure 6 we give the interesting rules. The transition rules introducing external actions such as (l-halt) and (l-disc) are subject to judgements of the form $\Sigma \vdash_{\mathsf{obs}} l : \mathbf{alive}$, requiring that l is alive ($\Sigma \vdash l : \mathbf{alive}$) and *accessible by the observer* ($l \in \mathbf{dom}(\Sigma_{\mathcal{O}})$). We employ three rules for scoping, the standard (l-rest), the standard but modified (l-open) which filters (unusable) links connected to *dead* nodes through the condition $\mathsf{U} = \mathsf{T} \cap \mathbf{dom}(\Sigma_{\mathcal{O}} \cup \Sigma_{\mathcal{H}})$, and the non-standard (l-rest-typ), which filters links between scope extruded locations and scoped locations in bound output labels.

With these actions we can now define in the standard manner a bisimulation equivalence between configurations, which can be used as the basis for contextual reasoning. Let us write

$$\Sigma \models M \approx_{int} N$$

to mean that there is a (weak) bisimulation between the configurations $\Sigma \triangleright M$ and $\Sigma \triangleright N$

Example 3 (Server Implementations Revisited). Consider the network:

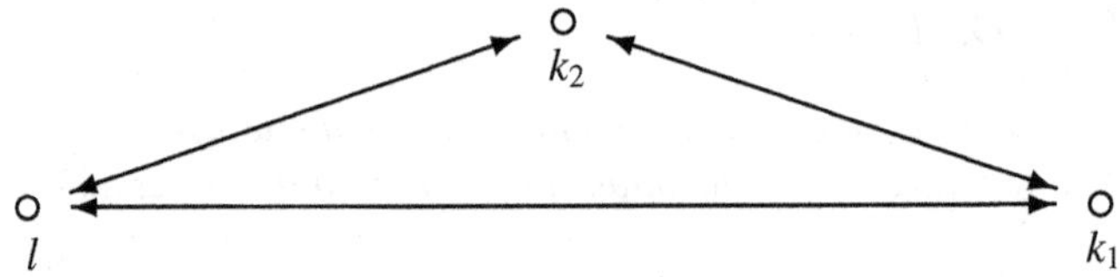

formally represented as $\Sigma = \langle \mathcal{N}, \mathcal{O}, \mathcal{H}\rangle$, where $\mathcal{N} = \{l, k_1, k_2\}$, $\mathcal{O} = \{l \leftrightarrow k_1,\ l \leftrightarrow k_2,\ k_1 \leftrightarrow k_2\}$ and $\mathcal{H} = \emptyset$. If we assume that the three server implementations presented earlier in the Introduction were running over Σ, we are able to formally argue that

$$\Sigma \models \mathsf{server} \not\approx_{int} \mathsf{servD} \not\approx_{int} \mathsf{servD2Rt}$$

To see this, it is sufficient to examine the behaviour of these systems subsequent to an actions such as $\xrightarrow{l \not\leftrightarrow k_1}$ and $\xrightarrow{\mathsf{kill}:k_1}$.

One can also use the lts to establish positive results. For example, for $\Sigma_{l,k} = \langle\{l, k\}, \{l \leftrightarrow k\}, \emptyset\rangle$, one can prove

$$\Sigma_{l,k} \models l[\![\mathsf{ping}\ k.\ a!\langle\rangle\ \mathsf{else}\ \mathbf{0}]\!] \approx_{int} k[\![\mathsf{go}\ l.a!\langle\rangle]\!]$$

Nevertheless, we can argue, at least informally, that this notion of equivalence is too *discriminating* and the lts labels too *intensional*, because we distinguish between configurations where the differences in behaviour are difficult to observe. Problems arise when there is an interplay between *hidden* nodes, links and dead nodes.

Table 6. *Main Operational Rules for DπF*

Assuming $\Sigma \vdash l : \mathbf{alive}$

(l-kill)

$$\frac{}{\Sigma \triangleright l[\![\mathsf{kill}]\!] \xrightarrow{\tau} (\Sigma - l) \triangleright l[\![\mathbf{0}]\!]}$$

(l-brk)

$$\frac{}{\Sigma \triangleright l[\![\mathsf{break}\ k]\!] \xrightarrow{\tau} \Sigma - (l \leftrightarrow k) \triangleright l[\![\mathbf{0}]\!]}\ \Sigma \vdash l \leftrightarrow k$$

(l-halt)

$$\frac{}{\Sigma \triangleright N \xrightarrow{\mathsf{kill}:l} (\Sigma - l) \triangleright N}\ \Sigma \vdash_{\mathsf{obs}} l : \mathbf{alive}$$

(l-disc)

$$\frac{}{\Sigma \triangleright N \xrightarrow{l \not\leftrightarrow k} \Sigma - (l \leftrightarrow k) \triangleright N}\ \Sigma \vdash_{\mathsf{obs}} l \leftrightarrow k$$

(l-open)

$$\frac{\Sigma + n : \mathrm{T} \triangleright N \xrightarrow{(\tilde{n}:\tilde{\mathrm{T}})l:a!\langle V\rangle} \Sigma' \triangleright N'}{\Sigma \triangleright (\nu n : \mathrm{T})N \xrightarrow{(n:\mathrm{U},\tilde{n}:\tilde{\mathrm{T}})l:a!\langle V\rangle} \Sigma' \triangleright N'}\ l, a \neq n \in V,\ \mathrm{U} = \mathrm{T} \cap \mathbf{dom}(\Sigma_{\mathcal{O}} \cup \Sigma_{\mathcal{H}})$$

(l-weak)

$$\frac{\Sigma + n : \mathrm{T} \triangleright N \xrightarrow{(\tilde{n}:\tilde{\mathrm{T}})l:a?(V)} \Sigma' \triangleright N'}{\Sigma \triangleright N \xrightarrow{(n:\mathrm{T},\tilde{n}:\tilde{\mathrm{T}})l:a?(V)} \Sigma' \triangleright N'}\ l, a \neq n \in V,\ (\Sigma + \tilde{n} : \tilde{\mathrm{T}}) \vdash_{\mathsf{obs}} \mathrm{T}$$

(l-rest-typ)

$$\frac{\Sigma + k : \mathrm{T} \triangleright N \xrightarrow{(\tilde{n}:\tilde{\mathrm{T}})l:a!\langle V\rangle} (\Sigma + \tilde{n} : \tilde{\mathrm{U}}) + k : \mathrm{U} \triangleright N'}{\Sigma \triangleright (\nu k : \mathrm{T})N \xrightarrow{(\tilde{n}:\tilde{\mathrm{U}})l:a!\langle V\rangle} \Sigma + \tilde{n} : \tilde{\mathrm{U}} \triangleright (\nu k : \mathrm{U})N'}\ l, a \neq k \in \mathbf{fn}(\tilde{\mathrm{T}})$$

(l-rest)

$$\frac{\Sigma + n : \mathrm{T} \triangleright N \xrightarrow{\mu} \Sigma' + n : \mathrm{U} \triangleright N'}{\Sigma \triangleright (\nu n : \mathrm{T})N \xrightarrow{\mu} \Sigma' \triangleright (\nu n : \mathrm{U})N'}\ n \notin \mathbf{fn}(\mu)$$

(l-par-ctxt)

$$\frac{\Sigma \triangleright N \xrightarrow{\mu} \Sigma' \triangleright N'}{\begin{array}{c}\Sigma \triangleright N|M \xrightarrow{\mu} \Sigma' \triangleright N'|M \\ \Sigma \triangleright M|N \xrightarrow{\mu} \Sigma' \triangleright M|N'\end{array}}\ \Sigma \vdash M$$

Example 4 (Inaccessible Network State). Let Σ be the network in which there is only one node, l, which is alive and consider the two systems

$$M_2 \Leftarrow (\nu k_1 : \{l\})\,(\nu k_2 : \{k_1\})\,(\nu k_3 : \{k_1, k_2\})\ l[\![a!\langle k_2, k_3\rangle.P]\!]$$
$$N_2 \Leftarrow (\nu k_1 : \{l\})\,(\nu k_2 : \{k_1\})\,(\nu k_3 : \{k_1\})\ l[\![a!\langle k_2, k_3\rangle.P]\!]$$

When M_2 and N_2 are running on Σ, the code $l[\![a!\langle k_2, k_3\rangle.P]\!]$, present in both M_2 and N_2, is effectively running on the following respective networks, due to the newly declared locations:

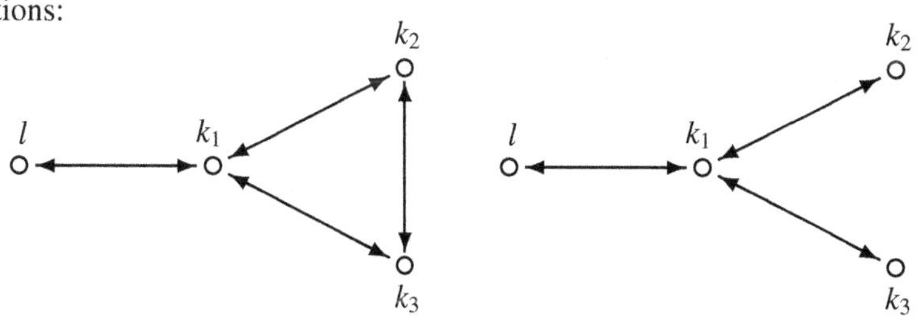

Using our lts, we determine that $\Sigma \models M_2 \not\approx_{int} N_2$ because the configurations give rise to *different* output actions:

$$\Sigma \triangleright M_2 \xrightarrow{(k_2:\emptyset,\, k_3:\{k_2\})l:a!\langle k_2,k_3\rangle} \Sigma + k_2:\emptyset + k_3:\{k_2\} \triangleright (\nu k_1:\{l, k_2, k_3\})\, l[\![P]\!]$$

$$\Sigma \triangleright N_2 \xrightarrow{(k_2:\emptyset,\, k_3:\emptyset)l:a!\langle k_2,k_3\rangle} \Sigma + k_2:\emptyset + k_3:\emptyset \triangleright (\nu k_1:\{l, k_2, k_3\})\, l[\![P]\!]$$

The difference lies in the type at which the location k_3 is exported: M_2 exports k_3 connected to k_2 whereas in N_2 exports a completely disconnected k_3.

However, if k_1 does not occur in P, then k_1 can never be scope extruded to the observer and thus k_2 and k_3 will remain inaccessible in both systems. This means that the presence (or absence) of the link $k_2 \leftrightarrow k_3$ can never be verified by the observer and thus there should be no observable difference between M_2 and N_2 running on Σ.

Example 5 (Interplay between Node and Link Failure). We consider the following three configurations together with the depiction of the respective networks over which the common located process $l[\![a!\langle k\rangle.P]\!]$ is running:

$$M_3^1 \Leftarrow \langle\{l, a\}, \{l_1 \leftrightarrow l_1\}, \emptyset\rangle \triangleright (\nu k:\mathtt{loc_d}[\{l\}])l[\![a!\langle k\rangle.P]\!] \quad :$$

$$M_3^2 \Leftarrow \langle\{l, a\}, \{l_1 \leftrightarrow l_1\}, \emptyset\rangle \triangleright (\nu k:\mathtt{loc_d}[\emptyset])l[\![a!\langle k\rangle.P]\!] \quad :$$

$$M_3^3 \Leftarrow \langle\{l, a\}, \{l_1 \leftrightarrow l_1\}, \emptyset\rangle \triangleright (\nu k:\mathtt{loc_a}[\emptyset])l[\![a!\langle k\rangle.P]\!] \quad :$$

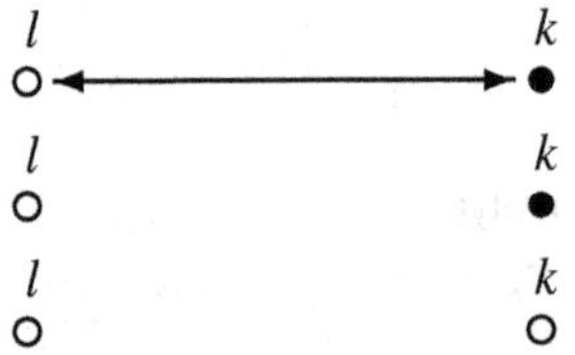

Intuitively, no observer can distinguish between these three configurations; even though some observer might obtain the scoped name k by inputting on channel a at l, it cannot determine the difference in the state of network. From rule (l-nping), we conclude that any attempt to ping k from l will yield the negative branch. However, such an observation does not give the observer enough information about whether it was caused by a node fault at k, a link fault between l and k or both. As a result, we would like to equate all three configuration. However, our lts specifies that all three configurations perform the output with different scope extrusion labels, namely:

$$\langle\{l\}, \{l \leftrightarrow l\}, \emptyset\rangle \triangleright M_3^1 \xrightarrow{(k:\mathtt{loc_d}[\{l\}])l:a!\langle k\rangle} \langle\{l\}, \{l \leftrightarrow l\}, \emptyset\rangle \triangleright l[\![P]\!]$$

$$\langle\{l\}, \{l \leftrightarrow l\}, \emptyset\rangle \triangleright M_3^2 \xrightarrow{(k:\mathtt{loc_d}[\emptyset])l:a!\langle k\rangle} \langle\{l\}, \{l \leftrightarrow l\}, \emptyset\rangle \triangleright l[\![P]\!]$$

$$\langle\{l\}, \{l \leftrightarrow l\}, \emptyset\rangle \triangleright M_3^3 \xrightarrow{(k:\mathtt{loc_a}[\emptyset])l:a!\langle k\rangle} \langle\{l\}, \{l \leftrightarrow l\}, \{k \leftrightarrow k\}\rangle \triangleright l[\![P]\!]$$

and as a result, these configurations are differentiated by $\approx_{int}$.

4 Reduction Barbed Congruence

The fundamental problem with the lts of the previous section is that when new locations are scope extruded, the associated information, coded in the types at which they are exported, is too detailed. The current actions carry too much *internal* information and hence, we need a revised form of action, which carry just the right amount of information.

However, before we plunge into our revision, it is best to have yardstick with respect to which we can calibrate the appropriateness of the revised labelled actions, and the resulting bisimulation equivalence. We adapt a well-known formulation of contextual equivalence to DπF, [13,11], called *reduction barbed congruence*. This relies on the notion of a *barb*, a collection of primitive observations which can be made on systems. Let us write $\Sigma \triangleright N \Downarrow_{a@l}$ to mean that an output on channel a at an accessible location l can be observed. Then, we would expect all reasonable behavioural equivalences to preserve these barbs. But the key idea in the definition is to use a notion of *contextual* relation over configurations, in which the contexts only have access to the *observable* part of the network.

Definition 3 (Contextual Relations). *A relation $\mathcal{R}$ over configurations is* contextual *if:*

(Parallel Systems)

- $\Sigma \triangleright M \,\mathcal{R}\, \Sigma' \triangleright N$ *and* $\Sigma \vdash_{obs} O$, $\Sigma' \vdash_{obs} O$ *implies* $-\ \Sigma \models M|O \,\mathcal{R}\, N|O$; $-\ \Sigma \models O|M \,\mathcal{R}\, O|N$

(Network Extensions)

- $\Sigma \triangleright M \,\mathcal{R}\, \Sigma' \triangleright N$ *and* $\Sigma \vdash_{obs} \mathtt{T}$, $\Sigma' \vdash_{obs} \mathtt{T}$, *$n$ fresh* *implies* $\Sigma{+}n{:}\mathtt{T} \models M \,\mathcal{R}\, N$

where $\Sigma \vdash_{obs} O$ and $\Sigma \vdash_{obs} \mathtt{T}$ restrict the observer O and connections of location types to accessible locations only.

Definition 4 (Reduction Barbed Congruence). *Let $\cong$ be the largest relation between configurations which is* contextual, *preserves* barbs *and is* reduction-closed.

Note that, apriori, this definition allows us to compare configurations which have different networks. However, it turns out that whenever $\Sigma \triangleright M \cong \Sigma' \triangleright N$, the external parts of Σ and Σ' must coincide. In the sequel, we abbreviate $\Sigma \triangleright M \cong \Sigma \triangleright N$, the cases where both networks are identical, to $\Sigma \models M \cong N$.

We now outline a revision of our labelled actions with the property that the resulting bisimulation equivalence coincides with the yardstick relation, $\cong$. The idea is to reuse the same actions but to simply change the types at which bound names appear. Currently, these are of the form $\mathtt{T} = \mathtt{ch}$ or $\mathtt{loc}_{\mathtt{S}}[\mathtt{C}]$, where the latter indicates the status of a location and its connectivity. We change these types to new types of the form $\mathtt{L}, \mathtt{K} = \{l_1 \leftrightarrow k_1, \ldots, l_i \leftrightarrow k_i\}$ where $\mathtt{L}, \mathtt{K}$ are linksets. these represent the new live nodes and links, which are made accessible to observers by the extrusion of the new location. Alternatively, this is the information which is added to the observable part of the network representation, Σ_O, as a result of the action.

The formal definition is given in Figure 7, which is expressed in terms of a function $\mathsf{lnk}(n : \mathtt{T}, \Sigma)$, the definition of which is relegated to the Appendix. Intuitively, if n is a channel ($\mathtt{T} = \mathtt{ch}$) or a dead location ($\mathtt{T} = \mathtt{loc}_{\mathtt{d}}[\mathtt{L}]$), $\mathsf{lnk}(n : \mathtt{T}, \Sigma)$ returns the empty link set $\emptyset$. Otherwise, when it is a live location ($\mathtt{T} = \mathtt{loc}_{\mathtt{a}}[\mathtt{C}]$), it constructs the linkset denoting the nodes and links that are made accessible by the addition of the new location $n : \mathtt{loc}_{\mathtt{a}}[\mathtt{C}]$ to the network Σ.

These revised actions give rise to a new bisimulation equivalence over configurations, $\approx$, and we use

$$\Sigma \models M \approx N$$

to mean that the configurations $\Sigma \triangleright M$ and $\Sigma \triangleright N$ are bisimilar.

Table 7. *The derived lts for DπF*

(l-deriv-1)
$$\frac{\Sigma \triangleright N \xrightarrow{\mu} \Sigma' \triangleright N'}{\Sigma \triangleright N \xmapsto{\mu} \Sigma' \triangleright N'} \; \mu \in \{\tau, \mathsf{kill} : l, l \leftrightarrow k\}$$

(l-deriv-2)
$$\frac{\Sigma \triangleright N \xrightarrow{(\tilde{n}:\tilde{\mathrm{T}})l:a!\langle V\rangle} \Sigma' \triangleright N'}{\Sigma \triangleright N \xmapsto{(\tilde{n}:\tilde{\mathrm{L}})l:a!\langle V\rangle} \Sigma' \triangleright N'} \; \tilde{\mathrm{L}} = \mathsf{lnk}(\tilde{n}:\tilde{\mathrm{T}}, \Sigma)$$

(l-deriv-3)
$$\frac{\Sigma \triangleright N \xrightarrow{(\tilde{n}:\tilde{\mathrm{T}})l:a?(V)} \Sigma' \triangleright N'}{\Sigma \triangleright N \xmapsto{(\tilde{n}:\tilde{\mathrm{L}})l:a?(V)} \Sigma' \triangleright N'} \; \tilde{\mathrm{L}} = \mathsf{lnk}(\tilde{n}:\tilde{\mathrm{T}}, \Sigma)$$

Example 6 (Derived bisimulations). Recall that, in Example 4, we had different actions for $\Sigma \triangleright M_2$ and $\Sigma \triangleright N_2$ because $\Sigma \triangleright M_2$ exported k_3 with a link to k_2 and $\Sigma \triangleright N_2$ did not. However, Σ contains only one accessible node, l, and extending it with the completely disconnected new node k_2 does not increase the set of accessible nodes, Σ_O. Furthermore, increasing $\Sigma + k_2 : \emptyset$ with a new node k_3, linked to the inaccessible k_2 (in the case of $\Sigma \triangleright M_2$) or completely disconnected (in the case of $\Sigma \triangleright N_2$), also leads to no increase in the accessible nodes. Correspondingly, the calculations of $\mathsf{lnk}(k_2 : \emptyset, \Sigma)$ and $\mathsf{lnk}(k_3 : \{k_2\}, \Sigma + k_2 : \emptyset)$ both lead to the empty linkset type. Formally, we get the same derived actions

$$\Sigma \triangleright M_2 \xmapsto{(k_2:\emptyset, k_3:\emptyset)l:a!\langle k_2, k_3\rangle} \Sigma + k_2 : \emptyset \; + k_3 : \{k_2\} \triangleright (\nu\, k_1 : \{l, k_2, k_3\})\, l[\![P]\!]$$
$$\Sigma \triangleright N_2 \xmapsto{(k_2:\emptyset, k_3:\emptyset)l:a!\langle k_2, k_3\rangle} \Sigma + k_2 : \emptyset \; + k_3 : \emptyset \triangleright (\nu\, k_1 : \{l, k_2, k_3\})\, l[\![P]\!]$$

Furthermore, if P contains no occurrence of k_1, we can go on to show $\Sigma \models M \approx N$.

On the other hand, if P is $a!\langle k_1\rangle$, the subsequent transitions are:-

$$\Sigma + k_2 : \emptyset \; + k_3 : \{k_2\} \triangleright (\nu\, k_1 : \{l, k_2, k_3\})\, l[\![P]\!] \xmapsto{(k_1:\mathrm{L})l:a!\langle k_1\rangle} \ldots$$
$$\Sigma + k_2 : \emptyset \; + k_3 : \emptyset \triangleright (\nu\, k_1 : \{l, k_2, k_3\})\, l[\![P]\!] \xmapsto{(k_1:\mathrm{K})l:a!\langle k_1\rangle} \ldots$$

where $\mathrm{L}/\mathrm{K} = \{k_2 \leftrightarrow k_3\}$. More specifically, L and K hold information directly related to k_1 such as $k_1 \leftrightarrow l$ together with information related to previously inaccessible nodes such as $k_2 \leftrightarrow k_3$, which has now become accessible as a result of exporting k_1. The first derived action $(k_1 : \mathrm{L})l : a!\langle k_1\rangle$ thus exports the extra (previously hidden) information $k_2 \leftrightarrow k_3$ in L and based on this discrepancy, we have $\Sigma \models M_2 \not\approx N_2$

Revisiting Example 5, the three different actions of M_3^1, M_3^2 and M_3^3 now converge to the same action $M_3^i \xmapsto{(k:\emptyset)l:a!\langle k\rangle} \ldots \triangleright l[\![P]\!]$, hence $\Sigma \models M_3^1 \approx M_3^2 \approx M_3^3$.

The main result of this paper can now be stated:

Theorem 1. *In DπF, $\Sigma \models M \approx N$ if and only if $\Sigma \models M \cong N$*

Proof. (Outline) In one direction, this involves showing that $\approx$ as a relation over configurations satisfies the defining properties of *reduction barbed congruence*. The main problem here is to show that $\approx$ is contextual, and in particular that $\Sigma \models M \approx N$ implies $\Sigma \models M|O \approx N|O$ for every O which only has access to the external (accessible) part of Σ. The overall structure of the proof is similar to the corresponding result in [10], Proposition 12, but the details are more complicated because of the presence of the network. We refer to the full paper, [8], for an elaborate presentation of the proofs.

The essential part of the converse is to show *Definability*, that is for every derived action, relative to a network Σ, there is an observer which only uses the external knowledge of Σ to completely characterises the effect of that action. These observers have already been constructed for simpler languages such as π-calculus, in [11], and Dπ, in [10]. Here the novelty is to be able to characterise the observable effect that actions have on a network.

5 Conclusions and Related Work

We have presented a simple extension of Dπ, in which there is an explicit representation of the state of the underlying network on which processes execute. Our main result is a *fully-abstract* bisimulation equivalence for reasoning about the behaviour of distributed processes in the presence of network configurations with *dead nodes*, *partial connectivity* and *dynamic network failures*. To the best of our knowledge, this is the first time system behaviour in the presence of *link* failure (*permanent* partial accessibility of nodes) has been investigated. It is also the first time that software observation of node and link failure has been investigated in a process calculus setting.

Application and Future Work: Our work is best viewed as a well-founded framework from which numerous variations could be considered such as unidirectional links, ping constructs that are *eventually* correct and transient failure. In our more immediate research, we intend to use our present results to develop a theory of *fault-tolerance* and to apply it to example systems from the literature such as [5]. As it currently stands, our work lends itself well to the study of distributed software that needs to be aware of the *dynamic* computing context in which it is executing; various examples can be drawn from ad-hoc networks, embedded systems and generic routing software. In these settings, the software typically *discovers* new parts of the neighbouring network *at runtime* and *updates* its knowledge of the network state with changes caused by failure.

Related Work: There have been a number of studies on process behaviour in the presence of *permanent node failure* only, amongst them [15], our point of departure. In this work, they developed bisimulation techniques for a distributed variant of CCS with location failure. Our work is also very close to the pioneering work [2,1]; their approach to developing reasoning tools is however quite different from ours. Rather than develop, justify and use bisimulations in the source language of interest, in their case π_l and π_{1l}, they propose a translation into a version of the π-calculus *without* locations, and use reasoning tools on the translations. But most importantly, they do show that for certain π_{1l} terms, it is sufficient to reason on these translations. The closest work to the study of link failure is [6], where distributed Linda-like programs are studied in the presence of connect and disconnect software primitives that dynamically change the accessibility of locations. The connect construct employed is however very powerful and can connect *any* two disconnected sites; this obviates the need for observer restricted views, thereby simplifying immensely the theory. Elsewhere, permanent location failure with hierarchical dependencies have been studied by Fournet *et al* [7]. Berger [3] was the first to study a π-calculus extension that models *transient* location failure with persistent code and communication failures, while Nestmann *et al* [14] employ a tailor-made process calculus to study standard results in distributed systems, such as [5].

References

1. Roberto M. Amadio. An asynchronous model of locality, failure, and process mobility. In *Proc. COORDINATION'97*, volume 1282, pages 374–391, Berlin, Germany, 1997. Springer-Verlag.
2. Roberto M. Amadio and Sanjiva Prasad. Localities and failures. *FSTTCS: Foundations of Software Technology and Theoretical Computer Science*, 14, 1994.
3. Martin Berger. Basic theory of reduction congruence for two timed asynchronous π-calculi. In *Proc. CONCUR'04*, 2004.
4. Luca Cardelli. Wide area computation. In *Proceedings of* 26th *ICALP*, Lecture Notes in Computer Science, pages 10–24. Springer-Verlag, 1999.
5. Tushar Deepak Chandra and Sam Toueg. Unreliable failure detectors for reliable distributed systems. *Journal of the ACM*, 43(2):225–267, March 1996.
6. Rocco De Nicola, Daniele Gorla, and Rosario Pugliese. Basic observables for a calulus for global computing. Technical report, Universita di Firenze, 2004.
7. Cedric Fournet, Georges Gonthier, Jean Jaques Levy, and Remy Didier. A calculus of mobile agents. *CONCUR 96*, LNCS 1119:406–421, August 1996.
8. Adrian Francalanza and Matthew Hennessy. Location and link failure in a distributed π-calculus. Technical report, 2005:01, University of Sussex, 2005.
9. R.J. van Glabbeek and U. Goltz. Equivalence notions for concurrent systems and refinement of actions. In *Proc. MFCS '89*, volume 379 of *lncs*, pages 237–248. Springer-Verlag, 1989.
10. Matthew Hennessy, Massimo Merro, and Julian Rathke. Towards a behavioural theory of access and mobility control in distributed systems. *Theoretical Computer Science*, 322:615–669, 2004.
11. Matthew Hennessy and Julian Rathke. Typed behavioural equivalences for processes in the presence of subtyping. *Mathematical Structures in Computer Science*, 14:651–684, 2004.
12. Matthew Hennessy and James Riely. Resource access control in systems of mobile agents. *Information and Computation*, 173:82–120, 2002.
13. K. Honda and N. Yoshida. On reduction-based process semantics. *Theoretical Computer Science*, 152(2):437–486, 1995.
14. Nestmann, Fuzzati, and Merro. Modeling consensus in a process calculus. In *CONCUR: 14th International Conference on Concurrency Theory*. LNCS, Springer-Verlag, 2003.
15. James Riely and Matthew Hennessy. Distributed processes and location failures. *Theoretical Computer Science*, 226:693–735, 2001.
16. Davide Sangiorgi and David Walker. *The π-calculus*. Cambridge University Press, 2001.

Comparing Two Approaches to Compensable Flow Composition

Roberto Bruni[1], Michael Butler[2], Carla Ferreira[3], Tony Hoare[4], Hernán Melgratti[1], and Ugo Montanari[1]

[1] Dipartimento di Informatica, Università di Pisa, Italy
[2] School of Electronics and Computer Science, University of Southamptom, UK
[3] Department of Computer Science, Technical University of Lisbon, Portugal
[4] Microsoft Research Cambridge, UK

Abstract. Web services composition is an emerging paradigm for the integration of long running business processes, attracting the interest of both Industry, in terms of XML-based standards for business description, and Academy, exploiting process description languages. The key challenging aspects to model are orchestration workflows, choreography of exchanged messages, fault handling, and transactional integrity with compensation mechanisms. Few recent proposals attempted to mitigate the explosion of XML-constructs in ad hoc standards by a careful selection of a small set of primitives related to the above aspects. This papers clarifies analogies and differences between two such recent process description languages: one based on interleaving trace semantics and the other on concurrent traces. We take advantage of their comparison to characterise and relate four different coordination policies for compensating parallel processes. Such policies differ on the way in which the abort of a process influences the execution of sibling processes, and whether compensation is distributed or centralised.

1 Introduction

Orchestration and choreography languages are tailored to the definition of web service composition. Typically, these languages provide, among others, programming primitives for the definition of business transactions, i.e., transactions that may require long periods of time to complete, also called *Long-Running Transactions* (LRTs). Moreover, they may be interactive and hence not able to be check-pointed. Consequently, LRTs cannot be based on locking (as usual for database transactions), but instead they rely on a weaker notion of atomicity based on *compensations* [8]. Compensations are activities programmed ad hoc to recover partial executions of transactional processes.

The existing babel of approaches developed along the years for orchestration and choreography building on WSDL [15] (WSCL [14], WSCI [13], BPML [3], WSFL [10], XLANG [16], BPEL4WS [2]) witnesses the need of languages for service integration with solid theoretical foundations. Several proposals have recently appeared in the literature focused on the formalisation of compensable processes using process calculi. They can be roughly divided into two types: (i) compensable flow composition [6, 5, 7] closer to the spirit of orchestration languages like BPEL4WS, where suitable process algebras are designed from the scratch to describe the possible flow of control among services; and

M. Abadi and L. de Alfaro (Eds.): CONCUR 2005, LNCS 3653, pp. 383–397, 2005.

(ii) interaction based compensations [1, 4, 9, 11], as suitable extensions of well-known name passing calculi, like the π-calculus and join-calculus, for describing transactional choreographies, where each service describes its possible interactions, and the actual composition takes place dynamically, i.e. when services interact.

In this paper we pursue the first approach, i.e., to study the abstract composition of services according to basic workflow shapes (sequential and parallel) and compensable transaction mechanisms (compensable activities, compensation scope, transaction scope, nesting). Nevertheless, we are not aimed at designing a new language but at comparing two main proposals, namely *compensating* CSP (cCSP) [7] and Sagas calculi [5]. Apart from stylistic differences (e.g., the trace semantics of cCSP and the big step SOS semantics of Sagas calculi), this comparison highlights the fact that such proposals account for different compensation policies when handling concurrent processes. First of all, we characterise such policies as the combination of two orthogonal strategies: (i) whether parallel flows are forced to interrupt their executions when a sibling process aborts; and (ii) whether compensation handling is centralised or distributed. The combination of such strategies gives rise to the following four policies:

1. *No interruption and centralised compensation.* All concurrent processes execute until completion, and only then they are compensated for if some abort.
2. *No interruption and distributed compensation.* All parallel flows execute until completion but, if needed, they compensate without waiting the completion of siblings.
3. *Coordinated interruption.* Parallel branches may be stopped when one flow aborts, but the activation of the compensation procedure is handled in a centralised way, i.e., all component flows have to be stopped, and only then the corresponding compensations are executed.
4. *Distributed interruption.* Flows, if needed, are interrupted and then their compensation procedures can be activated independently from the rest of the flows.

We show that all these policies can be defined by following either the cCSP approach or the Sagas style. Moreover, we note that the semantics of original cCSP corresponds to policy (3), while the two original semantics of Sagas Calculi, called Naïve and Revised, follow respectively policies (2) and (4). Finally, we compare the four alternatives (and hence the original semantics of both proposals) by relating the set of traces that each policy associates to a process. In particular, we show that these policies form a partial order of traces, where original cCSP and Naïve Sagas are more restrictive than Revised Sagas, but original cCSP is unrelated to Naïve Sagas.

Structure of the Paper. We start by recalling in § 2 the syntax and semantics of cCSP and Sagas from [5, 7]. Then, we outline the conceptual and stylistic similarities and differences between the two approaches in § 3. The more technical contribution starts in § 4, where we focus on the key aspects for the sequential case, by taking the corresponding fragments of the calculi associated with sequential processes, for which we prove the correspondence of both semantics by means of two straightforward encodings. The different policies implemented by the two approaches emerge in § 5, where we analyse the case of parallel processes in transactions. The formal comparison of compensation policies is summarised in § 6. Finally, in § 7 we draw some conclusions and discuss future work. Due to space limitation most proofs are omitted and some just sketched.

2 Background

In this section we summarise the basics of *Compensating* CSP (cCSP) proposed in [7] and of Sagas calculi from [5]. We focus on simplified versions by leaving out several features present in both proposals, like exception handling and nesting.

2.1 Compensating CSP

The set of cCSP processes is defined by the following grammar:

(STANDARD PROCESSES)

$$P,Q ::= \ A \mid P;Q \mid P|Q \mid SKIP \mid THROW \mid YIELD \mid [PP]$$

(COMPENSABLE PROCESSES)

$$PP,QQ ::= \ P \div Q \mid PP;QQ \mid PP|QQ \mid SKIPP \mid THROWW \mid YIELDD$$

A standard process is either a basic activity A from an alphabet Σ, the sequential composition $P;Q$ of processes, the parallel composition $P|Q$, the empty process *SKIP*, the raise of an interruption *THROW*, the yield to an interruption *YIELD*, or a transaction block $[PP]$. A basic compensable process is a compensation pair $P \div Q$ where P is an atomic process and Q is its compensation. Compensable processes can be composed either in sequence $PP;QQ$ or in parallel $PP|QQ$. The remaining processes are the compensable counterpart of the standard ones.

Figure 1 summarises the trace semantics of cCSP. A trace for a standard process is a string $s\langle\omega\rangle$, where $s \in \Sigma^*$ is said the *observable flow* and $\omega \in \Omega$ is the *final event*, with $\Omega = \{\checkmark, !, ?\}$, with $\Sigma \cap \Omega = \emptyset$ ($\checkmark$ stands for success, ! for fail, and ? for yield). The sequential composition $p;q$ concatenates the observable flows of p and q only when p terminates with success, otherwise it is p. The composition of two concurrent traces $p\langle\omega\rangle||q\langle\omega'\rangle$ corresponds to the set $p|||q$ of all possible interleavings of the observable flows, with final event $\omega\&\omega'$, where & is associative and commutative.

The definition for the traces of standard processes is straightforward. The most interesting one is that of a transaction block $[PP]$. Note that any trace of a compensable process PP is a pair $(p\langle\omega\rangle, p')$, where $p\langle\omega\rangle$ is the forward trace and p' is a compensation trace for p. Then, $[PP]$ selects all successful traces $p\langle\checkmark\rangle$ of PP, and the traces pp', corresponding to failed forward flows $p\langle!\rangle$ followed by their compensations p'.

When composing compensable traces in series, the forward trace corresponds to the sequential composition of the original forward traces, while the compensation trace starts by the second compensation followed by the first one. The parallel composition is defined as all possible interleavings of the forward and the backward flows, separately.

2.2 Sagas Calculi

We report here the two alternative semantics proposed in [5] for parallel Sagas, namely the *naïve* and *revised* versions. The main difference between the two semantics is that the latter allows the interruption of flow executions when a transaction fails. The set of parallel Sagas is given by the following grammar:

COMPOSITION OF STANDARD TRACES

Sequential $\begin{cases} p\langle\checkmark\rangle;q = pq \\ p\langle\omega\rangle;q = p\langle\omega\rangle \text{ when } \omega \neq \checkmark \end{cases}$

Parallel $p\langle\omega\rangle||q\langle\omega'\rangle = \{r\langle\omega\&\omega'\rangle | r \in (p|||q)\}$, where

ω	!	!	!	?	?	✓
ω'	!	?	✓	?	✓	✓
$\omega\&\omega'$	!	!	!	?	?	✓

and $\begin{cases} p|||\langle\rangle = \{p\} \\ \langle\rangle|||q = \{q\} \\ \langle x\rangle p|||\langle y\rangle q = \{\langle x\rangle r | r \in (p|||\langle y\rangle q)\} \cup \{\langle y\rangle r | r \in (\langle x\rangle p|||q)\} \end{cases}$

TRACES OF STANDARD PROCESSES

$$A =_{\text{traces}} \{\langle A, \checkmark\rangle\} \quad \text{for } A \in \Sigma$$
$$P;Q =_{\text{traces}} \{p;q | p \in P \wedge q \in Q\}$$
$$P|Q =_{\text{traces}} \{r | r \in (p||q) \wedge p \in P \wedge q \in Q\}$$
$$[PP] =_{\text{traces}} \{pp' | (p\langle !\rangle, p') \in PP\} \cup \{p\langle\checkmark\rangle | (p\langle\checkmark\rangle, p') \in PP\}$$
$$SKIP =_{\text{traces}} \{\langle\checkmark\rangle\}$$
$$THROW =_{\text{traces}} \{\langle !\rangle\}$$
$$YIELD =_{\text{traces}} \{\langle ?\rangle\}$$

COMPOSITION OF COMPENSABLE TRACES

Sequential $\begin{cases} (p\langle\checkmark\rangle, p');(q,q') = (pq, q';p') \\ (p\langle\omega\rangle, p');(q,q') = (p\langle\omega\rangle, p') \text{ when } \omega \neq \checkmark \end{cases}$

Parallel $(p,p')||(q,q') = \{(r,r') | r \in (p||q) \wedge r' \in (p'||q')\}$

Compensation pair $\begin{cases} p\langle\checkmark\rangle \div q = (p\langle\checkmark\rangle, q) \\ p\langle\omega\rangle \div q = (p\langle\omega\rangle, \langle\checkmark\rangle) \text{ when } \omega \neq \checkmark \end{cases}$

TRACES OF COMPENSABLE PROCESSES

$$P \div Q =_{\text{traces}} \{(\langle ?\rangle, \langle\checkmark\rangle)\} \cup \{p \div q | p \in P \wedge q \in Q\}$$
$$PP;QQ =_{\text{traces}} \{pp;qq | pp \in PP \wedge qq \in QQ\}$$
$$PP|QQ =_{\text{traces}} \{rr | rr \in (pp||qq) \wedge pp \in PP \wedge qq \in QQ\}$$
$$SKIPP =_{\text{traces}} SKIP \div SKIP =_{\text{traces}} \{(\langle ?\rangle, \langle\checkmark\rangle), (\langle\checkmark\rangle, \langle\checkmark\rangle)\}$$
$$THROWW =_{\text{traces}} THROW \div SKIP =_{\text{traces}} \{(\langle ?\rangle, \langle\checkmark\rangle), (\langle !\rangle, \langle\checkmark\rangle)\}$$
$$YIELDD =_{\text{traces}} YIELD \div SKIP =_{\text{traces}} \{(\langle ?\rangle, \langle\checkmark\rangle)\}$$

Fig. 1. Trace semantics of cCSP

$$
\begin{array}{lll}
(\text{STEP}) & X ::= 0 \mid A \mid A \div B \\
(\text{PROCESS}) & P ::= X \mid P;P \mid P|P \\
(\text{SAGA}) & S ::= \{[P]\}
\end{array}
$$

A saga S encloses a process P in a transaction scope. Each step in P corresponds either to an activity A or a compensated activity $A \div B$, where A is the activity of the normal flow and B its compensation. The term 0 represents the inert process, $P;P$ stands for the sequential composition of processes, and $P|P$ for the parallel composition.

To reduce the number of rules, the semantics of Sagas is defined up-to structural congruence over processes given by the following axioms:

$$
\begin{array}{lll}
A \div 0 \equiv A & 0;P \equiv P;0 \equiv P & (P;Q);R \equiv P;(Q;R) \\
P|Q \equiv Q|P & P|0 \equiv P & P|(Q|R) \equiv (P|Q)|R
\end{array}
$$

Moreover, activities are assumed to be named differently. The set of possible results for the execution of a saga is $\mathcal{R} = \{\boxdot, \boxtimes, \boxast\}$, where $\boxdot$ stands for *commit*, $\boxtimes$ for (compensated) *abort*, and $\boxast$ for *abnormal termination* (when the compensation procedure fails). We let $\square$ to range over $\mathcal{R}$. The execution of a sequential saga is described in terms of a context Γ, i.e., a partial function $\Gamma : \mathcal{A} \to \{\boxtimes, \boxdot\}$ that maps any activity to the result obtained with its execution. Activities can only commit or abort (they do not terminate abnormally). A particular function Γ is written $A_1 \mapsto \square_1, \ldots, A_n \mapsto \square_n$, where $A_i \neq A_j$ for all $i \neq j$. (Note that ',' stands for the disjoint union of partial functions).

The semantics of a saga S is given by a relation $\Gamma \vdash S \xrightarrow{\alpha} \square$, which denotes that the execution of S produces $\square$ when the atomic activities behave like Γ. The observation α describes the actual flow of control occurring when executing S under the context Γ. The flow α is a process whose activities have no compensations. The auxiliary relation $\Gamma \vdash \langle P, \beta \rangle \xrightarrow{\alpha} \langle \square, \beta' \rangle$ describes the behaviour of a process P within a saga that already installed the compensation β (but β itself contains no compensation). When P is executed inside a saga, it can either commit, abort, or fail, but additionally, it can change the compensations to β', for instance by installing new activities.

Naïve Semantics. The naïve semantics for a parallel saga is shown in Figure 2(a). Rule (S-ACT) stands for the successful execution of the compensated activity $A \div B$ that installs B in front of β. Rules (S-CMP) and (F-CMP) describe the execution of $A \div B$ when A fails. Both rules activate the compensation β (premises of the rules). In particular, (S-CMP) stands for the successful compensation, while rule (F-CMP) handles the failure of the compensation procedure. Rule (S-STEP) describes the behaviour of a process $P;Q$ when the step P commits. In such case, Q is executed with the compensation installed by P. Rule (A-STEP) handles the case in which $P;Q$ is stopped because P aborts or ends abnormally. Rule (SAGA) states that the execution of a saga $\{[P]\}$ runs P in a thread that initially has no compensations. The rules described above give the semantics for the sequential case, while the remaining rules define the naïve semantics of parallel composition. Rule (S-PAR) deals with the successful execution of both branches, while the remaining rules handle the cases in which at least one branch fails.

Revised Semantics. The revised semantics avoids the unnecessary execution of activities in the forward flow when the saga fails. This is achieved by stopping the execution of the forward flow when some activity fails. For this reason, the execution of a process may also finish with: (i) $\overline{\boxtimes}$, i.e. the execution is forced to compensate and the compensation is successful, and (ii) $\overline{\boxast}$, i.e., the execution is forced to compensate and the compensation procedure fails. The associative and commutative operator $\wedge$ expresses the result obtained by combining the execution of two parallel branches (see Figure 3). Note that $\wedge$ is not defined when one operand is $\boxdot$ and the other is not. In fact, it is not possible for a branch to commit when the other aborts or fails: in $P|Q$ when P can commit but Q aborts, then P is forced to compensate.

For the revised semantics, all rules for the sequential case are as in Figure 2(b), but considering for rule (A-STEP) the side condition $\sigma \in \{\boxtimes, \boxast, \overline{\boxtimes}, \overline{\boxast}\}$), and for rule (SAGA) the side condition $\square \in \{\boxdot, \boxtimes, \boxast\}$. In addition, rules in Figure 2(b) describe the behaviour of concurrent processes. Rule (FORCED-ABT) forces the activation of the compensation before executing P, which will produce a forced termination $\overline{\boxtimes}$ or $\overline{\boxast}$. Rule (S-PAR) is

(ZERO)

$$\Gamma \vdash \langle 0,\beta\rangle \xrightarrow{0} \langle \boxdot,\beta\rangle$$

(S-ACT)

$$A \mapsto \boxdot, \Gamma \vdash \langle A \div B,\beta\rangle \xrightarrow{A} \langle \boxdot, B;\beta\rangle$$

(S-CMP)

$$\frac{\Gamma \vdash \langle \beta,0\rangle \xrightarrow{\alpha} \langle \boxdot,0\rangle}{A \mapsto \boxtimes, \Gamma \vdash \langle A \div B,\beta\rangle \xrightarrow{\alpha} \langle \boxtimes,0\rangle}$$

(F-CMP)

$$\frac{\Gamma \vdash \langle \beta,0\rangle \xrightarrow{\alpha} \langle \boxtimes,0\rangle}{A \mapsto \boxtimes, \Gamma \vdash \langle A \div B,\beta\rangle \xrightarrow{\alpha} \langle \boxast,0\rangle}$$

(S-STEP)

$$\frac{\Gamma \vdash \langle P,\beta\rangle \xrightarrow{\alpha} \langle \boxdot,\beta''\rangle \quad \Gamma \vdash \langle Q,\beta''\rangle \xrightarrow{\alpha'} \langle \Box,\beta'\rangle}{\Gamma \vdash \langle P;Q,\beta\rangle \xrightarrow{\alpha;\alpha'} \langle \Box,\beta'\rangle}$$

(A-STEP)

$$\frac{\Gamma \vdash \langle P,\beta\rangle \xrightarrow{\alpha} \langle \sigma,0\rangle}{\Gamma \vdash \langle P;Q,\beta\rangle \xrightarrow{\alpha} \langle \sigma,0\rangle} \qquad \sigma \in \{\boxtimes,\boxast\}$$

(SAGA)

$$\frac{\Gamma \vdash \langle P,0\rangle \xrightarrow{\alpha} \langle \Box,\beta\rangle}{\Gamma \vdash \{[P]\} \xrightarrow{\alpha} \Box}$$

(S-PAR)

$$\frac{\Gamma \vdash \langle P,0\rangle \xrightarrow{\alpha} \langle \boxdot,\beta'\rangle \quad \Gamma \vdash \langle Q,0\rangle \xrightarrow{\alpha'} \langle \boxdot,\beta''\rangle}{\Gamma \vdash \langle P|Q,\beta\rangle \xrightarrow{\alpha|\alpha'} \langle \boxdot,(\beta'|\beta'');\beta\rangle}$$

(F-PAR-NAÏVE-1)

$$\frac{\Gamma \vdash \langle P,0\rangle \xrightarrow{\alpha} \langle \boxtimes,0\rangle \quad \Gamma \vdash \langle Q,0\rangle \xrightarrow{\alpha'} \langle \boxtimes,0\rangle \quad \Gamma \vdash \langle \beta,0\rangle \xrightarrow{\alpha''} \langle \Box_1,0\rangle}{\Gamma \vdash \langle P|Q,\beta\rangle \xrightarrow{(\alpha|\alpha');\alpha''} \langle \Box_2,0\rangle} \qquad \Box_2 = \begin{cases} \boxtimes \text{ if } \Box_1 = \boxdot \\ \boxast \text{ otherwise} \end{cases}$$

(F-PAR-NAÏVE-2)

$$\frac{\Gamma \vdash \langle P,0\rangle \xrightarrow{\alpha} \langle \boxast,0\rangle \quad \Gamma \vdash \langle Q,0\rangle \xrightarrow{\alpha'} \langle \boxdot,\beta'\rangle \quad \Gamma \vdash \langle \beta',0\rangle \xrightarrow{\alpha''} \langle \Box,0\rangle}{\Gamma \vdash \langle P|Q,\beta\rangle \xrightarrow{\alpha|(\alpha';\alpha'')} \langle \boxast,0\rangle}$$

(F-PAR-NAÏVE-3)

$$\frac{\Gamma \vdash \langle P,0\rangle \xrightarrow{\alpha} \langle \boxast,0\rangle \quad \Gamma \vdash \langle Q,0\rangle \xrightarrow{\alpha'} \langle \sigma,0\rangle}{\Gamma \vdash \langle P|Q,\beta\rangle \xrightarrow{(\alpha|\alpha')} \langle \boxast,0\rangle} \quad \textit{with } \sigma \in \{\boxtimes,\boxast\}$$

(F-PAR-NAÏVE-4A)

$$\frac{\Gamma \vdash \langle P,0\rangle \xrightarrow{\alpha} \langle \boxdot,\beta'\rangle \quad \Gamma \vdash \langle Q,0\rangle \xrightarrow{\alpha'} \langle \boxtimes,0\rangle \quad \Gamma \vdash \langle \beta',0\rangle \xrightarrow{\alpha''} \langle \boxtimes,0\rangle}{\Gamma \vdash \langle P|Q,\beta\rangle \xrightarrow{(\alpha;\alpha'')|\alpha'} \langle \boxast,0\rangle}$$

(F-PAR-NAÏVE-4B)

$$\frac{\Gamma \vdash \langle P,0\rangle \xrightarrow{\alpha} \langle \boxdot,\beta'\rangle \quad \Gamma \vdash \langle Q,0\rangle \xrightarrow{\alpha'} \langle \boxtimes,0\rangle \quad \Gamma \vdash \langle \beta',0\rangle \xrightarrow{\alpha''} \langle \boxdot,0\rangle \quad \Gamma \vdash \langle \beta,0\rangle \xrightarrow{\alpha'''} \langle \Box_1,0\rangle}{\Gamma \vdash \langle P|Q,\beta\rangle \xrightarrow{((\alpha;\alpha'')|\alpha');\alpha'''} \langle \Box_2,0\rangle} \qquad \Box_2 = \begin{cases} \boxtimes \text{ if } \Box_1 = \boxdot \\ \boxast \text{ otherwise} \end{cases}$$

(a) Naïve semantics of parallel Sagas.

(FORCED-ABT)

$$\frac{\Gamma \vdash \langle \beta,0\rangle \xrightarrow{\alpha} \langle \Box_1,0\rangle}{\Gamma \vdash \langle P,\beta\rangle \xrightarrow{\alpha} \langle \Box_2,0\rangle} \quad \Box_2 = \begin{cases} \overline{\boxtimes} \text{ if } \Box_1 = \boxdot \\ \overline{\boxast} \text{ otherwise} \end{cases}$$

(S-PAR)

$$\frac{\Gamma \vdash \langle P,0\rangle \xrightarrow{\alpha} \langle \boxdot,\beta'\rangle \quad \Gamma \vdash \langle Q,0\rangle \xrightarrow{\alpha'} \langle \boxdot,\beta''\rangle}{\Gamma \vdash \langle P|Q,\beta\rangle \xrightarrow{\alpha|\alpha'} \langle \boxdot,(\beta'|\beta'');\beta\rangle}$$

(F-PAR)

$$\frac{\Gamma \vdash \langle P,0\rangle \xrightarrow{\alpha} \langle \sigma_1,0\rangle \quad \Gamma \vdash \langle Q,0\rangle \xrightarrow{\alpha} \langle \sigma_2,0\rangle}{\Gamma \vdash \langle P|Q,\beta\rangle \xrightarrow{\alpha|\alpha'} \langle \sigma_1 \wedge \sigma_2,0\rangle} \qquad \begin{cases} \sigma_1 \in \{\boxast,\overline{\boxast}\} \\ \sigma_2 \in \{\boxtimes,\boxast,\overline{\boxtimes},\overline{\boxast}\} \end{cases}$$

(C-PAR)

$$\frac{\Gamma \vdash \langle P,0\rangle \xrightarrow{\alpha} \langle \sigma_1,0\rangle \quad \Gamma \vdash \langle Q,0\rangle \xrightarrow{\alpha'} \langle \sigma_2,0\rangle \quad \Gamma \vdash \langle \beta,0\rangle \xrightarrow{\gamma} \langle \Box_1,0\rangle}{\Gamma \vdash \langle P|Q,\beta\rangle \xrightarrow{(\alpha|\alpha');\gamma} \langle \sigma_1 \wedge \sigma_2 \wedge \Box_2,0\rangle} \qquad \sigma_1,\sigma_2 \in \{\boxtimes,\overline{\boxtimes}\} \text{ and } \Box_2 = \begin{cases} \overline{\boxtimes} \text{ if } \Box_1 = \boxdot \\ \overline{\boxast} \text{ otherwise} \end{cases}$$

(b) Revised semantics of parallel Sagas.

Fig. 2. Concurrent semantics of Sagas

$\wedge$	$\boxdot$	$\boxtimes$	$\boxast$	$\overline{\boxtimes}$	$\overline{\boxast}$
$\boxdot$	$\boxdot$	—	—	—	—
$\boxtimes$	—	$\boxtimes$	$\boxast$	$\boxtimes$	$\boxast$
$\boxast$	—	$\boxast$	$\boxast$	$\boxast$	$\boxast$
$\overline{\boxtimes}$	—	$\boxtimes$	$\boxast$	$\overline{\boxtimes}$	$\overline{\boxast}$
$\overline{\boxast}$	—	$\boxast$	$\boxast$	$\overline{\boxast}$	$\overline{\boxast}$

Fig. 3. The operator $\wedge$

the same as in the naïve semantics, while the rollback of a branch is handled by (F-PAR) and (C-PAR). Rule (C-PAR) handles the case in which both P and Q are successfully compensated for, while (F-PAR) handles the failure of the compensation procedure.

An interesting aspect on the revised semantics is that rule (SAGA) requires P to end with $\boxdot$, $\boxtimes$ or $\boxast$, but not with forced termination. This implies that a saga aborts if and only if (at least) one activity aborts.

3 cCSP vs Sagas Calculi

In this section we try to enucleate the main conceptual differences between the two approaches and to give an informal account of the underlying different policies for business process design and execution.

Executions of Activities. An activity A is always successful in cCSP. Instead, the execution of activities in Sagas depends on a particular execution context Γ, which allows to evaluate the semantics of a process according to different scenarios.

Aborted Activities vs Programmable Abort. In cCSP the special primitive *THROW* introduces programmable aborts. Instead, the abort of a saga is caused by the abort of an activity in the scenario Γ. Thus, the primitive *THROW* roughly corresponds to a Sagas activity that always fails in any Γ.

Yielding to Interrupt. In cCSP the yielding to interrupt is explicitly programmed by using the special primitive *YIELD*. Instead, in Sagas the yielding to interrupt is wired in the semantics rules and cannot be programmed.

Failed Compensations. Different from Sagas calculi, the abort of and the successful compensation of a transaction block in cCSP is silent to the parent process, i.e., there is no possibility to distinguish this case from the situation in which the forward flow complete successfully. Although not reported in § 2, Sagas calculi provide the primitive **try** S **or** P in [5], which allows to activates P when S aborts and it is compensated successfully.

Interleaving vs Concurrent Traces. The semantics of a cCSP process is given by listing all possible executions that differ on the interleaving of their concurrent activities. Instead, in the Sagas calculi computations are described up-to interleavings. Note that any label α in a reduction denotes a set of possible executions.

Compensation of Parallel Processes. As described in § 1, the most important distinction of both proposal is when defining the compensation for $P|Q$, since they use different compensation policies. This distinction is formalised in § 5

Nesting. The primitive $P \div Q$ of cCSP allow for the nesting of transactions. The Sagas counterpart is called nested Sagas and it is presented in [5], which provides two different kinds of compensations called *default compensations* and *programmed compensation*. The latter is equivalent to the cCSP primitive. The common fragment to cCSP and Sagas we shall discuss does not allow nesting, and therefore only compensable activities $A \div B$ will be considered.

Adequacy of the Semantics. Although not described here, correctness of cCSP semantics is stated in terms of self-cancelling properties. That is, when assuming compensations to be perfect, it is shown that the execution of a transaction is equivalent to its forward flow or to *SKIP*. In Sagas, the meaning of the execution of a transaction is shown by suitable adequacy theorems, which are more precise but less intuitive and more complex to express than the self-cancelling properties.

In the rest of the paper we shall focus on the formal comparison of the sequential and parallel fragments of the two calculi, leaving to future work the treatment of the last two items from the above list (nesting and adequacy). The yielding modality and parallel compensations are discussed in detail in § 5, while all the remaining items are relevant also for the sequential fragment in § 4.

4 The Sequential Case

In this section we focus on the subset of sequential processes and we show that both semantics coincide by giving two encodings. Sequential cCSP is obtained by restricting the syntax of compensable processes as follow.

$$PP, QQ ::= \; A \div B \mid PP;QQ \mid SKIPP \mid THROWW \mid YIELDD$$

Note that instead of having $P \div Q$, we only allow basic activities to be compensated by basic activities. Sequential Sagas is obtained by forbidding the parallel composition of processes $P|P$. We denote by $\mathsf{cCSP}_{\mathsf{seq}}$ the set of sequential cCSP processes, and by $\mathsf{Sagas}_{\mathsf{seq}}$ the set of sequential Sagas processes.

4.1 Encoding $\mathsf{cCSP}_{\mathsf{seq}}$ into $\mathsf{Sagas}_{\mathsf{seq}}$

The main idea is that any process $PP \in \mathsf{cCSP}_{\mathsf{seq}}$ is associated with both a saga process $P \in \mathsf{Sagas}_{\mathsf{seq}}$ and a particular environment $\Gamma \in \nabla$ in which all activities of P commits (∇ stands for the set of all possible environments). Moreover, the *THROWW* primitive is represented by a fresh activity that aborts in Γ. The last subtlety is that all activities in P have to be named differently, for this reason the encoding assures activities in P to have different names. Formally, the encoding is given by the following function

$$[\![\_]\!] : \mathsf{cCSP}_{\mathsf{seq}} \rightarrow \mathsf{Sagas}_{\mathsf{seq}} \times \nabla$$

which is defined in terms of the auxiliary function (used to assure activity names to be different)

$$[\![\text{-}]\!]_{\text{-}} : \mathsf{cCSP_{seq}} \times \mathbb{N}^* \rightarrow \mathsf{Sagas_{seq}} \times \nabla$$

The encoding is defined by letting $[\![PP]\!] \;=\; [\![PP]\!]_0$, with:

$$
\begin{aligned}
[\![A \div B]\!]_\sigma &= A_\sigma \div B_\sigma, \{A_\sigma \mapsto \boxdot, B_\sigma \mapsto \boxdot\}\\
[\![PP_1; PP_2]\!]_\sigma &= P_1; P_2, \Gamma_1 \uplus \Gamma_2 \quad s.t.\ [\![PP_i]\!]_{\sigma.i} = P_i, \Gamma_i \quad \text{for } i = 1,2\\
[\![SKIPP]\!]_\sigma &= [\![YIELDD]\!]_\sigma = 0, \emptyset \qquad [\![THROWW]\!]_\sigma = \mathsf{T}_\sigma, \{\mathsf{T}_\sigma \mapsto \boxtimes\}
\end{aligned}
$$

Notation 1. *We let $\llcorner\alpha\lrcorner$ be obtained from α by removing all the subscripts σ from activities and by considering* 0 *as SKIP. Given a saga S, we let $\mathcal{A}(S) = \{A \mid A \text{ occurs in } S\}$ be the set of its activities and $|S|$ be its* forward flow, *which is obtained by replacing the pattern $A \div B$ by A everywhere in S (i.e., removing all compensations).*

Theorem 4.1. *Let $[\![PP]\!] = P, \Gamma$. If $\Gamma \vdash \{[P]\} \xrightarrow{\alpha} \Box$, then $\llcorner\alpha\lrcorner =_{\mathsf{traces}} [PP]$.*

Proof (Sketch). The proof is by induction on the structure of PP, showing that one of the following conditions holds (for any β and Γ' s.t. $\Gamma' \vdash \langle\beta, 0\rangle \xrightarrow{\beta} \langle\boxdot, 0\rangle$):

- $\Gamma, \Gamma' \vdash \langle P, \beta\rangle \xrightarrow{\alpha} \langle\boxdot, \beta'; \beta\rangle$ and $PP = \{(p\langle\checkmark\rangle, p') | p\langle\checkmark\rangle \in \llcorner\alpha\lrcorner \wedge p' \in \llcorner\beta'\lrcorner\} \cup T$, where T is the set of all yielding traces $(q\langle ?\rangle, q'\langle\checkmark\rangle)$ s.t. q and q' have the same length and q is a prefix of a trace in $\llcorner\alpha\lrcorner$ and q' is prefix of a trace in $\llcorner\beta\lrcorner$.
- $\Gamma, \Gamma' \vdash \langle P, \beta\rangle \xrightarrow{\alpha;\alpha';\beta} \langle\boxtimes, 0\rangle$ s.t. $\mathcal{A}(\alpha) \subseteq \mathcal{A}(|P|) \wedge \mathcal{A}(\alpha') \cap \mathcal{A}(|P|) = \emptyset$, and $PP = \{(p\langle !\rangle, p') | p\langle\checkmark\rangle \in \llcorner\alpha\lrcorner \wedge p' \in \llcorner\alpha'\lrcorner\} \cup T$, where T is defined as before. □

4.2 Encoding $\mathsf{Sagas_{seq}}$ into $\mathsf{cCSP_{seq}}$

Any process $P \in \mathsf{Sagas_{seq}}$ represents a set of processes $PP \in \mathsf{cCSP_{seq}}$, one for any possible environment $\Gamma \in \nabla$. Hence, the encoding is defined as follow:

$$[\![\text{-}]\!]_{\text{-}} : \mathsf{Sagas_{seq}} \times \nabla \rightarrow \mathsf{cCSP_{seq}}$$

$$
\begin{aligned}
[\![0]\!]_\Gamma &= SKIPP & \qquad [\![P; Q]\!]_\Gamma &= [\![P]\!]_\Gamma; [\![Q]\!]_\Gamma\\
[\![A]\!]_{A \mapsto \boxdot, \Gamma} &= A & [\![A]\!]_{A \mapsto \boxtimes, \Gamma} &= THROWW\\
[\![A \div B]\!]_{A \mapsto \boxdot, B \mapsto \boxdot, \Gamma} &= A \div B & [\![A \div B]\!]_{A \mapsto \boxtimes, \Gamma} &= THROWW
\end{aligned}
$$

Note that the encoding for a compensation pair is defined only when the compensation B is an activity that commits, because the fragment of cCSP we are considering does not allow *THROW* in compensation pairs. Hence, we shall account only for contexts Γ that never make a saga to terminate abnormally (by adequacy results in [12, 5]).

Theorem 4.2. *Let Γ be an environment, $P \in \mathsf{Sagas_{seq}}$, and $[\![P]\!]_\Gamma = PP$. If $\Gamma \vdash \{[P]\} \xrightarrow{\alpha} \Box$, then $\llcorner\alpha\lrcorner =_{\mathsf{traces}} [PP]$.*

5 Alternative Semantics for Parallel Compensations

In this section we formally characterise the four compensation policies mentioned in § 1.

Notation 2. *We write* $\mathsf{cCSP}_{\mathsf{par}i}$ *and* $\mathsf{Sagas}_{\mathsf{par}i}$ *to denote the* cCSP *and* Sagas *semantics when considering the strategy* $i = 1,\ldots,4$, *as enumerated in § 1.*

In all remaining sections assume the encoding functions extended as follow

$$[\![PP_1|PP_2]\!]_\sigma = P_1|P_2,\Gamma_1 \uplus \Gamma_2 \quad s.t.\ [\![PP_i]\!]_{\sigma.i} = P_i,\Gamma_i \quad \text{for } i = 1,2$$
$$[\![P|Q]\!]_\Gamma = [\![P]\!]_\Gamma | [\![Q]\!]_\Gamma$$

5.1 No Interruption and Centralised Compensation

The desired behaviour for a parallel transaction when assuming no interruption and centralised compensation can be illustrated with the following law for $\mathsf{cCSP}_{\mathsf{par1}}$:

$$[A \div A' \mid B \div B' \mid THROWW] =_{\mathsf{traces}} (A|B);(A'|B')$$

The forward flow $A|B$ is executed completely before the compensation $A'|B'$. Moreover, all activities in the forward flow are observed even though their execution could be avoided in a clever system (since the transaction will fail anyway).

Trace Semantics. The trace semantics for this case is obtained by redefining the traces of compensation pairs and parallel composition. Since parallel branches do not yield to an interrupt, the definition for a compensation pair is simplified as follow:

$$A \div B =_{\mathsf{traces}} \{p \div q | p \in A \wedge q \in B\} =_{\mathsf{traces}} \{(\langle A,\checkmark\rangle,\langle B,\checkmark\rangle)\}$$

We remove from the original definition the possibility for a compensation pair to yield to an interrupt before executing the forward flow A. On the other hand, the traces for parallel composition $P|Q$ consider only the traces of P and Q that have finished either successfully or with a failure, but not those yielding to an interruption, i.e.,

$$p\langle\omega\rangle||q\langle\omega'\rangle = \{r\langle\omega\&\omega'\rangle | r \in (p|||q) \wedge \omega,\omega' \in \{\checkmark,!\}\}$$

Since we do not allow interruption, *YIELDD* has no effects and, hence, we let $YIELDD =_{\mathsf{traces}} SKIPP =_{\mathsf{traces}} \{(\langle\checkmark\rangle,\langle\checkmark\rangle)\}$. Moreover, $THROWW =_{\mathsf{traces}} \{(\langle !\rangle,\langle\checkmark\rangle)\}$.

SOS Semantics. The SOS semantics for the case of no interruption and centralised compensation is in Figure 4. The main differences with the rules in Figure 2(a) is that the activation of the compensation procedure is left to the rule (SAGA) and not to (F-ACT). Note also that the result for $P|Q$ is given by & (not by $\wedge$ as in § 2.2), which is analogous to the trace semantics.

Correspondence. The following results assure the correspondence between the two semantics.

Theorem 5.1. *Let* $PP \in \mathsf{cCSP}_{\mathsf{par1}}$ *and* $[\![PP]\!] = P,\Gamma$, *with* $P \in \mathsf{Sagas}_{\mathsf{par1}}$. *If* $\Gamma \vdash \{[P]\} \xrightarrow{\alpha} \square$, *then* $\llcorner\alpha\lrcorner =_{\mathsf{traces}} [PP]$.

Theorem 5.2. *Let* Γ *be an environment,* $P \in \mathsf{Sagas}_{\mathsf{par1}}$, *and* $[\![P]\!]_\Gamma = PP$, *with* $PP \in \mathsf{cCSP}_{\mathsf{par1}}$. *If* $\Gamma \vdash \{[P]\} \xrightarrow{\alpha} \square$, *then* $\llcorner\alpha\lrcorner =_{\mathsf{traces}} [PP]$.

(ZERO)

$$\Gamma \vdash \langle 0, \beta \rangle \xrightarrow{0} \langle \boxdot, \beta \rangle$$

(F-ACT)

$$A \mapsto \boxtimes, \Gamma \vdash \langle A \div B, \beta \rangle \xrightarrow{0} \langle \boxtimes, \beta \rangle$$

(A-STEP)

$$\frac{\Gamma \vdash \langle P, \beta \rangle \xrightarrow{\alpha} \langle \boxtimes, \beta' \rangle}{\Gamma \vdash \langle P; Q, \beta \rangle \xrightarrow{\alpha} \langle \boxtimes, \beta' \rangle}$$

(CMT-SAGA)

$$\frac{\Gamma \vdash \langle P, 0 \rangle \xrightarrow{\alpha} \langle \boxdot, \beta \rangle}{\Gamma \vdash \{[P]\} \xrightarrow{\alpha} \boxdot}$$

(FAILED-SAGA)

$$\frac{\Gamma \vdash \langle P, 0 \rangle \xrightarrow{\alpha} \langle \boxtimes, \beta \rangle \quad \Gamma \vdash \langle \beta, 0 \rangle \xrightarrow{\beta'} \langle \boxtimes, 0 \rangle}{\Gamma \vdash \{[P]\} \xrightarrow{\alpha;\beta'} \boxast}$$

(S-ACT)

$$A \mapsto \boxdot, \Gamma \vdash \langle A \div B, \beta \rangle \xrightarrow{A} \langle \boxdot, B; \beta \rangle$$

(S-STEP)

$$\frac{\Gamma \vdash \langle P, \beta \rangle \xrightarrow{\alpha} \langle \boxdot, \beta'' \rangle \quad \Gamma \vdash \langle Q, \beta'' \rangle \xrightarrow{\alpha'} \langle \Box, \beta' \rangle}{\Gamma \vdash \langle P; Q, \beta \rangle \xrightarrow{\alpha;\alpha'} \langle \Box, \beta' \rangle}$$

(PAR)

$$\frac{\Gamma \vdash \langle P, 0 \rangle \xrightarrow{\alpha_1} \langle \Box_1, \beta_1 \rangle \quad \Gamma \vdash \langle Q, 0 \rangle \xrightarrow{\alpha_2} \langle \Box_2, \beta_2 \rangle}{\Gamma \vdash \langle P|Q, \beta \rangle \xrightarrow{\alpha_1|\alpha_2} \langle \Box_1 \& \Box_2, \beta_1|\beta_2; \beta \rangle}$$

where $\boxdot \& \boxdot = \boxdot, \boxdot \& \boxtimes = \boxtimes, and\, \boxtimes \& \boxtimes = \boxtimes$

(ABORTED-SAGA)

$$\frac{\Gamma \vdash \langle P, 0 \rangle \xrightarrow{\alpha} \langle \boxtimes, \beta \rangle \quad \Gamma \vdash \langle \beta, 0 \rangle \xrightarrow{\beta} \langle \boxdot, 0 \rangle}{\Gamma \vdash \{[P]\} \xrightarrow{\alpha;\beta} \boxtimes}$$

Fig. 4. SOS for no interruption and centralised compensation

5.2 No Interruption and Distributed Compensation

As aforementioned, a distributed procedure for compensating parallel branches may allow the execution of activities of the backward flow even when parts of the forward flow are still in execution. As an example, the following law should hold in $\mathsf{cCSP}_{\mathsf{par2}}$ (i.e., by assuming no interruption and distributed compensation):

$$[A \div A' \mid B \div B' \mid THROWW] =_{\mathsf{traces}} A; A'|B; B'$$

Note that the forward flows A and B are executed entirely, but parallel branches are independently compensated for. For example, A' can be executed even before B.

Trace Semantics. As for the previous case, the traces of a compensation pair do not have yielding behaviours, and *SKIPP*, *YIELDD* and *THROWW* are defined analogously. Instead, the parallel composition of traces is as follow

$$\begin{aligned}(p\langle\checkmark\rangle, p')||(q\langle\checkmark\rangle, q') &= \{(r\langle\checkmark\rangle, r'\langle\checkmark\rangle) | r \in (p|||q) \wedge r'\langle\checkmark\rangle \in (p'||q')\} \\ &\quad \cup \{(r\langle ? \rangle, \langle\checkmark\rangle) | r\langle\checkmark\rangle \in (pp'||qq')\} \\ (p\langle\omega\rangle, p')||(q\langle\omega'\rangle, q') &= \{(r\langle\omega\&\omega'\rangle, \langle\checkmark\rangle) | r\langle\checkmark\rangle \in (pp'||qq')\} \quad \text{if} \quad \omega\&\omega' \in \{!, ?\}\end{aligned}$$

Note that the parallel composition of two successful traces contains all the interleavings of the forward flows compensated with the interleavings of the original compensations, and a set of yielding traces. Yielding traces stand for the behaviours of processes $PP|QQ$ in case they are composed in parallel with a process that fails, for instance

$PP|QQ|THROWW$. Finally, the parallel composition when at least one trace ends with ? or ! is defined as the interleavings of the original compensated flows.

SOS Semantics. This case corresponds to the naïve semantics described in § 2.2.

Correspondence. Different from previous cases, for a saga $\{[P]\}$ and an environment Γ there can be several α_i s.t. $\Gamma \vdash \{[P]\} \xrightarrow{\alpha_i} \square$. For instance, consider $P = A_1 \div B_1 | A_2 \div B_2 | F_1$ and $\Gamma = A_1 \mapsto \boxdot, A_2 \mapsto \boxdot, B_1 \mapsto \boxdot, B_2 \mapsto \boxdot, F_1 \mapsto \boxtimes$. Then, it is easy to check that $\Gamma \vdash \{[P]\} \xrightarrow{\alpha_i} \boxtimes$ for $\alpha_1 = A_1;B_1|A_2;B_2$ and $\alpha_2 = (A_1|A_2);(B_1|B_2)$, depending on whether P is considered either as $(A_1 \div B_1 | A_2 \div B_2)|F_1$ or as $A_1 \div B_1 | (A_2 \div B_2 | F_1)$. Nevertheless, note that the result $\square$ is always unique by results in [5].

We note $\Gamma \vdash \{[P]\} \xrightarrow{\kappa} \square$, where $\kappa = \{\alpha_i | \Gamma \vdash \{[P]\} \xrightarrow{\alpha_i} \square\}$ and let

$$\llcorner \kappa \lrcorner =_{\mathsf{traces}} \bigcup_{\alpha_i \in \kappa} \llcorner \alpha_i \lrcorner$$

Theorem 5.3. *Let $PP \in \mathsf{cCSP}_{\mathsf{par2}}$ and $[\![PP]\!] = P, \Gamma$, with $P \in \mathsf{Sagas}_{\mathsf{par2}}$. If $\Gamma \vdash \{[P]\} \xrightarrow{\kappa} \square$, then $\llcorner \kappa \lrcorner =_{\mathsf{traces}} [PP]$.*

Theorem 5.4. *Let Γ be an environment, $P \in \mathsf{Sagas}_{\mathsf{par2}}$, and $[\![P]\!]_\Gamma = PP$, with $PP \in \mathsf{cCSP}_{\mathsf{par2}}$. If $\Gamma \vdash \{[P]\} \xrightarrow{\kappa} \square$, then $\llcorner \kappa \lrcorner =_{\mathsf{traces}} [PP]$.*

5.3 Interruption and Centralised Compensation

When considering interruption, the main idea is to avoid the execution of steps by stopping the forward flow as soon as an activity fails. Nevertheless, in a distributed setting we cannot expect processes to be stopped immediately. The law we would like to prove when using this strategy is the following.

$$[A \div A' \mid B \div B' \mid THROWW] =_{\mathsf{traces}} SKIP \cup (A;A') \cup (B;B') \cup (A|B);(A'|B')$$

The first three terms show that parallel branches can be aborted even before starting their execution when one process fails (i.e., *THROWW*). Instead, the last term of the right hand side means that compensation is centralised.

Trace Semantics. The case of interruption and centralised compensation corresponds to the original proposal of the trace semantics summarised in § 2.1.

SOS Semantics. The SOS semantics for this strategy is obtained by adding forced termination to the rules corresponding to the policy of no interruption and centralised compensation (shown in Figure 4). In order to achieve that, rules in Figure 4 are extended with the additional rule

$$(\text{FORCED-ABT}) \qquad \Gamma \vdash \langle P, \beta \rangle \xrightarrow{0} \langle \overline{\boxdot}, \beta \rangle$$

which introduces forced termination. In this case, it is enough to consider one result, which we note $\overline{\boxdot}$. Moreover we extend the definition of & used in rule (PAR), as follow $\overline{\boxdot} \& \overline{\boxdot} = \overline{\boxdot}$, $\overline{\boxdot} \& \boxdot = \overline{\boxdot}$, $\overline{\boxdot} \& \boxtimes = \boxtimes$. (Note that this definition makes the operator & isomorphic in both the trace and the SOS semantics).

Correspondence. As for the previous cases, we have the following correspondence results for $\mathsf{cCSP}_{\mathsf{par3}}$ and $\mathsf{Sagas}_{\mathsf{par3}}$

Theorem 5.5. *Let $PP \in \mathsf{cCSP}_{\mathsf{par3}}$ and $[\![PP]\!] = P, \Gamma$, with $P \in \mathsf{Sagas}_{\mathsf{par3}}$. If $\Gamma \vdash \{[P]\} \xrightarrow{\kappa} \Box$, then $\llcorner\kappa\lrcorner =_{\mathsf{traces}} [PP]$.*

Theorem 5.6. *Let Γ be an environment, $P \in \mathsf{Sagas}_{\mathsf{par3}}$, and $[\![P]\!]_\Gamma = PP$, with $PP \in \mathsf{cCSP}_{\mathsf{par3}}$. If $\Gamma \vdash \{[P]\} \xrightarrow{\kappa} \Box$, then $\llcorner\kappa\lrcorner =_{\mathsf{traces}} [PP]$.*

5.4 Interruption and Distributed Compensation

This policy can be illustrated by the following equality in $\mathsf{cCSP}_{\mathsf{par4}}$:

$$[A \div A'|B \div B'|THROWW] =_{\mathsf{traces}} SKIP \cup (A;A') \cup (B;B') \cup (A;A')|(B;B')$$

The difference with the policy reported in § 5.3 relies in the last term of the summation in the right hand side of the equality. In fact, the last term of the above equality shows that the compensation is handled in a distributed way. The remaining terms stand for the cases in which the forward flow is stopped before completion.

Trace Semantics. The trace semantics for this policy is obtained from the original one (see Figure 1) by changing the definition for the parallel composition of traces as in § 5.2, i.e.,

$$\begin{aligned}(p\langle\checkmark\rangle, p')||(q\langle\checkmark\rangle, q') &= \{(r\langle\checkmark\rangle, r'\langle\checkmark\rangle) | r \in (p|||q) \wedge r'\langle\checkmark\rangle \in (p'||q')\}\\ &\quad \cup\{(r\langle ?\rangle, \langle\checkmark\rangle) | r\langle\checkmark\rangle \in (pp'||qq')\}\\ (p\langle\omega\rangle, p')||(q\langle\omega'\rangle, q') &= \{(r\langle\omega\&\omega'\rangle, \langle\checkmark\rangle) | r\langle\checkmark\rangle \in (pp'||qq')\} \quad \text{if} \quad \omega\&\omega' \in \{!, ?\}\end{aligned}$$

SOS Semantics. This strategy corresponds to the original revised semantics of parallel Sagas (Figure 2(b)).

Correspondence. The following results state the correspondence between the trace and SOS semantics for this policy.

Theorem 5.7. *Let $PP \in \mathsf{cCSP}_{\mathsf{par4}}$ and $[\![PP]\!] = P, \Gamma$, with $P \in \mathsf{Sagas}_{\mathsf{par4}}$. If $\Gamma \vdash \{[P]\} \xrightarrow{\kappa} \Box$, then $\llcorner\kappa\lrcorner =_{\mathsf{traces}} [PP]$.*

Theorem 5.8. *Let Γ be an environment, $P \in \mathsf{Sagas}_{\mathsf{par3}}$, and $[\![P]\!]_\Gamma = PP$, with $PP \in \mathsf{cCSP}_{\mathsf{par3}}$. If $\Gamma \vdash \{[P]\} \xrightarrow{\kappa} \Box$, then $\llcorner\kappa\lrcorner =_{\mathsf{traces}} [PP]$.*

6 Relation of the Proposed Semantics

The four strategies presented in § 5 correspond to alternative implementations for the compensation mechanism. In this section, we analyse the relation among such policies. The following result states the relation among the traces of a transaction $[PP]$ accordingly to the four possible semantics for compensating parallel processes.

Theorem 6.1. *Let $[PP]$ be a parallel* cCSP *process, and let $[PP]_{\mathsf{cCSP}_{\mathsf{par}i}}$ denote the traces of $[PP]$ when considering the strategy $i = 1,...,4$. Then, the four trace semantics satisfy the following diagram*

$$\begin{array}{lccccl} & [PP]_{\mathsf{cCSP}_{\mathsf{par1}}} & \xrightarrow{\subseteq} & [PP]_{\mathsf{cCSP}_{\mathsf{par2}}} & & \text{Naïve Sagas} \\ & \downarrow\subseteq & & \downarrow\subseteq & & \\ \text{Original cCSP} & [PP]_{\mathsf{cCSP}_{\mathsf{par3}}} & \xrightarrow{\subseteq} & [PP]_{\mathsf{cCSP}_{\mathsf{par4}}} & & \text{Revised Sagas} \end{array}$$

Proof (Sketch). The proof for any inclusion follows by showing (by induction on the structure of PP) that any trace in $PP_{\mathsf{cCSP}_{\mathsf{par}i}}$ corresponds with a trace in $PP_{\mathsf{cCSP}_{\mathsf{par}j}}$. For instance, that

- $(p\langle\checkmark\rangle, p') \in PP_{\mathsf{cCSP}_{\mathsf{par1}}} \quad\Rightarrow\quad (p\langle\checkmark\rangle, p') \in PP_{\mathsf{cCSP}_{\mathsf{par2}}}$
- $(p\langle!\rangle, p'p'') \in PP_{\mathsf{cCSP}_{\mathsf{par1}}} \quad\Rightarrow\quad (pp'\langle!\rangle, p'') \in PP_{\mathsf{cCSP}_{\mathsf{par2}}}$. □

Note that the above diagram does not include $[PP]_{\mathsf{cCSP}_{\mathsf{par2}}} \subseteq [PP]_{\mathsf{cCSP}_{\mathsf{par3}}}$ nor $[PP]_{\mathsf{cCSP}_{\mathsf{par3}}} \subseteq [PP]_{\mathsf{cCSP}_{\mathsf{par2}}}$. In fact, it is easy to check that there are processes $[PP]$ for which none of them holds. For instance, consider $P = [A \div A'; B \div B' | C \div C' | THROWW]$. Note that $p = \langle A, B, B', A', C, C', \checkmark\rangle \in P_{\mathsf{cCSP}_{\mathsf{par2}}}$, but $p \notin P_{\mathsf{cCSP}_{\mathsf{par3}}}$, since compensations A' and B' take place before C. On the other hand, note that $q = \langle\checkmark\rangle \in P_{\mathsf{cCSP}_{\mathsf{par3}}}$, but $q \notin P_{\mathsf{cCSP}_{\mathsf{par2}}}$ since the forward flow is required to execute until termination.

The above result makes incomparable the semantics of original cCSP and naïve Sagas. On the other hand, it shows that the revised version of Sagas allows more traces than cCSP, and hence it is less restrictive on which are the acceptable executions of processes. Nevertheless, the distributed compensation mechanism of $\mathsf{cCSP}_{\mathsf{par4}}$ includes a "guessing mechanisms" that allows branches on the forward flow to compensate even before an activity aborts. For instance, $[A \div A'; THROWW | B \div B']$ has the trace $p = \langle B; B'; A; A'\rangle$. Since A is executed after B, p stands for an execution in which the branch $B \div B'$ starts its compensation before $THROWW$ is reached. Although this is an acceptable and valid execution of the above transaction, it is hard to imagine a plausible implementation of such a mechanism, which suggests that a more realistic policy relies in between cCSP and revised Sagas.

7 Final Remarks

We have compared two recent formal approaches to the modelling of compensable flow composition, that have been proposed independently in [5, 7]. For the sequential case we have shown that the two frameworks essentially coincide by providing fully abstract encodings. For the parallel case we have observed that the two approaches followed different compensation policies, and that up to four different choices were possible for activating compensations in parallel branches. We have shown that each alternative can be formalised by adjusting the semantics of the two calculi. Finally we have related all different policies by showing that they form a partial order of trace models.

Our more ambitious research programme is to extend the comparison to deal with more advanced features, like nesting, joint transactions, message passing and action refinement. To this end, the research presented here has been valuable in deepening our understanding of the phenomenon of a compensable parallel transaction and the range of available design options.

Acknowledgements. Research supported by the project HPRN-CT-2002-00275 SEGRAVIS. We thank Microsoft Research (Cambridge) for hosting two workshops at which the ideas behind the paper were initiated and discussed. We also thank the anonymous referees for their helpful comments.

References

1. L. Bocchi, C. Laneve, and G. Zavattaro. A calculus for long-running transactions. In E. Najm, U. Nestmann, and P. Stevens, editors, *Proceedings of FMOODS 2003, 6th IFIP International Conference on Formal Methods for Open-Object Based Distributed Systems*, volume 2884 of *Lect. Notes in Comput. Sci.*, pages 124–138. Springer Verlag, 2003.
2. BPEL Specification (v.1.1). `http://www.ibm.com/developerworks/library/ws-bpel`.
3. Business Process Modeling Language (BPML). `http://www.bpmi.org/BPML.htm`.
4. R. Bruni, H. Melgratti, and U. Montanari. Nested commits for mobile calculi: extending Join. In J.-J. Lévy, E. Mayr, and J. Mitchell, editors, *Proceedings of the 3rd IFIP-TCS 2004, 3rd IFIP Intl. Conference on Theoretical Computer Science*, pages 569–582. Kluwer Academic Publishers, 2004.
5. R. Bruni, H. Melgratti, and U. Montanari. Theoretical foundations for compensations in flow composition languages. In *Proceedings of POPL 2005, 32nd ACM SIGPLAN-SIGACT Symposium on Principles of Programming Languages*, pages 209–220. ACM Press, 2005.
6. M. Butler and C. Ferreira. An operational semantics for StAC, a language for modelling long-running business transactions. In R. De Nicola, G. Ferrari, and G. Meredith, editors, *Proceedings of Coordination 2004*, volume 2949 of *Lect. Notes in Comput. Sci.*, pages 87–104. Springer Verlag, 2004.
7. M. Butler, T. Hoare, and C. Ferreira. A trace semantics for long-running transactions. In A. Abdallah, C.B. Jones, and J. Sanders, editors, *Proceedings of 25 Years of CSP*, volume 3525 of *Lect. Notes in Comput. Sci.*, pages 133–150. Springer Verlag, 2005.
8. H. Garcia-Molina and K. Salem. Sagas. In U. Dayal and I.L. Traiger, editors, *Proceedings of the ACM Special Interest Group on Management of Data Annual Conference*, pages 249–259. ACM Press, 1987.
9. C. Laneve and G. Zavattaro. Foundations of web transactions. In V. Sassone, editor, *Proceedings of FoSSaCS 2005, 8th International Conference on Foundations of Software Science and Computational Structures*, volume 3441 of *Lect. Notes in Comput. Sci.*, pages 282–298. Springer Verlag, 2005.
10. F. Leymann. WSFL Specification (v.1.0). `http://www-306.ibm.com/software/solutions/webservices/pdf/WSFL.pdf`, May 2001.
11. M. Mazzara and R. Lucchi. A framework for generic error handling in business processes. In M. Bravetti and G. Zavattaro, editors, *Proceedings of WS-FM 2004, 1st International Workshop on Web Services and Formal Methods*, 2004. To appear as ENTCS.
12. H. Melgratti. *Models and Languages for Global Computing Transaction*. PhD thesis, Computer Science Department, University of Pisa, 2005. Submitted.
13. Web Service Choreography Interface (WSCI) 1.0. `http://www.w3.org/TR/wsci`.
14. Web Services Conversation Language (WSCL) 1.0. `http://www.w3.org/TR/wscl10/`.
15. Web Service Description Language (WSDL). `http://www.w3.org/TR/wsdl`.
16. Web Services for Business Process Design (XLANG). `http://www.gotdotnet.com/team/xml_wsspecs/xlang-c/default.htm`.

Transactions in RCCS

Vincent Danos[1] and Jean Krivine[2,*]

[1] CNRS & Université Paris 7
[2] INRIA Rocquencourt & Université Paris 6
Jean.Krivine@inria.fr

Abstract. We propose a formalisation of the notion of transaction, using a variant of CCS, RCCS, that distinguishes reversible and irreversible actions, and incorporates a distributed backtrack mechanism. Any weakly correct implementation of a transaction in CCS, once embedded in RCCS, automatically obtains a correct one. We show examples where this method allows for a more concise implementation and a simpler proof of correctness.

1 Introduction

Transactions involve participants trying to reach for an agreement. Participants don't have usually a complete view of their context, nor of its possible evolutions. All they can do, is engage in a series of interactions, and decide, based on what they learn from this exploration, whether their requirements are met, and whether they want to commit themselves to the transaction.

A basic condition to meet in the design of a transaction is that whenever there is a solution, some evolution may find it *(i)*. This is intuitively saying that, given a complete view of the system, it is possible to schedule participants so as to reach any extant solution. One also has to ask that participants don't come to wrong decisions, actually committing to a transaction, while their requirements are not met *(ii)*, and in addition one wants participants to always find a agreement when one is possible *(iii)*.

In designing a transaction, it is usually a relatively easy task to cater for conditions *(i)* and *(ii)*. Why is this ? Because one has a pretty firm grasp of the local knowledge of any participant, it becomes therefore easy to verify, at any time, whether this local knowledge is compatible with the participant requirements. In essence, one asks that the exploration process inherent to the transaction makes no mistakes and knows how to tell a solution when it finds one.

It seems much harder, however, to deal with condition *(iii)*, because potential deadlocks, or more generally undue partial commitments, resulting from the exploration process, are hard to detect and to prevent. In examples, condition *(iii)* is often met by allowing some controlled form of backtracking, so that the transaction never gets stuck in an exploration. We set up here a framework where conditions *(i)* and *(ii)* are clearly separated from condition *(iii)*, and prove that the latter can indeed always be successfully handled by backtracking.

* Corresponding author.

M. Abadi and L. de Alfaro (Eds.): CONCUR 2005, LNCS 3653, pp. 398–412, 2005.

Specifically, we propose a formalisation of transactions using RCCS, a variant of CCS [1], based on a distinction between reversible and irreversible actions [2]. It is often a delicate point to justify one's choice of a formalism, however, we have here two good reasons for ours. First, CCS has been widely adopted as a basis for analysing concurrent systems. Second our variant of CCS provides exactly what we need here, namely a controlled and distributed backtracking mechanism. Importantly, the syntax of RCCS stays close to CCS, since backtracking stays hidden from the programmer, except for the distinction between reversible and irreversible actions. Thus, our choice seems to provide a suitable testbed to prove the result we have in mind. We are also confident that the idea, once well understood in CCS, will extend to π-calculus [3].

A transactional system is specified simply as a labelled transition system where each completed transaction is represented as an atomic transition. An RCCS process is then said to be a correct implementation if it is weakly bisimilar to its specification, where only irreversible actions —corresponding to commits in the transaction— are observable. In examples, the notion of participant is always clear, and so we have not made it a part of the current formalisation, even though it fixes a minimum level of distribution for the implementation.

With our formalisation in place, condition *(i)* translates as a weak simulation property restricted to causal CCS traces, while *(ii)* translates naturally into a 'no bad states' condition. None of these conditions enforces the absence of deadlocks. We show that whenever a CCS process checks *(i)* and *(ii)*, the corresponding RCCS process also checks *(iii)*, and as a result is weakly bisimilar to the specification. A crucial point is that the RCCS backtracking mechanism only reaches states that could be reached forwardly, else condition *(ii)* would be no longer satisfied, and reaches them all, else condition *(iii)* would no longer be satisfied either [2]. The significance of the result lies in that it allows sometimes both for a more concise code, since all the needed backtracking stays implicit, and for a simpler correctness proof, since there is less to prove.

The paper is organised as follows. First we recall briefly the definitions of RCCS, then we turn to the study of causal computation traces, which we characterise via a syntactic relation on their labels. We then state our formalisation of the implementation of a transactional system, and move on to the proof of our main result, based on the use of causal traces. We also show that causal traces are necessary. The paper ends with some examples, and a discussion of the merits of the method, and of the various trade-offs one can imagine between a concise code, an easy proof and an efficient implementation. Related work and perspectives are discussed in the conclusion.

2 RCCS

2.1 Syntax and Transitions

The syntax of RCCS starts with a distinction between two kinds of actions: *reversible* actions will be written τ, a, $\bar{a}$, ..., while *irreversible* ones will be written $\underline{\tau}$, $\underline{a}$, $\underline{\bar{a}}$, ..., and it is understood that these subsets are disjoint. The rest of the syntax is given in Figure 1.

Processes of the form $m \triangleright p$ are called *threads*, where m is a memory used to keep track of the thread past interactions. Memories are organised as stacks, and we will write $\leq$ for the associated *prefix ordering*, and $<$ for the strict version. We write $m \in r$, when m is the memory of some thread in r, $m \lessdot r$ when there is an $m' \in r$ such that $m \leq m'$, and $\mathcal{M}(r)$ for the set of memories m such that $m \lessdot r$. Together with the syntax one has a set of rules for deriving transitions,

$$\begin{array}{llr} m & := \langle\rangle,\ \langle 1\rangle.m,\ \langle 2\rangle.m,\ \langle *, \alpha, p\rangle.m,\ \langle m, \alpha, p\rangle.m,\ \langle\circ\rangle.m & \text{Memories} \\ r & := m \triangleright p,\ r \mid r,\ (a)r & \text{RCCS processes} \\ p & := 0,\ \sum \alpha_i.p_i,\ p \mid p,\ (a)p & \text{CCS processes} \end{array}$$

Fig. 1. RCCS Syntax

each of which bears a label $\mu : \zeta$. The first component, μ, is either a memory, in which case one says the transition is *unary*, or a pair of memories, in which case one says the transition is *binary*. The second component, ζ, either reads α, in which case one says the transition is *forward*, or α_*, in which case α has to be reversible, and one speaks of a *backward* transition.

We write μ_t for the memories labelling a given transition t, indicating the threads responsible for the transition. Thread transitions and synchronisation rules are given in Figure 2.

$$\text{act}\ \frac{}{m \triangleright \alpha.p + q \xrightarrow{m:\alpha} \langle *, \alpha, q\rangle \cdot m \triangleright p} \qquad \frac{}{\langle *, \alpha, q\rangle \cdot m \triangleright p \xrightarrow{m:\alpha_*} m \triangleright a.p + q}\ \text{act}_*$$

$$\underline{\text{act}}\ \frac{}{m \triangleright \underline{\alpha}.p + q \xrightarrow{m:\underline{\alpha}} \langle\circ\rangle \cdot m \triangleright p}$$

$$\text{com}\ \frac{r \xrightarrow{m_1:\alpha} r' \qquad s \xrightarrow{m_2:\bar{\alpha}} s'}{r \mid s \xrightarrow{m_1,m_2:\tau} r'_{m_2@m_1} \mid s'_{m_1@m_2}} \qquad \frac{r \xrightarrow{m_1:\alpha_*} r' \qquad s \xrightarrow{m_2:\bar{\alpha}_*} s'}{r_{m_2@m_1} \mid s_{m_1@m_2} \xrightarrow{m_1,m_2:\tau_*} r' \mid s'}\ \text{com}_*$$

$$\underline{\text{com}}\ \frac{r \xrightarrow{m_1:\underline{\alpha}} r' \qquad s \xrightarrow{m_2:\underline{\bar{\alpha}}} s'}{r \mid s \xrightarrow{m_1,m_2:\underline{\tau}} r' \mid s'}$$

Fig. 2. Thread transitions and Synchronisations

The first two rules act and act_* concern reversible actions. The corresponding memory $\langle *, \alpha, q\rangle.m$ is called a *semi-synch*. The yet unknown partner, written $*$, may be identified later in the synchronisation rules com and com_*. Specifically, given a process r and memories m_1, m_2, we write $r_{m_2@m_1}$ for the process obtained by replacing in r all semi-synchs $\langle *, \alpha, q\rangle.m_1$ with $\langle m_2, \alpha, q\rangle.m_1$, which is then called a *synch*.

$$\text{par-l}\ \frac{r \xrightarrow{\mu:\zeta} r'}{r \mid s \xrightarrow{\mu:\zeta} r' \mid s} \qquad \frac{r \xrightarrow{\mu:\zeta} r'}{s \mid r \xrightarrow{\mu:\zeta} s \mid r'}\ \text{par-r}$$

$$\text{res}\ \frac{r \xrightarrow{\mu:\zeta} r' \quad \zeta \not\ni a}{(a)r \xrightarrow{\mu:\zeta} (a)r'} \qquad \frac{r_1 \equiv r \xrightarrow{\mu:\zeta} r' \equiv r'_1}{r_1 \xrightarrow{\mu:\zeta} r'_1}\ \equiv$$

Fig. 3. Contextual transitions

Note that in a synch, the memory of a thread is used as its name. We will introduce early in the next section a *coherence* condition on processes which makes sure that this naming scheme stays injective. As a consequence, once a thread s with memory m_1 has used com, its memory is instantiated, and the resulting $s_{m_1 @ m_2}$ cannot undo the synchronisation alone, it has to use rule com_*. This will be referred to as the *lock effect.*

The third transition rule, act concerns irreversible actions. In this case there is no need to remember anything, so one uses instead a placeholder $\langle\circ\rangle$. For the same reason, there is no rule inverse to the irreversible synchronisation com, and no longer a need to instantiate r' and s' in the right hand side of the rule. When all actions are taken to be irreversible, RCCS essentially becomes CCS.

Contextual rules are given in Figure 3. These are as usual, except for ($\equiv$) which uses the congruence generated by the following rules:

$$m \triangleright (p \mid q) \equiv \langle 1\rangle.m \triangleright p \mid \langle 2\rangle.m \triangleright q \tag{1}$$

$$m \triangleright (a)p \equiv (a)\, m \triangleright p \tag{2}$$

where the last rule assumes a doesn't occur in m. Process summation is taken to be associative and commutative, and CCS processes are taken up to α-equivalence. Perhaps unusually, and because memories are using the syntactic product structure to record forks, as can be seen from the first clause of $\equiv$'s definition, the parallel product is not taken to be commutative or associative.

Memories of the form $\langle i\rangle.m$ with $i \in \{1, 2\}$ will be called *forks.* Just as in the case of a synch, there is a lock effect, as it is impossible for a thread to backtrack a fork alone.

2.2 Traces and Equivalence

Define a *trace* to be a sequence of composable transitions. Say a trace is *forward* if it only uses forward transitions. Write $r \rightarrow^\star s$ when there is a trace from r to s in RCCS, and likewise $p \rightarrow^\star q$ when there is a trace from p to q in CCS.

A first thing we can say is that our calculus is a decoration of CCS. Indeed, one has the following forgetful map ϕ from RCCS to CCS:

$$\begin{aligned} \phi(m \triangleright p) &= p \\ \phi(r \mid s) &= \phi(r) \mid \phi(s) \\ \phi((a)r) &= (a)\phi(r) \end{aligned}$$

The forgetful map ϕ is easily seen to extend to traces:[3]

Proposition 1. *If $p \rightarrow^\star q$ and $\phi(r) = p$, then $r \rightarrow^\star s$ for some s such that $q = \phi(s)$.*

Conversely, the backtracking mechanism is consistent in the following sense:

Proposition 2. *If $\langle\rangle \triangleright p \rightarrow^\star r$, then $p \rightarrow^\star \phi(r)$.*

One also has that, when all actions are reversible, any two traces with same source and target are *equivalent*, in the sense that one can be rearranged so as to obtain the other by commuting concurrent actions.[4]

As said, when all actions are irreversible in r, it behaves as a CCS process, while in the opposite case, when all actions are reversible, the set of processes reachable from r is invariant along any trace. Interesting behaviours arise in the middle ground, when some, but not all actions are reversible. This is where one typically finds transactional processes, and to understand them, we need first to understand causal dependencies between transitions, and how these reflect as a partial order over memories. This is what we do now.

3 Causality

Thereafter, we will assume all processes to be coherent, in the sense that their memories do reflect some past. Specifically, we define a process r to be *coherent* if for some p, $\langle\rangle \triangleright p \rightarrow^* r$. As a consequence, no memory $m \sqsubseteq r$ occurs twice in r, and for any transition t, μ_t can be safely handled with set-based notations. The restriction to coherent processes also has the following consequence:

Lemma 1. *Backtracking is noetherian and confluent.*

Proof. Any backward transition decreases the total memory size, so backward traces are bounded, and it is enough to prove local confluence to conclude to the second point. This in turn, downs to proving that any two distinct backward transitions t, t' with the same source are concurrent, which means $\mu_t \cap \mu_{t'}$ is empty. This is indeed the case, since the lock effect applies, because naming is injective on coherent processes. □

Further consequences of the coherence requirement are that: $\mathcal{M}(r)$ is closed under the *mating relation*, $\sim$, here defined as the least reflexive relation over memories such that:

---

[3] As was pointed out by the referees, α-conversion is sometimes needed. Suppose one wants to simulate in RCCS the reduction of $a.(a)(a \mid \bar{a})$:

$$\langle\rangle \triangleright a.(a)(a \mid \bar{a}) \rightarrow \langle *, a\rangle \triangleright (a)(a \mid \bar{a}) \equiv \langle *, a\rangle \triangleright (b)(b \mid \bar{b}) \equiv (b)\langle *, a\rangle \triangleright (b \mid \bar{b}) \equiv$$
$$(b)(\langle 0\rangle\langle *, a\rangle \triangleright b \mid \langle 1\rangle\langle *, a\rangle \triangleright \bar{b}) \rightarrow (b)(\langle\langle 1\rangle\langle *, a\rangle, b\rangle\langle 0\rangle\langle *, a\rangle \triangleright 0 \mid \langle\langle 0\rangle\langle *, a\rangle, \bar{b}\rangle\langle 1\rangle\langle *, a\rangle \triangleright 0)$$

as one sees, this is only possible if α-conversion is used in the second step, else the side-condition in the congruence rule (2) would forbid the next one.

[4] Further details can be found in the paper where these basic properties of RCCS were established [2].

— $\langle m, \alpha, p\rangle.m' \sim \langle m', \bar{\alpha}, q\rangle.m$
— $\langle i\rangle.m \sim \langle j\rangle.m$

and that mates are *co-scoped*, meaning if m occurs in the scope of some restriction (x), and x occurs in m, then m's mate, if any, is in the scope of the same (x). Note that $\sim$ is an equivalence relation over $\mathcal{M}(r)$, each class having either two elements in the case of synchs and forks, or one in the case of semi-synchs.

3.1 Causal Traces

There is a natural notion of causality between transitions in a same trace, which corresponds to structural dependency in CCS [4,5].

Definition 1. *Let $t_1; \ldots; t_n$ be a forward trace. One says t_i is a direct cause of t_k, if there is $m_i \in \mu_{t_i}$ and $m_k \in \mu_{t_k}$ such that $m_i < m_k$. The causality relation $<$ over transitions occurring in a same trace σ is the transitive closure of the direct cause relation.*

One says a trace σ is in *t-causal form* if $\sigma = \sigma_0; t; \sigma_1$ and for all $t' \in \sigma_0$, $t' < t$. When t is the last transition in σ, one simply says σ is in *causal form*.

Up to equivalence, any forward trace can be put in causal form with respect to any transition:

Lemma 2. *Let σ be a forward trace, and let t be a transition in σ, there exists an equivalent trace σ' such that σ' is in t-causal form.*

Proof. It is enough to prove the statement when σ ends with t. Let t' be the rightmost transition in σ, distinct from t, and not causing t, if any. This t' commutes to its successor in σ, say t''. Indeed, if not, then by definition it causes t'', and then by transitivity, also t. One concludes by an easy induction. □

3.2 Locked Memories

Let us for a moment put aside the notion of causality between transitions explained above. An irreversible action taken by a process may have a domino-effect on some other memories, and prevent them from being undone.

Let us say that a memory m in $\mathcal{M}(r)$ is *locked* if for all $r \rightarrow^* r'$, $m \lessdot r'$, and write $\mathcal{B}(r)$ for the set of memories locked in r. Clearly, $\langle\rangle \in \mathcal{B}(r)$, if $\langle\circ\rangle.m' \lessdot r$, then $\langle\circ\rangle.m' \in \mathcal{B}(r)$, and for all $r \rightarrow^* r'$, $\mathcal{B}(r) \subseteq \mathcal{B}(r')$.

Say a process r is *initial*, when all its memories are locked, that is to say when $\mathcal{M}(r) = \mathcal{B}(r)$, and write ι for the restriction of ϕ to initial processes. Thereafter, whenever we write $\iota(r)$, it is understood that r is initial. On such initial processes the forgetful map ϕ does not forget anything useful. This can be put in a form that generalises proposition 2.

Proposition 3. *If r is initial and $r \rightarrow^* s$, then $\iota(r) \rightarrow^* \phi(s)$.*

What we want now is a more convenient description of $\mathcal{B}(r)$, explaining how $\mathcal{B}(r)$ is generated by irreversible actions. This description can be construed as a procedure for collecting locked memories which have become useless.

Define $\prec := (\sim;<;\sim)^+$, where $\sim$ is the mating relation over memories. This new relation over memories is meant to express the causal dependencies at the level of memories.

We will write $m \preceq m'$, when $m \prec m'$ or $m \sim m'$. Because memory size decreases under $<$, $\prec$ is a strict finite partial order. Note also that $\mathcal{M}(r)$ is downward closed under $\prec$, since it is downward closed under $<$, and closed under $\sim$ (by the coherence condition). The same is true of $\mathcal{B}(r)$:

Lemma 3. *For all m, m', r: $m \prec m', m' \in \mathcal{B}(r) \Rightarrow m \in \mathcal{B}(r)$.*

Proof. It is enough to remark that $\mathcal{B}(r)$ is closed under the mate relation, because of the lock effect on forks and synchs, and downward closed under $<$, since if $m_1 < m_2$, m_1 always persists longer than m_2 along any trace. □

Corollary 1. *For all m, r, $\exists m' : m \preceq \langle\circ\rangle.m' \Rightarrow m \in \mathcal{B}(r)$.*

Proof. Either $m \sim \langle\circ\rangle.m'$, in which case m is also of the form $\langle\circ\rangle.m''$, and we are done, or $m \prec \langle\circ\rangle.m'$ and then the conclusion follows from lemma 3. □

One also has a converse to the corollary above, namely for all $m \neq \langle\rangle$, and r, if $m \in \mathcal{B}(r)$ then there is an m' such that $m \preceq \langle\circ\rangle.m'$. This says that our procedure is exhaustive, but we don't need this in the rest of the paper.

3.3 Causality and Irreversibility

Now that we have obtained our syntactic characterisation of locked memories, we turn back to causal traces and see that the two notions are intimately related.

Lemma 4. *Let t and t' be two forward transitions in a same trace, then $t < t'$ iff there is $m \in \mu_t$ and $m' \in \mu_{t'}$ such that $m \prec m'$.*

Proof. $\Rightarrow$: by induction on $t < t'$.

If t is a direct cause of t' then, by definition there is $m \in \mu_t$ and $m' \in \mu_{t'}$ such that $m < m'$, and so $m \prec m'$. Suppose now $t < t''$ and t'' is a direct cause of t'. If t'' is a semi-synch, the reasoning is easy. If not, then $\mu_{t''} = \{m_0'', m_1''\}$ and by induction there is m in μ_t such that $m \prec m_0''$, say, and m' in $\mu_{t'}$ such that one of m_0'' and m_1'' is $< m'$. If it is m_0'', again it is easy to conclude. Else, let r be the target of t''. We have that $\langle m_1'', \alpha, p\rangle.m_0'' \sqsubseteq r$ and $\langle m_0'', \bar{\alpha}, p'\rangle.m_1'' \sqsubseteq r$ for some α, p, p'. We have $\langle m_0'', \bar{\alpha}, p'\rangle.m_1'' \leq m'$, which implies $\langle m_1'', \alpha, p\rangle.m_0'' \preceq m'$, since $\langle m_1'', \alpha, p\rangle.m_0'' \sim \langle m_0'', \bar{\alpha}, p'\rangle.m_1''$. So we have $m_0'' \prec m'$ and hence $m \prec m'$.
$\Leftarrow$: by induction on $m \prec m'$.

If $m < m'$ we have that t is a direct cause of t'. If not, there exists m'' such that $m \prec m''$ for some $m'' \sim m'$ such that $m < m'$, and then we are in one of the following cases.

- $m'' = \langle m_0, \alpha, p\rangle.m_1$ is a synch: this implies that m' and m'' were created by some transition t'' with $\mu_{t''} = \{m_0, m_1\}$; and by the hypothesis, $m < m' = \langle m_1, \bar{\alpha}, p'\rangle.m_0$, so we have $t \leq t''$. Since $m' \in \mu_{t'}$ we have also $t'' < t'$, hence $t < t'$.

- $m'' = \langle i \rangle.m_0$ is a fork: in that case, we remark that if $\langle i \rangle.m_0$ occurs in the label of some transition in a trace, then m_0 does not. This is because we use only guarded choice, *e.g.*, we cannot have $m \rhd (p \mid q) + p'$. So $m < \langle j \rangle.m_0$, which implies $m < m_0$, and therefore $m < \langle i \rangle.m_0$ and $t < t'$.

The inductive case is obvious. □

From this we infer that all memories involved in transitions which have caused an irreversible action are locked.

Lemma 5. *Let σ be a forward trace with target r, and t_k be an irreversible transition in σ, then for all $t < t_k$, and $m \in \mu_t$, $m \in \mathcal{B}(r)$.*

Proof. Suppose t_k reads $r' \xrightarrow{\mu:\alpha} r''$ for some α irreversible. Pick $t < t_k$, there are $m \in \mu_t$ and $m_k \in \mu$ such that $m \prec m_k$ (by lemma 4, $\Rightarrow$). Besides, $m_k \in \mathcal{B}(r'')$, since by definition of an irreversible transition $\langle \circ \rangle.m_k \sqsubseteq r''$. Therefore, $m \in \mathcal{B}(r'')$ (by lemma 3), and $m \in \mathcal{B}(r)$, because $\mathcal{B}(r'') \subseteq \mathcal{B}(r)$. If $\mu_t = \{m, m'\}$, then one also has $m' \in \mathcal{B}(r)$ because of the lock effect. □

4 Transactions

With our causality lemmas in place, we turn now to the formalisation of transactional systems. The idea driving the definition, is that a successful transaction starts in a given state, which here we take as initial (in the technical sense that it cannot go backward), then proceeds to a series of reversible actions taken by the various participants, exploring the state space, and finally commits to an irreversible change. When all the preliminary reversible actions are actually involved in the success, in that they cause the last irreversible action, one says the transaction is minimal.

It is interesting to compare the notion of minimal transaction with the ACID requirements (Atomicity, Consistency, Isolation, and Durability) used in database management systems. In ACID terms, minimal transactions correspond to single logical operations, starting in a consistent state, proceeding then to a sequence of sub-atomic steps, which are committed only at the end, so as to ensure atomicity and consistency of the final state. The durability of the transaction is ensured by the fact that no backward transition is possible in the final state (because it is initial). On the other hand, the notion of isolation makes sense only in the context of shared-memory models, and doesn't have a direct analog in our process-algebraic approach.

Definition 2. *A forward trace $\theta = t_1; \ldots; t_n : r \to^* s$ is* transactional, *or simply a* transaction, *if r is initial, t_n is irreversible, and t_i is reversible for $i < n$. If s is also initial, one says the transaction is* minimal.

Lemma 6. *A transaction θ is minimal iff it is in causal form.*

Proof. If θ is not in causal form for t_n, let t_i be the rightmost transition such that $t_i \not< t_n$. Then for all $j > i$, $t_i \not< t_j$, so no $m \in \mu_{t_i}$ is a strict prefix of an

m' in μ_{t_j} (by lemma 4, $\Leftarrow$), and we can commute t_i with all t_js, obtaining a equivalent trace, ending with t_i. Since t_i is reversible, one can now go backward, and hence r_n is not initial, so θ is not minimal.

Conversely, suppose $\theta : r_0 \to^* r_n$ is in causal form, t_n is its last transition, and a backward transition t_b is possible after t_n. We show that for all i, $\mu_{t_b} \cap \mu_{t_i} = \emptyset$. Consider first the case of t_n. If μ_{t_b} and μ_{t_n} have a proper intersection, by the lock effect, these must be equal, and this is impossible since t_n is irreversible. Next, consider t_i, $i < n$. Again $\mu_{t_b} = \mu_{t_i}$ if they intersect at all. Suppose now t_i is binary, and $\mu_{t_i} = \{m_i, m_i'\}$, since $t_i < t_n$ (because θ is causal), $m_i, m_i' \prec m_n$ for some $m_n \in \mu_{t_n}$ (by lemma 4, $\Rightarrow$), so one of m_i, m_i', say $m_i < m \preceq m_n$ for some $m \in \mathcal{M}(r_n)$. The only possibility is that t_b undoes m, but then $m \in \mathcal{B}(r_n)$ (by lemma 3), since $m_n \in \mathcal{B}(r_n)$ (because t_n is irreversible), so this is not possible. The case where t_i is unary is similar. Now, if μ_{t_b} has an empty intersection with all μ_{t_i}, t_b commutes to all t_i, and this contradicts the fact that r_0 is initial. So no backward t_b is possible, which means indeed θ is minimal. □

4.1 Causal Encoding

We first define a notion of *causal encoding* between a labelled transition system, representing the specification, and a CCS process. This notion is based on the idea that one does not observe all CCS actions, but only a specific subset K, which we will later interpret as irreversible actions in RCCS.

We write respectively $\to^*$, and $\to_k^*$ for CCS traces with no labels in K, and CCS traces with no labels in K, except the last one $k \in K$.

We also extend the notion of a causal trace to CCS, by saying that a CCS trace is in causal form if it is the projection of an RCCS trace in causal form.

Finally, when p is a CCS process, we write $\mathcal{T}(p)$ for the labelled transition system associated to p, and $\mathcal{S}(p)$ for its state space. Likewise, if r is an RCCS process, we write $\mathcal{T}(r)$ for the labelled transition system associated to r, where the memories μ in labels $\mu : \zeta$ are dropped, and write $\mathcal{S}(r)$ for its state space.

Definition 3. *Let $\mathcal{S} = (S, s_0, L, \to)$ be an LTS, p_0 be a CCS process, and $\Phi \subseteq L \times K$ be a binary relation. A relation $\mathcal{R}_\Phi$ over $S \times \mathcal{S}(p_0)$ is said to be a causal encoding with respect to $\mathcal{S}$, p_0, and Φ if:*

1. $s_0 \; \mathcal{R}_\Phi \; p_0$
2. ***(Causal simulation)*** *if $s \; \mathcal{R}_\Phi \; p$ then, for all $s \to_l s'$, there exists $p \to_k^* p'$ in causal form, such that $s' \; \mathcal{R}_\Phi \; p'$, and $l \; \Phi \; k$.*
3. ***(No bad states)*** *if $s \; \mathcal{R}_\Phi \; p$ then, for all $p \to_k^* p'$ in causal form, there exists $s \to_l s'$, such that $s' \; \mathcal{R}_\Phi \; p'$ and $l \; \Phi \; k$.*

A first thing worth noticing, is that one asks in the second condition traces $p \to_k^* p'$ to be causal. The idea is that non causal traces may backtrack, once p_0 is seen as an RCCS process, and thus may induce behaviours that the specification cannot match. We will see later in an example that the theorem below does not hold if one relaxes this requirement, and allows for $\mathcal{S}$ actions to be matched also by non causal traces.

Dually, the third condition deals only with $\rightarrow_k^*$ traces, and not with general transitions of the form $p \rightarrow p'$. Therefore, the notion of causal encoding leaves the possibility that some unobservable traces in $\mathcal{T}(p_0)$ are leading to deadlocks or partial choices. By asking that only traces corresponding to successful explorations be matched by the specification, we obtain a stronger theorem. In fact, without this relaxation, $\mathcal{R}_\Phi$ would be a weak Φ-bisimulation (see definition right below) and the theorem would become completely uninteresting.

4.2 Weak Φ-Bisimilarity

The notion of causal encoding has a degree of flexibility, in that the two transition systems don't have to use the same set of labels. To manage the correspondence between labels, we use a relation over labels, written Φ, to screen off actions which we don't want to observe, and relate those we want to observe. The corresponding notion of weak bisimilarity, called weak Φ-bisimilarity is defined below.

Definition 4. *Let $\mathcal{S} = (S, s_0, \rightarrow, L)$, and $\mathcal{S}' = (S', s_0', \rightarrow', L')$ be labelled transition systems, and let Φ be be a relation over $L \times L'$.*

Define the range of Φ as $r(\Phi) := \{l' \in L' \mid \exists l \in L,\ l\ \Phi\ l'\}$, write Φ^{-1} for the inverse relation, and define S/Φ to the labelled transition system obtained by substituting silent actions τ to actions $l \notin r(\Phi^{-1})$ in $\mathcal{S}$.

One says $\mathcal{S}$ and $\mathcal{S}'$ are weak Φ-bisimilar *if $\mathcal{S}/\Phi$ and $\mathcal{S}'/\Phi^{-1}$ are weak bisimilar.*

In the particular case where Φ is the identity relation, $\mathcal{S}/\Phi = \mathcal{S}$, and weak Φ-bisimilarity is weak bisimilarity.

4.3 The Main Result

We may proceed to the theorem now.

Theorem 1. *Let $\mathcal{S} = (S, s_0, L, \rightarrow)$ be an LTS, p_0 be CCS process, $\Phi \subseteq L \times K$ be a binary relation, and $\mathcal{R}_\Phi$ be a causal encoding with respect to $\mathcal{S}$, p_0, and Φ, then $\mathcal{S}$ and $\mathcal{T}(\langle\rangle \triangleright p_0)$, where actions in K are chosen to be irreversible in RCCS, are weak Φ-bisimilar.*

Proof. Set $s \approx r := \exists r' : r \rightarrow^* r'\ \&\ s\ \mathcal{R}_\Phi\ \iota(r')$. We want to prove that $\approx$ is a weak Φ-bisimulation (with the obvious definition). Clearly $s_0 \approx r_0$, since by definition, $r_0 = \langle\rangle \triangleright p_0$, so $\iota(\langle\rangle \triangleright p_0) = p_0$, and $s_0\ \mathcal{R}_\Phi\ p_0$. We distinguish now three cases.

- Suppose $s \approx r$ and $s \rightarrow_l s'$.

We know that for some r', $r \rightarrow^* r'$ and $s\ \mathcal{R}_\Phi\ \iota(r')$. Since $\mathcal{R}_\Phi$ satisfies the 'causal simulation' property, there is a causal CCS trace $\iota(r') \rightarrow_k^* p$ such that $s'\ \mathcal{R}_\Phi\ p$ and $l\ \Phi\ k$. Then there is an RCCS trace $r' \rightarrow_k^* r''$ with $\phi(r') = \iota(r')$, and $\phi(r'') = p$ (by proposition 1). By definition, this trace is also in causal form, and so is a minimal transaction (by lemma 6, $\Leftarrow$). So $\iota(r'') = p$, $s' \mathcal{R}_\Phi \iota(r'')$, hence $s' \approx r''$.

– Suppose $s \approx r$ and $r \rightarrow_k^* r'$.[5]

Again for some r'', $r \rightarrow^* r''$ and $s \; \mathcal{R}_\Phi \; \iota(r'')$. By backtracking, one sees the trace $r \rightarrow_k^* r'$ is equivalent to $r \rightarrow^* r''' \rightarrow^* r \rightarrow_k^* r'$, where $r''' \rightarrow^* r \rightarrow_k^* r'$ is forward, and r''' is initial (by lemma 1). Hence $r''' \rightarrow^* r \rightarrow_k^* r'$ is a transaction, call it θ. Now, $r''' = r''$ (again by lemma 1). We may now put the transaction $\theta : r'' \rightarrow_k^* r'$ in causal form for its last transition t_k (by lemma 2), and obtain $r'' \rightarrow_k^* r_0' \rightarrow^* r'$, where $\theta' : r'' \rightarrow_k^* r_0'$ is minimal, *i.e.*, r_0' is initial (by lemma 6, $\Leftarrow$). So, $r'' \rightarrow_k^* r_0'$ projects to a CCS trace $\iota(r'') \rightarrow_k^* \iota(r_0')$, also in causal form (by proposition 3). Now, $\mathcal{R}_\Phi$ satisfies the 'no bad state' property, therefore, for some s', $s \rightarrow_l s'$ with $s' \; \mathcal{R}_\Phi \; \iota(r_0')$ and $l \; \Phi \; k$. By backtracking, $r' \rightarrow^* r_0'$, hence $s' \approx r'$.

– Finally, suppose $s \approx r$ and $r \rightarrow^* r'$.

By backtracking, $r' \rightarrow^* r$, and again $r \rightarrow^* r''$ for some initial r'', so $r' \rightarrow^* r''$, and $s \approx r'$. □

4.4 Causal Traces Are Needed

The reader may perhaps wonder whether the theorem still holds if one drops the causality requirements on traces in the simulation property. It does not. Compare the transition systems, $\mathcal{S}$ and $\mathcal{P}(p_0)$:

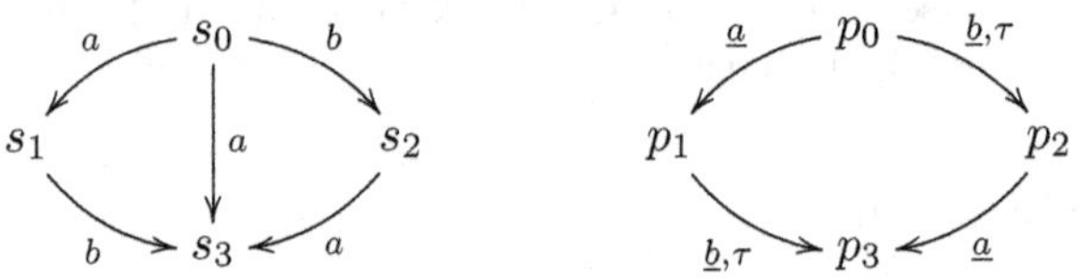

with $p_0 = \underline{a}.0 \mid (\underline{b}.0 + \tau.0)$, $p_1 := 0 \mid (\underline{b}.0 + \tau.0)$, $p_2 := \underline{a}.0 \mid 0$, and $p_3 := 0 \mid 0$.

Clearly the relation $\mathcal{R}_\Phi := \{(s_i; p_i), \, i = 0,1,2,3\}$ defines a 'non-causal' encoding with respect to $\mathcal{S}$ and p_0, and $\Phi := \{(a; \underline{a}), (b; \underline{b})\}$. And, just as clearly, the simulation property does not hold for causal traces since no causal trace starting from p_0 can match $s_0 \rightarrow_a s_3$.

On the RCCS side, the relation $\approx$, defined in the proof of the theorem, fails to be a weak Φ-bisimulation between $\mathcal{S}$ and $\langle\rangle \triangleright p_0$. In fact, $\langle\rangle \triangleright p_0$ is weak Φ-bisimilar to $\underline{a}.0 \mid \underline{b}.0$ which is not weak Φ-bisimilar to $\mathcal{S}$, so there is no such bisimulation at all.

5 Discussion

There is an amusing analogy between the method we propose and simulated annealing techniques which physicists developed in the 80s, and which turned out to be useful in some optimisation problems [6]. In essence, one has to walk a complicated space on the search for some optimum, and the task is hard

[5] One may take this trace to be of length one, but it doesn't help.

enough so that no up front computation is feasible (in the analogy centralised scheduling is not possible). The idea, then, is to base the search on inexpensive and overoptimistic cues, *e.g.*, the gradient of the function to minimise (a role played in the analogy by the CCS process), which one follows most of the time, except for some computation steps picked with a small probability, where one does random moves in the search space (a role played here by backtracking, combined with the inherent non-determinism of forward transitions).

Having said that, the purpose of this section is to illustrate our theorem with two basic examples of transactional systems, and discuss whether the theorem might have some merits and when. Ideally, the theorem should lead to shorter and more intuitive CCS code, and easier proofs. Recursive definitions can be incorporated to RCCS, and so we will use them freely in the following.

5.1 Dining Philosophers

We begin with the timeless example of the dining philosophers. There are a certain number of philosophers, say n, eating or thinking. So, $n = E + T$, where T is the set of thinking philosophers, and E the set of eating philosophers. Philosopher i may stop eating at any time, and conversely philosopher i may start eating but he needs two chopsticks for this. The trouble is, he is sharing one chopstick with $i-1$, and one with $i+1$.[6] This translates into the following system:

$$\begin{array}{l} E + \{i\}, T \rightarrow_{t_i} E, T + \{i\} \\ E, T + \{i-1, i, i+1\} \rightarrow_{e_i} E + \{i\}, T + \{i-1, i+1\} \end{array}$$

On the CCS side, we clearly want one process for each philosopher,[7] and need to make sure a transaction θ_i corresponding to the latter transition may only commit after the acquisition of two chopsticks. Here is a simple CCS encoding (where we already have underlined the irreversible actions):

$$\begin{array}{ll} \mathrm{THINK}_i & := cs_i.\underline{e}_{i+1}.\mathrm{EAT}_i + cs_{i+1}.\underline{e}_i.\mathrm{EAT}_i \\ \mathrm{EAT}_i & := \underline{t}_i.(\mathrm{THINK}_i \mid \mathrm{STICK}_i \mid \mathrm{STICK}_{i+1}) \\ \mathrm{STICK}_i & := \overline{cs}_i.0 + \bar{\underline{e}}_i.0 \\ \mathrm{PHIL}_{E,T} & := \prod_{i \in T} \mathrm{THINK}_i \mid \prod_{j \in E} \mathrm{EAT}_j \mid \prod_{u \in U} \mathrm{STICK}_u \end{array}$$

where $U := T - \{i, i+1 \mid i \in E\}$ is the set of unused chopsticks. Set $\Phi := \{(e_i, \underline{\tau}), (t_i, \underline{t}_i)\}$, and define $\mathcal{R}_\Phi$ as:

$$(E,T)\ \mathcal{R}_\Phi\ S_{E,T} := (cs_1)(\underline{e}_1) \cdots (cs_n)(\underline{e}_n)\mathrm{PHIL}_{E,T}$$

It is easy to verify that $\mathcal{R}_\Phi$ is a causal encoding. Causal simulation downs to exhibiting causal traces for:

$$\begin{array}{l} S_{E+\{i\},T} \rightarrow^*_{\underline{t}_i} S_{E,T+\{i\}} \\ S_{E,T+\{i-1,i,i+1\}} \rightarrow^*_{\underline{\tau}} S_{E+\{i\},T\{i-1,i+1\}} \end{array}$$

[6] Addition is taken modulo n.

[7] As said in the introduction, the level of distribution of the implementation one is looking for is usually quite clear in specific examples.

One finds exactly one causal trace ending with $\underline{t}_i$ in the first case, and two symmetrical causal traces, depending on which chopstick i grabs first. Verifying the other condition amounts to showing that for any causal trace with source $S_{E,T}$, there exists a corresponding transition in the specification LTS. That is to say, one has to verify that if $S_{E,T} \rightarrow^*_{\underline{\tau}} p$, then $p \equiv S_{E+i,T-i}$ for some i, and if $S_{E,T} \rightarrow^*_{\underline{t}_i} p$ we have $p \equiv S_{E-\{i\},T+\{i\}}$. As said, for a given i, the causal traces leading to $\underline{\tau}$ are symmetric so we already checked the property. Furthermore, there is only one causal trace leading to $\underline{t}_i$, so again we know the answer.

To handle backtrack explicitly, one would need a modification such as:

$$\begin{aligned}\mathrm{THINK}'_i := cs_i.(\tau.(\mathrm{STICK}_i \mid \mathrm{THINK}_i) + \underline{e}_{i+1}.\mathrm{EAT}_i)\\ +cs_{i+1}.(\tau.(\mathrm{STICK}_{i+1} \mid \mathrm{THINK}_i) + \underline{e}_i.\mathrm{EAT}_i)\end{aligned}$$

Not only is the code larger and not as immediately intuitive, but one has more to prove, and with a larger transactional system, where deeper exploration is needed, it would be even more so.

5.2 Choices

The object of this second example is to contrast the expressiveness of RCCS with that of CCS. We start with a system of agents indexed by a set I, where each agent is capable of emitting a vote, and the problem is to enforce that no more than $c_0 \leq |I|$ votes are actually emitted. The corresponding transition system is:

$$V_c(J + \{i\}) \rightarrow_{v_i} V_{c-1}(J)$$

where $0 < c$, $J \subset I$, together with the initial state $V_{c_0}(I)$. One may think of a simple implementation in CCS:

$$\begin{aligned}P_c(J) &:= (l)\big(\prod_{i\in J} A_i(l, \underline{v}_i) \mid \prod_{1\leq i\leq c} l.0\big)\\ A_i(l, \underline{v}_i) &:= \bar{l}.\underline{v}_i.0\end{aligned}$$

This system has no deadlocks, and for a while, the encoding may seem correct. But really it is not, as can be seen already in the case $c_0 = 1$ and $I = \{1, 2\}$. In that case the specification is no other than the *external* choice $v_1 + v_2$, and yet, in the corresponding process $P_1(I)$ one can move silently to a state where only v_1 (or v_2) is possible. Actually $P_1(I)$ is bisimilar to $\tau.\underline{v}_1 + \tau.\underline{v}_2$, and is the traditional non-divergent encoding of internal choice, which is not weakly bisimilar to the specification.

However, it is correct enough so that we can apply our theorem. To see this, take for $\mathcal{R}_\Phi$ the pairs of the form $(V_c(J), P_c(J))$, with $v_i \,\Phi\, \underline{v}_i$ for all $i \in I$. It is easy to check for the 'no bad state' and 'causal simulation' properties at once, since there is only one causal trace of the form $P_c(J + \{i\}) \rightarrow^*_{\underline{v}_i} p$, and for this trace $p \equiv P_{c-1}(J)$.

As in the preceding example, one could also directly define a weakly bisimilar encoding by modifying the behaviour of A_i:

$$A'_i(l, \underline{v}_i) := \bar{l}.(\underline{v}_i.0 + \tau.(A_i(l, \underline{v}_i) \mid l.0))$$

Again, the complete weak bisimulation has to be proved, and that is harder [7]. In a way, RCCS gets the best of both worlds, in that the code is as simple as the non-divergent encoding (actually it is the same encoding), while at the same time, the behaviour is fully correct. Another point worth observing, is that both the modified code and the RCCS code are divergent (*i.e.*, may loop). This is not because we are clumsy, Palamidessi and Herescu have shown that any solution has to be divergent [8].

6 Conclusion

We have presented a formalisation of the notion of transaction based on RCCS where reversible actions are distinguished from irreversible or commit actions. One interest of this formalisation is that one may prove that relatively straightforward correctness conditions on a CCS process with respect to a given specification, will ensure that the corresponding RCCS process is fully correct with respect to the same specification. We believe the method does have some interesting applications, and the consideration of simple examples in the last section gives some more credence to that, since we have found code which was shorter and easier to understand, and definitely simpler to prove correct.

An interesting question is to relate the present approach with the representation of transactional processes by means of zero-safe nets [9]. These are used to screen off traces leading to deadlocks, and retain only those which are decomposable as minimal transactions. Implementations in Join-calculus using resets, and processes monitoring running transactions [10], should be compared with the implicit backtracking mechanism inherent to RCCS.

There are also important transaction concepts which are not addressed here, such as compensations, during which participants may jump to some rally point in their state space, using a compensation. In so doing, they do not necessarily forget all what they learned during the interaction, and thus may not go back to their exact initial state. This mechanism is certainly useful, and was already studied in the context of process algebras [11,12]. Nested transactions are not considered either [13]. Whether a revision of the fundamentals of RCCS including compensations or nested transactions is possible, remains to be seen.

A further problem not addressed here, is the question of efficiency. By including in the picture some quantitative semantics, either by timeouts or probabilities, to control backtrack, would give means to evaluate the efficiency of the code one obtains. Then, an interesting question would be to find general conditions for efficiency, perhaps based on an analysis of the distribution of the causality chains in a transaction.

Acknowledgements. The authors wish to thank the referees for many useful suggestions, and specifically for drawing their attention to the need of including α-conversion in the structural equivalence over CCS processes.

References

1. Robin Milner. *Communication and Concurrency.* International Series on Computer Science. Prentice Hall, 1989.
2. Vincent Danos and Jean Krivine. Reversible communicating systems. In *Proceedings of CONCUR'04*, volume 3170 of *LNCS*, pages 292–307. Springer, September 2004.
3. Robin Milner. *Communicating and mobile systems: the π-calculus.* Cambridge University Press, Cambridge, 1999.
4. Gérard Boudol and Ilaria Castellani. Permutation of transitions: An event structure semantics for CCS and SCCS. In *Linear Time, Branching Time and Partial Order in Logics and Models for Concurrency*, volume 354 of *LNCS*, pages 411–427. Springer, 1989.
5. Pierpaolo Degano and Corrado Priami. Non interleaving semantics for mobile processes. In *Automata, Languages and Programming*, volume 944 of *LNCS*, pages 660–667. Springer, 1995.
6. V. Cerny. Thermodynamical approach to the traveling salesman problem: An efficient simulation algorithm. *J. Opt. Theory Appl.*, 45(1), 1985.
7. Uwe Nestmann and Benjamin C. Pierce. Decoding choice encodings. In *Proceedings of CONCUR'96*, volume 1119 of *LNCS*, pages 179–194. Springer, 1996.
8. Catuscia Palamidessi and Oltea Mihaela Herescu. A randomized encoding of the π-calculus with mixed choice. *Theoretical Computer Science*, 2004. To appear.
9. Roberto Bruni and Ugo Montanari. Zero-safe nets: Comparing the collective and individual token approaches. *Information and Computation*, 156(1–2), 2000.
10. Roberto Bruni, Cosimo Laneve, and Ugo Montanari. Orchestrating transactions in join calculus. In *Proceedings of CONCUR'02*, volume 2421 of *LNCS*, pages 321–336. Springer, 2002.
11. Jan A. Bergstra, Alban Ponse, and Jos van Wamel. Process algebra with backtracking. In *Proceedings of the REX School/Symposium*, volume 803 of *LNCS*, pages 46–91. Springer, 1994.
12. Laura Bocchi, Cosimo Laneve, and Gianluigi Zavattaro. A calculus for long running transactions. In *Proceedings of FMOODS 2003*, volume 2884 of *LNCS*, pages 124–138. Springer, 2003.
13. Roberto Bruni, Hernán Melgratti, and Ugo Montanari. Nested commits for mobile calculi: extending Join. In *Proceedings of IFIP-TCS'04*, pages 569–582, 2004.

Two-Player Nonzero-Sum ω-Regular Games

Krishnendu Chatterjee

Dept. of EECS, University of California, Berkeley
c_krish@eecs.berkeley.edu

Abstract. We study infinite stochastic games played by two-players on a finite graph with goals specified by sets of infinite traces. The games are *concurrent* (each player simultaneously and independently chooses an action at each round), *stochastic* (the next state is determined by a probability distribution depending on the current state and the chosen actions), *infinite* (the game continues for an infinite number of rounds), *nonzero-sum* (the players' goals are not necessarily conflicting), and undiscounted. We show that if each player has an ω-regular objective expressed as a parity objective, then there exists an ε-Nash equilibrium, for every $\varepsilon > 0$. However, exact Nash equilibria need not exist. We study the complexity of finding values (payoff profile) of an ε-Nash equilibrium. We show that the values of an ε-Nash equilibrium in nonzero-sum concurrent parity games can be computed by solving the following two simpler problems: computing the values of zero-sum (the goals of the players are strictly conflicting) concurrent parity games and computing ε-Nash equilibrium values of nonzero-sum concurrent games with reachability objectives. As a consequence we establish that values of an ε-Nash equilibrium can be computed in TFNP (total functional NP), and hence in EXPTIME.

1 Introduction

Stochastic Games. Non-cooperative games provide a natural framework to model interactions between agents [12,14]. The simplest class of non-cooperative games consists of the "one-step" games — games with single interaction between the agents after which the game ends and the payoffs are decided (e.g., matrix games). However, a wide class of games progress over time and in stateful manner, and the current game depends on the history of interactions. Infinite *stochastic games* [16,8] are a natural model for such games. A stochastic game is played over a finite *state space* and is played in rounds. In concurrent games, in each round, each player chooses an action from a finite set of available actions, simultaneously and independently of other players. The game proceeds to a new state according to a probabilistic transition relation (stochastic transition matrix) based on the current state and the joint actions of the players. Concurrent games subsume the simpler class of *turn-based games*, where at every state at most one player can choose between multiple actions. In verification and control of finite state reactive systems such games proceed for infinite rounds, generating an infinite sequence of states, called the *outcome* of the game. The players receive a payoff based on a payoff function that maps every outcome to a real number.

M. Abadi and L. de Alfaro (Eds.): CONCUR 2005, LNCS 3653, pp. 413–427, 2005.

Objectives. Payoffs are generally Borel measurable functions [11]. The payoff set for each player is a Borel set B_i in the Cantor topology on S^ω (where S is the set of states), and player i gets payoff 1 if the outcome of the game is in B_i, and 0 otherwise. In verification, payoff functions are usually index sets of *ω-regular languages*. The ω-regular languages generalize the classical regular languages to infinite strings, they occur in low levels of the Borel hierarchy (they are in $\Sigma_3 \cap \Pi_3$), and they form a robust and expressive language for determining payoffs for commonly used specifications. The simplest ω-regular objectives correspond to safety ("closed sets") and reachability ("open sets") objectives.

Zero-Sum Games. Games may be *zero-sum*, where two players have directly conflicting objectives and the payoff of one player is one minus the payoff of the other, or *nonzero-sum*, where each player has a prescribed payoff function based on the outcome of the game. The fundamental question for games is the existence of equilibrium values. For zero-sum games, this involves showing a *determinacy* theorem that states that the expected optimum value obtained by player 1 is exactly one minus the expected optimum value obtained by player 2. For one-step zero-sum games, this is von Neumann's minmax theorem [21]. For infinite games, the existence of such equilibria is not obvious, in fact, by using the axiom of choice, one can construct games for which determinacy does not hold. However, a remarkable result by Martin [11] shows that all stochastic zero-sum games with Borel payoffs are determined.

Nonzero-Sum Games. For nonzero-sum games, the fundamental equilibrium concept is a *Nash equilibrium* [10], that is, a strategy profile such that no player can gain by deviating from the profile, assuming the other player continues playing the strategy in the profile. Again, for one-step games, the existence of such equilibria is guaranteed by Nash's theorem [10]. However, the existence of Nash equilibria in infinite games is not immediate: Nash's theorem holds for finite bimatrix games, but in case of stochastic games, the strategy space is not compact. The existence of Nash equilibria is known only in very special cases of stochastic games. In fact, Nash equilibria may not exist, and the best one can hope for is an ε-Nash equilibrium for all $\varepsilon > 0$, where an ε-Nash equilibrium is a strategy profile where unilateral deviation can only increase the payoff of a player by at most ε. Exact Nash equilibria do exist in discounted stochastic games [9]. For concurrent nonzero-sum games with payoffs defined by Borel sets, surprisingly little is known. Secchi and Sudderth [15] showed that exact Nash equilibria do exist when all players have payoffs defined by closed sets ("safety objectives"). In the case of open sets ("reachability objectives"), the existence of ε-Nash equilibrium for every $\varepsilon > 0$, has been established in [5]. The above results hold even in the case of n-player games. In an important recent result in stochastic game theory, Vieille shows the existence of ε-Nash equilibrium, for every $\varepsilon > 0$, in two-player nonzero-sum concurrent games with limit-average payoff [19,20]. The existence of ε-Nash equilibrium in two-player concurrent games with objectives in higher levels of Borel hierarchy has been an intriguing open problem.

Result and Proof Techniques. In this paper we show that ε-Nash equilibrium exists, for every $\varepsilon > 0$, for two-player concurrent games with ω-regular objectives. However, exact Nash equilibria need not exist. For two-player concurrent games our result extends the existence of ε-Nash equilibrium from the lowest level of Borel hierarchy (open and closed sets) to ω-regular objectives that lie in the higher levels of Borel hierarchy; and our result for ω-regular objectives parallels Vieille's result for limit-average objectives. Our result is organized as follows:

1. In Section 3 we first show the existence of ε-Nash equilibrium, for every $\varepsilon > 0$, for a sub-class of concurrent games, namely single strongly connected component (Sscc) games, with ω-regular objectives.
2. We extend the above result to all concurrent games in Section 4.

The result for Sscc games involves the following key ideas:

- We identify four sufficient conditions that ensure existence of ε-Nash equilibrium, for every $\varepsilon > 0$, in Sscc games.
- We then show that if the sufficient conditions are not satisfied, then the game can be reduced to a nonzero-sum game with reachability objectives, with some desired properties. The result is proved by generalizing a result from [2] and using a fragment of analysis of Vieille [19].
- The existence of ε-Nash equilibrium, for all $\varepsilon > 0$, in the original game is then established by the use of *punishing or spoiling strategies.*

Complexity of ε-Nash Equilibrium. Computing the values of a Nash equilibria, when it exists, is another challenging problem [13,22]. For one-step zero-sum games, equilibrium values and strategies can be computed in polynomial time (by reduction to linear programming) [12]. For one-step nonzero-sum games, no polynomial time algorithm is known to compute an exact Nash equilibrium in two-player games [13]. In case of zero-sum concurrent games with ω-regular objectives several algorithms are known to compute values with in ε-approximation [7,2]. Since the values can be irrational, ε-approximation is the best one can achieve. From the computational aspects, a desirable property of an existence proof of Nash equilibrium is its ease of algorithmic analysis. We show that our proof for existence of ε-Nash equilibrium is completely constructive and algorithmic. Our proof shows that the computation of values of an ε-Nash equilibrium in two-player concurrent games with parity objectives can be reduced to the following two simpler problems:

1. Computing values of zero-sum concurrent games with parity objectives.
2. Computing values of some special ε-Nash equilibrium of nonzero-sum concurrent games with reachability objectives.

Since zero-sum games are special cases of nonzero-sum games, computing ε-Nash equilibrium in nonzero-sum games are at least as hard as solving the optimum values in zero-sum games. Our result shows that the extra cost of computing ε-Nash equilibrium for ω-regular objectives is no more than solving some special ε-Nash equilibrium of games with reachability objectives. We then prove that the equilibrium values of an ε-Nash equilibrium can be computed in TFNP (total functional NP) and hence in EXPTIME. Our result matches the best known complexity bound for the simpler case of turn-based games [5].

2 Definitions

Notation. For a countable set A, a *probability distribution* on A is a function $\delta : A \mapsto [0,1]$ such that $\sum_{a \in A} \delta(a) = 1$. We denote the set of probability distributions on A by $\mathcal{D}(A)$. Given a distribution $\delta \in \mathcal{D}(A)$, we denote by $\mathrm{Supp}(\delta) = \{x \in A \mid \delta(x) > 0\}$ the *support* of δ.

Definition 1 (Concurrent games). *A (two-player)* concurrent game structure *$\mathcal{G} = \langle S, Moves, \Gamma_1, \Gamma_2, \delta \rangle$ consists of the following components:*

- *A finite state space S and a finite set $Moves$ of moves.*
- *Two move assignments $\Gamma_1, \Gamma_2 \colon S \mapsto 2^{Moves} \setminus \emptyset$. For $i \in \{1,2\}$, assignment Γ_i associates with each state $s \in S$ the non-empty set $\Gamma_i(s) \subseteq Moves$ of moves available to player i at state s.*
- *A probabilistic transition function $\delta : S \times Moves \times Moves \to \mathcal{D}(S)$, that gives the probability $\delta(s, a_1, a_2)(t)$ of a transition from s to t when player 1 plays a_1 and player 2 plays a_2, for all $s, t \in S$ and $a_1 \in \Gamma_1(s)$, $a_2 \in \Gamma_2(s)$.* ∎

A special class of concurrent game structures are Markov decision processes (MDPs). A concurrent game structure is a Markov decision process (MDP) if there exists an $i \in \{1,2\}$ such that at every state s, $|\Gamma_i(s)| = 1$. In other words, MDPs are one-player stochastic games: only one player has a non-trivial choice of moves and for the other player the choice of the moves are fixed.

We define the size of the game structure $\mathcal{G}$ to be equal to the size of the transition function δ; specifically, $|\mathcal{G}| = \sum_{s \in S} \sum_{a \in \Gamma_1(s)} \sum_{b \in \Gamma_2(s)} \sum_{t \in S} |\delta(s,a,b)(t)|$, where $|\delta(s,a,b)(t)|$ denotes the space to specify the probability distribution. At every state $s \in S$, player 1 chooses a move $a_1 \in \Gamma_1(s)$, and simultaneously and independently player 2 chooses a move $a_2 \in \Gamma_2(s)$. The game then proceeds to the successor state t with probability $\delta(s, a_1, a_2)(t)$, for all $t \in S$. A state s is called an *absorbing state* if for all $a_1 \in \Gamma_1(s)$ and $a_2 \in \Gamma_2(s)$ we have $\delta(s, a_1, a_2)(s) = 1$. In other words, at s for all choices of moves of the players the next state is always s. Each player chooses her strategy independently and secretly from the other player, and is only interested in maximizing her own payoff. For all states $s \in S$ and moves $a_1 \in \Gamma_1(s)$ and $a_2 \in \Gamma_2(s)$, we indicate by $\mathrm{Dest}(s, a_1, a_2) = \mathrm{Supp}(\delta(s, a_1, a_2))$ the set of possible successors of s when moves a_1, a_2 are selected.

A *path* or a *play* ω of $\mathcal{G}$ is an infinite sequence $\omega = \langle s_0, s_1, s_2, \ldots \rangle$ of states in S such that for all $k \geq 0$, there are moves $a_1^k \in \Gamma_1(s_k)$ and $a_2^k \in \Gamma_2(s_k)$ with $\delta(s_k, a_1^k, a_2^k)(s_{k+1}) > 0$. We denote by Ω the set of all paths and by Ω_s the set of all paths $\omega = \langle s_0, s_1, s_2, \ldots \rangle$ such that $s_0 = s$, i.e., the set of plays starting from state s.

Randomized Strategies. A *selector* ξ for player $i \in \{1,2\}$ is a function $\xi : S \mapsto \mathcal{D}(Moves)$ such that for all $s \in S$ and $a \in Moves$, if $\xi(s)(a) > 0$ then $a \in \Gamma_i(s)$. We denote by Λ_i the set of all selectors for player $i \in \{1,2\}$. A *strategy* for player 1 is a function $\sigma : S^+ \to \Lambda_1$ that associates with every finite non-empty sequence of states, representing the history of the play so far, a selector. Similarly we define strategies π for player 2. A memoryless strategy is independent of the history of the play and depends only on the current state. Memoryless strategies coincide with selectors, and we often write σ for the selector corresponding to a memoryless strategy σ. We denote by Σ and Π the set of all strategies for player 1 and player 2, respectively.

Once the starting state s and the strategies σ and π for the two players have been chosen, the game is reduced to an ordinary stochastic process. Hence, the probabilities of events are uniquely defined, where an *event* $\mathcal{A} \subseteq \Omega_s$ is a measurable set of paths. For an event $\mathcal{A} \subseteq \Omega_s$, we denote by $\Pr_s^{\sigma,\pi}(\mathcal{A})$ the probability that a path belongs to $\mathcal{A}$ when the game starts from s and the players follow the strategies σ and π.

Objectives. An *objective* for a player in a game $\mathcal{G}$ is a set $\mathcal{W} \subseteq \Omega$ of infinite paths. We consider the following objectives.

- *Reachability objective.* For a set $R \subseteq S$ of *target* states, the Reachability objective is defined as $\text{Reach}(R) = \{ \langle s_0, s_1, s_2, \ldots \rangle \in \Omega \mid \exists k \in \mathbb{N}.\ s_k \in R \}$.
- *Safety objective.* For a set $F \subseteq S$ of *safe* states, the Safety objective is defined as $\text{Safe}(F) = \{ \langle s_0, s_1, s_2, \ldots \rangle \in \Omega \mid \forall k \in \mathbb{N}.\ s_k \in F \}$. Note that $\Omega \setminus \text{Reach}(R) = \text{Safe}(S \setminus R)$. Hence the reachability objective with target set R is complementary to the safety objective with safe set $S \setminus R$.
- *Parity objective.* Given $d \in \mathbb{N}$, we write $[d]$ for the set $\{0, 1, 2, \ldots, d\}$ and $[d]_+$ for the set $\{1, 2, \ldots, d\}$. Let $p : S \mapsto [d]$ be a function that assigns a *priority* $p(s)$ to every state $s \in S$, where $d \in \mathbb{N}$. For an infinite path $\omega = \langle s_0, s_1, s_2, \ldots \rangle \in \Omega$, we define $\text{Inf}(\omega) = \{ i \in [d] \mid p(s_k) = i \text{ for infinitely many } k \geq 0 \}$. The *parity objective* is defined as $\text{Parity}(p) = \{ \omega \in \Omega \mid \min\big(\text{Inf}(\omega)\big) \text{ is even} \}$. Informally we say that a path ω satisfies the parity objective, $\text{Parity}(p)$, if $\omega \in \text{Parity}(p)$.

The ability to solve games with parity objectives suffices for solving games with arbitrary ω-regular objectives, since every ω-regular objective can be specified as a parity objective [17].

A concurrent nonzero-sum parity game consists of a game structure $\mathcal{G}$ and two priority functions p_1 and p_2 for player 1 and player 2, respectively. The objectives of player 1 and player 2 are $\text{Parity}(p_1)$ and $\text{Parity}(p_2)$, respectively. We write Ψ for an arbitrary parity objective. We write the objectives of player 1 and player 2 as Ψ_1 and Ψ_2, respectively, where Ψ_1 and Ψ_2 are arbitrary ω-regular objectives formalized as parity objectives. We also use Ψ_1 to denote the set of paths $\omega \in \Omega$ such that $\omega \in \text{Parity}(p_1)$. Similarly we write Ψ_2 to denote the set of paths $\text{Parity}(p_2)$. Given a state s we write Ψ_{1s} to denote $\Omega_s \cap \Psi_1$ and similarly we write Ψ_{2s} to denote $\Omega_s \cap \Psi_2$. We also write Ψ_s to denote $\Omega_s \cap \Psi$. Given a parity objective Ψ, the set of paths Ψ_s is measurable for any choice of strategies for the two players [18]. Hence, the probability that a path satisfies objective Ψ starting from state $s \in S$ under strategies σ, π for the two players is $\Pr_s^{\sigma,\pi}(\Psi_s)$.

Concurrent Nonzero-Sum Games. A concurrent nonzero-sum game consists of a concurrent game structure $\mathcal{G}$ and objectives Ψ_1 and Ψ_2 for player 1 and player 2, respectively. A concurrent game is zero-sum if the objectives of the players are complementary, i.e., $\Psi_1 = \Omega \setminus \Psi_2$. The zero-sum values for the players in concurrent games with objectives Ψ_1 and Ψ_2, for player 1 and player 2, respectively, are defined as follows.

Definition 2 (Zero-sum values). *Let $\mathcal{G}$ be a concurrent game structure with objectives Ψ_1 and Ψ_2 for player 1 and player 2, respectively. Given a state $s \in S$ we call the maximal probability with which player 1 can ensure that Ψ_1 holds from s against any strategy of player 2 is the* zero-sum value *of player 1 at s. The zero-sum value for player 2 is defined symmetrically. Formally, the zero-sum value for player 1 and player 2 are given by functions $\langle\langle 1\rangle\rangle_{val}(\Psi_1) : S \mapsto [0,1]$ and $\langle\langle 2\rangle\rangle_{val}(\Psi_2) : S \mapsto [0,1]$, defined for all $s \in S$ by*

$$\langle\langle 1\rangle\rangle_{val}(\Psi_1)(s) = \sup_{\sigma\in\Sigma}\inf_{\pi\in\Pi} \Pr_s^{\sigma,\pi}(\Psi_{1s}); \qquad \langle\langle 2\rangle\rangle_{val}(\Psi_2)(s) = \sup_{\pi\in\Pi}\inf_{\sigma\in\Sigma} \Pr_s^{\sigma,\pi}(\Psi_{2s}). \blacksquare$$

Concurrent zero-sum games satisfy a *quantitative* version of determinacy [11], stating that for all parity objectives Ψ_1 and Ψ_2, such that $\Psi_1 = \Omega \setminus \Psi_2$, and all $s \in S$, we have $\langle\langle 1\rangle\rangle_{val}(\Psi_1)(s) + \langle\langle 2\rangle\rangle_{val}(\Psi_2)(s) = 1$. A strategy σ for player 1 is *optimal* with respect to objective Ψ, if for all $s \in S$ we have $\inf_{\pi\in\Pi} \Pr_s^{\sigma,\pi}(\Psi_s) = \langle\langle 1\rangle\rangle_{val}(\Psi)(s)$. For $\varepsilon > 0$, a strategy σ for player 1 is *ε-optimal* with respect to objective Ψ, if for all $s \in S$ we have $\inf_{\pi\in\Pi} \Pr_s^{\sigma,\pi}(\Psi_s) \geq \langle\langle 1\rangle\rangle_{val}(\Psi)(s) - \varepsilon$. We define optimal and ε-optimal strategies for player 2 symmetrically. Note that the quantitative determinacy of concurrent zero-sum games is equivalent to the existence of ε-optimal strategies for both players for all $\varepsilon > 0$, at all states $s \in S$.

Definition 3 (Cooperative value). *Given a concurrent game structure $\mathcal{G}$ and an objective Ψ we define the* cooperative value *at a state $s \in S$ as the maximal probability with which player 1 and player 2 can cooperate to satisfy the objective Ψ at s. Formally, the cooperative value is given by the function $\langle\langle 1,2\rangle\rangle_{val}(\Psi) : S \mapsto [0,1]$, defined for all $s \in S$ by $\langle\langle 1,2\rangle\rangle_{val}(\Psi)(s) = \sup_{(\sigma,\pi)\in\Sigma\times\Pi} \Pr_s^{\sigma,\pi}(\Psi_s)$.* $\blacksquare$

Note that the computation of the cooperative value function $\langle\langle 1,2\rangle\rangle_{val}(\Psi)$ can be interpreted as the computation of a value function in a MDP with objective Ψ, where player 1 and player 2 cooperatively choose strategies.

Definition 4 (ε-Nash equilibrium). *Let $\mathcal{G}$ be a concurrent game structure and let the objectives for player 1 and player 2 be Ψ_1 and Ψ_2, respectively. For $\varepsilon \geq 0$, a strategy profile $(\sigma^*, \pi^*) \in \Sigma \times \Pi$ is an ε-Nash equilibrium for a state $s \in S$ iff the following two conditions hold:*

$$\sup_{\sigma\in\Sigma} \Pr_s^{\sigma,\pi^*}(\Psi_{1s}) \leq \Pr_s^{\sigma^*,\pi^*}(\Psi_{1s}) + \varepsilon; \qquad \sup_{\pi\in\Pi} \Pr_s^{\sigma^*,\pi}(\Psi_{2s}) \leq \Pr_s^{\sigma^*,\pi^*}(\Psi_{2s}) + \varepsilon.$$

An exact Nash equilibrium is an ε-Nash equilibrium with $\varepsilon = 0$. $\blacksquare$

It may be noted that in case of zero-sum concurrent games with parity objectives optimal strategies need not exist, and only existence of ε-optimal strategies can be guaranteed, for all $\varepsilon > 0$ [6]. Hence in the general case of nonzero-sum concurrent games with parity objectives Nash equilibrium need not exist, and existence of ε-Nash equilibrium, for all $\varepsilon > 0$, is the best one can achieve.

Definition 5 (ε-optimal and ε-spoiling strategies). *Given a nonzero-sum concurrent game with objective Ψ_1 for player 1 and Ψ_2 for player 2, a strategy σ_ε is ε-optimal if it is ε-optimal with respect to objective Ψ_1, and a strategy $\overline{\sigma}_\varepsilon$ is ε-spoiling if it is ε-optimal with respect to objective $\overline{\Psi_2} = \Omega \setminus \Psi_2$. The ε-optimal and ε-spoiling strategies for player 2 are defined similarly. We denote by Σ_ε and Π_ε the set of ε-optimal strategies for player 1 and player 2, respectively. Similarly, we denote by $\overline{\Sigma_\varepsilon}$ and $\overline{\Pi_\varepsilon}$ the set of ε-spoiling strategies for player 1 and player 2, respectively.* ∎

The determinacy of concurrent games with parity objectives ensures that for all $\varepsilon > 0$, the sets $\Sigma_\varepsilon, \Pi_\varepsilon, \overline{\Sigma_\varepsilon}$ and $\overline{\Pi_\varepsilon}$ are non-empty.

3 Sscc Games

In this section we prove the existence of ε-Nash equilibrium for all $\varepsilon > 0$, in a subclass of concurrent games, namely, single strongly connected component games. In the next section we generalize the existence of ε-Nash equilibrium, for all $\varepsilon > 0$, to all concurrent games using the result of this section. Given a game structure $\mathcal{G}$ we define a underlying graph $G_\mathcal{G}$ of $\mathcal{G}$.

Definition 6 (Graph of a game structure $\mathcal{G}$). *Given a concurrent game structure $\mathcal{G} = \langle S, Moves, \Gamma_1, \Gamma_2, \delta \rangle$ the graph of the game structure $\mathcal{G}$ is a directed graph $G_\mathcal{G} = (S_\mathcal{G}, E_\mathcal{G})$ that is defined as follows:*

- *$S_\mathcal{G} = S$, i.e., the set of states of $G_\mathcal{G}$ is same as the state space of $\mathcal{G}$.*
- *$E_\mathcal{G} = \{ (s,t) \mid \exists\, a_1 \in \Gamma_1(s), \exists\, a_2 \in \Gamma_2(s).\ t \in \mathrm{Dest}(s, a_1, a_2) \}$.* ∎

Definition 7 (Single strongly connected component (Sscc) game structures). *Let $\mathcal{G}$ be a concurrent game structure with parity objectives $\Psi_1 = Parity(p_1)$ and $\Psi_2 = Parity(p_2)$ for player 1 and player 2, respectively. Let $G_\mathcal{G}$ be the graph of $\mathcal{G}$. We call $\mathcal{G}$ a single strongly connected component (Sscc) game structure if the graph $G_\mathcal{G}$ satisfy the following conditions:*

- *The state space $S_\mathcal{G}$ can be partitioned into three sets: C, U, T, with $T = \{ t_{00}, t_{10}, t_{01}, t_{11} \}$.*
- *C is a strongly connected component in the graph $G_\mathcal{G}$.*
- *The states $t_{ij} \in T$ are absorbing states, for $i,j \in \{ 0,1 \}$. The priority function for the states in T are as follows: $p_1(t_{ij}) = i$ and $p_2(t_{ij}) = j$, for $i,j \in \{ 0,1 \}$. Note that at state t_{00} objective of both the players are satisfied; at state t_{01} only player 1's objective is satisfied; at state t_{10} only player 2's objective is satisfied and at state t_{11} none of the players objective is satisfied.*

- *For every state $s \in U$ we have $|\Gamma_i(s)| = 1$ for $i \in \{1,2\}$ and $(\{s\} \times S_{\mathcal{G}}) \cap E_{\mathcal{G}} \subseteq \{s\} \times T$. In other words, at states in U there is no non-trivial choice of moves for the players and thus for any state s in U the game proceeds to the set T according to the probability distribution of the transition function δ at s.*
- *$C \times (S_{\mathcal{G}} \setminus C) \cap E_{\mathcal{G}} \subseteq C \times U$, i.e., the edges out of C end at a state in U. We also require that $(C \times U) \cap E_{\mathcal{G}} \neq \emptyset$.* ∎

Reduction Gadget. Let $\mathcal{G}$ be a SSCC game structure with parity objectives Ψ_1 and Ψ_2 for player 1 and player 2, respectively. Suppose for all $\varepsilon > 0$, there is an ε-Nash equilibrium $(\sigma_\varepsilon^*, \pi_\varepsilon^*)$ at s, with $x_1(s) = \lim_{\varepsilon \to 0} \Pr_s^{\sigma_\varepsilon^*, \pi_\varepsilon^*}(\Psi_{1s})$ and $x_2(s) = \lim_{\varepsilon \to 0} \Pr_s^{\sigma_\varepsilon^*, \pi_\varepsilon^*}(\Psi_{2s})$. Consider the gadget $\mathrm{gad}(s)$ to replace s as follows:

- Without loss of generality let $x_1(s) \leq x_2(s)$ (when $x_2(s) \leq x_1(s)$ the gadget is symmetric). Then gadget to replace s is as follows: $\Gamma_1(s) = \{a\}$, $\Gamma_2(s) = \{b\}$, and

$$\delta(s,a,b)(t_{00}) = x_1(s), \qquad \delta(s,a,b)(t_{10}) = x_2(s) - x_1(s),$$
$$\delta(s,a,b)(t_{11}) = 1 - x_2(s), \quad \delta(s,a,b)(t_{01}) = 0,$$

where t_{ij} are as defined in Definition 7.

The construction ensures that at state s the set $\{t_{00}, t_{01}\}$ of states is reached with probability $x_1(s)$, i.e., player 1's objective is satisfied with probability $x_1(s)$, and the set $\{t_{00}, t_{10}\}$ of states is reached with probability $x_2(s)$, i.e., player 2's objective is satisfied with probability $x_2(s)$.

Proposition 1 states that if existence of ε-Nash equilibrium is established at a state s, then state s can be replaced by the gadget $\mathrm{gad}(s)$ and to prove existence of ε-Nash equilibrium in the original game it suffices to prove existence of ε-Nash equilibrium in the transformed game with the gadget $\mathrm{gad}(s)$ replacing state s.

Proposition 1. *Let $\mathcal{G}$ be a SSCC game structure with parity objectives Ψ_1 and Ψ_2 for player 1 and player 2, respectively. Suppose for every $\varepsilon > 0$, there is an ε-Nash equilibrium $(\sigma_\varepsilon^*, \pi_\varepsilon^*)$ at s, with $x_1(s) = \lim_{\varepsilon \to 0} \Pr_s^{\sigma_\varepsilon^*, \pi_\varepsilon^*}(\Psi_{1s})$ and $x_2(s) = \lim_{\varepsilon \to 0} \Pr_s^{\sigma_\varepsilon^*, \pi_\varepsilon^*}(\Psi_{2s})$. The game structure $\mathcal{G}$ can be transformed to a game structure $\mathcal{G}'$ by replacing the state s with the gadget $\mathrm{gad}(s)$ such that if there is an ε-Nash equilibrium in the transformed game structure $\mathcal{G}'$ for all states in $\mathcal{G}'$, for all $\varepsilon > 0$, then there is an ε-Nash equilibrium in the original game structure $\mathcal{G}$ for all states in $\mathcal{G}$, for all $\varepsilon > 0$.* ∎

The result follows from the observation that player 1 and player 2 can switch to strategies $(\sigma_\varepsilon^*, \pi_\varepsilon^*)$ when the game reaches s.

Four Properties (P1-P4). Let $\mathcal{G}$ be a SSCC game structure with parity objectives Ψ_1 and Ψ_2 for player 1 and player 2, respectively. We define four properties (P1-P4) for a state $s \in C$ as follows:

(P1) $\langle\langle 1,2 \rangle\rangle_{val}(\Psi_1 \cap \Psi_2)(s) = 1$; **(P2)** $\langle\langle 1 \rangle\rangle_{val}(\Psi_1)(s) = 1$;
(P3) $\langle\langle 2 \rangle\rangle_{val}(\Psi_2)(s) = 1$; **(P4)** $\langle\langle 1 \rangle\rangle_{val}(\Psi_1)(s) = 0$ and $\langle\langle 2 \rangle\rangle_{val}(\Psi_2)(s) = 0$.

Lemma 1. *Let $\mathcal{G}$ be a* Sscc *game structure with parity objectives Ψ_1 and Ψ_2 for player 1 and player 2, respectively. If any of the four properties (P1-P4) hold for a state $s \in C$, then for every $\varepsilon > 0$, there is an ε-Nash equilibrium (σ^*, π^*) for the state $s \in C$.*

Proof.
1. Suppose there is a state $s \in C$ such that $\langle\langle 1,2 \rangle\rangle_{val}(\Psi_1 \cap \Psi_2)(s) = 1$, then there is a strategy profile (σ^*, π^*) such that $\Pr_s^{\sigma^*,\pi^*}(\Psi_{1s}) = 1$ and $\Pr_s^{\sigma^*,\pi^*}(\Psi_{2s}) = 1$. Since 1 is the maximum payoff a player can achieve, clearly (σ^*, π^*) is a Nash equilibrium at s.
2. Suppose there is a state $s \in C$ such that $\langle\langle 1 \rangle\rangle_{val}(\Psi_1)(s) = 1$. Then for every $\varepsilon > 0$, there is an ε-optimal strategy σ_ε for player 1 such that $\inf_{\pi \in \Pi} \Pr_s^{\sigma_\varepsilon,\pi}(\Psi_{1s}) \geq 1 - \varepsilon$. Consider a strategy π^* such that $\Pr_s^{\sigma_\varepsilon,\pi^*}(\Psi_{2s}) \geq \sup_{\pi \in \Pi} \Pr_s^{\sigma_\varepsilon,\pi}(\Psi_{2s}) - \varepsilon$. In other words, we fix an ε-optimal strategy σ_ε for player 1 and a strategy π^* for player 2 that ensures player 2 the maximal probability to satisfy Ψ_2 against the strategy σ_ε, within ε-precision. Thus we have $\sup_{\sigma \in \Sigma} \Pr_s^{\sigma,\pi^*}(\Psi_{1s}) \leq 1 \leq \Pr_s^{\sigma_\varepsilon,\pi^*}(\Psi_{1s}) + \varepsilon$ and $\sup_{\pi \in \Pi} \Pr_s^{\sigma_\varepsilon,\pi}(\Psi_{2s}) \leq \Pr_s^{\sigma_\varepsilon,\pi^*}(\Psi_{2s}) + \varepsilon$. Hence (σ^*, π^*) is an ε-Nash equilibrium at s, where $\sigma^* = \sigma_\varepsilon$. The proof for the case when we have a state s such that $\langle\langle 2 \rangle\rangle_{val}(\Psi_2)(s) = 1$ is symmetric.
3. Suppose there is a state $s \in C$ such that $\langle\langle 1 \rangle\rangle_{val}(\Psi_1)(s) = 0$ and $\langle\langle 2 \rangle\rangle_{val}(\Psi_2)(s) = 0$. Then consider ε-spoiling strategy pair $(\overline{\sigma_\varepsilon}, \overline{\pi_\varepsilon}) \in \overline{\Sigma_\varepsilon} \times \overline{\Pi_\varepsilon}$. Since $\overline{\sigma_\varepsilon}$ and $\overline{\pi_\varepsilon}$ are ε-spoiling strategies it follows that $\sup_{\pi \in \Pi} \Pr_s^{\overline{\sigma_\varepsilon},\pi}(\Psi_{2s}) \leq \varepsilon$ and $\sup_{\sigma \in \Sigma} \Pr_s^{\sigma,\overline{\pi_\varepsilon}}(\Psi_{1s}) \leq \varepsilon$. Hence $(\sigma^*, \pi^*) = (\sigma_\varepsilon, \pi_\varepsilon)$ is an ε-Nash equilibrium at s. ∎

Let $W_1 = \{ t_{00}, t_{01} \}$ and $W_2 = \{ t_{00}, t_{10} \}$. We consider a nonzero-sum reachability game $\mathcal{G}_R$ on the Sscc game structure $\mathcal{G}$, such that the objectives for player 1 and player 2 are Reach(W_1) and Reach(W_2), respectively. The following key lemma states that if properties (P1-P4) do not hold for every state s in C, then there exists an ε-Nash equilibrium in the game $\mathcal{G}_R$ such that the values of the ε-Nash equilibrium is greater than the respective zero-sum values of the original game. The proof idea is as follows: with the assumption that properties (P1-P4) do not hold for every state in C we establish the existence of ε-optimal strategies σ_ε and π_ε such that $\Pr_s^{\sigma_\varepsilon,\pi_\varepsilon}(\text{Reach}(U)) = 1$, for all states $s \in C$, as $\varepsilon \to 0$. The above fact and a fragment of analysis of Vieille [19] enables us to establish the following lemma. The proof of the lemma is non-trivial, and requires involved construction of *punishing* ε-optimal strategies (details available in [1]).

Lemma 2. *Let $\mathcal{G}$ be a* Sscc *game structure with parity objectives Ψ_1 and Ψ_2 for player 1 and player 2, respectively. If properties (P1-P4) do not hold for every state $s \in C$, then for every $\varepsilon > 0$, there is an ε-Nash equilibrium (σ^*, π^*) in the nonzero-sum reachability game $\mathcal{G}_R$, and there exists $k \in \mathbb{N}$ such that*

1. *$\Pr_s^{\sigma^*,\pi^*}(\mathit{Reach}^k(U)) \geq 1 - \varepsilon$; where $\mathit{Reach}^k(U)$ denotes reachability to U in k steps, i.e., $\mathit{Reach}^k(U) = \{ \langle s_0, s_1, s_2, \ldots \rangle \in \Omega \mid \exists i.\ 0 \leq i \leq k.\ s_i \in U \}$;*
2. *for all plays $\omega = \langle s_0, s_1, s_2, \ldots \rangle \in \text{Outcome}(s, \sigma^*, \pi^*)$, if $\omega_k = \langle s_0, s_1, \ldots, s_k \rangle$ and $s_0 = s$, then (a) $\Pr_s^{\sigma^*,\pi^*}(\mathit{Reach}(W_1) \mid \omega_k) \geq \langle\langle 1 \rangle\rangle_{val}(\Psi_1)(s_k) - \varepsilon$; and (b) $\Pr_s^{\sigma^*,\pi^*}(\mathit{Reach}(W_2) \mid \omega_k) \geq \langle\langle 2 \rangle\rangle_{val}(\Psi_2)(s_k) - \varepsilon$.*

Lemma 3. *Let $\mathcal{G}$ be a* SSCC *game structure with parity objective Ψ_1 for player 1 and Ψ_2 for player 2. If for every state $s \in C$ the properties (P1-P4) do not hold, then for every $\varepsilon > 0$, there is an ε-Nash equilibrium for every state $s \in C$.*

Proof. Fix arbitrary $\varepsilon > 0$, and we show that there is an 3ε-Nash equilibrium for every state $s \in C$. Since ε is arbitrary the result follows. Let (σ^*, π^*) be an ε-Nash equilibrium of the reachability game $\mathcal{G}_R$ as specified in Lemma 2. Consider the strategy σ_ε^* for player 1 defined as follows:

$$\sigma_\varepsilon^*(s_0, s_1 \ldots, s_l) = \begin{cases} \sigma^*(s_0, s_1, \ldots, s_l) & \text{if } l < k \\ \overline{\sigma}_\varepsilon(s_0, s_1, \ldots, s_l) & \text{if } l \geq k \end{cases}$$

where k of Lemma 2 is used and $\overline{\sigma}_\varepsilon \in \overline{\Sigma_\varepsilon}$, i.e., player 1 plays σ^* for k steps and then switches to an ε-spoiling strategy $\overline{\sigma}_\varepsilon$. Similarly, we define the strategy π_ε^* for player 2. Since $\Pr_s^{\sigma^*,\pi^*}(\text{Reach}^k(U)) \geq 1 - \varepsilon$, we have that

$$\Pr_s^{\sigma_\varepsilon^*,\pi_\varepsilon^*}(\Psi_{1s}) \geq \Pr_s^{\sigma^*,\pi^*}(\text{Reach}(W_1)) - \varepsilon; \qquad \Pr_s^{\sigma_\varepsilon^*,\pi_\varepsilon^*}(\Psi_{2s}) \geq \Pr_s^{\sigma^*,\pi^*}(\text{Reach}(W_2)) - \varepsilon.$$

Recall that (σ^*, π^*) is an ε-Nash equilibrium of the reachability game such that for all plays $\omega = \langle s_0, s_1, s_2, \ldots \rangle \in \text{Outcome}(s, \sigma^*, \pi^*)$, if $\omega_k = \langle s_0, s_1, \ldots, s_k \rangle$ and $s_0 = s$, then $\Pr_s^{\sigma^*,\pi^*}(\text{Reach}(W_1) \mid \omega_k) \geq \langle\!\langle 1 \rangle\!\rangle_{val}(\Psi_1)(s_k) - \varepsilon$ and $\Pr_s^{\sigma^*,\pi^*}(\text{Reach}(W_2) \mid \omega_k) \geq \langle\!\langle 2 \rangle\!\rangle_{val}(\Psi_2)(s_k) - \varepsilon$. Since the players play an ε-spoiling strategy after k-steps it follows that

$$\sup_{\sigma \in \Sigma} \Pr_s^{\sigma,\pi_\varepsilon^*}(\Psi_{1s}) \leq \Pr_s^{\sigma^*,\pi^*}(\text{Reach}(W_1)) + 2\varepsilon \leq \Pr_s^{\sigma_\varepsilon^*,\pi_\varepsilon^*}(\Psi_{1s}) + 3\varepsilon;$$

$$\sup_{\pi \in \Pi} \Pr_s^{\sigma_\varepsilon^*,\pi}(\Psi_{2s}) \leq \Pr_s^{\sigma^*,\pi^*}(\text{Reach}(W_2)) + 2\varepsilon \leq \Pr_s^{\sigma_\varepsilon^*,\pi_\varepsilon^*}(\Psi_{2s}) + 3\varepsilon.$$

Hence it follows that $(\sigma_\varepsilon^*, \pi_\varepsilon^*)$ is an 3ε-Nash equilibrium. ∎

Theorem 1 (ε-Nash equilibrium in SSCC **game).** *Let $\mathcal{G}$ be a* SSCC *game structure with parity objective Ψ_1 for player 1 and Ψ_2 for player 2. For every $\varepsilon > 0$, there is an ε-Nash equilibrium for every state $s \in C$.*

Proof. If for every state $s \in C$, the properties (P1-P4) do not hold, then the result follows from Lemma 3. Otherwise, there is a state $s \in C$, such that one of the properties (P1-P4) hold at s, and then by Lemma 1, for every $\varepsilon > 0$, there is an ε-Nash equilibrium at state s. By Proposition 1 we can replace s by the gadget $\text{gad}(s)$. This breaks C into smaller strongly connected components. We can then proceed recursively on the smaller strongly connected components in a bottom-up order. The idea is as follows: consider the transformed game $\mathcal{G}'$ with s replaced by $\text{gad}(s)$. Observe that in the graph $G_{\mathcal{G}'}$ edges out of s end in T, and after replacing s by $\text{gad}(s)$ it belongs to the set U. Consider a lowest strongly connected component $C_1 \subset C$ in the gamegraph $\mathcal{G}'$, i.e., in the graph $G_{\mathcal{G}'}$ there is no edge from C_1 to a state in $C \setminus (C_1 \cup \{s\})$. We consider two cases.

1. If for every state $s_1 \in C_1$, the properties (P1-P4) do not hold, and then from Lemma 3 we conclude that for all $\varepsilon > 0$, ε-Nash equilibrium exists for all states $s_1 \in C_1$.
2. Else for some state $s_1 \in C_1$, one of the properties (P1-P4) hold at s_1, and then using the result of Lemma 1, s_1 can be replaced by $\text{gad}(s_1)$ and we proceed recursively.

Hence we conclude (by induction on the size of the components) that for all $\varepsilon > 0$, ε-Nash equilibrium exists for every state $s_1 \in C_1$. By Proposition 1 every state $s_1 \in C_1$ can be replaced by the gadget $\text{gad}(s_1)$. This gives a smaller SCC game and we proceed in bottom-up fashion to establish the desired result. ∎

4 Existence of ε-Nash Equilibrium

In this section we show that for all nonzero-sum concurrent game structures $\mathcal{G}$, with ω-regular objectives specified as parity objectives Ψ_1 and Ψ_2 for player 1 and player 2, respectively, for every $\varepsilon > 0$, there exists an ε-Nash equilibrium for every state s of game $\mathcal{G}$. The proof follows from an inductive argument: by induction on the size of the state space of $\mathcal{G}$ and by application of Theorem 1. We assume without loss of generality that there are four special states $\{ t_{00}, t_{01}, t_{10}, t_{11} \}$ in $\mathcal{G}$, as defined in Definition 7.

Lemma 4. *Let $\mathcal{G}$ be a concurrent game structure with parity objectives Ψ_1 and Ψ_2 for player 1 and player 2, respectively. Let $G_{\mathcal{G}}$ be the graph of $\mathcal{G}$ and* TC *be a terminal strongly connected component in $G_{\mathcal{G}}$. Then for every $\varepsilon > 0$, there is an ε-Nash equilibrium for every state $s \in$ TC.*

Proof. The proof is by induction on the size of TC. It is easy to argue when $|\text{TC}| = 1$, i.e., TC consists of an absorbing state. Consider the sub-game induced by the set of states TC and call the sub-game $\mathcal{G}_{\text{TC}}$.

- Suppose there is a state $s \in \text{TC}$ such that $\langle\langle 1 \rangle\rangle_{val}(\Psi_1)(s) = 1$. Then fix an ε-optimal strategy σ for player 1 and let π be an ε-optimal strategy for player 2 against σ. Then (σ, π) is an ε-Nash equilibrium. We can replace s by the gadget described in Proposition 1. This will break TC into (possibly many) smaller strongly connected components. By induction hypothesis, Theorem 1 and the bottom-up evaluation procedure described in Theorem 1 it follows that ε-Nash equilibrium exists at every state in TC. Similar arguments hold if there is a state $s \in \text{TC}$ such that $\langle\langle 2 \rangle\rangle_{val}(\Psi_2)(s) = 1$.
- Suppose for every state $s \in \text{TC}$ we have $\langle\langle 1 \rangle\rangle_{val}(\Psi_1)(s) < 1$ and $\langle\langle 2 \rangle\rangle_{val}(\Psi_2)(s) < 1$. It follows from Corollary 1 of [6] that in a zero-sum concurrent game with ω-regular objectives if for every state s we have $\langle\langle 1 \rangle\rangle_{val}(\Psi_1)(s) < 1$, then for every state s in the game we have $\langle\langle 1 \rangle\rangle_{val}(\Psi_1)(s) = 0$, i.e., if the zero-sum value is positive for player 1 at some state, then there exists a state s where the zero-sum value is 1. Hence it follows from the above condition that for all states $s \in \text{TC}$ we have $\langle\langle 1 \rangle\rangle_{val}(\Psi_1)(s) = 0$ and $\langle\langle 2 \rangle\rangle_{val}(\Psi_2)(s) = 0$. Let $\overline{\pi}_\varepsilon$ be an ε-spoiling strategy for

player 2 and $\overline{\sigma}_\varepsilon$ be an ε-spoiling strategy for player 1. Hence we have the following inequalities: $\sup_{\sigma \in \Sigma} \Pr_s^{\sigma, \overline{\pi}_\varepsilon}(\Psi_{1s}) \leq \varepsilon$ and $\sup_{\pi \in \Pi} \Pr_s^{\overline{\sigma}_\varepsilon, \pi}(\Psi_{2s}) \leq \varepsilon$. Hence we have $(\overline{\sigma}_\varepsilon, \overline{\pi}_\varepsilon)$ is an ε-Nash equilibrium for all states $s \in$ TC. ∎

Theorem 2 (ε-Nash equilibrium). *Let $\mathcal{G}$ be a concurrent game structure with parity objectives Ψ_1 and Ψ_2 for player 1 and player 2, respectively. For every $\varepsilon > 0$, there is an ε-Nash equilibrium for every state $s \in S$.*

Proof. Let $G_{\mathcal{G}}$ be the graph of $\mathcal{G}$. It follows from Lemma 4 that for every state s in a terminal strongly connected component of $G_{\mathcal{G}}$ there is an ε-Nash equilibrium, for all $\varepsilon > 0$. By Proposition 1 we can replace every state s of a terminal strongly connected component by the gadget gad(s). For the rest of the strongly connected components we proceed in a bottom-up order as follows: consider a strongly connected component C when all the strongly connected component below it are replaced by the gadgets of Proposition 1. The sub-game induced by C and the gadgets of the strongly connected components below C form a Sscc game. By Theorem 1 we have there is an ε-Nash equilibrium for every state $s \in C$, for all $\varepsilon > 0$. ∎

5 Computational Complexity

In this section we show how to compute the values of an ε-Nash equilibrium of Sscc games within ε-precision. We prove that every case of the existence proof of ε-Nash equilibrium is constructive and computable. It may be noted that even in the case of zero-sum concurrent games with parity objectives the values can be irrational (for an example see [7]). Hence, one can only achieve ε-approximation of the values in the general case of nonzero-sum concurrent parity games. It follows from the inductive argument of Theorem 2 that the values of an ε-Nash equilibrium for nonzero-sum concurrent games with parity objectives can be computed by $|S|$-iterations of a procedure to compute ε-Nash equilibrium values for Sscc games.

Complexity of ε-Nash Equilibrium. To analyze the complexity of computing values of an ε-Nash equilibrium in Sscc games we consider the following cases:

1. Case 1. Compute the values of ε-Nash equilibrium when the property P1 is satisfied for some state s.
2. Case 2. Compute the values of ε-Nash equilibrium when the property P4 is satisfied for some state s.
3. Case 3. Compute the values of ε-Nash equilibrium when the property P2 or P3 is satisfied for some state s.
4. Case 4. Compute the values of some special ε-Nash equilibrium of Sscc games with reachability objectives.

We analyze the above cases below.

1. Case 1. Given Ψ_1 and Ψ_2 are parity objectives, the objective $\Psi_1 \cap \Psi_2$ is a Streett objective [17]. To analyze the computation of $\sup_{(\sigma,\pi)\in\Sigma\times\Pi} \Pr_s^{\sigma,\pi}(\Psi_1 \cap \Psi_2)$, observe that this is equivalent to the computation of values of MDPs where player 1 and player 2 cooperate to achieve the objective $\Psi_1 \cap \Psi_2$. Hence the computation reduces to computing values in a MDP with Streett objective, which can be done in polynomial time [3].
2. Case 2. After the computation of the zero-sum values $\langle\langle 1\rangle\rangle_{val}(\Psi_1)(\cdot)$ and $\langle\langle 2\rangle\rangle_{val}(\Psi_2)(\cdot)$, it is easy to determine if there is a state s such that $\langle\langle 1\rangle\rangle_{val}(\Psi_1)(s) = 0$ and $\langle\langle 2\rangle\rangle_{val}(\Psi_2)(s) = 0$. Hence Case 2 can be solved by computing the zero-sum values for player 1 and player 2.
3. Case 3. Given the zero-sum values for player 1 and player 2, we describe a polynomial time procedure to determine the values of an ε-Nash equilibrium when property P2 or P3 is satisfied. We prove the result for the case when property P2 is satisfied and the result for the case when property P3 is satisfied is symmetric. Consider the set $W = \{ s \mid \langle\langle 1\rangle\rangle_{val}(\Psi_1)(s) = 1 \}$ of states that have zero-sum value 1 for player 1. Since property P2 is satisfied, we have $W \cap C \neq \emptyset$. Given a state $s \in W$, consider the set $\mathrm{SafeAct}(s) = \{a \in \Gamma_1(s) \mid \forall\, b \in \Gamma_2(s).\ \mathrm{Dest}(s,a,b) \subseteq W\}$ of moves for player 1 that ensures that the set W is never left. Consider a reduced sub-game $\mathcal{G}'$ induced by W such that at every state $s \in W$ the available moves for player 1 is $\mathrm{SafeAct}(s)$. Let Σ' be the set of strategies such that player 1 plays only moves in $\mathrm{SafeAct}(s)$ for every state $s \in W$, i.e., the set of strategies in $\mathcal{G}'$. We compute the values $\langle\langle 1,2\rangle\rangle_{val}(\Psi_1 \cap \Psi_2)(s) = \sup_{(\sigma,\pi)\in\Sigma'\times\Pi} \Pr_s^{\sigma,\pi}(\Psi_1 \cap \Psi_2)$. It may be noted that there exists ε-optimal strategy σ_ε in the original game such that for every strategy $\pi \in \Pi$ we have $\Pr_s^{\sigma_\varepsilon,\pi}(\Psi_1 \cap \mathrm{Safe}(W)) \geq 1-\varepsilon$, for all states $s \in W$. Hence it follows that

$$\begin{aligned}\Pr_s^{\sigma_\varepsilon,\pi}(\Psi_2) &\leq \Pr_s^{\sigma_\varepsilon,\pi}(\Psi_1 \cap \Psi_2 \cap \mathrm{Safe}(W)) + \varepsilon \\ &\leq \sup_{(\sigma,\pi)\in\Sigma'\times\Pi} \Pr_s^{\sigma,\pi}(\Psi_1 \cap \Psi_2) + \varepsilon. \end{aligned} \tag{1}$$

   - If for some state $s \in W \cap C$ we have $\langle\langle 1,2\rangle\rangle_{val}(\Psi_1 \cap \Psi_2)(s) = 1$, then property P1 is satisfied and then Case 1 is followed.
   - Else for every state $s \in W \cap C$ we have $\langle\langle 1,2\rangle\rangle_{val}(\Psi_1 \cap \Psi_2)(s) < 1$. It follows from property of MDPs that for any ω-regular objective Ψ, the maximum probability to satisfy Ψ is equal to the maximum probability of reaching the set of states where the value is 1. Hence we have

$$\sup_{(\sigma,\pi)\in\Sigma'\times\Pi} \Pr_s^{\sigma,\pi}(\Psi_1 \cap \Psi_2) = \sup_{(\sigma,\pi)\in\Sigma'\times\Pi} \Pr_s^{\sigma,\pi}(\mathrm{Reach}(t_{00})) \tag{2}$$

   We show that for every state $s \in W \cap C$, the profile $(1, \langle\langle 1,2\rangle\rangle_{val}(\Psi_1 \cap \Psi_2)(s))$ is the values of an ε-Nash equilibrium profile, for all $\varepsilon > 0$. Let $(\widehat{\sigma}, \widehat{\pi})$ be a memoryless strategy profile such that $\Pr_s^{\widehat{\sigma},\widehat{\pi}}(\mathrm{Reach}(t_{00})) = \langle\langle 1,2\rangle\rangle_{val}(\Psi_1 \cap \Psi_2)(s)$, for all $s \in W \cap C$. The existence of such a memoryless strategy profile follows from [4]. For any $\varepsilon > 0$, let $k \in \mathbb{N}$ be such that $\Pr_s^{\widehat{\sigma},\widehat{\pi}}(\text{Reach}^k(t_{OO})) \geq \langle\langle 1,2\rangle\rangle_{val}(\Psi_1 \cap \Psi_2)(s) - \varepsilon$. The strategy profile (σ^*, π^*) is described as follows:

$$\sigma^*(s_0, s_1, \ldots, s_l) = \begin{cases} \widehat{\sigma}(s_0, s_1, \ldots, s_k) & l < k \\ \sigma_\varepsilon(s_0, s_1, \ldots, s_k) & l \geq k \end{cases}$$

where $\sigma_\varepsilon \in \Sigma_\varepsilon$ and $\pi^* = \widehat{\pi}$. Given strategy σ^*, for any strategy π the play never leaves W within k steps, since $\widehat{\sigma} \in \Sigma'$. Since $\sigma_\varepsilon \in \Sigma_\varepsilon$ and for every state $s \in W$ we have $\langle\langle 1\rangle\rangle_{val}(\Psi_1)(s) = 1$ it follows that $\Pr_s^{\sigma^*,\pi^*}(\Psi_1) \geq 1 - \varepsilon$. Since σ^* follows $\widehat{\sigma}$ for k steps, it follows that $\Pr_s^{\sigma^*,\pi^*}(\Psi_2) \geq \Pr_s^{\sigma^*,\pi^*}(\text{Reach}(t_{OO})) - \varepsilon$. It follows from equation 1 and 2 that $\sup_{\pi \in \Pi} \Pr_s^{\sigma^*,\pi}(\Psi_2) \leq \Pr_s^{\sigma^*,\pi^*}(\text{Reach}(t_{OO})) + \varepsilon$. Hence it follows that $(1, \langle\langle 1,2\rangle\rangle_{val}(\Psi_1 \cap \Psi_2)(s))$ is an ε-Nash equilibrium value profile for all states $s \in W \cap C$, for all $\varepsilon > 0$.

It follows from above that the values of an ε-Nash equilibrium of states $s \in C$ can be computed by a polynomial procedure and solving the zero-sum values for player 1 and player 2 when Case 1, Case 2 or Case 3 is satisfied. The analysis of Case 4 involves solving some special ε-Nash equilibrium values of the game $\mathcal{G}_R$ with reachability objectives. The existence of polynomial witness and polynomial time verification procedure for Case 4 follows from the results similar to [5] (details in [1]).

Let $\mathbf{ZS}(\mathcal{G}, \Psi, \varepsilon)$ denote the time complexity of an algorithm to compute the zero-sum values of a concurrent game structure $\mathcal{G}$ within ε-precision, for a parity objective Ψ. Let $\mathbf{NZReach}(\mathcal{G}, \varepsilon, \Psi_1^R, \Psi_2^R)$ denote the time complexity of an algorithm to compute the values of an ε-Nash equilibrium, greater than some specified value, of a concurrent game structure $\mathcal{G}$ with reachability objectives Ψ_1^R and Ψ_2^R for player 1 and player 2, respectively. It follows from [2] and [5] that there exist $\mathbf{ZS}(\mathcal{G}, \varepsilon, \Psi)$ and $\mathbf{NZReach}(\mathcal{G}, \varepsilon, \Psi_1^R, \Psi_2^R)$ that are in the complexity class TFNP, for all constants $\varepsilon > 0$. The above analysis yields the next Theorem.

Theorem 3 (Complexity of ε-Nash equilibrium).

1. *The values of an ε-Nash equilibrium of a nonzero-sum concurrent game structure $\mathcal{G}$ with parity objectives Ψ_1 and Ψ_2 for player 1 and player 2, respectively, can be computed in time*

$$O\big(n \cdot (\mathbf{ZS}(\mathcal{G}, \varepsilon, \Psi_1) + \mathbf{ZS}(\mathcal{G}, \varepsilon, \Psi_2) + \mathbf{NZReach}(\mathcal{G}, \varepsilon, \Psi_1^R, \Psi_2^R))\big) + O\big(p(|\mathcal{G}|)\big)$$

where p is a polynomial function and $n = |S|$ is the size of the state space.

2. *For all constants $\varepsilon > 0$, the values of an ε-Nash equilibrium of nonzero-sum concurrent games with parity objectives can be computed in TFNP; and hence in EXPTIME.*

The existence of ε-Nash equilibrium, for all $\varepsilon > 0$, for higher levels of Borel hierarchy than ω-regular objectives, and for ω-regular objectives for more than two-players are interesting open problems.

Acknowledgments. I am grateful to Tom Henzinger and Luca de Alfaro for several insights on concurrent ω-regular games. I thank Rupak Majumdar for interesting discussions. I am deeply indebted to Nicollas Vieille for several key insights of his results that he gave me. This research was supported in part by the ONR grant N00014-02-1-0671, the AFOSR MURI grant F49620-00-1-0327, and the NSF grant CCR-0225610.

References

1. K. Chatterjee. Two-player nonzero-sum ω-regular games. 2004. Technical Report: UCB/CSD-04-1364.
2. K. Chatterjee, L. de Alfaro, and T.A. Henzinger. The complexity of quantitative concurrent parity games. 2004. Technical Report: UCB/CSD-04-1354.
3. K. Chatterjee, L. de Alfaro, and T.A. Henzinger. The complexity of stochastic Rabin and Streett games. 2004. Technical Report: UCB/CSD-04-1355.
4. K. Chatterjee, L. de Alfaro, and T.A. Henzinger. Trading memory for randomness. In *QEST 04*. IEEE Computer Society Press, 2004.
5. K. Chatterjee, R. Majumdar, and M. Jurdziński. On Nash equilibria in stochastic games. In *CSL 04*, pages 26–40. LNCS, 2004.
6. L. de Alfaro and T.A. Henzinger. Concurrent omega-regular games. In *LICS 00*, pages 141–154. IEEE Computer Society Press, 2000.
7. L. de Alfaro and R. Majumdar. Quantitative solution of omega-regular games. In *STOC 01*, pages 675–683. ACM Press, 2001.
8. J. Filar and K. Vrieze. *Competitive Markov Decision Processes*. Springer-Verlag, 1997.
9. A.M. Fink. Equilibrium in a stochastic n-person game. *Journal of Science of Hiroshima University*, 28:89–93, 1964.
10. J.F. Nash Jr. Equilibrium points in n-person games. *Proceedings of the National Academny of Sciences USA*, 36:48–49, 1950.
11. D.A. Martin. The determinacy of Blackwell games. *The Journal of Symbolic Logic*, 63(4):1565–1581, 1998.
12. G. Owen. *Game Theory*. Academic Press, 1995.
13. C.H. Papadimitriou. On the complexity of the parity argument and other inefficient proofs of existence. *JCSS*, 48(3):498–532, 1994.
14. C.H. Papadimitriou. Algorithms, games, and the internet. In *STOC 01*, pages 749–753. ACM Press, 2001.
15. P. Secchi and W.D. Sudderth. Stay-in-a-set games. *International Journal of Game Theory*, 30:479–490, 2001.
16. L.S. Shapley. Stochastic games. *Proc. Nat. Acad. Sci. USA*, 39:1095–1100, 1953.
17. W. Thomas. Languages, automata, and logic. In *Handbook of Formal Languages*, volume 3, Beyond Words, chapter 7, pages 389–455. Springer, 1997.
18. M.Y. Vardi. Automatic verification of probabilistic concurrent finite-state systems. In *STOC 85*, pages 327–338. IEEE Computer Society Press, 1985.
19. N. Vieille. Two player stochastic games I: a reduction. *Israel Journal of Mathematics*, 119:55–91, 2000.
20. N. Vieille. Two player stochastic games II: the case of recursive games. *Israel Journal of Mathematics*, 119:93–126, 2000.
21. J. von Neumann and O. Morgenstern. *Theory of games and economic behavior*. Princeton University Press, 1947.
22. B. von Stengel. Computing equilibria for two-person games. *Chapter 45, Handbook of Game Theory*, 3:1723–1759, 2002.

Games Where You Can Play Optimally Without Any Memory*

Hugo Gimbert and Wiesław Zielonka

Université Paris 7 and CNRS, LIAFA, case 7014,
2, place Jussieu, 75251 Paris Cedex 05, France
{hugo, zielonka}@liafa.jussieu.fr

Abstract. Reactive systems are often modelled as two person antagonistic games where one player represents the system while his adversary represents the environment. Undoubtedly, the most popular games in this context are parity games and their cousins (Rabin, Streett and Muller games). Recently however also games with other types of payments, like discounted or mean-payoff [5,6], previously used only in economic context, entered into the area of system modelling and verification. The most outstanding property of parity, mean-payoff and discounted games is the existence of optimal positional (memoryless) strategies for both players. This observation raises two questions: (1) can we characterise the family of payoff mappings for which there always exist optimal positional strategies for both players and (2) are there other payoff mappings with practical or theoretical interest and admitting optimal positional strategies. This paper provides a complete answer to the first question by presenting a simple necessary and sufficient condition on payoff mapping guaranteeing the existence of optimal positional strategies. As a corollary to this result we show the following remarkable property of payoff mappings: if both players have optimal positional strategies when playing solitary one-player games then also they have optimal positional strategies for two-player games.

1 Introduction

We investigate deterministic games of infinite duration played on finite graphs. We suppose that there are only two players, called Max and Min, with exactly opposite interests. The games are played in the following way. Let G be a finite graph such that each vertex is controlled either by player Max or by player Min. Initially, a pebble is put on some vertex of G. At each step of the play, the player controlling the vertex with the pebble chooses an outgoing edge and moves the pebble along it to the next vertex. Players interact in this way an infinite number of times and a play of the game is simply an infinite path traversed by the pebble.

* This research was supported by European Research Training Network: Games and Automata for Synthesis and Validation and ACI Sécurité Informatique 2003-22 VERSYDIS.

M. Abadi and L. de Alfaro (Eds.): CONCUR 2005, LNCS 3653, pp. 428–442, 2005.

We assume that the edges of G are coloured by elements of a set C of colours. Thus a play yields an infinite sequence of visited colours and it is this sequence that is used to determine the amount of money paid by player Min to player Max; namely we assume that there is a payoff mapping that maps each infinite sequence of colours to the set $\mathbb{R} \cup \{\pm\infty\}$ of extended reals. The objective of player Max is to maximise the outcome of the game while player Min will seek to minimise it. Players plan their actions and such plans are called strategies. Thus a strategy indicates which move to choose in a given situation and this decision may depend on the whole history of previous moves.

For several well-known games: parity, mean-payoff, discounted games, both players can play optimally using particularly simple positional (or memoryless) strategies; their moves depend then only on the current vertex and all previous history is irrelevant [8,12,7,14]. (In fact, for all three payoffs cited above, if the state and action spaces are finite then even more general perfect information stochastic games have optimal deterministic positional strategies). In computer science, the most popular of these games is the parity game used in model-checking and μ-calculus while discounted and mean-payoff games were studied mainly in economics, see however [5,6].

Games with optimal positional strategies are of much interest in computer science since to implement such strategies no memory is needed, which saves computational resources and there is an ongoing quest for new positionally optimal games, especially on push-down graphs [2,1,11,9].

Recently, Colcombet and Niwiński [4] have shown that for infinite graphs if the payoff takes only values 0 and 1 and is prefix independent (the finite prefix of a play has not influence on the payoff value) then only parity games have positional optimal strategies.

While in our paper we consider only games over finite graphs, contrary to [4] we allow general real valued payoff and do not impose any supplementary restriction (like prefix independence). In the previous paper [10] we provided necessary conditions for a payoff mapping guaranteeing the existence of optimal positional strategies. These conditions were robust enough to hold for all popular positional payoffs as well as for several new ones. Nevertheless, there are some trivial positional payoff mappings that do not satisfy the criteria of [10]. In the present paper we improve on the result of [10] by giving a complete characterisation of positional payoff mappings, i.e. we provide conditions that are both sufficient and necessary.

As an application, we describe how to construct, by means of priorities, new positional payoff mappings. As a particular case, we obtain a positional payoff mapping for which both the parity and mean-payoff games are just special cases. This example may be of interest by itself combining qualitative criteria expressed by parity condition with quantitative measures expressed by mean-payoff. Note that recently another combination of parity and mean-payoff games was proposed in [3], however the payoff of [3] happens to be very different from ours, in particular it is not positional.

2 Games, Arenas, Preferences and Optimal Strategies

For any set C, we write C^*, C^+, C^ω to denote respectively the sets of finite, finite non-empty and infinite words over C. In general, for $X \subset C^*$, $X^* = \sum_{i=0}^{\infty} X^i$ is the usual Kleene iteration operation.

We begin by defining arenas where our players meet to confront each other. Let us fix a set C of *colours*. An *arena* coloured by C is a triple

$$G = (S_{\text{Max}}, S_{\text{Min}}, E),$$

where S_{Max} and S_{Min} are two disjoint sets of states and E is the set of coloured transitions. More specifically, if $S = S_{\text{Max}} \cup S_{\text{Min}}$ is the set of all states then $E \subset S \times C \times S$. For a transition $e = (s, c, t) \in E$, the states s, t and the colour c are respectively called the *source*, the *target* and the *colour* of e and we note $\text{source}(e) = s$, $\text{target}(e) = t$ and $\text{colour}(e) = c$. For a state $s \in S$, $sE = \{e \in E \mid \text{source}(e) = s\}$ is the set of transitions outgoing from s.

Throughout this paper, we always assume that arenas have finitely many states and transitions and that each state has at least one outgoing transition.

A *path* in G is a finite or infinite sequence of transitions $p = e_0e_1e_2\ldots$ such that, for all $i \geq 0$, $\text{target}(e_i) = \text{source}(e_{i+1})$. The source $\text{source}(p)$ of p is the source of the first transition e_0. If p is finite then $\text{target}(p)$ is the target of the last transition in p. It is convenient to assume that for each state s there exists an empty path λ_s with no transitions and such that $\text{source}(\lambda_s) = \text{target}(\lambda_s) = s$. The set of finite paths in G, including the empty paths, is denoted P_G^*.

Two players Max and Min play on the arena G in the following way: if the current game position is a state $s \in S_P$ controlled by player $P \in \{\text{Max}, \text{Min}\}$ then player P chooses an outgoing transition $e \in sE$ and the state $\text{target}(e)$ becomes the new game position. If the initial position is s then in this way the players traverse an infinite path $p = e_0e_1e_2\ldots$ in G such that $\text{source}(p) = s$. In the sequel, finite and infinite paths in G are called often (finite and infinite) *plays*.

Every play $p = e_0e_1e_2\ldots$ generates a sequence

$$\text{colour}(p) = \text{colour}(e_0)\,\text{colour}(e_1)\,\text{colour}(e_2)\ldots$$

of visited colours; we call $\text{colour}(p)$ the *colour* of p (i.e. a colour of a play is a sequence of colours rather than a colour).

Players express their preferences for the game outcomes by means of preference relations.

A *preference relation* over a set C of colours is a binary complete, reflexive and transitive relation over the set C^ω of infinite colour sequences (complete means here that for all $x, y \in C^\omega$ either $x \sqsubseteq y$ or $y \sqsubseteq x$). Thus $\sqsubseteq$ is in fact a complete preorder relation over infinite colour sequences.

Intuitively, if $x \sqsubseteq y$ then the player whose preference relation is $\sqsubseteq$ appreciates the sequence y at least as much as the sequence x. On the other hand, if $x \sqsubseteq y$ and $y \sqsubseteq x$ then the outcomes x and y have the same value for our player, we shall say that x and y are *equivalent for* $\sqsubseteq$. By $\sqsubseteq^{-1}$ by denote the inverse of $\sqsubseteq$, $x \sqsubseteq^{-1} y$ iff $y \sqsubseteq x$.

We shall write $x \sqsubset y$ to denote that $x \sqsubseteq y$ but not $y \sqsubseteq x$.

A two-person game is a triple $(G, \sqsubseteq_{\text{Max}}, \sqsubseteq_{\text{Min}})$, where G is a finite arena and $\sqsubseteq_{\text{Max}}, \sqsubseteq_{\text{Min}}$ are preference relations for players Max and Min. The obvious aim of each player is to obtain the most favourable for him infinite colour sequence.

We will investigate only antagonistic games where the preference relation for player Min is just the inverse of the preference relation of player Max. One of the preference relations being redundant in this case, *antagonistic games* (or simply *games* in the sequel) are just pairs $(G, \sqsubseteq)$, where $\sqsubseteq$ is the preference relation of player Max and G a finite arena.

Most often preference relations are introduced by means of *payoff* or utility mappings. Such a mapping $u : C^\omega \to \mathbb{R} \cup \{-\infty, +\infty\}$ maps infinite colour sequences to extended real numbers. If u is the payoff mapping of player Max for example and the game outcome is an infinite colour sequence $x \in C^\omega$ then player Max receives the payoff $u(x)$. A payoff mapping u induces a natural preference relation $\sqsubseteq_u$ compatible with u and defined by $x \sqsubseteq_u y$ iff $u(x) \leq u(y)$.

Although in game theory preference relations are slightly less employed than payoff mappings they are still standard, for example preference relations are largely used in the popular textbook of Osborne and Rubinstein [13]. We have chosen here to base our exposition on preference relations rather than on payoffs for several reasons: first of all the proofs are more comprehensive when written in the language of preference relations, secondly, one really does not need precise payoff values unless the so-called ϵ-optimal strategies are considered which is not the case in this paper, finally, for some preference relations it would be artificial, cumbersome and counterintuitive to define a corresponding payoff mapping (while, as noted before, the converse is always true, a payoff defines immediately a preference relation).

Intuitively, a strategy of a player is a method he uses to choose his moves during the play. Thus for each finite play p that arrives at a state controlled by player P, $\text{target}(p) \in S_P$, the strategy indicates a transition with the source in the state $\text{target}(p)$ to be taken by player P after p. Therefore in general a *strategy for player* P is a mapping

$$\sigma_P : \{p \in P_G^* \mid \text{target}(p) \in S_P\} \to E,$$

such that $\sigma_P(p) \in sE$ if $s = \text{target}(p)$.

A finite or infinite play $p = e_0 e_1 e_2 \ldots$ is said to be *consistent* with the strategy σ_P if whenever $\text{target}(e_i) \in S_P$ then $e_{i+1} = \sigma_P(e_0 \ldots e_i)$ and moreover $e_0 = \sigma_P(\lambda_s)$ if $s = \text{source}(p) \in \sigma_P$.

A *positional* (or memoryless) strategy for player P is a mapping $\sigma_P : S_P \to E$ such that for all $s \in S_P$, $\sigma_P(s) \in sE$. Using such a strategy σ_P, after a finite play p with $\text{target}(p) \in V_P$ player P chooses the transition $\sigma_P(\text{target}(p))$, i.e. the chosen transition depends only on the current game position. Our interest in positional strategies is motivated by the fact that they are especially easy to implement, no memory of the past history is needed.

In the sequel σ and τ, possibly with subscripts or superscripts, will always denote strategies for players Max and Min respectively.

Given a state t and strategies σ and τ for players Max and Min, there exists a unique play in G, denoted by $p_G(t, \sigma, \tau)$, with source t consistent with both σ and τ.

Strategies $\sigma^\#$ and $\tau^\#$ are called *optimal* if for all states $s \in S$ and all strategies σ and τ of both players

$$\mathrm{colour}(p_G(s, \sigma, \tau^\#)) \sqsubseteq \mathrm{colour}(p_G(s, \sigma^\#, \tau^\#)) \sqsubseteq \mathrm{colour}(p_G(s, \sigma^\#, \tau)) . \quad (1)$$

Inequalities above mean that players Max and Min have no incentive to deviate unilaterally from their optimal strategies.

It is easy to see that if $(\sigma_1^\#, \tau_1^\#)$ and $(\sigma_2^\#, \tau_2^\#)$ are pairs of optimal strategies then $(\sigma_1^\#, \tau_2^\#)$ and $(\sigma_2^\#, \tau_1^\#)$ are optimal and in fact $\mathrm{colour}(p_G(s, \sigma_1^\#, \tau_1^\#)))$ and $\mathrm{colour}(p_G(s, \sigma_2^\#, \tau_2^\#)))$ are equivalent for $\sqsubseteq$.

3 Preferences Relations with Optimal Positional Strategies

The main aim of this section it to provide a complete characterisation of preference relations for which both players have optimal positional strategies for all games on finite arenas.

Let $\mathrm{Rec}(C)$ be the family of recognizable subsets of C^* (C can be infinite and then $L \in \mathrm{Rec}(C)$ means that there exists a finite subset B of C such that L a recognizable subset of B^*). For any language of finite words $L \subset C^*$, $\mathrm{Pref}(L)$ will stand for the set of all prefixes of the words in L. We define an operator $[\cdot]$ that associates with each language $L \subset C^*$ of finite words a set $[L] \subset C^\omega$ of infinite words:

$$[L] = \{x \in C^\omega \mid \text{every finite prefix of } x \text{ is in } \mathrm{Pref}(L)\} .$$

We extend the preference relation $\sqsubseteq$ to subsets of C^ω: for $X, Y \subset C^\omega$,

$$X \sqsubseteq Y \quad \text{iff} \quad \forall x \in X, \exists y \in Y, x \sqsubseteq y .$$

Obviously, for $x \in C^\omega$ and $Y \subset C^\omega$, $x \sqsubseteq Y$ and $Y \sqsubseteq x$ stand for $\{x\} \sqsubseteq Y$ and $Y \sqsubseteq \{x\}$ respectively. We write also

$$X \sqsubset Y \quad \text{iff} \quad \exists y \in Y, \forall x \in X, x \sqsubset y .$$

Definition 1. *A preference relation $\sqsubseteq$ is said to be* monotone *if for all recognizable sets $M, N \in \mathrm{Rec}(C)$,*

$$\exists x \in C^*, [xM] \sqsubset [xN] \implies \forall y \in C^*, [yM] \sqsubseteq [yN] .$$

A preference relation $\sqsubseteq$ is said to be selective *if for each finite word $x \in C^*$ and all recognizable languages $M, N, K \in \mathrm{Rec}(C)$,*

$$[x(M \cup N)^* K] \sqsubseteq [xM^*] \cup [xN^*] \cup [xK] .$$

Now we are ready to state the main result of this paper.

Theorem 2. *Given a preference relation $\sqsubseteq$, both players have optimal positional strategies for all games $(G, \sqsubseteq)$ over finite arenas G if and only if the relations $\sqsubseteq$ and its inverse $\sqsubseteq^{-1}$ are monotone and selective.*

Before proceeding to the proof of Theorem 2 it can be useful to convey some intuitions behind the definitions of monotone and selective properties.

Roughly speaking, a preference relation of Max is monotone if at each moment during the play the optimal choice of player Max between two possible futures does not depend on the preceding finite play. For example, consider the payoff function u defined on the set $C = \mathbb{R}$ of colours by the formula

$$u(x_1 x_2 \ldots) = \sup_{n \in \mathbb{N}} \frac{1}{n} \sum_{k=1}^{n} x_k, \tag{2}$$

where $x_1 x_2 \ldots$ is an infinite sequence of real numbers. Consider the finite sequences $x = 0000$ and $y = 1111$ and the infinite sequences $v = 2000\ldots = 20^\omega$ and $w = 1111\ldots = 1^\omega$. Then $u(xv) < u(xw)$ while $u(yw) < u(yv)$, hence the preference relation $\sqsubseteq_u$ associated with u is not monotone. This means that player Max has no optimal positional strategy in the one-player arena depicted on the left of Fig 1, if Max plays optimally the transition to take at state z depends on whether he arrives from s or from t. It is worth to note that the payoff (2) is selective.

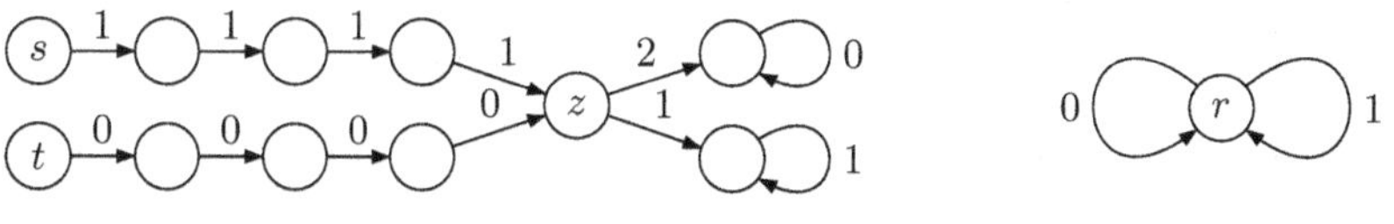

Fig. 1. When playing on the left arena using the non-monotone payoff (2), or playing on the right arena using the non-selective payoff "wins 1 if the colours 0 and 1 appear infinitely often and 0 otherwise" player Max has no optimal positional strategies.

The selective property expresses the fact that player Max cannot improve his payoff by switching between different behaviors. Typical non selective payoff is provided by the Muller condition. Let u be the payoff function for $C = \{0, 1\}$ defined by $u(x_0 x_1 \ldots) = 1$ if the colours 0 and 1 occur infinitely often, otherwise the payoff is 0. This payoff mapping is monotone (as are all payoffs that do not depend on finite prefixes) but is not selective. It is clear that when Max plays with this payoff on the one-player arena depicted on the right of Fig 1 then he should alternate infinitely often between the two transitions to maximize his payoff.

We begin the proof of Theorem 2 by noting the following trivial property of the operator $[\cdot]$:

Lemma 3. *For all* $L, M \subset C^*$, $[L \cup M] = [L] \cup [M]$.

A finite (non-deterministic) automaton over C is a tuple $\mathcal{A} = (Q, i, F, \Delta)$, where Q is a finite set of states, $i \in Q$ the initial state, $F \subset Q$ the set of final states and $\Delta \subset Q \times C \times Q$ is the transition relation. A path in $\mathcal{A}$ is a path in the one-player arena $(Q, \emptyset, \Delta)$ that we can construct from $\mathcal{A}$ and the notions of source, target and colour of a path are defined as for arenas. So, in this terminology, the language recognized by $\mathcal{A}$ is simply the set $\{\text{colour}(p) \mid p \text{ is a finite path in } \mathcal{A} \text{ such that source}(p) = i \text{ and target}(p) \in F\}$. The automaton $\mathcal{A}$ is said to be *co-accessible* if from any state there is a (possibly empty) path to a final state.

Lemma 4. *Let* $\mathcal{A} = (Q, i, F, \Delta)$ *be a co-accessible finite automaton recognizing a language* $L \subset C^*$. *Then*

$$[L] = \{\text{colour}(p) \mid p \textit{ is an infinite path in } \mathcal{A} \textit{ with } \text{source}(p) = i\}.$$

Proof. Let $p = e_0 e_1 e_2 \ldots$ be an infinite path in $\mathcal{A}$, where $\forall j, e_j \in \Delta$ and $\text{source}(e_0) = i$. Since $\mathcal{A}$ is co-accessible, for every n there is a path from the state $\text{target}(e_n)$ to a final state. Therefore the finite word $\text{colour}(e_0 \ldots e_n)$ is a prefix of some word recognized by $\mathcal{A}$. Hence $\text{colour}(p) \in [L]$.

Conversely, let $x = c_0 c_1 c_2 \cdots \in [L]$. Let T be the directed tree defined as follows. The vertices of T are finite paths q in $\mathcal{A}$ such that $\text{colour}(q)$ is a prefix of x and $\text{source}(q) = i$. There is an edge from a vertex q of T to a vertex q' iff there is a transition $e \in \Delta$ such that $q' = qe$. The root of T is the empty path λ_i with the source and target i. Clearly, T is infinite since x is infinite and the degree of vertices of T is bounded by the cardinality of Δ. Hence, by the Koenig Lemma, there exists an infinite path in T starting from the root λ_i. This infinite path corresponds to an infinite path in $\mathcal{A}$ coloured by x. □

It turns out that already for one-player games controlled by player Max to guarantee that Max has an optimal positional strategy it is necessary for his preference relation $\sqsubseteq$ to be monotone and selective:

Lemma 5. *Suppose that player* Max *has optimal positional strategies for all games* $(G, \sqsubseteq)$ *over finite one-player arenas* $G = (S_{\text{Max}}, \emptyset, E)$, *where he controls all states. Then* $\sqsubseteq$ *is monotone and selective.*

Proof. We want to use finite automata as one-player arenas with all states controlled by player Max. Technically however, this raises a problem since we require that arenas have always at least one outgoing transition for each state s and this condition may fail for automata. For this reason we introduce the following notion.

For any finite automaton $\mathcal{A} = (Q, i, F, \Delta)$, a state $s \in Q$ is said to be *essential* if there exists an infinite path in $\mathcal{A}$ with source s. A transition is essential if its target is essential. Note that for any essential state s there is at least one essential transition with source s and any infinite path in $\mathcal{A}$ traverses uniquely essential states and transitions. Moreover, by Lemma 4, if $\mathcal{A}$ is co-accessible and recognizes

L then $[L] \neq \emptyset$ iff the initial state is essential. By arena($\mathcal{A}$) we shall denote the arena $(Q', \emptyset, \Delta')$, where Q' and Δ' are respectively the sets of essential states and essential transitions of $\mathcal{A}$.

Suppose that $\sqsubseteq$ satisfies the hypothesis of our lemma. We show first that $\sqsubseteq$ is monotone. Let $x, y \in C^*$ and $M, N \in \mathrm{Rec}(C)$ and

$$[xM] \sqsubset [xN] \ . \tag{3}$$

We shall prove that this implies

$$[yM] \sqsubseteq [yN] \ . \tag{4}$$

Let $\mathcal{A}_x$ and $\mathcal{A}_y$ be the usual deterministic co-accessible automata recognizing the one-word languages $\{x\}$ and $\{y\}$. Let $\mathcal{A}_M, \mathcal{A}_N$ be finite co-accessible automata recognizing respectively M, N. Without loss of generality we can assume that neither $\mathcal{A}_M$ nor $\mathcal{A}_N$ has a transition with the initial state as the target.

If $[M]$ is empty then (4) holds trivially. Thus we can assume that $[M]$ and $[N]$ are non-empty and the initial states of $\mathcal{A}_M$ and $\mathcal{A}_N$ are essential.

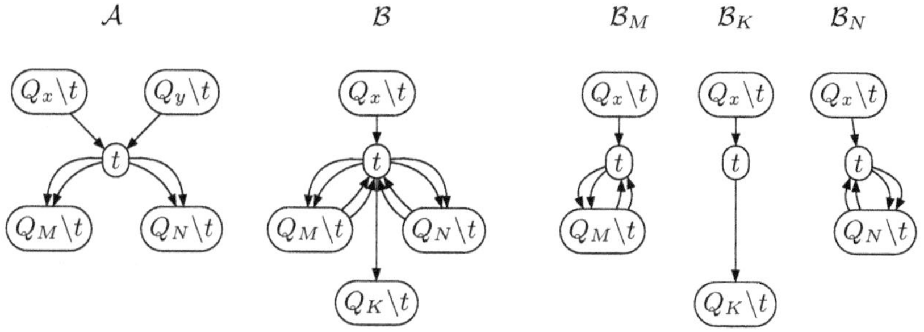

Fig. 2. Automaton $\mathcal{A}$ used to prove that $\sqsubseteq$ is monotone is obtained by "gluing" together the final states of $\mathcal{A}_x$ and $\mathcal{A}_y$ with initial states of $\mathcal{A}_M$ and $\mathcal{A}_N$. Q_x, Q_y, Q_M, Q_N are the states of the corresponding automata. Automaton $\mathcal{B}$ used to prove that $\sqsubseteq$ is selective is obtained by "gluing" together the final state of $\mathcal{A}_x$, the initial and the final states of $\mathcal{A}_M$ and $\mathcal{A}_N$ and the initial state of $\mathcal{A}_K$.

From automata $\mathcal{A}_x, \mathcal{A}_y, \mathcal{A}_M, \mathcal{A}_N$ we obtain a new automaton $\mathcal{A}$ by identifying the following four states: the final state of $\mathcal{A}_x$, the final state of $\mathcal{A}_y$, the initial state of $\mathcal{A}_M$ and the initial state of $\mathcal{A}_N$. We note t the state obtained in this way. The transitions of $\mathcal{A}_x$ and $\mathcal{A}_y$ with target in the final state have target t in $\mathcal{A}$ while the transitions of $\mathcal{A}_M, \mathcal{A}_N$ with the source in the initial state have source t in $\mathcal{A}$. All the other states and transitions remain unchanged in $\mathcal{A}$, see Fig 2. The final states of $\mathcal{A}_M$ and $\mathcal{A}_N$ are final in $\mathcal{A}$ while the initial state of $\mathcal{A}_x$ is initial in $\mathcal{A}$. Note that since $\mathcal{A}_M$ and $\mathcal{A}_N$ are co-accessible $\mathcal{A}$ is also co-accessible. Moreover, $\mathcal{A}$ recognizes the language $x(M \cup N)$ (since we have assumed that no transition of $\mathcal{A}_M$ and $\mathcal{A}_N$ returns to the initial state).

Let $\sigma^{\#}$ be an optimal positional strategy of player Max in the game (arena($\mathcal{A}$), u). Then, by Lemma 4 applied to $\mathcal{A}$, the set of plays in arena($\mathcal{A}$) starting from the initial state of $\mathcal{A}$ is $[x(M \cup N)]$, which is equal to $[xM] \cup [xN]$ by Lemma 3. Let p be the unique infinite play in arena($\mathcal{A}$) with source in the initial state of $\mathcal{A}$ and consistent with the strategy $\sigma^{\#}$. Then by optimality of $\sigma^{\#}$, $[xM] \cup [xN] \sqsubseteq \text{colour}(p)$ implying, by (3), $\text{colour}(p) \notin [xM]$.

Therefore, play p reaching the state t takes a transition leading to the states of $\mathcal{A}_N$ (Fig. 2) and stays forever in $\mathcal{A}_N$ in the sequel. In other words, we can conclude that $\sigma^{\#}(t)$ is a transition of $\mathcal{A}_N$.

Now let us examine the unique infinite play q in arena($\mathcal{A}$) consistent with $\sigma^{\#}$ and starting at the initial state of $\mathcal{A}_y$. Since q is consistent with $\sigma^{\#}$ and $\sigma^{\#}(t)$ is a transition of $\mathcal{A}_N$, play q traverses first the states of automaton $\mathcal{A}_y$ and next the states of $\mathcal{A}_N$.

Since from all the states traversed by q we can reach in $\mathcal{A}$ the final states of $\mathcal{A}_N$, we have

$$\text{colour}(q) \in [yN] \ . \tag{5}$$

On the other hand, for the same reasons as for $\mathcal{A}$ but now with the initial state of A_y, the optimality of $\sigma^{\#}$ yields $[yM] \cup [yN] \sqsubseteq \text{colour}(q)$. This and (5) imply immediately (4).

It remains to prove that $\sqsubseteq$ is selective. Let $x \in C^*$, $M, N, K \in \text{Rec}(C)$. Without loss of generality we can assume that M and N do not contain the empty word and choose the automata $\mathcal{A}_M$ and $\mathcal{A}_N$ recognizing M and N to be co-accessible, with one initial and one final state and with no transition returning to the initial state and no transition leaving the final state. Let A_K be a co-accessible automaton recognizing K with no transition returning to its initial state. We glue together the final states of automata $\mathcal{A}_x, \mathcal{A}_M, \mathcal{A}_N$ and the initial states of $\mathcal{A}_M, \mathcal{A}_N, \mathcal{A}_K$. The resulting state is called t. Taking the initial state from $\mathcal{A}_x$ and the final states from $\mathcal{A}_K$ we obtain an automaton $\mathcal{B}$.

Let $\sigma^{\#}$ be an optimal positional strategy of player Max in the game (arena($\mathcal{B}$), $\sqsubseteq$). Let p be the infinite play consistent with $\sigma^{\#}$ and with the initial state of $\mathcal{B}$ as the source. Automaton $\mathcal{B}$ is co-accessible and recognizes the language $x(M \cup N)^*K$, therefore, by Lemma 4 and optimality of $\sigma^{\#}$,

$$[x(M \cup N)^*K] \sqsubseteq \text{colour}(p) \ . \tag{6}$$

Since $\sigma^{\#}$ is positional, each time p traverses the state t, $\sigma^{\#}$ chooses the same outgoing transition. This means that p is an infinite path in one of the three co-accessible automata $\mathcal{B}_M, \mathcal{B}_N, B_K$ depicted on Fig. 2. By Lemma 4, $\text{colour}(p) \sqsubseteq [xM^*] \cup [xN^*] \cup [xK]$. This and (6) imply that u is selective. □

With each arena G with a state set S and a transition set E we associate the *index* n_G of G defined as $n_G = |E| - |S|$. Note that since in arenas each state has at least one outgoing transition the index is always non-negative. The proof of Theorem 2 will be carried on by induction on the value of n_G and the decisive inductive step is provided by the following lemma.

Lemma 6. *Let G be an arena and $\sqsubseteq$ a monotone and selective preference relation. Suppose that players* Max *and* Min *have optimal positional strategies in all games $(H, \sqsubseteq)$ over the arenas H such that $n_H < n_G$. Then* Max *has an optimal positional strategy in the game $(G, \sqsubseteq)$.*

Proof. Let $G = (S_{\text{Max}}, S_{\text{Min}}, E)$ and let $\sqsubseteq$ be monotone and selective. If for every $t \in S_{\text{Max}}$ there is only one transition with the source t then Max has never any choice and he has therefore a unique strategy which is positional and optimal.

Suppose now that there exists a state $t \in S_{\text{Max}}$ such that $|tE| > 1$. Fix a partition of tE into two disjoint non-empty sets A_0, A_1. We define two new arenas $G_i = (S_{\text{Max}}, S_{\text{Min}}, E_i)$, $i = 0, 1$, where $E_i = E \setminus A_{1-i}$. In other words, G_i is obtained by removing from G the transitions with the source t not belonging to A_i. Since $n_{G_i} < n_G$ we can apply the hypothesis of our lemma to the games $\mathbf{G}_i = (G_i, \sqsubseteq)$ to conclude that in both games $\mathbf{G}_i$ players Max and Min have optimal positional strategies $\sigma_i^\#$, $\tau_i^\#$ respectively. Let us note $\mathbf{G} = (G, \sqsubseteq)$ the initial game over G.

Let $M_i \subset C^*$ be the set of finite colour sequences colour(p) of all finite plays p in G_i that are consistent with strategy $\tau_i^\#$ and have source and target t.

To see that $M_i \in \text{Rec}(C)$, we can build a finite automaton with the same state space as for the arena G_i, we keep also all transitions of G_i that have the source in the set S_{Max}, however for each state $s \in S_{\text{Min}}$ controlled by player Min we keep only one outgoing transition, namely the transition $\tau_i^\#(s) \in sE_i$ chosen by the strategy $\tau_i^\#$. Then M_i is the set of words recognized by such an automaton if we take t as the initial and the final state.

Now we define the sets $K_i \subset C^*$, $i = 0, 1$ consisting of colours colour(p) of all finite plays p in the arena G_i that have source t and are consistent with $\tau_i^\#$ (but can end in any state of G_i). Again it should be obvious that $K_i \in \text{Rec}(C)$.

The monotonicity of $\sqsubseteq$ implies that either $\forall x \in C^*, [xK_0] \sqsubseteq [xK_1]$ or $\forall x \in C^*, [xK_1] \sqsubseteq [xK_0]$ Since the former condition is symmetric to the latter, without loss of generality, we can assume that

$$\forall x \in C^*, [xK_1] \sqsubseteq [xK_0] \ . \tag{7}$$

Let us set

$$\sigma^\# = \sigma_0^\# \ . \tag{8}$$

We shall show that, if (7) holds then strategy $\sigma^\#$ is not only optimal for player Max in the game $\mathbf{G}_0$ but it is also optimal for him in $\mathbf{G}$. It is clear that $\sigma^\#$ is a well-defined positional strategy for Max in the game $\mathbf{G}$. To finish the proof of Lemma 6 we should construct a strategy $\tau^\#$ for player Min such that $(\sigma^\#, \tau^\#)$ is a couple of optimal strategies. However, contrary to $\sigma^\#$, to implement the strategy $\tau^\#$ player Min will need some finite memory.

We define first a mapping $h : P_G^* \to \{0, 1\}$ that assigns to each finite play $p \in P_G^*$ in G a one bit value $h(p)$:

$$h(p) = \begin{cases} 0 & \text{if either } p \text{ does not contain any transition with the source } t \text{ or} \\ & \text{the last transition of } p \text{ with the source } t \text{ belongs to } A_0, \\ 1 & \text{if the last transition of } p \text{ with the source } t \text{ belongs to } A_1. \end{cases}$$

Then the strategy $\tau^{\#}$ of Min in $\mathbf{G}$ is defined by

$$\tau^{\#}(p) = \begin{cases} \tau_0^{\#}(\text{target}(p)) & \text{if } h(p) = 0, \\ \tau_1^{\#}(\text{target}(p)) & \text{if } h(p) = 1, \end{cases}$$

for finite plays p with target$(p) \in S_{\text{Min}}$. In other words, playing in $\mathbf{G}$ player Min applies either his optimal strategy $\tau_0^{\#}$ from the game $\mathbf{G}_0$ or his optimal strategy $\tau_1^{\#}$ from the game $\mathbf{G}_1$ depending on the value $h(p)$. Initially, before the first visit to t, player Min uses the strategy $\tau_0^{\#}$. After the first visit to t the choice between $\tau_0^{\#}$ and $\tau_1^{\#}$ depends on the transition chosen by his adversary Max at the last visit to t, if the chosen transition was in A_0 then player Min uses the strategy $\tau_0^{\#}$, otherwise, if Max took a transition of A_1 then player Min plays according to $\tau_1^{\#}$. The intuition behind the definition of $\tau^{\#}$ is the following: If at the last visit to t player Max has chosen a outgoing transition from A_0 then this means that the play from this moment onward is like a play in $\mathbf{G}_0$ and therefore player Min tries to respond using his optimal strategy from $\mathbf{G}_0$. Symmetrically, if at the last visit to t player Max has chosen an outgoing transition from A_1 then from this moment onward the play is like a play in $\mathbf{G}_1$ and player Min tries to counter with his optimal strategy from $\mathbf{G}_1$.

It should be clear that the strategy $\tau^{\#}$ needs in fact just two valued memory $\{0, 1\}$ for player Min to remember if during the last visit to t a transition of A_0 or a transition of A_1 was chosen by his adversary. This memory is initialised to 0 and updated only when the state t is visited.

We shall prove that $(\sigma^{\#}, \tau^{\#})$ is a couple of optimal strategies in $\mathbf{G}$, i.e. (1) holds for any strategies σ, τ of players Max and Min and any initial state s.

In the sequel we shall write frequently $p \sqsubseteq q$ for infinite plays p and q as an abbreviation of colour$(p) \sqsubseteq$ colour(q).

Let τ be any strategy for player Min in the game $\mathbf{G}$ and let τ_0 be its restriction to the set $P^*_{G_0}$ of finite plays in the arena G_0. Clearly τ_0 is a valid strategy of Min over the arena G_0. Then for any state s of G

$$\begin{aligned} p_G(s, \sigma^{\#}, \tau^{\#}) &= p_{G_0}(s, \sigma_0^{\#}, \tau_0^{\#}) && \text{by definition of } \sigma^{\#} \text{ and } \tau^{\#}, \\ &\sqsubseteq p_{G_0}(s, \sigma_0^{\#}, \tau_0) && \text{by optimality of } (\sigma_0^{\#}, \tau_0^{\#}) \text{ in } \mathbf{G}_0, \\ &= p_G(s, \sigma^{\#}, \tau) && \text{by definition of } \sigma^{\#} \text{ and } \tau_0, \end{aligned}$$

which concludes the proof of the right hand side inequality in (1).

Now let σ be any strategy for player Max in $\mathbf{G}$ and s any state of G. There are two cases to examine depending on whether the play $p_G(s, \sigma, \tau^{\#})$ traverses t or not.

Case 1: $p_G(s, \sigma, \tau^{\#})$ does not traverse the state t.

In this case, according to the definition of $\tau^{\#}$, player Min uses in fact all the time during this play the strategy $\tau_0^{\#}$, never switching to $\tau_1^{\#}$.

Let us take any strategy σ_0 for player Max which is defined exactly as σ for all finite plays with the target different from t while for plays with target

t the strategy σ_0 chooses always a transition of A_0. The last condition implies that σ_0 is also a valid strategy over the arena G_0. Moreover, since $p_G(s,\sigma,\tau^\#)$ never traverses t the strategies σ and σ_0 choose the same transitions for all finite prefixes of $p_G(s,\sigma,\tau^\#)$ with the target the state controlled by player Max, therefore $p_G(s,\sigma,\tau^\#) = p_{G_0}(s,\sigma_0,\tau_0^\#)$. However, $p_{G_0}(s,\sigma_0,\tau_0^\#) \sqsubseteq p_{G_0}(s,\sigma_0^\#,\tau_0^\#) = p_G(s,\sigma^\#,\tau^\#)$, where the first inequality follows from optimality of $\sigma_0^\#,\tau_0^\#$ in $\mathbf{G}_0$ while the last equality is just the consequence of (8) and definition $\tau^\#$. Therefore, $p_G(s,\sigma,\tau^\#) \sqsubseteq p_G(s,\sigma^\#,\tau^\#)$, i.e. the left-hand side of (1) holds in this case.

Case 2: $p_G(s,\sigma,\tau^\#)$ traverses the state t.
Let p' be the shortest finite play such that p' is a prefix of $p_G(s,\sigma,\tau^\#)$ and $\mathrm{target}(p') = t$. Note that by the definition of $\tau^\#$ it follows that p' is in fact consistent with $\tau_0^\#$. Let $\mathrm{colour}(p') = x$.

Then by definition of x, M_0, M_1, K_0 and K_1, any prefix of $\mathrm{colour}(p_G(s,\sigma,\tau^\#))$ longer than x belongs to the set $x(M_0 \cup M_1)^*(K_0 \cup K_1)$, hence

$$
\begin{aligned}
\mathrm{colour}(p_G(s,\sigma,\tau^\#)) &\in [x(M_0 \cup M_1)^*(K_0 \cup K_1)] \\
&\sqsubseteq [x(M_0)^*] \cup [x(M_1)^*] \cup [x(K_0 \cup K_1)] && \text{since } \sqsubseteq \text{ is selective,} \\
&\sqsubseteq [x(M_0)^*] \cup [x(M_1)^*] \cup [xK_0] \cup [xK_1] && \text{by Lemma 3,} \\
&\sqsubseteq [xK_0] \cup [xK_1] && \text{since } (M_i)^* \subset K_i, \\
&\sqsubseteq [xK_0] && \text{by (7).}
\end{aligned}
\tag{9}
$$

Let us define a new transition set $\delta \subset E$, where E is the the set of transitions of the arena G: for any state r of G the set of transitions with source r under δ is defined by:

$$
r\delta = \begin{cases} A_0 & \text{if } r = t, \\ rE & \text{if } r \in S_{\mathrm{Max}} \setminus \{t\}, \\ \tau_0^\#(r) & \text{if } r \in S_{\mathrm{Min}}. \end{cases} \tag{10}
$$

Let Q be the set of states of G that are accessible from t under δ. Take a finite automaton $\mathcal{D}$ with the initial state t, the set of states Q all of which are final and the transition relation δ restricted to Q.

Automaton $\mathcal{D}$ is co-accessible, recognizes the language K_0 and therefore, by Lemma 4, $[K_0]$ is precisely the set of colour sequences $\mathrm{colour}(q)$ of infinite plays q with source t that are consistent with $\tau_0^\#$.

Let U be the set of all colour sequences $\mathrm{colour}(q')$ of infinite plays q' in G_0 with source s that are consistent with $\tau_0^\#$. Then $x[K_0] \subset U$ implying that

$$
x[K_0] \sqsubseteq U \sqsubseteq \mathrm{colour}(p_{G_0}(s,\sigma_0^\#,\tau_0^\#)), \tag{11}
$$

where the last inequality follows from optimality of $\sigma_0^\#$ in the game $\mathbf{G}_0$. But, by definition of $\sigma^\#$ and $\tau^\#$, we get $p_{G_0}(s,\sigma_0^\#,\tau_0^\#) = p_G(s,\sigma^\#,\tau^\#)$, which together with (9) and (11) yield $p_G(s,\sigma,\tau^\#) \sqsubseteq p_G(s,\sigma^\#,\tau^\#)$ terminating the proof of the left hand-side of (1) in this case. □

Proof. of Theorem 2. Note that, due to symmetry, we can permute players Max and Min and replace the preference relation $\sqsubseteq$ by $\sqsubseteq^{-1}$ in Lemmas 5 and 6. Since, clearly, players have optimal positional strategies for the preference relation $\sqsubseteq$ iff they have optimal positional strategies with the preference $\sqsubseteq^{-1}$ under the permutation (in fact these are the same strategies), Lemma 5 shows that to be monotone and selective for $\sqsubseteq$ and $\sqsubseteq^{-1}$ is necessary for the existence of optimal positional strategies.

Now Lemma 6 allows us to apply a trivial induction over the arena index to conclude immediately that these conditions are also sufficient. □

The following corollary turns out to be much more useful in practice than Theorem 2 itself.

Corollary 7. *Suppose that $\sqsubseteq$ is such that for each finite arena $G = (S_{\text{Max}}, S_{\text{Min}}, E)$ controlled by one player, i.e. such that either $S_{\text{Max}} = \emptyset$ or $S_{\text{Min}} = \emptyset$, the player controlling all states of G has an optimal positional strategy in the game $(G, \sqsubseteq)$. Then for all finite two-player arenas G both players have optimal positional strategies in the games $(G, \sqsubseteq)$.*

Proof. By Lemma 5 if both players have optimal positional strategies on one-player games then $\sqsubseteq$ and $\sqsubseteq^{-1}$ are monotone and selective and then, by Theorem 2, they have optimal positional strategies on all two-person games on finite arenas. □

4 An Example: Priority Mean-Payoff Games

The interest in Corollary 7 stems from the fact that often it is quite trivial to verify if a given preference relation is positional for one-player games. To illustrate this point let us consider mean-payoff games [7]. Here colours are real numbers and for an infinite sequence $r_1 r_2 \dots$ of elements of $\mathbb{R}$ the payoff is calculated by $\limsup_{n\to\infty} \frac{1}{n}\sum_{i=1}^{n} r_i$. Suppose that G is an arena controlled by player Max. Take in G a simple cycle (in the sense of graph theory) with the maximal mean value. It is easy to see that any other infinite play in G cannot supply a payoff greater than the mean-payoff over this cycle. Thus the optimal positional strategy for player Max is to go as quickly as possible to this maximum payoff cycle and next go round this cycle forever. Clearly, player Min has also optimal positional strategies for all arenas where he controls all states and Corollary 7 allows us to conclude that in mean-payoff games both players have optimal positional strategies.

As a more sophisticated example illustrating Corollary 7 we introduce here *priority mean-payoff games.* Let $C = \{0, \dots, k\} \times \mathbb{R}$ be the set of colours, where for each couple $(m, r) \in \{0, \dots, k\} \times \mathbb{R}$ the non-negative integer m is called the *priority* and r is a real-valued reward. The payoff for an infinite sequence $x = (m_1, r_1), (m_2, r_2), \dots$ of colours is calculated in the following way: let $k = \limsup_{i\to\infty} m_i$ be the maximal priority appearing infinitely often in x and let $i_1 < i_2 < \dots$ be the infinite sequence of all positions in x with the priority k, i.e. $k = m_{i_1} = m_{i_2} = \dots$. Then the priority mean-payoff is calculated as the mean payoff of the corresponding subsequence $r_{i_1} r_{i_2} \ldots$ of real rewards, $\limsup_{t\to\infty} \frac{1}{t}\sum_{n=1}^{t} r_{i_n}$. In other words priorities are used here to select an appropriate subsequence of real rewards for which the mean-payoff mapping is applied subsequently.

This payoff, rather contrived at first sight, is in fact a common natural generalization of mean-payoff and parity payoffs. On the one hand, we recover simple mean-payoff games if there is only one priority. On the other hand, if we allow only a subset of colours consisting of couples (m, r) such that r is 1 if m is odd and r is 0 for m even then the rewards associated with the maximal priority are constant and we just obtain the parity game coded in an unusual manner.

Instead of proving immediately that the priority mean-payoff mapping admits optimal positional strategies let us generalize it slightly before.

Let $u_0, \ldots, u_k$ be payoff mappings on the set C of colours. We define a payoff mapping u on the set $\mathcal{B} = \{0, \ldots, k\} \times C$ of colours which we shall call *priority product* of $u_0, \ldots, u_k$. In the sequel we call the elements of $\{0, \ldots, k\}$ priorities. Let $x = (p_1, c_1), (p_2, c_2), \ldots \in \mathcal{B}^\omega$ be an infinite colour sequence of elements of $\mathcal{B}$. Define priority(x) to be the highest priority appearing infinitely often in x: priority$(x) = \limsup_{i\to\infty} p_i$.

Let $(j_m)_{m=0}^{\infty}$ be the sequence of positions in x with priority priority(x), priority$(x) = p_{j_1} = p_{j_2} = p_{j_3} = \ldots$. Then the priority product gives us the payoff

$$u(x) = u_m(c_{j_1} c_{j_2} c_{j_3} \ldots), \quad \text{where } m = \text{priority}(x) .$$

A payoff mapping u is said to be *prefix-independent* if $\forall x \in C^*$, $\forall y \in C^\omega$, $u(xy) = u(y)$.

Lemma 8. *If u_i, $i = 0, \ldots, k$, are prefix-independent and admit all optimal positional strategies for both players for all games on finite arenas then their priority product u admits optimal positional strategies for both players on all finite arenas.*

Note first that the priority product of several mean-payoff mappings is just the priority mean-payoff mapping. Thus Lemma 8 implies that on finite arenas priority mean-payoff mapping admits optimal positional strategies for both players.

Proof. We prove that, under the conditions of Lemma 8, player Max has optimal positional strategies on one-player arenas. Let G be such an arena. For each simple cycle in G we can calculate the value of the payoff u for the play that turns round the cycle forever. Let a be the maximal payoff calculated in this way and c the cycle giving this value. We prove that for any infinite play p on G, $u(\text{colour}(p)) \leq a$, which means that an optimal strategy for player Max is to go to as quickly as possible to the cycle c and turn round c forever. This strategy is positional. Thus let p be any infinite path in G and let m be the maximal priority appearing infinitely often in p. This implies that in G there exists at least one simple cycle with the maximal priority m. Let b be the maximum payoff of u over all simple cycles with the maximal priority m, this quantity is well-defined since we noted that such cycles exist. It is not difficult to observe that $u(\text{colour}(p)) \leq b$, but $b \leq a$ just by the definition of a.

The proof for arenas controlled by player Min is symmetrical and Corollary 7 applies. □

References

1. A. Bouquet, O. Serre, and I. Walukiewicz. Pushdown games with unboundedness and regular conditions. In *FSTTCS*, volume 2380 of *LNCS*, pages 88–99, 2003.
2. T. Cachat, J. Duparc, and W. Thomas. Solving pushdown games with a Σ_3 winning condition. In *CSL*, volume 2471 of *LNCS*, pages 322–336, 2002.
3. K. Chatterjee, T.A. Henzinger, and M. Jurdziński. Mean-payoff parity games. In *LICS*, 2005. to appear.
4. T. Colcombet and D. Niwiński. On the positional determinacy of edge-labeled games. submitted.
5. L. de Alfaro, M. Faella, T. A. Henzinger, Rupak Majumdar, and Mariëlle Stoelinga. Model checking discounted temporal properties. In *TACAS 2004*, volume 2988 of *LNCS*, pages 77–92. Springer, 2004.
6. L. de Alfaro, T. A. Henzinger, and Rupak Majumdar. Discounting the future in systems theory. In *ICALP 2003*, volume 2719 of *LNCS*, pages 1022–1037. Springer, 2003.
7. A. Ehrenfeucht and J. Mycielski. Positional strategies for mean payoff games. *Intern. J. of Game Theory*, 8:109–113, 1979.
8. E.A. Emerson and C. Jutla. Tree automata, μ-calculus and determinacy. In *FOCS'91*, pages 368–377. IEEE Computer Society Press, 1991.
9. H. Gimbert. Parity and exploration games on infinite graphs. In *Computer Science Logic 2004*, volume 3210 of *LNCS*, pages 56–70. Springer, 2004.
10. H. Gimbert and W. Zielonka. When can you play positionally? In *Mathematical Foundations of Computer Science 2004*, volume 3153 of *LNCS*, pages 686–697. Springer, 2004.
11. E. Grädel. Positional determinacy of infinite games. In *STACS*, volume 2996 of *LNCS*, pages 4–18. Springer, 2004.
12. A.W. Mostowski. Games with forbidden positions. Technical Report 78, Uniwersytet Gdański, Instytut Matematyki, 1991.
13. M. J. Osborne and A. Rubinstein. *A Course in Game Theory*. The MIT Press, 2002.
14. L. S. Shapley. Stochastic games. *Proceedings Nat. Acad. of Science USA*, 39:1095–1100, 1953.

On Implementation of Global Concurrent Systems with Local Asynchronous Controllers

Blaise Genest

Department of Computer Science, Warwick, Coventry, CV4 7AL, UK

Abstract. The classical modelization of concurrent system behaviors is based on observing execution sequences of global states. This model is intuitively simple and enjoys a variety of mathematical tools, e.g. finite automata, helping verifying concurrent systems. On the other hand, parallel composition of local controllers are needed when dealing with the actual implementation of concurrent models. A well known tool for turning global observation into local controllers is Zielonka's theorem, and its derivatives. We give here another algorithm, simpler and cheaper than Zielonka's theorem, in the case where the events observed do not include communication but only local asynchronous actions. In a developer point of view, it means that she does not have to explicitly specify the messages needed, which will be added (if allowed) automatically by the implementation algorithm.

1 Introduction

Specifying the behavior of software systems in such a way that formal methods can be applied and validation tasks can be automated, is a challenging goal. While research has brought strong results and tools for simple systems, complex systems still lack powerful techniques. For instance, concurrent systems such as message passing systems are still hard to cope with.

One of the challenging problem concerning concurrent systems is to design parallel algorithms. The problem is that it is easy to think in a sequential way, and to observe and model the global behavior of such a system. On the other hand, it is much harder to build local controllers, that is controllers that have only a local view of the behaviors. They have to deal with partial information, consisting of local behaviors plus information brought by messages from other processes. One method used for the implementation is to automatically turn, when possible, a global specification into a set of local controllers. Zielonka's theorem [22] states that the regular models that can be implemented by local controllers in term of asynchronous automata are exactly those closed by commutation. This theorem was further used and extended to give local controllers in term of communicating automata, with channels either bounded [18,11,12], or existentially-bounded [9] (that is a set of bounded executions suffices to represent up to commutation every execution of the system, even the unbounded ones [13,14,9]). This method has several major drawbacks. The first one is that the complexity of these Zielonka-based theorems is of several exponents [11]. Moreover, the implementation obtained in terms of communicating automata

M. Abadi and L. de Alfaro (Eds.): CONCUR 2005, LNCS 3653, pp. 443–457, 2005.

has unavoidable deadlocks, which is unacceptable for an implementation. Last, but not least, it forces the designer to provide every single message that will be needed: forgetting a message can compromise the implementability of a specification. These messages are used as support for passing information with control data (or gossiping in the terminology of [18,11]).

Our starting point is to implement a FIFO, **deadlock-free communicating automata**, with possibly more messages than specified by a regular set of executions. Of course, using all channels for messages is neither interesting (every system could be sequentialized, thus implemented), nor wanted (the less messages, channels and synchronizations used, the better), nor possible (some channel might not be available, as a direct communication from a PDA to a satellite). Thus, an architecture is set once for all, by means of a set of couples of processes, standing for the directed available channels. Since the implementation algorithm can add messages, we assume that no message is provided by the specification, even if we could technically express them. The specification is thus given by a finite automaton, whose transitions are labeled by local actions. Until this point, the background is general enough to use either synchronous or asynchronous messages, and to use open or closed systems. For instance, an action of a synchronous system would be a tuple of local actions (possibly the null action), one for each process. Here, we consider asynchronous systems that are closed, modeling communicating protocols, where every action is associated with one process. We want to obtain a deadlock-free communicating automaton such that the projection on local actions of its set of (partial) executions is exactly the language given as specification. Thus, every state is considered as final, for both the specification and the implementation. This non trivial restriction is natural when deadlocks are forbidden. Like Zielonka's theorem, the closure under a (semi) commutation related to the architecture is necessary. But unlike it, it is not always sufficient, due to the deadlock-free requirement.

Results: We first show that in the subcase where one process (the boss) can send messages to any other process (possibly via other processes), then an easy implementation exists as soon as the specification is closed by commutation.

We then give two different notions of deadlock-freeness (strong and weak), together with algorithms to test their implementability in the general setting. *Strong deadlock-freeness* allows only choices that are local, which we translate for the specification into the forward diamond property [6]. A linear size implementation can then be obtained. *Weak deadlock-freeness* allows global-choices (that is, choices involving the decision from several processes), which can be really tricky to implement. Nonetheless, we show the decidability of the weak deadlock-free implementability too, which yields an implementation exponential in the number of global choices. More precisely, we show that there are finitely many decisions to make, enabling us to test them all to find a potential unpredictable choice. The implementation is obtained by ruling out the global choices at the beginning of the implementation, and then by using the small implementation obtained in case there are only local-choices. It is worth noting that usually, the number of global choices is restricted, which limits the use of the expansive step of ruling out the global choices. We also define *very weak deadlock-freeness*, but argue against it, even though the algorithm for implementability is easier than for the weak deadlock freeness. We give examples that separate these three deadlock-free notions in section 3.3.

Related Work: Other papers deal with deadlock-free implementation. [1,3] give an algorithm for the implementation only when no information can be exchanged by processes, avoiding many protocols from being implementable. Moreover, [8,2] consider only local specifications (local-choice CMSC-graph [10] and a local flavor of EMSO logic), unlike the global specification in our paper. In the non FIFO case (two messages with different contents can overtake each other), Petri nets implementation can be used [5], allowing much more systems to be implemented. However unwanted scenarios can be implied.

Several papers were also published considering open systems. Synchronous open systems become quickly undecidable due to undecidability for partial information games [20], both if the specification is global [19,17] or local [15]. This basic undecidability result cannot be translated to the asynchronous case, so decidability is more likely: some promising results in restricted cases were published, as [7,16].

2 Preliminaries

Until the end of the paper, we consider that the set $\mathcal{P}$ of processes is fixed. We want to implement a global specification $\mathcal{S}$ by a set $\mathcal{A} = (\mathcal{A}_p)_{p \in \mathcal{P}}$ of local controllers for process p, using some communicating channels Ch.

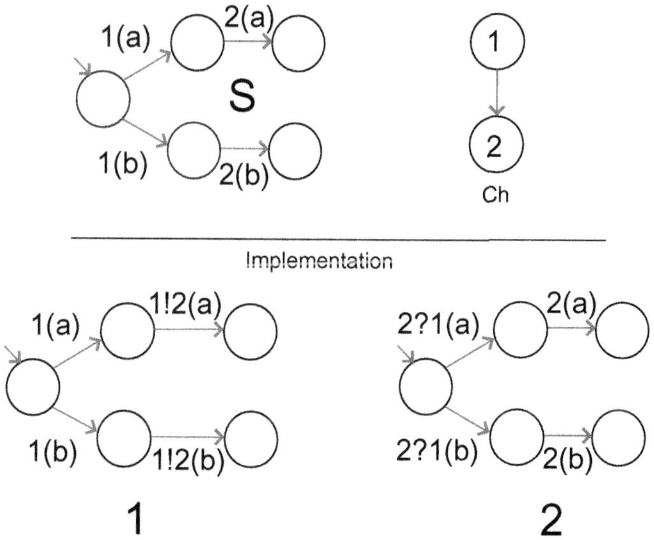

Fig. 1. An example of a specification S, an architecture Ch, and a communicating finite-state machine (CFM) on processes $\{1,2\}$

A specification is given by an automaton $\mathcal{S}$, whose transitions are labeled by local events $p(a)$, meaning that process $p \in \mathcal{P}$ does the action a. Here, we think that the specification to implement does not provide the messages yet. Indeed, it is the task of the implementation to find which messages are to be sent. Actually, the specification stands for the possibilities of executions, which is an arena the system should never exit. That is, $u \in \mathcal{L}(\mathcal{S})$ means that there exists a path labeled by u in $\mathcal{S}$ (we consider that every state of $\mathcal{S}$ is final).

We now define our target model, communicating finite state machines, which are restricted since every state is considered as final.

A communicating finite-state machine (CFM) $\mathcal{A} = (\mathcal{A}_p)_{p\in\mathcal{P}}$ [4] consists of finite automata $\mathcal{A}_p$ associated with processes $p \in \mathcal{P}$, that communicate over unbounded, error-free, FIFO channels. With each pair $(p,q) \in \mathcal{P}^2$ of distinct processes we associate a channel $C_{p,q}$. The content of a channel is a word over a finite alphabet $\mathcal{C}$. Each $\mathcal{A}_p$ is described by a tuple $\mathcal{A}_p = (S_p, A_p, \rightarrow_p)$ consisting of a set of local states S_p, a set of actions name A_p, and a transition relation $\rightarrow_p \subseteq S_p \times A_p \times S_p$. An action of $\mathcal{A}_p$ is either a local action $p(a)$, a send $p!q(a)$ or a receive $p?q(a)$, with $p, q \in \mathcal{P}$. Sending message $p!q(a)$ means that a is appended to the channel $C_{p,q}$. Receiving message $p?q(a)$ means that a must be the first message in $C_{q,p}$, which will be then removed from $C_{q,p}$. The function P associates an event with its process: $P(p(a)) = P(p!q(a)) = P(p?q(a)) = p$ for all $p, q \in \mathcal{P}$. Every computation begins in the initial state s^0, where $s^0 \in \prod_{p\in\mathcal{P}} S_p$.

A run of a CFM is a word x such that for all $p \in \mathcal{P}$, the projection of x on events of process p is a run of A_p, and such that any receive $p?q(a)$ is enabled, that is the first letter of $C_{q,p}$ before $p?q(a)$ is a. We say that a run is successful if every channel is empty at the end of the run. Moreover, we say that a CFM is *very weakly deadlock-free* if every run can be extended to a successful run. The set of successful runs generated by $\mathcal{A}$ is denoted $\mathcal{L}(\mathcal{A})$, the language of $\mathcal{A}$. With this definition of run, a CFM satisfies the FIFO restriction, that is, the n-th send event s from p to q is received by the n-th receive r from p to q. Thus, we call (s,r) a message if s and r are the n-th send and receive on the same channel, and define a mapping $m(s) = r$ and an order $s <_m r$ iff (s,r) is a message. Let x be a run of a CFM. The process order of x is $a <_p b$ if $P(a) = P(b) = p \in \mathcal{P}$ and a appears before b in x. The visual order $<$ of x is the transitive closure of $\bigcup_p <_p \cup <_m$. For every set of event X of x, we denote $\text{Future}(X) = \{z \mid y < z$ for some $y \in X\}$.

An architecture is a graph $(\mathcal{P}, Ch)$ where $\mathcal{P}$ is the set of processes and $Ch \subseteq \mathcal{P} \times \mathcal{P}$ is the set of directed channels. The channels which can be used have to be provided as an architecture since some channel might not be available (there is no way to talk to a sensor designed only to send some information, nor to send a message directly to a satellite with a small device). We call q a child of p for $(p,q) \in Ch$. We assume that for all $p \in \mathcal{P}$, $(p,p) \in Ch$. We will prove later that we can assume without loss of generality that $(\mathcal{P}, Ch)$ is an acyclic graph closed by transitivity. We thus call a process p minimal for Ch if there is no process $q \neq p$ with $(q,p) \in Ch$.

3 Implementability

3.1 Properties for Implementability

Given a specification $\mathcal{S}$, we want to obtain, when possible, a deadlock-free communicating automaton $\mathcal{A}$ on processes $\mathcal{P}$, which uses only the channels Ch, such that the projection $\pi(\mathcal{L}(\mathcal{A}))$ of $\mathcal{L}(\mathcal{A})$ on local actions $\{p(a) \mid p \in \mathcal{P}, a \in \Sigma\}$ equals $\mathcal{L}(\mathcal{S})$. We will consider several deadlock-free restrictions, but all will respect the very weak condition at least. The size $|\mathcal{P}|$ of $\mathcal{P}$ is the number of processes. The size $|\mathcal{A}|$ of an automaton $\mathcal{A}$ is its number of nodes. The size $|\mathcal{A}|$ of a CFM $\mathcal{A} = (\mathcal{A}_p)$ is $|\mathcal{A}| = \sum_{p \in \mathcal{P}} |\mathcal{A}_p|$.

We show now that we can assume without loss of generality that Ch is closed by transitivity, that is $Ch = Ch^*$. If two processes p, q are such that $(p,q) \in Ch^*$, then any implementation $\mathcal{A}$ for $Ch \cup (p,q)$ can be translated into an implementation $\mathcal{A}'$ for Ch. Let $p_0 \cdots p_n$ be some sequence of processes with $(p_i, p_{i+1}) \in Ch$ and $p_0 = p, p_n = q$. It suffices to change every action $p!q(a)$ into $p!p_1(fw,a)$ (for every a, (fw,a) is a new symbol meaning forward a), and $q?p(a)$ into $q?p_{n-1}(fw,a)$. Moreover, simple loops are added on every state of processes $p_i, i \in \{1, \cdots, n-1\}$, labeled by $p_i?p_{i-1}(fw,a)$ then $p_i!p_{i+1}(fw,a)$. Obtaining an implementation for Ch from an implementation $\mathcal{A}$ for Ch^* is of size at most $|\mathcal{P}||\mathcal{A}|$. Hence, from now on, we will assume that Ch is closed by transitivity.

We show now that we can assume without loss of generality that Ch is loop-free (remember that Ch is closed by transitivity). If two processes $p \neq q$ are such that $(p,q) \in Ch$ and $(q,p) \in Ch$, then any implementation $\mathcal{A}$ for $\mathcal{P} \setminus q$, where every action $q(a)$ is replaced by an action $p(r,a)$, can be translated into an implementation for $\mathcal{P}$. It suffices to change every actions $p(r,a)$ in $\mathcal{A}$ into two actions $p!q(a), p?q(ack)$. Moreover, the process q is easily made of loops $q?p(a), q(a), q!p(ack)$. The aim of the acknowledgements ack is to ensure the good timing of actions with respect to p and q. Obtaining an implementation for $\mathcal{P}$ from an implementation $\mathcal{A}$ for $\mathcal{P} \setminus q$ is of size at most $|\mathcal{P}||\mathcal{A}|$.

Moreover, the specification $\mathcal{S}$ can be assumed to be closed by the semi-commutation: $ab \rightarrowtail ba$ if $(P(a), P(b)) \notin Ch$ (see [6] for a formal definition of semi commutation). First, notice that for any CFM $\mathcal{A}$, if $uxyv \in \mathcal{L}(\mathcal{A})$ and $y \notin \text{Future}(x)$, then $uyxv \in \mathcal{L}(\mathcal{A})$. Let $\mathcal{S}$ be a specification not closed by semi $\rightarrowtail$ commutation: there is $uabv \in \mathcal{S}$ with $ab \rightarrowtail ba$ and $ubav \notin \mathcal{S}$. Assume by contradiction that there exists an implementation $\mathcal{A}$ of $\mathcal{S}$. Then $u'awbv' \in \mathcal{L}(\mathcal{A})$ with $\pi(u'awbv') = uabv$. Let $w = w_b w'$ with w_b in the past of b. Since b is not in the future of w', $u'aw_b bw'v' \in \mathcal{L}(\mathcal{A})$. We have that $w_b \cap \text{Future}(a) = \emptyset$, else there would exist in w a sequence of messages from a to b, which is not possible since $(P(a), P(b)) \notin Ch$ and Ch is closed by transitivity. So $u'w_b abw'v' \in \mathcal{L}(\mathcal{A})$, hence $u'w_b baw'v' \in \mathcal{L}(\mathcal{A})$, so $\pi(u'w_b baw'v') = uabv \in \mathcal{S}$, which is false. Hence, being closed by semi commutation is a necessary condition for being implementable.

We thus consider for the rest of the paper that $\mathcal{S}$, **given as minimal and deterministic**, is diamond. That is if there exist 3 states r, s, t with $r \xrightarrow{a} s \xrightarrow{b} t$ and $ab \rightarrowtail ba$, then there exists also a fourth state s' with $r \xrightarrow{b} s' \xrightarrow{a} t$, which translates the semi-commutation [6].

3.2 An Easy Subcase

Here, we give a subcase where the diamond property is enough to ensure the implementability. We do not need it for solving the general problem, but it is an easy implementation which stands for a good first example.

Namely, in case where there is a unique minimal process for Ch called $boss$, then any specification is implementable. The idea is that $boss$ makes the choices and dictates their behaviors to other processes.

Proposition 1. *If $\mathcal{S}$ is an automaton whose language is closed by semi $\rightarrowtail$-commutation, and there is a unique minimal process boss for Ch, then $\mathcal{S}$ is implementable by a CFM of size $O(|\mathcal{S}| \cdot |\mathcal{P}|!)$.*

Proof. We define now $\mathcal{A}_p$ for $p \neq boss$ as a program, which can be easily turned into an automaton.

while(true)
{ wait until $p?boss(a)$;
If $a = top(q)$ then $p!q(top)$;
If $a = wait(Q)$ then for all $q \in Q, p?q(top)$;
If $a = do(b)$ then b; }

We define now the automaton for boss. It is built upon $\mathcal{S}$, with two differences. A memory is kept recording the ordering of the last event on each process. More formally, let $\prec$ be an order on $\mathcal{P}$. After each transition labeled by an event on process p, the order $\prec$ is updated such that the restriction of $\prec$ on $\mathcal{P} \setminus \{p\}$ is kept, and for all $q \neq p$, $q \prec p$. In the initial state, the order $1 \prec \cdots \prec n$ is chosen (but any other is fine).

Consider a transition labeled by a with $P(a) = p$, from a state with an order $\prec$ between the processes. Let Q be the set of processes q with $p \prec q$ and $(q, p) \in Ch$. Now, we replace this transition labeled by a by a sequence of transitions $boss!q(top(p))$ for all $q \in Q$, then $boss!p(wait(Q))$, then $boss!p(do(a))$.

We have easily that $\pi_{boss!p(do(a))}(\mathcal{L}(\mathcal{A})) = \mathcal{L}(\mathcal{S})$, so it is closed by semi-commutation. Now, we can prove easily that $\pi_{boss!p(do(a))}(\mathcal{L}(\mathcal{A})) = \pi(\mathcal{L}(\mathcal{A}))$. □

3.3 Several Deadlock-Free Restrictions

If the implementation seems really easy in the case where there is a boss, many problems can arise in the case where there are several minimal processes in Ch.

Consider first the specification $\mathcal{S}_0$ made of three states $\{s_1, s_2, s_3\}$ with $s_1 \xrightarrow{p(a)} s_2$ and $s_1 \xrightarrow{q(b)} s_3$, with p, q two distinct minimal processes of Ch. While $\mathcal{S}_0$ satisfies the diamond property, it is not implementable in this architecture. The reason is that p and q can act separately, and since they have no common information (they are minimal in Ch), they can also act in the same time in any implementation, yielding the execution $p(a)q(b)$ which is not in the specification. When there is a process r with $(r, p) \in Ch$ and $(r, q) \in Ch$, then r can choose between p and q and inform either p or q (but not both) that it has to act, which is exactly what happens when there is a unique minimal process in Ch.

When a choice between 3 processes is involved, then a solution can be much difficult to obtain. Consider an architecture with 6 processes $\{1,2,3,4,5,6\}$ with $Ch = \{(1,4),(1,5),(2,4),(2,6),(3,5),(3,6)\}$, that is every pair of processes from $\{4,5,6\}$ has a common ancestor, but there is no common ancestor to $\{4,5,6\}$. Assume that the specification $\mathcal{S}_1$ allows $4(a)5(a)$, $5(a)6(a)$ or $4(a)6(a)$ up to commutation but not $4(a)5(a)6(a)$. Since every state of $\mathcal{S}_1$ is final, we have $\mathcal{L}(\mathcal{S}_1) = \{\epsilon, 4(a), 5(a), 6(a), 4(a)5(a), 5(a)6(a), 4(a)6(a)\}$ (up to commutation). There is a way to implement $\mathcal{S}_1$ with a very weakly deadlock free CFM $\mathcal{A}$. Processes $1,2,3$ guess two processes among $4,5,6$ and send this guess to their children (two processes among $4,5,6$). Process $p \in \{4,5,6\}$ does a if and only if the two guesses it received are the same (we could deal with some difference too) and contain p. We indeed have $\mathcal{L}(\mathcal{A}) = \mathcal{L}(\mathcal{S}_1)$. Moreover, $\mathcal{A}$ is very weakly deadlock-free because every message is received (the channels are empty) and the state reached is final. The problem is that if the guesses $1,2,3$ are not coherent (which is usually the case), then the CFM sends its messages and no local action happens, which is a kind of deadlock as well, even though it is allowed since $\epsilon \in \mathcal{L}(\mathcal{S}_1)$. We think this is due to a weakness of the (very weakly) deadlock-freeness as it is defined, and we propose two alternatives in our context where $\pi(\mathcal{L}(\mathcal{A})) = \mathcal{L}(\mathcal{S})$.

Definition 1. *A very weakly deadlock-free CFM is strongly deadlock-free if for every run x, if there exists an accepting run y with $\pi(y) = \pi(x)a$, then x can be extended into an accepting run xz with $\pi(z) = a$.*

A very weakly deadlock-free CFM is weakly deadlock-free if for every run x, if there exists an accepting run y with $\pi(y) = \pi(x)a$, then x can be extended into an accepting run.

The difference between the two definitions is that if a word x can be extended in k different ways in $\mathcal{S}$, then any run of a strongly deadlock-free CFM implementing x must be extendable in k different ways, while a weakly deadlock-free CFM must be extendable in at least one way. Strong deadlock-freeness is more restrictive than weak deadlock-freeness, but also easier to implement.

First, it is easy to show that the specification $\mathcal{S}_1$ defined above cannot be implemented by a weakly deadlock-free CFM, and hence neither by a strongly deadlock-free CFM. Then, consider the same architecture as for $\mathcal{S}_1$, that is $\mathcal{P} = \{1,2,3,4,5,6\}$ with $Ch = \{(1,4),(1,5),(2,4),(2,6),(3,5),(3,6)\}$. This time, let $\mathcal{S}_2 = \{4(a)5(a)6(b), 4(a)5(b)6(a), 4(b)5(a)6(a), 4(b)5(b)6(b)\}$ (up to commutation). Consider the following CFM $\mathcal{A}$: Process i guesses a bit b_i, where $i \in \{1,2,3\}$. It sends b_i to its two children. Each process $j \in \{4,5,6\}$ checks if the two bits it received from its two parents are equal. If yes, then it does b, else it does a. Either the three bits are equal, thus the CFM yields the execution $4(b)5(b)6(b)$ (up to commutation), or two bits are equal, let say $b_1 = b_2$, and then 4 does b, while $5,6$ does a. The CFM $\mathcal{A}$ is not strongly deadlock-free since the run x where $1,2,3$ have sent their bit can be extended in only one way, while $\pi(x) = \epsilon$ can be extended in many other ways. But $\mathcal{A}$ is weakly deadlock-free. While strong deadlock-freeness usually suffices, it sometimes forbids implementing legitimate specifications. For instance, the specification $\mathcal{S}_2$ corresponds to an election of two or none processes among three (or distributed mutual exclusion).

The proposition 2 shows that no strongly deadlock-free CFM can implement $\mathcal{S}_2$. First, let us define the forward diamond property:

Definition 2. *A deterministic and diamond automaton $\mathcal{S}$ fulfills the forward diamond property if for every states r, s, s' with $r \xrightarrow{a} s$, $r \xrightarrow{b} s'$ and $ab \rightarrowtail ba$ or $ba \rightarrowtail ab$ (that is $P(a) \neq P(b)$ since Ch is acyclic), there exists a fourth state t with $r \xrightarrow{a} s \xrightarrow{b} t$ and $r \xrightarrow{b} s' \xrightarrow{a} t$.*

Notice that $\mathcal{S}_2$ does not fulfill the forward diamond property.

Proposition 2. *Let $\mathcal{S}$ be a deterministic and diamond specification. If $\mathcal{S}$ is implemented by a strongly deadlock-free CFM $\mathcal{A}$, then $\mathcal{S}$ fulfills the forward diamond property.*

Proof. By contradiction, assume that $\mathcal{S}$ is implemented by a strongly deadlock-free CFM $\mathcal{A}$ and that there exists $r \xrightarrow{a} s$, $r \xrightarrow{b} s'$ and $(P(a), P(b)) \notin Ch$ but there is no transition labeled by b coming from s (else, by the diamond (non forward) property, there would be a transition labeled by q coming from s' as well). Let x be a run of $\mathcal{S}$ stopping in r. Since $xa \in \mathcal{L}(\mathcal{S})$ and $\mathcal{A}$ is an implementation of $\mathcal{S}$, there exists a run va of $\mathcal{A}$ with $\pi(v) = x$. Since $\mathcal{A}$ is strongly deadlock-free, there exists w with $\pi(w) = \epsilon$ and vwb is a run of $\mathcal{A}$. Let $w = w_b w'$ with w_b the past of b. The word $vw_b b$ is also an execution of $\mathcal{A}$. Since $(P(a), P(b)) \notin Ch$, $w_b b$ contains no events on p with $(p, P(b)) \notin Ch$. The projection of $vaw_b b$ on p with $(p, P(b)) \notin Ch$ is the same as the projection of va, which is an execution on p. The projection of $vaw_b b$ on q with $(q, P(b)) \in Ch$ is the same as the projection of $vw_b b$, which is an execution on q. So $vaw_b b$ is an execution of $\mathcal{A}$ which means that $\pi(vaw_b b) = xab \in \mathcal{L}(\mathcal{S})$, a contradiction. □

Last, notice that the proof of proposition 1 builds a weakly deadlock-free CFM. There are cases where it cannot be made strongly deadlock-free because of the proposition 2.

4 Strongly Deadlock-Free Implementation

We show in this section that proposition 2 is an equivalence, namely that $\mathcal{S}$ fulfills the forward diamond properties if and only if it is implementable by a strongly deadlock-free CFM.

We first build the communicating automaton $\mathcal{A}_\mathcal{S} = (\mathcal{A}_p)_{p \in \mathcal{P}}$ we use for the implementation, based on the automaton $\mathcal{S}$. For each process p, we let $\mathcal{S}_p$ be the accessible nodes of $\mathcal{S}$ from the initial node by any action of processes $\{q \mid (q, p) \in Ch\}$ (recall that $(p, p) \in Ch$). We then define $\mathcal{A}_p$ from the automaton $\mathcal{S}_p$, where the labels $a \in \Sigma_q, q \neq p$ of the transitions are replaced by $p?q(a)$. Furthermore, every transition labeled by $a \in \Sigma_p$ is replaced by a sequence of transitions labeled by a then by $p!q(a)$ for all $(p, q) \in Ch$. That is, when an action is done on p, then p informs each of its children. Conversely, the projection of $u \in \mathcal{A}_\mathcal{S}$ on p defines a run in $\mathcal{S}_p$.

Proposition 3. *Let $\mathcal{S}$ be a deterministic specification. If $\mathcal{S}$ fulfills the diamond and forward diamond properties, then $\mathcal{S}$ is implementable, and one of its strongly deadlock-free implementation is $\mathcal{A}_{\mathcal{S}}$, of size $O(|\mathcal{P}| \cdot |\mathcal{S}|)$.*

Proof. We let $\mathcal{A} = \mathcal{A}_{\mathcal{S}}$. We show that $\pi(\mathcal{L}(\mathcal{A})) = \mathcal{L}(\mathcal{S})$, and that $\mathcal{A}$ is strongly deadlock-free. Notice that both diamond properties hold for $\mathcal{S}_p, p \in \mathcal{P}$.

$\mathcal{L}(\mathcal{S})$ is included into $\pi(\mathcal{L}(\mathcal{A}))$. Let $u \in \mathcal{L}(\mathcal{S})$. We define an execution v by replacing every action $p(a)$ by a sequence of actions $p(a), p!q(a), q?p(a)$ for all $(p,q) \in Ch$. We thus have $\pi(v) = u$.

We show now that $v \in \mathcal{L}(\mathcal{A})$, which ends the proof of $\mathcal{L}(\mathcal{S}) \subseteq \pi(\mathcal{L}(\mathcal{A}))$. Let $p \in \mathcal{P}$. Let $u \rightarrowtail u_p u'$ with u_p containing every event of u on p or on $(q,p) \in Ch$, and none on other processes. Since $\mathcal{S}$ is closed by commutation, $u_p u' \in \mathcal{L}(\mathcal{S})$, and thus $u_p \in \mathcal{L}(\mathcal{S}_p)$. The execution of $\mathcal{A}_p$ which corresponds to u_p is exactly the projection v_p of v on p. Thus for all p, $v_p \in \mathcal{L}(\mathcal{A}_p)$, that is $v \in \mathcal{L}(\mathcal{A})$.

$\pi(\mathcal{L}(\mathcal{A}))$ is included into $\mathcal{L}(\mathcal{S})$. Let $u \in \mathcal{L}(\mathcal{A})$. Assume by contradiction that $v = \pi(u)$ is not an execution of $\mathcal{S}$. Let $v = v'p(a)w$ with v' the longest prefix with $v' \in \mathcal{L}(\mathcal{S})$. We let t be the state of $\mathcal{S}$ where the path labeled by v' ends. We define $v' \rightarrowtail v'_p v''$, with v'_p containing every event of v' on p or on $(q,p) \in Ch$, and none on other processes. Since $\mathcal{S}$ is diamond, $v'_p v'' \in \mathcal{L}(\mathcal{S})$ labels a path in $\mathcal{S}$ which ends in t. Moreover, $v'_p \in \mathcal{L}(\mathcal{S}_p)$, and let s be the state reached by the path labeled by v'_p. That is, $s \xrightarrow{v''} t$.

Let u_p be the projection of u on p, which belongs to $\mathcal{L}(\mathcal{A}_p)$, and w_p be the associated execution of $\mathcal{L}(\mathcal{S}_p)$. Notice that v'_p may not be a prefix of w_p since p may hear (receive the messages) about actions of an ancestor process much later than when it did happen. Anyway, it is a prefix of some equivalent run of w_p because of the FIFO condition. Hence, since $\mathcal{S}_p$ is closed by semi commutation, $w_p \in \mathcal{L}(\mathcal{S})$, and $w_p \rightarrowtail v'_p p(a) x$, there is a transition from s labeled by $p(a)$ in $\mathcal{S}_p$, so in $\mathcal{S}$.

Applying inductively the forward diamond property of $\mathcal{S}$ to s, to the transition labeled by $p(a)$, and to those leading to t and labeled by an event on a process not in p or in $(q,p) \in Ch$, we get a transition from t labeled by $p(a)$ in $\mathcal{S}$. This means $v'p(a) \in \mathcal{L}(\mathcal{S})$, contradicting the maximality of v'. So $\pi(\mathcal{L}(\mathcal{A})) = \mathcal{L}(\mathcal{S})$.

$\mathcal{A}$ is very weakly deadlock-free. Considering $\mathcal{L}(\mathcal{A})$ is closed by prefix, the only reason for $\mathcal{A}$ to have a very weak deadlock would be not to be able to receive some message $p!q(a)$ sent. We show that this is not possible.

Assume that there is a partial execution u of $\mathcal{A}$ with an unreceived send event $c = p!q(a)$. We choose c to be the minimal unreceived send in u sent by the smallest process possible. We show that $u\,d$ is also a partial execution, with d the receive $q?p(a)$.

Let u_q be the projection of u on q, which belongs to $\mathcal{A}_q$, and w_q be the associated execution in $\mathcal{S}_q$. Let $w_q \rightarrowtail w_p w'$ with w_p containing all events on process p or on $(k,p) \in Ch$. Because every send sent by any $k \neq p, (k,p) \in Ch$ is already received (by minimality of c), w_p contains exactly all the events of u on $k \neq p, (k,p) \in Ch$, and by FIFO, all the events until c on p.

Since u contains the send c, it means that there exists a prefix $u'_p c$ of the projection of u on p. Let $w'_p p(a)$ be the execution of $\mathcal{S}_p$ associated with $u'_p c$. We have $w_p \rightarrowtail w'_p x$, that is $w_q \rightarrowtail w'_p y$. By the diamond property of $\mathcal{S}_q$, we have states s, t with $s_0 \xrightarrow{w'_p} s \rightarrow^* t$ and $s_0 \xrightarrow{w_q} t$. Consider now that c is enabled after u'_p, so $p(a)$ is enabled after w'_p, so after s.

Applying the forward diamond property inductively in $\mathcal{S}_q$, to the transition labeled by $p(a)$, and the sequence of transitions leading to t (labeled by an event on a process different that p), $p(a)$ is enabled after t. The meaning in $\mathcal{A}_q$ is that d can be received by q after the projection of u on q, that is $u\,d$ is a partial execution of $\mathcal{A}$.

$\mathcal{A}$ is strongly deadlock-free. By the very construction of $\mathcal{A}$, if an execution x is such that $\pi(x)a \in \mathcal{S}$, then a transition labeled by a on $P(a)$ is possible after x. □

Remark 1. 1. Figure 1 depicts a specification and its corresponding implementation given by proposition 3.
2. One definition of a deterministic CFM is that if $\pi(x) = \pi(y)$ for two runs x, y of a CFM, then x and y are equal up to commutation. It makes sense in our case since only the projection on local events matters. Then any deterministic implementation needs to be strongly-deadlock free.
3. The CFM obtained in proposition 3 is deterministic for the determinacy definition of [11]. That is, each automaton $\mathcal{A}_p$ is deterministic, and there is no node r with two transitions $r \xrightarrow{p!q(a)} s$ and $r \xrightarrow{p!q(b)} s$ labeled by different messages data $a \neq b$.
4. The CFM obtained is not universally bounded. That is, there are specifications for which for every b, the implementation obtained has a run which uses more than b messages in some channel at one time.
5. The existential boundedness is defined in [13] (see also [14,9]). The CFM obtained in proposition 3 is not existentially bounded. Anyway, it is easy to obtain a strongly deadlock-free implementation which is existentially 1 bounded (but it is not of linear size). It suffices for a process p to simulate every process q with $(q, p) \in Ch$. For every state where two messages from different processes can be received (that is the two simulated states are not stuck), the transition receiving the message from the lower process (for Ch) can be deleted. It makes the CFM even more deterministic. The diamond property on $\mathcal{S}$ will allow process p to receive this message later, when the higher process will be stuck waiting for the same message, preserving the deadlock-freeness.

5 Weakly Deadlock-Free Implementation

5.1 Global Choices

The challenge with weakly deadlock-free implementation is that global choices (choices involving the decision from several processes) are possible. In contrast, being forward diamond means that every choice in the specification can be made locally by one process. The strategy we use to solve the weakly deadlock-free implementability is to make a precomputation on the specification (if possible) to have a forward diamond specification. Hence, we can use the strongly deadlock-free implementation, whose algorithm is fast and produce small implementations.

The important step in our algorithm is proposition 5 which states that the number of global choices is finite. Then proposition 6 states that there exists a finite number of different ways to take a decision, implying they can all be tested. A crucial hypothesis for proposition 5 is to choose $\mathcal{S}$ deterministic, hence we will assume that it is the case from now on (we can anyway determinize and minimize the specification, preserving the diamond property).

First, we give a syntactical characterization of global choices. We denote by $L(s)$ the language of $\mathcal{S}$ with initial node s. We denote by L_Q the projection of L on set of processes Q, where Q is such that if $q \in Q$ and $(p, q) \in Ch$, then $p \in Q$. In particular, if L satisfies the diamond property, L_Q is the accessible part of L by events in Q. This is the case for $L(s)$ for every node s of $\mathcal{S}$.

Definition 3. *A transition $s \xrightarrow{\tau} t$ is a global choice if $L_Q(s) \neq L_Q(t)$ for $Q = \{k \mid (P(\tau), k) \notin Ch\}$. We denote by $\mathcal{G}$ the set of global choices.*

Notice that $\mathcal{S}$ satisfies the forward diamond property iff $\mathcal{G} = \emptyset$.

First, we can test for global choice involving two process p, q without common ancestor. If such global choices exist, no implementation is possible since p and q cannot take a coherent decision.

Proposition 4. *Assume that a transition $s \xrightarrow{\tau} t$ is such that $L_K(s) \neq L_K(t)$ with $K = \{q \mid \nexists k, (k, q) \in Ch \wedge (k, P(\tau)) \in Ch\}$. Then $\mathcal{S}$ is not (very) weakly deadlock-free implementable.*

Proof. By contradiction, assume that $\mathcal{A}$ is a very weak deadlock-free implementation of $\mathcal{S}$. Let $u \in \mathcal{L}(\mathcal{S})$ such that this execution ends in the state s. We decompose u in u_1, u_2, with $u_1 = \pi_K(u)$. Let $v \in L_K(s) \setminus L_K(t)$. So $u_1u_2v, u_1u_2\tau \in \mathcal{L}(\mathcal{S})$, but $u_1u_2\tau v \notin \mathcal{L}(\mathcal{S})$, neither $u_2\tau u_1 v \notin \mathcal{L}(\mathcal{S})$ (by semi commutation of $\mathcal{S}$). So there exists $wxy, w'x'\tau \in \mathcal{L}(\mathcal{A})$, with $\pi(w) = \pi(w') = u_1$, $\pi(x) = \pi(x') = u_2$, $\pi(y) = v$, and $wy = \pi_K(xwy)$. We have wy is a partial execution of the processes in K since they cannot receive any message from other processes. In the same line, $x'\tau$ is a partial execution of $\mathcal{A}$. Hence $x'\tau wy$ is a partial execution of $\mathcal{A}$. Since $\mathcal{A}$ is a very weakly deadlock-free implementation of $\mathcal{S}$, we have $\pi(x'\tau wy) = u_2\tau u_1 v \in \mathcal{L}(\mathcal{S})$, a contradiction. □

5.2 A Finite Number of Decisions

We prove here that there is no loop around a global choice. That is, there is only a finite number of "questions" whether to take a choice or not.

Proposition 5. *Let $\mathcal{S}$ be a deterministic automaton that fulfills the diamond property. There is no loop $s \xrightarrow{\tau} t \xrightarrow{y} s$ with $(s \xrightarrow{\tau} t) \in \mathcal{G}$ a global choice.*

Proof. Since $s \xrightarrow{\tau} t$ is a global choice, there exists $x \in L_Q(s), x \notin L_Q(t)$ with $Q = \{k \mid (P(\tau), k) \notin Ch\}$. Now, for z the projection of y on Q, we have $y \rightarrowtail zz'$. We can merge τ with z', and renaming s, we obtain $s \xrightarrow{z'} t \xrightarrow{z} s$. We thus have the semi commutation $z'x \rightarrowtail xz'$ and $z'z \rightarrowtail zz'$. Because of the diamond property, $x \in L_Q(s)$ for the new s, and still $x \notin L_Q(t)$. Hence $s \neq t$.

Since $z'z \rightarrowtail zz'$, applying the diamond property, we obtain a state s' with $s \xrightarrow{z} s' \xrightarrow{z'} s$. Because $z'x \in L(s')$, $z'x \rightarrowtail xz'$ and the diamond property, $x \in L_Q(s')$. This means $s' \neq t$. The fact that $s' \neq s$ comes from the determinacy of $\mathcal{S}$, since $s' \xrightarrow{z'} s$ and $s \xrightarrow{z'} t$ with $s \neq t$. Assume by induction that we have constructed n different states s_n in this way. Then since $z'z \rightarrowtail zz'$, applying the diamond property, we obtain a state s_{n+1} with $s_n \xrightarrow{z} s_{n+1} \xrightarrow{z'} s_n$. Since $x \in L_Q(s_n)$ by induction hypothesis, and $z'x \rightarrowtail xz'$, we have $x \in L_Q(s_{n+1})$. So $s_{n+1} \neq t$. Assume that $s_{n+1} = s_i$. Then $s_i \xrightarrow{z'} s_{n+1}$. But we have already $s_i \xrightarrow{z'} s_{i-1}$. So by determinacy, $s_{n+1} = s_{i-1}$ as well. We come to a contradiction when $s_{n+1} = s$ means that $s_{n+1} = t$ by determinacy, which is known to be false.

We can iterate this to obtain an infinite number of nodes, using the diamond property and the determinacy, which is a contradiction with the finiteness of the automaton. □

Since the number of decisions to make is finite, they can be made once at the beginning, as a subset $G \subseteq \mathcal{G}$ of the global choices which can be used. However, not every subset can be chosen. Let $\mathcal{S}^G$ be the specification obtained from $\mathcal{S}$ by deleting every global choice not in $\mathcal{G}$. We say that G is compatible if:

- There exists $G \subseteq H$ with $\mathcal{S}^H$ diamond and forward diamond (a transition of $\mathcal{S}^H$ may be a global choice of $\mathcal{S}$ but is not in $\mathcal{S}^H$).
- Every $x \in \mathcal{L}(\mathcal{S}^G)$ that cannot be extended in $\mathcal{S}^G$ cannot be extended in $\mathcal{S}$ either.

We denote by $\mathcal{F}$ the set of compatible sets $G \subseteq \mathcal{G}$. Let $\mathcal{F}_p$ denote the set of projections of subsets of $\mathcal{F}$ on process p. We can easily compute $(\mathcal{F}_p)_{p \in \mathcal{P}}$.

5.3 Implementing Locally the Global Choices

Process p shall choose one set of global choices it can use among $\mathcal{F}_p$. If it could choose a set outside, then it would lead to an implementation which is not weakly deadlock-free (because a run cannot be extended), or which breaks the requirement $\mathcal{L}(\mathcal{A}) = \mathcal{L}(\mathcal{S})$.

First, we test whether $\bigcup_{G \in \mathcal{F}} \mathcal{L}(\mathcal{S}^G) = \mathcal{L}(\mathcal{S})$, else every implementation $\mathcal{A}$ will satisfy $\pi(\mathcal{L}(\mathcal{A})) \subseteq \bigcup_{G \in \mathcal{F}} \mathcal{L}(\mathcal{S}^G) \subsetneq \mathcal{L}(\mathcal{S})$: $\mathcal{S}$ cannot be implemented.

To help processes choosing locally a global choice among $\mathcal{F}$ (and not a combination of choices which is not in $\mathcal{F}$), they are helped by information sent by their ancestors. We can model the choices made by a function *choice* which associates each process p and each tuple of information sent to a set of $\mathcal{F}_p$ which the process p will execute if it receives the information. Of course, this function depends for p only on the information sent by ancestors of p. Let I_p be the set of different information that can be sent by process p. Let $I = I_1 \times \cdots \times I_n$ be the set of tuples of information.

We then say that $\mathcal{F}$ is implementable with I information if there exists a function *choice* as described above, such that:

- for every tuple $i \in I$, let $f(i) = \bigcup_{p \in \mathcal{P}} choice(p)(i)$,
- for every tuple $i \in I$ of information sent, $f(i) \in \mathcal{F}$, that is every global choice made by *choice* is compatible.
- $\bigcup_i \mathcal{L}(\mathcal{S}^{f(i)}) = \mathcal{L}(\mathcal{S})$, that is we get the whole language of $\mathcal{S}$ by implementing the function *choice*.

Notice that *choice* is defined by $f : I \to \mathcal{F}$ with $f(i) = \bigcup_{p \in \mathcal{P}} choice(p)(i)$. We show here that the information I can be limited. We can assume without loss of generality that minimal processes only send some information.

Proposition 6. *If $\mathcal{F}$ is implementable, then it is implementable with* $\log(|\mathcal{F}|)$ *bits of information sent by every minimal process p.*

Proof. Since $\mathcal{F}$ is implementable, there are a set of information I and $f : I \to \mathcal{F}$ which implements $\mathcal{G}$. Assume that $|I_1| > |\mathcal{F}| = n_0$ different information on process 1. We want to show that some information x is useless, that is the restriction $f|_{I \setminus \{x\}}$ still implements $\mathcal{G}$. We partition the space into n_0 pigeon holes: A tuple of information $i \in I$ is in the pigeon hole $f(i)$.

Obviously, if $\bigcup_{i \in I \setminus x} \mathcal{L}(\mathcal{S}^{f(i)}) = \mathcal{L}(\mathcal{S})$, then we can forget the information $x \in I_1$. In particular, it is the case if every pigeon hole which contains a tuple using x contains also a tuple not using x. Assume by contradiction that this is not the case. So for all information $x \in I_1$, there exists a pigeon hole which contains only information whose first component is x. Applying Dirichlet's pigeon hole lemma, since there are $n_0 < |I_1|$ pigeon holes, there is a pigeon hole associated with two different information, a contradiction. □

We can thus test if $\mathcal{F}$ is implementable or not by testing every function of choice f using information $|I_p| = |\mathcal{F}| \leq 2^{|\mathcal{G}|}$ for each minimal process p (there are at most $|\mathcal{F}|^{|\mathcal{F}|^{|\mathcal{P}|}}$ such functions), telling us whether $\mathcal{S}$ is weakly deadlock-free implementable or not. It gives us the following theorem:

Theorem 1. *Let $\mathcal{S}$ be a deterministic and diamond specification. It is decidable to test whether a specification $\mathcal{S}$ is weakly deadlock-free implementable. The complexity is EXPSPACE($m|\mathcal{G}|$) and the implementation obtained is of size at most $O(|\mathcal{P}| \cdot |\mathcal{S}| \cdot 2^{m|\mathcal{G}|})$, where $|\mathcal{G}| \leq |\mathcal{S}|$ is the number of global choices and $m \leq |\mathcal{P}|$ the number of minimal processes.*

Proof. If $\mathcal{F}$ is implementable by f using information $|I_p| = |\mathcal{F}|$ for each minimal process p, then a weakly deadlock-free implementation is obtained in two steps. The first step is that every minimal process guesses $\log(|\mathcal{F}|) \leq |\mathcal{G}|$ bits of information and sends it to each of its children. Then every process q computes $G = f(q)(i)$. The second step is for process q to run the CFM obtained as in section 4 from the specification $\mathcal{S}_q^G$. Every CFM $\mathcal{A}^i$ obtained from the information $i \in I$ is weakly deadlock-free and satisfies $\pi(\mathcal{L}(\mathcal{A}^i)) \subseteq \mathcal{L}(\mathcal{S})$ by the definition of $\mathcal{G}$. Moreover, $\mathcal{G}$ is implemented by f, which means that $\bigcup_{i \in I} \pi(\mathcal{L}(\mathcal{A}^i)) = \mathcal{L}(\mathcal{S})$. □

Remark 2. We can show that transitions $s \xrightarrow{\mathcal{T}} t$ with $L_Q(s) \neq L_Q(t)$ (cf proposition 4) are the only reasons a specification may not be *very weakly deadlock-free implementable*, which gives a polynomial time algorithm to test implementability. If there is no such transition, each minimal process guesses a subset $G \in \mathcal{G}$. A process does nothing if the guesses of its parents are not consistent, else it runs the implementation of section 4 on S^G. The implementation obtained is also of size at most $O(|\mathcal{P}| \cdot |\mathcal{S}| \cdot 2^{m|\mathcal{G}|})$.

6 Conclusion

Unlike the deadlock-free implementability of global specifications when no message can be added (but data can) for which no result but heuristics are known [8], the implementability of a global specification $\mathcal{S}$ is decidable when messages can be added.

- The *very weak deadlock-free* implementability can be tested in PTIME and the implementation obtained is of exponential size. However, this deadlock-free restriction is too weak since the implementation is allowed to stop, while actions can still happen according to the specification.
- The *strong deadlock-free* implementability can be tested in PTIME and yields an implementation of size $O(|\mathcal{P}||\mathcal{S}|)$. The implementation enjoys many good properties, while it doesn't compromise any deterministic implementation. For instance, the *usb* protocol [21] is strongly deadlock-free implementable since it does not involve global choices.
- The *weak deadlock-freeness* allows global choices, contrary to the strong deadlock-freeness. Its much more involved implementation yields a single exponential size implementation. However, our algorithm becomes tractable for really small number of global choices, which we think is the case in real-life examples. In the unlikely case where there are a lot of global choices, the help from the user can still be asked, by highlighting the global choices, asking if they are really needed, and if yes, asking for a redesign of the specification to explain how these choices can be locally taken.

Acknowledgement. I would like to thank Anca Muscholl, Doron Peled, Igor Walukiewicz for fruitful discussions and an annonymous referee for his comments.

References

1. R. Alur, K. Etessami, and M. Yannakakis. Realizability and verification of MSC graphs. In *ICALP'01*, LNCS 2076, pp.797-808, 2001.
2. B. Bollig and M. Leucker. Message-Passing Automata are expressively equivalent to EMSO Logic. In *CONCUR'04*, LNCS 3170, pp. 146-160, 2004.

3. N. Baudru and R. Morin. Safe implementability of regular message sequence chart specifications. In *SNPD'03*, pp 210–217. ACIS, 2003.
4. D. Brand and P. Zafiropulo. On communicating finite-state machines. *Journal of the ACM*, 30(2):pp.323-342, 1983.
5. B. Caillaud, P. Darondeau, L. Hélouët, and G. Lesventes. HMSCs as partial specifications... with PNs as completions. In *Modeling and Verification of Parallel Processes, 4th Summer School, MOVEP 2000*, Nantes, France 2000.
6. V. Diekert and G. Rozenberg, editors. *The Book of Traces*. World Scientific, Singapore, 1995.
7. P. Gastin, B. Lerman, M. Zeitoun. Distributed Games with Causal Memory Are Decidable for Series-Parallel Systems. In *FSTTCS'04*, LNCS 3328, pp. 275-286, 2004.
8. B. Genest. Compositional Message Sequence Charts (CMSCs) are better to Implement than MSCs. In *TACAS'05*, LNCS , pp. 429-444, 2005.
9. B. Genest, D. Kuske and A. Muscholl. A Kleene Theorem and Model Checking for a Class of Communicating Automata. In *DLT'04*, LNCS 3340, pp. 30-48, 2004.
10. E. Gunter, A. Muscholl, and D. Peled. Compositional Message Sequence Charts. In *TACAS'01*, LNCS 2031, pp. 496–511, 2001. Journal version *International Journal on Software Tools for Technology Transfer (STTT)* 5(1): 78-89 (2003).
11. J. G. Henriksen, M. Mukund, K. Narayan Kumar, M. Sohoni and P. Thiagarajan. A Theory of Regular MSC Languages. To appear in *Information and Computation*, available at http://www.comp.nus.edu.sg/~thiagu/public_papers/icregmsc.pdf.
12. D. Kuske. Regular sets of infinite message sequence charts. In *Information and Computation 187*, Academic Press, pp.80-109, 2003.
13. M. Lohrey and A. Muscholl. Bounded MSC communication. *Information and Computation*, (189):135–263, 2004.
14. P. Madhusudan and B. Meenakshi. Beyond Message Sequence Graphs. In *FSTTCS'01*, LNCS 2245, pp. 256-267, 2001.
15. P. Madhusudan and P.S. Thiagarajan. Distributed Controller Synthesis for Local Specifications. In *ICALP'01*, LNCS 2076, pp. 396-407,2001.
16. P. Madhusudan and P.S. Thiagarajan. A Decidable Class of Asynchronous Distributed Controllers. In *CONCUR'02*, LNCS 2421, pp. 145-160, 2002.
17. S. Mohalik and I. Walukiewicz. Distributed Games. In *FSTTCS'03*, LNCS 2914, pp. 338-351, 2003.
18. M. Mukund, K. Narayan Kumar and M. Sohoni. Synthesizing Distributed Finite-State Systems from MSCs. In *CONCUR 2000*, LNCS 1877 , pp. 521-535, 2000.
19. A. Pnueli and R. Rosner. Distributed Reactive Systems Are Hard to Synthesize. In *FOCS 1990*, pp. 746-757, 1990.
20. J.H. Reif. The Complexity of Two-player Games of Incomplete Information. *J. Comp. Sys. Sci. 29*, pp 274-301, 1984.
21. USB 1.1 specification, available at http://www.usb.org/developers/docs/usbspec.zip
22. W. Zielonka. Note on finite asynchronous automata, R.A.I.R.O. *Informatique Théorique et Applications*, 21:pp.99-135, 1987.

Defining Fairness

Hagen Völzer[1], Daniele Varacca[2], and Ekkart Kindler[3,*]

[1] University of Lübeck, Germany
voelzer@tcs.uni-luebeck.de
[2] Imperial College London, UK
varacca@doc.ic.ac.uk
[3] University of Paderborn, Germany
kindler@uni-paderborn.de

Abstract. We propose a definition for the class of all fairness properties of a given system. We provide independent characterizations in terms of topology, language theory and game theory. All popular notions of fairness from the literature satisfy our definition. Moreover our class is closed under union and countable intersection, and it is, in a sense, the maximal class having this property. On the way, we characterize a class of liveness properties, called *constructive liveness*, which is interesting by itself because it is also closed under union and countable intersection. Furthermore, we characterize some subclasses of liveness that are closed under arbitrary intersection.

1 Introduction

The distinction of *safety* and *liveness* properties, first proposed by Lamport [10] and later formalized by Lamport [11] and Alpern and Schneider [2], is now well-established in the specification, analysis, and verification of *reactive systems* [6]. The main reasons for the success of these concepts is their natural and convincing intuition, their stringent mathematical formalization, and the fact that every property can be expressed as the conjunction of a safety and a liveness property (see [7] for a survey). In particular, it turned out that safety properties are the closed sets and liveness properties are the dense sets in the natural topology of runs [2].

The distinction of safety and liveness is also reflected in the operational model of a reactive system: Some sort of state machine or transition system defines the set of all possible runs of the system, which is a safety property. In order to guarantee something to happen at all and to guarantee that some particular choices will eventually be made, there is an additional liveness property. That liveness property is usually called the *fairness assumption* of the reactive system.

Fairness usually means that a particular choice is taken sufficiently often provided that it is sufficiently often possible [3]. Depending on the interpretation of 'choice', 'sufficiently often', and 'possible', many different fairness notions arise (cf. e.g. [13,4,8]).

* D. Varacca acknowledges a support from the EPSRC grant GR/T04724/01.

M. Abadi and L. de Alfaro (Eds.): CONCUR 2005, LNCS 3653, pp. 458–472, 2005.

In contrast to safety and liveness properties, there is no satisfactory characterization of fairness. Apt, Francez, and Katz [3] gave some criteria that must be met by fairness. Following Lamport [12], we think that their most important criterion is that a fairness assumption must be *machine closed*[1] with respect to (w.r.t.) the safety property defined by the underlying transition system. This, basically, means that fairness is imposed in such a way to the transition system that the system 'cannot paint itself into a corner' [3]; i. e., whatever the system does, it is possible to continue in such a way that the fairness assumption is met. However, machine closedness does not exclude some properties that, we think, should not be considered to be fairness properties. For example, consider the two properties:

P_1: Transition t is always eventually taken if it is always eventually enabled.
P_2: Transition t is eventually henceforth never taken.

While P_1 (called *strong fairness* w.r.t. t) is a typical fairness assumption that enforces a transition to be taken sufficiently often, P_2 rather prevents a particular choice (transition t) from being taken sufficiently often. P_2 is therefore not a fairness property from our point of view. However, both properties are machine closed with respect to any safety property[2].

Another issue is that fairness should be closed under intersection, i.e., the intersection of finitely many, or better: countably many, fairness assumptions should be a fairness assumption. This is because fairness assumptions are usually imposed stepwise and componentwise, e.g., with respect to a particular process or with respect to a particular transition. The fairness assumption for the system is then the intersection of all fairness assumptions for its components.

Machine-closure is not sufficient to guarantee closure under intersection: The intersection of P_1 and P_2 is the empty set in some systems, and the empty set is not machine closed w.r.t. any nonempty safety property. Kwiatkowska [9] proposes a definition of fairness[3] that is closed under countable intersection. However, many popular fairness notions, such as strong fairness are not covered by her definition.

We propose a definition of fairness that refines machine-closure and excludes properties like P_2 that prohibits a choice to be taken sufficiently often. Roughly, a fairness property w.r.t. a system is a property that can be realized by a scheduler that always eventually gets control over the system. We show that fairness is then closed under union and countable intersection and that popular fairness notions satisfy our definition. We give independent characterizations in terms of game theory, language theory, and topology. It turns out that fairness as we define it coincides with the *co-meager sets* of the natural topology of runs, a subclass of

---

[1] *Machine closedness* was originally called *feasibility*. The term *machine closedness* was introduced in [1].

[2] P_2 also meets the other criteria of Apt, Francez, and Katz [3].

[3] Kwiatkowska [9] works on the domain of Mazurkiewicz traces. She defines a fairness property for a system to be a G_δ set of maximal traces that is machine closed w.r.t. the safety property of the system.

the dense sets. Co-meager sets are 'large', which in our context means that they, besides of possibly enforcing some choices, also leave enough choices.

2 Preliminaries

Runs. A *run* is a nonempty finite or infinite sequence over some fixed countable set Σ of *states*. Σ^+, Σ^ω, and $\Sigma^\infty = \Sigma^+ \cup \Sigma^\omega$ denote the set of all *finite runs*, *infinite runs*, and of all *runs* respectively. We will use the symbols α, β for denoting finite runs, and x, y for arbitrary runs. The length of a run x is denoted by $|x|$ ($= \omega$ if x is infinite). Concatenation of sequences is denoted by juxtaposition; $\sqsubseteq$ denotes the usual (reflexive) *prefix order* on sequences. Two runs x and x' are *compatible*, if $x \sqsubseteq x'$ or $x' \sqsubseteq x$. By $x\!\uparrow = \{y \mid x \sqsubseteq y\}$ and $x\!\downarrow = \{y \mid y \sqsubseteq x\}$ we denote the set of all *extensions* and *prefixes* of a run x respectively. The least upper bound of a sequence $(\alpha_i)_{i=0,1,\ldots}$ of finite runs where $\alpha_i \sqsubseteq \alpha_{i+1}$ is denoted by $\sup_i \alpha_i$. For a run $x = s_0, s_1, \ldots$ and a position i where $0 \leq i < |x|$ of x, x_i denotes the i-th prefix $s_0, \ldots, s_i$ of x.

Temporal Properties. A *temporal property* (*property* for short) is a set $E \subseteq \Sigma^\infty$; E is *finitary* if $E \subseteq \Sigma^+$, and *infinitary* if $E \subseteq \Sigma^\omega$. Sometimes (e.g. [2,14]), a temporal property is defined to be a subset of Σ^ω. That results in the underlying topology having nicer properties[4]. However, that needs finite runs to be ruled out a priori or to be mimicked by infinite runs, e.g., by repeating the last state infinitely often. Moreover, including finite runs gives rise to a more natural generalization to other domains such as non-sequential runs (cf. Sect. 6). We say that some run x *satisfies* a property E if $x \in E$, otherwise we say that x *violates* E. A property S is a *safety property* if for any run x violating S, there exists a finite prefix α of x that violates S and each extension of a run violating S violates S as well, i.e.:

$$\forall x \notin S : \exists \alpha \sqsubseteq x : \alpha\!\uparrow \cap S = \varnothing.$$

Safety properties are exactly those sets S that are *downward-closed* and *complete*, where the former means $x \in S$ and $y \sqsubseteq x$ implies $y \in S$ and the latter $\alpha_i \in S$ for $i \in \mathbb{N}$ with $\alpha_i \sqsubseteq \alpha_{i+1}$ implies $\sup_i \alpha_i \in S$. A property E is *live in* a finite run α if there exists a run $x \in E$ such that $\alpha \sqsubseteq x$. A property E is *live* (or a *liveness property*) if E is live in every $\alpha \in \Sigma^+$. Let S be a safety property. E is *live w.r.t.* S (or (S, E) is *machine closed*) if $E \cap S$ is live in every $\alpha \in \Sigma^+ \cap S$.

Σ^+ and Σ^ω are simple examples of liveness properties. The empty set $\varnothing = \Sigma^\omega \cap \Sigma^+$ is not a liveness property, which shows that liveness properties are not closed under finite intersection. It is easy to see that for a liveness property E, every property $E' \supseteq E$ is also a liveness property. No property except Σ^∞ is a safety and a liveness property.

[4] The natural topology on Σ^ω is metrizable while the natural topology on Σ^∞ does not satisfy the separation axiom T_1.

Basic Notions from General Topology. A *topology* on a nonempty set Ω is a family $\mathscr{T} \subseteq 2^{\Omega}$ that is closed under union and finite intersection such that $\Omega, \varnothing \in \mathscr{T}$. The elements of $\mathscr{T}$ are called *open sets.* A family $\mathscr{B} \subseteq \mathscr{T}$ is a *base* for $\mathscr{T}$ if every open set $G \in \mathscr{T}$ is the union of members of $\mathscr{B}$. The complement of an open set is called a *closed set.* The *closure* of a set $X \subseteq \Omega$, denoted by $\overline{X}$, is the smallest closed set that contains X. A set X is closed if and only if $X = \overline{X}$. A set X is *dense* if $\overline{X} = \Omega$. A G_δ *set* is a set that is the intersection of countably many open sets. Let $X \subseteq \Omega$ be a nonempty set. The family $\mathscr{T}_X = \{G \cap X \mid G \in \mathscr{T}\}$ is a topology, called the *relativization* of $\mathscr{T}$ to X.

Scott Topology. The *Scott topology* on Σ^∞ is the family of sets G such that

$$\forall x \in G : \exists \alpha \sqsubseteq x : \alpha\!\uparrow\, \subseteq G.$$

The family $\{\alpha\!\uparrow \mid \alpha \in \Sigma^+\}$ is a basis for the Scott topology. Note that open sets are generated by finitary properties Q by $G = Q\!\uparrow\, = \bigcup_{\alpha \in Q} \alpha\!\uparrow$, i.e., there is an exact correspondence between open sets and finitary properties. Open sets can therefore be interpreted as *observations* that can be recognized in finite time.

It is easy to see that safety properties are exactly the closed sets and that liveness properties are exactly the dense sets of the Scott topology. It follows that each property E is the intersection of a safety property and a liveness property [2], viz. $E = \overline{E} \cap \mathrm{lex}(E)$ where $\overline{E}$ is the smallest safety property that contains E, and $\mathrm{lex}(E)$ is the *liveness extension* of E, defined by

$$\mathrm{lex}(E) = E \cup \neg\overline{E} = E \cup \bigcup_{\alpha\uparrow \cap E = \varnothing} \alpha\!\uparrow.$$

Temporal Operators. Manna and Pnueli [14] define four operators that construct temporal properties from finitary properties. While they consider only sets $E \subseteq \Sigma^\omega$ as temporal properties, we generalize their operators here to our setting in a natural way. Let Q be a finitary property. Define $\mathrm{A}(Q) = \{x \mid \forall i < |x| : x_i \in Q\}$, $\mathrm{E}(Q) = \{x \mid \exists i : x_i \in Q\}$, $\mathrm{R}(Q) = \{x \mid \forall i < |x| : \exists j \geq i : x_j \in Q\}$, and $\mathrm{P}(Q) = \{x \mid \exists i : \forall j : i \leq j < |x| : x_j \in Q\}$. Properties of the form $\mathrm{A}(Q)$ are exactly the safety properties. Properties of the form $\mathrm{E}(Q)$, $\mathrm{R}(Q)$, and $\mathrm{P}(Q)$ are called *guarantee*, *recurrence*, and *persistence properties* respectively. It is easy to see that guarantee properties are exactly the open sets (where Q is the corresponding observation). We have $\neg\mathrm{A}(Q) = \mathrm{E}(\neg Q)$, $\neg\mathrm{E}(Q) = \mathrm{A}(\neg Q)$, $\neg\mathrm{R}(Q) = \mathrm{P}(\neg Q)$, and $\neg\mathrm{P}(Q) = \mathrm{R}(\neg Q)$ where $\neg\cdot$ denotes the complement w.r.t. the appropriate universe. Since $\mathrm{A}(Q) = \mathrm{R}(\mathrm{A}(Q) \cap \Sigma^+)$ and $\mathrm{E}(Q) = \mathrm{R}(\mathrm{E}(Q) \cap \Sigma^+)$, we have that each safety property and each guarantee property is a recurrence property. Similarly, each safety and each guarantee property is also a persistence property. We will use a simple linear-time temporal logic with the modalities $\Diamond$ and $\Box$ to be interpreted on finite and infinite runs in their usual meaning. The properties $\Box\,\varphi$, $\Diamond\,\varphi$, $\Box\Diamond\,\varphi$, and $\Diamond\Box\,\varphi$ are simple examples of safety, guarantee, recurrence, and persistence properties respectively where φ denotes any state property.

3 Constructive Liveness

Fairness is always defined with respect to a particular system, where a system can be seen as a safety property. In this section, we define fairness with respect to the system where every transition is possible at any time, i.e., with respect to the safety property Σ^∞. The generalization to arbitrary safety properties will be a simple step, which we take in Sect. 4. Fairness properties with respect to Σ^∞ are special liveness properties, which we call *constructive liveness*. Constructive liveness is interesting by itself because it is closed under union and countable intersection. We give three independent characterizations of constructive liveness: a game-theoretic, a language-theoretic, and a topological characterization. Additional proofs can be found in the full version of this paper [17].

3.1 A Game-Theoretic View

Fairness may enforce that a particular choice is taken sufficiently often while it must not prevent any other choice from being taken sufficiently often. This can be formalized by thinking of a party, which we will call the *scheduler*, that enforces a choice to be taken sufficiently often while it cannot prevent other choices from being taken by another party, called the *opponent*. Fairness properties (or here: constructive liveness properties) are those properties that can be realized by the scheduler regardless of the behavior of the opponent. In detail: We view runs now as the result of an infinite interaction between the *scheduler* and the *opponent*. The opponent starts by performing a nonempty sequence α_0. The scheduler then appends a finite, possibly empty, sequence of states yielding a finite run α_1 such that $\alpha_0 \sqsubseteq \alpha_1$. Now it is the turn of the opponent again, which also appends a finite, possibly empty, sequence and so on. The result of this interaction is the run $x = \sup_i \alpha_i$. A liveness property is *constructive* if, regardless of what the opponent does, the scheduler can guarantee that a run is obtained that satisfies the property. This game is similar to the *Banach-Mazur game* (see [5], cf. Sect. 3.4).

Definition 1. *A* play *on Σ is an infinite sequence of finite runs $(\alpha_i)_{i\in\mathbb{N}}$, such that $\alpha_i \sqsubseteq \alpha_{i+1}$. Given a play $(\alpha_i)_{i\in\mathbb{N}}$, we say that the scheduler* wins *the play for the game with* target *$E \subseteq \Sigma^\infty$ if $\sup_i \alpha_i \in E$. Otherwise the opponent wins. A* strategy *(for the scheduler) is a mapping[5] $f : \Sigma^+ \to \Sigma^+$ such that $\alpha \sqsubseteq f(\alpha)$ for all $\alpha \in \Sigma^+$. A strategy f is* progressive *if $f(\alpha) \neq \alpha$ for all $\alpha \in \Sigma^+$. A play $(\alpha_i)_{i\in\mathbb{N}}$ is f-*compliant *if for every i, $f(\alpha_{2i}) = \alpha_{2i+1}$. A run x is f-*compliant *if it is the result of an f-compliant play $(\alpha_i)_{i\in\mathbb{N}}$, i.e., $x = \sup_i \alpha_i$. The set of all f-compliant runs is denoted by R_f. A strategy f is* winning *for E if $R_f \subseteq E$.*

Note that a finite run α is f-compliant if and only if $f(\alpha) = \alpha$. Therefore, all f-compliant runs are infinite if f is progressive. We could indeed restrict to consider progressive strategies, as the following result shows.

[5] Considering strategies that depend on the full history of the play does not increase their power in the game considered here.

Lemma 1. *There exists a winning strategy for E if and only if there exists a progressive winning strategy for $E \cap \Sigma^\omega$.*

Proof. Let f be a winning strategy for E. Let $\beta \in \Sigma^+$ be any finite run and define $f'(\alpha) = f(\alpha)\beta$. Then $R_{f'} \subseteq R_f \subseteq E$. Moreover $R_{f'} \subseteq \Sigma^\omega$ and hence f' is also winning for $E \cap \Sigma^\omega$. The converse is trivial. □

However, we will use non-progressive strategies to neatly characterize some interesting subclasses of liveness.

It is easy to see that, for every strategy f, the property R_f is a liveness property. Therefore, if a target E has a winning strategy, it is a liveness property. This justifies the following definition.

Definition 2. *A property E is called* constructive liveness property *if there exists a winning strategy for E.*

Corollary 1. *A property E is a constructive liveness property if and only if $E \cap \Sigma^\omega$ is a constructive liveness property.*

Corollary 1 is a direct consequence of Lemma 1. We now get:

Proposition 1. *The family of constructive liveness properties is closed under union and countable intersection.*

Proof. Closure under union is trivial. Let E_i be a constructive liveness property and f_i a progressive winning strategy for E_i for each $i \in \mathbb{N}$. Define for $\alpha \in \Sigma^+$ with $|\alpha| = k$: $f(\alpha) = f_k(f_{k-1}(\dots f_0(\alpha)\dots))$. It is straight-forward to check that f is a winning strategy for $\bigcap_{i\in\mathbb{N}} E_i$. □

Σ^ω is a constructive liveness property, while Σ^+ is a liveness property but not constructive because the opponent can enforce the outcome of the play to be infinite. Similarly for any run x, the property $\{\alpha x \mid \alpha \in \Sigma^+\}$ is a liveness property but not constructive. The property $\Box \Diamond \varphi$ is a constructive liveness property while $\Diamond \Box \varphi$ is a liveness property but not constructive—for any non-trivial state property φ. More examples for constructive liveness properties are $\Box(\varphi \Rightarrow \Diamond \psi)$, $\Diamond \Box \varphi \Rightarrow \Box \Diamond \psi$, and $\Box \Diamond \varphi \Rightarrow \Box \Diamond \psi$.

Call a run *periodic* if it is of the form $\alpha\beta^\omega$ for $\alpha, \beta \in \Sigma^+$ and *aperiodic* otherwise. The set of aperiodic runs is a constructive liveness property while the set of periodic runs is a liveness property but not constructive; f defined by $f(\alpha) = \alpha s^k r$ where $k = |\alpha|, s, r \in \Sigma, s \neq r$ is a winning strategy for aperiodic runs.

3.2 A Language-Theoretic View

In this section, we study what guarantee, recurrence, and persistence properties are constructive liveness properties. (Recall that a safety property is a liveness property only if it equals Σ^∞.) Furthermore, we derive an independent characterization of constructive liveness that is based on recurrence properties.

Proposition 2. *Let Q be a finitary property.*

1. $\mathrm{E}(Q)$ *is a liveness property if and only if Q is a* pseudo-liveness property, *that is, for each $\alpha \in \Sigma^+$ exists an $x \in Q$ that is compatible with α.*
2. $\mathrm{R}(Q)$ *is a liveness property if and only if Q is a liveness property.*
3. $\mathrm{P}(Q)$ *is a liveness property if and only if Q is a liveness property.*

It is easy to check that each live guarantee as well as each live recurrence property is constructive. More precisely, live recurrence properties correspond to the runs complying with *idempotent* strategies, i.e., strategies f that satisfy $f(f(\alpha)) = f(\alpha)$ for all $\alpha \in \Sigma^+$. Live guarantee properties correspond to the runs complying with *stable* strategies, i.e., strategies f that satisfy $f(\alpha) \sqsubseteq \beta \Rightarrow f(\beta) = \beta$ for all $\alpha, \beta \in \Sigma^+$. Each stable strategy is idempotent.

Proposition 3. *We have:*

1. $\{\mathrm{E}(Q) \mid Q$ *is a pseudo-liveness property*$\} = \{R_f \mid f$ *is a stable strategy*$\}$ *and*
2. $\{\mathrm{R}(Q) \mid Q$ *is a liveness property*$\} = \{R_f \mid f$ *is an idempotent strategy*$\}$.

It follows from Prop. 3 that each property that contains a live guarantee property or a live recurrence property is a constructive liveness property. We show now that live persistence properties are in general not constructive.

Proposition 4. *A live persistence property is constructive if and only if it contains a live guarantee property.*

We have shown that each property that contains a live recurrence property is a constructive liveness property. The converse does not hold. However, we can give a characterization of constructive liveness in terms of recurrence properties if we restrict ourselves to the infinitary subset of a recurrence property in the spirit of Corollary 1. Define $\mathrm{R}^\omega(Q) = \mathrm{R}(Q) \cap \Sigma^\omega$, i.e., $\mathrm{R}^\omega(Q)$ consists of all runs that have infinitely many prefixes in Q. A property is called *infinitary recurrence property* if it is of the form $\mathrm{R}^\omega(Q)$. Infinitary recurrence properties are closed under countable intersection (and finite union) [14]. In contrast, recurrence properties are not closed under finite intersection.

Proposition 5. *The family of live infinitary recurrence properties is closed under finite union and countable intersection.*

We obtain the following characterization of constructive liveness.

Proposition 6. *A property is a constructive liveness property if and only if it contains a live infinitary recurrence property.*

Proof. The claim is part of the more general Thm. 1 below. □

The property $\Diamond\varphi$ is a live guarantee property, $\Box\Diamond\varphi$ is a live recurrence property and hence, $\Box\Diamond\varphi\cap\Sigma^\omega$ ('infinitely often φ') is a live infinitary recurrence property.

3.3 A Topological View

In this section, we characterize constructive liveness in terms of dense G_δ sets. As we have stated, a dense open set is a live guarantee property. Such a property has a nice intuition: It requires one finite observation to be made. Often it is natural to require countably many finite observations to be made. This corresponds to the intersection of countably many dense open sets, which is again dense in our topology:

Proposition 7. *A property E is a dense G_δ set if and only if it is the intersection of countably many dense open sets.*

Topological spaces that satisfy Prop. 7 are called *Baire spaces*.

Corollary 2. *The family of dense G_δ sets is closed under finite union and countable intersection.*

Each G_δ set E is, like any open set, *upward-closed*, i.e., $x \in E$ and $x \sqsubseteq y$ implies $y \in E$. Recurrence properties are therefore not G_δ sets in general. However, they are related as follows.

Proposition 8. *E is a G_δ set if and only if $E = \mathrm{E}(Q) \cup \mathrm{R}^\omega(Q')$ for some finitary Q and Q'.*

In particular, each infinitary recurrence property is a G_δ set. Furthermore, $\mathrm{lex}(E)$ is a dense open set if E is open and a dense G_δ set if E is a G_δ set. We define now two more classes of liveness properties.

Definition 3. *A property is an* open-liveness property *if it contains a dense open set. A property is a* G_δ-liveness property *if it contains a dense G_δ set.*

An open-liveness property is a property satisfying

$$\forall \alpha \in \Sigma^+ : \exists \beta : \alpha \sqsubseteq \beta \wedge \beta\!\uparrow \subseteq E.$$

Examples of open-liveness properties are $\Diamond \varphi \Rightarrow \Diamond \psi$ and $\Box \Diamond \varphi \Rightarrow \Diamond \psi$ if ψ is nonempty. E is a dense open set if and only if $E = \mathrm{lex}(\mathrm{E}(Q))$ for some finitary Q. Due to Prop. 7, a property is a G_δ-liveness property if and only if it is the intersection of countably many open-liveness properties.

G_δ-liveness properties have another topological characterization—they are the *co-meager* sets of our topology: In a topological space, we say that a set is *nowhere dense* if its closure does not contain any nonempty open set. A set is *meager*, if it is the countable union of nowhere dense sets. The complement of a meager set is called *co-meager* (or *residual*).

Proposition 9 (E.g. [15], page 41). *In a Baire space, a set is co-meager if and only if it contains a dense G_δ set.*

Co-meagerness is a topological notion of 'largeness' of a set. The class of co-meager sets shares many properties with the class of sets of measure 1 [15], which are the 'large' sets in probability theory. We prove now that our three views on constructive liveness coincide.

Theorem 1. *Let E be a temporal property. The following statements are equivalent:*

1. *E is a constructive liveness property.*
2. *E contains a live infinitary recurrence property.*
3. *E is a G_δ-liveness property.*

Proof.

1. ⇒ 2. Let f be a progressive winning strategy for E. It is easy to check that $R_f = \mathrm{R}(f(\Sigma^+)) \cap \Sigma^\omega$.
2. ⇒ 3. Each infinitary recurrence property is a G_δ set due to Prop. 8.
3. ⇒ 1. Each open-liveness property is constructive (Prop. 3.1). Since constructive liveness is closed under countable intersection, each G_δ-liveness property is constructive as well. □

Fig. 1.a shows the relationships between the subfamilies of constructive liveness.

3.4 A Maximality Result

We would like to argue that constructive liveness is the most permissive definition that suits our purposes, i.e., it is in some sense maximal among all the subclasses of liveness that are closed under countable intersection. We are not able to prove such a result. However we are able to prove that it is maximal if we restrict to *determinate* sets.

Definition 4. *A* counter strategy *(for the opponent) is a pair $g = (\alpha, f)$ of a finite run $\alpha \in \Sigma^+$ and a strategy f; g is* progressive *if f is progressive. A play $(\alpha_i)_{i \in \mathrm{N}}$ is g-*compliant *if $\alpha_0 = \alpha$ and for every i, $f(\alpha_{2i+1}) = \alpha_{2i+2}$. A run x is said to be g-compliant if it is the result of a g-compliant play $(\alpha_i)_{i \in \mathrm{N}}$, i.e., $x = \sup_i \alpha_i$. The set of all g-compliant runs is denoted by R_g. A counter strategy g is* winning *for target E if $R_g \subseteq \neg E$. We say that E is* determinate *if it has either a winning strategy or a winning counter strategy.*

Determinate sets have been studied in the classical theory of Banach-Mazur games. In the standard definition of a Banach-Mazur game, both players must play progressively and strategies may also depend on the full history of the previous play. However, in our setting, both definitions characterize the same class of sets (see [5]). In particular

Proposition 10. *E is determinate if and only if $E \cap \Sigma^\omega$ is determinate in the Banach-Mazur game.*

Using the axiom of choice, it is possible to show the existence of indeterminate sets. Nevertheless, the class of determinate sets is quite general. For instance, every *Borel set* of the natural topology[6] on Σ^ω is determinate in the Banach-Mazur game (see [5]), where the family of *Borel sets* of a topology is the smallest family of sets that contains the open sets and is closed under countable union and complementation. It easily follows from Prop. 10 that each Borel set of the Scott topology is determinate. In particular, this means that the class of determinate sets contains all properties that can be expressed by Büchi automata and hence all properties that can be expressed by common linear-time temporal logics.

We show now the maximality of constructive liveness within the determinate sets. Note that each constructive liveness property is determinate.

Theorem 2. *The family of constructive liveness properties is the largest family of determinate liveness properties that contains all dense* G_δ *sets and is closed under finite intersection.*

Proof. Consider a determinate set E that is not a constructive liveness property. E must therefore have a winning counter strategy $g = (\alpha_0, f)$. Note that R_f is a constructive liveness property. We claim that $R_f \cap E$ is not dense: Consider the finite run α_0. Since g is a winning counter strategy, any extension of α_0 into R_f is in $\neg E$. Therefore, there is no extension of α_0 into $R_f \cap E$ and hence $R_f \cap E$ is not dense. Since R_f is constructive, it contains a dense G_δ set L. It follows that $L \cap E$ is not a liveness property. Hence no non-constructive determinate liveness property can be added to the dense G_δ sets without losing closedness under finite intersection. □

Note that we have a complete proof strategy for showing that a determinate set is a constructive liveness property or not: Either display a winning strategy for the scheduler or a winning counter strategy for the opponent.

4 Defining Fairness

We consider now an arbitrary system, represented by a safety property S. We are interested in properties $E \subseteq S$ of the system under consideration. These properties are equipped with the Scott topology relativized to S. Liveness of a property F w.r.t. S is exactly density of $F \cap S$ in the Scott topology relative to S. We now define fairness properties in S analogously to constructive liveness. All notions and theorems from Sect. 3 easily carry over to the relativized case.

Definition 5. *Let S be a safety property, F a temporal property, and let $S^\top = \{x \in S \mid x\!\uparrow \cap S = \{x\}\}$ denote the set maximal runs w.r.t. S. A strategy f is* closed in S *if $\alpha \in S \Rightarrow f(\alpha) \in S$ for all $\alpha \in \Sigma^+$; f is* progressive in S *if $f(\alpha) = \alpha \Rightarrow \alpha \in S^\top$; f is a* winning strategy for F in S *if f is closed in S and $R_f \cap S \subseteq F$. F is a* fairness property *for S if there is a winning strategy for*

[6] This means the Cantor topology on Σ^ω, which coincides with the Scott topology on Σ^∞ relativized to Σ^ω.

F in S. A fairness notion *is a mapping that maps each safety property S to a fairness property for S.*

Clearly, each fairness property for S is live w.r.t. S, moreover:

Theorem 3. *The family of fairness properties for S is closed under union and countable intersection.*

Theorem 4. *The following statements are equivalent:*

1. *F is a fairness property for S.*
2. *There exists a finitary Q such that $F' = \mathrm{R}(Q) \cap S^{\top} \subseteq F$ and F' is live w.r.t. S.*
3. *There exists a G_δ set E such that $F' = E \cap S \subseteq F$ and F' is live w.r.t. S.*

Note that statement 3 is equivalent with F being co-meager in the Scott topology relativized to S.

Theorem 5. *The family of all fairness properties w.r.t. S is the largest family of live determinate properties w.r.t. S that contains the live G_δ sets w.r.t. S and that is closed under finite intersection.*

Note that E being a liveness property does not imply that E is live w.r.t. S, nor does the converse hold. However for the converse case we have: If E is live w.r.t. S then $E \cup \neg S$ is a liveness property that is live w.r.t. S. Therefore, it is neither necessary nor wrong to think of fairness properties as liveness properties, i.e., we would not gain or lose anything if we additionally required that a fairness property for S has to be a liveness property.

4.1 Examination of Popular Fairness Notions

We show now that our definition of fairness covers popular fairness notions in the literature. To check this, one can use the following proposition. Define $\mathrm{lex}_S(E)$ to be the *liveness extension of E relative to S* by

$$\mathrm{lex}_S(E) = E \cup \bigcup_{\alpha \in S, \alpha\uparrow \cap E \cap S = \varnothing} \alpha\uparrow .$$

Proposition 11. *If E is a constructive liveness property, then (any superset of) $\mathrm{lex}_S(E)$ is a fairness property for S.*

Define a *transition* to be a relation $t \subseteq \Sigma \times \Sigma$ over states. Let S be a safety property and $x = s_0, s_1, \ldots \in S$. Transition t is *enabled* in S at position i of x if there exists a state s such that $x_i s \in S$ and $(s_i, s) \in t$; t is *taken* at position i if $(s_i, s_{i+1}) \in t$. The following examples of fairness notions can be checked by using Prop. 11, but it is also easy to define a winning strategy in each case. The following list cannot be exhaustive due to lack of space. We also omit here the references to the papers where the fairness notions were introduced. Those can be found in the full version of this paper [17].

1. Maximality w.r.t. a transition t defined as $\Box(\text{enabled}_S(t) \Rightarrow \exists t' : \Diamond\,\text{taken}(t'))$ is a fairness notion.
2. Weak and strong fairness w.r.t. a transition t defined as $\Diamond\Box\,\text{enabled}_S(t) \Rightarrow \Box\Diamond\,\text{taken}(t)$ and $\Box\Diamond\,\text{enabled}_S(t) \Rightarrow \Box\Diamond\,\text{taken}(t)$ respectively are fairness notions. Weak and strong fairness w.r.t. words is similar.
3. Let $\varphi \subseteq \Sigma$ be a state property. Say that φ is *enabled* in S at a position i of a run x if there is a state $s \in \varphi$ such that $x_i s \in S$. State fairness w.r.t. φ defined as $\Box\Diamond\,\text{enabled}_S(\varphi) \Rightarrow \Box\Diamond\,\varphi$ is a fairness notion.
4. Extreme fairness w.r.t. a transition t and a state property φ defined as $\Box\Diamond(\varphi \wedge \text{enabled}_S(t)) \Rightarrow \Box\Diamond(\varphi \wedge \text{taken}(t))$ is a fairness notion. The notion of α-fairness is similar.
5. Say that a transition t is k-*enabled* in S at position i of x if there is a finite sequence α with $|\alpha| \leq k$ such that $x_i\alpha \in S$ and $x_i\alpha$ enables t; k-fairness w.r.t. t defined as $\Box\Diamond\,\text{enabled}_S(k,t) \Rightarrow \Box\Diamond\,\text{taken}(t)$ is a fairness notion.
6. Say that a transition t is ∞-*enabled* in S at position i of x if there exists a k such that t is k-enabled at i; ∞-fairness w.r.t. t (called *hyperfairness* in [12]) defined as $\Box\Diamond\,\text{enabled}_S(\infty,t) \Rightarrow \Box\Diamond\,\text{taken}(t)$ equals $\text{lex}_S(\Box\Diamond\,\text{taken}(t))$ and is therefore a fairness notion. Note that ∞-fairness is not the intersection of all k-fairness for $k \in \mathbb{N}$.
7. Unconditional fairness, defined as $\Box\Diamond\,\text{taken}(t)$ is not a fairness notion because it is not live w.r.t. all S.
8. Say that a transition t is k-*taken* at position i of a run x if t is taken at a position $j \leq i+k$ in x. The property $\Box\,\text{enabled}_S(t) \Rightarrow \text{taken}(k,t)$ is in general not a fairness property for S since it is a safety property and only live w.r.t. S if it coincides with S.
9. Let $y \in \Sigma^\omega$. Say that y is *enabled* in S at a position i of a run x if $x_i y \in S$; it is *taken* at i if $x = x_i y$. The property $\Box\Diamond\,\text{enabled}_S(y) \Rightarrow \Diamond\,\text{taken}(y)$ is live w.r.t. S but not a fairness property in general. Similarly, $\text{lex}_S(\Diamond\Box\,\varphi)$ is not a fairness property in general.
10. Finitary fairness w.r.t. a transition t, which is defined as $\bigcup_k \Box(\text{enabled}_S(t) \Rightarrow \text{taken}(k,t))$ is live w.r.t. S but not a fairness property. A winning counter strategy is defined by $f(\alpha) = \alpha s^k$ where $k = |\alpha|, s \in \Sigma$. Note that finitary fairness w.r.t. t is in conflict with the intersection of countably many strong fairness requirements (w.r.t. transitions $t_i, i \in \mathbb{N}$).

5 A Complete Lattice of Liveness Properties

The family of fairness properties for a given S and in particular the family of constructive liveness properties is not closed under arbitrary intersection. In particular, there is not a strongest fairness property in general.

Proposition 12. *Constructive liveness is not closed under arbitrary intersection.*

Proof. The property $\neg\{x\}$ is a constructive liveness property for each run x. $\bigcap_{x\in\Sigma^\infty} \neg\{x\} = \varnothing$ is not a liveness property. $\Box$

In this section, we identify a subclass of constructive liveness that is closed under arbitrary union and intersection, i.e., it forms a complete lattice. Therefore it possesses a strongest and a weakest property. We develop the theory here for constructive liveness. Analogous results can be obtained for fairness w.r.t. a given safety property. We start with the definition of two families of liveness properties which have been mentioned by Alpern and Schneider [2], where *absolute liveness* was introduced earlier by Sistla [16].

Definition 6. *A temporal property E is a* uniform liveness property *if there exists an x such that $\alpha x \in E$ for all $\alpha \in \Sigma^+$. E is an* absolute liveness property *if $E \neq \varnothing$ and $x \in E \Rightarrow \alpha x \in E$ for all $\alpha \in \Sigma^+$.*

Each absolute liveness property is a uniform liveness property and each uniform liveness property is a liveness property. Moreover:

Proposition 13. *A property is a uniform liveness property if and only if it contains an absolute liveness property.*

Both properties, $\Box \Diamond \varphi$ and $\Diamond \Box \varphi$ are absolute and hence uniform liveness properties. Absolute and uniform liveness properties are closed under union but not under finite intersection.

Definition 7. *Let E be a temporal property.*

1. *E is an* open-uniform liveness property *if there exists a finite run β such that $\alpha\beta\uparrow \subseteq E$ for all $\alpha \in \Sigma^+$.*
2. *E is a* G_δ-uniform liveness property *if it is the intersection of countably many open-uniform liveness properties.*
3. *E is a* G_δ-absolute liveness property *if it is the intersection of countably many absolute and open sets.*

Proposition 14.

1. *Each open-uniform liveness property is a uniform open-liveness property.*
2. *Each G_δ-uniform liveness property is a uniform G_δ-liveness property.*
3. *Each G_δ-absolute liveness property is an absolute G_δ set.*

An example of an absolute open set is $\Diamond \varphi$. The properties $\Box \Diamond \varphi$ and $\Box(\varphi \Rightarrow \Diamond \psi)$ are G_δ-uniform liveness properties; $\Diamond \Box \varphi$ is uniform but not G_δ-uniform. The converse of Prop. 14.1 and 2 does not hold. Consider, for example, the property $E = \bigcap_{k \in \mathbb{N}} (s^k \Rightarrow \Diamond r^k)$ for $s, r \in \Sigma$. E is a uniform open-liveness property, the witness for uniformity being the infinite sequence r^ω. However, it is not an open-uniform liveness property.

Proposition 15.

1. *A property is an open-uniform liveness property if and only if it contains an absolute and open set.*
2. *A property is a G_δ-uniform liveness property if and only if it contains a G_δ-absolute liveness property.*

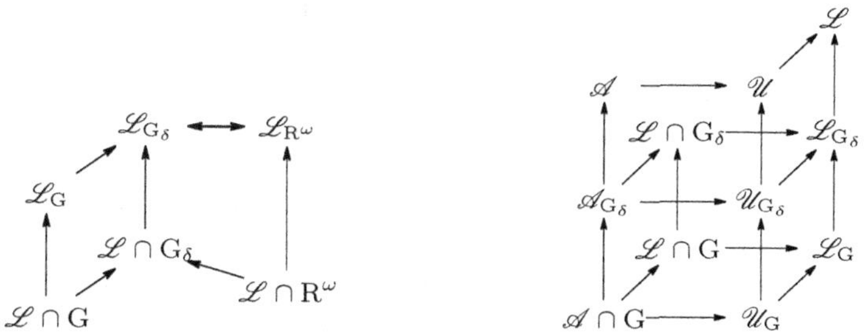

(a) Constructive liveness (b) Absolute and uniform liveness

Fig. 1. Relationships between various subclasses of liveness: An arrow denotes inclusion. $\mathscr{L}$, G, and R^ω denote the family of liveness properties, open sets, and infinitary recurrence properties respectively. $\mathscr{L}_{\mathscr{F}}$ denotes the family of sets that contain a dense set from the family $\mathscr{F}$. By $\mathscr{A}$, $\mathscr{U}$, $\mathscr{A}_{\mathrm{G}_\delta}$, $\mathscr{U}_{\mathrm{G}}$, and $\mathscr{U}_{\mathrm{G}_\delta}$ we denote the absolute, uniform, G_δ-absolute, open-uniform, and G_δ-uniform liveness properties respectively.

Proposition 16. *The family of* G_δ*-absolute liveness properties is closed under arbitrary intersection.*

Proof. Consider the property

$$\hat{E} = \{x \mid \forall\alpha\exists\beta : \beta\alpha \sqsubseteq x\} = \bigcap_{\alpha\in\Sigma^+} E(\alpha) \text{ where } E(\alpha) = \{x \mid \exists\beta : \beta\alpha \sqsubseteq x\}.$$

$\hat{E}$ is a G_δ-absolute liveness property because each $E(\alpha)$ is an absolute open set. Furthermore, each G_δ-absolute liveness property E contains $\hat{E}$: Let $E = \bigcap_{i\in\mathbb{N}} G_i$ where G_i is an absolute open set. Let $x \in \hat{E}$. Consider a G_i and a $y \in G_i$. Since G_i is absolute and open, there exists $\beta \sqsubseteq y$ such that $\alpha\beta\uparrow \subseteq G_i$ for all $\alpha \in \Sigma^+$. Since $x \in \hat{E}$, there is an α' such that $\alpha'\beta \sqsubseteq x$. Hence $x \in G_i$. □

Proposition 17. *The family of* G_δ*-uniform liveness properties is closed under arbitrary union and intersection.*

Proof. Closedness under union is trivial. Closedness under intersection follows from Props. 15.2 and 16. □

Fig. 1.b shows the inclusion of the defined families.

6 Conclusion

For this presentation, we have restricted ourselves to sequential runs. But our definitions and results can be generalized to non-sequential runs. In topological terms, the results can be generalized to any Baire space and, in particular, to the Scott topology of ω-algebraic domains. Since the configurations of an event structure form an ω-algebraic domain, our results immediately carry over to event structures. However, the game-theoretic point of view could allow us to refine fairness in a non-sequential setting. The details remain to be worked out.

Apt, Francez, and Katz [3] proposed that fairness should be machine-closed w.r.t. the safety property of the system. We refined this to exclude some properties that should not be called fairness properties from our point of view. We did not consider their other two criteria: *equivalence robustness* and *liveness enhancement*. Equivalence robustness is an issue when concurrency plays an important role in the modeling of the reactive system. That issue is then best dealt with in the domain of non-sequential runs. Since our results carry over to these domains, equivalence robustness is orthogonal to our definition of fairness. Liveness enhancement refers to the view that every system is equipped with the basic assumption of maximality with respect to every transition. Liveness enhancement means that fairness should be strictly stronger than this basic assumption—at least with respect to some safety property. Liveness enhancement is also orthogonal to our definition and can be additionally used when relevant.

References

1. M. Abadi and L. Lamport. The existence of refinement mappings. *Theoretical Computer Science*, 82:253–284, 1991.
2. B. Alpern and F. B. Schneider. Defining liveness. *IPL*, 21:181–185, Oct. 1985.
3. K. R. Apt, N. Francez, and S. Katz. Appraising fairness in languages for distributed programming. *Distributed Computing*, 2:226–241, 1988.
4. N. Francez. *Fairness*. Springer, 1986.
5. E. Grädel. Positional determinacy of infinite games. In *STACS*, pp. 4–18, 2004.
6. D. Harel and A. Pnueli. On the development of reactive systems. In K. Apt (ed.), *Logics and Models of Concurrent Systems*, pp. 477–498. Springer-Verlag, 1985.
7. E. Kindler. Safety and liveness properties: A survey. *EATCS Bulletin* 53, 1994.
8. M. Z. Kwiatkowska. Survey of fairness notions. *Information and Software Technology*, 31(7):371–386, 1989.
9. M. Z. Kwiatkowska. On topological characterization of behavioural properties. *Topology and Category Theory in Computer Science*, Oxford Univ. Press, 1991.
10. L. Lamport. Proving the correctness of multiprocess programs. *IEEE Transactions on Software Engineering*, SE-3(2):125–143, Mar. 1977.
11. L. Lamport. Formal foundation for specification and verification. *Distributed Systems: Methods and Tools for Specification, LNCS* 190. Springer-Verlag, 1985.
12. L. Lamport. Fairness and hyperfairness. *Distr. Computing*, 13(4):239–245, 2000.
13. D. Lehmann, A. Pnueli, and J. Stavi. Impartiality, justice, and fairness: The ethics of concurrent termination. In ICALP, *LNCS* 115, pp. 264–277. Springer, 1981.
14. Z. Manna and A. Pnueli. A hierarchy of temporal properties. In *9th PODC*, pp. 377–408. ACM, 1990.
15. J. C. Oxtoby. *Measure and Category. A Survey of the Analogies between Topological and Measure Spaces.* Springer-Verlag, 1971.
16. A. P. Sistla. On characterization of safety and liveness properties in temporal logic. In *4th PODC*, pp. 39–48. ACM, 1985.
17. H. Völzer, D. Varacca, and E. Kindler. Defining Fairness. SIIM Technical Report SIIM-TR-A-05-18, Universität zu Lübeck, 2005.

Regular Symbolic Analysis of Dynamic Networks of Pushdown Systems

Ahmed Bouajjani[1], Markus Müller-Olm[2], and Tayssir Touili[1]

[1] LIAFA, University of Paris 7, 2 place Jussieu, 75251 Paris cedex 5, France
[2] Universität Dortmund, FB 4, LS 5,Baroper Str. 301, 44221 Dortmund, Germany

Abstract. We introduce two abstract models for multithreaded programs based on dynamic networks of pushdown systems. We address the problem of symbolic reachability analysis for these models. More precisely, we consider the problem of computing effective representations of their reachability sets using finite-state automata. We show that, while forward reachability sets are not regular in general, backward reachability sets starting from regular sets of configurations are always regular. We provide algorithms for computing backward reachability sets using word/tree automata, and show how these algorithms can be applied for flow analysis of multithreaded programs.

1 Introduction

Multithreaded programs are an important class of programs, in which parallelism is used routinely in practice. Parallel programming in general is known to be difficult and error prone, and multithreaded programs are no exception. Therefore, the design of methods and techniques for automatic analysis of such programs is an important and a quite challenging issue. For that, we need to define formal models which are adequate for modelling multithreaded programs, and for which it is possible to construct automatic analysis algorithms.

In recent related work, complete analysis algorithms for abstract classes of parallel programs have been studied by several researchers. Mayr [13] establishes a number of decidability and undecidability results for process classes in the so-called PRS (process rewrite system) hierarchy. PRS are able to model sequential as well as parallel phenomena. In fact, they can be seen as combinations of pushdown systems and Petri nets (defined in a term rewriting setting using prefix and multiset rewrite rules). Following the automata-based approach for the symbolic verification of pushdown systems [2,11], Lugiez and Schnoebelen [12] show how to use tree automata for reachability analysis of PA processes [1], a particularly well-known class in the PRS hierarchy. Their paper has inspired further work that applies tree automata techniques to analysis of more expressive models [6,7,3,4,19]. Another line of research generalizes fixpoint-based techniques as common in flow analysis to analysis of similar models of parallel programs [18,14,15]. Both approaches can be used to solve bitvector problems, a certain type of simple but important data-flow-analysis problems, for flow graph systems with parallel calls of procedures, or, equivalently, parbegin/parend-blocks interprocedurally [9,10,18]. While [9,10] reduce the problem to reachability analysis of PA-processes, [18] uses fixpoint-based techniques.

M. Abadi and L. de Alfaro (Eds.): CONCUR 2005, LNCS 3653, pp. 473–487, 2005.

Unfortunately, these results do *not* cover interprocedural analysis of multithreaded programs because commands that start new threads cannot adequately be modelled by parallel calls. In a multithreaded program such a command typically returns immediately (see, e.g., the JAVA or POSIX thread API). Therefore the father of a new thread can pursue its execution concurrently to its son and can even terminate or return to its caller while the son is still alive. In contrast, a parallel call returns only when and if all its component processes have terminated, which is a fundamentally different behavior. Indeed we show in Sect. 2 that in presence of procedures, multithreaded programs can have trace languages different from that of any program with parallel calls.

The goal of this paper is to adapt the automata-based approach mentioned above to interprocedural (reachability) analysis of multithreaded programs. For this purpose we propose two models of multithreaded programs, show how to perform reachability analysis for them with automata-theoretic constructions, and discuss their utility for modelling and analysing multithreaded and other classes of parallel programs.

In Sect. 2 we introduce *Dynamic Pushdown Networks (DPNs)* as a basic model of multithreaded programs. Intuitively, a DPN is a network of pushdown processes that run independently in parallel. Each process can create new members of the network as a side effect of a pushdown transition. DPNs thus model a network of threads each of which can perform basic actions, call (recursively) procedures, and *spawn* new processes. We show that while forward reachability of DPNs does not preserve regularity of configuration sets in general, it still preserves context-freeness (Sect. 4). Backward reachability in contrast preserves regularity and we show how to compute the backward reachability set of a regular set of configurations by means of a saturation algorithm in polynomial time (Sect. 4). We also show that DPN allow us to solve bitvector problems interprocedurally for multithreaded programs (Sect. 3), contrary to previously used models in the literature such as PA processes (Sect. 2).

We extend DPNs to *Constrained DPNs (CDPN)* in Sect. 5, a model that combines (indeed even extends) the modelling power of both DPNs and PA (and even the so-called PAD [13]). The new idea is that enabledness of a transition for a process can be made dependent on a *constraint* which is a regular pattern among the sequence of control states of its sons. We require constraints to be *stable* in the sense that further evolution of the sons cannot invalidate a constraint. We show that otherwise we lose the property that backward reachability preserves regularity. Transition rules with stable constraints increase the expressive power considerably over DPNs. In particular they allow us to model, in addition to thread creation and procedure calls, also parallel calls and various types of join commands among other things. It also allows us to return information back from procedures called in parallel to their caller which cannot be handled in PA and not even in PAD. Constrained DPNs inherit from DPNs that forward reachability does not preserve regularity. Therefore, we consider here backward reachability only. We show that the set of configurations that can reach a given regular set of configurations of a CDPN can again be computed by a saturation algorithm. As configurations of CDPNs are given by unbounded width trees rather than by words as in the DPN case—the tree structure captures the father-son relationship—we resort to hedge automata here [8]. The construction is nontrivial and its justification uses in a subtle manner the assumption about the stability of the constraints in the system definition. While the overall complexity of this procedure is exponential—we indeed prove a PSPACE lower bound—it is exponential only in the number of different constraints used in the rules of the given CDPN, and just polynomial in the other problem parameters. Therefore, if the number of different constraints is bounded, we obtain a polynomial-time analysis algorithm. This in particular holds if we just model (in addition to spawn operations), parallel calls, a fixed selection of join commands, or a combination of these. Due to lack of space, proofs are omitted. They can be found in [5].

2 Dynamic Pushdown Networks

A *Dynamic Pushdown Network* (DPN) is a tuple $M = (Act, P, \Gamma, \Delta)$, where Act is a finite set of visible *actions*, P is a finite set of *control states*, Γ is a finite set of *stack symbols* disjoint from P, and Δ is a finite set of transition rules of the following forms: either (a) $p\gamma \overset{a}{\hookrightarrow} p_1 w_1$, or (b) $p\gamma \overset{a}{\hookrightarrow} p_1 w_1 \rhd p_2 w_2$, where $p, p_1, p_2 \in P$, $a \in Act$, $\gamma \in \Gamma$, and $w_1, w_2 \in \Gamma^*$. A DPN can be seen as a collection of identical sequential processes running in parallel, each of them being able to (1) perform pushdown operations and to (2) create processes in the network. Synchronization is not allowed between processes.

A configuration of a DPN M (also called M-configuration) is a word over the alphabet $\Sigma = P \cup \Gamma$ starting with a symbol in P. An M-configuration can be seen as a sequence of (sub)words in $P\Gamma^*$ each of them corresponding to the configuration of one of the processes running in parallel in the network. Let $Conf_M$ be the set of all M-configurations.

For every $a \in Act$, we define $\xrightarrow{a}_M$ to be the smallest relation in $Conf_M \times Conf_M$ s.t. $\forall u, v \in Conf_M$, $u \xrightarrow{a}_M v$ iff (1) there is a rule $p\gamma \overset{a}{\hookrightarrow} p_1 w_1$ in Δ s.t. $u = u_1 p\gamma u_2$ and $v = u_1 p_1 w_1 u_2$, or (2) there is a rule $p\gamma \overset{a}{\hookrightarrow} p_1 w_1 \rhd p_2 w_2$ in Δ s.t. $u = u_1 p\gamma u_2$ and $v = u_1 p_2 w_2 p_1 w_1 u_2$. We write $u \rightarrow_M v$ if there exists $a \in Act$ s.t. $u \xrightarrow{a}_M v$.

The semantics above says that rules of the form (a) correspond precisely to pushdown operations (manipulation of the top of the stack) which can be applied anywhere in the configuration (i.e., by any of the processes in the network): if a process is at control state p and has γ as topmost stack symbol, then it can move to control state p_1 and replace γ by w_1 at the top of its stack. Rules of the form (b) allow in addition the creation of new processes: a process with control state p and topmost stack symbol γ can (1) move to state p_1 and modify its stack by replacing γ with w_1, and moreover, (2) create (to its left) a process which starts its execution at the initial configuration $p_2 w_2$.

Given a configuration c, the set of immediate predecessors (resp. successors) of c is $\mathsf{pre}_M(c) = \{c' \in C \,:\, c' \rightarrow_M c\}$ (resp. $\mathsf{post}_M(c) = \{c' \in C \,:\, c \rightarrow_M c'\}$). These notations can be generalized straightforwardly to sets of configurations. Let pre^*_M (resp. post^*_M) denote the reflexive-transitive closure of pre_M (resp. post_M). We omit the subscript M when it is understood from the context. Given $\Delta' \subseteq \Delta$, we use $\mathsf{pre}_{\Delta'}$ (resp. $\mathsf{post}_{\Delta'}$) to denote immediate predecessors (resp. successors) using a rule in Δ'. Then, $\mathsf{pre}^*_{\Delta'}$ and $\mathsf{post}^*_{\Delta'}$ denote the corresponding reflexive-transitive closures. Furthermore, $\mathsf{Traces}_M(c) = \{w \in Act^* \,:\, \exists c'.\, c \xrightarrow{w}_M c'\}$ is the set of traces generated by c.

DPN vs. PA Processes: DPNs allow to model multithreaded programs where creation of threads is done using spawn commands (see Sect. 3). This is not the case for other formalisms used in the literature for modelling parallel programs like PA [1]:[1]

Theorem 1. *Let* $\mathcal{L} = \bigcup\{a^n(b^{n'} \otimes (c^m d^{m'})) : n \geq n' \geq 0,\ m \geq m' \geq 0\}$, *where* $\otimes$ *denotes the shuffle (or interleaving) operator defined as usual. Then:*

a) There is a DPN M and an M-configuration c such that $\mathsf{Traces}_M(c) = \mathcal{L}$.
b) There is no PA system Δ *and no process variable A such that* $\mathsf{Traces}_\Delta(A) = \mathcal{L}$.

Hence, PA processes are inadequate for capturing the behavior of multithreaded programs with spawn-like creation of threads. It also follows from the proof that trace sets of DPNs cannot be captured by the type of constraint systems used as semantic reference point in the constraint-based approach [18,14,15]. Therefore, the methods of [9,10,18,15,14] for interprocedural analysis of flow graphs with parallel calls do not carry over immediately to multithreaded programs. These inadequacy results are rather strong because any interesting process equivalence would imply equality of traces.

3 Program Analysis Based on DPN

We show hereafter how DPNs can be used to model multithreaded programs and how our results on symbolic reachability analysis can be used in flow analysis of these programs. This is inspired by Esparza et. al. [9,10].

Flow Graph Systems: As common in program analysis we assume that the program is given by a flow graph system. Let **Proc** be a finite set of procedure names containing **Main**. We assume that the program operates on a set $\mathbf{X} = \{\mathbf{x}_1, \ldots, \mathbf{x}_k\}$ of global variables. We consider the following types of basic statements: assignment statements, $\mathbf{x}_i := e$, where $\mathbf{x}_i \in \mathbf{X}$ and e is some expression; call of a single procedure, $\mathsf{call}(\pi)$, where $\pi \in \mathbf{Proc}$; and spawn of a new thread, $\mathsf{spawn}(\pi)$, where $\pi \in \mathbf{Proc}$. The intuitive meaning of assignment statements and calls is obvious. The spawn command $\mathsf{spawn}(\pi)$ models creation of a new independent thread. Like the call $\mathsf{call}(\pi)$, $\mathsf{spawn}(\pi)$ starts an instance of procedure π. In contrast to a call, however, the spawn command returns immediately such that the newly created instance of π runs as a new thread concurrently to the statements that are executed after the spawn. Let **Stmt** be the set of basic statements.

The control flow of each procedure $\pi \in \mathbf{Proc}$ is described by a control flow graph $G_\pi = (N_\pi, E_\pi, e_\pi, x_\pi)$, where N_π is a finite set of program points of procedure π; $E_\pi \subseteq N_\pi \times \mathbf{Stmt} \times N_\pi$ is a finite set of edges annotated by basic statements; $e_\pi \in N_\pi$ is the entry point of π; and $x_\pi \in N_\pi$ is the exit point of π. We assume that the sets of program points of different procedures are disjoint, $N_\pi \cap N_{\pi'} = \emptyset$ if $\pi, \pi' \in \mathbf{Proc}$, $\pi \neq \pi'$, and agree that $N = \bigcup_{\pi \in \mathbf{Proc}} N_\pi$ and $E = \bigcup_{\pi \in \mathbf{Proc}} E_\pi$.

[1] PA corresponds to processes definable by a set of rewrite rules of the form $A \to t$ where A is a process variable, and t is a term built from process variables, sequential composition, and asynchronous parallel composition.

From Flow Graph Systems to DPN: From a given flow graph system as above we construct a DPN $M = (Act, P, \Gamma, \Delta)$ that captures its operational semantics:

- The actions are given by the assignments that appear in the flow graph system; a special symbol τ is used to signify steps in which no assignment is executed: $Act = \{\mathbf{x} := e \mid \exists u, v : (u, \mathbf{x} := e, v) \in E\} \cup \{\tau\}$;
- we have just one artificial control state #: $P = \{\#\}$;
- we work with a stack of program points; the topmost stack symbol is the current program point of the current procedure, the other stack symbols are the return points of its callers: $\Gamma = N$;
- the transition rules in Δ describe computation steps of the flow graph system:
  1. for every assignment edge $(u, x := e, v) \in E$ we put the rule $\#u \overset{x:=e}{\hookrightarrow} \#v$ to Δ;
  2. for every call edge $(u, \mathsf{call}(\pi), v) \in E$ we put the rule $\#u \overset{\tau}{\hookrightarrow} \#e_\pi v$ to Δ;
  3. for every spawn-edge $(u, \mathsf{spawn}(\pi), v) \in E$ we put the rule $\#u \overset{\tau}{\hookrightarrow} \#v \rhd \#e_\pi$ to Δ,
  4. for each procedure $\pi \in \mathbf{Proc}$, we put the rule $\#x_\pi \overset{\tau}{\hookrightarrow} \#$ to Δ. This rule describes the return from procedure π.

Note that it is possible to extend the semantics above in order to handle local procedure variables and return values from procedure calls. For that, we assume as usual that data values are mapped into a finite abstract domain using standard techniques such as predicate abstraction. Then, abstract values of local variables can be encoded in the stack alphabet and abstract return values can be encoded in the control states.

Solving Bitvector Problems: The operational semantics given above can be used for solving bitvector problems. In order to ease comparison with [10] we discuss detection of live (global) variables. Other bitvector problems can be solved in a similar fashion. Informally, a variable $\mathbf{x} \in \mathbf{X}$ is *live* at a program point $u \in N$ if there is an execution from u in which $\mathbf{x}$ is used before it is over-written. We restrict attention to *reachable* configurations and use a similar definition and notation as Esparza and Podelski [10]. Thus, we define: program variable $\mathbf{x}$ is *live* at a program point $u \in N$ if there is a transition sequence $\#e_{\mathbf{Main}} \xrightarrow{\sigma_1} c_1 \xrightarrow{\sigma_2} c_2 \xrightarrow{\mathbf{y}:=e} c_3$ such that: (1) u is *active* in configuration c_1, i.e., appears as the topmost stack symbol of one of the parallel pushdown processes in the network described by c_1; (2) σ_2 is a sequence of statements that do not modify $\mathbf{x}$ (i.e., do not write to $\mathbf{x}$); and (3) e is an expression in which $\mathbf{x}$ is used.

We denote the set of configurations c in which u is active by At_u, the set of assignments in the given program that modify $\mathbf{x}$ by $\mathsf{Mod}_\mathbf{x} \subseteq Act$, and the set of assignments in the program in which $\mathbf{x}$ is used by $\mathsf{Use}_\mathbf{x} \subseteq Act$. Moreover, we write Δ_A for the set of rules of Δ with an action in a subset $A \subseteq Act$: $\Delta_A = \{(p\gamma \overset{a}{\hookrightarrow} w) \in \Delta \mid a \in A\}$. Using this notation it is not hard to see that $\mathbf{x}$ is live at u if and only if

$$\#e_{\mathbf{Main}} \in \mathsf{pre}^*(\mathsf{At}_u \cap \mathsf{pre}^*_{\Delta_{Act \setminus \mathsf{Mod}_\mathbf{x}}}(\mathsf{pre}_{\Delta_{\mathsf{Use}_\mathbf{x}}}(Conf_M)))$$

Then, our results concerning backward reachability analysis of DPN given in the next section (see Theorem 3 and Note 1) can be used to decide this property.

4 Reachability Analysis for DPN

We consider the problem of computing representations of the post* and pre* images of given sets of configurations. We are interested in the case that sets of configurations are effectively given using automata-based representations.

Computing post* Images: We show first that post* does not preserve regularity in general. Consider indeed the DPN $M = (\{a\},\{p\},\{\gamma_1,\gamma_2\},\{p\gamma_1 \overset{a}{\hookrightarrow} p\gamma_1\gamma_1 \rhd p\gamma_2\})$. It is easy to see that $\mathsf{post}^*_M(\{p\gamma_1\}) = \{(p\gamma_2)^n p\gamma_1^{n+1} \,:\, n \geq 0\}$, which is clearly nonregular.

Proposition 1. *There is a DPN M, and a configuration c of M, such that* $\mathsf{post}^*(c)$ *is not a regular set of configurations.*

We prove, however, that post* preserves context-freeness:

Theorem 2. *For every DPN M and any context-free set C of M-configurations, the set* $\mathsf{post}^*(C)$ *is context-free and effectively constructible in polynomial time.*

Computing pre* Images: We show now that pre* preserves regularity. Let M be a DPN and $\mathcal{A}$ be an automaton recognizing a set of M-configurations. We define a polynomial-time algorithm allowing to construct an automaton $\mathcal{A}_{\mathsf{pre}^*}$ s.t. $L(\mathcal{A}_{\mathsf{pre}^*}) = \mathsf{pre}^*_M(L(\mathcal{A}))$. For technical reasons, we require that $\mathcal{A}$ is in a special form we define below.

M-Automata: Let $M = (Act, P, \Gamma, \Delta)$ be a DPN. A finite automaton $\mathcal{A} = (S, \Sigma, \delta, s^0, F)$ is an M-automaton if the following conditions hold:

1. $\Sigma = P \cup \Gamma$ is the finite alphabet,
2. the set of states is partitioned into two sets, $S = S_c \cup S_s$, $S_c \cap S_s = \emptyset$,
3. for every $s \in S_c$ and every $p \in P$, there is a (unique and distinguished) state $s_p \in S_s$,
4. there is a relation $\delta' \subseteq S_s \times \Gamma \times (S_s \setminus \{s_p \,:\, s \in S_c, p \in P\}) \cup S_s \times \{\varepsilon\} \times S_c$ such that $\delta = \delta' \cup \{(s, p, s_p) \,:\, s \in S_c, p \in P\}$,
5. the initial state $s^0 \in S_c$, and
6. $F \subseteq S$ is the set of final states.

For $\sigma \in \Sigma \cup \{\varepsilon\}$ and $s, s' \in S$, we write $s \xrightarrow{\sigma}_\delta s'$ in lieu of $(s, \sigma, s') \in \delta$. We extend this notation in the obvious manner to sequences of symbols: (1) $\forall s \in S.\ s \xrightarrow{\varepsilon}_\delta s$, and (2) $\forall s, s' \in S.\ \forall \sigma \in \Sigma \cup \{\varepsilon\}.\ \forall w \in \Sigma^*.\ s \xrightarrow{\sigma w}_\delta s'$ iff $\exists s'' \in S.\ s \xrightarrow{\sigma}_\delta s''$ and $s'' \xrightarrow{w}_\delta s'$.

Note that requirement (4) codes a number of conditions on δ: (1) each $s \in S_c$ has s_p as its unique p-successor and has no Γ-transitions, (2) s is the only predecessor of s_p, (3) only ε-moves from states in S_s lead to states $s \in S_c$, (4) states $s \in S_s$ do not have p-successors, for any $p \in P$. So, every path in an M-automaton (starting from the initial state) is the concatenation of paths of the form $s \xrightarrow{p}_\delta s_p \xrightarrow{w}_\delta t \xrightarrow{\varepsilon}_\delta s'$ where $s, s' \in S_c$, $p \in P$, $w \in \Gamma^*$, and all states in the path $s_p \xrightarrow{w}_\delta t$ are in S_s. Note that for every finite automaton $\mathcal{A}$ over the alphabet $P \cup \Gamma$ such that $L(\mathcal{A}) \subseteq Conf_M$, it is possible to construct an M-automaton recognizing the same language.

Constructing the Automaton $\mathcal{A}_{\mathsf{pre}^*}$*:* Let M be a DPN and $\mathcal{A} = (S, \Sigma, \delta, s^0, F)$ be an M-automaton. The construction of $\mathcal{A}_{\mathsf{pre}^*}$ is in the same spirit as the ones for single pushdown systems (see [2]). It consists in adding iteratively new transitions to the automaton $\mathcal{A}$ according to *saturation* rules (reflecting the backward application of the transition rules in the system), while the set of states remains unchanged. Therefore, we define $\mathcal{A}_{\mathsf{pre}^*}$ to be the finite-state automaton $(S, \Sigma, \delta', s^0, F)$, where δ' is the smallest relation which contains δ (i.e., $\delta \subseteq \delta'$) and satisfies the following conditions:

$R1$: If $(p\gamma \overset{a}{\hookrightarrow} p_1 w_1) \in \Delta$ and $s \xrightarrow{p_1 w_1}_{\delta'} s'$, for $s, s' \in S$, then $(s_p, \gamma, s') \in \delta'$.
$R2$: If $(p\gamma \overset{a}{\hookrightarrow} p_1 w_1 \rhd p_2 w_2) \in \Delta$ and $s \xrightarrow{p_2 w_2 p_1 w_1}_{\delta'} s'$, for $s, s' \in S$, then $(s_p, \gamma, s') \in \delta'$.

The relation δ' can be computed as the limit of an increasing sequence of relations obtained by adding transitions to δ that are required by one of the implications above. This procedure terminates after a polynomial number of steps since only a polynomial number of transitions can potentially be added.

Let us explain intuitively the role of the saturation rule (R_1). Consider a path in the automaton of the form $s \xrightarrow{p_1 w_1} s'$. This means, by definition of M-automata, that s is necessarily in S_c and that we have $s \xrightarrow{p_1} s_{p_1} \xrightarrow{w_1} s'$. Then, the rule consists in adding to the automaton the transition $s_p \xrightarrow{\gamma} s'$. Since by definition of M-automata we have $s \xrightarrow{p} s_p$, we obtain a path $s \xrightarrow{p\gamma} s'$ in the automaton. Therefore, if a configuration $u_1 p_1 w_1 u_2$ is recognized by a run $s^0 \xrightarrow{u_1} s \xrightarrow{p_1 w_1} s' \xrightarrow{u_2} s_F$, then its predecessor $u_1 p\gamma u_2$ is also recognized due to the new transition by the run $s^0 \xrightarrow{u_1} s \xrightarrow{p\gamma} s' \xrightarrow{u_2} s_F$. The role of (R_2) is similar.

Theorem 3. $L(\mathcal{A}_{\mathsf{pre}^*}) = \mathsf{pre}^*_M(L(\mathcal{A}))$.

Note 1. For the sake of completeness, we mention that for every DPN M, and every M-automaton $\mathcal{A}$, the sets $\mathsf{pre}_M(\mathcal{A})$ and $\mathsf{post}_M(\mathcal{A})$ are regular and effectively constructible. The constructions are quite straightforward. For pre_M we take two copies of $\mathcal{A}$. The first copy provides the initial state and the second copy the final states. We then apply the saturation rules to the first copy of the automaton, but let all new transitions lead from states of the first copy to states of the second copy. The post_M construction is similar (it needs adding a finite number of intermediary states).

5 Constrained DPN

We consider in this section an extension of the DPN model introduced in Section 2. In addition to the ability of performing spawn operation as previously, processes are now allowed to observe the control states of their children (processes they have created in the past). This is relevant in particular for handling return values and some kinds of *join* statements between parallel processes. To achieve that, we define a model where the application of a transition rule by some process is conditioned by a (regular language) constraint on the sequence of control states of its children. We need however to impose a *stability* condition (defined below) on the constraints in order to have a model which can be analysed by means of finite-state automata representations. We show later that we lose regularity of the reachability sets if we relax the stability condition.

Stable Regular Languages: Let Σ be a finite alphabet and let $\rho \subseteq \Sigma \times \Sigma$ be a binary relation over Σ. Then, a set of symbols $S \subseteq \Sigma$ is ρ-*stable* iff $\forall s \in S.\ \forall t \in \Sigma.\ (s,t) \in$

$\rho \Rightarrow t \in S$. A ρ-stable regular language over Σ is a subset of Σ^* which is definable by a regular expression of the form:

$$e ::= S, \text{ a } \rho\text{-stable set} \mid e+e \mid e \cdot e \mid e^*$$

We can prove straightforwardly by induction on the structure of regular expressions:

Lemma 1. *Let $\phi \subseteq \Sigma^*$ be a ρ-stable regular language, let $u,v \in \Sigma^*$, and let $a \in \Sigma$ such that $uav \in \phi$. Then, for every $b \in \Sigma$, $(a,b) \in \rho$ implies that $ubv \in \phi$.*

Definition of the Models: A *Constrained Dynamic Pushdown Network* (CDPN) is a tuple $M = (Act, P, \Gamma, \Delta)$, where Act is a finite set of visible *actions*, P is a finite set of *control states*, Γ is a finite set of *stack symbols* disjoint from P, and Δ is a finite set of transition rules of the following forms: either (a) $\phi : p\gamma \overset{a}{\hookrightarrow} p_1 w_1$, or (b) $\phi : p\gamma \overset{a}{\hookrightarrow} p_1 w_1 \rhd p_2 w_2$, where $p, p_1, p_2 \in P$, $a \in Act$, $\gamma \in \Gamma$, $w_1, w_2 \in \Gamma^*$, and ϕ is a ρ_Δ-stable regular language over P, with $\rho_\Delta = \{(p,p') \in P \times P :$ there is a rule $\psi : p\delta \overset{a}{\hookrightarrow} p'u$ or $\psi : p\delta \overset{a}{\hookrightarrow} p'u \rhd p''v$ in $\Delta\}$.

A CDPN consists of a collection of identical sequential processes running in parallel, each of them being modeled as a pushdown system which is able to (1) manipulate its own stack using pushdown rules of the form (a), (2) create a new process (which becomes its youngest son) using rules of the form (b), and (3) observe, under some conditions, the states of its children (processes it created in the past): each transition rule is constrained by the fact that the sequence of control states of the children (given in the decreasing order of their age) must belong to the specified language ϕ.

Since we need to refer to the children of each process, a configuration of a CDPN can be naturally seen as a tree where each vertex is annotated with the configuration of some sequential process (pushdown system), and where the structure corresponds to the relation father-son. Notice that such a tree may have an arbitrary width. We define hereafter a class of terms describing such configurations and we define a transition relation between such terms.

M-Terms: Let $X = \{x_1, \ldots, x_n\}$ be a set of variables. We define the set $\mathcal{T}[X]$ of M-terms over $P \cup \Gamma \cup X$ inductively as follows:

- $X \subseteq \mathcal{T}[X]$,
- If $t \in \mathcal{T}[X]$ and $\gamma \in \Gamma$, then $\gamma(t) \in \mathcal{T}[X]$,
- If $t_1, \ldots, t_n \in \mathcal{T}[X]$ and $p \in P$, then $p(t_1, \ldots, t_n) \in \mathcal{T}[X]$, for $n \geq 0$.

Note that in the last item of this definition, n can be 0 (i.e., p is on a leaf). In that case, we write $p()$ or simply p to represent the corresponding term.

Terms in $\mathcal{T}[\emptyset]$ are called *ground terms*, and will also be denoted by $\mathcal{T}$. A term in $\mathcal{T}[X]$ is linear if each variable occurs at most once. A *context* C is a linear term. Let $t_1, \ldots, t_n$ be n ground terms. Then $C[t_1, \ldots, t_n]$ is the ground term obtained by substituting in C the occurrence of the variable x_i with the term t_i, for $1 \leq i \leq n$.

A term in $\mathcal{T}[X]$ can be seen as a rooted labeled tree of arbitrary width, where (1) an internal node is either of arity 1 (has one successor) if it is labeled with a stack symbol $\gamma \in \Gamma$, or it has an arbitrary arity if it is labeled with a state $p \in P$, and (2) where the leaves are labeled with either variables $x \in X$, or with states $p \in P$.

M-Configurations: We define M-configurations to be the ground M-terms (terms in $\mathcal{T}[X]$ without variables). Given n ground terms $t_1, \ldots, t_n$, the term $\gamma_m \cdots \gamma_1 p(t_1, \ldots, t_n)$ represents a configuration where (1) the common ancestor to all processes is at local control state p and has $\gamma_1 \cdots \gamma_m$ as stack content, where γ_1 is the topmost stack symbol, and (2) this process has n children, the ith of which is described, together with all of its descendants, by the term t_i, for $i = 1, \ldots, n$. A ground term of the form $\gamma_m \cdots \gamma_1 p$ corresponds to the case of one single process without children.

Transition Relation: Given a CDPN M, we define a transition relation $\rightarrow_M$ between M-configurations. We introduce first a notation. Given a configuration t of one of the forms $\gamma_m \cdots \gamma_1 p(t_1, \ldots, t_n)$ or $\gamma_m \cdots \gamma_1 p$, we define $\mathcal{S}(t)$ to be the control state p, i.e., $\mathcal{S}(t)$ is the local control state of the topmost process represented in t. Then, $\rightarrow_M$ is the smallest relation between M-configurations such that:

– If $(\phi : p\gamma \overset{a}{\hookrightarrow} p_1 w_1) \in \Delta$ and $\mathcal{S}(t_1) \cdots \mathcal{S}(t_n) \in \phi$, then

$$C\big[\gamma p(t_1, \ldots, t_n)\big] \rightarrow_M C\big[w_1^R p_1(t_1, \ldots, t_n)\big]$$

– If $(\phi : p\gamma \overset{a}{\hookrightarrow} p_1 w_1 \rhd p_2 w_2) \in \Delta$ and $\mathcal{S}(t_1) \cdots \mathcal{S}(t_n) \in \phi$, then

$$C\big[\gamma p(t_1, \ldots, t_n)\big] \rightarrow_M C\big[w_1^R p_1(t_1, \ldots, t_n, w_2^R p_2)\big]$$

where w^R denotes the reverse word (mirror image) of w. The notions of post, pre, post*, and pre* are defined as usual.

Modelling Power: Since CDPN generalize DPN, the modelling of programs with spawn operations given in Section 3 is still valid for CDPN. Moreover, stable constraints as preconditions of transition rules increase tremendously the modelling power of our formalism. We discuss some applications in this section.

Parallel Calls: In the data-flow analysis scenario, we can use constraints, e.g., in order to accommodate parallel call commands as another basic primitive for creation of parallelism in addition to spawn commands. A parallel call, $\mathsf{pcall}(\pi, \pi')$ with $\pi, \pi' \in \mathbf{Proc}$ starts an instance of procedure π and an instance of π' and runs them in parallel. It terminates if and when both these instances terminate.

Assume that we extend the flow-graph model of Section 3 by allowing parallel calls as another type of basic statement. In the CDPN model we capture the operational semantics of an edge $(u, \mathsf{pcall}(\pi, \pi'), v)$ as follows: we start two new threads for π and π' and ensure by a transition rule with an appropriate constraint that we can move to v only after both these threads have terminated. For that, both threads indicate termination by moving to a special new "terminated" control state $\natural$ when they see a special new stack symbol \$ that we put at the bottom of their stack upon thread creation. Thus, we have the following rules for modelling $(u, \mathsf{pcall}(\pi, \pi'), v)$:

$$P^* : \#u \overset{\tau}{\hookrightarrow} \#\gamma_1 \rhd \#e_\pi\$ \qquad P^* : \#\gamma_1 \overset{\tau}{\hookrightarrow} \#\gamma_2 \rhd \#e_{\pi'}\$ \qquad P^*\natural^2 : \#\gamma_2 \overset{\tau}{\hookrightarrow} \#v$$

where γ_1, γ_2 are two auxiliary stack symbols chosen fresh for each parallel call. Moreover, the rule $P^* : \#\$ \overset{\tau}{\hookrightarrow} \natural$ allows a thread to move to the state $\natural$ once it has terminated.

Join Statements: Besides parallel calls we can also model different types of join-commands. We use the same technique as above for making termination visible to the father of threads: we now use the rule $\#u \overset{\tau}{\hookrightarrow} \#v \rhd \#e_p\$$ to describe the behavior of a spawn edge $(u, \mathsf{spawn}(p), v) \in E$. Thus, we mark the bottom of the stack with the special symbol \$. We also use the rule $P^* : \#\$ \overset{\tau}{\hookrightarrow} \natural$ from above to make termination visible in the control state. This allows us to describe the operational semantics of different types of join-command such as for instance (1) $\mathsf{join}_\forall$: proceed if all threads directly created by the current thread have terminated, and (2) $\mathsf{join}_{\exists k}$: proceed if at least k among the threads directly created by the current thread have terminated.

The behavior of an edge (u, j, v) where j is one of the join commands from above is modelled by the rule $\phi : \#u \overset{\tau}{\hookrightarrow} \#v$ where $\phi = \natural^*$ for $j = \mathsf{join}_\forall$, and $\phi = (P^*\natural)^k P^*$ for $j = \mathsf{join}_{\exists k}$. Obviously, these constraints are stable.

Return Values: We can distinguish between different termination conditions by using more than one terminated control state and use regular patterns of such control states in constraints in the father process. This allows us, for instance, to return information back to the caller from procedures called in parallel. Therefore, the modelling power of CDPNs exceeds that of PA and even that of PAD [2] [13]: While in a PAD process (like in a DPN process) we can use control states to return information back to a caller in a normal procedure call, there is no such mechanism for parallel calls. The modelling power for calls and parallel calls is thus more symmetric for CDPNs than for PAD.

Observing Execution Phases: Finally, as we allow *stable* constraints, a creator of a thread can react on situations in which the created thread has achieved some progress already but is not necessarily terminated yet. As an example, let us assume that a process F (the father) creates a number of worker threads that sequentially go through a number of phases, say phases $1, \ldots, n$, before termination. For modelling the worker threads we use new control states from a hierarchy $P_0 \supset P_1 \supset \ldots \supset P_n = \emptyset$ of control states such that a worker thread is in phase i if and only if its control state is in $P_{i-1} \setminus P_i$. This means a worker thread has finished phase i if and only if its control state belongs to P_i. Then, the sets P_i are stable and can be used as building blocks for constraints in transitions of F. Hence, process F can react on situations like "all worker threads have finished phase i" by using the constraint P_i^*, "there is a worker thread that has finished phase i and all other worker threads have finished phase j" by the constraint $P_j^* P_i P_j^*$, etc.

6 Backward Reachability Analysis of CDPN

Symbolic Representations: We use hedge automata (unbounded width tree automata) [8] to represent infinite sets of CDPN configurations. Let $M = (Act, P, \Gamma, \Delta)$ be a CDPN. An *M-tree automaton* is a tuple $\mathcal{A} = (Q, \delta, F)$, where Q is a set of states, F is the set of final states, and δ is a set of rules of either the form (1) $\gamma(q) \to q'$, where $\gamma \in \Gamma$, and $q, q' \in Q$, or (2) $p(L) \to q$, where L is a regular language over Q, $p \in P$, and $q \in Q$.

In order to define the language recognized by $\mathcal{A}$, we define a *move relation* $\to_\delta$ between terms over $P \cup \Gamma \cup Q$: for every two terms t and t', we have $t \to_\delta t'$ iff there exist

[2] PAD extends PA by allowing rewrite rules of the form $A \cdot B \to t$.

a context C and a rule $r \in \delta$ such that $t = C[s]$, $t' = C[s']$, and (1) either $r = \gamma(q) \to q'$, $s = \gamma(q)$, and $s' = q'$, or (2) $r = p(L) \to q$, $s = p(q_1, \dots, q_n)$, $q_1 \cdots q_n \in L$, and $s' = q$.

Let $\xrightarrow{*}_\delta$ denote the reflexive-transitive closure of $\to_\delta$. A term $t \in \mathcal{T}$ is accepted by $q \in Q$ if $t \xrightarrow{*}_\delta q$. Let $L_q^\delta = \{t \in \mathcal{T} \,:\, t \xrightarrow{*}_\delta q\}$. A term t is accepted by $\mathcal{A}$ if there exists a state $q \in F$ such that $t \xrightarrow{*}_\delta q$. Let $L(\mathcal{A})$ be the set of all terms accepted by $\mathcal{A}$.

A straightforward adaptation of the proofs in [8] allows to show that:

Theorem 4. *The class of M-tree automata is closed under boolean operations. Moreover, the emptiness problem of M-tree automata is decidable.*

Computing pre* **Images:** Let $M = (Act, P, \Gamma, \Delta)$ be a CDPN and let $\mathcal{A} = (Q, \delta, F)$ be an M-tree automaton. We present hereafter an algorithm that allows us to construct an M-tree automaton $\mathcal{A}_{\mathsf{pre}^*}$ recognizing the pre*-image of $L(\mathcal{A})$. The construction proceeds (similarly to Section 4) by adding new transitions to the original automaton $\mathcal{A}$ corresponding to the backward application of transition rules. In order to deal with the constraints in the transition rules, we need to extend the original automaton.

Propagating Control States: Remember that, by definition of CDPN terms, the configuration of each process is encoded bottom-up in the tree (reading first the control state, and then the stack contents starting from its topmost symbol). Since constraints in CDPN transition rules refer to control states of the children processes, and since hedge automata can check only constraints on immediate successors in trees (which correspond in our case to the bottom symbols in the stacks of the children processes), we need to propagate upward the informations about the control states through the stacks. Therefore, the first step of our construction consists in defining a new automaton $\mathcal{A}_P = (Q_P, \delta_P, F_P)$ such that $L(\mathcal{A}_P) = L(\mathcal{A})$, and where states of Q are labelled by control states $p \in P$. This automaton is given by: $Q_P = Q \times P$, $F_P = F \times P$, and δ_P is the smallest set of rules such that:

- if $p(L) \to s \in \delta$, then $p(L') \to (s, p) \in \delta_P$, where L' is obtained by substituting in the words of L every occurrence of a state $s \in Q$ by $\{(s, p) \mid p \in P\}$;
- if $\gamma(s) \to s' \in \delta$, then for every $p \in P$, $\gamma((s, p)) \to (s', p) \in \delta_P$.

Lemma 2. *$L(\mathcal{A}_P) = L(\mathcal{A})$, and for every $t \in \mathcal{T}$, $t \xrightarrow{*}_{\delta_P} (s, p)$ iff $t \xrightarrow{*}_\delta s$ and $\mathcal{S}(t) = p$.*

Note 2. To avoid confusion, we use in the sequel $p, p', p_1, p_2, \dots$ to denote elements of P, $s, s', s_1, s_2, \dots,$ to denote states of $\mathcal{A}$, and $q, q', q_1, q_2, \dots$ to denote states of $\mathcal{A}_P$.

From Constraints over P to Constraints over Q_P: Given a constraint ϕ and n terms $t_1, \dots, t_n$ such that $t_i \xrightarrow{*}_{\delta_P} q_i$ for $1 \leq i \leq n$, we need also to be able to get the information whether $\mathcal{S}(t_1) \cdots \mathcal{S}(t_n) \in \phi$ from the states $q_1, \dots, q_n$. For that, we associate with each constraint ϕ over P a constraint $\langle \phi \rangle$ over Q_P such that $\mathcal{S}(t_1) \cdots \mathcal{S}(t_n) \in \phi$ if and only if $q_1 \cdots q_n \in \langle \phi \rangle$. The definition of $\langle \phi \rangle$ is straightforward by induction on the structure of regular expressions for stable languages: (1) $\langle S \rangle = \{(s, p) \,:\, s \in Q, p \in S\}$, (2) $\langle \phi_1 \cdot \phi_2 \rangle = \langle \phi_1 \rangle \cdot \langle \phi_2 \rangle$, (3) $\langle \phi_1 + \phi_2 \rangle = \langle \phi_1 \rangle + \langle \phi_2 \rangle$, and (4) $\langle \phi^* \rangle = \langle \phi \rangle^*$.

Closed Set of Constraints: During the construction of the automaton, new transition rules of the form $p(L') \rightarrow q$ are added where L' are languages which are built from languages L appearing in the rules of the original automaton $\mathcal{A}$, and constraints ϕ appearing in the transition rules of the CDPN M, using intersection and right-quotient operations. Intersections $L \cap \langle\phi\rangle$ allow us to check that the guarding constraint for the application of a transition rule is satisfied at the considered position in the tree. Right-quotients $Lq^{-1} = \{w : wq \in L\}$ allow us to get immediate predecessors by a spawn operation of trees where the children of the spawning process are recognized by a sequence of states in L, and the youngest son among these children (i.e., the one created by the spawn operation and which is the right-most one in the list of children) is recognized by the state q. Then, let us define Λ to be the smallest family of languages over Q_P such that:

- If $(p(L) \rightarrow q) \in \delta_P$, then $L \in \Lambda$.
- If $L \in \Lambda$, and $(\phi : p\gamma \overset{a}{\hookrightarrow} p_1 w_1 \rhd p_2 w_2) \in \Delta$, then $L \cap \langle\phi\rangle \in \Lambda$.
- If $L \in \Lambda$ and $q \in Q_P$, then $Lq^{-1} \in \Lambda$.

Lemma 3. *The family Λ is finite. Assuming that all languages and constraints appearing in rules δ_P and Δ are given by backward-deterministic finite-state automata of size at most K, the number of elements of Λ is in $O(K^{n+1})$ where n is the number of different constraints appearing in the rules of Δ.*

Constructing $\mathcal{A}_{\mathsf{pre}^*}$: We define $\mathcal{A}_{\mathsf{pre}^*}$ to be the M-tree automaton (Q', δ', F') such that (1) $Q' = Q_P \cup \{q_p^L : p \in P, L \in \Lambda\}$, (2) $F' = F_P$, and (3) δ' is the smallest set of rules such that $\delta'_0 = \delta_P \cup \{p(L) \rightarrow q_p^L : p \in P, L \in \Lambda\} \subseteq \delta'$ and:

R_1: If $(\phi : p\gamma \overset{a}{\hookrightarrow} p'w) \in \Delta$, $p'(L) \rightarrow q \in \delta'_0$, and $w^R(q) \xrightarrow{*}_{\delta'} q'$, then $\left(\gamma(q_p^{L\cap\langle\phi\rangle}) \rightarrow q'\right) \in \delta'$.

R_2: If $(\phi : p\gamma \overset{a}{\hookrightarrow} p'w_1 \rhd p''w_2) \in \Delta$, $p'(L) \rightarrow q'' \in \delta'_0$, $w_1^R(q'') \xrightarrow{*}_{\delta'} q'$, and $w_2^R(p'') \xrightarrow{*}_{\delta'} q$,

$$\text{then } \left(\gamma(q_p^{Lq^{-1}\cap\langle\phi\rangle}) \rightarrow q'\right) \in \delta'.$$

Note that the states q_p^L, for $p \in P$, and $L \in \Lambda$, are added to the automaton in order to recognize precisely all the terms having p at the root and such that the sequence of children of the root is recognized by a sequence of states in the language L. Note also that all the transitions added by the construction are Γ-transitions, and therefore they do not add P-transitions to the automaton.

The set of rules δ' can be computed iteratively as the limit of an increasing sequence $\delta'_0 \subseteq \delta'_1 \cdots$ such that δ'_{i+1} contains at most one transition more than δ'_i added by applying either (R_1) or (R_2). Note that δ' is necessarily finite since (by Lemma 3) the number of triples (γ, q_p^L, q), for $\gamma \in \Gamma$, $p \in P$, $L \in \Lambda$, and $q \in Q'$ is finite.

Lemma 4. *For every $q \in Q_P$, $L_q^{\delta'} = \mathsf{pre}^*(L_q^{\delta_P})$.*

The lemma above says that the construction ensures that every state recognizes the set of all predecessors of its original language (i.e., in the automaton before saturation). Let us give some intuitive explanations about the role of the saturation rules, and let us consider the rule (R_1) (since the role of (R_2) is similar). Consider a term $w^R p'(t_1, \ldots, t_n)$

such that $t_i \xrightarrow{*}_{\mathcal{B}'} q_i$, for $i \in \{1,\dots,n\}$. Assume that $p'(L) \rightarrow q$ is a rule of the automaton. This means that after recognizing each of the terms t_i and labelling their roots by the states q_i, the automaton can label the term $p'(t_1,\dots,t_n)$ by q if the sequence $q_1 \cdots q_n$ is in L. Assume furthermore that $w^R(q) \xrightarrow{*}_{\mathcal{B}'} q'$. This means that the automaton can proceed by reading upward the word w and label the term $w^R p'(t_1,\dots,t_n)$ by q'. Therefore, if $(\phi : p\gamma \overset{a}{\hookrightarrow} p'w)$ is a transition rule of the system, and if the sequence of control states $\mathcal{S}(t_1)\cdots\mathcal{S}(t_n)$ is in ϕ, then we must add the term $\gamma p(t_1,\dots,t_n)$ (which is the immediate predecessor of $w^R p'(t_1,\dots,t_n)$ by the transition rule) to the language of q' (to say that this term is a predecessor of some term which was recognized by q' in the original automaton). This is achieved by applying the saturation rule which adds to the automaton the transition $(\gamma(q_p^{L\cap\langle\phi\rangle}) \rightarrow q')$. The justification of this is in fact subtle. First, if $\mathcal{S}(t_1)\cdots\mathcal{S}(t_n) \in \phi$, we must have $q_1 \cdots q_n \in \langle\phi\rangle$. Since states recognize predecessors of terms in their original language, each state q_i is a pair (s_i, p'_i) such that $p'_i = \mathcal{S}(t'_i)$ for some t'_i such that $t_i \in \mathsf{pre}^*(t'_i)$. Now, here is the point where the stability property of ϕ plays a crucial role: it ensures that backward transitions cannot make a term satisfy new constraints (or equivalently, that forward transitions cannot falsify a constraint). Therefore, since $\mathcal{S}(t_1)\cdots\mathcal{S}(t_n) \in \phi$, we must have also $\mathcal{S}(t'_1)\cdots\mathcal{S}(t'_n) \in \phi$, which implies that $q_1 \cdots q_n \in \langle\phi\rangle$. On the other hand, assume that $\mathcal{S}(t_1)\cdots\mathcal{S}(t_n) \notin \phi$ but $q_1 \cdots q_n \in \langle\phi\rangle$ because $\mathcal{S}(t'_1)\cdots\mathcal{S}(t'_n) \in \phi$. We can show that $\gamma p(t_1,\dots,t_n)$ is actually in the pre^* image of the original language. Indeed, it is possible in this case to start by rewriting each term t_i to its successor t'_i, which makes the transition rule $(\phi : p\gamma \overset{a}{\hookrightarrow} p'w)$ applicable.

Theorem 5. *For every CDPN M, and for every M-tree automaton $\mathcal{A}$, we can construct an M-tree automaton $\mathcal{A}_{\mathsf{pre}^*}$ such that $L(\mathcal{A}_{\mathsf{pre}^*}) = \mathsf{pre}^*(L(\mathcal{A}))$.*

Note 3. It is easy to show that, given an M-tree automaton $\mathcal{A}$, the set $\mathsf{pre}_M(\mathcal{A})$ (and in fact also the set $\mathsf{post}_M(\mathcal{A})$) is an effectively M-tree automata definable set.

Then, based on the modelling described in Sections 3 and 5, we can apply Theorems 5 and 4 to check reachability properties and solve flow analysis problems (such as bitvector problems) for multithreaded programs.

Complexity Issues: By Lemma 3, we know that the size of the automaton $\mathcal{A}_{\mathsf{pre}^*}$ is at most exponential in the number of constraints appearing in the given CDPN. In fact, we can prove the following PSPACE lower bound by a reduction of the satisfiability problem for quantified Boolean formulas (QBF).

Theorem 6. *It is at least PSPACE-hard to decide for a given CDPN M, a regular set of M-configurations R and an M-configuration c, whether $c \in \mathsf{pre}^*(R)$ or not.*

Despite the hardness result above, in many interesting cases, we only need a *fixed* number of constraints, which leads to polynomial analysis algorithms. For instance, this is the case when only trivial constraints (i.e., of the form P^*) are used, which corresponds to the case of DPN models. Also, to model parallel calls only one additional constraint is needed, namely $P^*\natural^2$, as we have seen in Section 5. Similarly, we only need one additional constraint for each type of join statement such as $\mathsf{join}_\forall$ or $\mathsf{join}_{\exists k}$. Note that the automata for these constraints can easily be defined by backward deterministic automata of very small sizes. Also for typical properties such as bitvector problems (see

Section 3), the initial automaton is always the one recognizing the set of all configurations. Therefore, for an important fragment of CDPN which subsumes (in modelling power) existing formalisms such as PA and PAD, and allows us in addition to model spawn operations, our construction leads to a polynomial analysis algorithm.

However, when return values from parallel processes are taken into account, our construction becomes exponential in the number of used abstract data values. This price is unavoidable since dealing with an unfixed domain of return values is precisely the feature which makes our model complex (see the proof of Theorem 6). Such complexity does not appear for weaker models such as PA or PAD (which have polynomial analysis algorithms [12,10,6]) since they cannot handle return values from parallel processes.

Relaxing Stability: We end this section by mentioning the fact that relaxing the stability condition on the constraints appearing in the transition rules of CDPN leads to a model for which pre^* images are not regular in general.

Theorem 7. *There exists a CDPN M with nonstable constraints, and a regular set T of M-configurations such that $\mathsf{pre}^*_M(T)$ is not definable by an M-tree automaton.*

Actually, we can define M s.t. all its transition rules are of the form $\phi : p\gamma \hookrightarrow p'\gamma$ (i.e., without stack manipulation and dynamic creation of processes), and where ϕ is of the simple form pP^*, for $p \in P$. This shows that it is hard to relax the stability condition in the definition of CDPN without losing the property that pre^* preserves regularity.

7 Conclusion

We have defined new formalisms (DPN and CDPN), based on word/term rewrite systems, allowing to model adequately spawn-like commands in multithreaded programs. We have shown that (1) they are more suitable for modelling these commands than previously proposed formalisms (such as PA and PAD), and that (2) they subsume in fact in modelling power these models (concerning CDPN), and allow to handle features these models cannot handle such as return values from parallel processes, various join commands, etc.

We have defined automata-based techniques for computing backward reachability sets of our models. In the case of the basic model of DPN, word automata can be used for this purpose and the construction is simple. In the case of CDPN where constraints on the children are used, the problem of reachability analysis becomes much more delicate. The condition of stability we impose in CDPN on the constraints (guards) appearing in the transition rules seems to be necessary in order to have regular backward reachability sets. Concerning complexity, our construction is exponential in the number of different constraints used in the model, but significant classes of parallel programs can be modelled using a fixed number of constraints (often representable using small automata), and therefore they can be analysed in polynomial time.

Future work includes the extension of our models and our approach to handle synchronisation between parallel processes. Of course, the reachability analysis becomes undecidable in general, but reasonable classes of programs with particular synchronisation policies can be considered (see e.g., [16]), and generic frameworks for defining abstractions (and refining them) can be developed based on our models and our techniques, e.g., following the approaches of [3,4,14]. We think also that our techniques could be used to handle models which extend those considered in this paper by allowing a bounded number of context switches, in the spirit of the approach of [17].

References

1. J. Baeten and W. Weijland. Process algebra. In *Cambridge Tracts in Theoretical Computer Science*, volume 18, 1990.
2. A. Bouajjani, J. Esparza, and O. Maler. Reachability Analysis of Pushdown Automata: Application to Model Checking. In *CONCUR'97*. LNCS 1243, 1997.
3. A. Bouajjani, J. Esparza, and T. Touili. A generic approach to the static analysis of concurrent programs with procedures. In *POPL'03*. ACM, 2003.
4. A. Bouajjani, J. Esparza, and T. Touili. Reachability Analysis of Synchronised PA systems. In *INFINITY'04*. to appear in ENTCS, 2004.
5. A. Bouajjani, M. Müller-Olm, and T. Touili. Regular Symbolic Analysis of Dynamic Networks of Pushdown Processes. Technical report, LIAFA lab No 2005-05, and University of Dortmund No 798, June 2005.
6. A. Bouajjani and T. Touili. Reachability Analysis of Process Rewrite Systems. In *FSTTCS'03*. LNCS 2914, 2003.
7. A. Bouajjani and T. Touili. On Computing Reachability Sets of Process Rewrite Systems. In *RTA'05*. LNCS, 2005.
8. A. Bruggemann-Klein, M. Murata, and D. Wood. Regular tree and regular hedge languages over unranked alphabets. Research report, 2001.
9. J. Esparza and J. Knoop. An automata-theoretic approach to interprocedural data-flow analysis. In *FoSSaCS'99*, volume 1578 of *LNCS*, 1999.
10. J. Esparza and A. Podelski. Efficient algorithms for pre* and post* on interprocedural parallel flow graphs. In *POPL'00*. ACM, 2000.
11. A. Finkel, B. Willems, and P. Wolper. A Direct Symbolic Approach to Model Checking Pushdown Systems. In *Infinity'97, ENTCS 9*. Elsevier Sci. Pub., 1997.
12. D. Lugiez and P. Schnoebelen. The regular viewpoint on PA-processes. *Theoretical Computer Science*, 274(1-2):89–115, 2002.
13. R. Mayr. Decidability and Complexity of Model Checking Problems for Infinite-State Systems. Phd. thesis, Technical University Munich, 1998.
14. M. Müller-Olm. Variations on Constants. Habilitationsschrift, Fachbereich Informatik, Universität Dortmund, 2002.
15. M. Müller-Olm. Precise interprocedural dependence analysis of parallel programs. *Theoretical Computer Science*, 311:325–388, 2004.
16. S. Qadeer, S. Rajamani, and J. Rehof. Procedure Summaries for Model Checking Multithreaded Software. In *POPL'04*, 2004.
17. S. Qadeer and J. Rehof. Context-Bounded Model-Checking of Concurrent Software. In *TACAS'05*. LNCS 3440, 2005.
18. H. Seidl and B. Steffen. Constraint-based inter-procedural analysis of parallel programs. In *ESOP'2000*. LNCS 1782, 2000.
19. T. Touili. Dealing with communication for dynamic multithreaded recursive programs. In *1st VISSAS workshop*, March 2005. Invited Paper.

Termination Analysis of Integer Linear Loops*

Aaron R. Bradley, Zohar Manna, and Henny B. Sipma

Computer Science Department,
Stanford University,
Stanford, CA 94305-9045
{arbrad, zm, sipma}@theory.stanford.edu

Abstract. Usually, ranking function synthesis and invariant generation over a loop with integer variables involves abstracting the loop to have real variables. Integer division and modulo arithmetic must be soundly abstracted away so that the analysis over the abstracted loop is sound for the original loop. Consequently, the analysis loses precision. In contrast, we introduce a technique for handling loops over integer variables directly. The resulting analysis is more precise than previous analyses.

1 Introduction

Proving termination of program loops is necessary for ensuring the correct behavior of embedded systems and safety critical software. It is also required when proving general temporal properties of infinite state programs (*e.g.*, [9,12,14]). The traditional method for proving loop termination is by proving that some function of the program variables is well-founded within the loop. Such a function is called a ranking function.

Discovering ranking functions is thus one way of automating termination proofs. Colón and Sipma describe the synthesis of linear ranking functions over linear loops using polyhedra [3,4]. In [13], Podelski and Rybalchenko specialize the technique to a restricted class of single-path imperative loops without initial conditions. Their method is complete for this class. The authors generalize these results in [1] to general linear loops: loops that contain multiple paths and that have a nontrivial initial condition. Ranking functions can be lexicographic and have supporting invariants simultaneously generated, yet the method is still complete. The primary feature linking these analyses is that loop variables are assumed to range over the reals, $\mathbb{R}$. On loops in which variables range over the integers, $\mathbb{Z}$, or the nonnegative integers, $\mathbb{Z}^*$, and which include integer division or modulo arithmetic, real-based analyses are weak. They must abstract away this arithmetic to maintain soundness. Yet loops may terminate precisely because of the behavior of integer arithmetic.

* This research was supported in part by NSF grants CCR-01-21403, CCR-02-20134, CCR-02-09237, CNS-0411363, and CCF-0430102, by ARO grant DAAD19-01-1-0723, and by NAVY/ONR contract N00014-03-1-0939. The first author was additionally supported by a Sang Samuel Wang Stanford Graduate Fellowship.

M. Abadi and L. de Alfaro (Eds.): CONCUR 2005, LNCS 3653, pp. 488–502, 2005.

Our main contribution is a technique for synthesizing linear ranking functions with supporting linear invariants over *integer linear loops*, which allow integer division and modulo arithmetic. The technique treats the integer variables without abstraction, so that the resulting analysis is guaranteed to find a linear ranking function with a specified number of supporting linear (inductive) invariants, if one exists.

Linear inequality invariant generation is a related task. Abstract interpretation [7,8] is the classical approach to invariant generation, while recently, the constraint-based approach [2] has been proposed. We show how to adapt the ranking function synthesis method to generate linear inequality invariants with a fixed number of conjuncts over integer linear loops. The analysis finds stronger invariants than a real-variable analysis, although at high computational cost.

Our technique is characteristically constraint-based: it solves directly for a set of expressions that satisfy the ranking function and invariant *verification conditions* — the constraints — generated by the loop. The focus of our paper, then, is the method for solving such constraint systems exactly when the loop has integer variables. While real analyses (*e.g.*, [2,3,13,1,6]) exploit the *dual* of a constraint system to solve for the ranking function or invariants, an integer analysis cannot be so formulated: an integer constraint system does not have a known dual. Our analysis is based on two observations. First, integer linear loops, which allow integer division and modulo arithmetic, may be converted to equivalent *Presburger loops*, in which all formulae are Presburger formulae. Second, one can in principle enumerate all linear functions of the program state with integer (or, equivalently, rational) coefficients. Determining if each such function is a ranking function is decidable, as the verification conditions can be encoded in Presburger arithmetic [15,5]. A similar argument works for generating invariants. Thus, enumeration provides a complete, although prohibitively expensive, procedure.

Instead, we propose a *region-based* search. A *region* is a collection of intervals over which the *parameters* of the problem — the unknown coefficients of the linear function — may take their values. Thus, a region represents an infinite set of functions, one for each rational point that it contains. Regions are enumerated in such a way that examining the corners of regions is equivalent to naive enumeration. But a *feasibility check* can determine that no function in the region can be a ranking function (or an inductive invariant), pruning the region and all its functions in one step. For invariant generation, a *subsumption check* avoids regions that contain only assertions weaker than already discovered invariants. The feasibility and subsumption checks are motivated by ideas from the numerical constraint satisfaction community (see, *e.g.*, [11]). We demonstrate that they are powerful in practice, making an intractable problem tractable.

The rest of the paper is organized as follows. Section 2 introduces our loop abstraction and basic concepts. Section 3 describes our synthesis technique for termination analysis. Section 4 adapts the technique for invariant generation. Section 5 presents empirical evidence showing the effectiveness of the technique. Finally, Section 6 concludes.

```
uint x > 0
while 2x > 1 do
    x := x - x/2
done
```
(a)

$$\begin{array}{l}\texttt{uint}\ x\\ \theta:\ x>0\\ \tau_1:\ 2x>1 \wedge x' = x - \frac{x}{2}\end{array}$$
(b)

Fig. 1. Loop ZERO written in an **(a)** imperative form and **(b)** as an integer linear loop

2 Preliminaries

This section introduces our loop abstraction and basic concepts.

Definition 1 (Integer Variable). A program variable x has type `int` if its domain is the integers $\mathbb{Z}$ or `uint` if its domain is the nonnegative integers $\mathbb{Z}^*$.

Definition 2 (Integer Linear Formula). An *integer linear term* is either c, cx, $c_1\frac{E}{c_2}$ (division), or $c_1(E\%c_2)$ (modulus), for constants $c, c_1 \in \mathbb{Z}$, positive constant $c_2 \in \mathbb{Z}^+$, variable x of type `uint` or `int`, and *integer linear expression* E. An *integer linear expression* is the summation of *integer linear terms.*

An *integer linear atom* is the comparison $E_1 \bowtie E_2$ of two integer linear expressions, for $\bowtie \in \{<, \leq, =, \neq, \geq, >\}$. An *integer linear formula* is a Boolean combination of *integer linear atoms.*

Definition 3 (Integer Linear Loop). An *integer linear loop* L : $\langle \mathcal{V}_{\mathbb{Z}}, \mathcal{V}_{\mathbb{Z}^*}, \theta, \mathcal{T}\rangle$ consists of variables $\mathcal{V}_{\mathbb{Z}}$ of type `int`, variables $\mathcal{V}_{\mathbb{Z}^*}$ of type `uint`, *initial condition* θ, and set of *transitions* $\mathcal{T}$. We refer to $\mathcal{V}_{\mathbb{Z}} \cup \mathcal{V}_{\mathbb{Z}^*}$ as $\mathcal{V}$.

θ is an integer linear formula over $\mathcal{V}$ expressing what is true before entering the loop. Each transition $\tau \in \mathcal{T}$ is an integer linear formula over $\mathcal{V} \cup \mathcal{V}'$, where the primed versions of variables indicate their values in the next state.

Integer linear loops allow modeling nondeterminism, both in the update of variables (*e.g.*, via inequality constraints or no constraints on the next state value of a variable) and in the execution of transitions (*e.g.*, when guards are not disjoint).

Example 1. Figure 1 shows the loop ZERO as an imperative loop and as an integer linear loop. If $x = 1$, then $\frac{x}{2} = 0$ so that x does not decrease; thus, ZERO does not terminate.

If x is a variable ranging over $\mathbb{R}$, the loop terminates: the transition simplifies to $x' = \frac{x}{2}$ so that x eventually reaches $\frac{1}{2}$ or below. Thus, abstracting this loop to the reals results in an unsound termination analysis.

Our synthesis technique is based on deciding validity of Presburger arithmetic formulae; hence, we need to transform away division and modulo operators.

Definition 4 (Presburger Formula). A *Presburger formula* is an integer linear formula that does not involve division or modulo arithmetic. Given an integer linear formula $\mathcal{A}$, $\mathcal{P}(\mathcal{A})$ is an equivalent Presburger formula. $\mathcal{P}(\mathcal{A})$ is defined recursively in Figure 2, where $\mathcal{P}(\mathcal{A}) = \mathcal{A}$ if neither rule applies.

$$\mathcal{P}(\mathcal{A}[c_1\tfrac{E}{c_2}]) = \bigvee_{b\in[0..c_2-1]} (\exists a)\left(\begin{array}{l}[c_2a+b=E\wedge E\geq 0\wedge \mathcal{P}(\mathcal{A}[c_1a])]\\ \vee\ [c_2a-b=E\wedge E\leq 0\wedge \mathcal{P}(\mathcal{A}[c_1a])]\end{array}\right)$$

$$\mathcal{P}(\mathcal{A}[c_1(E\%c_2)]) = \bigvee_{b\in[0..c_2-1]} (\exists a)\left(\begin{array}{l}[c_2a+b=E\wedge E\geq 0\wedge \mathcal{P}(\mathcal{A}[c_1b])]\\ \vee\ [c_2a-b=E\wedge E\leq 0\wedge \mathcal{P}(\mathcal{A}[-c_1b])]\end{array}\right)$$

Fig. 2. $\mathcal{P}(\mathcal{A})$ is recursively applied to remove division and modulo operators from $\mathcal{A}$

Definition 5 (Presburger Loop). A loop L is a *Presburger loop* if all of its formulae are Presburger formulae.

Example 2. Consider the formula defining τ_1 of ZERO.

$$\mathcal{P}(\tau_1) = \mathcal{P}(2x>1\wedge x'=x-\frac{x}{2}) = \begin{array}{l}(\exists a)[2a=x\wedge x'=x-a]\\ \vee\ (\exists a)[2a+1=x\wedge x'=x-a]\end{array}$$

The formula is simplified according to the `uint` type of x.

Definition 6 (Linear Inductive Invariant). A *linear inductive invariant* φ for loop $L : \langle \mathcal{V}_{\mathbb{Z}}, \mathcal{V}_{\mathbb{Z}^*}, \theta, \mathcal{T}\rangle$ is a finite conjunction of affine formulae $\bigwedge_j(c_{j,1}x_1 + \cdots + c_{j,n}x_n + c_{j,n+1} \geq 0)$ over $\mathcal{V} = \{x_1,\ldots,x_n\}$ with integer coefficients $c_{j,i} \in \mathbb{Z}$ that satisfies the following verification conditions:

Initiation $(\forall\mathcal{V})[\theta \rightarrow \varphi]$
Consecution $(\forall\tau \in \mathcal{T})(\forall\mathcal{V},\mathcal{V}')[(\varphi\wedge\tau) \rightarrow \varphi']$

φ' is the formula in which each variable is primed.

Definition 7 (Linear Ranking Function). A *linear ranking function* δ with *supporting linear invariant* φ for loop $L : \langle \mathcal{V}_{\mathbb{Z}}, \mathcal{V}_{\mathbb{Z}^*}, \theta, \mathcal{T}\rangle$ is an affine expression $c_1x_1 + \cdots + c_nx_n + c_{n+1}$ over $\mathcal{V} = \{x_1,\ldots,x_n\}$ with integer coefficients $c_i \in \mathbb{Z}$ that satisfies the following verification conditions:

Bounded $(\forall\tau \in \mathcal{T})(\forall\mathcal{V},\mathcal{V}')[(\varphi\wedge\tau) \rightarrow \delta \geq 0]$
Ranking $(\forall\tau \in \mathcal{T})(\forall\mathcal{V},\mathcal{V}')[(\varphi\wedge\tau) \rightarrow \delta' < \delta]$

Example 3. Consider loop ONE in Figure 3(**a**). Figure 3(**b**) presents the loop as a Presburger loop. Writing the existentially quantified variables as actual loop variables reveals that a Presburger loop may be written without quantification, as in Figure 3(**c**). The type of a new variable depends on whether the replaced expression ranges over $\mathbb{Z}$, $\mathbb{Z}^*$, or $-\mathbb{Z}^*$.

We show that the function $\delta(x,y) = x+y$ is a ranking function with supporting invariant $x \geq 1$. The verification conditions have been trivially simplified for ease of presentation. Note that $\mathcal{V}\cup\mathcal{V}'$ are universally quantified and that they range over $\mathbb{Z}^*$.

$$\begin{array}{l}\texttt{uint}\ x, y\\ \theta:\ x > 0 \wedge x\%2 = 0\\ \tau_1:\ x\%2 = 0 \wedge x' = x - \frac{x}{2} \wedge y' = y\\ \tau_2:\ x\%3 = 0 \wedge x' = x - 2 \wedge y' = y\\ \tau_3:\ y > x \wedge x' = x \wedge y' = y - x\end{array}$$

(a)

$$\begin{array}{l}\texttt{uint}\ x, y\\ \theta:\ (\exists a)[x > 0 \wedge 2a = x]\\ \tau_1:\ (\exists a)[2a = x \wedge x' = x - a \wedge y' = y]\\ \tau_2:\ (\exists a)[3a = x \wedge x' = x - 2 \wedge y' = y]\\ \tau_3:\ y > x \wedge x' = x \wedge y' = y - x\end{array}$$

(b)

$$\begin{array}{l}\texttt{uint}\ x, y, a\\ \theta:\ x > 0 \wedge 2a = x\\ \tau_1:\ 2a = x \wedge x' = x - a \wedge y' = y\\ \tau_2:\ 3a = x \wedge x' = x - 2 \wedge y' = y\\ \tau_3:\ y > x \wedge x' = x \wedge y' = y - x\end{array}$$

(c)

Fig. 3. **(a)** Loop ONE and **(b)**, **(c)** two ways of writing ONE as a Presburger loop

$$\begin{array}{ll}x > 0 \wedge 2a = x \ \rightarrow\ x \geq 1 & \}\ \text{Initiation}\\ \tau_1:\ x \geq 1 \wedge 2a = x \ \rightarrow\ x - a \geq 1 & \\ \tau_2:\ x \geq 1 \wedge 3a = x \ \rightarrow\ x - 2 \geq 1 & \text{Consecution}\\ \tau_3:\ x \geq 1 \ \rightarrow\ x \geq 1 & \\ \tau_1:\ x \geq 1 \wedge 2a = x \ \rightarrow\ x + y \geq 0 & \\ \tau_2:\ x \geq 1 \wedge 3a = x \ \rightarrow\ x + y \geq 0 & \text{Bounded}\\ \tau_3:\ x \geq 1 \wedge y > x \ \rightarrow\ x + y \geq 0 & \\ \tau_1:\ x \geq 1 \wedge 2a = x \ \rightarrow\ (x - a) + y < x + y & \\ \tau_2:\ x \geq 1 \wedge 3a = x \ \rightarrow\ (x - 2) + y < x + y & \text{Ranking}\\ \tau_3:\ x \geq 1 \wedge y > x \ \rightarrow\ x + (y - x) < x + y & \end{array}$$

The verification conditions are all valid, so ONE terminates on all input.

3 Termination

Existence of a ranking function for a loop L proves that L terminates. In principle, to find a linear ranking function with supporting linear invariant of some size, one can enumerate pairs of functions and invariants with integer coefficients, check whether each satisfies Definitions 6 and 7, and stop when one pair is found. This enumeration is sufficient to find any linear ranking function with supporting linear invariant in which all coefficients are rational. Of course, if no such function exists, then the enumeration does not terminate. It trivially allows synthesis over linear loops, as all formulae can be expressed in Presburger arithmetic. However, it is impractical.

We describe an alternate version of enumeration in which an infinite sets of pairs of functions and assertions, none of which is a ranking function with supporting invariant, can be pruned in a single step. The technique is based on searching for a valid instantiation of a *ranking function synthesis template.*

Definition 8 (Template Assertion). A *template expression* over $\mathcal{V} = \{x_1, \ldots, x_n\}$ is an expression $c_1x_1 + \cdots + c_nx_n + c_{n+1}$ with unknown coefficients c_i. Letting $\mathbf{x} = (x_1, \ldots, x_n, 1)^{\mathrm{T}}$ be a homogeneous vector, we write

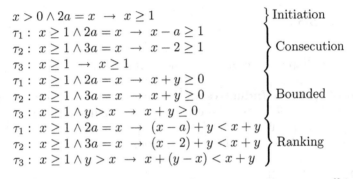

$\mathbf{c}^{\mathrm{T}}\mathbf{x} = (c_1, \ldots, c_n, c_{n+1})(x_1, \ldots, x_n, 1)^{\mathrm{T}}$, with unknown coefficients $\mathbf{c}$. A *template assertion* is a conjunctive assertion $\bigwedge_i \mathbf{c_i}^{\mathrm{T}}\mathbf{x} \geq 0$, or $\mathbf{C}\mathbf{x} \geq 0$, with unknown coefficient matrix $\mathbf{C}$.

Definition 9 (Ranking Function Synthesis Template). Given loop $L : \langle \mathcal{V}_{\mathbb{Z}}, \mathcal{V}_{\mathbb{Z}^*}, \theta, \mathcal{T} \rangle$ and the desired size of the supporting invariant *isz*, the *ranking function synthesis template* is

$$\varphi: \begin{array}{lr} \theta \to \mathbf{I}\mathbf{x} \geq 0 & \text{(initiation)} \\ \wedge \bigwedge_{\tau \in \mathcal{T}} [(\mathbf{I}\mathbf{x} \geq 0 \wedge \tau) \to \mathbf{I}\mathbf{x}' \geq 0] & \text{(consecution)} \\ \wedge \bigwedge_{\tau \in \mathcal{T}} [(\mathbf{I}\mathbf{x} \geq 0 \wedge \tau) \to \mathbf{r}^{\mathrm{T}}\mathbf{x} \geq 0] & \text{(bounded)} \\ \wedge \bigwedge_{\tau \in \mathcal{T}} [(\mathbf{I}\mathbf{x} \geq 0 \wedge \tau) \to \mathbf{r}^{\mathrm{T}}\mathbf{x}' < \mathbf{r}^{\mathrm{T}}\mathbf{x}] & \text{(ranking)} \end{array}$$

where $\mathbf{I}$ is an $(n+1) \times isz$ matrix representing the unknown coefficients of the supporting invariants, and $\mathbf{r}$ is an $(n+1)$-vector representing the unknown coefficients of the ranking function. The elements of $\mathbf{I}$ and $\mathbf{r}$ are the *parameters* of the synthesis template, collectively referred to as P. A synthesis template with parameters P is written $\varphi[P]$.

To prove the existence of a ranking function supported by invariants for a loop L, it suffices to prove the validity of $(\exists P)(\forall \mathbf{x}, \mathbf{x}')\varphi[P]$. This assertion is not a Presburger formula, as it involves multiplication of elements of P and $\mathbf{x}$. We propose a search for a solution $\widetilde{P}$ such that $(\forall \mathbf{x}, \mathbf{x}')\varphi[\widetilde{P}]$, which is a Presburger formula if L is a Presburger loop, is valid. Later, we show that it is sometimes useful to split the parameters P into two sets P_1 and P_2, where the parameters in P_2 are not involved in any multiplication with $\mathbf{x}$, and search for the solution $\widetilde{P_1}$ to P_1 such that $(\exists P_2)(\forall \mathbf{x}, \mathbf{x}')\varphi[\widetilde{P_1}, P_2]$ is valid.

Example 4. Consider loop ONE. $i_1 x + i_2 y + i_3 \geq 0$ is a 1-conjunct invariant template, and $r_1 x + r_2 y + r_3$ is a ranking function template. The conjunction of the verification conditions of Example 3 is the instantiation of the synthesis template for ONE in which $i_1 = 1,\ i_2 = 0,\ i_3 = -1,\ r_1 = 1,\ r_2 = 1,\ r_3 = 0$.

Definition 10 (Parameter Region and Corner). For parameter set P, a *parameter region* R is a hyper-rectangle of dimension $|P|$ assigning a closed interval from $\mathbb{R}$ to each parameter in P. A *corner* of a region is an extreme point: each parameter is assigned either the lower or upper bound of its interval. The *lower corner* is the extreme point in which each parameter is assigned its lower bound.

A parameter region R represents an infinite number of possible instantiations of a synthesis template $\varphi[P]$. Each rational point $r \in R$ corresponds to an integer instantiation of P, $\widetilde{P}$. Specifically, r corresponds to the integer point $\widetilde{P}$ such that the GCD of the coordinates of $\widetilde{P}$ is 1 and $\widetilde{P}$ is a scalar multiple of r. We write that $\widetilde{P} \in R$ if there is some rational point $r \in R$ such that r corresponds to $\widetilde{P}$.

```
let TERMINATES L isz =
  let φ[P] = TEMPLATE L isz in
  let queue = {(1, [−1, 1]^|P|)} in
  while |queue| > 0 do
    let d, R = CHOOSE queue in
    if FEASIBLE φ R then begin
      if CORNER_SOLUTION φ R then raise Terminates;
      if d ≤ D · |P| then
        let l, r = BISECT R in
        ADD {(d + 1, l), (d + 1, r)} queue
    end
  done;
  raise Unknown
```

Fig. 4. The function TERMINATES returns **Terminates** if a ranking function with a supporting invariant is discovered

Definition 11 (Feasible Region). Given synthesis template $\varphi[P]$, region R for P is *feasible* if it may contain a solution point.

Figure 4 presents the outline of the method. First, a synthesis template with supporting invariant template of size *isz* is constructed. P is the set of parameters. A search queue is initialized to contain a tuple $(1, [-1,1]^{|P|})$ expressing that the search is at depth 1 and the *region* under consideration is $[-1,1]^{|P|}$. While this queue is not empty, some pair is chosen. The selected region is checked for *feasibility*; if it is infeasible, it is pruned. If it is feasible, a *corner* of the region is checked by instantiating the template and checking validity. If it is not a solution and the maximum depth, given by parameter D, has not been reached, the region is bisected along some dimension, and each half is added to the queue. We now present the details.

We start with the *feasibility* check. While a region R represents an infinite number of possible instantiations of a synthesis template $\varphi[P]$, we want to determine the feasibility of R by checking the validity of only a finite number of Presburger formulae. We proceed by forming $2^{|\mathcal{V}_{\mathbb{Z}} \cup \mathcal{V}'_{\mathbb{Z}}|}$ *quadrant completions* of φ, $\widehat{\varphi}$, each of which forces each variable of $\mathcal{V}_{\mathbb{Z}} \cup \mathcal{V}'_{\mathbb{Z}}$ to range over either $\mathbb{Z}^*$ or $-\mathbb{Z}^*$. For each completion $\widehat{\varphi}$, we form a *relaxation* of $\widehat{\varphi}$ over R, $\widehat{\varphi}_R$. If any one of these relaxed instantiations is invalid, then R does not contain a solution.

Definition 12 (Quadrant Completion). Given loop $L : \langle \mathcal{V}_{\mathbb{Z}}, \mathcal{V}_{\mathbb{Z}^*}, \theta, \mathcal{T} \rangle$ and synthesis template φ, a *quadrant completion* $\widehat{\varphi}$ of φ has the form

$$\left(\bigwedge_{x \in \mathcal{V}_{\mathbb{Z}}} (x \bowtie_x 0 \ \wedge \ x' \bowtie_{x'} 0) \right) \ \rightarrow \ \varphi,$$

where each $\bowtie \in \{\leq, \geq\}$; *i.e.*, each $x \in \mathcal{V}_{\mathbb{Z}}$ and $x' \in \mathcal{V}'_{\mathbb{Z}}$ is forced to be either nonnegative or nonpositive.

Definition 13 (Relaxation). Consider loop $L : \langle \mathcal{V}_{\mathbb{Z}}, \mathcal{V}_{\mathbb{Z}^*}, \theta, \mathcal{T} \rangle$, quadrant completion $\widehat{\varphi}[P]$ of $\varphi[P]$ expressed in negation normal form and with all minus signs eliminated by rearrangement, and region $R : [\mathbf{l}, \mathbf{u}]$ for P. The *relaxation* of $\widehat{\varphi}$ over R is the assertion $\widehat{\varphi}_R$ in which each inequality $\alpha \geq \beta$ of $\widehat{\varphi}[P]$ is replaced by $\overline{\alpha} \geq \underline{\beta}$. $\overline{\alpha}$ is obtained by replacing each term of the form p, where $p \in P$ and $\ell \leq p \leq u$ in R, with u and each term of the form px with ux if $\widehat{\varphi}[P]$ requires $x \geq 0$ and ℓx otherwise. Similarly $\underline{\beta}$ is obtained by replacing each term of the form p with ℓ and each term of the form px with ℓx if $\widehat{\varphi}[P]$ requires $x \geq 0$ and ux otherwise.

Lemma 1 (Feasible Region). *Consider synthesis template $\varphi[P]$ and region R for P. If for some quadrant completion $\widehat{\varphi}$ of φ, $(\forall \mathbf{x}, \mathbf{x}')\widehat{\varphi}_R$ is invalid, then R is infeasible.*

Definition 14 (Corner Solution). Given synthesis template $\varphi[P]$ and the corner $\widetilde{P} \in R$ for P, $\widetilde{P}$ is a *corner solution* if $\varphi[\widetilde{P}]$ is valid.

Theorem 1 (Sound and Complete). *Consider loop $L : \langle \mathcal{V}_{\mathbb{Z}}, \mathcal{V}_{\mathbb{Z}^*}, \theta, \mathcal{T} \rangle$, supporting invariant size isz, and maximum search depth parameter D. Suppose that* BISECT *always bisects one of the widest dimensions of a region and that* CORNER_SOLUTION *always chooses the lower corner of a region. Then L has a linear ranking function with supporting isz-conjunct linear invariant, expressed so that all coefficients are integers in $[-2^{D-1}, 2^{D-1})$, if and only if* (TERMINATES *L isz*) *returns* **Terminates**.

Soundness is immediate: TERMINATES reports success only if it finds a solution, which by construction of the synthesis template obeys the verification conditions of Definitions 6 and 7.

Completeness (relative to the maximum search depth) is also fairly straightforward. First, every rational invariant and ranking function may be represented such that all coefficients lie in $[-1, 1]$ and the denominators of coefficients are powers of 2. Second, if BISECT and CORNER_SOLUTION satisfy the stated restrictions, then every combination of such coefficients, with coefficient denominators up to 2^{D-1} and numerators in $[-2^{D-1}, 2^{D-1})$, appears as a corner. Converting these rational coefficients to integers results in integer coefficients in $[-2^{D-1}, 2^{D-1})$. Finally, Lemma 1 ensures that no region containing a solution is pruned.

It is easy to see that alternately running TERMINATES and incrementing the maximum depth results in a complete procedure: it is guaranteed to find a linear ranking function with its specified number of supporting invariants, in which coefficients are rational, if one exists. However, this procedure is not guaranteed to terminate when a solution does not exist, as the following example demonstrates.

Example 5. Consider applying the alternating procedure to ZERO. Consider checking the feasibility of a region R in which the coefficient of x and the constant offset are both positive intervals; that is, $R = [\ell_1, u_1] \times [\ell_2, u_2]$ for $\ell_1, u_1, \ell_2, u_2 > 0$. Clearly, any instance of $r_1 x + r_2$ in R is bounded from below,

$$\begin{array}{l} \texttt{uint}\ x, y \\ \theta:\ x > 0 \wedge x\%2 = 0 \wedge y < 100 \\ \tau_1:\ x\%2 = 0 \wedge x' = x - \frac{x}{2} \wedge y' = y \\ \tau_2:\ x\%2 = 0 \wedge y < 100 - \frac{x}{2} \wedge x' = x \wedge y' = y + \frac{x}{2} \end{array}$$

Fig. 5. Loop with large constants

as $x \geq 0$. This region is also feasible: at worst, $x = 1$ so that $x' = x$, yet then $\ell_1 x' + \ell_2 = \ell_1 x + \ell_2 < u_1 x + u_2$, so that the relaxation $\widehat{\varphi}_R$ is valid. An infinite number of such regions is encountered during an unbounded search.

We conclude this section on termination by noting that one useful variation is possible. Constant parameters (*e.g.*, r_2 of $r_1 x + r_2$) that appear in ranking function synthesis templates may be existentially quantified. Consider loop $L : \langle \mathcal{V}_\mathbb{Z}, \mathcal{V}_{\mathbb{Z}^*}, \theta, \mathcal{T} \rangle$. Letting $\mathbf{x} = (x_1, \ldots, x_n)^\mathrm{T}$ for $x_i \in \mathcal{V}$, the ranking function synthesis template is then

$$(\exists \mathbf{i}, r)(\forall \mathbf{x}, \mathbf{x}') \begin{bmatrix} \theta \rightarrow \mathbf{Ix} + \mathbf{i} \geq 0 \\ \wedge \bigwedge_{\tau \in \mathcal{T}} [(\mathbf{Ix} + \mathbf{i} \geq 0 \wedge \tau) \rightarrow \mathbf{Ix}' + \mathbf{i} \geq 0] \\ \wedge \bigwedge_{\tau \in \mathcal{T}} [(\mathbf{Ix} + \mathbf{i} \geq 0 \wedge \tau) \rightarrow \mathbf{r}^\mathrm{T}\mathbf{x} + r \geq 0] \\ \wedge \bigwedge_{\tau \in \mathcal{T}} [(\mathbf{Ix} + \mathbf{i} \geq 0 \wedge \tau) \rightarrow \mathbf{r}^\mathrm{T}\mathbf{x}' < \mathbf{r}^\mathrm{T}\mathbf{x}] \end{bmatrix}$$

When $\mathbf{I}$ and $\mathbf{r}$ are instantiated, the formula is decidable, although the quantifier alternation increases the difficulty of the instance.

Example 6. Consider the loop in Figure 5. $x - y + 99$ is a ranking function supported by the invariants $x \geq 1$ and $y \leq 99$. Without quantifying the constant coefficients, the search must continue to depth 8; however, with quantification, the search finds a solution at depth 2.

4 Invariant Generation

In this section, we adapt the technique to invariant generation. The primary challenge in invariant generation, relative to ranking function synthesis, is to avoid discovering invariants weaker than those already known. We adapt the region-based technique to invariant generation by introducing a region-subsumption check, which may prune a region in which all assertions are subsumed by those already found.

Definition 15 (Invariant Synthesis Template). Given a loop L : $\langle \mathcal{V}_\mathbb{Z}, \mathcal{V}_{\mathbb{Z}^*}, \theta, \mathcal{T} \rangle$ and the desired size of the conjunctive invariant *isz*, the *invariant synthesis template* is

$$\varphi: \begin{array}{ll} \theta \rightarrow \mathbf{Ix} \geq 0 & \text{(initiation)} \\ \wedge \bigwedge_{\tau \in \mathcal{T}} [(\mathbf{Ix} \geq 0 \wedge \tau) \rightarrow \mathbf{Ix}' \geq 0] & \text{(consecution)} \end{array}$$

where $\mathbf{I}$ is an $(n+1) \times isz$ matrix representing the unknown coefficients of the invariant. The elements of $\mathbf{I}$ are the *parameters*, which we refer to collectively as P, of the template.

As with the termination analysis, solutions are integer instantiations $\widetilde{P}$ of P such that $(\forall \mathbf{x}, \mathbf{x}')\varphi[\widetilde{P}]$ is valid. However, generating invariants requires reporting all discovered solutions, rather than halting after finding a solution. Invariants are common, yet many are weak. The termination analysis prunes many regions containing invariants because they do not support a ranking function. No such criterion exists here. Instead, the invariant generation method may prune a region if all of its assertions are *subsumed by* already discovered invariants.

Definition 16 (Subsumed Region). Consider invariant template $\mathbf{Ix} \geq 0$, region R for $\mathbf{I}$, and the set of known invariants K. R is a *subsumed region* if every instantiation of $\mathbf{Ix} \geq 0$ from R is subsumed by $\bigwedge K$.

Definition 17 (Subsumption Template). Consider known invariants K and invariant template $\mathbf{Ix} \geq 0$. Then

$$\left(\bigwedge K\right) \rightarrow \mathbf{Ix} \geq 0$$

is the *subsumption template* for $\mathbf{Ix} \geq 0$.

Definition 18 (Strengthening). Consider loop $L : \langle \mathcal{V}_{\mathbb{Z}}, \mathcal{V}_{\mathbb{Z}^*}, \theta, \mathcal{T} \rangle$, quadrant completion $\widehat{\psi}[P]$ of subsumption template $\psi[P]$, and region $R : [\mathbf{l}, \mathbf{u}]$ for P. The *strengthening* of $\widehat{\psi}$ is the assertion $\widehat{\psi}^R$ in which each inequality $\alpha \geq 0$ of $\widehat{\psi}[P]$ containing parameterized terms is replaced by $\underline{\alpha} \geq 0$, and other literals are unchanged. $\underline{\alpha}$ is obtained by replacing each term of the form p, where $p \in P$ and $\ell \leq p \leq u$ in R, with ℓ and each term of the form px with ℓx if $\widehat{\psi}[P]$ requires $x \geq 0$ and ux otherwise.

Lemma 2 (Subsumed Region). *Consider known invariants K, subsumption template $\psi[P]$, and region R for P. If for all quadrant completions $\widehat{\psi}$ of ψ, $(\forall \mathbf{x})\widehat{\psi}^R$ is valid, then R is a subsumed region.*

Figure 6 shows the function INVARIANTS. It is similar in structure to TERMINATES, except that it returns the discovered invariants after it has searched the space defined by the maximum depth parameter D. The function CORNER_SOLUTION returns None if the corner of R is not a solution, and Some I otherwise. Discovered invariants are recorded in K. SUBSUMED implements the subsumption check.

Theorem 2 (Sound and Complete). *Consider loop $L : \langle \mathcal{V}_{\mathbb{Z}}, \mathcal{V}_{\mathbb{Z}^*}, \theta, \mathcal{T} \rangle$, invariant size isz, and maximum search depth parameter D. Suppose that*

```
let INVARIANTS L isz =
  let φ[P] = TEMPLATE L isz in
  let K = {} in
  let queue = {(1, [−1, 1]^|P|)} in
  while |queue| > 0 do
    let d, R = CHOOSE queue in
    if (FEASIBLE φ R) ∧ ¬(SUBSUMED φ R K) then begin
      begin
        match CORNER_SOLUTION φ R with
        | Some I  →  ADD I K
        | None    →  ()
      end;
      if d ≤ D · |P| then
        let l, r = BISECT R in
        ADD {(d + 1, l), (d + 1, r)} queue
    end
  done;
  K
```

Fig. 6. The function INVARIANTS returns a set of invariants of L

BISECT *always bisects one of the widest dimensions of a region and that* CORNER_SOLUTION *always chooses the lower corner of a region. Then L has a linear isz-conjunct invariant I, expressed so that all coefficients are integers in* $[-2^{D-1}, 2^{D-1})$, *if and only if the conjunction of the set returned by* (INVARIANTS L *isz*) *implies I.*

Proving soundness and completeness is again straightforward, given Lemma 2. As with TERMINATES, the procedure that alternately runs INVARIANTS and increases its maximum depth will find any linear inductive invariant with rational coefficients, unless a stronger one has been found. This procedure is not guaranteed to terminate.

Example 7. Consider ZERO again and any region $R = [\ell_1, u_1] \times [\ell_2, u_2]$ in which $\ell_1, u_1 \geq 0$, $\ell_2 = -u_1$, and $u_2 = -\ell_1$. The corner instantiation $\ell_1 x + u_2 \geq 0$ (*e.g.*, $4x - 4 \geq 0$) is an invariant of ZERO. It is also the strongest invariant in the region, yet it trivially subsumes $x \geq 1$, as they are equivalent. But in the strengthening $\widehat{\psi}^R$ in which $x \geq 1$ is known, $\ell_1 x + \ell_2 = \ell_1 x - u_1 = \ell_1 x - (\ell_1 + \epsilon)$, for some $\epsilon > 0$. At $x = 1$, $\ell_1 x - (\ell_1 + \epsilon) = \ell_1(1) - \ell_1 - \epsilon = -\epsilon \not\geq 0$, so that $\widehat{\psi}^R$ is invalid and R is not pruned as subsumed. An infinite number of such regions is encountered during an unbounded search.

5 Empirical Observations

In this section, we examine the behavior of TERMINATES and INVARIANTS on a set of loops. We prototyped TERMINATES and INVARIANTS in O'Caml, using the OMEGA TEST [16] to decide validity of Presburger formulae.

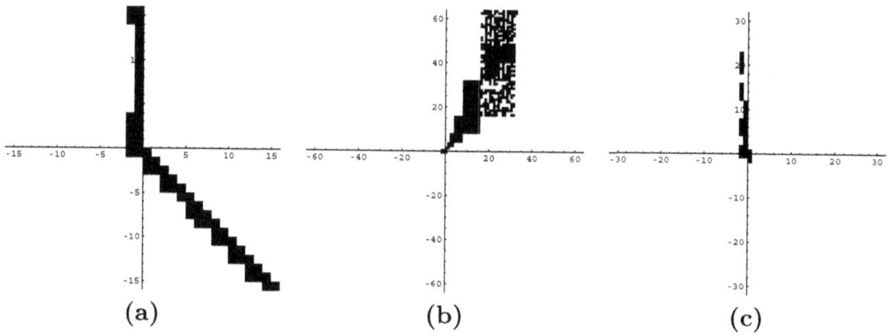

Fig. 7. Feasible regions explored during search

$$\begin{array}{l}\texttt{int}\ i, j, k\\ \theta:\ \top\\ \tau_1:\ i + 17j + 33k > 0 \wedge i' = i + 16 \wedge j' = j - 1 \wedge k' = k\\ \tau_2:\ i + 17j + 33k > 0 \wedge i' = i + 32 \wedge j' = j \wedge k' = k - 1\end{array}$$

Fig. 8. Loop with large coefficients

When INVARIANTS is applied to loop ZERO with a maximum search depth of 5, it can potentially search over two thousand regions. It actually searches approximately 8% of the regions. Figure 7(a) shows the feasible regions encountered during the search. To represent feasible regions pictorially, regions are normalized to have integer bounds. Regions farther from the origin occur later in the search. INVARIANTS focuses on the invariant *true*, represented by the vertical line of regions, and the invariant $x \geq 1$, indicated by the diagonal group.

The loop in Figure 8 has the obvious ranking function $i + 17j + 33k$. We analyze it to force a deep search: finding it requires searching to a depth of 7, resulting in over four million possible regions. TERMINATES finds the solution after searching under three thousand regions. Figure 7(b) shows the feasible regions encountered during the search. As the search focuses on a coefficient of 1 for i, the graph shows the projection for the coefficients of j and k.

Figure 9(a) presents a loop that does not have a linear ranking function. When the transitions are strengthened with the invariants discovered during a depth-two search (*e.g.*, $s \geq 1$), running TERMINATES to a depth of 6 reveals that the loop does not have a linear ranking function supported by that set of invariants. That is, no region is skipped because of depth, proving the nonexistence of

$$\begin{array}{l}\texttt{uint}\ x, s\\ \theta:\ s = 1\\ \tau_1:\ x > 100 \wedge s \neq 1 \wedge x' = x - 10 \wedge s' = s - 1\\ \tau_2:\ x \leq 100 \wedge x' = x + 11 \wedge s' = s + 1\end{array}$$

(a)

$$\begin{array}{l}\texttt{uint}\ x, y\\ \theta:\ x = 0 \wedge y > 10\\ \tau_1:\ x' = x + 1 \wedge y' = y + 7\\ \tau_2:\ x' = \frac{y}{7} \wedge y' = y\end{array}$$

(b)

Fig. 9. (a) Loop without linear ranking function. (b) Loop SEVEN

Table 1. Summary of experiments. (T) indicates termination analysis; (I) indicates invariant generation. **Time** is in seconds. The **Regions** column indicates the percentage of the search space explored; for searches terminating at depth 2, this percentage is too variable to state.

Loop	Time	Depth	Regions	Loop	Time	Depth	Regions
ONE (T)	20s	2	—	Fig. 5 (T)	5s	2	—
ZERO (I)	1s	5	8%	Fig. 8 (T)	100s	7	.07%
Fig. 9(**a**) (T)	1s	6	1%	Fig. 9(**b**) (I)	45s	5	5%

```
uint i, n, m1, m2, p
θ: p = 0
for i = 1 to n do
   if m1%2 = 1 then
      p := p + m2
   m1 := m1/2
   m2 := 2 * m2
done
```

(**a**)

$$
\begin{array}{l}
\texttt{uint}\ i, n, m_1, m_2, p \\
[\texttt{uint}\ M, M_0] \\
\theta:\ p = 0 \wedge i = 1 \wedge [M = M_0] \\
\tau_1:\ \left(\begin{array}{l} i \le n \wedge m_1\%2 = 0 \wedge i' = i + 1 \wedge n' = n \\ \wedge\ m_1' = m_1/2 \wedge m_2' = 2m_2 \wedge p' = p \\ [\wedge\ M' = M \wedge M_0' = M_0] \end{array}\right) \\
\tau_2:\ \left(\begin{array}{l} i \le n \wedge m_1\%2 = 1 \wedge i' = i + 1 \wedge n' = n \\ \wedge\ m_1' = m_1/2 \wedge m_2' = 2m_2 \wedge p' = p + m_2 \\ [\wedge\ M' = M - m_2 \wedge M_0' = M_0] \end{array}\right)
\end{array}
$$

(**b**)

Fig. 10. (a) Multiplication of two n-bit binary numbers m_1 and m_2 into $2n$-bit product p, where multiplication and division by 2 and modulo arithmetic model bit manipulation. **(b)** Integer linear loop form, in which M and M_0 have been introduced to track m_1m_2. Augmenting variables and assertions are in brackets.

a linear ranking function (relative to the discovered supporting invariants). In this search, about 1% of possible regions are examined. Figure 7(**c**) shows the examined feasible regions for the coefficients of x and s.

Running INVARIANTS to a depth of 5 on the loop in Figure 9(**b**) reveals the two invariants $y \geq 11$ and $7x \leq y$. The search examines approximately 5% of the possible regions and produces about 15 invariants. Disabling the subsumption check results in examining about a third of the possible regions and producing over ten thousand invariants.

Table 1 summarizes these results.

Finally, we describe the application of our method to a simple hardware multiplication algorithm [10]. Figure 10 presents the algorithm for multiplying two n-bit nonnegative integers, m_1 and m_2, into $2n$-bit product register p. Actually, m_2 is a $2n$-bit register, but its left half is initially 0. As we would like to verify facts about multiplication, which we cannot model explicitly, we introduce tracking variables M and M_0. The variable M tracks the changes to m_1m_2 as the algorithm progresses, while M_0 records M's initial value. After transforming Figure 10(**a**) to an integer linear loop, we calculate

$$
\begin{aligned}
M' &= m_1'm_2' = \tfrac{m_1}{2}(2m_2) \\
&= \begin{cases} m_1m_2 = M & \text{if } m_1\%2 = 0 \\ \frac{m_1-1}{2}(2m_2) = m_1m_2 - m_2 = M - m_2 & \text{if } m_1\%2 = 1 \end{cases}
\end{aligned}
$$

and augment the loop as in Figure 10(**b**). Termination is trivial. Invariant generation of 1-conjunct invariants produces the two invariants $p + M \leq M_0$ and $p + M \geq M_0$, so that $p = M_0 - M$, proving correctness.

6 Conclusion

We presented a technique for synthesizing linear ranking functions with supporting linear invariants and generating linear invariants of loops with integer variables. Unlike previous work, the technique handles integer variables directly, yet remains complete. Thus, it is more precise than previous analyses.

Several parameters of TERMINATES and INVARIANTS are left open for heuristics, including the criterion for choosing the dimension to bisect and the method of choosing regions from the queue. Even with heuristics, analyses over integer variables cannot scale to the size of problems that real-variable analyses can handle, while many integer loops can be soundly and effectively analyzed by real-variable techniques. Thus, future work includes developing an analysis system that identifies when the stronger integer-based analyses are required. Handling mixed-variable loops, in which only some variables are integers, would also be of value.

Acknowledgments. We thank Sriram Sankaranarayanan and the reviewers for their insightful comments.

References

1. BRADLEY, A. R., MANNA, Z., AND SIPMA, H. B. Linear ranking with reachability. In *CAV* (2005). To appear.
2. COLÓN, M., SANKARANARAYANAN, S., AND SIPMA, H. Linear invariant generation using non-linear constraint solving. In *CAV* (2003), pp. 420–433.
3. COLÓN, M., AND SIPMA, H. Synthesis of linear ranking functions. In *TACAS* (2001), pp. 67–81.
4. COLÓN, M., AND SIPMA, H. Practical methods for proving program termination. In *CAV* (2002), pp. 442–454.
5. COOPER, D. C. Theorem proving in arithmetic without multiplication. *Machine Intelligence 7* (1972), 91–100.
6. COUSOT, P. Proving program invariance and termination by parametric abstraction, lagrangian relaxation and semidefinite programming. In *VMCAI* (2005), pp. 1–24.
7. COUSOT, P., AND COUSOT, R. Abstract Interpretation: A unified lattice model for static analysis of programs by construction or approximation of fixpoints. In *ACM Principles of Programming Languages* (1977), pp. 238–252.
8. COUSOT, P., AND HALBWACHS, N. Automatic discovery of linear restraints among the variables of a program. In *ACM Principles of Programming Languages* (Jan. 1978), pp. 84–97.
9. H. B. SIPMA, T. E. URIBE, AND Z. MANNA. Deductive model checking. In *CAV* (1996), pp. 209–219.

10. Hennessy, J. L., and Patterson, D. A. *Computer organization and design (2nd ed.): the hardware/software interface.* Morgan Kaufmann Publishers Inc., 1998.
11. Hentenryck, P. V., Michel, L., and Benhamou, F. Newton - constraint programming over nonlinear constraints. *Sci. Comput. Program.* (1998), 83–118.
12. Manna, Z., Browne, A., Sipma, H., and Uribe, T. E. Visual abstractions for temporal verification. In *Algebraic Methodology and Software Technology* (1998), pp. 28–41.
13. Podelski, A., and Rybalchenko, A. A complete method for the synthesis of linear ranking functions. In *VMCAI* (2004), pp. 239–251.
14. Podelski, A., and Rybalchenko, A. Transition invariants. In *LICS* (2004), pp. 32–41.
15. Presburger, M. Ueber die vollstaendigkeit eines gewissen systems der arithmetik ganzer zahlen, in welchem die addition als einzige operation hervortritt. *Comptes Rendus du I congrs de Mathmaticiens des Pays Slaves* (1929), 92–101.
16. Pugh, W. The Omega test: a fast and practical integer programming algorithm for dependence analysis. *Communications of the ACM 35* (1992), 102–114.

A Practical Application of Geometric Semantics to Static Analysis of Concurrent Programs

Eric Goubault[1] and Emmanuel Haucourt[2]

[1] LIST (CEA - Technologies Avancées),
DTSI-SOL, CEA F91191 Gif-sur-Yvette Cedex
Eric.Goubault@cea.fr
[2] Preuves, Programmation, Systèmes,
Université Paris 7, 175 rue Chevaleret, F75013
haucourt@cea.fr

Abstract. In this paper we show how to compress efficiently the state-space of a concurrent system (here applied to a simple shared memory model, but this is no way limited to that model). The technology used here is based on research on geometric semantics by the authors and collaborators [1]. It has been implemented in a abstract interpretation based static analyzer (ALCOOL), and we show some preliminary results and benchmarks.

1 Introduction and Related Work

The aim of this paper is to show how to infer some important properties of concurrent and distributed systems using geometric ideas[1]. The algorithms we describe in this paper have been implemented in a prototype "ALCOOL" briefly benchmarked and explained in Section 4, as well as in appendix A.

A class of examples arises from a toy langage manipulating semaphores. Using Dijkstra's notation [2], we consider processes to be sequences of locking operations Pa on semaphores a and unlocking operations Va. In the example where two processes share two resources a and b: $T1 = Pa.Pb.Vb.Va$ in parallel with $T2 = Pb.Pa.Va.Vb$, the geometric model is the "Swiss flag", Fig. 1, regarded as a subset of $\mathbb{R}^2$ with the componentwise partial order $(x_1, y_1) \leq (x_2, y_2)$ if $x_1 \leq y_1$ and $x_2 \leq y_2$. The (interior of the) horizontal dashed rectangle comprises global states that are such that T_1 and T_2 both hold a lock on a: this is impossible by the very definition of a binary semaphore. Similarly, the (interior of the) vertical rectangle consists of states violating the mutual exclusion property on b. Therefore both dashed rectangles form the *forbidden region*, which is the complement of the space X of (legal) states. This space with the inherited partial order provides us with a particular po-space X [3],[4], as defined in Sect. 2. This view can be generalized to more general counting semaphores, i.e. resources that can be shared by some $k > 1$ but not $k+1$ processes (see Figure 3 for the case $k = 2$ and three processes). Moreover, legal execution paths, called *dipaths*, are

[1] Work partially funded by EDF under grant CEA/EDF 1-5-163 CE.

M. Abadi and L. de Alfaro (Eds.): CONCUR 2005, LNCS 3653, pp. 503–517, 2005.

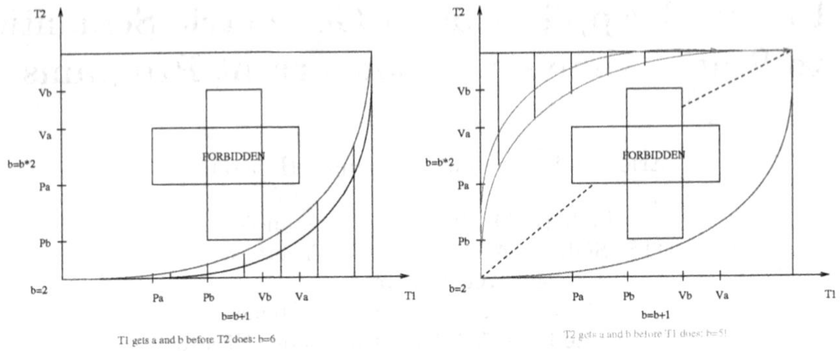

Fig. 1. Essential schedules for the swiss flag

increasing maps from the po-space $\boldsymbol{I}$ (the unit segment with its natural order) to X. The partial order on X thus reflects (at least) the time ordering on all possible execution paths. Many different execution paths have the same global effect: In the "Swiss Flag" example, for any execution path shaped like the one at the left of Figure 1, T_1 gets hold of locks a and b before T_2 does. This implies that for the actual assignments on variable b that we have chosen in this example: T_1 does $b := b + 1$ and T_2 does $b = b * 2$, starting with an initial value of 2, all execution paths below the hole will end up with the value $b = 6$, since T_1 will do $b = 2 + 1 = 3$ and then only after will T_2 do $b = 3 * 2 = 6$. In fact, there are only two essentially different execution paths from the initial point $(0, 0)$ to the final point $(1, 1)$, that fully determine the computer-scientific behaviour of the system. See picture at the right hand side of Figure 1). These are in fact the only two classes of dipaths from $(0, 0)$ to $(1, 1)$ modulo "continuous deformations" that do not reverse time, i.e., up to *dihomotopy* as defined in [5]. This fact is indeed general, and is not at all limited to the example. For determining the possible outcome of a concurrent program (modelled in a suitable way, as for our PV programs), only the dihomotopy classes of dipaths count.

Other interesting dipaths, in our example space, start in the initial point $(0, 0)$ and end in a deadlock, or start in the unreachable point and end in $(1, 1)$ see the dashed paths on Figure 1.

In general, one of the important invariants of a concurrent system is its *fundamental category* [6],[7], defined in Section 3.1, classifiying dipaths between any pair of points up to dihomotopy, i.e, a directed version of the fundamental groupoid of a topological space. In nice cases, the relevant information in the fundamental category is essentially finite. This is shown using a construction based on categories of fractions [8], as developped in [1] and [9]. The formalism developped in these last two papers allows to decompose the fundamental category (or the state-space) into big chunks as the regions 1 to 10 in Figure 2. Basically, inside these regions, or components, nothing important happens. This produces the following compressed state-space on which, using general results of [1], one can read all temporal properties as pictured in Figure 2 (with two views, one geometric, the other, algebraic). The graph of the right hand side

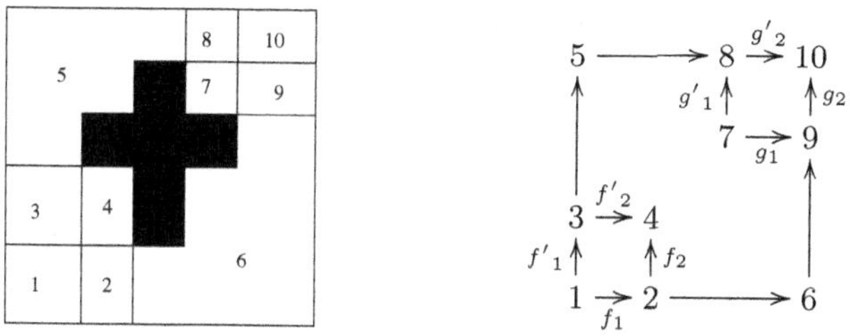

Fig. 2. The components of the Swiss flag

should be understood as generating a category [10], where morphisms represent classes of paths of execution, such that we have relations ${g'}_2 \circ {g'}_1 = g_2 \circ g_1$ and ${f'}_2 \circ {f'}_1 = f_2 \circ f_1$ (compare with e.g. [11]). In some sense, this so-called category of components finitely presents the fundamental category and the essential properties of the state-space, that can be used in a static analysis based verification tool.

Some comparisons between what this type of approach should buy us with other state-space reduction techniques such as persistent sets [12],[13], stubborn sets [14],[15], Petri nets based techniques [16] etc. have been made in [7]. In this paper, we develop this line of research a bit further, giving actual algorithms to compute this component category in relevant cases, implementing them and benchmarking them.

In Section 3.2, we give an algorithm to find the components, and to enumerate the "essential traces", i.e. the traces of execution modulo dihomotopy, which correspond, on a fragment of the model, to finding representatives of the Mazurkiewicz traces [17]. This in turn can be used to compute efficiently an abstraction of the collecting semantics of parallel processes, as used in abstract interpreters [18]. This is described in Section 4. The implementation of this algorithm is for the time being rather crude, but still, one can fully handle the case of 9 philosophers, and effectively compress its state-space and its set of essential schedules (which in this case is very large anyway). This is the base of the static analyzer ALCOOL we have been developping for EDF (the main French electricity provider), that we briefly describe at the end of this section.

We should end up this introductory section by saying that this state-space reduction technique is entirely orthogonal to other techniques like *symbolic model-checking* as developped in e.g. [19],[20],[21] or like abstraction based techniques. A combination of good abstractions with this algorithm should improve performances a lot. Last but not least, other geometric criteria for state-space reduction are currently being developped, one which looks extremely promising being [22].

2 Models of Concurrent Computation

The main idea (see [23] for instance) is to model a *discrete* concurrency problem in a *continuous geometric* set-up: A system of n concurrent processes will be represented as a subset of Euclidean space $\mathbb{R}^n$. Each coordinate axis corresponds to one of the processes. The state of the system corresponds to a point in $\mathbb{R}^n$, whose i'th coordinate describes the state (or "local time") of the i'th processor. An execution is then a *continuous increasing path* within the subset from an initial state to a final state.

A more general framework on which this paper is based is defined below (see [5]):

Definition 1.

1. *A po-space is a topological space X with a (global) closed partial order $\leq$ (i.e. $\leq$ is a closed subset of $X \times X$).*
2. *A dimap $f : X \to Y$ between po-spaces X and Y is a continuous map that respects the partial orders (is non-decreasing).*
3. *A dipath $f : \boldsymbol{I} \to X$ is a dimap whose source is the interval $\boldsymbol{I}$ with the usual order.*

Po-spaces and dimaps form a category. To a certain degree, our methods apply to the more general categories of lpo-spaces [5] , of flows [24] and of *d*-spaces [25].

We start with a very simplistic language, in order to explain the concepts. We will point out in Section 4 that this can be extended to more realistic languages, as used in ALCOOL.

$$Proc_d = \epsilon \mid Pa.Proc_d \mid Va.Proc_d$$

(ϵ being the empty string, a being any object of $\mathcal{O}$, defined as a binary semaphore: $s(a) = 1$ or as a counting semaphore initialized to k: $s(a) = k$). A PV program is any parallel combination of these PV processes, $Prog = Proc \quad | \quad (Prog \mid Prog)$. The typical example in shared memory concurrent programs is $\mathcal{O}$ being the set of shared variables and for all $a \in \mathcal{O}$, $s(a) = 1$. The P action is putting a lock and the V action is relinquishing it. We will suppose in the sequel that any given process can only access once an object before releasing it.

Supposing that the length of the strings X_i $(1 \leq i \leq n)$, denoting n processes in parallel in this language, are integers l_i, the semantics of $Prog$ is included in $[0, l_1] \times \cdots \times [0, l_n]$. A description of $[\![Prog]\!]$ can be given by describing inductively what should be digged into this n-rectangle (the semantics is given in terms of the set of forbidden hyper-rectangles). The semantics of our language can be described by the simple rule, $[k_1, r_1] \times \cdots \times [k_n, r_n] \in [\![X_1 \mid \cdots \mid X_n]\!]$ if there is a partition of $\{1, \cdots, n\}$ into $U \cup V$ with $card(U) = s(a) + 1$ for some object a with, $X_i(k_i) = Pa$, $X_i(r_i) = Va$ for $i \in U$ and $k_j = 0$, $r_j = l_j$ for $j \in V$.

3 Essential Schedules

3.1 A Bit of Theory

Equivalence of dipaths, as used in the examples of Figure 1, is modelled by the notion of dihomotopy, a directed version of standard homotopy [26]. They describe accurately, in a continuous model, a generalized notion of "commutation of actions", and make available some powerful tools from algebraic topology (see [6], [27], [5] for surveys).

Dihomotopies between dipaths f and g (with fixed extremities α and β in X) are dimaps $H : \boldsymbol{I} \times I \to X$ such that for all $x \in \boldsymbol{I}$, $t \in I$, $H(x,0) = f(x)$, $H(x,1) = g(x)$, $H(0,t) = \alpha$, $H(1,t) = \beta$. Notice that here I carries the equality as order contrarily to $\boldsymbol{I}$ (another definition can be given [25], but which is equivalent in all the cases dealt with in this paper).

A dihomotopy is to be understood as a 1-parameter family of dimaps without order requirements in the second I-coordinate[2]. Now, we can define the main object of study of this paper, the fundamental category, which contains all relevant information for the study of traces of execution:

Definition 2. *The fundamental category is the category $\boldsymbol{\pi}_1(X)$ with:*

- *as objects: the points of X,*
- *as morphisms, the dihomotopy classes of dipaths: a morphism from x to y is a dihomotopy class $[f]$ of a dipath f from x to y.*

Concatenation of dipaths factors over dihomotopy and yields the composition of morphisms in the fundamental category. A dimap $f : X \to Y$ between po-spaces induces a functor $f_\# : \boldsymbol{\pi}_1(X) \to \boldsymbol{\pi}_1(Y)$, and we obtain thus a functor $\boldsymbol{\pi}_1$ from the category of po-spaces to the category of categories.

We formally invert some "inessential" morphisms in the fundamental category, as in [1], [9], to obtain a "compressed" component category. For instance, for a binary semaphore taken by two processes, we will obtain the category generated by the graph of Figure 6. In the case of three processes trying to get hold of a counting semaphore initialized to two (geometric semantics given by Figure 3), we would get the component category pictured in Figure 4: each of the 26 subcubes delineated by the green planes are components, and there is one morphism from each of these to neighbouring ones (in the directed order). Every four neighbours having a segment in common have their four "neighbouring" morphisms commute.

3.2 Inductive Computation

In the case of the geometric semantics of the toy PV language we chose, all these component categories are in fact generated by 2-dimensional precubical sets (graphs plus a notion of 2-cell, filling some of the rectangular holes in the graph):

Definition 3. *A 2-dimensional precubical set is given by*

$$(X_0, X_1, X_2, (\partial_0^0, \partial_1^0, \partial_0^1, \partial_1^1 : X_2 \to X_1), (\partial_0^0, \partial_0^1 : X_1 \to X_0))$$

such that $\partial_i^k \circ \partial_j^l = \partial_{j-1}^l \circ \partial_i^k$ for $i < j$ and $k = 0, 1$, $l = 0, 1$. ∂_0^1 and ∂_1^1 (respectively ∂_0^0, ∂_1^0) are called end (respectively start) boundary operators.

[2] This is slightly different for d-spaces, but coincides in important cases.

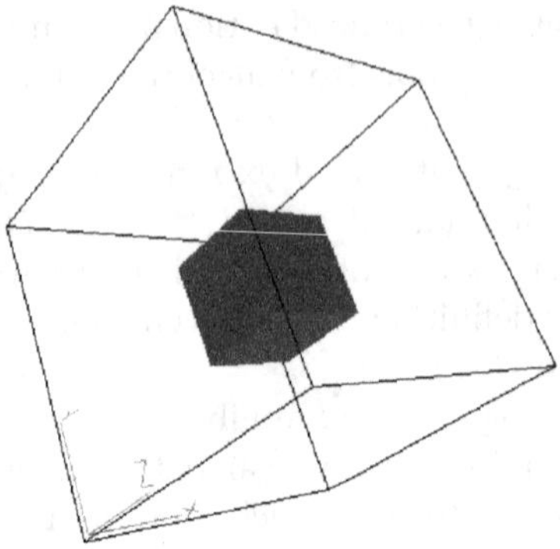

Fig. 3. Geometric semantics of a counting semaphore initialized to 2

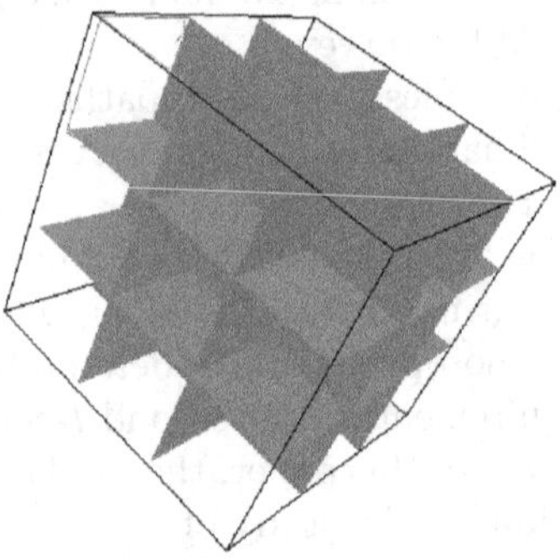

Fig. 4. Its component category

More general versions of these precubical sets have been used to model concurrent processes [6]. These 2-dimensional precubical sets are somehow the analogues of asynchronous transition systems [28], [29]. Elements of X_n $(n = 0, 1, 2)$ are called n-transitions. A simple example of a 2-dimensional pre-cubical set (which should represent a in parallel with b) is given below:

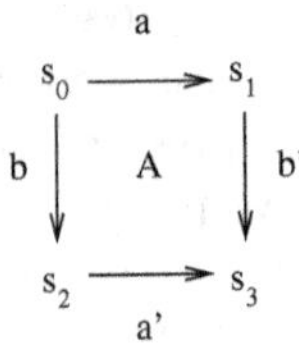

where A is a 2-transition, a, b, a', b' are 1-transitions and s_0, s_1, s_2 and s_3 are all 0-transitions (or states). We have $\partial_0^0(A) = a$, $\partial_0^1(A) = a'$, $\partial_1^0(A) = b$, $\partial_1^1(A) = b'$, $\partial_0^0(a) = \partial_0^0(b) = s_0$, $\partial_0^1(a) = s_1 = \partial_0^0(b')$, $\partial_0^1(b) = \partial_0^0(a') = s_2$ and $\partial_1^1(b') = \partial_1^1(a') = s_3$. One can readily check the commutation rules of the definition, for instance, $\partial_0^0\partial_1^1(A) = \partial_0^0(b') = s_1 = \partial_0^1(a) = \partial_0^1\partial_0^0(A)$. We should think in the sequel, of A as representing the independance of a and b.

Example. We know from [1] that the po-space and the component category corresponding to the PV program (where **a** is a binary semaphore) $A = Pa.Va$ in parallel with $B = Pa.Va$ are those pictured at Figure 5, respectively, of Figure 6.

As a matter of fact, the precubical set (here of dimension 1, since there is no relation between morphisms here) corresponding to this component category can be pictured as in Figure 7.

Intuition of the Inductive Algorithm. Now, what if we dig in a new hole in the po-space of Figure 5? We get the po-space pictured in Figure 8 and should obtain the component category (where solid squares represent relations) pictured in Figure 9. This po-space corresponds to the PV program $A = Pa.Va.Pb.Vb$ in

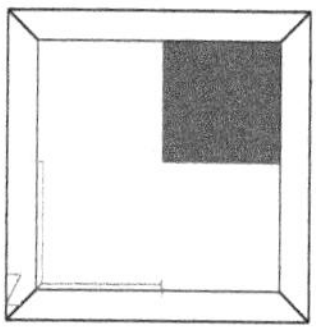

Fig. 5. Po-space corresponding to a simple PV program

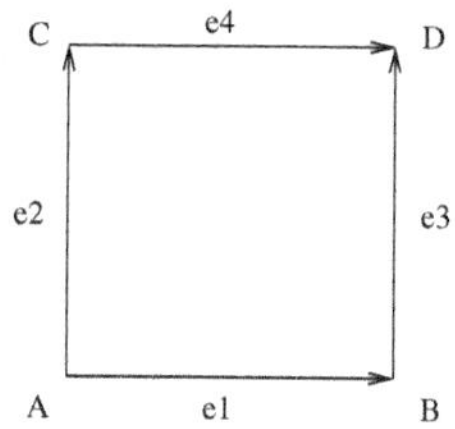

Fig. 6. Its component category

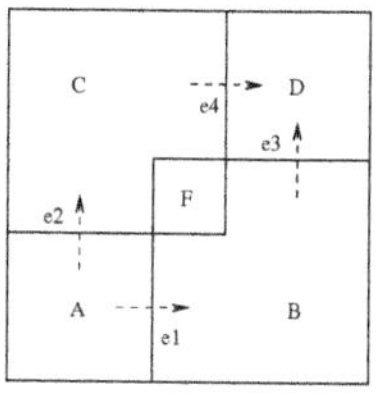

Fig. 7. The components, geometrically

parallel with $B = Pb.Vb.Pa.Va$ and the component category corresponds to the precubical set of dimension 2, pictured "geometrically" in Figure 10. The idea is that digging a new hole, creates new isothetic hyperplanes, coming out from the min and max points of this hole. These hyperplanes cut the previous components into new components; the orthogonal of these hyperplanes will create new edges in the component graph, or morphisms in the component category. A new phenomenon here is that the intersection of two hyperplanes (here lines), which give a codimension 2 linear variety in general (here, points), correspond to relations between newly created morphisms. Here, in Figure 10, F_2 is the new hole. The morphisms of the component category for the only hole F_1 are denoted here by f_1, f_2, f_3 and f_4. We see[3] in Figure 10 that we have two codimension 2 varieties of interest, namely the two intersections $e_1 \cap f_2$ and $e_3 \cap f_4$ which give the two relations, hence the two 2-cells of the component category, pictured in Figure 9.

In the case of the 3 philosophers problem, $A = Pa.Pb.Va.Vb$ parallel $B = Pb.Pc.Vb.Vc$ parallel $C = Pc.Pa.Vc.Va$, we get the very nice component category pictured in Figure 11 for instance, where the central point represents both the deadlocking and the unreachable regions.

Inductive Computation - the Algorithm. We start inductively by a component category of $[0,1]^n \backslash R$, generated by a 2-dimensional precubical set, that we write in short as $(Y_0, Y_1, Y_2, \delta^0, \delta^1)$. We define a new structure $(Z_0, Z_1, Z_2, \partial^0, \partial^1)$ as follows, which will generate (an "approximation" of) the component category of $U \backslash R$:

- $Z_0 = \{A \cap B \mid A \in X_0, B \in Y_0, A \cap B \neq \emptyset\}$
- $Z_1 = \begin{array}{l}\{A \cap f \mid A \in X_0, f \in Y_1, A \cap f \neq \emptyset\}\\ \cup\{e \cap B \mid e \in X_1, B \in Y_0, e \cap B \neq \emptyset\}\end{array}$
- $Z_2 = \begin{array}{l}\{e \cap f \mid e \in X_1, f \in Y_1, e \cap f \neq \emptyset\}\\ \cup\{R \cap B \mid R \in X_2, B \in Y_0, R \cap B \neq \emptyset\}\\ \cup\{A \cap S \mid A \in X_0, S \in Y_2, A \cap S \neq \emptyset\}\end{array}$

[3] The intersection $a \cap b$ in this figure are denoted by the pair a, b.

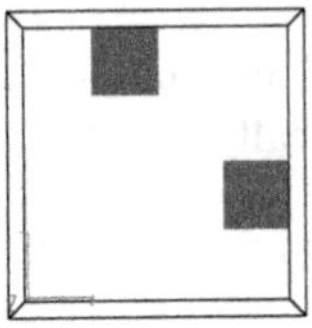

Fig. 8. Po-space with two incomparable holes

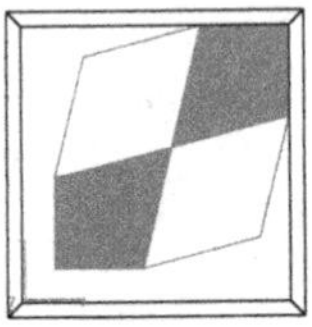

Fig. 9. Component category (squares are relations)

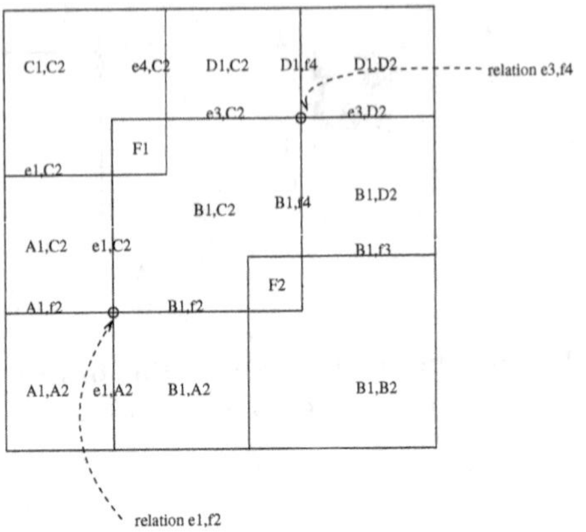

Fig. 10. The precubical set corresponding to the component category, geometrically

$\partial_*^* : Z_1 \to Z_0$ are defined by:

- $\partial_0^0(A \cap f) = A \cap \delta_0^0(f)$,
- $\partial_0^1(A \cap f) = A \cap \delta_0^1(f)$,
- $\partial_0^0(e \cap B) = d_0^0(e) \cap B$,
- $\partial_0^1(e \cap B) = d_0^1(e) \cap B$.

$\partial_*^* : Z_2 \to Z_1$ are defined by:

- $\partial_0^0(e \cap f) = d_0^0(e) \cap f$,
- $\partial_1^0(e \cap f) = e \cap \delta_0^0(f)$,
- $\partial_0^1(e \cap f) = d_0^1(e) \cap f$,
- $\partial_1^1(e \cap f) = e \cap \delta_0^1(f)$,
- $\partial_l^k(R \cap B) = d_l^k(R) \cap B$, $k, l = 0, 1$,
- $\partial_l^k(A \cap S) = A \cap \delta_l^k(S)$.

One can show that this gives an "over-approximation" of the component category in general, i.e. that one will get a compressed state-space, which might not be as optimal as the component category defined in [1]. Similarly, one can check easily that this, applied to the case of Figure 8 starting with the case of Figure 6 gives the right result of Figure 10.

3.3 Syntactic Lift

From the component category, we can deduce the maximal morphisms (or equivalently, the equivalences classes of maximal dipaths, or put it differently the maximal essential traces), basically from some traversing of the underlying graph modulo 2 cells. In the case of the maximal dipaths modulo dihomotopy for the 3 philosophers, we find 7 paths, the $3! = 6$ non-deadlocking paths, 3 of which are represented as blue lines in Figures 11, 12 and 13, one deadlocking path.

Now, we want to get back from these "continuous" paths to "discrete" paths. This "discrete" path should be an interleaving path corresponding to this idealized execution, which can then be analyzed by any standard sequential analyzer.

We remark, essentially by [1], that (1): every component has a trivial $\overrightarrow{\pi}_1$ and (2): there exists a path (unique) from the *minimum* (or infimum in general) from a component to the minimum of the next component (essentially by the lifting property). Given the morphisms of the component category, we compute:

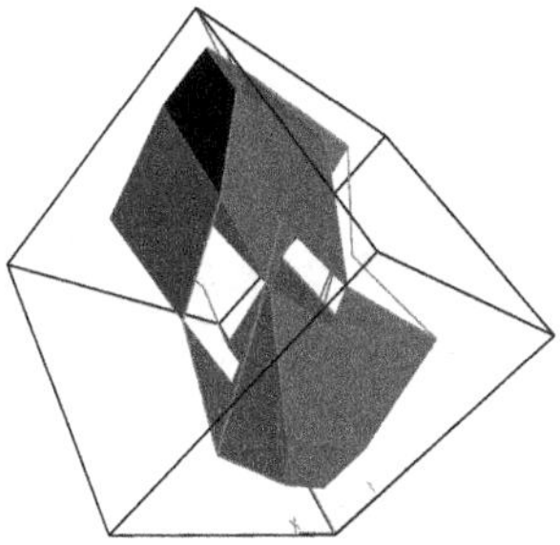

Fig. 11. Paths (1)

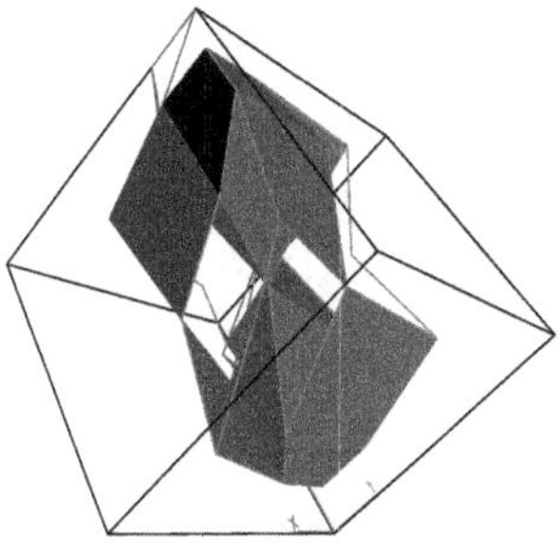

Fig. 12. Paths (2)

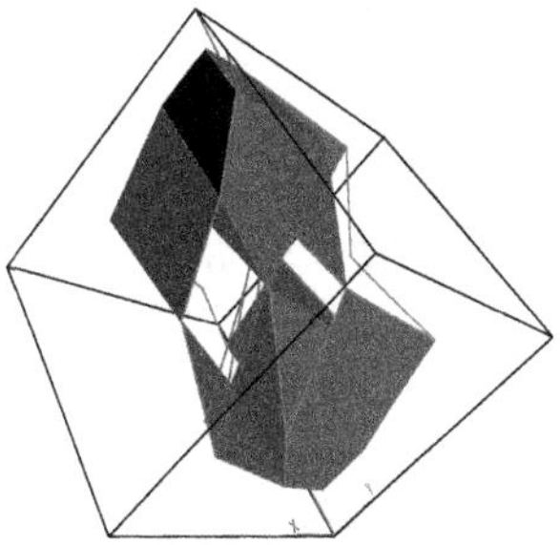

Fig. 13. Paths (3)

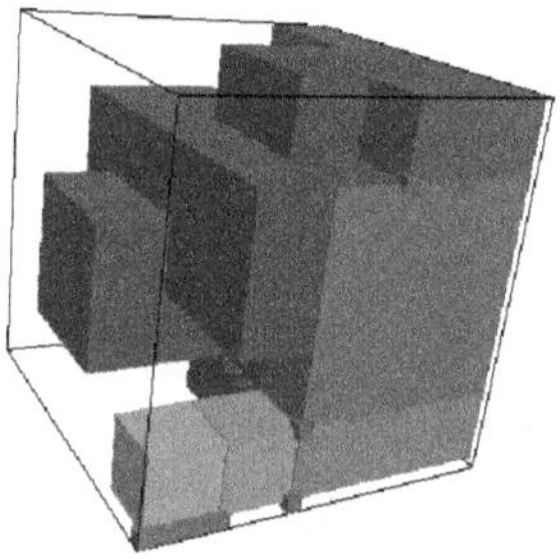

Fig. 14. First step

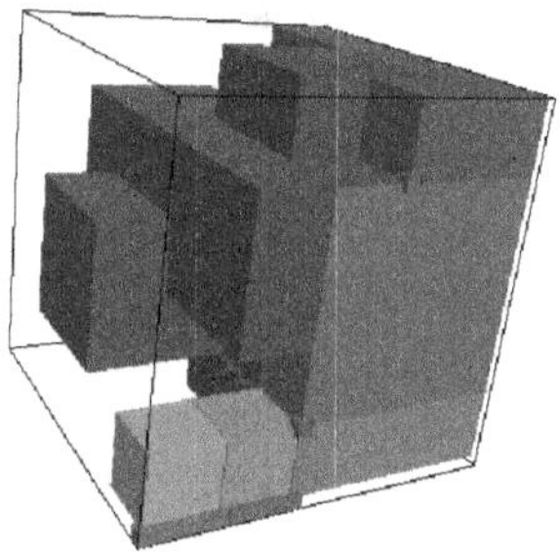

Fig. 15. Second step

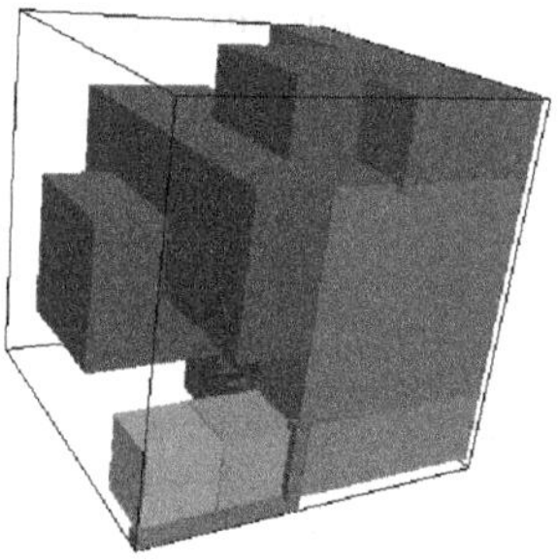

Fig. 16. Third step

- (a) the infimum of the components (i.e. of hyperrectangles minus the forbidden region)
- (b) the *program* comprising the possible executions between the minimum of a component, and the minimum of the next
- (c) we use the interleaving semantics for finding *just one path* in this program (using (1), in a very economical manner)

We exemplify this in Figures 14, 15, 16, 17, 18 and 19 for the 3 philosophers' problem. Forbidden regions are represented in blue, and components are represented from green to red, in a graded manner. We represent only maximal paths in the component category as sequences of such components in these figures.

Point (c) is done by taking any interleaving path for some program, extracted from *Prog* in a very easy manner, using the coordinates of the two consecutive infima points (represented as red dots) as intervals, in each coordinate, or equivalently for each process, of instructions to fire (this is represented as red chunks). The first step of the lifting is (Figure 14) amounts to interpreting `0 | 0 | P(c)` in context $sem(c) = 1$, $sem(b) = 1$, and $sem(a) = 1$. We use the notation $sem(x) = k$ to express that x is a semaphore which can be taken (by P) by at most k processes. This describes the state of our concurrent machine. The 2nd, 3rd, 4th, 5th and 6th steps are respectively described in Figures 15, 16, 17, 18 and 19.

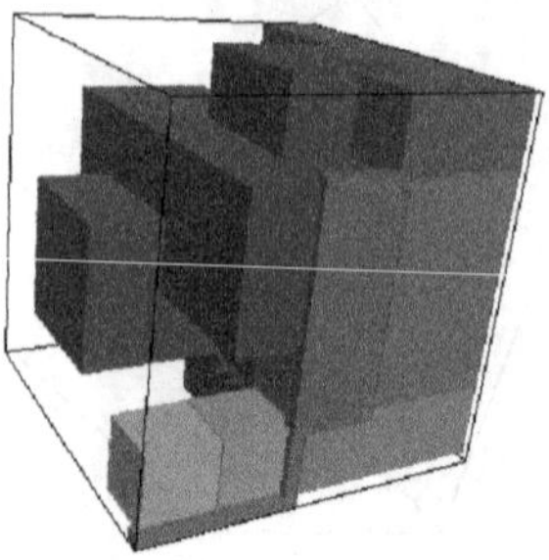

Fig. 17. Fourth step

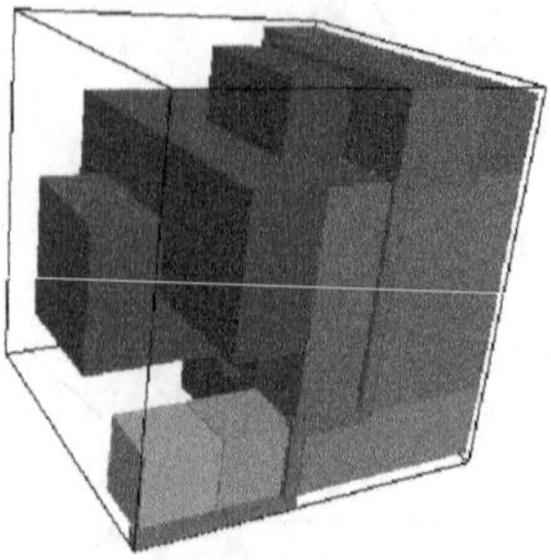

Fig. 18. Fifth step

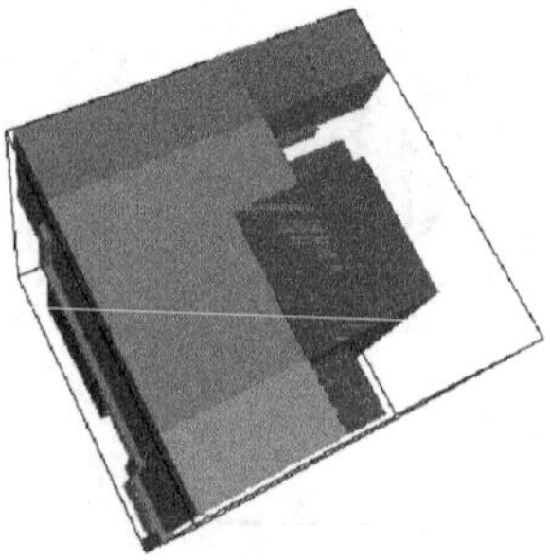

Fig. 19. Sixth step

The final interleaving representative is given at Figure 20 and corresponds to[4]:

$$P_3(c).P_3(a).P_2(b).V_3(c).P_2(c).V_2(b).V_2(c).V_3(a).P_1(a).P_1(b).V_1(a).V_1(b).$$

4 Application to Static Analysis

A static analyzer (ALCOOL) based on these principles has been implemented, it consists of about 25000 lines of C. It relies on Hans Boehm garbage collector [30] for memory allocation and QT for the graphical user interface. ALCOOL analyzes programs written in a high-level language, to be described elsewhere, extending the one of Section 2: binary semaphores, general counting semaphores but also synchronisation barriers and bounded and unbounded FIFO message passing queues (with various blocking/unblocking policies for sending and receiving) are modelled. Numeric variables are allowed, and guards (tests) are allowed in non-deterministic choices. General expressions on variables are understood, as well as iteration schemes. As such, this language is not far from the level of expressiveness of PROMELA [31], with a different syntax, aimed at the particular geometric models we have developped. A comparison with PROMELA, and SPIN, will be published elsewhere. An example of the syntax can be found in appendix A. The analyzer first represents an abstraction of the set of forbidden regions (as products of intervals in some subspace of R^n), from the syntax of the program to analyze. It then computes inductively, using the algorithm presented in Section 3.2, the component category, as a 2-dimensional precubical set both geometrically (meaning that the objects, morphisms and relations are represented as their corresponding 0-, 1- and 2-codimensional geometric varieties) and combinatorially, using the boundary operators. It represents internally also the duals of the boundary operators, the "coboundary" operators, mapping each i-dimensional object to the $(i+1)$-dimensional objects it is the boundary of. Using these coboundary operators for edges, and a simple depth-first or breadth-first traversal of the underlying graph, it can determine the maximal

[4] Where we put the number of the process which takes the step as a subscript of the P and V actions.

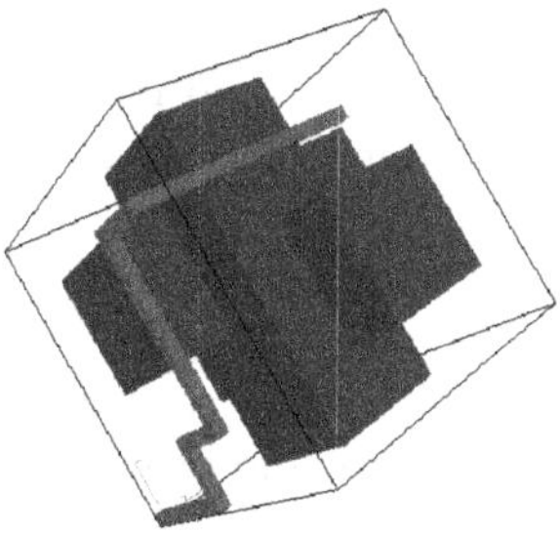

Fig. 20. The interleaving representative

dipaths modulo 2-cells (modulo dihomotopy), that is, the essential paths. From the essential paths, it determines using a simple abstract interpreter [32] (using intervals of values again), an over-approximation of the local invariants of the program. It has then to iterate this process again, since knowing more about the values of the variables at each reachable state, enables to qualify more precisely whether all the synchronisation that have been modelled as forbidden regions are actually done (because of the guards of the choices for instance). More about the look and feel of the analyzer can be found in appendix A. The analyzer has been applied to a variety of academic examples. For instance, the enumeration of the compressed state space of the n-philosophers' problem is shown for different values of n, on a standard PC with 512Mb of memory and 1GHz clock:

n	time	mem	# o	# m	# r	# p	#s	# t
3	0.38s	$\leq$ 10 Mb	27	48	18	6	576	1475
4	0.43s	$\leq$ 15 Mb	85	200	132	24	3966	13450
5	0.69	19 Mb	263	770	730	120	27265	113938
6	3.49	23 Mb	807	2832	3516	720	184876	914019
7	96.76s	42 Mb	2467	10094	15484	5040	?	?
8	1656.9s	100Mb	7533	35216	64312	40320	?	?
9	13739s	319Mo	22995	120924	256158	362880	~2996970*	~22698700*

where # o, # m and # r denote respectively the number of objects, morphisms and relations of the component category, # p is the number of maximal terminating paths (not counting the deadlocking path for instance) and # s (respectively # t) is the number of states (respectively transitions) used in the translation of the n-philosophers' problem for SPIN with the partial-order reduction package (in PROMELA) of [33][5]. For the 9 philosophers' problem, we have only an estimate $\sim \ldots^*$, using the bit state hashing reduction technique.

This analyzer has also been applied to a real industrial example, for the french electricity provider EDF. The code to analyze was a 100000 lines program written in C, comprising a dozen threads running on top of the VXWORKS op-

[5] Some other implementations of the n-philosophers' problem may find different numbers of states and transitions: our experience is that it can vary from 1 to 10.

erating system. These threads communicate through FIFO queues, and synchronize using several dozens of semaphores and monitors. First, this code has been translated in the ALCOOL language (an extract of a typical example is given in Appendix A). This can now be done using the tool MIEL, by Jean-Michel Collart (CEA/LIST), which will be described elsewhere. The first analysis has been made using a handmade translation, taking into account a subgroup of six processes, accounting for 1966 lines of process algebra code, much like the ones shown in Appendix A. The analyzer could prove (using some restrictive assumptions though) that there is no deadlock, no loss of message in 497.43 seconds, for a maximal memory consumption of 47 Mb. In order to do this, it enumerated the class of execution paths (about 6.2 Mb in textual form) and interpret them using a simple interval abstract interpreter.

5 Conclusion and Future Work

We have described a first step towards using geometric invariants for efficient static analysis of concurrent programs. Much work is still to do. For instance, the computation of components is still sub-optimal (in size). We could also use static/dynamic segment trees to improve the computation of intersections, or simpler geometric constraints to prune the intersection search. For the computation of morphisms in the component category, we could think of getting some help from the first homology group. We can also approximate relations using some techniques used in persistent sets [34] for instance. On the longer run, we think that the consideration of higher-dimensional analogues of the fundamental category (see [6] and in particular [35]) should help us having smaller retracts of the state space. We should also point out that some other methods used to compress the state space being entirely orthogonal to our technique, we should combine the latter with symbolic methods, use of symmetry, on the fly traversal etc. We would also like to generalize our current ALCOOL analyzer so that it can deal with more general temporal logic formulas. For the time being, loops (and non-deterministic branchings) are interpreted in a simplistic way, by just unravelling them. We are currently trying to see if we can extend our method to local po-spaces [5] directly.

Acknowledgments. We used Geomview, see the Web page `http://freeabel.geom.umn.--edu/software/download/geomview.html/` to make the 3D pictures of this article (in a fully automated way, from ALCOOL). Acknowledgments are due to Fabrice Derepas for his help with comparing ALCOOL with SPIN. Acknowledgments to Jean-Michel Collart (CEA), Alain Ourghanlian and Jean-Baptiste Chabannes (EDF).

References

1. Fajstrup, L., Goubault, E., Haucourt, E., Raussen, M.: Components of the fundamental category. Applied Categorical Structures (2004)
2. Dijkstra, E.: Cooperating Sequential Processes. Academic Press (1968)

3. Nachbin, L.: Topology and Order. Van Nostrand, Princeton (1965)
4. Johnstone, P.T.: Stone Spaces. Cambridge University Press (1982)
5. Fajstrup, L., Goubault, E., Raussen, M.: Algebraic topology and concurrency. submitted to Theoretical Computer Science, also technical report, Aalborg University (1999)
6. Goubault, E.: Some geometric perspectives in concurrency theory. Homology Homotopy and Applications (2003)
7. Goubault, E., Raussen, M.: Dihomotopy as a tool in state space analysis. In Rajsbaum, S., ed.: LATIN 2002: Theoretical Informatics. Volume 2286 of Lect. Notes Comput. Sci., Cancun, Mexico, Springer-Verlag (2002) 16 – 37
8. Gabriel, P., Zisman, M.: Calculus of fractions and homotopy theory. Number 35 in Ergebnisse der Mathematik und ihrer Grenzgebiete. Springer Verlag (1967)
9. Haucourt, E.: A framework for component categories. ENTCS (to appear, 2005)
10. Mac Lane, S.: Categories for the working mathematician. Springer-Verlag (1971)
11. Gaucher, P., Goubault, E.: Topological deformation of higher dimensional automata. Technical report, arXiv:math.AT/010760, to appear in HHA (2001)
12. Godefroid, P., Peled, D., Staskauskas, M.: Using partial-order methods in the formal validation of industrial concurrent programs. IEEE Transactions on Software Engineering **22** (1996) 496–507
13. Godefroid, P., Holzmann, G.J., Pirottin, D.: State-space caching revisited. In: Formal Methods and System Design. Volume 7., Kluwer Academic Publishers (1995) 1–15
14. Valmari, A.: A stubborn attack on state explosion. In: Proc. of CAV'90, Springer Verlag, LNCS (1990)
15. Valmari, A.: Eliminating redundant interleavings during concurrent program verification. In: Proc. of PARLE. Volume 366., Springer-Verlag, Lecture Notes in Computer Science (1989) 89–103
16. Melzer, S., Roemer, S.: Deadlock checking using net unfoldings. In: Proc. of Computer Aided Verification, Springer-Verlag (1997)
17. Mazurkiewicz, A.: Basic notions of trace theory. In: Lecture notes for the REX summer school in temporal logic, Springer-Verlag (1988)
18. Cousot, P., Cousot, R.: Abstract interpretation: A unified lattice model for static analysis of programs by construction of approximations of fixed points. Principles of Programming Languages 4 (1977) 238–252
19. Boigelot, B., Godefroid, P.: Model checking in practice: An analysis of the access.bus protocol using spin. In: Proceedings of Formal Methods Europe'96. Volume 1051., Springer-Verlag, Lecture Notes in Computer Science (1996) 465–478
20. Burch, J.R., Clarke, E.M., McMillan, K.L., Dill, D.L., Hwang, L.J.: Symbolic model checking: 10^{20} states and beyond. In: Proc. of the Fifth Annual IEEE Symposium on Logic and Computer Science, IEEE Press (1990) 428–439
21. Garavel, H., Jorgensen, M., Mateescu, R., Pecheur, C., Sighireanu, M., Vivien, B.: Cadp'97 – status, applications and perspectives. Technical report, Inria Alpes (1997)
22. Raussen, M.: Deadlocks and dihomotopy in mutual exclusion models. Technical report, Aalborg University (2005) available at http://www.math.aau.dk/index_en.html.
23. Carson, S., Reynolds, P.: The geometry of semaphore programs. ACM TOPLAS **9** (1987) 25–53
24. Gaucher, P.: A convenient category for the homotopy theory of concurrency. preprint available at math.AT/0201252 (2002)

25. Grandis, M.: Directed homotopy theory, I. the fundamental category. Cahiers Top. Gom. Diff. Catg, to appear, Preliminary version: Dip. Mat. Univ. Genova, Preprint 443 (2001)
26. Spanier, E.J.: Algebraic Topology. McGraw Hill (1966)
27. Goubault, E.: Geometry and concurrency: A users' guide. Mathematical Structures in Computer Science (2000)
28. Goubault, E.: Cubical sets are generalized transition systems. Technical report, pre-proceedings of CMCIM'02, also available at http://www.di.ens.fr/˜goubault (2001)
29. Fahrenberg, U.: A category of higher-dimensional automata. In: Foundations of Software Science and Computation Structures (FOSSACS) : 8th International Conference. LNCS, Springer (2005) to appear.
30. Boehm, H.: Bounding space usage of conservative garbage collector. In: Principles Of Programing Language. (2002) see http://www.hpl.hp.com/personal/Hans_Boehm/gc/.
31. Holzmann, G.J.: SPIN Model Checker : The Primer and Reference Manual. Addison Wesley (2003)
32. Cousot, P., Cousot, R.: Comparison of the Galois connection and widening/narrowing approaches to abstract interpretation. JTASPEFL '91, Bordeaux. BIGRE **74** (1991) 107–110
33. Demartini, C., Iosif, R., Sisto, R.: Modeling and validation of java multithreading applications using spin. In: SPIN Workshop. (1998)
34. Godefroid, P., Wolper, P.: Using partial orders for the efficient verification of deadlock freedom and safety properties. In: Proc. of the Third Workshop on Computer Aided Verification. Volume 575., Springer-Verlag, Lecture Notes in Computer Science (1991) 417–428
35. Grandis, M.: The shape of a category up to directed homotopy. Technical Report preprint 509, Dip. Mat. Univ. Genova (2004) available at http://www.dima.unige.it/∼grandis/rec.public_grandis.html.

A ALCOOL Analyzer

Let us give a simple example, in the language used by ALCOOL. Here we define two FIFO queues containing at most one entry, x and y, and two semaphores z and evt. `INIT` is a reserved keyword for initializing, before starting any process (see PROMELA) the context of execution. `@(a,5)` stands for setting value 5 to variable `a`. We can also use general interval expressions, such as `[0,2]`. `PROG` is a reserved keyword to express which are the processes put in parallel. `R(x,z)` stands for (blocking) receive on channel `x`, and put the received value in z (value "protected" by semaphore `z`). `A+[x=0]-B` stands for: do `A` is guard (here `x=0`) is true, otherwise, do `B`. The definition of `automate` as a "matrix" of actions times events is typical of actuation and control software. `S(x,7)` stands for (non-blocking) send on channel `x`, of value 7.

```
#fifo x
#fifo y
#sem z
#sem evt
```

```
INIT=@(a,5).@(z,0).@(evt,[0,2])
PROG=automate|tache

act1=R(x,z).@(z,z*2)
act2=R(y,z).@(z,z*3+1)
act3=Pa.@(a,1).Va
ligneA=act1+[a=0]-(act2+[a=1]-(act3+[a=2]-))
ligneB=act2+[a=0]-(act3+[a=1]-(act1+[a=2]-))
ligneC=act3+[a=0]-(act1+[a=1]-(act2+[a=2]-))
matrice=ligneA+[evt=0]-(ligneB+[evt=1]-(ligneC+[evt=2]-))
automate=matrice.automate

tache=S(x,7).S(y,9).Pa.@(a,0).Va.Pa.@(a,2).Va
```

Verification of Qualitative $\mathbb{Z}$ Constraints

Stéphane Demri and Régis Gascon

LSV/CNRS UMR 8643 & INRIA Futurs projet SECSI & ENS Cachan,
61, av. Pdt. Wilson, 94235 Cachan Cedex, France
{demri, gascon}@lsv.ens-cachan.fr

Abstract. We introduce an LTL-like logic with atomic formulae built over a constraint language interpreting variables in $\mathbb{Z}$. The constraint language includes periodicity constraints, comparison constraints of the form $x = y$ and $x < y$, it is closed under Boolean operations and it admits a restricted form of existential quantification. This is the largest set of qualitative constraints over $\mathbb{Z}$ known so far, shown to admit a decidable LTL extension. Such constraints are those used for instance in calendar formalisms or in abstractions of counter automata by using congruences modulo some power of two. Indeed, various programming languages perform arithmetic operators modulo some integer. We show that the satisfiability and model-checking problems (with respect to an appropriate class of constraint automata) for this logic are decidable in polynomial space improving significantly known results about its strict fragments. As a by-product, LTL model-checking over integral relational automata is proved complete for polynomial space which contrasts with the known undecidability of its CTL counterpart.

1 Introduction

Model-Checking Infinite-State Systems. The verification of systems with an infinite amount of states has benefited from the numerous decidable model-checking problems for infinite-state systems, including timed automata [AD94], infinite transition graphs [Cau03], or subclasses of counter systems (see e.g. [CJ98]). Even though decidability can be obtained via numerous proof techniques (finite partition of the infinite domain, well-structured systems, Presburger definable reachability sets, reduction to the second-order theory of the binary tree), showing undecidability of model-checking for some classes of infinite-state systems is often easy. After all, the halting problem for Minsky machines is already undecidable. Decidability is more difficult to establish and it can be sometimes regained by naturally restricting the class of models (see e.g. the flatness condition in [CJ98]) or by considering fragments of the specification language (to consider only reachability or repeated reachability for instance).

Systems with Variables Interpreted in $\mathbb{Z}$. Structures with a finite set of control states augmented with a finite set of variables interpreted either in $\mathbb{Z}$ or in $\mathbb{N}$ (counters) are operational models of numerous infinite-state systems, including broadcast protocols (see e.g. [EFM99, FL02]). The class of counter machines

M. Abadi and L. de Alfaro (Eds.): CONCUR 2005, LNCS 3653, pp. 518–532, 2005.

has numerous undecidable model-checking problems such as the reachability problem but many classes of counter systems have been shown to be decidable: reversal-bounded multicounter machines [Iba78], flat counter systems with affine update functions forming a finite monoid [Boi98, FL02, BFLP03], flat counter systems [CJ98] (weaker class of Presburger guards but no condition on the monoid) and constraint automata with qualitative constraints on $\mathbb{Z}$ [DD03].

Our Motivation. Constraint automata with qualitative constraints on $\mathbb{Z}$ are quite attractive operational models since they can be viewed as abstractions of counter automata where incrementations and decrementations are abstracted by operations modulo some power of two. Common programming languages perform arithmetic operators for integer types modulo 2^k [MOS05], typically k is either 32 or 64. For example, $x = y+1$ can be abstracted by $x \equiv_{2^k} y+1 \wedge y < x$. Such an abstraction is well-suited to check safety properties about the original counter system. In the paper, we study a class of constraint automata with a language of qualitative constraints as rich as possible and a companion LTL-like logic to perform model-checking on such operational models. Our framework should be able to deal both with abstractions modulo (see e.g. [CGL94, LS01]) and with integer periodicity constraints used in logical formalisms to deal with calendars [LM01], i.e. constraints of the form $x \equiv_k y + c$. By a qualitative constraint, we mean for instance a constraint that is interpreted as a non-deterministic binary relation, like $x < y$ and $x \equiv_{2^k} y + 5$ (the relationship between x and y is not sharp).

Our Contribution. We introduce a version of constraint LTL over the constraint language IPC*, whose expressions are Boolean combinations of IPC^{++} constraints from [Dem04] and constraints of the form $x < y$. The language IPC^{++} is already closed under Boolean operators and first-order quantification. No constraint of the form $x < y$ occurs in the scope of a quantifier. Otherwise incrementation is definable and it leads to undecidability of the logic. So, as shown in this paper, adding the single type of constraints $x < y$ leads to many technical complications, but not to undecidability. We call CLTL(IPC*) the specification language built over IPC* constraints. We also introduce the class of IPC*-automata defined as finite-state automata with transitions labelled by CLTL(IPC*) formula à la Wolper [Wol83]. Such structures can be viewed as labelled transition systems obtained by abstraction of counter automata.

Constraint LTL over IPC^{++} is shown to be in PSPACE in [Dem04] whereas constraint LTL over constraints of the form either $x = y$ or $x < y$ is also shown to be in PSPACE in [DD03]. Both proofs use reductions to the emptiness problem for Büchi automata following the approach in [VW94]. However, the proofs are of different nature: in [Dem04] the complexity upper bound is obtained by a finite model property argument whereas in [DD03] approximations of classes of symbolic models are considered because some formulae can generate non ω-regular classes of symbolic models. We show that model-checking and satisfiability problems for the logic CLTL(IPC*) are decidable (which was open so far) and moreover in PSPACE (PSPACE-hardness is easy). The proof substantially generalizes what is done for constraint LTL over the domain $\langle \mathbb{Z}, <, = \rangle$ by considering both new constraints of the form $x \leq d$, $d \in \mathbb{Z}$ and integer periodicity constraints. The optimal treatment of constants occurring in such constraints is our main technical contribution. As a corollary, we establish that LTL model-checking over integral relational automata [Čer94] is PSPACE-complete. Hence, even though IPC* is a powerful language of qualitative constraints, the PSPACE upper bound is preserved in CLTL(IPC*). To our opinion, we provide a definite complexity characterization of LTL with qualitative constraints over $\mathbb{Z}$.

Related Work. Reachability problems for subclasses of counter systems have been addressed for instance in [Iba78, CJ98, FL02, BFLP03] (see also richer questions in [BEM97, JKMS04]). In our work, we have a full LTL-like language, not restricted to reachability questions, used as a specification language and no restriction on the structure of the models. However, atomic formulae of the specification language are qualitative constraints. If we give up the decidability requirement, LTL over Presburger constraints can be found in [BEH95, CC00].

Constraint LTL over concrete domains (not only restricted to $\mathbb{Z}$) has been considered in [WZ00, BC02, DD03, GKK$^+$03, Dem04] where often PSPACE-completeness is shown. The idea of building LTL over a language of constraints, although already present in first-order temporal logics, stems from the use of concrete domains for description logics, see e.g. [Lut04]. The language CLTL(IPC*) extends the different LTL-like fragments from [Čer94, LM01, DD03, Dem04] (past-time operators can be added for free in our formalism thanks to [GK03]). The class of IPC*-automata introduced in the paper generalizes the class of integral relational automata from [Čer94] (see details in [DG05]).

Integer periodicity constraints, a special class of Presburger constraints, have found applications in many formalisms such as abstractions with congruences modulo an integer of the form 2^k (see e.g. [CGL94, MOS05]), logical formalisms dealing with calendars (see e.g. [LM01]), DATALOG with integer periodicity constraints [TC98] and in real-time logics [AH94].

Omitted proofs can be found in [DG05].

2 The Logic CLTL(IPC*)

2.1 Language of Constraints

Let $V = \{x_0, x_1, \ldots\}$ be a countably infinite set of variables (in some places for ease of presentation, V will denote a particular finite set of variables). The language of constraints p is defined by the following grammar:

$$p ::= pmod \mid x < y \mid p \wedge p \mid \neg p$$

$$pmod ::= x \equiv_k [c_1, c_2] \mid x \equiv_k y + [c_1, c_2] \mid x = y \mid x < d \mid x = d \mid pmod \wedge pmod \mid \neg pmod \mid \exists x \; pmod$$

where $x, y \in V$, $k \in \mathbb{N} \setminus \{0\}$, $c_1, c_2 \in \mathbb{N}$ and $d \in \mathbb{Z}$. This language is denoted by IPC*. We write IPC^{++} to denote its restriction to constraints ranged over by *pmod*, and $\mathrm{Z^c}$ its restriction to constraints of the form either $x \sim y$ or $x \sim d$. The symbol $\sim$ is used to mean either $=$ or $<$. The language Z is the restriction of $\mathrm{Z^c}$ to constraints of the form $x \sim y$. We define a valuation v as a map $v : V \rightarrow \mathbb{Z}$ and the satisfaction relation $v \models_\star p$ is defined as follows in the standard way:

- $v \models_\star x \sim y \overset{\text{def}}{\Leftrightarrow} v(x) \sim v(y)$; $v \models_\star x \sim d \overset{\text{def}}{\Leftrightarrow} v(x) \sim d$;
- $v \models_\star x \equiv_k [c_1, c_2] \overset{\text{def}}{\Leftrightarrow} v(x)$ is equal to c modulo k for some $c_1 \leq c \leq c_2$;
- $v \models_\star x \equiv_k y + [c_1, c_2] \overset{\text{def}}{\Leftrightarrow} v(x) - v(y)$ is equal to c modulo k for some $c_1 \leq c \leq c_2$;
- $v \models_\star p \wedge p' \overset{\text{def}}{\Leftrightarrow} v \models_\star p$ and $v \models_\star p'$; $v \models_\star \neg p \overset{\text{def}}{\Leftrightarrow}$ not $v \models_\star p$;
- $v \models_\star \exists x\ p \overset{\text{def}}{\Leftrightarrow}$ there is $z \in \mathbb{Z}$ such that $v[x \leftarrow z] \models_\star p$ where $v[x \leftarrow z](x') = v(x')$ if $x \neq x'$ and $v[x \leftarrow z](x) = z$.

We recall that x is equal to y modulo k if there is $z \in \mathbb{Z}$ such that $x - y = k \times z$. We write $x \equiv_k c$ instead of $x \equiv_k [c, c]$, $x \equiv_k y + c$ instead of $x \equiv_k y + [c, c]$ and $v \models_\star X$ where X is a set of IPC*-constraints, whenever $v \models_\star p$ for every $p \in X$.

A constraint p is satisfiable iff there is a valuation v such that $v \models_\star p$. Two constraints are equivalent iff they are satisfied by the same valuations.

Lemma 1. *(I) The satisfiability problem for* IPC* *is* PSPACE*-complete. (II) Every constraint in* IPC* *admits an equivalent quantifier-free constraint in* IPC*.

Hence, IPC* is a quite well understood fragment of Presburger arithmetic.

2.2 Logical Language

We consider the linear-time temporal logic CLTL(IPC*) whose atomic formulae are defined from constraints in IPC*. The atomic formulae are of the form $p[x_1 \leftarrow \mathsf{X}^{i_1} x_{j_1}, \ldots, x_r \leftarrow \mathsf{X}^{i_r} x_{j_r}]$, where p is a constraint of IPC* with free variables $x_1 \ldots x_r$. We substitute each occurrence of the variable x_l with $\mathsf{X}^{i_l} x_{j_l}$, which corresponds to the variable x_{j_l} preceded by i_l next symbols. Each expression of the form $\mathsf{X}^{\beta} x_\alpha$ is called a term and represents the value of the variable x_α at the βth next state. Here are examples of atomic formulae: $\mathsf{X}y \equiv_{2^{32}} x + 1$ and $x < \mathsf{X}y$.

The set of CLTL(IPC*) formulae ϕ is defined by

$$\phi ::= p[x_1 \leftarrow \mathsf{X}^{i_1} x_{j_1}, \ldots, x_r \leftarrow \mathsf{X}^{i_r} x_{j_r}] \mid \neg\phi \mid \phi \wedge \phi \mid \mathsf{X}\phi \mid \phi \mathsf{U} \phi,$$

where p belongs to IPC*. The operators next (X) and until (U) are the classical operators used in temporal logics. In the language, all the integers are encoded with a binary representation (this is important for complexity considerations). Given a set of constraints X included in IPC*, we write CLTL(X) to denote the restriction of CLTL(IPC*) in which the atomic constraints are built over elements of X.

A model $\sigma : \mathbb{N} \times V \rightarrow \mathbb{Z}$ for CLTL(IPC*) is an ω-sequence of valuations. The satisfaction relation is defined as follows (we omit the Boolean cases):

- $\sigma, i \models p[x_1 \leftarrow \mathsf{X}^{i_1} x_{j_1}, \ldots, x_r \leftarrow \mathsf{X}^{i_r} x_{j_r}]$ iff $[x_1 \leftarrow \sigma(i + i_1, x_{j_1}), \ldots, x_r \leftarrow \sigma(i + i_r, x_{j_r})] \models_\star p$;
- $\sigma, i \models \mathsf{X}\phi$ iff $\sigma, i + 1 \models \phi$;
- $\sigma, i \models \phi \mathsf{U} \phi'$ iff there is $j \geq i$ s.t. $\sigma, j \models \phi'$ and for every $i \leq l < j$, $\sigma, l \models \phi$.

By definition, CLTL(IPC*)-models interpret variables but not propositional variables. However, it is easy to encode propositional variables by using atomic formulae of the form $x = 0$ where x is a new variable introduced for this purpose.

2.3 Satisfiability and Model-Checking Problems

We recall below the problems we are interested in.

Satisfiability Problem for CLTL(IPC*): Given a CLTL(IPC*) formula ϕ, is there a model σ such that $\sigma, 0 \models \phi$?

If we extend IPC* to allow constraints of the form $x < y$ in the scope of $\exists$, then the satisfiability problem for the corresponding constraint LTL-like logic is undecidable since the successor relation is then definable and the halting problem for Minsky machines can be easily encoded.

The model-checking problem rests on IPC*-automata which are constraint automata. An IPC*-automaton $\mathcal{A}$ is defined as a Büchi automaton over the infinite alphabet composed of CLTL(IPC*) formulae. In an IPC*-automaton, letters on transitions may induce constraints between the variables of the current state and the variables of the next state as done in [CC00]. Hence, guards and update functions are expressed in the same formalism. We are however a bit more general since we allow formulae on transitions as done in [Wol83]. As an illustration, we present an IPC*-automaton in Fig. 1 which is an abstraction of the pay-phone controller from [CC00, Example 1] (x is the number of quarters which have been inserted and y measures the total communication time). Incrementation of a variable z is abstracted by $\mathsf{X}z \equiv_{2^{32}} z + 1 \wedge \mathsf{X}z > z$. The formula $\phi_{=}$ denotes $\mathsf{X}x = x \wedge \mathsf{X}y = y$. Messages are omitted because they are irrelevant here (simplifications are then possible).

Model-Checking Problem for CLTL(IPC*): Given an IPC*-automaton $\mathcal{A}$ and a CLTL(IPC*) formula ϕ, are there a symbolic ω-word $v = \phi_0 \cdot \phi_1 \cdot \ldots$ accepted

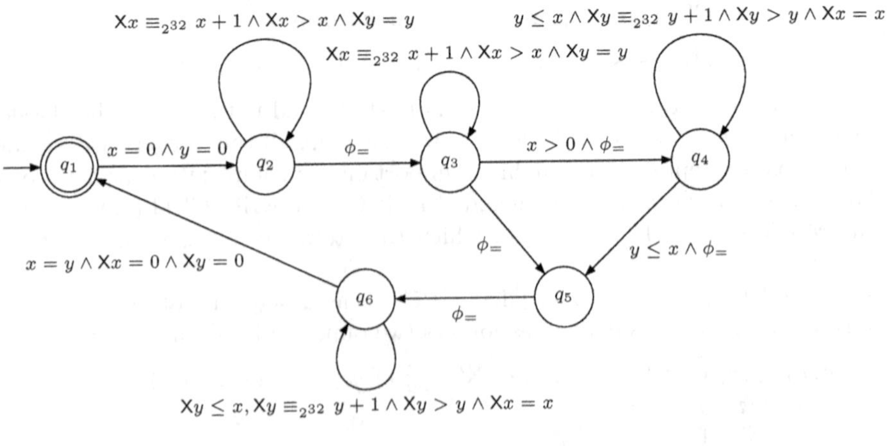

Fig. 1. An IPC*-automaton

by $\mathcal{A}$ and a model σ (a realization of v) such that $\sigma, 0 \models \phi$ and for every $i \geq 0$, $\sigma, i \models \phi_i$?

The satisfiability problem and the model-checking problem are reducible to each other in logspace following techniques from [SC85], by possibly introducing a new variable. In the following sections, we prove results for the satisfiability problem but they also extend to the model-checking problem.

The equivalence problem for Extended Single-String automata [LM01] can be encoded as a model-checking problem for CLTL(IPC*) [Dem04]. Furthermore, the model-checking problem for integral relational automata restricted to the LTL fragment of CCTL* introduced in [Čer94] is a subproblem of the model-checking problem for CLTL(IPC*) (see details in [DG05]). The model-checking problem for CLTL(IPC^{++}) (resp. CLTL(Z)) is shown to be PSPACE-complete in [Dem04] (resp. in [DD03]). However, the proof for IPC^{++} uses an ω-regular property of the set of models that does not hold when we introduce constraints of the form $x < y$. The problem for CLTL(Z^c) is shown to be in EXPSPACE in [DD03] by a translation into CLTL(Z) that increases exponentially the size of formulae (with a binary encoding of the natural numbers).

A restricted IPC*-automaton is defined as an IPC*-automaton such that the labels on transitions are Boolean combinations of atomic formulae with terms of the form x and $\mathsf{X}x$ (see Fig. 1). The logic CCTL*(IPC*) (constraint CTL* over IPC* constraints) is defined as the extension of CLTL(IPC*) with the path quantifiers $\exists$ and $\forall$ but restricted to atomic formulae with no variables in V preceded by X. The models of CCTL*(IPC*) are the configuration graphs of restricted IPC*-automata. The satisfaction relation $\mathcal{A}, \langle q, \overline{x} \rangle \models \phi$ is defined in the usual way. The model-checking problem for CCTL*(IPC*) takes as inputs a restricted IPC*-automaton $\mathcal{A}$, an initial configuration $\langle q, \overline{0} \rangle$ (q is a control state and $\overline{0}$ is the initial valuation with null values for the variables) and a CCTL*(IPC*) formula ϕ and checks whether $\mathcal{A}, \langle q, \overline{0} \rangle \models \phi$. Full CCTL*(IPC*) model-checking can be shown to be undecidable by using developments in [DG05] and [Čer94] (even its CTL-like fragment) and one can show that its LTL fragment is decidable in polynomial space, a new result not captured by [Čer94].

3 Properties of the Constraint Language

In this section, we establish results about the constraint language underlying the logic CLTL(IPC*). In order to define automata that recognize symbolic representations of CLTL(IPC*)-models, the valuations v of the form $V \to \mathbb{Z}$ are represented by symbolic valuations. Given a finite set X of IPC* constraints, typically the set of constraints occurring in a given CLTL(IPC*) formula, we introduce the following notations:

- K is the lcm of $k_1, \ldots, k_n$ where periodicity constraints with relations $\equiv_{k_1}$, $\ldots$, $\equiv_{k_n}$ occur in X. Observe that $|K|$ is in $\mathcal{O}(|k_1| + \cdots + |k_n|)$.
- C is the set of constants d occurring in constraints of the form $x \sim d$.
- m is the minimal element of C and M is its maximal element.

- C' denotes the set of constants $\{m, m-1, \ldots, M\}$. The cardinality of C' is in $\mathcal{O}(2^{|m|+|M|})$ and each element of C' can be binary encoded in binary representation with $\mathcal{O}(|m|+|M|)$ bits.
- V is the finite set of variables occurring in X.

In the remaining, we assume that the above objects are always defined (possibly by adding dummy valid constraints in order to make the sets non-empty).

A maximally consistent set Y of $\mathrm{Z^c}$ constraints with respect to V and C is a set of $\mathrm{Z^c}$ constraints using only the variables from V and the constants from C such that there is a valuation $v : V \to \mathbb{Z}$ verifying $v \models_\star Y$ and for any proper extension Z of Y, there is no valuation $v' : V \to \mathbb{Z}$ verifying $v' \models_\star Z$. A valuation is abstracted by three disjoint finite sets of IPC* constraints like regions for timed automata.

Definition 1. *Given a finite set X of* IPC* *constraints, a symbolic valuation sv is a triple $\langle Y_1, Y_2, Y_3 \rangle$ such that*

- *Y_1 is a maximally consistent set of $\mathrm{Z^c}$ constraints wrt V and C.*
- *Y_2 is a set of constraints of the form $x = d$ with $x \in V$ and $d \in C' \setminus C$. Each $x \in V$ occurs at most in one constraint of the form $x = d$ in Y_2. Moreover, for every $x \in V$, $(x = d) \in Y_2$ for some unique $d \in C' \setminus C$ iff for every $d' \in C$, $(x = d') \notin Y_1$ and $\{m < x, x < M\} \subseteq Y_1$.*
- *Y_3 is a set of constraints of the form $x \equiv_K c$ with $x \in V$ and $0 \leq c \leq K-1$. Each $x \in V$ occurs exactly in one constraint of the form $x \equiv_K c$ in Y_3.*

A consequence of Definition 1 is that in a symbolic valuation $sv = \langle Y_1, Y_2, Y_3 \rangle$, no constraint occurs in more than one set. That is why, given an IPC* constraint p, we write $p \in sv$ instead of $p \in Y_1 \cup Y_2 \cup Y_3$. A symbolic valuation is satisfiable iff there is a valuation $v : V \to \mathbb{Z}$ such that $v \models_\star Y_1 \cup Y_2 \cup Y_3$.

Lemma 2. *Let X be a finite set of* IPC* *constraints and $sv = \langle Y_1, Y_2, Y_3 \rangle$ be a triple composed of* IPC* *constraints such that Y_1 is a set of $\mathrm{Z^c}$ constraints built over V and C, Y_2 is a set of $\mathrm{Z^c}$ constraints of cardinality at most $|V|$ built over V and $C' \setminus C$, Y_3 is a set of constraints of the form $x \equiv_K c$ of cardinality $|V|$. Checking whether sv is a satisfiable symbolic valuation can be done in polynomial-time in the sum of the respective size of X and sv.*

Maximal consistency of Y_1 can be checked in polynomial-time by using developments from [Čer94, Lemma 5.5]. Indeed, given a set Y of $\mathrm{Z^c}$ constraints built over V and C, a graph G_Y can be built such that Y is maximally consistent wrt V and C iff G_Y satisfies the conditions below. G_Y is a structure $\langle V \cup C, \xrightarrow{=}, \xrightarrow{<} \rangle$ such that $n \xrightarrow{\sim} n' \stackrel{\text{def}}{\Leftrightarrow} n \sim n'$ belongs to Y. Following [Čer94, Lemma 5.5], Y is maximally consistent iff G_Y satisfies the conditions below:

(MC1) For all n, n', either $n \xrightarrow{\sim} n'$ or $n' \xrightarrow{\sim} n$ for some $\sim \in \{<, =\}$.
(MC2) $\xrightarrow{=}$ is a congruence relation compatible with $\xrightarrow{<}$.
(MC3) There is no path $n_0 \xrightarrow{\sim_0} n_1 \xrightarrow{\sim_1} \ldots \xrightarrow{\sim_{\alpha-1}} n_\alpha$ with $n_0 = n_\alpha$ and $<$ occurs in $\{\sim_0, \sim_1, \ldots, \sim_{\alpha-1}\}$.

(MC4) For all $d_1, d_2 \in C$, $d_1 \sim d_2$ implies $d_1 \overset{\sim}{\rightarrow} d_2$.

(MC5) For all d_1, d_2 with $d_1 \leq d_2$, there is no path $n_0 \overset{\sim_0}{\rightarrow} n_1 \overset{\sim_1}{\rightarrow} \ldots \overset{\sim_{\alpha-1}}{\longrightarrow} n_\alpha$ with $n_0 = d_1$ and $n_\alpha = d_2$ such that the cardinality of $\{i :\sim_i$ equals $<, 1 \leq i \leq \alpha - 1\}$ is strictly more than $d_2 - d_1$.

The symbolic representations of valuations contain the relevant information to evaluate constraints.

Lemma 3. *Let X be a finite set of* IPC* *constraints. (I) For every valuation $v : V \rightarrow \mathbb{Z}$ there is a unique symbolic valuation $sv(v) = \langle Y_1, Y_2, Y_3 \rangle$ such that $v \models_\star Y_1 \cup Y_2 \cup Y_3$. (II) For all valuations v, v' such that $sv(v) = sv(v')$ and for every $p \in X$, $v \models_\star p$ iff $v' \models_\star p$.*

The proof of (I) is by an easy verification whereas (II) is shown by structural induction on p similarly to the proof of [Dem04, Lemma 1]. By Lemma 3, a symbolic valuation is an equivalence class of valuations.

Given a symbolic valuation sv and p a constraint, we write $sv \models_{\text{symb}} p \overset{\text{def}}{\Leftrightarrow}$ for every valuation v such that $sv(v) = sv$, $v \models_\star p$.

Lemma 4. *The problem of checking whether $sv \models_{\text{symb}} p$ is* PSPACE-*complete (given that the syntactic resources used in p are included in those used for the symbolic valuation sv).*

4 Satisfiable ω-Sequences of Symbolic Valuations

Given a CLTL(IPC*) formula ϕ, we write IPC$^\star(\phi)$ to denote the set of IPC* constraints p such that some atomic formula of the form $p[x_1 \leftarrow \mathsf{X}^{i_1} x_{j_1}, \ldots, x_r \leftarrow \mathsf{X}^{i_r} x_{j_r}]$ occurs in ϕ. To IPC$^\star(\phi)$ we associate the objects relative to any finite set of IPC* constraints. The set V denotes the set of variables occurring in ϕ. We write $|\phi|_\mathsf{X}$ to denote the maximal natural number i such that $\mathsf{X}^i x$ occurs in ϕ for some variable x. $|\phi|_\mathsf{X}$ is called the X-length of ϕ. Without any loss of generality, we can assume that $|\phi|_\mathsf{X} \geq 1$. In the following, we assume that $V = \{x_1, \ldots, x_s\}$ and $|\phi|_\mathsf{X} = l$. We write Terms(ϕ) to denote the set of terms of the form $\mathsf{X}^\beta x_\alpha$ with $\beta \in \{0, \ldots, l\}$ and $\alpha \in \{1, \ldots, s\}$.

Let V' be a set of variables of cardinality $|\text{Terms}(\phi)|$ and $f : \text{Terms}(\phi) \rightarrow V'$ be an unspecified bijection such that f and f^{-1} can be computed in polynomial time. By extension, for every atomic subformula p of ϕ, $f(p)$ is obtained from p by replacing each occurrence of $\mathsf{X}^\beta x_\alpha$ by $f(\mathsf{X}^\beta x_\alpha)$. The map f^{-1} is used in a similar fashion. A symbolic valuation wrt ϕ is a symbolic valuation built over the set of variables V', C and K.

We say that a pair $\langle \langle Y_1, Y_2, Y_3 \rangle, \langle Y_1', Y_2', Y_3' \rangle \rangle$ of symbolic valuations wrt ϕ is one-step consistent $\overset{\text{def}}{\Leftrightarrow}$

1. $f(\mathsf{X}^j x_i) \sim f(\mathsf{X}^{j'} x_{i'}) \in Y_1$ and $j, j' \geq 1$ imply $f(\mathsf{X}^{j-1} x_i) \sim f(\mathsf{X}^{j'-1} x_{i'}) \in Y_1'$,
2. $f(\mathsf{X}^j x_i) \sim d \in Y_1 \cup Y_2$ and $j \geq 1$ imply $f(\mathsf{X}^{j-1} x_i) \sim d \in Y_1' \cup Y_2'$,
3. $f(\mathsf{X}^j x_i) \equiv_K c \in Y_3$ and $j \geq 1$ imply $f(\mathsf{X}^{j-1} x_i) \equiv_K c \in Y_3'$.

An ω-sequence ρ of satisfiable symbolic valuations wrt ϕ is one-step consistent $\overset{\text{def}}{\Leftrightarrow}$ for every $j \in \mathbb{N}$, $\langle \rho(j), \rho(j+1) \rangle$ is one-step consistent. A model for ρ is defined as a CLTL(IPC*)-model σ such that for all $j \in \mathbb{N}$ and $p \in \rho(j)$, $\sigma, j \models f^{-1}(p)$. In order to simplify the future developments, we write ρ_f to denote the ω-sequence obtained from ρ by substituting each occurrence of some variable x by $f^{-1}(x)$.

One-step consistent ω-sequences of symbolic valuations wrt ϕ define abstractions of models for ϕ. We represent a one-step consistent sequence ρ as an infinite labeled structure $G_\rho = \langle (V \cup C') \times \mathbb{N}, \overset{\equiv}{\rightarrow}, \overset{\lesssim}{\rightarrow}, mod \rangle$ where $mod : (V \cup C') \times \mathbb{N} \rightarrow \{0, \ldots, K-1\}$:

$$
\begin{array}{ll}
\langle x, i \rangle \overset{\sim}{\rightarrow} \langle y, j \rangle & \text{iff either } i \leq j \text{ and } x \sim \mathsf{X}^{j-i} y \in \rho_f(i) \\
 & \quad \text{or } i > j \text{ and } \mathsf{X}^{i-j} x \sim y \in \rho_f(j), \\
\langle x, i \rangle \overset{\equiv}{\rightarrow} \langle d, j \rangle & \text{iff } x = d \ \in \rho_f(i), \\
\langle d, i \rangle \overset{\equiv}{\rightarrow} \langle x, j \rangle & \text{iff } x = d \ \in \rho_f(j), \\
\langle x, i \rangle \overset{\lesssim}{\rightarrow} \langle d, j \rangle & \text{iff there is } d' \sim d \text{ such that } x \sim' d' \ \in \rho_f(i) \text{ and } < \in \{\sim, \sim'\}, \\
\langle d, i \rangle \overset{\lesssim}{\rightarrow} \langle x, j \rangle & \text{iff there is } d \sim d' \text{ such that } d' \sim' x \ \in \rho_f(j) \text{ and } < \in \{\sim, \sim'\}, \\
\langle d_1, i \rangle \overset{\sim}{\rightarrow} \langle d_2, j \rangle & \text{iff } d_1 \sim d_2, \\
mod(\langle x, i \rangle) = c & \text{iff } x \equiv_K c \in \rho_f(i) \text{ and } mod(\langle d, i \rangle) = c \text{ iff } d \equiv_K c.
\end{array}
$$

for all $x, y \in V$, $d_1, d_2 \in C$ and $i, j \in \mathbb{N}$ such that $|i - j| \leq l$. By construction of G_ρ, the variables and constants are treated in a similar fashion. It is worth observing that G_ρ is well-defined because ρ is one-step consistent. The construction ensures that the "local" representation of every $\rho(i)$ verifies the conditions (MC1) to (MC5) of Sect. 3.

In the following, we say that a vertex represents the constant d if it is of the form $\langle d, i \rangle$ for some i. The level of a node $n = \langle a, t \rangle$ in G_ρ is t, and is denoted by lev(n). There is some redundancy in G_ρ for the nodes of the form $\langle d, i \rangle$. However, this is useful to establish strict relationships between ρ and G_ρ.

Example 1. Assuming that $C = \{2, 4\}$, $K = 2$, $V' = \{x, x'\}$ ($f(x) = x$ and $f(\mathsf{X}x) = x'$) and $l = 1$, let us define the sequence $\rho = sv^0 \cdot (sv^1 \cdot sv^2)^\omega$ where $sv^0 = \langle Y_1^0, Y_2^0, Y_3^0 \rangle$ such that $Y_1^0 = \{x = x, x' = x', x < x', 2 < x, x < 4, x' = 4, x' > 2\}$, $Y_2^0 = \{x = 3\}$ and $Y_3^0 = \{x \equiv_2 1, x' \equiv_2 0\}$. The symbolic valuation $sv^1 = \langle Y_1^1, Y_2^1, Y_3^1 \rangle$ satisfies: $Y_1^1 = (Y_1^0 \setminus \{2 < x, x < 4, x' = 4, x' > 2\}) \cup \{4 < x, 4 < x'\}$, $Y_2^1 = \emptyset$ and $Y_3^1 = \{x \equiv_2 0, x' \equiv_2 1\}$. The symbolic valuation $sv^2 = \langle Y_1^2, Y_2^2, Y_3^2 \rangle$ verifies $Y_1^2 = Y_1^1$, $Y_2^2 = Y_2^1$ and $Y_3^2 = Y_3^0$. The graph G_ρ is presented in Fig. 2. In order to simplify the representation, closure by transitivity for $\overset{\lesssim}{\rightarrow}$ and the fact that $\overset{\equiv}{\rightarrow}$ is a congruence are omitted. The function mod is directly encoded in the node label.

A path in G_ρ is a sequence (possible infinite) of the form $n_0 \overset{\sim_0}{\rightarrow} n_1 \overset{\sim_1}{\rightarrow} n_2 \overset{\sim_2}{\rightarrow} \ldots$. For any finite path $w = n_0 \overset{\sim_0}{\rightarrow} n_1 \overset{\sim_1}{\rightarrow} n_2 \overset{\sim_2}{\rightarrow} \ldots \overset{\sim_{\alpha-1}}{\longrightarrow} n_\alpha$, its strict length $slen(w)$ is the cardinality of $\{i : 0 \leq i \leq \alpha - 1, \sim_i \text{ equals } <\}$. When w has a strict length greater than 1, we say that w is strict. A finite path w such that $n_0 = n_\alpha$ is called a cycle. The strict length between two nodes n_1 and n_2, written $slen(n_1, n_2)$, is the least upper bound of the strict lengths of finite paths between n_1 and n_2. By

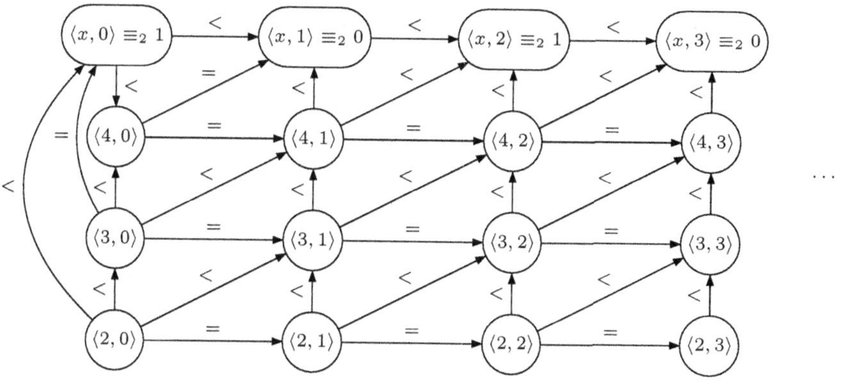

Fig. 2. A graph G_ρ

convention, if there is no path between n_1 and n_2, $slen(n_1, n_2)$ takes the value $-\infty$. In Fig. 2, $slen(\langle 2,2\rangle, \langle x,3\rangle) = 4$.

In Lemma 5 below, the one-step consistency of ρ implies global constraints on its graph representation that already hold true locally. By a global constraint, we mean a constraint on the whole graph and not only on the local representation of a single symbolic valuation or on two successive satisfiable symbolic valuations.

Lemma 5. *Let ρ be a one-step consistent sequence.*

(I) *G_ρ has no strict cycle.*
(II) *If there is a finite path w starting at $\langle d, i\rangle$ and ending at the node n of level j, then: if w is strict then $\langle d, j\rangle \xrightarrow{<} n$, otherwise $\langle d, j\rangle \xrightarrow{=} n$.*
(III) *If there is a finite path w starting at the node n of level j and ending at $\langle d, i\rangle$, then: if w is strict then $n \xrightarrow{<} \langle d, j\rangle$, otherwise $n \xrightarrow{=} \langle d, j\rangle$.*

Corollary 1. *Let ρ be a one-step consistent sequence and G_ρ its graph representation. Then, for all nodes $\langle d_1, i\rangle$ and $\langle d_2, j\rangle$ in G_ρ representing constants such that $d_1 \leq d_2$, $slen(\langle d_1, i\rangle, \langle d_2, j\rangle) = d_2 - d_1$.*

So far, we have stated properties about the graph G_ρ. Below, we establish simple conditions on G_ρ equivalent to the existence of a model for ρ. An edge-respecting labeling for G_ρ is a map $lab : (V \cup C') \times \mathbb{N} \rightarrow \mathbb{Z}$ such that for all nodes n_1, n_2, $n_1 \xrightarrow{\sim} n_2$ implies $lab(n_1) \sim lab(n_2)$ and for every node n, $lab(n) \equiv_K mod(n)$. Additionally, lab is said to be strict if for every $\langle d, i\rangle$ in G_ρ, $lab(\langle d, i\rangle) = d$.

Lemma 6. *A one-step consistent sequence ρ has a model iff G_ρ has a strict edge-respecting labeling.*

The proof is quite direct by unfolding the definitions. A refinement is possible.

Lemma 7. *A one-step consistent sequence ρ has a model iff G_ρ has an edge-respecting labeling (not necessarily strict).*

Lemmas 6 and 7 state correspondences between ρ and its graphical representation G_ρ. However, we need a more abstract characterization of the one-step consistent sequences admitting a model (see Lemma 8 below).

Lemma 8. *Let ρ be a one-step consistent sequence. The graph G_ρ has an edge-respecting labeling iff for all nodes n_1, n_2 in G_ρ, $slen(n_1, n_2) < \omega$.*

By construction of G_ρ, for all nodes $\langle d_1, i\rangle$ and $\langle d_2, j\rangle$ representing constants such that $d_1 \leq d_2$, $slen(\langle d_1, i\rangle, \langle d_2, j\rangle) = d_2 - d_1$ (see Corollary 1). That is why, in Lemma 8, there is no additional constraint for nodes of the graph representing constants.

Lemma 8 characterizes the set of sequences having a model but what we really need is to recognize them with automata. The main difficulty rests on the fact that the set of satisfiable one-step consistent ω-sequences of satisfiable symbolic valuations is not ω-regular, a consequence of [DD03] for the fragment CLTL(Z). In order to approximate this class of sequences, we define below a condition $(\mathcal{C})$ shown to be ω-regular such that for every one-step consistent ω-sequence ρ of satisfiable symbolic valuations that is ultimately periodic, ρ has a model iff G_ρ satisfies $(\mathcal{C})$.

An infinite forward (resp. backward) path in G_ρ is defined as a sequence $w : \mathbb{N} \rightarrow (V \cup C') \times \mathbb{N}$ such that: for every $i \in \mathbb{N}$, there is an edge $w(i) \xrightarrow{\sim} w(i+1)$ (resp. $w(i+1) \xrightarrow{\sim} w(i)$) in G_ρ and if $\mathrm{lev}(w(i)) = j$, then $\mathrm{lev}(w(i+1)) \geq j+1$. The path w is infinitely often strict $\overset{\text{def}}{\Leftrightarrow}$ for every $i \geq 0$, there is $j \geq i$ such that $w(j) \xrightarrow{\lneq} w(j+1)$ (resp. $w(j+1) \xrightarrow{\lneq} w(j)$). The condition $(\mathcal{C})$ on the graph G_ρ is: there *do not* exist vertices n_1 and n_2 in G_ρ with $|\mathrm{lev}(n_1) - \mathrm{lev}(n_2)| \leq l$ satisfying

(AP1) there is an infinite forward path w_{for} from n_1,
(AP2) there is an infinite backward path w_{back} from n_2,
(AP3) either w_{for} or w_{back} is infinitely often strict, and
(AP4) for all $i, j \in \mathbb{N}$, whenever $|\mathrm{lev}(w_{\mathrm{for}}(i)) - \mathrm{lev}(w_{\mathrm{back}}(j))| \leq l$, $w_{\mathrm{for}}(i) \xrightarrow{\lneq} w_{\mathrm{back}}(j)$ in G_ρ.

We say an infinite word is ultimately periodic if it is of the form $\tau \cdot \delta^\omega$ for some finite words τ and δ.

Lemma 9. *Let ρ be one-step consistent ω-sequence of satisfiable symbolic valuations that is ultimately periodic. Then ρ admits a model iff G_ρ satisfies $(\mathcal{C})$.*

Thanks to the way G_ρ is built from ρ, $(\mathcal{C})$ does not explicitly mention the constants in C' and the constraints of the form $x \equiv_K c$. Hence, Lemma 9 can be proved as [DD03, Lemma 6.2]: the map *mod* in G_ρ is ignored and a uniform treatment for all nodes in $(V \cup C') \times \mathbb{N}$ is provided. In [DD03, Lemma 6.2], there are no nodes of the form $C' \times \mathbb{N}$ but we take into account their specificity in our construction of G_ρ. If ρ admits a model then by Lemma 8 it satisfies the condition $(\mathcal{C})$. Conversely, let $\rho = \tau \cdot \delta^\omega$ be an ultimately periodic one-step consistent ω-sequence. We can show that if ρ has no model then it does not satisfy $(\mathcal{C})$. By Lemma 8, if ρ has no model, then there exist two vertices n_1 and n_2 such that $slen(n_1, n_2) = \omega$. One can construct a finite path w between

n_1 and n_2 long enough so that paths w_{for} and w_{back} satisfying the conditions (AP1)–(AP4) can be constructed, witnessing that G_ρ does not satisfy $(\mathcal{C})$. The construction of w_{for} and w_{back} from w uses the fact that ρ is ultimately periodic by repeating infinitely finite subpaths. The construction of such infinite paths can be done smoothly by using the properties established in this section (see e.g. Lemma 5). As the proof is not essentially different from [DD03, Lemma 6.2] modulo slight changes mentioned above, we omit it here.

5 Büchi Automata and PSPACE Upper Bound

Based on the previous results and following the approach in [VW94], we show that given a CLTL(IPC*) formula ϕ, one can build a standard Büchi automaton $\mathcal{A}_\phi$ such that ϕ is CLTL(IPC*) satisfiable iff $\mathrm{L}(\mathcal{A}_\phi)$ is non-empty. Moreover, we establish that emptiness of $\mathrm{L}(\mathcal{A}_\phi)$ can be checked in polynomial space in $|\phi|$. From the technical viewpoint, the construction of $\mathcal{A}_\phi$ as the intersection of three Büchi automata can be done quite smoothly thanks to the previous results. In the following, V, V', C and C' are the sets of variables and constants associated to ϕ as defined in Sect. 4. Moreover, K, m and M are constants with their usual meaning and we use the map $f : \mathrm{Terms}(\phi) \rightarrow V'$ as previously.

Unlike LTL, the language recognized by the Büchi automaton $\mathcal{A}_\phi$ is not a set of models but rather a set of symbolic models. We write Σ to denote the set of satisfiable symbolic valuations wrt ϕ. A symbolic model for ϕ is an ω-sequence $\rho : \mathbb{N} \rightarrow \Sigma$. We write $\rho \models' \phi$ where the symbolic satisfaction relation $\models'$ is defined as $\models$ except at the atomic level: $\rho, i \models' p \overset{\mathrm{def}}{\Leftrightarrow} \rho(i) \models_{\mathrm{symb}} f(p)$ where $\models_{\mathrm{symb}}$ is the satisfaction relation between symbolic valuations and constraints.

By Lemma 4 and by using standard techniques for LTL [VW94], checking whether there is a symbolic model ρ satisfying $\rho \models' \phi$ can be done in PSPACE (see more details below). Since every model for ϕ generates a unique symbolic model for ϕ, we obtain the result below.

Lemma 10. *A* CLTL(IPC*) *formula ϕ is satisfiable iff there is a one-step consistent symbolic valuation ρ such that $\rho \models' \phi$ and ρ has a model.*

All the following automata are built over the alphabet Σ which is of exponential size in $|\phi|$. The automaton $\mathcal{A}_\phi$ is formally defined as the intersection $\mathcal{A}_{\mathrm{LTL}} \cap \mathcal{A}_{\mathrm{1cons}} \cap \mathcal{A}_{\mathcal{C}}$ of Büchi automata where $\mathrm{L}(\mathcal{A}_{\mathrm{LTL}})$ is the set of symbolic models satisfying ϕ, $\mathrm{L}(\mathcal{A}_{\mathrm{1cons}})$ is the set of one-step consistent sequences of satisfiable symbolic valuations, $\mathrm{L}(\mathcal{A}_{\mathcal{C}})$ is the set of sequences of symbolic valuations verifying $(\mathcal{C})$. We briefly explain below how these automata are built. The automaton $\mathcal{A}_{\mathrm{LTL}}$ is obtained from [VW94] with a difference for atomic formulae. We define $cl(\phi)$ the closure of ϕ as usual, and an atom of ϕ is a maximally consistent subset of $cl(\phi)$. We define $\mathcal{A}_{\mathrm{LTL}} = (Q, Q_0, \rightarrow, F)$ as the generalized Büchi automaton below:

- Q is the set of atoms of ϕ and $Q_0 = \{X \in Q : \phi \in X\}$,
- $X \overset{sv}{\rightarrow} Y$ iff

(atomic constraints) for every atomic formula p in X, $sv \models_{\text{symb}} f(p)$,
(one step) for every $\mathsf{X}\psi \in cl(\phi)$, $\mathsf{X}\psi \in X$ iff $\psi \in Y$,

– let $\{\psi_1 \mathsf{U} \varphi_1, \ldots, \psi_r \mathsf{U} \varphi_r\}$ be the set of until formulas in $cl(\phi)$. We pose F equal to $\{F_1, \ldots, F_r\}$ with for every $i \in \{1, \ldots, r\}$, $F_i = \{X \in Q : \psi_i \mathsf{U} \varphi_i \notin X \text{or } \varphi_i \in X\}$.

By Lemma 4, the condition about atomic formulae can be checked in PSPACE. Hence, the transition relation can be computed in PSPACE.

We define $\mathcal{A}_{1\text{cons}} = \langle Q, Q_0, \rightarrow, F \rangle$ as a Büchi automaton such that $Q = Q_0 = F = Q = \Sigma$ and the transition relation satisfies: $sv \xrightarrow{sv''} sv' \overset{\text{def}}{\Leftrightarrow} \langle sv, sv' \rangle$ is one-step consistent and $sv' = sv''$. Since checking whether a symbolic valuation is satisfiable can be done in P (Lemma 2) and checking whether a pair of symbolic valuations is one-step consistent can be also done in P, the transition relation of $\mathcal{A}_{1\text{cons}}$ can be computed in P.

It remains to define $\mathcal{A}_{\mathcal{C}}$ that recognizes ω-sequences of symbolic valuations satisfying ($\mathcal{C}$). As done in [DD03], instead of building $\mathcal{A}_{\mathcal{C}}$, it is easier to construct the Büchi automaton $\mathcal{A}_{\mathcal{C}}^{\neg}$ that recognizes the complement language of $\mathrm{L}(\mathcal{A}_{\mathcal{C}})$. The automaton $\mathcal{A}_{\mathcal{C}}^{\neg}$ is essentially the automaton $\mathcal{B}$ defined in [DD03, page 20] except that we work with a different type of alphabet. We need to consider vertices in the graph that represent constants in C and equality between constants does not need to be explicitly present in the symbolic valuations (see details in [DG05]).

Lemma 11. *A* CLTL(IPC*) *formula* ϕ *is satisfiable iff* $\mathrm{L}(\mathcal{A}_\phi)$ *is non-empty.*

The proof of this lemma is similar to [DD03, Lemma 6.3]. The main trick is to observe that if $\mathrm{L}(\mathcal{A}_\phi)$ is non-empty then $\mathcal{A}_\phi$ accepts an ultimately periodic ω-sequence so that Lemma 9 can be applied. Since given a formula ϕ we can effectively construct $\mathcal{A}_\phi$ and check whether $\mathrm{L}(\mathcal{A}_\phi)$ is empty, the model-checking and satisfiability problems for CLTL(IPC*) are decidable. We also have all the arguments to establish the PSPACE upper bound by using subtle arguments from complexity theory and [Saf89].

Theorem 1. *The satisfiability problem for* CLTL(IPC*) *is* PSPACE*-complete.*

All the temporal operators in CLTL(IPC*) are definable in monadic second order logic (MSO) and by using [GK03], it is immediate that any extension of CLTL(IPC*) obtained by adding a finite amount of MSO-definable temporal operators remains in PSPACE. Only the automaton $\mathcal{A}_{\text{LTL}}$ needs to be updated.

Corollary 2. *The model-checking problem for integral relational automata restricted to the LTL fragment of CCTL* introduced in [Čer94] is in* PSPACE.

6 Conclusion

In the paper, we have introduced the logic CLTL(IPC*) extending formalisms in [Čer94, LM01, DD03, Dem04] and we have shown that both model-checking over IPC*-automata and satisfiability are decidable in polynomial space. The proof heavily relies on a translation into the emptiness problem for standard

Büchi automata and on the approximation of non ω-regular sets of symbolic models. As a by-product, the model checking problem over the integral relational automata defined in [Čer94] is also PSPACE-complete when restricted to its LTL fragment. The logic CLTL(IPC*) supports a rich class of constraints including those of the form $x < y$ unlike periodicity constraints from [Dem04] (which are quite useful to compare absolute dates) and comparison with constants unlike logics shown in PSPACE in [DD03]. Abstraction of counter automata by performing reasoning modulo can be encoded in CLTL(IPC*) thanks to the presence of integer periodicity constraints.

To conclude, we mention a few open problems that are worth investigating.

- CTL* for integral relational automata is undecidable [Čer94] whereas we have shown that its LTL fragment is PSPACE-complete. It is interesting to design other decidable fragments of CTL* strictly more expressive than Boolean combinations of LTL formulae.
- The decidability status of constraint LTL over the domain $\langle\{0,1\}^*, \subseteq\rangle$ is open either with the subword relation or with the prefix relation. Constraint LTL over the domain $\langle\{0\}^*, \subseteq\rangle$ is already equivalent to constraint LTL over $\langle\mathbb{N}, <, =\rangle$ that is a strict fragment of CLTL(IPC*).
- The decidability status of CLTL(IPC*) extended with constraints of the form $3x + 2\mathsf{X}y \equiv_5 3$ is open. They are considered in [MOS05] but not integrated in any LTL-like language.

References

[AD94] R. Alur and D. Dill. A theory of timed automata. *TCS*, 126:183–235, 1994.

[AH94] R. Alur and Th. Henzinger. A really temporal logic. *JACM*, 41(1):181–204, 1994.

[BC02] Ph. Balbiani and J.F. Condotta. Computational complexity of propositional linear temporal logics based on qualitative spatial or temporal reasoning. In *FroCoS'02*, volume 2309 of *LNAI*, pages 162–173. Springer, 2002.

[BEH95] A. Bouajjani, R. Echahed, and P. Habermehl. On the verification problem of nonregular properties for nonregular processes. In *LICS'95*, pages 123–133, 1995.

[BEM97] A. Bouajjani, J. Esparza, and O. Maler. Reachability analysis of pushdown automata: application to model-checking. In *CONCUR'97*, volume 1243 of *LNCS*, pages 135–150. Springer, 1997.

[BFLP03] S. Bardin, A. Finkel, J. Leroux, and L. Petrucci. FAST: Fast Acceleration of Symbolic Transition systems. In *CAV'03*, volume 2725 of *LNCS*, pages 118–121. Springer, 2003.

[Boi98] B. Boigelot. *Symbolic methods for exploring infinite state spaces*. PhD thesis, Université de Liège, 1998.

[Cau03] D. Caucal. On infinite transition graphs having a decidable monadic theory. *TCS*, 290:79–115, 2003.

[CC00] H. Comon and V. Cortier. Flatness is not a weakness. In *CSL'00*, volume 1862 of *LNCS*, pages 262–276. Springer, 2000.

[Čer94] K. Čerāns. Deciding properties of integral relational automata. In *ICALP*, volume 820 of *LNCS*, pages 35–46. Springer, 1994.

[CGL94] E. Clarke, O. Grumberg, and D. Long. Model checking and abstraction. *ACM Transactions on Programming Languages and Systems*, 16(5):1512–1542, 1994.

[CJ98] H. Comon and Y. Jurski. Multiple counters automata, safety analysis and Presburger arithmetic. In *CAV'98*, volume 1427 of *LNCS*, pages 268–279. Springer, 1998.

[DD03] S. Demri and D. D'Souza. An automata-theoretic approach to constraint LTL. Technical Report LSV-03-11, LSV, August 2003. 40 pages. An extended abstract appeared in Proc. of FSTTCS'02.

[Dem04] S. Demri. LTL over integer periodicity constraints. Technical Report LSV-04-6, LSV, February 2004. 35 pages. An extended abstract appeared in Proc. of FOSSACS'04.

[DG05] S. Demri and R. Gascon. Verification of qualitative $\mathbb{Z}$-constraints. Technical Report LSV-05-07, LSV, June 2005.

[EFM99] J. Esparza, A. Finkel, and R. Mayr. On the verification of broadcast protocols. In *LICS'99*, pages 352–359, 1999.

[FL02] A. Finkel and J. Leroux. How to compose Presburger accelerations: Applications to broadcast protocols. In *FST&TCS'02*, volume 2256 of *LNCS*, pages 145–156. Springer, 2002.

[GK03] P. Gastin and D. Kuske. Satisfiability and model checking for MSO-definable temporal logics are in PSPACE. In *CONCUR'03*, volume 2761 of *LNCS*, pages 222–236. Springer, 2003.

[GKK+03] D. Gabelaia, R. Kontchakov, A. Kurucz, F. Wolter, and M. Zakharyaschev. On the computational complexity of spatio-temporal logics. In *FLAIRS'03*, pages 460–464, 2003.

[Iba78] O. Ibarra. Reversal-bounded multicounter machines and their decision problems. *JACM*, 25(1):116–133, 1978.

[JKMS04] P. Jančar, A. Kučera, F. Moller, and Z. Sawa. DP lower bounds for equivalence-checking and model-checking of one-counter automata. *I & C*, (188):1–19, 2004.

[LM01] U. Dal Lago and A. Montanari. Calendars, time granularities, and automata. In *Int. Symposium on Spatial and Temporal Databases*, volume 2121 of *LNCS*, pages 279–298. Springer, Berlin, 2001.

[LS01] G. Logothetis and K. Schneider. Abstraction from counters: an application on real-time systems. In *TIME'01*, pages 214–223. IEEE, 2001.

[Lut04] C. Lutz. NEXPTIME-complete description logics with concrete domains. *ACM Transactions on Computational Logic*, 5(4):669–705, 2004.

[MOS05] M. Müller-Olm and H. Seidl. Analysis of modular arithmetic. In *ESOP'05*, LNCS. Springer, 2005.

[Saf89] S. Safra. *Complexity of Automata on Infinite Objects.* PhD thesis, The Weizmann Institute of Science, 1989.

[SC85] A. Sistla and E. Clarke. The complexity of propositional linear temporal logic. *JACM*, 32(3):733–749, 1985.

[TC98] D. Toman and J. Chomicki. Datalog with integer periodicity constraints. *Journal of Logic Programming*, 35(3):263–290, 1998.

[VW94] M. Vardi and P. Wolper. Reasoning about infinite computations. *I & C*, 115:1–37, 1994.

[Wol83] P. Wolper. Temporal logic can be more expressive. *I & C*, 56:72–99, 1983.

[WZ00] F. Wolter and M. Zakharyaschev. Spatio-temporal representation and reasoning based on RCC-8. In *KR'00*, pages 3–14, 2000.

Uniform Satisfiability Problem for Local Temporal Logics over Mazurkiewicz Traces*

Paul Gastin[1] and Dietrich Kuske[2]

[1] LSV, CNRS & ENS de Cachan,
61, Av. du Président Wilson, F-94235 Cachan Cedex, France
Paul.Gastin@lsv.ens-cachan.fr
[2] Institut für Informatik, Universität Leipzig,
Augustusplatz 10-11, D-04109 Leipzig, Germany
kuske@informatik.uni-leipzig.de

Abstract. We continue our study of the complexity of temporal logics over concurrent systems that can be described by Mazurkiewicz traces. In a previous paper (CONCUR 2003), we investigated the class of local and MSO definable temporal logics that capture all known temporal logics and we showed that the satisfiability problem for any such logic is in PSPACE (provided the dependence alphabet is fixed). In this paper, we concentrate on the uniform satisfiability problem: we consider the dependence alphabet (i.e., the architecture of the distributed system) as part of the input. We prove lower and upper bounds for the uniform satisfiability problem that depend on the number of monadic quantifier alternations present in the chosen MSO-modalities.

1 Introduction

Executions of distributed systems can be modeled as Mazurkiewicz traces [5] where the architecture of the system is mirrored by the dependence alphabet. Then a trace is a partial order execution of such a system. Over the past fifteen years, a lot of papers have been devoted to the study of temporal logics over partial orders and in particular over Mazurkiewicz traces (cf. [13,14,11,2,1,9,10,3,4]). This is motivated by the need for specification languages that are suited for concurrent systems where a property should not depend on the ordering between independent events. Hence logics over linearizations of behaviors are not adequate and logics over partial orders were developed. In particular local temporal logics are of interest here due to their good algorithmic properties. The common feature of these logics is that formulas are evaluated at single events corresponding to local views of processes. In [8], we proposed a unified treatment of all these local temporal logics very much in the spirit of [7]. Basically, a local temporal logic is given by a finite set of modality names. The semantics of any such modality name is described by a monadic second order (MSO) formula having a single

* Work partly supported by the DAAD-PROCOPE project Temporal and Quantitative Analysis of Distributed Systems.

M. Abadi and L. de Alfaro (Eds.): CONCUR 2005, LNCS 3653, pp. 533–547, 2005.

individual free variable. For any fixed dependence alphabet (i.e., architecture of a distributed system) we showed that the satisfiability problem of any such logic is in PSPACE. For (almost) all temporal logics considered in the literature so far, this was known before. Our contribution was a uniform proof that would also be applicable for not-yet-defined temporal logics.

A more realistic setting is the uniform satisfiability problem where both, the temporal formula and the architecture form the input. In other words, this uniform satisfiability problem for the local temporal logic TL asks whether a given property $\varphi \in$TL can be satisfied in a given architecture (Σ, D) (described as a trace alphabet). The paper at hand studies the complexity of this problem depending on the temporal logic TL. Recall that the semantics of the modality names of TL are given by MSO formulas. The complexity of the uniform satisfiability problem depends on the number of alternations of set quantifiers in these formulas. The bad news is that any quantifier alternation in the MSO-descriptions of the modalities adds an exponent to the space complexity. The good news is that local temporal logics considered in the literature do not have any alternation of set quantifiers and are, more precisely, definable in $\mathrm{M}\Delta^1_1$.

Section 2 defines and discusses the necessary concepts used in this paper. The following Section 3 proves an upper bound on the complexity of the uniform satisfiability problem. Our decision procedure makes crucial use of a locality theorem due to Schwentick & Bartelmann [12] that generalizes both, Hanf's and Gaifman's locality theorems. Section 4 presents, for any $n \in \mathbb{N}$, a local temporal logic whose uniform satisfiability is hard for n-fold exponential space. Examples of temporal logics that fall into our setting can be found in Sections 2 (where we discuss action based logics) and 5 that is devoted to process based logics, e.g., Thiagarajan's logic TrPTL from [13]. From our upper bound, it follows that any temporal logic from the literature has a uniform satisfiability problem whose space complexity is doubly exponential in the alphabet and polynomial in the formula.

Due to space limitations, we had to omit complete proofs as well as many more examples. They can be found in a technical report available on the web pages of the authors.

2 Preliminaries

Throughout this paper, we fix some countably infinite set N of *action names*. A *dependence alphabet* is a pair (Σ, D) where $\Sigma \subset \mathrm{N}$ is a set of action names and $D \subseteq \Sigma^2$ is a symmetric and reflexive relation on Σ. A *trace over* (Σ, D) is a labeled at most countably infinite partial order $(V, \leq, \lambda)$ such that $(V, \leq)$ is a partial order and $\lambda : V \to \Sigma$ is the labeling function satisfying for all $x, y \in V$

- $\downarrow x = \{z \in V \mid z \leq x\}$ is finite
- $(\lambda(x), \lambda(y)) \in D$ implies $x \leq y$ or $y \leq x$
- $x \lessdot y$ implies $(\lambda(x), \lambda(y)) \in D$,

where $\lessdot \; = \; < \setminus <^2$ is the immediate successor relation. The set $\mathbb{M}(\Sigma, D)$ comprises all finite traces while $\mathbb{R}(\Sigma, D)$ contains all traces over (Σ, D).

Trace concatenation is an operation $\cdot : \mathbb{M}(\Sigma, D) \times \mathbb{R}(\Sigma, D) \to \mathbb{R}(\Sigma, D)$ defined by $(V, \leq, \lambda) \cdot (V', \leq', \lambda') = (V \uplus V', (\leq \cup \leq' \cup E)^*, \lambda \cup \lambda')$ with $E = \{(v, v') \in V \times V' \mid (\lambda(v), \lambda'(v')) \in D\}$. Its restriction to finite traces is associative, i.e., $(\mathbb{M}(\Sigma, D), \cdot)$ is a monoid, called *trace monoid*.

We can identify a letter $a \in \Sigma$ with the trace $[a] = (\{0\}, \leq, \lambda)$ with $\lambda(0) = a$. In this sense, the trace monoid $\mathbb{M}(\Sigma, D)$ is generated by the set of letters $a \in \Sigma$. The canonical homomorphism $[.] : \Sigma^* \to \mathbb{M}(\Sigma, D)$ can be extended naturally to infinite words: for a (finite or infinite) word $u = a_0 a_1 \ldots$ with $a_i \in \Sigma$, the trace $[u] = (V, \sqsubseteq, \lambda)$ is given by $V = \{i \in \mathbb{N} \mid 0 \leq i < |u|\}$, $\sqsubseteq = E^*$ with $(i, j) \in E$ iff $i < j$ and $(a_i, a_j) \in D$, and $\lambda(i) = a_i$.

Formulas of the logic $\mathrm{MSO}(\mathrm{N}, \lessdot, \mathrm{fin})$ will be interpreted over traces. This logic is based on atomic propositions of the form $(\lambda(x) = a)$ for $a \in \mathrm{N}$, $x \lessdot y$, $x = y$, $x \in X$, and $\mathrm{fin}(X)$ for x, y individual variables and X a set variable. Intuitively, the formula $\mathrm{fin}(X)$ means that the set X is finite. Note that we do not allow the partial order $\leq$ to be used in our formulas. On one hand, the successor relation is sufficient since the partial order can be expressed using the successor. On the other hand, our upper bound proof relies on the fact that the Hasse diagram of any trace has bounded degree. The fragment $\mathrm{MSO}(\mathrm{N}, \lessdot)$ of $\mathrm{MSO}(\mathrm{N}, \lessdot, \mathrm{fin})$ consists of all formulas that do not mention the atomic proposition $\mathrm{fin}(X)$.

Example 2.1. Consider the following two formulas

$$\begin{aligned} \mathrm{upset}(x, X) &= \forall y (y \in X \leftrightarrow y = x \vee \exists z (z \in X \wedge z \lessdot y)) \text{ and} \\ \mathrm{downset}(x, X) &= \mathrm{fin}(X) \wedge \forall y (y \in X \leftrightarrow y = x \vee \exists z (z \in X \wedge y \lessdot z)) \,. \end{aligned}$$

of $\mathrm{MSO}(\mathrm{N}, \lessdot)$ and $\mathrm{MSO}(\mathrm{N}, \lessdot, \mathrm{fin})$, respectively. Then, for a trace $t = (V, \leq, \lambda)$ (over any finite dependence alphabet), $t \models \mathrm{upset}(x, X)$ iff $X = \{y \in V \mid x \leq y\}$ and $t \models \mathrm{downset}(x, X)$ iff $X = \{y \in V \mid y \leq x\}$. We could alternatively write the second of these formulas without the atomic proposition $\mathrm{fin}(X)$ at the expense of additional set quantifications. For later use, we prefer this version. It is not clear to us whether both, set quantifications and atomic propositions $\mathrm{fin}(X)$ can be avoided when expressing $\mathrm{downset}(x, X)$. In the following formulas, we will write $X = \downarrow x$ and $X = \uparrow x$ as a more intuitive abbreviation for the formulas $\mathrm{downset}(x, X)$ and $\mathrm{upset}(x, X)$.

An $\mathrm{MSO}(\mathrm{N}, \lessdot, \mathrm{fin})$-formula is an *$m$-ary modality* if it has m free set variables $X_1, \ldots, X_m$ and one free individual variable x.

Definition 2.2. *An* $\mathrm{MSO}(\mathrm{N}, \lessdot, \mathrm{fin})$-definable temporal logic *is given by*

- *a finite set B of modality names together with a mapping* $\mathrm{arity} : B \to \mathbb{N}$ *giving the arity of each modality name and*
- *a mapping* $[\![-]\!] : B \to \mathrm{MSO}(\mathrm{N}, \lessdot, \mathrm{fin})$ *such that $[\![M]\!]$ is an m-ary modality whenever* $\mathrm{arity}(M) = m$.

Then the syntax of the temporal logic $\mathrm{TL}(B)$ *is defined by the grammar*

$$\varphi ::= \sum_{M \in B} M(\underbrace{\varphi, \ldots, \varphi}_{\mathrm{arity}(M)}) + \sum_{a \in \mathrm{N}} a \,.$$

Let $t = (V, \leq, \lambda)$ be a trace over some finite dependence alphabet (Σ, D) and $\varphi \in \mathrm{TL}(B)$ a formula of $\mathrm{TL}(B)$. The semantics φ^t of φ in t is the set of positions in V where φ holds. The inductive definition is as follows. If $\varphi = a \in \mathrm{N}$, then $\varphi^t = \{x \in V \mid \lambda(x) = a\}$. If $\varphi = M(\varphi_1, \ldots, \varphi_m)$ where $M \in B$ is of arity $m \geq 0$, then

$$\varphi^t = \{p \in V \mid t \models [\![M]\!](\varphi_1^t, \ldots, \varphi_m^t, p)\}.$$

We also write $t, p \models \varphi$ for $p \in \varphi^t$.

For notational convenience and consistency, we consider elements of N as modality names as well and write $[\![a]\!] = (\lambda(x) = a)$ for $a \in \mathrm{N}$.

This definition of an MSO(N, $\lessdot$, fin)-definable temporal logic is very much in the style of [7]. It differs in as far as we allow set quantifications and the atomic proposition $\mathrm{fin}(X)$ in our modalities. On the other hand, we do not allow to use the order relation $\leq$ explicitly (but implicitly using set quantification).

Example 2.3. First, the boolean connectives negation and conjunction can be expressed by $[\![\neg]\!](X_1, x) = \neg(x \in X_1)$ and $[\![\wedge]\!](X_1, X_2, x) = (x \in X_1) \wedge (x \in X_2)$.

Existential next $\mathsf{EX}\,\varphi$ is one of the simplest temporal modality. Intuitively, $\mathsf{EX}\,\varphi$ means that there is an immediate successor of the current vertex where φ holds. Formally, we can set $[\![\mathsf{EX}]\!](X_1, x) = \exists y(x \lessdot y \wedge X_1(y))$ which is even a first-order formula.

The unary modality $\mathsf{Eco}\,\varphi$ ("*concurrent*") claims that φ holds for some vertex concurrent to the current vertex x. Thus, its semantics can be defined as

$$[\![\mathsf{Eco}]\!](X_1, x) = \exists X \exists Y \exists z((X = \uparrow x) \wedge (Y = \downarrow x) \wedge z \notin X \cup Y \wedge z \in X_1)\ .$$

Universal strict until $\varphi\ \mathsf{SU}\ \psi$ is a binary modality claiming the existence of a vertex y in the strict future of the current one x such that ψ holds at y and φ holds for all vertices strictly between x and y. Formally, $[\![\mathsf{SU}]\!](X_1, X_2, x)$ is given by

$$\begin{aligned}\exists X \exists H\ (X = \uparrow x) \wedge H \cap X_2 \neq \emptyset \wedge \forall y\\ (y \in H \leftrightarrow y \in X \setminus \{x\} \wedge \forall z \in X(z \lessdot y \rightarrow z \in \{x\} \cup (H \cap X_1))).\end{aligned}$$

The second line expresses that H contains precisely those nodes $y \in X \setminus \{x\}$ such that any vertex strictly between x and y belongs to X_1. Hence, by $H \cap X_2 \neq \emptyset$, there is one such vertex belonging to X_2. The classical non strict version of universal until is $\varphi\ \mathsf{U}\ \psi = \psi \vee (\varphi \wedge (\varphi\ \mathsf{SU}\ \psi))$.

Existential until $\varphi\ \mathsf{EU}\ \psi$ is another binary modality. It claims the existence of some finite path starting in the current node. At any node along this path, φ holds while ψ holds at the final node. Formally, we have

$$\begin{aligned}[\![\mathsf{EU}]\!](X_1, X_2, x) = \exists P,\quad & P \cap X_2 \neq \emptyset \wedge P \subseteq X_1 \cup X_2\\ & \wedge \forall z \in P,\ (z = x \vee \exists p \in P,\ p \lessdot z).\end{aligned}$$

For more examples, see [8] where most modalities met in the literature on local temporal logics for traces are expressed in terms of MSO(N, $\leq$)-modalities. As $\leq$ can be expressed using $\lessdot$, any of those formulas can be transformed into an equivalent one from MSO(N, $\lessdot$).

Uniform Satisfiability Problem for Temporal Logics. Let TL(B) be an MSO(N, $\lessdot$, fin)-definable temporal logic.

input: a finite dependence alphabet (Σ, D) and a formula φ of TL(B)
question: Is there a trace $t \in \mathbb{R}(\Sigma, D)$ and a position p in t with $t, p \models \varphi$?

In [8], we considered the non-uniform satisfiability problem for temporal logics definable in MSO(N, $\leq$) where the dependence alphabet (Σ, D) was fixed and not part of the input. By the above discussion, any MSO(N, $\lessdot$)-definable temporal logic is MSO(N, $\leq$)-definable. Hence [8, Thm. 9] translates into:

Theorem 2.4 ([8]). *The non-uniform satisfiability problem of any* MSO(N, $\lessdot$)*-definable temporal logic and any finite dependence alphabet* (Σ, D) *is in* PSPACE.

Analyzing the proof of this result, one obtains the following

Theorem 2.5 (cf. [8]). *For any* MSO(N, $\lessdot$)*-definable temporal logic, the uniform satisfiability problem is elementarily decidable.*

In this paper, we present a lower bound and a more precise upper bound for the uniform satisfiability problem. These bounds are expressed in terms of the number of monadic quantifier alternations in the formulas $[\![M]\!]$. Following [6], $\mathrm{M}\Sigma^1_n(\mathrm{N}, \lessdot, \mathrm{fin})$ comprises all MSO(N, $\lessdot$, fin)-formulae that are logically equivalent to one of the form $\exists\overrightarrow{X_1}\forall\overrightarrow{X_2}\ldots\exists/\forall\overrightarrow{X_n}\varphi$ where φ does not contain any second-order quantification. A formula belongs to $\mathrm{M}\Pi^1_n(\mathrm{N}, \lessdot, \mathrm{fin})$ iff its negation is an element of $\mathrm{M}\Sigma^1_n(\mathrm{N}, \lessdot, \mathrm{fin})$. Finally, $\mathrm{M}\Delta^1_n(\mathrm{N}, \lessdot, \mathrm{fin}) = \mathrm{M}\Sigma^1_n(\mathrm{N}, \lessdot, \mathrm{fin}) \cap \mathrm{M}\Pi^1_n(\mathrm{N}, \lessdot, \mathrm{fin})$. The fragments $\mathrm{M}\Sigma^1_n(\mathrm{N}, \lessdot)$ etc. are defined similarly. Finally, we write FO(N, $\lessdot$) for $\mathrm{M}\Delta^1_0(\mathrm{N}, \lessdot) = \mathrm{M}\Sigma^1_0(\mathrm{N}, \lessdot) = \mathrm{M}\Pi^1_0(\mathrm{N}, \lessdot)$, i.e., for those formulas that can be written without set quantification or fin(X). In this sense, we speak of $\mathrm{M}\Pi^1_n(\mathrm{N}, \lessdot, \mathrm{fin})$-definable temporal logics whenever all modalities $[\![M]\!]$ belong to $\mathrm{M}\Pi^1_n(\mathrm{N}, \lessdot, \mathrm{fin})$.

Example 2.6. We show that all the modalities EX, Eco, EU, and SU are actually definable in $\mathrm{M}\Delta^1_1(\mathrm{N}, \lessdot, \mathrm{fin})$. Above, we already gave $\mathrm{M}\Sigma^1_1(\mathrm{N}, \lessdot, \mathrm{fin})$-definitions for their semantics, so it remains to present equivalent $\mathrm{M}\Pi^1_1(\mathrm{N}, \lessdot, \mathrm{fin})$-formulas. This is trivial for EX since the FO(N, $\lessdot$)-formula $[\![\mathsf{EX}]\!]$ belongs to $\mathrm{M}\Delta^1_1(\mathrm{N}, \lessdot, \mathrm{fin})$. The negation of $[\![\mathsf{Eco}]\!]$ is equivalent to

$$\exists X \exists Y (X = \uparrow x \wedge Y = \downarrow x \wedge X_1 \subseteq X \cup Y)$$

stating that all nodes z satisfying φ are comparable with x.

To express $\neg[\![\mathsf{SU}]\!]$ by a formula in $\mathrm{M}\Sigma^1_1(\mathrm{N}, \lessdot)$ just replace $H \cap X_2 \neq \emptyset$ by $H \cap X_2 = \emptyset$ in the formula $[\![\mathsf{SU}]\!]$.

Next note that $\neg[\![\mathsf{EU}]\!]$ states that no path in X_1 starts in x and leads to a node in X_2. In other words, the connected component of $(\uparrow x \cap X_1, \lessdot)$ containing x does not contain any element with upper neighbor in X_2. This can be expressed by the following formula

$$\begin{aligned} \exists X \quad & \forall y \; (y \in X \leftrightarrow y \in X_1 \wedge (y = x \vee \exists z \; (z \in X \wedge z \lessdot y))) \\ & \wedge \forall z \; ((z = x \vee \exists y \; (y \in X \wedge y \lessdot z)) \rightarrow z \notin X_2). \end{aligned}$$

3 nEXPSPACE Upper Bound for $\mathbf{M\Delta^1_{n-1}}$(N, <, fin)-Logics

The function $\mathtt{tower} : \mathbb{N} \to \mathbb{N}$ is defined inductively by $\mathtt{tower}(0, m) = m$ and $\mathtt{tower}(\ell, m) = 2^{\mathtt{tower}(\ell-1,m)}$ for $\ell > 0$. It is the aim of this section to prove an upper bound for the uniform satisfiability problem sharper (and more general since it also deals with MSO(N, <, fin)-modalities) than that given in Theorem 2.5:

Theorem 3.1. *Let* TL *be some* $\mathrm{M}\Delta^1_n(\mathrm{N}, <, \mathrm{fin})$*-definable temporal logic. Then the uniform satisfiability problem for* TL *can be solved in space* $\mathtt{poly}(|\varphi|) \cdot \mathtt{tower}(n+1, \mathtt{poly}(|\Sigma|))$.

The decision procedure we propose refines ideas from [8]. The main ingredient are "modality automata" defined below. Let $w = a_0 a_1 \ldots$ be a word over Σ and $X_i \subseteq \omega$ be sets for $1 \le i \le m$. Then $(w, \overrightarrow{X})$ denotes the word $b_0 b_1 \ldots$ over $\Sigma \times \{0,1\}^m$ with $b_i = (a_i, x_i^1, x_i^2, \ldots, x_i^m)$ and $x_i^j = 1$ iff $i \in X_j$.

Definition 3.2. *Let* (Σ, D) *be a finite dependence alphabet and* α *an* m*-ary* MSO(N, <, fin)*-modality. A Büchi-automaton* $\mathcal{A}$ *over* $\Sigma \times 2^{m+1}$ *is called* modality automaton for (α, Σ, D) *if it accepts precisely those words* $(w, Y_0, Y_1, \ldots, Y_m)$ *such that the induced trace* $[w]$ *satisfies* $[w] \models \forall x(\alpha(Y_1, Y_2, \ldots, Y_m, x) \leftrightarrow Y_0(x))$.

Before we explain how to use modality automata to solve the uniform satisfiability problem, we fix some more notation: Let φ and ψ be TL(B)-formulas. Then top(φ) denotes the outermost modality name of φ. We write $\varphi \le \psi$ if φ is a subformula of ψ (this includes the case $\varphi = \psi$). Furthermore $\mathrm{Sub}(\psi) = \{\varphi \in \mathrm{TL}(B) \mid \varphi \le \psi\}$ is the set of subformulas of ψ. For an alphabet Σ, we will consider words of the form $(w, (Y_\varphi)_{\varphi \in \mathsf{Sub}(\psi)})$ with $w \in \Sigma^\omega$ and $Y_\varphi \subseteq \omega$, i.e., words over the extended alphabet $\Sigma_\psi = \Sigma \times \{0,1\}^{\mathsf{Sub}(\psi)}$. For a subformula $\varphi = M(\varphi_1, \ldots, \varphi_m) \le \psi$ and $\bar{w} = (w, (Y_\xi)_{\xi \le \psi}) \in \Sigma_\psi^\omega$, let $\bar{w}\restriction\varphi = (w, Y_\varphi, Y_{\varphi_1}, \ldots, Y_{\varphi_m})$.

Now let ξ be some TL(B)-formula and (Σ, D) some finite dependence alphabet. Furthermore, suppose we are given modality automata $\mathcal{A}_M$ for $([\![M]\!], \Sigma, D)$ with set of states Q_M. From these modality automata, we can construct an automaton $\mathcal{A}$ over Σ_ξ with set of states $Q = \prod_{\varphi \le \xi} Q_{\mathsf{top}(\varphi)}$ that has the following useful property (this construction follows [8] and can alternatively be found in the technical report):

Lemma 3.3. *Let* $\bar{w} = (w, (Y_\varphi)_{\varphi \le \xi}) \in \Sigma_\xi^\omega$. *Then,* $\bar{w}$ *is accepted by* $\mathcal{A}$ *if and only if for each* $\varphi \le \xi$ *we have* $Y_\varphi = \varphi^{[w]} = \{p \in \omega \mid [w], p \models \varphi\}$.

As an immediate consequence, we obtain

Proposition 3.4. *Let* $w \in \Sigma^\omega$. *Then there exists* $p \in \omega$ *with* $[w], p \models \xi$ *iff there exist* $Y_\varphi \subseteq \omega$ *for* $\varphi \le \xi$ *with* $Y_\xi \ne \emptyset$ *such that* $(w, (Y_\varphi)_{\varphi \le \xi})$ *is accepted by* $\mathcal{A}$.

Thus, the satisfiability of ξ is (essentially) equivalent to the emptiness problem for the automaton $\mathcal{A}$. To solve it, we only need to keep in memory three $|\xi|$-tuples of states of our modality automata. Thus, once the modality automata are computed, the satisfiability of ξ can be solved easily. To prove Thm. 3.1, we have to show that a modality automaton for an $M\Delta_n^1(\mathrm{N}, \lessdot, \mathrm{fin})$-definable modality can be constructed in space $\mathtt{tower}(n+1, \mathtt{poly}(|\Sigma|))$ (see Prop. 3.9). Our construction relies on a locality theorem by Schwentick & Bartelmann [12]. In essence, it says that a $\mathrm{FO}(\mathrm{N}, \lessdot)$-formula is effectively equivalent to the existence of some finite sets such that any sphere in the structure extended by these "colors" satisfies some first-order property (this is the reason why we consider spheres in traces in the following section). More precisely, this locality theorem holds for connected structures, only.[3] Therefore, from now on, we consider only rooted traces: Suppose there is $\# \in \Sigma$ with $\Sigma \times \{\#\} \subseteq D$. Then $\#\mathbb{M}(\Sigma, D)$ is the set of finite traces over (Σ, D) that have a least node labeled $\#$. Similarly, $\#\mathbb{R}(\Sigma, D)$ comprises all infinite traces over (Σ, D) with such a minimal node. We refer to the elements of $\#\mathbb{R}(\Sigma, D)$ as *rooted traces*. The *uniform rooted satisfiability problem for temporal logics* is the variant of the uniform satisfiability problem where we ask for the existence of some rooted trace. We only prove the above main result for this uniform rooted satisfiability problem, the general case can easily be derived.

3.1 Spheres

The *trace graph* of a trace $t = (V, \leq, \lambda)$ is the structure $G(t) = (V, \leq, \lessdot, (P_a)_{a\in\Sigma})$ given by $P_a = \lambda^{-1}(a)$. The *restriction* of a structure $\mathcal{M} = (W, \leq, \lessdot, (P_a)_{a\in\Sigma})$ to $X \subseteq W$ is the structure

$$\mathcal{M}{\restriction}X = (X, \leq \cap X^2, \lessdot \cap X^2, (P_a \cap X)_{a\in\Sigma}) .$$

If $\mathcal{M} = G(t)$ is a trace graph, $\mathcal{M}{\restriction}X$ need not be a trace graph itself. In particular, the relation $\lessdot$ in $\mathcal{M}{\restriction}X$ need not be the covering relation of $\leq$. A *path of length* n in $\mathcal{M}$ is a sequence $x_0, x_1, \ldots, x_n$ with $x_i \in W$ and $(x_i, x_{i+1}) \in (\lessdot \cup \gtrdot)$, i.e., consecutive elements are related by $\lessdot$ in any direction. For $x, y \in W$, the *distance* $d_{\mathcal{M}}(x, y)$ is the minimal length of a path $x_0, \ldots, x_n$ with $x = x_0$ and $y = x_n$. The distance is generalized to $x \in W$ and $U \subseteq W$ by $d_{\mathcal{M}}(x, U) = \min\{d_{\mathcal{M}}(x, y) \mid y \in U\}$. For $r \in \mathrm{N}$ and $U \subseteq W$, let $S_r(\mathcal{M}, U) = \{x \in W \mid d_{\mathcal{M}}(x, U) \leq r\}$ of all elements of W whose distance to U is at most r. Then the *sphere* $\mathrm{Sph}_r(\mathcal{M}, U)$ *around* U denotes the substructure $\mathcal{M}{\restriction}S_r(\mathcal{M}, U)$.

Let $t = (V, \leq, \lambda)$ be a trace and $U \subseteq V$. Then we write $\mathrm{Sph}_r(t, U)$ for $\mathrm{Sph}_r(G(t), U)$. Furthermore, for $a \in \mathrm{alph}(t)$, let $\mathrm{last}_a(t) = \max(\lambda^{-1}(a))$ be the $\leq$-maximal a-labeled node occurring in t. Let $\mathrm{last}(t) = \{\mathrm{last}_a(t) \mid a \in \mathrm{alph}(t)\}$ and for $r \in \mathrm{N}$, let $\mathrm{top}_r(t)$ be the structure $\mathrm{Sph}_r(t, \mathrm{last}(t))$, i.e., the restriction of $G(t)$ to those nodes from t whose distance to some maximal a-labeled node is at most r.

[3] Hanf and Gaifman proved similar locality theorems (cf. [6]). We could not use Hanf's theorem since there is no uniform bound for the degree of trace graphs independent from the dependence alphabet. Using Gaifman's theorem results in slightly more involved automata constructions (because of the disjointness condition) without improving the result.

Example 3.5. Let $\Sigma = \{a, b, c, d\}$ with $I = \{(b, d), (d, b), (a, c), (c, a)\}$ and consider the trace $s = [aabbcccbbbb]$. In Fig. 1, the trace graph of $s \cdot d$ is depicted in the first line. There, solid edges denote the covering relation $\lessdot$. Furthermore, black nodes are those in $\text{last}(sd)$. In the second picture, the structure $\text{top}_1(sd)$ is depicted. There, solid arrows have the same meaning as in the first picture, but the partial order relation $\leq$ is the reflexive and transitive closure of all arrows (including the dashed ones). If, in this second picture, we erase the d-labeled node, we obtain $\text{top}_1(s)$. Note the similarity of these pictures with those of Fig. 2 with $t = [ccbbaaabbbb]$: In particular, the covering relation restricted to $\text{top}_1(s)$ and $\text{top}_1(t)$ are equal, but they differ in $\text{top}_1(sd)$ and $\text{top}_1(td)$. Thus, although we are only interested in the relation $\lessdot$, in order to update this information, we also have to keep the order in the top sphere. The following lemma shows that this information is sufficient to compute $\text{top}_r(sd)$ from $\text{top}_r(s)$.

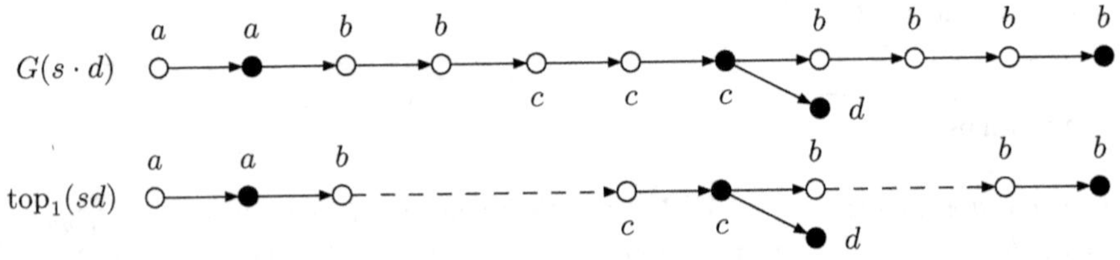

Fig. 1. Update of $\text{top}_1(s)$

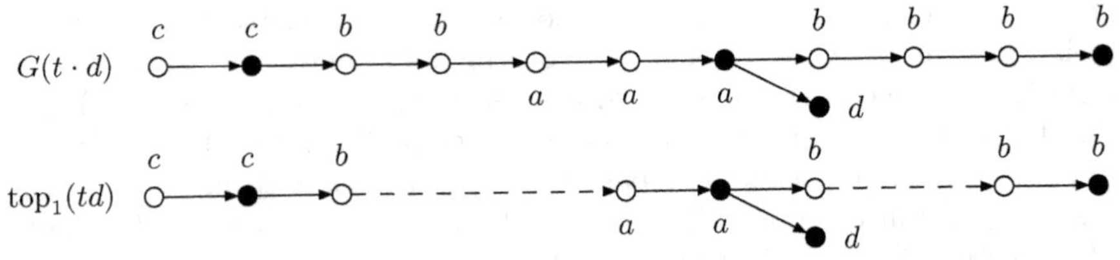

Fig. 2. Update of $\text{top}_1(t)$

Lemma 3.6. *Let s be a trace, $a \in \Sigma$, and $r \in \mathbb{N}$. Then $\text{top}_r(sa)$ is determined by $\text{top}_r(s)$ and the letter a.*

Let $w \in \Sigma^\infty$ and $t = [w] = (V, \leq, \lambda) \in \mathbb{R}(\Sigma, D)$. Fix also some $r \in \mathbb{N}$. A modality automaton will have to check properties of spheres of the form $\text{Sph}_r(t, x)$. For each $x \in V$, we can find a finite prefix u of w such that $\text{Sph}_r(t, x)$ is contained in $\text{top}_{2r}([u])$. From Lemma 3.6, the structures $\text{top}_{2r}([u])$ can be computed by an automaton. But we also need to determine when a vertex x in $\text{top}_{2r}([u])$ is such that $\text{Sph}_r(t, x)$ is contained in $\text{top}_{2r}([u])$. This is the purpose of the following definition and lemma.

Definition 3.7. *Let $s = (V, \leq, \lambda) \in \mathbb{M}(\Sigma, D)$ be a finite trace. Let $B \subseteq \Sigma$ and $r \in \mathbb{N}$. A vertex $x \in V$ is* r-critical *for (s, B) if $d_{G(s)}(x, \mathrm{last}(s)) \leq r$, and for all $(a, b) \in D \cap (\mathrm{alph}(s) \times B)$, if $d_{G(s)}(x, \mathrm{last}_a(s)) < r$ then $\mathrm{last}_a(s) < \mathrm{last}_c(s)$ for some $c \in \mathrm{alph}(s)$ with $(c, b) \in D$.*

Note that we can determine whether x is r-critical for (s, B) just knowing $\mathrm{top}_r(s)$ and B.

Lemma 3.8.

1. *Let $s = (V, \leq, \lambda) \in \mathbb{M}(\Sigma, D)$, $B \subseteq \Sigma$ and $r \in \mathbb{N}$. If a vertex $x \in V$ is r-critical for (s, B) then for all $t \in \mathbb{R}(\Sigma, D)$ with $\mathrm{alph}(t) \subseteq B$, we have $\mathrm{Sph}_r(st, x) = \mathrm{Sph}_r(\mathrm{top}_{2r}(s), x)$.*
2. *Let $w \in \Sigma^\infty$, $[w] = (V, \leq, \lambda) \in \mathbb{R}(\Sigma, D)$, $x \in V$ and $r \in \mathbb{N}$. There is a factorisation $w = uv$ with u finite such that x is r-critical for $([u], \mathrm{alph}(v))$.*

3.2 Construction of Modality Automata

For a k-ary $\mathrm{M}\Delta^1_n(\mathrm{N}, \lessdot, \mathrm{fin})$-modality α, the formula $\forall x(\alpha(Y_1, \ldots, Y_k, x) \leftrightarrow Y_0(x))$ belongs to $\mathrm{M}\Pi^1_n(\mathrm{N}, \lessdot, \mathrm{fin})$. Its kernel can be written as a Boolean combination of $\mathrm{FO}(\mathrm{N}, \lessdot)$-formulas $\varphi(X_1, \ldots, X_m)$ and formulas of the form $\mathrm{fin}(X)$. By [12, Theorem 3.2(2)], there are $\ell, r \in \mathbb{N}$ and a formula $\psi \in \mathrm{FO}(\mathrm{N}, \lessdot)$ with $h = m + \ell$ many free set variables $X_1, \ldots, X_{m+\ell}$ and one free individual variable y such that

- ψ is r-*local around* y (i.e., quantifications in ψ are restricted to nodes z with $d(y, z) \leq r$)
- for any finite dependence alphabet (Σ, D) and for any rooted trace $t = (V, \leq, \lambda) \in \#\mathbb{R}(\Sigma, D)$ together with m sets $X_1, \ldots, X_m$ contained in V, we have $(t, X_1, \ldots, X_m) \models \varphi$ iff $(t, X_1, \ldots, X_m) \models \exists X_{m+1} \ldots \exists X_{m+\ell}(\forall y\, \psi \wedge \bigwedge_{1 \leq i \leq \ell} \mathrm{fin}(X_{m+i}))$.

Let (Σ, D) be some finite dependence alphabet. We define a Büchi-automaton over the alphabet $\Sigma \times 2^h$ as follows. A state of this automaton is a tuple $q = (\mathrm{top}_{2r}(s), (X_i)_{1 \leq i \leq h}, B, C)$ where

- $s = (V, \leq, \lambda) \in \#\mathbb{M}(\Sigma, D)$ is some finite rooted trace and X_i is contained in $\mathrm{top}_{2r}(s)$ for $1 \leq i \leq h$,
- $B, C \subseteq \Sigma$, (the intuition is that B is used to guess the alphabet of the word that remains to be read and C is used to check the correctness of this guess)
- for any y in $\mathrm{top}_r(s)$ which is r-critical for (s, B), if we let Y_i be the intersection of X_i and $\mathrm{Sph}_r(\mathrm{top}_{2r}(s), y)$ for $1 \leq i \leq h$, then we have $\mathrm{Sph}_r(\mathrm{top}_{2r}(s), y) \models \psi(Y_1, \ldots, Y_h, y)$.

Based on this set of states Q and using Lemmas 3.6 and 3.8, we can then define a *sphere automaton* $\mathcal{A}(\Sigma, D, \psi)$ in space $2^{h|\Sigma|^{O(r)}}$ that checks, reading a word $\overline{w} = (w, X_1, \ldots, X_h)$ with $w \in \#\Sigma^\omega$ whether $([w], X_1, \ldots, X_h) \models \forall y \psi$. In this automaton, if we have a transition labeled $(a, x_1, \ldots, x_h)$ between states $q =$

$(\mathrm{top}_{2r}(s), (X_i)_{1\leq i\leq h}, B, C)$ and $q' = (\mathcal{M}', (X'_i)_{1\leq i\leq h}, B', C')$ then we have $\mathcal{M}' = \mathrm{top}_{2r}(sa)$, $B = B' \cup \{a\}$, $C' = C \setminus \{a\}$ if $C \neq \emptyset$ and $C' = B'$ otherwise, and for each $1 \leq i \leq \ell$, the set X'_i is obtained from X_i by removing the vertices in $\mathrm{top}_{2r}(s)$ that are no longer in $\mathrm{top}_{2r}(sa)$ and by adding a new vertex if $x_1 = 1$.

Note that the finiteness of a set X can be checked by a fixed automaton. Applying the usual Boolean operations and projections to these Büchi-automata, we obtain the following proposition which completes the proof of Theorem 3.1.

Proposition 3.9. *Let α be an $\mathrm{M}\Delta^1_n(\mathrm{N}, \lessdot)$-modality. Then the following problem can be solved in space* $\mathtt{tower}(n+1, \mathtt{poly}(|\Sigma|))$

input: *a finite dependence alphabet (Σ, D)*
output: *a modality automaton for (α, Σ, D).*

4 nEXPSPACE Lower Bound for $\mathrm{M}\Pi^1_{n+1}(\mathrm{N}, \lessdot)$-Logics

This section is devoted to the proof of

Theorem 4.1. *Let $n \in \mathbb{N}$. There is an $\mathrm{M}\Pi^1_{n+1}(\mathrm{N}, \lessdot)$-definable temporal logic TL_{n+1} such that its uniform satisfiability problem is* **nEXPSPACE**-*hard.*

Towards this aim, we will restrict ourselves to finite traces, the general result can easily be derived.

Idea of Proof and Notation: Let M be a deterministic Turing machine working in space $\mathtt{tower}(n, m)$ where m is the length of the input word. A configuration of M is described by a word $\triangleright\alpha q\beta\triangleleft$ (of length $\mathtt{tower}(n, m)$) over some alphabet Γ where q is the current state, $\alpha\beta$ is the tape contents and the head of M is on the first letter of β. We write $w \vdash w'$ if there is a transition of M from the configuration w to the configuration w'. To encode the computation $(w_0, w_1, \ldots, w_k)$ of M, we consider the word $c_{n+1}w_0d_{n+1}\, c_{n+1}w_1d_{n+1} \ldots c_{n+1}w_kd_{n+1}$ where c_{n+1} and d_{n+1} are new letters that act as delimiter. Now, to relate consecutive configurations, we will add counters that describe the index in the configuration (i.e., any configuration gets replaced by an alternating sequence of letters and counters). These counters will use additional letters and the number of additional letters used determines an upper bound of the value of these counters. Our main task in this section will be to encode counters that can count up to $\mathtt{tower}(n, m)$ using only linearly many new letters (in m). In a first step, we will encode these counters using new letters from an infinite set A. This will be achieved using in addition to the covering relation $\lessdot$ a relation $\prec$ that is an appropriate restriction of $\sqsubset$ from the previous section. Thus, in Section 4.1, we will describe encodings of successful computations of M as words using the relations $\lessdot$ and $\prec$. In the following Section 4.2, we will consider traces over some larger alphabet. This larger alphabet will allow us to replace the relation $\prec$ just using the covering relation $\lessdot$. Thus, we will be able to encode successful computations in traces. The remaining procedure (to be found in Section 4.3) is standard: from an input word v of length m, we will define a formula φ of the temporal logic TL (that we are going to construct from the Turing machine M) and an alphabet (Σ_m, D) of size $O(m)$ such that φ is satisfiable in $\mathbb{M}(\Sigma_m, D)$ iff M accepts the word v.

4.1 Encoding by Words

Notation. We fix some pairwise disjoint alphabets Γ (the "alphabet" of the Turing machine M), $B_i = \{0_i, 1_i\}$ and $C_i = \{c_i, d_i\}$ for $i > 0$ and we let $\Delta_i = \Gamma \cup \bigcup_{j\geq i}^{n} B_j \cup \bigcup_{j\geq i}^{n+1} C_j$. Furthermore, let A be an infinite set and $\Sigma = A \uplus \Delta_1$. For a set $E \subseteq \Sigma$ of letters, let $\Pi_E : \Sigma^* \to E^*$ be the projection to E (we will use this in particular for $E = B_i, A, \Gamma$). For Π_{B_i}, we write simply Π_i.

In this section, we consider formulas of the logic MSO$(\lessdot, \prec)$ that speak about words over the alphabet Σ. Atomic formulas are of the form $x \in X$, $\lambda(x) = a$ for $a \in \Delta_1$, $x \lessdot y$, and $x \prec y$. We define the semantics of $\prec$ by $w \models x \prec y$ iff

$$x < y \wedge (\lambda(x), \lambda(y) \in A \to \lambda(x) = \lambda(y)) \wedge \forall z(x < z < y \to \lambda(z) \notin \{\lambda(x), \lambda(y)\}).$$

We will freely use formulas like $\lambda(x) \in E$ for $E \subseteq \Delta_1$ meaning $\bigvee_{e\in E} \lambda(x) = e$. Note that formulas $\lambda(x) = a$ for $a \in A$ are not allowed, but we use $\lambda(x) \in A$ for $\neg(\lambda(x) \in \Delta_1)$.

Level 1 Counters: Let $K_1 = c_1(AB_1)^+ d_1$. The intuition is that a word $v = c_1 a_1 b_1 \cdots a_m b_m d_1$ is a counter whose value is $\Pi_1(v) \in B_1^m$ representing a number between 0 and $2^m - 1$.

Let L_1 be the set of words $v = u_0 v_1 u_1 \cdots v_k u_k \in \Delta_2^*(K_1 \Delta_2^*)^+$ with $v_i \in K_1$ and $u_i \in \Delta_2^*$ such that $\Pi_A(v_i)$ uses any letter at most once and $\Pi_A(v_i) = \Pi_A(v_j)$ for all $1 \leq i, j \leq k$. In other words, L_1 is the union of all languages $\Delta_2^*(c_1 a_1 B_1 \cdots a_m B_1 d_1 \Delta_2^*)^+$ where $a_1, \ldots, a_m$ is a sequence of pairwise distinct letters from A. Here the intuition is that a word $w \in L_1$ is a sequence of Δ_2 words separated by level 1 counters all using the same number m of bits for some $m > 0$.

Lemma 4.2. *The language L_1 can be defined in* FO$(\lessdot, \prec)$, *i.e., there is a sentence $\varphi_1 \in$* FO$(\lessdot, \prec)$ *such that $L_1 = \{w \in \Sigma^* \mid w \models \varphi_1\}$.*

Proof. First, one writes a formula expressing that a word belongs to $\Delta_2^*(K_1 \Delta_2^*)^+$. Since we can express that the letter at position x belongs to A (by saying that it does not belong to the finite set Δ_1), this is clearly possible. Next, one has to express that no factor from K_1 contains any letter from A more than once. If A was finite, this could be achieved by listing all these requirements. The problem caused by the infinity of A can be solved by saying that any position x with $\lambda(x) \in A$ is $\prec$-related to some d_1-position: $\forall x \exists y(\lambda(x) \in A \to \lambda(y) = d_1 \wedge x \prec y)$. Finally, factors from K_1 shall contain the same sequence of letters of A. By transitivity, it suffices to express this for consecutive such factors that start and end, resp., in positions x, z and x', z' with $\lambda(x) = \lambda(x') = c_1$, $\lambda(z) = \lambda(z') = d_1$, and $x \prec z \prec x' \prec z'$. Then, the formula requires that the relation $\prec$, restricted to the A-positions between x and z is an order-isomorphism (more precisely: $\prec$-isomorphism) onto the A-positions between x' and z'. □

Level ℓ Counters $(1 < \ell \leq n)$: Let K_ℓ be the set of words $v \in L_{\ell-1} \cap c_\ell(K_{\ell-1}B_\ell)^+ d_\ell$ such that if we write $v = c_\ell v_0 b_0 \cdots v_k b_k d_\ell$ with $v_i \in K_{\ell-1}$ and $b_i \in B_\ell$ then we have $\Pi_{\ell-1}(v_0) \in 0^+_{\ell-1}$, $\Pi_{\ell-1}(v_k) \in 1^+_{\ell-1}$, and $\Pi_{\ell-1}(v_{i+1}) = \mathrm{succ}(\Pi_{\ell-1}(v_i))$ for all $0 \leq i < k$, where succ denotes the successor for the lexicographic order. As above, the intuition is that a word $v \in K_\ell$ is a counter whose value is $\Pi_\ell(v) \in B^+_\ell$ representing an integer between 0 and $\mathtt{tower}(\ell, m)-1$ for some $m > 0$. Note that each bit b_i in a level ℓ counter is preceded by a level $\ell - 1$ counter v_i whose value is the index of this bit. Note also that words from K_ℓ use letters from $A \cup \bigcup_{1\leq i \leq \ell}(B_i \cup C_i)$, only.

Now, let $L_\ell = L_{\ell-1} \cap \Delta^*_{\ell+1}(K_\ell \Delta^*_{\ell+1})^+$. The intuition is that a word in L_ℓ represents a sequence of level ℓ counters all using the same number $\mathtt{tower}(\ell - 1, m)$ of bits for some $m > 0$.

Computation of the Turing Machine M: Recall that M is a deterministic Turing machine working in space $\mathtt{tower}(n, m)$ with m the length of the input.

Let K be the set of words $v \in L_n \cap c_{n+1}(K_n\Gamma)^+ d_{n+1}$ such that if we write $v = c_{n+1}v_0\gamma_0 \cdots v_k\gamma_k d_{n+1}$ with $v_i \in K_n$ and $\gamma_i \in \Gamma$ then $\Pi_n(v_0) \in 0^+_n$, $\Pi_n(v_k) \in 1^+_n$, and $\Pi_n(v_{i+1}) = \mathrm{succ}(\Pi_n(v_i))$ for all $0 \leq i < k$. As above, the intuition is that a word $v \in K$ describes a configuration of M whose value is $\Pi_\Gamma(v) \in \Gamma^+$. Note that each letter γ_i in a configuration is preceded by a level n counter v_i whose value is the index of this letter.

Now, let L be the set of words $w \in L_n \cap K^+$ such that if we write $w = w_0 w_1 \cdots w_k$ with $w_i \in K$ then we have $\Pi_\Gamma(w_i) \vdash \Pi_\Gamma(w_{i+1})$ for all $0 \leq i < k$. In other words, the language L is the set of encodings of computations of M.

Lemma 4.3. *The language L can be defined in $\mathrm{M}\Pi^1_{n+1}(\lessdot, \prec)$, i.e., there is a sentence $\psi \in \mathrm{M}\Pi^1_{n+1}(\lessdot, \prec)$ such that $L = \{w \in \Sigma^* \mid w \models \psi\}$.*

4.2 From Words to Traces

We consider a disjoint copy $\bar{A} = \{\bar{a} \mid a \in A\}$ of A and we let $\Sigma' = \Sigma \cup \{\dagger\} \cup \bar{A} \cup (\Sigma \times \Delta_1)$. The dependence relation D on Σ' is the least reflexive and symmetric relation such that elements of $\Sigma \cup \{\dagger\}$ are mutually dependent, $\bar{a}$ depends on a only (for $a \in A$), and (σ, δ) depends on σ and δ only. For simplicity, we write $\mathbb{M}$ for the trace monoid $\mathbb{M}(\Sigma', D)$.

Formulas in this section will mention the actions from $\Delta_1 \cup \{\dagger\} \cup (\Delta_1 \times \Delta_1)$ only. In this section, we will define a set $L' \subseteq \mathbb{M}$ definable in $\mathrm{MSO}(\mathrm{N}, \lessdot)$ such that $\Pi_\Sigma(L') = L$, the language from Lemma 4.3.

For $\sigma \in \Sigma$, we let $T(\sigma)$ be the unique trace having exactly one occurrence of each letter in $\{\sigma\} \times \Delta_1$. Define a homomorphism $\eta : \Sigma^* \to \mathbb{M}(\Sigma', D)$ by

$$\eta(\sigma) = \begin{cases} \bar{a}\,T(a)\,a\dagger\bar{a}\,T(a) & \text{if } \sigma = a \in A \\ \sigma\dagger T(\sigma) & \text{otherwise.} \end{cases}$$

For $\Delta_1 = \{\tau_1, \ldots, \tau_k\}$, the traces $\eta(a)$ and $\eta(\sigma)$ with $a \in A$ and $\sigma \in \Delta_1$ are depicted in Fig. 3. Note that for any $w \in \Sigma^*$, we have $\Pi_{\Sigma\cup\{\dagger\}}(\eta(w)) \in (\Sigma\dagger)^*$. The language L' that we will define here is precisely $\dagger\eta(L)$.

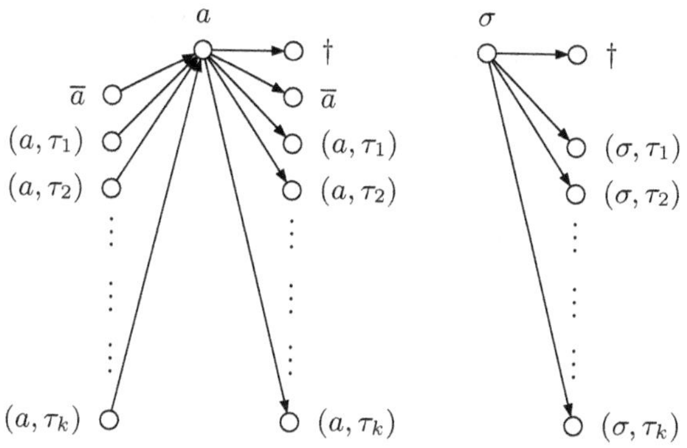

Fig. 3. The traces $\eta(a)$ and $\eta(\sigma)$

Lemma 4.4. *There is a formula $\varphi \in \mathrm{FO}(\mathrm{N}, \lessdot)$ such that a trace $t \in \mathbb{M}$ satisfies φ iff $t \in \dagger\eta(\Sigma^*)$*

Proof (Sketch). We construct $\varphi = \varphi_1 \wedge \varphi_2 \wedge \varphi_3$. The formula φ_1 ensures that $\Pi_{\Sigma\cup\{\dagger\}}(t) \in \dagger(\Sigma\dagger)^*$. The formula φ_2 ensures that any Σ-labeled node is the center of some factor $\eta(\sigma)$. This is easy if $\sigma \in \Delta_1$ since $\{\dagger\} \cup (\Delta_1 \times \Delta_1)$ is finite. For $\sigma \in A$, it turns out to be sufficient to require the existence of at least $|\Delta_1|+2$ many upper and lower neighbors. The formula φ_3 expresses that the whole trace is the disjoint union of these factors. □

For any word $w \in \Sigma^*$ we have $w = \Pi_\Sigma(t)$ where $t = \dagger\eta(w)$. Thus, the word w can be seen as a chain in the trace $t = \dagger\eta(w)$. The predicate $(\lambda(x) \in \Sigma)$ and the relations $\lessdot$ and $\prec$ of w can be expressed in t by $\mathrm{FO}(\mathrm{N}, \lessdot)$-formulas as follows:

$$\begin{aligned}(\lambda(x) \in \Sigma) &= \exists z, (x \lessdot z) \wedge (\lambda(z) = \dagger),\\ \mathrm{cover}(x, y) &= \exists z, (x \lessdot z \lessdot y) \wedge (\lambda(z) = \dagger),\\ \mathrm{nx}(x, y) &= \exists z_1 \exists z_2, (x \lessdot z_1 \lessdot y) \vee (x \lessdot z_1 \lessdot z_2 \lessdot y).\end{aligned}$$

More precisely, for $w \in \Sigma^*$, $t = \dagger\eta(w)$ and x, y in t with $\lambda(x), \lambda(y) \in \Sigma$, we have $x \lessdot y$ in w iff $t \models \mathrm{cover}(x, y)$, and $x \prec y$ in w iff $t \models \mathrm{nx}(x, y)$. This allows immediately to derive the following consequence since L is definable in $\mathrm{M}\Pi^1_{n+1}(\lessdot, \prec)$:

Proposition 4.5. *The language $\dagger\eta(L)$ is $\mathrm{M}\Pi^1_{n+1}(\mathrm{N}, \lessdot)$-definable, i.e., there is a sentence $\overline{\psi} \in \mathrm{M}\Pi^1_{n+1}(\mathrm{N}, \lessdot)$ such that $\dagger\eta(L) = \{t \in \mathbb{M} \mid t \models \overline{\psi}\}$.*

4.3 The Lower Bound

Proof (of Theorem 4.1). Recall that the deterministic Turing machine M works (with an input of length m) in space $\mathtt{tower}(n, m)$.

Consider the $\mathrm{M}\Pi^1_{n+1}$-definable temporal logic TL_{n+1} based on the modality SU, the usual boolean connectives, and the constant COMPUTATION with $[\![\mathrm{COMPUTATION}]\!] = \overline{\psi}$, the formula from Proposition 4.5 defining $\dagger\eta(L)$.

We denote by q_0 and q_1 the initial state and the accepting state of M respectively. We also denote by $\square$ the blank letter of the tape. Let $v = v_1 \cdots v_m$ be an input word of the Turing machine M and consider the formula INIT_v

$$\neg\Gamma \,\mathsf{SU}\, (\triangleright \wedge \neg\Gamma \,\mathsf{SU}\, (q_0 \wedge \neg\Gamma \,\mathsf{SU}\, (v_1 \wedge \cdots \neg\Gamma \,\mathsf{SU}\, (v_m \wedge (\neg\Gamma \vee \square) \,\mathsf{SU}\, \triangleleft) \cdots)))$$

which intuitively expresses the fact that the first configuration is actually the initial configuration of M on the input word v. Consider also the alphabets $\Sigma_m = A_m \cup \Delta_1 \subseteq \Sigma$ and $\Sigma'_m = \Sigma_m \cup \overline{A_m} \cup (\Sigma_m \times \Delta_1) \cup \{\dagger\}$ where $|A_m| = m$, $\overline{A_m} = \{\overline{a} \mid a \in A_m\}$ and the dependence relation D defined as above. We claim that v is accepted by M if and only if there is a trace in $\mathbb{M}(\Sigma_m, D)$ satisfying the formula $g_v = \mathrm{COMPUTATION} \wedge \mathrm{INIT}_v \wedge \top \,\mathsf{SU}\, q_1$. Therefore, the uniform satisfiability problem for TL_{n+1} is **nEXPSPACE**-hard. □

Remark 4.6. Note that all modalities of the logic TL_{n+1} are of arity at most two. Furthermore, the only binary temporal modality is SU. In our hardness proof, it is only used in the context $\neg\Gamma \,\mathsf{SU} -$, $(\neg\Gamma \vee \square) \,\mathsf{SU} -$ and $\top \,\mathsf{SU} -$. Thus, we could have replaced the binary modality SU by these three unary filter modalities in the style of [9]. Furthermore, the temporal logic could be deprived of constant formulas a for $a \notin \Gamma$ since they are not used in the hardness proof.

5 Process-Based $\mathrm{M}\Delta^1_1(\mathrm{N}, \lessdot, \mathrm{fin})$-Definable Logics

In Sect. 2, we showed that the modalities EX, Eco, EU, and SU can be dealt with in our framework. The technical report that this paper is based on shows that all modalities considered in the context of action based local temporal logics fall into our framework. Hence our upper bound shows that their uniform satisfiability problem can be solved in space $\mathtt{poly}(|\varphi|) \cdot \mathtt{tower}(2, \mathtt{poly}(|\Sigma|))$.

It is the aim of this final section to indicate that also Thiagarajan's logic TrPTL [13] can be dealt with in the setting of $\mathrm{M}\Delta^1_1(\mathrm{N}, \lessdot, \mathrm{fin})$-definable local temporal logics. The underlying idea of TrPTL is that the actions of the dependence alphabet are executed by independent processes. Communication between these processes is possible by the execution of joint actions. Hence, with any action $a \in \Sigma$, we associate a nonempty and finite set of processes $p(a) \subseteq \mathbb{N}$ in such a way that $(a, b) \in D$ iff $p(a) \cap p(b) \neq \emptyset$. This ensures that events performed by process i are linearly ordered in any trace t. With this additional information, one can define modalities that speak about the location of an action. The logic TrPTL is based on modalities $\mathcal{P}_i$, $\mathcal{O}_i$ and $\mathcal{U}_i$ ($i \in \mathbb{N}$) of arity 0, 1 and 2 respectively. Intuitively, $\mathcal{P}_i$ holds if the current vertex is located on process i and $\mathcal{O}_i\varphi$ means that φ holds at the first vertex of process i which is not below the current one. Finally, $\varphi\mathcal{U}_i\psi$ means that we have φ until ψ on the sequence of vertices located on process i and starting from the last vertex of process i which is below the current one.

We only explain how to handle $\mathcal{P}_i$, the remaining modalities are discussed in the technical report. The basic idea is that the index i is dealt with as an additional argument, i.e., $\mathcal{P}$ is considered to be of arity 1. The semantics of $\mathcal{P}$

is then given by the first-order formula $[\![\mathcal{P}]\!](X_1, x) = (x \in X_1)$. Then, given a concrete and finite dependence alphabet (Σ, D) together with a concrete function $p : \Sigma \to \mathbb{N}$, Thiagarajan's formula $\mathcal{P}_i$ is given by $\mathcal{P}(\bigvee_{a \in p^{-1}(i)} a)$. Thus, a temporal logic admitting modalities $\vee$ and $\mathcal{P}$ is able to simulate the modality $\mathcal{P}_i$. Similarly, we can deal with the other process based modalities.

References

1. B. Adsul and M. Sohoni. Complete and tractable local linear time temporal logics over traces. In *Proc. of ICALP'02*, number 2380 in LNCS, pages 926–937. Springer Verlag, 2002.
2. R. Alur, D. Peled, and W. Penczek. Model-checking of causality properties. In *Proc. of LICS'95*, pages 90–100. IEEE Computer Society Press, 1995.
3. V. Diekert and P. Gastin. Local temporal logic is expressively complete for cograph dependence alphabets. *Information and Computation*, 195:30–52, 2004.
4. V. Diekert and P. Gastin. Pure future local temporal logics are expressively complete for Mazurkiewicz traces. In *Proc. of LATIN'04*, number 2976 in LNCS, pages 232–241. Springer Verlag, 2004.
5. V. Diekert and G. Rozenberg, editors. *The Book of Traces*. World Scientific, Singapore, 1995.
6. H.-D. Ebbinghaus and J. Flum. *Finite Model Theory*. Springer Verlag, 1991.
7. D. Gabbay, I. Hodkinson, and M. Reynolds. *Temporal Logic*. Oxford University Press, 1994.
8. P. Gastin and D. Kuske. Satisfiability and model checking for MSO-definable temporal logics are in PSPACE. In *Proc. of CONCUR'03*, number 2761 in LNCS, pages 222–236. Springer Verlag, 2003.
9. P. Gastin and M. Mukund. An elementary expressively complete temporal logic for Mazurkiewicz traces. In *Proc. of ICALP'02*, number 2380 in LNCS, pages 938–949. Springer Verlag, 2002.
10. P. Gastin, M. Mukund, and K. Narayan Kumar. Local LTL with past constants is expressively complete for Mazurkiewicz traces. In *Proc. of MFCS'03*, number 2747 in LNCS, pages 429–438. Springer Verlag, 2003.
11. M. Mukund and P.S. Thiagarajan. Linear time temporal logics over Mazurkiewicz traces. In *Proc. of MFCS'96*, number 1113 in LNCS, pages 62–92. Springer Verlag, 1996.
12. Th. Schwentick and K. Bartelmann. Local normal forms for first-order logic with applications to games and automata. *Discrete Mathematics and Computer Science*, 3:109–124, 1999.
13. P.S. Thiagarajan. A trace based extension of linear time temporal logic. In *Proc. of LICS'94*, pages 438–447. IEEE Computer Society Press, 1994.
14. P.S. Thiagarajan. A trace consistent subset of PTL. In *Proc. of CONCUR'95*, number 962 in LNCS, pages 438–452. Springer Verlag, 1995.

Taming Interface Specifications*

Tiziana Margaria[1], A. Prasad Sistla[2], Bernhard Steffen[3], and Lenore D. Zuck[2]

[1] Georg-August-Universität Göttingen
margaria@informatik.uni-goettingen.de
[2] University of Illinois at Chicago
{sistla,lenore}@cs.uic.edu
[3] Universität Dortmund
Bernhard.Steffen@cs.uni-dortmund.de

Abstract. Software is often being assembled using third-party components where the developers have little knowledge of, and even less control over, the internals of the components comprising the overall system. One obstacle to composing agents is that current formal methods are mainly concerned with "closed" systems that are built from the ground up. Such systems are fully under the control of the user. Hence, problems arising from ill-specified components can be resolved by a close inspection of the systems. When composing systems using "off-the-shelf" components, this is often no longer the case.

The paper addresses the problem of *under-specification*, where an off-the-shelf component does only what it claims to do, however, it claims more behaviors than it actually has and that one wishes for, some of which may render it useless. Given such an under-specified module, we propose a method to automatically synthesize some safety properties from it that would tame its "bad" behaviors. The advantage of restricting to safety properties is that they are monitorable.

The safety properties are derived using an automata-theoretic approach. We show that, when restricting to ω-regular languages, there is no maximal safety property. For this case we construct a sequence of increasingly larger safety properties. We also show how to construct an infinite-state automata that can capture any safety property that is contained in the original specifications.

1 Introduction

The process of constructing software is undergoing rapid changes. Instead of a monolithic software development within an organization, increasingly, software is being assembled using third-party components (e.g., JavaBeans, .NET, etc.). The developers have little knowledge of, and even less control over, the internals of the components comprising the overall system.

One obstacle to composing agents is that current formal methods are mainly concerned with "closed" systems that are built from the ground up. Such systems are fully under the control of the user. Hence, problems arising from ill-specified components can

* This research was supported in part by NSF grants CCR-0205571 and CCR-0205363, and ONR grant N00014-99-1-0131

M. Abadi and L. de Alfaro (Eds.): CONCUR 2005, LNCS 3653, pp. 548–561, 2005.

be resolved by a close inspection of the systems. When composing agents using "off-the-shelf" ones, this is often no longer the case. Out of consideration for proprietary information, or in order to simplify presentation, companies may provide *incomplete specifications*. Worse, some agents may have no description at all except one that can be obtained by experimentation. Despite being ill-specified, "off-the-shelf" components might still be attractive enough so that the designer of a new service may wish to use them. In order to do so safely, the designer must be able to deal with the possibility that these components may exhibit undesired or unanticipated behavior, which could potentially compromise the correctness and security of the new system.

The main problem addressed in this paper is that of *under-specification*. As a simple example of the phenomenon, consider an interface specification that guarantees "after input *query* q is received, output $r = \mathit{response}(q)$ is produced." The designer of the interface probably meant a stronger specification, "after q is received, nothing else is produced until r is produced." Assume that the later version is sufficient and necessary to ensure the correctness of the entire system consisting of the module and the interface. Formal methods in general, and model checking in particular, are to fail in such situations since there is no algorithmic way to provide the model checker with the proper strengthening of the interface specification. Yet, under the assumption that interface specifications may be partial, there may exist a subset of the allowed behaviors that guarantees correctness, and one may still choose to use the component, provided deviations of the interface from this "good" set of behaviors can be detected at runtime.

Assume that we are given

- A finite-state *module* M, designed by our designer and accompanied by the full details of its implementation;
- An *interface specification* Φ_I for the external component interacting with the module M; and
- A *goal specification* Φ for the entire system which must be satisfied by the interaction between the module and the interface.

The *system* thus contains the composition of the module with the external component. The goal of the designer is to guarantee that the behavior of the system satisfies the goal specification Φ. Obviously, our underlying assumption is that the external component is helpful for the module, i.e., it computes things that the module cannot accomplish on its own. For example, if the module is a "general best buyer," and the external component has access to numerous bookstores which the module has no access to, the module uses the component to obtain the best book deals. However, the book buying component may be under-specified, thus, allow for behaviors for which the designer cannot guarantee the goal (while, of course, allow also for "good" behaviors, otherwise the designer will not be inclined to use it!).

The designer has a reason to believe that the real interface specification is more restricted than Φ_I, say it is $\Phi_I \wedge \phi$ for some ϕ. With this assumption, the designer can compose the module with the component so that Φ is guaranteed. If the property ϕ can be *run-time monitored*, i.e., if there is a simple module that runs synchronously with the system and watches for violations of ϕ, the designer can then go ahead and safely use the designed module as long as the monitor does not alarm.

Using a run-time monitor would allow the system to operate correctly as long as the external component satisfies ϕ. When it violates it, the run-time monitor alerts the user of the system that a violation occurred (and Φ is no longer guaranteed). However, this should not be viewed as a major obstacle – the applications intended are clearly not "safety critical" since no designer would use "black box" components inside a safety critical application. Such components can only be used in applications where a violation is tolerable. E.g., a leak of the credit card number, if caught in a timely manner, allows the holder of the credit card to alert the credit company and avoid bogus charges.

In this paper we focus on the problem of synthesizing a property ϕ that can be run-time monitored. In fact, we restrict the search to *safety* properties. Safety properties are those that can only be violated by a finite prefix. Hence, they can be monitored. In future work we will show how to synthesize the module M. Here, we restrict to the case where M is trivial. Thus, given Φ_I, we synthesize a safety property ϕ such that $\Phi_I \wedge \phi \rightarrow \Phi$.

We consider properties that are expressed as ω-sequences over a finite alphabet. Essentially, our synthesis problem reduces to that of finding safety properties that are contained in the property defined by $\Xi = \neg\Phi_I \vee \Phi$. While there is always *some* safety property ϕ that guarantees $\Phi_I \wedge \phi \rightarrow \Phi$ (e.g., the trivially false property), there is, in general no "maximal" one: Assume that Ξ is neither valid nor an obvious safety property. We show that when Ξ is ω-regular, then for every safety property ϕ_1 such that $\Phi_I \wedge \phi_1 \rightarrow \Phi$ there exists is a safety property $\phi_2 \neq \phi_1$ that is implied by ϕ_1 and that satisfies $\Phi_I \wedge \phi_2 \rightarrow \Phi$.

We compute a family of safety properties ϕ_k such that the higher k is, the more "accurate" and costly is the computation of ϕ_k. All these safety properties are given by deterministic finite state automata. As to be expected, the number of states of these automata increases linearly with k.

We also define a class of, possibly infinite-state, deterministic automata called *bounded automata* and show that the set of sequences accepted by bounded automata gives the desired safety property ϕ. We also prove a completeness result, showing that every safety property contained in the property defined by Ξ is accepted by some bounded automaton. In order for these automata to be useful, they need to be recursive, i.e., computable. With this in mind, we define *history-based recursive automata* that can be applied in practice.

The paper is organized as follows. Section 2 introduces the notation and definitions. Section 3 establishes the impossibility of finding a maximal safety properties for the case of ω-regular languages and contains the construction of the sequence of finite-state ω-automata for the synthesis of the desired safety property. Section 4 contains the definitions and results of our study of bounded automata. Section 5 compares our work with related work, and Section 6 contains discussion and concluding remarks.

2 Preliminaries

Sequences. Let S be a finite set. Let $\sigma = s_0, s_1, \ldots$ be a possibly infinite sequence over S. The length of σ, $|\sigma|$, is defined to be the number of elements in σ if σ is finite, and ω otherwise. We let ; denote the concatenation operator for sequences so that if

α_1 is a finite sequence and α_2 is a either a finite or a ω-sequence then $\alpha_1;\alpha_2$ is the concatenation of the two sequences in that order.

For integers i and j such that $0 \leq i \leq j < |\sigma|$, $\sigma[i,j]$ denotes the (finite) sequence $s_i, \ldots s_j$. A *prefix* of σ is any $\sigma[0,j]$ for $j < |\sigma|$. We denote the set of σ's prefixes by $Pref(\sigma)$. Given an integer i, $0 \leq i < |\sigma|$, we denote by $\sigma^{(i)}$ the *suffix* of σ that starts with s_i.

For an infinite sequence $\sigma : s_0, \ldots$, we denote by $\inf(\sigma)$ the set of S-elements that occur in σ infinitely many times, i.e., $\inf(\sigma) = \{s : s_i = s \text{ for infinitely many } i\text{'s}\}$.

Languages. A *language* L over a finite alphabet Σ is a set of finite or infinite sequences over Σ. When L consists only of infinite strings (sequences), we sometimes refer to it as an ω*-language*. For a language L, we denote the set of prefixes of L by $Pref(L)$, i.e.,

$$Pref(L) = \bigcup_{\sigma \in L} Pref(\sigma)$$

Following [6,2], an ω-language L is a *safety property* if for every $\sigma \in \Sigma^\infty$:

$$Pref(\sigma) \subseteq Pref(L) \implies \sigma \in L$$

i.e., L is a safety property if it is *limit closed* – for every ω-string σ, if every prefix of σ is a prefix of some L-string, then σ must be an L-string.

Safety properties play an important role in the results reported here.

Büchi Automata A *Büchi automaton* (NBA for short) $\mathcal{A}$ on infinite strings is described by a quintuple $(Q, \Sigma, \delta, q_0, F)$ where:

- Q is a finite set of states;
- Σ is a finite alphabet of symbols;
- $\delta \colon Q \times \Sigma \to 2^Q$ is a transition function;
- $q_0 \in Q$ is an initial state; and
- $F \subseteq Q$ is a set of accepting states.

The *generalized transition function* $\delta^* : Q \times \Sigma^* \to 2^Q$ is defined in the usual way, i.e., for every state q, $\delta^*(q, \epsilon) = \{q\}$, and for any $\sigma \in \Sigma^*$ and $a \in \Sigma$, $\delta^*(q, \sigma; a) = \bigcup_{q' \in \delta^*(q,\sigma)} \delta(q', a)$.

If for every $(q, a) \in Q \times \Sigma$, $|\delta(q, a)| = 1$, then $\mathcal{A}$ is called a *deterministic* Büchi automaton (or DBA for short).

Let $\sigma : a_1, \ldots$ be an infinite sequence over Σ. A *run* r *of* $\mathcal{A}$ on σ is an infinite sequence $q^0, \ldots$ over Q such that:

- $q^0 = q_0$;
- for every $i > 0$, $q^i \in \delta(q^{i-1}, a_i)$;

A run r is *accepting* if $\inf(r) \cap F \neq \emptyset$. The automaton $\mathcal{A}$ *accepts* the ω-string σ if it has an accepting run over σ (for the case of DBAs, the automaton has a single run over σ). The *language accepted by* $\mathcal{A}$, denoted by $L(\mathcal{A})$, is the set of ω-strings that $\mathcal{A}$ accepts. A language L' is called ω*-regular* if it is an ω-language that is accepted by some (possibly non-deterministic) Büchi automaton.

A Büchi automaton $\mathcal{A}$ can also be used to define a *regular automaton* that is just like $\mathcal{A}$, only the acceptance condition of a run r is that its last state is accepting. We denote the regular language accepted by the regular version of $\mathcal{A}$ by $L_f(\mathcal{A})$.

3 Synthesis of Safety Properties by Finite-State Automata

As described in Section 1, given an interface specification Φ_I of a readily available off-the-shelf reactive component and a desired goal specification Φ, we wish to derive a safety property ϕ so that $\Phi_I \wedge \phi \rightarrow \Phi$. We assume that both Φ_I and Φ are given by temporal logic formulas. Our methods, however, can also be applied to the case where Φ_I and Φ are described by ω-automata. As before, denote $\Xi = \neg\Phi_I \vee \Phi$. Obviously, any safety property ϕ such that $\phi \rightarrow \Xi$ is a satisfies our requirements.

In this section we describe how to obtain ϕ as deterministic automaton. The advantage of obtaining the required ϕ as a deterministic automaton is that it can be directly used to monitor the execution of the module: The automaton simply runs on the executions of the module and a violation of the safety property by the execution is indicated by the automaton entering a "bad" state. In this section we restrict to ω-automata, for which, as we show, only a limited set of safety properties can be derived. To overcome this limitation we present, in the next section, automata that are not necessarily finite-state and study their power.

Using the methods of [13,3], we first obtain a Büchi automaton $\mathcal{A}$ whose language is the set of ω-strings satisfying Ξ. Thus, we reduce the problem to that of obtaining a deterministic automaton whose language is a safety property that is contained in $L(\mathcal{A})$. Roughly speaking, we start with the automaton that accepts Ξ, and construct a family of automata, indexed by some integer k, each accepting a sequence that satisfies Ξ where an accepting state is realized in every block of k consecutive states.

Example 1. Suppose an off-the-shelf *permission manager* that receives requests by a user and grants appropriate permissions, e.g., authorizations to access different resources. Assume there are two types of requests, r_1 and r_2, with two corresponding grants, g_1 and g_2 respectively. The permission manager guarantees that every request is eventually responded by granting of the corresponding permission. Thus Φ_I is:

$$\Box(r_1 \rightarrow \Diamond g_1) \wedge \Box(r_2 \rightarrow \Diamond g_2)$$

Assume a user who wishes to use e component and who requires that a r_1 request receives a higher priority than a r_2 request, at the possibly cost of ignoring an r_2 request, i.e., that an r_1 should be granted before any potentially pending r_2 requests are granted. Thus, the goal Φ of the user is:

$$\Box(r_1 \rightarrow (\neg g_2)\,\mathcal{U}\,g_1)$$

where $\mathcal{U}$ is the temporal "until" operator.

Note user's requirement for r_1 is stronger than that guaranteed by the component, while the user's requirement for r_2 is weaker.

The user can construct a monitor that monitors for violations of a safety property that is contained in $(\neg\Phi_I \vee \Phi)$, e.g., of the property:

$$\Box(r_1 \rightarrow (\neg g_2)\,\mathcal{W}\,g_1)$$

where $\mathcal{W}$ is the unless (weak until) temporal operator. Thus, the property does not require g_1 to hold after r_1 (but does require that as long as g_1 doesn't hold, neither does g_2).

3.1 Derivation of a Safety Property Using Büchi Automata

Ideally, given a property described by a Büchi automaton $\mathcal{A}$, we would like to synthesize the *maximal* safety property that is contained in $L(\mathcal{A})$. However, as the following lemma shows, if $L(\mathcal{A})$ is not already a safety property, then there exists no maximal safety property in it that can be accepted by a Büchi automaton. The proof of this lemma is given at the end of this subsection.

Lemma 1. *Let $\mathcal{A}$ be a Büchi automaton and assume $L(\mathcal{A})$ is not a safety property. Then for every safety property $L' \subset L(\mathcal{A})$, there exists a safety property L'' such that $L' \subset L'' \subset L(\mathcal{A})$. Moreover, if L' is ω-regular then so is L''.*

In the following, we construct from a given Büchi automaton $\mathcal{A}$ and an integer k, an automaton $\mathcal{A}_k$ that accepts those sequences in $L(\mathcal{A})$ that have an accepting $\mathcal{A}$-run in which an accepting state appears in every k-length block of consecutive states, thus $L(\mathcal{A}_k) \subseteq L(\mathcal{A})$ is a safety property.

Assume a Büchi automaton $\mathcal{A} :\ = (Q_A, \Sigma, \delta_A, q_A^0, F_A)$. Let $k > 0$ be an integer. We first define an ω-language $L_k(\mathcal{A})$, that is a subset of $L(\mathcal{A})$, where every string has an accepting run where accepting (F_A) states appear at least every k states from the beginning. Formally,

$$\begin{aligned} L_k(\mathcal{A}) \ = \ \{\sigma \in L(\mathcal{A}) : & \text{ for some accepting } \mathcal{A}\text{-run } r : q0, \ldots \text{ over } \sigma, \\ & \text{for every } i \geq 0, r[i \times k, ((i+1) \times k) - 1] \cap F_A \neq \emptyset\} \end{aligned}$$

Note that

$$\bigcup_{k>0} L_k(\mathcal{A}) \subseteq L(\mathcal{A})$$

This containment may, in general, be strict.

In general, $L_k(\mathcal{A})$ may not be contained in $L_{k+1}(\mathcal{A})$. However, it is not difficult to show that, if $k' \geq 2k - 1$ then $L_k(\mathcal{A}) \subseteq L_{k'}(\mathcal{A})$. As a consequence, by increasing k, we can get larger and larger safety properties contained in $L(\mathcal{A})$.

We next describe the construction of a DBA $\mathcal{A}_k$ that accepts the language $L_k(\mathcal{A})$. The construction of the automaton is an extension of the standard subset construction combined with partitioning the input into segments of length k. The segment partitioning is done by means of a modulo k counter. The automaton $\mathcal{A}_k$ simulates the possible runs of $\mathcal{A}$ on the input, and maintains the set of states that $\mathcal{A}$ may be at after reading each prefix. With each such state, $\mathcal{A}_k$ also keeps a bit, called *accepting state* bit, which indicates if an accepting state had been reached since the beginning of the most recent input segment.

Let $R = F_A \times \{1\} \cup (Q_A \setminus F_A) \times \{0, 1\}$. Fix some $k > 0$. Define the Büchi automaton $\mathcal{A}_k = (Q', \Sigma, \delta', q'_0, F')$ where:

- $Q' = 2^R \times \{0, 1, ..., k-1\}$;
- $q'_0 = \begin{cases} (\{(q_A^0, 0)\}, k-1) \text{ if } q_A^0 \notin F_A \\ (\{(q_A^0, 1)\}, k-1) \text{ otherwise} \end{cases}$
- F' is the set of all Q''s states whose first coordinate is non-empty, i.e., $F' = (2^R - \emptyset) \times \{0, 1, ..., k-1\}$

To define δ', we use two auxiliary transition functions $\beta, \gamma : 2^R \times \Sigma \rightarrow 2^R$ defined below. The function β captures the behavior of $\mathcal{A}_k$ within a segment: Note that the first coordinate of a state $q' \in Q'$ is a set of the form $\{(q_i, b_i) : 1 \leq i \leq m\}$ where each q_i is a state $\mathcal{A}$ can be in after reading a prefix, and b_i is the accepting bit which is 1 iff an accepting state was reached since the beginning of that segment. After reading an input letter s from a state q', $\mathcal{A}_k$ reaches all the states $\mathcal{A}$ reaches from q_i after reading s (i.e., $\delta(q_i, s)$), and the accepting bit is 1 if either it was 1 before (i.e., $b_i = 1$), or the state that is reached is accepting. Let β: $2^R \times \Sigma \rightarrow 2^R$ be defined by:

$$\beta(\cup_{i=1}^m \{(q_i, b_i)\}, s) = \{(q, b) : \exists i. 1 \leq i \leq m \wedge q \in \delta(q_i, s) \wedge b \leftrightarrow (q \in F_A \vee b_i = 1)\}$$

The second auxiliary transition system, γ: $2^R \times \Sigma \rightarrow 2^R$, captures the behavior of $\mathcal{A}$ when moving in between segments. It is similar to β, only that it restricts moves between segments to be only from states whose b_i is 1.

$$\gamma(\cup_{i=1}^m \{(q_i, b_i)\}, s) = \{(q, b) : \exists i. 1 \leq i \leq m \wedge b_i = 1 \wedge q \in \delta(q_i, s) \wedge (b \leftrightarrow q \in F_A)\}$$

We now define δ'. For $c > 0$,

$$\delta'(\langle \cup_{i=1}^m \{(q_i, b_i)\}, c\rangle, s) = \{(\beta(\cup_{i=1}^m \{(q_i, b_i)\}, s), c - 1)\}$$

and for $c = 0$,

$$\delta'(\langle \cup_{i=1}^m \{(q_i, b_i)\}, 0\rangle, s) = \{(\gamma(\cup_{i=1}^m \{(q_i, b_i)\}, s), k - 1)\}$$

Lemma 2. *$L_k(\mathcal{A})$ is a safety property and $L(\mathcal{A}_k) = L_k(\mathcal{A})$.*

Proof. Note that in the automaton $\mathcal{A}_k$, there are no transitions from states in $Q' - F'$ to states in F'. Thus the states of the $\mathcal{A}_k$ are partitioned into *good* states (i.e., members of F') and *bad* states (i.e., members of $Q' - F'$), so that an input sequence is accepted by it iff the unique run of $\mathcal{A}_k$ on the input contains only good states. From [11] it follows that $L(\mathcal{A}_k)$ is a safety property. It remains to show that $L(\mathcal{A}_k) = L_k(\mathcal{A})$.

$\supseteq$: Assume $\sigma \in L_k(\mathcal{A})$. Thus, there exists an accepting $\mathcal{A}$-run $r = q^0, \ldots$ such that for each $j \geq 0$, $r[jk, (j+1)k] \cap F_A \neq \emptyset$. Let $\hat{r} : (R_0, c_0), (R_1, c_1), \ldots$ be the $\mathcal{A}_k$-run on σ. For every i, let $Q_i \subseteq Q_A$ be the set $\{q : (q, b) \in R_i$ for $b = 0$ or $b = 1\}$;i.e., Q_i is the set consisting of projections of each pair in R_i on its first component. By a simple induction, it can be shown that for $i \geq 0$, $q^i \in Q_i$. Since each Q_i is non-empty, $\hat{r}$ is an accepting run of $\mathcal{A}_k$. It therefore follows that $\sigma \in L(\mathcal{A}_k)$.

$\subseteq$: Assume $\sigma = s_1, \ldots$ is in $L(\mathcal{A}_k)$. Let $\hat{r} : (R_0, c_0), (R_1, c_1), \ldots$ be $\mathcal{A}_k$'s run on σ. For every i, let $Q_i \subseteq Q_A$ be the set $\{q : (q, b) \in R_i$ for $b = 0$ or $b = 1\}$. Since $\hat{r}$ is accepting, $Q_i \neq \emptyset$ for every $i \geq 0$. Define an infinite tree whose nodes are elements of the form $(q, j) \in Q_A \times \mathbb{N}$. The root of the tree is $(q_A^0, 0)$. For a tree node $n = (q, j)$, the children of n are the nodes $(n', j+1)$ such that $n' \in \delta_A(q, s_{j+1}) \cap Q_{j+1}$. Note that since $\hat{r}$ is an accepting $\mathcal{A}_k$-run, this tree is an infinite tree. Since it is finitely branching, form Köning's lemma, it follows that the tree has an infinite path r which is an $\mathcal{A}$-run. Moreover, from the way the accepting bits b_j are updated, it follows that, for every $i \geq 0$, the finite sequence $r[ik, (i+1)k]$ contains at least one occurrence of an F_A-state. Consequently, r is an accepting$\mathcal{A}$- run. It therefore follows that $\sigma \in L_k(\mathcal{A})$. □

Note. There are alternate ways of deriving safety properties contained in $L(\mathcal{A})$. We chose the one above for its relative simplicity.
We can now prove Lemma 1:

Proof (of Lemma 1). Assume $L' \subset L(\mathcal{A})$ is a safety property. Since $L(\mathcal{A})$ is not a safety property, there exists some $\sigma \in \Sigma^\omega \setminus L(\mathcal{A})$ such that $Pref(\sigma) \subseteq Pref(L(\mathcal{A})))$. Since $L' \subset L(\mathcal{A})$, it is the case, σ is not in L'. Since L' is safety property, there exists some $\alpha \in Pref(\sigma)$ which is a bad prefix for L', i.e., $\alpha\Sigma^\omega \cap L' = \emptyset$. Consider now the set $L_\alpha = \alpha\Sigma^\omega \cap L(\mathcal{A})$ of the $L(\mathcal{A})$ ω-strings with prefix α. The set L_α is an infinite ω-regular set. Let $\mathcal{B}$ be the Büchi automaton that accepts it, i.e., $L(\mathcal{B}) = L_\alpha$. Let k be an integer greater than or equal to the number of states in $\mathcal{B}$, and consider the language $L_k(\mathcal{B})$. From Lemma 2 it follows that $L_k(\mathcal{B})$ is a ω-regular safety property contained in L_α. Since k is at least as large as the number of states of $\mathcal{B}$, $L_k(\mathcal{B}) \neq \emptyset$. Since L' and $L_k(\mathcal{B})$ are safety properties, from [11], we see that $L'' = L' \cup L_k(\mathcal{B})$ is also a safety property. From the fact that L' and $L_k(\mathcal{B})$ are disjoint subsets of $L(\mathcal{A})$ and $L_k(\mathcal{B}) \neq \emptyset$, it follows that $L' \subset L'' \subset L(\mathcal{A})$. Note that since ω-languages are closed under union, it follows that if L' is ω-regular then so is L''. □

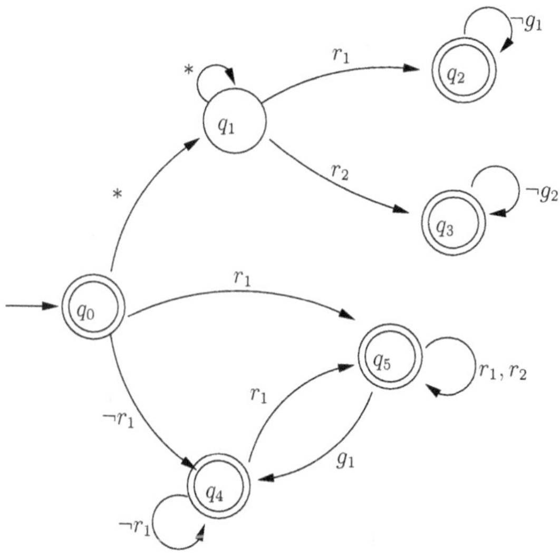

Fig. 1. Automaton for $\neg\Phi_I \vee \Phi$

In Fig 1 we give the automaton $\mathcal{A}$ for the property $\neg\Phi_I \vee \Phi$ for the permission manager example,i.e., example 1. Notice that this is a non-deterministic Buchi automaton. All double circles indicate accepting states and the state with an incoming edge from outside is the initial state. The input alphabet is $\{r_1, g_1, r_2, g_2\}$. The $*$ symbol on an input transition indicates that this transition can take place on any input symbol, i.e., it represents four transitions corresponding to each of the input symbols. The $\neg g_1$ symbol

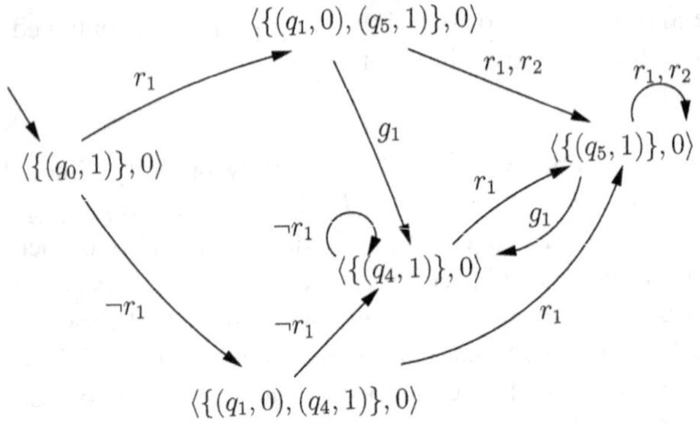

Fig. 2. Our safety property: the $k = 1$ approximation

on a transition indicates that this transition can take place on any input symbol other than g_1, thus it represents three transitions. The symbols $\neg g_2, \neg r_1$ are similarly used.

In Fig. 2 we see the $k = 1$ approximation for our permission manager example, i.e., the automaton $\mathcal{A}_1$. This is a deterministic automaton. Each state of this automaton has the structure as given in the definition. There is an additional state, not shown in the figure, which is $\langle\emptyset, 0\rangle$. All unspecified transitions in the figure go to this state. For example, there is a transition from the state $\langle\{(q_5, 1)\}, 0\rangle$ to the state on input g_2. All states excepting $\langle\emptyset, 0\rangle$ are accepting states. It is not difficult to see that $L(\mathcal{A}) = L(\mathcal{A}_1)$. Note that this does not contradict Lemma 1 since $L(\mathcal{A})$ is a safety property.

4 Synthesis of Safety Properties by Bounded Automata

Section 3 describes the construction of deterministic finite state automata that synthesize safety properties contained in $L(\mathcal{A})$. It is often the case that "interesting" safety properties that are contained in $L(\mathcal{A})$ cannot be captured by finite state automata. For example, suppose that $L(\mathcal{A})$ is the set of ω-strings over $\{a, b\}$ where a appears infinitely often. Using the construction of Section 3, each $L(\mathcal{A}_k)$ requires that the number of bs between successive occurrences of a be bounded by a constant. Thus, they all rule out, e.g., a sequence where the number of b's between the ith and the $(i + 1)^{st}$ occurrence of a is i. On the other hand, an infinite state automaton that dynamically changes the bound on the number of input symbols before an acceptance state of $\mathcal{A}$ occurs on a run, can accept such a sequence.

Let $\mathcal{A} = (Q_A, \Sigma, \delta_A, q_A^0, F_A)$ be a Büchi automaton which we fix for this section. We generalize the construction of Subsection 3.1 using a class of infinite-state automata called *bounded automata*, and show that the language accepted by each bounded automaton is a safety property that is contained in $L(\mathcal{A})$. We also prove the converse, showing that every safety property contained in $L(\mathcal{A})$ is accepted by some bounded automaton.

Assume some (possibly infinite) set Y_B. A *bounded automaton* $\mathcal{B}$ is described by a tuple $(Q_B, \Sigma, \delta_B, q_B^0, F_B)$ where:

- $Q_B \subseteq Y_B \times 2^{Q_A \times \{0,1\}} \times (\mathbb{N} \cup \{\infty\})$ is a set of *states*;
- Σ is a finite *alphabet*;
- $\delta_B \colon Q_B \times \Sigma \rightarrow Q_B$ is a *transition function*. We further require that for every $\langle r, C, i \rangle, \langle r', C', i' \rangle \in Q_B$ and $a \in \Sigma$, if $\delta_B(\langle r, C, i \rangle, a) = \langle r', C', i' \rangle$ then the following all hold:
  - If $i = \infty$ then $i' = \infty$.
  - If $i' < i$ then $C' = \{(q', b') : \exists.(q, b) \in C$ such that $q' \in \delta_A(q, a) \wedge (b' = 1) \Leftrightarrow (b = 1 \vee q' \in F_A)\}$.
  - If $i' \geq i$ then $C' = \{(q', b') : \exists.(q, 1) \in C$ such that $q' \in \delta_A(q, a) \wedge (b = 1 \Leftrightarrow q' \in F_A)\}$.
- q_B^0 is the initial state, and it is required to be of the form $(r, \{(q_A^0, b)\}, i)$ where $b' = 1 \Leftrightarrow q_A^0 \in F_A$ and $i \neq \infty$.
- $F_B = \{\langle r, C, i \rangle : C \neq \emptyset \wedge i \neq \infty\}$.

It is to be noted that the range of δ_B is Q_B (and not 2^{Q_B}). This is done to make the notation simple and it also makes a bounded automaton as a deterministic automaton. A run of $\mathcal{B}$, an accepting run, and the language accepted by $\mathcal{B}$ are defined just in the case of Büchi automata.

The definition δ_B implies that once the second component of a state in a run is empty, it remains so. Similarly, if the third component of a state in a run is ∞, then it remains so. Thus, once a run enters a state in $Q_B \setminus F_B$, it remains there. (It thus follows that it suffices to define a run as accepting if it never reaches a $Q_B \setminus F_B$-state.) From [11] it follows that:

Lemma 3. *For a bounded automata $\mathcal{B}$, $L(\mathcal{B})$ is a safety property.*

Intuitively, given an input string, $\mathcal{B}$ simulates $\mathcal{A}$. Suppose $\mathcal{B}$ reaches a state $\langle r, C, i \rangle$. For each $(q, b) \in C$, q is a state $\mathcal{A}$ reaches on some run on the input seen thus far. The integer i is an upper bound on the number of steps before an accepting state of $\mathcal{A}$ is reached on some run. There are two types of transitions in δ_B— *decreasing* and *non-decreasing* transitions— denoting, respectively, those transitions that decrease i and those that do not. In case of decreasing transitions, C is updated to be the successor states of the corresponding runs of $\mathcal{A}$. In the case of non-decreasing transitions, only those runs containing an accepting state of $\mathcal{A}$, since the last occurrence of a non-decreasing transition, are considered for updating C. The bit b for each $(q, b) \in C$ records whether an accepting state has been reached since the last occurrence of a non-decreasing transition.

Let α be a finite string over Σ. If $\delta_B^*(q_B^0, \alpha) = \langle r, C, i \rangle$, then for every infinite string $\sigma \in L(\mathcal{B})$ such that $\alpha \in \mathit{Pref}(\sigma)$, for some $j \leq i$, $\delta_A^*(q_A^0, \sigma_{|\alpha|+j}) \cap F_A \neq \emptyset$ (where σ_j denotes the prefix of σ of length j). Thus, i is an upper bound on the number of inputs before an accepting state is going to appear after α is read on some run of $\mathcal{A}$. From the description of the operation of $\mathcal{B}$, given above, it is not difficult to show the following lemma.

Lemma 4. *For any bounded automaton $\mathcal{B}$, $L(\mathcal{B}) \subseteq L(\mathcal{A})$.*

Proof. Let $\sigma = s_1, \ldots$ be a string in $L(\mathcal{B})$. Let $u = \langle r_0, C_0, i_0 \rangle, \ldots, \langle r_j, C_j, i_j \rangle, \ldots$ be the (unique) run of $\mathcal{B}$ on σ. For each $j \geq 0$, let $C_j = (Q_j, b_j)$. As in the proof of Lemma 1, define an infinite tree whose nodes are elements of the form $(q, j) \in Q_A \times \mathbb{N}$. The root of the tree is $(q_A^0, 0)$. For a tree node $n = (q, j)$, where $j \geq 0$, the children of n are the nodes $(n', j+1)$ such that $n' \in \delta_A(q, s_{j+1}) \cap Q_{j+1}$. This tree is infinite and hence has an infinite path. Every such path defines a run of $\mathcal{A}$ on σ. Let k_j be the number of non-decreasing transitions of $\mathcal{B}$ that occur in the finite run $u[0, j]$. From our earlier discussion, it should be easy to see that every path of length j from the root node of the above tree contains at least k_j nodes of the form (q', l) where $q' \in F_A$. Since the run u has infinite number of non-decreasing transitions appearing in it, it is the case that every infinite path in the tree contains infinite nodes of the form (q', l) where $q' \in F_A$. Hence each such path gives an accepting run of $\mathcal{A}$ on σ. Since there exists at least one such path, we see that $\sigma \in L(\mathcal{A})$. □

We next show that for every safety property in $L(\mathcal{A})$ there exists a bounded automaton that accepts it.

Recall that for a Büchi automaton $\mathcal{A}$, $L_f(\mathcal{A})$ is the regular language defined by the regular version of $\mathcal{A}$. Let $S \subseteq L(\mathcal{A})$ be a safety property. Note that every sequence in S has infinite number of prefixes that are in $L_f(\mathcal{A})$. For a sequence $\sigma \in S$ and $\alpha \in \mathit{Pref}(\sigma)$, let $\mathit{min\_idx}(\sigma, \alpha) = \min\{|\beta| : \alpha; \beta \in L_f(\mathcal{A}) \cap \mathit{Pref}(\sigma)\}$. Note that if $\alpha \in L_f(\mathcal{A}) \cap \mathit{Pref}(\sigma)$, then $\mathit{min\_idx}(\sigma, \alpha) = 0$.

For any finite string $\alpha \in \Sigma^*$, let $Z(\alpha, S) = \{\mathit{min\_idx}(\sigma, \alpha) : \sigma \in S \text{ and } \alpha \in \mathit{Pref}(\sigma)\}$. Obviously, if $\alpha \in L_f(\mathcal{A}) \cap \mathit{Pref}(S)$, then $Z(\alpha, S) = \{0\}$. Also, if $\alpha \notin \mathit{Pref}(S)$ then $Z(\alpha, S) = \emptyset$. The following lemma establishes that $Z(\alpha, S)$ is always finite.

Lemma 5. *For any $\alpha \in \Sigma^*$, $Z(\alpha, S)$ is finite.*

Proof. From the comments above it suffices to prove the claim for the case when $\alpha \in \mathit{Pref}(S) \setminus L_f(\mathcal{A})$. Assume, by way of contradiction, that $Z(\alpha, S)$ is infinite. Since Σ is a finite set, it follows that there exists some $a_0 \in \Sigma$ such that $Z(\alpha a_0, S)$ is an infinite, hence $\alpha_1 = \alpha; a_0 \notin L_f(\mathcal{A})$. We can repeat this observation inductively, and obtain an infinite sequence of finite sequences $\alpha = \alpha_0, a_1, \ldots$ such that for every $i \geq 0$, $\alpha_{i+1} = \alpha_i; a_i$ for some $a_i \in \Sigma$, $Z(\alpha_i, S)$ is infinite, and $\alpha_i \notin L_f(\mathcal{A})$. Let $\beta \in \Sigma^\omega$ be the limit sequence of the α_i's. Since for every i, $\alpha_i \in \mathit{Pref}(S)$, and S is a safety property, it follows that $\beta \in S$. All the prefixes of β of length greater than $|\alpha|$ are not in $L_f(\mathcal{A})$. Consequently, $\beta \notin L(\mathcal{A})$. It therefore follows that $S \not\subseteq L(\mathcal{A})$, which is a contradiction. □

For $\alpha \in \Sigma^*$, let $\mathit{idx}(\alpha, S) = \max_{i \in Z(\alpha, S)} i$. If $Z(\alpha, S)$ is empty, we define $\mathit{idx}(\alpha, S) = \infty$. Thus, $\mathit{idx}(\alpha, S) \in \mathbb{N}$ iff $\alpha \in \mathit{Pref}(S)$. With a safety property $S \subseteq L(\mathcal{A})$, we associate a bounded automaton $\mathcal{D} = (Q_D, \Sigma, \delta_D, q_D^0, F_D)$ where:

- Q_D consists of triples of the form $\langle \alpha, C, i \rangle$ where $\alpha \in \Sigma^*$, $C \subseteq Q_A \times \{0, 1\}$, and $i = \mathit{idx}(\alpha, S)$;
- For every $\langle \alpha, C, i \rangle \in Q_D$ and $a \in \Sigma$, $\delta_D(\langle \alpha, C, i \rangle, a) = \langle \alpha', C', i' \rangle$ implies $\alpha' = \alpha; a$.
- q_D^0 is the triple $\langle \epsilon, (q_A^0, b), \mathit{idx}(\epsilon, S) \rangle$ where ϵ is the empty sequence and $b = 1 \Leftrightarrow q_A^0 \in F_A$;

For $\alpha \in \Sigma^*$, it is easy to see that $\delta_D^*(q_D^0, \alpha)$ is of the form $(\alpha, C, idx(\alpha, S))$. Moreover, if $\alpha \in Pref(S)$, then $C \neq \emptyset$ and $i \neq \infty$. Thus, after having read any prefix of a S-sequence, $\mathcal{D}$ is in a $F_{\mathcal{D}}$-state. Thus, $S \subseteq L(\mathcal{D})$. Conversely, if $\sigma \notin S$, then there exists some $\alpha \in Pref(\sigma) \setminus Pref(S)$. In this case, the state reached by $\mathcal{D}$ after reading α is of the form (α, C, ∞), and thus $\sigma \notin L(\mathcal{D})$. We thus have:

Lemma 6. $L(\mathcal{D}) = S$.

The following theorem follows from Lemma 4 and Lemma 6:

Theorem 1 (Completeness). *Let $\mathcal{A}$ be a Büchi automaton. Then every safety property $S \subseteq L(\mathcal{A})$ is accepted by some bounded automaton.*

Recursive and History Based Automata. We have shown that the class of languages accepted by bounded automata is exactly the class of safety properties contained in $L(\mathcal{A})$. We say that a bounded automaton $\mathcal{B} = (Q_B, \Sigma, \delta_B, q_B^0, F_B)$ is *recursive* if the set Q_B is recursive and δ_B is a computable function. It is to be noted that only recursive bounded automata are useful. It is not difficult to see that the automata $\mathcal{A}_k$ that we defined in Subsection 3.1 are recursive bounded automata as each of these is a finite state automaton. Recall that, in these automata, k is the length of the segments into which the input string is divided. We can generalize the automata A_k, so that it starts with an initial value of k and increases the value of k dynamically; that is, it increases the lengths of the segments according to some computable function f, so that $f(i)$ is the length of the ith segment.

We can now define a class of recursive bounded automata, called *history based automata*: Let $f\colon \Sigma^* \times 2^{Q_A \times \{0,1\}} \to (\mathbb{N} \cup \{\infty\})$ be some computable function. A *history based automaton with respect to* f is the bounded automaton $\mathcal{B}_f = (Q_B, \Sigma, \delta_B, q_B^0, F_B)$ where $Q_B = \{(\alpha, C, f(\alpha, C)) : \alpha \in \Sigma^*,\ C \subseteq Q_A \times \{0,1\}\}$. Note that $\mathcal{B}_f$ is uniquely defined. Essentially, the bound in each state of $\mathcal{B}_f$ is defined by the recursive function f. It is not difficult to show that every recursive bounded automaton is homomorphic to a history based automaton.

5 Related Work

Some of the techniques we employ are somewhat reminiscent of techniques used for verifying that a safety property described by a state machine satisfies a correctness specification given by an automaton or temporal logic. For example, simulation relations/state-functions together with well-founded mappings [5,1,12] have been proposed in the literature for this purpose. Our bounded automata use a form of well-founded mappings in the form of positive integer values that are components of each state. (This is as it should be, since we need to use some counters to ensure that an accepting state eventually appears.) However, here we are not trying to establish the correctness of a given safety property defined by a state machine, but rather, we are deriving safety properties that are contained in the language of an automaton.

In [7,8] Larsen et.al. propose a method for turning an implicit specification of a component into an explicit one. I.e., given a context specification (in their case a process algebraic expression with a hole, where the desired components needs to be plugged in) and an overall specification, they fully automatically derive a temporal safety property characterizing the set of all implementations which, together with the given context, satisfy the overall specification. While this technique has been developed for component synthesis, it can also be used for synthesizing optimal monitors in a setting where the interface specification Φ_I and the goal specification Φ are both safety properties. In this paper, we do not make any assumptions on Φ_I and Φ. They can be arbitrary properties specified in temporal logic or by automata. We are aiming at exploiting liveness guarantees of external components (contexts), in order to establish liveness properties of the overall system under certain additional safety assumptions, which we can run time check (monitor). This allows us to guarantee that the overall system is as live as the context, as long as the constructed monitor does not cause an alarm.

Perhaps closest to our work in motivation is the work in [10]. The approach taken there, however, is that of considering the interaction between the module and the interface as a 2-player game, where the interface has a winning strategy if it can guarantee that no matter what the module does, Φ is met while maintaining Φ_I. Run-time monitoring is used to verify that the interface has a winning strategy.

There has been much work done in the literature on monitoring violations of safety properties in distributed systems. In these works, the safety property is typically explicitly specified by the user. Our work is more on deriving safety properties from component specifications than developing algorithms for monitoring given safety properties. In this sense, the approach to use safety properties for monitoring that have been automatically derived by observation using techniques adapted from automata learning (see [4]) is closer in spirit to the proposal here. Much attention has since been spent in optimizing the automatic learning of the monitors [9]. However, the learned monitors play a different role: whereas the learned monitors are good, but by no means complete, sensors for detecting unexpected anomalies, the monitors derived with the techniques of this paper *imply* the specifying property as long as the guarantees of the component provider are true.

6 Conclusions and Discussion

In this paper, we considered the problem of customizing a given, off-the-shelf, reactive component to user requirements. In this process, we assume that the reactive module's external behavior is specified by a formula Φ_I and the desired goal specifications is given by a formula Φ. Both Φ_I and Φ can be arbitrary properties, i.e. , they need not be safety properties. We presented methods for obtaining a safety specification ϕ so that $\Phi_I \wedge \phi \rightarrow \Phi$. Our methods obtain ϕ as a deterministic (possibly infinite state) automaton. This automaton can be used to monitor execution of the off-the-shelf component so that it does not violate ϕ and hence satisfies the goal specification Φ.

There are a number of issues that need to be further addressed. When the desired property is given by a finite state automaton, then monitoring executions can be done in real time, i.e., each successive state change of the automaton can be done within a constant time that only depends on the size of the automaton but not on the length of the computation, i.e., the history seen thus far. On the other hand, when ϕ is given by an infinite state automaton, real time change in the state of the automaton may not always be achievable. For example, we defined a class of infinite state automata, called history based automata, that divide the input into segments and ensure that an appropriate liveness condition is satisfied in each segment. In these automata, the lengths of successive segments can vary dynamically and are computed as functions of the history using a computable function. In such cases, one has to ensure that the computation of the length of the next segment does not take too long a time. Of course, one can compute lengths of successive segments by simple functions such as increasing the lengths by a constant factor, etc. These and other issues need to be further investigated. We also need to further investigate practical cases where these techniques can be applied.

References

1. M. Abadi and L. Lamport. The existence of state mappings. In *Proceedings of the ACM Symposium on Logic in Computer Science*, 1988.
2. B. Alpern and F. Schneider. Defining liveness. *Information Processing Letters*, 21:181–185, 1985.
3. E. A. Emerson and A. P. Sistla. Triple exponential decision procedure for the logic ctl*. In *Workshop on the Logics of Program, Carnegie-Mellon University*, 1983.
4. H. Hungar and B. Steffen. Behavior-based model construction. *STTT*, 6(1):4–14, 2004.
5. B. Jonsson. Compositional verification of distributed systems. In *Proceedings of the 6th ACM Symposium on Principles of Distributed Computing*, 1987.
6. L. Lamport. Logical foundation, distributed systems- methods and tools for specification. *Springer-Verlag Lecture Notes in Computer Science*, 190, 1985.
7. K. Larsen. Ideal specification formalisms = expressivity + compositionality + decidability + testability + ... In *Invited Lecture at CONCUR 1990, LNCS 458*, 1990.
8. K. Larsen. The expressive power of implicit specifications. In *ICALP 1991, LNCS 510*, 1991.
9. T. Margaria, H. Raffelt, and B. Steffen. Knowledge-based relevance filtering for efficient system-level test-based model generation (to appear). *Innovations in Systems and Software Engineering, a NASA Journal, Springer Verlag.*
10. A. Pnueli, A. Zaks, and L. D. Zuck. Monitoring interfaces for faults. In *Proceedings of the 5th Workshop on Runtime Verification (RV'05)*, 2005. To appear in a special issue of ENTCS.
11. A. P. Sistla. On characterization of safety and liveness properties in temporal logic. In *Proceedings of the ACM Symposium on Principle of Distributed Computing*, 1985.
12. A. P. Sistla. Proving correctness with respect to nondeterministic safety specifications. *Information Processing Letters*, 39:45–49, 1991.
13. M. Vardi, P. Wolper, and A. P. Sistla. Reasoning about infinite computations. In *Proceedings of IEEE Symposium on Foundations of Computer Science*, 1983.

Synthesis of Distributed Systems from Knowledge-Based Specifications*,**

Ron van der Meyden[1] and Thomas Wilke[2]

[1] School of Computer Science and Engineering,
University of New South Wales & National ICT Australia
meyden@nicta.com.au

[2] Institut für Informatik, Christian-Albrechts-Universität zu Kiel
wilke@ti.informatik.uni-kiel.de

Abstract. We consider the problem of synthesizing protocols in a distributed setting satisfying specifications phrased in the logic of linear time *and* knowledge. On the one hand, we show that synthesis is already undecidable in environments with just two agents, one of which observes every aspect of the system state and one of which observes nothing of it. This falsifies a conjecture of van der Meyden and Vardi from CONCUR'96. On the other hand, we prove that synthesis is decidable in broadcast environments, verifying a conjecture of van der Meyden and Vardi from the same paper, and we show that for specifications that are positive in the knowledge modalities the synthesis problem can be reduced to the same problem for formulas without knowledge modalities. After adapting Pnueli and Rosner's decidability result on synthesis for linear temporal logic specifications in hierarchical environments, we obtain that, in our setting, synthesis is decidable for specifications positive in the knowledge modalities when restricted to hierarchical environments. We conclude the decidability in hierarchical systems of a property closely related to nondeducibility on strategies, a notion that has been studied in computer security.

1 Introduction

In program synthesis, one starts with a specification of a system and attempts to derive a program that implements this specification. This problem is particularly challenging in the context of *open systems*, which are required to respond appropriately to a sequence of inputs provided by an environment that is not under the full control of the program to be synthesized. A specification of an open system is said to be *realizable* if there exists a protocol with the property that the specification is satisfied, whatever the behaviour of the environment. A problem that has received significant attention is the synthesis of open systems

* Work supported by a grant from the Australian Research Council. National ICT Australia is funded through the Australian Government's *Backing Australia's Ability* initiative, in part through the Australian Research Council.

** A full version of this paper is available at http://www.cse.unsw.edu.au/~meyden/research/unsw-cse-tr-0504.pdf

M. Abadi and L. de Alfaro (Eds.): CONCUR 2005, LNCS 3653, pp. 562–576, 2005.

from temporal logic specifications [2,1,4,10,8,15,16,18,21,19]. It has been shown that, under certain circumstances, the synthesis process can be automated.

Often, designers of concurrent systems reason informally but explicitly not just about time, but also about the uncertainty that systems components have about the global state of the system. One finds statements such as "if process X knows that the transaction will be aborted, it should rollback its local contribution and terminate immediately." Such assertions can be made formal in the logic of knowledge [6]. A variety of distributed protocols have been studied using the logic of knowledge, and it has been argued that such an approach leads to a more perspicuous presentation of the design, and to implementations in which components are optimal in their use of information—see [6] for many citations.

The logic of knowledge also provides expressive capabilities useful for the specification of information flow in security protocols [7,13]. For example, the Dining Cryptographers protocol [3] provides a mechanism for a sender to communicate a message anonymously. This can be specified in the logic of knowledge by the requirement that all parties come to know a fact p, but all agents except the sender should not come to know the identity of the sender [13].

A common assumption in both types of applications of the logic of knowledge is that agents have *perfect recall* of their observations, i.e., that they keep a complete record of all events they have observed, and determine what they know using this complete record. This assumption is of particular relevance both when optimal use of information acquired is a design concern, and when we wish to determine the capabilities of the most powerful possible adversary in a security analysis. Realizability of specifications in the logic of knowledge and linear time under the assumption of perfect recall has been studied by van der Meyden and Vardi [14]. They showed that the realizability problem is decidable for such specifications in the context of an open system involving a single agent.

In general, realizability for specifications in the logic of knowledge and time is undecidable when there is more than one agent, because the problem is already undecidable even for two-agent systems and specifications involving only linear-time temporal operators, by results of Pnueli and Rosner [17]. However, a number of cases have been identified where multi-agent temporal specifications are decidable. Pnueli and Rosner identify a class of architectures for process communication as yielding a decidable case for synthesis from linear-time temporal logic specification. One example in this class is pipelines, in which communication is constrained to occur along a chain of processes. The characterization of the decidable cases has recently been refined [9].

These positive results for realizability from temporal specifications led van der Meyden and Vardi to conjecture that similar results could be found for specifications in the logic of knowledge and time. In particular, they proposed that *hierarchical systems* and *broadcast* systems might be cases where realizability of specifications in the logic of knowledge and linear time could be found to be decidable. Hierarchical systems are systems in which agents can be linearly ordered in such a way that each agent in the sequence observes (hence knows) at least as much as the preceding agents. An example of an hierarchical system is a system of three agents with security clearances to read unclassified, secret and top-secret documents, respectively (where a security clearance implies a capability to read documents at or below the security level.)[1] Broadcast systems are systems in which agents maintain a private state, information about which they can communicate to other agents, but only by a broadcast to all other agents, which is synchronous in the sense that all agents receive a broadcast at the same time. It has been shown that these assumptions lead to lowered complexity of a variety of problems in the logic of knowledge (e.g., a logic of knowledge and propositional quantification goes from being highly undecidable to decidable and axiomatizable in hierarchical systems [5], and implementations of knowledge based programs go from having a highly complex structure to being finite state in broadcast environments [12]) so the conjecture that they might make realizability decidable is reasonable.

We provide in this paper a complete resolution of van der Meyden and Vardi's conjectures. In the case of broadcast systems, we show that the conjecture is true. On the contrary, the conjecture concerning hierarchical systems is false: realizability for specifications in the logic of knowledge and linear time is undecidable in hierarchical systems with two or more agents. On the positive side, however, we identify a special class of formulas: those in which the knowledge operators have only positive occurrences, and show that for such formulas the realizability problem can be reduced to a problem of realizability of specifications in linear-time temporal logic. This result enables known cases of decidable realizability problems for linear-time temporal logic to be transferred to give decidable cases of realizability for the logic of knowledge and linear time. In particular, we show that realizability of linear-time temporal logic formulas is decidable in hierarchical systems, so the reduction yields the decidability of realizability of positive specifications in the logic of linear time and knowledge in hierarchical systems. As an application of this result, we establish the decidability of a property closely related to the notion of "nondeducibility on strategies" [20] from the computer security literature.

2 Basic Definitions and Main Result

In this section we lay out the definition of the synthesis problem we study, provide an example that illustrates how it may express the type of information flow property that has been studied in the computer security literature, and state the main results of the paper.

2.1 The Logic of Linear Time and Knowledge

We fix a finite set *Prop* of propositional variables and a finite number n of agents, which are simply numbered 1 through n. The formulas of the logic of linear time and knowledge is built from the elements of *Prop* using boolean connectives, the usual temporal operators X and U and the unary operators K_i for $i \in [n]$.

[1] This definition differs slightly from the definition of hierarchical system shown by Pnueli and Rosner to yield a decidable class of architectures.

For convenience, for each $i \in [n]$ the operator L_i is also allowed; it is the dual of K_i and an abbreviation for $\neg\mathsf{K}_i\neg$. Similarly, G (always) and F (eventually) and R (release, dual to U) are allowed.

A formula is said to be *positive* if every occurrence of a knowledge operator K_i is under an even number of negations.

An *interpreted system* is a tuple $\mathcal{I} = (\mathcal{R}, \{\sim_i\}_{i\in[n]}, \pi)$ where $\mathcal{R}$ is a set of so-called *runs*, $\pi\colon \mathcal{R}\times\mathbf{N} \to 2^{Prop}$ is an *interpretation function* which assigns to each *point* (r, m) of a run the propositions that hold true in it, and $\{\sim_i\}_{i\in[n]}$ is a family of *indistinguishability relations* on the points of all runs. Each indistinguishability relation $\sim_i$ is required to be an equivalence relation; the relation $\sim_i$ relates the points that are indistinguishable by agent i.

Given a point (r, m) of an interpreted system $\mathcal{I}$, we define what it means for a formula φ in the logic of linear time and knowledge to hold at this point, denoted $\mathcal{I}, (r, m) \models \varphi$:

- $\mathcal{I}, (r, m) \models p$ if $p \in \pi(r, m)$,
- $\mathcal{I}, (r, m) \models \mathsf{X}\psi$ if $\mathcal{I}, (r, m + 1) \models \psi$,
- $\mathcal{I}, (r, m) \models \psi \mathbin{\mathsf{U}} \chi$ if there exists $m' \geq m$ such that $\mathcal{I}, (r, l) \models \psi$ for all l with $m \leq l < m'$ and $\mathcal{I}, (r, m') \models \chi$,
- $\mathcal{I}, (r, m) \models \mathsf{K}_i\psi$ if $\mathcal{I}, (r', m') \models \psi$ for all (r', m') with $(r, m) \sim_i (r', m')$.

The boolean connectives are dealt with as usual.

We write $\mathcal{I}, r \models \varphi$ if $\mathcal{I}, (r, 0) \models \varphi$ and $\mathcal{I} \models \varphi$ if $\mathcal{I}, r \models \varphi$ for all runs r of $\mathcal{I}$.

2.2 Systems with Perfect Recall in Finite-State Environments

A *signature* of size n is a family $\{ACT_i\}_{i\in\{e,1,\dots,n\}}$ where each set ACT_i is a finite, non-empty set of actions for the *environment* e or *agent* $i \in [n]$. The set of *joint actions* of such a signature is defined by $ACT = ACT_e \times ACT_1 \times \cdots \times ACT_n$. When $\boldsymbol{a}$ denotes a joint action, we write $\boldsymbol{a}_i$ for the action of agent i in $\boldsymbol{a}$.

An *environment* over a signature as just described is a tuple

$$\mathcal{E} = (S, I, P_e, \tau, \{O_i\}_{i\in[n]}, Prop, \pi) \tag{1}$$

where S is a finite set of *states*, $I \subseteq S$ is the set of *initial states*, $P_e\colon S \to 2^{ACT_e}$ is the *protocol of the environment*, which says which actions can be performed by the environment in a given state, $\tau\colon ACT \to (S \to S)$ is the *transition function*, which, for every joint action $\boldsymbol{a}$ specifies a transition function $\tau(\boldsymbol{a})$, $\{O_i\}_{i\in[n]}$ is a family of *observation functions* $O_i\colon S \to \mathcal{O}$ for some set $\mathcal{O}$ of *observations*, *Prop* is a finite set of propositions, and $\pi_e\colon S \to 2^{Prop}$ is an *interpretation function* which assigns to each state the propositions that hold in it.

We require $P_e(s) \neq \emptyset$ for each $s \in S$. We also note that $\tau(\boldsymbol{a})(s)$ needs only be defined if $\boldsymbol{a}_e \in P_e(s)$.

A *run* of such an environment is an infinite sequence $s_0, s_1, s_2, \dots$ such that $s_0 \in I$ and such that for all m there exists $\boldsymbol{a} \in ACT$ with $\boldsymbol{a}_e \in P_e(s_m)$ and $\tau(\boldsymbol{a})(s_m) = s_{m+1}$. When r denotes such a run and (r, m) is a point, we set $r(m) = s_m$.

To obtain an interpreted system, we set $\pi(r,m) = \pi_e(r(m))$ for every point (r,m). Further, we let $O_i(r,m) = O_i(r(0))O_i(r(1))\ldots O_i(r(m))$ for every agent i and call $O_i(r,m)$ the *local state* of agent i at point (r,m). Using this notation, we define $\sim_i$ by $(r,m) \sim_i (r',m')$ iff $O_i(r,m) = O_i(r',m')$. (Note that this implies $m = m'$.) This indistinguishability relation is called *synchronous perfect recall.* The resulting interpreted system is denoted $\mathcal{I}(\mathcal{E})$.

2.3 Protocols, Realizability, Synthesis Problem

Assume we are given an environment $\mathcal{E}$ as above. A *protocol* for agent i is a function $P_i\colon \mathcal{O}^+ \to ACT_i$. A *joint protocol* is a family $\boldsymbol{P} = \{P_i\}_{i\in[n]}$ where each P_i is a protocol for agent i. Given such a protocol and a run r in the environment, we say r is *consistent* with the protocol if for every m there exists $a \in ACT_e$ such that $r(m+1) = \tau(a, P_1(O_1(r,m)),\ldots,P_n(O_n(r,m)))(r(m))$. The interpreted system which is obtained from $\mathcal{I}(\mathcal{E})$ by restricting its runs to runs consistent with $\boldsymbol{P}$ is denoted $\mathcal{I}(\mathcal{E},\boldsymbol{P})$.

We say a formula φ is *realizable* in an environment $\mathcal{E}$ if there exists a joint protocol $\boldsymbol{P}$ such that $\mathcal{I}(\mathcal{E},\boldsymbol{P}) \models \varphi$. The *synthesis problem* is to determine whether a given formula is realizable in a given environment.

2.4 Hierarchical and Broadcast Environments

Hierarchical environments [5] are those in which for all states s and agents $i \in [n-1]$, we have that $O_i(s) = O_i(t)$ implies $O_{i+1}(s) = O_{i+1}(t)$. Intuitively, this means that each agent in the sequence observes not more than the preceding agent. Clearly the same property holds for the indistinguishability relations on points derived using the assumption of perfect recall. The name derives from the fact that the equivalence classes of these relations form a hierarchically nested collection of sets.

Say that agent i is *omniscient* if for all states s, we have $O_i(s) = s$, i.e., the complete state is observable to the agent. Say that agent i is *blind* if for all states s, we have $O_i(s) = \bot$, for some fixed value $\bot$. Clearly, a system with agent 1 omniscient and agent 2 blind is hierarchical. This type of simple hierarchical environment will play a rôle in our undecidability result, Theorem 1.

Broadcast environments [12] model situations in which agents may maintain private information, but where the only means by which this information can be communicated is by synchronous simultaneous broadcast to all agents.

Our definition of broadcast environment in this paper will be slightly more general than that in [12]. Formally, we define a broadcast environment to be an environment $\mathcal{E} = (S, I, P_e, \tau, \{O_i\}_{i\in[n]}, Prop, \pi)$ of a specific structure, determined by the following ingredients:

- a finite set S_0 of *shared states,*
- a *common observation function* O_c with domain S_0,
- an *action interpretation function* $\tau_0\colon ACT \to (S_0 \to S_0)$,
- an *environment action function* $f\colon S_0 \to 2^{ACT_e}$,
- for each agent i, a set S_i of *private states,* and
- for each agent i, an *action interpretation function* $\tau_i\colon ACT_i \to (S_i \to S_i)$.

The environment $\mathcal{E}$ is now determined by $S = S_0 \times S_1 \times \cdots \times S_n$ and

$$O_i((s_0, \ldots, s_n)) = (O_c(s_0), s_i) \ , \tag{2}$$

$$P_e((s_0, \ldots, s_n)) = f(s_0) \ , \tag{3}$$

$$\tau(\boldsymbol{a})((s_0, s_1, \ldots, s_n)) = (\tau_0(\boldsymbol{a})(s_0), \tau_1(\boldsymbol{a}_1)(s_1), \ldots, \tau_n(\boldsymbol{a}_n)(s_n)) \ . \tag{4}$$

Observe that these definitions guarantee that (1) the private state s_i of agent i is observable and modifiable only by agent i, (2) agent i's actions depend on agent i's private state and the shared state only, (3) the protocol of the environment may depend on the shared state only.

For notational convenience, if $s = (s_0, \ldots, s_n)$ denotes a state, we will often write $\boldsymbol{p}_i(s)$ to denote agent i's private state s_i.

2.5 A Security Example

Realizability of specifications in the logic of linear time and knowledge may be used to express a type of information flow property similar to those studied in the computer security literature. Consider a system with two agents High and Low, subject to a security policy that permits High to observe any information belonging to Low, but does not permit any information known only to High to flow to Low. If the system has been designed in an insecure fashion, and contains a "covert channel" that enables unintended information flow, High and Low may be able to collude to ensure that Low comes to know some secret belonging to High. (Concretely, such collusion may come about if Low has managed to place a Trojan Horse program at High.) We show how to formulate a version of this question as a realizability problem.

Let $\mathcal{E}$ be an environment with agents H (High) and L (Low) describing the possible states of the system we wish to analyse for unintended information flows. We may capture the assumption that information is permitted to flow from Low to High by defining states the observation functions by $O_H(s) = (O_L(s), P_H(s))$, where $O_L(s)$ is Low's observation in s and $P_H(s)$ is additional private information observable to High but not to Low. Note that this makes the environment hierarchical with respect to the ordering H, L on the agents. Suppose that p is a proposition whose value depends only on $P_H(s)$, and is moreover unaffected by the agents' actions. Then we may phrase the question "Can High and Low collude to reliably pass the information p from High to Low?" as the problem of whether the formula $\mathsf{F}(\mathsf{K}_L p \vee \mathsf{K}_L \neg p)$ is realizable.

This question is closely related to, but somewhat stronger than, the notion of "(non)deducibility on strategies" of Wittbold and Johnson [20]. It can be shown that deducibility on strategies corresponds to the formula $\mathsf{F}(\mathsf{K}_L(p) \vee \mathsf{K}_L(\neg p))$ being true on *some* run, rather than *all* runs, as required by our definition of realizability, with Low acting passively rather than having a choice of protocol. Realizability of the branching time formula $\mathsf{EF}(\mathsf{K}_L(p) \vee \mathsf{K}_L(\neg p))$, (where the path quantifier $E\varphi$ means that φ is true on some computation path) would correspond more directly to deducibility on strategies. Nevertheless, realizability of $\mathsf{F}(\mathsf{K}_L(p) \vee \mathsf{K}_L(\neg p))$ does seem to correspond to an interesting and intuitive security notion, which we call *strong deducibility on strategies* in the sequel.

2.6 Main Results

We start with the theorem stating that the synthesis problem is undecidable in hierarchical environments. The proof is given in Section 4.

Theorem 1. *The synthesis problem for distributed systems with respect to specifications in the logic of linear time and knowledge is undecidable in an environment with two agents, the first being omniscient, the second being blind. In particular, it is undecidable in hierarchical environments.*

Our proof yields an even stronger statement: The problem remains undecidable for the case where the protocol of the blind agent is fixed (so only the protocol for the omniscient agent needs to be synthesized) and the specification does not contain the omniscient agent's knowledge operator (but does contain the blind agent's knowledge operator).

For broadcast systems, however, it turns out that synthesis is decidable. The following result, proved in Section 3, is by a reduction to the case of a single agent.

Theorem 2. *The synthesis problem for specifications in the logic of linear time and knowledge is decidable in broadcast environments.*

As stated before, we can moreover get to decidable cases when we restrict the syntax of the specifications. Such results are based on the following theorem, which is proved in Section 5.

Theorem 3. *For positive specifications φ in the logic of linear time and knowledge, and environments E, there exists an effective construction of a formula φ' of linear time temporal logic and an environment E' such that φ is realizable in E iff φ' is realizable in E'.*

Moreover, if E is hierarchical, then so is E'.

As the synthesis problem for distributed systems with respect to specifications in the logic of linear time is decidable in hierarchical systems (see below), we obtain:

Corollary 4. *The synthesis problem for positive specifications in the logic of linear time and knowledge is decidable in hierarchical environments.*

Noting that $\mathsf{F}(\mathsf{K}_L p \vee \mathsf{K}_L \neg p)$ is a positive formula, we obtain the following result concerning the notion from computer security of Section 2.5.

Corollary 5. *Strong deducibility on strategies is decidable in hierarchical environments.*

Our definition of hierarchical systems and the definition of pipelines shown by Pnueli and Rosner [17] to yield a decidable case of realizability for linear-time logic specifications in multi-agent systems are similar in spirit, but differ in some key respects. (Our definition is adjusted to the knowledge-based setting, that is, hierarchies are specified in terms of observation functions, whereas Pnueli and Rosner use a definition which is expressed in terms of properties of the architecture of the system in question.) We therefore also prove that realizability of linear-time logic specifications is decidable in hierarchical systems, closely following Pnueli and Rosner's arguments.

Theorem 6. *The synthesis problem for distributed systems with respect to specifications in the logic of linear time is decidable in hierarchical systems.*

3 Broadcast Environments

In this section we describe the major steps of Theorem 2, by means of a reduction to the synthesis problem for specifications in the logic of linear time and knowledge in single agent environments, which is decidable by the results of [14].

The following notion is useful for the proof that the reduction works. Define an *isomorphism of interpreted systems* $\mathcal{I} = (\mathcal{R}, \{\sim_i\}_{i\in[n]}, \pi)$ and $\mathcal{I}' = (\mathcal{R}', \{\sim_i'\}_{i\in[n]}, \pi')$ to be a bijection f between the runs of $\mathcal{I}$ and the runs of $\mathcal{I}'$ such that (1) $\pi(r,k) = \pi'(f(r),k)$ for all $r \in \mathcal{R}$, and $k \in \mathbf{N}$ and (2) $(r,n) \sim_i (r',n')$ iff $(f(r),n) \sim_i' (f(r'),n')$, for all runs $r, r \in \mathcal{R}$, $k, k' \in \mathbf{N}$ and agents i. We say $\mathcal{I}$ and $\mathcal{I}'$ are *isomorphic*, denoted $\mathcal{I} \cong \mathcal{I}'$, if there exists an isomorphism from $\mathcal{I}$ to $\mathcal{I}'$.

The following can be shown by a straightforward induction on the construction of the formula.

Lemma 7. *If f is an isomorphism of interpreted systems $\mathcal{I}$ and $\mathcal{I}'$, then for all formulas φ of the logic of linear time and knowledge, runs r of $\mathcal{I}$ and times k, we have $\mathcal{I}, (r,k) \models \varphi$ iff $\mathcal{I}', (f(r),k) \models \varphi$.*

To prove Theorem 2, we break the reduction into two stages. Since we synthesize a deterministic protocol for each agent and transitions of agents' private state depend only on their choices of action, we can always derive an agent's private state from its initial private state and the sequence of observations it has made of the shared state. This is formalised in the following construction.

Given a broadcast environment $\mathcal{E}$, define the environment

$$\mathcal{E}' = (S', I', P_e', \tau', \{O_i'\}_{i\in[n]}, \mathit{Prop}, \pi') \tag{5}$$

over the same signature by

$$S' = \{0,1\} \times S \ , \qquad I' = \{0\} \times I \ , \tag{6}$$

$$\pi'((x,s)) = \pi(s) \ , \qquad P_e'((x,s)) = P_e(s) \ , \tag{7}$$

$$O_i'((0,s)) = (O_c(s), \boldsymbol{p}_i(s)) \ , \qquad O_i'((1,s)) = O_c(s) \ , \tag{8}$$

$$\tau'(\boldsymbol{a})((x,s)) = (1, \tau(\boldsymbol{a})(s)) \ . \tag{9}$$

So $\mathcal{E}'$ is just like $\mathcal{E}$ with the only difference that all but the initial observation of the private state is suppressed.

The fact that we have defined protocols to be deterministic (and that the semantics for knowledge assumes implicitly that the protocol being executed is common knowledge) plays a critical role in the following result.

Lemma 8. *Let φ be a formula of the logic of linear time and knowledge. Then φ is realizable in $\mathcal{E}$ iff φ is realizable in $\mathcal{E}'$.*

Proof (sketched). For each protocol $\boldsymbol{P}$ for $\mathcal{E}$, we define a protocol $\boldsymbol{P}{\downarrow}$ for $\mathcal{E}'$, and for each protocol $\boldsymbol{P}'$ for $\mathcal{E}'$ we define a protocol $\boldsymbol{P}{\uparrow}$such that $\mathcal{I}(\mathcal{E}, \boldsymbol{P}) \cong \mathcal{I}(\mathcal{E}', \boldsymbol{P}{\downarrow})$ and $\mathcal{I}(\mathcal{E}', \boldsymbol{P}') \cong \mathcal{I}(\mathcal{E}, \boldsymbol{P}{\uparrow})$. From Lemma 7, we can then conclude that any formula φ is realizable in $\mathcal{E}$ iff φ is realizable in $\mathcal{E}'$.

The transformation from $\mathcal{E}$ to $\mathcal{E}'$ shows that (with respect to each deterministic joint protocol) an agent's knowledge is completely determined by a sequence of the form $O_i(s_0)O_c(s_1)\ldots O_c(s_k)$, where $s_0, \ldots, s_k$ is a sequence of states of E. In a second step, we show how the remaining dependency on $O_i(s_0)$ can be eliminated by a further transformation. The basic idea is that we add a component to the state space in order to have a memory of the initial state of E at the start of the run and make the actions depend on this. Formally, we proceed as follows.

Let $I_i = \{s_i \mid (s_0, s_1, \ldots, s_n) \in I\}$ be the set of possible initial private states of agent i in E. We define an environment $E^c = (S^c, I^c, P^c_e, \tau^c, O^c_c, Prop^c, \pi^c)$ with a single agent that we call c, signature defined by

$$ACT^c_e = ACT_e \ , \qquad ACT^c_c = (I_1 \to ACT_1) \times \ldots \times (I_n \to ACT_n) \ , \tag{10}$$

and components defined by

$$S^c = I \times S' \ , \qquad I^c = \{(s, (0, s)) \mid s \in I\} \ , \tag{11}$$

$$P^c_e((s,t)) = P'_e(t) \ , \qquad Prop^c = Prop \cup \{p_{i,x} \mid i \in [n], \ x \in I_i\} \ , \tag{12}$$

$$O^c_c((s,(x,t))) = O_c(t) \ , \tag{13}$$

and $\tau^c((\boldsymbol{a}_e, (\alpha_1, \ldots, \alpha_n)))((s,t)) = (s, \tau'((\boldsymbol{a}_e, \alpha_1(\boldsymbol{p}_1(s)), \ldots, \alpha_n(\boldsymbol{p}_n(s))))(t))$. Given a formula φ of the logic of linear time and knowledge, define φ^c to be the formula obtained, recursively, by replacing each subformula of the form $\mathsf{K}_i\psi$ by

$$\bigwedge_{x \in I_i} (p_{i,x} \to K_c(p_{i,x} \to \psi^c)) \ . \tag{14}$$

Then we can prove the following.

Lemma 9. *If φ is a formula of the logic of linear time and knowledge, then φ is realizable in E' iff φ^c is realizable in E^c.*

Proof (sketched). First note that we can convert a system $\mathcal{I}(E^c, P^c)$ to a system $\mathcal{I}_n(E^c, P^c)$ for n agents by defining the equivalence relations $\sim^c_i$ on points in the usual way, using the functions O^c_i on points, defined by $O^c_i(r,k) = \boldsymbol{p}^c_i(r(0)) \cdot O^c_c(r,k)$, where $\boldsymbol{p}^c_i((s,t)) = \boldsymbol{p}_i(s)$.

We first show that for every protocol $\boldsymbol{P}^c$ for c we can find a protocol $\boldsymbol{P}'$ for $\mathcal{E}'$ such that $\mathcal{I}_n(E^c, P^c) \cong \mathcal{I}(E', \boldsymbol{P}')$, and vice versa.

We then show by an induction on the construction of the formula ψ that $\mathcal{I}_n(E^c, P^c), (r,k) \models \mathsf{K}_i\psi$ iff $\mathcal{I}(E^c, P^c), (r,k) \models \bigwedge_{x \in I_i} (p_{i,x} \to \mathsf{K}_c(p_{i,x} \to \psi^c))$, which yields the result, when we take Lemma 7 into account.

Combining these two lemmas, the transformation from E to E' to E^c reduces the realizability problem for the multi-agent broadcast environment E to a problem of realizability in a single agent environment E^c, which is decidable by results of van der Meyden and Vardi [12].

We note that this result plays essentially on the determinism of the evolution of the private states. If we were to add a source of non-determinism, e.g., independent inputs to the agents, then, using techniques from [17], one could show that the realizability problem would be undecidable already for linear-time temporal logic formulas.

4 Undecidability for Temporal *and* Knowledge Formulas

In this section we sketch the proof of Theorem 1, for which we need background on lossy counter machines. For technical reasons, our set-up differs slightly from the one in [11].

A *complete counter machine with forbidden state* is a tuple $L=(Q, k, q_I, q_f, \Delta)$ where Q is a finite set of *states,* k is a natural number, the number of *counters* of the machine, $q_I \in Q$ is the *initial state* of L, $q_f \in Q$, and $\Delta \subseteq (Q \times \{0, \dots, k-1\} \times Q) \cup (Q \times \{0, \dots, k-1\} \times Q \times Q)$ is the set of *commands.* We require that $(q, 0, q_f) \in \Delta$ for every $q \in Q$ (justifying the term "complete").

A *configuration* of such a counter machine is a tuple $(q, r_0, \dots, r_{k-1})$ where q is a state and $r_j \in \mathbf{N}$ for all $j < k$, representing the values of the counters.

To define lossy semantics, we start with the definition of three binary relations on $(Q \cup \bar{Q} \cup \Delta) \times \mathbf{N}^k$ where $\overline{Q}$ is an isomorphic copy of Q. Given a state $q \in Q$, its isomorphic copy is denoted $\overline{q}$. First, for every $q \in Q$, we let $(q, r_0, \dots, r_{k-1}) \rightarrow^{al} (\gamma, r'_0, \dots, r'_{k-1})$ if γ is a command starting with q and $r'_j \le r_j$ for all $j < k$.

Second, we let $(\gamma, r_0, \dots, r_{k-1}) \rightarrow^{am} (\overline{q'}, r'_0, \dots, r'_{k-1})$ if

1. $\gamma = (q, j, q')$, $0 < r'_j \le r_j + 1$ and $r'_{j'} \le r_{j'}$ for all $j' \ne j$,
2. $\gamma = (q, j, q_1, q_2)$, $r_j > 0$, $q' = q_1$, $r'_j \le r_j - 1$, and $r'_{j'} \le r_{j'}$ for all $j' \ne j$, or
3. $\gamma = (q, j, q_1, q_2)$, $r_j = 0$, $q' = q_2$, and $r'_{j'} \le r_{j'}$ for all j'.

And, third, we let $(\overline{q}, r_0, \dots, r_{k-1}) \rightarrow^{aal} (q', r'_0, \dots, r'_{k-1})$ if $(q, r_0, \dots, r_{k-1}) \rightarrow^{l} (q', r'_0, \dots, r'_{k-1})$.

Next, we set $\Rightarrow \; = \; \rightarrow^{al} \circ \rightarrow^{am} \circ \rightarrow^{aal}$ and define a *lossy run* of a counter machine to be a sequence $s_0 \Rightarrow s_1 \Rightarrow s_2 \Rightarrow \dots$ of configurations. It is called an *infinite run* if the sequence is infinite.

Theorem 10 ([11]). *The following problem is undecidable. Given a complete counter machine L with forbidden state q_f, is there a number n such that there exists an infinite lossy run of L starting with the configuration $(q_I, 0, \dots, 0, n)$ and never going through state q_f.*

There is another relation we will also need in the proof to follow. This relation is denoted $\rightarrow^{am'}$. It is different from $\rightarrow^{am}$ in that 2. and 3. above are simply replaced by $\gamma = (q, j, q_1, q_2)$, $q' \in \{q_1, q_2\}$ and $r'_{j'} \le r_{j'}$ for all $j' < k$. In particular, we have $\rightarrow^{am} \subseteq \rightarrow^{am'}$.

We say $s_0, s_1, s_2, \dots$ is a *refined computation* of the given machine if $s_0 \rightarrow^{al} s_1 \rightarrow^{am} s_2 \rightarrow^{aal} s_3 \rightarrow^{al} s_4 \rightarrow^{am} s_5 \rightarrow^{aal} s_6 \rightarrow^{al} \dots$. We say it is a *refined weak computation* if $s_0 \rightarrow^{al} s_1 \rightarrow^{am'} s_2 \rightarrow^{aal} s_3 \rightarrow^{al} s_4 \rightarrow^{am'} s_5 \rightarrow^{aal} s_6 \rightarrow^{al} \dots$

The important observations here are:

1. A refined weak computation $s_0, s_1, s_2, \dots$ is a refined computation iff for every m with $s_{3m+1} = ((q, j, q_1, q_2), r_0, \dots, r_{k-1})$ and $s_{3m+2} = (q', r'_0, \dots, r'_{k-1})$ we have $q' = q_2$ if $r_j = 0$ and else $q' = q_1$ and $r'_j < r_j$.
2. There is an infinite computation starting with $(q_I, 0, \dots, 0, n)$ for some n iff there is an infinite refined weak computation $s_0, s_1, s_2, \dots$ starting with $(q_I, 0, \dots, 0, n)$ and satisfying the above requirement.

We prove Theorem 1 by reducing the problem from Corollary 10 (in the variant from the previous remark) to the realizability problem. This will yield the desired result. To this end, let L be a complete k-counter machine with forbidden state as above. We construct an environment $\mathcal{E}$ with two agents and a formula φ in the language of linear time and knowledge such that there exists a joint protocol $\boldsymbol{P}$ realizing φ in $\mathcal{E}$ iff there exists a natural number n such that there exists an infinite run of L starting with $(q_I, 0, \dots, 0, n)$ and avoiding q_f.

We call the two agents by the names A and B, where agent A is omniscient and agent B is blind. We construct the environment $\mathcal{E}$ in such a way that for each joint protocol $\boldsymbol{P}$ we can view $\mathcal{I}(\mathcal{E}, \boldsymbol{P})$ as a refined weak computation of L. In addition, we will construct φ in such a way that $\mathcal{I}(\mathcal{E}, \boldsymbol{P}) \models \varphi$ iff this sequence is a refined computation and never goes through q_f.

To be able to view $\mathcal{I}(\mathcal{E}, \boldsymbol{P})$ as a refined computation of L, we simply consider, for each m, the set of all states a run of $\mathcal{I}(\mathcal{E}, \boldsymbol{P})$ can be in. This gives us a multiset of states of $\mathcal{E}$ in a natural way, and with each such multiset we will associate an element of a refined computation.

Our environment operates in two phases. In the first phase, the environment uses nondeterminism to generate the initial configuration of the machine, that is, the number n counter $k-1$ gets assigned in the initial configuration. In the second phase, the refined computation of L is simulated.

The important point is the following. There needs to be some "coordination" between the individual runs of $\mathcal{I}(\mathcal{E}, \boldsymbol{P})$ so as to ensure that, for instance, the decision to switch from the first to the second phase is made at the same time for all runs. This is where agent B comes into the picture. Since B is blind, if B decides to perform an action corresponding to switch from the first to the second phase, it will take this decision at the same point in time of all runs. Similarly, if we want to check that the value of a counter is 0, this can be checked by the knowledge operator for agent B, which can quantify over all runs, because B is blind. Agent A is used for "individual" actions, in particular, to model lossiness.

The actual number of runs, hence distinguishable points, may in general be infinite, but since choice of action is based only on the prefixes, at each moment of time, there will be a finite number of equivalence classes of points for agent A. We use the number of these distinct equivalence classes to represent the values of the counters. To distinguish different counters we use different states, that is, depending on the current state of a point of an equivalence class, this class will be counted for a certain counter or not.

The environment has the following state set:

$$S = \{\mathit{spawn}, \mathit{stable}, \mathit{trash}, c_0, \ldots, c_{k-1}, d_0, \ldots, d_{k-1}\} \cup Q \cup \overline{Q} \cup \Delta \tag{15}$$

where $\overline{Q}$ is a disjoint copy of Q. The state *spawn* is the initial state. The states *spawn* and *stable* are the states of the *first phase* whereas the other states are the states of the second phase. We also set $\pi_e(s) = s$ for every $s \in S$, that is, we have a proposition for each state expressing that the system is in that state.

Let $\boldsymbol{P}$ be any joint protocol and let $\mathcal{I}(\mathcal{E}, \boldsymbol{P}) = (\mathcal{R}, \pi, \{\sim_i\}_{i\in[n]})$. For each m, let $\mathcal{R}_m$ be the set of prefixes of elements from $\mathcal{R}$ of length m and let M_m be the multi-set of all end states of the elements from $\mathcal{R}_m$.

Now, assume a sequence $s_0, s_1, s_2, \ldots$ is a refined weak computation starting with $s_0 = (q_I, 0, \ldots, 0, n)$. Then there will be a joint protocol $\boldsymbol{P}$ such that the following holds.

First, for every $m \leq n$ and s different from *spawn* and *stable*, we will have:

$$M_m(\mathit{spawn}) = 1 \ , \qquad M_m(\mathit{stable}) = m \ , \qquad M_m(s) = 0 \ . \tag{16}$$

And for all $m \geq 0$ with $s_m = (\alpha, r_0, \ldots, r_{k-1})$ and every $\alpha' \in Q \cup \Delta \cup \overline{Q}$ different from α, we will have:

$$M_{n+m}(\mathit{spawn}) = 0 \ , \qquad M_{n+m}(\mathit{stable}) = 0 \ , \qquad M_{n+m}(\alpha) = 1 \ , \tag{17}$$

$$M_{n+m}(\alpha') = 0 \ , \qquad M_{n+m}(c_j) = r_i \ . \tag{18}$$

That means, in particular, that the number of occurrences of state c_j corresponds exactly to the value of counter j. In the above, we haven't said anything about the states d_j and the state *trash*. The latter is simply used as a dummy state if we want to discontinue a run. The former are used as indicator variables to have some control over the lossiness. In our construction, if we want to decrement a counter we could simply switch from c_i to *trash*. What we do is to transition from c_i to d_i and then to *trash*; as a consequence we can specify in a formula that a decrement for counter i has occurred.

For the above claim, the converse will also hold true. That is, for every system induced by a joint protocol, there will be a sequence as above satisfying the specified conditions, with one exception. There will also be a system where, for every m and any state s different from *spawn* and *stable*, $M_m(\mathit{spawn}) = 1$, $M_m(\mathit{stable}) = m$, and $M_m(s) = 0$. That is, the second phase will never be started in that system.

Since, by (12) and (13) the environment is constructed so that at each moment of time at most one element α of $Q \cup \Delta \cup \overline{Q}$ can occur, and the agent B has synchronous perfect recall but is blind, the formula $\mathsf{L}_B\alpha$ says that α is the unique such element occurring at the current time. Similarly, $\mathsf{L}_B c_i$ says that there is at least one prefix of length equal to the current time ending in state c_i.

Taking all this into account, in order to make the reduction work, we will only have to choose our formula φ to be the conjunction of the three formulas. The first conjunct is $\mathsf{FL}_B q_I$ which rules out the last system, which never gets to the second phase. The second conjunct ist

$$\bigwedge_{(q,j,q_1,q_2)\in\Delta} \mathsf{G}((q,j,q_1,q_2) \to ((\mathsf{K}_B\neg c_i \to \mathsf{XL}_B\overline{q_2}) \wedge (\mathsf{L}_B c_j \to \mathsf{X}(\mathsf{L}_B\overline{q_1} \wedge \mathsf{L}_B d_j))) \ ,$$

which takes care of the condition from the observation on weak refined computations. And the thrid conjunct is $\bigwedge \mathsf{GK}_B\neg q_f$; it makes sure we get a run avoiding q_f. Note that this formula refers only to agent B's knowledge: we do not need the knowledge modality for agent A. What remains to be specified are the actions and the transitions. This can be dealt with easily.

5 A Reduction for Positive Formulas

We now define the reduction promised in Theorem 3, and prove its correctness.

Let $\mathcal{E}$ be an environment for n agents and φ a positive formula. We construct an environment E' and a formula φ' in the language of linear time (without knowledge operators) such that φ is realizable in $\mathcal{E}$ iff φ' is realizable in $\mathcal{E}'$. Moreover, we will be able to derive a protocol realizing φ in $\mathcal{E}$ from a protocol realizing φ' in $\mathcal{E}'$ in a straightforward way (just by forgetting).

The idea is that in the new system in each state each agent has to say which of his knowledge subformulas he thinks are true by choosing a corresponding action. That the agent's choices are indeed correct will then be verified by modifying φ appropriately. To describe E' we need some more notation. For every $i \in [n]$ we let Φ_i be the set of subformulas of φ of the form $\mathsf{K}_i\psi$ and Φ^* the union of all these sets.

We first describe the sets of actions for $\mathcal{E}'$, which are denoted by ACT'_e, $ACT'_1, \ldots, ACT'_n$. We set $ACT'_e = ACT_e$ and $ACT'_i = ACT_i \times 2^{\Phi_i}$ for every $i \in [n]$. The system $\mathcal{E}'$ is given by $\mathcal{E}' = (S \times 2^{\Phi^*}, I', P'_e, \tau', \{O'_i\}_{i\in[n]}, P', \pi'_e)$ where the individual components are defined by

$$I' = \{(s_I, \emptyset) \mid s_I \in I\} \ , \qquad O'_i((s,\Psi)) = O_i(s) \ , \tag{19}$$

$$P' = P \cup \{p_\psi \mid \psi \in \Phi^*\} \ , \qquad \pi'_e((s,\Psi)) = \pi_e(s) \cup \{p_\psi \mid \psi \in \Psi\} \ , \tag{20}$$

and $\tau'(a_e, (a_1, \Psi_1), \ldots, (a_n, \Psi_n)) = (\tau(a, a_1, \ldots, a_n), \Psi_1 \cup \cdots \cup \Psi_n)$.

To obtain the new specification φ', we proceed as follows. First, we define the *flattened variant* of a formula ψ, denoted $\overline{\psi}$. The formula $\overline{\psi}$ is the temporal formula obtained from ψ by substituting every maximal knowledge subformula ψ' by $\mathsf{X}p_{\psi'}$. For example, if ψ is $\mathsf{K}_1\mathsf{K}_2 p \to \mathsf{GK}_1 q$ then $\overline{\psi}$ is $(\mathsf{X}p_{\mathsf{K}_1\mathsf{K}_2 p}) \to \mathsf{GX}p_{\mathsf{K}_1 q}$.

Now, the new specification simply says that whenever agent i claims $\mathsf{K}_i\psi$ is true it is, in fact, true and uses flattened variants of the knowledge formulas:

$$\varphi' = \overline{\varphi} \wedge \bigwedge_{i\in[n], \mathsf{K}_i\psi\in\Phi_i} \mathsf{G}(\mathsf{X}p_{\mathsf{K}_i\psi} \to \overline{\psi}) \ . \tag{21}$$

We will also write χ for the big conjunction on the right-hand side. The use of the X-operator is due to the fact that the claims about valid subformulas an agent makes by carrying out an action are only available in the environment in the next state. We omit the proof of correctness of the above construction.

6 Conclusion

We have shown that there exist classes of environments and formulas (broadcast, or hierarchical environments and positive formulas) for which synthesis from specifications in the logic of linear time and knowledge is decidable. These results suggest several directions for further research. One is to obtain a more general characterization of the decidable cases, as has been done for temporal specifications [9]. There are also good reasons to explore versions of these problems where the temporal logic used is for branching time rather than linear time. In particular, results on branching-time versions would be directly applicable to classical security notions such as deducibility on strategies, which we have closely appromixated but not precisely captured with our notion of strong deducibility on strategies. Where such notions are found to be decidable, it is moreover of interest to find precise complexities and develop specially tailored decision procedures for the automation of security analysis. Another potential area of application is the compilation of knowledge-based programs [6]. Finally, our assumption that the protocols synthesized are deterministic should also be relaxed, particularly as it is often the case that security is attained by creative use of non-determinism.

References

1. A. Arnold, A. Vincent, and I. Walukiewicz. Games for synthesis of controlers with partial observation. *Theoretical Computer Science*, 303(1):7–34, 2003.
2. P. C. Attie, A. Arora, and E. A. Emerson. Synthesis of fault-tolerant concurrent programs. *ACM Transactions on Programming Languages and Systems*, 26(1):125–1851, 2004.
3. D. Chaum. The dining cryptographers problem: unconditional sender and recipient untraceability. *J., Cryptology*, (1):65–75, 1988.
4. E.A. Emerson and E.M. Clarke. Using branching time logic to synthesize synchronization skeletons. *Science of Computer Programming*, 2:241–266, 1982.
5. K. Engelhardt, R. van der Meyden, and K. Su. Modal logics with a hierarchy of local propositional quantifiers. In P. Balbiani, N. Suzuki, F. Wolter, and M. Zakharyaschev, editors, *Advances in Modal Logic*, volume 4, pages 9–30. World Scientific, 2003.
6. R. Fagin, J. Y. Halpern, Y. Moses, and M. Y. Vardi. *Reasoning about Knowledge*. MIT Press, 1995.
7. J. Y. Halpern and K. O'Neill. Anonymity and information hiding in multiagent systems. In *Proceedings of the 16th IEEE Computer Security Foundations Workshop*, pages 75–88, 2003.
8. O. Kupferman and M.Y. Vardi. Synthesis with incomplete informatio. In *2nd International Conference on Temporal Logic*, pages 91–106, Manchester, July 1997.

9. P. Madhusudan. *Control and Synthesis of Open Reactive Systems.* PhD thesis, University of Madras, Nov 2001.
10. Z. Manna and P. Wolper. Synthesis of communicating processes from temporal logic specifications. *ACM Transactions on Programming Languages and Systems*, 6(1):68–93, January 1984.
11. Richard Mayr. Undecidable problems in unreliable computations. *Theoretical Computer Science*, 297(1–3):337–354, March 2003.
12. R. van der Meyden. Finite state implementations of knowledge-based programs. In *Proceedings of the Conference on Foundations of Software Technology and Theoretical Computer Science*, Springer LNCS No. 1180, pages 262–273, Hyderabad, India, December 1996.
13. R. van der Meyden and K. Su. Symbolic model checking the knowledge of the dining cryptographers. In *Proc. 17th IEEE Computer Security Foundations Workshop*, pages 280–291, June 2004.
14. R. van der Meyden and M. Y. Vardi. Synthesis from knowledge-based specifications. In *CONCUR'98, 9th International Conf. on Concurrency Theory*, Springer LNCS No. 1466, pages 34–49, Sept 1998.
15. A. Pnueli and R. Rosner. On the synthesis of a reactive module. In *Proc. 16th ACM Symp. on Principles of Programming Languages*, Austin, January 1989.
16. A. Pnueli and R. Rosner. On the synthesis of an asynchronous reactive module. In *Proc. 16th Int. Colloquium on Automata, Languages and Programming*, volume 372, pages 652–671. Lecture Notes in Computer Science, Springer-Verlag, July 1989.
17. A. Pnueli and R. Rosner. Distributed reactive systems are hard to synthesize. In *Proc. 31st IEEE Symp. on Foundation of Computer Science*, pages 746–757, 1990.
18. M.Y. Vardi. An automata-theoretic approach to fair realizability and synthesis. In P. Wolper, editor, *Computer Aided Verification, Proc. 7th Int'l Conf.*, volume 939 of *Lecture Notes in Computer Science*, pages 267–292. Springer-Verlag, Berlin, 1995.
19. I. Walukiewicz. A landscape with games in the background. In *Proc. IEEE Symp. on Logic In computer Science*, pages 356–366, 2004.
20. D.M. Wittbold, J.T.and Johnson. Information flow in nondeterministic systems. In *Proc. IEEE Symp. on Research in Security and Privacy*, pages 144–161, 1990.
21. H. Wong-Toi and D.L. Dill. Synthesizing processes and schedulers from temporal specifications. In E.M. Clarke and R.P. Kurshan, editors, *Computer-Aided Verification'90*, volume 3 of *DIMACS Series in Discrete Mathematics and Theoretical Computer Science*, pages 177–186. AMS, 1991.

Author Index

Lecture Notes in Computer Science

For information about Vols. 1–3526

please contact your bookseller or Springer

Vol. 3654: S. Jajodia, D. Wijesekera (Eds.), Data and Applications Security XIX. X, 353 pages. 2005.

Vol. 3653: M. Abadi, L.de Alfaro (Eds.), CONCUR 2005 – Concurrency Theory. XIV, 578 pages. 2005.

Vol. 3649: W.M.P. van der Aalst, B. Benatallah, F. Casati, F. Curbera (Eds.), Business Process Management. XII, 472 pages. 2005.

Vol. 3639: P. Godefroid (Ed.), Model Checking Software. XI, 289 pages. 2005.

Vol. 3638: A. Butz, B. Fisher, A. Krüger, P. Olivier (Eds.), Smart Graphics. XI, 269 pages. 2005.

Vol. 3634: L. Ong (Ed.), Computer Science Logic. XI, 567 pages. 2005.

Vol. 3633: C. Bauzer Medeiros, M. Egenhofer, E. Bertino (Eds.), Advances in Spatial and Temporal Databases. XIII, 433 pages. 2005.

Vol. 3632: R. Nieuwenhuis (Ed.), Automated Deduction – CADE-20. XIII, 459 pages. 2005. (Subseries LNAI).

Vol. 3627: C. Jacob, M.L. Pilat, P.J. Bentley, J. Timmis (Eds.), Artificial Immune Systems. XII, 500 pages. 2005.

Vol. 3626: B. Ganter, G. Stumme, R. Wille (Eds.), Formal Concept Analysis. X, 349 pages. 2005. (Subseries LNAI).

Vol. 3625: S. Kramer, B. Pfahringer (Eds.), Inductive Logic Programming. XIII, 427 pages. 2005. (Subseries LNAI).

Vol. 3624: C. Chekuri, K. Jansen, J.D.P. Rolim, L. Trevisan (Eds.), Approximation, Randomization and Combinatorial Optimization. XI, 495 pages. 2005.

Vol. 3623: M. Liśkiewicz, R. Reischuk (Eds.), Fundamentals of Computation Theory. XV, 576 pages. 2005.

Vol. 3621: V. Shoup (Ed.), Advances in Cryptology – CRYPTO 2005. XI, 568 pages. 2005.

Vol. 3620: H. Muñoz-Avila, F. Ricci (Eds.), Case-Based Reasoning Research and Development. XV, 654 pages. 2005. (Subseries LNAI).

Vol. 3619: X. Lu, W. Zhao (Eds.), Networking and Mobile Computing. XXIV, 1299 pages. 2005.

Vol. 3615: B. Ludäscher, L. Raschid (Eds.), Data Integration in the Life Sciences. XII, 344 pages. 2005. (Subseries LNBI).

Vol. 3608: F. Dehne, A. López-Ortiz, J.-R. Sack (Eds.), Algorithms and Data Structures. XIV, 446 pages. 2005.

Vol. 3607: J.-D. Zucker, L. Saitta (Eds.), Abstraction, Reformulation and Approximation. XII, 376 pages. 2005. (Subseries LNAI).

Vol. 3606: V. Malyshkin (Ed.), Parallel Computing Technologies. XII, 470 pages. 2005.

Vol. 3603: J. Hurd, T. Melham (Eds.), Theorem Proving in Higher Order Logics. IX, 409 pages. 2005.

Vol. 3602: R. Eigenmann, Z. Li, S.P. Midkiff (Eds.), Languages and Compilers for High Performance Computing. IX, 486 pages. 2005.

Vol. 3599: U. Aßmann, M. Aksit, A. Rensink (Eds.), Model Driven Architecture. X, 235 pages. 2005.

Vol. 3598: H. Murakami, H. Nakashima, H. Tokuda, M. Yasumura, Ubiquitous Computing Systems. XIII, 275 pages. 2005.

Vol. 3597: S. Shimojo, S. Ichii, T.W. Ling, K.-H. Song (Eds.), Web and Communication Technologies and Internet-Related Social Issues - HSI 2005. XIX, 368 pages. 2005.

Vol. 3596: F. Dau, M.-L. Mugnier, G. Stumme (Eds.), Conceptual Structures: Common Semantics for Sharing Knowledge. XI, 467 pages. 2005. (Subseries LNAI).

Vol. 3595: L. Wang (Ed.), Computing and Combinatorics. XVI, 995 pages. 2005.

Vol. 3594: J.C. Setubal, S. Verjovski-Almeida (Eds.), Advances in Bioinformatics and Computational Biology. XIV, 258 pages. 2005. (Subseries LNBI).

Vol. 3592: S. Katsikas, J. Lopez, G. Pernul (Eds.), Trust, Privacy and Security in Digital Business. XII, 332 pages. 2005.

Vol. 3587: P. Perner, A. Imiya (Eds.), Machine Learning and Data Mining in Pattern Recognition. XVII, 695 pages. 2005. (Subseries LNAI).

Vol. 3586: A.P. Black (Ed.), ECOOP 2005 - Object-Oriented Programming. XVII, 631 pages. 2005.

Vol. 3584: X. Li, S. Wang, Z.Y. Dong (Eds.), Advanced Data Mining and Applications. XIX, 835 pages. 2005. (Subseries LNAI).

Vol. 3583: R.W. H. Lau, Q. Li, R. Cheung, W. Liu (Eds.), Advances in Web-Based Learning – ICWL 2005. XIV, 420 pages. 2005.

Vol. 3582: J. Fitzgerald, I.J. Hayes, A. Tarlecki (Eds.), FM 2005: Formal Methods. XIV, 558 pages. 2005.

Vol. 3581: S. Miksch, J. Hunter, E. Keravnou (Eds.), Artificial Intelligence in Medicine. XVII, 547 pages. 2005. (Subseries LNAI).

Vol. 3580: L. Caires, G.F. Italiano, L. Monteiro, C. Palamidessi, M. Yung (Eds.), Automata, Languages and Programming. XXV, 1477 pages. 2005.

Vol. 3579: D. Lowe, M. Gaedke (Eds.), Web Engineering. XXII, 633 pages. 2005.

Vol. 3578: M. Gallagher, J. Hogan, F. Maire (Eds.), Intelligent Data Engineering and Automated Learning - IDEAL 2005. XVI, 599 pages. 2005.

Vol. 3577: R. Falcone, S. Barber, J. Sabater-Mir, M.P. Singh (Eds.), Trusting Agents for Trusting Electronic Societies. VIII, 235 pages. 2005. (Subseries LNAI).

Vol. 3576: K. Etessami, S.K. Rajamani (Eds.), Computer Aided Verification. XV, 564 pages. 2005.

Vol. 3575: S. Wermter, G. Palm, M. Elshaw (Eds.), Biomimetic Neural Learning for Intelligent Robots. IX, 383 pages. 2005. (Subseries LNAI).

Vol. 3574: C. Boyd, J.M. González Nieto (Eds.), Information Security and Privacy. XIII, 586 pages. 2005.

Vol. 3573: S. Etalle (Ed.), Logic Based Program Synthesis and Transformation. VIII, 279 pages. 2005.

Vol. 3572: C. De Felice, A. Restivo (Eds.), Developments in Language Theory. XI, 409 pages. 2005.

Vol. 3571: L. Godo (Ed.), Symbolic and Quantitative Approaches to Reasoning with Uncertainty. XVI, 1028 pages. 2005. (Subseries LNAI).

Vol. 3570: A. S. Patrick, M. Yung (Eds.), Financial Cryptography and Data Security. XII, 376 pages. 2005.

Vol. 3569: F. Bacchus, T. Walsh (Eds.), Theory and Applications of Satisfiability Testing. XII, 492 pages. 2005.

Vol. 3568: W.-K. Leow, M.S. Lew, T.-S. Chua, W.-Y. Ma, L. Chaisorn, E.M. Bakker (Eds.), Image and Video Retrieval. XVII, 672 pages. 2005.

Vol. 3567: M. Jackson, D. Nelson, S. Stirk (Eds.), Database: Enterprise, Skills and Innovation. XII, 185 pages. 2005.

Vol. 3566: J.-P. Banâtre, P. Fradet, J.-L. Giavitto, O. Michel (Eds.), Unconventional Programming Paradigms. XI, 367 pages. 2005.

Vol. 3565: G.E. Christensen, M. Sonka (Eds.), Information Processing in Medical Imaging. XXI, 777 pages. 2005.

Vol. 3564: N. Eisinger, J. Małuszyński (Eds.), Reasoning Web. IX, 319 pages. 2005.

Vol. 3562: J. Mira, J.R. Álvarez (Eds.), Artificial Intelligence and Knowledge Engineering Applications: A Bioinspired Approach, Part II. XXIV, 636 pages. 2005.

Vol. 3561: J. Mira, J.R. Álvarez (Eds.), Mechanisms, Symbols, and Models Underlying Cognition, Part I. XXIV, 532 pages. 2005.

Vol. 3560: V.K. Prasanna, S. Iyengar, P.G. Spirakis, M. Welsh (Eds.), Distributed Computing in Sensor Systems. XV, 423 pages. 2005.

Vol. 3559: P. Auer, R. Meir (Eds.), Learning Theory. XI, 692 pages. 2005. (Subseries LNAI).

Vol. 3558: V. Torra, Y. Narukawa, S. Miyamoto (Eds.), Modeling Decisions for Artificial Intelligence. XII, 470 pages. 2005. (Subseries LNAI).

Vol. 3557: H. Gilbert, H. Handschuh (Eds.), Fast Software Encryption. XI, 443 pages. 2005.

Vol. 3556: H. Baumeister, M. Marchesi, M. Holcombe (Eds.), Extreme Programming and Agile Processes in Software Engineering. XIV, 332 pages. 2005.

Vol. 3555: T. Vardanega, A.J. Wellings (Eds.), Reliable Software Technology – Ada-Europe 2005. XV, 273 pages. 2005.

Vol. 3554: A. Dey, B. Kokinov, D. Leake, R. Turner (Eds.), Modeling and Using Context. XIV, 572 pages. 2005. (Subseries LNAI).

Vol. 3553: T.D. Hämäläinen, A.D. Pimentel, J. Takala, S. Vassiliadis (Eds.), Embedded Computer Systems: Architectures, Modeling, and Simulation. XV, 476 pages. 2005.

Vol. 3552: H. de Meer, N. Bhatti (Eds.), Quality of Service – IWQoS 2005. XVIII, 400 pages. 2005.

Vol. 3551: T. Härder, W. Lehner (Eds.), Data Management in a Connected World. XIX, 371 pages. 2005.

Vol. 3548: K. Julisch, C. Kruegel (Eds.), Intrusion and Malware Detection and Vulnerability Assessment. X, 241 pages. 2005.

Vol. 3547: F. Bomarius, S. Komi-Sirviö (Eds.), Product Focused Software Process Improvement. XIII, 588 pages. 2005.

Vol. 3546: T. Kanade, A. Jain, N.K. Ratha (Eds.), Audio- and Video-Based Biometric Person Authentication. XX, 1134 pages. 2005.

Vol. 3544: T. Higashino (Ed.), Principles of Distributed Systems. XII, 460 pages. 2005.

Vol. 3543: L. Kutvonen, N. Alonistioti (Eds.), Distributed Applications and Interoperable Systems. XI, 235 pages. 2005.

Vol. 3542: H.H. Hoos, D.G. Mitchell (Eds.), Theory and Applications of Satisfiability Testing. XIII, 393 pages. 2005.

Vol. 3541: N.C. Oza, R. Polikar, J. Kittler, F. Roli (Eds.), Multiple Classifier Systems. XII, 430 pages. 2005.

Vol. 3540: H. Kalviainen, J. Parkkinen, A. Kaarna (Eds.), Image Analysis. XXII, 1270 pages. 2005.

Vol. 3539: K. Morik, J.-F. Boulicaut, A. Siebes (Eds.), Local Pattern Detection. XI, 233 pages. 2005. (Subseries LNAI).

Vol. 3538: L. Ardissono, P. Brna, A. Mitrovic (Eds.), User Modeling 2005. XVI, 533 pages. 2005. (Subseries LNAI).

Vol. 3537: A. Apostolico, M. Crochemore, K. Park (Eds.), Combinatorial Pattern Matching. XI, 444 pages. 2005.

Vol. 3536: G. Ciardo, P. Darondeau (Eds.), Applications and Theory of Petri Nets 2005. XI, 470 pages. 2005.

Vol. 3535: M. Steffen, G. Zavattaro (Eds.), Formal Methods for Open Object-Based Distributed Systems. X, 323 pages. 2005.

Vol. 3534: S. Spaccapietra, E. Zimányi (Eds.), Journal on Data Semantics III. XI, 213 pages. 2005.

Vol. 3533: M. Ali, F. Esposito (Eds.), Innovations in Applied Artificial Intelligence. XX, 858 pages. 2005. (Subseries LNAI).

Vol. 3532: A. Gómez-Pérez, J. Euzenat (Eds.), The Semantic Web: Research and Applications. XV, 728 pages. 2005.

Vol. 3531: J. Ioannidis, A. Keromytis, M. Yung (Eds.), Applied Cryptography and Network Security. XI, 530 pages. 2005.

Vol. 3530: A. Prinz, R. Reed, J. Reed (Eds.), SDL 2005: Model Driven. XI, 361 pages. 2005.

Vol. 3528: P.S. Szczepaniak, J. Kacprzyk, A. Niewiadomski (Eds.), Advances in Web Intelligence. XVII, 513 pages. 2005. (Subseries LNAI).

Vol. 3527: R. Morrison, F. Oquendo (Eds.), Software Architecture. XII, 263 pages. 2005.